Commentary on
EXODUS

Commentary on
EXODUS

GEORGE BUSH

kregel
PUBLICATIONS

Grand Rapids, MI 49501

Commentary on Exodus, by George Bush.

Published in 1993 by Kregel Publications, a division of Kregel, Inc., P.O. Box 2607, Grand Rapids, MI 49501.

Cover Design: Alan G. Hartman

Library of Congress Cataloging-in-Publication Data

Bush, George, 1796-1859.
   [Notes, critical and practical, on the book of Exodus]
   Commentary on Exodus / George Bush.
     p.   cm.
   Orginally published: Notes, critical and practical, on the book of Exodus. New York: M. H. Newman, 1843.
   1. Bible. O.T. Exodus—Commentaries. I. Bible. O.T. Exodus. English. Authorized. 1993. II. Title.
BS1245.3.B875   1993   222'.1207—dc20   92-39337
                                                        CIP

ISBN 0-8254-2181-0 (paperback)
ISBN 0-8254-2182-9 (deluxe hardback)

      1 2 3 4 5 year / printing 97 96 95 94 93

Printed in the United States of America

CONTENTS

INTRODUCTION

§ 1. *Title, Author, Scope, &c.*

THE designation given in our version to the second book of the Pentateuch, viz. 'Exodus,' is derived directly from the Greek εξοδος, *exodos*, varying only by the Latinised termination *us* for *os*. The import of the term is that of *going forth, emigration, departure*, and is significant of the principal event recorded in it, to wit, the departure of the children of Israel from Egypt. According to Hebrew usage, though no where in the text itself, it is called ואלה שמות *ve-ëlleh shemoth, and these are the names*, from the initial words of the book. This phrase, however, is sometimes abbreviated by the Jewish writers to the simple term שמות *shemoth, the names*.

That the authorship of this book is rightly ascribed to Moses, is proved by the arguments which go to ascertain the entire Pentateuch as the production of his hand. These are so fully detailed in our Introduction to Genesis, that it will be unnecessary to repeat them here. But we have in addition still more explicit evidence on this point. Moses testifies of himself, Ex. 24. 4, that he 'wrote all the words of the Lord,' commanded him on a certain occasion, which words are contained in this book. Our Savior, also, when citing, Mark 12. 26, a certain passage from this book, calls it 'the book of Moses.' And again, Luke 20. 37, he says, ' Now that the dead are raised, even Moses showed at the bush.' It is moreover to be observed that the books of the Old Testament are spoken of in the New, Luke 15. 31, as divided into two grand classes, 'Moses and the prophets,' and in v. 16, 'the law and the prophets ;' so that all the Scriptures, besides 'the prophets,' were written by Moses ; in other words, the four books of the 'law' were written by him. There remains, therefore, no room for doubt that Moses wrote the book of Exodus, and if any thing more were necessary to establish its canonical character, it would be found in the fact mentioned by Rivet, that twenty-five passages are quoted from it by Christ and his Apostles in express terms, and nineteen as to the sense.

As to the general scope of the book, it is plainly to preserve the memorial of the great facts of the national history of Israel in its earlier periods, to wit, their deliverance from Egypt, the kindness and faithfulness of God in their subsequent preservation in the wilderness, the delivery of the Law, and the establishment of a new and peculiar system of worship. All the particulars connected with these several events are given in the fullest and most interesting detail, and in such a manner as to compel in the reader the recognition of an overruling Providence at every step of the narration. There is perhaps no book in the Bible that records such an illustrious series of miracles, or that keeps the divine agency so constantly before the mind's eye. Nor are the moral lessons which it teaches less prominent and striking. We find the Apostle Paul, 1 Cor. 10. 11, after having adverted to the course of Israel's experience as a nation, immediately adding, 'Now all these things happened unto them for ensamples; and they are written for our admonition, upon whom the ends of the world are come.' No sooner had he adverted to their privileges than he describes their chastisements, as inflicted to the intent that we should not so imitate their sin, as to provoke a visitation of the same vengeance. Indeed their whole history forms one grand prediction and outline of human redemption, and of the lot of the church. In the servitude of Israel we behold a lively image of the bondage to sin and Satan in which the unregenerate are held captive. In the deliverance from Egypt is foreshown their redemption from this horrid thraldom ; and the journey through the wilderness is a graphic program of a Christian's journey through life to his final inheritance in the heavenly Canaan. So also, without minute specification, the manna of which the Israelites ate, and the rock of which they drank, as well as the brazen serpent by which they were healed, were severally typical of corresponding particulars under the Christian economy. Add to this, that under the sacrifices, and ceremonial service of the Mosaic institute, were described the distinguishing features of the more spiritual worship of the Gospel.

It is necessary to bear in mind, if we would adequately understand the drift of the peculiar institutions which we find prescribed in the pages of this book, that the grand design of Heaven was to form the Israelites into a distinct and independent people, and to unite them in one great political and ecclesiastical body of whom Jehovah himself was to be the ackowledged head, constituting what is familiarly known as the *Jewish Theocracy*. But upon this unique kind of polity, which never had a parallel in the case of any other nation on earth, we have reserved a more extended train of remark in the Introduction to the Second Volume of this work, where the reader will find the whole subject amply discussed.

§ 2. *Time occupied by the History, Divisions, &c.*

The period embraced by the history will be seen from the following computation :—

	Years.
From death of Joseph to birth of Moses,	60
From birth of Moses to departure from Egypt,	81
From departure from Egypt to Tabernacle erected,	1
	142

Some make the period from the death of Joseph to the birth of Moses to be 63 years, which will increase the sum total to 145 years, but the difference is too slight to make it necessary to state the grounds of either calculation. It is to be observed, however, that nearly the whole book is occupied in the detail of the events which occurred in the last year of the period above mentioned.

According to the Jewish arrangement this book is divided into eleven פרשות *parashoth*, or larger divisions, and twenty סדרים *siderim*, or smaller divisions

In our Bibles it is divided into forty chapters, which, according to the different subjects treated, may be classified as follows:—

I. The oppression of the Israelites in Egypt, ch. 1.

II. The birth and early life of Moses, ch. 2.

III. The legation of Moses, ch. 3, 4. 1—29.

IV. The mission of Moses, and the infliction of the first eight plagues, ch. 4. 29—10. 21.

V. The institution of the Passover, ch. 12. 1—21.

VI. The conclusion of the ten plagues, ch. 10. 21—12. 21—31.

VII. The exodus, ch. 12. 31—37, and 40—42.

VIII. The wanderings in the wilderness, from Rameses in Egypt to Mount Sinai, ch. 12. 37—40 to ch. 19. 1, 2.

IX. Moses called up into the mount, and the preparation of the people for the renewing of the Covenant, ch. 19.

X. The moral law delivered, ch. 20.

XI. The judicial and ceremonial law delivered, ch. 21—31.

XII. The idolatry of the Israelites, and their punishment with the renewal of the Covenant, ch. 32—34.

XIII. The offerings for and the construction of the tabernacle, ch. 35—39.

XIV. The tabernacle erected, and covered by the cloud of the divine Presence, ch. 40.

§ 3. *Commentators.*

Throughout the great mass of biblical criticism and exposition embodied in our own and foreign languages, there are comparatively few works devoted to the book of Exodus alone ; nor is it always from these that the student or commentator can expect to derive the most valuable aid. For the most part, the commentaries which embrace either the whole Scriptures, or extended portions of them, are the store-houses from whence the materials of exegetical illustration are to be sought. Of these the Critici Sacri, the Synopsis of Pool, the Scholia of Rosenmuller, the Annotations of Leclerc, Ainsworth, and Patrick, will always hold the chief rank in the estimation of the scholar, next to the Ancient Versions and Targums contained in Walton's Polyglot. These accordingly have been always at hand, as a constant tribunal of reference, through every stage of the progress of the present work. But it is obvious at a glance, that so vast is the variety of subjects necessarily brought under review in the course of this book, that no one class of authorities will by any means suffice for its adequate elucidation. Philology, Geography, Antiquities, History, Architecture, the arts of Sculpture, Engraving, Dyeing, Weaving, Embroidering, to say nothing of the peculiar system of Law, Jurisprudence, and Worship, enjoined upon the Israelites, all prefer their claims for more or less of illustration at the hands of him who assumes the task of expounding in order the chapters of Exodus. It would scarcely be possible, therefore, to enumerate all the works which have gone to constitute the apparatus for the present undertaking, without citing the entire list of biblical helps appended to the Introduction to the Notes on Genesis, besides a great multitude of others which are there omitted. In fact, we know of no book in the Bible that demands so great a diversity of material for its exposition as the second book of the Pentateuch. How far the various and voluminous sources of information, to which the author has had access, have been made available to his grand purpose in the execution of the present work, is a question that awaits the decision of his readers. A very minute specification might invite a more critical comparison, and present a more palpable contrast, between his advantages and his achievement, than would redound to the credit of his work. At the same time, he cannot in candor confess to any conscious lack of effort to do the utmost justice to every part of his self-imposed labor—if that may be called a labor, which has proved, from beginning to end, an unfailing source of pleasure.

The following catalogue is not given as complete, but merely as indicating, in addition to those already specified, the most important collateral aids to a full critical and ethical developement of the sense of this remarkable book.

I. *Jewish and Christiano-Rabbinical Commentators.*

R. SALOMONIS JARCHI, dicti RASCHI, Commentarius Hebraicus, in quinque Libros Mosis, Latine versus atque Notis Critics ae philologicis illustratus a JOH. FREDERICO BREITHAUPTO. Gothæ, 1713. 4to.

Jarchi, or Raschi, as he is usually called from combining, according to Hebrew usage, the three initial letters of his name (רשי), is generally placed by the Jews at the head of their commentators. They call him ' the great light ' and ' the holy mouth,' from the value attached to his learned comments on the Law and the Prophets. These I have found occasionally to contain some happy verbal criticisms, and in the account of the construction of the tabernacle, in particular, his remarks are plain, common-sense, and valuable ; but in the main he indulges in the characteristic silly conceits of the Rabbins, and his style, with all the aid it derives from Breithaupt's excellent notes and paraphrases, is so obscure as to render him of little service to one who cares not for words without meaning. He was a native of Troyes in Champagne, and died, A. D. 1180.

R. ISAACI ABARBANELIS Commentarius in Pentateuchum Mosis, curâ Henrici J. Van Banshuisen. Hanoviæ, 1710. Folio.

Rabbi Abarbanel, or Abravanel, as the name is sometimes written, was a Portuguese Jew, who flourished in the fifteenth century, and wrote commentaries on the Pentateuch, the whole of the Prophets, and some other books of Scripture. He also is highly esteemed by his countrymen, and though an exceedingly bitter enemy of Christianity, yet Father Simon says of him, 'We may, in my opinion, reap more advantage in Scripture-translation from R. Isaac Abravanel, than from any other Jew. He has written in an elegant and perspicuous style, although he is too copious and sometimes affects rhetoric more than strict fidelity to the sacred text.' As the volume abovementioned came into my hands only at a very advanced stage of my own work, I have been unable to make any *direct* use of it. Through the medium of Rosenmuller and Cartwright, however, his remarks have occasionally found their way into my Notes.

CHRISTOPHORI CARTWRIGHT Electa Targumico-Rabbinica ; sive Annotationes in Exodum ex triplici Targum. Lond. 1653. 8vo.

This is a valuable work, purely critical, made up almost entirely of materials drawn from the Rabbinical commentaries and the Chaldee and other ancient versions. It is used much oftener than quoted by Rosenmuller.

AINSWORTH'S (H.) Annotations upon the Second Book of Moses, called Exodus. Lond. 1639. Fol.

This is the second part of the author's invaluable work on the Pentateuch. It is rich in pertinent citations from Jewish sources, and in that kind of verbal criticism which consists in laying open the *usus loquendi* of the original is entirely without a parallel.

LIGHTFOOT'S Handful of Gleanings out of the Book of Exodus. Works (Pitman's Ed. in 13 vols.), Vol. II. p. 351—409.

This is a collection of remarks critical, chronological, historical, and talmudical upon detached portions of Exodus. As in all Lightfoot's works, some of his observations are of considerable value, others of very little.

II. *Christian Commentators.*

WILLETT'S Hexapla in Exodum ; that is, a sixfold commentary upon the Book of Exodus, according to the Method propounded in the Hexapla upon Genesis. Lond. 1608. Folio.

A voluminous and tedious Commentary, but not without its value, especially as embodying and usually confuting the interpretations of the Romanists. He compares also the various versions and deduces doctrinal and moral inferences.

RIVETI'S (ANDR.) Opera Theologica. Rotterdam, 1651. 2 Tom. Folio.

The first of these huge volumes contains the author's Exercitations on Genesis and Exodus. They are very elaborate and generally judicious, but marked with the prolixity of the seventeenth century. At the present day they are merely commentaries for commentators.

HOPKINS' (WM.) Corrected Translation of Exodus, with Notes critical and explanatory. Lond. 1784. 4to.

Said to be a work of little value.

III. *Miscellaneous and Illustrative Works.*

PICTORIAL BIBLE with Wood-cuts and Original Notes. Lond. 1836-8. 3 vols. Roy. 8vo.

For a character of this very valuable work see the Preface to my Notes on Genesis. The ' Pictorial History of Palestine,' now in course of publication by the same author, is a work of similar character, and abounding with rich materials for illustrating the Old Testament history.

BUDDICOM'S Christian Exodus, or the Deliverance of the Israelites from Egypt, practically considered in a series of Discourses. Lond. 1839. 2 vols. 12mo.

BÄHR'S Symbolik des Mosaischen Cultus (Symbolism of the Mosaic Worship). Heidelb. 1837—9. 8vo.

An exceedingly curious and valuable work, entering into the most profound researches respecting the symbolical character of the Tabernacle and Temple ritual.

GRAVES' (RICH.) Lectures on the Four Last Books of the Pentateuch. Lond. 1815, 2 vols. 8vo.

FABER'S (G. S.) Horæ Mosaicæ ; or a Dissertation on the Credibility and Theology of the Pentateuch. Lond. 1818. 2 vols. 8vo.

The leading object of this work is to establish the authenticity of the Pentateuch, by pointing out the coincidence of its facts and statements with the remains of profane antiquity, and their connexion with Christianity. It is a production of great value to the biblical student.

—— Treatise on the Patriarchal, Levitical, and Christian Dispensations. Lond. 1823. 2 vols. 8vo.

This Treatise exhibits all the strong masculine sense, and extensive classical erudition that distinguish the author, but from its greater license of hypothesis in particular parts is perhaps generally less esteemed than the 'Horæ Mosaicæ' mentioned above. The attentive reader, however, cannot but derive from it many very important ideas on the subject of sacred antiquity. His refutation of some of Warburton's bold positions is eminently successful.

OUTRAM's (WM.) Two Dissertations on Sacrifices; translated by Allen. Lond. 1817. 8vo.

A standard work on the subject of which it treats.

MICHAELIS' (J. D.) Commentaries on the Laws of Moses; translated by Smith. Lond. 1814. 4 vols. 8vo.

The value of this, the main work of its author, depends upon the degree to which it is imbued with the genius of Orientalism, and the sagacity discovered in tracing the connexion between the institutions of Moses and the various influences of climate, manners, hereditary usages, and other national characteristics which may be supposed to have governed their adoption. Its great fault is its treating the Mosaic jurisprudence and ritual as if it originated with Moses rather than with God. It is also occasionally disfigured with a levity and grossness very unsuited to its subject. Yet it throws too much light on the wisdom and design of the Levitical code not to be on the whole a very valuable, as well as very interesting work.

ROBINSON's (Prof. E.) Biblical Researches in Palestine, Mount Sinai, and Arabia Petræa. A Journal of Travels in the year 1838, by E. Robinson, and E. Smith; undertaken in reference to Biblical Geography; with new Maps and Plans. New York, 1841. 3 vols. 8vo.

From no source have I experienced greater regret in looking back upon the execution of my task, than in not having been able, from the late date of its publication, to avail myself of the rich topographical treasures contained in this work. In all that relates to the geography of the land of Goshen, the region of the Israelites' sojourn in Egypt; to the route from thence to the Red Sea; to the passage of that sea; to the wilderness of Sin; and to the interesting localities of the Sinai tract, the researches of the American travellers have settled a multitude of disputed points, and in fact opened a new era in the progress of Biblical geography. The very maps themselves are sufficient to have produced this result, even had the matter of the journal been wanting. Both together form a noble contribution to the cause of sacred science, of which the age and the country that have given birth to it may well be proud. The portion of the work which treats of Palestine I have not yet seen, though I am assured by the author that it contains more of *discovery* than any other.

NOW ᵃ these *are* the names of the children of Israel, which

ᵃ Gen. 46. 8.—ch. 6. 14.

Chapter 1

The prominent subject of the book upon whi ch we now enter, as intimated by its title, is the wonderful deliverance of the nati on of Israel from their bondage in Egypt. But as this and all the great events in the history of that people were matters of express prediction and promise on the part of God ; the sacred writer commences his narrative with a virtual commentary on the promise made to Abraham, Gen. 15. 5, that his seed should from small beginnings eventually become as numerous as the stars of heaven and as the sands on the sea shore. Though the migration of Jacob's family from Canaan to Egypt, and the oppression to which they were subjected, would seem to have threatened the complete frustration of the divine purposes in regard to the increase of Abraham's seed, yet the writer shows that notwithstanding it was but a mere handful of that seed that was sown in the adverse soil of Egypt, yet the harvest which sprung from it was vast beyond conception, and such as to illustrate the divine veracity in the most glorious manner. Many interesting incidents had no doubt occurred between the death of Joseph and the incipient bondage of Israel; but these are passed over in silence because they did not bear particularly upon the fulfilment of any special prediction. But God would have nothing lost that was essential to the proof of his faithfulness in his covenant relations. He deems it of more im-

---

came into Egypt; every man and his household came with Jacob.

2 Reuben, Simeon, Levi, and Judah,

3 Issachar, Zebulun, and Benjamin,

---

portance to confirm faith than to gratify curiosity.

1. *Now these are the names.* Heb. ואלה שמות *ve-elleh shemoth, and these are the names.* The use of the Hebrew copulative ו *and* is peculiar. Though its ordinary office in a continuous narrative is that of a *connective,* yet it frequently occurs at the beginning of a book where it can have no reference to any thing preceding, as Est. 1. 1, ' *Now* it came to pass.' Heb. *And* it came to pass. Compare Ruth 1. 1, Ezek. 1. 1. Here, however, as well as in the commencement of the two following books, it is probably to be taken in its connective sense, indicating the continuation of the foregoing narrative. The books of Moses appear not to have been orginally divided, as at present, into five separate portions, but to have constituted one unbroken volume. This is inferred from the manner in which the writings of Moses are quoted in the New Testament, where no such distinction is recognized. See Luke 16. 31. ——¶ *Which came.* Heb. הבאים *hab-baim, which* (were) *coming.* See Note on Gen. 46. 8.——¶ *Every man and his household.* Heb. איש וביתו *ish u-betho, every one and his house.* Chal. ' Every one and the men of his household.' On this frequent sense of the term ' house' see Note on v. 21. Gr. εκαστος πανυικι, *each with his whole household.*

2–4. *Reuben, Simeon,* &c. In this enumeration the sons of the handmaids are reckoned last, which accounts for

4 Dan, and Naphtali, Gad, and Asher.

5 And all the souls that came out of the loins of Jacob were b seventy

b Gen. 46. 26, 27.—ver. 20. Deut. 10. 22.

souls: for Joseph was in Egypt *already*.

6 And c Joseph died, and all his brethren, and all that generation.

c Gen. 50. 26.   Acts. 7. 15.

Benjamin's occupying the seventh place instead of the eleventh. The frequent mention of the names of the twelve patriarchs in the sacred history lays a foundation for the numerous allusions in the sacred writings to this as a mystical number applied to the church of the New Testament. Thus in Rev. 7. 5—8, mention is made of the *twelve* tribes of Israel, and of *twelve* thousand sealed out of every tribe ; ch. 12. 1, of the *twelve* stars upon the woman's crown ; ch. 21. 12—14, of the *twelve* gates, and *twelve* foundations of the heavenly city, the New Jerusalem ; where it may be observed that the jasper foundation, the precious stone in the breast-plate in which Benjamin's name was written, Ex. 28. 20, is the first in order. Moses also in Deut. 33. 12, assigns Benjamin his blessing before his elder brother Joseph.

5. *All the souls that came out of the loins of Jacob.* Heb. כל נפש יצאי ירך יעקב *kol nephesh yotzeë yerek Yaakob, all the soul* (collect. sing.) *of the proceeders-out-of the thigh of Jacob ;* the usual idiom for expressing physical generation.——¶ *Seventy souls.* That is, persons. See Note on Gen. 14. 21. By comparing this passage with Gen. 46. 27, it appears that the whole number, exclusive of Jacob himself, amounted to 66 ; including him to 67 ; so that Joseph with his two sons are necessary to make up the complement. If it be objected that this mode of enumeration represents Jacob as coming out of his own thigh, we refer in reply to the Note on a similar phraseology, Gen. 35. 22, 26. The Sept. version, which transfers the final clause of this verse to the beginning of it, states the number at 75, which is followed by Stephen, Acts

7. 14. For an explanation of this apparent discrepancy, see Note on Gen. 46. 27.——¶ *For Joseph was in Egypt already ;* and therefore is to be excepted from the number that came into Egypt, though not from the number of Jacob's descendants. Chal. ' With Joseph, who was in Egypt.'

6. *And Joseph died,* &c. After attaining to the age of 110 years, during 80 of which he was a ruler in Egypt. Of his sepulture nothing is here said ; but we learn elsewhere that his remains, as well as those of his brethren, were carried out of Egypt and buried in Sychem in the land of Canaan, Exod. 13. 19. Acts, 7. 16.——¶ *All that generation.* Not only the whole generation of Joseph's kindred, but all the men of that age, Egyptians as well as Israelites. Compare Gen. 6. 9. Generations are mortal as well as individuals, nor can the nearest relations keep each other alive. The term of their existence, as well as the bounds of their habitation, is set by God himself. A very considerable lapse of time however is implied in this expression, as Levi lived to the age of 137, and consequently survived Joseph by 27 years. The passage forms a natural introduction to the ensuing history of the great change that occurred in the condition of the Israelites under the next reign. During the long period of the sojourning of Joseph and his brethren in Egypt nothing transpired to mar the peace and prosperity which they there enjoyed, or to prevent the men of that generation passing off the stage in silent succession, till a new race had imperceptibly sprung up to occupy their places. Eccl. 1. 4, ' One generation passeth away, and another generation cometh.'

7 ¶ d And the children of Israel were fruitful, and increased abundantly, and multiplied, and waxed

dGen. 46. 3. Deut. 26. 5. Ps. 105. 24. Acts 7. 17.

exceeding mighty; and the land was filled with them.

8 Now there e arose up a new

e Acts 7. 18.

7. *Were fruitful.* Heb. פָּרוּ *paru*, a term often applied to the vigorous fructification of trees and plants, and implying here that none of the Israelitish women were barren; they began early and continued long in bearing, and not unfrequently perhaps brought forth more than one at a birth. Gr. ηυξηθησαν, *were augmented.*——¶ *Increased abundantly.* Heb. יִשְׁרְצוּ *yishretzu, bred swiftly, like fishes,* or reptiles. See Note on Gen. 1. 20. Gr. επληθυνθησαν, *were multiplied.* Vulg. 'Quasi germinantes multiplicati sunt,' *as it were springing up were multiplied.*——¶ *Multiplied.* Heb. יִרְבּוּ *yirbu,* became numerous. Gr. χυδαιοι εγενοντο, *became diffusely abundant.*—— ¶ *Waxed exceeding mighty.* Heb. וַיַּעַצְמוּ *yaatzmu,* became strong. Gr. κατισχυον, *prevailed.* The accumulation of these nearly synonimous terms gives the utmost intensity to the writer's meaning, and conveys the idea of amazing and unparalleled increase. This is elsewhere abundantly confirmed. It was 430 years from the call of Abraham to the deliverance from Egypt, during the first 215 of which the promised seed increased to but 70 souls, but during the latter half of the same period these 70 were multiplied, Num. 1. 46, to 600,000 fighting men; and if to these we add the women, the children, and the aged, the whole number probably amounted to upwards of two millions! Well then does the psalmist say, Ps. 105. 24, that ' he increased his people greatly, and made them stronger than their enemies.' See also Deut. 26. 5.

8. *There arose up a new king over Egypt.* Gr. ανεστη βασιλευς ετερος, *there arose up another king.* This rendering is somewhat remarkable, as the literal translation of חָדָשׁ is not ετερος, an-

other, but καινος, *new.* It probably implies a king of *another* race, of a different dynasty, one who came to the throne, not by regular succession, but in consequence of intestine revolution or foreign conquest. This interpretation seems to be warranted by the analogous usage of the word 'new' in the following and numerous other passages; Deut. 32. 17, 'They sacrificed unto devils, not to God; to gods whom they knew not, to *new* gods that came newly up;' i. e. to strange gods, to exotic deities. Judg. 5. 8, 'They chose *new* gods;' i. e. other or strange gods, the gods of the heathen. So Mark, 16. 17, 'They shall speak with *new* tongues;' i. e. with foreign tongues, the languages of other people. The informations of profane history on this point are exceedingly vague and meagre, but it is contended by some writers, that it was about this time that Egypt was invaded and occupied by a powerful Asiatic people, whose rulers formed the dynasty of *shepherd-kings,* of whom so much is said in Manetho, Herodotus, and others. Josephus also (Ant. L. II. c. 9. § 1.) expressly affirms that the Israelites were oppressed by the Egyptians after the death of Joseph, ' *the government having been transferred to another family.*' But even were this point involved in far less obscurity than it is, it would comport but little with our plan to enter into its discussion. Matters of mere historical interest, of which the Scriptures say nothing, come rather within the province of the anti-quarian than of the commentator.—— ¶ *Which knew not Joseph.* That is, who regarded not, who appreciated not. A like phraseology occurs Judg. 2. 10, 'And there arose another generation which *knew not* the Lord, neither the

king over Egypt, which knew not Joseph.

---

works which he had done for Israel.' That is, which did not *gratefully acknowledge* the Lord,· or his various works of mercy towards them. The memory of the name and services of so eminent a benefactor could not but have been preserved among the nation, and must, as a matter of report, have come to the ears of the king, but it is a peculiarity of words of *knowledge*, in the Hebrew, that they imply also the exercise of the *affections.* Thus, Ps. 1. 6, ' The Lord *knoweth* the way of the righteous,' i. e. loveth. Ps. 31. 7, ' Thou hast *known* my soul in adversities ;' i. e. thou hast tenderly regarded. Prov. 24. 23, ' It is not good to *have respect* of persons in judgment.' Heb. ' to *know* persons.' Job. 34. 19, ' How much less to him that accepteth not the persons of princes, nor *regardeth* the rich more than the poor.' Heb. ' nor *knoweth the rich.*' It was probably in this sense that the new king is said not to have *known* Joseph, and this is less to be wondered at if, as suggested above, he was of a foreign nation and another dynasty. The Chal. renders it, ' Who confirmed not the decree of Joseph,' i. e. according to Fagius, either that he totally disregarded all the ordinances and enactments which Joseph had originated, and introduced universal innovation ; or that he utterly broke through all the compacts and covenants existing between Joseph as the representative of Israel, and the Pharaoh who then filled the throne, and began cruelly to oppress a people whom his predecessor had sworn to protect and befriend. Both the Targum of Jonathan and that of Jerusalem adhere to the former sense ; ' Who considered not Joseph, nor walked in his statutes.' The comment of Rabbi Solomon probably brings us still nearer to the true sense, ' Who acted

9 And he said unto his people Behold, ᶠthe people of the children

ᶠ Ps. 105. 24.

as if he did not know him.' It is doubtless to be set down to the account of an exemplary modesty in Joseph that no more effectual means had been adopted to secure among the Egyptians the abiding memory and acknowledgment of his great services to that people. Had he been of an aspiring spirit, covetous of present or posthumous fame ; had he sought great things for himself or his kindred, we cannot question but that monuments and various other memorials would have transmitted his name to posterity as an illustrious benefactor of his adopted country. But no prompting of this nature appears to have swayed the bosom of Joseph. As his hopes were fixed upon the possession of the promised inheritance, he seems to have accounted it sufficient simply to enjoy, for the time being, the hospitality of a foreign prince, till the destined period of removal should arrive, without multiplying the ties which would then have to be broken. But just in proportion as *he* was little anxious and aspiring on this score, was the ingratitude and forgetfulness of the Egyptians the more culpable. It is only the basest spirit of the world that will take occasion, from the lowliness of the claims of an eminent public servant, to bury in speedy oblivion the remembrance of his services. Yet his was but the lot of thousands, whose noblest benefactions to their fellow men have been repaid with the most ungrateful neglect. The poor man by his wisdom delivereth the city, yet no man remembereth that same poor man. Could we find a national conscience, we might look for national gratitude.

9. *He said unto his people.* To his people in the persons of their representatives, his counsellors.——¶ *Behold, the people of the children of Israel.* Heb.

of Israel *are* more and mightier than we.

10 g Come on, let us h deal wisely with them, lest they multiply, and

g Ps. 10. 2. & 83. 3, 4. h Job. 5. 13. Ps. 105. 25. Prov. 16. 25. & 21. 30. Acts. 7. 19.

עַם בְּנֵי יִשְׂרָאֵל *am benë Yisrael.* This is rendered in most of the ancient versions as in ours ; but Aben Ezra remarks, with undoubted correctness, that עַם *people* is not here in the construct state, but in apposition with בְּנֵי *children*, so as to require the rendering, 'the people, the children of Israel.' A distinctive and not conjunctive accent is placed upon *people.*——¶ *More and mightier.* Heb. רַב וְעָצוּם *rab ve-atzum, many and mighty* beyond us. They had become mightier by becoming more ; that is, not perhaps absolutely more ; not so as to outnumber the population of all Egypt ; but more in proportion to the space occupied ; more within any given limits. ' He speaks,' says Trapp, ' as if he had looked through a multiplying glass ;' and it is scarcely extravagant to say, that such a multiplying glass was in fact the promise given to Abraham. By others, the words have been regarded as a false pretext for reducing the Israelites to bondage. But this we think less probable.

10. *Let us deal wisely with them.* Heb. נִתְחַכְּמָה לוֹ *nithhakkemah lo, let us deal wisely against him* (collect. sing. for plur.) ; i. e. cunningly, craftily ; let us devise some method of oppressing them, of preventing their enormous increase, and at the same time avoid the show of oppression and downright tyranny, and the danger arising from their great physical force. Gr. κατασοφισωμεθα, *let us outwit them.* Vulg. Sapiente opprimamus eum, *let us wisely oppress him* (*them*). Chal. ' Let us deal wisely against them.' The original term חכם *hakam*, is used for the most part in a good sense for *acting wisely, skilfully, prudently*, yet it occasionally carries with it the import of *cunning*,

it come to pass, that, when there falleth out any war, they join also unto our enemies, and fight against us, and *so* get them up out of the land.

subtlety, wiliness, and in Ps. 105. 20, in reference to this very event, we find the equivalent term הִתְנַכֵּל *hithnakkel,* from נכל *to contrive deceitfully or insidiously,* 'He turned their hearts to hate his people, to *deal subtilely* with his servants.' The *wisdom* here proposed to be employed was the wisdom of the serpent; but with men of reprobate minds, governed solely by the corrupt spirit of this world, whatever measures tend to promote their own interests and circumvent their opponents, is dignified by the epithet *wise*, though it be found when judged by a purer standard, to be in reality nothing less than the very *policy of hell.* So easily is language perverted, and made a sanction for the most iniquitous proceedings.——¶ *Lest they multiply,* &c. That is, lest they *continue* to multiply, and become more and mightier still. It is obvious, however, that the mere multiplication of the Israelites was no just ground of alarm, so long as they were well used and no provocation given them to turn against the people with whom they dwelt. They were a peaceful race of shepherds, who looked upon themselves as mere temporary sojourners in Egypt, and who would therefore be the last to engage in plots and insurrections against the government. The promises given them by God, and the hopes which they entertained as a nation, were the strongest security which the Egyptians could have that nothing was to be apprehended from them on the score of rebellion. Indeed, a nation so evidently favored of Heaven, instead of being regarded as a source of danger, could not but prove a bulwark of defence to the country, if treated as friends. But the wicked fear where no fear is, and when intent upon

11 Therefore they did set over them taskmasters, [i] to afflict them with their [k] burdens. And they built for Pharaoh treasure-cities, Pithom, [l] and Raamses.

[i] Gen. 15. 13. ch. 3. 7. Deut. 26. 6.

[k] ch. 2. 11. & 5. 4, 5. Ps. 81. 6. [l] Gen. 47. 11.

oppression or wrong they will feign occasions for it, and pretend the existence in others of the same evil purposes which they cherish themselves. Looking through the flimsy veil with which their real motives were covered, we see plainly that hatred of their religion, envy at their prosperity, and a covetous desire of possessing their riches, prompted the oppressors of Israel to these nefarious counsels. But it should not be forgotten on the other hand, that the *truly wise* counsels of God in reference to his own people lay deeper than those of their enemies. It is clear from various intimations in the sacred writers, as Josh. 24. 14. Ezek. 20. 5—8, and 23. 8, that the chosen people were beginning to lapse into the idolatry of Egypt, which justly subjected them to the hardships which they were now made to endure ; and the train of events was now also to be laid which was to result in their deliverance from the house of bondage. Their covenant God had a rich blessing in store for them, but he determines, by the antecedent bitterness of their lot, to enhance its sweetness when it came.——¶ *When there falleth out any war.* Heb. תקראנה מלחמה *tikrenah milhamah.* The original here presents a grammatical anomaly in point of concord, the verb ' falleth out,' being in the plural, while the substantive, ' war,' is in the singular. Such instances occur where it is the object of the writer to give at once a collective and distributive sense to the term employed. This import of the phrase our translators have endeavored to intimate by introducing, very properly, the epithet ' any,' which does not occur in the Hebrew. A usage precisely similar is met with in the following passages ; Ps. 119. 103, ' How *sweet are*

thy words unto my taste ;' i. e. all and singular of thy words. Prov. 28. 1, ' The *wicked flee* when no man pursueth ;' i. e. the wicked, one and all, flee. So also 1 Tim. 2. 15, ' Notwithstanding *she* shall be saved in child-bearing, if *they* continue in faith, and charity, and holiness.'

11. *Set over them task-masters,* or, tax-gatherers. Heb. וישימו עליו שרי מסים *va-yasimu alauv sarë missim, and they placed over him* (collect. sing.) *masters of burdens.* The original is frequently used to denote *tribute,* but here, and occasionally elsewhere, it doubtless has the sense of *tasks, burdens, onerous services,* such as were probably imposed upon those who could not or would not pay the appointed tribute. The term therefore which primarily signified *tribute* was employed to denote its substitute or equivalent *service.* Gr. εργων επιστατας, *masters of works.* Chal. ' Princes or prefects evil-entreating (them).' Syr. ' Worst of rulers.' Targ. Jon. ' Prefects who made them to serve.'——¶ *To afflict them with their burdens.* Heb. ענתו בסבלתם *annotho be-siblotham, to humble him* (collect. sing.) *with their burdens ;* i. e. with the burdens of their imposing ; the suffix ' their' having reference to the Egyptians and not the Israelites. It is worthy of notice that the term ענה *anah, afflict,* here used is the very term in which God had predicted to Abraham, hundreds of years before the hard lots of his seed ; Gen. 15. 13, ' And they shall *afflict* (ועני *ve-innu*) them four hundred years.' Their purpose evidently was by their severe exactions of tribute and labor not only to afflict and impoverish them, but utterly to break down their spirits, to destroy their energy, and thus eventually to check their prodigious increase. With this view they

were suddenly reduced to a state of vassalage ; they were declared to be the absolute property of the crown ; and the whole of the male population being told off into companies, was employed night and day under their task-masters, upon public works, and driven like cattle into the fields. They were compelled to dig clay, to make bricks, to bear burdens, and to build cities, whilst at the same time no doubt the greatest cruelties were exercised towards them. Of this period of the Jewish history, Josephus thus speaks : ' And having, in length of time, forgotten the benefits they had received from Joseph, particularly the crown being now come into another family, they became very abusive to the Israelites, and contrived many ways of afflicting them ; for they enjoined them to cut a great number of channels for the river, and to build walls for their cities, and ramparts that they might restrain the river, and hinder its waters from stagnating, upon its running over its own banks. They set them also to build pyramids ; and by all this wore them out, and forced them to learn all sorts of mechanical arts, and to accustom themselves to hard labor.' All this was done under the expectation that multitudes of them would perish from over exertion, whilst all would become so enfeebled as that the progress of population would be effectually checked. But as usual where men set themselves to counteract the fixed purposes of God, the result proved directly contrary to their anticipations. When the language of his decree is, ' Increase and multiply,' it is equally idle and impious for the edict of puny mortals to proclaim, ' Abstain and be diminished.'——
¶ *And they built treasure cities.* Heb. דריבן ערי מסכנות, *va-yiben arë miskenoth, and he built* (collect. sing.) *cities of store,* as the phrase is rendered 2 Chron. 16. 4, ' And they smote Ijon, and Dan, and Abel-maim, and all the *store-cities* (מסכנות *miskenoth*) of

Naphtali ;' and 17. 12, ' And Jehoshaphat waxed great exceedingly ; and he built in Judah castles, and *cities of store* (מסכנות *miskenoth*).' Different versions, however, present different renderings, among which are *store-houses, granaries, fortresses,* and *walled towns.* The Chal. has ' Cities of the house of treasure ;' i. e. cities in which treasures are deposited ; but what kind of treasures we are not informed. Probably they were cities that served not so much for places where the king laid up his riches, as for depots and granaries for corn. Syr. and Arab. ' Store-houses for corn.' This is confirmed by 2 Chron. 32. 28, from which we learn that Hezekiah caused the erection of ' *store-houses* (מסכנות *miskenoth*) for the increase of corn, and wine, and oil.' The Gr. renders it by πολεις οχυρας, *fortified cities,* not because this is the primary meaning of the original words, but because it was proper and customary that cities which were to be made repositories for the safe keeping of any articles whatever should be enclosed by walls and strongly fortified. Large armies were no doubt subsisted even in times of peace by the kings of Egypt, which would make such depots necessary ; and perhaps the very force required to carry into execution the measures against the Israelites would lead to the erection of these places as public stores. The Vulg. has ' urbes tabernaculorum,' *cities of tabernacles,* undoubtedly from mistaking the original for משכנות *mishkenoth,* which signifies *tabernacles.*——
¶ *Pithom and Raamses.* The Jerus. Targ. makes these places to be *Tanis* and *Pelusium ;* but nothing certain can be determined respecting their site. As the land of Goshen, however, is called ' the land of Rameses,' Gen. 47. 11, there is reason to believe that the latter town was in that land, to which it gave or from which it received its name. See Professor Stuart's Course of Hebrew Study, Vol. II., Excursus II., which con-

12 But the more they afflicted them, the more they multiplied and grew. And they were grieved because of the children of Israel.

13 And the Egyptians made the children of Israel to serve with rigour.

14 And they ᵐmade their lives

m ch. 2. 23. & 6. 9. Numb 20. 15. Acts 7. 19, 34.

tains a very able and interesting view of the topography of Goshen.

12. *The more they afflicted them*, &c. Heb. כאשר רענו אתו *ka-asher ye-annu otho*, *according as they afflicted him* (collect. sing.), *so he multiplied and so he brake forth* (into a multitude). The latter verb יפרץ *yiphrotz* is the same as that which occurs Gen. 28. 14, to denote a rapid and, as it were, a *bursting* increase and diffusion ; ' Thou shalt *spread abroad* (תפרץ *tiphrotz*) to the west, and to the east, and to the north, and to the south.' The historian's words depict to us the conflict between the favor of God and the cruelty of the Egyptian king. The more his people suffered from the tyranny of their masters, the more prolific the women proved to be, thus showing, that ' there is no wisdom nor understanding nor counsel against the Lord.' Some commentators have been disposed to resort to natural causes to account for this amazing increase, but we are satisfied with the solution offered by the words of the promise, Gen. 15. 5, ' Look now toward heaven and tell the stars, if thou be able to number them—so shall thy seed be.'——¶ *They were grieved because of the children of Israel.* Heb. יקצו *yakutzu*. The leading idea is doubtless that of mingled *chagrin* and *abhorrence*. Finding that, in spite of all their efforts, the people continued to increase, they were filled with inward vexation, and there was something *irksome* in the very thought of the hated race of Israel. Chal. ' There was tribulation (vexation) to the Egyptians by reason of the children of Israel.' Gr. εβδελυσσοντο, *they were abominated*, just as one is said to be ' scandalized' by that which *is* a cause of offence ; they

regarded the Israelites as an abomination. The import of the original word may be gathered from its use in the following connexions. Gen. 27. 46, ' I am *weary* (קצתי) of my life, because of the daughters of Heth.' Num. 21. 5, ' Our soul *loatheth* (קצה) this light bread.' Lev. 20. 23, ' They committed all these things, and therefore I *abhorred* (אקץ) them.' A passage still more to the point occurs Num. 22. 3, where a like cause of vexation is hinted at ; ' And Moab was sore afraid of the people, because they were many ; and Moab *was distressed* (וירקץ) because of the children of Israel ;' where Ainsworth renders, as in Gen. 27. 46, ' was irked.'

13. *With rigor.* Heb. בפרך *bepharek*, *with fierceness.* Gr. βια, *with force.* Chal. ' With hardness.' From the original פרך *pherek* comes the Latin *ferox* and the English *fierce.* The Israelites were subsequently prohibited from ruling in this manner over their brethren, Lev. 25. 46, ' But over your brethren, the children of Israel, ye shall not rule one over another *with rigor* (בפרך *bepherek*) ;' i. e. without mercy. So far were the pretended fears of the Egyptians from working within them the least sentiment of clemency, that they were evidently goaded on by the frustration of their hopes, to a still more relentless course of oppression. Wicked men are slow to be taught, when their mad schemes are defeated, that God fights against them ; and even if such a thought now and then glances upon their minds, they seem to be stung and exasperated by it, to rush on yet more recklessly in the way of rebellion. This is strikingly evident from the sequel of the present narrative.

14. *Made their lives bitter*, &c. Gr

καrωδυνων αυτων rην ζωην, *made sorrow-ful their life.* 'Of a bad man it is said, in the East, ' He makes the lives of his servants bitter.' Also, ' Ah! the fellow: the heart of his wife is made bitter.' ' My soul is bitter.' ' My heart is like the bitter tree.'—*Roberts.* The intensity of their hardships could not well be better expressed, for as nothing is sweeter than life, it is only the ex-tremest misery that can render exist-ence itself grievous and burdensome. ——¶ *In mortar.* Heb. בחמר *behomer;* more properly ' in clay' of which bricks are made. This is considered by some as subversive of the statement of Josephus, that the pyramids were built by the Israelites, as it is well known that they are constructed of *stone,* in-stead of *brick.* But all the pyramids are not of stone, as in the province of Fayoum, the ancient Arsinoe, as also at Dashour and Saccara, pyramids of sun-dried brick are still found in a remarkable degree of preservation. Yet even if they were all of them stone structures, it is not a legitimate con-clusion that because the Hebrews work-ed in brick, they therefore did not work in stone also. After all, however, the agency of the Israelites in rearing the pyramids is a point on which nothing positive can be asserted, although it is no doubt safe to affirm that, *if* the pyramids were built during the bondage of the Is-raelites, they were engaged upon them, and indeed upon all the public works which were then undertaken. Prisoners and slaves would seem to have been generally employed in such labors ; for it was the proud boast of some of the princes of that country, that no Egyptian hand had labored in the greatest of their works. ' What masses were employ-ed, and how profusely human life was wasted, is evinced by the statement in a previous note, that Necho worked away 100,000 lives in the attempt to cut a canal from the Nile to the Red Sea. Things are much the same now

in the same country. Mehemet Ali, the Pasha of Egypt, obliged 150,000 men, chiefly Arabs from Upper Egypt, to work on his canal connecting the Nile with the sea at Alexandria: 20,000 of the number perished during the progress of the work. A new canal was in pro-gress when Carne was at Alexandria. That writer says : ' The bed of the canal presented a novel spectacle, being filled with a vast number of Arabs of various colors, toiling in the intense heat of the day, while their Egyptian (?) task-masters, with whips in their hands, watched the progress of their la-bor. It was a just and lively repre-sentation of the children of Israel forced to toil by their oppressive masters of old. The wages Mahmoud allowed to these unfortunate people, whom he had obliged to quit their homes and families in Upper Egypt, were only a penny a day and a ration of bread.' (' Letters from the East,' p. 71, 72.) Thus were the lives of the Israelites ' made bit-ter with hard bondage.' '—*Pict. Bib* ——¶ *In all manner of hard service in the field.* That is, in all kinds of agri-cultural labor. We may here remark, that although the condition of the He-brews in Egypt at this time was one of bondage, yet it does not appear to have been that of *house-slaves* or *personal servants.* It was rather a servitude which consisted in being subject to very grievous and excessive exactions im-posed by public authority. They were slaves to the *state* rather than to in-dividuals. In this respect their bondage differed very considerably from that which is unhappily common in our own country. It resembled more the con-dition of the *serfs* or *vassals* of feudal times, who held their lands at the pleasure of their lords, and who were subject to any exactions of rent or labor at the will of the baron. It appears clear from Ex. 12. 38, that the Hebrews as a body had continued to hold prop-erty of their own, though heavy bur-

bitter with hard bondage, [n] in mortar, and in brick, and in all manner of service in the field : all their

n Ps. 81. 6.

dens had been laid upon them ; and the accounts given elsewhere of the offerings and presents made to the tabernacle, &c., make it evident that the nation as such had not been reduced to precisely *that kind of slavery* with which we are familiar in modern times. They had only been subject to severe and oppressive demands of service, in behalf of the king of Egypt and his officers. Still it was a state of cruel suffering to which an innocent people, against the faith of covenants, were condemned, and such as could not but in the end draw down the judgments of Heaven. But let us not forget the wise and ultimately beneficent purposes which these afflictions were designed to subserve. To the suffering Israelites they were at once *penal* and *disciplinary.* One great end to be attained by them was, that they might be inspired with so deep an abhorrence of the land of their oppressions, that the prospect of returning to Canaan should become more and more refreshing to their hearts, and that when once embarked in the journey thither, they might, remembering the wormwood and the gall, feel no desire to retrace their steps, and fix themselves again in the house of bondage. And as the ensuing narrative acquaints us with the fact, that notwithstanding all their previous calamities, many of them, during the sojourn in the wilderness, did actually project a return to Egypt, we can easily conjecture what would have been the case had they lived in ease, in fulness, and in pleasure, in the place of their sojourn.

15. *The king of Egypt spake to the Hebrew midwives.* Finding himself baffled in his first scheme of open and atrocious wrong, he now resorts to a secret stratagem of a more bloody character to compass his ends. This re-

service wherein they made them serve *was* with rigour.

15 ¶ And the king of Egypt spake to the Hebrew midwives (of which

quires to be somewhat more particularly considered. The original word for ' midwives' (מילדת *meyalledoth*) is not a substantive, but a participle, signifying *those who cause to bring forth,* and the words, according to several of the ancient versions, and some modern critics, may be rendered, ' And the king spake to those who made or aided the Hebrew women to bring forth ;' thus understanding from the original ' midwives of the Hebrew women,' instead of ' Hebrew midwives.' The construction certainly renders it in a degree doubtful whether they were Egyptian or Hebrew women. On the one hand it is difficult to suppose that the king should have entrusted such an order to Hebrew women. Could he have supposed that they would conspire with him in an attempt to extinguish their own race ? And when they excused themselves by the plea mentioned v. 19, could he have relied implicitly on their word, without suspecting fraud, had they been Israelitish women ? Yet he seems to have admitted the truth of their statement without the slightest hesitation. This was natural, provided the women were Egyptians, but less so if they were not. It is indeed said, ver. 17, that these women ' feared God,' and consequently refused to obey the royal mandate ; from which it is inferred that they must have been Hebrew women. But the original ' Elohim' is here preceded by the article, and may, it is said, be rendered ' the gods,' i. e. the powers above ; implying merely such a belief in a divine being and a superintending providence, as was perhaps generally prevalent in this early age of the world. But then, on the other hand, (1.) The more obvious import of the text leads us to understand Hebrew women as

the name of one *was* Shiphrah, and the name of the other Puah ;)
16 And he said, When ye do the office of a midwife to the Hebrew

women, and see *them* upon the stools ; if it *be* a son, then ye shall kill him ; but if it *be* a daughter, then she shall live.

---

meant, whether we regard the construction of the original, or of the translation. Doubtless there *were* Hebrew women capable of employing themselves in this service in behalf of their kindred, and if Egyptian women had been procured, it would have excited suspicion at once, and perhaps prevented their access to them. (2) It cannot be denied that the character given of them, v. 17, as 'fearers of God,' applies more naturally to Hebrew women, who had been instructed in the religion of their fathers. The phrase, we think, is indicative of *general character*, and not of any sudden dread with which they may have been smitten on this occasion. Being habitually under the influence of a salutary fear of God, they could not be persuaded for a moment to entertain the thought of such horrid cruelty, though they may have been restrained, from motives of policy, from expressly saying to the king at the time that they would have no hand in the perpetration of such a deed. (3) Their names are purely Hebraic and not Egyptian. (4) As to the improbability of Pharaoh's selecting Hebrew women to be the instruments of such a cruel scheme against their own flesh and blood, it may be replied that the same reason held against his appointing Hebrew officers over their own countrymen, which yet we find he actually did, Ex. 5. 14. On the whole, therefore, we cannot but conclude that the midwives were Hebrew and not Egyptian women, notwithstanding that Josephus affirms the contrary.—¶ *The name of the one was Shiphrah,* &c. Two individuals only are mentioned, but as this number would be wholly inadequate to the service of so many thousand Israelites, it is with great reason supposed, that Shiphrah and Puah were

the chief persons of the profession, having the direction of the rest. We learn from Plutarch, that some of the nations of antiquity had schools established among them where females were taught the obstetrical art. This was perhaps the office of these two individuals.
16. *See them upon the stools.* Heb. עַל הָאָבְנָיִם *al ha-obnayim, upon the stones.* Commentators have been much divided in opinion as to the nature and use of the objects intended by the term here translated *stools*, but which is literally *stones*. It would seem perhaps at first view, that they were some contrivance for procuring a more easy delivery for women in labor. But besides that, stone-seats were obviously very unfit for such a purpose, the Heb. word in Ex. 7. 19, signifies *a vessel of stone for holding water, a trough*. A far more probable interpretation, therefore, is made out by referring the pronoun ' them,' which it will be observed is not in the original, not to the *mothers*, but to the *children ;* ' When ye see the new-born children laid in the troughs or vessels of stone, for the purpose of being washed, ye shall destroy the boys.' A passage from the travels of Thevenot seems to confirm this construction: ' The kings of Persia are so afraid of being deprived of that power which they abuse, and are so apprehensive of being dethroned, that they destroy the children of their female relations, when they are brought to bed of boys, *by putting them into an earthen trough*, where they suffer them to starve ;' that is, probably, under pretence of preparing to wash them, they let them pine away or destroy them in the water. This view of the meaning represents the midwives above spoken of, as acting in the capacity of *superintendents, for they are not*

17 But the midwives o feared God, and did not p as the king of Egypt commanded them, but saved the men-children alive.

18 And the king of Egypt called for the midwives, and said unto them, Why have ye done this thing, and have saved the men-children alive?

o Prov. 16. 6. p Dan. 3. 16, 18. & 6. 13. Acts 5. 29.

19 And q the midwives said unto Pharaoh, Because the Hebrew women *are* not as the Egyptian women; for they *are* lively, and are delivered ere the midwives come in unto them.

20 r Therefore God dealt well with the midwives; and the people multiplied, and waxed very mighty.

q See Josh. 2. 4, &c. 2 Sam. 17. 19, 20. r Prov. 11. 18. Eccles. 8. 12. Isai. 3. 10. Hebr. 6. 10.

supposed to place the children on the 'stools,' but to examine them after they are placed there by others. It is evident that if they actually assisted at the birth, the sex of the infant would be known without the necessity of inspecting its person during its ablutions at the trough.——¶ *If it be a son,* &c. The reason of the order is obvious; the state had nothing to apprehend on the score of insurrection from the weaker sex, and as they were fairer than the daughters of Egypt, they would naturally be preserved, with a view to their finally becoming inmates of the harems of their lords.

17. *The midwives feared God,* &c. Their faith shines conspicuous in this, for they must have been aware that it was dangerous to incur the king's wrath by disobeying his orders. Tyrants are not wont to suffer their decrees to be disregarded with impunity, and it was no doubt at the peril of their lives that they gave way to the dictates of piety towards God rather than comply with the injunction of the king.

19. *Because the Hebrew women are lively,* &c. Heb. הָיוֹת *ha-yoth;* i. e. quick and strong in bearing; being possessed of greater natural vigor and robustness of constitution. It is well known that women inured to hard labor have but little pain in child-bearing, compared with those who are accustomed to an easier mode of life. It is worthy of note also that the original here is the term usually applied to *wild beasts* (see Note on Gen. 1. 24),

and the latent implication may be, that they brought forth somewhat after the manner of the beasts of the forest, without requiring any obstetrical aid. This assertion of the midwives was doubtless true in itself, although not the whole truth; but the withholding a part of the truth from those who would take advantage of the whole to injure or destroy the innocent, is not only lawful but laudable.

20. *God dealt well with the midwives.* We may doubtless fairly infer from this that, in some way not expressly recorded, they were favored with special tokens of the divine approbation for the conduct they had evinced. At the same time, the fact of granting to the Israelites such a continued extraordinary multiplication was in itself a 'dealing well' with the midwives. They were no doubt many of them mothers themselves, and they could not but rejoice in the preservation and the increase of their families, nor could the general favor thus bestowed upon the nation fail to redound to them. Indeed, we are strongly inclined to consider the final clause of this verse as perfectly synonimous with the expression 'made them houses,' in the next. The connexion between the two will be obvious from the remarks that immediately follow. In the mean time let us not fail to observe, that an upright and exemplary conduct, by whomsoever displayed, may be of the most eminent service to a whole community. Even a few feeble but right-minded women may, without their dreaming of

21 And it came to pass, because the midwives feared God, ˢthat he made them houses.

ˢ See 1 Sam. 2. 35. 2 Sam. 7. 11, 13, 27, 29. 1 Kings 2. 24. & 11. 38. Ps. 127. 1.

the effects of their deportment, be silently working out the welfare of the state to which they belong.

21. *And it came to pass, because,* &c. The original will easily admit a slight variation in the rendering of this paragraph, which, if we mistake not, will throw light upon the whole context ; ' And it came to pass, because the midwives feared God, and (because) he made them houses (i. e. increased the progeny of the children of Israel), *that* Pharaoh charged all his people saying,' &c. It is important for the English reader to be informed that the original for ' them' is in the *masculine* and not in the *feminine* gender ; so that, without a violent grammatical anomaly, it cannot so properly or primarily be referred to the midwives, as to the families of Israel at large. If the expression, moreover, refers strictly to the midwives, it would have been more natural to insert it in the preceding verse, as explanatory of the manner in which God ' dealt well' with them ; ' Therefore God dealt well with the midwives, *and made them houses.*' But this is not the construction. There is nothing to illustrate his ' dealing well' with them but his multiplying the nation, and as this is the undoubted import of the phrase ' made them houses,' we cannot but consider the two clauses as essentially synonimous. At the same time, there is perhaps no good reason to doubt that the *houses* or *families* of the midwives were intended to be especially, but not exclusively, referred to. *Their* houses shared in a signal manner in the general prosperity. We may now, having endeavored to fix the connexion of the context, consider with more precision the import of the phrase ' made them houses.' We

22 And Pharaoh charged all his people, saying, ᵗEvery son that is born ye shall cast into the river, and every daughter ye shall save alive.

ᵗ Acts 7. 19.

have in the Note on Gen. 16. 2, detailed at length the ideal connexion between *building* and *the begetting of children.* In the scriptural idiom a *house* is a *family,* as the ' house of Judah,' ' the house of Benjamin,' the house of David,' &c., and *to build or make one a house* is to confer upon him a numerous posterity. To the examples there adduced, the following may be added, 2 Sam. 7. 11, ' The Lord telleth thee that he will *make thee an house* (ברת יעשה לך ;' i. e. will give thee a long line of descendants. 1 Kings, 2. 24, ' Now, therefore, as the Lord liveth, which hath established me, and set me on the throne of David my father, and who has *made me an house* (עשה לי ברת), as he promised, &c.,' i. e. given me a prosperous family. The phraseology might be still farther confirmed, but the above will be sufficient to show that the 'blessing' intended was that of a *numerous increase,* and not of a *material habitation,* or any thing of that nature, as some have supposed.

22. *Charged all his people, saying,* &c., leaving it no more to the care of the midwives alone. Frustrated in his former device, the king is now urged on to a higher pitch of enormity, and discarding all secret stratagems for effecting his object, commands *all* his people indiscriminately to destroy the Hebrew male children wherever they should find them. The execution of this bloody command would no doubt lead to scenes of barbarity and cruelty at which every tender feeling of our nature revolts with an inward shudder. Helpless babes would be mercilessly torn from their mothers' arms, and if they did not follow their dear offspring, as they were ruthlessly thrown into the Nile, it was

only because their religious sentiments were stronger than their maternal instincts. But we read, in a subsequent part of the history, a fearful requital of this sanguinary transaction, when Pharaoh and his Egyptian host were overwhelmed in the waters of the Red Sea. 'Righteous art thou, O Lord, because thou hast judged thus.'

REMARKS.—(1, 2.) In the history of the church, it is the special aim of the Spirit to present its humble beginnings in strong contrast with the abundant increase and ample prosperity of its more advanced periods.

(7.) The land of enemies, and the scene of the most grinding oppression, is easily rendered in the providence of God a nursery for the increase of his church.

(8.) Peculiar blessings from God, and fierce opposition from worldly powers, are not unfrequently connected in the lot of the church on earth.

(8.) The people of God would have experienced less ill treatment at the hands of civil governments, were the national benefits which they are instrumental in procuring better appreciated and remembered.

(8, 9.) The prosperity of the righteous is doubtless an eye-sore to evil-minded oppressors ; but those who task their invention to devise methods of affliction are dealing wisely to compass their own destruction. Eccl. 7. 16, 'Make not thyself over wise : why shouldest thou destroy thyself ?'

(10.) Much of the *real* suffering of the saints in all ages has been inflicted on the ground of *hypothetical* offences. 'Lest when there falleth out,' &c.

(11.) Counsels of wickedness ripen rapidly into acts and practices of cruelty.

(13, 14.) The favor of God toward his children in affliction, is often the signal for their oppressors to load them with new burdens of anguish.

(15.) How fiendish is the policy which would employ the tender and susceptible nature of woman in executing deeds of blood !

(17.) The true fear of God will deter the weakest creatures who are capable of cherishing it, from the commission of sin, and when the command of man is put in competition with the command of God, they will boldly say with the intrepid disciples, Acts, 4. 19, 'Whether it be right in the sight of God to hearken unto you more than unto God, judge ye.'

(20.) Even in this world a supreme regard to the will of God seldom goes unrewarded. This reward is sometimes entailed as a precious legacy to generations yet unborn.

(22.) Relentless persecutors proceed from secret subtilty to open cruelty, and downright murder is the resource when other stratagems have failed of effecting their object.

Chapter 2

To what extent the murderous edict mentioned at the close of the foregoing chapter was carried, or how long it continued in force, we are not informed. But when we consider that the love of offspring was an absorbing passion with the Israelites, inasmuch as all their future hopes depended upon and were connected with the possession of a numerous issue, we can easily conceive the horror that must have hung over that ill-fated people so long as the bloody statute remained unrepealed. Yet now, at this very time, when men in their weak counsels proposed utterly to root up the vine of Israel, which had already spread its branches so widely and borne such abundant fruit, it pleased God to call into existence the future Deliverer, and to make the very evils to which his infancy was exposed, the means of his preparation for that high office, which was, in a distant day, to devolve upon him. This remarkable event in the history of oppressed Israel it is the object of the present chapter to relate.

CHAPTER II.

AND there went ᵃa man of the house of Levi, and took *to wife* a daughter of Levi.

ᵃ ch. 6. 20. Numb. 26. 59. 1 Chron. 23. 14.

2 And the woman conceived and bare a son; and ᵇwhen she saw him that he *was a* goodly *child*, she hid him three months.

ᵇ Acts 7. 20. Hebr. 11. 23.

---

1. *And there went· a man,* &c., Heb. דרלך *va-yelek.* According to Calvin, *there had gone ;* implying that the marriage had taken place some time previous to the royal order for the drowning of the male-children. Certain it is that Aaron was three years old at the birth of Moses, and we have no intimation that *his* infancy was in any way exposed to peril. As such an order would naturally be executed with most severity immediately upon its being issued, and as Aaron's infancy was unmolested, it seems a fair presumption that the edict came forth not far from the birth-time of Moses ; so that the pluperfect rendering of the verb may perhaps be considered the most correct. The verb 'to go,' by a peculiarity of idiom in the original, is frequently employed in a sense including not the idea of locomotion, but simply that of *commencing, or entering upon, an action or enterprise ;* thus, Gen. 35. 22, ' And it came to pass, when Israel dwelt in that land, that Reuben *went* and lay with Bilhah his father's concubine.' Deut. 31. 1, ' And Moses *went* and spake these words unto all Israel.' Hos. 3. 1, ' Then said the Lord unto me, *Go*, yet love a woman beloved of her friend.' The word in such connexions may not improperly be considered as an expletive. Something similar occurs in the New Testament, Eph. 2. 17, ' And *came* and preached peace to you.' So also 1 Pet 3. 19, ' By which also he *went* and preached unto the spirits in prison.'—The name of the man here mentioned was Amram, the son of Kohath, the son of Levi, Ex. 6. 16—20, and the name of the woman whom he took to wife was Jochebed, the sister of Kohath, and consequently the aunt of Amram, Ex. 6. 20. Num. 26.

19. Marriage connexions between kindred thus nearly related was afterwards forbidden under the law, Lev. 18. 12, but more indulgence was granted in this and other respects in the early and unsettled state of the commonwealth.

2. *And the woman conceived.* The anxiety and apprehension naturally incident to the delicate situation in which Jochebed found herself, must have been aggravated by terrors more dreadful than the prospective pangs of child-birth, or the loss of life itself. As a wife and a mother in Israel, she was looking and longing for the birth of another man-child ; but that fond expectation was as often dashed by the bitter reflection, that an order had gone forth which would in all probability consign her son, if she should bear one, to the jaws of the devouring crocodile of the Nile. Yet it would seem not improbable from the apostle's words, Heb. 11. 23, that some extraordinary presentiments in the minds of his parents accompanied the birth of this illustrious child, and strengthened the faith under which he was hidden for three months from the rage of the Egyptian dragon, which stood eager for his prey as soon as it should see the light, Rev. 12. 4.——
¶ *When she saw him, that he was a goodly child.* Heb. טוב *tob,* good. The original term, as remarked on Gen. 39. 6, is used to denote bodily endowments, as well as the qualities of the heart, and its import may be learned from the corresponding Gr. phrase employed by Stephen, Acts, 7. 20, αστειος τῳ Θιῳ, *fair to God,* i. e. divinely or exceedingly fair. In Heb. 11. 23, the epithet is the same (αστειον) but rendered ' proper.' The implication obviously is, that an extraordinary beauty distinguished the

3 And when she could not longer hide him, she took for him an ark of bulrushes, and daubed it with slime and with pitch, and put the

---

smiling babe that now reposed in his mother's arms. To the fond eye of maternal affection *every* child is lovely, and we can only account for the strong language used here and elsewhere in regard to Moses, by supposing that his infant features possessed a grace and comeliness that were perhaps without a parallel. We must recognize in this a special providence, for there is no doubt that the uncommon beauty of the child was a strong motive with the parents for so anxiously aiming to secure it from harm. This is clearly intimated in the words of the apostle, Heb. 11. 23, ' By faith Moses, when he was born, was hid three months of his parents, because they saw that he was a proper child,' &c. It may be supposed moreover that this circumstance was ordered by providence in order to afford to Pharoah's daughter a stronger motive for preserving the child. But the dearer the comfort the greater the care, and under their present circumstances we can easily imagine that every lovely lineament in the countenance of her child would weave a new fold of anguished anxiety in her own face as she gazed upon it, and thought of the jeopardy to which he was exposed. For the space of three months she was permitted, through her precautions, from day to day to fondle and nourish the helpless babe, though her heart trembled at the sound of every tread while so employed, just as the miser dreads the noise of approaching footsteps while surveying and counting over his hoarded wealth. But at the end of that period, the rigor of the search on the part of her enemies convinced her that farther concealment would be impracticable, and that she must part with her treasure.

3. *She took for him an ark of bulrushes*, &c. Heb. גמא תבת *tabath gomë, ark of bulrush.* The Egyptian papyrus.

The original term is derived from a verb signifying *to swallow, to sup up, to drink,* and is so named from its remarkably *absorbing* the water where it grows, as appears from Job. 8. 11, ' Can the *rush* (גמא *gomë*) grow up without mire ?' It is a plant growing on the banks of the Nile, and in marshy grounds. The stalk is of a vivid green, of a triangular form, and tapering towards the top. At present it is rarely found more than ten feet long, about two feet or little more of the lower part of the stalk being covered with hollow sharp-pointed leaves which overlap each other like scales, and fortify the most exposed part of the stem. It terminates in a tuft or crown of small grassy filaments, each about a foot long. Near the middle each of these filaments parts into four, and in the point of partition are four branches of flowers, the termination of which is not unlike an ear of wheat in form, but is in fact a soft silky husk. This singular vegetable was used for a variety of purposes, the principal of which was the structure of boats and the manufacture of paper. In regard to the first, we are told by Pliny that a piece of the acacia-tree was put in the bottom to serve as a keel, to which the plants were joined lengthwise, being first sewed together, then gathered up at stem and stern, and made fast by means of a ligature. These vessels are still to be seen on the engraven stones and other monuments of Egyptian antiquity. According to Dr. Shaw, the vessels of bulrushes or papyrus mentioned in sacred and profane history were no other than large fabrics of the same kind with that of Moses, which from the introduction of plank and stronger materials, are now laid aside The prophet's words, Is. 18. 2, ' That sendeth ambassadors by the sea, even in *vessels of bulrushes* upon the waters,'

child therein; and she laid *it* in the flags by the river's brink.

---

are supposed to allude to the same kind of sailing craft. Pliny takes notice of the ' naves papyraceas armentaque Nili;' *ships made of the papyrus, and the equipments of the Nile ;* and Lucan, the poet has, ' Conseritur bibula Memphitis cymba papyro,' *the Memphian (or Egyptian) boat is made of the thirsty papyrus,* where the epithet ' bibula,' *drinking, soaking, thirsty* is particularly remarkable, as corresponding with great exactness to the nature of the plant, and to its Hebrew name. The Egyptian bulrush or papyrus required much water for its growth ; when therefore the river on whose banks it grew was reduced, it perished sooner than other plants. This explains Job, 8. 11, where the circumstance is referred to as an image of transient prosperity.—— ¶ *Daubed it with slime and with pitch.* Heb. בחמר *ba-hemor, with bitumen,* or mineral pitch. See Note on Gen. 11. 3. The '*bitumen*' cemented the rushes or reeds together, the pitch served to keep out the water. ' There seems to be considerable analogy between the ark or boat in which Moses was deposited, and the curious vessels which are at the present day employed in crossing the Tigris. They are perfectly circular in shape, and are made with the leaves of the date-palm, forming a kind of basket-work, which is rendered impervious to the water by being thickly coated with bitumen.' *Pict. Bib.*——¶ *Laid it in the flags.* Heb. בסוף *bassuph, in the sea-weed, or sedge.* The *suph* was probably a general term for sea or river-weed. The Red Sea is always called, in the Scriptures ים סוף *yam suph,* or *the weedy-sea,* as some suppose, from the great variety of marine vegetables which grow in it, and which at low water are left in great quantities upon the shores. But see Note on Ex. 13. 18.

4 c And his sister stood afar off, to wit what would be done to him.

c ch. 15. 20. Numb. 26. 59.

---

4. *And his sister stood afar off,* &c. His sister Miriam undoubtedly, as we have no account of his having any other. She was unquestionably older than Aaron, or she would have been unfit for such an office on this occasion. The incident makes it plain that the little ark, though made water-tight, was not deposited on the bosom of the river, where it would be borne away by the current, but on the margin of the stream, where perhaps the finder would infer that it had lodged, after having floated down from above. Throughout the whole of this transaction, which was no doubt supernaturally suggested, no mention is made of the father. That every thing was done with his privity and consent we cannot doubt, for the apostle couples both the parents in his encomium on their faith ; but the case was probably one in which the faith of the mother was more decided and active than that of the father, and has therefore more prominence given it in the sacred narrative. The proceeding detailed is a beautiful illustration of the connexion which should always exist between the diligent use of means and a pious trust in Providence. Instead of sitting down in sullen despair, or passive reliance on divine interposition, every thing is done which can be done by human agency to secure the wished-for result. The careful mother pitches every seam and chink of the frail vehicle as anxiously as if its precious deposit were to owe its preservation solely to her care and diligence. Nor even yet does she think she has done enough. Miriam her daughter must go, and at a distance watch the event, and strange would it be if she did not herself in the mean time take a station where she could watch the watcher. And here we behold all the parties standing precisely

5 ¶ And the ᵈ daughter of Pharaoh
came down to wash *herself* at the
river; and her maidens walked
along by the river's side : and
when she saw the ark among the

ᵈ Acts 7. 21.

flags, she sent her maid to fetch it.
6 And when she had opened *it.*
she saw the child : and behold, the
babe wept. And she had compassion on him, and said, This *is*
one of the Hebrew's children.

upon the line where the province of human sagacity, foresight, and industry
ends, and providential succor begins.
The mother has done her part. The
rushes, the slime, and the pitch were
her prudent and necessary preparations ;
and the great God has been at the same
time preparing *his* materials, and ar-
ranging *his* instruments. He causes
every thing to concur, not by miraculous
influence, but by the simple and natural
operation of second causes, to bring
about the issue designed in his counsels
from everlasting. The state of the
weather, the flux of the current, the
promenade of Pharaoh's daughter, the
state of her feelings, the steps of her
attendants, are all so overruled at that
particular juncture, as to lead to the
discovery, the rescue, and the disposal
of the child ! But let us not anticipate
the thread of the story.

5. *The daughter of Pharoah came*
down to wash herself at the river. Heb.
עַל הַיְאֹר *al ha-yeor,* at or *by the river.*
Gr. επι τον ποταμον, to be translated in
the same manner, implying that the
washing, which was probably a religious
ablution, and not a proper bathing,
was performed just at the *river's brink.*
The washing of Naaman the Syrian,
on the other hand, is said to have been
in the Jordan (בירדן *ba-yarden*) and
not *at* it, because he entered further into
the stream. We advert to the phraseology here principally for the purpose
of showing the relation of the Gr. rendering to a parallel passage in Rev. 9.
14, ' Loose the four angels which are
bound *at* (επι *at,* not *in*) the great river
Euphrates ;' i. e. the four angels which
nad hitherto been providentially restrained or confined *in the vicinity* of

the great river Euphrates. ' Angels'
here is a symbolical term for the *na-*
tions or *people* over which they are represented in prophecy as presiding.
See Dan. 10. 3. The import of the command is, that those obstructions which
had hitherto opposed the issuing forth
and the desolating spread of four great
political powers in the region bordering
upon the Euphrates, should now be removed and free scope given them.
These powers were the origin of the
Ottoman empire, which, as it was announced by the sixth trumpet, was to
be destroyed by the sixth vial. Rev.
16. 12.——¶ *She sent her maid to take*
it. Heb. ותקחה *vattikkaheha, and took*
it ; i. e. she took it by the hand of her
maid ; by which term is meant the
maid who more immediately waited
upon her, as the word (אמתה) is different from that (נערתיה) translated
' maidens.'

6. *She saw the child : and behold, the*
babe wept. Rather according to the
Heb. ' And she saw him, the child ; and
behold a male-infant weeping !' The
Eng. word ' babe,' as it does not dis-
criminate the sex, is not an exact or
adequate rendering of the original נער
naar, which strictly denotes a *male*
child, and is here used expressly for
that purpose.——¶ *She had compassion*
on him. Or, Heb. תחמל *tahmol, mer-*
cifully spared him. If there be an object in nature more calculated than any
other to interest and affect the susceptible heart of woman, it was that which
now presented itself to the eye of this
Egyptian princess—a beautiful infant,
deserted by its parents, exposed to the
most imminent peril, and expressing by
the moving testimony of tears its sense

7 Then said his sister to Pharaoh's daughter, Shall I go, and call to thee a nurse of the Hebrew women, that she may nurse the child for thee?

8 And Pharaoh's daughter said to her, Go. And the maid went and called the child's mother.

9 And Pharaoh's daughter said unto her, Take this child away and nurse it for me and I will give *thee* thy wages. And the woman took the child and nursed it.

10 And the child grew, and she brought him unto Pharaoh's daughter, and he became e her son. And she called his name Moses: and she said, Because I drew him out of the water.

e Acts 7. 21.

---

of that misery of which it had not yet acquired the consciousness. The story told itself. The situation in which the child was found explained the cruel occasion. The covenant-sign which he carried engraven on his flesh, declared to whom he belonged, and notwithstanding the scruples which must have arisen from his parentage, his outcast condition made an irresistible appeal to the bosom of Pharaoh's daughter.

7. *Then said his sister*, &c. Who no doubt came up and joined the train, as if by accident. If she had not been previously instructed by her mother what to say on the contingency of such an occurrence as now actually took place, we cannot but refer this suggestion on the part of a little girl to an immediate inward prompting from above. How else should it have entered her thoughts to propose making the *mother* of the exposed infant its *nurse?* Can we fail to acknowledge the secret hand of the Lord of hosts, ' who is wonderful in counsel and excellent in working?'

9. *Take this child away and nurse it for me*, &c. No mere human writer could here have well forborne to dilate in glowing terms on the transports of the happy mother as she again clasped her beloved babe to her bosom, free from the fear of having him again torn from her. What a joyful change! The fond mother permitted to do that for princely hire and under royal protection which she would have given her life for the privilege of doing for nothing, could she have done it with safety to her

child! ' I will give thee thy wages.' Wages, indeed! What ' wages' would not *she* have given for the extacy she now enjoyed in the prospect of acting the mother to the son of her womb! What sentiments of adoring wonder and grateful praise must have thrilled her heart in view of the overwhelming goodness so kindly and unexpectedly vouchsafed to her from the God of all comfort!

10. *She brought him*, &c. At what age the future deliverer of Israel was transferred from the care of his mother to the palace and the court of Egypt, we are not informed. It would seem from the history that he was old enough to have learnt the principles of his ancestral religion, in which his mother would not fail to instruct him; and though it was somewhat of a renewed trial to her to part with her son, under the apprehension that the influence of a heathen and hostile court might alienate his tender mind from the love of God and his people, yet she would doubtless infer from the past incidents of his life that something great was in store for him, and that the same tutelary providence which had watched over his infancy, would make his childhood and youth and mature age its special care. He came accordingly into the relation of an adopted son to Pharaoh's daughter, and was by her, for an end of which she little dreamed, ' trained up in all the wisdom of the Egyptians.' As the book of Revelation is constructed with a continual or running reference to the events of the Old Testament history,

11 ¶ And it came to pass in those days, ᶠ when Moses was grown, that he went out unto his brethren,

ᶠ Acts 7. 23, 24. Hebr. 11. 24, 25, 26.

we cannot doubt that there is a real though covert allusion to the history of Moses in the vision, Ch. 12, of the dragon, the sun-clad woman, and the child to which she gave birth. The dragon's standing before the woman ready to devour her child as soon as it should be born, is strikingly in analogy with the bloody edict of Pharaoh, whom the prophets denominate the Egyptian dragon, Ezek. 29. 3, while the child's being caught up to God and his throne, has an equally distinct reference to the wonderful preservation and elevation of Moses as here described.——¶ *She called his name Moses.* Heb. משה *Mosheh*, from the verb משה *mashah*, *to draw out*, a term occurring Ps. 18. 16, ' He sent from above, he took me ; he *drew me* (ימשני *yamsheni*) out of many waters ;' where the Psalmist seems to liken his preservation to that of Moses, unless indeed, which we rather incline to believe, he is giving an allegorical history of the church from its earlier periods, and has here a designed but mystic allusion to the very person and deliverance of Moses, in whose preservation that of Israel was concentrated. It has indeed been a matter of dispute among critics whether the name were truly of Hebrew or Egyptian origin. Yet the former is most probable, as a Hebrew etymology seems to be designedly given it by the sacred writer. Although the Egyptians did not speak the Hebrew language, yet as it appears from Ex. 11. 2, that the two people lived in a great measure intermingled together, the language of each might have been to a considerable extent understood by the other ; and in the present case it would not be unnatural that a Hebrew child should have bestowed upon it a Hebrew name.

and looked on their ᵍ burdens : and he spied an Egyptian smiting an Hebrew, one of his brethren.

ᵍ ch. 1. 11.

11. *When Moses was grown.* Heb. רגדל *yigdal, had become great,* not in stature only, but in repute, influence, and consideration at court. This is in several unequivocal instances the force of the original, and it is said of him by Stephen that he ' was mighty both in word and deed,' as well as that he had attained the full age of forty years. ——¶ *Went out unto his brethren, and looked on their burdens.* Heb. וירא בסבלתם *va-yar besiblotham.* Gr. κατανοησας τον πονον αυτων, *considered their labor.* Chal. ' Saw their servitude.' Verbs of the senses often imply in the Scripture idiom a connected working of the emotions or affections of the heart. Here ' looking upon' is *viewing with sympathy and compassion, having his heart touched with the spectacle.* Gen. 29. 32, ' And Leah conceived and bare a son, and she called his name Reuben : for she said, surely the Lord hath *looked upon* my afflictions ;' i. e. hath mercifully regarded. Eccl. 1. 16, ' My heart *had great experience* of wisdom and knowledge ;' Heb. ' My heart *saw* wisdom and knowledge.' Eccl. 2. 1, ' I said in my heart, go to now, I will prove thee with mirth, therefore *enjoy* pleasure ;' Heb. ' *see* pleasure.' Ps. 118. 7. ' Therefore shall I *see* (my desire) *upon* them that hate me.' We must regard this as the incipient working of that noble spirit which finally prompted Moses to forego the honors of the court of Egypt, and cast in his lot with the despised people of Israel. Ease and affluence generally tend to deaden the sensibilities of the heart to the wants and woes of others. But Moses seems never to have forgotten his extraction, nor to have lost his sympathies with the chosen race. He remembered that the oppressed and suffering Israelites

were his nearest and dearest relations, and though now ignorant perhaps of the part which he was destined to act in their deliverance, he was unable to relish a solitary selfish joy, while *they* were eating the bread and drinking the water of affliction. He therefore goes out to look upon their misery, or as Stephen says, Acts, 7. 23, ' It came into his heart to visit his brethren,' and though for the present he can neither remove nor alleviate it, yet he is determined to evince his willingness to be a partaker in it. But the most fitting commentary upon this passage is found in the words of the apostle, Heb. 11. 23—26, ' By faith Moses, when he was come to years, refused to be called the son of Pharaoh's daughter ; choosing rather to suffer affliction with the people of God, than to enjoy the pleasures of sin for a season ; esteeming the reproach of Christ greater riches than the treasures in Egypt: for he had respect unto the recompense of the reward.' By his ' refusing to be called the son of Pharaoh's daughter,' we are not probably to understand that he rejected *the nominal appellation*, but according to the true force of the orignal, which has reference rather to *the reality of things* than to their *denomination*, he refused to be *treated* as her son, he *positively declined* all the honor and aggrandizement which was implied in that relation. This was his deliberate choice, and perhaps no man was ever called to make a choice under circumstances more trying, or made one which redounded more to his credit and glory than this of Moses. It is to be remembered that he was at this time of mature age, ' full forty years old,' says Stephen. He had reached the grand climacteric of life, all his faculties perfectly ripened, and his judgment calm, unclouded, and dispassionate. Were not this the case, had he been now just emerging from youth, with all the sanguine and enthusiastic ardor of dawning manhood upon

him, it might have been regarded as the effect of a rash excitement, as a sudden sally of the buoyant temperament of his age, and one which he would afterwards have regretted or condemned. Had it occurred later in life, when the powers and energies of his mind were on the wane, when the pursuits of ambition and the prospects of pleasure had vanished, it might have been stigmatized as the act of an old worn-out courtier, whose disgusted satiety of this world's good had driven him to the sorry refuge of seeking something better in another. It might easily have been characterised as the mean compromise of a man in his dotage with an uneasy conscience, for having squandered his youthful prime and his manly meridian in the service of the world to the neglect of his Maker. But every such imputation is cut off by the facts of the case. It was not a step prompted by the precipitate ardor of youth, nor one dictated by the timid or sordid policy of age. It was a decision formed under circumstances in which *deep principle*, and not a *passionate impulse*, must have been the ruling motive ; for while in a worldly sense he had nothing to hope from a transfer of himself, he had, on the other hand, every thing to lose. We have only to appeal to our knowledge of human nature to learn the difficulty, and consequently the virtue, of such a sacrifice as Moses now made. When we compare the respective states of the Egyptian and the Israelitish people, it would seem to human view that the lot of the meanest Egyptian was preferable to that of the highest Israelite. Yet Moses voluntarily gave up the one for the other ; ' the honors of the palace for the ignominy of the brick-yard.' Though he was the adopted son of Pharaoh's daughter, and, for aught that appears to the contrary, was the presumptive heir to the crown, yet he refused not to come down from this preeminent distinction, and to cast in his lot with the despised and embondaged seed of Jacob. History affords us some few instances where kings have laid aside their purple and abdicated their thrones. But in all such cases they have descended to a rank in private life which was surrounded by ease, affluence, and continued respectability ; so that their sacrifices were relieved by many countervailing considerations. But Moses descended from the dignity of a court to the degradation of a slave. What was there in the vaunted condescension of Dioclesian or Charles the Vth. to be compared with this? And where, in all the annals of time, shall we find *such* a surrender made from *such* motives?——

¶ *Spied an Egyptian smiting an Hebrew.* Probably one of the task-masters. As the original word for *smiting* (מכה *makkeh*) is the same with that rendered *slew* (יך *yak*) in the next verse, it is to be presumed that the Egyptian was actually attempting to kill the Hebrew, and that had it not been for the intervention of Moses, he would have effected his purpose. Thus Ps. 136. 17, ' To him which *smote* (מכה *makkeh*) great kings ;' i. e. that slew. It is important to view this incident in connexion with what Stephen says of it, Acts, 7. 23—25, ' And when he was full forty years old, it came into his heart to visit his brethren the children of Israel. And seeing one of them suffer wrong, he defended him, and avenged him that was oppressed, and smote the Egyptian : for he supposed his brethren would have understood how that God by his hand would deliver them : but they understood not.' It is undoubtedly to be supposed that Moses was now acting under a divine commission, and that an immediate impulse from the Spirit of God prompted him to the deed here recorded. This is to be inferred from the words of Stephen, ' for he supposed his brethren would have understood how that God by his hand would deliver them ;' implying that Moses himself

understood this to be the fact. It is however worthy of note that Diodorus Siculus informs us that a law existed in Egypt, which might have been at this time in force. ' That whoever saw his fellow-creature either killed by another, or violently assaulted, and did not either apprehend the murderer, or rescue the oppressed if he could ; or if he could not, made not an information thereof to the magistrate, himself should be put to death.' For aught that can be affirmed to the contrary, Moses might have been warranted on this ground alone in proceeding to the extremity he did. The act however cannot be pleaded as a precedent on occasions that are not similar. It bore a striking resemblance to the conduct of Phineas on another occasion, Num. 25. 7, 13, a conduct which was certainly approved of God. If it be objected that the secrecy observed by Moses both in performing the act and in disposing of the body, is scarcely consistent with the idea of his being empowered by the call and authority of God to execute his pleasure on this occasion, it may be observed, that as his calling, though clear to himself, had not yet been publicly manifested or accredited, it was fitting that a temporary concealment should be drawn over the present occurrence. Thus Ehud, Judg. 3. 21, though moved by an influence from above, slew Eglon king of Moab in a private chamber ; and Gideon, Judg. 6. 27, before his office of deliverer was publicly known, demolished the altar of Baal by night. Again, if it be asked what reason Moses had to suppose that his brethren would have understood that he was acting by a divine commission, it may be answered, 'that the marvellous circumstances of his birth and preservation, and subsequent training in the court of Pharaoh, were doubtless matters well known and much talked of among the nation of Israel, from which they might reasonably infer that he was raised up for some extraordi

12 And he looked this way and that way, and when he saw that *there was* no man, he h slew the Egyptian, and hid him in the sand.

13 And i when he went out the second day, behold, two men of the Hebrews strove together: and he said to him that did the wrong,

h Acts 7. 24. i Acts 7. 26.

Wherefore smitest thou thy fellow?

14 And he said, k Who made thee a prince and a judge over us? intendest thou to kill me, as thou killedst the Egyptian? And Moses feared, and said, Surely this thing is known.

k Acts 7. 27, 28.

---

nary end. It was *before* this time, that Stephen's testimony assures us he had ' become mighty in words and in deeds.' And when he was seen to come forth *alone*, and take vengeance on one of their oppressors, it might have been presumed that he regarded himself as directed by God in what he had undertaken. But the result showed that the expectation of being recognized in his true character was premature.

12. *He looked this way and that way*, &c. Evidently implying that he was not exempt from some inward wavering of spirit in thus entering upon his mission. But if oppression maketh a wise man mad, we may easily perceive that his natural indignation, joined to a conscious impulse from above, was sufficient to urge him forward to the act recorded.

13. *Behold, two men of the Hebrews strove together*. Heb. נצים *nitzim*, *fighting*. Whatever were the occasion of this unhappy contest, it must have been mortifying to Moses to behold it. As if they had not enemies enough in their common cruel taskmasters, they fall into strife with each other! Alas, that sufferings in common should fail to unite the professing people of God in the strictest bonds of brotherhood.——

¶ *He said to him that did the wrong*. Heb. לרשע *larasha*, *to the wicked one*. The Gr. however renders very correctly by τῷ ἀδικοῦντι, *to the wrong-doer*, and Stephen confirms the same version, Acts, 7. 26, ' Sirs, ye are brethren, why *do ye wrong* (ἀδικεῖτε) one to another?' In the case of the offending Egyptian

Moses administered reproof by a mortal blow, but he tries to gain a contending brother by mild and gentle means. In the former instance he acted more as a judge; in the present, as a peace maker. His question has indeed the air of being sternly proposed, but there was nothing in it which could not or should not have been said by one Israelite to another; and we ought never to think it going beyond the bounds of charity or duty, where we are satisfied on which side the wrong lies, to call an offender to account by an equally plain interrogation. Every man should look upon himself as at least so far appointed a guardian of the general interests of justice and of right as to expostulate in pointed terms with the injurious and overbearing.

14. *Who made thee a prince and a judge over us?* Heb. ' Who set thee for a man a prince and a judge over us?' Moses intended merely to administer a mild and friendly reproof, and yet how roughly is his admonition received. The man could not easily have given a plainer testimony of his guilt than by such a choleric reply. What authority did Moses assume in thus gently reproving a manifest outrage? Does one need a commission to perform an act of real kindness, and to endeavor to make friends of apparent enemies? Yet how boldly does he challenge his authority as if he were imperious and presuming. It is rare virtue ingenuously to confess our faults and to receive correction with meekness!——¶ *Intendest thou to kill me, as thou killedst the Egyptian?* Heb. הלהרגני אתה אמר

15 Now when Pharaoh heard this thing, he sought to slay Moses. But ¹ Moses fled from the face of Pharaoh, and dwelt in the land of Midian: and he sat down by ᵐ a well.

¹ Acts 7. 29. Hebr. 11. 27.

ᵐ Gen. 24. 11. & 29. 2.

halhorgani attah omer, sayest thou to kill me? See Note on Gen. 20. 11. We here behold a striking specimen of the base constructions which an ill mind will put upon the best words and actions. What right had he to charge Moses with a murderous intention? He had indeed slain an Egyptian, but an Egyptian was not a Hebrew, nor had he any grounds to suppose that Moses would go farther than the provocation warranted. The occasion called simply for a reproof, and a reproof was the head and front of his offending; yet the aggressor would turn away the force of his rebuke by pretending that he aimed at nothing less than his life! Besides, why should he cast the slaying of the Egyptian in Moses' teeth, when he had really done it from his regard to his own countrymen? Should not this quarrelsome Hebrew have taken it rather as a proof of Moses' favorable feelings towards himself than as an evidence of a wish to harm him? If he had not loved the Hebrews would he have dispatched one of their enemies? But reason and humanity speak in vain to those whom a guilty conscience leads to pervert the wisest and the kindest counsels.——¶ *Surely this thing is known ;* i. e. his slaying the Egyptian. Heb. הדבר *haddabar, this word.* See Note on Gen. 15. 1. Moses was satisfied from this that the Hebrew whom he had liberated the day before by slaying the Egyptian, had divulged the circumstance, and not doubting that it would soon come to the ears of the king, began to be in dread of his life.

15. *When Pharaoh heard this thing,* &c. He soon learnt that his fears were well founded. Pharaoh was apprised of the fact of his having put an Egyptian to death, and Moses was at once marked as the victim of his wrath. This was perhaps not so much with a view to avenge the death of a single individual of the Egyptian race, as because Moses had by this act discovered himself to be a friend and favorer of the oppressed Israelites, and given the king reason to suspect that he was secretly cherishing the purpose of one day attempting to effect their liberation. His only safety therefore was in flight. This would subject him to great trials and privations, and had his heart been less firmly fixed in the great purpose which he had adopted, he would have sought rather to make his peace with the king, his benefactor, and to retain his place at court. But he had made his election, and now chose rather to wander through dreary deserts than to be reconciled to the enemies of his people. The providence which thus withdrew the destined agent of deliverance from the field of action in the very outset of his work, would seem at first view extremely mysterious and adverse. But infinite wisdom saw that he needed a quite different training from that which he would receive in a luxurious court, in order to fit him for the hard services which awaited him. He sends him to school therefore for forty years in the desert to qualify him the better for leading his people through *their* forty years sojourn in the desert. 'God,' says Henry, 'fetches a wide compass in his plans, but his eye is continually upon the grand point at which he aims.'—It is not to be supposed that there is any real discrepancy between this passage and Heb. 11. 27, 'By faith he forsook Egypt, not fearing the wrath of the king.' The Apostle alludes not to his flight into Midian, but to his final departure from Egypt at

16 ⁿ Now the priest of Midian had seven daughters : ᵒ and they came and drew *water*, and filled the troughs to water their father's flock.

ⁿ ch. 3. 1. ᵒ Gen. 24. 11. & 29. 10. 1 Sam. 9. 11.

the head of the children of Israel.——
¶ *Dwelt in the land of Midian.* Heb.
רשב *yesheb, sat down;* the same word in the original with that applied in the ensuing clause to his seating himself by the well. Probably in both cases the time implied is that of his *first arrival* in Midian, the one referring us in general to the *country* in which he stopped on his route, the other to the *particular place* which was the scene of the incidents subsequently related. Coming to that land he *halted* in his sojourning, and finding a refreshing well of water he *sat down* or *tarried* a longer time than usual by the side of it. Otherwise we seem to be forced to the awkward construction that the dwelling mentioned in our translation, which implies somewhat of a permanent abode, was *prior* to his *sitting by the well*, which evidently is not the sense of the passage.
—Midian was a country in Arabia Petræa, deriving its name from Midian, the fourth son of Abraham by Keturah. It was situated on the south of the Dead Sea and the land of Moab, and probably comprehended the whole country, as far south as the Red Sea. It is at least certain, that if the country of Midian did not actually reach to Sinai, there were colonies of the Midianites who settled near that mount, and who also gave the surrounding districts the name of the ' Land of Midian.' Among those emigrants who preserved the worship of God in comparative purity when lost amongst their countrymen in the north, was Jethro, with whose family Moses here comes into connexion.

16. *The priest of Midian had seven daughters.* Heb. כהן *kohen.* Chal. ' The prince of Midian.' The original word signifies ' prince ' as well as

17 And the shepherds came and drove them away : but Moses stood up and helped them, and ᴾ watered their flock.

ᴾ Gen. 29. 10.

' priest,' as is shown in the Note on Gen. 41. 18, and accordingly in the early ages of the world both these offices were often united in one and the same person. The humble occupation of his daughters will be no objection to this view of the title, if the difference between ancient and modern customs be duly considered. See Note on Gen. 48. 45. Nearly all the ancient versions, besides the Chaldee, adhere to the sense of ' priest ;' but whether he were the priest of a true or false religion, is not so clear. Being in all probability descended from Midian the son of Abraham by Keturah, it is perhaps most reasonable to infer that he retained the leading doctrines of the faith of his great progenitor, though possibly corrupted in some measure by the admixture of errors originating in the surrounding systems of heathen idolatry. From what we are subsequently informed of Jethro, he seems to have possessed a knowledge of the true God, and to have been imbued with sentiments of piety; and this supposition is strengthened when we consider the improbability of Moses' entering into a marriage alliance with the family of an idolater.

17. *The shepherds came and drove them away.* Heb. רגרשום *yegareshum,* where the pronominal suffix answering to ' them' is in the masculine, and not in the feminine gender ; from which we are doubtless to understand that the daughters of Reuel were accompanied by men-servants who were under their direction. It would be strange indeed for a company of unprotected females to be thus employed, and equally strange, if they were without assistance, tha, such savage rudeness should be prac-

18 And when they came to q Reuel their father, he said, How *is it that* ye are come so soon to-day?

19 And they said, An Egyptian delivered us out of the hand of the shepherds, and also drew wa-

q Numb. 10. 29. ch. 3. 1. & 4. 18. & 18. 1. &c.

ter enough for us, and watered the flock.

20 And he said unto his daughters, And where *is* he? why *is* it *that* ye have left the man? call him, that he may r eat bread.

r Gen. 31. 54. & 43. 25.

---

tised toward them by the shepherds. See Note on Gen. 29. 3.——¶ *Moses stood up and helped them.* Heb. רקם ‎ וירשען ‎ *yakom va-yoshian, arose and saved them.* Gr. ερρυσατο αυτας, *delivered them.* Here again we are probably required to suppose a fact not expressly mentioned in the sacred record, viz. that Moses travelled with attendants. Joining his servants with those of Reuel, a party was formed sufficiently strong to overpower the shepherd-boors who had so rudely attempted to drive away the flocks of the young women.——¶ *Watered their flock.* Heb. צאנם ‎ *tzonam.* Helped to water them. Here too the pronominal suffix ' their' is in the masculine gender.

18. *Came to Reuel their father.* The assignment of the names Reuel, or Raguel (Num. 10. 29), Jethro and Hobab, to the proper persons is no easy matter. It is supposed by many that Jethro and Reuel were but different names of the same person. Others consider Reuel as the father of Jethro, and the grand-father of the maidens here spoken of, but called their father in conformity to a very common idiom in the original, of which see examples, Gen. 31. 43. 2 Sam. 19. 25. 2 Kings, 14. 3. 16. 2. 18. 3. So Targ. Jon. ' They came to Reguel, their father's father.' But as Reuel seems obviously to have been the same person as the priest of Midian, who had the seven daughters, an office which he probably would not have held had his father been alive, and as he is the one who is said v. 21, to have given Moses his daughter to wife, an act more appropriate to a father than to a grand-father, provided both were living, as it

is clear they were if they were different persons; we cannot but give a decided preference to the former opinion, which makes Jethro and Reuel the same person, but, for reasons now unknown to us, called by different names. As to Hobab, mentioned afterwards, Num. 10. 29, he is expressly affirmed to be the son of Reuel (Raguel) ' Moses' father-in-law,' which would seem to preclude all controversy on the subject. But see Note in loc.——¶ *How is it that ye are come so soon to-day.* Heb. מהרתן בא ‎ *miharten bo, hastened to come.*

19. *An Egyptian delivered us,* &c. This they inferred from his speech and dress, or they had learned from his own mouth the country from which he came —— ¶ *Drew (water) enough for us.* Heb. דלה דלה ‎ *daloh dalah, drawing drew.* The word ' enough' is inserted in our translation in order to bring the expression somewhat nearer to the emphasis of the original.

20. *Why is it that ye have left the man?* It is not, we presume, to be construed as a breach of propriety on the part of the daughters, that they did not invite Moses home to their father's house. It would have had a very questionable air had they introduced a stranger into the paternal mansion without any previous notice to its proper head. On the contrary, they demean themselves with all the decorous reserve appropriate to their sex. It does not appear even that they solicited protection, but modestly received it; and when rendered they rather looked their thanks than uttered them. This was sufficient, for no noble or sensible mind, like that of Moses, would be in danger

21 And Moses was content to dwell with the man : and he gave Moses ˢZipporah his daughter.

ˢ ch. 4. 25. & 18. 2.

22 And she bare *him* a son, and he called his name ᵗGershom ; for he said, I have been ᵘa stranger in a strange land.

ᵗ ch. 18. 3.   ᵘ Acts 7. 29. Hebr. 11. 13, 14.

of interpreting the instincts of maidenly reserve into an ungrateful return for generous services. But what they failed to say to Moses himself they no doubt said *for* him to their father, and were happy to be able, under his sanction, to express their thanks by ministering all in their power to his comfort as a guest. ——¶ *That he may eat bread.* That is, partake of an entertainment. See Note on Gen. 21. 14.

21. *Moses was content to dwell with the man.* Heb. רִיאֶל *yoel, was willing ;* or perhaps more strictly, *prevailed upon himself, adopted the resolution.* The word occurs in the following passages ; Gen. 18. 27, ' Behold now I *have taken upon me* to speak unto the Lord ;' i. e. have persuaded myself. Josh. 7. 7, ' Would to God *we had been content,* and dwelt on the other side Jordan ;' i. e. had prevailed upon ourselves. Judg. 19. 6, ' *Be content,* I pray thee, and tarry all night ;' i. e. consent. 2 Sam. 7. 29, ' Therefore now *let it please thee* to bless the house of thy servant ;' i. e. be thou willing. With characteristic brevity, Moses says nothing of the previous proposition and negotiation which led to this arrangement, but the simple fact of the compact to remain is alone mentioned. The nature of the services he was to perform is not here specified, as it was in the case of Jacob in similar circumstances, but we learn from the opening of the ensuing chapter, what might be inferred from the manners and habits of those pastoral tribes, that the humble occupation of a shepherd was that in which the illustrious exile now consented to engage. Being thus brought into daily intimacy with kindred minds, it was natural that his intercourse with Jethro's family should result, as it did,

in a union with one of the daughters. ——¶ *He gave Moses Zipporah his daughter ;* to whom reference is made Numb. 12. 1, ' And Miriam and Aaron spake against Moses because of the Ethiopian woman whom he had married ; for he had married an Ethiopian.' The original has ' Cushite' instead of ' Ethiopian,' not, probably, because her family was descended from Cush, or that she had the features and complexion of the modern Ethiopian race, but simply from the fact that they inhabited a country to which the name of Cush or Ethiopia was applied. See Pict. Bib. p. 137.

22. *He called his name Gershom,* &c. Heb. גֵרְשֹׁם *gēreshom,* which appears to be a compound made up of גֵר *gēr, stranger,* and שָׁם *sham, there.* Others take the final syllable שָׁם to be an adjective derived from the root שָׁמַם *shamam, to be desolate,* implying a *lonely* or *desolate stranger.* The import however of this member of the word is of little consequence, as its main significancy is concentrated in that of *stranger* conveyed by the other. The Gr. version here adds : ' And she conceived again and bare a second son ; and he called his name Eliezer, saying, For the God of my father is my helper, and hath delivered me from the hand of Pharaoh.' This addition, which is transferred also into the Vulg., was borrowed from Ex. 18. 4, where nearly the same words occur. The birth of a second son is also expressly mentioned in this connexion by Stephen, Acts, 7. 29, ' Then fled Moses at this saying, and was a stranger in the land of Midian, *where he begat two sons.*' At what period of Moses' forty years sojourning in Midian his marriage with Zipporah, or the birth

23 ¶ And it came to pass, ˣ in process of time, that the king of Egypt died: and the children of Israel ʸ sighed by reason of the bondage, and they cried; and ᶻ their

ˣ ch. 7. 7. Acts 7. 30. ʸ Numb. 20. 16. Deut. 26. 7. Ps. 12. 5. ᶻ Gen. 18. 20. ch. 3. 9. & 22. 23, 27. Deut. 24. 15. James 5. 4.

cry came up unto God, by reason of the bondage.

24 And God ᵃ heard their groaning, and God ᵇ remembered his ᶜ covenant with Abraham, with Isaac, and with Jacob.

ᵃ ch. 6. 5. ᵇ ch. 6. 5. Ps. 105. 8, 42. & 106 45. ᶜ Gen. 15. 14. & 46. 4.

of his children took place, we have no means of ascertaining. From the incident mentioned, Ex. 4. 24, 25, it has generally been supposed that the children were then young, as one of them was circumcised on that occasion by his mother. But it strikes us as extremely improbable that Moses should have deferred his marriage for near forty years after entering Midian, or that being married shortly after that time, so long an interval should have elapsed before he became a father. It is to be remembered that he was at the time mentioned, ch. 4. 24, 25, on the way to Egypt, and is it conceivable that he was *then* the father of two small children? True indeed it is said, Ex. 4. 20, ' that he took his wife and his sons and set them upon an ass, and returned to Egypt,' from which it is argued that the sons must have been mere children, or they could not have been carried, with their mother, on a single ass. But this objection will be obviated in our note on that passage, and as the advanced age of the eldest son at this time is an important item in our interpretation of the context in question, we are forced for the present to lay great stress on the intrinsic probability that Moses was both married and begat one at least of his two sons very early during his residence in Midian.

23. *It came to pass in process of time.* Heb. בימים הרבים ההם *ba-yamim ha-rabbim hahem, in those many days.* Gr. μετα δε τας ημερας τας πολλας εκεινας, *after those many days.* On this phraseology Ainsworth remarks that the Heb. ב *in* is here rightly translated by the

Gr. μετα, *after,* as is clear from Num. 28. 26, ' After your weeks (בשבעתיכם *in your weeks*),' and elsewhere. So in the New Testament, Mark, 13. 24, ' *In* those days' is parallelled by Mat. 24. 29, ' *After* the tribulation of those days.' But it is perhaps sufficient to understand by the phrase simply that *in the course* and *towards the latter part* of the forty years of Moses' sojourn in Midian the king of Egypt died. As to the *precise* date of the event, it was not important that we should be informed of it.——

¶ *Sighed by reason of the bondage.* The time was now fast approaching in which the Most High had proposed to visit and redeem his people, and still no symptoms of favor as yet are perceived. On the contrary, though Egypt had changed its sovereign in the mean time, yet the seed of Jacob experienced no mitigation of their distress. Every change which they had undergone was rather a change from evil to worse, till at length their calamities are represented, like the blood of murdered Abel as having a voice and crying to heaven for vengeance.

24. *God remembered his covenant, &c.* There is a pitch of oppression which will not fail to awaken the wrath of heaven. The groans and tears extorted by violent wrong, especially if they come from humbled and penitent hearts, will pierce the ear of God, and prove a presage of deliverance. ' Cum latera duplicantur Moses adest,' *when the bricks are doubled, Moses is at hand* Yet it seems that in the present case it was not solely from a regard to their miseries that God determined to inter.

23 And God ᵈlooked upon the children of Israel, and God ᵉhad respect unto *them.*

ᵈch. 4. 31.   1 Sam. 1. 11.   2 Sam. 16. 12.
Luke 1. 25.

ᵉch. 3. 7.

fere. His own faithfulness was at stake. He remembered his covenant, and his covenant is his engagement. To the three patriarchs here mentioned he had solemnly bound himself to enlarge, to prosper, and to bless their seed, and after the lapse of a certain period to bring them out of bondage and plant them in the land of promise. As this period had now nearly expired, and the enemies of Israel by making their condition to the utmost degree intolerable were doing what in them lay to crush and exterminate the race, and thus counteract the fulfilment of the divine promises, the God of Abraham, of Isaac, and of Jacob saw that it was time to awake, and make bare his arm, lest his word should fail for evermore. What is meant by God's ' remembering' his covenant we have explained in the Note on Gen. 8. 1. It is an *effective* remembrance evinced by the *performance* of some special act of his care. We may understand it the better by conceiving of its opposite. God is said to *forget* or *not to remember*, when he fails to assist or deliver. And in like manner his *looking upon* a people is the opposite of *turning his back* upon them, and the term for one of the most fearful forms of the divine judgments.

25. *God had respect unto them.* Heb. ידע *yeda, knew* them. That is, compassionately regarded them, tenderly cared for them. On the peculiar import of the word ' know,' see Note on Ex. 1. 8.

REMARKS.—(1.) The doctrine of a special overruling providence is no where more impressively taught than in the early history of Moses ; and in contrasting the perils which surrounded his infancy with the security and comfort with which we can rear our own offspring, we have abundant grounds of gratitude. Yet it should not be forgotten that whatever care we may exercise for our little ones, or whatever guardianship we may afford them, they as really require the preserving mercy of heaven when reposing in their cradles or sporting in our parlors, as did Moses when enclosed in his ark of bulrushes and exposed to the waves or the ravenous tenants of the Nile.

(2.) It is doing no violence to the spirit of the sacred text to conceive of our heavenly Father as saying to the believer when presenting his infant-offspring in baptism, ' Take this child away and nurse it for me, and I will give thee thy wages.' Take him out of the pollution that is in the world through sin, and bring him up in the nurture and admonition of the Lord. Take him from the many perils which beset him by the lusts of the flesh, the pride of life, and the malice of Satan, and establish him in faith, hope, and love, as a devoted servant of the Savior, and verily thou shalt by no means lose thy reward.

(3.) What a powerful principle is true faith ! And how illustrious the exhibition of it in the choice of Moses ! We know how hardly men are persuaded to resign a *little* wealth, to forego a *little* honor, to resign the *faintest* prospect of rank and power. Yet Moses freely gave up *all* that was tempting in this respect, as a noble sacrifice of sense to faith ! Several of the circumstances which rendered this sacrifice so remarkable have been already considered. Consider in addition, that there were other than selfish objections to be overcome. Pharaoh's daughter had strong claims on the gratitude of Moses. He was a poor foundling, rescued from the peril of a watery grave, by the kindness of his benefactor ; and no one acquainted with the sympathy and tenderness of woman's heart needs to be told, how strong is the attachment formed for a helpless infant thus strangely and unexpectedly thrown upon her hands. A deep and affectionate interest would inevitably spring up in her bosom towards her orphan charge, an interest all the deeper and stronger from having no children of her own. Now can we suppose that Moses when he had attained to years of reflection and was made acquainted with the events of his history, could have been insensible to what he owed to his preserver? Would it not be a mighty struggle to tear himself away from one who had been a mother to him from his infancy; who had watched with kind solicitude over his advances from childhood to youth, and from youth to manhood; whose heart had exulted to note his expanding intellect as he grew learned in all the wisdom of the Egyptians, and to see him entitling himself by his intrinsic merit to the station to which he had been fortuitously raised? Shall he then summon up an iron resolve, sunder the ties that bound him to his earliest benefactor, and bid her adieu for ever? Shall he do this when *in* doing it he would seem to be resigning the only hope of aiding and of finally emancipating his brethren? For if he would consent to be called the son of his patroness, retaining his place in the court, and watching the events of providence, some opportunity might at length occur for effecting an object so near his heart. But we see the conviction of present duty outweighing every other consideration, and triumphing over the promptings of affection and the dictates of worldly policy. So complete is the dominion of Faith over his whole soul that he resolves to take the momentous step, though assured that he should thereby plunge into affliction and incur reproach. But the afflictions anticipated were the 'afflictions of the people of God,' and the reproach incurred 'the reproach of Christ,' and these he well knew would be *sanctified* to any one who should encounter them for conscience sake.

Chapter 3

Of the events which marked the history of Moses during the forty years of his residence in the land of Midian, the Scriptures have furnished us with no detailed account. As Moses is himself the historian of his own life, it is reasonable to infer from his silence that the period was not distinguished by any occurrences sufficiently important in his view to deserve a record. His days probably passed quietly away in the wonted discharge of his duties as a shepherd, and the shepherd too of another man's flock. His situation was no doubt favorable to contemplation and communion with God. He could scarcely fail to make progress in that divine knowledge which would do more to qualify him for his future mission than all the learning he had acquired in Egypt. The life too which he led was happily adapted to work within him that hardihood of constitution and character, of which he would afterwards stand so much in need, and of which the sequel of his story affords us so many striking instances. Still, it could not but be a severe trial of his faith to find year after year elapsing, and the prime and vigor of his age apparently wearing away, while no tokens from above indicated that the great work of his vocation was any nearer at hand. Yet he seems meekly to have endured as seeing Him who is invisible, and to have evinced that true wisdom which consists in waiting for and following the call of heaven, instead of running before it. It was evidently no part of his design to hold up for admiration his own example of submissive patience, yet the Holy Spirit is

CHAPTER III.

NOW Moses kept the flock of Jethro his father-in-law, a the priest of Midian: and he led the

a ch. 2. 16.

---

not restrained from presenting his conduct in such a light as will suggest the most useful lessons to all succeeding ages.

1. *Now Moses kept the flock of Jethro.* Heb. צֹאן אֶת רֹעֶה הָיָה *hayah roeh eth tzon, was feeding the flock,* or *acting the shepherd towards.* See Note on Gen. 37. 2. He who is before, Ex. 2. 18, called Reuel, is here denominated Jethro. Our reasons for thinking them the same person have already been given. In Num. 10. 29, he is called Raguel, and is expressly said to have been the father of Hobab.—There is no doubt a very marked contrast between Moses in the court of Egypt, making his abode in a palace, and surrounded with all the splendors of royalty, and Moses a humble hireling shepherd, leading his flocks over the rough places of the desert, sleeping often in the open air, exposed to heat and to cold, to weariness and watchings, and living upon the coarsest fare. But as we know that he had voluntarily and deliberately made the exchange of one condition for the other, and as we know too the motives by which he had been governed in doing it, it would be no matter of surprise could we be assured, as was doubtless the fact, that he was as truly happy while thus traversing the rocky region of Midian, his tent his only shelter, as when treading the marble pavements of Egyptian halls, or reposing on couches of state, with a crowd of menials prompt to do his pleasure. As it was from a supreme regard to the glory of God that he had entered this humble sphere, so God was not unmindful of the sacrifices he had made, nor did he leave him without witness of his special favor. Desert

flock to the back side of the desert, and came to b the mountain of God *even* to Horeb.

b ch. 18. 5.   1 Kings 19. 8.

---

and lonely places have often been those which God has selected for the most signal displays of himself to his servants ; nor is it superfluous to remark, that such manifestations are usually made, as here, not to the idle or slothful, but to those who are busied in the duties of their calling.——¶ *He led the flock to the back side of the desert,* &c Gr. υπο τον ερημον, *under the wilderness.* Vulg. ' Ad interiora deserti,' *to the interior parts of the desert.* Chal. ' To the place of fair pasturage in the desert.' The expression is probably equivalent to a great way into the desert.—— ¶ *Came to the mountain of God,* so called, not so much from its great height, as tall cedars are called cedars of God, &c. (see Note on Gen. 23. 6), as by anticipation, from several very remarkable events having afterward occurred upon this memorable mount tending to confer upon it a sacred character. It was here (1.) that God appeared to Moses in the bush ; (2.) that he manifested his glory at the delivery of the law ; (3.) that Moses with his rod brought water out of the rock ; (4.) that by lifting up his hands he made Joshua to prevail against Amelek ; (5.) that he fasted twice forty days and forty nights ; (6.) that from hence he brought the two tables of the law ; and (7.) that Elijah was vouchsafed a glorious vision. The Chal. renders it, ' the mount where the Glory of the Lord was revealed.' ——¶ *Even to Horeb.* Heb. חֹרֵב *horeb,* i. e. *dryness,* from the character of the soil ; it being a dry, sterile, bleak, rocky region. The names ' Horeb' and ' Sinai' are interchanged in the Scriptures : and modern travellers give such varied accounts of them, that we are left in great uncertainty with regard to their original

2 And c the Angel of the LORD appeared unto him in a flame of fire out of the midst of a bush;

c Deut. 33. 16. Isai. 63. 9. Acts 7. 30.

and he looked, and behold, the bush burned with fire, and the bush *was* not consumed.

position. They may be considered as parts of one vast eminence in the midst of the surrounding desert, the upper region of which forms an irregular circle of thirty or forty miles in diameter. This region contains the highest mountains of the peninsula, whose shagged and pointed peaks, and steep and shattered sides, render it clearly distinguishable from all the rest of the country in view. Abrupt cliffs of granite, from six to eight hundred feet in height, whose surface is blackened by the sun, surround the avenues leading to the elevated region, to which the name of Sinai, at the present day, is specifically applied. The cliffs enclose the mountain on three sides, leaving the east and north-east sides only, towards the gulf of Akaba, more open to the view. Further information respecting this remarkable mountainous tract will be given in tracing the course of the children of Israel in their march from Egypt to Canaan.

2. *The angel of the Lord appeared unto him,* &c. Of the scriptural import of the word 'angel' we have given a somewhat extended view in the Note on Gen. 16. 7, with which compare Note on Gen. 24. 7. It is properly a term of' *office,* and not of *nature,* and is used to denote not only human and spiritual *messengers,* but also any of the impersonal agents, such as winds, fires, pestilences, remarkable dispensations, &c., which serve as a *medium* to make known the divine will, or to illustrate the divine operation in nature or providence. In fact, one of the most frequent uses of the term is as a *personification of divine judgments.* Thus 2 Kings, 19. 35, 'And it came to pass that the Angel of the Lord went out and smote in the camp of the Assyrians an hundred

four score and five thousand.' The effect here described is very generally conceded to have been produced by a *pestilential wind* of the desert, which is personified, and termed an *angel.* So the pestilence which occurred in consequence of David's numbering the people, 2 Sam. 24. 15, 16, in like manner represented as the work of *an angel.* The destruction of the first-born in Egypt, Ex. 12. 23, 29, is doubtless to be viewed in the same light. Though cut off by the direct supernatural judgment ot the Most High, yet the agency is personified and represented as a *destroying angel.* The language of the Psalmist, Ps. 78. 49, undoubtedly requires the same construction; ' He cast upon them the fierceness of his anger, wrath and indignation and trouble *by sending evil angels* among them;' i. e. the judgments of the plagues. In the New Testament the same mode of speech occurs, Acts, 12. 23, ' And immediately *the angel of the Lord* smote him, because he gave not God the glory, and he was eaten ot worms, and gave up the ghost.' Here the judgment itself, the fatal disease with which Herod died, was the angel intended in the text. But if such language was used in reference to *vindictive judgments* extraordinarily inflicted, there is no reason to doubt that *merciful visitations,* or in fact any kind of rare, *wonderful,* and *astounding* occurrences that happen somewhat out of the ordinary course of providence, should be set forth in a similar figurative or symbolical diction. Thus when it is said, Dan. 6. 22, that ' God had sent his *Angel* and shut the lions' mouths, that they should not hurt Daniel,' it is not necessary to understand the literal presence of an angel, or spiritual being, but simply, that by the special interposition or influence of the Almighty, the ravenous beasts were restrained from acting according to their instincts. The principle on which this interpretation rests is well expressed by Reland (Dissert. de Samarit. 7. § 7.), ' That with whatever instrument God unites his own virtue, so as to animate it, and to work in, with, and by it, that instrument is called *an angel.*' Accordingly, even a dream, a vision, a voice from heaven, may be so denominated. But the appellation seems to be in a particular manner bestowed upon the *theophanies*, or special divine manifestations of which we so frequently read in the Old Testament as made to the patriarchs and prophets. The *Shekinah*, or visible material symbol of glory, is undoubtedly, in repeated instances, called *the angel of the Lord*, inasmuch as it was the medium or vehicle through which the Divinity was pleased to reveal himself to the outward senses. Thus the Shekinah in the pillar of cloud and fire which guided the march of the Israelites is called, Ex. 14. 19, *the angel of the Lord*. At the same time, in all such cases an intelligent agent, a spiritual being, or, in other words, Jehovah himself, is doubtless to be considered as really but invisibly present in and associated with the visible emblem. Thus, in the present instance, the *appearance*, the preternatural light or fire in the burning bush, we suppose to be what is truly and primarily meant by the *angel of the Lord;* but it is clear from the sequel that in and under this outward symbol there was present the divine personage who styles himself, v. 6, ' the God of Abraham, of Isaac, and of Jacob,' and who is also, v. 7, expressly called ' Jehovah' (Lord). This is still farther manifest from Deut. 33. 16, where Moses, in blessing the tribes in the name of the Lord, invokes upon Joseph ' the good will of him *that dwelt in the bush.*' Still farther confirmation of this view will be given as we proceed.——¶ *In a flame of fire out of the*

midst of a bush. This appeared to Moses a natural fire burning with great vehemence in the midst of the bush, yet we may suppose it to have been the supernatural fiery splendor which constituted the Shekinah, the symbol of the divine presence. The Hebrew word for ' bush,' (properly *bramble bush*) is סְנֶה *seneh*, and from the ' bush' here mentioned, in connexion with the divine appearance, the Jewish writers, not improbably, suppose that this mountain and desert were afterwards called by the Israelites ' Mount *Sinai*,' and the ' wilderness of *Sinai*.' Thus in Pirke Eliezer, ch. 41, ' From the beginning of the world this Mount was called Horeb, and when God appeared unto Moses out of the midst of the bramble-bush, from the name of the bramble (Seneh) it was called Sinai.'—The incident which so much excited the wonder of Moses is generally supposed to have been designed as a representation of the condition of the Israelites in Egypt. ' The burning bush,' says Philo, ' was a symbol of the oppressed, and the flaming fire of the oppressors ; that what was burning but not consumed, did portend that these who were afflicted by the violence of their enemies should not perish ; and that the attempts of their enemies should be frustrated ; and that the present troubles of the afflicted should have a good issue.' There they were oppressed and cruelly treated, bound down with bondage, and suffering every grievance that malice could devise and power effect to wear out their strength and diminish their numbers. They were in a furnace of fire, and in themselves but as briars and thorns compared with those that kindled it. But they were nevertheless not destroyed ; nay, they were still flourishing ; the nation continued to shoot forth vigorous branches, and a numerous offspring surrounded them in spite of their enemies. And whence this wonder, this apparent contradiction to the common

3 And Moses said, I will now turn aside, and see this ^d great sight, why the bush is not burnt.

4 And when the LORD saw that

^d Ps. 111. 2. Acts 7. 31.

he turned aside to see, God called ^e unto him out of the midst of the bush, and said, Moses, Moses! And he said, Here *am* I.

^e Deut. 33. 16.

course of nature? It was because God was in the midst of them. He, the imperishable and eternal God, who now appeared to Moses in the bush, burning but unburnt, and who afterwards walked with his three faithful servants in the burning fiery furnace of Nebuchadnezzar, was continually with his oppressed people, and *therefore* they were not consumed. But farther, it will be no stretch of fancy if we consider the appearance of the bush as an emblem of the *present* condition of the children of Israel. They are at this day strangers in foreign lands. They have been in circumstances which, according to the common operation of merely human and political causes, would have long ago amalgamated them entirely with other nations, and made them vanish, as a people, from the earth. But they are at this day a distinct and separate people; they have survived the lapse of ages, which have swept away others far more numerous and powerful; they are scattered over the face of the whole earth, and yet their national character and name are preserved, and even their visages declare their origin. And why is this burning bush of the house of Israel yet unconsumed? It is because God is with them. He remembers his covenant with their fathers. He has further mercy in store for them. ' There shall yet come out of Zion the Deliverer, and shall turn away ungodliness from Jacob.' They shall again be grafted into their own olive-tree, for God is able to graft them in again, and his gifts and callings are without repentance. But again, this appearance may be considered as an apt emblem of the condition of even the spiritual church of Christ. Against himself and the cause of his gospel

did ' the kings of the earth set themselves, and the rulers take counsel together.' And ever since have the world and the devil been striving to crush his people, and to root out the memoria. of them from the earth. Often have his witnesses prophesied in sackcloth, and often have his people suffered bonds and imprisonment and death for their religion. Yet it remains, and is still a light shining in a dark place. This is because that God is with his church God is in the midst of her, and there fore she is not moved. ' When thou passest through the waters, I will be with thee; and through the rivers, they shall not overflow thee; when thou walkest through the fire thou shalt not be burned; neither shall the flame kindle upon thee.' She is built upon a rock and the gates of hell shall not prevail against her. Her great head has declared, ' Lo I am with you always even unto the end of the world.' And herein consists the stability, perpetuity, and increase of the church.

3. *Why the bush is not consumed.* Heb. רבער לֹא *lo yibar*, *is not eaten up*; i. e. burnt up, entirely consumed, for that it was *apparently burning* we are expressly informed in v. 2. A fire in the Scriptures is frequently said to ' eat' as Lev. 6. 10, ' And take up the ashes which the fire hath *consumed ;*' Heb. ' hath eaten,' Ps. 50. 3, ' Our God shall come and shall not keep silence: a fire shall *devour* before him, and it shall be very tempestuous round about him.' It was matter of astonishment to Moses that this was not the effect in the present instance.

4. *When the Lord saw that he turned aside to see, he called unto him,* &c. As if to reward the religious awe and

5 And he said, Draw not nigh hither: f put off thy shoes from off thy feet; for the place whereon thou standest *is* holy ground.

f ch. 19. 12.   Josh. 5. 15.   Acts 7. 33.

dread, and the sanctified curiosity, with which his spirit was touched. The phraseology shows that the term ' Lord' here is used interchangeably with 'Angel,' carrying with it the idea of something visible, or in other words of the Shekinah. God might have called to him without any such tokens of reverence on the part of Moses, but he does not see fit to make his communications to heedless minds. ' The desire of Moses to be taught,' says Calvin, ' as indicated by his drawing near, is especially worthy of note. It often happens that God meets us in vain because we perversely spurn so great a grace. Let us learn from the example of Moses, as often as God, by any sign, invites us to himself, sedulously to attend, nor stifle the offered light by our sluggishness.' The vouchsafement of visions of this nature was never intended to inspire a fruitless wonder or alarm in the minds of holy men. They were always subservient to some great moral end, and for the most part were attended with some express instructions in which the beholder was deeply concerned. It had now been a long time since any such personal intercourse with the Deity had been enjoyed by any of the chosen people. No instance of the kind is recorded as having taken place since God was pleased to speak to Jacob to encourage him to go down into Egypt ; but now after a lapse of two hundred years God again condescends to appear and to converse with Moses, in order to encourage him to go back to the same country to bring his people out of it. We are ready to say that those favored men of old were happy in being permitted to enjoy such immediate intercourse with God ; but happier are we who enjoy the full revelation of the pre-

cious gospel. Whatever they heard, they heard not the things which have come to our ears. Whatever were the promises given to them, we are in possession of better. Whatever the covenant made with the fathers, a better one has been established with us their spiritual descendants. Whatever the encouragement granted to them, we have still greater afforded to us in every part of the work which we have to do, in every trial and danger to which we may be exposed. Let us then hear the voice of God speaking to us in the gospel, where no phenomenon of fire intimidates our spirits. Let us hearken in faith to all its declarations, and yield implicit obedience to all its commands. ——¶ *Here am I.* A common expression indicative of readiness to hearken or obey. See Note on Gen. 22. 1.

5. *Draw not nigh hither.* That is, approach not any nearer than thou art. The scrutiny of mere curiosity was repelled ; an undue familiarity was not permitted ; a deep and awful reverence was enjoined. He was forbidden to approach too nigh unto God. The deepest awe which can possibly fill the soul is called for when a worm of the dust is admitted to stand within the precincts of the divine presence. We are indeed favored to live under a milder dispensation than was Moses, one under which we are not only bidden ' to draw nigh unto God,' but assured that ' he will draw nigh unto us.' We do not now draw nigh unto a burning bush or a flaming mount, but to a mercy seat to which we are commanded to come with filial boldness to obtain all needed grace. Yet even here there is nothing to warrant an unhallowed familiarity, nothing to abate the most profound reverence and godly fear when we enter

into the audience-chamber of the King of kings.——¶ *Put off thy shoes from off thy feet.* By *shoe* here is meant the leathern or wooden sole attached to the bottom of the foot by ' shoe-latchets' passing round the instep and ancle. See Note on Gen. 18. 4. Jerus. Targ. סנדלך *sandelok, thy sandal.* ' The reverence indicated by putting off the covering of the feet is still prevalent in the East. The Orientals throw off their slippers on all those occasions when we should take off our hats. They never uncover their heads, any more than we our feet. It would every where, whether among Christians, Moslems, or Pagans, be considered in the highest degree irreverent for a person to enter a church, a temple, or a mosque, with his feet covered ; and we shall observe that the priests under the law officiated with bare feet. And not only is this form of showing respect exhibited in religious observances, but in the common intercourse of life. Few things inspire an Oriental with deeper disgust, than for a person to enter his room with shoes or boots on, regarding such conduct both as an insult to himself and a pollution to his apartment. These usages influence the costume of the head and feet. The former, being never uncovered, is in general shaven, and the head-dress generally is such that it could not be replaced without some degree of trouble ; while for the feet they have loose and easy slippers, which may be thrown off and resumed with the least possible degree of inconvenience.' *Pict. Bib.* —— ¶ *The place whereon thou standest is holy ground.* Heb. אדמת קדש *admath kodesh, ground of holiness ;* i. e. sanctified by the presence and manifestation of the Deity, who makes the heavens, the earth, the sanctuary, or whatever place it be in which his glory is revealed, to be accounted ' holy,' and therefore to be occupied with devout reverence by his worshippers. Accordingly the mount on which

Christ was transfigured, 2 Pet. 1, 18. is called the ' holy mount.' A ' holiness' of this kind, founded solely upon divine appointment, and not upon the intrinsic nature of the subject, is termed ' relative' in contradistinction from ' positive,' or ' absolute,' and ceases when the occasion creating it ceases. The same direction was afterwards given to Joshua, the successor of Moses, on a somewhat similar occasion, Josh. 6. 15, ' Loose thy shoe from off thy foot, for the place whereon thou standest is holy.' That is, it was made temporarily holy by the divine manifestation there witnessed. We are not indeed in the Scriptures taught the intrinsic holiness of places, but there is no doubt that the *spirit* of this command enjoins upon us a peculiar awe and reverence of feeling whenever we enter a house of worship or any other place, where God is considered to be especially present. The impression that ' God is here' ought ever to have a solemnizing effect upon our minds, and repress every thing like carelessness, listlessness, or levity. Had we a proper sense of the divine majesty resting upon our spirits, would it be possible that we could give way to that profane heedlessness of mind which often steals upon us ? Would one short hour's attendance betray us into slumber ? Would a crowd of worldly or sensual thoughts intrude into our minds ? Could the eye find leisure to roam over the assembly and upon the dress or deportment of others ? Could a scornful or simpering countenance by significant smiles communicate its contemptuous or frivolous emotions to another ? Assuredly not. God is as truly, though not as visibly, in the midst of his worshipping assemblies, as he was in the burning bush at Horeb, and our most appropriate sentiments on such occasions are those which would utter themselves in the reverential language of Jacob at Bethel, ' How dreadful is this place !'

6 Moreover he said, g I *am* the God of thy father, the God of Abraham, the God of Isaac, and the God of Jacob. And Moses hid

g Gen. 28. 13. ver. 15. ch. 4. 5. Matt. 22. 32. Mark 12. 26. Luke 20. 37. Acts 7. 32.

his face; for h he was afraid to look upon God.
7 ¶ And the LORD said, I have surely seen the affliction of my peo-

h So 1 Kings 19. 13. Isai. 6. 1, 5. Neh. 9. 9. Ps. 106. 44. Acts 7. 34.

6. *Moreover, he said, I am the God of thy father.* That is, of each one of thy fathers, even Abraham, and Isaac, &c. The term here is usually understood of Moses' immediate father, Amram, but it is with more probability to be considered as a collective singular, equivalent to ' fathers.' Accordingly it is rendered in Stephen's version of this event, Acts 7, 32, ' I am the God of thy *fathers.*' A like sense, we presume, is to be given to the expression, Ex. 15. 2, ' He is my God, and I will prepare him an habitation; my *father's* God, and I will exalt him;' i. e. the God of my ancestors in general. We suppose the true import of the passage before us would be better expressed by the rendering; ' I am the God of thy fathers, (even) the God of Abraham, &c.' This is obviously confirmed by v. 15 of this chapter. While the Most High repressed presumption in Moses, and enjoined reverence, he encouraged him by reassuring him of that relation into which he had entered with the nation of Israel in the persons of their fathers. This declaration was made in order to assure Moses that even in the present oppressed state of his nation in Egypt, he had not forgotten them, or his relation to them as a God in covenant. This would be an unspeakable consolation to Moses, to find himself addressed by that God of whose appearances and promises to his fathers he had often heard, and to know that his heart was as kindly affected to him as it ever had been to his venerated ancestors. How comforting beyond measure to the Christian, in his more favored moments, to be assured that the God of all the good who have ever lived is his God, and equally pledged by his

covenant faithfulness, to show to *him* the same loving kindness that he showed to them!——¶ *Moses hid his face, for he was afraid to look upon God.* Or rather perhaps, parenthetically, according to the Heb. accents, ' And Moses hid his face (because he was afraid) from looking upon God.' A more literal rendering of the last words (אֶל הָאֱלֹהִים *el haelohim*) is *to* or *towards God,* or *towards the Elohim,* as the article is prefixed, which is not the common usage. It would seem that the term ' Elohim' here is intended to signify simply *that which was visible,* the outward symbol representing the essential Godhead, ' which no man hath seen nor can see.' The Chal. has correctly, ' He feared to look towards the Glory of God;' i. e. towards the overpowering brightness of the Shekinah, in which God manifested his presence. The effect described is what might have been anticipated. A consciously sinful creature may well fear and tremble when God comes to visit him, even though on a purpose of mercy. It is ignorance of God, not intimate communion with him, that begets an unhallowed familiarity. The angels, who know him best and adore him most profoundly, are most sensible of the infinite distance between him and them, and are therefore represented as ' covering their faces with their wings' when standing in his awful presence.

7. *I have surely seen the affliction,* &c. Heb. רָאֹה רָאִיתִי *raoh raithi, seeing I have seen,* i. e. have intently considered. Arab. ' Have regarded.' Thus Ps. 106. 44, ' Nevertheless he *regarded* their affliction when he heard their cry.' Heb. ' He *saw* (וַיַּרְא) their affliction.'
——¶ *By reason of their task-masters*

ple which *are* in Egypt, and i have heard their cry k by reason of their taskmasters; for l I know their sorrows:

i ch. 2. 23, 24.　k ch. 1. 11.　l Gen. 18. 21. ch. 2. 25.

Heb. נֹגְשָׂיו *nogesauv, his task-masters ;* the whole people spoken of as one man, according to common usage. The original for *task-masters,* though of equivalent import, is not the same word with that so rendered, ch. 1. 11, but properly signifies *exacters,* translated in Job, 39. 7, *driver,* and in Zech. 9. 8, *oppressor.* The Gr. has εργοδιωκται, *workmasters,* and the Chal. ' Those who cause them to serve.'——¶ *I know their sorrows.* Heb. מַכְאֹבָיו *makobauv, his sorrows,* collect. sing. as before. For the import of ' know,' see Note on Ex. 1. 8. Hos. 13. 5, presents a parallel phraseology, ' I did *know* thee in the wilderness, in the land of great drought ;' i. e. I compassionately knew thee ; I knew thee so as to succor thee.

8. *I am come down to deliver them.* Heb. לְהַצִּילוֹ *lehatzilo, to deliver him,* collect. sing. In strict propriety of speech neither ascent nor descent can be predicated of the Omnipresent Being, but in adaptation to our modes of conceiving of the divine acts, God is said to ' come down' when he puts forth in the sight of men such striking exhibitions of his power, either for grace or judgment, as shall constitute an indubitable token of his special presence. It may be remarked, moreover, that whenever the Most High is said, in the sacred volume, to ' descend,' some signal event of his providence is uniformly represented as following. Thus, when he is said to have resolved to ' go down' and see the sins of Sodom, the fearful overthrow of their city quickly ensued; when he ' came down' to thwart the building of Babel, the confusion of tongues followed, as it were, upon his footsteps; and when, in the narrative before us, he announces his purpose of descending in behalf of

8 And m I am come down to n deliver them out of the hand of the Egyptians, and to bring them up out of that land, o unto a good land,

m Gen. 11. 5, 7. & 18. 21. & 50. 24.　n ch. 6. 6, 8. & 12. 51.　o Deut. 1. 25. & 8. 7, 8, 9.

his people, their miraculous deliverance, with deserved vengeance upon Egypt, is the memorable result.——¶ *Unto a good land and a large.* Not indeed a land very large in itself, but large in comparison with their territory in Goshen, and of sufficient extent to contain with ease all the population of that race which was destined to inherit it. ——¶ *Unto a land flowing with milk and honey.* An abundance of milk and honey indicates a country rich in pasturage and flowers, of which the one is evinced by the teeming udders of the flocks and herds, and the other by large quantities of wild or cultivated honey. That this description held literally good of the land of promise, there is the most unquestionable evidence, not only from the declarations of Scripture, Deut. 8. 8. 32. 13. Judg. 14. 8. 1 Sam. 14. 25, 26. Ps. 81. 17, but even from what we know in modern times of the soil, climate, and productions of Palestine. But if this should be thought too rigid an interpretation of the words, ' milk' may be understood to denote all kinds of *necessary food,* and ' honey,' whatever is peculiarly *agreeable to the palate,* so that this expression, so often applied to the land of Canaan, may be simply intended to characterise *a very fruitful and pleasant country,* abounding in all the products necessary to the *subsistence of life,* and rich in the dainties which minister to *the gratification of the taste.* See the emphatic commendation of the soil, productions, &c. of the promised land, Deut. 8. 7—9. The same proverbial expression of plenty is familiar to the classic writers. Thus Euripides, Bac. v. 142, ' The field flows with milk, with wine, and with the nectar of bees.' The enemies of reve-

and a large, unto a land ᴾ flowing with milk and honey ; unto the place of ᑫ the Canaanites, and the Hittites, and the Amorites, and the Perrizzites, and the Hivites, and the Jebusites.

ᴾ ver. 17. ch. 13. 5. & 33. 3. Numb. 13. 27. Deut. 26. 9, 15. Jer. 11. 5. & 32. 22. Ezek. 20 6. ᑫ Gen. 15. 18.

lation have drawn arguments from the present neglected state of some parts of Palestine, to invalidate the statements of the sacred historians, who represent it as one of the most delightful spots upon the face of the earth. In this, however, they have not only utterly failed, but by drawing the attention of modern travellers on the subject, have unwittingly contributed towards the illustration and confirmation of the sacred records. The land has, indeed, suffered under the blighting dominion of the Saracens, Turks, and Egyptians ; agriculture has been neglected ; and an air of desolation has crept over its once luxuriant hills and dales, but the traces of its original fertility and beauty are far from being wholly obliterated. We may infer, from the following passages from the pens of eminent travellers, what Palestine was in a state of prosperity. ' We left the road,' says D'Arvieux, ' to avoid the Arabs, whom it is always disagreeable to meet with, and reached by a side path the summit of a mountain, where we found a beautiful plain. It must be confessed, that if we could live secure in this country, it would be the most agreeable residence in the world, partly on account of the pleasing diversity of mountains and valleys, partly on account of the salubrious air which we breathe there, and which is at all times filled with balsamic odors from the wild flowers of these valleys, and from the aromatic herbs on the hills.' Dr. E. D. Clarke, speaking of the appearance of the country between Sychem and Jerusalem, says, ' A sight of this territory alone, can

9 Now therefore, behold, ʳ the cry of the children of Israel is come unto me : and I have also seen the ˢ oppression wherewith the Egyptians oppress them.

10 ᵗ Come now therefore, and I will send thee unto Pharaoh, that ʳ ch. 2. 23. ˢ ch. 1. 11, 13, 14 22. ᵗ Ps. 105. 26. Micah. 6. 4.

convey any adequate idea of its surprising produce : it is truly the Eden of the East, rejoicing in the abundance of its wealth. The effect of this upon the people was strikingly portrayed in every countenance. Under a wise and beneficent government, the produce of the Holy Land would exceed all calculation. Its perennial harvests ; the salubrity of its air ; its limpid springs ; its rivers, lakes, and matchless plains ; its hills and valleys ; all these, added to the serenity of the climate, prove this land to be indeed ' a field which the Lord hath blessed : God hath given it of the dew of heaven, and the fatness of the earth, and plenty of corn and wine!'——¶ *Canaanites, Hittites, Amorites,* &c. All singular in the original, *Canaanite, Hittite,* &c., and so in innumerable other instances.

9. *Now therefore behold the cry,* &c. The Most High repeats this declaration from v. 7, in order to give stronger assurance to Moses that he will be with him and not suffer him to go upon a fruitless embassy. His truth, his justice, his mercy were all concerned in the liberation of his people. Such cruelties as they had suffered at the hands of the Egyptians would have awaked his vindictive providence in behalf of *any* people, and armed it against their oppressors. How much more when the sufferers were *his own* chosen people, whom he had taken under his special covenant care, whom he had sworn to protect, to befriend, to bless.

10. *Come now therefore,* &c. Heb. ‏וְעַתָּה לְכָה‎ *ve-attah lekah, and now go.* The secret impulse under which Moses

thou mayest bring forth my people, the children of Israel, out of Egypt.

11 ¶ And Moses said unto God,

---

had formerly acted, in his incipient essays towards the deliverance of his people, ch. 2. 11, now becomes an open call and a full commission ; and he whom the Israelites, Acts, 7. 35, ' refused saying, Who made thee a ruler and a judge ? the same did God send to be a ruler and a deliverer by the hand of the angel which appeared to him in the bush.' The divine Speaker here passes from promises and assurances to commands. Moses is now required to address himself to the work which God had destined him to perform. He dealt kindly with his servant in thus strengthening and animating him with these precious hopes of success. Nothing could have been laid to his charge had he waved all such preliminary encouragements, and sternly bid him go forward without any intimations as to the result of his mission. But our merciful God deals more graciously with human infirmity. He excites a more prompt and cheerful obedience by assuring his servants of a happy issue to all the work in which they engage for him. He thus leaves our perverse and selfish and refractory hearts utterly without excuse, if we decline his service.

11. *And Moses said unto God, Who am I*, &c. Calling to mind the lively interest which Moses had formerly evinced in behalf of his people, and the ready zeal with which he had entered upon the redress of their wrongs, we should no doubt at first suppose that his inmost heart would have responded to the divine call, and that he would have discovered an almost eager promptitude to enter upon so congenial a service. But no ; he is appalled by the appointment. He cannot believe himself **equal to it, or worthy of it.** Forty

---

u Who *am* I, that I should go unto Pharaoh, and that I should bring forth the children of Israel out of Egypt ?

u See ch. 6. 12. 1 Sam. 18. 18. Isai. 6. 5. 8. Jer. 1. 6.

---

years before, in the ardor of comparative youth, he had made such an attempt, and failed. He shrinks back therefore from it now. But we are not to suppose that it was altogether from the recollection of the past that he declined the present service. He was in many respects a different man now from what he was then. He had long been leading a retired, quiet, and contemplative life, and had gained a deeper knowledge of God and of himself. He had greater experience of the dispositions and motives of men, and had grown in humility and a diffidence of his own powers. He could better estimate the magnitude and difficulty of the work. He could better understand the weight of opposition which would arise from a powerful king and a mighty nation ; and he might also well expect to have again to encounter fear or unwillingness in his own people. Now also he would feel that he could have no protection or favor from Pharaoh's daughter, and obscure as he was in Midian, he looked upon himself as altogether insufficient and incompetent for so great an undertaking. That his backwardness was excusable no one will affirm, yet it is probably no more than justice to Moses to say, that his reply did not flow from a positively disobedient spirit, like that which prompted Jonah to flee from the presence of the Lord, but from a profoundly humble sense of his own unworthiness and incompetence for such an arduous trust. From a similar consciousness, Isaiah shrunk from the duty to which he was called of being the Lord's messenger, saying, ' I am a man of unclean lips ;' and Jeremiah was led to exclaim ' Ah, Lord God ! behold I cannot speak

12 And he said, ˣ Certainly I will be with thee; and this *shall be* a

ˣ Gen. 31. 3. Deut. 31. 23. Josh. 1. 5. Rom. 8. 31.

for I am a child.' Paul also was actuated by the same feeling when he anxiously enquired, ' Who is sufficient for these things?' A due degree of distrust in ourselves is no doubt always proper, but we should not forget, that as there is a sinful pride which urges men to seek stations and employments to which they have no just pretensions, so there is a sinful humility which shrinks from the call of God, and which under the guise of self denial, or the affectation of under-valuing and debasing our own persons and qualities, indirectly charges God with foolishness in choosing instruments unsuited to his work. Let us ever aim then to observe a happy medium between self-complacency and self-disparagement. As it is God's prerogative to send by whom he will send, so he will never fail to qualify his emissaries for the errand on which he dispatches them. His commission is sufficient to empower the weakest man for the most arduous service.

12. *And he said, Certainly I will be with thee.* Chal. ' My Word shall be for thy help.' It no doubt for the most part holds true, that those who are in reality the best fitted for the peculiar work of God are usually prone to esteem themselves the least so ; yet the promised presence of Jehovah is sufficient to silence every plea which would prevent the humble-minded from going forward in any prescribed deliverance, reformation, or change in the church or the world. No other than this simple consideration is afforded in order to remove the misgivings of Moses. It was of no consequence who he was, or what he could do, as long as Omnipotence led the way before him. We render the highest honor to God when relying on his proffered aid, we seek no ground of

token ᴢᴜᴏ thee, that I have sent thee : when thou hast brought forth the people out of Egypt, ye shall serve God upon this mountain.

confidence out of himself, when in the deep sense of our own impotence we count it enough that he is with us and for us.——¶ *This shall be a token unto thee that I have sent thee.* Heb. זה לך האות *zeh leka haoth, this shall be to thee a sign.* These words are understood by most of the Rabbinical commentators to refer to the supernatural appearance which Moses was now called to witness in the burning bush. According to this mode of interpretation there is a two-fold assurance conveyed to him in the two several clauses of this verse ; first, that God would be with him, and protect him in his embassy to Pharaoh. Of this fact he might regard the spectacle before him as a sign or token ; for as he saw the burning bush subservient to the divine pleasure without being consumed, so he might be confident of being enabled to execute the commission assigned to him without personal harm. Secondly that when this was accomplished, when he had delivered his message to Pharaoh, and brought out the people from Egypt, then both he and all the host of Israel should serve God, by oblations of sacrifice and praise, upon that very mountain where he now stood. The mass of modern interpreters, however, understand the token here spoken of, to refer, not to the vision of the divine glory in the burning bush, but to the *actual future result* of the mission now devolved upon Moses : the *sign* promised was no other than the *event itself,* which was predicted ; q. d. ' Go now and try, and you shall find, *by the event,* that I have sent you.' Of these interpretations the former is more agreeable to the Hebrew accents, which indicate a marked distinction between the former and the latter clauses of the verse ; and it seems

13 And Moses said unto God, Behold, *when* I come unto the children of Israel, and shall say unto them, The God of your fathers hath sent me unto you ; and they shall say to me, What *is* his name ? what shall I say unto them ?

14 And God said unto Moses, I AM THAT I AM : and he said Thus shalt thou say unto the chil-

also better to accord with our ordinary conceptions of the use of a sign, which is understood to be something addressed to the *outward senses* rather than to the *faith* of the recipient, and is of course naturally regarded rather as a cause, help, or confirmation of faith, than its *object*. The latter view of the passage, however, it must be admitted, is strongly corroborated by Isaiah, 7. 14. ' Therefore the Lord himself shall give you a sign ; Behold a virgin shall conceive and bear a son, and shall call his name Immanuel.' Here both the sign and the thing promised are future. But, the point is one which after all we must leave undecided.

13. *Behold, when I come*, &c. The diffidence of Moses is not yet overcome. Still doubting and irresolute, he ventures to urge another difficulty in the words of this verse. He supposes that his own people will rigidly interrogate him by way of sifting the authority under which he acts, and will particularly require of him an account of the *nature, character*, and *attributes* of the Being whose commission he bore. This is undoubtedly the true sense of the term *name* in this connexion. It is not so much the *common title* by which he was known that they would wish to learn— for it is supposed by the wording of the text that he would announce him as ' the God of Abraham, of Isaac, and of Jacob'—as the *new* and *significant denomination*, which he might be expected to assume on this occasion. The people were well aware by tradition that whenever God had been pleased to honor any of their ancestors with a new revelation, it was his wont, in order to give it greater weight, to assume a new **characteristic denomination, expressive**

mainly of that attribute which served as a security for the fulfilment of the promise. Thus when he appeared to Abraham, Gen. 17. 1, and promised him a son in his old age, he announced himself as *El Shaddai, God Almighty*, infinitely *able* to accomplish all his purposes. So also we find the occasional titles *Most High, Ancient of Days, Jah*, &c. In like manner, Moses took it for granted that on an occasion so momentous as the present, they would expect the announcement of some new and appropriate name, which should carry in its import a kind of pledge for the performance of all that he was pleased to promise.

14. *God said unto Moses, I am that I am.* Heb. אהיה אשר אהיה *ehyeh asher ehyeh*, literally, *I will be that I will be*. The Gr. resolves it, εγω ειμι ο ων, *I am he that is*, or *the Existing One*. Arab. ' The Eternal who passeth not away.' A somewhat similar denomination occurs, Rev. 1. 4, where John invokes grace and peace ' from Him which is and which was, and which is to come,' which is supposed to be a paraphrase or exposition of the name יהוה *Yehovah*, a word derived from the same root היה *hayah*, and of kindred import with the phrase before us. See Note on Ex. 6. 3. The title, ' I am that I am,' properly denotes the underived, eternal, and unchangeable existence of the great Being to whom it is applied, carrying in it also the implication that He, in distinction from all others, is the one only true God, the God who really *is*, while all the pretended deities of the Egyptians and other nations were *a vanity, a nonentity, a lie*. It implies, moreover, as founded upon the immutability of the Divine nature, the certain and

dren of Israel, y I AM hath sent
me unto you.

15 And God said moreover unto
Moses, Thus shalt thou say unto
the children of Israel, The LORD

y ch. 6. 3. John 8. 58. 2 Cor. 1. 20. Hebr.
13. 8. Rev. 1. 4.

God of your fathers, the God of
Abraham, the God of Isaac, and
the God of Jacob, hath sent me
unto you: this *is* z my name for
ever, and this *is* my memorial unto
all generations.

z Ps. 135. 13. Hos. 12. 5.

faithful performance of every promise
which he had uttered, so that whatever
he had bound himself by covenant to
do for Abraham, for Isaac, and for Jacob, he pledges himself by the annunciation of this august title to make the
same good to their seed. ' I am that
(which) I will be, and I will be that
(which) I am; the same yesterday, to-
day, and for ever.' We see then the
purport of the passage. ' If they shall
ask, what is he? by what name is he
known? what are the nature and attributes of him who, as thou sayest, has
sent thee to bring us out of Egypt? tell
them that thou art commissioned by
him who describes his own nature by
saying I AM THAT I AM; I am the eternal, self-existent, and immutable Being;
the only being who can say, that he always will be what he always has been.'
——¶ I AM *hath sent me unto you.*
Heb. אֶהְיֶה *ehyeh, I will be*; a proper
future, but having the force of the *continuous present.* The first person of
the verb of existence is here used as a
noun substantive, and made the nominative to another verb in the third person. This is indeed a striking grammatical anomaly, but it arises out of
the nature of the subject. When God
speaks of himself it is no matter of
wonder that he should disregard all
grammatical rules, for adequate expressions come not within the compass of
any language or any possible form of
speech. The Targ. of Jonathan thus
feebly halts towards a fitting phraseology, ' The That-was and Hereafter-
will-be hath sent me unto you.' And
here we cannot but be reminded of the
remarkable words of our Savior, John,

8. 58, ' Before Abraham was, *I am*.'
The expression is so strikingly parallel, that we know not how to resist the
conclusion that there was a real though
mysterious identity in the essential nature of the two speakers, so that whatever was meant by Jehovah in saying
to Moses, ' I am hath sent me to you,'
the same was meant by the saying of
Jesus, ' Before Abraham was, I am.'
And thus the Jews would appear to have
understood it, for they immediately took
up stones to cast at him, as being guilty
of the highest blasphemy in thus appropriating to himself the incommunicable
name of God.

15. *This is my memorial unto all
generations.* Heb. זִכְרִי *zikri.* The
name or character by which I will be
remembered, celebrated, and invoked
in all time to come. Accordingly, in
allusion to this declaration, we have
Hos. 12. 5, ' Even the Lord (Jehovah)
God of Hosts; the Lord (Jehovah) is
his *memorial*.' Ps. 135, ' Thy name, O
Lord, (Jehovah,) endureth for ever;
and thy *memorial*, O Lord, (Jehovah,)
unto all generations.' The words were
evidently adapted, as they were doubtless intended, to bring the chosen people to a devout recognition of God as
emphatically and pre-eminently the God
of their race, and to wake up to more
lively actings that faith which had become dormant under the pressure of
long continued affliction. Their protracted bondage, though it had not utterly extinguished the light of the great
truth respecting the divine Being and
his perfections, yet had no doubt very
much obscured it. They had lost the
practical sense of their covenant rela

16 Go, and ᵃgather the elders of Israel together, and say unto them, The LORD God of your fathers, the God of Abraham, of Isaac, and of Jacob, appeared unto me, saying,

ᵃ ch. 4. 29.

ᵇ I have surely visited you, and *seen* that which is done to you in Egypt: 17 And I have said, ᶜ I will bring you up out of the affliction of Egypt;

ᵇ Gen. 50. 24. ch. 2, 25. &   ᵈ Luke 1. 68.
ᶜ Gen. 15. 14, 16. ver. 8.

tion to Jehovah, and yet as this was the only true spring of all active faith, hope, and obedience, it was important that they should be freshly instructed on this head, and taught continually to speak of and to trust in God as the God of their fathers, who would never be unfaithful to his engagements.. Moses, therefore, by reminding them of this endearing title of the Most High, would be in fact furnishing them with a constant memorial of their own mercies.

16. *Gather the elders of Israel together.* Gr. την γερουσιαν των υιων Ισραηλ, *the senate or eldership of the children of Israel;* not so much *all* the aged men of the congregation of Israel, as the *elders in office,* the persons of principal note and influence in the tribes, teachers and rulers; men who were qualified by age, experience, and wisdom, to preside over the affairs of the nation, and who it appears were usually employed as organs of communication between Moses and the body of the people. Thus when Moses and Aaron are said, ch. 12. 3, to have been commanded 'to speak unto *all the congregation of Israel,* saying,' &c. we find that in the account of the execution of this order, v. 21, 'Moses called for *all the elders of Israel,* and said unto them,' &c. See Note on Gen. 24. 2—4. As the distinction of tribes was undoubtedly kept up among the Israelites in Egypt, and as it is clear from Num. 2, and elsewhere, that each of the tribes had one or more presiding or ruling chiefs called elders, who formed collectively, at least in after times, the great counsel of the nation, it was to these individuals, as the natural heads and representatives of the rest, that

Moses in the first instance was commanded to go, and summon them together to a general assembly, when he would announce to them the fact and the object of his mission. The release of Israel was to be demanded of the king in the general name of the whole people, and this required the consent and concurrence of the entire body of their rulers, the proper organs of the national voice. When *they* were informed of the fact and convinced of the reality of Moses' mission, they would of course exert all their influence in preparing the people for the crisis before them.——¶ *I have surely visited you and* seen, &c. Heb. פקד פקדתי *pakod pakadti, visiting I have visited.* That is, I have so absolutely purposed and decreed to deliver you from Egypt, that it may be said to be already done. Although the word 'seen' is supplied in our version, it is not indispensably necessary to complete the sense; as the import of the preceding verb includes the idea of *judicial* or *penal visitation,* as well as *merciful.* To *visit the doings* of any one is plainly to *punish* them. The phrase therefore expresssively conveys the assurance of visiting the Israelites *in mercy* and their oppressors *in judgment.*

17. *And I have said I will bring,* &c. That is, I have resolved. See Note on Gen. 1. 3. The term 'affliction' here will appear very appropriate upon comparing this with the original promise given to Abraham, Gen. 15. 13, 'Know of a surety that thy seed shall be a stranger in a land that is not theirs, and shall serve them; and they shall *afflict* them four hundred years.' From this *affliction* they were now to be delivered,

unto the land of the Canaanites, and the Hittites, and the Amorites, and the Perizzites, and the Hivites, and the Jebusites, unto a land flowing with milk and honey.

18 And d they shall hearken to thy voice ; and e thou shalt come, thou and the elders of Israel, unto the king of Egypt, and ye shall say unto

d ch. 4. 31.   e ch. 5. 1, 3.

him, The LORD God of the Hebrews hath f met with us ; and now let us go (we beseech thee) three day's journey into the wilderness, that we may sacrifice to the LORD our God.

19 ¶ And I am sure that the king of Egypt g will not let you go, no, not by a mighty hand.

f Numb. 23. 3, 4, 15, 16.   g ch. 5. 2. & 7. 4.

---

and in order to stimulate their minds with the incentive of hope, the Most High recites a list of nations of whose territories they were to come into possession, and lest moreover they should be discouraged by the recollection that several of the patriarchs had been formerly driven out of that land by famine, he gives them adequate assurance on that head by telling them that it is 'a land flowing with milk and honey.'

18. *And they shall hearken to thy voice.* That is, shall believingly and obediently hearken. See Note on Gen. 16. 2. This assurance on the part of God was peculiarly seasonable and precious. The Israelites had been so long depressed and dispirited by their bondage, that they would naturally be slow to entertain any thoughts of deliverance, and a cordial willingness to use the means, encounter the difficulties, and face the dangers requisite for that purpose, could only be effected by a powerful divine influence on their hearts; and that influence God here engages to put forth. Such an assurance is the grand encouragement of all good men engaged in declaring useful and saving truths or commanding laborious duties to their fellow men. Their best words will be unregarded, their utmost efforts will fail, unless the Lord himself infuse a vital efficacy into them, and give the hearing ear and the yielding heart to their auditors.——¶ *The Lord God of the Hebrews hath met with us.* Heb. נקרה *nikrah, has been made to occur.* The allusion is plainly to the *visible*

token of the divine presence which had been manifested, and they say ' hath met with *us*,' though Moses alone had witnessed it, from his constructive identity, as leader, with the people, and from its having been vouchsafed for their benefit as well as his. The Gr. and the Vulg. both render, ' hath called us.'——¶ *Let us go three days' journey into the wilderness,* &c. Neither Moses nor he in whose name he spoke, can be justly charged with falsehood or prevarication in uttering this language. The utmost that can be alleged is, that he did not tell the *whole* truth, and this it cannot be shown that he was bound to do. See on this subject the Note on Gen. 12. 13. The command to make this request of Pharaoh shows, that it may sometimes be the way of true wisdom to seek that as a favor, which may at the same time be claimed as a right.

19. *I am sure that the king of Egypt will not let you go.* Heb. לא יתן אתכם להלך *lo yitten ethkem lahalok, will not give you to go.* See Note on Gen. 20. 6. God announces beforehand that their first application will be unavailing, in order that they may not be disheartened by the repulse, and give up the enterprise as hopeless. Let it not be thought, however, derogatory to the divine glory thus to send men advisedly upon a bootless errand ; for the result would tend far more strikingly to illustrate the equity of the subsequent proceedings of providence in extorting, with tremendous judgments, that which had been unjustly

20 And I will ^hstretch out my hand, and smite Egypt with ⁱall my wonders which I will do in the midst thereof: and ^kafter that he will let you go.

21 And ^lI will give this people favour in the sight of the Egyptians;

^h ch. 6. 6. & 7. 5. & 9. 15. ⁱ ch. 7. 3. & 11. 9. Deut. 6. 22. Neh. 9. 10. Ps. 105. 27. & 135. 9. Jer. 32. 20. Acts 7. 36. See ch. 7. to ch. 13. ^k ch. 12. 31. ^l ch. 11. 3. & 12. 36. Ps. 106. 46. Prov. 16. 7.

and it shall come to pass, that, when ye go, ye shall not go empty :

22 ^mBut every woman shall borrow of her neighbour, and of her that sojourneth in her house, jewels of silver, and jewels of gold, and raiment : and ye shall put *them* upon your sons, and upon your daughters ; and ⁿye shall spoil the Egyptians.

^m Gen. 15. 14. ch. 11. 2. & 12. 35, 36. ⁿ Job 27. 17. Prov. 13. 22. Ezek. 39. 10.

and impiously withheld. As the request was in itself simple and reasonable, his refusal to comply with it would disclose his real character, and show how truly he and his people deserved all the wrath that they were afterwards made to feel. ——¶ *No, not by a mighty hand.* That is, he will at first resist and rebel, notwithstanding all the demonstrations of my great power against him; but at length he shall yield, as is declared in the next verse. Or it may be rendered, with the Gr. and Vulg. 'Unless by a strong hand.'

20. *And I will stretch out mine hand,* &c. Heb. וְשָׁלַחְתִּי *veshalahti, and I will send out.* Chal. ' And I will send the stroke of my strength.' The connective particle ו *and* may as properly here be rendered *but* or *therefore ;* as if the design were to point to the *opposition* which God was to make to Pharaoh's resistance ; or to indicate the *reason* of his stretching forth his hand ; ' *Therefore* will I stretch forth my hand, because Pharaoh will not yield to my demand without it. I will see whose hand is the stronger, his or mine.'

21. *I will give this people favor in the sight of the Egyptians.* Here again we perceive that God has his eye upon the ancient promise, Gen. 15. 14, ' And also that nation whom they shall serve, will I judge : and afterward shall they come out *with great substance.*' He allures his people by an accumulation of promises, that they may engage in the work before them with more alac-

rity and vigor. He not only assures them of liberty, but of riches. But this could be accomplished only by turning the hostile hearts of the Egyptians to a posture of clemency and generosity, and this he engages to do. The words, however, ' I will give this people favor,' are not to be understood as intimating that he would *conciliate towards them the affection* of their enemies. Undoubtedly the reverse of this was the case, particularly at the time when the promised favor was shown them ; for they were then trembling for their lives under the repeated inflictions of the plagues ; but the meaning is, that God would so overrule their dispositions towards his people that they should bestow upon them *marked expressions of favor,* they should be induced to *treat them as if they loved them,* though in reality they hated them as the procuring cause of all their troubles. Such an absolute control over the fiercest spirits of the enemies of his church shows that when God allows them to rage it is for the wisest purposes of discipline to his people. As he *could* soften them in a moment, if he does not do so, it is because he sees it better that license should be afforded them for a season.

22. *Every woman shall borrow of her neighbor,* &c. Heb. שָׁאֲלָה *shaalah. shall ask.* For a somewhat extended view of the moral character of this transaction see Note on Ex. 12. 35. We shall there see that when God commanded the Israelites to possess them-

CHAPTER IV.

AND Moses answered and said, But, behold, they will not be-

selves of the jewels and raiment of their enemies, and to ' spoil' them, they did not take them by rapine and stealth, but as *spoils* voluntarily given up to them by the Egyptians; in a word, that there is no ground in the import of the original for accusing the Israelites of fraud or injustice. Without anticipating the fuller canvassing the subject which we there propose, we may here remark, that the term ' borrow' has been somewhat unhappily adopted in our translation, as it implies a *promise of return*. But this is not the sense of the original שָׁאַל *shaal*. This signifies *to ask, demand, petition, request,* and is the very word employed Ps. 2. 8, ' *Ask* (שְׁאַל *sheal*) of me the heathen for thine inheritance,' &c.; although in two passages, Ex. 22. 14, and 2 Kings, 6. 5, it cannot perhaps be doubted that its import is that of *borrowing*. But for. *borrow* in the more strict and genuine sense of the word, the Heb. has entirely another term לָוָה *lavah*, which occurs among other places, Deut. 28. 12, ' Thou shalt lend unto many nations, and thou shalt not *borrow* (הִלְוִיתָ *hilvitha*).' Neh. 5. 4, ' There were also that said, We have *borrowed* (לָוִינוּ *lavinu*) money for the king's tribute.' Prov. 22. 7, ' The *borrower* (מַלְוֶה *malveh*) is servant to the lender.' Is. 24. 2, ' And t shall be, as with the lender, so with the *borrower* (מַלְוֶה *malveh*).'——¶ *Of her that sojourneth in her house.* Heb. מִגָּרַת בֵּיתָהּ *miggarath bethah.* Gr. σνσκηνον αντης, *her fellow-dweller.* Chal. ' From her who is a near neighbor to her house.' But this is not an exact rendering of the Heb. nor does it differ sufficiently from the preceding term. The original properly signifies *an in-dweller*, as in Job, 19. 15, ' They that dwell in mine house (גָּרֵי בֵיתִי *garë bëthi*), and my maids count me for a

lieve me, nor hearken unto my voice: for they will say, The LORD hath not appeared unto thee.

stranger.' The implication would seem to be, that the Egyptians in some cases occupied tenements which belonged to the Israelites, or at any rate that they lived very closely intermingled together, a circumstance which gave them a better opportunity to despoil their oppressors of their effects.——¶ *Jewels of silver and jewels of gold.'* Heb. כְּלֵי *kelë.* The present rendering no doubt restricts too much the meaning of the original, which properly includes *vessels, implements, utensils,* of any kind made of gold or silver. The term is here equivalent to *valuable effects.* These they were to ' put upon their sons and upon their daughters,' by which would naturally be understood from our translation, that they were to put them upon their children *as ornaments.* But would the sons wear female ornaments? A much more probable supposition is, that they were to *lay* them upon the young people *as a burden to be carried.* If the original term meant nothing but *jewels,* the former interpretation would no doubt be entirely plausible. But we have seen that it includes every kind of gold and silver articles. They were therefore put upon their sons and daughters, not to be *worn*, but to be *carried.*

Chapter 4

1. *Moses answered and said, But behold, they will not believe me.* Heb. וְהֵן *ve-hen, and behold.* The Gr. we incline to believe has the most correct rendering εαν, *if,* making it a *hypothetical* instead of an *absolute* affirmation of Moses. Thus too the Arab, ' Perhaps they will not believe me.' The original term is expressly so rendered, Jer. 3. 1, ' They say *if* (הֵן *hen*) a man put away his wife, and she go from him,' &c. It cannot indeed be questioned

2 And the LORD said unto him, What *is* that in thy hand ? And he said, ª A rod.

3 And he said, Cast it on the ground. And he cast it on the ground, and it became a serpent: and Moses fled from before it.

---

that Moses was reluctant to be employed on the embassy to Pharaoh and intended in these words to urge an objection, but the phraseology appears to present it in a *conditional* form. Otherwise, it may be asked, on what authority did he make the assertion? How did he know that the elders would not believe him, when God had expressly assured him, ch. 3. 18, that they would? Would he adventure upon such a pointed contradiction of the words of Jehovah?

2. *What is that in thine hand?* The drift of this question is simply to wake up and direct Moses' attention to the miracle about to be wrought. It is as if he had said, 'Take particular notice, and see that there is no illusion in the matter. Be sure that what you see is really what you take it to be.' When God questions his creatures it is not for the sake of *learning*, but of *teaching*. —¶ *And he said, a rod.* Heb. מטה *matteh, a rod*, or *staff*, as it is rendered Gen. 38. 18; i. e. such a rod or crook as is used by shepherds in tending their flocks. Thus Mic. 7. 14, 'Feed thy people *with thy rod* the flock of thine heritage.' In v. 20, it is called the 'rod of God' from the miraculous effects which it was instrumental in working. Comp. v. 20.

3. *And it became a serpent.* Heb. יהי לנחש *yehi lenahash, it became to a serpent*. It will probably answer all the demands of the text to consider this as simply a miraculous sign intended to authenticate the mission of Moses. We are not required to seek or assign a reason why this particular sign was adopted rather than any other, yet we may without extravagance suppose that there *was* some intrinsic adaptedness in the sign selected to the purpose of

its exhibition. In what this consisted it may not be easy confidently to affirm. Calvin suggests with great plausibility, that the drift of it was to intimate the formidableness of Moses to Pharaoh, notwithstanding his comparatively abject and despised condition. The staff was the ensign of the shepherd's calling, and what to human view more contemptible than a rustic keeper of sheep coming forth from the desert, where he had been accustomed to encounter only wild beasts of prey, and oppose his simple crook to the sceptre of a powerful king? Would not this be a very significant mode of teaching that however destitute of human means of intimidation, the shepherd of Midian should notwithstanding be rendered dreadful to a throned oppressor, when the rude staff that he carried in his hand should be a more destructive instrument than a thousand swords? His own affrightment on the occasion would tend to give him a deeper sense of the hidden power of that terror which Omnipotence could strike into the inmost spirit of his adversary, and he could not but infer that there was no need of numerous forces or great preparations when he carried in his hand an implement the bare sight of which was able to smite the monarch with consternation. It may be proper, however, to observe that the Jewish commentators are disposed to consider the serpent as representing Pharaoh rather than Moses. As the original נחש *nahash*, as remarked on Gen. 3. 1, is occasionally interchanged with תנין *tannin, dragon*, the very word in fact which occurs Ex. 7. 10, 'And Aaron cast down his rod before Pharaoh and before his servants, and it became a *serpent* (תנין *tannin*),' and as Pharaoh, king of

4 And the LORD said unto Moses, Put forth thy hand, and take it by the tail. And he put forth his hand, and caught it, and it became a rod in his hand:

5 That they may b believe that c the LORD God of their fathers, the God of Abraham, the God of Isaac,

b ch. 19. 9.   c ch. 3. 15.

and the God of Jacob, hath appeared unto thee.

6 ¶ And the LORD said furthermore unto him, Put now thine hand into thy bosom. And he put his hand into his bosom: and when he took it out, behold, his hand *was* leprous d as snow.

d Numb. 12. 10.   2 Kings 5. 27.

Egypt, is termed, Ezek. 29. 3, ' The great *dragon* (תנים *tannim*) that lieth in the midst of his rivers,' they suggest hat thé rod converted into this reptile-nonster, (perhaps the *crocodile*, as ightfoot believes), was designed to represent Pharaoh in all the terrors of his cruelty and oppression ; while on the other hand his being seized by the hand of Moses, and converted into an innocuous rod, indicated the ease with which, under the mighty working of God, he should be subdued, despoiled of his power to harm, and even brought to confess himself to be at the mercy of Moses, as a rod is wielded by the hand of its possessor. Thus, Eliezer, a Jewish commentator : ' As the serpent biteth and killeth the sons of Adam, so Pharaoh and his people did bite and kill the Israelites ; but he was turned and made like a dry stick.'

5. *That they may believe*, &c. The sentence is apparently imperfect, requiring some such preliminary clause, as ' Do this, that they may believe, &c.' For a similar omission, and the manner in which it is to be supplied, compare Mark, 14. 49, ' I was daily with you in the temple teaching, and ye took me not : but the Scriptures must be fulfilled,' with Matt. 26. 55, 56, ' I sat daily with you teaching in the temple, and ye laid no hold on me. But all this was done, that the Scriptures of the prophets might be fulfilled.' The miracle was not only exhibited on this occasion to Moses, but the power conferred upon him of working it himself, both for the purpose of acquiring credence among the Israel-

ites, and of overawing the obstinacy of Pharaoh. The incident goes evidently on the ground that miracles are a certain and satisfactory proof of the divinity of the mission and doctrine of a prophet. They constitute the proper credentials of one sent of God. They are a divine testimony both to the commission of the messenger and to the truth of the message. The principle on which miracles are wrought is clear ly and distinctly recognised in the words of the woman of Sarepta to the prophet who had raised her son to life, 1 Kings, 17. 24, ' Now by this I know thou art a man of God, and that the word of the Lord by thy mouth is truth.' This is the language of nature and of common sense.

6. *Put now thine hand into thy bosom*, &c. That is, into the open part of the tunic, a long outer robe, above the girdle. The drift of this second sign was similar to that of the first, for with these miraculous voices ' God speaketh once, yea twice,' though it is too often the case that ' man regardeth it not.' As far as the intrinsic significancy of the sign is concerned, it was evidently calculated to teach that whatever is now vigorous, vital, and flourishing may at once be withered at the nod of Omnipotence ; and again with equal facility restored to its pristine condition. The effect of a leprosy was to banish the subject of it from the abodes of men to solitary seclusion. As far as the miracle had relation to the person of Moses, an emblematic leprosy was upon him when he went out as a shunned and

7 And he said, Put thine hand into thy bosom again. And he put his hand into his bosom again, and plucked it out of his bosom, and behold, e it was turned again as his *other* flesh.

e Deut. 32. 39. Numb. 12. 13, 14. 2 Kings 5. 14. Matt. 8. 3.

hated fugitive from the palace of Pharaoh, and led his flock over the rough, sandy, and arid places of the Midian desert, and among sapless thorns and thickets. After passing forty years in this desolate state, cast out as a withered branch, without name, without repute, without power, he suddenly recovers all he had lost, and comes forth as a messenger of God, clothed in all the honors of a divine commission. With a slight modification, the same sign may be considered as shadowing forth the contrast between the condition of the Israelites, wasted and worn out in their bondage, and the state of prosperity and glory to which they were about to be raised as the elect people of Heaven. This view is sufficient to show the pertinency of the sign, without requiring us to fix upon any more recondite import. It was plainly adapted to teach the general salutary lesson, that every thing human stands or falls, flourishes or fades, according to the good pleasure of God; that it is his prerogative to weaken and abase the stout, the hardy, the lofty, and his to restore the decayed and fallen to life, activity, and vigor.——¶ *Leprous as snow.* As snow is not leprous, reference must be intended to the color of the flesh. Accordingly the Chal. has correctly, ' As white as snow.' This was the worst kind of leprosy, in which the body not only assumes the hue of dead and bloodless flesh, but becomes covered with white scales, attended with a most tormenting itch.

8. *If they will not hearken to the voice of the first sign,* That is, to the im-

8 And it shall come to pass, if they will not believe thee, neither hearken to the voice of the first sign, that they will believe the voice of the latter sign.

9 And it shall come to pass, if they will not believe also these two signs, neither hearken unto thy

port, meaning, drift, of the first sign. See Note upon the sense of the word ' voice,' Gen. 21. 17. The sign is said to have a ' voice,' because it speaks that to the eye which words do to the ear. On the contrary, that which is addressed to the ear is sometimes represented as if exhibited to the eye; thus Gal. 3. 1, ' Before whose eyes' Jesus Christ hath been evidently set forth crucified among you;' i. e. who have heard this fact declared in the preaching of the gospel. The Psalmist probably alludes to the phraseology of the text, Ps. 105. 27, ' They showed his signs among them.' Heb. ' They showed the *words* of his signs.' They were words spoken to the ear of reason, if not of sense.——¶ *They will believe the voice of the latter sign.* This is not perhaps to be understood as a positive affirmation, for the next verse intimates the possibility that they may require still farther evidence. The words appear designed to express the *intrinsic adaptedness* of the signs to produce belief, or the effect which might be *reasonably anticipated* from their exhibition. The circumstance strikingly shows the extent of the divine indulgence. The perverse rejection of the first sign alone would clearly show them unworthy of being favored with another. But God multiplies mercies, even when judgments are most richly deserved. He gives sign upon sign, as well as line upon line.

9. *Take of the water of the river.* That is, of the river Nile. This, it would appear, was a miracle to be wrought for the confirmation of Moses' calling

voice, that thou shalt take of the water of the river, and pour *it* upon the dry *land* : and f the water which thou takest out of the river shall become blood upon the dry *land.*

f ch. 7. 19.

10 ¶ And Moses said unto the Lord, O my Lord, I *am* not eloquent, neither heretofore, nor since thou hast spoken unto thy servant: but g I *am* slow of speech, and of a slow tongue.

g ch. 6. 12. Jer. 1. 6.

before the Israelites and not before the Egyptians, for in that mentioned, ch. 7. 17, the waters *in* the river were to be turned into blood, here the water *taken out* of the river. The sign imported, perhaps, that the time was now at hand when God would judge the Egyptians for the death of the Hebrew infants, whose blood they had shed in the waters.

10. *O my Lord, I am not eloquent.* Heb. אִישׁ דְּבָרִים *ish debarim, a man of words.* Thus, Job, 11. 2, ' A man of lips,' i. e. a talkative man ; Eng. ' a man full of talk.' Job, 22. 8, ' Man of arm ;' i. e. mighty man. Ps. 140. 11, ' man of tongue ;' i. e. prattler, or, perhaps, slanderer. The Gr. has ουκ ικανος ειμι, *I am not sufficient.* We cannot but wonder at the backwardness of Moses, although we are forced to admire the fidelity of the historian in thus frankly recording his own incredulity and perverseness. Though it is doubtless true that nothing becomes a man so much as humility, yet diffidence may degenerate into distrust, and carry us into a criminal disobedience of the positive commands of God. He who calls us into the field of action can give us both wisdom and strength to perform the work which he has laid upon us. When Moses expressed his inherent inability to execute the mighty charge, he did well ; but when he resisted the appointment, after so many promises and signs, he failed in his duty, and betrayed a spirit of the most culpable unbelief. But even this was borne with. —— ¶ *Neither heretofore, nor since thou hast spoken.* Heb. ' Since yesterday, and since the third day.' A usual form of speech to intimate time past in

general. See Note on Gen. 31. 2. Some have supposed that Moses labored under a natural defect of utterance, and that he declined the commanded service from an apprehension that the effect of his message might be defeated in the delivery of it. He is supposed therefore to intimate in the present passage, that as the infirmity of which he speaks had been of long standing, and as he perceived no alteration in himself for the better in this respect during the present interview, he knew not any reason to think that the difficulty was likely to be obviated ; for if at this time, while God was speaking to him, who had power at once to remove all impediment of speech, his defective articulation continued, much more was it likely to continue afterward. But whether his objection was founded upon this, or upon the want of that ready and copious command of language which constitutes the powerful orator, we have not the means of ascertaining. He was soon however taught that he who made the mouth could make it eloquent.—— ¶ *Slow of speech and of a slow tongue.* Heb. כבד פה וכבד לשׁון *kebad peh u kebad lashon, heavy of mouth and heavy of tongue.* Gr. ' Of a small voice and of a slow tongue.' Chal. ' Of a heavy speech and of a deep tongue.' As the words are rendered in our translation, it would be difficult, perhaps, to mark the distinction between 'slow of speech,' and ' of a slow tongue ;' but from the the force of the original we gather, that the former is more appropriate to an imperfect elocution, occasioned by some defect in the action of the organs of speech ; the latter, to a want of aptness

11 And the LORD said unto him,
ⁿ Who hath made man's mouth? or
who maketh the dumb, or deaf, or
the seeing, or the blind? have not
I the LORD?

12 Now therefore go, and I will be
ⁱ with thy mouth, and teach thee
what thou shalt say.

h Ps. 94. 9.　　ⁱ Isai. 50. 4.　Jer. 1. 9.　Matt.
10. 19.　Mark 13. 11.　Luke 12. 11, 12. & 21.
14, 15.

13 And he said, O my Lord, ᵏ send,
I pray thee, by the hand *of him
whom* thou wilt send.

14 And the anger of the LORD was
kindled against Moses, and he said.
Is not Aaron the Levite thy brother?
I know that he can speak well. And
also, behold, ˡ he cometh forth to
meet thee: and when he seeth
thee, he will be glad in his heart.

ᵏ Jonah 1. 3.　ˡ ver. 27.　1 Sam. 10. 2, 3, 5.

or felicity in adapting one's expressions
to the ideas which he wishes to convey. The latter phrase occurs, Exek.
3. 5, 6, where it is rendered, ' hard language,' i. e. obscure, requiring interpretation, as it is immediately added,
' whose words thou canst not understand.' There is perhaps an intimation
that in the long lapse of forty years he
had almost lost the true pronunciation
of the Egyptian language.

11. *Who hath made man's mouth.*
Heb. מִי שָׂם פֶּה לָאָדָם *mi sam peh le-
adam, who put the mouth to man,* or, *to
Adam?* Targ. Jon. ' Who is he who
placed the utterance of speech in the
mouth of Adam the first man?' Arab.
' Who created pronunciation to man?'
By this appeal to Moses respecting the
origin of the human faculties, God would
have him to infer, that he who bestowed
them upon the first man could, with infinite ease, endow him with those which
were lacking and remedy those which
were imperfect.

13. *O my Lord, send I pray thee,* &c.
Chal. and Targ. Jerus. ' Send now by
the hand of him who is worthy to be
sent.' Gr. ' Choose another able man
whom thou wilt send.' By the Heb.
idiom the term ' hand' is used to denote
any kind of instrumentality or ministry; thus Ex. 9. 35, ' As the Lord had
spoken by Moses,' Heb. ' *By the hand*
of Moses.' 2 Kings, 17. 13, ' Yet the
Lord testified against Israel by all the
prophets.' Heb. ' *By the hand* of all
prophets.' Is. 64. 7, ' And has con-

sumed us because of our iniquities.'
Heb. ' *By the hand* of our iniquities.'—
The reluctance of Moses to engage in
the work is not yet overcome. And
who can wonder that the anger of the
Lord was kindled against him? Had
an earthly monarch been thus rudely
treated by one of his subjects, whom he
chose to honor by sending him as his
representative to a foreign court, would
he not have been justified in spurning
the man from his presence, and conferring the high distinction upon some one
else? So, had God taken Moses at his
word, and entirely discarded him from
the honorable service to which he was
thus called, he would only have treated
him as he deserved. But the divine for
bearance was not yet exhausted.

14. *Is not Aaron the Levite thy brother*
The literal rendering of this clause is
' Is not Aaron thy brother the Levite?'
which we cannot but understand as implying, that in consequence of Moses'
unbelieving waywardness on this occa
sion, the distinguishing honor of the
priesthood, and of being the official
head of the house of Levi, the person in
whom the dignity of that name should
be especially centred, which would
otherwise have been bestowed upon
him, should now be conferred upon his
brother Aaron, and perpetuated in his
family. In this fact the expression of
the Lord's anger consisted. Otherwise
how was Aaron any more ' the Levite
than Moses? We find accordingly the
forfeited privilege of Moses thus so

15 And ^mthou shalt speak unto him, and ⁿput words in his mouth:

m ch. 7. 1, 2. n Numb. 22. 38. & 23. 5, 12, 16. Deut. 18. 18. Isai. 51. 16. Jer. 1. 9.

and I will be with thy mouth, and with his mouth, and ^owill teach you what ye shall do.

o Deut. 5. 31.

cured to Aaron, 1 Chron. 23. 13, ' And Aaron was separated that he should sanctify the most holy things, he and his sons for ever, to burn incense before the Lord, to minister unto him, and to bless his name for ever.' This, we suppose would have been the honor of Moses, had he yielded a ready obedience to the divine mandate. The event teaches us that those who decline the labor and hazard connected with the call of God to a special service, may thereby forfeit and forego a blessing of which they little dream.——¶ *I know that he can speak well.* Heb. רבר ידבר כי *ki dabbēr yedabbēr, that speaking he will speak.*——¶ *Behold, he cometh forth to meet thee.* This was plainly the annunciation of a *future* event. As Moses had not hitherto thought of leaving Midian, nor had yet started upon his journey thence, if Aaron was now on his way to meet his brother, it must lave been in consequence of a divine suggestion, for from no other source could he have had any information that he *should meet* him. Yet no one can question that God, from his foresight of Moses' departure from Midian, might have put it into the heart of Aaron to go forth anticipating an interview with one who was dear to him by nature, and whom, after an absence of forty years he would be very desirous to see. The hearts of the different agents are often moved to the same work at a great distance from each other. It would seem that the Most High was simultaneously drawing Aaron with one hand from Egypt, and Moses with the other from Midian. The vision ought undoubtedly at once to have impelled Moses forward to a compliance with the divine injunction ; but as Omniscience saw the result from the beginning, he pro-

vided a new stimulus to his apathy in the promise of meeting his brother in the desert, whom he determined by a secret impulse to lead forth for that purpose. In a manner somewhat analogous Ananias was directed in a vision to go and meet Saul of Tarsus, Acts, 9. 17, in order to be an instrument of opening his eyes and confirming his faith. This favor the perverse importunity of Moses extorted from God, but he, in the plenitude of his goodness, determined to elicit from the fault of his servant new matter of grace ; as it is his to bring light out of darkness. In saying that he knew that Aaron would be ' glad in his heart' upon meeting his brother, he designs perhaps to administer a covert reproof to the tardiness of Moses ; q. d. ' Aaron is coming forth with alacrity, and shall hail thee with joy and exhilaration of spirits, whilst thou, restrained by sinful distrust and weighed down with sadness, canst scarcely drag thyself forward to a meeting.'

15. *And thou shalt speak unto him,* &c. The Lord in these words declares that he will not admit his plea of, ' I pray thee have me excused,' and yet so does it as to consult his servant's honor against his will. When he might justly have substituted another in his room, he still condescends to employ him, and though he divides the office, and joins Aaron in commission with him, he endows his reluctant emissary with the highest dignity. While Aaron was to supply by his native ready utterance, the deficiency of Moses in this respect, the latter was to convey to his brother, *as from God himself,* the instructions and directions which should from time to time be given him.——¶ *I will be with thy mouth, and with his mouth*

16 And he shall be thy spokesman unto the people : and he shall be, *even* he shall be to thee instead of a mouth, and p thou shalt be to him instead of God.

17 And thou shalt take q this rod in thy hand, wherewith thou shalt do signs.

p ch. 7. 1. & 18. 19.   q ver. 2.

Chal. 'My Word shall be with thy mouth and with his mouth.' Gr. ' I will open thy mouth and his mouth.' Even Aaron himself, however eloquent, could not speak to the purpose unless God was with his mouth. The possession of the best gifts does not supersede the necessity of divine assistance.

16. *He shall be to thee instead of a mouth, and thou shalt be to him instead of God.* Chal. ' He shall speak for thee with the people, and shall be thine interpreter, and thou shalt be as a prince (רֵב *rab*) unto him.' Jerus. Targ. ' Thou shalt be to him a master inquiring doctrine from before the Lord.' Gr. and Vulg. Thou shalt be to him in things pertaining to God ;' the very phrase which Paul employs, Heb. 5. 1, ' For every high priest taken from among men, is ordained for men *in things pertaining to God.*' How strikingly does this illustrate the Apostle's declaration that ' the gifts and callings of God are without repentance.' We see a *persevering beneficence* towards Moses, that fills us with amazement. When we should rather expect that the fire which had spared the bush would consume the recusant, we behold a continued triumph of mercy over judgment.

17. *Thou shalt take this rod in thine hand.* Gr. ' This rod which was turned into a serpent, shalt thou take,' &c. The end of his mission was to be accomplished rather · by *acting* than by *speaking*, and he is commanded to take with him his shepherd's rod, not only as an instrument for working wonders, and an ensign of authority, but also as

18 ¶ And Moses went, and returned to Jethro his father-in-law, and said unto him, Let me go, I pray thee, and return unto my brethren which *are* in Egypt, and see whether they be yet alive. And Jethro said to Moses, Go in peace.

---

a memento of the mean condition out of which he had been called, and as a means of pouring deeper contempt upon the state and pomp of Pharaoh. In like manner on a subsequent occasion the simple sling of David was made to put to shame the ponderous armor of Goliath. The more humble the guise in which we go against the enemies of God, the more signal the glory of their defeat.

18. *Moses went and returned to Jethro.* Heb. אֶל יֶתֶר *el Yether*, to Jether ; but in the close of the verse ' Jethro,' as usual. Thus the person who in Nehem. 6. 12, is called ' Geshem,' is in v. 6, called ' Gashmu.' Moses was prompted by a sense of justice and decency to acquaint his father-in-law with his intention to leave Midian and go into Egypt ; but he saw fit to conceal from Jethro the errand upon which God had sent him, lest he should endeavor to hinder or discourage him from so difficult and dangerous an enterprise. In this conduct the piety and prudence of Moses are equally conspicuous with his modesty and humility. He determines to guard against all temptations to disobedience, and at the same time not to indulge in a vain-glorious ostentation of the high honor conferred upon him. This part of Moses' conduct is a striking proof that the privilege of being admitted to near communion with God will never generate a contemptuous disregard for those whom we are bound in the relations of life to honor.——¶ *Go in peace.* Gr. 'Go prospering ;' an invocation of general welfare. See Note on Gen. 29, 6.—37. 4.

19 And the LORD said unto Moses in Midian, Go, return into Egypt: for ʳall the men are dead which sought thy life.

r ch. 2. 15, 23.   Matt. 2. 20.

20 And Moses took his wife, and his sons, and set them upon an ass, and he returned to the land of Egypt.   And Moses took ˢthe rod of God in his hand.

s ch. 17. 9.   Numb. 20. 8, 9.

19. *And the Lord said.* Aben Ezra says, and we think with great probability, that this should be rendered in the pluperfect tense, 'The Lord *had* said; i. e. on some other occasion not particularly specified.   He observes moreover that as a general rule events are not recorded by the sacred writers in the exact order in which they occurred.——¶ *The men are dead which sought thy life.* Heb. מבקשים את נפשך *mebakshim eth naphsheka, which (were) seeking thy soul.*   On the sense of the word 'soul,' see Note on Gen. 2, 7. Chal. 'Which sought to kill thee.'   The phrase, 'to seek the soul' is sometimes used in a good sense, as Ps. 142, 4. (Heb.) 'No man sought my soul;' (Eng.) 'No man *cared for* my soul;' yet it usually signifies seeking with a murderous intent, thus explained 1 Kings, 19, 10. 'And they seek my life (soul) *to take it away.*'   This declaration would remove a fear which it was natural that Moses should feel, though we do not learn that he expressed it. A grand obstacle would meet him on the very threshold, should the blood formerly shed by him be required at his hand.   God therefore allays all his fears on this head by assuring him that no avengers of that deed were now alive to trouble him.   It is probable that the information thus conveyed to him was important to be given to Jethro in order to obtain his consent to his son-in-law's departure.   It is scarcely to be supposed that he would have bestowed his daughter upon a wandering stranger without being made acquainted with the leading events of his previous history; nor after his being an inmate of his house for forty years, would he be

willing to see him and his daughter rush into danger without some prospect of escape.   His scruples would be of course removed by the assurance of a heavenly call, accompanied by the promise of a happy issue.

20. *Moses took his wife and his sons,* &c.   Thus clearly intimating the purpose of a final departure from Midian, and of a permanent settlement in Egypt. The single ass for his family shows an humble equipment for a messenger of God, but the Gr. has τα υποξυγια, *the beasts of burden,* and the Hebrew usage in this particular as illustrated in the Note on Gen. 24, 10, will show that we are not necessarily shut up to the precise letter of the narrative.   This is confirmed by the following extract from the 'Pict. Hist. of Palestine,' page 184. 'The original narrative speaks but of one ass, 'set them upon an ass;' but, as it seems preposterous to suppose that there was but one ass for them all, it is likely that, as often happens, the singular is here put for the plural; and that the meaning is, 'he set every one of them upon an ass.'   We do not recollect any modern instance of asses being employed in a journey across this desert, whereas the present is far from being the only ancient instance.   In fact, there seem to have been, in very ancient times, greater facilities for travel across this desert than at present.   Perhaps it was not so desolate as now; although even now we believe that during the winter and early spring it might be crossed on asses.   Then there seem also to have been caravanserais in districts where no one now expects to find such a convenience; and that the way across this and other deserts was com-

21 And the LORD said unto Moses,
When thou goest to return into
Egypt, see *that* thou do all those
wonders before Pharaoh which I

t ch. 3. 20.

have put in thine hand: but ᵘ I
will harden his heart, that he shall
not let the people go.

u ch. 7. 3, 13. & 9. 12, 35. & 10. 1. & 14. 8
Deut. 2. 30. Josh. 11. 20. Isai. 63. 17 John
12. 40. Rom. 9. 18.

paratively safe appears from numerous instances, such as the journeys of the patriarchs to Egypt, those of Eliezer and Jacob to Mesopotomia, and this of Moses to Egypt from the eastern gulf, with his wife and two children. Indeed, if there were no attendants with this party, it would seem that the wife of Moses returned to Midian with her two sons, unaccompanied by any man. We think it very possible, however, that there may have been attendants, although the Scriptural narrative has no intimation to that effect. However, the absence of any acts of robbery, or of the fear of any such acts, from those who crossed the deserts in all the early Hebrew history, is a remarkable circumstance when we consider the acts of constant violence upon travellers which now take place, and the strong apprehensions with which a journey across any of the Arabian or Syrian deserts is now regarded.'——¶ *Returned to the land of Egypt.* That is, took up his journey *towards* the land of Egypt. See Note on Gen. 22, 3.——¶ *Took the rod of God in his hand.* Chal. ' The rod by which miracles were to be wrought.' This staff is called ' the rod of God,' partly because it was appropriated to God's special service to be the instrument of all his glorious works ; and partly to show that whatever was done by it was not effected by any intrinsic virtue in the rod itself or in the hand of Moses which wielded it, but solely by the power of God, who was pleased, for the greater confusion of his enemies, to employ so mean an instrument. It would seem that there was a designed though latent antithesis between the poorness of his equipage and the dignity conferred upon him by the mystic

rod which he bore in his hand. The outward eye, as he passed along, beheld only an humble wayfarer clad in coarse habiliments, and slowly moving by the side of the beasts, loaded with the burden of his wife and children, but in the simple staff that supported his steps slept the hidden virtue of Omnipotence itself! It had but to be waved in the air and the salubrious Nile run a river of blood, and hail and pestilence and lightning and thunders waited upon its movements ! What sceptre of royalty ever invested its possessor with such a grandeur !

21. *And the Lord said unto Moses,* &c. Moses has not as yet given an exact recital of the various miracles which he was commanded to work, but from the language of his verse we cannot doubt that all the successive prodigies of power of which we read in the sequel had been previously enjoined, and the process of the whole affair accurately made known. This was in order to prepare him for the issue, lest upon a first and second abortive attempt he should despair of moving the mind of Pharaoh, and renounce his rod and his calling together. Here therefore God exhorts him to hold on in persevering constancy and not desist from his work till every item of the divine injunctions had been complied with. Let him not suppose that his failure in the first instance to gain his point would be owing simply to an *evil accident ;* nor let him deem that a puny mortal could safely treat miraculous agency as a mockery. On the contrary, he was to carry with him the assurance that whatever was the immediate result, however adverse it might *seem* to the deliverance of his people, the hand of

God was in it all, for the stout heart of the king was to be brought down by repeated blows, and the whole train of events so ordered that he should be magnificently triumphed over. This is indicated still more plainly in what follows.——¶ *Which I have put in thine hand.* Which I have put in thy power; which I have enabled and authorized thee to perform before him.——¶ *I will harden his heart.* Heb. אחזק את לבו *ehazzek eth libbo, I will strengthen his heart.* Thus the Most High precludes the possibility of ascribing the result to any thing unforeseen or fortuitous; or of supposing that he could not, if he pleased, have curbed the tyrant's arrogance and brought him to submit in a moment. Pharaoh will not hold out in rebellion because he *could* not be subdued, but because infinite wisdom had great ends to accomplish in suffering him to prolong his obstinacy. But as the language here employed is liable to be wrested widely from its legitimate meaning, it will be necessary to weigh it with more than ordinary precision. It is worthy of remark that the Heb. text in speaking of the ' hardening' of Pharaoh's heart, employs in different parts of the narrative three distinct words differing from each other by a marked diversity of import, but which are all indiscriminately rendered in the common version by ' harden.' These are חזק *hazak, to strengthen, confirm;* כבד *kabad, to make heavy;* and קשה *kashah, to make hard,* in the sense of *difficult, intractable, rigid* or *stiff.* The whole number of passages in which Pharaoh's heart is said to have been ' hardened' is nineteen, in thirteen of which the term employed is ' *hazak ;*' in five, ' *kabad ;*' and in one ' *kashah.*' The passage before us belongs to the former class ; ' I will harden (אחזק *ehazzek*) his heart ;' i. e. I will make strong, firm, determined. The original properly signifies *to brace* or *tighten up,* in opposition to a state of *relaxation,*

remission, yielding. Thus Is. 35, 3, ' Strengthen ye the weak hands and *confirm* the feeble knees.' In its legitimate import it is applied rather to the vigorous tension of a man's courage or resolution than to the obduration of the moral sensibilities. Its prevailing sense may be gathered from the following passages : Jer. 23. 14, ' They *strengthen* also the hands of evil-doers, that none doth return from his wickedness ;' i. e. they make them more determined. Judg. 9, 24, ' And upon the men of Shechem which *aided* him in the killing of his brethren. Heb. ' which *strengthened* him ;' i. e. instigated him. Is. 41. 7, ' So the carpenter *encouraged* the goldsmith ;' i. e. urged on. 2 Chron. 26. 8, ' And his name spread abroad, for he *strengthened himself* exceedingly ;' i. e. he acted with great vigor, conquering all obstacles by the energy of his character. When God therefore is represented as saying, ' I will harden (strengthen) Pharoah's heart,' the language implies simply, that the course of events should be so ordered that, without any *positive divine influence* exerted upon him, the haughty king should take occasion to *confirm himself* in his disregard of the counsels of the Most High, and instead of being bowed and humbled by the displays of Omnipotence should array himself in a posture of more *determined resistance* to the mandate of Jehovah. This God is said to have *done* because he *permitted it to be done.* A similar instance is related in Deut. 2. 30, ' But Sihon king of Heshbon would not let us pass by him : for the Lord thy God *hardened his spirit,* and made his heart obstinate, that he might deliver him into thy hand, as appeareth this day.' So also Josh. 11. 20, ' For it was of the Lord to *harden their hearts* that they should come against Israel in battle, that he might destroy them utterly.' Yet in the present instance it is expressly said, ch. 9. 34, that Pharaoh *hardened his*

22 And thou shalt say unto Pharaoh, Thus saith the Lord, ˣ Israel *is* my son, ʸ *even* my first-born.

23 And I say unto thee, Let my son go, that he may serve me: and if

ˣ Hos. 11. 1. Rom. 9. 4. 2 Cor. 6. 18. ʸ Jer. 31. 9. James 1. 18.

thou refuse to let him go, behold, ᶻ I will slay thy son, *even* thy first-born.

24 ¶ And it came to pass by the way in the inn, that the Lord ᵃ met him, and sought to ᵇ kill him.

ᶻ ch. 11. 5. & 12. 29. ᵃ Numb. 22. 22. ᵇ Gen. 17. 14.

---

own heart; and the exhortation of the Psalmist is, Ps. 95. 8, ' *Harden not your hearts,* as in the provocation,' as though it were a voluntary act in those in whom it takes place with which God could be by no means chargeable. The expression involves no difficulty provided the ordinary *usus loquendi* be borne in mind.

22. *Israel is my son, even my first-born.* That is, beloved and favored beyond other nations; dear to me as a first-born child. Thus Hos. 11. 1, ' When Israel was a child, then I loved him and called *my son* out of Egypt.' ' Israel' is here a collective denomination for all the natural seed of Jacob, who are called God's ' son' as a title of favor, and his ' first-born' as a note of honorable relationship, pointing to their pre-eminence above all other nations. For as the first-born in a family was consecrated to God as his peculiar portion, so were the children of Israel adopted from among the nations as a peculiar treasure above all people, Ex. 19. 5, from whom was appointed to descend, according to the flesh, the Messiah, ' the first-born of every creature.' The epithet ' first-born' is at once a term of dignity and of endearment. Thus Ps. 89. 26, 27, ' He shall cry unto me, Thou art my Father, my God, the Rock of my salvation. Also I will make him *my first-born,* higher than the king's of the earth.' This is a mutual recognition of the privileges of adoption.—— ¶ *Let my son go.* He is *my* son, not yours; he comes under allegiance to another lord; you are not to claim or exercise jurisdiction over him.

23. *And I say unto thee, Let my son*

go, &c. These, it would seem, were the words not of Moses, but of God speaking through the person of Moses. Such, at least, is the usual and more obvious interpretation; yet there is a remarkable apparent change of persons in passing from the 22d to the 23d verse, and if it were possible to conceive of the words being spoken at the same time to Moses himself on the principle announced, Is. 8. 18, ' Behold, I and the children whom the Lord hath given me are for signs and for wonders in Israel,' it would seem to afford an easier explication of the remarkable incident mentioned in the two next verses, which comes in a manner so abrupt and almost unaccountable in this connexion. It would certainly tend to inspire Moses with a deeper impression of the fearful consequences of Pharaoh's refusing compliance with the divine mandate, had he himself barely escaped the loss of his own son by reason of his neglect to fulfil an express injunction of heaven. May it not then be supposed that there is involved in the address to Pharaoh an intimation also to Moses himself of danger to his first-born, if he neglected longer to circumcise him, and put him into that condition in which he could acceptably serve the God of his fathers? By circumcising his son he would put him virtually into the same relation to God as the nation of Israel would be in when ' let go' by Pharaoh from their bondage, and brought to worship and serve him in the wilderness.

24. *It came to pass by the way in the inn.* Heb. בַּמָּלוֹן *bammalon, in the lodging-place.* For the true import of this expression see Note on Gen. 42. 27.

It would appear that they had not yet reached the place of their final destination, though they may have entered within the bounds of Egypt. Comp. v. 20.——¶ *The Lord met him.* That is, met him in the tokens of displeasure. Gr. and Chal. ' The angel of the Lord met him.' It is undoubtedly clear from many passages of the sacred narrative, that the term ' Lord' (Jehovah) is synonymous with the ' angel of the Lord,' and that ' angel of the Lord' is used to denote the *supernatural manifestation of the Deity by means of some visible or sensible symbol.*—— ¶ *Sought to kill him.* That is, made a show of intending to kill him; manifested alarming signs of wrath, probably by visiting him with some threatening disease. Language like this must of course be understood in consistency with what we know of the divine attributes. He in whose hands our breath is has no occasion to *seek* to take away the life of any of his creatures. The being which he originated he can at any instant extinguish. The phrase is doubtless advisedly chosen to indicate a *delay*, a *respite*, on the part of the Most High, as if he were *reluctant* to enter upon the work of judgment. But who is to be understood by the pronoun ' him' in this connexion? Was it Moses himself or his first-born son, who was the subject of the menacing judgment? The Arabic version of Saadias has ' he rushed upon his son,' and as, according to the view suggested above, the first-born of Moses was the subject last spoken of, we see no objection to consider that as the true construction. At the same time, it may be properly said that Moses himself was put in peril in the person of his son. See Note on Gen. 9. 25. The probability we think is, that there was some criminal delay in Moses in respect both to this rite and to the prosecution of his mission, and that it pleased God, in accordance with his conditional denunciation above mentioned, v. 23, to visit his son with some alarming sickness which threatened to prove fatal. In the note on Ex. 2. 22 we adverted to the very great improbability of Moses being the father of a *very young* child at the time when he set out for Egypt, which was forty years after he first entered Midian. How much *more* improbable is it that his eldest son was now an infant or a little child? We cannot but infer from the narrative, ch. 2. 15—22, that Moses married shortly after entering the family of Jethro, and that the birth of his first-born occurred in all probability within the usual period of such an event. If so, and if his circumcision had been deferred to the present time, instead of being now an infant or a child, he must have been a full grown man of upwards of thirty years of age. And if this be admitted we can see an ample reason for the divine displeasure manifested on this occasion. It was not a delay of a few months, but of many years, that elicited such tokens of judgment; and if it be asked why this expression of anger was reserved to the present time; why it vented itself rather at this particular juncture than at any other, we can only suggest in reply that it was with a view to give it a *typical* or *symbolical* import; to bring it into connexion with the threatening against Pharaoh, in order that Moses might have a more impressive sense of the danger of disobeying the commands of Heaven. There would seem, at any rate, to be some link of connexion between this incident and the previous address to Moses, v. 22, 23, and if any other can be suggested more probable, we have no interest in adhering to our proposed interpretation, although it is one that does not, that we perceive, offer any violence to the text. The reader who refers to Rosenmuller's Commentary will see that it has long been doubted to whom to refer the pronouns relative.

25 Then Zipporah took ^c a sharp stone, and cut off the foreskin of her

^c Josh. 5. 2, 3.

son, and cast *it* at his feet, and said Surely a bloody husband *art* thou to me.

---

25. *Then Zipporah took a sharp stone,* &c. . That is, a knife made of a stone sharpened. That such instruments were in use at this early period, may be inferred from Josh. 5. 2, ' The Lord said unto Joshua, make thee *sharp knives,* (Heb. ' knives of stones') and circumcise again the children of Israel ;' where the Chal. has ' sharp razors ;' and the Gr. ' stone knives.' Thus Herodotus, describing the preparations for embalming a dead body, says, ' they cut around the hips with a *sharp Ethiopic stone.*'— ' Flints and other hard stones formed the tools and cutting instruments of almost all nations before the art of working iron was discovered. We find such instruments still in use among savages, and discover them occasionally buried in different parts of Europe and Asia, showing the universality of their use when the people were ignorant of iron. They were no doubt formed, as savages form them at present ; that is, they were shaped and sharpened on a kind of grindstone, until, at a great expense of time, labor, and patience, they were brought to the desired figure. They were then fitted to a handle, and used nearly in the same way as we use our instruments and tools of iron. From the act of Zipporah, we are, however, not authorized to infer that instruments and tools of metal were not common at the time and in the neighborhood before us. We shall soon have occasion to see the contrary. The fact seems to be, that Zipporah knew that sharp stones were exclusively used in Egypt and elsewhere, in making incisions on the human person ; and she therefore either used such an instrument, or employed in its room one of the flints with which the region they were traversing is abundantly strewed.' *Pict. Bible.* As the danger apprehended was imme-

diately averted upon the circumcision of their son, it is plain that the delay of this ordinance was its procuring cause, although we are not informed whether the parents learned this from an express revelation, or from the course of their own reflections. There is doubtless something abhorrent to our ideas of propriety in the mother's performing this rite upon an adult son, but against this we must set the whole strength of the evidence that he *was* adult, that he was the *first-born,* and also the fact that it was a *mother* complying with a divine requisition, and that among a people and in a state of society whose sentiments and usages were very different from ours.——¶ *Cast it at his feet.* Heb. ותגע לרגליו *vattigga leraglauv, made it to touch his feet.* Chal. ' Brought it near before him.' Gr. ' She fell at his feet.' Jerus. Targ. ' She laid it at the feet of the destroyer.' The clause is difficult of explication. By the mass of commentators, Zipporah is supposed to have cast the prepuce, or circumcised foreskin, of her son, besmeared with blood, at the feet of Moses, and in a reproachful and angry manner to have addressed him in the words immediately following. Others, however, with perhaps equal plausibility, suppose it to mean, that she made it to touch his feet, or rather his legs, in the act of cutting, for the original term is by no means that which is ordinarily employed to signify *casting* or *throwing down.* The true interpretation is doubtless to be determined by the ensuing words. ——¶ *Surely a bloody husband art thou to me.* Heb. חתן דמים אתה לי *hathan damim attah li, a spouse,* or *bridegroom, of bloods art thou to me.* Here again the interpreter finds himself encompassed with difficulties. The question that almost defies solution is, whether these

26 So he let him go: then she ₁aid, A bloody husband *thou art*, because of the circumcision.

27 ¶ And the LORD said to Aaron, Go into the wilderness ᵈ to meet

ᵈ ver. 14.

words are to be considered as addressed to Moses or to her son. By those who adopt the common construction, and suppose Moses himself to have been the person endangered, and the child an infant, Zipporah is understood as virtually saying ; ' Behold *the* evidence of my intense affection towards thee. I have jeoparded the life of my babe as the ransom for thine. In order to free thee from danger, and, as it were, to espouse thee to myself anew, to make thee once more a bridegroom, I have not shunned to shed the blood of this dear child, even under perilous circumstances, when the hardships of the journey may render the operation fatal.' But a far preferable construction, in our opinion, is to consider the words as addressed to the son, now grown up, from his being *espoused*, as it were, to God by the seal of circumcision. Aben Ezra remarks, ' It is the custom of women to call a son when he is circumcised *a spouse* (חתן *hathan*).' Kimchi in his Lexicon, under חתן concurs in the same view, which is also adopted by Schindler, Spencer, Mede, and others. The idea that Zipporah intended to upbraid her husband with the cruelty of the rite which his religion required him to perform, seems hardly tenable ; for as she was a Midianitess, and so a daughter of Abraham by Keturah, it is not easy to imagine her altogether a stranger to the ceremony of circumcision, which had been from the earliest ages perpetuated in all the branches of the Abrahamic race, and is even observed by the followers of Mohammed at the present day, not as an institution of the prophet himself, but as an ancient rite received from Ishmael.

26. *So he let him go.* Heb. ירף ממנו *₁ereph mimmenu, he slackened from* ₁m. That is, God desisted from the

further effects of his displeasure. The signs of his anger ceased when the occasion ceased. Jerus. Targ. ' The Destroyer let him go.' The phrase is taken from the act of relaxing a vigorous grasp. The original term is similarly applied, 1 Chron. 21. 15, ' And he said unto the angel that destroyed, It is enough *stay* (ירף *hereph, relax, remit*) now thine hand.' So also Josh. 10. 6, ' And the men of Gibeon ˙sent unto Joshua to the camp to Gilgal, saying, *slack* (ירף *hereph*) not thine hand from thy servants, &c.' Notwithstanding all the obscurity that envelopes the transaction here recorded, we learn from it, .(1) That God takes notice of and is much displeased with the sins of his own people, and that the putting away of their sins is indispensably necessary to the removal of the divine judgments. (2) That no circumstances of prudence or conveniency can ever with propriety be urged as an excuse for neglecting a clearly commanded duty, especially the observance of sacramental ordinances. (3) That he who is to be the interpreter of the law to others ought in all points to be blameless, and in all things conformed to the law himself. (4) That when God has procured the proper respect to his revealed will, the controversy between him and the offender is at an end ; the object of his government being not so much to avenge himself as to amend the criminal.—From Ex. 18. 2, it would seem that Zipporah and her sons were sent back to his father-in-law where they remained till Jethro brought them to Moses in the wilderness.

27. *The Lord said unto Aaron,* &c. The scene of domestic danger and distress described above is speedily followed by another of a pleasanter kind, viz., the interview between the two brothers in the wilderness. The present

Moses. And he went, and met him in ᵉ the mount of God, and kissed him.

28 And Moses ᶠ told Aaron all the words of the Lᴏʀᴅ who had sent

ᵉ ch. 3. 1.   ᶠ ver. 15, 16.

him, and all the ᵍ signs which he had commanded him.

29 ¶ And Moses and Aaron ʰ went, and gathered together all the elders of the children of Israel.

ᵍ ver. 8, 9.   ʰ ch. 3. 16.

phrase however should rather be rendered ' The Lord *had* said,' for the command had no doubt reached him some time previous, as Moses was yet in the neighborhood of the sacred mount where the vision appeared. Although the command is recited in the most general terms, ' Go into the wilderness,' yet we cannot doubt that detailed directions as to the *particular place* where he should meet his brother accompanied it.—— ¶ *He went and met him in the mount of God.* That is, in or at Horeb, called the ' Mount of God' for the reasons stated in the Note on Ex. 3. 1. Chal. ' In the mount where the Glory of the Lord had been revealed.' Aaron was now eighty-three years of age, though we are wholly unacquainted with his previous history. We have every reason to believe, however, from the fact that God selected him as the companion of Moses in so arduous an enterprise, and from his subsequent conduct and station, that his character was one of no ordinary stamp. While residing in Egypt he had been making progress in knowledge, in moral worth, and in influence among his countrymen. Like his brother, he had been maturing for the great work in which he was now to engage.——¶ *And kissed him.* In remarking upon the interview between Joseph and Jacob, Gen. 46. 29, we observed that the phrase ' he fell on his neck' might be understood of both; and in like manner we cannot question but that the embrace of Moses and Aaron was mutual. Accordingly the Gr. renders it, ' They kissed each other.'

28. *And Moses told Aaron all the words*, &c. To Moses it must have been highly gratifying, after a sojourn

of forty years among strangers, to meet his own brother, to receive from him the welcome tidings of his family and nation, and to impart to his friendly ear the story of his own life during so long an interval. On the other hand, what pleasure must it have afforded to Aaron, to learn from the mouth of his brother the great designs of providence respecting themselves and their people? With what overflowings of heart would they join in a fraternal embrace and mingle their sighs and tears? With what ardor would their united prayers and vows and praises ascend to heaven? How confirmed the faith, how forward the zeal of each, strengthened and stimulated by that of the other? Well may they go on their way rejoicing. They are following God, and they must prosper.

29. *Moses and Aaron went and gathered together.* We do not learn that any doubt or hesitancy was evinced on the part of Aaron. Convinced by the intimations he had himself received, and by the scene of wonders which Moses had related to him, he is ready to go with his brother on their momentous errand, and as if to indicate the alacrity with which they now proceeded forward, passing in silence over all the intermediate details of their journey, we all at once find them in the midst of their countrymen. Before this, however, possibly before the meeting of the two brothers at Horeb, Moses had directed his wife and sons to return to his father-in-law Jethro. He doubtless had good reasons for this step, though we are left in ignorance what they were. At what time and under what circumstances they met again, we shall see in a subsequent part of the history.

30 ⁱ And Aaron spake all the words
which the Lord had spoken unto
Moses, and did the signs in the
sight of the people.
31 And the people ^k believed : and
when they heard that the Lord had
^l visited the children of Israel, and
that he ^m had looked upon their affliction, then ⁿ they bowed their
heads and worshipped.

ⁱ ver. 16.   ^k ch. 3. 18. ver. 8, 9.   ^l ch. 3. 16.   ^m ch. 2. 25. & 3. 7.   ⁿ Gen. 24. 26. ch. 12. 27. 1 Chron. 29. 20.

30. *And Aaron spake*, &c. Having
assembled the elders Aaron begins, according to the divine appointment, v.
16, to act as ' spokesman' in delivering
the message, while Moses at the same
time, in the discharge of *his* appropriate
office, performs the miraculous signs
which were to be a seal of his commission. There can be no doubt that
the rendering of our version, which
ascribes the working of the signs to
Aaron is erroneous. The pronoun ' he'
should be inserted before ' did the signs,'
to indicate that Moses and not Aaron
is the true subject of the verb. Comp.
v. 21.——¶ *In the sight of the people.*
As nothing has been hitherto said of
the ' people,' but only of the ' elders,'
we must either understand this of the
elders alone, called ' people' in virtue
of their representative character, or else
we must suppose that a considerable
body of the people, such as could be
conveniently assembled, were present
with the elders who acted in their
name. The same remark is to be made
respecting the term ' people' in the next
verse. The former is perhaps the most
probable interpretation, not only because that mode of speech is common,
but because the act of solemn worship
that ensued appears to have taken place
in a meeting ; and if so, it must have
been a meeting of a select number, and
not of the whole nation, who cannot be
supposed to have been convened on the
occasion. The result was such as God
had foretold, Ex. 3. 18. The return of
Moses after his long exile, in company
with his brother whom they well knew
and highly esteemed ; the cheering nature of the message addressed to them
in the name of the great I AM ; the con-

vincing demonstrations of the divine
power in the miracles which they had
witnessed ; all conspired to produce in
their breasts the deepest emotions of
wonder and joy ; a strong confidence in
God ; and an assurance that he was indeed about to show them mercy. In
testimony of this, and as a solemn act
of reverential gratitude, the whole assembly bowed their heads and worshipped. They accounted it not sufficient
merely to ponder in their hearts these
signal tokens of the divine interposition in their behalf, but were prompted
to give expression to their feelings by
appropriate outward signs. Such external acts of reverence are indeed of
comparatively little account in the eyes
of him who weighs the spirits, but as
they are helps to our infirmities, and go
to show more fully the *entireness* of
our devotion to our heavenly benefactor,
they are always acceptable in his sight
when springing from the proper motive.
——¶ *And when they heard.* Heb.
וישמעו *va-yishme-u, and they heard.*
Gr. και επιστευσαν ὁ λαος και εχαρη, *and
the people believed and rejoiced,* that
the Lord, &c. That an import analogous to this, viz., that of a *joyful hearing*, is conveyed by the original term
would appear from 2 Kings, 20. 13,
' And Hezekiah *hearkened* unto them,'
which in the parallel passage, Is. 39. 2,
is rendered, ' And Hezekiah *was glad* of
them.' We have before had occasion to
remark that verbs of the senses frequently imply the exercise of the affections.
See Note on Gen. 21. 17.——¶ *Had visited.*
Had visited in mercy. See Note on Gen.
21. 1. Chal. 'Had remembered.'——¶ *Looked upon the affliction.* Compassionately regarded. See Note on Ex. 2. 11.

CHAPTER V.

AND afterward Moses and Aaron went in, and told Pharaoh, Thus saith the Lord God of Israel, Let my people go, that they may hold a a feast unto me in the wilderness.

ᵃ ch. 10. 9.

Chapter 5

The present chapter ushers in the history of the controversy between God and Pharaoh, and its fearful issue in the utter destruction of the daring rebel who had presumed to set himself in array against his Maker. While the incidents mentioned in the close of the preceding chapter were transpiring, Pharaoh was sitting proudly and securely on his throne, surrounded by his obedient subjects, and wholly ignorant of the portentous movement which was taking place in the midst of the wretched bondsmen to whom he was wringing out the waters of a full cup of affliction. He had heard, indeed, of Moses and his singular history. He had been told of his living so long at the court of his predecessor, as the adopted son of the daughter of the king; of his high character and attainments, and his great influence among his countrymen; of his strange abandonment of his conspicuous station, and of the circumstances which led to his flight from Egypt. But if he were still living, he supposed him to be an insignificant exile in some foreign land from which he would never dare again to return. Little did he think that this outcast Israelite was now so near him, having come in the strength of Omnipotence to rescue the oppressed from his grasp and to overwhelm him and his host in utter destruction.

1. *Moses and Aaron went in and told Pharaoh*, &c. They were doubtless accompanied on this occasion by a number of the elders of Israel, to give more weight and solemnity to the demand. Comp. Ex. 3. 18.——¶ *Thus saith the Lord God of Israel.* Moses in addressing the elders of Israel is directed to call God ' the God of their fathers;' but in addressing Pharaoh the title employed is, ' the God of Israel,' and this is the first time the title occurs in that connexion in the Scriptures. He is indeed in Gen. 33. 20, called ' the God of Israel,' the *person*, but here it is Israel, the *people*. Though now a poor, afflicted, and despised people, yet ' God is not ashamed to be called their God.' As such he commands Pharaoh to let them go. Whatever claim their oppressor had set up to their persons or services, it was a downright and daring usurpation which God, their rightful Lord and Sovereign, would not tolerate for a moment. Here therefore he moves towards their deliverance, and may be considered as virtually saying in the language of the prophet, Is. 52. 5, 6, ' Now therefore, what have I here, saith the Lord, that my people is taken away for nought? they that rule over them make them to howl, saith the Lord. Therefore my people shall know my name : therefore they shall know in that day that I am he that doth speak : behold it is I.'——¶ *That they may hold a feast unto me.* Heb. יחגּוּ *yahogu*. The primary import of the original word חגג *hagag* is to *dance*, rendered, Ps. 107. 27, ' reel too and fro,' probably from the fact that the staggering motion of men in a ship, tossed by a tempest, resembled that of *dancers*. In a secondary sense, it is applied to *keeping a feast religiously*, which was marked by eating, drinking, *dancing*, and mirth. The term is here, therefore, used synecdochally for all the attendant ceremonies of a sacred festival, in which *worship* and *sacrifice* were prominent; for which reason the phrase is rendered by the Chal. ' that they may *sacrifice* before me.'——¶ *In the wilderness.* A retired place was rendered proper from the peculiar religious usages of the He-

2 And Pharaoh said, b Who *is* the
LORD, that I should obey his voice
to let Israel go? I know not the
LORD, c neither will I let Israel go.
3 And they said, d The God of the

b 2 Kings 18. 35.   Job 21. 15.   c ch. 3. 19.
d ch. 3. 18.

Hebrews hath met with us: let us
go, we pray thee, three days' journey into the desert, and sacrifice unto the LORD our God; lest he fall
upon us with pestilence, or with the
sword.

---

drews, which were different from those
practised or allowed among the Egyptians.

2. *Who is the Lord*, &c. Rather,
'Who is Jehovah?—I know not Jehovah.' There is a special reason why
this title should here be rendered, ver-
batim, 'Jehovah,' rather than 'Lord,'
viz. that it is mentioned as the *peculiar
name* of the God of Israel, whereas the
title 'Lord,' was common to the heathen deities, many of them being called
'Baalim,' or 'Lords.' This makes Pharaoh's answer more emphatic, 'Who is
Jehovah?'—a name of which he had
never before heard. Chal. 'The name
of Jehovah is not revealed to me, that I
should obey his word.' Targ. Jon. 'I
have not found in the book of the angels
(gods) the name of Jehovah written: I
fear him not.' The reply of Pharaoh
is, upon the best construction, marked
by a tone of insolence and contempt for
which we can find no excuse. Yet it
would perhaps be unjust to charge upon
him an *intentional* act of impiety, for
he was no doubt a worshipper of the
gods of Egypt. But he would intimate
that he considered Moses and Aaron as
the setters-forth of a strange god, whose
claims he would not deign to admit.
That the poor outcast slaves, who existed by his sufferance, and labored for
his pleasure, should have a God of such
authority as to prescribe laws for him,
was not to be endured. It is as if he
had said, 'Who is this unheard-of deity
that you call 'Lord?' What greater
or better is he than my gods? What
have I to do with him? Why should I
care for him? He is not the God whom
I serve?' From the degraded and de-

spised character of the people of Israel,
he no doubt formed his estimate of the
God whom they professed to serve, and
concluded that he was no more entitled
to reverence as a deity, than they were
to respect as a people.——¶ *That I
should obey his voice.* Heb. אשמע בקלו
*eshma bekolo, should hearken to his
voice.* See Note on Gen. 16. 3.

3. *The God of the Hebrews hath met
with us.* Heb. נקרא עלינו *nikra alenu,*
lit. *is called upon us,* i. e. is invoked
and worshipped by us. And accordingly the Chal. has, 'The God of the Jews
is invoked upon us.' But the other versions vary. Gr. 'The God of the Hebrews hath called us.' Syr. 'The God
of the Hebrews has appeared unto us.'
Arab. 'The command of the God of the
Hebrews is come unto us.' It is on the
whole most probable that נקרא *nikra,*
is used by change of letters for נקרה
nikrah, hath met, the very phrase which
occurs Ex. 3. 18.——¶ *Let us go three
days' journey,* &c. Instead of reproaching Pharaoh, or threatening him with
the judgments of heaven, they adopt a
style of humble and respectful entreaty,
'We pray thee;' at the same time
representing that the journey they proposed was not a project formed among
themselves, but a measure enjoined
upon them by the God of their nation,
and one which they dared not decline.
In saying this it is true they dissem-
ble the design of forsaking Egypt altogether, perhaps with a view to learn
from the manner in which he treated a
smaller request, what prospect of success they would have in urging a greater. In this they stated no falsehood,
but merely concealed a part of the

4 And the king of Egypt said unto them, Wherefore do ye, Moses and Aaron, let the people from their works? get you unto your ᵉ burdens.

ᵉ ch. 1. 11.

truth.—As to the moral character of this part of their conduct see Note on Gen. 12. 13.——¶ *Lest he fall upon us with pestilence*, &c. Heb. בדבר *badde-ber*. Gr. μη ποτε συναντηση ημιν θανατος η φονος, *lest death or slaughter meet us*. The original word for ' pestilence' is here, as in numerous cases elsewhere, rendered in the Gr. by θανατος *death*. Thus Levit. 26. 25, ' I will send the *pestilence* among you.' Gr. ' *the death*.' Deut. 28. 21, ' The Lord shall make the *pestilence* cleave unto thee.' Gr. ' *the death*.' Ezek. 33. 27, ' They that be in the forts and in the caves shall die of the *pestilence*.' Gr. of ' *the death*.' This usage, a parallel to which occurs in the Chaldee paraphrase, is transferred to the New Testament, and is of great importance to the right understanding of the following passages ; Rev. 2. 23, ' I will kill her children with *death ;*' i. e. with pestilence, by which is sometimes meant any kind of premature or violent death ; death out of the common course of nature. Rev. 6. 8, ' And power was given unto them over the fourth part of the earth to kill with the sword, and with hunger (famine), and with *death* (i. e. pestilence), and with the beasts of the earth.' So also, probably, Rev. 21. 4, ' And God shall wipe away all tears from their eyes; and there shall be no more *death ;*' i. e. violent death; death occasioned by sudden and fatal casualties or judgments ; for that this portion of Scripture does not describe a state of happiness in which its subjects shall be absolutely immortal may be gathered from the language of Isaiah, ch. 65. 19, 20, referring to the same future period ; ' And the voice of weeping shall be no more heard in her, nor the voice of crying. There shall be no more thence an infant of days, nor an old man that hath not filled his days ; for the child *shall die* an hundred years old ; but the sinner being an hundred years old, shall be accursed.'— This intimation of danger to themselves in case of their neglecting to comply with the divine injunction, would administer a seasonable hint to Pharaoh. For if he were a God so jealous of his honor as to punish his own people for such a delinquency, even when they were forcibly prevented from obeying, how much reason had he to fear the visitations of his wrath, if he openly bade him defiance ? It was evidently no very great thing for Pharaoh to have yielded, had he complied with the request of Moses and Aaron. Considering the benefits he had derived from the labors of the Israelites, he might well have allowed them this short respite for a religious service. But when men's pride and passions are roused, reason and humanity might as well make their plea to the deaf adder as to them.

4. *Wherefore do ye let the people from their works ?* That is, why do ye *hinder*, or, literally, *cause to desist*. Gr. ινατι διαστρεφετε τον λαον, *wherefore do ye divert*, or *turn away, the people* from their works? It will be observed that Pharaoh takes no notice of what Moses and Aaron had said to him respecting the liberation of the people, but treats them merely as the disturbers of the peace of his kingdom, and as endeavoring to excite sedition among his subjects. The same thing was laid to the charge of Christ and the apostles ; Luke, 23. 2, ' And they began to accuse him, saying, We found this fellow perverting the nation, and forbidding to give tribute to Cæsar.' Acts, 24. 5 ' For we have found this man a pestilent fellow and a mover of sedition among all the Jews throughout the world.'——¶ *Get you unto your bur-*

5 And Pharaoh said, Behold, the people of the land now *are* ᶠ many, and ye make them rest from their burdens.

6 And Pharaoh commanded the same day the ᵍ taskmasters of

ᶠ ch. 1. 7, 9.   ᵍ ch. 1. 11.

the people, and their officers, saying,

7 Ye shall no more give the people straw to make brick, as heretofore: let them go and gather straw for themselves.

---

dens, &c. This command was probably designed more expressly for the elders who had accompanied Moses and Aaron, though he would perhaps intimate at the same time that if the brothers were where they ought to be, they would be bearing their part of the burdens.

5. *The people of the land now are many,* &c. As if he should say, 'If the people are already increased to such a multitude, notwithstanding all the methods taken to prevent it, how much more numerous and formidable will they soon become if suffered to cease from their labor.' Vulg. 'You see that the multitude is increased; how much more, if you give them rest from their works?' Or, the number of the people may be alluded to in order to hint at the greatness of the damage done to the state by the interruption of the labors of so large a body of men. Some of the Jewish commentators give it still a different shade of meaning, viz. that it was absolutely necessary to keep so great a multitude busily employed, lest they should engage in plots of insurrection.

6. *The task-masters of the people and their officers.* These 'task-masters,' lit. 'exactors,' constituting the highest grade of officers, were Egyptians appointed to exact labor of the Israelites. But those termed 'officers,' appear, v. 14—16, to have been Israelites set over their brethren. The latter term is rendered in the Gr. 'Scribes,' i. e. probably men who executed written decrees, or rendered written accounts of their official services, answering with cons'derable exactness to our modern 'sheriffs.' It is, however, certain that they were under-officers to the task-masters.

7. *Ye shall no more give the people straw,* &c. Commentators have doubted for what particular purpose straw was made use of by the Egyptians in making brick, some supposing it to be employed for fuel in burning the brick, and others that it was cut or chopt fine and mixed with the clay to give more consistency and firmness to the brick when taken from the kiln. The probability is that it was used for both purposes. The Gr. term αχυρον, by which the Heb. חבן is here rendered, signifying properly *straw* instead of *chaff*, occurs in Mat. 3. 12. 'He will gather his wheat into the garner; but he will burn up the *chaff* (straw) with unquenchable fire;' intimating that when the wheat was separated, the straw was of no farther use, except as fuel for fires. Kypke, in his note on this passage, has the following observation: 'The Jews and other nations burnt straw and stubble, instead of wood, in cooking their meats, in *heating their furnaces*, and in othei uses:' for which he cites the Symposi acks of Plutarch; 'Those who melt gold work it by a fire *kindled with straw.*' The same thing is to be inferred from the words of Christ, Mat. 6. 30, 'Wherefore if God so clothe the grass of the field which to-day is, and to-morrow is *cast into the oven*, shall he not much more,' &c. On which Grotius quotes the words of Ulpian the Roman lawyer in a definition of fuel; 'In some regions, as for instance in Egypt, where reeds and the papyrus plant are burnt for fuel, the common appellation 'wood' includes certain species of herbs and thorns and other vegetables. This is accounted for from the fact, that in

8 And the tale of the bricks which they did make heretofore, ye shall lay upon them ; ye shall not diminish *aught* thereof ; for they *be* idle; therefore they cry, saying,

Let us go *and* sacrifice to our God. 9 Let there more work be laid upon the men, that they may labour therein : and let them not regard vain words.

---

most of the eastern countries wood is so extremely scarce, that various species of dried vegetables, grass, straw, flowers, and furze, constitute their principal articles of fuel. But that straw, on the other hand, was used in the composition of brick in Egypt, is evident from the reports of modern travellers. Thus Dr. Shaw, speaking of the bricks found in one of the Egyptian pyramids, says, ' The composition is only a mixture of clay, mud, and *straw*, slightly blended and kneaded together.' Baumgarten, another traveller, speaking of Cairo in Egypt, says, 'The houses for the most part are of brick *mixt with straw* to make them firm. Sir John Chardin tells us, ' That eastern bricks are made of clay, well moistened with water, and *mixed with straw*, which, according to their way of getting the grain out of the ear, is cut into small pieces by a machine which they make use of instead of a flail for thrashing.' —— ¶ *As heretofore.* Literally, 'As yesterday and the third day.' See Note on Gen. 31 2. Hitherto those who labored in the brick-fields had been furnished all the materials for their work, not only the clay of which the bricks were made, but the straw with which they were compacted. But the present order was a great grievance, as much of the time which should have been employed in making the bricks was now consumed in seeking for straw. And this burden must have become more heavy every day, in proportion as the straw thus hunted up became scarce in the neighborhood of the brick-fields. But in all this the lot of the Israelites seems intended to illustrate a frequent law of providence, viz., that the burden of affliction presses the heavier, the

nearer the approach of deliverance. His people are not prepared for the destined relief till their cup of woe is full, and all help is entirely despaired of except from heaven.

8. *The tale of the bricks,* &c. That is, the number, the amount of the bricks. This was the very refinement of cruelty to require the end and yet deny the means.——¶ *For they be idle.* A charge than which nothing could be more unreasonable or untrue. The cities they built for Pharaoh, and the other fruits of their labors, were witnesses for them that they were not idle, though it is not unlikely that many of these public works were so intrinsically useless, like the pyramids, that it was little better than idleness to be employed about them ; yet diligently employed they certainly were, and he thus basely misrepresents them, that he might have a pretence for increasing their burdens.

9. *Let there more work be laid upon the men.* Heb. תכבד העבדה *tikbad ha-abodah, let the work be heavy* upon the men; which if they performed they would be broken down by it, while if they failed to perform it, they would be punished. So fearful is the alternative which iron-hearted oppression leaves to its poor victims !——¶ *Let them not regard vain words.* Heb. דברי שקר *dibrë shaker, words of lying. Vanity* and *falsehood,* according to the Hebrew idiom, are often used interchangeably for each other. See Note on Ex. 20. 7 If the phrase is to be understood in the sense given it by our translation, it is a directly impious and slanderous imputation upon the words of God, as vain, empty, and delusive. But as the original for ' words,' is often equivalent to ' things,' (See Note on Gen. 15. 1.),

10 ¶ And the taskmasters of the people went out, and their officers, and they spake to the people, saying, Thus saith Pharaoh, I will not give you straw.

11 Go ye, get you straw where ye can find it: yet not aught of your work shall be diminished.

12 So the people were scattered abroad throughout all the land of Egypt, to gather stubble instead of straw.

13 And the taskmasters hasted *them*, saying, Fulfil your works, *your* daily tasks, as when there was straw.

---

the import may be that they were not to indulge themselves in vain hopes, dreams, and aspirations. The Heb. term for *regard* (שָׁעָה *shaah*) when used in the sense of *having respect* to a person or thing is usually followed by אֶל *el*, עַל *al*, or לְ *l* signifying *to*, as Gen. 4. 4, 'And God *had respect unto Abel* (וַיִּשַׁע אֶל הֶבֶל *va-yisha el Hebel*) and to his offering.' But when constructed with the preposition בְּ *b, in*, as here, it signifies rather *to meditate* or *to ponder orally* upon any thing, as Ps. 119. 117, וְאֶשְׁעָה בְחֻקֶּיךָ תָמִיד *ve-esha behukkeka tamid, and I will meditate in thy statutes continually.* Accordingly the Gr. renders the present passage, 'Let them care for these words, and let them not care for vain words.' Chal. 'Let them be occupied in it (the work), and let them not be occupied in idle words.' Syr. 'Let them think upon it (the work), and not think upon vain words.' Arab. 'Let them be occupied in it, and not occupy themselves in vain things.' The sense undoubtedly is, that they were to give themselves unremittingly to their work, and not to cherish any vain, wild, illusory hopes, whether the product of their own minds, or suggested to them by others.

10. *I will not give you straw.* I will not allow it to be given. The *taskmasters* were probably Egyptians, while the *officers* were native Israelites. The message would be as grievous to the one as it probably was acceptable to the other.

12. *So the people were scattered abroad.* This dispersion, however, would at least have the effect to make Pharaoh's barbarous usage of his bondmen extensively known, and perhaps to cause them to be pitied and somewhat aided by their compassionate neighbors.——
¶ *To gather stubble instead of straw.* 'We are so much in the habit of associating the making of bricks with burning, that the common reader fails to discover that the straw could be for any other use than to burn the bricks. Without disputing that the Egyptians did sometimes burn their bricks, the evidence of ancient remains in their country and the existing customs of the East leave little room to doubt that the use of the straw was to mix with and compact the mass of clay used in making sun-dried bricks, such as we have noticed in the notes on Babylon and on the pyramids. Bricks of this sort are still commonly made in Egypt; and their ancient use in the same country is evinced by the brick pyramids at Dashoor and Faioum. That they were never in the fire is shown by the fact that the straw which enters into their composition has sustained no injury or discoloration. Such bricks are very durable in dry climates like Egypt, but would soon be ruined if exposed to much rain. Herodotus observed it as one of the customs in which the Egyptians were unlike other nations, that they kneaded their clay with their hands, and their dough with their feet.'—*Pict. Bib.*

13. *The task-masters hasted* them. Heb. אָצִים *atzim* (were) *urgent, pressing.* Chal. 'Drove them.' As the task-masters exercised a more especial superintendance over the 'officers,' it is pro-

14 And the officers of the children of Israel, which Pharaoh's task-masters had set over them, were beaten, *and* demanded, Wherefore have ye not fulfilled your task in making brick, both yesterday and to-day, as heretofore?

15 ¶ Then the officers of the children of Israel came and cried unto Pharaoh, saying, Wherefore dealest thou thus with thy servants?

16 There is no straw given unto thy servants, and they say to us,

---

bable that the latter are to be understood by the expletive 'them' in this connexion. This appears still more obvious in comparing the next verse. ——¶ *Fulfil your works,* your *daily tasks.* Heb. דבר יום ביומו *debar yom beyomo, the matter of a day in his day.* Gr. τα καθηκοντα καθ' 'ημεραν, *the things appropriate to every day.*

14. *The officers of the children of Israel.* That is, not so much the officers that were *over* the children of Israel, but the officers that were by birth *of* the children of Israel. Accordingly the Gr. has, 'The scribes of the lineage of the sons of Israel.'——¶ *Were beaten, and demanded.* Heb. יכו לאמר *yukku lëmor, were beaten, saying.* 'This is quite oriental. We need only allude to China, which has aptly been said to be governed by the stick. In Persia also the stick is in continual action. Men of all ranks and ages are continually liable to be beaten. It is by no means a rare occurrence for the highest and most trusted persons in the state, in a moment of displeasure or caprice in their royal master, to be handed over to the beaters of carpets, who thrash them with their sticks as if they were dogs. The same practice descends through all ranks; and it has often made the writer's heart ache to see respectable, and even venerable white-bearded men chastised by the menials and messengers of great persons, on their own account, with a brutality which would in this country subject a man to judicial punishment if exercised upon his ass or horse. Thus, beating comes to be regarded by all as among the common evils to which life is inci-

dent. Instances are mentioned of persons who, being wealthy, and knowing that attempts would be made to extort money from them by beating, have inured themselves, by self-inflicted blows, to bear the worst without being shaken. The consequence of all this is, that personal chastisement is in those countries not considered a disgrace, but simply a misfortune, limited to the pain inflicted, or to the degree of displeasure on the part of a superior which it may be understood to indicate. A great minister of state, who was beaten yesterday, does not hold his head less erect, and is not less courted or respected to-day, if he still retains his place and influence at court; and if his great master condescends, on second thoughts, to invest his bruised person with a robe of honor, and to speak a few words of kindness or compliment, the former punishment is considered by all parties to be more than adequately compensated.'—*Pict. Bib.*

15. *Then the officers came and cried unto Pharaoh,* &c. Supposing perhaps that this rigor had been imposed upon them by the task-masters, without Pharaoh's order, and therefore having hope of obtaining redress. But, alas! theirs was a case of which it might well be said in the language of the preacher, Ecc. 1. 1, 'I returned and considered all the oppressions that are done under the sun; and behold the tears of such as were oppressed, and they had no comforter; and on the side of their oppressors there was power; but they had no comforter.'

16. *The fault is in thine own people* Heb. חטאת עמך *hattath ammeka, thy*

Make brick: and behold, thy servants *are* beaten; but the fault *is* in thine own people.

17 But he said, Ye *are* idle, *ye are* idle: therefore ye say, Let us go, *and* do sacrifice to the LORD.

18 Go therefore now, *and* work: for there shall no straw be given you, yet shall ye deliver the tale of bricks.

19 And the officers of the children of Israel did see *that* they *were* in evil *case*, after it was said, Ye shall not minish *aught* from your bricks of your daily task.

---

people has sinned, or *done wrong ;* or considering חטאת a noun, *this is the sin of thy people*. The true meaning of the clause is not easily determined, as it is by no means obvious whether the phrase 'thy people' is to be referred to the Israelites or to the Egyptians. Those who adopt the former construction suppose the Israelites are called Pharaoh's people in order to work upon his compassion. But even in this case there is some discrepancy of interpretation. The words may be understood as a complaint of the officers that *they* were beaten, though *the people* (the Israelites) were the offenders, if any. On another, and on the whole a better construction, the sense will be; ' Behold thy servants are beaten, and yet the fault really lies at the door of thine own people (the Egyptians), who refuse to furnish them straw.' According to this the Chal. has, ' Thy people sinneth against them.' Leclerc, however, intimates that the phrase, ' the fault is in thine own people,' is equivalent to saying the fault is charged, imputed, to thine own people (the Israelites), and punishment inflicted upon them accordingly, though with vast injustice. This is somewhat countenanced by the Gr. Syr. and Vulg. which all render substantially, ' Thou injurest thy people,' i. e. the Israelites. We are still left in some degree of suspense as to the true import.

17, 18. *But he said, Ye are idle, ye are idle*, &c. Thus affording a sample of the grossest tyranny, which generally thinks it sufficient to answer reasonable complaints by redoubled abuse and crimination, and by increasing the burdens which call them forth. To a

certain extent indeed there was ground for Pharaoh's words; that is to say, they recognize the fact, that being idle is oftentimes the occasion of indulging vain and evil thoughts, and cherishing visionary projects. Had it been true, as he professed to think, that the Israelites had not work enough to do, nothing would have been more likely than that they should have devised some such excursion as he here charges upon them, under the plea of religious service. Thus the worldly wisdom and base insinuations of the king of Egypt, though grossly false and injurious in the present case, may yet teach us the useful lesson, that increased diligence in our daily work is one of the best remedies for a roving imagination and ungovernable thoughts. Let those that suffer from such temptations set themselves diligently to work at some employment useful to man and honorable to God. The less time they allow their hands to be idle, the less will be the risk of their thoughts leading them astray.

19. *The officers—did see that they were in evil* case. Heb. ברע *in evil.* Moses and Aaron are here made to experience the lot that sometimes befalls good men in the best of causes. Their well-meant efforts but increase the hardships they were intended to remedy. The mission which had not long before so exhilarated the minds of the people and filled them with eager anticipations of deliverance, now proves the occasion of new miseries and persecutions. Bad as their condition had been before the two brothers came among them with their promises and their wonderful

20 ¶ And they met Moses and Aaron, who stood in the way, as they came forth from Pharaoh :

21 ʰ And they said unto them, The Lord look upon you, and judge ; because ye have made our savour to be abhorred in the eyes of Pharaoh, and in the eyes of his servants, to

ʰ ch. 6. 9.

put a sword in their hand to slay us.

22 And Moses returned unto the Lord, and said, Lord, wherefore hast thou *so* evil-entreated this people ? why *is* it *that* thou hast sent me ?

23 For since I came to Pharaoh to speak in thy name, he hath done evil to this people : neither hast thou delivered thy people at all.

signs, it was not to be compared to the intolerable hardships which the vindictive despot, in consequence of this mission, laid upon them. For the fancied invasion of his royal prerogative and the wound given to his pride, he avenges himself upon the bleeding shoulders of the poor vassals who could not redress themselves and who durst not complain.

20. *And they met Moses and Aaron, who stood in the way, as they came forth from Pharaoh.* They doubtless having stationed themselves at some convenient stand on the way-side, where they could speedily learn the result of the interview.

21. *The Lord look upon you,* &c. The crimination of Moses and Aaron on this occasion was clearly as unjust and unreasonable as that of Pharaoh had been well deserved. They had given the best evidence of their devotedness to the interests of their countrymen, and of their zeal for their emancipation, and yet, from the *accidental* issues of their enterprise, they are reproached as accessaries to their slavery. But some allowance is to be made for their rashness on the principle mentioned by the Preacher, that 'oppression will drive a wise man mad,' so that he shall speak unadvisedly with his lips, and sometimes mistake a true friend for a bitter enemy. But let public benefactors learn from this, that they must expect to be tried, not only by the malice of declared opponents, but also by the unjust and unkind reflections of those from whom they had a right to

hope for better things.——¶ *Put a sword in their hands to slay us.* That is, give them a plausible pretext for destroying us. A proverbial expression.

22. *And Moses returned,* &c. Or rather perhaps 'turned unto the Lord,' i. e. mentally, for we can conceive of no *local* return expressed by the term. He was evidently unprepared for this issue of the transaction, though he had been assured by God himself, that Pharaoh would not, till driven to the utmost extremity, consent to the departure of the Israelites. While he could not but be grieved to the heart to perceive that his efforts to serve his brethren had only contributed to plunge them deeper in distress, yet he was doubtless strongly sensible of the wrong that was done to him by their keen reproaches. But instead of retorting upon them in terms of equal harshness, he has immediate recourse to God and to him he pours out his complaint in a pathetic expostulation.——¶ *Wherefore hast thou so evil entreated this people?* That is, why hast thou *suffered them to be so evilly treated,* as is evident from the tenor of the next verse. But as we have seen before, this is entirely according to prevailing usage in the Scripture to represent God as doing that which he sovereignly permits to be done. Thus the petition in the Lord's Prayer, 'Lead us not into temptation,' is to be understood, not of any supposable direct and positive act on the part of God, but simply of *sufferance* and *permission*: 'Do not suffer us to be led into temptation.' Moses was evidently at a loss how to

CHAPTER VI.

THEN the Lord said unto Moses, Now shalt thou see what I will do to Pharaoh: for ^a with a strong hand shall he let them go, and with

a strong hand ^b shall he drive them out of his land.

2 And God spake unto Moses, and said unto him, I *am* the Lord:

---

^a ch. 3. 19.

^b ch. 11. 1. & 12. 31, 33, 39.

---

reconcile the adverse providence with the promise and the commission which he had received. He had indeed been taught to anticipate Pharaoh's refusal to let the people go, but he was taken by surprise on finding their burdens increased. It seemed to him that his mission was utterly abortive, and that thus far not one step had been taken towards their deliverance. But guided by the light of his experience, and that of thousands of others in subsequent times, *we* can put a more discreet construction upon this apparently mysterious style of dispensation. To *us* it is not a strange spectacle to see the most merciful counsels of God ushered in by a train of events apparently the most disastrous; to see his dearest servants reduced to the utmost straits just when he is ready to appear for their deliverance; and to witness the best directed endeavors for men's conviction and conversion, but exasperating their corruptions, confirming their prejudices, hardening their hearts, and sealing them up under unbelief. This result is suffered to take place in infinite wisdom that we may learn to cease from man, and that the divine interpositions may be more endeared to the hearts of those that wait for them.

Chapter 6

1. *Then the Lord said unto Moses,* &c. That is, in answer to the complaining tenor of his address mentioned at the close of the preceding chapter, to which this verse properly belongs. It is somewhat singular, indeed, that it should have been separated from it, for with this verse ends the fourteenth section, or Sabbath day's reading of the Law; a division very clearly marked in

the Hebrew Scriptures.—The murmuring spirit in which Moses appealed to God might have been justly met by a stern rebuke. But in the tone of gentleness and kindness in which this answer is couched we read no reproach of the infirmity, not to say perverseness, which had appeared in Moses' language. Thus long-suffering and indulgent is the Father of mercies towards his offending children. By an emphatic repetition of the promise before given, Ex. 3. 20, he silences the complaints of his servant and assures him not only of ultimate but speedy success in his embassy to the king.——¶ *Now shalt thou see.* Your seeing this result shall not long be delayed. The words perhaps imply a *tacit* reproof of his former incredulity; q. d. I perceive you are slow to believe what I assured you, ch. 3. 19, 20, I would do to Pharaoh. Therefore you shall very shortly have evidence that will convince you.——¶ *With a strong hand shall he let them go,* &c. The 'strong hand' here mentioned is to be understood both of God and of Pharaoh. Pharaoh should by the sudden exercise of his kingly power and with great urgency send them forth out of Egypt; but to this he should himself be compelled by the 'strong hand' of God put forth in the terrific judgments of the plagues. The language of the promise, it will be observed, becomes more intense in the final clause. He shall not only be brought at last to *consent* to the departure of Israel, but shall be impelled himself by the pressure of the divine judgments to *urge* and *hasten* it with the utmost vehemence.

2. *And God spake unto Moses,* &c Whether this is to be regarded as a

3 And I appeared unto Abraham, unto Isaac, and unto Jacob by *the name of* c God Almighty, but by

c Gen. 17 1. & 35. 11. & 48. 3.

my name d JEHOVAH was I not known to them.

d ch. 3. 14. Ps. 68. 4. & 83. 18   John 8. 58 Rev. 1. 4.

continuation of the address commenced in the preceding verse, or whether it was spoken to Moses on some subsequent occasion, is not easily determined. However this may be, the drift of the words is undoubtedly to show the sure foundation on which the fulfilment of the promise of deliverance rested. To this end he begins by declaring himself under the significant name of 'Jehovah,' by which he designed hereafter to be more especially recognized as the covenant God of their race. Hitherto the august title of 'Lord God Almighty' (El Shaddai) had been that with which they had been most familiar, and which had afforded the grand sanction and security to all his promises. In their various wanderings, weaknesses, and distresses, they had been encouraged to trust in a Being *omnipotent* to protect them, *all-sufficient* to supply their wants. But their posterity were henceforth to know him by another name, under a new character, even the incommunicable name 'Jehovah,' which denotes eternal unchangeable self-existence; deriving nothing from any, but conferring upon all, life, and breath, and all things; who is above all, through all, and in all; 'the same yesterday, to day, and for ever.' This glorious name he puts significantly in contrast with that by which he was known to Abraham, Isaac, and Jacob, in order to minister to his people a more abundant ground of hope and confidence.

3. *By my name* JEHOVAH *was I not known to them.* Gr. 'My name 'Lord' I did not manifest unto them.' Chal. 'My name 'Adonai' I showed not.' A twofold mode of interpretation divides into two classes the great mass of commentators upon this passage. (1.) It is maintained by some that the words are

to be understood in their most exact and literal import, as teaching that the name 'Jehovah' was utterly unknown to the ancient patriarchs, and was first revealed to Moses at the burning bush, where, when he asked the name which he should announce to Israel, God declared himself by the sacred denomination 'I am that I am,' which is of the same origin and import with 'Jehovah,' and said moreover of the title 'Jehovah,' 'this is my *name* for ever, and this is my *memorial* unto all generations.' The advocates of this opinion, in answer to the objection that the name in question must have been known long before this, as it occurs in repeated instances in the course of the book of Genesis, reply, that as there is no evidence that the book of Genesis was written till after the divine appearance at Horeb, when this title was first revealed, the mere fact of Moses' making use of the name 'Jehovah' in that book is no sufficient proof that the name was known to those of whom he writes, any more than his mention of a place called 'Dan' in the time of Abraham, Gen. 14. 14, proves that the place was at that time known by this name, whereas it was then called 'Laish.' They contend farther, that as Moses wrote for the benefit of those of his own age and their posterity, it was specially fitting, that in writing the history of the Israelitish race from its earliest period, he should proleptically employ that peculiar name by which the Most High would be known as *their God,* the very same God who brought them out of Egypt, and who, a little before that deliverance, had made this his name known to them as that by which he would especially be called in memory of that great event. As to the passages where the patriarchs are represented as expressly addressing the Lord by his title ' Jehovah,' as for instance, Gen. 15. 2, these, they say, are corrupted in the original text, and that later writers have substituted ' Jehovah' for ' Elohim or ' Adonai,' which Moses undoubtedly wrote, and this hypothesis, it must be confessed, is somewhat favored by the variation of several of the ancient versions from the present Hebrew reading. See Geddes' Critical Remarks on this passage, who observes, that ' if the name 'Jehovah' were known before it was here communicated to Moses, and were the common appellation of the God of the patriarchs, the question of Moses, Ex. 3. 13, was needless, was impertinent ; for God had before told him, v. 6, that he was ' the God of his (Moses') fathers, the God of Abraham, the God of Isaac, and the God of Jacob.' It is clear then that Moses, by asking, what was the name of this same God of his fathers, knew not that he had any particular name ; and that particular ' Jehovah' is now, for the first time, made known as the peculiar God of the Israelitic nation.' These are the principal arguments adduced in favor of the first hypothesis. (2.) Others, and we think for better reasons, understand the words as implying, not that the literal name ' Jehovah' was unknown to the ancient fathers who preceded Moses, but that its true, full, and complete import—its force, burden, and pregnant significancy, was not before known ; whereas now and hereafter, the chosen people should come to understand this august name, not in the letter merely, but in the actual realization of all which it implied. The name ' Jehovah,' as before remarked, natively denotes not only God's eternal existence, but also his unchangeable truth and omnipotent power, which give being to his promises by the actual performance of them. Now, although Abraham, Isaac, and Jacob, had received promises, yet they had not enjoyed the things promised. They believed in these things, but they had not lived to see the actual accomplishment of them ; they had not experimentally known them. The time, however, was now come, when God was to be known by his name ' Jehovah,' in the doing of what he had before decreed, and the fulfilling of what he had before promised. Accordingly in the words immediately following, which may be regarded as exegetical of the title under consideration, God goes on to assure them that he will make good his promise by establishing his covenant. Agreeably to this mode of interpretation it appears from other passages that God is said to make himself known under the high designation of ' Jehovah' by bringing to pass the grand predicted events of his providence. Thus, Ex. 7. 5, ' And that the Egyptians shall know that I am Jehovah, when I stretch forth my hand upon Egypt.' Again, v. 17, ' Thou shalt know that I am Jehovah ; for I will strike with the rod that is in thine hand upon the rivers, and they shalt be turned into blood.' Ezek. 28. 22, ' And they shall know that I am the Lord (Jehovah) when I shall have executed judgments in her and shall be sanctified in her.' It may be observed, moreover, that the Lord is not called ' Jehovah' till after he had finished the work of creation, Gen. 2. 4 ; and in like manner Christ, having fulfilled all things pertaining to our redemption, which is the new creation, manifested himself under the same significant name, not in its letter but in its interpretation, when he declared himself, Rev. 1. 8, 17, 18, to be ' the Alpha and the Omega, the beginning and the ending, the Lord who is, and who was, and who is to come, even the Almighty.' The words of Moses, therefore, it is contended, are not to be understood as an *absolute* but a *comparative* negative ; for that the literal name ' Jehovah' was known to the patriarchs, is indubitable, from the fol

4 e And I have also established
my covenant with them, f to give
them the land of Canaan, the land
of their pilgrimage, wherein they
were strangers.

5 And g I have also heard the
groaning of the children of Israel,
whom the Egyptians keep in bondage : and I have remembered my
covenant.

6 Wherefore say unto the children
of Israel, h I *am* the Lord, and i I

will bring you out from under the
burdens of the Egyptians, and I will
rid you out of their bondage, and I
will k redeem you with a stretched-
out arm, and with great judgments :

7 And I will l take you to me for a
people, and m I will be to you a
God : and ye shall know that I *am*
the Lord your God, which bringeth you out n from under the burdens of the Egyptians.

e Gen. 15. 18. & 17. 4, 7.   f Gen. 17. 8. &
28 4.   g ch. 2. 24.   h ver. 2, 8, 29.   i ch. 3.
17. & 7. 4.   Deut. 26. 8.   Ps. 81. 6. & 136.
11, 12.

k ch. 15. 13.   Deut. 7. 8.   1 Chron. 17. 21.
Neh. 1. 10. l Deut. 4. 20. & 7. 6. & 14. 2. & 26.
18. 2 Sam. 7. 24. m Gen. 17. 7, 8. ch. 29. 45, 46.
Deut. 29. 13. Rev. 21. 7. n ch. 5. 4, 5. Ps. 81. 6.

lowing passages ; Gen. 9. 26, Noah in
his benediction of Shem says, ' Blessed
be the Lord (Jehovah) God of Shem.'
Gen. 15. 2, 'And Abraham said, Lord
(Jehovah or Jehovih) God, what wilt
thou give me ?' Gen. 22. 14, 'And Abraham called the name of that place Je-
hovah-jireh.' Certainly then the name
' Jehovah' must have been known to
him. And so also to Isaac, Gen. 27, 7 ;
and to Jacob, Gen. 28. 20, 21. Such
comparative modes of speech are not
unfrequent in the Scriptures. Thus Jer.
7. 22, 23, ' For I spake not unto your
fathers, nor commanded them in the
day that I brought them out of the land
of Egypt, concerning burnt-offerings or
sacrifices. But this thing commanded
I them, saying, Obey my voice, and I
will be your God, and ye shall be my
people ;' i. e. I gave no commandment
respecting *ritual* duties compared with
the importance which I attached to
moral duties. Otherwise it is evident
that the language of the Most High militates with the recorded facts in the
sacred history.

4. *I have also established my covenant
with them.* Heb. הקימתי *hakimothi,*
have made to stand, have erected.——
¶ *To give them.* That is, not in their
own persons, but in their posterity.

5. *I have remembered my covenant.*
That is, I still bear in vivid remem-

brance my covenant entered into with
Abraham, Gen. 15. 10. 11, and confirmed
with solemn rites, in which I promised
that I would judge that nation which
should afflict his seed.

6, 7. *I am the Lord* (Jehovah), *and I
will bring you out—will rid—will redeem—will take,* &c. These verbs are
all, in the original, in the past instead
of the future tense, denoting the *absolute certainty* of the accomplishment
of the things promised, though for the
present they were merely in futurition.
But where God becomes a covenant 'Jehovah' to any soul or any people, the
unfailing effect is to put his every promise into being, and it should not be
forgotten that in Christ, under the Gospel, he becomes emphatically such to
his church. Here the precious and glorious titles ' El Shaddai' and 'Jehovah,'
power and *performance,* are sweetly
combined in the person of him in whom
the promises are all yea and amen.——
¶ *With a stretched-out arm.* The word
here rendered ' stretched-out,' may also
be rendered ' lifted up,' or ' high,' as it
is in fact by the Chal. and Latin Vulgate. The expression is borrowed from
the circumstance of men's *stretching
out* and *lifting up* their arms and hands
with a view to strike their enemies
with greater force. In order to which,
it was usual in those Eastern countries

8 And I will bring you in unto the land, concerning the which I did ° swear to give it to Abraham, to Isaac, and to Jacob ; and I will give it you for an heritage : I *am* the LORD.

9 ¶ And Moses spake so unto the children of Israel : P but they hearkened not unto Moses, for anguish of spirit, and for cruel bondage.

10 And the LORD spake unto Moses, saying,

11 Go in, speak unto Pharaoh king of Egypt, that he let the children of Israel go out of his land.

° Gen. 15. 18. & 26. 3. & 28. 13. & 35. 12.   P ch. 5. 21.

---

where their outer garments were of a loose and flowing kind, to fling them aside that they might not hinder or weaken the effect of the intended blow. It is in allusion to this that the expression ' making bare his holy arm,' is applied to the Most High, Is. 54. 10, in speaking of the inflictions of his wrath upon his enemies.

8. *Concerning the which I did swear to give it.* Heb. אֶת יָדִי נָשָׂאתִי *nasathi eth yadi, have lifted up my hand;* an expression taken from the common custom of elevating the hand to heaven when taking an oath. Dan. 12. 7, ' And I heard the man clothed in linen, which was upon the waters of the river, when he *held up his right hand* and his left hand unto heaven, and *sware*, &c.' See Deut. 32. 40. Is. 62. 8.

9. *They hearkened not unto Moses for anguish of spirit, and from cruel bondage.* Heb. רוּחַ מִקֹּצֶר *mikkotzer ruah, for shortness, or straitness of spirit.* That is, from extreme dejection and discouragement of soul, mingled with irritation and impatience. That this is the force of the original will appear from the usage in the following passages. Prov. 14. 29, ' He that is slow to wrath is of great understanding; but he that is *hasty of spirit* (Heb. רוּחַ קְצַר *ketzar ruah*) exalteth folly.' Job, 21. 4, ' And if it were so, why should not my spirit be *troubled* (Heb. תִּקְצַר *tiktzar, shortened*).' Numb. 21. 4, ' And the soul of the people was much *discouraged* (Heb. תִּקְצַר *shortened*) by reason of the way.' Judg. 16. 16, ' And it came to pass, when she pressed him

daily with her words, and urged him, so that his soul was *vexed* (Heb. תִּקְצַר *shortened*) unto death.' The Gr. renders it ' from feeble-mindedness,' the same word in effect and nearly in form as that which occurs, 1 Thes. 5. 14, ' Comfort the *feeble-minded*.' It is to this period probably that allusion is had, Ex. 14. 12, ' Is not this the word that we did tell thee in Egypt, saying, Let us alone that we may serve the Egyptians, for it had been better for us to serve the Egyptians than that we should die in the wilderness ;' which words in the Samaritan version are inserted in this place. To such a pitch of disheartening anguish had their sufferings wrought them that they chose to have all farther proceedings relative to their deliverance stayed. So heavy was their affliction, and so grievously had they been of late disappointed, that they can neither believe nor hope any longer ; and the message now delivered by Moses was like a charming song upon the ear of a deaf or dead man. So strongly does a sense of wretchedness oppose the cordial reception of promises and encouragements. Even the comforts to which they are entitled, and which God has expressly provided for them, do the disconsolate put far from them under the pressure of their griefs. ' To whom he said, This is the rest wherewith ye may cause the weary to rest; and this is the refreshing: yet they would not.' Is. 28. 12.

10, 11. *And the Lord spake unto Moses,* &c. The narrative proceeds to inform us with what still farther indulgence

12 And Moses spake before the Lord, saying, Behold, the children of Israel have q not hearkened unto me; how then shall Pharaoh hear

q ver. 9.

me, r who *am* of uncircumcised lips?

13 And the Lord spake unto Moses, and unto Aaron, and gave them

r ver. 30. ch. 4. 10. Jer. 1. 6.

God treated the backwardness of his people to welcome the tidings of deliverance. He still moved forwards in his measures for their relief, as if he heard not or heeded not their unbelieving complaints, and remonstrances, and groans. That perverseness which would a thousand times have wearied out all human forbearance, is still graciously borne with by the long-suffering of heaven. But that which is mercy to Israel is wrath to Pharaoh, although the punishment which is ripening even for him is not to be inflicted without farther warnings. When the Lord is about to visit with judgments, we see him advancing as with slow and reluctant steps. On the contrary, when misery is to be relieved, benefits conferred, or sins forgiven, the blessing makes haste as it were, to spend itself upon its objects. But when the wicked are to be dealt with, justice seems to regret the necessity under which it is laid to maintain itself, and the sinner is not destroyed till the equity of his condemnation is manifest, and every thing around him calls for vengeance.

12. *And Moses spake before the Lord,* &c. It would seem that Moses had caught, in some measure, the spirit of despondency which reigned among his brethren. He speaks as one discouraged and timidly shrinking from what appears to him a hopeless service. Reasoning from the less to the greater, he is ready to conclude the cause to be desperate. If the Israelites themselves, who were so deeply interested in the burden of his message, turned a deaf ear to it, how little ground had he to hope for a hearing from Pharaoh? Would he not, in the pride and insolence of his spirit, spurn a message which required

him to bow down his loftiness and humbly submit to the authority of a Being whom he did not acknowledge, and in so doing to honor a people whom he despised? More especially was he led to distrust his success when' he called to mind his own infirmity in speaking This objection God had indeed sufficiently overruled on a former occasion, but in the depth of his dejection he pleads it again, forgetting the sufficiency of grace to overcome the defects of nature. In these circumstances, with a leader disheartened and broken down in spirit and a people sunk in utter despondency, what hope remained of deliverance to Israel, had not God himself taken the accomplishment of the whole work into his own hands? But his strength is made perfect in man's weakness.——¶ *Who am of uncircumcised lips.* Chal. 'Of an heavy speech.' Gr. αλογος, *without speech.* As among the Jews the circumcision of any part denoted its perfection, so on the other hand uncircumcision was used to signify its defectiveness or inaptitude to the purposes for which it was designed. Thus the prophet says of the Jews, Jer. 6. 10, that 'their ear was uncircumcised,' and adds the explanation of it, ' because they cannot hearken.' Again, ch. 9. 26, he tells us that ' the house of Israel were uncircumcised in heart,' i. e. would not understand and learn their duty. In like manner ' uncircumcised lips' in the passage before us must mean a person who was a bad speaker and wanting eloquence. Syr. ' Mine is a stammering tongue.'

13. *The Lord spake unto Moses and unto Aaron, and gave them a charge,* &c. Aaron is here again joined in commission with Moses, and the debate

a charge unto the children of Israel, and unto Pharaoh king of Egypt, to bring the children of Israel out of the land of Egypt.

14 ¶ These *be* the heads of their fathers' houses: ⁵ The sons of Reuben the first-born of Israel; Hanoch, and Pallu, Hezron, and Carmi: these *be* the families of Reuben.

15 ᵗ And the sons of Simeon; Jemuel, and Jamin, and Ohad, and Jachin, and Zohar, and Shaul the son of a Canaanitish woman: these *are* the families of Simeon.

16 ¶ And these *are* the names of ᵘ the sons of Levi, according to

ˢ Gen. 46. 9. 1 Chron. 5. 3.   ᵗ 1 Chron. 4. 24.
Gen. 46. 10. ᵘ Gen. 46. 11.   Numb. 3. 17
1 Chron. 6. 1, 16.

their generations; Gershon, and Kohath, and Merari.   And the years of the life of Levi *were* an hundred thirty and seven years.

17 ˣ The sons of Gershon; Libni, and Shimi, according to their families.

18 And ʸ the sons of Kohath; Amram, and Izhar, and Hebron, and Uzziel: and the years of the life of Kohath *were* an hundred thirty and three years.

19 And ᶻ the sons of Merari; Mahali and Mushi: these *are* the families of Levi, according to their generations.

ˣ 1 Chron. 6. 17. & 23. 7.   ʸ Numb. 26. 57.
1 Chron. 6. 2, 18.   ᶻ 1 Chron. 6. 19. & 23. 21.

ended by the interposition of the divine *authority*. A solemn *charge* is given to both which, upon their allegiance, they are required to execute with all possible expedition and fidelity. 'Where the word of a king is, there is power,' and the repetition of baffled arguments is suitably cut short by the voice of the Most High speaking in majesty. It is not clear that the words of this verse are to be understood as the answer to what Moses had said in the verse before. They seem to be rather a brief recapitulation of what had been said in the three preceding verses. As he was about to interrupt the thread of the narrative by the insertion of a genealogical table, he here repeats the general fact of Moses and Aaron having received a charge to go into the presence of Pharaoh and renew their demand of the dismission of the people. The historian thus indicates the posture of things at that particular stage of the business where the continuity of his story is broken.

14. *These be the heads*, &c. Gr. αρχηγοι, *chiefs, captains, governors.* 'Their houses,' i. e. the houses of Moses and Aaron. The design of introducing this genealogical record in its present con-

nexion, is to point out distinctly the stock and lineage of Moses and Aaron. As one of these was to be the great Legislator and Prophet, and the other the High Priest of the peculiar people, it might be of very great importance in after ages to have their true descent authenticated beyond a doubt.——¶ *The sons of Reuben,* &c. As Reuben and Simeon were elder than Levi, from whom Moses and Aaron derived their pedigree, it seemed to be proper to state the rank which their progenitor held, in the order of birth, among the sons of Jacob.

16. *According to their generations.* The force of this expression may, perhaps, be better conceived by its being paraphrased thus: 'These are the names of the sons of Levi, *viewed in connexion with the respective lines of descendants proceeding from them.*'——¶ *The years of the life of Levi,* &c. Levi was four years elder than Joseph, consequently he was 43 when he came into Egypt, Joseph being then 39; was 114 at the death of Joseph, whom he survived 23 years; lived after coming into Egypt 94 years, and died 41 years before the birth of Moses, and 121 before the exode from Egypt. His age is per-

20 And ᵃ Amram took him Jochebed his father's sister to wife ; and
she bare him Aaron and Moses.
And the years of the life of Amram
were an hundred and thirty and
seven years.

21 ¶ And ᵇ the sons of Izhar ; Korah, and Nepheg, and Zichri.

22 And ᶜ the sons of Uzziel ; Mi-
shael, and Elzaphan, and Zithri.

23 And Aaron took him Elisheba
daughter of ᵈ Amminadab, sister of
Naashon to wife ; and she bare him
ᵉ Nadab and Abihu, Eleazar and
Ithamar.

24 And the ᶠ sons of Korah ; Assir,
and Elkanah, and Abiasaph : these
are are the families of the Korhites.

ᵃ ch. 2. 1, 2. Numb. 26. 59. ᵇ Numb. 16. 1.
1 Chron. 6. 37, 38. ᶜ Lev. 10. 4. Numb. 3. 30.
ᵈ Ruth 4 19, 20. 1 Chron. 2. 10. Matt. 1. 4.
ᵉ Lev. 10. 1. Numb. 3. 2. & 26. 60. 1 Chron.
6. 3. & 24. 1. ᶠ Numb. 26. 11.

---

25 And Eleazar, Aaron's son, took
him *one* of the daughters of Putiel
to wife ; and ᵍ she bare him Phine-
has : these *are* the heads of the fathers of the Levites, according to
their families.

26 These *are* that Aaron and Moses, ʰ to whom the Lᴏʀᴅ said,
Bring out the children of Israel
from the land of Egypt according
to their ⁱ armies.

27 These *are* they which ᵏ spake
to Pharaoh king of Egypt, ˡ to bring
out the children of Israel from
Egypt : these *are* that Moses and
Aaron.

28 ¶ And it came to pass on the
day *when* the Lᴏʀᴅ spake unto Moses in the land of Egypt,

ᵍ Numb. 25. 7, 11. Josh. 24. 33. ʰ ver. 13.
ⁱ ch. 7. 4. & 12. 17, 51. Numb. 33. 1. ᵏ ch.
5. 1, 3. & 7. 10. ˡ ver. 13. ch. 32. 7. & 33. 1.
Ps. 77. 20.

---

haps expressly stated in order to afford
aid toward settling the precise time of
the fulfilment of the prophecy made to
Abraham, Gen. 15. 13. It is moreover
worthy of notice, that the promise made
to Abraham, Gen. 15. 16, that the Israelites should be delivered out of Egypt
' in the fourth generation' was strictly
fulfilled. Moses was the son of Amram,
the son of Kohath, the son of Levi, the
son of Jacob. Jacob went down into
Egypt, and Moses was in the fourth
generation from him.

20. *Amram took him Jochebed his
father's sister to wife*. It is obvious
that in giving this genealogical record
Moses is very far from being prompted
by a vain-glorious wish to laud his ancestry ; for he not only inserts in the
list the names of those whose characters disgraced it, but he openly declares
himself to be the offspring of a connexion which was afterwards expressly
forbidden under the law, and which was
probably even now regarded as doing
some violence to the dictates of nature.
Comp. Lev. 18. 12. Numb. 26. 59. We

may learn, however, from the circum
stances of the parentage of Moses and
Aaron, that the evil or equivocal conduct of progenitors does not always
avail to preclude their having a seed
which shall stand high in the favor of
God.

23. *Aaron took him Elisheba*. Gr.
Ελιζαβετ, *Elizabeth*. She was of the
tribe of Judah, being sister to Naashon,
a prince of that tribe. While Moses
thus dwells particularly on the genealogy of Aaron, he modestly passes over
his own in silence. Had he been a man
of ambition, or his institutions been of
his own devising, he would never have
given this precedence to his brother's
family over his own.

26. *These are that Aaron and Moses.*
Heb. הוא אהרן ומשה *hu Aharon u
Mosheh, this is that Aaron and Moses.*
The words of this and the following
verse are merely a more minute speci
fication of the persons of Moses an
Aaron, without being in the least de-
signed as a note of self-commendation.
We see rather a tacit intimation of the

29 That the LORD spake unto Moses, saying, m I *am* the LORD: n speak thou unto Pharaoh king of Egypt all that I say unto thee.

30 And Moses said before the LORD, Behold, o I *am* of uncircumcised lips, and how shall Pharaoh hearken unto me ?

m ver. 2. n ver. 11. ch. 7. 2. o ver. 12. ch. 4. 10.

---

distinguishing grace of heaven in raising up two individuals from the humblest ranks of life, and entrusting them with the dignified service of delivering Israel from the hand of Pharaoh.——¶ *According to their armies.* That is, their tribes, now grown so numerous as to form each an army. There seems to be intended also an oblique antithesis between these armies of Israel, and the two inconsiderable men who were appointed to lead them ; as if he would insinuate that they were called to a work to which they were in themselves totally inadequate, and one which they could never have performed without being miraculously aided and endowed from heaven.

29. *Saying, I am the Lord* (Jehovah). Nothing more could be really needed to countervail the fears and misgivings of Moses than this assurance. The name 'Jehovah,' carries enough in its import to support his ministers in their severest trials and most arduous labors.

Chapter 7

1. *I have made thee a god to Pharaoh.* Heb. אלהים נתתיך *nathattika elohim, I have given thee a god ;* i. e. set, ordained, appointed ; according to a common usage of the original נתן *to give*, of which see Note on Gen. 1. 17. Chal. ' I have set thee a prince or master (רב *rab*).' Arab. ' I have made thee a lord.' See Note on Ex. 4. 10. Moses was to be God's representative in this affair, as magistrates are called *gods*

CHAPTER VII.

AND the LORD said unto Moses, See, I have made thee a a god to Pharaoh : and Aaron thy brother shall be b thy prophet.

2 Thou c shalt speak all that I command thee : and Aaron thy brother shall speak unto Pharaoh, that he

a ch. 4. 16. Jer. 1. 10. b ch. 4. 16. c ch 4. 15.

---

because they are God's vicegerents. He was authorized to speak and act in God's name, doing that which was above the ordinary power of nature, and commissioned to demand obedience from a sovereign prince.——¶ *Aaron shall be thy prophet.* Chal. 'Thine interpreter.' See Note on Gen. 28. 7. 'A man who is afraid to go into the presence of a king, or a governor, or a great man, will seek an interview with the minister, or some principal character ; and should he be much alarmed, it will be said, ' Fear not, friend ; I will make you *as a god* to the king.' 'What! are you afraid of the collector ? fear not ; you will be *as a god* to him.' ' Yes, yes, that upstart was once much afraid of the great ones ; but now he is like a *god* among them.' *Roberts.* Moses himself was to be an oracle, and Aaron a mouth, to Pharaoh. Aaron was to be to Moses what Moses himself was to God. The Most High does not scruple to clothe his humblest servants with a kind of divinity when he would make them oracles to his people or instruments of wrath to his enemies.

2. *Thou shalt speak,* &c. That is, to Aaron. When men speak by God's command they are to keep back no part of his message. Although the name of Aaron is not always expressly mentioned in connexion with that of Moses throughout the ensuing narrative, yet it is to be inferred, from the charge now given, that the two brothers uniformly went into the presence of Pharaoh together.

send the children of Israel out of
his land.

3 And d I will harden Pharaoh's
heart, and e multiply my f signs
and my wonders in the land of
Egypt.

4 But Pharaoh shall not hearken
unto you, g that I may lay my hand
upon Egypt, and bring forth mine
armies, *and* my people the children

d ch. 4. 21.   e ch. 11. 9.   f ch. 4. 7   g ch. 10.
1. & 11. 9.

of Israel, out of the land of Egypt,
h by great judgments.

5 And the Egyptians i shall know
that I *am* the LORD, when I k stretch
forth mine hand upon Egypt, and
bring out the children of Israel
from among them.

6 And Moses and Aaron l did as
the LORD commanded them, so
did they.

h ch. 6. 6.   i ver. 17. ch. 8. 22. & 14. 4, 18.
Ps. 9. 16.   k ch. 3. 20.   l ver. 2.

3. *I will harden Pharaoh's heart*, &c.
As in the former instance, ch. 4. 15, 21,
God announced to Moses the result, of
which his message would be the *occasion*, not the *cause*, so here also he expressly informs him that the course
which he should pursue with Pharaoh
would but serve to 'harden his heart,'
and set him with more obstinacy than
ever against letting Israel go. The consequence would be, that it would become necessary to display before the
Egyptians multiplied and still more
striking exhibitions of the divine majesty and power.——¶ *My wonders.*
Heb. מרפתי *mophethai.* The original
comes from the root רפה *yaphah*, to
persuade. It therefore properly implies
a *persuasive fact, event*, or *sign*, effected to produce conviction and to lead to
faith and obedience, whether the wonder
be strictly miraculous or not.

4. *But Pharaoh shall not hearken
unto you.* Heb. לא ישמע *lo yishma,
will not hear ;* i. e. will not obediently
give heed to you. The received mode of
rendering, ' *shall* not hearken,' puts upon the passage an *imperative* air which
the original does not warrant, or at least
require. It is merely a *predictive* sentence.——¶ *That I may lay mine hand.*
Heb. ונתתי ידי *ve-nathatti eth yadi,
and I will give mine hand.* Chal. ' And
will lay the stroke of my strength (i. e.
my powerful plague) upon the land of
Egypt.'——¶ *Bring forth mine armies*,
and *my people.* Rather, according to
the original, ' Mine hosts, even my

people,' as the copulative ' and' is wanting.

5. *The Egyptians shall know*, &c.
The great end at which God aims by
his penal judgments upon the world, is
to make himself known to the children
of men. His messengers may be despised, contradicted, and opposed, but
it should be a satisfaction to them to be
assured that the divine word shall so
far prosper in that whereunto it is sent,
that *God shall finally be glorified* in the
issue of their embassy. They shall not
in the end have reason to say that they
have labored in vain, though they would
rejoice to have been made the instru
ments of mercies rather than of judgments.

6. *Moses and Aaron did*, &c. These
words contain merely a general affirmation that Moses and Aaron, according
to what was required of them, delivered
all the words, and performed all the
miracles which are afterward recorded
in their various minute details. The
statement is not prompted by a spirit
of self-complacent boasting, but as Moses had before frankly recorded his sinful backwardness to engage in the Lord's
service, it was no more than proper that
he should pay this tribute to his subsequent prompt fidelity. It is in effect
the same testimony which is given by
the Psalmist, Ps. 105. 28, ' They (Moses
and Aaron) rebelled not against his
word,' provided this was spoken of
Moses and Aaron, which may be doubt
ed. **See Note on Ex. 9. 14—16.**

7 And Moses *was* ᵐ fourscore years old, and Aaron fourscore and three years old, when they spake unto Pharaoh.

8 ¶ And the Lᴏʀᴅ spake unto Moses, and unto Aaron, saying,

9 When Pharaoh shall speak unto you, saying, ⁿ Shew a miracle for you: then thou shalt say unto Aaron, ᵒ Take thy rod, and cast *it* before Pharaoh, *and* it shall become a serpent.

ᵐ Deut. 29. 5. & 31. 2. & 34. 7. Acts 7. 23, 30. ⁿ Isai. 7. 11. John 2. 18. & 6. 30.

10 ¶ And Moses and Aaron went in unto Pharaoh, and they did so ᵖ as the Lord had commanded: and Aaron cast down his rod before Pharaoh, and before his servants, and it �q became a serpent.

ᵒ ch. 4. 2, 17. ᵖ ver. 9. q ch. 4. 3.

7. *Moses was fourscore years old*, &c. They both therefore had, in the eyes of their countrymen, all the venerableness attached to age, and their years would inspire confidence that they would do nothing rashly. Pharaoh also might be expected to consider with more respect a message delivered by men of such a reverend and patriarchal demeanor. At the same time, it went to display the divine hand more illustriously, that two such grey headed old men, should be selected to manage a business of such an immensely arduous nature; as no degree of vigor of constitution could prevent them from feeling and evincing *some* of the infirmities of age.

9. *Show a miracle for you.* Heb. תְנוּ לָכֶם מוֹפֵת *tenu lakem mophëth, give a miracle for yourselves.* The tone is *supposed* to be supercilious and haughty, as though it were much more important for *their* sakes than for *his* that a miracle should be wrought. It is taken for granted however that Pharaoh would demand a *miraculous* testimony in proof of their commission from God. The implication involved in this is plainly, that such a demand is in itself *reasonable;* and although Pharaoh probably had no desire to be convinced, but was rather in hopes that no miracle would be wrought, and thus his disobedience be justified to himself, yet it is obvious that the Scriptures go all along on the admitted principle that the performance *of miracles is the true seal of a divine commission.* See on this subject the Note on Ex. 4. 5. Those who profess to speak to men in the name of God may expect to have their authority sifted, and though they may not now be able to silence cavils by the exhibition of miraculous power, yet they may, by a pure doctrine and a blameless life, leave objectors without excuse.——¶ *And it shall become a serpent.* Heb. רהר לְתַנִּין *yehi letannin, it shall be to a serpent;* i. e. a large serpent, a dragon (Gr. δρακων, *a dragon*). On the import of the original word תַנִּין *tannin,* see Note on Gen. 1. 21. The word here is not the same with that which occurs ch. 4. 3, though, in some instances, probably synonymous with it. It is not unlikely that the rod was changed into a *crocodile,* an animal abounding in Egypt, and apparently spoken of, in some cases, as an emblem of its persecuting rulers. Ps. 74. 13, 'Thou didst divide the sea by thy strength (the Red Sea): thou brakest the heads of the *dragons* (Heb. תנרים *tanninim*) in the waters;' i. e. thou destroyedst the Egyptian power. See also Ezek. 29. 3.

10. *Aaron cast down his rod,* &c. Though not expressly asserted, yet it is to be presumed, that a sign was demanded by Pharaoh. The command to Moses and Aaron to work the miracle was predicated on the contingency of Pharaoh's asking it, and we must presume that this condition occurred. But the sacred writers study the extremest brevity upon all points that do not positively *require* specification. Up to this point Moses and Aaron had simply

11 Then Pharaoh also ʳ called the wise men, and ˢ the sorcerers: now the magicians of Egypt, they also ᵗ did in like manner with their enchantments.

ʳ Gen. 41. 8.   ˢ 2 Tim. 3. 8.   ᵗ ver. 22. ch. 8. 7, 18.

delivered their *message*, their *instructions*, to Pharaoh; the time had now come for them to produce their *credentials*.

11. *Pharaoh called the wise men.* Heb. חכמים *hakamim*, from חכם *hakam*, *to be wise*, *to act wisely*; and applied in its adjective form by the orientals to those that practised magical arts and incantations, from their being supposed to *know* more, to be *wiser*, than the mass of men. The Gr. here has σοφιστας, *sophists*; i. e. philosophers, or professors of science.—— ¶ *Sorcerers.* Heb. מכשפים *mekash-shephim*, from כשף *kashaph*, *to use inchantments for magical purposes*; equivalent to *sorcerers*, *jugglers*, *wizards*. Gr. φαρμακους, *conjurors by drugs*. ——¶ *Magicians.* Heb. הרטמים *hartummim*. On this word see Note on Gen. 41. 8. It is here evidently used in a *general* sense, comprehending under it the *wise men* and the *sorcerers* mentioned above, from whom the *magicians* were not a different class. The Gr. renders the term variously by εξηγηται *interpreters* or *explainers* of something secret, επαοιδοι, *inchanters*, and φαρμακοι, *drug-sorcerers*. In the Lat. it is often explained by *genethliaci* or *sapientes nativitatum*, *casters-up of nativities*, and is joined with *astrologers* and *soothsayers*, Dan. 1. 20.—2. 10, 27.—4. 7.

Having thus defined, as well as we are able, the import of the original terms, two important questions naturally suggest themselves for consideration;—(1) What was Pharaoh's design in calling these magicians into his presence? and (2) What do we learn from the sacred text that they actually *did*? The subject is one which has been very largely discussed and very variously understood, and at best is encompassed with difficulties of no easy solution. One of the most elaborate and satisfactory of the numerous tractates to which this part of the Mosaic history has given rise, is that of Farmer in his 'Dissertation on Miracles,' a work which has supplied us with many important hints in the ensuing remarks.

First, as to Pharaoh's *design* in sending for the magicians, there is no good reason for supposing that the object was to engage the gods of Egypt to work miracles in *direct opposition* to the God of Israel, and thereby to invalidate Moses' divine commission. In that case they would obviously have endeavored to *counteract* the aim of Jehovah and not to *promote* it. Instead of joining with the God of the Hebrews in bringing down heavier judgments and adding to the direful plagues already inflicted, they would have sought to have had them diminished and removed. Instead of desiring them to turn more water into blood, they would have besought them to restore the corrupted waters to their natural state. Instead of entreating them to multiply frogs, their prayer would have been for them to be removed or destroyed, as it would certainly be as easy to do the one as the other. The fact seems to have been, that Pharaoh's first thought was that Moses was nothing more than a magician, and that he sent for *his* magicians in order to learn from them whether the sign given by Moses was truly supernatural, or only such as their art was able to accomplish. The question therefore was not whether the gods of Egypt were superior to the God of Israel, or whether evil spirits could perform greater miracles than those which Moses performed by the assistance of Jehovah; but whether the works of Moses were proper proofs that the God of Israel was Je-hovah, the only sovereign of nature, and consequently whether Moses was acting by his commission. This was to be determined by the result of their efforts to perform the same extraordinary acts as Moses did ; and had they succeeded, the effect would have been the same as if Baal had answered his votaries by fire ; it would have followed of course that Moses, whatever he might pre-tend, was a magician only, and not a divinely commissioned messenger, and also that Jehovah was not the only sovereign of nature. Having been sum-moned therefore for this purpose into the royal presence, the question arises,

Secondly, as to the true nature of the magicians' performances. Were they real miracles, and if so by what power effected ? Or were they nothing more than dextrous feats of juggling or sleight of hand? On these points various opin-ions have been held, each supported by an array of reasoning more or less plau-sible. Some have supposed that the magicians were aided by evil spirits in the performance of the miracles ; and that these spirits were allowed by God to exercise a supernatural power up to a certain point, when they were sud-denly arrested and confounded in their impotency, and made to give a more signal triumph to the cause of Omnipo-tence and truth. But to this it is we think validly objected that the Scrip-tures, properly understood, never ascribe to evil spirits the power of working *real miracles*. Whatever wonders they may be capable of effecting, a *miracle* strict-ly so termed, invariably requires and im-plies a *divine interposition*, as other-wise it would be difficult to conceive how a miracle should be a proof of a commission from God. Others there-fore have supposed that although the magicians pretended to have communi-cation with evil spirits and employed their arts accordingly, yet that God was pleased to interpose in concurrence with their enchantments, and work a real miracle, contrary perhaps to their ex-pectations ; while yet his design was by working a still greater one on the side of Moses and Aaron, to show the *vast superiority* of his power over theirs. This they would infer of course when they saw for instance Aaron's rod swal-lowing up their own, and consequently both they and Pharaoh would be inex-cusable in refusing to acknowledge the agency of Omnipotence. But to this again it may be replied, that the proof thus adduced was not absolutely con-clusive to their minds, that no power but that of Jehovah could work mira-cles. How was the transformation of Moses' rod a demonstration of his be-ing sent by Jehovah, when the magicians apparently produced the very same cre-dentials of a supernatural ability? Nay, the magicians, in the first contest, if a real miracle was wrought on their side no matter by what power, would appear not only to have imitated, but to have exceeded Moses ; having the advantage over him in the *number* of their mira-cles. For to human view they turned not only one rod into a serpent, which was all that Moses had hitherto done, but they turned their several rods into serpents. Now why was Moses to be credited on account of a single miracle, if it were contradicted and overborne by several miracles fully equal to it ? After the conversion of the rods, it is true, Moses' serpent swallowed up those of the magicians ; but this after victory, however splendid, could not retrieve the credit of the former defeat. It could not establish the validity of the proof, from the change of his rod, which he had appealed to in the beginning as a de-cisive testimony in favor of his claims. We seem therefore to be shut up to the necessity of seeking for a still more satisfactory solution of the difficulties involved in the case of the Egyptian ma-gicians. Our conclusion, on the whole, is the same with that of Dr. Dwight, as expressed in his 'Theology' (Serm. LX, on the Miracles of Christ), that the magicians wrought no miracles. All that they did was to busy themselves with *their enchantments*, by which every man now knows that, although the weak and credulous may be deceived, miracles cannot possibly be accomplished.

We proceed, therefore, to state the grounds of this interpretation, and in doing it we regret that, from its depending so entirely upon the idiomatic structure of the Hebrew, the mere English reader will not perhaps be able fully to appreciate its force. We will endeavor to make it, however, if not demonstrable, at least intelligible.—It is a canon of interpretation of frequent use in the exposition of the sacred writings, that verbs of action sometimes signify merely the *will* and *endeavor* to do the action in question. Thus Ezek. 24. 13, 'I have *purified* thee, and thou wast not purged ;' i. e. I have endeavored, used means, been at pains, to purify thee. John 5. 44, 'How can ye believe which *receive* honor one of another;' i. e. endeavor to receive. Rom. 2. 4. 'The goodness of God *leadeth* thee to repentance ;' i. e. endeavors or tends to lead thee. Amos, 9. 3, 'Though they be *hid* from my sight in the bottom of the sea ;' i. e. though they aim to be hid. 1 Cor. 10. 33, ' I *please* all men ;' i. e. endeavor to please. Gal. 5. 4, 'Whosoever of you are *justified* by the law ;' i. e. seek and endeavor to be justified. Ps. 69. 4, ' They that *destroy* me are mighty ;' i. e. that endeavor to destroy me. Eng. ' That *would* destroy me.' Acts, 7. 26, 'And *set them at one* again ;' i. e. wished and endeavored. Eng. ' *would* have set them.' The passage before us we consider as exhibiting a usage entirely analogous. 'They also did in like manner with their enchantments,' i. e. they endeavored to do in like manner ; just as in ch. 8. 18, it is said, 'And the magicians did so with their enchantments to bring forth lice,

but *they could not* ;' the words being precisely the same in both instances. Adopting this construction, we suppose that the former clause of verse 12 should be rendered, ' For they cast down every man his rod, *that* they might become serpents ;' which the Hebrew reader will perceive to be a rendering precisely parallel to that which occurs ch. 6. 11, ' Speak unto Pharaoh *that* he let the children of Israel go ;' Heb. '*And* he shall let go.' So also ch. 7. 2, ' Shall speak unto Pharaoh, *that* he send ;' Heb. '*And* he shall send.' The magicians cast down their rods that they might undergo a similar transmutation with that of Moses, but it is not expressly said that *were* so changed, and we therefore incline to place their discomfiture in the loss of their rods, those instruments with which they had vainly hoped to compete with Moses. If it be contended that there was some kind of change produced on the magicians' rods, but that it was effected by feats of juggling, or legerdemain, and amounted in fact merely to an optical illusion, we do not particularly object to this construction, inasmuch as it admits our main position, that there was no *real miracle* wrought by or through the magicians. Perhaps on the whole it may be considered as the most probable hypothesis ; especially as the narrative does not require us to understand all these various incidents as having occurred at one and the same interview. It seems that it was *after* the miracle wrought upon Aaron's rod that the magicians were called for by Pharaoh, and as they would learn from the summons itself the object for which they were called into the royal presence, as well as the character of the miracle that had been wrought, they would of course have time to make all the necessary preparations for playing off an illusion upon the senses of the spectators by their *semblances of serpents*.

12 For they cast down every man his rod, and they became serpents: but Aaron's rod swallowed up their rods.

13 And he hardened Pharaoh's heart that he hearkened not unto them; ^u as the LORD had said.

14 ¶ And the LORD said unto Moses, ^x Pharaoh's heart *is* hardened, he refuseth to let the people go.

15 Get thee unto Pharaoh in the

morning; lo, he goeth out unto the water, and thou shalt stand by the river's brink against he come: and ^y the rod which was turned to a serpent shalt thou take in thine hand.

16 And thou shalt say unto him, ^z The LORD God of the Hebrews hath sent me unto thee, saying, Let my people go, ^a that they may serve me in the wilderness: and behold, hitherto thou wouldest not hear.

u ch. 4. 21. ver. 4.   x ch. 8. 15. & 10. 1, 20, 27.

y ch. 4. 2, 3. & ver. 10.   z ch. 3. 18.   a ch. 3 12. 18. & 5. 1, 3.

13. *And he hardened Pharaoh's heart.* Heb. ויחזק לב פרעה *va-yehezak lëb Pharoh, and the heart of Pharaoh waxed strong, or hardened itself.* The expression in the original is precisely the same with that which occurs v. 22, of this chapter, and is there rendered, 'And Pharaoh's heart was hardened.' Why it is translated differently here, it is not easy to say.

14. *Is hardened.* Heb. כבד *kabëd, is heavy;* an instance of the unhappy usage by which our translators have uniformly employed the word 'harden' to represent several different words in the original. See Note on Ex. 4. 21.

15. *Get thee unto Pharaoh,* &c. We here enter upon the account of the ten successive plagues, to which the Most High had recourse in order to humble and break the refractory spirit of Pharaoh. Hitherto a miracle had been wrought, but no judgment inflicted. The conversion of the rod into a serpent had given proof of the tremendous power with which God's messengers were armed, but no injury having ensued, no conviction or relenting had been produced. Another step was therefore now to be taken in the progress of the divine visitations. The rod was now to begin its *chastising* work, and though remaining unchanged to become a *rod of scorpions* to the whole nation. As if there were a probability that he would not be admitted into the pres-

ence-chamber, or room of state, where audience was usually given to embassadors, he is directed to meet him by the river's brink, whither he was in the habit of resorting in the morning, either to perform his ablutions or his devotions, or both; as there is clear evidence that the Nile was anciently deified as the source of the fertility of the soil of Egypt, and that it had its appointed priests, festivals, and sacrifices. Indeed at the present day, under the sterner system of the Moslem religion, the reverence entertained for the Nile exhibits a tendency towards the same superstitious regard, as it is called 'the Most Holy River,' and its benefits are still celebrated by a variety of religious rites. As this river was to be the subject of the first plague, Moses was ordered to meet Pharaoh on its banks and there, with the intimidating rod in his hand which had so recently triumphed over the rods of the magicians, to give him a new summons to surrender, and in case of a refusal to announce the coming judgment. He would thus have no possible pretence for ascribing the effect, when it came, to any other than the true cause. It was affording him, moreover, another fair opportunity to forego his obstinacy and comply with the divine mandate, for God is longsuffering; not willing that any should perish, but that all should come to the knowledge of the truth.

17 Thus saith the LORD, in this b thou shalt know that I *am* the Lord: behold, I will smite with the

b ch. 5. 2. ver. 5.

rod that *is* in my hand upon the waters which *are* in the river, and c they shall be turned d to blood.

c ch. 4. 9.   d Rev. 16. 4, 6.

17. *In this shalt thou know*, &c. Heb. בְזֹאת *bezoth, in* or *by this;* i. e. this miracle about to be wrought. Pharaoh had before, ch. 5. 2, contemptuously asked, 'Who is the Lord, that I should obey his voice to let Israel go? I know not the Lord, neither will I let Israel go.' He was now to be instructed to his cost on this head.——¶ *I will smite with the rod that is in mine hand.* As these are probably to be considered the words of Jehovah himself they present a striking example of the phraseology by which an agent is said to do that which he commands or procures to be done. The smiting rod was said to be in God's hand, because it was in the hand of Moses who was acting by his orders and in his name. Thus, Hos. 8. 12, 'I have written to him the great things of my law;' i. e. have ordered or procured them to be written. Yet it is proper to observe that the Jewish and many Christian commentators consider these as more truly the words of Moses speaking in the name of God, whose representative he was expressly declared to be to Pharaoh, v. 1. The rod was literally in the hand of Aaron, but Moses, they contend, might properly say it was in *his* hand because he was principal in the affair and merely used the ministry of Aaron in performing the miraculous works. Compare Mark, 15. 45, 'And when he (Pilate) knew it of the centurion, he *gave* the body to Joseph;' with Mat. 27. 58, ' Then Pilate *commanded the body to be delivered.*' As the sense is plain, it is not very material to whom the words are most immediately referred. Throughout the transaction God, Moses, and Aaron acted in such entire concert that they are considered as one, though all the *efficiency* exerted is of course to be referred exclusively to Om-

nipotence.——¶ *They shall be turned to blood.* As precisely the same expression in the original occurs Joel, 3. 4 'The moon shall be *turned into blood,* where all that can be understood is that it should be *turned into the color of blood,* some have supposed that nothing more is meant in the present case than that the waters were to be made to assume a preternatural *red and blood-like color.* This, they intimate, may have been done by miraculously impregnating the water with some substance capable of producing that effect, and which should render it at the same time destructive to animal life. But the case is very different in regard to a solid and a fluid body ; as also in respect to a high ly figurative mode of speech appropriate to prophecy, and the language of simple historical narrative. As to the change of the moon, we perceive at once that nothing more than an *optical* illusion is the effect intended to be described ; but in the case of the river, if the text declares it, no good reason can be assigned why the mass of waters should not be converted to *real blood* as well as to any other fluid substance, since it is an operation equally easy to Omnipotence, and since we can much more readily conceive of a river of blood becoming *putrescent* than of common water, which had merely undergone discoloration. We are constrained therefore to take the words in their literal sense as announcing that Pharaoh and his people should behold their delicious and venerated river become a vast rolling stream of blood, pure blood, no doubt florid and high-colored, exhibiting a spectacle which *they* could not contemplate, nor *we* conceive, without emotions of horror. But of the *actual miracle* the sequel informs us more particularly.

18 And the fish that *is* in the river shall die, and the river shall stink: and the Egyptians shall e loathe to drink of the water of the river.

19 ¶ And the LORD spake unto Moses, Say unto Aaron, Take thy rod, and f stretch out thine hand upon the waters of Egpyt, upon their streams, upon their rivers, and upon their ponds, and upon all their pools of water, that they may be-

e ver. 24. f ch. 8. 5, 6, 16. & 9. 22. & 10. 12, 21. & 14. 21, 26.

come blood: and *that* there may be blood throughout all the land of Egypt, both in *vessels of* wood, and in *vessels of* stone.

20 And Moses and Aaron did so, as the LORD commanded; and he g lifted up the rod and smote the waters that *were* in the river, in the sight of Pharaoh, and in the sight of his servants; and all the h waters that *were* in the river were turned into blood.

g ch. 17. 5.   h Ps. 78. 44. & 105. 29.

---

18. *The fish that is in the river shall die.* 'We remember the fish which we did eat in Egypt freely,' said the murmuring Israelites in the wilderness, Num. 11. 5; from which it is obvious that fish constituted no small part of the food of the country. But the changing of the waters was to be the death of the fish, so that the means of satisfying hunger as well as of quenching thirst would be abridged to them.——¶ *Shall loathe to drink of the water.* Heb. נִלְאוּ לִשְׁתּוֹת *nilu lishtoth, shall be wearied to drink;* i. e. wearied by digging round about the river for water. The original comprehensively expresses both the distasteful loathesomeness of the bloody water and the trouble and pains to which they were subjected in obtaining that which was pure. Gr. 'They shall not be able to drink the water of the river.'

19. *Stretch out thine hand,* &c. The fearful plague was not to be confined to the river. By stretching out his arm, and waving his rod in different directions over the land, the judgment was to become, as it were, universal. The various branches of the Nile, the canals derived from it, the ponds and reservoirs, all were to exhibit the spectacle of the same hideous and nauseous transformation!——¶ *In* vessels of *wood and in* vessels of *stone.* Heb. 'In woods and in stones;' by which is probably meant not so much the vessels in domestic use, as the cisterns, tanks, and

other larger receptacles constructed of wood or stone for the purpose of containing the water which run into them on the overflowing of the Nile. As they have no rain in Egypt, and the water of their wells is very bad, the river was their great dependence for water.

20. *And Moses and Aaron did so,* &c. The event answered to he prediction and the performance of Moses and Aaron. That noble river, the pride and ornament of their country, which alone gave fertility to its soil and beauty to its scenery, now no longer pours its native refreshing stream along its banks, but flows in thickened blood, casting up its perished inhabitants, and tainting the air with its noisome stench! In order to appreciate more justly the appalling nature of this judgment, we must bear in mind, not only the *fertilizing* properties of the Nile, but the deliciousness of its waters as a beverage. By the universal consent of all who have drank of this river, it is unrivalled in this respect by any waters in the world which are not medicinal. Such is its character now, and such doubtless it was then. How terrible the privation for a whole people to be thus deprived at once of the blessing and the luxury of such a river! But the event teaches us how easily an avenging God can not only cut off our most necessary supplies, but also convert our choicest comforts to our greatest

21 And the fish that *was* in the river died; and the river stank, and the Egyptians [i] could not drink of the water of the river; and there was blood throughout all the land of Egypt.

22 [k] And the magicians of Egypt did so with their enchantments: and Pharaoh's heart was hardened, neither did he hearken unto them; [l] as the LORD had said.

23 And Pharaoh turned and went

i ver. 18.   k ver. 11.

into his house, neither did he set his heart to this also.

24 And all the Egyptians digged round about the river for water to drink; for they could not drink of the water of the river.

25 And seven days were fulfilled after that the LORD had smitten the river.

CHAPTER VIII.

AND the LORD, spake unto Moses, Go unto Pharaoh, and say

l ver. 3.

plagues. And not only so. We see in this judgment the marks of a twofold retribution; first, for idolatry, and secondly, for cruelty. The river of Egypt was the idol of Egypt. They vainly boasted that by reason of their river they were independent of the rains of heaven. They paid to that cherished stream the homage which was due to its Creator. They ascribed to it the blessings which they owed to him. It was fitting therefore that he should 'smite it in the seven streams thereof;' that he should make that a loathing, a scourge, and a curse, which they had made an idol. 'Men are sure to be punished most and soonest in that which they make a corrival with God.' *Bp. Hall.* But this was not all. It was a significant as well as a righteous plague. They had stained the waters of that river with the blood of the Hebrew innocents, and now he gave them blood to drink, for they were worthy, Rev. 16. 6. Its cruel lord is now punished by seeing its channel filled, from shore to shore, with one crimson tide! So signally are the instruments of sin often made the instruments of punishment!

22. *The magicians did so with their enchantments.* That is, as before, attempted to do so. It will be observed that nothing is said of the *effect* of the magicians' attempt to imitate this miracle. Whether they succeeded in multiplying the bloody fluid is not affirmed,

though even if they did, it was evidently on so small a scale, as not to afford any plausible pretext for disparaging the unspeakably greater miracle of Moses. As Moses had already turned the running and standing waters of Egypt into blood, they could only procure small quantities by digging below the surface. But what was this compared with the *immensity* of the work wrought by Moses? Indeed the shallowness of their pretences was palpable in their proposing to show their skill by increasing an evil which was already intolerable. If they had had any confidence in their own art they would rather have attempted to turn the blood into water than the reverse. But they chose to ape the miracle of Moses, and though there is no evidence of their succeeding even in this, yet the result went to harden still farther the obdurate heart of Pharaoh.

24. *The Egyptians digged round about,* &c. Probably they found so much as barely sufficed for the wants of existence, though at the expense of great labor and fatigue. The fact affords an affecting proof, how in the midst of wrath God remembers mercy. The people must indeed suffer for the perverseness of their rulers, but the righteous judge tempers the strokes which yet he does not spare.

Chapter 8

From the last verse of the previous

unto him, Thus saith the LORD, Let my people go a that they may serve me.

2 And if thou b refuse to let *them* go, behold, I will smite all thy borders with c frogs :

3 And the river shall bring forth

a ch. 3. 12, 18. b ch. 7. 14. & 9. 2. c Rev. 16. 13.

---

frogs abundantly, which shall go up and come into thine house, and into d thy bed-chamber, and upon thy bed, and into the house of thy servants, and upon thy people, and into thine ovens, and into thy kneading troughs :

d Ps. 105. 30.

---

chapter it appears that the first plague was of a week's continuance. So long a time was probably necessary to give the judgment its full effect. Had it lasted but a day or two, it might have been referred to some casualty which did not require the admission of a supernatural agency. But when they perceived the river rolling its bloody tide day after day, and the nauseous pestilential vapors still increasing upon them and poisoning the air which they breathed, and all in accordance with what Moses had announced, they would be rendered doubly inexcusable if they refused to acknowledge the working of Omnipotence. Whatever may have been its influence upon the nation at large, it seems to have produced no salutary effect upon Pharaoh or his court ; yet at the end of that time God was pleased to remove the calamity, and grant a short respite to king and people, that they might reflect upon the awful phenomenon, and peradventure be led to humble themselves before him. Yet the narrative informs us that the deliverance from the curse, like the curse itself,— the forbearance, as well as the judgments, of the Almighty—only served to prolong and aggravate their wickedness. A second plague is therefore now to be denounced.

1. *Let my people go that they may serve me.* Heb. ורעבדני *va-yaabdeni, and they shall serve me.* But the rendering of the particle ו *ve* by ' that' is undoubtedly correct, and goes to confirm our interpretation of Ex. 7. 11, 12, where the same form of expression occurs. Examples of similar usage are al-

most innumerable in the original Scriptures.

2. *Behold, I will smite all thy borders* Heb. הנה אנכי נגף *hinnëh anoki nogëph, behold I smiting ;* i. e. just about to smite, as Gen. 6. 13, 'Behold, I will destroy.' Heb. 'Behold I destroying ;' according to a very frequent import of the present participle. The term ' borders' in scriptural usage does not merely denote the *limits, coasts,* or *boundaries* of a country, but in a larger sense its *regions, districts,* or *provinces* in general.

3. *The river shall bring forth frogs abundantly.* Heb. שרץ צפרדעים *sharatz tzephardeïm, shall swarm or crawl (with) frogs.* On the force of the original term, see Note on Gen. 1. 20. The emphatic phraseology of the text shows that nothing would be able to debar the access of these loathsome intruders into every nook and corner of the habitations of men. No doors, locks, or bolts ; no walls, gates, or fences, should preclude their entrance. The circumstance of their coming up into the 'bed-chambers,' and into the 'ovens,' and 'kneading-troughs,' needs explanation to those whose domestic economy is so different from that of the ancient nations. *Their* lodgings were not in *upper stories,* but recesses on the ground floor ; and their *ovens* were not like ours built on the side of a chimney, and adjacent to a fire-place, where the glowing heat would fright away the frogs ; but they dug a hole in the ground, in which they placed an earthen pot, which having sufficiently heated they put their cakes upon the inside to be baked. To

4 And the frogs shall come up both on thee, and upon thy people, and upon all thy servants.

5 ¶ And the LORD spake unto Moses, Say unto Aaron, e Stretch forth thine hand with thy rod over the streams, over the rivers, and over the ponds, and cause frogs to

e ch. 7. 19.

come up upon the land of Egypt.

6 And Aaron stretched out his hand over the waters of Egypt; and f the frogs came up, and covered the land of Egypt.

7 g And the magicians did so with their enchantments, and brought up frogs upon the land of Egypt.

f Ps. 78. 45. & 105. 30.   g ch. 7. 11.

find such places full of frogs when they came to heat them in order to bake their bread, and to find these loathsome creatures in their beds when they sought repose, must have been disgusting and distressing beyond measure. The fact that these noxious vermin were thus prompted to forego their natural habits, and instead of confining themselves to the waters and moist soils, to spread over the country and make their way to the most frequented and driest places, indicates the countless numbers in which they came forth; and this is still more confirmed by the immense heaps of their carcasses which ultimately corrupted the land. It is observable also that as the frog was one of the sacred animals of the Egyptians, the objects of their superstition became here, as in other instances, the instruments of their punishment. Indeed every line of the narrative of the plagues seems to have a point and force which, without some considerable acquaintance with the condition and usages of ancient Egypt, cannot be properly appreciated.

5. *And the Lord spake unto Moses,* &c. Of the reception which Pharaoh gave to the present threatening, Moses gives us no account, leaving it to be inferred from the facts which ensued. From these it is obvious that he treated the message either with open or silent contempt. He probably scorned the idea of being terrified at a swarm of frogs— creatures loathsome indeed but despicably harmless. Nothing remained therefore but for Moses to execute his com-

mission, and show the haughty monarch that the Lord of the universe could easily arm the most contemptible of his creatures to the intolerable annoyance or the utter destruction of himself and his hosts.

6. *The frogs came up, and covered the land.* Heb. 'And the frog came up,' collect. sing. for plur. The word of command has but to be uttered, and the Lord's armies make their appearance in countless myriads. Shoals of leaping, croaking, filthy frogs on their land, in their houses, in their beds, in their food! What a distressing and nauseous plague! Many delicate persons and children shudder at the sight of one as it suddenly leaps across their path. What must have been the condition of a people thus visited and pursued wherever they went by swarming multitudes of these loathsome vermin!

7. *The magicians did so with their enchantments, and brought up frogs.* Or, Heb. וְיַעֲלוּ *va-yaalu, that they might bring up ;* i. e. the magicians *attempted* to do so, *that* they might bring up ; precisely the same mode of speech with that, v. 1, ' *that* they might serve me.' As in the two former cases, so here also we see no positive evidence that the magicians did any thing more than go through certain preliminary ceremonies of jugglery which may perhaps have deceived the senses of the spectators. or they might have obtained them from among the multitudes produced by Moses and Aaron. See Note on Ex. 7 11, 12.

8 ¶ Then Pharaoh called for Moses and Aaron, and said, h Entreat the LORD that he may take away the frogs from me, and from my people: and I will let the people

h ch. 9. 28. & 10. 17. Numb. 21. 7. 1 Kings 13. 6. Acts 8. 24.

go, that they may do sacrifice unto the LORD.

9 And Moses said unto Pharaoh, Glory over me: when shall I entreat for thee and for thy servants, and for thy people, to destroy the frogs from thee, and thy houses,

---

8. *Then Pharaoh called for Moses and Aaron,* &c. Symptoms of relenting begin at length to show themselves. The plague was too formidable to be despised, too mighty to be resisted, too extensive to be remedied. In the case of the waters turned into blood there was some mitigation of the scourge. They *could* procure pure water, though with great labor, by digging around the river. But from the plague of the frogs there was no respite or relief. In their houses, in their beds, at their tables, they were incessantly infested by these hated intruders. Whatever quantities of them were killed, besides infecting the air by their stench, their places were instantly made good by increased numbers, so that the very lives of the sufferers must have been a weariness to them. The judgment in its extremity is no longer endurable. Pharaoh is compelled to intercede for its removal. He who drove Moses and Aaron from him in wrath, with the angry words, 'Wherefore do ye Moses and Aaron let the people from their works; get you unto your burdens,' now sends for them in fear, alters his voice, and begs that they would entreat the Lord for him. He is now glad to be beholden to the mercy of that God of whom he had before spoken with the utmost disdain. The request to Moses and Aaron he backs with the promise to let the people go, in which perhaps he was *at the time* sincere; as much so undoubtedly as sinners usually are in the promises to God that are extorted from them under the pressure of the heavy hand of his judgments. But in this, as in a thousand similar cases, time soon showed how little depend-

ence was to be placed upon such promises.——¶ *That he may take away.* Heb. ודסר *vayaser, and he shall take away;* the same form of expression with that adverted to above. So also in the close of the verse, '*that* they may do sacrifice.' Heb. '*And* they shall do sacrifice.' Thus also where one Evangelist, Mark, 12. 17, has, '*And* the inheritance shall be ours;' another, Luke, 20. 4, has, '*That* the inheritance may be ours.'

9. *Glory over me.* Heb. התפאר עלי *hithpaër alai, have the honor over me.* Moses by these words seems to indicate so much satisfaction and joy at the least sign of relenting on the part of Pharaoh, that he is ready to humble himself in his presence, disclaiming, as it were, and foregoing the honor and pre-eminence which naturally accrued to him from the performance of such mighty works, and laying them at the feet of Pharaoh. So obsequious indeed does he profess himself in view of the hopeful change which had taken place in the king's mind, that he willingly gives him the honor of appointing a time when he should entreat the Lord for the removal of the plague. Gr. 'Appoint unto me when I shall pray.' Chal. 'Ask for thee a powerful work, and give thou the time.' The incident suggests an important practical hint. The ministers of God should be ever prompt to greet with joy the slightest symptoms of relenting in those to whom they may have been the occasion of suffering, whether bodily or mental. Indeed, a benevolent mind will be so rejoiced with such indications, that he will readily exchange the language and the air of sternness and severity for the most condescend-

that they may remain in the river
only ?

10 And he said, To-morrow. And
he said, *Be it* according to thy
word : that thou mayest know that
i *there is* none like unto the LORD
our God.

11 And the frogs shall depart

i ch. 9. 14. Deut. 33. 26. 2 Sam. 7. 22.
1 Chron. 17. 20. Ps. 86. 8. Isai. 46. 9. Jer.
10. 6, 7.

from thee, and from thy houses,
and from thy servants, and from
thy people ; they shall remain in
the river only.

12 And Moses and Aaron went
out from Pharaoh : and Moses
k cried unto the LORD, because of
the frogs which he had brought
against Pharaoh.

k ver. 30. ch. 9. 33. & 10. 18. & 32. 11. James
5. 16, 17, 18.

ing deportment, in order to encourage
the incipient workings of a godly sorrow.——¶ *That they may remain in the
river only.* Not that they should be
removed by being transferred from the
land to the river, but that they should
be henceforth *confined* to the river, and
not suffered to infest the land any more.
This is the true import of the original.
Those that were already on the land
died and were gathered in heaps.

10. *And he said, To-morrow.* Heb.
למחר *lemahor, against to-morrow.* It
is perhaps a natural query why Pharaoh did not demand an *instantaneous*
cessation of the plague ? To this it
may be replied, that he was possibly
desirous of seeing whether the frogs
might not disappear of themselves in
the meantime. If so, he would have
some show of reason to doubt whether
they were really the product of supernatural agency, or had *chanced* to appear in such countless numbers. We
may suppose moreover that it was to
meet some such latent misgiving in his
mind that Moses had given him the option of the time that he should fix for
the withdrawment of the plague. He
would leave no ground for suspicion that
the miracle was owing to any other than
supernatural agency. Add to this as
another reason for the delay of a day,
that Pharaoh may have supposed from
the past that some time would be requisite for prayer and consultation of
the Deity on the part of Moses, which
he was disposed, as a reasonable thing,

to allow.——¶ *That thou mayest know,*
&c. These words declare to us the grand
design of all the dispensations, whether
of judgment or mercy, of the Most High,
that he may be convinced that ' there
is none like unto the Lord our God ;'
none so wise, so good, so mighty ; none
so formidable as an enemy, none so desirable as a friend. Nothing would more
tend to produce this impression on his
mind than the circumstance of his being
permitted *himself* to assign the time for
the removal of the frogs, and then to
see the event punctually accomplished.

12. *Cried unto the Lord because of
the frogs.* Heb. על דבר *al debar, upon
the word* (or matter) of the frogs ; i. e.
on the subject of the frogs, in regard to
them. See Note on Gen. 15. 1. From
the force of the original for ' cried'
(יצעק *yitzak*) it is to be at least inferred that Moses prayed with great
earnestness and intensity of spirit, if
not with special energy of utterance.
Though the word has a primary reference to the use of the voice, yet in Ex.
14. 15, it is evidently employed where
nothing more than a fervent *mental* petition is intended. 'Wherefore *criest
thou* (תצעק *titzak*) unto me ?' See
Note in loc.——¶ *Which he had brought
against Pharaoh.* Heb. אשר שם לפרעה
*asher sam le-Pharoh, which he had put
to Pharaoh ;* i. e. proposed, appointed
to Pharaoh. In other words, he made
supplication to the Lord relative to the
removal of the frogs on the conditions
which he had *fixed, settled,* or *agreed to*

13 And the LORD did according to the word of Moses: and the frogs died out of the houses, out of the villages, and out of the fields.

14 And they gathered them together upon heaps: and the land stank.

15 But when Pharaoh saw that

there was ¹ respite, ᵐ he hardened his heart, and hearkened not unto them; as the LORD had said.

16 ¶ And the LORD said unto Moses, Say unto Aaron, Stretch out thy rod, and smite the dust of the

¹ Eccles. 8. 11. ᵐ ch. 7. 14.

with Pharaoh. This sense of the word is rather more agreeable to the original, and equally so, we think, to the context.

13. *Out of the villages.* Rather according to the Heb. 'out of the courts.' The term חֲצֵרֹת *hatzeroth* is indeed occasionally applied to 'villages;' but its primary sense is that of an *open court or area, a place walled or fenced round.* This is probably the meaning here. The writer's design seems to be to say, that the frogs first deserted the houses, then the court-yards or enclosed grounds about the houses, and lastly the open fields.

14. *They gathered them together upon heaps.* Heb. 'Gathered them together, heaps, heaps.' See Note on Gen. 14. 10. They were now delivered from the principal calamity, but they still had a most offensive evil to endure to keep Pharaoh in mind of his promise. Being obliged to gather together the dead frogs in heaps, the number and size of such masses of putrifying matter were so great as to fill the whole air with an odor that was intolerable.

15. *When Pharaoh saw that there was respite.* Heb. הָרְוָחָה *harevahah*, a *breathing.* Gr. αναψυξις, a *refreshing*, as rendered, Acts, 3. 10, 'When the times of *refreshing* (αναψυξεως) shall come from the presence of the Lord.' The usual effect of the intermission of divine judgments upon obstinate offenders is here strikingly displayed. 'Let favor be showed to the wicked, yet will he not learn righteousness: in the land of uprightness will he deal unjustly, and will not behold the majesty of the Lord.' Is. 26. 10. The

respite granted in order to lead the rebellious king to repentance, serves but to embolden him in the career of disobedience, and harden his heart afresh. Without considering either what he had lately felt, or what he had reason to fear, he utterly disregards his promise, and settles down again into a posture of impious defiance of the wrath of heaven. How exact the counterpart which this conduct finds in that of sinners awakened and aroused by some startling appeal of Providence or of the Holy Spirit. No more striking picture of this perverseness has ever been furnished than that which we find in the words of the Psalmist, Ps. 78. 34—42. 'When he slew them, then they sought him: and they returned and inquired early after God. And they remembered that God was their Rock, and the high God their Redeemer. Nevertheless they did flatter him with their mouth, and they lied unto him with their tongues. For their heart was not right with him, neither were they steadfast in his covenant. How oft did they provoke him in the wilderness, and grieve him in the desert! Yea, they turned back and tempted God, and limited the Holy One of Israel. They remembered not his hand, nor the day when he delivered them from the enemy.'

16. *Stretch out thy rod.* The judgment now to be inflicted was to be inflicted without any previous warning. On the other hand, the fourth and fifth were preceded by a warning, while the sixth was not; again, the seventh and eighth were announced, but not so the ninth; under the tenth the people were

land, that it may become lice throughout all the land of Egypt.

17 And they did so; for Aaron stretched out his hand with his rod, and smote the dust of the earth, and [n] it became lice in man and in beast: all the dust of the land became lice throughout all the land of Egypt.

[n] Ps. 105. 31.

sent away. God was under no obligations to make known his purposes to Pharaoh before hand, and from his gross abuse of the respite granted him, he had no reason to be surprised if another plague of tenfold severity, or of utter destructiveness should suddenly burst forth upon him. But though God sees fit again to 'correct' him without warning, yet it is 'with measure, lest he should be brought to nothing.'

17. *It became lice*, &c. Heb. כנם *kinnim*. Gr. σκνιφες, *gnats*. Of the real instrument by which the third plague was effected, we are inclined to adopt, as most probable, the view given by the Editor of the Pictorial Bible. 'The Septuagint renders the Hebrew word כנם *kinnim*, by σκνιφες, which means the mosquito gnat; and this rendering is entitled to great respect, when we recollect that the translators lived in Egypt. It is also confirmed by Origen and Jerome, who, with the Septuagint, form perhaps the best mass of authority on such a point which it is possible to possess. Gesenius, Dr. Boothroyd, and others, concur in this view of the word; but it is certain that the generality of interpreters agree with the common translation, which perhaps may be accounted for by the fact, that the noisome parasite is better known in the West than the mosquito, although, happily, neither of them are so generally familiar as in the East. The writer has had some experience in different countries of the misery and continual irritation which the mosquito-gnat occasions, and can say, without the least hesitation, that of all insect plagues there is none which he should think so intolerable. The activity of these insects, their small size, their insatiable thirst for blood, and the power of their sting, which enable them to run riot not only on the exposed parts of the person, but on those that are thinly covered, as the legs, almost render existence a calamity during the seasons in which they most abound. The painful sensation which their sting produces, and the intolerable and protracted itching which ensues, with the combined torture resulting from the infliction of fresh stings while the former are still smarting, is scarcely less distressing to the mind than to the body. To secure sleep at night, the inhabitants of the countries infested by these insects are obliged to shelter themselves under mosquito-nets or curtains; and it deserves to be mentioned that this precaution was used by the ancient Egyptians. There is a remarkable passage on this subject in Herodotus. After mentioning how the country is infested by gnats, he says that as the wind will not allow these insects to ascend to any considerable elevation, the inhabitants of Upper Egypt sleep in turrets to avoid these tormentors; but that in lower Egypt the people sleep securely underneath their nets with which they fish by day, and which they spread over their beds at night. This has puzzled translators and others; but it is a fact that mosquitoes and other flies will not pass through nets, the meshes of which are much more than large enough to admit them. This is practically known in some parts of Italy, where the inhabitants use net window-curtains which freely admit the air while they exclude gnats and flies. How severely this calamity was felt is evinced by the fact that the Egyptians and other nations of antiquity had gods whose especial

18 And º the magicians did so with their enchantments to bring forth

º ch. 7. 11.

province it was to protect them from these and other 'flies.' The 'Baalzebub,' or 'god of flies,' so often mentioned in Scripture, was a deity of this description. We read also of towns near lakes and marshy grounds (where these insects particularly abound) being deserted on account of this nuisance, as well as of important military undertakings being relinquished. As the mosquitoes breed in marshy soil, and particularly in moist rice-grounds, where such exist, the annual overflowing of the Nile renders Egypt but too favorable to their production. They accordingly appear in immense swarms, and the testimony of travellers concur in declaring that there is no country, in the old continent at least, where the mosquito-gnats are so numerous and voracious as in Egypt, or where the pain of their wound and the consequent smart and itching are so acute. We have abstained from describing them, as their general appearance and habits do not differ from those of the common gnat; but there is no comparison in the degree of annoyance which they occasion. The Egyptian gnat is rather small. It is ash-colored, with white spots on the articulation of the legs. It may be objected to the view of the text which we have taken, that it detracts from the miraculous nature of the visitation to suppose it connected with insects which Egypt *naturally* produces in such abundance. But this objection equally applies to ' lice,' which swarm there to such a degree that it is difficult for the most cleanly persons to keep themselves wholly free from them. If we take either reading, it is only necessary to conclude (which the text expressly states) that the creatures were brought in swarms most extraordinary even in Egypt, and perhaps that

lice, but they ᴘ could not : so there were lice upon man, and upon beast.

ᴘ Luke 10. 18.   2 Tim. 3. 8, 9.

they were brought thus abundantly at a time of the year when they do not usually abound.' *Pict. Bib.*

18. *The magicians did so,* &c.—*but could not.* That is, they tried the utmost of their skill to imitate the miracle, but they could not. The motives which led them at first to engage in the contest with Moses, the shame of desisting, and some slight appearances of success in their former attempts, prompted them still to carry on their imposture in the present instance. But all was unavailing. With all their skill in magic, and with all their dexterity in deceiving the spectators, they could not even succeed so far as they had already done in producing a specious counterfeit of the work of Moses. Had they hitherto performed real miracles, how came they to be baffled now? It cannot be a greater miracle to produce lice or gnats, than to turn rods into serpents, water into blood, or to create frogs. It is indeed often said that they were now laid under *restraint.* But it does not appear, from the text, that they were laid under any other restraint than that which arose from the impracticability of the thing itself compared with their other performances. The vermin now produced were so minute that it is inconceivable that any human artifice should even *appear* to produce them. Besides in all the former instances the magicians knew beforehand what they were to undertake, and had time for preparation. But now, as the plague came without warning, they had no opportunity for contriving any expedient for imitating or impeaching the act of Moses. And had they been allowed time, how was it possible for them to make it appear, that they produced these creatures by which they themselves and all the country were al-

19 Then the magicians said unto
Pharaoh, This *is* ꟼ the finger of
God: and Pharaoh's ʳ heart was
hardened, and he hearkened not
unto them; as the Lᴏʀᴅ had said.
20 ¶ And the Lᴏʀᴅ said unto Moses, ˢ Rise up early in the morning,

ꟼ 1 Sam. 6. 3, 9. Ps. 8. 3. Matt. 12. 28. Luke
11. 20.   ʳ ver. 15.   ˢ ch. 7. 15.

ready covered? What then was more
natural than that the abortiveness of
their present attempts should be expressly mentioned, and that too without implying that they had *really* succeeded in any former instance?

19. *This is the finger of God.* That
is, the special work and power of God;
who is said, after the manner of men,
to do things by his hand or 'finger;' Ps.
8. 4.—102. 26.—109. 27.—1 Sam. 6. 9. To
this phraseology Christ had reference
when he refuted those who withstood
his miracles, as these magicians did
Moses; Luke, 11. 20, 'If I with *the
finger of God* cast out devils;' which
another Evangelist expresses thus; 'If
I cast out devils by the *Spirit of God.*' It
may well be doubted, however, whether
by this acknowledgment the magicians
intended to award any honor to Moses
and Aaron, or even to the true God.
The original expression as uttered by
them, may have reference not to Jehovah, but to the divinities worshipped in
Egypt; so that it is simply equivalent
to saying, that were it not for the invisible agency of the gods (Elohim),
Moses and Aaron were no better workers of wonders than themselves, but
that in some way unaccountable they
were frustrated in their attempts. This
was the best apology they could make
for their own failure of success, and to
prevent Pharoah from reproaching them
with the want of skill in their profession.—— ¶ *And Pharaoh's heart was
hardened.* How clearly does it appear
from this, that unbelief will sometimes
survive the refutation of the lies by

and stand before Pharaoh; (lo, he
cometh forth to the water;) and
say unto him, Thus saith the Lᴏʀᴅ,
ᵗ Let my people go, that they may
serve me:
21 Else, if thou wilt not let my
people go, behold, I will send
swarms *of flies* upon thee, and up-

ᵗ ver. 1.

which it is nourished. Who would
not have thought that this confession
of the magicians, which was a virtual
avowal of the impotency of their craft,
together with the striking displeasure
of the Almighty, manifested in the new
calamity visited upon him, would have
made the haughty monarch at least begin to waver in his resolution? But no.
We still read the affecting record of
his perverseness and his guilt, showing
that he grew more and more obstinate.
'Though thou shouldest bray a fool in
a mortar with a pestle, yet will not his
foolishness depart from him.'

20. *Rise up early in the morning,
and stand before Pharaoh,* &c. The
servant of God was not to be behind-
hand with the earliest morning visitation of Pharaoh to the god of his idolatry, nor was he to be daunted or deterred by what had happened from again
meeting him face to face, and renewing
his inexorable demands. Proud and imperious and exasperated as he was, he
was again to be challenged in the name
of the Most High, to let the captives go
free, and in case of his refusal, to prepare to encounter another detachment
of the Lord's armies, no less fierce and
formidable than that from which he had
just been delivered — provided indeed
he *were* delivered from it, which is not
expressly stated. Jehovah had but to
'hiss for the fly,' and the winged insect hosts would be present, in countless multitudes, to execute his orders.

21. *I will send swarms* of flies *upon
thee,* &c. Heb. עָרֹב *arob, a mixture,* or
mixed swarm; i. e. probably of flies,

on thy servants, and upon thy people, and into thy houses : and the houses of the Egyptians shall be full of swarms *of flies*, and also the ground whereon they *are*.

---

wasps, hornets, and other vexatious and stinging insects. It will be observed that 'flies' in our version, being printed in Italics, is not in the original, nor is it easy to ascertain precisely what kind of *swarm* or *mixture* formed the constituents of the fourth plague. The original term, עֲרֹב *arob*, applied in Ex. 12. 38, to men, and rendered, 'a mixed multitude,' comes from עָרַב *to mingle*, and is understood by most of the Jewish interpreters to imply *a mixed multitude of noisome beasts*. Thus, Targ. Jer. 'A mixed swarm of wild beasts.' Chal. 'A mixed swarm of wild beasts of the field.' Josephus, 'Various sorts of pestilential creatures.' Rab. Solomon, 'All kinds of venomous animals, as serpents and scorpions.' Aben Ezra, 'All the wild beasts intermingled together, as lions, bears, and leopards.' The Sept. however, renders it by κυομυιαν, *dog-fly*, from its biting, an insect that fastens its teeth so deep in the flesh, and sticks so very close, that it oftentimes makes cattle-run mad. The etymology of the word leads us, on the whole, to regard as probably true the rendering given Ps. 78. 45, , 'He sent (עָרֹב *arob*) *divers sorts of flies* among them which devoured them;' so that it was not one particular kind, but all sorts of vexatious, winged creatures of the smaller tribes, mingled together in one prodigious swarm. It must be admitted, however, that there is so striking a similarity between this and what we have *supposed* to be the preceding plague, as to give some countenance to the suggestion of the Editor of the Pictorial Bible. ' As the word *Arob* implies a mixture, the Vulgate has translated it 'all sorts of flies,' and from thence our version ' swarms of flies,' where it is to be observed that 'flies,' in Italics, is not in the original. We are left to conjecture what kind of fly is meant, or whether, indeed, the plague consisted in flies at all. The language of the 24th verse is remarkable : ' The land was corrupted by reason of the swarm,' which could hardly apply to any 'fly,' properly so called. If also we refer to Ps. 78. 45, we see the *Arob* is described as *devouring* the Egyptians, which is an act that seems inapplicable to a fly. Upon the whole, we strongly incline to the opinion which has found some able supporters of late years, that the Egyptian beetle (*blatta Ægyptiaca*) is denoted in this place. The beetle, which is almost every where a nuisance, is particularly abundant and offensive in Egypt, and all the circumstances which the Scriptures in different places intimates concerning the *Arob*, applies with much accuracy to this species. It devours every thing that comes in its way, even clothes, books, and plants, and does not hesitate to inflict severe bites on man. If also we conceive that one object of these plagues was to chastise the Egyptians through their own idols, there is no creature of its class which could be more fitly employed than this insect. What precise place it filled in the religious system of that remarkable people has never, we believe, been exactly determined ; but that it occupied a conspicuous place among their sacred creatures seems to be evinced by the fact, that there is scarcely any figure which occurs more frequently in Egyptian sculpture and painting. Visiters to the British Museum may satisfy themselves of this fact, and they will also observe a remarkable colossal figure of a beetle in greenish colored granite. Figures of beetles cut in green-colored stone occur very frequently in the ancient tombs of Egypt. They are generally plain ; but some have hieroglyphic

22 And ᵘ I will sever in that day the land of Goshen, in which my people dwell, that no swarms *of flies* shall be there; to the end thou mayest know that I *am* the LORD, in the midst of the earth.

ᵘ ch. 9. 4, 6, 26. & 10. 23. & 11. 6, 7. & 12. 13.

23 And I will put a division between my people and thy people: to-morrow shall this sign be.

24 And the LORD did so: and. ˣ there came a grievous swarm *of flies* into the house of Pharaoh, and

ˣ Ps. 78. 45. & 105. 31.

figures cut on their backs, and others have been found with human heads. The Egyptian beetle is about the size of the common beetle, and its general color is also black. It is chiefly distinguished by having a broad white band upon the anterior margin of its oval corslet.' *Pict. Bible.* The reader will perceive that the real nature of this judgment is still a matter of great uncertainty, and one on which we can scarcely obtain even a balance of probabilities.——¶ *The ground upon which they are.* It is not clear to what the pronoun 'they' refers. If it be to the mixed swarm, it would seem to carry the implication that they were some kind of *ground reptiles*, probably of the smaller species, and if this were so, it favors the above interpretation of *beetles* more decisively than any thing that has been yet offered.

22. *And I will sever.* Heb. הפלרתי *hiphlëthi, I will marvellously sever ;* i. e. will separate and exempt in a marvellous manner. Accordingly, the Gr. renders it, 'I will marvellously glorify, or miraculously honor ;' the same word which occurs Luke, 5. 2, 6, 'And they were all amazed, and *glorified* God.' The Heb. term occurs, Ps. 4. 3, 'Know that the Lord *hath set apart* him that is godly for himself ;' i. e. hath gloriously or honorably distinguished, discriminated, appropriated him that is godly. Again, Ex. 33. 16, ' So shall we be *separated,* I and thy people, from all the people that are upon the face of the earth.' Gr. ' Shall be more glorious.' Compare Wisd. 18. 8, speaking of this event; 'For wherewith thou didst punish our adversaries, by the same thou

didst *glorify* us whom thou hadst called.'——¶ *I will put a division.* Heb. שמתי פדת *samti peduth, I will put or set redemption.* Ps. 111. 9, 'He sent *redemption* unto his people.' The Gr. renders it by διαστολη *division,* or *distinction,* the same word which occurs Rom. 3. 22, ' The righteousness of God which is by faith of Jesus Christ unto all and upon all them that believe: for there is no *difference* (διαστολη).' Hitherto the plagues appear to have been common to the Egyptians and Hebrews. We can easily understand that the latter were included in these visitations, to punish them for their partially favoring the idolatries of Egypt, and for their unbelief. But as this may have contributed to prevent the Egyptians from seeing the finger of God in the previous plagues, a distinction was henceforth to be made, and the land of Goshen to be exempted from the calamities still impending. It was a ' division' strikingly illustrative of that final diversity of allotment which awaits the two great classes of men, the righteous and the wicked, in the great day of discrimination. It may be remarked that as the preceding verse announces the severing of the land of Goshen from the rest of Egypt, some of the Jewish commentators understand by this verse not a mere repetition of the former, but an assurance that if ever any of the Israelites should chance to be in any other part of Egypt, they should *there* also remain uninjured by the plague.

24. *There came a grievous swarm.* Heb. ערב כבד *arob kabëd, a heavy swarm.* The epithet in the original may apply either to the *grievousness*

into his servants' houses, and into
all the land of Egypt: the land was
corrupted by reason of the swarm
of flies.

25 ¶ And Pharaoh called for Moses, and for Aaron, and said, Go ye,
sacrifice to your God in the land.

26 And Moses said, It is not meet

so to do; for we shall sacrifice y the
abomination of the Egyptians to
the LORD our God: Lo, shall we
sacrifice the abomination of the
Egyptians before their eyes, and
will they not stone us?

y Gen. 43. 32. & 46. 34.   Deut. 7. 25, 26. &
12. 31

of the plague considered in its *effects*,
or to the *vast numbers* of the insects by
which it was brought about. See Note
on Gen. 50. 9.——¶ *The land was corrupted;* or Heb. 'destroyed,' as the
word often signifies. See Note on Gen.
6. 13. By the land we are probably to
understand the 'inhabitants of the land,'
who were destroyed in the sense of being reduced to the greatest extremities,
and of suffering an annoyance that was
almost beyond endurance, in addition
to which probably many of them actually perished in consequence of the inflammation produced by the bites or
stings of the venomous insects. The
original word, however, is often used to
signify the afflictive and wasting effects
of a judgment which at the same time
falls short of actually extinguishing life.
Thus the Psalmist says of this and the
preceding plague of frogs, Ps. 78. 45,
'He sent divers sorts of flies among
them, which *devoured them* (יאכלם
yokelum); and frogs which *destroyed
them* (תשחיתם *tashhithëm, corrupted
them*).' It is probably to this judgment
more especially that the author of the
Book of Wisdom alludes when he says,
ch. 16. 8—10, 'And indeed thou madest
thine enemies to confess that it is thou
who deliverest from all evil: For them
the bitings of grasshoppers and flies
killed, neither was there found any remedy for their life: for they were worthy to be punished by such. But thy
sons not the very teeth of venomous
dragons overcame, for thy mercy was
ever by them.' It is, however, but fair
to remark that some commentators of
note suppose that the 'corruption' or

'destruction' of the land here mentioned
was the spoiling, devouring, or consuming of the fruits of the land, the herbage,
the young grain, the pasture grounds,
&c. If the plague consisted of swarms
of *beetles*, this is not an improbable supposition.

25. *Go ye, sacrifice to your God in the
land.* It is evident that each successive
plague thus far exceeded in intensity
that which went before it, and so griev
ous was the present, that with a view
to its removal Pharaoh sent for Moses
and Aaron and proposed to them a *compromise.* Unable to bear the tormenting scourge, and yet unwilling to resign
his grasp of his Hebrew bondmen, he
flatters himself that by *a half-way measure* he may secure himself from injury
in both respects. He consents that they
should sacrifice to their God, provided
they would do it in the land of Egypt.

26. *Moses said, It is not meet so to do.*
Heb. לא נכון לעשות כן *lo nakon laas-
oth kën, it is not appointed, ordained,
constituted, so to do.* The reply of Moses was prompt and decided. He knew
his duty too well thus to depart, in the
least degree, from the strict import of
his instructions. Implicit obedience was
his only rule of conduct, and by adhering in the most inflexible manner to the
expressed will of Jehovah, the name of
Moses has come down to the latest generation honored by the testimony of
pre-eminent *fidelity*—'Moses was *faithful* in all his house.' Far from accepting this concession, he tells Pharaoh
there is no alternative. His *entire requisition* must be complied with, or it
would amount to nothing. He more-

27 We will go ᶻ three days' journey into the wilderness, and sacrifice to the LORD our God, as ª he shall command us.

ᶻ ch. 3. 18.   ª ch. 3. 12.

28 And Pharaoh said, I will let you go, that ye may sacrifice to the LORD your God in the wilderness: only ye shall not go very far away: ᵇ entreat for me.

ᵇ ver. 8. ch. 9. 28.   1 Kings 13. 6.

over condescends to state the reason *why* it is impossible to listen to such a proposal. He in effect presents his objections in the form of a dilemma: If we sacrifice here, we must do it either after the manner of the Egyptians, or of the Israelites. If after *their* manner, that would be an abomination to the Lord our God; if after our own manner, that would be an abomination to them, and they will stone us; for they will not endure to see us slay those animals for sacrifice, which they adore as deities. Chal. 'For the beasts which the Egyptians worship, shall we offer for sacrifice; lo, shall we offer for sacrifice the beasts which the Egyptians worship?'

27. *As he shall command us.* The Israelites knew not, therefore, precisely in what manner they should serve the Lord, till they came to the place appointed. So Moses says, ch. 10. 26, 'We know not with what we must serve the Lord until we come thither.'

28. *Only ye shall not go very far away.* The haughty monarch still shrinks from an *unconditional* submission to the mandate of heaven. He will yield the former point, and allow them to go out of Egypt, but then they must agree not to go *very far away,*—a stipulation of which the object evidently was to keep them still within his reach. In this, and still more clearly in the subsequent incidents, the king betrays his suspicion that under the plea of going into the wilderness to worship their God, the real intention of the Hebrews was to make their escape from his power altogether. Indeed it must be admitted that the *real* question before Pharaoh was not merely the ostensible matter, whether the Hebrews were to be allow-

ed a week's holiday, to go and hold their feast in the desert, but whether he was henceforth to lose entirely so considerable and so useful a part of the population of the kingdom. This was the Egyptian view of the question; to which is to be added the apprehension that becoming thus independent of their control, they might one day resolve themselves into a very dangerous hostile power on the frontiers, whether in the desert as pastoral nomades, or as a settled people in Palestine. Viewing the matter thus, as the Egyptian king unquestionably did, his conduct, though no more excusable, is somewhat less surprising. It goes to illustrate his position to bear in mind, that he could say *he* had not brought them into bondage. They had labored for a century in the public service; whence the king, or few Egyptians then living, had ever known them otherwise than as bondsmen, and few, if any Hebrews then living, could remember when they were free. In these circumstances it may justly be doubted whether there is now any state having bondsmen, however acquired, which would consent to part with them on much easier terms than the urgent compulsion to which God had recourse with Pharaoh. Corrupt human nature has ever shown an inveterate pertinacity in holding on to a usurped dominion over a nation or community of slaves. No matter how clear their *right* to be free, or how great the injustice or oppression of detaining them in bondage, yet for the most part men will 'harden their hearts,' just as did Pharaoh, in resisting the claims of justice, and will resign their *asserted* possessions only with their lives.

29 And Moses said, Behold, I go out from· thee, and I will entreat the LORD that the swarms *of flies* may depart from Pharaoh, from his servants, and from his people, to-morrow: but let not Pharaoh c deal deceitfully any more, in not letting the people go to sacrifice to the LORD.

30 And Moses went out from Pharaoh, and d entreated the LORD:

31 And the LORD did according to the word of Moses: and he removed the swarms *of flies* from Pharaoh, from his servants, and from his people; there remained not one.

c ver. 15. d ver. 12.

32 And Pharaoh e hardened his heart at this time also, neither would he let the people go.

CHAPTER IX.

THEN the LORD said unto Moses, a Go in unto Pharaoh, and tell him, Thus saith the LORD God of the Hebrews, Let my people go, that they may serve me.

2 For if thou b refuse to let *them* go, and wilt hold them still.

3 Behold, the c hand of the LORD is upon thy cattle which *is* in the field, upon the horses, upon the asses, upon the camels, upon the oxen, and upon the sheep: *there shall be* a very grievous murrain.

e ver. 15. ch. 4. 21. a ch. 8. 1. b ch. 8. 2. c ch. 7. 4.

29—32. *I will entreat the Lord.* As Pharaoh had appended to his proposal a request that Moses would intercede for him with the Lord for the removal of the plague, he expresses his readiness to do so, but he at the same time bids him beware of acting any more deceitfully with the Lord or his servants. Those that have once been perfidious are justly liable to suspicion, and therefore have no grounds to take it ill that they are admonished on this score in regard to the future. With what propriety Moses exhorted Pharaoh to beware of violating his promise again appears from the sequel. No sooner was this calamity over-past, than like a bent bow the spirit of the king sprung back to its former habitual obstinacy, and heedless of the admonition and of his own word, he refused to let the people go.

Chapter 9

In four successive plagues of constantly increasing severity had Pharaoh already been made to feel the lighting down of the heavy arm of the divine indignation, without yet being brought to submit to the mandate of heaven. He consequently yet stands a mark for the arrows from Jehovah's quiver. His last recent breach of faith was so gross an affront both to God and to Moses, that we might have looked for the infliction of another judgment without the least premonition. But warning is here given of another plague of still more deadly nature than any of the preceding, in case he should persist in refusing to let the people go. Would that his compliance had spared the historian the necessity of relating any thing but the *threatening!* But alas! we pass directly into the narrative of its *execution.*

2. *Wilt hold them still.* Heb. מחזיק בם *mahazik bam, strengthenest upon them ;* i. e. forcibly detaining them.

3. *Behold, the hand of the Lord is upon the cattle,* &c. Heb. יד יהוה הויה *yad Yehovah hoyah, the hand of the Lord (is) being* (i. e. made to be) *upon the cattle,* &c. Carrying still the *future* import which so frequently pertains to the present participle. The plague in this instance was to come *directly* from the hand of the Lord, without the intermediate wielding or waving of Aaron's rod.——¶ *A very grievous murrain.* Heb. דבר כבד מאד *deber kabed meod, a pestilence very heavy;* i. e. a very great and general mortality, as

4 And d the LORD shall sever between the cattle of Israel, and the
cattle of Egypt: and there shall
nothing die of all *that is* the children's of Israel.

5 And the LORD appointed a set

d ch. 8. 22.

time, saying, To-morrow the LORD
shall do this thing in the land.

6 And the LORD did that thing on
the morrow, and e all the cattle of
Egypt died: but of the cattle of the
children of Israel died not one.

e Ps. 78. 50.

appears from v. 6. The original word
for ' murrain,' when applied to men, is
translated 'pestilence,' and is rendered
in the Gr. both here and elsewhere, by
θανατος, *death*. See Note on Ex. 5. 3. Our
English word ' murrain' comes either
from the French *mourir, to die,* or from
the Greek μαραινω, *to grow lean, to
waste away*. It is with us applied to a
a particular contagious disease among
cattle, the symptoms of which are a
hanging down and swelling of the head,
abundance of gum in the eyes, rattling
in the throat, difficulty of breathing,
palpitation of the heart, staggering, a
hot breath, and a shining tongue; all
which symptoms prove that a general
inflammation has taken place. But as
no particular disorder is here specified,
mortality would have been a better rendering. There was a peculiar affliction
in the judgment of the murrain, not only
from the Egyptians being dependent on
their animals in various ways for their
sustenance and comfort, but also from
their being compelled to witness their
excruciating sufferings without the power of affording relief. The poor beasts
themselves were guiltless of wrong, yet
having their being under a constitution
in which they are a sort of appendage
to man, they are made subject to suffering by reason of his sin, or as Jeremiah
expresses it, ch. 12. 4, 'For the wickedness of the land, the beasts are consumed.' This infliction therefore was
a trial to Pharaoh and the Egyptians
whether they would be at all wrought
upon by a view of the *effects* of their
sin as evinced in the sufferings of the
unoffending brute creation. At the same
time, in order to impress them still more

forcibly with the displeasure of God
against them, the Israelites, whom they
so much despised and oppressed, were
entirely exempt from this calamity.

5. *To-morrow the Lord shall do this
thing in the land*. The fixing of the
time in this manner would make the
judgment when it came the more remarkable. '*We* know not what any day
will bring forth, and therefore cannot
say what we will do to-morrow, but
God can.' *Henry*.

6. *All the cattle of Egypt died*. That
is, some of all sorts; not absolutely
each and every one; for we find, v. 19,
25, some remaining which were smitten
by a subsequent plague. This peculiar
usage of the word ' all,' as denoting
some of all kinds, instead of the *absolute totality* of the number spoken of,
is of great importance to a right understanding of the sacred Scriptures
throughout. Thus, 1 Tim. 2. 4, 'Who
will have *all* men to be saved, and to
come unto a knowledge of the truth;'
i. e. all classes and ranks of men; for
he had just before exhorted that prayers
should be made for ' kings and for all
that are in authority;' implying, that
as no order of men are placed without
the pale of salvation, so none should
be left out of the supplications of the
saints. In like manner it is to be observed, that while in v. 25, of this chapter it is said that ' the hail smote *every*
herb of the field,' in ch. 10. 15, we are
told that the locusts ate ' every herb of
the land *which the hail had left*.' For
a full and interesting illustration of this
phraseology, see J. P. Smith's Geology
and Scripture Compared, p. 247, in respect to the universality of the deluge.

7 And Pharaoh sent, and behold, there was not one of the cattle of the Israelites dead. And f the heart of Pharaoh was hardened, and he did not let the people go.

8 ¶ And the LORD said unto Moses and unto Aaron, Take to you handfuls of ashes of the furnace, and let Moses sprinkle it toward the heaven in the sight of Pharaoh.

9 And it shall become small dust

f ch. 7. 14. & 8. 32.

in all the land of Egypt, and shall be g a boil breaking forth *with* blains upon man, and upon beast, throughout all the land of Egypt.

10 And they took ashes of the furnace, and stood before Pharaoh; and Moses sprinkled it up toward heaven : and it became h a boil breaking forth *with* blains upon man, and upon beast.

g Rev. 16. 2.　h Deut. 28. 27.

---

7. *And Pharaoh sent,* &c. This shows that he was at least somewhat impressed by the plague as a calamity of very marvellous operation. His sending to ascertain the fact of the Israelites' exemption indicates that he was not satisfied with reports to that effect. But whether the result of the mission convinced him that the hand of God was in the affliction or not, it is clear that no permanent good impression was made upon him. His heart remained still unsoftened, and he refused to let Israel go.

8. *Take to you handfuls of ashes of the furnace,* &c. Something similar to this is still to be recognized in the maledictory usages of the East. 'When the magicians pronounce an imprecation on an individual, a village, or a country, they take ashes of cow's dung (or from a common fire,) and *throw them in the air,* saying to the objects of their displeasure, such a sickness, or such a curse, shall surely come upon you.' *Roberts.* The obstinacy of Pharaoh under such an accumulation of calls, warnings, and judgments was becoming continually a sin of a more and more aggravated character, and it was therefore fitting that the punishments it incurred should also be of a growing intensity. As the ravages of the pestilence that had wasted their flocks and herds had proved unavailing, a plague was now to be sent that should seize their bodies and touch them to the quick. The Heb. term for 'ashes,' as

it comes from a root signifying 'to blow,' properly denotes the fine cinereal particles which are carried off in the dense clouds of smoke arising from a furnace. The original for 'furnace' signifies also a 'lime-kiln or brick-kiln;' and as these were among the instruments of oppression to the Israelites, it was fitting that they should be converted to a means of chastisement to the Egyptians, for God oftentimes makes men to recognize their sin in their punishment.

9. *It shall become dust,* &c.; i. e. it shall by a miraculous diffusion become a fine cinder-like sleet floating in the atmosphere above the surface of the earth like a cloud of dust which does not subside, and wherever it lights upon the persons of men causing a 'boil breaking forth with blains.' Heb. 'boil budding, germinating, or efflorescing with pustules or blisters.' The original term for 'boil,' שחין *shehin,* denotes *an inflammation,* which gives us the true sense of the obsolete word 'blains,' accompanied with a sense of tormenting heat, which first produces a morbid tumor, and then a malignant ulcer. In Job, 2. 7, 8, the word occurs in the sense of a *burning itch* or an *inflamed scab,* which Job could not remove with his nails, and was therefore obliged to make use of a potsherd, or fragment of a broken earthen vessel, for the purpose. In the case of the Egyptians, the 'Shehin' was of a still more virulent nature,

11 And the i magicians could not stand before Moses, because of the boil: for the boil was upon the magicians, and upon all the Egyptians.

12 And the LORD hardened the heart of Pharaoh, and he hearkened not unto them; k as the LORD had spoken unto Moses.

13 ¶ And the LORD said unto Mo-

l ch. 8. 18, 19.   2 Tim. 3. 9.   k ch. 4. 21.

ses, l Rise up early in the morning, and stand before Pharaoh, and say unto him, Thus saith the LORD God of the Hebrews, Let my people go, that they may serve me.

14 For I will at this time send all my plagues upon thine heart, and upon thy servants, and upon thy people: m that thou mayest know that *there is* none like me in all the earth.

l ch. 8. 20.   m ch. 8. 10.

so that they were in fact visited with a treble punishment at once, viz. aching boils, nauseous ulcers, and burning itch. To this severe plague the threatening of Moses, Deut. 28. 27, obviously has reference; 'The Lord will smite thee with the *botch of Egypt*, and with the emerods, and with the scab, and with the itch whereof thou canst not be healed.' The Gr. renders it by ελκος, *ulcer*, which occurs, Rev. 16. 2, which in our version is translated ' noisome and grievous sore.' The judgment of the first vïal, therefore, considered in the letter, was similar to that of the sixth plague of Egypt.

11. *The magicians could not stand before Moses.* They had probably hitherto continued to linger about the person of Pharaoh, confirming him in his obstinate refusal to let the people go, and pretending that though Moses had thus far performed works beyond their skill, yet they should doubtless be too hard for him at last; but now, being seized with these loathsome and painful ulcers, they were utterly confounded, and quitting the court in disgrace, were henceforth no more heard of. See an allusion to this part of the sacred history, 2 Tim. 3. 8, 9.

12. *And the Lord hardened the heart of Pharaoh.* Heb. רחזק *yehazzëk.* On the import of the term, see Note on Ex. 4. 21. God had there threatened that he *would* harden Pharaoh's heart, but we do not, until we come to the present passage, find it expressly said that he

did harden it. Here, it is true, the effect is ascribed to the divine agency, but after what we have remarked at so much length on this subject in that place, the reader will scarcely be in danger of putting a wrong construction on the words. It is not to be understood that God, by a positive act, *created* any hardness of heart in Pharaoh, or that he immediately put forth any influence to render him callous and incapable of right feeling. He had before hardened his own heart by resisting both the grace and the wrath of heaven, and nothing more is meant by the expression before us, than that God was pleased to leave him under the control of his own strong delusions, and so to order the events of his providence as to make him more and more obstinate. In no other sense did God harden his heart, than by permitting him to rush forward in precisely such a course of rebellion as would issue in his hardening his own heart. But even this was a fearful judgment, and one that speaks awfully to those who do violence to their own consciences and sin with a high hand.

14. *I will send all my plagues upon thine heart.* In again repeating his demand for his people's deliverance, and his threatenings against Pharaoh's disobedience, the Most High makes a startling and terrible declaration. If lesser judgments do not do their work, God will send greater. Moses is charged to tell Pharaoh that, in the plagues that remained to be inflicted there would be

15 For now I will ⁿ stretch out my hand, that I may smite thee

ⁿ ch. 3. 20.

and thy people with pestilence; and thou shalt be cut off from the earth.

---

a kind of concentrated terribleness, so that each one should come upon him as if with the accumulated weight of all the rest. What he had already experienced was indeed grievous, but it should be nothing compared to what was to follow. They were to be such plagues as should not only endanger the body, but *smite the heart, the inner man.* They should penetrate the inward spirit with such indescribable pangs of terror, that it would seem as if the whole magazine of heaven's vengeance were opened upon him and his people. This seems to be what is intended by the language—' I will at this time send all my plagues upon thine heart,' where we are probably to understand by 'this time,' the time occupied by the whole ensuing course of judgments that should finally end in the utter destruction of Pharaoh.

15. *For now I will stretch out my hand that I may smite,* &c. Heb. כי עתה שלחתי את ידי ואך *ki attah shalahti eth yadi va-ak, for now have I sent forth my hand and smitten.* The true construction is somewhat ambiguous. The verbs in the original undoubtedly require a *past* rendering, though the Greek, with our own and several other versions, give the *future.* But it does not appear in what sense Pharaoh and his people could be said to have been cut off by *pestilence,* as they were drowned in the Red Sea, unless the term be taken in the general sense of *mortality,* to which it is probably a valid objection, that the original has the definite article (בהדבר=בדבר *by the pestilence*) implying a *particular* pestilence. At the same time, if it be applied to the past, it is evident that it must be understood in a *qualified* and *hypothetical* rather than in an *absolute* sense; for Pharaoh had not yet been *really* cut off from the earth. But

the idiom of the original will easily admit of this *conditional* import of the passage, and we may consider the meaning of the divine speaker as fairly represented by the following paraphrase, which is largely sustained by Rabbinical and other critical authorities: 'For I *had, or could have, stretched* out my hand (i. e. in the plague of the murrain which destroyed so many of the beasts, and could easily have numbered thee among its victims,) and I *had* (potentially, though not in actual fact) smitten thee and thy people with (that) pestilence, and thou *wert* (as good as) *cut off* from the earth.' On the same principle it is said, Luke, 5. 6, ' They enclosed a great multitude of fishes ; *and their net brake ;*' i. e. if we may so express it, the net, *considered in itself,* brake, but was kept whole by the power of God ; for had it *actually* broken, the fish would have escaped, whereas it is said, 'they filled both the ships, so that they began to sink.' In like manner, if we mistake not, it is said, Ps. 105. 26—28, ' He sent Moses his servant ; and Aaron whom he had chosen. They showed his signs among them, and wonders in the land of Ham. He sent darkness and made it dark ; and they rebelled not against his word.' That is, there was such an intrinsic moral power in these miracles to beget belief, to work submission and compliance ; they were in themselves so convincing, so overpowering, so absolutely charged with demonstration ; that the writer speaks as if it would be an abuse of language in him, equal to the abuse of reason in them, not to admit the actual working of the legitimate effect. He says, therefore, that 'they (the Egyptians) rebelled not against his word,' because the word came attended with such a flood of evidence that there was

16 And in very deed for ᵒ this *cause* have I raised thee up, for to shew *in* thee my power; and that

ᵒ Rom. 9. 17. See ch. 14. 17. Prov. 16. 4. 1 Pet. 2. 9.

my name may be declared throughout all the earth.

17 As yet exaltest thou thyself against my people, that thou wilt not let them go ?

a kind of moral paradox, or absurdity, or impossibility in supposing that it did not produce obedience, although such was indeed the fact. In the passage before us we conceive that God designs to assure Pharaoh, that considering his liability to have been cut off by the preceding plague, he may regard himself as having been in effect a dead man; 'nevertheless,' says he, 'for this cause have I raised thee up.' Heb. 'Have I *made thee to stand ;*' i. e. have preserved thee safe in the midst of danger, 'for to show in thee, &c.' The word translated 'raised up' does not signify *to bring into existence*, but *to cause to stand, to make to continue.* Thus, 1 Kings, 15. 4, 'Nevertheless for David's sake did the Lord his God give him a lamp in Jerusalem, to set up his son after him, and *to establish* Jerusalem.' Heb. 'To make to stand,' i. e. to preserve. Prov. 29. 4, 'The king by judgment *establisheth* the land.' Heb. ' Makes to stand ;' i. e. renders safe. So also Ex. 21. 21, 'If he continue a day or two.' Heb. ' If he *stand* a day or two ;' i. e. survive. Paul, however, in quoting this passage, Rom. 9. 17, employs the term ' raised up,' which will occasion no difficulty, if it be borne in mind that a person may be said to be 'raised up' who is preserved alive when in danger of dying, a usage of the word which occurs James, 5. 15. 'And the prayer of faith shall save the sick, and the Lord *shall raise him up.*' It was in this sense of being *spared from imminent destruction* that Pharaoh was raised up. Among the ancient versions the Chal. has 'For now it was near before me (i. e. it lacked but little) that I had sent out the stroke of my strength and thou hadst been consumed.' Arab. 'Because if I had given

a loose to my power, I should have destroyed thee and thy people, and thou wouldst have been eradicated ; but I have reserved, &c.' Taking the words in this sense we may gather, (1) That however men may forget or disregard former judgments, God remembers them, and that sooner or later he will remember his enemies of them. (2) That as a preservative against future tokens of divine displeasure, we do well to call often to mind the plagues and destructions from which we have very narrowly, and through the forbearance of heaven, escaped.

16. *To show in thee my power.* Heb. הַרְאֹתְךָ אֶת כֹּחִי *harotheka eth kohi, to make thee see my power.* This is the strictly literal rendering, which is intimated by the word ' in' in our translation being printed in Italics. The Gr. however has εν σοι, *in thee*, which Paul also adopts, Rom. 9. 17, leaving us to infer that it is the true sense. Consequently הַרְאֹתְךָ *harotheka, make thee to see*, is an elliptical mode of expression for הַרְאֹת בָּךְ *haroth beka, show in or by thee ;* and instances of similar usage are easily adducible. Thus Gen. 30. 20, ' Now will my husband *dwell (with) me* (יִזְבְּלֵנִי *yizbeleni* for רִזְבָּל עִמִּי *yizbal immi*).' Ps. 5. 4, 'Neither shall evil *dwell (with) thee* (יְגֻרְךָ *yegureka* for יָגוּר עִמָּךְ *yegur immeka*).' Prov. 8. 36, 'He that *sinneth (against) me* (חֹטְאִי *hotei* for חֹטֵא בִי *hote bi*) wrongeth his own soul.'

17. *Exaltest thou thyself against my people ?* Heb. מִסְתּוֹלֵל *mistolël*, from the root סָלַל *salal, to elevate* or *cast up.* The present term is the participle of Hithpael, or the *reflexive* voice, and seems to denote that *self-elevation* which resembles a rampart made to oppose an

18 Behold, to-morrow about this time I will cause it to rain a very grievous hail, such as hath not been in Egypt since the foundation thereof even until now.

19 Send therefore now, *and* gather thy cattle, and all that thou hast in the field : *for upon* every man and beast which shall be found in the field, and shall not be brought home, the hail shall come down upon them, and they shall die.

20 He that feared the word of the Lord among the servants of Pharaoh made his servants and his cattle flee into the houses :

21 And he that regarded not the word of the Lord left his servants and his cattle in the field.

---

enemy. Gr. εμποιη, *thou insultest.* Chal. *id.* Syr. 'Thou detainest.' Arab. 'Thou hinderest.' Although Pharaoh was a powerful monarch, and God's people a poor, degraded, and enslaved race, yet it was to be to his ruin that he exalted himself against them, inasmuch as it was virtually exalting himself against God. No power is too high to be called to account for lording it despotically over ' the people of the saints of the Most High.'

18. *To-morrow about this time.* Gr. 'At this same hour.' The time is thus accurately specified, that the effect, when it occurred, might not be attributed to chance.——¶ *I will cause it to rain a very grievous hail.* As rain is exceedingly rare, and hail almost unknown in Egypt, so formidable a hailstorm as that predicted, would be one of the greatest marvels that could occur in a climate like that of Egypt. A heavy fall of snow in July, would not be so great a phenomenon in our own country, as a heavy hail-storm at any time in Egypt.——¶ *Since the foundation thereof.* Heb. למן היום הוסדה *lemin hayom hivvasedah, since the day of its being founded.* That is, since its first being inhabited ; otherwise expressed, v. 24, 'since it became a nation.' The Gr. however renders it, 'From the day of its being created,' i. e. physically created. It was at any rate to be a storm such as never had had a precedent in that country, and for the reason, that the occasion of it had never had a precedent. But unparalleled judg-ments may be expected to overtake unparalleled offenders.

19. *Send therefore now, and gather,* &c. Heb. העז *haëz, gather speedily,* denoting an action to be performed with the utmost expedition, as is explained in the ensuing verse, ' made to flee.' With characteristic clemency the Lord couples with the prediction a gracious warning, to as many as will heed it, to send and gather their servants and cattle out of the field, and place them under shelter before the appointed time arrived. So unwilling is God that any should perish that even in the midst of impending wrath, he kindly provides and points out a way of escape.

21. *He that regarded not the word.* Heb. לא שם לבו *lo sam libbo, that set not his heart* to the word. Although there were some, even among the servants of Pharaoh, who had been sufficiently wrought upon by the former plagues to tremble at God's word, yet there were others, and they probably the majority, who partook of the spirit of their master, and would not believe, though the event thus far, had in every instance proved the truth of Moses' predictions. One would have thought that even if there were a *peradventure* that the calamity might come, they would have chosen the safer side, and housed their cattle for so short a time, rather than leave the poor creatures exposed to perish in the tempest ; but they were so fool-hardy as in defiance of the truth of Moses and the power of God to risk the consequences.

22 ¶ And the LORD said unto Moses, Stretch forth thine hand toward heaven, that there may be p hail in all the land of Egypt, upon man, and upon beast, and upon every herb of the field, throughout the land of Egypt.

23 And Moses stretched forth his

p Rev. 16. 21.

rod toward heaven, and q the LORD sent thunder and hail, and the fire ran along upon the ground: and the LORD rained hail upon the land of Egypt.

24 So there was hail, and fire mingled with the hail, very griev-

q Josh. 10. 11. Ps. 18. 13. & 78. 47. & 105. 32 & 148. 8. Isa. 30. 30. Ezek. 38. 22. Rev. 8. 7.

---

23. *The Lord sent thunder and hail.* Heb. נתן קלת וברד *nathan koloth u-barad, gave voices and hail.* The Lord's 'voice,' is an expression often used as equivalent to 'thunder.' See Note on Gen. 3. 8. Thus Rev. 6. 1, 'And I heard as it were the *noise* (φωνη, *voice*) of *thunder.*' Rev. 10. 3, 'And when he had cried (the) seven *thunders* uttered their *voices.*'——¶ *The fire ran along upon the ground.* Heb. ארצה *aretzah, towards the earth.* This is the exact rendering, and there can be no doubt that the fire meant was the *lightning* that accompanied the hail. The Psalmist thus speaks of this judgment, Ps. 78. 47, 48, 'He destroyed their vines and their sycamore-trees with frost. He gave up their cattle also to the hail and their flocks to *hot thunderbolts.*' To this seventh plague of Egypt is compared the effect of the seventh vial of the Apocalypse; Rev. 16. 17—21, 'And the seventh angel poured out his vial into the air ... and there were voices, and thunderings, and lightnings; and there was a great earthquake, such as was not since men were upon the earth ... and there fell upon men a great hail out of heaven, every stone about the weight of a talent;' where in the mention of the hail-stones there is an allusion probably to the passage of Joshua, ch. 10. 11, 'The Lord cast down great stones from heaven upon them unto Azekah, and they died: they were more which died with hail-stones than they whom the children of Israel slew with the sword.'

24. *Fire mingled with the hail.* Heb.

אש מתלקחת בתוך הברד *esh mithlak-kahath bethok habbarad, fire catching hold, infolding, involving itself in the midst of the hail.* The words are no doubt intended to depict a complication of elemental terrors which it is not easy distinctly to conceive. Amid peals of deep and portentous thunder, the lightning gleamed with terrific flashes, and at the same time a tremendous hail-storm poured its fury over a land of which the inhabitants had probably never before witnessed or heard of a similar phenomenon. If a violent tempest or tornado is an appalling occurrence in countries where they are not uncommon, what overwhelming dread must this have produced in Egypt! How could they but imagine that heaven and earth were mingling together in wild confusion! And then, when its fury had somewhat abated, to behold the desolations it had caused! Men and cattle killed and promiscuously scattered over the fields—all kinds of trees, plants, and grain battered down and destroyed—and the whole face of the ground appearing to have been swept by the besom of destruction! And yet, to enhance the wonder still more, in the land of Goshen not a solitary vestige of the wide-spreading havoc was to be seen. Here all nature was smiling unruffled in its usual fertility and beauty. What a contrast between the verdant fields and tranquil flocks of the one region, and the fearful spectacle of scathing and ruin in the other! 'And my people shall dwell in a peaceable habitation, and in sure dwellings, and

ous, such as there was none like it in all the land of Egypt since it became a nation.

25 And the hail smote throughout all the land of Egypt all that *was* in the field, both man and beast, and the hail ʳ smote every herb of the field and brake every tree of the field.

26 ˢ Only in the land of Goshen, where the children of Israel *were*, was there no hail.

r Ps. 105. 33. s ch. 8. 22. & 9. 4, 6. & 10. 23. & 11. 7. & 12. 13. Isai. 32. 18, 19.

27 ¶ And Pharaoh sent and called for Moses and Aaron, and said unto them, ᵗ I have sinned this time: ᵘ the LORD *is* righteous, and I and my people *are* wicked.

28 ˣ Entreat the LORD (for *it is* enough) that there be no *more* mighty thunderings and hail; and I will let you go, and ye shall stay no longer.

t ch. 10. 16. u 2 Chron. 12. 6. Ps. 129. 4 & 145. 17. Lam. 1. 18. Dan. 9. 14. x ch. 8 8, 28. & 10. 17. Acts 8. 24.

in quiet resting-places, when it shall hail, coming down on the forest; and the city shall be utterly abased.' No wonder that the visitation should, for a time at least, have overpowered the obduracy of Pharaoh, and prompted him to send in haste for Moses and Aaron, and address them in the language of the humbled penitent.

25. *The hail smote every herb of the field.* That is, some of all sorts, as is evident from Ex. 10. 15. Thus, Acts, 10. 12, 'Wherein were *all manner* of four-footed beasts of the earth.' Gr. παντα τα τετραποδα, *all four-footed beasts.*

27, 28. *I have sinned this time.* As it can hardly be supposed that Pharaoh intended to limit this confession of his sin to the present instance of his unbelief, we are no doubt authorized to extend the import of the phrase ' this time' to the whole course of his disobedience during the occurrence of the preceding plagues. This sense of the phrase strikingly confirms the interpretation put upon it in v. 14, as implying the time of a future series of judgments. Overcome by the tremendous display of the divine indignation which he had just witnessed, and which had proved fatal to many of his subjects, he confessed himself on the wrong side in his contest with the God of the Hebrews, declares that he has sinned in standing it out so long, and owns the equity of God's proceedings against him: 'The Lord is right-

eous, and I and my people are wicked. Under the pressure of his convictions he humbles himself still farther, and entreats that this direful plague may at once be stayed, promising without any qualification that the people shall be dismissed. Perhaps he sincerely felt and intended all that he said at the time as the terror of the rod often extorts penitent acknowledgments from those that have no penitent affections; but the result proved that he knew little of the plague of his own heart, whatever he had been compelled to know of the plague of God's hand. Moses, however, though he evidently placed no reliance upon his promise, v. 30, did not hesitate to listen to his request, and engaged at once to obtain a cessation of the storm; thus teaching us that even those of whom we have little hopes, and who will probably soon repent of their repentance are still to be prayed for and admonished.——¶ *Righteous*, &c. Heb. הצדיק *hatz-tzaddik, the righteous one* — הרשעים *hareshaim, the sinners;* thus showing that the original is far more emphatic than our translation. It was equivalent to saying that he and his people fully deserved all that had been brought upon them.——¶ *Mighty thunderings.* Heb. קלת אלהים *koloth Elohim, voices of God;* i. e. loud and deafening peals of thunder, called voices or thunderings of God as ' mountains of God' are large and lofty mountains.

29 And Moses said unto him, As soon as I am gone out of the city, I will ʸ spread abroad my hands unto the Lᴏʀᴅ; *and* the thunder shall cease, neither shall there be any more hail; that thou mayest know how that the ᶻ earth *is* the Lᴏʀᴅ's.

30 But as for thee and thy servants, ᵃ I know that ye will not yet fear the Lᴏʀᴅ God.

31 And the flax and the barley was smitten: ᵇ for the barley *was* in the ear, and the flax *was* bolled.

32 But the wheat and the rye

y 1 Kings 8. 22, 38. Ps. 143. 6. Isai. 1. 15.
z Ps. 24. 1. 1 Cor. 10. 26, 28. a Isai. 26. 10.
b Ruth 1. 22. & 2. 23.

were not smitten: for they *were* not grown up.

33 And Moses went out of the city from Pharaoh, and ᶜ spread abroad his hands unto the Lᴏʀᴅ: and the thunders and hail ceased, and the rain was not poured upon the earth.

34 And when Pharaoh saw that the rain and the hail and the thunders were ceased, he sinned yet more, and hardened his heart, he and his servants.

35 And ᵈ the heart of Pharaoh was hardened, neither would he let the children of Israel go; as the Lᴏʀᴅ had spoken by Moses.

c ver. 29. ch. 8. 12. d ch. 4. 21.

See Note on Gen. 23. 6.——¶ *Shall stay no longer.* Heb. לֹא תֹסִפוּן לַעֲמֹד *lo tosiphun laamod, shall not add to stand.* Chal. 'I will detain you no longer.'

29. *As soon as I am gone out of the city.* He would retire from the city not only for purposes of privacy, in his intercession with God, but also to show that he was not afraid to expose himself to the action of the elements in the open field. By thus venturing forth in the midst of the tempest with a perfect confidence of impunity, Moses gave to Pharaoh a striking proof that he was the special object of the divine protection, and consequently that his message ought to be diligently heeded.—— ¶ *That thou mayest know,* &c. That is, that thou mayest be convinced that the God of the Hebrews is no local deity like the fancied gods of Egypt, but the absolute and universal Sovereign, holding sway over all creatures, controlling the elements, and making every department of nature obsequious to his will. ' See what various methods God uses to bring men to their proper senses. Judgments are sent, and judgments removed, and all for the same end, to make men know that the Lord reigns.' *Henry.*

31. *The flax was bolled.* That is, podded. Heb. הַפִּשְׁתָּה גִּבְעֹל *happishtah gibol.* The original word occurs

only here, and its true import is not easily fixed. Nearly all the ancient versions understand it as intimating a stage of maturity in the flax in which it was past flowering. We think it probable that the genuine scope of the Heb. term expresses the formation of that small globous fruit, pod, or capsule on the top of the stalk of flax which succeeds the flower, and contains the seed. Gr. 'The flax was in seed, or seeding.' The Egyptians sowed all sorts of grain soon after the waters of the Nile had subsided; but flax and barley being of more rapid growth would at any given time be more forward than wheat and rye, which explains the circumstance mentioned in the text. The interval between the two harvests is usually about a month.

34, 35. *The thunders and the hail ceased.* The prayer of Moses was in this case invested with a power like that of Elias, and the two witnesses of the Apocalypse, James, 5. 17, 18. Rev. 11. 6, to open and shut heaven, and yet the mercy now accorded to Pharaoh tended as little to soften his heart as the previous judgment had done. As if the sun which now shone forth in the clear sky and hardened the soaked and saturated earth had produced a similar effect upon his heart, he is merely em-

CHAPTER X.

AND the LORD said unto Moses, Go in unto Pharaoh: a for I have hardened his heart, and the heart of his servants; b that I might shew these my signs before him: 2 And that c thou mayest tell in the ears of thy son, and of thy son's son, what things I have wrought in Egypt, and my signs which I have

a ch. 4. 21. & 7. 14. b ch. 7. 4. c Deut. 4. 9. Ps. 44. 1. & 71. 18. & 78. 5, &c. Joel. 1. 3.

boldened by this respite of wrath to persist in a course of more determined rebellion. Yet the language of the text implies that this increased hardness of heart was an increased measure of guilt: 'He sinned yet more and more, and hardened his heart;' i. e. sinned by hardening his heart. God's foretelling the result, therefore, and permitting it, did not go to lessen his criminality.

Chapter 10

1. *Go in unto Pharaoh.* That is, to renew the demand so often made and so often resisted ; though this is not in so many words asserted in the text. We infer what Moses was *ordered* to say from what he *did* say. Wicked men are sometimes to be admonished even where there is no hope that they will be amended. But while the divine message was to be repeated, and new tokens of the vengeance of God denounced as shortly to appear before Pharaoh and his people, an additional reason is assigned for the fearful proceedings thus far and thenceforth recorded. God had providentially and permissively hardened the hearts of Pharaoh and his servants, in order to take occasion from the event for the display of such signs and miracles as would furnish a lesson never to be forgotten to his own people and to their posterity to the latest generation. And not to them only, for as the charge is given more immediately, though not exclu-

done among them; that ye may know how that I *am* the LORD. 3 And Moses and Aaron came in unto Pharaoh, and said unto him, Thus saith the LORD God of the Hebrews, How long wilt thou refuse to d humble thyself before me? Let my people go, that they may serve me.

d 1 Kings 21. 29. 2 Chron. 7. 14. & 34. 27. Job 42. 6. Jer. 13. 18. James 4. 10. 1 Pet. 5. 6.

sively to Moses, we may understand it as an intimation, that these miraculous inflictions were to be recorded and thus made in his writings a perpetual source of instruction, and admonition to the end of the world. This use they are in fact serving at this moment. Wherever the word of God is published abroad in the earth, there are these signal events made known, and there are they operating to impress the hearts of the children of men with an awful sense of the greatness of God and the danger of provoking him to jealousy.——¶ *Before him.* Heb. בקרבו *bekirbo, in the midst of him;* where the person of the king stands for the body of his people collectively. See Note on Gen. 14. 10. Gr. 'That yet my signs may come επ' αυτους *upon them.*' Chal. 'That I might set my signs in the midst of them ;' i. e. of Pharaoh and his people. Syr. 'That I might do these my signs among them.'

3. *How long wilt thou refuse to humble thyself before me?* Gr. εως τινος ου βουλει ευτραπηναι με; *how long wilt thou not reverence me?* This is the grand controversy of God with sinners, that they refuse at his bidding to humble themselves in penitent prostration before him. But to this point they must come at last, and the more voluntarily it is done the better. Pharaoh had indeed on former occasions made some pretences to humbling himself, but as he was neither sincere nor constant in it, it passed for nothing in God's esteem,

4 Else, if thou refuse to let my people go, behold, to-morrow will I bring the ᵉ locusts into thy coast:

5 And they shall cover the face of the earth, that one cannot be able to see the earth: and ᶠthey shall eat the residue of that which is escaped, which remaineth unto you from the hail, and shall eat every tree

ᵉ Prov. 30. 27. Rom. 9. 3. ᶠ ch. 9. 32. Joel. 1. 4. & 2. 25.

which groweth for you out of the field:

6 And they ᵍ shall fill thy houses, and the houses of all thy servants, and the houses of all the Egyptians; which neither thy fathers, nor thy fathers' fathers have seen, since the day that they were upon the earth unto this day. And he turned himself, and went out from Pharaoh.

ᵍ ch. 8. 3, 21.

and he is here addressed as if it were a duty which he had never yet performed in the least degree. Let us learn from this how little value God puts upon those religious acts in which the *heart* is wanting.

4, 5. To-morrow will I bring the locusts into thy coast. Heb. הנני מביא מחר ארבה *hinneni mëbi mahar arbeh, behold me bringing to-morrow the locust;* collect. sing. for plur. The original word for *locust* (ארבה *arbeh*) is derived from רבה *rabah, to be multiplied,* or *increased.* It carries, therefore, the import of *prodigious numbers,* Judg. 6. 5, Jer. 46. 23, and on this account immense swarms of locusts stand in the figurative style of the prophets for *multitudinous armies of men.* Thus when the fifth angel sounded his trumpet, Rev. 9. 3, 'There came out of the smoke of the bottomless pit *locusts* upon earth,' denoting the countless hordes of Saracens which arose in the commencement of the seventh century under Mohammed, and overran and depopulated a great portion of Christendom.——¶ *They shall cover the face of the earth.* Heb. את עין הארץ *eth ayin haaretz, the eye of the earth.* The phraseology is singular, but it is probably by metonymy of the faculty for the object, denoting that the *sight,* the *visibility,* of the earth should be hidden by the dense masses and layers of locusts. A phraseology of perhaps a similar import occurs, Zech. 5 6, in the description of the symbolical ephah; 'This is their *resemblance*

through all the earth.' Heb. 'This is their *eye* through all the earth;' i. e. their aspect, their visible appearance. So also possibly Zech. 3. 9, 'Upon one stone shall be seven *eyes;*' i. e. a sevenfold aspect; it shall have the property of presenting under different circumstances seven distinct phases.—Swarms of this devouring insect had often before been the scourge of Egypt, but he was told that this irruption of them should be beyond all former precedent, and that their numbers, size, and voracity should be such, that they would eat up every vegetable production in the land. The wheat and the rye, it is clear, had escaped the ravages of the hail, ch. 9. 32, but they were now to be swept away by the locust, and whatever trees had been left with leaves upon their branches were now to be stript bare. ——¶ *Which neither thy fathers nor thy fathers' fathers have seen;* i. e. the like of which for numbers and ravages thy fathers have never seen; not that they had never seen locusts at all before.

6. He turned himself and went out. Seeing no reason to anticipate any better reception of his message than before. *Words* had hitherto passed between them without producing the desired results. Moses now left it with God to deal with him mainly by *acts.* It is a fearful point which the sinner has reached, when the messenger of God thinks it of very little consequence what his answer may be

7 And Pharaoh's servants said unto him, How long shall this man be ʰ a snare unto us? Let the men go, that they may serve the LORD their God: knowest thou not yet that Egypt is destroyed?

8 And Moses and Aaron were brought again unto Pharaoh: and he said unto them, Go, serve the

ʰ ch. 23. 33. Josh. 23. 13. 1 Sam. 18. 21. Eccles. 7. 26. 1 Cor. 7. 35.

LORD your God: *but* who *are* they that shall go?

9 And Moses said, We will go with our young and with our old, with our sons and with our daughters, with our flocks and with our herds will we go: for ⁱ we *must hold* a feast unto the LORD.

10 And he said unto them, Let the LORD be so with you, as I will

ⁱ ch. 5. 1.

7. *And Pharaoh's servants said unto him.* That is, the principal men that were about him, his nobles and counsellors. After the loss and devastation which the preceding plague had occasioned, they ventured to remonstrate.——¶ *How long shall this* man *be a snare unto us?* How long shall he prove the cause of leading us into fresh calamities? As, however, there is no separate word in the original to answer to 'man,' some have supposed the meaning to be, 'how long shall this thing, this affair, be a snare to us?' And with this the Gr. coincides, εως τινος εσται τουτο ημιν σκωλον, *how long shall this scandal be to us?* But were this the true sense, the original would doubtless be זאת *zoth* instead of זה *zeh*, which latter is the proper designation of a *person* instead of a *thing*. Our version is correct.——¶ *Knowest thou not yet that Egypt is destroyed?* Hast thou not yet evidence enough from the calamities experienced, especially by the ravages of the late hail-storm, that the whole country is just upon the verge of destruction? If his own courtiers and counsellors were of this opinion, the king could not but infer that in the course he was now pursuing, he was no longer sustained by the general consent of the Egyptian people, who now lamented his obstinacy, and had become desirous that, as the least of many evils, the demand of the Israelites should be complied with. This consideration was **not without its weight with the king.**

Perceiving the feeling that was entertained by his court and his subjects, he resolved so far to comply with their wishes as to have Moses and Aaron sent for and brought back, that he might at least ostensibly appear disposed to treat with them anew.——¶ *But who are they that shall go?* Heb. מי ומי ההלכים *mi va-mi haholekim, who and who (are) going?* The repetition of the interrogative is emphatic, implying that he was to specify with the utmost distinctness who were to go, and who, if any, were to stay behind. Moses in reply tells him plainly that they were to serve God with their *all*; that their wives and their children, their flocks and their herds, without any exception or reservation, must go with them.

10. *And he said unto them, Let the Lord,* &c. This bold and positive declaration of Moses was too much for Pharaoh. Greatly exasperated by this uncompromising statement he answers in a style of mingled irony and wrath, 'Let the Lord do with you as I will let you go;' q. d. 'If this be the proposed condition of your going, that you take your little ones with you, then may the God whom you serve favor you as much with his presence as I do with my consent, and no more. In this case your prospects are sorry indeed.' It is a very strong and emphatic mode of denying them the permission which they sought.——¶ *Look to it, for evil is before you.* It is doubted by commentators whether this is to be understood as a *threatening*

let you go, and your little ones : look *to it ;* for evil is before you.

11 Not so: go now ye *that are* men, and serve the LORD; for that ye did desire. And they were driven out from Pharaoh's presence.

12 ¶ And the LORD said unto Moses, k Stretch out thine hand over the land of Egypt for the locusts,

k ch. 7. 19.

that they may come up upon the land of Egypt, and ¹ eat every herb of the land, *even* all that the hail hath left.

13 And Moses stretched forth his rod over the land of Egypt, and the LORD brought an east wind upon the land all that day, and all *that* night: *and* when it was morning, the east wind brought the locusts,

l ver. 4. 5.

of evil to happen to them, or as an *accusation* of evil intended by them. Probably the words will admit the union of both senses ; 'You are harboring an *evil* design, and are exposing yourselves to the *evil* of a corresponding punishment.' Gr. 'See that mischief is proposed by you.' Vulg. 'Who doubteth but that you intend very wickedly ?' Chal. 'See how the evil which you were thinking to do shall return to your own faces.'

11. *Not so.* I do not consent to your going on these conditions.——¶ *Go now ye that are men.* 'Leave your women and children behind as a pledge for your safe return, and then you have my consent that the ' men,' all the adults of the congregation, should go, for this is the fair interpretation of your request ; thus only did I understand it ; thus far only will I comply with it.' Yet it is difficult to say what authority he had for such an assertion, as the foregoing narrative attributes no expression to Moses which would seem fairly capable of such a construction. It is possible he intended to say, that *that must have been Moses' meaning* when he asked permission to sacrifice unto Jehovah. But he had no right to attribute a sense to Moses' words which Moses did not design to convey, and then act as if it were the true sense.——¶ *And they were driven out from Pharaoh's presence.* Heb. אתם וירגש *va-yegaresh otham, and one drove them out ;* an instance of the phraseology in which a

verb active is used indefinitely in the third person singular for the plural passive. See Note on Gen. 16. 14. 'Among natives of rank, when a person is very importunate or troublesome, when he presses for something which the former are not willing to grant, he is told to begone. Should he still persist, the servants are called, and the order is given, 'Drive that fellow out.' He is then seized by the *neck,* or taken by the *hands,* and *dragged* from the premises ; he all the time *screaming* and *bawling* as if they were taking his *life.* Thus to be driven out is the greatest indignity which can be offered, and nothing but the most violent rage will induce a superior to have recourse to it.' *Roberts*

12. *For the locusts, that they may come up.* Heb. וירעל בארבה *ba-arbeh va-yaal, for the locust, that he may come up ;* collect. sing.

13. *The Lord brought an east wind upon the land.* Heb. נהג *nihag, conducted.* The word is remarkable, as it has the import of *guiding, leading, directing one's course.* The wind may be said to blow where it listeth; but then it listeth or chooseth only as God has ordered it. At his command it blows one day to bring up locusts, and on the next another to sweep them away. Though locusts are common in Arabia, they are comparatively rare in Egypt ; the Red Sea forming a sort of barrier against them, as they are not formed for crossing seas, or for long flights. Yet on the present occasion they were

14 And ᵐ the locusts went up over all the land of Egypt, and rest-

ᵐ Ps. 78. 46. & 105. 34.

ed in all the coasts of Egypt: very grievous *were they ;* ⁿ before them

ⁿ Joel 2. 2.

enabled, by the aid of a 'strong east wind,' to cross that sea from Arabia, which was another remarkable circumstance, as the winds which prevalently blow in Egypt are six months from the south, and six months from the north. ——¶ *Brought the locusts.* Heb. נשׂא *nasa, bore up, supported, sustained.* Syr. and Vulg. ' The burning rushing wind raised the locusts.' Considering what Pharaoh and his people had already suffered from the preceding plagues, this additional one must have been beyond measure afflictive. The dearth and desolation were now complete. Every leaf and blade of grass left from the previous ravages of the hail, were now devoured. It is difficult to conceive the devastating effects that follow when a cloud of hungry locusts, comes upon a country. They devour to the very root and bark, so that it is a long time before vegetation can be renewed. The account which M. Volney (Travels in Syria, vol. 1. p. 188) gives of the devastations of these insects, contains a striking illustration of this passage :— 'Their quantity is incredible to all who have not themselves witnessed their astonishing numbers ; the whole earth is covered with them for the space of several leagues. The noise they make in browsing on the trees and herbage may be heard at a great distance, and resembles that of an army plundering in secret. The Tartars themselves are a less destructive enemy than these little animals. One would imagine that fire had followed their progress. Wherever their myriads spread, the verdure of the country disappears ; trees and plants stripped of their leaves and reduced to their naked boughs and stems, cause the dreary image of winter to succeed in an instant to the rich scenery of spring. When these clouds of lo-

custs take their flight, to surmount any obstacles, or to traverse more rapidly a desert soil, the heavens may literally be said to be obscured with them.' To this may be added the narrative of a similar visitation in the Canary Islands described by an eye-witness, about two centuries ago. 'The air was so full of them, that I could not eat in my chamber without a candle ; all the houses being full of them, even the stables, barns, chambers, garrets, and cellars I caused cannon-powder and sulphur to be burnt to expel them, but all to no purpose ; for when the door was opened an infinite number came in, and the others went out, fluttering about ; and it was a troublesome thing when a man went abroad to be hit on the face by those creatures, so that there was no opening one's mouth but some would get in. Yet all this was nothing, for when we were to eat, these creatures gave us no respite ; and when we cut a bit of meat, we cut a locust with it ; and when a man opened his mouth to put in a morsel, he was sure to chew one of them. I have seen them at night, when they sit to rest them, that the roads were four inches thick of them, one upon another ; so that the horses would not trample over them, but as they were put on with much lashing, pricking up their ears, snorting and treading fearfully. The wheels of our carts and the feet of our horses bruising these creatures, there came forth from them such a stench as not only offended the nose, but the brain. I was not able to endure it, but was forced to wash my nose with vinegar, and hold a handkerchief dipped in it continually at my nostrils.' *Gallaudet's Life of Moses,* vol. 1. p. 114, See also 'Scrip. Illust.' p. 551

14. *The locusts went up over all the land.* From the following passages in

there were no such locusts as they, neither after them shall be such.

15 For they º covered the face of the whole earth, so that the land was darkened; and they ᴾ did eat every herb of the land, and all the fruit of the trees which the hail had left: and there remained not any green thing in the trees, or in

º ver. 5.　ᴾ Ps. 105. 35.

the herbs of the field, through all the land of Egypt.

16 ¶ Then Pharaoh called for Moses and Aaron in haste; and he said, �q I have sinned against the LORD your God, and against you.

17 Now therefore forgive, I pray thee, my sin only this once, and ʳ entreat the LORD your God that

q ch. 9. 27.　ʳ ch. 9. 28.　1 Kings 13. 6.

the Psalms some have thought that the locusts were accompanied by countless swarms of caterpillars. Ps. 78. 46, 'He gave also their increase unto the caterpillar, and their labor unto the locust.' Ps. 105. 34, 'He spake, and the locusts came, and the caterpillars, and that without number.' But it is now generally admitted that the original terms merely imply *different species* of locusts.——¶ *Before them there were*, &c. This has been thought to be inconsistent with Joel, 2. 2, when in speaking of an invading army of locusts the prophet says, 'A great people and a strong; there hath not been ever the like, neither shall be any more after it, even to the years of many generations.' To this Abarbanel, the Jewish critic, answers, that Moses' words are to be understood of the country of Egypt only; that there never was before and never was to be again such a plague of locusts *there*. But Rosenmuller contends that this is no more than a common hyperbolical and proverbial mode of speech, which is not to be pressed to the utmost strictness of its import. He adduces the following instances of parallel usage. 2 Kings, 18. 5, 'He (Hezekiah) trusted in the Lord God of Israel; so that after him was none like him among all the kings of Judah, nor any that were before him.' 2 Kings, 23. 25, 'And like unto him (Josiah) was there no king before him, that turned to the Lord with all his heart, and with all his soul, and with all his might, according to all the law of Moses; nei-

ther after him arose there any like him.' Here indeed it is not easy to see how the same thing could consistently be said of these two different kings, except on the ground of the correctness of Rosenmuller's remark. On the same principle we are perhaps to interpret the two prophetical declarations of Daniel and our Savior; Dan. 12. 1, 'And at that time shall Michael stand up, the great prince which standeth for the children of thy people: and there shall be a time of trouble, such as never.was since there was a nation even to that same time.' Mat. 24. 21, 'For there shall be great tribulation, such as was not since the beginning of the world to this time, no, nor ever shall be.' It may indeed be affirmed that the two predictions refer to the same time, which is indeed possible, though not certain.

15. *Covered the face of the whole earth.* Heb. עין כל הארץ *ayin kol haaretz, the eye of the whole earth.* See Note on v. 5.——¶ *The land was dark-ened.* Heb. ארץ *eretz*, the same word as in the preceding clause. Either the surface of the ground was so covered as to be hidden from sight, so making the phrase exegetical of the preceding; or, which is preferable, the immense clouds of them in the air intercepted the sun's rays, and thus darkened the land. Chal. 'They covered all the land so that the sun-beams could not pierce to it, and the land was obscured.'

16, 17. *Then Pharaoh called.* Heb. רמהר לקרא *yemaher likro, hastened to call.* So formidable was this calamity

he may take away from me this death only.

18 And he s went out from Pharaoh, and entreated the LORD.

19 And the LORD turned a mighty strong west wind which took away the locusts, and cast them t into the

s ch. 8. 30.　t Joel. 2. 20.

Red sea: there remained not one locust in all the coasts of Egypt.

20 But the LORD u hardened Pharaoh's heart, so that he would not let the children of Israel go.

21 ¶ And the LORD said unto Moses, x Stretch out thine hand toward

u ch. 4. 21. & 11. 10.　x ch. 9. 22.

that although Pharaoh had previously driven Moses and Aaron from his presence, yet he is now constrained to send for them again, to avow his fault, and to beg for one reprieve more. His confession now has more the air of unfeigned repentance than on any former occasion. He acknowledges that he had sinned against God and his servants, humbly asks their forgiveness, and sues for their intercession. Only let him be forgiven *this once*, only let him be delivered from *this* death, and there should be no more cause for complaint. Alas! there are but too many who upon reading this will be reminded of something similar in their own case; too many who will recollect in the hour of sickness and in the fear of death, to have prayed to be delivered *only this once*, with promises of amendment, but who yet upon recovery have returned, Pharaoh-like, to their former impenitence, worldliness, and sin. But let it not be forgotten that these repeated lapses and broken vows are all the while swelling our guilt to fearful dimensions, and making us more and more ripe for a sudden destruction.——¶ *This death.* That is, *this deadly plague.* Thus, 2 Kings, 4. 40, 'And they cried out and said, O thou man of God, there is *death* in the pot;' i. e. something *deadly.* The plague of the locusts was in itself deadly in the sense of *having been destructive;* but it is probable that Pharaoh alluded rather to its *apprehended* consequences. He may have supposed, that famine and pestilence causing a general mortality would follow in the train of the ravages of the locusts.

However this may be, he deprecates the plague of locusts more than the plague of his own heart, which was much more deadly. But this is one of the thousand cases continually occurring, where men are more anxious to be delivered from their troubles than their sins, and cry upon their beds only from acuteness of bodily pain or fear of hell They shrink and writhe under the consequences of their transgressions, but they do not hate and repent of the transgressions themselves.

19. *The Lord turned a mighty strong west wind.* Heb. רוח ים חזק מאד *ruah yam hazak meod, a sea-wind strong exceedingly.* The Hebrews denominated the West from the Mediterranean sea, which lay to the west of Palestine. ——¶ *Cast them.* Heb. יתקעהו *yith-kaëhu, fastened them;* i. e. they were so cast or driven into the sea, that as to the event, it was as if they had been 'fastened,' like a tent which is pitched and fast nailed to the ground. This complete removal of the locusts was as miraculous as the bringing them on.—— ¶ *Into the Red Sea.* Heb. ים סוף *yam suph, Sea of Suph,* or *weedy sea, sea of rushes,* from the great quantities of seaweeds and flags which abound upon its shores. It is called 'Red Sea' from its bordering upon the country of Edom, which, in the Hebrew tongue signifies ' red.'

21. *Even darkness which may be felt.* Heb. וימש חשך *va-yamesh hoshek, that one may feel darkness;* the same word in the original with that used to express the 'darkness' which covered the deep at the time of the six days' creation.

heaven, that there may be darkness over the land of Egypt, even darkness *which* may be felt.

22 And Moses stretched forth his hand toward heaven: and there

was a ʸ thick darkness in all the land of Egypt three days:

23 They saw not one another, neither rose any from his place for

y Ps. 105. 28.

It was a darkness consisting of thick, clammy fogs, of vapors and exhalations so condensed that they might almost be perceived by the organs of touch. Some commentators, supposing that human life could not be sustained an hour in such a medium, imagine that instead of 'darkness that may be felt,' the Heb. phrase may signify a darkness in which men went groping and feeling about for every thing they wanted. But something of a hyperbolical character may be allowed for expressions of this kind, which are not to be pared to the quick. Considering that the sun was one of the deities of Egypt, and that in that country *any* darkening of his light in the day time is an extremely rare occurrence, we may imagine the consternation that would sieze upon the inhabitants at such a phenomenon. The cloud of locusts which had previously darkened the land were nothing compared with this. It was truly 'an horror of thick darkness.'

22. *There was a thick darkness.* Heb. חשך אפלה *hoshek aphëlah, darkness of obscurity or gloom;* i. e. a darkness of preternatural density. The expression in the original is peculiarly emphatic, and is, therefore, rendered in the Gr. by three words, 'darkness, thick blackness, and tempestuous gloom.' The description which the author of the Book of Wisdom, chap. 17. 2, 3, 21, gives of their inward terrors and consternation may not be altogether conjectural: 'They were not only prisoners of darkness and fettered with the bonds of a long night, but were horribly astonished likewise and troubled with strange apparitions.' Compare with Moses' account of the ninth plague, the woe of the fifth apocalyptic vial, Rev. 16.

10, 'And the fifth angel poured out his vial upon the seat of the beast, and his kingdom was full of darkness ; and they gnawed their tongues for anguish.'

23. *Neither rose any from his place.* Heb. מתחתיו *mittahtav, from that which was under him.* Gr. εκ της κοιτης αυτου, *from his bed.* The meaning probably is, that no one went out of his house to attend to his usual business. It is probable too that they were prevented by the heavy and humid state of the atmosphere from availing themselves of any kind of artificial light. So Wisdom, chap. 17. 5, 'No power of fire might give light.' We can scarcely conceive a more distressing situation ; yet as Pharaoh and his people had rebelled against the light of God's word, conveyed to them by Moses, it was a righteous thing with God thus to punish them with a sensible pre-intimation of that 'blackness of darkness' which enters into the misery of the damned.——
¶ *The children of Israel had light in their dwellings.* Again God put a marked difference between his enemies and his people. Well is it said of this miracle in the apocryphal book above quoted, ch. 17. 20, 21, 'The whole world shined with clear light, and none were hindered in their labor ; over them only (the Egyptians) was spread a heavy night, an image of that darkness which should afterwards receive them : but yet were they unto themselves more grievous than the darkness !' In allusion, perhaps, to the gracious discrimination here spoken of we find the promise, Is. 60. 1, 2, 'Arise, shine ; for thy light is come, and the glory of the Lord is risen upon thee. For behold, darkness shall cover the earth and gross darkness the people, but the Lord shall

three days: ᶻbut all the children of Israel had light in their dwellings.

24 ¶ And Pharaoh called unto Moses, and ᵃsaid, Go ye, serve the LORD: only let your flocks and your herds be stayed: let your ᵇlittle ones also go with you.

25 And Moses said, Thou must give us also sacrifices, and burnt-

ᶻ ch. 8. 22.　ᵃ ver. 8.　ᵇ ver. 10.

offerings, that we may sacrifice unto the LORD our God.

26 Our cattle also shall go with us; there shall not an hoof be left behind; for thereof must we take to serve the LORD our God; and we know not with what we must serve the LORD, until we come thither.

27 ¶ But the LORD ᶜhardened

ᶜ ver. 20. ch. 4. 21. & 14. 4, 8.

arise upon thee, and his glory shall be seen upon thee.' Yet a greater difference will hereafter be made between the righteous and the wicked, between those that fear God, and those that fear him not. While the light of his countenance and theʳ glory of his heaven shall exhilarate and rejoice the former, in that state which needs not sun or moon to enlighten it, the wicked shall endure the total loss of day, and dwell darkling in perpetual night. There is even now an earnest of the final diversity of lot. The darkness of ignorance and sin enshrouds the one, and the night of nature clouds all their perceptions; while the bright shining of the sun of righteousness sheds its kindly and refreshing beams upon the other.

24. *And Pharaoh called unto Moses.* That is, after the lapse of three days of darkness.——¶ *Go ye, serve the Lord, only let the flocks,* &c. The visitation of the darkness, so well calculated to appal and terrify the Egyptians, compelled the king to relax his previous determination. Still he is bent on a compromise. He will now permit the children also to go, but the flocks and the herds must be stayed behind as a security for their return. Thus it is that sinners are disposed to make terms with the Almighty, instead of yielding cheerfully to *all* his demands. They will consent, under the pressure of judgments, to part with *some* of their sins, but not all. They would rather retain them all, if they could do it consistent-ɪy with their hope of heaven. If they

do part with any, it is with the utmost reluctance, like the mariner who casts his goods overboard to lighten his ship and keep it from sinking. But while Pharaoh would plead for some abatement, and shrinks from obeying the Lord *wholly,* Moses, instead of receding an iota from his previous demand, grows bolder as the crisis approaches, and declares that not only shall the children go, but also that there shall not an ' hoof be left behind.'

25. *Thou must give us also sacrifices.* Heb. תִתֵּן בְּיָדֵנוּ *titten be-yadenu, shalt give in, or into, our hands.* It is not probably to be understood from this that Moses demanded that animals for sacrifice should be given to them from the flocks and herds of the Egyptians, but that he should freely *allow them to take their own ;* that he should throw no obstacle in the way of their taking their stock of cattle with them. To give into their hands, therefore, is equivalent to leaving in their power and at their disposal. This is evident from the drift of the next verse.

26. *Not an hoof be left behind.* The exact and punctilious obedience of Moses to every item of the divine commandment is here displayed, as an example from following which we should be deterred by no persecution or tyranny of men. The ' not leaving an hoof behind' intimated their full and complete egress from Egyptian bondage, leaving nothing to tempt them to return.

27. *He would not let them go.* Heᴅ

Pharaoh's heart, and he would not let them go.

28 And Pharaoh said unto him, Get thee from me, take heed to thyself, see my face no more: for in *that* day thou seest my face, thou shalt die.

29 And Moses said, Thou hast

אבֹה לֹא *lo abah, was not willing, was not persuaded, did not consent*, to let them go. This word, strongly indicative of the *wilfulness* of the king, occurs here for the first time in the whole narrative.

28. *Get thee from me*, &c. ' Has a servant, an agent, or an officer, deeply offended his superior, he will say to him, ' Take care never to see my face again ; for on the day you do that, evil shall come upon you.' ' Begone, and in future never look in this *face*,' pointing to his own.' *Roberts*. The firmness of Moses exasperated Pharaoh beyond measure. He here shows himself frantic with disappointment and rage. He not only dismisses the unwelcome messenger with indignation, from his court, but forbids, upon pain of death, the beholding his face again. A desperate madness and an impotent malice are alike conspicuous in this angry order. Had he not had abundant evidence that Moses could plague him without seeing his face ? Had he not had time to discover that an almighty power was working with Moses, and that it was idle to threaten *him* with death, who was the special charge of Omnipotence ? But to what length of daring impiety will not a hardened heart bring the presumptuous rebel !

29. *I will see thy face again no more.* It is a sad farewell when God, in the persons of his servants, refuses any more to see the face of the wicked ; especially if in so doing he yields to their desires. For the manner in which this is to be reconciled with the subsequent history, see Note on Ex. 11. 1—3.

---

spoken well, [d] I will see thy face again no more.

CHAPTER XI.

AND the LORD said unto Moses, Yet will I bring one plague *more* upon Pharaoh, and upon Egypt; afterwards he will let you

[d] Hebr. 11. 27.

Chapter 11

1. *And the Lord said unto Moses.* Rather perhaps, 'The Lord *had said* unto Moses.' From v. 8, it appears that Moses, after announcing the eighth plague, went out from Pharaoh in great anger, and yet previously in ch. 10. 29, he is represented as saying to Pharaoh, 'I will see thy face again no more.' It is consequently to be inferred that the present judgment was denounced to the king before the close of the last-mentioned interview, and the information respecting it communicated to Moses some time previous to that interview. The true construction undoubtedly is to consider the first three verses of this chapter as a mere parenthesis, and to connect ch. 11. 4, with ch. 10. 29, as a continuation of the same train of narrative. Otherwise there is very great confusion in the incidents detailed. The connexion between this and the last verse of the preceding chapter is undoubtedly very close, however loose at first sight it may appear. Moses does in effect in these words state the ground of the confident and peremptory tone which he assumed in his reply to Pharaoh. They give us to understand that it was not of his own motion that he then intimated that that should be their last interview; for we cannot suppose that it was optional with Moses whether to continue or to break off the negociations with Pharaoh. Unless divinely instructed to the contrary, how did he know but that God would have him carry another message to the king in despite of his lordly interdict ? From this passage we learn that he *was* thus in-

go hence : ᵃ when he shall let *you* go, he shall surely thrust you out hence altogether.

2 Speak now in the ears of the

ᵃ ch. 12. 31, 33, 39.

structed,—that God had informed him that the contest with Pharaoh was just about to close,—that with one plague more he would complete the deliverance of Israel.——¶ *Yet will I bring one plague more upon Pharaoh.* Fearful and wonderful had been the plagues which the Lord had already brought upon Egypt, but before Moses retires from the royal presence he has one more, and but one, judgment to denounce to the incorrigible king. It was of portentous import, and might well make the ears of the haughty rebel to tingle. The solemn manner in which it is announced to Moses reminds us that whatever awful succession of plagues we may have thus far endured, God may still have one in reserve which shall do more execution than all the preceding.

2. *Speak now in the ears of the people, and let every man borrow,* &c. Heb. ישׁאלו *yishalu, ask, demand.* On the import of the term see Note on Ex. 3. 22. We are by no means satisfied that Moses was required to *command* the people to practise the device here mentioned. We regard it rather, as far as *they* were concerned, as the mere *prediction* of a fact which should occur. Moses, we conceive, was here directed as a private individual, and probably in a covert manner (whence the Gr. has, ' speak therefore *privily* in the ears ;' i. e. in a *private*, not in a *public*, capacity), to start the suggestion among the people that the present was a favorable opportunity to obtain some measure of that remuneration for years of unrequited service to which they were justly entitled. The grounds of this proceeding are given in the ensuing verse, which is to be taken in immediate connection with what goes before,

people, and let every man borrow of his neighbour, and every woman of her neighbour, ᵇ jewels of silver, and jewels of gold.

ᵇ ch. 3. 22. & 12. 35.

as a statement of the reason which existed to give countenance and secure success to the measure proposed. Both Moses and the people were now in high estimation with the Egyptians, from its having been so clearly evinced that they were the special objects of a divine interposition, and accounting this as a providential intimation they were led to avail themselves of the favorable impressions of their enemies to obtain a partial redress for their wrongs. As to the true import of the original word for ' borrow,' it is, as before remarked, ch. 3. 22, that of *asking, demanding, soliciting*, without expressly implying a promise of restoration, although it cannot be denied that there are cases where it legitimately imports the act of *borrowing*, as Ex. 22. 14, 2 Kings 6. 5. But in the present instance it is obvious that the Egyptians were as voluntary and as forward in giving as the Israelites were in receiving, there being no bribe which they were not willing to offer in order to free themselves from the presence of men whom they regarded as the cause of their calamities, and the natural effect of the terrible inflictions which they had just sustained, would be, for the time, to render the precious things which the Hebrews required of small value in their sight. When we consider for how long a period the Israelites had been impoverished that the Egyptians might be enriched, and that now being about to quit the land of their sojourning with only so much of their effects as they could ' bind up in their clothes upon their shoulders,' all the property which they left behind would naturally fall into the hands of their oppressors, we cannot deem it inconsistent with the divine perfections that

3 c And the LORD gave the people favour in the sight of the Egyptians. Moreover, the man d Moses *was* very great in the land of Egypt, in the sight of Pharaoh's servants, and in the sight of the people.

4 And Moses said, Thus saith the LORD, e About midnight will I go out into the midst of Egypt.

5 And f all the first-born in the land of Egypt shall die, from the first-born of Pharaoh that sitteth upon his throne, even unto the first-born of the maid-servant that *is* behind the mill; and all the first-born of beasts.

c ch. 3. 21. & 12. 36. Ps. 106. 46. d 2 Sam. 7. 9. Esther 9. 4. e ch. 12. 12, 23, 29. Amos 5. 17.

f ch. 12. 12, 29. Amos 4. 10.

this mode of possessing themselves of their dues should be suggested to an injured people. They took no more than they received, they received no more than they demanded, and they demanded no more than that to which they were justly entitled. Josephus says, 'They also honored the Hebrews with *gifts,* some in order to get them to depart quickly, and others on account of their neighborhood and the friendship they had with them.' It is evident from ch. 12. 35, 36, that this account of the borrowing of the jewels is inserted here by anticipation, as the fact did not occur till some time afterward. This confirms still farther the idea above suggested that these verses are parenthetical.

3. *The Lord gave the people favor,* &c. The influence which should produce the effect here described was too signal and marvellous not to be ascribed directly to a divine source. The Psalmist informs us Ps. 105. 25, that the hearts of the Egyptians were turned to hate the chosen people, and here we find the secret agency of heaven controlling the spirits of his enemies, and prompting them to bestow favors where they might rather be expected to vent malice. But God very often mollifies the hearts which he does not sanctify, and realizes to his afflicted people what is said, Ps. 106. 46, 'He made them also to be pitied of all them that carried them captive.' By the same working of his overruling providence he made Moses also 'great' in the esteem of the people of Egypt, and

thus rendered the reverence and awe which his miracles had inspired tributary to the enriching his people. The 'servants' and the 'people' here spoken of are undoubtedly both to be understood of the Egyptians.

4. *And Moses said.* That is, to Pharaoh, in continuation of ch. 10. 29, before he left the royal presence.—— ¶ *About midnight will I go out,* &c. Heb. אֲנִי יֹצֵא *ani yotzë, I going out ;* the present future participle. Chal. 'I will be revealed in the midst of Egypt.' Arab. 'I will make my Angel to walk through the country of Egypt.' God was now to go forth, as he is elsewhere said to come down, in the execution of his judgments. The language represents God himself as the immediate author of the tremendous calamity about to be inflicted. Hitherto he had plagued Egypt by means and instruments : ' Stretch out thine hand ;' ' Say unto Aaron, Stretch forth thine hand with thy rod.' But now it is, 'I will go out into the midst of Egypt.' As mercies coming immediately from the hand of our heavenly Father are sweeter and better than those that are communicated through the medium of the creature ; so the judgments issuing directly from the stores of the divine wrath, are more terrible and overwhelming than those which come through any created agency.

5. *All the first-born in the land of Egypt shall die.* It is scarcely possible to conceive a denunciation fraught with elements of more terror than this. Had the whole Egyptian nation been doomed

to utter extinction, it would indeed have been a judgment of greater magnitude, and have produced a deeper impression upon those that should have beheld it; but then one part of the people would not have survived to experience the anguish of being so fearfully separated from the other. As it was, it was to be attended with the most heart-rending aggravations. It was to be a blow which should wound there where the heart is most susceptible. The pride, the hope, the joy of every family was to be taken from them. The bitterness of fathers and mothers for their first-born is proverbial. Here were Egyptian parents soon to be found weeping for their children 'because they were not.' It was to be a woe without alleviation and without remedy. He that is sick may be restored. A body emaciated or ulcerated, maimed or enfeebled, may again recover soundness and strength. But what kindly process can reanimate the breathless clay, and give back to the arms of mourning affection an only son, a first-born, stricken with death! Hope, the last refuge and remedy under other evils, was here to be cut up by the roots. Again, the blow was to be struck at midnight, when none could see the hand that inflicted it, and most were reposing in quiet sleep. Had this sleep been silently and insensibly exchanged for the sleep of death, the circumstances would have been less overwhelmingly awful. But it was not to be so. Although for three days and nights previously they had been enveloped in thick darkness, and none had ¬isen up from their places, yet now they were to be aroused from their beds to render what fruitless aid they could to their expiring children, and to mourn over their slain. What consternation and woe could be equal to this? To be prematurely awakened out of sleep by the dying groans of a near relative suddenly smitten; to be presented with the ghastly image of death in a darling

object lately seen and enjoyed in perfect health; to be forced to the acknowledgment of the great and holy Lord God by such a fearful demonstration of his presence and power! But this was not all. The universality of the woe was to be such as greatly to enhance its horrors. From every house the cry of misery was to burst forth. The mighty leveller was to invade all ranks and conditions. The prince and the peasant, the master and the slave, were alike to confess the destructiveness of his march. And then to crown the whole was the keen reflection, that all this accumulated distress *might have been prevented.* How would they now condemn their desperate madness in provoking a power which had so often and so forcibly warned them of their danger? If Pharaoh were not past feeling, how dreadful must have been the pangs which he felt in the thought that after attempting to destroy, by unheard of cruelties, an innocent and helpless race of strangers, he had now ruined his own country by his obstinate perseverance in impiety and folly? With what anguish must he have beheld his own hopes blasted in their dearest object, the heir of his throne and empire, because he regarded not the claims of humanity in the treatment of his vassals? But see the judgment more fully considered in the Note on Ex. 12. 29.——¶ *From the first-born of Pharaoh that sitteth upon his throne.* That is, the first-born whose right it would have been to sit upon the throne of the kingdom as a successor to his father. Modern interpreters for the most part refer the expression 'that sitteth upon his throne' to Pharaoh, but the Targums of Onkelos and Jonathan understand it of the heir apparent—qui sessurus est super thronum regni ejus, *who is to sit upon the throne of his kingdom.*—— ¶ *The maid-servant that is behind the mill.* 'Most families,' says Shaw (Travels, p. 231) speaking of the Moors in Barbary, 'grind their wheat and barley

6 g And there shall be a great cry throughout all the land of Egypt, such as there was none like it, nor shall be like it any more.

7 h But against any of the children of Israel i shall not a dog move his tongue, against man or beast: that ye may know how that the LORD

g ch. 12. 30. Amos 5. 17. h ch. 8. 22. i Josh. 10. 21.

---

doth put a difference between the Egyptians and Israel.

8 And k all these thy servants shall come down unto me, and bow down themselves unto me, saying, Get thee out, and all the people that follow thee; and after that I will go out. And he went out from Pharaoh in a great anger.

k ch. 12. 33.

---

at home, having two portable millstones for that purpose; the uppermost of which is turned round by a small handle of wood or iron that is placed in the rim. When this stone is large, or expedition is required, then a second person is called in to assist; and as it is usual for the women alone to be concerned in this employment, who seat themselves over against each other with the millstones between them, we may see not only the propriety of the expression, Ex. 11. 5, of ‘sitting behind the mill,’ but the force of another, Mat. 24. 40, that ‘two women shall be grinding at the mill, the one shall be taken, and the other left.’ Sir John Chardin also remarks, that ‘they are female slaves who are generally employed in the East at these hand-mills; that this work is extremely laborious, and esteemed the lowest employment in the house.’ Thus, we find a translation from the highest honor to the lowest degradation described in the following terms, Is. 47. 1, 2, ‘Come down and sit in the dust, O virgin, daughter of Babylon, sit on the ground—*take the millstones and grind meal.*’

6. *And there shall be a great cry.* A cry of lamentation and mourning, and anguish, a loud and universal wailing, such as never was and never should be paralleled in that land. The latter clause of the verse is probably to be interpreted on the same principle with that of ch. 10. 14.

7. *Shall not a dog move his tongue.* A proverbial expression for the most

profound tranquillity, implying that nothing should occur to harm or affright them; they should abide in peace and safety.—— ¶ *Doth put a difference.* Heb. יפלה *yapleh, wonderfully distinguisheth.* See Note on Ex. 8. 22.

8. *Shall come down unto me, and bow down themselves unto me, saying,* &c. Moses has thus recited the words of God’s message to Pharaoh, but here he begins to speak in his own person, announcing the speedy submission of Pharaoh’s servants to *him,* and their humble and earnest request that he should ‘depart out of their coasts.’ At the same time, we must bear in mind that Moses says this in his *representative* character, and that it is *to the Most High in Moses* that this submission was to be made. It is indeed wonderful to see God thus identifying himself with a creature of clay who speaks in his name, and yet it is unquestionable that the Scriptures afford repeated instances of the same usage of speech.——¶ *All the people that follow thee.* Heb. אשר ברגליך *asher beraglëka, who are at thy feet.* An expressive phrase, of which see the import explained in the Notes on Gen. 49. 10, and Judg. 4. 10. Gr. ‘Whom thou leadest.’ Chal. ‘Who are with thee.’ Vulg. ‘Who are subject to thee.’ Aben Ezra, ‘Who are in thy power.’ Jarchi, ‘Who follow thy counsel and thy steps.’——¶ *Went out from Pharaoh in a great anger.* Heb. בחרי אף *bohori aph, in a heat of anger.* His indignation was justly moved at the repeated falsehoods of the king, at his

9 And the LORD said unto Moses,
l Pharaoh shall not hearken unto
you; that m my wonders may be
multiplied in the land of Egypt.
10 And Moses and Aaron did all

l ch. 3. 19. & 7. 4. & 10. 1.   m ch. 7. 3.

these wonders before Pharaoh;
n and the LORD hardened Pharaoh's
heart, so that he would not let the
children of Israel go out of his
land.

n ch. 10. 20, 27.   Rom. 2. 5. & 9. 22.

mercenary and cruel disposition, and at
the insolent manner in which he had
himself been treated by him. But it
was mainly in view of the indignity
put upon the messages of God that his
spirit was stirred. He saw in him a
proud, obstinate, audacious opposer of
the God of heaven, one who had resisted
warnings and convictions, judgments
and mercies ; one who would not yield
to the divine authority to save all the
first-born of his kingdom, and who was
now rushing headlong to his ruin. No
wonder that he was provoked with a
holy indignation at his enormous sin,
and angered, as our Savior himself
afterwards was, 'at the hardness of his
heart.' But it was a being angry and
sinning not. 'To be angry at nothing
but sin, is the way not to sin in anger.'
Henry.

9, 10. *And the Lord said unto Moses,* &c. Rather, 'The Lord *had said.*'
These two concluding verses appear to
be designed as a kind of general recapitulation of the main incidents of the
preceding narrative, of which the scope
is to inform the reader that every thing
took place just as God had predicted.
In obedience to the divine command
Moses and Aaron had performed all
their wonders before the king and his
court, and yet according to the previous
intimation, Pharaoh had turned a deaf
ear, and presented an obdurate heart, to
all these exhibitions and appeals, most
stubbornly refusing to let the people go
from under his yoke. It was proper to
make this statement to preclude any
lurking impression that such an amazing
demonstration of divine power had been
put forth *in vain,* or that Omnipotence
had been *baffled* in the contest. Far from

it. Every thing had resulted just as God
had foretold. The incredulity and obstinacy of men is sometimes made known
beforehand, that it may not be a surprise or a stumbling-block when it happens.

Chapter 12

We have in the present chapter an
account of the execution of the fearful
judgment threatened in the preceding,
and in that event of the removal of the
last obstacle in the way of the exit of
the Israelites from Egypt. The slaughter of the first-born ended for the present
the controversy with Pharaoh, though
his subsequent infatuation brought the
final stroke of justice upon him in his
overthrow in the Red Sea. Previously
however to detailing the incidents of
this awful providence, the historian
pauses to give us an account of the institution of the Passover, which God
himself ordained, not only as a present
means of safety to his own people while
the judgment went through the land,
but also as a permanent memorial of
the event of their deliverance. As such
the ordinance is perhaps the most remarkable of all the festivals of the Jewish church, and that which is more frequently mentioned in the New Testament than any other. It consisted of
three parts ; (1) The killing and eating
of the paschal lamb. (2) The sprinkling of the blood upon the door-posts,
spoken of as a distinct thing, Heb. 11.
28, and peculiar to the first passover.
(3) The feast of unleavened bread for
seven days following. The details will
come before us as we proceed, to which
will be appended suitable moral reflections at the close.

CHAPTER XII.

AND the LORD spake unto Moses and Aaron in the land of Egypt, saying,

2 a This month *shall be* unto you the beginning of months: it *shall*

be the first month of the year to you.

3 ¶ Speak ye unto all the congregation of Israel, saying, In the tenth *day* of this month they shall take to them every man a lamb according to the house of *their* fathers, a lamb for an house:

a ch. 13. 4. Deut. 16. 1.

---

1. *And the Lord spake*, &c. Better rendered 'the Lord *had* spoken,' for this order was given anterior to Moses' last interview with Pharaoh, and probably prior to the three days' darkness, as is inferrible from the fact of the paschal lamb being required to be made ready the fourth day before it was killed. We suppose, therefore, that the above direction was given to Moses on the ninth or tenth day of the month when the Passover was immediately provided ; then followed the three days' darkness ; on the thirteenth Moses appeared for the last time before Pharaoh ; and on the fourteenth the Passover was eaten.

2. *This month shall be unto you the beginning of months.* Heb. ראש חדשים *rosh hodoshim, the head of months ;* not only first in order, but highest in estimation ; the chief and most excellent month of the year. This month had formerly been reckoned the seventh, but was henceforth to stand the first of the *ecclesiastical* year, while the *civil* year remained unaltered, commencing in Tisri or September. Thus Josephus : 'Moses appointed that Nisan should be the first month ; so that this month began the year, *as to all the solemnities they observed in honor of God*, although they preserved the original order of the mónths as to buying and selling, and other ordinary affairs.' This year had formerly begun from the middle of September ; it was henceforward to begin from the middle of March. This alteration of style was the special appointment of God, whose prerogative Antichrist usurps when he ' thinks to change times and laws.'

3. *Speak ye unto all the congregation of Israel.* Upon retiring from Pharaoh's presence Moses had undoubtedly withdrawn to the land of Goshen to make arrangements for the departure of his people, which he now saw to be close at hand. They had probably been gathering thither by degrees, and unconsciously perhaps forming themselves into an immense caravan, ready to move at an hour's warning. It is consequently to the 'congregation,' the assembled mass of Israel, that the order is here given, and there can be no doubt that the judgments recently exercised upon the Egyptians, with the manner in which their own affairs had been conducted, had for the present made the Israelites very tractable, and disposed them to receive and follow the directions of Moses with the utmost deference and respect The order for observing a religious ordinance in such circumstances as the Israelites were now in, in the midst of the hurry and bustle of their preparations for departure, teaches us that whatever the urgency of the business or cares that occupy us, still the claims of religion are paramount, and that *nothing* should crowd out the duties of worship and devotion from our minds.——¶ *Take to them every man a lamb.* Heb. שה *seh*, which implies either a *lamb* or a *kid*, as appears from v. 5.——¶ *According to the house of their fathers.* The whole host of Israel was divided into twelve *tribes ;* these tribes into *families ;* and the families into *houses ;* the last being composed of particular individuals. In one family, therefore, there might be several *houses.*

4 And if the household be too little for the lamb, let him and his neighbour next unto his house take it according to the number of the souls: every man according to his eating shall make your count for the lamb.

5 Your lamb shall be b without

b Lev. 22. 19, 20, 21. Mal. 1. 8, 14. Hebr. 9. 14. 1 Pet. 1. 19.

blemish, a male of the first year: ye shall take it out from the sheep or from the goats:

6 And ye shall keep it up until the c fourteenth day of the same month: and the whole assembly of the congregation of Israel shall kill it in the evening.

c Lev. 23. 5. Numb. 9. 3. & 28. 16. Deut. 16. 1, 6.

---

4. *According to the number of the souls.* As to the requisite number necessary to constitute what was termed the 'paschal society,' which Moses does not specify, some light is gathered from the following passage of Josephus: (J. W. B. 6. ch. 9. § 3.) 'These high-priests did so upon the coming of that feast which is called the Passover, when they slay their sacrifices, from the ninth hour till the eleventh; but so that a company of *not less than ten* belonged to every sacrifice: (for it is not lawful for them to feast singly by themselves;) and many of us are *twenty in a company.*' ——¶ *Every man according to his eating.* Heb. ארש לפי אכלו *ish lephi oklo, every man according to the mouth of his eating.* That is, in making out a suitable number to participate of the lamb, or form the paschal society, ye shall include every one who is capable of eating a certain quantity, to the exception of the sick, the very aged, and the very young. This quantity the Jewish writers say was to be equal to the size of an olive.

5. *Without blemish.* Heb. תמים *tamim, perfect;* i. e. entire, whole, sound, having neither defect nor redundancy of parts, unsoundness of members, or deformity of aspect. See this more fully explained, Lev. 22. 21—24. This has a typical reference to Christ, who is called, 1 Pet. 1. 19, 'A Lamb without blemish and without spot.'——¶ *A male of the first year.* Heb. בן שנה *ben shanah, son of a year.* A male, as being accounted more excellent than a female,

Mal. 1. 14; and of the first year, because it retains during that period its lamb-like harmlessness and simplicity. The phrase implies rather a lamb that falls somewhat short of a full year, than one that has reached it. It was probably taken at the age when its flesh was most tender and grateful.

6. *Ye shall keep it up.* Heb. והיה לכם למשמרת *ve-hayah lakem lemish-mereth, it shall be to you for a keeping, or reservation.* It was to be singled out from the rest of the flock on the tenth day of the month, and kept apart till the fourteenth, when it was to be slain.—— ¶ *The whole assembly of the congregation shall kill it.* Not that the whole assembly of the congregation were to kill one lamb, but each house their several lambs. As this however was to be done throughout the whole congregation, at the same time, it is spoken of as a single act, and the collective singular for the plural employed.——¶ *Shall kill it in the evening.* Heb. בין הערבים *ben ha-ar-bayim, between the two evenings.* That is, in the afternoon between the time of the sun's beginning to decline, which was called the first evening, and that of his setting, which was termed the second. The usual time doubtless was the middle point between noon and sunset, or about three o'clock in the afternoon. Thus Josephus, speaking of the Passover: 'They slay their sacrifices from the ninth hour (three o'clock) to the eleventh, (five o'clock.)' Thus also the Talmud: "They slew the daily (evening) sacrifice at the eighth hour

7 And they shall take of the blood, and strike *it* on the two side-posts, and on the upper door-post of the houses, wherein they shall eat it.

8 And they shall eat the flesh in that night, roast with fire, and ᵈ unleavened bread; *and* with bitter *herbs* they shall eat it.

ᵈ ch. 34. 25.　Deut. 16. 3.　Numb. 9. 11. 1 Cor. 5. 8.

---

and a-half, (or half past two,) and of-fered it up at the ninth hour and a-half, (or half past three.) But on the eve of the Passover they slew it at the seventh hour and a half, (or half past one,) and offered it up at the eighth hour and a half, (or half past two.)' And Maimonides informs us that the paschal lamb was slain and offered up immediately after the usual time of killing and offering up the evening sacrifice. In like manner our blessed Lord, who is the 'true Passover slain for us,' was condemned soon after the sixth hour, John, 19. 14; i. e. after our twelve at noon, and he died soon after the ninth hour, Mat. 27. 46. 50; i. e. after our three in the afternoon.

7. *Strike it on the two side-posts.* Which was done by means of the hyssop-branch. This was to be done as a mark of safety, a token of deliverance, that the destroying angel, when passing through the land to slay the first-born of the Egyptians, might see and *pass over* the houses of the Israelites, and spare their families. They were sinners as well as the Egyptians, and God might *justly* have punished them for their sins by taking away the lives of their first-born. But he was pleased to show them mercy, and accept the life of a lamb as a substitute. Its blood was the signal of this, and all who obeyed the command of God and relied on his protection, were secure from the stroke of the aveng'r. Nothing could be a more significant and striking emblem of the application of Christ's blood to the guilty conscience as the sole means of deliverance from the wrath to come. In him we have redemption through his blood. His is the true ' blood of sprinkling, which speaketh

better things than the blood of Abel.' It is better than the blood of the Pass-over-lamb, for it effects for us a far greater deliverance than that of the Israelites; it redeems us from the bondage of Satan and sin, from the fear of death and hell.——¶ *On the upper door-post of the houses.* Heb. עַל הַמַּשְׁקוֹף *al hammashkoph;* i. e. the lintel, or that part of the door-frame which lies across the door-posts over head. The Hebrew word in its radical signification denotes *looking,* and may here imply a part of the door-frame which was peculiarly *prominent* and *conspicuous,* which would naturally *be looked at.* Others, however, suppose, with perhaps more plausibility, that the term carries the import of *looking through,* and implies that the Egyptian houses had *lattices* or *windows* over their doors, through which it was customary for the inmates to look upon hearing a knock. It was not to be sprinkled upon the threshold, perhaps out of regard to its typical import, to intimate that the blood of Christ is not to be trodden under foot, or counted by any as an unholy thing.

8. *Roast with fire.* Because it could sooner be made ready by roasting than by boiling. This circumstance constituted a marked difference between the Passover-lamb and all the other peace-offerings, the flesh of which was usually boiled, in order to be eaten both by the people and the priests, as something additional even at the paschal solemnity. Wherefore in 2 Chron. 35. 13, the two kinds of offerings are accurately distinguished: 'And they roasted the passover with fire according to the ordinance: but the other holy offerings sod they in pots, and in caldrons, and in pans.' Whether any more satisfactory

9 Eat not of it raw, nor sodden at all with water, but e roast *with*

e Deut. 16. 7.

fire; his head with his legs, and with the purtenance thereof.

---

moral reason can be assigned for this order, than that the extremity of our Savior's sufferings from the fire of God's wrath might be thereby affectingly depicted, we pretend not to say.——¶ *With unleavened bread.* This also was ordered for the sake of expedition, Deut. 16. 3, as both Abraham and Lot, in preparing a hasty meal for their visiters, caused unleavened cakes to be made. The original term is supposed to be derived from a word signifying to *press, squeeze,* or *compress,* and is applied to bread destitute of the fermenting matter, because it has its parts closely *compressed* together, and becomes what we commonly call *heavy.* So, on the other hand, our English word 'leaven,' is formed from the French ' levain,' which is derived from the verb ' lever,' *to raise up,* the effect produced upon dough by *leaven* rendering the bread *light* and *spongy.* The use of unleavened bread as a perpetual observance in the paschal celebration may have been designed to remind the chosen people of their leaving Egypt in such haste as to be obliged to carry their unleavened dough with them. It is also not unreasonably to be inferred from one or two passages in the New Testament, that a mystical meaning was couched under this circumstance. Leaven is a *species of corruption,* caused by fermentation, and tending to putrefaction. For this reason it is said of our Savior, Luke, 12. 1, 'He began to say unto his disciples first of all, Beware ye of the *leaven* of the Pharisees, which is hypocrisy.' Paul also in 1 Cor. 5. 7, 8, says, 'Purge out therefore the *old leaven ;* for Christ our passover is sacrificed for us; therefore let us keep the feast, not with the old *leaven,* neither with the *leaven* of malice and wickedness; but with the *unleavened bread* of sincerity and truth.'——¶ *With*

bitter herbs. Heb. מררים *merorim,* *bitters,* or *bitternesses.* That is, with bitter things, bitter ingredients ; alluding doubtless to herbs, such as *succory,* or *wild lettuce,* as it is rendered in the Vulgate, although some commentators have imagined that not herbs, but a *bitter* or *sour sauce,* like that mentioned by the Evangelist in which Jesus dipped the sop which he gave to Judas, John, 13. 26, is meant. But this is less likely, as the Talmudists enumerate the different species of herbs allowed to be eaten with the paschal lamb, among which were the *lettuce,* the *endive,* the *horehound,* &c. In modern times, in England and some other northern countries, we are told that *horse-radish* is used. The Israelites were probably commanded to eat these bitter herbs on this occasion in remembrance of their afflictions in Egypt, where their lives had been made *bitter.*

9. *Eat not of it raw.* That is, half-roasted, or superficially done, having some of the blood remaining in it. With the express prohibition, Gen. 9. 4, against eating blood before them, they scarcely needed to be warned against eating flesh absolutely *raw.* But in the hurry with which the first passover was observed, and with so great a number of paschal lambs, it might easily happen that some of them would be but imperfectly done, unless specially admonished on that score.——¶ *Nor sodden at all with water.* Not boiled at all. *Sodden* is the past participle of *seethe,* *to boil.* Should it be deemed superfluous to say ' sodden, or boiled, *with water,'* there being no other way supposable in which the flesh of animals would be boiled, it may be observed in reply, that the Heb. word בשל *bashal* is applied both to *roasting* and *boiling,* and Moses, in order to take away the

10 fAnd ye shall let nothing of it remain until the morning: and that which remaineth of it until the morning ye shall burn with fire.

f ch. 23. 18. & 34. 25.

11 ¶And thus ye shall eat it; *with* your loins girded, your shoes on your feet, and your staff in your hand: and ye shall eat it in haste; g it *is* the LORD's passover.

g Deut. 16. 5.

---

ambiguity, adds the specification 'with water;' as also in naming its opposite in the next clause, he says, 'roast *with fire.*——¶ *With the purtenance thereof.* Heb. קרבו עַל *al kirbo, with his midst, or inwards ;* meaning that the lamb was to be roasted whole and entire. Neither the head nor the legs were to be separated, nor the intestines removed. It may be supposed however that these last simply included the *heart, lungs, liver, kidneys,* &c. and not the intestinal canal.

1. *Ye shall let nothing of it remain.* Lest it should be appropriated to a superstitious use, and also to prevent putrefaction; for it was not meet that a thing offered to God should be subjected to corruption, which in such hot countries it must speedily undergo. Thus the body of our Lord 'saw no corruption,' Ps. 16. 10, Acts, 2. 17, and it was his body which was prefigured by the paschal lamb.

11. *With your loins girded.* 'That is, as persons prepared for a journey. The inhabitants of the East usually wear long and loose dresses, which, however convenient in postures of ease and repose, would form a serious obstruction in walking or in any laborious exertion, were not some expedients resorted to, such as those which we find noticed in Scripture. Thus the Persians and Turks, when journeying on horseback tuck their skirts into a large pair of trousers, as the poorer sort also do when travelling on foot. But the usage of the Arabs, who do not generally use trousers, is more analogous to the practice described in the Bible by 'girding up the loins.' It consists in drawing up the skirts of the vest and fastening

them to the girdle, so as to leave the leg and knee unembarrassed when in motion. An Arab's dress consists generally of a coarse shirt and a woollen mantle. The shirt, which is very wide and loose, is compressed about the waist by a strong girdle generally of leather, the cloak being worn loose on ordinary occasions. But in journeying or other exertion, the cloak also is usually confined by a girdle to which the skirts are drawn up and fastened. When manual exertion is required, the long hanging sleeves of the skirt are also disposed of by the ends of both being tied together and thrown over the neck, the sleeves themselves being at the same time tucked high up the arm.' *Pict. Bib.*—— ¶ *Shoes on your feet.* 'This was another circumstance of preparation for a journey. At the present time Orientals do not, under ordinary circumstances, eat with their shoes or sandals on their feet, nor indeed do they wear them indoors at all. This arises not only from the ceremonial politeness connected with the act of sitting unshod; but from the fear of soiling the fine carpets with which their rooms are covered. Besides, as they sit on the ground cross-legged, or on their heels, shoes or sandals on their feet would be inconvenient. To eat therefore with sandalled or shod feet is as decided a mark of preparation for a journey as could well be indicated. But perhaps a still better illustration is derived from the fact, that the ancient Egyptians, like the modern Arabs, did not ordinarily wear either shoes or sandals. In their sculptures and paintings very few figures occur with sandalled feet; and as we may presume, that in the course of 215 yea s

12 For I h will pass through the land of Egypt this night, and will smite all the first-born in the land

h ch. 11. 4, 5.   Amos 5. 17.

of Egypt, both man and beast: and i against all the gods of Egypt I will execute judgment: k I *am* the LORD.

i Numb. 33. 4.   k ch. 6, 2.

the Israelites had adopted this and other customs of the Egyptians, we may understand that (except by the priests) sandals were only used during journeys, which would render their eating the passover with sandalled feet, a still stronger mark of preparation than even the previous alternative.' *Pict. Bible.* It does not appear that the directions given in this verse were held to be binding in the subsequent observance of the paschal rite. It is clear, at least, that our Savior and his Apostles celebrated the Passover in a *sitting* or *recumbent* posture, denoting ease and security, the contrary of the urgent haste of the Israelites on this occasion.——¶ *It is the Lord's passover.* Heb. פסח *pesah*, *leap*, or *transition*. So called from the figurative destroying angel's *passing over* the blood-marked houses of the Israelites. The legitimate signification of the original is to *leap* or *skip over.* A phraseology constructed with reference to this incident occurs Amos, 7. 8, ' I will not pass by them any more ;' i. e. I will not grant them exemption any more ; intimating how often he had passed by them, as now, while his judgments were abroad. Gr. πασχα.

12. *I will pass through the land of Egypt.* That is, in the infliction of my wrath. Chal, 'I will reveal myself in the land of Egypt.' Arab. 'I will make manifest my Angel.' Thus Amos, 5. 17, 'And in all vineyards shall be wailing ; for *I will pass through thee,* saith the Lord ;' i. e. in desolating judgment.——¶ *Against all the gods of Egypt I will execute judgment.* Heb. בכל אלהים *bekol Elohim*, by which may be meant not only the objects of their idolatrous worship, but also the *princes* or *grandees* of the nation. Probably the most appropriate sense of the term is the

general one of *powers, principalities, dignities,* whatever in fine constituted the grand objects of their dependence, whether divine or human. Arab. 'All the objects of adoration.' These should all, by the stupendous judgments of this night, be turned to confusion together, and their votaries covered with indelible shame. What could be a more signal infliction upon the gods of Egypt than the complete exposure of their impotence to aid their worshippers in a time of need? We have elsewhere but a single allusion to this incident of the divine visitation, and that is not of a nature to afford us any help to a more minute explanation. Num. 33. 4, 'For the Egyptians buried all their first-born, which the Lord had smitten among them ; upon their *gods* also the Lord executed judgments.' There is a tradition among the Jewish doctors, which may be well founded, that the *idols* or the Egyptians were on that night demolished. Thus Pirke Eliezer, ch. 48, 'When Israel came out of Egypt, what did the holy blessed God do? He threw down all the images of their abominations, and they were broken in pieces. Targ. Jon. 'Their molten images were dissolved and melted down, their images of stone were dashed in pieces, their images made of earth were crumbled into bits, and their wooden ones reduced to ashes.' Artapanus in Prep. Evang. of Eusebius, l. 9. c. 27, goes so far as to affirm, that most of the Egyptian temples were overthrown on this occasion and from the allusion in Isaiah, ch. 19. 1, to the idols of Egypt being *moved* at the Lord's presence, the idea is perhaps not ill founded. It would be a singular fact should the truth prove to be that the traces of violent wrenchings and disruptions, now so evident in the

13 And the blood shall be to you for a token upon the houses where ye *are:* and when I see the blood, I will pass over you, and the plague shall not be upon you to destroy *you,* when I smite the land of Egypt.

14 And this day shall be unto you ¹ for a memorial; and ye shall keep it a ᵐ feast to the Lord throughout your generations: ye shall keep it a feast ⁿ by an ordinance for- ever.

¹ ch. 13. 9.   ᵐ Lev. 23. 4, 5.   2 Kings 23. 21.
ⁿ ver. 24. 43. & ch. 13. 10.

massy ruins of the temples of Upper and Lower Egypt, should have happen- ed at the very time of which we are now speaking.

13. *When I see the blood, I will pass over you.* Heb. פסחתי *pasahti;* the original word from which פסח *pesah, passover* is derived, and a different one from that rendered ' pass through,' in the preceding verse. Gr. σκεπασω υμας, *I will protect you.* Chal. I will com- miseràte, or spare you.'——¶ *To des- troy you.* Heb. למשחרת *lemashith, for a corruption or destruction.——* ¶ *Ye shall keep it a feast to the Lord.* Heb. חגתם אתו חג *haggothem otho hag, ye shall festivally keep it a feast.* ——¶ *By an ordinance for ever.* Heb. חקת עולם *hukkath olam, a statute of eternity;* one to be observed as long as the legal economy should subsist.

15. *Seven days shall ye eat,* &c. That is, seven days commencing on the day after the killing of the passover, or the fifteenth day of the month. The feast of unleavened bread was in fact a distinct ordinance from the passover, though following immediately upon it. This law respecting the feast of unleavened bread, though given *before* the depar- ture from Egypt, seems not to have gone into effect till *after* it.——¶ *Ye shall put away.* Heb. תשביתו *tashbi- thu, ye shall cause to cease.* Gr. αφα- νιειτε, *ye shall abolish or cause to dis- appear.* 'This was probably to com- memorate the fact that the Israelites left Egypt in such haste, that they had no opportunity to leaven their dough (v. 39), and were consequently obliged, ın the first instance, to eat unleavened cakes, (Deut. 16. 3). The present in-

junction is even now attended to by modern Jews with the most scrupulous precision. The master of the family searches every corner of the house with a candle, lest any crumb of leavened bread should remain, and whatever is found is committed to the fire ; and after all, apprehending that some may still remain, he prays to God that, if any leaven be still in the house, it may be- come like the dust of the ground. Ex- traordinary precautions are also used in preparing the unleavened bread, lest there should be any thing like leaven mixed with it, or any kind of fermenta- tion take place in it. See Jennings' ' Jewish Antiquities.' Two distinct words are employed to signify 'leaven' in this verse, the former of which שאר *seor,* properly imports *leaving* or *re- mainder,* and is rendered by Ainsworth, the most exact of all translators, 'old leaven,' to which Paul alludes, 1 Cor. 5· 7, 'Purge out therefore the *old leaven,'* &c. The other חומץ *hometz,* is so called from a word signifying *sourness.* The terms, perhaps, have allusion to a two-fold species of spiritual leaven, the one hidden and secret, or hypocrisy, Luke, 12. 1, the other *open malice* and *wickedness,* Cor. 5. 8, or *wicked persons,* as David, Ps. 71. 4, calls the malicious and unrighteous man, חומץ *hometz, a leavener,* though rendered in our trans- lation 'cruel man.' Thus also Ps. 73. 21, he terms the heart infected with er- ror and filled with vexation, 'leavened,' although our version has 'grieved.'—— ¶ *That soul shall be cut off.* Shall be excommunicated from the society and privileges of the chosen people, either by the public act of the proper officers,

15 ᵒSeven days shall ye eat un-leavened bread; even the first day ye shall put away leaven out of your houses: for whosoever eateth leavened bread, from the first day until the seventh day, ᵖthat soul shall be cut off from Israel.

16 And in the first day *there shall be* ᑫan holy convocation, and in the seventh day there shall be a holy convocation to you: no manner of work shall be done in them, save *that* which every man must eat, that only may be done of you.

17 And ye shall observe *the feast of* unleavened bread; for ʳin this self-same day have I brought your armies out of the land of Egypt: therefore shall ye observe this day in your generations by an ordinance for ever.

ᵒch. 13. 6, 7. & 23. 15. & 34. 18, 25. Lev. 23. 5, 6. Numb. 28. 17. Deut. 16. 3, 8. 1 Cor. 5. 7. ᵖGen. 17. 14. Numb. 9. 13. ᑫLev. 23. 7, 8. Numb. 28. 18, 25. ʳch. 13. 3.

18 ¶ ˢIn the first *month*, on the fourteenth day of the month at even, ye shall eat unleavened bread, un-til the one and twentieth day of the month at even.

19 ᵗSeven days shall there be no leaven found in your houses: for whosoever eateth that which is leavened, ᵘeven that soul shall be cut off from the congregation of Israel, whether he be a stranger, or born in the land.

20 Ye shall eat nothing leavened: in all your habitations shall ye eat unleavened bread.

21 ¶ Then Moses called for all the elders of Israel, and said unto them, ˣDraw out, and take you a lamb, according to your families, and kill the passover.

ˢLev. 23. 5. Numb. 28. 16. ᵗExod. 23. 15. & 34. 18. Deut. 16. 3. 1 Cor. 5. 7, 8. ᵘNumb. 9. 13. ˣver. 3. Numb. 9. 4. Josh. 5. 10. 2 Kings 23. 21. Ezra 6. 20. Matt. 26. 18, 19. Mark 14. 12,—16. Luke 22. 7, &c.

---

or by the direct hand of God himself. See Note on Gen. 17. 14.

16. *An holy convocation.* Heb. מקרא קדש *mikra kodesh, a convocation of holiness.* By the prohibition of secular work, it appears that these days were to be regarded as proper sabbaths, with the exception that on these days meat might be dressed, which was unlawful on the Sabbath, Ex. 16. 23, 24. The original for 'convocation' comes from a verb קרא *kara,* signifying *to call, to make proclamation,* and implies the summoning the people together by the sound of the trumpet, as is intimated Num. 10. 2, 'Make thee two trumpets of silver—that thou mayest use them for the *calling* of the people ;' the same word as that here rendered ' convoca-tion.'——¶ *Save that which every man must eat.* Heb. כל נפש *kol nephesh, every soul ;* i. e. every person. See Note on Gen. 14. 21.

17. *In this self same day.* Heb. בעצם היום הזה *be etzem hă-yom hazzeh, in*

the strength or bone of this day. See Note on Gen. 7. 13.——¶ *Have I brought,* &c. As the deliverance of the Israel-ites had not yet been actually accom-plished, this phraseology is doubtless adopted on the ground of the certainty of the event in the view of the divine mind, and as the matter of his promise.

18. *Ye shall eat.* Ye shall begin to eat.

19. *Whether he be a stranger or born in the land.* As ' strangers,' strictly so called, or foreigners, were not permitted to partake of the Passover unless pre-viously converted and circumcised, v. 43, 44, the word must here be under-stood of gentile proselytes in contra-distinction from native-born Israelites.

21. *Draw out and take you a lamb.* Heb. משכו *mishk'u.* Draw out from the folds. Of this word, which is fre-quently employed in the sense of *draft-ing* or *making a levy,* see a full expla-nation in the Note on Judg. 4. 6.—— ¶ *Kill the passover.* That is, the lamb

22 ʸ And ye shall take a bunch of hyssop, and dip *it* in the blood that *is* in the bason, and ᶻ strike the lintel and the two side-posts with the blood that *is* in the bason : and none of you shall go out at the door of his house until the morning.

23 ᵃ For the LORD will pass through to smite the Egyptians; and when he seeth the blood upon the lintel, and on the two side-posts, the LORD will pass over the door, and ᵇ will not suffer ᶜ the destroyer to

y Hebr. 11. 28. z ver. 7. a ver. 12. 13. b Ezek. 9. 6. Rev. 7. 3. & 9. 4. c 2 Sam. 24. 16. 1 Cor. 10. 10. Hebr. 11. 28.

come in unto your houses to smite *you.*

24 And ye shall observe this thing for an ordinance to thee and to thy sons for ever.

25 And it shall come to pass, when ye be come to the land which the LORD will give you, ᵈ according as he hath promised, that ye shall keep this service.

26 ᵉ And it shall come to pass, when your children shall say unto you, What mean ye by this service?

d ch. 3. 8, 17. e ch. 13. 8, 14. Deut. 32. 7. Josh. 4. 6. Ps. 78. 6.

---

of the Passover; the animal slain being called, by a figure of speech, by the name of the institution of which it constituted a leading feature. In accordance with this, we often meet with the phrase 'to eat the Passover,' 'to prepare the Passover,' &c.; and in like manner the word ' covenant' is used for the sacrifice offered in making the covenant; the 'rock' that followed the Israelites 'was Christ;' and the 'bread and wine' of the sacrament are the ' body and blood' of Christ.

22. *Ye shall take a branch of hyssop.* A plant growing about a foot and a half high, having bushy stalks, terminated by spikes of flowers, and leaves of an aromatic smell, and warm, pungent taste. It grows in great plenty on the mountains near Jerusalem. From its growing in bunches, and putting out many suckers from a single root, it was well adapted to the purpose here mentioned, as also for purifications of different kinds.——¶ *None of you shall go out.* This injunction seems also peculiar to this first Passover, as the reason for it did not exist afterwards. In allusion to this language the prophet says, Isa. 26. 20, 'Come, my people, enter thou into thy chambers, and shut thy doors about thee; hide thyself as it were for a little moment, until the indignation be overpast.' Those who ex-

pect God's salvation must abide by the terms on which he has declared it his purpose to grant it.

23. *When he seeth the blood,* &c. No destroyer can smite unless God first grant him a commission. And the Most High always recognises his own mark upon those who bear it, and while they are 'passed over' and spared in the visitation of his wrath, all others must expect to fall under the stroke of his breath.——¶ *Will not suffer the destroyer to come in,* &c. By this is generally understood *a destroying angel.* But as the term 'angel' is often employed figuratively as a personification of divine judgments, we have no question that this is the preferable sense here. But as the subject has already been fully discussed in another place (Note on Ex. 3. 2.), it will be unnecessary to recite the arguments again in connexion with this passage.

25. *Ye shall keep this service.* That is, with the exception of those circumstances of the ordinance which in their own nature were confined to the first instance of its celebration.

26. *When your children say unto you, What mean ye by this service?* Heb מה העברה הזאת לכם *mah ha-abodah hazzoth lakem, what this service to you?* i. e. what does it signify? The annual observance of this ceremony was well

27 That ye shall say, f It *is* the sacrifice of the LORD's passover, who passed over the houses of the children of Israel in Egypt, when he smote the Egyptians, and delivered our houses. And the people g bowed the head and worshipped.

28 And the children of Israel went away, and h did as the LORD had

f ver. 11.   g ch. 4. 31.   h Hebr. 11. 28.

commanded Moses and Aaron, so did they.

29 ¶ i And it came to pass, that at midnight k the LORD smote all the first-born in the land of Egypt, l from the first-born of Pharaoh that sat on his throne, unto the first-born of the captive that *was* in the

i ch. 11. 4. k Numb. 8. 17. & 33. 4. Ps. 78. 51. & 105. 36. & 135. 8. & 136. 10. l ch. 4. 23. & 11. 5.

calculated to secure the perpetual remembrance of the events which it celebrated. The various rites and usages connected with it were so peculiar, they made such an inroad upon the ordinary routine of domestic life, that the curiosity of children would be naturally arrested, and they would be led to inquire into the reasons of such strange proceedings. This would afford to parents the opportunity to acquaint their offspring with the origin and import of the solemn service, and to impart to them all those related instructions which were so important to be received into their opening minds. The inquisitiveness of children when it flows in this channel, prompting them to learn the reasons of religious services and the meaning of the various solemn ordinances which they behold, is always to be encouraged. Indeed we see not how pious parents at this day can take their children to witness the common ordinances of the Christian Church, viz. baptism and the Lord's supper, and consider their duty discharged without explaining to them the nature of those solemn rites, and endeavoring to impress upon their minds the duties and obligations which they involve.

27. *The people bowed the head and worshipped.* That is, when all these informations and instructions were communicated to them by the elders; for it seems from v. 21, that Moses' address was made to the people through the elders.

28. *And the children of Israel went away and did as the Lord commanded.* This was a very proper sequel to the professions implied in their bowing and worshipping. Unless followed by a prompt and candid obedience our acts of external reverence are a 'bodily exercise that profiteth little.'

29. *At midnight the Lord smote all the first-born,* &c. Had this judgment been executed by an angel, it would have been natural for the writer here to have said that the angel went forth at midnight and smote all the first-born of the Egyptians, both of men and cattle. But it is ascribed directly to the Most High himself, as no doubt it is to be understood. Indeed it is difficult, if not impossible, to conceive of such an effect wrought at one and the same time all over Egypt by the agency of a single angel. We are obliged to conceive of him in this work as passing from house to house in at least successive moments of time, and as we may suppose that there were many thousands slain, we see not how they could all have been said to perish at the hour of midnight, as they undoubtedly did. On the whole there can be no question we think that the judgment in v. 23, is personified. But how shall we adequately conceive of the complicated horrors of that fearful night? The groans of the dying, mingled with the shrieks of the living, broke in upon the stillness of the night, and from the imperial palace to the **poorest hovel, lamentation and mourn-**

dungeon; and all the first-born of cattle.

30 And Pharaoh rose up in the night, he, and all his servants, and all the Egyptians; and there was a ^mgreat cry in Egypt: for *there was* not a house where *there was* not one dead.

m ch. 11. 6. Prov. 21. 13. Amos 5. 17. Jam. 2. 13.

ing and woe were heard throughout the length and breadth of the land! Three days and three nights previously they had been wrapped in gloomy darkness, even darkness which might be felt, and no one had risen up that night from his place. But now they were aroused from their beds to render what aid they could, though all in vain, to their expiring children and brothers and sisters. The blow was universal and irresistible. There was no discharge in that warfare, and no respect of persons in the indiscriminate destruction of the appointed victims. All the first-born, from man in the vigor of manhood to the infant which had just been born, died in that hour of death. The stay, the comfort, the delight of every family was annihilated at a single stroke! And how natural was it for them in such a scene of carnage to fancy that they were all doomed to destruction, and that the work of death would not cease till they had all perished? But let us not fail to recognise the righteous retribution, as well as the awful terrors of the Almighty in this visitation. The Egyptians had killed the children of the Lord's people, and now their own children die before their eyes. Israelitish mothers had wept over the cruel deaths of their infants, and now Egyptian mothers wept for the same woe. Upwards of eighty years before had that persecution begun, but the Lord visits the iniquities of the fathers upon the third and fourth generation of them that hate him, and now the day of his vengeance and recompense was come. The cry of these slaughtered innocents had risen up, 'How long, O Lord holy and true, dost thou not judge and avenge our blood?' A book of remembrance had

been written, space for repentance had been afforded, warnings had been given; but all had been unavailing, and now nought remained but that justice should do its desolating work. And similar will the issue be with those who after their impenitent hearts treasure up wrath against the day of wrath. If they turn not he will whet his glittering sword, and a great ransom will not then deliver them.

30. *Not a house where there was not one dead.* As it is somewhat difficult to suppose that in *every* house in Egypt every first-born child was still alive, the present expression is probably to be taken with some qualification. We may either suppose ' house' in this case equivalent to ' family,' or the phrase may be classed with those *absolute* modes of speech which are yet to be understood *comparatively.* We have already noticed a striking usage of this kind in what is said of 'all the cattle,' and 'all the herbs,' in ch. 10. 15. In fact the universal negative or affirmative terms 'none' and 'all' are very frequently to be understood with exceptions, especially when such exceptions are so few as scarcely to deserve notice when compared with the cases in which the proposition holds good. Thus it is said, Ps. 53. 3, 'There is none that doeth good;' i. e. scarcely any one. So Jer 5. 1, 'Run ye to and fro through the streets of Jerusalem, and see now, and know, and seek in the broad places thereof, if ye can find a man, if there be any that executeth judgment, that seeketh the truth;' which has a strong negative implication, and yet we cannot doubt that there were actually pious men then living in Jerusalem, especially the prophets. On the same princi-

31 ¶ And [n] he called for Moses and Aaron by night, and said, Rise up, *and* get you forth from among my people, [o] both ye and the children of Israel: and go, serve the LORD, as ye have said.

32 [p] Also take your flocks and your herds, as ye have said, and be gone: and [q] bless me also.

33 [r] And the Egyptians were urgent upon the people, that they might send them out of the land in haste; for they said, [s] We *be* all dead *men.*

[n] ch. 11. 1. Ps. 105. 38. [o] ch. 10. 9. [p] ch. 10. 26. [q] Gen. 27. 34. [r] ch. 11. 8. Ps 105. 38 [s] Gen. 20. 3.

ple it is said 1 Sam. 25. 1, 'And Samuel died; and all the Israelites were gathered together and lamented him, and buried him;' i. e. the body of the nation; not in the most literal sense every individual. In like manner, John, 12. 19, 'The Pharisees therefore said among themselves, Perceive ye how ye avail nothing? behold, the world is gone after him:' i. e. the great mass of the people. We may suppose therefore that all that is implied in the present case is, that nearly every house in Egypt had one or more slain in it.

31. *Called for Moses and Aaron.* As Moses had before this withdrawn from the presence of Pharaoh, with the determination to see his face no more, this must be understood to mean that Pharaoh sent his servants or deputies to Moses and Aaron, and thus communicated his message to them. See Note on Gen. 49. 1. This was a striking fulfilment of Moses' previous declaration, ch. 11. 8, and clearly proving that he then spake under a divine impulse; 'And all these thy servants shall come down unto me, and bow down themselves unto me, saying, Get thee out, and all the people that follow thee.'

32. *Also take your flocks*, &c. Pharaoh's pride is now effectually humbled, and he surrenders at discretion. He yields unreservedly to all that Moses had insisted on, and even betrays so much of a guilty conscience as to beg an interest in his prayers; for this is evidently to be understood by the request that Moses would bless him also. He desired that Moses would bless him by invoking the blessing of God upon him. Chal. 'Pray for me also,' Arab. 'Cause me to receive indulgence.' The oppressor is here taught that the Israel of God is not only a *blessed*, but a *blessing* people, and that it is highly desirable to have the benefit of their intercessions. Yet the sequel shows clearly that even now he was not penitent. He submitted not in heart, nor sincerely humbled himself before God. He let them go by constraint and most unwillingly. He would still have held out if he had dared, and he yielded only because he could oppose no longer. He made a forced show of obedience, but his heart was as hard and rebellious as ever.

33. *And the Egyptians were urgent.* Heb. ותחזק מצרים *vattehezak Mitzraim, and Egypt was strong upon them;* the same word in the original with that which is, for the most part, applied to the *hardening* (strengthening) of Pharaoh's heart, implying a most vehement, pressing urgency. Gr. κατεβιαζοντο. Ps 105. 38, 'Egypt was glad when they departed: for the fear of them fell upon them.' Jerus. Targ. 'The Egyptians said, If Israel tarry one hour, lo, all the Egyptians are dead men.' For ought they knew, the plague they had experienced might be but the precursor of another still more dreadful, that would sweep off the whole population in a mass. 'When death comes into our houses, it is seasonable for us to think of our own mortality. Are our relations dead? It is easy to infer thence that we are dying, and in effect already dead men.' *Henry.*

34 And the people took their dough before it was leavened, their kneading troughs being bound up in their clothes upon their shoulders. 35 And the children of Israel did according to the word of Moses: and they borrowed of the Egyptians ^tjewels of silver, and jewels of gold, and raiment.

t ch. 3. 22. & 11. 2.

34. *Their kneading-troughs being bound up,* &c. Heb. מִשְׁאֲרֹתָם *misharotham,* prop. *relics.* Targ. Jon. 'What was left of the unleavened bread and the bitter herbs;' with which Jarchi concurs. The Gr. varies, rendering it τα φυραματα, *lumps of dough,* for which it is not easy to determine their authority. The Hebrew term is supposed to signify both the *dough* and the *vessel* in which it was contained; and it is probable that the dough was wrapped in some kind of covering cloth, or thrown into some kind of sack, as the word rendered 'clothes' denotes any thing which covers a substance, or wherein it is wrapped. Arab. 'Their cold mass of dough being bound up in towels, and put on their shoulders.' We learn indeed from the reports of modern travellers that the vessels which some of the oriental tribes make use of for kneading the unleavened cakes while travelling in the desert, are *small wooden bowls,* in which they both knead their bread, and afterward serve up their provisions when cooked; yet Dr. Pocock informs us that the Arabs not unfrequently carry their dough in something else, and gives a description of a *round leather coverlid,* which they lay on the ground, and from off which they eat, having a number of rings round it, by which it is drawn together with a chain, terminating in a hook to hang it by. This is drawn together, and they sometimes carry in it their *meal made into dough;* and in this manner they bring it full of bread; and when the repast is over, carry it all away at once. Which of these two kinds of vessels is meant in this place cannot easily be ascertained, but there is no question that some other **term than 'kneading-troughs' ought to** be adopted. The habit is very natural of identifying oriental utensils with our own when the same name is given to both, although the ideas thus acquired are often extremely incorrect.

35. *They borrowed of the Egyptians jewels,* &c. 'Dr. Boothroyd, instead of borrow, translates 'ask.' Dr. A. Clarke says, 'request, demand, require.' The Israelites wished to go three days' journey into the wilderness, that they might hold a feast unto the Lord. When the Orientals go to their sacred festivals, they always put on their *best jewels.* Not to appear before the gods in such a way, they consider would be disgraceful to themselves and displeasing to the deities. A person, whose clothes or jewels are indifferent, will *borrow* of his richer neighbors; and nothing is more common than to see poor people standing before the temples, or engaged in sacred ceremonies, well adorned with jewels. The almost pauper bride or bridegroom at a marriage may often be seen decked with gems of the most costly kind, which have been *borrowed* for the occasion. It fully accords therefore, with the idea of what is due at a sacred or social feast, to be thus adorned in their best attire. Under these circumstances, it would be perfectly easy to *borrow* of the Egyptians their jewels, as they themselves, in their festivals, would doubtless wear the same things. It is also recorded the Lord gave them 'favor in the sight of the Egyptians. It does not appear to have been *fully* known to the Hebrews, that they were going finally to leave Egypt: they might expect to return; and it is almost certain that, if their oppressors had known they were not to return, they would not have *lent* them their jewels.' *Roberts*

36 ᵘ And the LORD gave the people favour in the sight of the Egyptians, so that they lent unto them *such things as they required :* and ˣ they spoiled the Egyptians.

37 ¶ And ʸ the children of Israel

ᵘ ch. 3. 21. & 11. 3.   ˣ Gen. 15. 14. ch. 3. 22. Ps. 105. 37.   ʸ Numb. 33. 3, 5.

---

36. *They lent unto them.* Heb. וַיַּשְׁאִלֻם *va-yashilum, caused them to ask.* That is, their deportment toward the Israelites was such, they were so extremely anxious for their departure, and evinced such a promptitude in furthering it, that a *strong inducement* was held out to them to *ask* for the articles which they received.——¶ *Spoiled the Egyptians.* This was in fulfilment of the promise made to Abraham, Gen. 15. 14, 'They shall come out with great substance.' Israel came into Egypt few in numbers, weak, and indigent; but they go out from the land of their oppressors greatly increased, mighty, and formidable; laden with the spoils of their cruel oppressors, the well-earned reward of the labors of many years, and of much sorrow. In allusion, perhaps, to this event, God says by the prophet Ezekiel, ch. 39. 10, 'And they shall *spoil* those that *spoiled* them, and rob them that robbed them, saith the Lord God.' See Note on Ex. 3. 22.

37. *Journeyed from Rameses to Succoth.* Heb. יִסְעוּ *yisu.* The primitive meaning of נָסַע *nasa,* is *to pluck out, to pull up or out,* being especially applied to *pulling up* the stakes or pins by which the tents of the nomades were fastened to the earth, and which was done by the way of preparing for migration to another place. Hence the secondary meaning of *departing, journeying, proceeding,* &c. Rameses was one of those cities which the Israelites, ch. 1. 11, are said to have built for Pharaoh. It was probably in the land of Goshen, and was made on this occasion the place of general rendezvous before their departure. Professor Stuart has

journeyed from ᶻ Rameses to Succoth, about ᵃ six hundred thousand on foot *that were* men, beside children.

38 And a mixed multitude went up also with them ; and flocks, and herds, *even* very much cattle.

ᶻ Gen. 47. 11.   ᵃ Gen. 12. 2. & 46. 3. ch. 38. 26.   Numb. 1. 46. & 11. 21.

---

given very plausible reasons for believing that this place occupied the site of the ruins of Aboukeyshid, lying about half way, or forty miles from Suez. Succoth signifies *tents* or *tent-places,* and does not necessarily imply the existence of a *town* of this name in ancient times ; at any rate, no remains of such an one are found at the present time in the desert, or any of the routes from the Nile to Suez. Nothing more is necessary than to suppose Succoth to be an ordinary *encamping-place* for caravans between Rameses (Aboukeyshid) and Suez, for those who took the direct route. The original word comes from a root signifying to *hide, cover, defend,* and this was the design of those temporary tenements made of the boughs of trees, in which the Israelites lodged at this station, and in memory of which they were required, as a standing ordinance, to keep the 'feast of tabernacles' once every year.——¶ *About six hundred thousand men.* Heb. גִּבֹּרִם *geborim, strong men.* If we compute the whole number of Israelites, male and female, adult persons and children, and allow the proportion of four to one between the number of the whole nation and those who were fit to bear arms, it will give an aggregate of two millions four hundred thousand souls which went out of Egypt with Moses and Aaron. Of this immense multitude the Psalmist says, Ps. 105. 37, ' He brought them forth also with silver and gold: and there was not one feeble person among all their tribes.'

38. *A mixed multitude.* Heb. עֵרֶב רַב *ereb rab, a great mixture ;* a multitude composed of strangers, partly

39 And they baked unleavened cakes of the dough which they brought forth out of Egypt, for it was not leavened : because b they were thrust out of Egypt, and could not tarry, neither had they prepared for themselves any victual.

40 ¶ Now the sojourning of the children of Israel who dwelt in Egypt, *was* c four hundred and thirty years.

b ch. 6. 1. & 11. 1. & ver. 33.   c Gen. 15. 13. Acts 7. 6.   Gal. 3. 17.

41 And it came to pass, at the end of the four hundred and thirty years, even the self-same day it came to pass, that all d the hosts of the LORD went out from the land of Egypt.

42 It *is* e a night to be much observed unto the LORD, for bringing them out from the land of Egypt : this *is* that night of the LORD to be observed of all the children of Israel in their generations.

d ch. 7. 4. & ver. 51.   e See Deut. 16. 6.

Egyptians, and partly natives of other countries, who had been prevailed upon by the miracles wrought in behalf of the Israelites, and from other motives, to embark with them in the present enterprise of leaving Egypt. Thus Zech. 8. 23, 'In those days it shall come to pass that ten men shall take hold out of all languages of the nations, even shall take hold of the skirt of him that is a Jew, saying, We will go with you, for we have heard that God is with you.' It can hardly be supposed, however, that the major part of them were prompted by considerations so creditable to their piety. Self-interest was, no doubt, the moving spring with the great mass. Some of them were probably Egyptians of the poorer class, who were in hopes to better their condition in some way, or had other good reasons for leaving Egypt. Others were perhaps foreign slaves belonging both to the Hebrews and Egyptians, who were glad to take the opportunity of escaping with the Israelites. Others again were a mere rude restless mob, a company of hangers-on, that followed the crowd they scarcely knew why, perhaps made up of such vagabonds, adventurers, and debtors, as could no longer stay safely in Egypt. Whoever or whatever they were, the Israelites were no better for their presence, and like thousands in all ages that turn their faces towards Zion, and run well for a time, when

they came to experience a little of the hardships of the way, they quitted the people of God and returned to Egypt.

40. *Now the sojourning,* &c. The following is a more accurate version of the original ; 'Now the sojourning of the children of Israel which they sojourned in Egypt was four hundred and twenty years.' The date of this event is to be reckoned probably from the time that Abraham received the promise, Gen. 15. 13, which makes just 430 years, as detailed in the Note in loc. From the time that Jacob and his sons came into Egypt to that of the deliverance, was only 215 years. The phrase, 'children of Israel,' is to be taken therefore in a somewhat larger sense than usual, as equivalent to 'Hebrews,' and of them it might properly be said, that they were sojourners in a land that was not theirs, either Canaan or Egypt, for the space of time here mentioned. Unless we consider the words as comprehending their fathers, Abraham, Isaac, and Jacob, we cannot include in them Israel himself, who was the person that brought them into Egypt, and lived there with his family for the space of seventeen years.

41. *Even the self-same day.* Implying probably that the time corresponded *to a day* with the period predicted.

42. *A night to be much observed.* Heb. לֵיל שִׁמֻּרִים *lēl shimmurim, a night of observations.* That is, a night to be

43 ¶ And the LORD said unto Moses and Aaron, This *is* f the ordinance of the passover: there shall no stranger eat thereof:

44 But every man's servant that is bought for money, when thou hast g circumcised him, then shall he eat thereof.

45 h A foreigner, and a hired servant, shall not eat thereof.

46 In one house shall it be eaten; thou shalt not carry forth aught of the flesh abroad out of the house: i neither shall ye break a bone thereof.

47 k All the congregation of Israel shall keep it.

f Numb. 9. 14. g Gen. 17. 12, 13. h Lev. 22. 10. i Numb. 9. 12. John 19. 33, 36. k ver. 6. Numb. 9. 13.

48 And, when a stranger shall sojourn with thee, and will keep the passover to the LORD, let all his males be circumcised, and then let him come near and keep it; and he shall be as one that is born in the land: for no uncircumcised person shall eat thereof.

49 m One law shall be to him that is home-born, and unto the stranger that sojourneth among you.

50 Thus did all the children of Israel; as the LORD commanded Moses and Aaron, so did they.

51 n And it came to pass the selfsame day, *that* the LORD did bring the children of Israel out of the land of Egypt o by their armies.

l Numb. 9. 14. m Numb. 9. 14. & 15. 15, 16. Gal. 3. 28. n ver. 41. o ch. 6. 26.

accounted peculiarly memorable, bringing with it the recollection of an event never to be forgotten, and awakening sentiments of unfeigned gratitude to their Almighty Deliverer.

43. *The Lord said.* Rather, 'the Lord *had* said,' probably on the same occasion as that on which he instituted the Passover; at any rate, at some time previous to the departure from Egypt.
——¶ *There shall no stranger eat thereof.* That is, while he continues a stranger or alien, unproselyted and uncircumcised. By parity of reasoning it is to be supposed that all who had proved themselves *apostate* from their religion were in like manner to be interdicted.

45. *A foreigner.* Heb. תושב *toshab,* a dweller, an inhabitant. This was a term applied to those pious gentiles who, without embracing the Jewish religion, renounced idolatry and took up their abode with the chosen people— a privilege which was not allowed to foreigners who still continued idolaters. Maimonides observes of such persons, that they might dwell in any part of Judea except Jerusalem, from which they

were excluded on account of its preeminent sanctity.

46. *In one house shall it be eaten.* That is, each paschal lamb was to be eaten by the requisite company or number, and consequently not divided into two or more parts to be eaten in different houses, but all that ate of it were to eat together in one house. This was for the sake of fellowship, that they might rejoice together, and edify one another while eating of it. Chal. 'In one society shall ye eat it.'——¶ *Neither shall ye break a bone thereof.* There is something in this precept which doubtless has a prospective reference to Christ our Passover, of whom the Evangelist tells us, John, 19. 33—36, that his legs were providentially prevented from being broken, in order 'that the Scriptures might be fulfilled, A bone of him shall not be broken.' So the Psalmist, Ps. 34. 20. 'He keepeth all his bones; not one of them is broken.'

49. *One law shall be to him,* &c. The enlarged and liberal spirit of the Hebrew system appears very strikingly in these regulations. Any stranger might be incorporated into the nation by con-

forming to the rites of their religion, and thereby become entitled to all the privileges of the native-born Jew. In order to this, it was proper that they should make themselves debtors to the law in its burthens, for in God's economy *privileges* and *duties* always go together. The provision was calculated at the same time to afford hope to the Gentile and to moderate the self-complacency of the Israelite.

REMARKS.—A positive institution so directly from heaven, and one so closely connected by typical relations with an event of infinitely greater importance, as the Passover, may well be supposed to be fraught with a richness of moral import demanding the most serious attention.

1. The ordinance may be viewed in reference to the *discriminating* circumstances in which it was established. God was now about to make a terrible display of his righteous indignation. The destroying angel had, as it were, received his commission, and stood prepared to pass through Egypt. But a people in covenant with the Lord, and to whom his mercy was promised; who had avouched him for their God, and cried to him for deliverance, were mingled with the multitude of Egypt; and amid the terrors of the approaching desolation, how could they escape? Some mode must be devised by which the angel, as he went his midnight round of death, might know that the Lord had put a difference between the Egyptians and Israel; so that while one was smitten, the other might be left in safety. A lamb therefore was to be slain; its blood to be sprinkled upon the lintels and side-posts of their doors; and the Lord promised that when he saw the blood, he would stay the plague from destroying them. In like manner the sentence of death has gone forth against an ungodly world. But in the midst of its condemned transgressors there is a covenant people whom he has

engaged to spare. How then shall the distinction be made between them and the careless, godless world, who mock at and neglect the warnings and denunciations of heaven? The Israel of God is composed of fallen, guilty creatures, who are by nature the children of wrath, even as others. In themselves considered they do not *deserve* exemption, and are placed in the pathway of the divine anger, as the dwellers in Goshen would have been, if they had remained unmarked for safety. But lo! the Paschal Lamb is slain! The Lord Christ by his one oblation of himself once offered, makes a full, perfect, and sufficient sacrifice and satisfaction for the sins of the whole world. He lays down his life for the sheep. They are sprinkled by his blood, sealed by his spirit, and interested by faith in the blessings of his covenant. When the Lord therefore proceeds to execute judgment upon impenitent transgressors, he views them as they are in Christ Jesus, looks in mercy towards them, and saves them from eternal death. Would we avoid the doom?—let us have recourse to the remedy. The blood of the lamb did not save the Israelites by being shed, but by being sprinkled. In the same manner, it is not the blood of Christ as shed on Calvary, but as sprinkled on the soul, that saves us from the wrath to come. We must, as it were, dip the hyssop in the blood, and by faith apply it to our own hearts and consciences, or we can have no benefit from it, no interest in it.

2. We may consider the *essential qualities of the victim*, and the manner in which it was to be treated. (1.) It was to be a lamb, the most innocent and gentle of all animals—in the idea and language of all nations, but another name for gentleness, harmlessness, and simplicity. This meek and unresisting creature was to be early removed from its fond mother's side, deprived of liberty, and destined to bleed by the sacri-

ficing knife. Who can think of its plaintive bleating during the days of separation, without emotion? What Israelitish heart so insensible as not to be melted at the thought, that his own life, and the comfort of his family, were to cost the life of that inoffensive little creature whom he had shut up for the slaughter, and which, in unsuspecting confidence, licked the hand lifted to shed its blood? (2.) It was to be a lamb of the first year, and without blemish. If it bore the mark of any deformity, or even of any defect, it would have been a forbidden sacrifice, as well as a victim unfit to represent the Lamb slain for sinners from the foundation of the world. How beautiful is the harmony between the type and the antitype! 'We are redeemed with the precious blood of Christ, as of a lamb without blemish and without spot.' (3.) It was to be set apart four days before it was slain ; not only to mark the previous designation of Christ, to be a sacrifice, but perhaps also, as has been suggested, to foreshow that he should, during the four last days of his life, be examined at different tribunals to ascertain whether there was the smallest flaw in his character, that so his bitterest enemies might all be constrained to attest his innocence, and thereby unwittingly to declare, that he was fit to be a sacrifice for the sins of the whole world. (4.) When slain and prepared, the lamb was to be eaten by *all* the Israelites at the same time, and by each party in one house. The victim was slain for all, because all were partners in the same danger, and all were to be indebted to the same mode of deliverance. And it was not to be divided and carried to different houses, when two households joined in one lamb, in order to keep up the idea of *unity* in the general observance of the ceremony. The nation appears, therefore, in the paschal solemnity as a beautiful and instructive representation of the great, united, harmonious family

of God, who are 'one body, one spirit, and are called in one hope of their calling ;' 'who have one Lord, one faith, one baptism.'

3. We may consider the *attendant circumstances* of the institution. (1.) The passover was to be eaten with unleavened bread and bitter herbs. The herbs were meant primarily to awaken the remembrance of the bitter bondage to which they had been subject in Egypt ; but besides this they were intended to show the necessity of penitence for sin, and to shadow forth the hardships and trials which await along the chequered path of the Lord's pilgrims in their journey to the Canaan of rest. And it is as impossible spiritually to partake of Jesus Christ, the Paschal Lamb of our salvation, without abiding godly sorrow for sin, and a sacred resolve to take up our cross and bear it cheerfully in the trials of life, as it is to bring light and darkness, east and west together. Equally impossible is it to partake of the mercies of the Son of God, while the leaven of any iniquity is indulged and cherished within our hearts. Let not Demas imagine that he may embrace the world, and hold the Savior. Let not Ananias and Sapphira suppose that they may keep back any part of that which they have solemnly dedicated to God, and yet be his true friends and servants. Let every one that nameth the name of Christ, as the refuge of his soul, depart from iniquity. As the scrupulous Israelites searched with lighted candles every hidden corner and dark recess of their houses for any latent particle of leaven, so let our language be, 'Search me, O God, and know my heart; try me, and know my thoughts, and see if there be any wicked way in me, and lead me in the way everlasting.' (2.) It was to be eaten in a standing posture with their loins girded, their shoes on their feet, and their staves in their hands, ready to depart at a moment's warning. These

CHAPTER XIII.

A ND the LORD spake unto Moses, saying,

2 ᵃ Sanctify unto me all the first·

ᵃ ver. 12. 13, 15. ch. 22. 29, 30. & 34. 19
Lev. 27. 26. Numb. 3. 13. & 8. 16, 17. & 18.
15. Deut. 15. 19. Luke 2. 23.

were to them memorial circumstances, connected with the haste and suddenness of their exit. But to us they speak an emphatic language; 'Arise ye and depart, for this is not your rest.' 'Here we have no abiding city, but look for one to come.' 'Now we desire a better country, even an heavenly.' 'Arise, and let us go hence.' (3.) Not a bone of the paschal lamb was to be broken. The primary moral drift of the injunction seems to be, that what has once been offered to God is not to be unnecessarily disfigured or mangled. The blood must be shed, for that was the seal of the covenant; the flesh might be eaten for it was given for the sustenance of man's life; but the bones forming no part either of food or sacrifice, were to be left in their original state till consumed by fire with the remainder of the flesh, if any remained, in the morning. At the same time we cannot doubt that there was an ulterior allusion in this commanded circumstance of the paschal rite. 'But when the soldiers came to Jesus, and saw that he was dead already, they broke not his legs.' It is clear from what follows, that the Evangelist regarded the precept of the law as a prophecy of Christ; 'For these things are done that the Scripture should be fulfilled, A bone of him shall not be broken;' as if a special Providence had watched over the crucifixion of the Savior to secure his sacred person from maiming, and thus bring about the fulfilment of the prediction.

Chapter 13

1. *And the Lord spake unto Moses.* From v. 15, it would appear that this precept was founded upon the fact of the preservation of Israel's first-born when the first-born of the Egyptians were slain. To perpetuate the remem-

brance of that remarkable event, and in token of their gratitude for it, their first-born, in all ages, were to be consecrated to God as his peculiar portion, and if re-appropriated to themselves, it could only be done on the ground of certain redemptions prescribed in v. 13.

2. *Sanctify unto me all the first-born,* &c. Let them be *set apart, consecrated hallowed* to me. See the import of the term more fully explained in the Note on Gen. 2. 3. God, as the universal Creator, is of course the universal Proprietor of all his creatures, and might justly lay claim to the most absolute and unreserved dedication of *all* the progeny of men and brutes to himself. But in the present case he was pleased to restrict this *more peculiar sanctification* to the first-born, as being especially his on the ground of their protection and exemption from the destroying judgment which had swept off the first-born of the Egyptians. As he had in this fact shown to them a distinguishing mercy, he was pleased to make it the occasion of a standing acknowledgment to that effect on the part of his people. As he had spared their first-born, who were the joy, the hope, and the stay of their families, so it was fitting, as an evidence of their grateful love to their heavenly benefactor, that they should recognise as paramount his title to what he had graciously spared them, and should cheerfully resign to him who is First and Best, what was dearest and most valuable to themselves. And it is by this test that we are to determine the measure of our love to God. Does he stand so high in our affections that we are willing for his sake to part with what we love best in this world? It is only by losing sight of all the claims of infinite beneficence, and becoming deaf to the dictates of every tender and gen-

born, whatsoever openeth the womb among the children of Israel, *both* of man and of beast: it *is* mine.

3 ¶ And Moses said unto the people, ᵇRemember this day, in which ye came out from Egypt, out of the

ᵇ ch. 12. 42. Deut. 16. 3.

house of bondage; for ᶜ by strength of hand the LORD brought you out from this *place:* ᵈ there shall no leavened bread be eaten.

4 ᵉ This day came ye out, in the month Abib.

ᶜ ch. 6. 1.   ᵈ ch. 12. 8.   ᵉ ch. 23. 15. & 34 18. Deut. 16. 1.

---

erous emotion, that we can suffer ourselves to offer to the Most High the blind, the maimed, or the halt for sacrifice, or to serve him with that which costs us nothing. In accordance with this character of *sanctity* pertaining to the first-born, the redeemed in heaven are called ' the church of the *first-born,*' and Christ himself is the '*first-born* among many brethren.' We find indeed that at a subsequent period, Num. 3. 12, the divine Lawgiver saw fit to ordain a commutation, by which one whole tribe out of the twelve came into the room of the first-born of every tribe, as an order of priests to minister to him in holy things, which was otherwise one of the rights of primogeniture ; and at any time the privilege of redemption was allowed in certain terms, Num. 18. 15—17; but neither of these provisions were to operate in such a way as to weaken the force of the moral considerations connected with the ordinance.

3. *Remember this day,* &c. Heb. זכור *zakor,* which has the import not merely of *mental recollection,* but of *actual celebration,* or of some kind of public proceeding which should serve as a perpetuating memorial of a particular event. See Note on Ex. 20. 8. The reason of this was not merely the favor shown to them in such a signal deliverance, but the display it involved of the divine interposition, and obviously the more of God and of his power there is in any deliverance, the more memorable it is.——¶ *Out of the house of bondage.* Heb. מבית עבדים *mibbeth abadim, out of the house of servants ;* i. e. from a condition of the most severe and de-

grading bondage ; for which reason they are said elsewhere to have been brought forth ' from the furnace of iron ;' Deut. 4. 20. 1 Kings, 8. 51. Jer. 11. 4.——¶ *By strength of hand,* &c. Heb. בחזק יד *behozek yad.* As God had previously announced to Moses, Ex. 3. 19, ' I am sure that the king of Egypt will not let you go, no, not by a *strong hand* (ביד חזקה *beyad hazakah*),' where the accompanying note shows that the meaning is, *except* or *unless* by a strong hand. As the original term is the same as that applied in several instances to the *hardening* of Pharaoh's heart (see Note on Ex. 4, 21.), there is a tacit antithetical allusion to that event, implying that however *hard* or *strong* the impious king made his heart, God made his hand still *stronger.* This is one of those nice shades of meaning which cannot well be conveyed in a translation. See Note on Ex. 12. 33.——¶ *There shall no leavened bread be eaten.* This mode of rendering overlooks the true syntactical structure of the sentence, which is to be read thus ; 'Remember this day in which ye came out from Egypt, out of the house of bondage ; for by strength of hand the Lord brought you out of this place (so) that there should no unleavened bread be eaten ;' i. e. under such circumstances as gave rise to the ordinance that no unleavened bread should be eaten.

4. *In the month Abib.* That is, in the month of *green corn,* which is the true import of the word *Abib.* The Chaldee name of this month was *Nisan,* corresponding to part of our March and part of April. See Note on Ex. 9. 31. Gr.

5 ¶ And it shall be when the LORD shall f bring thee into the land of the Canaanites, and the Hittites, and the Amorites, and the Hivites, and the Jebusites, which he g sware unto thy fathers to give thee, a land flowing with milk and honey; h that thou shalt keep this service in this month.

6 i Seven days shalt thou eat unleavened bread, and in the seventh day *shall be* a feast to the LORD.

7 Unleavened bread shall be eat-

f ch. 3. 8.   g ch. 6. 8.   h ch. 12. 25, 26.   i ch. 12. 15, 16.

en seven days: and there shall k no leavened bread be seen with thee, neither shall there be leaven seen with thee in all thy quarters.

8 ¶ And thou shalt l shew thy son in that day, saying, *This is done* because of that *which* the LORD did unto me when I came forth out of Egypt.

9 And it shall be for m a sign unto thee upon thine hand, and for a memorial between thine eyes; that

k ch. 12. 19.   l ver. 14. ch. 12. 26.   m See ver. 16. ch. 12. 14.   Numb. 15. 39.   Deut. 6 8. & 11. 18.   Prov. 1. 9.   Isai. 49. 16.   Jer. 22. 24.   Matt. 23. 5.

Vulg. Chal. and Sam. 'In the month of new fruits.' Syr. 'In the month of flowers.' Arab. ' In the month when corn has ears.'

5. *When the Lord shall bring,* &c. Provision is here made for the permanent remembrance of the great event of the nation's exodus from Egypt. The present injunction prescribes the observance of the rite after their settlement in the land of promise, and we learn that they kept only one passover during their forty years sojourn in the wilderness. It was omitted probably because circumcision was omitted during that time, which was an indispensable prerequisite to the passover.

8. *Thou shalt show thy son,* &c. The most sedulous care in instructing their children in the rites and ceremonies of their religion, and in the reasons on which they were founded, is frequently enjoined upon parents throughout the Mosaic narrative. The Psalmist also speaks of it, Ps. 78. 5—8, as a positive institution among his people ; ' For he established a testimony in Jacob, and appointed a law in Israel, which he commanded our fathers, that they should make them known to their children: That the generation to come might know them, even the children which should be born : who should arise and declare them to their children : that they might

set their hope in God, and not forget the works of God, but keep his commandments : and might not be as their fathers, a stubborn and rebellious generation ; a generation that set not their heart aright, and whose spirit was not steadfast with God.' No one can fail to infer from this the great importance of acquainting children at an early age with the leading stories of sacred writ, and familiarising their minds with the moral lessons which they are designed to teach. It is a debt which we owe to the honor of God and to the benefit of their souls, to tell them of the great things which God has in former ages, or in our own age, done for his church, or is still doing. Nor should parents consider themselves released from this duty because their children can read these narratives for themselves, or hear them recited and explained by Sunday School teachers. They are things *to be talked about* in the family circle, which is the grand nursery of God's appointment for the training of the infant mind, and where the tender heart of childhood is most easily to be reached.

9. *It shall be for a sign unto thee upon thine hand,* &c. It may be doubted whether this is to be understood as a mere metaphorical expression or as a literal injunction. The Jewish commentators are generally of opinion that the

the LORD's law may be in thy mouth : for with a strong hand hath the LORD brought thee out of Egypt.

10 ⁿ Thou shalt therefore keep this ordinance in his season from year to year.

11 ¶ And it shall be when the LORD shall bring thee into the land

ⁿ ch. 12. 14, 24.

words of the precept concerning the sanctification of the first-born were to be written on shreds of linen or parchment, and worn on their wrists and foreheads. These where the 'Phylacteries,' or *scrolls of parchment*, with portions of the law written upon them, of which our Savior speaks, Mat. 23. 5, as distinguishing, when made uncommonly broad, the hypocritical Scribes and Pharisees. It is not improbable, however, that the precept here is only figurative, implying that the remembrance of God's goodness should be continually cherished, that it should no more be lost sight of than is an object appended to the hand or hanging between the eyes. Thus Prov. 3. 3, 'Bind them about thy neck ; write them upon the table of thine heart ;' i. e. have them in perpetual remembrance. That this was a proverbial mode of speech appears from the following passages among others, Hag. 2. 23, 'In that day will I make thee *as a signet ;* for I have chosen thee, saith the Lord.' Cant. 8. 6, 'Set me *as a seal* upon thy heart, as a seal upon thine arm.' Comp. Deut. 6. 6—9, with Note.——¶ *That the Lord's law may be in thy mouth.* That is, that it may be familiar to thee ; that thou mayest frequently speak of it, both in order to affect thine own heart, and to instruct others. See Note on Josh. 1. 8.

10. *From year to year.* Heb. מימים רמימה *mi-yamim yamimah, from days onward to days.* An instance of the frequent usage by which *days* is employed for *years*, particularly in the language of prophecy. Chal. 'From time to time.' This throws light upon the words of Dan. 4. 25, 35, written also in Chaldaic, 'Seven *times* shall pass over thee ;' i. e. seven years.

of the Canaanites, as he sware unto thee and to thy fathers, and shall give it thee ;

12 º That thou shalt set apart unto the LORD all that openeth the matrix ; and every firstling that cometh of a beast which thou hast, the males *shall be* the LORD's.

º ver. 2. ch. 22. 29, & 34. 19. Lev. 27. 26. Numb. 8. 17. & 18. 15. Deut. 15. 19. Ezek. 44. 30.

11. *And it shall be,* &c. We have here a repetition, with some additional circumstances, of the precept respecting the separation and dedication of the first-born to God, after they should have become fixed in the land of their destined inheritance. During their sojourn in the desert the strict observance of this and some other of their national laws appears to have been dispensed with.

12. *Thou shalt set apart.* Heb. העברת *ha-abarta, thou shalt make to pass over;* i. e. from thine own power and possession ; thou shalt make a transfer of it. This term, therefore, may be considered as explanatory of the term 'sanctify,' v. 2.—— ¶ *That openeth the matrix.* The Hebrew expression is the same with that in v. 2.——¶ *And every firstling.* Rather 'even every firstling,' as the precept, as here repeated, has respect primarily to the first-born of beasts, and not of men. The firstlings of clean beasts, such as calves, lambs, and kids, if males, were to be dedicated to God, and used in sacrifice. These were not to be redeemed. Their blood must be sprinkled on the altar, and their fat consumed upon it ; while their flesh belonged to the priest, who used it as his share of the sacrifice, Num. 18. 17, 18. But the first born of unclean beasts, as the ass's colt, for instance,

13 And P every firstling of an ass thou shalt redeem with a lamb; and if thou wilt not redeem it, then thou shalt break his neck: and all the first-born of man among thy children q shalt thou redeem.

P ch. 34. 20. Numb. 18. 15, 16. q Numb. 3. 46, 47. & 18. 15, 16.

though due to God in virtue of this law of consecration, yet, as they could not be offered in sacrifice, were either to be redeemed or killed. Comp. Num. 18. 15.

13. *Every firstling of an ass thou shalt redeem with a lamb.* Or with a kid, as the original equally signifies. This lamb or kid was to be given to the Lord through the priest, Num. 18. 8, 15, and then the owner of the ass might appropriate it to his own use, which otherwise he would not be at liberty to do. There is no doubt that the spirit of the law applied also to other animals, as the horse, the camel, &c., but the ass alone is specified, because the Israelites had scarcely any other beast of burden, and if they had, one species would serve as a representative of all others.——¶ *Thou shalt break his neck.* Heb. עָרַפְתּוֹ *araphto.* The original is defined in the Lexicon *to break the neck,* but it seems more properly to express the act of *decollation,* or *cutting off the neck* (i. e. *the head*), in which sense it is plainly used, Deut. 21. 4, 'And the elders of that city shall *strike off the heifer's neck* (עָרְפוּ *arephu*) there in the valley.' Is. 66. 3, 'He that sacrificeth a lamb, as if he *cut off a dog's neck* (עֹרֵף *oreph*).' The reason of the law was undoubtedly this, that whatever had been once solemnly devoted to God was ever after to be considered as clothed with such a peculiar sanctity as forbade its being put to any other use. —— ¶ *All the first-born of man among thy children shalt thou redeem.* The law of this redemption is more specifically given Num. 18. 16, where it

14 ¶ r And it shall be when thy son asketh thee in time to come, saying, What *is* this? that thou shalt say unto him, s By strength of hand the LORD brought us out from Egypt, from the house of bondage:

r ch. 12. 26. Deut. 6. 20. Josh. 4. 6, 21. s ver. 3,

appears that it was fixed at five shekels. Comp. also Num. 3. 46, 47. The redemption of a child took place when it was a month old. If it died sooner, the parents were not obliged to redeem it It died as it were to God, to whom it previously belonged.

14. *It shall be when thy son asketh thee,* &c. Again the duty of instructing children in the import of these sacred rites is inculcated. It is supposed that when they saw all the firstlings thus devoted, they would ask the meaning of it, and this their parents were required to explain to them, teaching them that God's special claim to their first-born and all their firstlings, was founded in his gracious preservation of *them* from the sword of the destroying angel. This feature of the Mosaic economy was calculated to have a powerful practical effect upon the eldest sons of every family; for when they were taught that they themselves had been redeemed by their parents according to the divine appointment, they could scarcely fail to perceive that peculiar obligations rested upon them to walk worthy of that hallowed preeminence with which they were invested in God's estimation. But if this was the impression produced by this statute on the minds of Jewish children, how should Christians be affected with the consideration, that they have been redeemed, not with corruptible things, as silver and gold, like the first-born of Israel, but with the precious blood of Christ, as of a lamb without blemish and without spot? —— ¶ *By strength of hand the Lord brought us out of Egypt.* This

15 And it came to pass, when Pharaoh would hardly let us go, that ᵗ the LORD slew all the first-born in the land of Egypt, both the first-born of man, and the first-born of beast: therefore I sacrifice to the LORD all that openeth the matrix, being males; but all the first-born of my children I redeem.

16 And it shall be for ᵘ a token upon thy hand, and for frontlets be-

tween thine eyes: for by strength of hand the LORD brought us forth out of Egypt.

17 ¶ And it came to pass, when Pharaoh had let the people go, that God led them not *through* the way of the land of the Philistines, although that *was* near; for God said, Lest peradventure the people ˣ repent when they see war, and ʸ they return to Egypt:

ᵗ ch. 12. 29.　ᵘ ver. 9.

ˣ ch. 14. 11, 12. Numb. 14. 1,—4. ʸ Deut. 17. 16.

allusion to 'the strong hand' by which the Lord brought his people out of Egypt occurs again and again, in order the more to magnify the power of God by setting it in contrast with the opposition that was made to it. To the latest generations of Israel the language here cited was to be used, and it will be observed that it is a mode of speech which teaches the children to consider whatever was done to their *fathers* as in effect done to *themselves;* they were to conceive themselves as having existed in the persons of their progenitors. Accordingly the Psalmist says, Ps. 66. 6. 'They went through the flood on foot: there did *we* rejoice in him.' Hos. 12. 4. 'He found him in Bethel, and there he spake with *us*.' In accordance with this, the Hebrew canons say, ' That throughout all generations a man is bound to show (demean) himself as if he in person came out from the bondage of Egypt, as it is written, *And he brought* us *out*, &c. And for this cause the holy blessed God hath commanded in the law, *and then shalt remember that* THOU *wast a servant,*' Deut. 15. 5.

15. *When Pharaoh would hardly let us go.* Heb. 'When Pharaoh hardened (himself) against sending us out.'

16. *It shall be for a token upon thine hand.* This is to be considered as a continuation of the instruction which parents were to give to their children, and not directly the words of Moses or of God. They were, after explaining

the grounds of the institution in question, to enjoin upon them to cherish the memory of the great event with the most sacred fidelity.——¶ *Frontlets between thine eyes.* These were parchment labels containing several passages of the law, worn upon the forehead and the left arm; called from the Greek φυλακτηρια *observatories* or *preservatories,* from a root signifying to *keep, guard, preserve.* A fuller account of them is given hereafter. See Note on Deut. 6. 8. The remark made on v. 9, is applicable here also, viz. that nothing more is necessarily implied by this language, than that they were to have these things as familiar to their minds and lips *as if* they were literally appended in the form of frontlets and phylacteries to their heads or arms.

17. *And it came to pass,* &c. As Palestine was the country which formed the final destination of Israel, and as they were now on their march thither, we should naturally suppose that the shortest and easiest route would have been selected. This was a route laying along the coast of the Mediterranean, and forming to this day the usual caravan track from Egypt to Gaza. Travelling by this road they might easily have accomplished the distance in five days, had infinite wisdom no special purposes to effect by a longer delay. But the nearest way to rest is not always that which God sees to be best for his people, and the sequel shows us that in the

present instance there was ample reason for a departure from the usual route. To say nothing of the divine purposes relative to the drowning of the Egyptians in the Red Sea, and the humbling and proving of the Israelites by a protracted sojourn in the wilderness, they could not enter Canaan by the direct route without encountering the Philistines, who then occupied all its southern borders. These Philistines were a powerful and warlike nation, between whom and the Israelites there seems to have been an ancient grudge existing, from a circumstance mentioned 1 Chron. 7. 21, 22, 'And Zabad his son, and Shuthelah his son, and Ezer, and Elead, whom the men of Gath (Philistines) that were born in that land slew, because they came down to take away their cattle. And Ephraim, their father, mourned many days, and his brethren came to comfort him.' God could indeed with infinite ease have crushed all opposition from this or any other quarter, and have carried his people triumphantly through every obstacle, as he had abundantly shown in bringing them out of Egypt. But he saw fit to make no useless display of miraculous power, or exempt his people from the necessity of using the ordinary means of avoiding danger, notwithstanding his omnipotence was pledged to their defence. He therefore uses all the precaution of a wise and provident leader, as if apprehensive that his people, however numerous, being but little accustomed to the use of arms, and just emerging from a state of enervating servitude, would be unable, at the first onset, to face an active foe, and therefore deemed it necessary to inure them gradually to warlike exercises before exposing them to the perils of battle. To avoid, therefore, the perils which were to be anticipated in this quarter, Moses is directed to take another far more circuitous and difficult route ' by the way of the wilderness of the Red Sea.' We

say that Moses was *directed* in this, for the circumstances clearly evince that he could have been no self-appointed lawgiver, leading forth the Israelites from Egypt of his own motion, but that he all along acted under divine dictation and control. Bad as the alternative was of passing through the territories of the Philistines, yet in the eye of mere human prudence, the other was scarcely more feasible. Moses had long fed the flocks of Jethro in that very desert, and he must have been well aware that it afforded no resources for the subsistence of such a vast host of men, women, and children, and cattle, as he was now leading thither. Had he not then been acting under a divine commission, we can see that he had merely a choice of difficulties both apparently insurmountable ; on the one hand, war, without any reasonable prospect of success ; on the other, starvation in the desert. With this alternative before him, would not any worldly politician have preferred fighting to starving? At any rate, how can it be imagined that if Moses possessed one half the talent which his enemies concede to him, he could have entertained such a project as that of conducting the Israelites out of Egypt, without previously well considering whither he would lead them? Nothing affords a solution of the course which he took on this occasion but the fact that he was supernaturally directed in every movement, and with this key to his conduct all his plain. It was God's will that the Red Sea route should be taken, because he foresaw that if the other were taken, the Israelites instead of standing the shock of war would have retreated ignominiously before the enemy, and have sought refuge in that very bondage from which they had so recently escaped, and by which they had become so unfitted for warlike encounters. The hard bondage in mortar and brick, and in all manner of rigorous and degrading service in the field, was not the school

18 But God z led the people about, *through* the way of the wilderness

z ch. 14. 2. Numb. 33. 6, &c.

of the Red sea: and the children of Israel went up harnessed out of the land of Egypt.

in which the lessons of ardent courage and overcoming enterprise were to be learned. Slavery necessarily and fearfully debases the mind, and makes it incapable of great or noble exertion. The iron of such a state had entered deeply into the souls, no less than it painfully galled the limbs, of the Israelites. That the result *would have been* precisely what is here intimated, no one can doubt who considers what the fact actually *was* when their spirit came to be put to the test at the subsequent periods of their history. The report of the faithless spies threw them into a panic of fear, and prompted them to cry out, 'Would God that we had died in the land of Egypt, or would God that we had died in this wilderness.' Thus too when the armies of Pharaoh pursued them and the Red Sea lay before them, they exclaimed in an agony of alarm, 'Is not this the word that we did tell thee in Egypt saying, Let us alone that we may serve the Egyptians.' So also on experiencing the first pressure of want, they cried, 'Would that we had died by the hand of the Lord in the land of Egypt, when we sat by the flesh-pots, and when we did eat bread to the full.' These then were not combatants who could be depended upon to open for themselves a way through the armies of the Philistines, and God who knew the frame of their spirits much better than they did themselves, graciously spared them a conflict to which he saw they were unequal. In like manner the infinitely wise and gracious God consults the weakness of his people in the earlier stages of their Christian course, and spares them the trials and contests which would be too much for them. His mercy tempers their burdens to their strength, and *gradually* accustoms his soldiers and servants to the diffi-

culties of their warfare. They are first trained to contend with weaker enemies before they are called to encounter stronger ones, and by having their graces *exercised* rather than *oppressed*, they are enabled to go on from strength to strength, till they are finally qualified to wield the whole armor of God. In the mean time he who will not over-drive the tender lambs lest they should die of fatigue, expressly assures us that he will not suffer us to be tempted above that we are able to bear, and that as our day is so shall our strength be also.

18. *The Red Sea.* As this is one of the most remarkable waters mentioned in the geography of the Scriptures, it may be proper here to give a more particular description of its general features. This we do in the words of the Editor of the *Pict. Bible.* ' It occupies a basin, in general deep and rocky, and extends about 1160 miles in length, from north to south, with a mean breadth which may be stated at 120 miles. Throughout this great extent it does not receive the waters of a single river. The western coast is of a bolder character, and has a greater depth of water than the eastern. The gulf abounds in sunken rocks, sand-banks, and small islands, together with numerous coral-reefs, which in some places rise above the water to the height of ten fathoms. The bottom is covered abundantly with the same substance, as well as with marine plants, which in calm weather give that appearance of submarine forests and verdant meadows to which the sea probably owes its Hebrew name of Yam Suph (see Nóte on chap. 2. 3.), as well as its present Arab name of Bahr Souf· Burckhardt observes, that the coral is red in the inlet of Akaba, and white in that of Suez. The remarkably beautiful appearance which this sea exhibits

has attracted notice in all ages; and among its other characteristics, the far more than ordinary phosphorescence of its waters has been mentioned with peculiar admiration. The width of the gulf contracts towards its extremities, and at its mouth is considerably narrower than in any other part. The strait of Bab-el-Mandeb is there formed, and does not exceed fourteen miles in breadth; beside which it is divided, at the distance of three miles from the Arabian shore, by the island of Perim. The high land of Africa and the peak of Azab give a remarkably bold appearance to the shore in this part. At its northern extremity the Red Sea separates into two minor gulfs or inlets, which inclose between them the peninsula of Sinai. The easternmost of these is that of Akaba or Ailah, called by the Greeks and Romans Ælanites; this is only about half the extent of the other, and is rendered very dangerous by shoals and coral-reefs. The westernmost gulf is called the gulf of Suez, anciently, Heeropolites: the ancient and modern names of both inlets being from towns that formerly did, or do now, stand at their extremities. It is the latter, the western gulf, which was crossed by the Hebrews. It is about 160 miles in length, with a mean breadth of about thirty miles, narrowing very much at its northern extremity. The mean depth of its water is from nine to fourteen fathoms, with a sandy bottom; and it is of much safer navigation than the other. There are many indications which place it beyond a doubt that the Arabian Gulf was formerly much more extensive and deeper than at present. One of the most certain proofs of this is, that cities, which were formerly mentioned as sea-ports, are now considerably inland. This is particularly the case in the Gulf of Suez, where the shore is unusually low. That the sea formerly extended more northward than at present, there is much reason to conclude, not only

from the marine appearances of the now dry soil, but from this fact, among others, that Kolsoum, which was formerly a port, is now three-quarters of a mile inland. There is certainly nothing in the appearance of the soil about the isthmus of Suez to discountenance the hypothesis that the Red Sea was formerly no other than a strait uniting the Mediterranean with the Indian Ocean; and that the isthmus which is now interposed between the Red Sea and the Mediterranean was formed by drifts of sand from the adjoining deserts. This, however, is an hypothesis: but there is nothing hypothetical in the statement that the gulf once extended more to the north than at present; and this fact is of importance, because it enables us to see that nothing less than a miraculous interposition of the Divine Power could have enabled the Israelites to cross the bay even at the highest of the points which has been selected by those who perhaps were influenced by the wish to diminish the force of the miracle, or to account for it on natural principles.'——.

¶ *Went up harnessed.* Heb. חמשׁים *hamushim.* Marg. 'By five in a rank.' But this cannot well be considered the true rendering, for at this rate if we allow the ranks to be but three feet asunder, the 600,000 fighting men alone would have formed a procession sixty miles in length; and if we add to them the remainder of the host, the line would have extended, by the direct route, from Egypt quite into the limits of the land of Canaan. The Greek renders it, ' in the fifth generation;' but plainly erroneously, as the promise to Abraham, Gen. 15. 16, was, that they should come out in the *fourth* generation. Other versions render it diversely by 'marching in array'—'in military order'—'armed' —'well panoplied'—'girded'—'marshalled by fives'—'by fifties,' &c. It is certain that the original Hebrew term involves the sense of 'five,' but upon what circumstance the allusion is founded it

19 And Moses took the bones of Joseph with him: for he had straitly sworn the children of Israel, saying, ᵃGod will surely visit you; and ye shall carry up my bones away hence with you.

20 ¶ And ᵇthey took their jour-

ᵃ Gen. 50. 25.   Josh. 24. 32.   Acts 7. 16.
ᵇ Numb. 33. 6.

ney from Succoth, and encamped in Etham, in the edge of the wilderness.

21 And ᶜthe LORD went before them by day in a pillar of a cloud,

ᶜ ch. 14. 19, 24. & 40. 38.   Numb. 9. 15. & 10. 34. & 14. 14. Deut. 1. 33.   Neh. 9. 12, 19. Ps. 78. 14.   & 99. 7. & 105. 39.   Isai. 4. 5. 1 Cor. 10. 1.

---

is extremely difficult to determine. Perhaps the most probable supposition is that it includes both the import of their being in some way arranged into *five* grand divisions or squadrons, and of their being well appointed and equipped for expedite travelling, going forth not in a confused and tumultuary manner like timorous fugitives, but every one duly trussed and girded up so as to cause no impediment to others, and the whole body moving on in the style of an orderly and well marshalled army. When viewed in this aspect the spectacle must have been most imposing, and we can see with what peculiar propriety it is said, that Israel went out *with a high hand.*

19. *Moses took the bones of Joseph with him.* Joseph had expressly ordered, Gen. 50. 25, 26, that his bones should be carried up from Egypt when God should visit them, and their doing it now was not only a performance of the oath sworn by their fathers to Joseph, but an acknowledgment of God's faithful accomplishment of his promises. From the speech of Stephen, Acts, 7. 16, it is to be inferred that the bones of all the rest of the patriarchs were also at this time conveyed out of Egypt; each tribe, doubtless, taking charge of the bones of its own patriarch.

20. *Encamped in Etham in the edge of the wilderness.* We are not perhaps to suppose either in this or many other cases, that the places which are named are the *only* places at which they rested. In the present instance, if Succoth were about half way between Rameses and Suez, the second stage of their jour-

ney must have been at least forty miles, which is certainly too much to be accomplished in one day by such an immense cavalcade as that of the Israelites. Twenty miles a day for them would be severe driving. As the country was a desert, travelling would be hard; hours of refreshment and repose were needed ; the beasts must have had time to collect their food from the grass and shrubs of the desert ; and many of them being heavily burdened, they could move only, when they did move, with great slowness. With these considerations before us, we may perhaps safely infer that Etham was the third rather than the second encampment. The halting places of caravans are, in these desert regions, so much determined by the presence of wells, that in connexion with the circumstance of its being situated on the 'edge of the wilderness,' there is not much difficulty in concluding that Etham is the same place as the modern Adjeroud, which forms the third stage of the pilgrim's caravan to Mecca, and where there is an old fortress, a small village, and a copious well of indifferent water. This place is about eleven miles to the north-west of Suez, and is, in fact, near to the 'edge' of the wilderness, which extends around the north-eastern and eastern side of the Gulf of Suez. The journey to this point had been almost entirely over a desert, the surface of which is composed of hard gravel, often strewed with pebbles.

21. *The Lord went before them by day in a pillar of a cloud,* &c. Heb. בְּעַמּוּד עָנָן *be-ammud anan.* The orig-

to lead them the way; and by night in a pillar of fire, to give them light: to go by day and night.

22 He took not away the pillar of the cloud by day, nor the pillar of fire by night, *from* before the people.

---

inal comes from the root עמד *amad, to stand,* and imports, undoubtedly, an upright standing mass of cloud, resembling a column or pillar in a building, it being the same term as that employed in reference to the two supporting pillars of the edifice overthrown by Samson. Still it may be doubted whether this resemblance was very exact, for as it appears from Ps. 105. 39, that it was spread out at the base so as to cover as with a canopy the whole host of Israel, shading them from the intense heat of the sun, the height of the pillar, if it bore any proportion to such a base, must have been immense, as an encampment for 2,400,000 men would require a space of ground of nearly twelve miles square. We imagine, therefore, that in external appearance it approached near to the form of an ascending column of smoke, with a widely extended base, and shooting up to an inconceivable height in the heavens. Some have supposed that the pillar of cloud and the pillar of fire were two distinct pillars, but the hypothesis is scarcely necessary; one might have answered both purposes. This pillar-cloud was a striking emblem of the divine *protection* and *guidance* to the chosen people in their sojournings, and we find very significant allusions to it in the following passages, Is. 4. 5, 6, 'For the Lord will create upon every dwelling-place of Mount Zion and upon her assemblies a cloud and smoke by day, and the shining of a flaming fire by night; for upon all the glory there shall be a defence. And there shall be a tabernacle for a shadow in the day-time from the heat, and a place of refuge and for a covert from storm and from rain.' This predicts the same favored period of the church with that described by the inspired writer, Rev. 7. 15, 16, 'And he that sitteth on the throne shall

dwell among them. They shall hunger no more, neither thirst any more; neither shall the sun light on them, nor any heat;' i. e. they shall have the symbols of the divine presence with them as the Israelites had in the wilderness, only in a far more glorious manner; and while they shall be shadowed, as were the chosen people, from the burning rays of the sun, they shall be exempted from their privations; they shall not complain of hunger or thirst. It is evident that this cloudy pillar was the seat or habitation of the divine presence, and therefore, in one sense, his throne, from which oracles were given forth to the people. See Deut. 31. 15.

REMARKS ON THE PILLAR OF CLOUD.

Under the strong conviction that this extraordinary phenomenon has not hitherto been duly appreciated *as a visible symbol of the Divine Presence,* we are induced to add some remarks upon the purposes which, in that character, it was designed to answer. Of its uses as a guiding signal to the chosen tribes in their march through the wilderness, we have, both here and elsewhere, the clearest intimations. Thus, Ps. 78. 14, 'In the day-time also he led them with a cloud, and all the night with a light of fire.' So also Neh. 9. 12, 'Moreover thou leddest them in the day by a cloudy pillar; and in the night by a pillar of fire, to give them light in the way wherein they should go.' In what particular manner this twofold office of a pillar of cloud by day and of fire by night, could be performed by one and the same aerial column, is not entirely obvious. Whether the whole mass of cloud which was opaque by day became luminous by night; or whether there was a rending at night of the outer dark body of the cloud and the consequent disclosure of an interior splendor, which was enveloped and concealed from view during the day, has never been satisfactorily determined. We are inclined on the whole to adopt the latter opinion, not only because it strikes us as affording a more easy and consistent interpretation of the letter of various passages in which it is spoken of, but also because it harmonises better with what we conceive to have been the *substance* of this sublime symbolical *shadow;* on both which points we shall be more full in our subsequent annotations. This inwrapped inner splendor, which appeared at night, we suppose to have been that which is more appropriately termed 'the Glory of the Lord,' and this 'Glory' is said occasionally to have appeared in the day time, particularly when God would convey to his people an expression of his displeasure on account of their transgressions, or when he would strike them with a trembling awe of his majesty, as at the giving of the Law from Sinai, where the Glory of the Lord appeared as a devouring fire on the summit of the mount. Comp. Ex. 16. 10. Num. 16. 42. In like manner it appears that when the two sons of Aaron, Nabab and Abihu, offended by strange fire in their offerings, a fatal flash from the cloudy pillar instantaneously extinguished their lives. We cannot doubt, therefore, that this majestic pillar of cloud was intended to serve as the Shekinah, or visible representative of Jehovah, dwelling in the midst of the chosen people.

This, if we mistake not, will be placed still farther beyond the reach of question, upon considering the names by which it is designated. In the passage before us, ch. 13. 21, instead of the phraseology of the text, 'the Lord went before them,' the Targ. Jon. has, 'The Glory of the Shekinah went before them.'

The Arab. 'The Angel of the Lord went before them.' This latter mode of rendering is to be especially noticed, as we shall find it confirmed by the sacred writer himself, Ex. 14. 19, 'And the *angel of God* which went before the camp of Israel, removed, and went behind them; and the *pillar of cloud* went from before their face and stood behind them.' Here it is evident that that which in one clause of the verse is called the 'pillar of the cloud,' is in another called the 'angel of God.' The grounds of this phraseology we have already explained in the Note on Ex. 3. 2, from which it appears that the term 'Angel' is employed to denote any kind of agency, personal or impersonal, by which the divine will or working is made manifest. Accordingly, as the visible phenomenon of the burning bush is called the 'angel of the Lord,' which was on that occasion but another name for the Shekinah, so we find the Shekinah again under another aspect, viz. that of the cloudy pillar, expressly called by the same designation, Ex. 23. 20—23, 'Behold, I send an Angel before thee, to keep thee in the way, and to bring thee into the place which I have prepared. Beware of him, and obey his voice, provoke him not; for he will not pardon your transgressions: for my name is in him. But if thou shalt indeed obey his voice, and do all that I speak; then I will be an enemy unto thine enemies, and an adversary unto thine adversaries. For mine Angel shall go before thee, and bring thee in unto the Amorites, and the Hittites, and the Perizzites, and the Canaanites, and the Hivites, and the Jebusites; and I will cut them off.' This Angel, we cannot question, was the visible Shekinah in the pillar of cloud; and it is to the same manifested personage that allusion is had in what is said, Is. 63. 8, 9, of the 'Angel of the divine presence,' who was afflicted in all the affliction of his people, and who in his love and in his pity redeemed them, bearing and carrying them all the days of old. Again, the allusion is the same, Mal. 3. 1, 'Behold, I will send my messenger, and he shall prepare the way before me : and the Lord, whom ye seek, shall suddenly come to his temple, even the *messenger* (i. e. the Angel) *of the covenant*, whom ye delight in : behold, he shall come, saith the Lord of hosts.' Here it is clear that the 'Lord' and the 'Angel of the covenant' are identical, and no one doubts that this is a prediction of the coming of Christ heralded by John the Baptist. Consequently, Christ of the New Testament, and the 'Angel' or 'Jehovah' of the Old, are one and the same. But to return to the passage last quoted from Exodus, as the 'name' of God is but another term for his *nature*, the import is, that the divine nature, that is, the divine power, efficacy, authority, majesty, and omniscience would be associated with the external visible symbol. To all practical purposes, therefore, this cloudy pillar was to them the 'Angel-Jehovah,' the God of their nation, and they were to look up to that sublime and awful column as a visible embodiment of their covenant God, as an ever present witness, and feel as if a thousand eyes were peering out of the midst of it upon them, from which not even their slightest word or deed could be hidden. Indeed this view of the cloudy pillar as a kind of watch-tower of the Almighty, an aerial Mizpeh, or 'place of espial,' is expressly recognised in the remarkable passage, Ex. 14. 24, 25, 'And it came to pass, that in the morning-watch the Lord looked unto the host of the Egyptians through the pillar of fire and of the cloud, and troubled the host of the Egyptians, and took off their chariot-wheels, that they drave them heavily ; so that the Egyptians said, Let us flee from the face of Israel ; for the Lord fighteth for them against the Egyptians.' We shall hereafter have occasion to

notice, throughout the whole tenor of the Mosaic narrative, that this wondrous symbol is the very object which is to be understood, in innumerable instances, by the title 'Lord' (Jehovah), to which 'Angel of the Lord,' or rather 'Angel-Jehovah' is perfectly tantamount. This is plainly the idea conveyed by the language of the text which has given rise to these remarks ; 'The Lord went before them in a pillar of cloud,' &c., where we do not perceive that to the minds of the ancient readers of the Hebrew Scriptures the term 'Lord' would convey any other idea than that of the visible phenomenon by, in, and through which the divine attributes were manifested. So again Deut. 1. 32, 33, 'Yet in this thing ye did not believe the Lord your God, who went in the way before you, to search you out a place to pitch your tents in, in fire by night, to show you by what way ye should go, and in a cloud by day.' It was this *visible Deity* which was intended in all such phrases as 'before the Lord,' 'from the Lord,' 'unto the Lord,' &c., where the circumstances compel us to affix somewhat of a *local* idea to the expression.

But another important view of the subject is afforded by the fact, that it was this visible symbol of Jehovah which was the *oracle* of the chosen people. It was the Shekinah, the Glory, enthroned in the pillar of cloud, but afterwards removed into the most holy place of the tabernacle and temple, which issued commands and delivered responses to the congregation. Thus Ps. 99. 6, 7, 'They called upon the Lord, and he answered them. He spake unto them in the cloudy pillar.' A still more remarkable passage to the same effect occurs Ex. 33. 9—11, which we give with the omission of the Italics gratuitously introduced into the English version ; 'And it came to pass, as Moses entered into the tabernacle, the cloudy pillar descended, and stood at the door of the tabernacle, and talked with Moses. And all the people saw the cloudy pillar stand at the tabernacle-door : and all the people rose up and worshipped, every man in his tent-door. And the Lord spake unto Moses face to face, as a man speaketh unto his friend.' Here it is evident that 'cloudy pillar' and 'Lord' are used synonymously, and if the fact of such a usage in repeated instances be borne in mind, there will be no serious objection to the present mode of rendering v. 9, ' the Lord talked with Moses,' instead of simply ' it talked with Moses.' The phraseology, at any rate, is remarkable, and shows beyond question that the cloud of the Shekinah was the grand organ of communication to the covenant people. It was the *Speaker*, the *Word*, of the ancient economy ; and the place whence the oracles were uttered from the Shekinah, after it became enthroned in the sanctuary, was called דביר *debir*, *word-place*, from דבר *dabar*, *word*, to which, as every scholar knows, corresponds the Gr. Λογος, *word*, used by John in the commencement of his Gospel. Indeed, we are persuaded that it is only in the view above given of the import of the visible symbol of the cloudy pillar and the enshrined Glory, that we have the true clue to the Evangelist's meaning, which, if we understand it, is nothing less than an identification of Christ with the 'Jehovah,' or the *oracular presence*, the Shekinah, of the Old Testament. 'In the beginning,' i. e. under the old dispensation, 'was the Word,' the speaking, commanding, law-giving Shekinah; 'and the Word was with God, and the Word was God,' equivalent to what Moses says, 'My name is in him,' all divine attributes were to be considered as associated with and dwelling in the sensuous symbol ; 'And the Word was made flesh and dwelt among us,' the shadowy, but glorious symbol of the earlier economy at length became substantiated in human flesh, and as the incarnate Jehovah dwelt, or as the original has it (εσκηνωσεν) *tabernacled*, *shekinized* among us ; 'and we beheld his glory,' referring not to the intrinsic moral glory that distinguished his character, and that might be said to be seen whenever his person was seen, but rather to that special and overwhelming display of which John, Peter, and James were eye-witnesses on the mount of transfiguration, when there was a temporary rending or laying aside of the veil of his flesh, the cloud of his human nature, and a transient disclosure of the indwelling Shekinah, the glory of his Godhead. This was a preintimation to the senses of that ineffable light and splendor in which he will appear when he comes with the retinue of his saints to be the luminary of the New Jerusalem, which is to come down from God out of heaven. The whole scene seems to have been intended to afford a demonstration to the senses of the substantial identity of the person of the incarnate Redeemer with the manifested Jehovah of the Jewish dispensation. Consequently, whatever of essential divinity is indicated by the title 'Jehovah,' it is unquestionably to be considered as belonging to Christ. The proposal of Peter on this occasion to build three tabernacles, while it showed that the overpowering display had somewhat confused his mind, shows at the same time, by a natural association, the connexion in his thoughts of the *Shekinah* with a *tabernacle*. Here was the Shekinah, which he well knew had been used to abide in a tabernacle, but there was no tabernacle to receive it, and thence his proposition. It would be easy to prosecute this train of thought to a much greater extent, and accumulate proofs of our main position, but we must leave it to be followed out by ourselves or others under circumstances that will allow of more enlargement. We doubt not it is a field in which a rich harvest of Scripture elucidation is yet to be reaped.

CHAPTER XIV.

AND the Lord spake unto Moses, saying,

2 Speak unto the children of Israel, a that they turn and encamp

a ch. 13. 18.

before b Pi-hahiroth, between c Migdol and the sea, over against Baalzephon : before it shall ye encamp by the sea.

b Numb. 33. 7.   c Jer. 44. 1.

Chapter 14

The children of Israel had now arrived near the head of the Red Sea, and at the limit of the three days' journey into the wilderness, for which they had applied. It is therefore evident that their next move must decide their future course, and convey to the Egyptians, who doubtless kept a keen eye upon their movements, a clear and decisive intimation of their intentions. If they designed to do as they had all along declared to be their purpose, they would stay at this place and proceed to celebrate their intended feast to Jehovah ; but if they meant to escape altogether, they would resume their journey, and, passing by the head of the Red Sea, strike off into the desert. The march from Etham then, whatever direction it took, was to be a decisive move, and what that move was we are now to consider.

2. *Speak unto the children of Israel, that they turn*, &c. Heb. רשׁבו *yashubu*, from שׁוב, the usual meaning of which is *to return, turn back, go back again*, and so it is here rendered by Gesenius. But the circumstances of the case forbid this meaning except in a very limited degree. The import of the term undoubtedly is that of *turning off, deviating*, from the direct course, which would have been due east till they had rounded the upper extremity of the gulf. An ample confirmation of this sense of the term may be seen upon comparing Ezek. 35. 7. Zech. 7. 14—9. 8. Ps. 73. 10. The divine command now given to change the direction of their route must have been unexpected and surprising to all parties, and one which on any human principle of action would have appeared

utterly inexplicable. To be convinced of this we need only bring before us the topography of the region. About the head of the Gulf of Suez a desert plain extends for ten or twelve miles to the west and north of the city of that name. On the west this plain is bounded by the mountainous chain of Attaka, which comes down toward the sea in a north-western direction, contracting the breadth of the plain more and more, till it finally seems to shut it up by its termination at Ras-el-Attaka, twelve miles below Suez. But on approaching this point ample room is found to pass beyond ; and on passing beyond, we find ourselves in a broad alluvial plain, forming the mouth of the valley of Bedea. This plain is on the other or southern side nearly shut up by the termination of another chain of these mountains, which extend between the Nile and the western shore of the Red Sea. Any further progress in this direction would be impossible to a large army, especially one encumbered with flocks and herds, with women, children, and baggage. The valley of Bedea, which opens to the Red Sea in the broad plain abovementioned, narrows as it proceeds westward towards the Nile. It forms a fine roadway between the Nile and the Red Sea, and as such has in all ages been one of the most frequented routes in all the country, being travelled by all parties and caravans desirous of proceeding from the neighborhood of Cairo, or places to the south of Cairo, to Suez, or the region lying beyond the head of the gulf. Now, the Hebrew host being at Etham, and their next step from thence being of the utmost importance, they were directed, not—as might obviously have been expected—to pass round the head of the Gulf into the Sinai peninsula, but to proceed southward, between the mountains of Attaka and the *western* shore of the Gulf, and, after passing the Ras-el-Attaka, to encamp in the plain into which the valley of Bedea opens. But the question recurs, why bring them down this way, and make the passage of the Red Sea necessary, when they might so much more easily have got into the peninsula of Sinai by going round the Gulf?—why lead them out of their way to 'entangle' and 'shut them in' between the mountains and the sea? The answer to this is given in v. 3, 4. It was to give Pharaoh an additional inducement to follow them to his own destruction, by his knowledge of the advantage which their embarrassed position would give him over them. The overthrow of the Egyptian host was the contemplated result of this movement; and by this overthrow not only did the Egyptians receive their complete and final punishment, but the immediate security and future success of the Israelites were greatly assisted by it. For we learn from many passages of Scripture, that the neighboring tribes and natives were too much alarmed and intimidated by this stupendous event to think of any hostile encounter, the single instance of the Amalekites excepted. But of this more in the sequel.——¶ *Before Pihahiroth.* Heb. לִפְנֵי פִּי הַחִירֹת *liphnë pi hahiroth*, more properly written in English in the form of 'Pi-ha-hiroth.' 'There is not a more minute specification of locality in the Bible than that which the text affords; and one is led to think that it was thus carefully pointed out, in order to render it manifest that the passage could not there be effected by less than a miracle; or, in other words, to preclude those attempts to account for it on natural grounds which have actually resulted from the memory of the spot thus distinctly denoted being now lost Not one of the

names now exists. It perhaps throws some light on the passage to read the word Pi-ha-hiroth not as a proper name, but as a descriptive epithet. *Hiroth* means a valley, a confined pass, or a defile among mountains; *pi* signifies 'mouth,' or 'entrance;' *ha* is merely the definite article *the*, or of the: so that we may read the word *Pi-ha-hiroth*, as 'the entrance of the valley or pass.' It would thus denote, as we may take it, the pass or strip of land along the western shore of the gulf, between the mountains which skirt the sea, and the sea itself. It is certain that they crossed from the western to the eastern shore; and as this valley between the mountains and the sea commences nearly at the extremity of the gulf, the Hebrews must have encamped along its 'mouth' or entrance, if the sea were nearly then as it is now; and there they would have been effectually 'shut in' between the mountains, the desert, and the sea. The same result arises if we read Pi-hahiroth as a proper name, and apply it to the mountains which confine the valley at its entrance, the present name of which, *Addagi*, 'deliverance,' may be supposed to commemorate the passage of the Red Sea, and therefore to have superseded some previous name. This opinion is the more probable, because the flanks of the Hebrew host would have been exposed to the Egyptians whilst marching into the sea, if we place the point of passage any where above this valley, in which the mountains protected the right flank, and the sea the left. Here their rear only would be exposed, and accordingly we read only of their rear being protected by the pillar of cloud, which implies that their flanks needed no protection. We also think that it has not been sufficiently considered that an encampment consisting of about two millions of people must have covered a vast extent of ground; and wherever they encamped so as to face the sea, their camp must

3 For Pharaoh will say of the children of Israel, ^d They *are* en- | tangled in the land, the wilderness hath shut them in.

d Ps. 71. 11.

have stretched along the shore for the extent of several miles, particularly if they were hemmed in between the sea and the mountains as we would conjecture ; and if then when thus stretched out in one extensive line from north to south along the western shore of the gulf, the southern part of the body commenced the move into the dried passage in the sea, it necessarily follows that the point of passage must have been many miles below the termination of the inlet. This argument is conclusive to our minds that, consistently with their encampment along the sea coast, they must have passed many miles to the south of the end of the gulf, wherever the gulf then ended ; and even if it terminated much more to the south than at present, we are still disposed to consider this position of the camp as the most probable, because most consistent with the ' shutting in,' the ' entangling,' and the other circumstances, which imply that, when the Egyptian host took them in the rear, their only way to escape was through the sea.' *Pict. Bible.*
——¶ *Between Migdol and the sea over against Baal-zepher.* It is impossible to attain to any certainty in the location of these places, nor in fact is it clear what precise idea is to be affixed to the term ' before' in this connexion. We may doubtless be satisfied that the several places mentioned were all within the distance of ten or twelve miles of each other, and probably all in sight to some part of the host, which in a valley of no great width must have spread over at least that extent. Professor Stuart (Course of Heb. Study, Exc. IV.) thinks that Migdol is identical with the modern Ber Suez, or well of Suez. 'This is a small place, strongly fortified in modern times, in order to secure the

privilege of water for Suez. It is about three miles west from Suez ; and in this low sandy plain, it must be altogether in view. If now in ancient times there was a similar castle or fortification at this well, (a thing altogether probable, considering the nearness of predatory Arabian Nomades), then *Migdol* was an appropriate name for the place. For although the regular Hebrew word for *tower* is מִגְדָּל *migdal*, yet מִגְדֹּל *migdol*, from its derivation, seems to be altogether an equivalent for מִגְדָּל *migdal;* and therefore to mean *tower, fortified place.*'
3. *Pharaoh will say of the children of Israel.* Heb. אָמַר לִבְנֵי יִשְׂרָאֵל *amar libnë Yisraël, will say to the children of Israel ;* i. e. as to, respecting, the children of Israel. See this sense of the particle ' to' illustrated in the Note on Gen. 20. 2. Gr. περὶ τῶν υἱῶν.——¶ *They are entangled.* Heb. נְבֻכִים *nebukim*, from בּוּךְ *buk*, to be perplexed, to wander about in perplexity, whether physically or mentally. Gr. πλανῶνται, *they rove about.* The term occurs Est. 3. 15, 'The city of Shushan was *perplexed ;*' and also Joel. 1. 18, 'The herds of cattle are *perplexed*, because they have no pasture.' This sudden turn on the part of the Israelites would naturally lead Pharaoh to conclude that they had mistaken their way, and knew not what to do. But their *apparent* infatuation was the means of producing in him a *real* infatuation, which prompted him to pursue them to his ruin.——¶ *The wilderness hath shut them in.* The host of Israel having entered this narrow pass between the mountains on one side, and the sea on the other, Pharaoh would suppose that by cutting off their retreat in the rear, they would have no means of escape except through the sea and

4 And e I will harden Pharaoh's heart, that he shall follow after them; and I f will be honoured upon Pharaoh, and upon all his host; g that the Egyptians may know that I *am* the LORD. And they did so.

e ch. 4. 21. & 7. 3. f ch. 9. 16. ver. 17, 18. Rom. 9. 17, 22, 23. g ch, 7, 5.

5 ¶ And it was told the king of Egypt that the people fled: and h the heart of Pharaoh and of his servants was turned against the people, and they said, Why have we done this, that we have let Israel go from serving us?

b Ps. 105. 25.

---

this of course did not enter his thoughts. 'What seems to tend to the church's ruin, is often overruled to the ruin of the church's enemies.' *Henry.*

4. *I will be honored upon Pharaoh, and upon all his host.* Heb. אכבדה *ikkabedah, I will be glorified.* The ultimate scope to which all the counsels of Pharaoh were to be overruled is here stated; viz. the bringing of a larger measure of glory to the great name of God. This is in fact the end of all his judgments upon wicked men. As all creatures are made for his honor and glory, if they do not willingly and cordially render him his due, he will extort it from them in the righteous doom to which he condemns them. Comp. Ezek. 38. 22, 23.——¶ *And they did so.* That is, the Israelites did as they had been commanded relative to changing their route.

5. *It was told the king that the people had fled.* Pharaoh could not be ignorant that the Israelites had left Egypt, for the avowed purpose of holding a sacrifice in the desert, as they had gone out with his permission, and their departure had been hastened by his own people. But this he seems not to have regarded as a 'flight.' He is now, however, informed that they had 'fled;' i. e. that they discovered a very different intention from that of going three days' journey into the wilderness and returning again, as he had been led to expect. He now understood that they had no intention of returning. It was in this sense that Pharaoh learned that they had 'fled.' He probably received his

information from some of the mixt multitude who returned upon the route being changed, for which they could see no reason, and therefore concluded it not safe to trust themselves longer to such an uncertain guidance.——¶ *And the heart of Pharaoh and of his servants was turned,* &c. This inexorable monarch was left in a previous chapter stricken with terror and dismay at the death of the first-born. We saw him overpowered by that signal display of divine wrath against him, and inwardly constrained to send away the Israelites in haste out of his dominions. We could fain have hoped that the terrible chastisement he had already experienced would have been sufficient to humble the pride of his spirit, and bring him in penitence and prayer to the footstool of divine mercy. Bnt, alas! the power of a reprobate sense shows itself as strong as ever. Every conviction and alarm had passed away from his obdurate mind, like breath from the polished surface of a mirror. He repented indeed, but only that he had let them go. He repented that he had been obedient to the command of God, and he would retract his permission. Pride, resentment, avarice, reassumed their empire over his heart, and goaded him on to the mad attempt to recover his escaping captives. His subjects, so far as they had a profitable interest in the labors of the Israelites, would naturally share in the feelings of the king, and the intimation of loss would not fail to alarm those who had 'lent' to the Hebrews their 'jewels of silver and jewels

6 And he made ready his chariot, and took his people with him :

7 And he took [i] six hundred chosen chariots, and all the chariots of Egypt, and captains over every one of them.

8 And the LORD [k] hardened the heart of Pharaoh king of Egypt, and he pursued after the children of Israel : and [l] the children of Israel went out with an high hand.

9 But the [m] Egyptians pursued after them (all the horses *and* chariots of Pharaoh, and his horsemen, and his army) and overtook them encamping by the sea, beside Pi-hahiroth, before Baal-zephon.

[i] ch. 15. 4. [k] ver. 4. [l] ch. 6. 1. & 13. 9. Numb. 33. 3. [m] ch. 15. 9. Josh. 24. 6.

of gold,' and who by this time had found leisure to think that they had too easily parted with their wealth. Thus it is that the wicked show themselves as prone to repent of their well-doing as the righteous of their ill-doing.

6. *He made ready his chariot.* Heb.

וַיֶּאְסֹר אֶת רִכְבּוֹ *va-yesor eth rikbo,* *joined or bound his chariot;* i. e. the horses to the chariot. Gr. εζευξε *yoked.* The word 'chariot,' though in the singular, is to be understood in a plural sense. He ordered all his chariots to be got ready. The same term in the next verse is also singular.

EGYPTIAN WAR CHARIOT.

7. *Went out with an high hand.* That is, openly, boldly, powerfully, in the full view of the Egyptians, and with the air not of a company of renegadoes, but of a mighty army. So to sin with a high hand,' Num. 15. 30, is to sin openly, fearlessly, and audaciously.

9. *Overtook them encamping by the sea.* Upon this passage the Editor of the Pictorial History of Palestine re-

10 ¶ And when Pharaoh drew nigh, the children of Israel lifted up their eyes, and behold, the Egyptians marched after them; and

they were sore afraid: and the children of Israel [n] cried out unto the LORD.

[n] Josh. 24. 7. Neh. 9. 9. Ps. 34. 17. & 107. 6.

---

marks, 'We do not agree with those who think that the king of Egypt came upon the encamped Hebrews through the valley of Bedea, in the plain at the mouth of which they were encamped. As he was so glad to find how they had 'entangled themselves in the land,' he was not likely to take a course which would deprive him of all the advantages derivable from their apparent oversight. This he would do by coming upon them through the valley of Bedea, for this would have left open to them the alternative of escaping from their position by the way they entered; whereas, by coming the same way they had come, he shut up that door of escape; and if they fled before him, left them no other visible resource but to march up the valley of Bedea, back to Egypt, before the Egyptian troops. That this was really the advantage to himself which the king saw in their position, and that it was his object to drive them before him back to Egypt through this valley, or to destroy them if they offered to resist, we have not the least doubt: and it is unlikely that he would take any road but that which would enable him to secure these benefits.' To this view of the subject we do not object as far as the *main body* of Pharaoh's army is concerned. They would no doubt pursue the Hebrew caravan in the same route which it travelled, but as the Egyptians doubtless kept themselves informed of every movement of the Israelites, we would suggest the probability that a *detachment* of Pharaoh's forces took their march through the valley of Tih, in order to intercept their escape through that avenue. They would thus be effectually hemmed in on every side, and no possible mode of extrication remained for them, unless

the sea opened to let them pass through it. The Egyptians being satisfied that they had secured their prey, and that it was impossible for their fugitive bondsmen to escape, were in no haste to assail them. They were themselves also probably wearied by their rapid march. They therefore encamped for the night —for it was towards evening when they arrived—intending, no doubt, to give effect to their intentions in the morning.

10. *And when Pharaoh drew nigh,* &c. However much reason we have before had to wonder at the obstinacy and unbelief of Pharaoh, we have here occasion to vent our astonishment at the unbelief of those in whom we should least expect it. The sight of their old oppressors struck the Israelites with terror. Pervaded by a general panic, their faith and their courage seemed to desert them at once. They deplored the rash adventure in which they had engaged, and their servile minds looked back with regret and envy upon the enslaved condition under which they had so recently sighed. But wherefore did they now give way to fear? Could they not look back upon the wonders which God had wrought for them so short a time before? Could they not remember the recent death of all the first-born in Egypt? Could they not fix their eye on the pillar of cloud, and encourage themselves in that immediate token of God's presence with them and his care for them? True indeed, they were in a strait, a very great strait, and their peril was imminent. They were surrounded with dangers on all sides. The mountains, the sea, the pursuing hosts of Egypt pressed close upon them on every hand. In ordinary circumstances there was no doubt, occasion for the greatest

11 °And they said unto Moses, Because *there were* no graves in Egypt, hast thou taken us away to die in the wilderness? Wherefore hast thou dealt thus with us, to carry us forth out of Egypt?

° Ps. 106. 7, 8.

alarm. But they were not in ordinary circumstances. They had lately witnessed a series of most extraordinary proofs that God had taken up their cause. They knew, moreover, that it was the same God who had so miraculously appeared in their behalf, and brought them out of Egypt, that had conducted them to the perilous position which they now occupied, and they were bound to believe that in all this he intended them good and not evil, and that his omnipotence would in some way make sure their rescue. Their fears therefore were groundless, and their complaints inexcusable. They showed in this too much of the spirit of Pharaoh himself. They were as forgetful of the Lord's mercies which they had experienced, as he of the judgments which he had suffered. The similarity however of our own conduct in trying circumstances should no doubt abate our surprise at the perverseness of Israel. Alas, how little can *we ourselves* exercise faith and trust, in *our own* dangers and troubles! How prone are *we* to forget our past mercies, how incapable to see our present help, how ready to count God our enemy when his providence frowns, and after all our experience of his truth to cry out, 'We shall one day perish?' Let then the spirit of self-reproof temper our condemnation of unbelieving Israel.

11. *And they said unto Moses, Because,* &c. Had the Israelites merely given way to the inward promptings of an ignoble fear, or confined the expression of it to one another, we should have been less disposed to condemn, although even then we should not have been able to excuse it. But when we see their fears exciting them to murmur against Moses, as the procuring cause of their distresses, we can scarcely prevent a feeling of the indignant from mingling with our surprise. It was at once an ebullition of rank injustice and ingratitude towards Moses, and a gross provocation of God, in obedience to whose orders he had taken every step towards their deliverance. We do not forget, although they did, that all his great interests were embarked with theirs in this enterprise. His lot was cast into the common lap. He had made a sacrifice unspeakably greater than any other individual of the immense congregation. His prospects, either for himself or his family, were no more bright or flattering than those of the obscurest Hebrew. If there were danger from the pursuing host of Pharaoh, his share, assuredly, was not less than that of any other man. He had rendered himself peculiarly obnoxious to the unrelenting tyrant, and must have been among the first victims of his resentment. In view of this treatment we feel that if others might be offended, Moses might burn; and yet in the midst of these trying circumstances, he affords us a noble example of the meekness and forbearance for which he was so distinguished. In the danger which appeared, and in the unreasonable and wicked complaining of the people against him, he stood unmoved. Far from remonstrating with them or vindicating himself, he discovered the most admirable composure of mind, aiming to comfort and encourage instead of chiding them, and assuring them that they had nothing to do but to remain quiet and wait. They need neither flee nor fight. That was the last time that the Egyptians should cause them either fear or trouble. The Lord should fight for them and they should soon see the unreasonableness

12 p *Is* not this the word that we did tell thee in Egypt, saying, Let us alone, that we may serve the Egyptians ? For *it had been* better for us to serve the Egyptians, than that we should die in the wilderness.

13 ¶ And Moses said unto the people, q Fear ye not, stand still,

p ch. 5. 21. & 6. 9. q 2 Chron. 20. 15, 17. Isai. 41. 10, 13, 14.

and see the salvation of the LORD, which he will shew to you to-day : for the Egyptians whom ye have seen to-day, ye shall see them again no more for ever.

14 r The LORD shall fight for you, and ye shall s hold your peace.

r ver. 25. Deut. 1. 30. & 3. 22. & 20. 4. Josh. 10. 14, 42. & 23. 3. 2 Chron. 20. 29. Neh. 4. 20. Isai. 31. 4. s Isai. 30. 15.

---

of their alarms, and be ashamed of their unjust suspicions and complaints.

12. *Is not this the word,* &c. We do not indeed previously read of their uttering these precise words, but this was the spirit, the drift, of their desponding expostulations with Moses and Aaron when they found their burdens increased. The language breathes the most deplorable sordidness and pusillanimity of soul, as if their spirits had been utterly broken down and crushed by their long bondage. Because their liberty was attended with some dangers and difficulties, they speak of it with virtual contempt, as if a state of servitude were to be preferred ! Had they possessed the generous spirits of *men,* they would have said it was better, if needs be, to die on the field of honor than to live in the chains of slavery. Why should the idea of a grave in the wilderness be so dreadful to them ? Why should they prefer to it a grave in Egypt ? It was but a grave at the worst ; only if they died now, they died at once ; died like men defending their lives, liberty, and families ; not pouring out their lives, drop by drop, under the whip of a cruel taskmaster. But slavery had done its work in extinguishing the nobler impulses of their nature, and the native unbelief and depravity of the human heart had put the finishing stroke to their perverseness.

13. *Fear ye not, stand still.* Heb. התיצבו *hithyatzebu, stand firm;* waver not stagger not, in your minds.——

¶ *See the salvation of the Lord.* That is, experience, enjoy the salvation. See on this peculiar use of the word ' see' the Note on Gen. 42. 1.——¶ *For the Egyptians whom ye have seen,* &c. Heb. 'For in what manner ye have seen the Egyptians to-day ye shall not add to see them any more for ever ;' i. e. ye shall not see them *alive* any more.

14. *Ye shall hold your peace.* Heb. תחרשון *taharishun, ye shall be silent ;* a term denoting here, as in many other instances, not so much a cessation from *noise* as from *action,* equivalent to remaining still, quiet, or inert. Thus, 2 Kings, 19. 11, 'Why *are ye the last* to bring the king back from his house ?' Heb. 'Why are ye *silent* from bringing,' &c. ; i. e. why are ye *negligent?* Ps. 83. 1, 'Keep not thou *silence,* O God ;' i. e. do not *forbear to act.* Ps. 5. 3, 'Our God shall come and not *keep silence;*' i. e. shall not *remain inactive.* By this usage of the term we are assisted in the interpretation of Rev. 8. 1, 'And when we had opened the seventh seal there was *slence* in heaven about the space of half an hour ;' i. e. there was a respite from action ; the various symbolical agents who had hitherto been so busily employed in the visionary heaven, came to a temporary pause, representing some epoch in the state of the church when a series of stirring and momentous events, a succession of wars and commotions, were followed by a profound, though not a lasting calm. Such is the import of the symbol, and

15 ¶ And the Lord said unto Moses, Wherefore criest thou unto me? Speak unto the children of Israel, that they go forward:

16 But t lift thou up thy rod, and stretch out thine hand over the sea,

t ver. 21, 26. ch. 7. 19.

and divide it: and the children of Israel shall go on dry *ground* through the midst of the sea.

17 And I, behold, I will u harden the hearts of the Egyptians, and they shall follow them: and I will

u ver. 8. ch. 7. 3.

it is the province of the prophetic expositor to ascertain from the records of history with what era of the church the vision corresponds. In the case before us, the prophet's words are strikingly pertinent, Isa. 30. 7, 'Therefore have I cried concerning this, Their strength is to sit still.'

15. *Wherefore criest thou unto me?* As nothing has been before said of Moses' crying or praying to the Lord in express words, we may suppose either that his crying on this occasion was in strong inward ejaculations and groanings, mingled perhaps with an undue perturbation of spirit, or that Moses is here addressed as the representative of the people; not as crying in his own person, but in that of the collective body of which he was the head. The first is the most probable supposition, and it naturally suggests the inquiry how it could be wrong for Moses to pray under these circumstances? Does not God himself say, Ps. 4. 15, 'Call upon me in the day of trouble; I will deliver thee and thou shalt glorify me.' To this it may be answered, that in the present case there was *no occasion* to cry to the Lord; for he had already manifested so decidedly that he was determined to deliver his people, that neither they nor Moses ought to have had a doubt about it. And again, this was *no time* for prayer. There was something else to be instantly done. It was the time for him and them to act. 'Speak unto the children of Israel that they go forward.' Let us remember that every thing is beautiful in its season. Times there often are when it is proper and necessary that we should enter our

chambers, and shut the door upon us, and commune with our own hearts and with God—often times when it might be well for us even to spend whole nights in prayer—often also sudden emergencies when we must cry with our whole souls to God. But there are other times when we are required to exert ourselves actively, and to show our faith in the promises of God by entering without fear or care or delay into the greatest straits and dangers.——¶ *Speak unto the children of Israel, that they go forward.* Though the sea was directly before them, and its depths seemed utterly to deny them a passage, yet as the power that *made* the sea bade them advance it was certain that he would either divide, or congeal, or exhaust it, so that it should offer no obstruction to their crossing. This is no strange language to the Christian. In the most difficult and appalling circumstances, the command is often to be heard by us, 'Go forward.' Though there may be mountains of opposition, or waves of trouble, or seas of danger, in the path of duty, yet the word is 'Go forward.' Faith has its most perfect work in the hour of darkness. Follow its guidance and ' a way shall be made in the sea, and a path in the mighty waters.'

16. *Lift thou up thy rod—and divide it.* Heb. בקעהו *bekaëhu, cleave it.* Gr. ρηξον αυτην, *rend it.* No efficacy of course is to be attributed on this or any former occasion to the rod, or even to Moses, in producing an effect to which Omnipotence alone was competent. But it was proper that Moses as an instrument should appear conspicuous in the transaction, in order that God might

x get me honour upon Pharaoh, and upon all his host, upon his chariots, and upon his horsemen.

18 And the Egyptians y shall know that I *am* the LORD, when I have gotten me honour upon Pharaoh, upon his chariots, and upon his horsemen.

19 ¶ And the angel of God z which went before the camp of Israel, removed, and went behind them; and the pillar of the cloud went from before their face, and stood behind them:

x ver. 4. y ver. 4. z ch. 13. 21. & 23. 20. & 32. 34. Numb. 20. 16. Isai. 63. 9.

20 And it came between the camp of the Egyptians and the camp of Israel; and a it was a cloud and darkness *to them*, but it gave light by night *to these:* so that the one came not near the other all the night.

21 And Moses b stretched out his hand over the sea; and the LORD caused the sea to go *back* by a strong east wind all that night, and c made the sea dry *land*, and the waters were d divided.

a See Isai. 8. 14. 2 Cor. 4. 3. b ver. 16 c Ps. 66. 6. d ch. 15. 8. Josh. 3. 16. & 4. 23. Neh. 9. 11. Ps. 74. 13. & 106. 9. & 114. 3. Isai. 63. 12.

---

thus give a new attestation, in the sight of the whole host, to the authority with which he was clothed, in order to secure for him a suitable degree of respect, honor, and obedience in all their subsequent relations.

19. *And the angel of God—removed,* &c. The Israelites were still in their encampment, waiting with trembling solicitude the crisis of their fate. What must have been their astonishment to see, all at once, the pillar of the cloud, which was in front of them, move round in silent majesty through the air, and take its place in their rear! 'The glory of the Lord became their rere-ward!' Yet it appears that some delay was still to occur before they began to enter upon the bed of the sea, as a strong east wind was to be raised, and by its action the waters so disposed of as to facilitate the passage. As to the relation of the terms 'Angel of God' and 'pillar of the cloud,' see the Remarks at the close of the preceding chapter.

20. *It was a cloud and darkness* to them, *but it gave light by night* to these. The supplementary words in our version show that the Hebrew here is elliptical. The sense, however, is undoubtedly correctly rendered. Chal. 'It was an obscure cloud to the Egyptians, but a light during all the night to the Israelites.'

Jerus. Targ. 'It was a cloud half lucid and half dark; the light gave light unto Israel, and the darkness gave darkness unto the Egyptians.' Thus the word and the providences of God have a two-fold aspect, a black and dark side towards sin and sinners, a bright and pleasant side towards those that are Israelites indeed. On the former the Most High looks frowningly in wrath; on the latter his countenance shines brightly with favor. That which is a savor of life unto life to the one, is a savor of death unto death to the other. The distinction thus made in this respect between the two hosts is a preintimation of the eternal distinction which will be made between the inheritance of the saints in light, and that utter darkness which will for ever be the portion of hypocrites.

21. *The Lord caused the sea to go* back *by a strong east wind.* Heb. ברוח קדים עזה *beruah kadim azzah.* The immediate effect of the stretching out of Moses' hand and wielding the potent rod, was not the division of the waters, but the raising of the wind, which thenceforward continued to blow through the rest of the night. The circumstance, as read in our version, creates some difficulty in reconciling every part of the narrative. Although the original does not *necessarily* imply that the wa-

22 And ᵉthe children of Israel
went into the midst of the sea

e ver. 29. ch. 15. 19. Numb. 33. 8. Ps. 66. 6.
& 78. 13. Isai. 63. 13. 1 Cor. 10. 1. Hebr. 11. 29.

ters 'went back' from the western shore
of the Gulf, inasmuch as there is no
word answering to ' back,' yet there is
the utmost probability that this was the
fact, as otherwise it would be more natural to say that the Lord caused the
waters ' to come,' than ' to go.' But
how is this to be reconciled with the inevitable effects of a strong east wind
acting upon the same mass of waters?
This would have been to drive the waters from the eastern and heap them up
to a great depth on the western side,
where the Israelites were to make their
entrance. As the sea was undoubtedly
cloven asunder by miraculous power
over and above any effect produced by
the wind, it would matter little to Omnipotence whether it was swollen most
on the eastern or western coast. But
from a comparison of all the incidents
we rather infer that the body of the
waters had been rolled up as it were by
the force of the wind from the western
to the eastern side of the sea, and that
it was through this agglomerated fluid
mass that the passage was opened. To
this view of the subject it will of course
be objected that the wind in question is
expressly said to have been the *east
wind*. But we reply that the original
term קדים *kadim*, has rather a generic
than a specific import, and denotes *any
uncommonly strong or violent wind*,
from whatever quarter it blows. Accordingly it is rendered by the Vulg. in
this very passage, 'a vehement and burning wind,' and Rosenmuller adduces the
following passages as confirming the
above interpretation: Ps. 48. 7, 'Thou
breakest the ships of Tarshish with an
east wind (קדים) ;' i. e. as expressly
rendered in the Gr. εν πνευματι βιαιω, *with
a violent wind*. Ezek. 27. 26, 'Thy row-
ers have brought thee into great waters:

upon the dry *ground:* and the waters *were* ᶠa wall unto them on their
right hand, and on their left.

f Hab. 3. 10.

the *east wind* (קדים) hath broken thee
in the midst of the seas ;' 1. e. any kind
of fierce and tempestuous wind. So Job,
27. 20, 21, speaking of the wicked rich
man; 'Terrors take hold on him as
waters, a tempest stealeth him away in
the night. The *east wind* (קדים) car-
rieth him away, and he departeth ; and
as a storm hurleth him out of his place.'
Here it can only be by a rhetorical figure
that any particular wind is specified.
The idea is obviously that of violent
wind in general. Comp. Jer. 18. 17, and
Is. 27. 8, in the latter of which places
קדים *east wind* is made synonymous
with רוח קשה *rough wind.*——¶ *Were
divided.* Heb. יבקעו *yibbake-u*, *were
cloven, were violently sundered ;* usually applied to the cleaving or splitting
of rocks, wood, the earth, or solid substances in general, and consequently a
term not well suited in itself to describe
the effects of the wind.

22. *The children of Israel went into,*
&c. From the calm and unimpassioned
tone of the narrative, we should scarcely
imagine that the writer was describing
one of the most stupendous miracles
ever wrought in the view, or for the
benefit, of mortals. While the immense
congregation stands in mute expectation, with its countless eyes fastened
on Moses and Aaron, whose movements
would be a signal for their own, these
venerated leaders advanced together into the untrodden path, and at once the
yielding waters divide, and contrary to
all the laws of fluids stand erect on
either hand like walls of solid ice! The
bed of the sea appears between them,
and lost in amazement on this high-
way of the Lord's ransomed they pass
through dry-shod and reach in safety the
opposite shore! 'The waters saw thee
O God, the waters saw thee; they were

23 ¶ And the Egyptians pursued, and went in after them, to the midst of the sea, *even* all Pharaoh's horses, his chariots, and his horsemen.

---

afraid: the depths also were troubled. Thy way is in the sea, and thy path in the great waters, and thy footsteps are not known. Thou leddest thy people like a flock by the hand of Moses and Aaron.' Ps. 77. 16—20.

23. *And the Egyptians pursued*, &c. It is by no means clear that the Egyptians knew or thought they were following the Israelites into the bed of the sea. Considering the darkness additional to that of the night, which had been super-induced between the pursuers and the pursued, it is not probable that they had any clear perception of the course in which they were moving, and least of all that they imagined themselves travelling on the bared bed of the divided waters. They could hear the noise of the flying host before them, and could see confusedly a little way about their feet, but in all likelihood were utterly unable to distinguish the localities around them, and may even have thought that they were following the Israelites up the valley of Bedea on their return to Egypt. But by the time the day broke they became aware of their condition, and a fearful discovery did it prove to them.

We may here remark that although the precise place of the Israelites' crossing the western Gulf of the Red Sea is by many writers placed higher up in the immediate vicinity of Suez, yet to our mind the evidence decidedly predominates in favor of a point some ten or twelve miles farther south. It is true that Niebuhr, Leclerc, Rosenmuller, Prof. Robinson, and others, advocate the claims of the former locality, but after the thorough canvassing of their arguments ·by the Editor of the Pictorial Bible, we cannot refuse our assent to the conclusions to which he comes in the following Note on Ex. 14. 2: 'Let us then proceed down the valley between the mountains and the sea, which we have supposed the Israelites to have taken. At the distance of about fifteen miles below Suez, occurs Ras (Cape) Addagi projecting into the sea, and which is formed by the termination of a cluster of hills about five miles in length, which now interpose *on the left* between the valley and the sea, so that the road in this part has mountains on either hand for several miles. Was the entrance of this defile the mouth of the *Hiroth*, or pass, before which the Hebrews encamped? The cape on the opposite coast is called Ras (Cape) Moses, and near this are the Fountains of Moses (Ain Mousa), which one of the most distinct traditions points out as the scene of the miracle. The claims of Ain Mousa above Suez in the present, and indeed in *any*, state of the gulf, are, that if the Israelites crossed here, they must have been more completely 'shut in' than at Suez, between the mountains, the wilderness, and the sea—that it is far enough from the bottom of the gulf to account for the Egyptians not going round to intercept them as they came up from the sea—that the waters being here deeper and broader, the miracle would be the more conspicuous and unquestionable, and at the same time the waters would be the more adequate to overwhelm the Egyptian host; while still the channel is not too broad for the Hebrew host to pass through in a single night. It is true that Dr. Shaw does not think the water deep enough even here; but there is every reason to conclude that the water was deeper formerly than at present, and the same objection certainly applies with still greater force to the passage at Suez. Let us however proceed southward, and having traversed the pass, and continued our course along the shore, we come to an expansion or bay, forming the mouth,

24 And it came to pass, that in the morning-watch *g* the LORD looked unto the host of the Egyptians

g See Ps. 77. 17, &c.

through the pillar of fire and of the cloud, and troubled the host of the Egyptians,

---

towards the Red Sea, of a valley or opening in the mountains, which is here called *Badea,* and also *Wady Tyh,* or ' the Valley of Wandering,' and which, under the various names of Wady Ramlia, Derb Towarek, Wady Jendeli, &c. extends from the Nile to the Red Sea, and through which a canal of communication seems to have formerly ran. Was this the Hiroth, or pass, before or in the mouth of which the Israelites encamped, and from which they afterwards made their famous passage? Many good authorities are of this opinion ; and it deserves to be mentioned that D'Anville and Major Rennel concur in fixing the town of Clysma at this spot. Certainly no body of men could be more effectually shut in than in this bay of Badea. There are many indications that an arm of the sea, now filled up, stretched a considerable way into the opening at this place, and must have prevented all further progress to the south; and if such progress had not been thus prevented, it would be so by the mountains of Ghobede, which bound the bay and valley on the south, and which, with their continuations, stand out so close to the sea as to preclude the continuation of the march along the shore. There was therefore no retreat but through the sea, or back to Egypt through the valley; and, on the hypothesis that there was then, as at present, a practicable road through this valley between the Red Sea and the Nile, we hazard a conjecture, that it was Pharaoh's intention to drive them back before him through this valley. As names and traditions, on one side of the sea, point the egress of the Hebrews at Ain Mousa—as, on the other side, the same authorities place the ingress at Badea—and as it is necessary to assume that the opening

was most extensive, we might hazard a conjecture that the whole opening extended from about Ain Mousa to opposite Badea. We must again repeat, however, that not the least stress is to be laid on the unsupported traditions of the natives. Ain Mousa is only one out of many places which they indicate as the point of passage. Perhaps the place which both Arabian and Egyptian traditions most strongly indicate is the large bay called *Birket Faroun* (Pharaoh's Pool), about the 29th parallel of latitude. The waters of this bay are in continual commotion, which the natives think to be occasioned by the unquiet spirits of the drowned. But the passage cannot reasonably be fixed here or any where else below Wady Gharendel at the lowest: for not only does the gulf from thence downward become too wide to have been crossed by such a body as the host of Israel in one night, but the shore, which till thereabout is low and sandy, then becomes rocky and mountainous, while that on the Egyptian side is still more impracticable—affording a convenient place neither for the ingress nor egress of such a multitude. Upon the whole, we should think the claims of Ain Mousa far preferable to those of Suez, and those of Badea at least equal to those of Ain Mousa.' *Pict. Bible.*

24. *In the morning watch.* The Jews divided the whole night from sun-setting till sun-rising, into three watches, consisting each of four hours. The morning watch began at two in the morning and ended about six.——¶ *Looked unto the host of the Egyptians through the pillar of fire and of the cloud.* Heb. בְּעַמּוּד *be-ammud; in or by the pillar;* i. e. by means of it. The original word for 'looked,' as applied to God, denotes

25 And took off their chariot-wheels, that they drave them heavily: so that the Egyptians said, Let us flee from the face of Israel; for the Lord ʰ fighteth for them against the Egyptians.

ʰ ver. 14.

not a simple and bare act of ocular inspection, but also a *positive putting forth* of some demonstration of wrath or mercy corresponding with the occasion. Thus Ps. 102. 19, 20, 'For he hath *looked down* from the height of his sanctuary; from heaven did the Lord behold the earth; to hear the groaning of the prisoner, to loose those that are appointed to death;' i. e. his *looking down* consisted in his interposition in behalf of the afflicted. Deut. 26. 15, '*Look down* from thy holy habitation, from ·heaven, and bless thy people ;' i. e. *look down* by blessing. So here the Lord's ' looking' is explained by what follows, viz. his 'troubling' them. We suppose the fact to have been that the side of the pillar of cloud toward the Egyptians was suddenly and for a few moments illuminated with a blaze of light, which coming as it were in a refulgent flash upon the dense darkness which had preceded, so frightened the horses of the pursuers that they rushed confusedly together, dashing the wheels of one chariot furiously against those of another, upsetting, breaking, and tearing them from their axles, while the horses themselves, floundering in pools, or sinking in quicksands, were thrown into inextricable confusion, and thus became an easy prey to the returning waves. In the mean time, as is evident from the words of the Psalmist, Ps. 77. 17, 18, the elements were wrought into a fearful commotion, which redoubled the horrors of the scene ; 'The clouds poured out water, the skies sent out a sound ; thine arrows also went abroad. The voice of thy thunder was in the heavens ; thy lightnings* lightened the

26 ¶ And the Lord said unto Moses, ⁱ Stretch out thine hand over the sea, that the waters may come again upon the Egyptians, upon their chariots, and upon their horsemen.

ⁱ ver. 16.

world ; the earth trembled and shook.' With this agrees the description of Josephus ; ' Showers of rain also came down from the sky, and dreadful thunder and lightning, with flashes of fire. Thunderbolts also were darted upon them ; nor was there any thing which God sends upon men as indications of his wrath, which did not happen at this time.' The complicated horrors of the scene can neither be described nor imagined. It was evident beyond all dispute that the Lord God Almighty fought against them, and the lighting down of his arm who could withstand ? Officers and soldiers, Pharaoh and his commanders, were alike terror-stricken, and one universal thrill of panic and dismay pervaded the host of the Egyptians. 'Let us flee,' was the cry that resounded in every direction, through the broken and trembling ranks, but, alas, it was now too late. All attempts at flight were vain. The day of forbearance was passed. The measure of their iniquity was full. The tyrant and his people had hardened themselves in rebellion against God till his patience was exhausted, and the day of vengeance was come. They are first frightened into despair, and then plunged into destruction. —— ¶ *The Egyptians said,* &c. Heb. ויאמר מצרים *va-yomer Mitzraim, Egypt,* or *the Egyptian, said, Let us flee ;* indicating that they were as unanimous in making this declaration, as if they had been but one man. But they were like persons oppressed with the nightmare in their sleep, who would fain fly from the impending danger that presses upon them, but cannot. An invisible power fixes them to the spot.

27 And Moses stretched forth his hand over the sea, and the sea [k]returned to his strength when the morning appeared; and the Egyptians fled against it; and the LORD [l]overthrew the Egyptians in the midst of the sea.

28 And [m]the waters returned, and [n]covered the chariots, and the horsemen, *and* all the host of Pharaoh that came into the sea after them: there remained not so much as one of them.

29 But [o]the children of Israel walked upon dry *land* in the midst of the sea; and the waters *were* a wall unto them on their right hand, and on their left.

30 Thus the LORD [p]saved Israel that day out of the hand of the Egyptians: and Israel [q]saw the Egyptians dead upon the sea-shore.

[k] Josh. 4. 18. [l] ch. 15. 1, 7 [m] Hab. 3. 8, 13. [n] Ps. 106. 11.

[o] ver. 22. Ps. 77. 20. & 78. 52, 53. [p] Ps. 106. 8, 10. [q] Ps. 58. 10. & 59. 10.

27. *And Moses stretched forth his hand*, &c. The rod of Moses is again stretched over the sea, and it returns to its strength. Those very waters which had guarded the passage of Israel, again obey the suspended law of gravitation, and rushing down upon the heads of the Egyptians with overwhelming force engulph them all beyond the power or possibility of escape. Prostrated by the fury of the resistless flood, wave after wave passing over them, they pierce the air with the shrieks of hopeless anguish, and in all their multitudes are buried beneath the deep, which roared in closing upon them like a ravenous beast over his prey. 'The sea covered them; they sank as lead in the mighty waters.' The same element is the defence of the one, and the destroyer of the other. Not an Israelite perished, not an Egyptian survived. What an awful retribution upon the incorrigible king and people who had hardened themselves against God, bidding defiance to his demands, his threatenings, his judgments! Here he lies with all his host, men, horses, and chariots, merged in one common watery grave, as a perpetual monument of the folly of rebellious man, and the just wrath of offended heaven!——¶ *The Lord overthrew the Egyptians*. Heb. ינער *yenaër*, *shook off*. That is, cast away, rid himself of. The force of the original may be better understood from the following examples of its use. Nehem. 5. 13, 'Also I *shook* my lap and said, So God *shake out* every man from his house that performeth not this promise, even thus be he *shaken out*.' Job, 38. 13 'That it might take hold of the ends of the earth that the wicked might be *shaken out* of it.' The same original word occurs, Ps. 136. 15, in allusion to this same event, though translated as here 'overthrow.' So absolutely and utterly was the power of this guilty nation now broken and destroyed, that although the camp of Israel was pitched within a little distance of Egypt, during the space of forty years, yet no pursuit was attempted against them, no future effort made to subdue and enslave them.

30. *Israel saw the Egyptians dead upon the sea-shore.* Heb. יראו את מצרים מת *yiru eth Mitzrayim mëth*, *saw Egypt*, or *the Egyptians*, *a corpse*; the whole nation spoken of as one individual. This was ordered at once for the greater disgrace of the Egyptians, and the greater triumph of the Israelites. However superstitiously nice and curious that people were in embalming and preserving the bodies of their great men, and whatever horror was inspired by their religion at the idea of lying unburied till their bodies were consumed, still that dreaded doom was here allotted them, and the utmost contempt thus poured upon the nobles of Egypt. In short, it was little else than

31 And Israel saw that great work which the LORD did upon the Egyptians: and the people feared the

dragging out the dead body of the slain Egyptian dragon from the waters and proclaiming over it, 'I will leave thee upon the land, I will cast thee forth upon the open field, and will cause all the fowls of the heaven to remain upon thee, and I will fill the beasts of the whole earth with thee.' Ezek. 32. 4. It is perhaps in allusion to this that we read, Rev. 19. 17, 18, 'And I saw an angel standing in the sun ; and he cried with a loud voice, saying to all the fowls that fly in the midst of heaven, Come, and gather yourselves together unto the supper of the great God ; that ye may eat the flesh of kings, and the flesh of captains, and the flesh of mighty men, and the flesh of horses, and of them that sit on them, and the flesh of all men, both free and bond, both small and great.' Such a result would also heighten the expression of the divine favor towards Israel, and more deeply affect their hearts with their great deliverance. They probably stripped the bodies of the slain, and thus possessed themselves of a mass of treasure which they were afterwards able to apply to the furnishing of the tabernacle. Nothing can be more striking than the manner in which these incidents are figuratively set forth by the Psalmist, Ps. 74. 13, 14, ' Thou didst divide the sea by thy strength: thou brakest the heads of the dragons in the waters. Thou brakest the heads of leviathan in pieces, and gavest him to be meat to the people inhabiting the wilderness.'

31. *Israel saw that great work.* Heb. את היד הגדלה *eth ha-yad haggedolah,* *that great hand ;* or as the Chal. expressively renders it, 'The power of the great hand.' The import is plainly that of an amazing display of the divine omnipotence. It was scarcely necessary to pray for them in the language

LORD, and r believed the LORD, and his servant Moses.

r ch. 4. 31. & 19. 9. Ps. 106. 12. John. 2. 11. & 11. 45.

of David, Ps. 109. 27, 'That they may know that *this is thy hand,* that thou, Lord, hast done it.' Conviction of this truth was now wrought in the depths of their souls. 'Deep answered unto deep.' The language is very emphatic, that they now began in earnest to 'fear the Lord and believe the Lord,' in view of the wonders of his mercy and his might, and to yield themselves more unreservedly to the guidance of his servant Moses. They were now profoundly ashamed of their former distrusts and murmurings, and doubtless were ready to conclude, from their present feelings, that they should never relapse into a complaining spirit or a disobedient conduct again. Infidelity and rebellion are, for a time at least, banished from their hearts, and ' while they believe his word, they sing his praise ;' although their subsequent demeanor showed that they were still capable of forgetting and slighting their heavenly benefactor.

Chapter 15

The preceding chapter having given us an account of the total overthrow and destruction of the Egyptians, we are informed in the present of the manner in which the signal victory was celebrated. The circumstances which called forth this grateful song of praise here recorded, were indeed unparalleled. We behold an immense congregation just rescued in a marvellous manner from the power of their enemies, standing upon the shores of a sea which was then rolling its waves in their usual course, waves which had so lately been made to stand as crystal walls on either side of a dry passage, and which had again rushed together in their might, overwhelming all the chariots, and horses, and footmen of Pharaoh. There they stand, seeing the shores of the sea

CHAPTER XV.

THEN sang ᵃ Moses and the children of Israel this song unto the LORD, a'nd spake, saying, I will

ᵃ Judg. 5. 1. 2 Sam. 22. 1. Ps. 106. 12.

ᵇ sing unto the LORD, for he hath triumphed gloriously; the horse and his rider hath he thrown into the sea.

ᵇ ver. 21.

strewed with the dead bodies of men and horses, with the broken pieces of chariots and weapons of war scattered in all directions, and all the other wrecks of that awful catastrophe. There they stand, safe and unhurt, not a feeble woman, not an infant child, not a hoof of cattle, not an article of property, lost—all monuments of the mighty power and distinguishing favor of their covenant God! Well may they lift up their voices and sing. Well may they bring the timbrel and harp to aid their voices in celebrating the praises of their great deliverer.—It may be remarked, by the way, that here, as in many other instances, the Old Testament narrative has afforded the ground for one of the most striking features of the symbolical scenery of the Apocalypse, ch. 15. 2, 3, 'And I saw as it were a sea of glass mingled with fire; and them that had gotten the victory over the beast, and over his image, and over his mark, and over the number of his name, stand on the sea of glass, having the harps of God. And they sing the song of Moses the servant of God, and the song of the lamb, saying, Great and marvellous are thy works, Lord God Almighty; just and true thy ways, thou King of saints.' The phrase 'on the sea of glass' is, undoubtedly, more correctly rendered 'by the sea of glass,' i. e. on the shores, while the mingling of the fire is perhaps in allusion to the pillar of fire which accompanied the march of the Israelites through the Red Sea, and whose terrific flashings mingled with the returning and roaring billows that overwhelmed the Egyptian hosts.

1. *Then sang Moses and the children of Israel this song*, &c. Heb. אָז יָשִׁיר *az yashir*, lit. *then will sing*. As the verb

in the original is in the future, perhaps the suggestion may not be wholly groundless, that it is hereby implied that this song was to serve as a model for the triumphant songs of the church in subsequent ages, somewhat as the Lord's prayer is designed as a model for the prayers of his disciples in every period of the world. Accordingly, we find it said of those, Rev. 15. 2, 3, who had obtained a victorious deliverance from the thraldom of the beast, that they sung *the song of Moses and the Lamb*, in evident allusion to the sublime pean here recorded. The present is the most ancient song extant in any language, as those ascribed to Linus, Musaeus, and Orpheus, have a date of three hundred years subsequent to this. Its poetical merits are of the very first order, as we might infer from the undoubted fact, that it was prompted by divine inspiration, to be sung on the spot, and probably on the very morning of the event which it celebrates. It is alike remarkable for its grandeur and simplicity, its touching pathos and its true sublime. It was probably sung in alternate strophes or strains, as was usual in all the sacred symphonies of the ancients.——¶ *I will sing*, &c. Intimating that although the song was to be sung by the whole company, yet each one was to appropriate the burden of it to himself individually. The triumph of Israel over the Egyptians did not resemble the usual triumphs of nation over nation, where the individual is overlooked and lost in the mass. Every thing here is peculiar and personal. Every Israelite for himself reflects with joy on his own chains now for ever broken. He seems to exult over his *own* tyrant-master now sub

2 The LORD *is* my strength and
ᶜsong, and he is become my salvation: he *is* my God, and I will

c Deut. 10. 21. Ps. 18. 2. & 22. 3. & 59. 17.
& 62. 6. & 109. 1. & 118. 14. & 140. 7. Isai.
12. 2. Hab. 3. 18, 19.

died under him, and hails his *own* personal liberty as fully recovered.——
¶ *Hath triumphed gloriously.* Heb.
גָּאֹה גָּאָה *gaoh gaah, excelling he excelleth*, or, *he is exceedingly exalted.* Gr.
ενδόξως γαρ δεδόξασται, *for he is gloriously glorified.* The leading idea of
the Hebrew term in this connexion is,
that of displaying *grandeur, preeminence, magnificence.* It is perhaps primarily applied, in a physical sense, to
corporeal objects which *grandly raise
and rear themselves up,* as towering
trees and swelling waves (Ezek. 47. 5);
and thence, in mental relations, denoting *elation, self-exaltation,* whether in
a good or bad sense. As used here in
reference to God there can be no mistake as to its import. Chal. 'He hath
exalted himself above the excellent
ones, and excellence is his.'——¶ *The
horse and his rider hath he thrown
into the sea.* Heb. רָמָה *ramah, violently cast, precipitated, projected;* a bold
and emphatic mode of expression, implying far more than if he had merely
said that he *suffered them to sink into
the sea.* The expression is strikingly
paralleled in Neh. 9. 11, ' Their persecutors thou *threwest* into the deeps, as
a stone into the mighty waters.' In
like manner the use of 'horse' and 'rider'
in the singular is more emphatic than
that of 'horses' and 'riders' in the plural. It marks strongly the suddenness,
the universality, the completeness, of
the destruction. The Egyptian cavalry, numerous and formidable, covering
the face of the ground, is represented
as in a moment, by a single effort, by
one blow, overthrown, overwhelmed,
as if they had been but *one* horse and
one rider.
 2. *The Lord is my strength and song.*

prepare him ᵈan habitation; my
ᵉfather's God, and I ᶠwill exalt
him.

d Gen. 28. 21, 22. 2 Sam. 7. 5. Ps. 132 5.
e ch. 3. 15, 16. f 2 Sam. 22. 47. Ps. 99 5. &
118. 28. Isai. 25. 1.

Heb. עָזִּי וְזִמְרָת יָהּ *ozzi ve-zimrath
Yah, my strength and my song is Jah;*
one of the distinguishing titles of the
Most High, a contraction of 'Jehovah,'
occurring here for the first time in the
Scriptures, and seldom met with except
in the poetical books. We find it Ps.
68. 4, 'Extol him that rideth upon the
heavens by his name Jah.' It enters
also into the composition of the Hebrew
phrase הַלְלוּ יָהּ *halleluyah,* i. e. ' Hal-
lelu,' *praise ye,* 'Jah,' *the Lord,* which
is retained by the Holy Spirit in Rev.
19. 1—4, 'And after these things I heard
a great voice of much people in heaven
saying, Alleluia, &c.' intimating, probably, by the use of a Hebrew word that
at the period alluded to in the prophecy,
the Jewish nation shall have become
united with the Christian church, and
shall be heard uttering the praises of
God in their own language. By con-
fessing that God was their 'strength,'
they virtually abjure from themselves
the glory of the recent triumph, ascribing it solely to the almighty power of
their great and gracious Deliverer. No
instrument is to divide the praise with
him. No power, no wisdom, is to be acknowledged but that of God alone.——
¶ *My song.* That is, the subject of it.
——¶ *My salvation.* That is, the author of it.——¶ *I will prepare him a
habitation.* Chal. ' I will build him a
sanctuary.' This, if the Chaldee interpretation be correct, is a prophetical
intimation of the rearing of the sacred
edifice of the tabernacle. Some, however maintain that the word comes from
a root signifying *to adorn,* in which
case the sense of the expression is, *I
will pay him becoming honor.* Thus
Jarchi; 'I will celebrate his beauty and
his praise to those that shall come into

3 The LORD *is* a man of g war:
the LORD *is* his h name.

4 iPharaoh's chariots and his host
hath· he cast into the sea: k his

g Ps. 24. 8. Rev. 19. 11. h ch. 6. 3. Ps.
83. 18. i ch. 14. 28. k ch. 14. 7.

chosen captains also are drowned
in the Red sea.

5 lThe depths have covered them:
m they sank into the bottom as a
stone.

l ch. 14. 28. m Neh. 9. 11.

the world.' Gr. δοξασω αυτον, *I will
glorify him.* As this honor, however,
was to consist mainly in the dedication
to him of a place of worship, both senses
of the term very nearly harmonize.——
¶ *My father's God.* Heb. אלהי אבי
Elohë abi, God of my father; col. sing.
implying the entire line of his paternal
ancestry. The whole strain of the writer is full of affectionate and appropriating recognition of God as *their* God.
'He whose greatness I adore is not a
strange God unknown till now, a deliverer or protector for a moment. No,
he is the ancient and covenant God of
my family; his goodness is from generation to generation. I have a thousand
domestic proofs of his constant, undi-
minished affection; and he is now making good to me only that which he
solemnly promised to my *forefathers.'*
Such is the purport of this grateful
strain.

3. *The Lord is a man of war.* Heb.
איש מלחמה *ish milhamah.* That is,
mighty in battle, the achiever of great
victories. Chal. 'A victor of wars.'
Gr. κυριος συντριβων πολεμους, *the Lord
breaking wars;* a rendering for which
it is difficult to account, and in respect
to which Cartwright has very plausibly
suggested that πολεμους *wars* is a corrupt reading for πολεμιους *enemies;* the
Lord is a breaker-down, a prostrater, of
all enemies. Some have thought there
was something degrading in a form of
expression which seemed to bring down
the Deity to the level of a mere mortal
hero; but it is to be borne in mind, that
the phrase is purely Hebraic, and one
of the most emphatic of which the language admits to denote *excellence* or
preeminence of prowess. Thus the

very same phrase occurs 1 Sam. 17. 33,
as an appellation of Goliath, 'For thou
art but a youth, and he איש מלחמה *a
man of war* from his youth;' i. e. distinguished for warlike prowess and skill
Thus also we find ' man of beauty' for
one exceedingly fair and comely; ' man
of words,' for an eloquent man; ' man
of arm,' for a mighty man, &c.——
¶ *The Lord is his name.* Heb. יהוה
שמו *Yehovah shemo, Jehovah his name.*
That is, he hath shown his *nature* to be
Jehovah, by causing that *actually to be*
which he had promised *should be.* It is
as if the speaker had said, 'I cannot
characterise the mighty Deliverer so
well as by his name Jehovah, that ineffable and mysterious title which implies
not only the *promise* but the *performance*
of every thing that relates to the
well-being and happiness of his people.'
See Note on Ex. 6. 3.

4. *Hath he cast into the sea.* Heb.
ירה *yarah ;* a term applied mostly to
the *casting, hurling,* or *discharging*
of darts or arrows. Accordingly Aben
Esra, a Jewish commentator, remarks
that it is designed here to imply, that
God cast the chariots and the hosts of
Pharaoh into the sea with as much swift-
ness and ease as one would emit an arrow from the bow.—— ¶ *His chosen
captains.* Heb. מבחר שלשיר *mibhar
shalishauv, the choice of his captains ;*
i. e. the prime, the flower, of his chieftains.

5. *Sank into the bottom as a stone.*
Words strikingly expressive of the utter
and remediless overthrow of the enemy.
So completely were they plunged into
the depth of the sea, that they could not
rise to the surface, being probably for
the most part encumbered with heavy

6 n Thy right hand, O LORD, is become glorious in power : thy right hand, O LORD, hath dashed in pieces the enemy.

7 And in the greatness of thine o excellency thou hast overthrown them that rose up against thee:

n Ps. 118. 15, 16.　o Deut. 33. 26.

thou sentest forth thy wrath, *which* p consumed them q as stubble.

8 And r with the blast of thy nostrils the waters were gathered together, s the floods stood upright as

p Ps. 59. 13.　q Isai. 5. 24. & 47. 14.　r ch. 14. 21.　2 Sam. 22. 16.　Job. 4. 9.　2 Thess. 2. 8　s Ps. 78. 13.　Hab. 3. 10.

---

armor, which would effectually prevent their rising or floating ; while the guilt of their sins weighed still more heavily upon them.

6. *Thy right hand*, &c. Another form of expression for God's omnipotence. The right hand, being naturally the strongest from being most employed, is used by an apt metaphor for the highest degree of power. It is to be remarked moreover, that the verb in the original is in the future—'shall dash in pieces'— a remark which applies in fact to most of the verbs throughout the hymn. The phraseology is so constructed as to carry with it the implication that what *had* happened on this occasion to the enemies of God *would happen* in like manner in all future time, as far as utter discomfiture and signal perdition was concerned. On the other hand, in v. 14, and elsewhere, the verbs rendered in the future are in Heb. in the past, to indicate the infallible certainty of the event foretold.

7. *Overthrow them that rose up against thee.* Heb. קָמֶיךָ *kameka, thy risers-up.* So near is the relation between God and his people, that he accounts what is done to them as done to himself.——¶ *Thou sentest forth thy wrath.* Like a dreadful projectile, thou didst direct thy wrath against the foes of Israel, scattering desolation and death. It quitted the guiding pillar of fire, like a flash of lightning or like the blighting blast of the desert, and as either withers the grass or shrinks up the standing corn, so did they fall prostrate before it, and perished under the stroke of divine vengeance. They were of no more

account in thy sight than the useless stubble which is consumed by the sweeping autumnal fire.

8. *With the blast of thy nostrils the waters were gathered,* &c. Heb. בְּרוּחַ אַפֶּךָ *beruah appëka,* with the wind, or spirit, of thine anger ; the same word in the original signifying both 'nostril' and ' anger ;' from the effect of anger in inflating the nostrils. This has respect to the stormy wind mentioned, ch. 14. 26, 27. Thus Job, 4. 9, 'By the blast of God they perish, and by the *breath of his nostrils* (מֵרוּחַ אַפּוֹ) are they consumed.' So it is said of the ' man of sin,' 2 Thes. 2. 8, that the Lord will 'consume him by *the spirit of his mouth.*' Nothing can be grander than the image here employed. It implies that the gathering together of the mighty waters was an immediate act of the divine power ; the poet representing the Deity as emitting from his inflated nostrils the wind which produced an effect never before, nor since, witnessed by man. ——¶ *The depths were congealed.* A strong poetical expression not to be understood literally, but denoting that the waters maintained themselves in an upright position, with as much stability as if they had been converted to a wall of ice. The whole verse presents a beautiful gradation of sense. The waters were not only arrested in their channel and ceased to flow, but were *gathered together;* and not only were they gathered together, but they were fixed for the time in a condition entirely contrary to their natural tendency, and made *to stand upright* like a wall of masonry, or as firmly as if they had been *solidly congealed.*

an heap, *and* the depths were congealed in the heart of the sea.

9 t The enemy said, I will pursue, I will overtake, I will u divide the spoil: my lust shall be satisfied upon them; I will draw my sword, mine hand shall destroy them.

t Judg. 5. 30.   u Gen. 49. 27.   Isai. 53. 12. Luke 11. 22.

---

9. *The enemy said, I will pursue*, &c. The destruction of the Egyptians was more remarkable by reason of the pride and insolence which they displayed, and their strong assurance of success. The contrast between the confidence and elation of the pursuit, and the shame and ignominy of their overthrow, is made very impressive. They will not only pursue, but they will overtake, and if they overtake they have no question but they shall overcome, and obtain such a decisive victory as to divide the spoil. Thus it is that men are often never more confident and presumptuous than when they stand upon the very brink of ruin.——¶ *My lust shall be satisfied upon them.* Heb. תמלאמו נפשי *timlaëmo naphshi, my soul shall be filled with them.* See upon this peculiar signification of the word 'soul' the Note on Gen. 23. 8. The sentence expresses not only an intense desire, but a ruthless determination, of vengeance. The mere infliction of summary punishment upon a fugitive people who had quitted his dominions in opposition to his will, is not sufficient to satisfy the rage and vindictiveness of his spirit. He would give them up to slaughter and glut his implacable malice upon them. He is goaded on by a savage thirst of blood, and by the ordinary retributions of Providence has in the issue blood given him to the full.——¶ *My hand shall destroy them.* Or, Heb. תורישמו *torishëmo yadi, my hand shall repossess them;* i. e. bring them back to slavery. The original term ירש *yarash* is very peculiar in its import. The sense

10 Thou didst x blow with thy wind, y the sea covered them: they sank as lead in the mighty waters.

11 z Who *is* like unto thee, O Lord, among the gods? who *is* like thee, a glorious in holiness,

x ch. 14. 21.   Ps. 147. 18.   y ver. 5. ch. 14. 28. z 2 Sam. 7. 22.   1 Kings 8. 23.   Ps. 71. 19. & 86. 8. & 89. 6, 8. Jer. 10. 6. & 49. 19. a Isai. 6. 3

of *possession* or *inheriting* is very evident in Num. 14. 24, 'Him will I bring into the land whereunto he went, and he shall *possess it* (דורשנה).' And yet in other cases the contrary sense of *disinheriting, dispossessing,* is equally obvious. Thus Num. 14. 12, 'I will smite them with the pestilence and *disinherit* (אורשנו) them.' Josh. 23. 5. 'And the Lord your God he shall expel them from before you, and *drive* (הרש) them from out of your sight.' So also Deut. 4. 38. Jud. 1. 19—29. This apparent anomaly is to be accounted for from the fact, that the original, particularly in Hiphil, signifies *to inherit or possess in consequence of dispossessing another,* so that it is plainly equivalent to *driving out;* and to this the sense of *destroying, extirpating,* is closely analogous. The Greek here renders by κυριευσει ἡ χειρ μου, *my hand shall have dominion, or lord it.* Chal. 'My hand shall exterminate them.' Vulg. 'My hand shall slay them.'

10. *Thou didst blow with thy wind.* It was a wind raised by special divine intervention, not by the ordinary operation of nature. It was God's wind distinctly and preeminently; such a wind as caused the waters to accumulate and remain for a time stationary, or as the sacred text expresses it, 'to be congealed in the heart of the sea.'

11. *Who is like unto thee, O Lord, among the gods?* Heb. באלם *ba-ëlim, among the mighties, among the potentates.* In these words the superiority is affirmed of the true God over all earthly princes and potentates, and over

fearful *in* praises, b doing wonders?

b Ps. 77. 14.

all the false and factitious gods of
Egypt. A contrast is presented between
the omnipotence of the former and the
impotence of the latter What were the
mightiest of men whose breath was in
their nostrils; what were all the animal and reptile divinities to which that
besotted people offered adoration, that
they should be so much as named in
comparison with the great and glorious
God of the Hebrews, the Being of be-
beings, the infinite, the almighty, the
eternal!——¶ *Glorious in holiness.* Heb.
נאדר בקדש *nedar bakkodesh.* Gr.
δεδοξασμενος εν αγιοις, *glorified in the
holy ones,* i. e. among the saints and
angels; or, *in the holy things;* i. e. in
holiness. God is glorious in that holiness and immaculate purity which constitute his perfection. It is an attribute which especially elicits the praises
of the angelic hosts in heaven, Is. 6. 3,
and which shone conspicuous on the
present occasion. His holiness, his hatred of sin, his wrath against obstinate
transgressors, never appeared more re-
splendently glorious than in the destruction of Pharaoh in the Red Sea.
The insanctified heart may not respond
to this character of the divine holiness,
but to the soul which has been enlightened from above and gifted with
a spiritual perception of the things of
God, nothing appears so truly, so tran-
scendently glorious, as this perfection
of the immaculate Jehovah. It is, in
fact, the crowning glory of the Godhead, and if it do not so appear to us,
we have reason to be concerned at its
relations to our character and destiny.
——¶ *Fearful in praises.* Heb. נורא
תהלת *nora tehilloth, terrible, awful,
reverend, as to praises,* i. e. in his
praiseworthy manifestations of himself.
Thus the Apostle, Philip. 4. 8, 'If there
be any *praise;*' i. e. any thing praise-

12 Thou stretchedst out c thy right
hand, the earth swallowed them.

c ver. 6.

worthy. Even in those displays of his
perfections, which are matter of joyful
praise to his people, he is dreadful and
terrible to his enemies; and the consideration of this fact should chasten
and solemnize the tone of all our lauda-
tory ascriptions. Though, we honor
him with praises on our tongues, we
should do it with an humble awe upon
our spirits.——¶ *Doing wonders.* Heb.
עשה פלא *oseh pelë, doing that which
is wonderful.* Gr. ποιων τερατα, *doing
signs or prodigies.* On the import of
the original term פלא *pelë,* see Note on
Judg. 13. 18, from which it will appear
that it denotes that which is *preeminently marvellous* or *miraculously wonderful.* How justly the poet ascribes
this character to Jehovah, the whole
scope of the inspired history is a continued proof. Indeed the entire series
of providential dispensations in the
world is a tissue of *works of wonder.*
But the children of Israel in their present circumstances would naturally have
their eye more especially upon that succession of *miraculous judgments* which
had visited and desolated the land of
Egypt, and so prepared the way for
their deliverance. We find a striking
echo to the sentiment of this passage
in the parallel language of Job, ch. 5. 9,
'Which doeth great things and unsearch-
able; *marvellous things* (נפלאות *niphlaoth*) without number.'

12. *The earth swallowed them.* This
is nothing more than a poetical hyperbole, varying or rather strengthening
the prior description of the Egyptians
being overwhelmed in the mighty waters. They were so completely sub-
merged and sunk to the bottom of the
sea, that they might be said to be *swallowed* up by its deep abysses. 'Earth,'
however, is here to be taken in its generic import as equivalent to 'globe,'

13 Thou in thy mercy hast ^dled forth the people *which* thou hast redeemed: thou hast guided *them* in thy strength unto ^ethy holy habitation.

^d Ps. 77. 15, 20. & 78. 52. & 80. 1. & 106. 9. Isai. 63. 12, 13. Jer. 2. 6. ^e Ps. 78. 54.

14 ^fThe people shall hear, *and* be afraid: ^g sorrow shall take hold on the inhabitants of Palestina.

^f Numb. 14. 14. Deut. 2. 25. Josh. 2. 9, 10. ^g Ps. 48. 6.

which does not regard the distinction of land and water. Thus Jon. 2. 6, 'I went down to the bottoms of the mountains ; the *earth* with her bars was about me forever ;' i. e. I was engulphed in the deep places of the earth.

13. *Thou in thy mercy hast led forth,* &c. The poet here passes, by a sudden but natural transition, from the destruction of the Egyptians to the deliverance of the Israelites. This is very appropriate, as it places the two grand aspects of the event in strong and immediate contrast, the one that of justice, the other of mercy. How impressively are both presented before the mind in this transcendent song. While on the one hand thousands of wretched beings who knew not God, but had mocked him with their idolatries and provoked him with their rebellion, had been suddenly hurled into the embraces of death, they on the other had been graciously exempted from harm, rescued from bondage, restored to freedom! Great and manifold indeed were the mercies of God to his chosen, and richly were they worthy of the highest celebration.—— ¶ *Thou hast guided them,* &c. Heb. נהלת *nehalta.* The original in its legitimate sense signifies to *guide gently, softly, and with care,* as a good shepherd does his flock. It is the word used by the prophet, Is. 40. 11, ' He shall gather the lambs with his arms, and carry them in his bosom, and *gently lead* those that are with young.' Very pertinent to this are the words of the Psalmist, Ps. 77. 20, 'Thou *leddest thy people like a flock* by the hand of Moses and Aaron.' The phrase in the present instance is indeed rendered in the past,

'thou *hast* guided,' as if their destination had been actually reached, yet the meaning obviously is, that they were now *being guided,* that they were on the way which led toward the land of promise where they were to dwell, and where God was to dwell with them. Whether any thing more definite and precise than a peculiar residence or indwelling in the land of Canaan in general be intended, it is not perhaps possible to determine. This is called God's habitation simply because it was Israel's habitation, among whom he had engaged to *tabernacle* or dwell.

14. *The people shall hear and be afraid,* &c. The high poetic afflatus under which this sublime triumphal song was composed is nearly akin to the spirit of prophecy, and the verse before us evidently points to the future results of this signal victory, in its bearings upon the devoted nations of Canaan. The very tidings of such a tremendous overthrow of the Egyptians would go so far towards terrifying and disheartening their other enemies, that it would render the conquest of them comparatively easy. Their spirits would sink at the idea of grappling with such a power as evidently fought for Israel, and this secret misgiving, though it might not entirely preclude resistance, would yet so far weaken it, as to make them very little formidable in their warfare. That this was a true prediction we see at once by referring to the subsequent history. Josh. 5. 1, 'And it came to pass, when all the kings of the Amorites which were on the side of Jordan westward, and all the kings of the Canaanites which were by the sea,

15 h Then i the dukes of Edom
shall be amazed ; k the mighty men
of Moab, trembling shall take hold
upon them ; l all the inhabitants of
Canaan shall melt away.

16 m Fear and dread shall fall

h Gen. 36. 40. i Deut. 2. 4. k Numb. 22.
3. Hab. 3. 7. l Josh. 5. 1. m Deut. 2. 25. &
11. 25. Josh. 2. 9.

upon them ; by the greatness of
thine arm they shall be *as* still n as
a stone; till thy people pass over,
O Lord, till the people pass over,
o *which* thou hast purchased.

n 1 Sam. 25. 37. o ch. 19. 5. Deut. 32. 9.
2 Sam. 7. 23. Ps. 74. 2. Isai. 43. 1, 3. & 51. 10
Jer. 31. 11. Tit. 2. 14. 1 Pet. 2. 9. 2 Pet.
2. 1.

---

heard that the Lord had dried up the
waters of Jordan from before the children of Israel, until we were passed
over, that their heart melted; neither
was there spirit in them any more, because of the children of Israel.'——
¶ *The inhabitants of Palestina.* That
is, the Philistines, from whom, although
they inhabited only a part of it, the
land of Palestine is supposed to have
derived its denomination. They were
not of the prophetically accursed seed
of Canaan, nor are they enumerated
among the nations devoted to extermination, whose territory God assigned to
the Hebrews. But they maintained a
hostile attitude towards the Israelites,
with whom they had many battles, and
after a long series of struggles they were
finally effectually subdued by David.

15. *The dukes of Edom shall be amazed.* Heb. אלופי אדום *alluphë Edom.*
On the import of the Heb. term 'alluph'
see Note on Gen. 36. 15, 16.——¶ *All
the inhabitants of Canaan shall melt
away.* Heb. נמגו *namogu;* a term to
be understood rather of the mental despondency, the sinking away of courage
and hope, than of the physical wasting
and consumption of the Canaanites before the victorious arms of Israel. How
accurately this depicts the result that
actually occurred is evident from the
parallel language, Josh. 2. 9—11, 'And
she said unto the men, I know that the
Lord hath given you the land, and that
your terror is fallen upon us, and that
all the inhabitants of the land *faint*
(נמגו *namogu*) because of you. For
we have heard how the Lord dried up

the water of the Red Sea for you, when
ye came out of Egypt ; and what ye did
unto the two kings of the Amorites
that were on the other side Jordan, Sihon and Og, whom ye utterly destroyed. And as soon as we had heard these
things, our hearts *did melt* (ימס *yim-
mas*), neither did there remain any more
courage in any man, because of you.'
Throughout the whole context the gra-
dations of distress are strikingly mark
ed. First, there is to be *fear* among the
people ; then *sorrow* is to overtake the
inhabitants of Palestine ; next, the
princes of Edom are to be *amazed* or
painfully disturbed ; then the Moab-
ites shall *tremble* with terror ; and,
finally, the hearts of Canaan shall *melt
away* with overwhelming dread of the
coming disasters.

16. *Fear and dread shall fall upon
them,* &c. This is but an expansion of
the sentiment of the last clause of the
preceding verse.. They should be so utterly overcome with consternation that
their energies should be paralyzed, and
they should be unable to offer any effectual resistance. But let not Israel
forget that 'it was not their own arm
which would get them the victory.' It
was to be by the greatness of God's
arm, by the direct intervention of his
power, that the inhabitants were thus
to be rendered impotent in their alarm.
——¶ *They shall be as still as a stone.*
Gr. απολιθωθητωσαν, *let them be turned
into stones,* equivalent to the English
phrase of being *petrified* with fear, grief,
astonishment, &c.——¶ *Till thy people
pass over.* That is, till the Israelites

17 Thou sha.t bring them in, and
p plant them in the mountain of
thine inheritance, *in* the place, O
Lord, *which* thou hast made for

p Ps. 44. 2. & 80. 8.

thee to dwell in; *in* the q sanctuary, O Lord, *which* thy hands have
established.

q Ps 78. 54.

pass over the desert and the limits of
the land of Canaan, and enter upon
their inheritance. The Jordan, however, is probably more especially intended, as the spirit of prophecy pervades the poem. Thus the Chal. 'Until the people, O Lord, shall have passed
over Arnon and the Jordan.' This was
only a less miracle than the passage of
the Red Sea, inasmuch as the channel
is narrower, and the transit unattend-
ed by the destruction of enemies.——
¶ *Which thou hast purchased.* Heb.
קנית *kanitha*, hast gotten, *acquired, become possessed of.* The original signifies *to obtain* either by purchase, by generation, or by any other mode of acquisition, but more especially the former.
Thus, Deut. 32. 6, 'Is not he thy father
that hath *bought* thee?' Ps. 74. 2, ' Remember thy congregation which thou
hast *purchased* of old;' and the Apostle,
2 Pet. 2. 1, speaks of such as 'deny the
Lord that *bought* them.' Chal. 'Which
thou hast redeemed.' Gr. ὁν εκτησω, *which
thou hast possessed.*

17. *Thou shalt bring them in.* This
glorious beginning of God's favor to
them was of such a nature, as to afford
an earnest of the full accomplishment
of all his purposed mercy. If notwithstanding their unworthiness and all the
difficulties that lay in the way of their
escape, he had thus with a high hand
brought them out of Egypt, might they
not be assured that he would *bring them
into Canaan?* For having so begun
would he not make an end?——¶ *Plant
them in the mountain of thine inheritance.* That is, thou shalt give them a
settled and firmly fixed inheritance; a
metaphor taken from trees which when
their roots are struck deeply into the

earth cannot without the greatest difficulty be plucked up. It predicts, therefore, a permanent and stable mode of
life, in opposition to the roving and mi-
gratory habits of a people who are ever
on the move. See the similitude beautifully expanded, Ps. 80. 8—16, no doubt
in direct allusion to the expression of
the present text ; 'Thou hast brought a
vine out of Egypt: thou hast cast out
the heathen and planted it. Thou pre-
paredst room before it, and didst cause
it to take deep root, and it filled the
land. The hills were covered with the
shadow of it, and the boughs thereof
were like the goodly cedars. She sent
out her boughs unto the sea, and her
branches unto the river.' By the 'mountain of thine inheritance' is doubtless
meant the mountainous country of Canaan, with, however, a more especial reference to Mount Zion, the site of the
Temple. The term 'mountain' is plainly applied to the whole land of promise
in the following passage: Deut. 3. 25,
'Let me go over, and see the good land
that is beyond Jordan, the *goodly mountain,* and Lebanon.' Comp. Ps. 78. 54,
'And he brought them to the border of
his sanctuary, even to this *mountain,*
which his right hand had purchased.'
The three clauses rise in striking gradation, according to the genius of Hebrew poetry. First we have the *mountain,* or the land of Canaan generally ;
it is then restricted to *the place,* the
particular spot, upon which the temple
of the Lord's habitation was built; and
lastly we have the *sanctuary* itself,
the seat and centre of that economy
which was so certainly to be ' established,' that it is spoken of as if already
done.

18 r The LORD shall reign for ever and ever.

19 For the s horse of Pharaoh went in with his chariots and with his horsemen into the sea, and t the LORD brought again the waters of the sea upon them : but the chil-

r Ps. 10. 16. & 29. 10. & 146. 10. Isai. 57. 15. s ch. 14. 23.   Prov. 21. 31.   t ch. 14. 28, 29.

18. *The Lord shall reign for ever and ever.* This sublime pean is here concluded with a burst of rapturous exultation in view of God's universal and everlasting dominion. Though they had seen an end of Pharaoh's reign, and were assured of the final extinction of those hostile powers with which they would yet have to contend, there was no period to be put to the ever-during reign of the blessed and only Potentate, King of kings and Lord of lords. This appears to have been a sort of chorus in which all the people joined.

19. *For the horse of Pharaoh,* &c. This verse, if a part of the song, contains what the Greeks call the *epiphonema*, which includes the whole subject of the piece like the first chorus. It is obvious that it is a mere iteration in condensed terms of the general theme of the ode, such as might easily be retained in the memory of each individual, and by him transmitted along the line of his descendants to the latest posterity. But we decidedly prefer to adopt the opinion of Rosenmuller, who supposes that the triumphal hymn properly closes with v. 18, and that this is to be joined to the two succeeding verses as a brief recapitulation in simple prosaic narrative of the grand incident which gave occasion to the song.

20. *And Miriam the prophetess, the sister of Aaron.* Gr. Μαοιαμ, *Mariam;* Lat. 'Maria ;' Eng. 'Mary'—all the same name. She is called the sister of Aaron rather than of Aaron and Moses together, simply for brevity's sake, from Aaron's being her elder brother, and

dren of Israel went on dry *land* in the midst of the sea.

20 ¶ And Miriam u the prophetess, x the sister of Aaron, y took a timbrel in her hand; and all the women went out after her, z with timbrels, and with dances.

u Judg. 4. 4.   1 Sam. 10. 5.   x Numb. 26. 59 y 1 Sam. 18. 6. z Judg. 11. 34. & 21. 21. 2 Sam 6. 16.   Ps. 68. 11, 25. & 149. 3. & 150. 4.

from her having lived with him in Egypt while Moses was absent in Midian. The character of 'prophetess' is ascribed to her probably from the fact that she in common with Moses and Aaron, and like Deborah, Huldah, and Anna, was made in some degree the organ of divine communications, as it is said, Mic. 6. 4, 'I sent before thee Moses, Aaron, and Miriam,' where the three appear to be placed in co-ordinate rank.   So also, Num. 12. 1, Aaron and Miriam are represented as saying together, 'Hath the Lord spoken only by Moses? hath he not spoken also by *us ?*' It is supposed, however, by some to mean here no more than a woman eminently skilled in music, as it is plain that the word ' prophesy' is in several instances in the Scriptures employed to denote the act of singing or of playing upon musical instruments.   Thus David, 1 Chron. 25. 1, set apart the sons of Asaph and others, 'Who should *prophesy* with harps, with psalteries, and with cymbals.' The word ' prophesy' is also supposed to be used in the sense of singing the praises of God, 1 Cor. 11. 5, ' But every woman that prayeth or *prophesieth* with her head uncovered dishonoreth her head ;' for that it cannot here signify to *communicate instruction* is to be inferred from 1 Cor. 14. 34, 'Let your women keep silence in the churches ; for it is not permitted unto them to speak.'   Probably both senses are to be included in the term.——¶ *Took a timbrel.* Heb. הֹף *toph,* from a root signifying *to strike,* *smite, beat.*   The original word occurs about twenty times in the Heb. Bible

21 And Miriam ª answered them, ᵇ Sing ye to the LORD, for he hath triumphed gloriously: the horse and his rider hath he thrown into the sea.

ª 1 Sam 18. 7. ᵇ ver. 1.

but our translators, with a disregard of uniformity which too often mars their version, have in about one half the cases rendered it by *timbrel*, and in the other by *tabret*, and in only one instance, Jer. 31. 4, does the margin present a choice of renderings. The instrument thus denominated is with great probability supposed to have been constructed of a hoop, sometimes furnished with pieces of brass to make a jingling noise, over which a membrane of parchment was stretched like the head of a drum; it was beat with the fingers, and answered very exactly to the tambourins of modern times. In allusion to this mode of playing upon the instrument, the prophet, Nah. 2. 7, compares women's beating upon their breasts in deep anguish to their 'tabering,' or playing upon the timbrel, where the epithet is to be understood not of ' doves,' but of ' maids,' in a preceding part of the verse. For a more particular account of this instrument see Note on Gen. 31. 27.——¶ *With dances.* Of the eastern mode of dancing Lady M. W. Montagu says; 'Their manner of dancing is certainly the same that Diana is said to have danced on the banks of the Eurotas. The great lady still leads the dance, and is followed by a troop of young girls, who imitate her steps, and if she sings, make up the chorus. The steps are varied according to the pleasure of her that leads the dance, but always in exact time.' Accordingly Miriam here led the dance, whose movements regulated the steps of her female associates. In like manner it is probable that David, 2 Sam. 6. 24, 25, when the ark was removed, danced not *alone* before the Lord, but led the dance in the same authoritative kind of way.

22 So Moses brought Israel from the Red sea, and they went out into the wilderness of ᶜ Shur; and they went three days in the wilderness, and found no water.

ᶜ Gen. 16. 7. & 25. 18.

21. *Miriam answered them.* The whole song was probably, as suggested above, sung alternately by the men and women ranged into two bands, and by Miriam's 'answering' the men (for the original for 'them' is masculine) is meant, undoubtedly, that she was precentrix, or leader of the choir to the women, as Moses was to the men; or, as the words immediately following, ' Sing ye to the Lord, &c.' appear to indicate that which formed the 'answer of Miriam' and her companions, it is not unlikely that these words constituted a kind of chorus which was repeated at the end of each of the preceding verses, as in Ps. 136, the words, ' For his mercy endureth for ever,' are repeated throughout the whole psalm.

22. *So Moses brought Israel,* &c. From the opinion already expressed respecting the place where the Israelites encamped, and at which they entered the sea, it is evident that we regard Ain Mousa as the place, on the eastern shore, where they came up from the bed of the waters, and where they witnessed the overthrow of their oppressors. It is certain that the local traditions of the inhabitants of Sinai confirm this view of the subject; and although undue weight should not be attached to such traditions, yet neither should they be entirely disregarded when they support conclusions otherwise probable. Travellers who have explored the locality inform us, that a number of green shrubs, springing from numerous hillocks, mark the landward approach to this place. Here are also a number of neglected palm-trees, grown thick and bushy for want of pruning. The springs which here rise out of the

23 ¶ And when they came to
d Marah, they could not drink of
d Numb. 33. 8.

the waters of Marah; for they
were bitter: therefore the name of
it was called Marah.

ground in various places, and give name
to the spot, are soon lost in the sands.
The water is of a brackish quality, in
consequence, probably of the springs
being so near the sea; but it is nevertheless cool and refreshing, and in these
waterless deserts affords a desirable
resting-place. The view from this place,
looking westward, is very beautiful, and
it deserves to be mentioned that not
only do the springs bear the name of
Moses, but the projecting headland below them, towards the sea, bears the
name of Ras Mousa, *Cape of Moses.*
On the opposite shore of the Gulf stands
in full view the *Cape of Deliverance,*
the two uniting their abiding and un-
shaken testimony to the judgments and
wonders of that memorable day. The
'wilderness of Sinai' is the name given
to the desert extending from Canaan in
a southern direction, and bordering upon
the territories of Egypt. In Num. 33.
8, it is said that 'they passed through
the midst of the sea into the wilderness,
and went three days in the wilderness
of Etham, and pitched in Marah.' By
comparing the passage now quoted with
Ex. 13. 20, it appears that the wilderness of Etham extended from the western side, quite round the northern point
of the Red Sea, and to a considerable
distance along its eastern shore, as it is
evident that the Israelites on emerging
from the sea entered into the same wilderness on the edge of which they had
encamped before passing it. We imagine therefore that Junius and Tremellius have given the correct rendering of
this verse; 'Then Moses ordered the
Israelites to depart from the weedy
(red) sea that they might go into the
desert of Shur; and having gone three
days through the desert (of Etham)
they found water.' According to this
version, the wilderness of Shur, in-

stead of being the same with that of
Etham, lay beyond it, and could only be
reached by a previous three days' travel
through it. It is said, that a clear trace
of the ancient appellation still remains
in the present name of *Sdur.* 'To this
day there is nearly opposite the Bay of
Bedea the bed of a winter torrent which
is called *Wady Sdur,* and the coast to
some distance northward also bears the
name of *Sdur.* It is fair therefore to
infer that the Hebrews emerged from
the bed of the Gulf somewhere between
Wady Sdur and *Ras Mousa.* Indeed,
the necessary breadth of the opening
made for their passage, would have
obliged them to spread over a considerable part of the extent between the two
points, which are distant about fifteen
miles from each other.' *Pict. Hist. of
Palestine.*

23. *And when they came to Marah
they could not drink,* &c. Departing
from Ain Mousa their road lay over a
desert region, sandy, gravelly, and stony, by turns. On their right hand, their
eyes rested on the deep blue waters of
the gulf so recently sundered for their
sake; while on their left was the mountain chain of El Ruhat, stretching away
to a greater distance from the shore as
the pilgrims advanced. In about nine
miles they entered an extensive desert
plain now called El Ati, white and painfully glaring to the eye. Proceeding
beyond this, the ground becomes hilly,
with sandhills near the coast. In all this
way, which it took them three days to
traverse, they found no water; but at
last they came to a well, the waters of
which were so bitter, that it bore the
name of Marah, *bitterness.* At present,
'as we do not know that there were
three complete days' journey, nor what
distance made a day's journey for such
a numerous and encumbered host, and

24 And the people ᵉ murmured against Moses saying, What shall we drink ?

ᵉ ch 16. 2. & 17. 3.

25 And he ᶠcried unto the LORD; and the LORD shewed him a tree, g *which* when he had cast into the

ᶠ ch. 14. 10. & 17. 4. Ps. 50. 15. g See 2 Kings 2. 21. & 4. 41.

are also not quite assured of the point from which to begin the computation, we are allowed a considerable latitude in looking for Marah. Proceeding, then, along the coast south by east, over a plain alternately gravelly, stony, and sandy, we find the country begins to be hilly, with sand-hills near the coast, and at last come to the barren bed of a winter-torrent, called Wady *Amarah* (just the same in sound and meaning as *Marah*), a few miles south of which there is a well called Howara, which both Niebuhr and Burckhardt concur in considering to be the Marah of Scripture. It is true that these travellers agree in fixing the passage of the Red Sea at Suez, from which this spot is fifty miles distant, and forty miles from Ain Mousa. The distance from either point would be a good three-days' journey for such a body as the Hebrew host, nor would the distance be too short, if we suppose them to have started from some point between Ain Mousa and Wady Sdur. Even Dr. Shaw, who places the starting point at or below Wady Sdur, does not fix Marah more than a few miles below Howara. We may therefore consider the evidence for Howara as good as for any place that has yet been indicated. The well there lies among rocks, about a hundred paces out of the road, and its water is so bitter that men cannot drink it, and even camels, unless very thirsty, refuse to taste it. It occurs on the customary road along the coast from Suez to Sinai, and Burckhardt observes that there is no other well absolutely bitter on the whole coast so far as Ras Mohammed at the extremity of the peninsula. He adds: 'The complaints of the bitterness of the water by the children of Israel, who had been accustomed to

the sweet water of the Nile, are such as may be daily heard from the Egyptian peasants and servants who travel in Arabia. Accustomed from their youth to the excellent water of the Nile, there is nothing they so much regret in countries distant from Egypt ; nor is there any eastern people who feel so keenly the want of good water as the present natives of Egypt.' (Tour in the Peninsula of Mount Sinai.)' *Pict. Bib.*

24. *And the people murmured against Moses, saying,* &c. We here behold an affecting instance, not merely of Hebrew, but of human instability. How soon, alas ! does the feeling of a little present distress convert the peans and hallelujahs of weak believers into sighs of murmuring and grief ! All that Moses, all that God had done for Israel is forgotten, the moment a scarcity of water is felt ! Strange that one unpalatable beverage at Marah should have obliterated all remembrance of the recent wonders of Egypt, and the still more recent miracles of the Red Sea ! Did it require greater power to make the waters of Marah palatable, than to make those of the sea passable ? But why should they murmur against Moses ? Had he conducted them thither of his own motion without himself being led by the guiding movement of the cloudy pillar ? Might he not therefore with the utmost propriety have remonstrated with them, as on a subsequent occasion, 'Your murmurings are not against me, but against the Lord.' Unreasonableness towards men cannot well fail to blend itself with impiety towards God.

25. *And he cried unto the Lord,* &c. The ingratitude of the people of his charge did not prevail to extingush in the breast of Moses the spirit of fervent

waters, the waters were made sweet: there he ʰ made for them a

ʰ See Josh. 24. 25.

intercession in their behalf. By following his example the servants of God may be taught, like him, the means of turning bitter into sweet.——¶ *The Lord showed him a tree.* Heb. ‏רורהו‎ ‏עץ‎ *yorehu ëtz*, *taught him a tree.* Gr. εδειξεν αυτω ξυλον, *showed him a wood.* It is clear that God by some special monition or suggestion indicated to Moses a peculiar kind of tree or wood, which when thrown into the fountain rendered the bitter waters sweet and fit for use. But it is not clear whether this was owing to some inherent curative properties in the tree itself, or whether its selection was entirely arbitrary, and the effect purely miraculous. On the one hand, unless we admit that it possessed some native efficacy this way, it is not easy to see why a particular kind of tree was pointed out to Moses, when *any* tree, or even his own rod, would have answered the purpose equally well. Again, there is no doubt that certain species of vegetable productions have this corrective property, and that they have been often employed for this purpose. A modern traveller in South America speaks of a shrub called *alum-bre*, a branch of which put into the muddy stream of the Magdalena, precipitated the mud and earth, leaving the water sweet and clear. The first discoverers of the Floridas are said to have corrected the stagnant and fetid waters they found there, by infusing into it branches of sassafras ; and it is understood that the first use of tea among the Chinese, was to correct the waters of their ponds and rivers. 'Since the publication of the first edition,' says Mr. Milman, in a note to his history of the Jews, 'some water from a fountain called that of Marah, but probably not the Howara of Burckhardt, has been

statute and an ordinance, and there ⁱ he proved them.

ⁱ ch. 16, 4. Deut. 8. 2, 16. Judg. 2. 22 & 3. 1, 4. Ps. 66. 10. & 81. 7.

brought to this country, and has been analyzed by a medical friend of the author. His statement is subjoined: 'The water has a slightly astringent bitterish taste. Chemical examination shows that these qualities are derived from the selenite or sulphate of lime which it holds in solution, and which is said to abound in the neighborhood. If, therefore, any vegetable substance containing oxalic acid (of which there are several instances) were thrown into it, the lime would speedily be precipitated, and the beverage rendered agreeable and wholesome.'' At the same time, however plausible this reasoning, it is certain that the tree had not *necessarily* any such virtue, for nothing is more common than for God to disguise the naked exhibition of supernatural power by the interposition of an *apparent* cause, while yet the true character of the event is obvious from the utter inadequacy of the ostensible cause to produce by itself the resulting effect. It may be remarked too that it is scarcely credible, that in the scanty and little diversified vegetation of this district, a tree of such virtues should have been hitherto undiscovered. But if it had been discovered, Moses would no doubt have been informed of it, and so the divine indication of the tree have been rendered needless. If the corrective qualities, moreover, were inherent, but were at this time first made known, it can scarcely be conceived that so valuable a discovery would ever have been forgotten or lost, and yet it is manifest that in after times the Hebrews had not the knowledge of any tree which could render bad water drinkable ; and the inhabitants of the desert have not only not preserved the knowledge of any such fact, but they have not discovered it

26 And said, k If thou wilt diligently hearken to the voice of the
LORD thy God, and wilt do that
which is right in his sight, and
wilt give ear to his command-

k Deut. 7. 12, 15.

ments, and keep all his statutes, I
will put none of these l diseases
upon thee, which I have brought
upon the Egyptians : for I *am* the
LORD m that healeth thee.

l Deut. 28. 27, 60.   m ch 23. 25.   Ps. 41. 3,
4. & 103. 3. & 147. 3.

in the thirty-five centuries which have
since elapsed. This is shown by the
inquiries of travellers, some of whom
were actuated by the wish of finding a
plant which would supersede the miracle. Burckhardt confesses that after numerous inquiries, he never could learn
that Arabs were acquainted with any
plant or tree possessing such qualities ;
and on the whole, we cannot but conclude that whatever the tree was, it had
no more *inherent* virtue in sweetening
the bitter well of Marah, than the salt
had which produced the same effect
when thrown by Elisha into the well of
Jericho. In this, as in many other similar cases, it is easier to understand and
believe the miracle itself than the best
explanations which have been given. It
is remarkable that the Jewish writers
generally are so far from recognizing
any inherent virtues in the tree, that
they on the contrary affirm that its quality was bitter, saying, 'It is the manner
of the blessed holy God to make that
which is bitter, sweet, by that which is
bitter.' The Targums call it the bitter
tree *Ardiphni*, supposed to be the Rho-
dodaphne, or *rose-laurel*.——¶ *There he
made for them a statute and an ordinance.* Heb. משמט ומשפט
*sham sam lo hok u-mishpot, there he ap-
pointed to him a statute and a judgment;* i. e. to the nation of Israel spoken
of as one person. The original word
הק *hok*, comes from a root הקק *hakak*,
signifying to *describe, delineate, mark
out, define* and properly implies a *definite decree, a prescribed rule, order,
or course of action.* The statute or decree here intended is evidently that contained in the ensuing verse in which

God, having now assumed his people
into a peculiar relation to himself, and
being about shortly to organize them
under a more settled polity, here gives
them a general intimation of the conditions on which they might expect to
be dealt with during their sojourn in the
wilderness, which he is pleased to denominate a 'statute.' We find the same
or a similar phraseology occurring elsewhere on occasions on which the covenant obligations of the chosen people
are, as it were, entered into and ratified
anew. Thus, Josh. 24. 25, 'So Joshua
made a covenant with the people that
day, and *set them (him) a statute* (הק)
and an ordinance in Shechem'; i. e.
made known to them the conditions on
which they might expect to enjoy the
divine favor. So also in the second
Psalm, the Son is represented as declaring or reciting the 'decree' (הק) ; i. e.
announcing the terms or conditions on
which he was to exercise the prerogatives of the King of Zion.——¶ *There
he proved them.* Heb. נסהו *nissahu,
proved, tried, tempted him ;* the same
word with that used in reference to the
trial of Abraham, Gen. 22. 1, on which
see Note. God now *proved* or *tried* the
Israelites by bringing them into circumstances where their patience and
faith would be put to the test.

26. *If thou wilt diligently hearken,*
&c. These words contain a more full
and distinct explanation of what was
implied in the ' statute and ordinance'
that he now appointed for them. They
were now to be put in a special manner
upon their good behavior, and informed
both what God would expect from them
and what they might expect from him.

27 ¶ ⁿ And they came to Elim, where *were* twelve wells of water,

ⁿ Numb. 33. 9.

and threescore and ten palm-trees: and they encamped there by the waters.

They were not to suppose that because he had thus signally favored and honored them, he would connive at their sins and exempt them from merited punishment. On the contrary, they were to know that if they were rebellious and disobedient, the very same plagues which they had seen inflicted upon their enemies should be brought upon them, as it is again expressly threatened Deut. 28. 60, 'He will bring upon thee all the diseases of Egypt, which thou wast afraid of, and they shall cleave unto thee.' God is no respecter of persons, and they were to assure themselves that a rebellious Israelite would fare no better than a rebellious Egyptian. This declaration of God to his people, made under the present affecting circumstances, seems to have been regarded as so important that the prophet Jeremiah, a thousand years afterwards, referred to it to show, that from the very earliest period of Israel's covenant relation to God, their sacrifices had been held as of no account compared with obedience, Jer. 7. 22, 23, 'For I spake not unto your fathers, nor commanded them in the day that I brought them out of the land of Egypt, concerning burnt-offerings or sacrifices: But this thing commanded I them, saying, Obey my voice, and I will be your God, and ye shall be my people: and walk ye in all the ways that I have commanded you, that it may be well unto you.' Nor is it less important for *us* at this day, to be assured that God will deal with us according as we demean ourselves towards to him. The retribution may not indeed be now so visibly marked by outward signals, but it will be no less real in secret visitations upon the spirit, in the conscious well or ill being of the inner man. And in many cases the frown or the smile of God will be evident in the dispen-

sations of his providence.——¶ *I am the Lord that healeth thee.* Heb. יהוה רפאך *Yehovah rophe'eka, Jehovah thy healer.* This word in scripture usage is applied to the soul as well as to the body, and implies the *forgiveness of sins.* Thus, Ps. 41. 4, 'Lord be merciful unto me and *heal* my soul, for I have sinned against thee.' So also where one Evangelist, Mat. 13. 15, has, 'Lest they should be converted and I should *heal* them,' another, Mark, 4. 12, has 'Lest they should be converted, and *their sins should be forgiven* them.' In like manner it will be perceived by reference to Mat. 9. 2—6, that Christ's *healing* and *forgiving sins*, in the case of the paralytic, are spoken of as nearly identical acts. Yet we cannot but think that there was still more in the incident and the language here recorded. We know that nothing was more common than for God to make outward actions and events a significant medium of conveying moral lessons. The present incident we regard of this character. God ordered in his providence that the Israelites should be brought to this bitter fountain, where an *occasion* should be afforded them of evincing and thus of learning the bitterness of their own hearts. And as he healed the waters by the miraculous exertion of his power, so he here tells them that he is the Lord who heals *them* also. He only can infuse a healing virtue into the embittered and empoisoned fountain of the human heart.

27. *They came to Elim where were,* &c. This spot is supposed, with sufficient probability, to be the same as that which now bears the name of Wady Gharendel, which is the largest of all the torrent-beds on the western side of the peninsula. It is about a mile broad, and extends away indefinitely to the north-east. This pleasant valley abounds in

CHAPTER XVI.

AND they ^a took their journey from Elim, and all the congregation of the children of Israel

a Numb. 33. 10, 11.

came unto the wilderness of ^b Sin, which *is* between Elim and Sinai, on the fifteenth day of the second month after their departing out of the land of Egypt.

b Ezek. 30. 15.

---

date or palm-trees, tamarisks, and acacias of different species. But the springs are not at present immediately in the common route, though a small rivulet of brackish water runs through the valley, rendering it one of the principal stations on the route to Sinai. Burckhardt says of it, 'If we admit *Bir Howara* to be the Marah of Exodus, then *Wady Gharendel* is probably Elim, with its wells and its date-trees ; an opinion entertained by Niebuhr. The non-existence at present of twelve wells at Gharendel, must not be considered as evidence against this conjecture ; for Niebuhr says that his companions obtained water here by digging to a very small depth; and there was a great plenty of it when I passed. Water, in fact, is readily found by digging, in every fertile valley in Arabia, and wells are thus easily formed, which are quickly filled up by the sands.'——¶ *Three score and ten palm-trees.* Or 'date-trees,' as the fruit of the palm is called *date.* The presence of the palm in the arid regions of the East is an unerring sign of water. It is a tree which rises to a great height ; the stalk is very strait, but knotty, and the centre, instead of being solid like the trunk of other trees, is filled with pith. The leaves are six or eight feet long, and when spread out, broad in proportion. It is crowned at the top with a large tuft of leaves which never fall off, but always continue in the same flourishing verdure. This tree attains its greatest vigor about thirty years after being planted, and continues in full vigor seventy years longer, bearing all this while every year about three or four hundred pounds weight of dates. This fruit grows below the leaves

in clusters, and is of a sweet and agreeable taste. The palm is put to an immense variety of uses in the East, and is to the inhabitants of that region incomparably the most important and valuable production of all the vegetable world. It forms therefore a suitable emblem of the righteous in their flourishing condition, Ps. 92. 12—14, and the bearing of its branches is a badge of victory; Rev. 7. 9, 'After this, I beheld, and lo ! a great number which no man could number... stood before the throne and before the Lamb, clothed with white robes, and *palms* (palm branches) in their hands,' &c.

Chapter 16

1. *And they took their journey from Elim,* &c. Upon comparing this account with that given Num. 10. 11, we find that previous to their reaching the wilderness of Sin, they came again upon the shore of the Red Sea, where, or at Elim, they must have abode for some time ; for as it was thirty days after leaving Egypt before they arrived at the wilderness of Sin, and we have not more than ten days accounted for at the previous stage, twenty days remain to be distributed between the two or three last stations. But it is obvious from other parts of the history, that the writer does not specify every place where they encamped, but only the most important, or those in which some remarkable incident occurred.——¶ *Came to the wilderness of Sin.* Heb. אֶל מִדְבַּר סִין *el midbar Sin.* No part of the history of the Israelites is more perplexing and obscure than that which relates to the topography of the places and stations mentioned on their route from

2 And the whole congregation of the children of Israel ᶜ murmured

ᶜ ch. 15. 24.   Ps. 106. 25.   1 Cor. 10. 10.

against Moses and Aaron in the wilderness:

3 And the children of Israel said

Egypt to Canaan. We cannot, at best, assure ourselves of any thing more than an approximation to the truth in most instances, and in many cases not even to that. As to the present passage, it is to be remarked that the Scriptures distinguish two *deserts of Sin*, one being written סִין *sin*, the other צִין *tzin*. The former is the one spoken of here, the latter in Deut. 32. 51. Num. 13. 21. —27. 14.—34. 3. Josh. 15. 3. Of the present we know little more than what is here said of it, that it lay between Elim and Sinai. What is implied in this may perhaps as probably be learned from the ensuing extract as from any other source. 'A chain of mountains called El Tyh stretches across the peninsula of Sinai, from the Gulf of Akaba, to near the coast of the Gulf of Suez. The common road, which we suppose the Israelites to have taken—and which they most obviously would take wherever they might have crossed between Suez and Birket Faroun—turns off from the shores of the gulf, southeast towards Sinai, after the extremity of these mountains towards the west has been rounded. We understand the desert of Sin to comprehend most of the space to be traversed between the point where the road turns off to within a few miles of Mount Serbal, which is the first of the larger mountains of the Sinai group. This is of course, from its situation, not a flat and uniform desert; but it is still a desolate wilderness, but more or less hilly and rocky, with valleys of various dimensions, but generally sandy or stony, strewed with the bones of camels, generally without plants or herbage, and also without water, except in the rainy season, when the valleys are traversed by the torrents that descend from the mountains. Burckhardt, who however says nothing

about the identity of this region with the desert of Sin, relates that while traversing it from Sinai, his party met several Arabs, who had started in the morning from the well of Morkha, and had ventured on the journey without water, *or the hope of finding any* till the following day, when they would reach Wady Feiran. Now Morkha is near the gulf at one extremity of this desert region, and Wady Feiran near Mount Serbal at the other, the distance between the two points being about thirty miles; and we suppose this to have been nearly the route of the Israelites. We do not mean to say that the desert of Sin was limited to the district we mention; we only attempt to define its limits in the direction of the journey, at the same time not denying that the term might be applicable to all the country between the shore of the gulf on the west, and the Sinai group on the east.' *Pict. Bib.*

2. *And the whole congregation murmured*, &c. Individual exceptions it may be presumed there were, but the great body of the host are to be considered as having been justly liable to the charge. They had now subsisted thirty days upon the provisions brought out of Egypt, and it may well be supposed that their stock was nearly, if not altogether exhausted. Two millions of people, encamped in a barren desert, and beginning to find themselves short of food, would be very easily pervaded by a general alarm lest the horrors of famine should soon be upon them. To exercise faith in these circumstances in opposition to the dictates of sense, was doubtless no easy matter. Accordingly finding themselves reduced to straits, their impatient spirits again utter the language of murmuring against Moses and Aaron, whom they invidiously accuse, if not of an express design to

starve them in the wilderness, yet with bringing them into circumstances where they had every reason to fear that this would be the actual result. It is scarcely possible to conceive any thing more ungrateful or perverse. Indeed their conduct was marked by the double brand of *impious* and *absurd*. It was very culpable towards God. This was neither the first nor greatest extremity to which they had been reduced, and out of which they had been delivered. That which they had experienced at the Red Sea was much greater. There they had become acquainted with God as one who never suffers those that hope in him to be confounded. Why therefore do they not trust in him now? why not resignedly commit themselves to him? He had promised to conduct them to Canaan, and he will keep his word. If they do not know where to obtain food, neither did they know how to pass the Red Sea; and yet they did pass it. So they were bound to believe that on this occasion he would not fail to supply their wants—that 'bread should be given and water should sure.' Again, a moment's thought will show us that their deportment was now less absurd than wicked. What ground had they for ascribing such base intentions to Moses and Aaron? Had they any more to eat than the rest? and were not they as much in danger of perishing as themselves? One would think that reason, as well as gratitude, must have become extinct in men who could in these circumstances have preferred such a charge. Yet this is not all. The very people who had seen all the first-born of Egypt slain in one night on their account, now virtually wish that they had themselves perished in like manner. The very people that had sighed and cried by reason of their bondage in that country, now magnify its plenty, because they had sat by the flesh-pots and ate bread to the full! How strange to hear them speak as if it had been better to drag out a wretched, degraded life and die a miserable death in Egypt, provided they could have plenty of food, than to live under the guidance of the heavenly pillar in the wilderness, with God himself for their almoner, simply because they find themselves pinched a little with hunger, as they had before been with thirst! After all we cannot well doubt that in their present distress they paint their former comforts in altogether too glowing colors. What they call plenty now, they probably did not call so then; but it is easy to over-estimate the past when men are disposed to aggravate to themselves or others the hardships of their present lot. It heightens, moreover, our sense of their unreasonable and guilty conduct, when we consider that they were really in no danger of dying for want in the wilderness so long as they had their flocks and herds with them. But, alas! we recognise in this, as in other instances of their perverseness, but too faithful a picture of our fallen nature. How prone are we to fret and murmur under any present inconvenience! That which troubles us for the moment is the greatest of all troubles. Past dangers and deliverances, past supports and comforts, are all forgotten. Our minds dwell upon present evil, and our tempers are irritable, fretful, and impatient. We quarrel it may be, with our best friends, and murmur in spirit, though not perhaps with our lips, against God. Even those who profess to be the only the spiritual seed of Abraham, may adopt the language of his literal seed, Ps. 106. 6, 7, 13, 14, 'We have sinned with our fathers, we have committed iniquity, we have done wickedly. Our fathers understood not thy wonders in Egypt; they remembered not the multitude of thy mercies; but provoked him at the sea, even at the Red Sea. They soon forgat his works, they waited not for his counsel: But lusted exceedingly in the wilderness, and tempted God in the desert.

unto them, d Would to God we had died by the hand of the LORD in the land of Egypt, e when we sat by the flesh-pots, *and* when we did eat bread to the full: for ye have brought us forth into this wilderness, to kill this whole assembly with hunger.

d Lam. 4. 9.　e Numb. 11. 4, 5.

4 ¶ Then said the LORD unto Moses, Behold, I will rain f bread from heaven for you; and the people shall go out and gather a certain rate every day, that I may g prove them whether they will walk in my law, or no.

f Ps. 78. 24, 25. & 105. 40.　John 6. 31, 32.
1 Cor. 10. 3.　g ch. 15. 25.　Deut 8. 2, 16.

——¶ *This whole assembly.* Heb. כל את הקהל הזה eth kol hakkahol hazzeh, *this whole church*, as the term is usually rendered in the Greek. Comp. Acts, 7, 'This is he that was *in the church* in the wilderness with the angel that spake to him, &c.'

4. *Then said the Lord unto Moses,* &c. Although the murmuring was not directly but only indirectly against God, yet he at once takes up the cause as his own. Instead, however, of expressing the resentment of an insulted sovereign and benefactor, he utters the gracious purpose of overcoming their evil with good, and of pouring down blessings instead of wrath upon the murmuring host. Complaining is to be silenced by complying, and men, unworthy of the meanest earthly fare have the promise of a daily supply of bread from heaven! But this, though not the manner of men, is the manner of God. He has gifts even for the rebellious, and the unspeakable gift of salvation through his Son was imparted in manifest contrariety to our deserts. He hath commended his love to us in that while we were yet sinners Christ died for us. Though we have rendered to him only disobedience, guilt, and unthankfulness, yet how have they been repaid? Not by a visitation of vengeance, not by an award of judgment, but by raining upon us the bread of life from heaven! As to the grand design of this miraculous provision the remarks of Henry are strikingly appropriate. 'Man being made out of the earth his maker has wisely ordered him food out of the earth, Ps. 104. 14.

But the people of Israel, typifying the church of the first-born that are written in heaven, and born from above, and being themselves under the conduct and government of heaven, receiving their charters, laws, and commissions from heaven, from heaven also received their food: their law being given by the disposition of angels, they did eat angels' food.' —— ¶ *I will rain bread.* Heb. ממטיר לחם mamtir lehem, *I am raining bread, or food;* i. e. about to rain; the same phraseology that occurs in announcing the rain of the deluge, Gen. 6. 13, 17.——¶ *A certain rate every day.* Heb. דבר יום ברומו debar yom beyomo, *the matter of a day in his day;* i. e. they were to collect on each day the portion necessary for that day, but no more. They were not to collect to day what would not be required till to-morrow. It was but another form of enjoining upon them the Savior's rule, 'Take no thought for to-morrow what ye shall eat or drink.' God would school them to simple-hearted dependence on his daily providence.——¶ *That I may prove them whether*, &c. That is, that I may afford them an occasion of testifying whether they will trust me and walk by faith in the absence of all human means of supply, or not. This lesson, or ' law,' though hard to learn, is one that God would have deeply engraven upon the hearts of his children in all ages. A state of constant conscious dependence upon him is the state to which he aims to bring all his people. And this, could we realize it aright, is a far *happier* state than any

5 And it shall come to pass, that on the sixth day they shall prepare *that* which they bring in ; and h it shall be twice as much as they gather daily.

6 And Moses and Aaron said unto all the children of Israel, i At even, then ye shall know that the LORD

h See ver. 22. Lev. 25. 21. i See ver. 12, 13.
& ch. 6. 7. Numb. 16. 28, 29, 30.

hath brought you out from the land of Egypt:

7 And in the morning, then ye shall see k the glory of the LORD: for that he heareth your murmurings against the LORD : And l what *are* we, that ye murmur against us ?

k See ver. 10. Isai. 35. 2. & 40. 5. John 11. 4, 40. l Numb. 16. 11.

other. How unspeakably kind and condescending in the great Father of all to assume upon himself the care of our interests, and relieve our minds from the oppressive load of anxiety which we so often suffer to weigh upon them ! Not that we are to deem ourselves exempted from the necessity of diligent exertion; not that we are to fold our hands in listless torpor, and call this an humble reliance on heaven; but having done what we can, we are not to be solicitous ; we are not to give way to unbelieving fears lest we should not be provided for. Our heavenly Father knoweth that we have need of these things. He will take care of his children, and let them not be surprised or stumbled if they should themselves painfully 'proved' on this score at more than one station of their wanderings in this wilderness world. The original term נסה *nasah, to tempt or try,* is the same as that applied elsewhere in similar connexions, and which is fully explained in the Note on Gen. 22. 1. The pronominal suffix, however, is not 'them,' as in our translation, but ' him,' representing the whole people as spoken of as one man.

5. *On the sixth day they shall prepare that which they bring in.* From this it appears that the manna gathered on the sixth day was not eaten in the form in which it was brought in. It was first bruised in a mortar, or ground in a mill, and then baked into bread. This process, whatever it was, was to be performed on the day before the sabbath,

that both their hands and their minds might be unencumbered with domestic cares during the season of worship. Whether the same or a similar preparation of the manna was necessary on the other days of the week, it is not possible to determine. The probability, we think, is that it was not.

6. *At even, then shall ye know,* &c. The Israelites had charged Moses and Aaron with bringing them out of Egypt as if from their own motion. Moses, therefore, here assures them, on the other hand, that they should soon have evidence that it was Jehovah, and not his servants, who had brought them out of the land of bondage.

7. *In the morning, then ye shall see the glory of the Lord.* That is, shall behold the cloudy pillar, the Shekinah, resplendent with a peculiar brightness and glory, as a signal of the Lord's special presence, both to hear your murmurings and to supply your wants. It appears that on several occasions the tumults of the people were assuaged by some visible change in the ordinary appearance of the pillar of cloud, betokening, perhaps, by a fierce and vehement glow the kindling of the divine displeasure. See Num. 12. 5—14, 10—16, 42. Or the phrase ' glory of the Lord' may be but another expression for the miraculous work, the sending of the manna, which so strikingly manifested his glory. Thus, in like manner, in reference to the miraculous work of Christ in raising Lazarus from the dead it is said, John, 11. 40, 'Said I not unto thee

8 And Moses said, *This shall be* when the LORD shall give you in the evening flesh to eat, and in the morning bread to the full; for that the LORD heareth your murmurings which ye murmur against him: and what *are* we? your murmurings *are* not against us, but ᵐ against the LORD.

9 ¶ And Moses spake unto Aaron, Say unto all the congregation oᵢ the children of Israel, ⁿ Come near

ᵐ See 1 Sam. 8. 7.   Luke 10. 16.   Rom. 13. 2.   ⁿ Numb. 16. 16.

---

that if thou wouldst believe thou shouldst see *the glory of God?*' i. e. the glorious work of God. So also Num. 14. 21, 22, 'glory' is used in a sense equivalent to *striking achievements of divine power;* 'But as truly as I live, all the earth shall be filled with the glory of the Lord. Because all those men which have seen my *glory,* and my miracles (or, *even* my miracles), &c., shall not see the land which I sware unto their fathers.' The first is doubtless the most primary and legitimate sense, as appears from v. 10; and we cannot question, from the ordinary import of the glowing or burning pillar of cloud, that the spectacle now predicted wʾas intended to intimate to them the fact of the divine displeasure, notwithstanding the purpose graciously to supply their wants. Thus the Jewish commentator Abrabanel; 'Their seeing the glory of the Lord is not to be understood of the bread, or the flesh he sent them, but of the fire which appeared to all the people to reprove them for their murmurings.'

8. *The Lord shall give you in the evening flesh to eat.* As God does not always withhold in displeasure, so he does not always grant in love. A promise of bread in the morning is precious information, but the addition of flesh to the full in the evening, and that very evening, wears rather the appearance of a threatening. When our desires exceed the bounds of wisdom they amount to lusts, and if God deigns to gratify our lusts it is very far from being a token for good. On the contrary, it is suspicious; it is ominous of a purpose to chastise us through the natural results of our own folly.——¶ *For that the*

Lord heareth, &c. These words confirm the idea suggested above, that the language of rebuke and threatening is intermingled with that of favor. Otherwise how can we understand it as a reason for supplying their wants, that he had heard their murmurings? Such a reason demanded a punishment rather than a favor; and we can have no doubt that while God intended to bestow upon them, in his own way, the requisite means of subsistence, he intended at the same time to make such a display of himself as would chasten, humble, and shame his people in view of their sinful deportment.—— ¶ *Your murmurings are not against us.* Not so much against us as against the Lord. So 1 Sam. 8. 7, 'For they have not rejected thee, but they have rejected me;' i. e. not so much thee as me. John, 12, 44, 'He that believeth on me, believeth not on me, but on him that sent me;' i. e. not so much on me. Chal. 'Your murmurings are not against us, but against the Word of the Lord.'

9. *Come near before the Lord.* That is, before the cloud in which the Lord's glorious presence was manifested, and which for the present constituted the Shekinah or habitation of the divine Majesty. The symbols of God's presence are repeatedly in the Scriptures called by his name. Thus Uzzah is said, 1 Chron. 13. 10, to have died 'before God;' whereas in 2 Sam. 6. 7, it is said, 'He died by the ark of God.' So the commandment, Ex. 23. 17, 'Three times in the year all thy males shall appear before the Lord God,' is to be understood of appearing before the tabernacle or temple, 'the place which the Lord did choose to put

before the LORD: for he hath heard your murmurings.

10 And it came to pass, as Aaron spake unto the whole congregation of the children of Israel, that they looked toward the wilderness, and behold, the glory of the LORD º appeared in the cloud.

11 ¶ And the LORD spake unto Moses, saying.

12 P I have heard the murmurings

º ver. 7. ch. 13. 21. Nuшb. 16. 19. 1 Kings 8. 10, 11. P ver. 8.

of the children of Israel; speak unto them, saying, ۹ At even ye shall eat flesh, and ʳ in the morning ye shall be filled with bread: and ye shall know that I *am* the LORD your God.

13 And it came to pass, that at even ˢ the quails came up, and covered the camp: and in the morning ᵗ the dew lay round about the host.

۹ ver. 6. ʳ ver. 7. ˢ Numb. 11. 31. Ps. 78. 27, 28. & 105. 40. ᵗ Numb. 11. 9.

his name there.' Deut. 12. 5, 6. Before this awful symbol they were now cited to appear, as before a tribunal.

10. *They looked toward the wilderness.* In the direction in which they were journeying, whither the cloud had probably moved in advance of the congregation.——¶ *The glory of the Lord appeared in the cloud.* Chal. 'The Glory of the Lord was revealed.' Arab. 'And lo, the Light of the Lord in the cloud.' That is, the Shekinah appeared in a new aspect. An unwonted glowing fiery brightness appeared in the guiding pillar, which on ordinary occasions presented to the eye merely an opaque towering mass of cloud, in which the divine Majesty was supposed to dwell, and did dwell. Its preternatural resplendent appearance was obviously a token of the displeasure of God towards his people. See Remarks above, p. 164 —168.

11, 12. *The Lord spake unto Moses,* &c. These two verses are undoubtedly designed to acquaint us with the source and authority of the annunciation which Moses gave v. 6, 7, and therefore the verb 'spake' should be rendered in the pluperfect tense, 'had spoken.' This makes the narrative clear, and supersedes the necessity for which some commentators contend, of transposing these verses so as to bring them in immediately after v. 3. —— ¶ *At even.* Heb. בֵּין הָעַרְבַּיִם *bĕn ha-arbayim, between*

the two evenings. Gr. το προς ἑσπεραν, *towards evening;* i. e. in the afternoon. See Note on Ex. 12. 6.

13. *At even the quails came up.* Heb. תַּעַל הַשְּׂלָו *taal hasselav, the quail* (collect. sing.) *came up.* The 'quail' is a bird of the gallinaceous kind, somewhat resembling the partridge. Hasselquist, speaking of the larger species of quail, says, 'It is of the size of the turtle-dove. I have met with it in the wilderness of Palestine near the shores of the Dead Sea and the Jordan, between Jordan and Jericho, and in the deserts of Arabia Petræa. If the food of the Israelites was a bird, this is certainly it; being so common in the places through which they passed.' Some commentators have supposed that the original word שְׂלָו *salav,* denoted a species of *locust,* which is well known to have constituted anciently an article of food among the inhabitants of that region, and which is in fact eaten by the Arabs of the present day. But to this it is an insuperable objection, that the Psalmist, in describing this particular food of the Israelites, says, Ps. 78. 27, 'He rained *flesh* also upon them as dust, and *feathered fowls* like as the sand of the sea.' They 'came up' from the Arabian Gulf, across which they fly in the spring in great numbers, and are often so fatigued after their passage, and fly so low, as to become an easy prey wherever they alight. Wisd. 19. 12, 'For quails came

14 And when the dew that lay was gone up, behold, upon the face of the wilderness *there lay* ᵘ a small round thing, *as* small as the hoar frost on the ground:

ᵘ Numb, 11. 7. Deut. 8. 3. Neh. 9. 15. Ps. 78. 24. & 105. 40.

15 And when the children of Israel saw *it*, they said one to another, It *is* manna : for they wist not what it *was*. And Moses said unto them, ˣ This *is* the bread which the Lᴏʀᴅ hath given you to eat.

ˣ John 6. 31, 49, 58. 1 Cor. 10. 3.

up unto them from the sea for their contentment.' Another miraculous supply of quails was granted to the Israelites about a year after this, of which we have a detailed account, Num. 11. 31—35. David probably alludes to both when he says, Ps. 105. 40, 'The people asked, and he brought *quails*, and satisfied them with the bread of heaven (the manna).' —— ¶ *The dew lay.* Heb. הרתה שכבת הטל hayethah shikbath hattal, *there was a laying (or layer) of dew.* Chal. 'There was a descent of dew.' Arab. 'There was a spreading of dew.'

14. *And when the dew that lay was gone up*, &c. Heb. ותעל שכבת הטל vattaal shikbath hattal, *and the layer of dew came up ;* i. e. appeared on the surface of the earth, without any special reference to its originating in the air, and much less without intending to convey the idea of its evaporation into the atmosphere, as our translation has erroneously rendered it. The phrase in the original is precisely the same with that applied to the quails, v. 13, ותעל השלו taal hasselav, *the quail came up;* i. e. made its appearance. There is no good reason for rendering the particle ו *and* by ' when' as is done in our version. The true meaning of the clause must be determined by what is more explicitly affirmed of the phenomenon, Num. 11. 9, 'And when the dew fell npon the camp in the night, the manna fell upon it ;' from which it does not appear that the ordinary dew first vanished away before the manna was seen. On the contrary, the substance resembling the hoar-frost lay *upon* the dew. It was perhaps imbedded thus in the morning

dew in order that a due degree of moisture might be imparted to it, and that it might be gathered clean and free from the dust or sand of the desert. It was made to fall ' upon the face of the wilderness,' or without the precincts of the camp, probably because the camp was not so clean a place for the purpose.— ¶ *A small round thing.* Heb. דק דק דק דק דק mehuspos, from the root דקק dakak, signifying *to beat small or fine, to comminute, to triturate ;* and hence as an adjective *small, minute, atom-like.* It would seem to have been a fine powdered substance, like flour, and perhaps a pretty large mixture of dew was necessary to give it sufficient coherence to enable them to gather it. As to the connected word מחספס *mehusphos,* though rendered *round,* it is of extremely uncertain sense, occurring no where else but here, and derived from an unknown root. From a comparison of the cognate dialects Castell elicits the sense of *beat, pounded, pulverised;* Gesenius that of *decorticatum* or something *pealed off;* i. e. *scaly, flaky;* and Michaelis that of *snow-like*, which latter Rosenmuller very confidently adopts as the true sense, particularly as it is immediately after compared to the *hoar-frost.* But it is still a field of conjecture.

15. *They said one to another, It is manna; for they wist not what it was.* Heb. מן הוא *man-hu.* The rendering in our translation is manifestly incorrect and contradictory, and should be exchanged for that in the margin, 'What is this ?' For how could the Israelites be ignorant what it was, if they at once declared it to be *manna ?* Josephus

says expressly that 'man' is a particle of interrogation, and so the Septuagint understands it—τι εστι τουτο, *what is this?* It is but proper to remark here, however, that another, and perhaps on the whole a better derivation of the term itself is given by most of the Jewish and many Christian critics. This is to trace its etymology to מנה *manah, to prepare, appoint, determine, apportion,* whence by apocope of the last letter מן *man,* the same as מנה *manah, a part, a portion, a prepared allowance.* Thus we find the latter employed, 1 Sam. 1. 4. 5, 'And when the time was that Elkanah offered, he gave to Peninnah his wife, and to all her sons and her daughters, *portions* (מנות *manoth*). But unto Hannah he gave a worthy *portion* (מנה *manah*) for he loved Hannah; but the Lord had shut up her womb.' 1 Sam. 9. 23, 'And Samuel said unto the cook, Bring the *portion* (מנה *manah*) which I gave thee, of which I said unto thee, Set it by thee.' Ps. 11. 6, 'This shall be the *portion* (מנת *menath*) of their cup.' That an abbreviation of the word from מנה *manah* to מן *man* should occur under the circumstances is very natural, as the next word begins with ה *h,* the very letter elided, and similar contractions in regard to the verb מנה *manah* are very common. Thus Ps. 61. 7, 'O *prepare* (מן *man*) mercy and truth for him.' Jonah, 1. 17, 'Now the Lord had *prepared* (ימן *yeman*) a great fish.' Dan. 1. 5, 'And the king *appointed* (ימן *yeman*) them a daily provision, &c.' As, therefore, both the form and the signification favor this etymology, there is, we conceive, little hazard in saying with the most learned of the Rabbins, that *man* signifies the food *appointed, prepared for,* and *doled out* to the children of Israel as their *portion.* Such a name was appropriate to this miraculous food, while there is something undignified, to say the least, in the idea that this supernatural aliment should always be called

'what,' simply because that, upon its first appearance, they said, 'what is it?' Although it is true that they did not distinctly know what it was when it appeared, and they had no particular name by which to express it, yet they had been assured by Moses, verse 12, that they should be satisfied with food, and they accordingly conjectured that what they saw was the *portion* intended for them from heaven, and applied to it the proper term for expressing that idea.—It can scarcely be necessary to inform the reader that attempts have been made to identify this manna with the natural juices or gums of certain trees or shrubs to which the name has been given. The strongest claim to identity applies to the substance called by the Arabs *mann,* of which the fullest account is given by Burckhardt (Tour in the Peninsula of Mount Sinai). Speaking of the Wady el Sheikh, to the north of Mount Serbal, he says, 'It is the only valley in the peninsula of Sinai where this tree grows, at present, in any great quantity; though small bushes of it are here and there met with in other parts. It is from the tarfa that the manna is obtained. This substance is called by the Bedouins *mann,* and accurately resembles the description of manna given in the Scriptures. In the month of June, it drops from the thorns of the tamarisk upon the fallen twigs, leaves, and thorns which always cover the ground beneath that tree in the natural state; the manna is collected before sunrise, when it is coagulated; but it dissolves as soon as the sun shines upon it. The Arabs clean away the leaves, dirt, etc., which adhere to it, boil it, strain it through a coarse piece of cloth, and put it in leathern skins: in this way they preserve it till the following year, and use it as they do honey, to pour over unleavened bread, or to dip their bread into. I could not learn that they ever made it into cakes or loaves. The manna is found only in years when copious rains have fallen; sometimes it is not produced at all. I saw none of it among the Arabs, but I obtained a small piece of the last year's produce, in the convent (of Mount Sinai) where, having been kept in the cool shade and moderate temperature of that place, it had become quite solid, and formed a small cake; it became soft when kept some time in the hand; if placed in the sun for five minutes, it dissolved; but when restored to a cool place, it became solid again in a quarter of an hour. In the season at which the Arabs gather it, it never acquires that state of hardness which will allow of its being pounded, as the Israelites are said to have done, in Num. 11. 8. Its color is a dirty yellow, and the piece which I saw was still mixed with bits of tamarisk leaves; its taste is agreeable, somewhat aromatic, and as sweet as honey. If eaten in any considerable quantity, it is said to be slightly purgative. The quantity of manna collected at present, even in seasons when the most copious rains fall, is trifling, perhaps not amounting to more than five or six hundred pounds. It is entirely consumed among the Bedouins, who consider it the greatest dainty which their country affords. The harvest is usually in June, and lasts for about six weeks.'—'The notion, however, that any species of vegetable gum is the manna of the Scriptures, appears so totally irreconcilable with the Mosaic narrative, that, notwithstanding the learned names which may be cited in support of the conjecture, it cannot be safely admitted as any explanation of the miracle. It is expressly said, that the manna was rained from heaven; that when the dew appeared, it also appeared lying on the surface of the ground, 'a small, round thing, as small as the hoar-frost,' 'like coriander seed, and its color like a pearl;' that it fell but six days in the week, and that a double quantity fell on the sixth day; that what was gathered on the first five days

became offensive and bred worms if kept above one day, while that which was gathered on the sixth day kept sweet for two days; that the people had never seen it before, which could not possibly be the case with either wild-honey or gum-arabic; that it was a substance which admitted of being ground in a handmill or pounded in a mortar, of being made into cakes and baked, and that it tasted like wafers made with honey; lastly, that it continued falling for the forty years that the Israelites abode in the wilderness, but ceased on their arriving at the borders of Canaan. To perpetuate the remembrance of the miracle, a pot of the manna was to be laid up by the side of the ark, which clearly indicates the extraordinary nature of the production. In no one respect does it correspond to the modern manna. The latter does not fall from heaven, it is not deposited with the dew, but exudes from the trees when punctured, and is to be found only in the particular spots where those trees abound; it could not, therefore, have supplied the Israelites with food in the more arid parts of the desert, where they most required it. The gums, moreover, flow only for about a month in the year; they neither admit of being ground, pounded, or baked; they do not breed worms; and they are not peculiar to the Arabian wilderness. Others have supposed the manna to have been a fat and thick honey-dew, and that this was the wild-honey which John the Baptist lived upon—a supposition worthy of being ranked with the monkish legend of St. John's bread, or the locust-tree, and equally showing an entire ignorance of the nature of the country. It requires the Israelites to have been constantly in the neighborhood of trees, in the midst of a wilderness often bare of all vegetation. Whatever the manna was, it was clearly a substitute for bread, and it is expressly called meat, or food. The abundant supply, the periodical suspen-

16 ¶ This *is* the thing which the LORD hath commanded, Gather of it every man according to his eating: yan omer for every man *according to* the number of your persons, take ye every man for *them* which *are* in his tents.

17 And the children of Israel did

y ver. 36.

so, and gathered, some more, some less.

18 And when they did mete *it* with an omer, zhe that gathered much had nothing over, and he that gathered little had no lack : they gathered every man according to his eating.

z 2 Cor. 8. 15.

sion of it, and the peculiarity attaching to the sixth day's supply, it must at all events be admitted, were preternatural facts, and facts not less extraordinary than that the substance also should be of an unknown and peculiar description. The credibility of the sacred narrative cannot receive the slightest addition of evidence from any attempt to explain the miracle by natural causes. That narrative would lead any plain reader to expect that the manna should no longer be found to exist, having ceased to fall upwards of 3,000 years. As to the fáct that the Arabs give that name to the juice of the *tarfa,* the value of their authority may be estimated by the pulpit of Moses and the footstep of Mohammed's camel. The cause of Revelation has less to fear from the assaults of open infidels, than from such ill-judged attempts of skeptical philosophers, to square the sacred narrative by their notions of probability. The giving of the manna was either a miracle or a fable. The proposed explanation makes it a mixture of both. It admits the fact of a divine interposition, yet insinuates that Moses gives an incorrect or embellished account of it. It requires us to believe, that the scripture history is at once true and a complete misrepresentation, and that the golden vase of manna was designed to perpetuate the simple fact, that the Israelites lived for forty years upon gum-arabic! The miracle, as related by Moses, is surely more credible than the explanation.' *Modern Traveller.*

16. *According to his eating.* Heb.

לפי אכלו *lephi oklo, according to the mouth of his eating;* i. e. as much as would be sufficient for his daily consumption. See Note on Ex. 12. 4.——— ¶ *An omer for every man.* Heb. עמר לגלגלת *omer laggulgoleth, an omer for an head;* the head being put for the whole person, as in Ex. 38. 26. An omer was about three quarts English measure.——¶ *According to the number of your persons.* Heb. מספר נפשתכם *mispar naphshothekem, the number of your souls.* See Note on Gen. 12. 5.

17. *Gathered some more, some less.* Heb. וילקטו המרבה והממעיט *yilketu hammarbeh ve-hammamit, they gathered, (both) he that multiplied and he that diminished;* correctly rendered, as to the sense, in our translation, 'some more, some less.' Paul, 2 Cor. 8. 13—15, thus alludes to this circumstance; 'For I mean not that other men be eased and ye burdened. But by an equality, that now at this time your abundance may be a supply for their wants, that their abundance also may be a supply for your wants; that there may be equality: As it is written, He that hath gathered much had nothing over; and he that had gathered little had no lack ;' from which it is inferred by some that when any one had gathered more than his due share he gave the overplus to those who had gathered less. Others however suppose that the whole quantity gathered by any one family was first put into a common mass and then measured out to the several individuals composing the household.

19 And Moses said, Let no man leave of it till the morning.

20 Notwithstanding, they hearkened not unto Moses; but some of them left of it until the morning, and it bred worms, and stank: and Moses was wroth with them.

21 And they gathered it every morning, every man according to his eating: and when the sun waxed hot it melted.

22 ¶ And it came to pass, *that* on the sixth day they gathered twice as much bread, two ómers for one *man :* and all the rulers of the congregation came and told Moses.

23 And he said unto them, This *is that* which the LORD hath said, To-morrow *is* ᵃthe rest of the holy sabbath unto the LORD: bake *that* which ye will bake *to-day*, and seethe that ye will seethe; and that which remaineth over, lay up for you to be kept until the morning.

ᵃ Gen. 2. 3. ch. 20. 8. & 31. 15. & 35. 3. Lev. 23. 3.

---

19. *Let no man leave of it.* It is not implied by this that every man was imperiously commanded to eat at all events every particle which he gathered; but that if any portion of it was left, instead of being reserved for future use, it should be immediately thrown away.

20. *It bred worms.* Heb. וירם תולעים *va-yarum tolaim, wormed worms, or bred abundantly, or crawled with worms.'*

22. *And it came to pass,* &c. If it be asked why this matter was brought to Moses, we know of no other answer than that the people were taken by surprise at the great quantity which they found that they had gathered. Finding upon measuring it, that upon the sixth day they had collected as much as two omers for a man, they had recourse to Moses to know what do to under the circumstances. His answer immediately follows. There is no reason that their surprise should surprise us, for although this fact of the fall of the double quantity of manna had been announced to Moses, v. 5, it does not appear that it had been previously declared to the people; or if the direction had been given to collect a double quantity on the sixth day, it does not appear that the *reason* of it had been declared.

23. *This is that which the Lord hath said.* That is, this double quantity on the sixth day is according to what the Lord hath said, v. 5, though, as before remarked, it had been said to Moses,

and not to the people.——¶ *Tomorrow is the rest of the holy sabbath unto the Lord.* Heb. שבתון שבת קדש ליהוה מחר, *shabbathon shabbath kodesh lahovah mahar, the sabbatism, the sabbath of holiness to the Lord, is tq-morrow.* That is, the season of *rest* or *cessation,* appointed at the creation to be kept holy to the Lord, as explained on Gen. 2. 3. But as the Heb. שבת *shabbath* is retained by the Holy Spirit in the form of the Gr. σαββατον, *sabbaton,* Mat. 12. 5, 8, so the apostle in Heb. 4. 9, employs the corresponding שבתון *shabbathon,* here used in the form of the Gr. σαββατισμος *sabbatismos,* which is by interpretation *rest.* Although the law was not yet given, yet it is clear that the sabbath had been previously observed. He does not say 'To-morrow shall or will be, but, to-morrow *is* the rest of the holy sabbath unto the Lord.' The institution is recognised as one already existing, but its observance is now in a manner renewed and enjoined with more express particularity, perhaps from its having fallen into much neglect among the Israelites. The present was in fact a very suitable occasion to remind them of its obligation; for they would now have an opportunity to notice the *miraculous* seal of regard which God was pleased to put upon it. ——¶ *Bake that which ye will bake to day,* &c. That is, bake or boil to-day whatever you wish to have so dressed

24 And they laid it up till the morning, as Moses bade: and it did not b stink, neither was there any worm therein.

25 And Moses said, Eat that to-day; for to-day *is* a sabbath unto the LORD; to-day ye shall not find it in the field.

26 c Six days ye shall gather it;

b ver. 20.　　c ch 20. 9, 10.

but on the seventh day, *which is* the sabbath, in it there shall be none.

27 ¶ And it came to pass, *that* there went out *some* of the people on the seventh day for to gather, and they found none.

28 And the LORD said unto Moses, How long d refuse ye to keep my commandments and my laws?

d 2 Kings 17. 14.　Ps. 78. 10, 22. & 106. 13.

for to-morrow's provision. In like manner, the spirit of the Christian as well as of the Mosaic economy requires that no work shall be done on the sabbath, which can as well be done the day before.

24. *And they laid it up,* &c. The result was now found to be directly the reverse of what had been experienced in a former case, v. 20, when a portion of it had been kept contrary to the divine precept. That which was laid by *in opposition* to a command, putrified and stank, while that which was kept *in obedience* to a command, remained pure and sweet.

26. *In it there shall be none.* On that day it should not fall. They were, therefore not to expect it, nor go out to gather it. This intermission of the manna on the seventh day was an irrefragable proof that it was not produced by natural causes ; and it would be a striking attestation to the sanctity which he had attached to that day. It is scarcely possible to avoid drawing the inference from this, that the attempt to procure for ourselves any advantage by doing on the holy sabbath the appropriate work of the week-time, will prove abortive. Every thing is beautiful, and we may add, prosperous, in its season, and only then.

27. *And it came to pass that there went out,* &c. There were probably some who were disposed to put Moses' words to the test, and ascertain from experiment whether his prediction would hold good. They were no doubt prompted by the same motives as those who

would fain satisfy themselves whether the manna would corrupt by being kept over till the next morning, and accordingly. laid by a portion for that purpose. There can be no question that this conduct in both cases was highly offensive to God, as it showed a practical distrust of his veracity.

28. *And the Lord said unto Moses,* &c. Moses himself was not disobedient, but he was the ruler of a disobedient people, and God charges the offence upon him with the rest, that he might the more warmly charge it upon them. The language would naturally have the effect to make him feel himself invested with a greater responsibility as to watching over the spirit and deportment of the people, whose collective person he sustained in his own.——¶ *Let no man go out of his place.* That is, out of the camp of Israel. It is not an absolute prohibition of all locomotion on the sabbath, as it was lawful to attend their holy convocations and their meetings in the synagogue, Lev. 23. 3. Acts, 15. 21. But they were especially interdicted on that day from going abroad in order to gather manna. The general rule adopted by the Jews in regard to travelling on the sabbath was, that the distance to be considered lawful should not extend beyond the suburbs of a city, which was ordinarily the space of two thousand cubits, or about three quarters of an English mile. Thus. Mount Olivet was a sabbath-day's journey from Jerusalem, which is known to have been about a mile.

29 See, for that the LORD hath given you the sabbath, therefore he giveth you on the sixth day the bread of two days: abide ye every man in his place, let no man go out of his place on the seventh day.

30 So the people rested on the seventh day.

31 And the house of Israel called the name thereof Manna: and e it *was* like coriander-seed, white; and the taste of it *was* like wafers *made* with honey.

32 ¶ And Moses said, This *is* the thing which the LORD commandeth,

e Numb. 11. 7, 8.

Fill an omer of it to be kept for your generations; that they may see the bread wherewith I have fed you in the wilderness, when I brought you forth from the land of Egypt.

33 And Moses said unto Aaron, f Take a pot, and put an omer full of manna therein, and lay it up before the LORD, to be kept for your generations.

34 As the LORD commanded Moses, so Aaron laid it up g before the Testimony, to be kept.

f Hebr. 9. 4. g ch. 25. 16, 21. & 40. 20. Numb. 17. 10. Deut. 10. 5. 1 Kings 8. 9

---

30. *So the people rested on the seventh day.* Not only on this particular sabbath, after being frustrated in seeking for manna, but also uniformly on the seventh day during the whole course of their sojourning. It is a virtual intimation of the restored regular observance and sanctification of the sabbath, which had previously no doubt, during the bondage, gone into desuetude.

31. *It was like coriander seed.* It resembled this seed in shape and size, but in color it is expressly said, Num. 11. 6, to have resembled the bdellium, which from this passage it is evident was white. When baked it is said, Num. 11. 8, to have had the taste of 'fresh oil.' But in its native state, when first collected, its taste is here intimated to have resembled that of honey-wafers.

32. *Fill an omer of it to be kept.* That the memory of signal mercies to one generation should be perpetuated for the benefit of another, is doubtless the principle on which this precept is founded. By a method which was in itself miraculous, God purposed that posterity should see the bread on which his people were sustained for forty years, and also how much was allotted for each man's portion. They would then be able to bear witness that their

fathers were neither stinted to hard fare nor to a short allowance, and could thus judge between God and Israel, whether they had most reason to murmur or be grateful.—The idea that the manna was a mere natural production, is amply refuted by this injunction. For where was the necessity or propriety of preserving a specimen of that which nature continued to produce?

33. *Take a pot,* &c. The original word, which occurs no where else but here, signifying simply a *pot* or *urn*, is rendered by the Sept. 'golden pot,' and this rendering is adopted by the apostle, Heb. 9. 4.——¶ *Lay it up before the Lord.* That is, before the Ark of the Testimony, the symbol of the divine presence, as is clearly evinced in the ensuing verse. This Ark was not indeed yet constructed, but the history was written and perhaps the command given after it *was* made, and the fact is introduced here out of its natural order, because the sacred writer would now conclude all that he had to say respecting the manna.

34. *Aaron laid it before the Testimony.* That is, before the Ark of the Testimony, which in this connexion is evidently equivalent to 'before the Lord' in the preceding verse. It is here called the 'testimony,' instead of the 'ark of

35 And the children of Israel did eat manna h forty years, i until they came to a land inhabited: they did eat manna, until they came unto the borders of the land of Canaan.

36 Now an omer *is* the tenth *part* of an ephah.

h Numb. 33. 38. Deut. 8. 2, 3. Neh. 9. 20, 21. John 6. 31, 49. i Josh. 5. 12. Neh. 9. 15.

---

the testimony,' its usual appellation, by the same kind of ellipsis by which 'covenant' is used Gen. 17. 10, for the 'sign of the covenant.' See Note in. loc.

35. *The children of Israel did eat manna forty years.* Notwithstanding all their provocations, which were gross and often repeated, yet the manna, the grand staple of their subsistence, never failed. We know not on the whole but the manna is fairly entitled to be considered the greatest of the Old Testament miracles. It was not in fact one miracle, but an astonishing combination of many. It was a regular supply of food, a substitute for corn, during nearly forty years. It fell around the camp of the Israelites regularly, in all places and at all seasons, during all their removals. The supply, which was regularly intermitted once in every week, was compensated by a double supply the preceding day. It became unfit for use if kept to the next day, and yet, once a week, it might be kept for two days. And when the miracle was about to be discontinued, as no longer necessary, a pot full of it was directed to be laid aside, and preserved as a memorial to future generations. All these marvellous circumstances are not mere abstract qualities of the manna, but *historical facts* — facts inseparably interwoven with the history of the chosen people. It is surely then an attempt of no common hardihood, though it has been made, to endeavor to bring this sublime set of miracles within the limit of a natural probability. But, in truth, **every effort made to explain away the**

CHAPTER XVII.

AND a all the congregation of the children of Israel journeyed from the wilderness of Sin, after their journeys, according to the commandment of the LORD, and pitched in Rephidim: and *there*

a ch. 16. 1. Numb. 33. 12, 14.

---

miracle as related by Moses, actually requires one as great, or greater, to fill its place, and we are therefore content to take the matter as we find it in the scriptural narrative.

Chapter 17

1. *And all the congregation — journeyed — and pitched in Rephidim.* From the station in the wilderness of Sin, where the manna began to fall, the Israelites continued their journey over a sandy and stony region, intersected by the beds of numerous torrents, which are perfectly dry except in the seasons of rain, when some of them are filled with water to the depth of ten or twelve feet. Except at that season water is scarce; and by the usual and nearest route, which is generally supposed to be that taken by the Israelites, water occurs only at two places before reaching Wady Feiran. Upon comparing the present narrative with the fuller details given Num. 33, we find that two stations, viz. Dophkah and Alush, are entirely omitted here, which are mentioned there as resting-places between the desert of Sin and Rephidim. The first of these is probably the Wady Naszeb, still a favorite station for travellers on account of the combined advantages of a well of good water and the shelter of a large impending rock. 'Shady spots like this,' says Burckhardt, 'are well known to the Arabs; and as the scanty foliage of the acacia, the only tree in which these valleys abound, affords no shade, they take advantage of such rocks, and regulate their journey in such a way as to be

was no water for the people to drink.

2 b Wherefore the people did chide with Moses, and said, Give us wa-

b Numb. 20. 3, 4.

able to reach them at noon, there to take their siesta'—a circumstance which reminds one of the satisfaction with which ' the shadow of a great rock in a weary land' is mentioned by the prophet, Is. 32. 2. The other station may have been at Wady Boodra, where there is a spring of good water, though from its being somewhat aside from the common road, and often choked with sand, it has escaped the notice of most travellers. The next rest of the host was at Rephidim, where no water could be found. The determination of this station is important from its bearing upon an alleged locality of modern times, which is said to contain the identical rock smitten by Moses for the supply of water to the Israelites. There is, we think, the greatest reason to question the truth of this tradition, though very ancient; but to go fully into the argument would require a more extended detail of particulars relative to the topography of the entire Sinai region, than our limits will allow. We must therefore content ourselves with referring the reader to the able discussions of the Pictorial Bible on the subject. He will there find abundant reason to believe that the tradition which makes the rock of Rephidim to be among the higher summits of Sinai, and at the very foot of Mount St. Catherine, where there is plenty of water, to be altogether erroneous.—— ¶ *According to the commandment of the Lord.* Heb. עַל פִּי רְהֹוָה *al pi Yehovah, at the mouth of Jehovah.* They are said to have journeyed at the 'mouth' or 'commandment' of the Lord, because they followed the direction of the cloudy pillar, pausing **when it paused, and moving when it**

ter that we may drink. And Moses said unto them, Why chide ye with me ? wherefore do ye c tempt the LORD ?

c Deut. 6. 16. Ps. 78. 18, 41. Isai. 7. 12. Matt. 4. 7. 1 Cor. 10. 9.

moved. That this is to be understood by the phrase ' commandment of the Lord,' is evident from Num. 9. 18, 19. '*At the commandment of the Lord* (עַל פִּי רְהֹוָה) the children of Israel journeyed, and at the commandment of the Lord they pitched: as long as the cloud abode upon the tabernacle they rested in their tents. And when the cloud tarried along upon the tabernacle many days, then the children of Israel kept the charge of the Lord, and journeyed not. And so it was, when the cloud was a few days upon the tabernacle; according to the commandment of the Lord they abode in their tents, and according to the commandment of the Lord they journeyed.' Though journeying by the commandment, or under the express guidance of the Lord, yet they are conducted to a scene of extreme trial and distress; showing that the mere fact of our being in the way of our duty is no certain security against the occurrence of trouble. God may have wise though inscrutable reasons for bringing his pilgrims from Sin to Rephidim, from hunger to thirst.

2. *The people did chide with Moses.* Heb. וַיָּרֶב *va-yareb*, from the root רוּב *rub* which signifies *to strive, contend, litigate,* usually by reproachful words, though sometimes by deeds, as Gen. 49. 23. Ex. 21. 18. 1 Sam. 16. 5. In this case the impatience and irritation of their spirits vented itself in violent reproaches against Moses, and they challenge him to supply them with water, as if he had the command of springs and rivers and could summon them up at will, and produce effects in the desert to which Omnipotence alone is equal. As on a former occasion, they now also mur-

3 And the people thirsted there for water; and the people d murmured against Moses, and said, Wherefore *is* this *that* thou hast brought us up out of Egypt to kill

d ch. 16. 2.

us and our children and our cattle with thirst.

4 And Moses e cried unto the LORD saying, What shall I do unto this people? they be almost ready to f stone me.

e ch. 14. 15. f 1 Sam. 30. 6. John 8. 59. & 10. 31.

mured against him for bringing them out of Egypt, as if, instead of delivering, he designed to slay them, their children, and cattle with thirst. Their rage and malice at length rose to such a pitch, that they were 'almost ready to stone him;' and yet we are to remember that they had been, a very short time before, supplied with food directly from the hand of God himself; they were feeding upon that food every day; and they were daily led by the miraculous pillar of cloud, which was a sensible token that the responsibility of their route rested not upon Moses, but upon God. Into such gross absurdities, as well as flagrant wrongs, do the fierce demands of appetite hurry sinful men, prompting them to act like madmen, casting about fire brands, arrows, and death, among their best friends. 'Though he had commanded the clouds from above, and opened the doors of heaven, and had rained down manna upon them to eat, and had given them of the corn of heaven. For all this they sinned still, and believed not for his wondrous works.' Yet in this complaining and murmuring multitude we see but an epitome of the race. Their conduct is but too faithful a picture of what large bodies of men are continually disposed to do, even to quarrel the most with those from whom they have received the greatest benefits, and to be ready to seek their death, as soon as they meet with the least disappointments of their desires. Thus it was in after ages with the divine Benefactor of the world. 'Many good works have I showed you from my Father; for

which of these works do ye stone me?' —— ¶ *And Moses said unto them,* &c. Under these trying circumstances, Moses retains his characteristic calmness. He indeed reproves them; he shows them upon whom their murmurings reflected; but he does not denounce them; he does not meet rage with rage; but simply expostulates with them upon the unreasonableness of chiding *with him* for a privation which he had no hand in producing.—— ¶ *Wherefore do ye tempt the Lord?* Why do ye tempt the Lord by distrusting his providential care and kindness, and by murmuring against his ministers? Why do ye act as if ye would *try him,* and see whether he will be provoked to come out in some severe judgment against you?

3. *To kill us and our children.* Heb. לְהָמִית אֹתִי וְאֶת בָּנַי *lehamith othi ve-eth banai, to kill me and my sons;* spoken of as one man. 'To kill' here is properly 'to make to die,' that is, to suffer to die; to bring into circumstances which would expose to death.

4. *And Moses cried unto the Lord, saying,* &c. The present was an emergency on which Moses might very properly adopt the Psalmist's motto, 'What time I am afraid I will trust in thee.' The torments of extreme thirst tend very much to work men up to desperation, and render their passions fierce and ungovernable. We cannot doubt that Moses was now in real peril of his life. But he had before this learned where his true refuge lay, and to that he betakes himself. He pours out his complaint to God as to a friend, a father, a guardian, a guide. He begs of him to direct him

5 And the LORD said unto Moses, g Go on before the people, and take with thee of the elders of Israel: and thy rod, wherewith h thou smotest the river, take in thine hand, and go.

g Ezek. 2. 6.   h ch. 7. 20. Numb. 20. 8.

6 i Behold, I will stand before thee there upon the rock in Horeb; and thou shalt smite the rock, and there shall come water out of it, that the people may drink.   And

i Numb. 20. 10, 11. Ps. 78. 15, 20. & 105. 41. & 114. 8. 1 Cor. 10. 4.

how to act in this emergency, for he is himself utterly at a loss. This is the true import of his words, 'What shall I do unto this people?' They imply nothing vindictive; they are not a question touching the manner in which he should most effectually *punish* them, but simply regard the proper deportment for him to observe under the circumstances. How unspeakable the comfort of having such a sanctuary and such an oracle to flee to when our motives are suspected, our good, evil spoken of, our conduct reviled, and our patience tried ! How favored is he whom the Lord hides in his pavilion from the strife of tongues !

5. *And the Lord said unto Moses,* &c. However much we have trembled for Moses in this extremity, we are prompted, on reading this verse, to tremble still more for those murmuring, unbelieving, rebellious Israelites. We hear the voice of God commanding his servant to take the ominous rod with which he had bruised and broken Egypt, and we anticipate that it is now to be an instrument of inflicting some fearful chastisement upon his guilty people. We can scarce repress an inward shudder in anticipation of the sequel. But how speedily are our apprehensions calmed ? The rod is to be assumed for a purpose of mercy and not of wrath. It is to smite, not a sinful people, but a flinty rock. It is to draw forth, not a stream of blood from the heart of the offender, but a stream of water to cool his tongue, and to restore his fainting frame. How involuntary the exclamation, ' Surely, O Lord, thy ways are not as our ways, nor thy thoughts as our thoughts !'——

¶ *Go on before the people.* Go even in the midst of their rage, and before their thirst is relieved; fear not to advance boldly at the head of the host, and trust to my arm for protection.——¶ *Take with thee of the elders.* As if the mass of the people had rendered themselves unworthy of being the spectators of such a glorious miracle.——¶ *And thy rod, wherewith thou smotest the river.* He does not say, ' the rod which was turned into a serpent,' or ' the rod with which thou didst work wonders,' but he makes special mention of the miracle wrought upon the waters of the Nile, because a somewhat similar one was now to be effected.

6. *Behold, I will stand before thee there.* That is, the cloudy pillar, the symbol of my presence, shall stand before thee there. Gr. 'I stand there before thou come to the rock.' It is implied that the cloud should go before, and stationing itself on the spot where the miracle was to be performed should await the arrival of Moses and the elders, just as the star pointed out the birth place of Christ.——¶ *Upon the rock in Horeb.* The arguments adduced above in relation to the true site of Rephidim, require that we should understand by 'Horeb' not so much a particular mountain as a mountainous district of considerable extent in which the Sinai group was situated.——¶ *Moses did so in the sight of the elders of Israel.* The elders therefore were the only eye-witnesses of the miracle of the smiting of the rock, which was performed in a retired place, pointed out by the station of the cloud, whence the waters flowed in copious streams to the camp.   The elders

Moses did so in the sight of the elders of Israel.

7 And he called the name of the place ^k Massah, and Meribah, because of the chiding of the children

^k Numb. 20: 13. Ps. 81. 7. & 95. 8. Hebr. 3. 8.

would be able satisfactorily to testify that there was previously no spring or reservoir of water in the place, and that the present supply was produced solely by the mighty power of God. In regard to the apostle's allusion to this incident, 1 Cor. 10. 1—3, the reader is referred to Mr. Barnes' Note on that passage.

7. *He called the name of the place Massah and Meribah.* 'Massah' signifies *temptation*, and 'Meribah' *chiding*, or *strife*. The latter word is rendered in the Greek version by παραπικρασμος, *bitter contention*, which in the English translation, Heb. 3. 8, is rendered 'provocation;' 'Harden not your hearts as in the *provocation*, in the day of temptation in the wilderness.'——¶ *Saying, Is the Lord among us or not?* It is not perhaps to be understood that they uttered with their lips these precise words, but such was *the language of their conduct.* In like manner when our Savior says, Mat. 12. 37, 'By thy *words* thou shalt be justified, and by thy *words* thou shalt be condemned,' his meaning is, that they shall be judged by *actions* which have the force of language; actions which *express* the truth as clearly as *words* could do it. *Temptation* of God and *contention* with his servants, are very closely connected together; and no provocation does God more highly resent, than to have his gracious presence with his people called in question.

8. *Then came Amalek, and fought with Israel;* implying that they came from some distance for this purpose, and consequently that Israel was not at this time encroaching upon their territories, and thus giving occasion for the **attack.** Hitherto nothing has been said

of Israel, and because they tempted the Lord, saying, Is the Lord among us, or not?

8 ¶ ^l Then came Amalek, and fought with Israel in Rephidim.

^l Gen. 36. 12. Numb. 24. 20. Deut. 25. 17. 1 Sam. 15. 2.

of the inhabitants of the Sinai peninsula; no clew accordingly has been furnished that might inform us how they were affected by the recent transactions, or with what feelings they regarded the advance of the vast Hebrew host into the finest part of the country. We now hear of them. It appears that not only the peninsula, but the adjoining deserts towards the south of Palestine, were occupied by an extensive and powerful tribe, of Bedouin habits, called Amalekites. The fine valley of Feiran was then doubtless, as now, the principal seat of those who occupied the peninsula; and indeed the Arabic historians preserve the tradition that the valley contained ancient towns and settlements of the Amalekites. There are some ruins of an old city which they say was *Faran* or *Paran*, and that it was founded by and belonged to the Amalekites; and they affirm that the numerous excavations in the mountains near, were the sepulchres of that people. (Makrizi in Burckhardt, p. 617.) *Feiran*, the name of this valley is undoubtedly the same as the *Paran* of the Scriptures, which we know is expressly applied to Mount Sinai, Deut. 33. 2. These Amalekites were the posterity of Esau, and were no doubt prompted in this assault by the hereditary hatred of that race which had become possessed of the birth-right and the blessing lost by their father. Their malice, which may be said to have run in the blood, was probably somewhat exasperated at this time by seeing the promises to Israel working towards an accomplishment. And they may have been aware, moreover, of the wealth, the spoils of Egypt, with which the

9 And Moses said unto ᵐ Joshua,
Choose us out men, and go out,
fight with Amalek: to-morrow I
will stand on the top of the hill
with ⁿ the rod of God in my hand,
10 So Joshua did as Moses had

ᵐ Called Jesus. Acts 7. 45. Hebr. 4. 8.
ⁿ ch. 4. 20.

Hebrews were now laden. But however this was, certain it is that we find
not the slightest hint of any provocation
given by the Israelites for the attack
now wantonly made upon them, which
it appears from Deut. 25. 18, was not
conducted in a style of open and manly
warfare, but in a mean and cowardly
manner, by falling upon their rear, and
smiting the faint and feeble who could
neither make resistance, nor escape;
'Remember what Amalek did unto thee
by the way, when ye were come forth
out of Egypt; how he met thee by the
way, and smote the hindmost of thee,
even all that were feeble behind thee,
when thou wast faint and weary: and
he feared not God.' The last clause is
emphatically added, because such an invasion of the chosen people under these
circumstances was a virtual defiance to
that power which had so lately destroyed the Egyptians. This fact explains
the deep resentment which God himself
expresses on the occasion, and which,
by a positive statute, he transmits to
Israel. 'Therefore it shall be, when the
Lord thy God hath given thee rest from
all thine enemies round about, in the
land which the Lord thy God giveth
thee for an inheritance to possess it,
that thou shalt blot out the remembrance of Amalek from under heaven;
thou shalt not forget it.' The same offence is accounted more or less heinous
in the eyes of heaven according to the
greater or less degrees of light against
which it is committed.

9. *And Moses said unto Joshua.*
Heb. יְהוֹשֻׁעַ *Yehoshua*, properly *Savior*,
from the root יָשַׁע *yasha, to save.* Gr.

said to him, and fought with Amalek; and Moses, Aaron, and Hur,
went up to the top of the hill.
11 And it came to pass, when Moses ᵒ held up his hand, that Israel
prevailed: and when he let down
his hand, Amalek prevailed.

ᵒ Jam. 5. 16.

Ιησους, *Jesus*, by which name Joshua is
twice called in the New Testament, viz.
Acts, 7. 45. Heb. 4. 8. In Num. 13. 9,
he is called 'Oshea.' The name of this
distinguished personage in the sacred
story here occurs for the first time, but
his courage and discretion had before this
become known to Moses, and he does
not hesitate, under divine suggestion,
to confide to him the conduct of this
first military action. Whether Moses
in this had an eye to his future station,
and designed to afford him an opportunity for that preliminary training
which his destined services would require, we know not; but we may safely say that God had such an end in
view, and accordingly now entered him
upon that course of action which should
best qualify him for the arduous duties
of his subsequent leadership of Israel.
He was now ordered to draw out a detachment of the choicest spirits from
the many thousands of Israel, and with
them to give battle on the morrow to
the Amalekites.——¶*And Moses, Aaron,
and Hur went up to the top of the hill.*
Of the Hur here mentioned we only know
from 1 Chron. 2. 18, that he was the son
of Caleb, the son of Hezron, the son of
Pharez, the son of Judah. But whether
this Caleb was the same with the faithful spy of that name, is more than can
be positively determined. These then
went to the summit of the hill, but for
a different purpose than merely that of
being idle spectators of the coming contest, as appears from the next verse.

11. *It came to pass, when Moses held
up his hand,* &c. It is not here expressly affirmed that Moses held any thing

in his hand, but as it is clear from v. 9, that he took 'the rod of God' with him, there can be no doubt that this was to be held up as a kind of banner or signal to be seen by the warring host below, and to operate as a continual incentive to their valor and prowess, while engaged in the contest. The sight of that wonder-working wand, which had already wrought such glorious things for them, which had summoned the plagues of Egypt, which had opened a path through the trackless waters, and which had so recently smitten the rock for their refreshment, could not fail to nerve their arms with new vigor every time their eye was turned towards it. Yet a moment's reflection would convince them, as it will us, that there was no intrinsic virtue in the rod to produce this effect; that it derived all its efficacy from the divine appointment, from its being a visible symbol of that unseen succor and strength which God was pleased to minister to his militant servants fighting his own battle and maintaining his glory. But it was evidently proper that, in order to secure the divine cooperation on such an occasion, fervent prayer should be united with external appliances; and accordingly we have every reason to believe that the uplifted rod was merely an accompaniment of the earnest intercessions which breathed from the lips and hearts of the venerable trio convened on the summit of the hill. Such also is the view taken of the incident by the Chal. and Jerus. Targums; 'When Moses held up his hands in prayer, the house of Israel prevailed; and when he let down his hands from prayer, the house of Amelek prevailed.' We have here then grouped together that hallowed combination of agencies which ought never to be separated, and in which safety and success are ever to be found; viz. the acknowledgment of heaven and the use of appointed means. The rod in the hand of Moses, and the sword in that of Joshua; the embattled host in the valley below, and the praying band on the mount above, all were necessary in the divine economy to the grand result. In vain had Moses prayed if Joshua had not fought; in vain had Joshua fought if Moses had not prayed. The whole narrative, however, conclusively shows, that God designed to teach Israel that the hand of Moses, with whom they had just been chiding, contributed more to their safety than their own hands; his rod more than their weapons; and accordingly the success fluctuates as he lifts up or lets down his hands. What can more strikingly illustrate the principle, that the triumphs of the church depend upon the prayers of its friends? Accordingly as they are more or less strong in faith and fervent in supplication, the victory wavers to their side or that of their enemies. And the same holds true of the individual. The lesson here intended to be taught is 'that men ought always to pray and not to faint;' it is, 'that men should pray every where, lifting up holy hands without wrath or doubting.' The Christian warfare will be attended with but little success, unless it be waged in the spirit and practice of unceasing, earnest prayer. And in this struggle let us be cheered by the consideration that we do not engage in this holy war unassisted and alone. The faithful servants of God, our brethren, have ascended the hill of spiritual prayer, and are imploring blessings upon our efforts. And not only so; he who marshals the ranks of the sacramental host, who leads them on to battle, and fights in their behalf, sustains another office equally important. He has gone up to the summit of the everlasting hills, and is there employed in prevalent intercessions for their success. A greater than Moses is mediating for them on the mount above, and *his* hands never grow heavy and weary, and faint. Of him it can never be said, that though the spirit is

12 But Moses' hands *were* heavy; and they took a stone, and put *it* under him, and he sat thereon: and Aaron and Hur stayed up his hands, the one on the one side, and the other on the other side; and his hands were steady until the going down of the sun.

13 And Joshua discomfited Amalek and his people with the edge of the sword.

14 And the LORD said unto Moses, p Write this *for* a memorial in a book, and rehearse *it* in the ears of Joshua : for q I will utterly put

P ch. 34. 27.   q Numb. 24. 20.   Deut. 25. 19. 1 Sam. 15. 3, 7. & 30. 1, 17.   2 Sam. 8. 12, Ezra 9. 14.

willing, the flesh is weak. ' He ever liveth to make intercession for us' — liveth in the spiritual undecaying vitality of his love, and the vigor of his advocacy for his people.

12. *Moses' hands were heavy.* That is, felt heavy to him, were wearied by being kept so long in the same uplifted posture. The infirmity of nature prevailed over the promptings of piety. In this emergency recourse is had to artificial supports. A stone is put under him for a seat, and Aaron and Hur become living stays for his arms. In performing this office, however, we do not suppose that both his hands were held up on either side at the same time; for in this case we cannot see but the arms of Aaron and Hur would eventually become as weary, and as much need support as those of Moses. The main object of holding up his arms was that the rod might be held up. This he no doubt shifted from time to time from one hand to the other, and Aaron and Hur each of them successively aided in holding that hand which was next to them, and thus relieved both him and each other. In our native feebleness and proneness to languish under the pressure of spiritual duties, recourse may be innocently had to adventitious aids in keeping alive the spirit of devotion.——¶ *Were steady until the going down of the sun.* Heb. אמונה *amunah, steadiness.* Even though thus supported, yet so long a continuance in one fixed posture must have been a severe trial to his patience, and it impressively shows us to what a test our pious perse-

verance may sometimes be brought. Of the occasions our consciences must judge, but there can be no doubt that circumstances do sometimes occur in Christian experience that call upon us for services equally trying to the flesh ; occasions when we should be unfaithful to our own souls did we not hold out in prayer and inward groanings far beyond the point where nature would plead for respite and repose.

13. *And Joshua discomfited Amalek and his people.* That is, the Amalekites and the people of other clans which had confederated with them in this assault Junius and Tremellius, however, make the latter clause exegetical of the former ; ' discomfited Amalek, *even* his people.'

14. *Write this for a memorial in a book,* &c. The memorandum or memorial which Moses was commanded to write, was undoubtedly the very words contained in the final clause of the verse, and therefore the Hebrew term translated ' for' should be rendered ' that ;' 'Write and rehearse it in the ears of Joshua *that* I will utterly put out,' &c. ——¶ *Rehearse it in the ears of Joshua.* This record was especially to be impressed, and, as it were, engraven, upon the memory of Joshua, inasmuch as he was the destined successor of Moses, as head of the chosen people, and it was all important for him to be informed what particular tribes or nations they were with whom the Israelites were not to make any treaties, but rather to devote to utter extermination. It would serve also as a very season-

out the remembrance of Amalek
from under heaven.

15 And Moses built an altar, and
called the name of it JEHOVAH-
nissi :

16 For he said, Because the LORD
hath sworn *that* the LORD *will
have* war with Amalek from generation to generation.

---

able pledge and assurance that he should
be victorious in the career of his future
wars against the enemies of God's people.——¶ *I will utterly put out the remembrance*, &c. Heb. מחה אמחה *ma-
hoh emheh, wiping I will wipe out.*
The denunciation is awfully emphatic.
It declares that in process of time Amalek should be totally ruined and rooted
out, that he should be remembered only
in history. This was but meting out to
them the measure of destruction which
they themselves had meditated against
Israel. Their language was that reported by the Psalmist, Ps. 83. 4, 'Come,
and let us cut them off from being a
nation ; that the name of Israel may be
no more in remembrance.' God therefore determines not only to disappoint
them in that, but to cut off *their* name.
It was to be known for the encouragement of Israel, whenever the Amalekites should be an annoyance to them,
that sentence had irrevocably gone forth
against them ; they were a doomed
people ; and the chosen race should not
fail at last to triumph over them. This
sentence was executed in part by Saul,
1 Sam. 15, and completely by David,
1 Sam. 30. 2 Sam. 1. 1.—8. 12, after
which we never read so much as the
name of Amalek. Thus are the cunning
taken in their own craftiness, and thus
are designs of violence and blood turned
back upon the heads of their contrivers.

15. *Called the name of it Jehovah-
nissi.* Heb. יהוה נסי *Yehovah nissi,
the Lord my banner.* This was a grateful acknowledgment to him to whom
the glory of the recent victory was due.
Instead of rearing a monument in honor
of Joshua or his brave associates, an
altar for sacrificial and thank-offerings
is erected to God, of which the most

important item was the inscription, or
rather, the appellation, by which it was
to be known. The original term נס
nës, signifying primarily *lifting up, exaltation,* is applied also to a *banner* or
ensign, such as were usually lifted up
conspicuously in a field of battle as a
rallying-point to the assembled hosts.
In bestowing the name ' Jehovah-nissi'
upon the altar, there is no doubt an
allusion to the lifting up of the rod
of God as a *banner* or *standard* in this
action. The victory was achieved, not
by their own prowess, but by the power
of Jehovah accompanying this uplifted
banner, and therefore in commemorat-
ing the result of the conflict it was
proper that they should recognise the
agency of the Most High evinced in
their behalf through his appointed symbol. It was, in fact, virtually adopting
the language of Israel in the Psalms,
'Not unto us, O Lord, not unto us ; but
unto thy name, give the glory.' 'We
will rejoice in thy salvation, and in the
name of our God will we *set up our
banners.*'

16. *Because the Lord hath sworn,*
&c. Heb. Because the hand עַל כֵּס
יָהּ *al kës Yah, upon the throne Yah.*
Very considerable doubt hangs over the
true interpretation of this clause. It
may be referred by the construction
either to the hand of Amalek, or to the
hand of the Lord. In the former case,
the import is; ' Because the hand of
Amalek is upon (or against) the throne
of heaven, therefore the Lord will have
war,' &c. In the latter, the Lord's
hand being upon the throne is equivalent to the taking an oath declarative
of a purpose of irrevocable hostility
toward Amalek in all generations. If
we adopt the former as the true sense,

CHAPTER XVIII.

WHEN ᵃ Jethro the priest of Midian, Moses' father-in-law,

ᵃ ch. 2. 16. & 3. 1.

the implication is, that the attack made by the Amalekites upon the Israelites while they were under the tutelary conduct of the cloudy pillar, was a virtual assault upon that sacred symbol itself, which they were taught to regard as the seat, throne, or dwelling-place of Jehovah. This is by no means an improbable interpretation, although it is certain that the older versions incline rather in favor of the other. Thus, Chal. 'With an oath this is spoken from the face of the terrible (one), whose majesty is upon the throne of glory ; that it shall come to pass that war shall be waged from the face of the Lord against the men of the house of Amalek ; that he may consume them from the generations of the world.' Arab. ' Now have I cause to swear by the throne, that the Lord shall have war against the Amalekites, &c.' Syr. ' Lo, the hand upon the throne, the war of the Lord with Amalek.' This idea is still more explicitly enounced in the old rabbinical work, Pirke Eliezer, c. 44, 'When God would root out and destroy all Amalek's seed, he stretched forth his right hand, and took hold on the throne of his glory, and sware to root out and destroy all Amalek's seed out of this world and out of the world to come.' The Greek renders as if the reading of their text was different from what it is at present ; 'And Moses built an altar to the Lord, and called the name of it, The Lord my refuge ; because with a hidden hand (secretly) the Lord will war against Amalek from generation to generation.' Vulg. ' Because the hand upon the throne of the Lord, and the war of the Lord, shall be against Amalek.' It would seem, perhaps, that some of these renderings must yield the true sense, and yet we are not entirely satisfied with any of

heard of all that ᵇ God had done for Moses, and for Israel his people,

ᵇ Ps. 44. 1. & 77. 14, 15. & 78. 4. & 105. 5, 43. & 106. 2, 8.

them. As it is clear that the lifting up of the rod in the hand of Moses was the prominent incident in the whole transaction, it is certainly natural to look for some allusion to that in the words of the present record. We would suggest then, with deference, whether the *hand of Moses* is not the hand intended in the passage. Because his hand was upon, or *towards*, as the original עַל *al* will admit, the heavens, or perhaps the cloudy pillar, which may have been near, and was perseveringly sustained in that direction, therefore the Lord assumes this contest as his own, and declares perpetual war against the devoted race who have ventured to provoke his hostility. How far the proposed construction goes to free the passage from obscurity must be left to the judgment of the reader.

Chapter 18

1. *When Jethro, the priest of Midian,* &c. Lightfoot, in accordance with Aben Ezra and Jarchi, is of opinion that this account of Jethro's visit to Moses is inserted out of its chronological order, which would require its collocation between the tenth and eleventh verses of the tenth chapter of Numbers. That it does not properly pertain to this part of the narrative, he argues, (1.) From the fact mentioned verse 12, that 'Jethro took burnt-offerings and sacrifices for God,' whereas the law respecting these offerings was not yet given. (2.) From that mentioned in v. 13. 16, that 'Moses sat to judge the people, and made them know the statutes of God and his law,' whereas these statutes and laws not having yet been promulgated, Moses himself could not know them. (3.) It appears from Deut. 1. 9—15, that the judges and rulers here mentioned, were

and that the LORD had brought Israel out of Egypt :

2 Then Jethro, Moses' father-in-law, took Zipporah, Moses' wife, c after he had sent her back,

3 And her d two sons ; of which the e name of the one *was* Gershom; (for he said, I have been an alien in a strange land :)

c ch. 4. 26.   d Acts 7. 29.   c ch. 2. 22.

4 And the name of the other *was* Eliezer; (for the God of my father, *said he, was* mine help, and delivered me from the sword of Pharaoh :)

5 And Jethro, Moses' father-in-law, came with his sons and his wife unto Moses into the wilderness, where he encamped at f the mount of God :

f ch. 3. 1, 12.

not appointed till after the departure from Sinai, and yet at this time they had not arrived at Sinai. The inference, therefore, plainly is, that this incident is transposed from its natural place in the order of the sacred story. The reason of the present arrangement, Lightfoot says, is to be sought for in the prophetic curse denounced against the Amalekites in the close of the preceding chapter; for as Jethro and his family were residing in the country of this devoted people, it was proper to afford the reader an intimation that he was not to be involved in their doom, and accordingly the incident of his visit to the camp of Israel, and his joining in the worship of the true God, is introduced in immediate connection with the mention of the curse; not that it actually occurred at that precise time, but to show that he once came, and evinced by his conduct that he was exempted from the denunciation. This view of the subject we consider on the whole the correct one. In regard to Jethro and his true relation to Moses, see Note on Ex. 2. 18.

2. *Then Jethro took,* &c. Neither time nor distance had alienated his affection for the husband of his daughter, of which he gives decisive evidence in undertaking the present journey. He does not satisfy himself with sending by the mouth of another his congratulations to his son-in-law, neither will he permit Zipporah and her sons to go unaccompanied, unprotected through the wilderness, but aged and infirm as he

is, choses himself to be their attendant and guardian. He had undoubtedly heard the report of the great and glorious things which had been wrought for the deliverance of Israel, and though as a Midianite he was not to share with them in the promised land, yet as a descendant of Abraham and a worshipper of Israel's God, he feels a deep interest in their welfare, and sympathises with them in the joy of their deliverance ——¶ *After he had sent her back.* That is, from the inn or lodging-place mentioned, Ex. 4. 26, where Moses' life had been endangered in the manner and for the reasons thus explained. He no doubt foresaw that the presence of his wife and children would be a hindrance instead of a help in the prosecution of his mission to Pharaoh.

3. *The name of the one was Gershom.* That is, *stranger there ;* alluding thereby not only to his own condition at the time, but designing it as a memorial also to his son of *his* condition, as a stranger and pilgrim on earth, as all his fathers were.

4. *The name of the other was Eliezer.* That is, *my God a help,* as immediately after explained.——¶ *Delivered me from the sword of Pharaoh.* The obvious deduction from this mode of rendering is, that this deliverance from the sword of Pharaoh is no other than his escape from the royal vengeance after slaying the Egyptian. But in this case it would have been more natural, while that event was fresh upon his mind, to bestow such a commemorative name upon the

6 And he said unto Moses, I thy father-in-law Jethro am come unto thee, and thy wife, and her two sons with her.

7 ¶ And Moses g went out to meet his father-in-law, and did obeisance, and h kissed him : and they asked

g Gen. 14. 17. & 18. 2. & 19. 1. 1 Kings 2. 19. h Gen. 29. 13. & 33. 4.

---

first born, rather than upon the *second;* and as the original will as well, if not better, admit of it, we prefer to render the verb in the future, 'The Lord is mine help and *will deliver* me from the sword of Pharaoh,' which he had reason to expect would be drawn against him in his attempt to bring Israel out of bondage. It is a name which is at once indicative of Moses' grateful acknowledgment of God's past mercies and of his faith in his future kindness. In this case, the child thus named was probably not the one which was circumcised by his mother at the place above mentioned.

6. *And he said unto Moses.* Not personally, but by messengers despatched before him to acquaint Moses with his coming. Thus in like manner by comparing Mat. 8. 5—8, with Luke 7. 3—6, it appears that what the centurion is represented as saying to Jesus,•was said to him by certain persons whom he had sent for the purpose. Accordingly the Gr. version of the present passage reads thus: 'And it was told Moses, saying, Lo, Jethro thy father-in-law cometh.' Vulg. 'He sent word to Moses.'

7. *Moses went out to meet his father-in-law.* The acquaintance which we have already formed with Moses assures us before hand of the reception with which he would greet his honored relative. Our anticipations are realized. Though a prophet and a judge in Israel, he does not forget the duties that grow out of his relations as a man. Instead of waiting in state till his visitors are

---

each other of *their* welfare ; and they came into the tent.

8 And Moses told his father-in-law all that the LORD had done unto Pharaoh, and to the Egyptians for Israel's sake, *and* all the travail that had come upon them by the way, and *how* the LORD i delivered them.

i Ps. 78. 42. & 81. 7. & 106. 10. & 107. 2.

---

admitted to pay their homage to the 'king in Jeshurun,' he goes forth with alacrity to meet them, and after the usual significant tokens of respect, to conduct them into his tent. However highly the providence of God may have advanced us in rank or authority, yet we are bound to give honor to whom honor is due, and never to look with disdain upon our kinsmen or others in an humbler sphere of life. No dignities conferred by God can exempt us from entertaining the sentiments or evincing the signs of natural affection.——¶ *They asked each other of their welfare.* Literally, ' they asked a man his neighbor of peace.' Of this phraseology see Note on Gen. 29. 6.—37. 5. 'Even the kind 'How-do-you's' that pass between them are taken notice of, as the expressions and improvements of mutual love and friendship.' *Henry.*

8. *Moses told his father all,* &c. The separation of near and dear friends even for a few days or weeks naturally calls up a thousand little topics of interest when they meet. What then must it have been for two such friends, such a father and such a son, to meet after an interval of many months, during which events of such stupendous character had occurred? — events supremely interesting to them, and destined to live in the memory of all coming generations. Were ever two individuals furnished with such a subject of conversation? If the most trifling incidents that befall a brother, a friend, a parent, a child, are full of interest to the parties concerned,

9 And Jethro rejoiced for all the goodness which the LORD had done to Israel, whom he had delivered out of the hand of the Egyptians.

10 And Jethro said, k Blessed *be* the LORD, who hath delivered you out of the hand of the Egyptians, and out of the hand of Pharaoh,

k Gen. 14. 20.   2 Sam. 18. 28.   Luke 1. 68.

who hath delivered the people from under the hand of the Egyptians.

11 Now I know that the LORD *is* l greater than all gods : m for in the thing wherein they dealt n proudly, *he was* above them.

l 2 Chron. 2. 5.   Ps. 95. 3. & 97. 9. & 135. 5.
m ch. 1. 10, 16, 22. & 5. 2, 7. & 14. 8, 18.
n 1 Sam. 2. 3.   Neh. 9. 10, 16, 29.   Job. 40. 11, 12.   Ps. 31. 23. & 119. 21.   Luke 1. 51.

what must have been the emotions of Jethro in listening to the wondrous narrative of Moses? Yet it was for this object, among others, that he came. He wished to learn more fully and particularly the events of which he had heard in a general and indefinite report ; and in this conversation we may see a specimen of those themes which are most grateful to a gracious heart. They are well characterised by the Psalmist, Ps. 145, 5—12, 'I will speak of the glorious honor of thy majesty, and of thy wondrous works. And men shall speak of the might of thy terrible acts : and I will declare thy greatness. They shall abundantly utter the memory of thy great goodness, and shall sing of thy righteousness. They shall speak of the glory of thy kingdom, and talk of thy power ; to make known to the sons of men his mighty acts, and the glorious majesty of his kingdom.'——¶ *All the travail that had come upon them.* Heb. אשר מצאתם *asher metzatham, which had found them.* For this sense of the original word, viz., *the happening of afflictions* to any one, see Note on Gen. 44. 34.

9.—10. *And Jethro rejoiced,* &c. The emotions excited in Jethro's breast by the narrative of Moses, soon rose above all personal or selfish regards, above the partiality of private friendship, above the tenderness of natural affection. His heart expands at the thought of the wonders wrought by the divine interposition in behalf of Israel. Though a Midianite, yet he is conscious of joy unfeigned in view of the goodness shown to a foreign people, while many of the Israelites themselves were murmuring under the sense of their privations and hardships. His joyful emotions, however, are not blind to the true source of the blessings which prompt them. He gives the glory to God, and not to Moses or to Israel. He who is the originating fountain of all good to his people is the ultimate object of their joy and their praise. We cannot without treachery to his glory and black ingratitude to his goodness stop short of him in our ascriptions.

11. *In the thing wherein they dealt proudly,* &c. Heb. בדבר אשר זדו עליהם *baddabar asher zadu alëhem, in the thing in which they (the Egyptians) dealt proudly towards or against them (the Israelites),* he was still too strong for them ; this last clause or something similar being necessary to supply the ellipsis. Compare Neh. 9. 10, which has a reference to this passage. Chal. 'In the thing wherein the Egyptians thought to judge Israel, in that they are judged.' The pronoun 'they' in the original is somewhat indefinite in construction, and may be supposed to include largely not only all the Egyptian princes and potentates, but also the magicians, the courtiers, and the common people. In spite of all their efforts and machinations, they were baffled, subdued, humbled, and Israel triumphantly rescued from their grasp. In like manner will he sooner or later show himself above every thing that opposes him or sets itself up in competition with him.

12 And Jethro, Moses' father-in-law, took a burnt-offering and sacrifices for God: and Aaron came, and all the elders of Israel to eat

12. *Took a burnt-offering and sacrifices for God.* The friendly interview issues in a solemn religious service, in which Aaron and all the elders of Israel are called to assist. By the latter term is to be understood *sacrifices of peace-offerings*, or *eucharistic oblations*, and of these the banquet was exclusively composed; for it was not lawful to eat of the *burnt-offerings*, which were to be consumed whole as a holocaust. Comp. Lev. 7. 15, with Lev. 1. 9. Having had communion with each other in joy and thankfulness, they now continue it in a feast and a sacrifice, in which it is probable, that Jethro, who was priest of Midian, and a worshipper of the true God, officiated. What could be more decorous or proper than that such a friendship as subsisted between these holy men, should be consecrated by an act of joint-worship?——¶ *To eat bread.* The usual term for *food.* Yet it is reasonably supposed that an opportunity was afforded to Jethro of seeing and tasting that wonderful bread from heaven by which Israel was now sustained.——¶ *Before God.* That is, before the glory of God appearing in the cloud, or perhaps before the tabernacle, which we suppose to have been now erected. But we need not, on this account, exclude the additional sense of eating soberly, thankfully, in the fear and to the glory, of God. This they no doubt did, and from the whole incident we gather an example well worthy of imitation. Let those who enjoy the delight of a happy meeting, again to mingle the sympathies of friendship and domestic affection, after a season of separation, not fail, while acknowledging the goodness of God, to offer up their united tribute of thanksgiving to the Author of all their mercies.

bread with Moses' father-in-law o before God.

13 ¶ And it came to pass on the

o Deut. 12. 7. 1 Chron. 29. 22. 1 Cor. 10. 18, 21, 31.

13. *And it came to pass on the morrow,* &c. Due attention having been paid to the rites of hospitality, the dictates of friendship, and the demands of filial duty, Moses re-enters next day upon the discharge of his public functions as lawgiver and judge. Although the presence of his father, and the recent arrival of his wife and children, would seem to have given him a good pretence for at least a short respite from his judicial labors, yet he resumed his task the very next day after their coming, as if acting under the full force of the conviction that ceremonious attentions must give place to necessary business. And this, as a general rule, is no doubt correct. The time, the talents, of the minister of God, whether ecclesiastical or civil, are not his own, they belong to his fellow men ; and if the burdens of such stations were duly considered, they would be much seldomer looked at with envy than they now are. The honors and emoluments are often wishfully eyed, while the thousand sacrifices of ease, of inclination, of health, of private attachment, are entirely overlooked. The anxious days, the sleepless nights, the painful toils, the causeless disaffection, the open odium, the secret aspersions, which one's official conduct incurs, are not taken into the account. Many would no doubt be eager to be Moses, sitting on high and judging the people ; but who would be Moses, oppressed and worn down by the burden of the multitude thronged around him 'from the morning unto the evening'? The narrative makes it plain that Moses did not spare himself the most onerous duties of his station. In so vast an assembly it is easy to conceive that the controversies and matters of reference would be very numerous,

morrow, that Moses sat to judge the people: and the people stood by Moses from the morning unto the evening.

14 And when Moses' father-in-law saw all that he did to the people, he said, What *is* this thing that thou doest to the people? Why sittest thou thyself alone, and all the people stand by thee from morning unto even?

15 And Moses said unto his father-in-law, Because [p] the people come unto me to inquire of God:

16 When they have [q] a matter they come unto me, and I judge between one and another, and I do [r] make *them* know the statutes of God, and his laws.

17 And Moses' father-in-law said unto him, The thing that thou doest *is* not good.

18 Thou wilt surely wear away, both thou, and this people that *is* with thee: for this thing *is* too heavy for thee; [s] thou art not able to perform it thyself alone.

[p] Lev. 24. 12. Numb. 15. 34.

[q] ch. 23. 7. &24. 14 Deut. 17. 8. 2 Sam. 15. 3. Job. 31. 13. Acts 18. 15. 1 Cor. 6. 1. [r] Lev. 24. 15. Numb. 15. 35. & 27. 6, &c. & 36. 6, 7, 8, 9. [s] Numb. 11. 14. 17. Deut. 1. 9, 12.

---

and as the appeal was directly to Moses, as the organ of God, it would be inevitable that the load of responsibility and toil should be almost too great for human endurance. Jethro accordingly, observing the weighty and fatiguing cares which thus devolved upon his son-in-law, was convinced that his physical powers would soon sink under such a burden, and ventured to expostulate with him in regard to it. The reply of Moses shows how anxious he was to do his duty, and make himself the servant of all, notwithstanding the unworthy returns which he often met with at their hands. He tells him that he found it necessary to perform this arduous service, because the people wished, through him, to ascertain the *will of God*, as the supreme authority in their concerns.——¶ *Come unto me to inquire of God.* Heb. לדרש אלהים *lidrosh Elohim, to seek God.* That is, to inquire of me what is the mind and will of God, in whose name and authority I both speak and act. The original implies, however, more than a bare 'seeking.' It is applied to an *anxious, studious, careful quest*, as in consulting an oracle. It is to seek any thing, or apply to any person with earnest and affectionate interest; and therefore is not improperly, though still inadequately rendered in our translation 'to inquire of.' Gr. *εκζητησαι κρισιν παρα τον Θεον, to seek judgment of God.* Chal. 'To seek doctrine from the face of the Lord.'

16. *When they have a matter.* Heb. כי יהיה להם דבר *ki yihyeh lahem dabar, when there is to them a word.* On this phraseology see Note on Gen. 15. 1. Gr. *αντιλογια, a controversy*, as also in Ex. 24. 14. Deut. 1. 12.——¶ *Between one and another.* Heb. בין איש ובין רעהו *bën ish u-bën reähu, between a man and between his fellow;* a frequent Hebrew idiom.——¶ *I do make* them *know.* Heb. הודעתי *hodati.* Gr. *συμβιβαζω αυτους, I instruct them;* a version confirmed by comparing 1 Cor. 2. 16, 'Who hath known the mind of the Lord, that he may *instruct* (*συμβιβασει*) him,' with Is. 40. 13, 'Who hath directed the Spirit of the Lord, or being his counsellor hath *taught him* (Heb. יודיענו. *yodiënu, hath made him know.* Gr. *συμβιβα αυτον, instructeth him.*

18. *Thou wilt surely wear away.* Heb. נבל תבל *nabol tibbol;* a similitude drawn from the leaf of a tree, which withers for want of moisture. In like manner the corroding care growing out of such a charge on the part of Moses would soon exhaust the vital powers; as Moses himself in effect afterward acknowledges, Deut. 1. 9, 12. The advice given

19 Hearken now unto my voice, I will give thee counsel, and t God shall be with thee: Be thou u for the people to God-ward, that thou mayest x bring the causes unto God: 20 And thou shalt y teach them ordinances and laws, and shalt shew them z the way wherein they must walk, and a the work that they must do.

21 Moreover, thou shalt provide out of all the people, b able men,

t ch. 3. 12. u ch. 4. 16. & 20. 19. Deut. 5. 5. x Numb. 27. 5. y Deut. 4. 1, 5. & 5. 1. & 6. 1, 2. & 7. 11. z Ps. 143. 8. a Deut. 1. 18. b ver. 25 Deut. 1. 15. 16. & 16. 18. 2 Chron. 19. 5.—10. Acts 3. 6.

such as c fear God, d men of truth, e hating covetousness; and place such over them to be rulers of thousands, and rulers of hundreds, rulers of fifties, and rulers of tens: 22 And let them judge the people f at all seasons: g and it shall be, that every great matter they shall bring unto thee, but every small matter they shall judge: so shall it be easier for thyself, and h they shall bear the burden with thee.

c Gen. 42. 18. 2 Sam. 23. 3. 2 Chron. 19. 9. d Ezek. 18. 8. e Deut. 16. 19. f ver. 26. g ver. 26. Lev. 24. 11. Numb. 15. 33. & 27. 2. & 36, 1. Deut. 1. 17. & 17. 8. h Numb 11. 17.

by Jethro, in its whole tenor, and the manner of it, is a fine illustration of his character. It shows him to have been a very intelligent, wise, conscientious, and modest man ; one of sound discretion, yet not disposed to dictate ; and especially careful to have the *will of God* ascertained, even if it should be found to run counter to his judgment.

19. *I will give thee counsel, and God shall be with thee.* That is, by following my counsel you may anticipate the divine blessing. Chal. ' The Word of the Lord shall be for thy help.' —— ¶ *Be thou for the people to God-ward.* Chal. 'Be thou inquiring doctrine from before the Lord.'——¶ *That thou mayest bring the causes unto God.* Act thou as mediator and interpreter with God, bringing the causes of the people before him, and in turn also reporting ' the ordinances and laws' which constitute his decisions in the matters referred to him. The two verses, 19, 20, declare the two-fold office which he was to sustain, viz. that of advocate in behalf of the people, and interpreter on the part of God.

21. *Provide out of all the people able men.* Heb. אנשי חיל *anshë hayil, men of might or force ;* i. e. men of vigorous, active, energetic character. See the import of the phrase explained,

Gen. 47. 6, where it is rendered 'men of activity,' while in 1 Chron. 26. 6, it is rendered 'mighty men of valor.' The leading sense is that of men of strong character, active, efficient men, possessing the qualities which in modern times we assign to those who are emphatically termed *good business men.* This was the first requisite. The second was that they should be men *fearing God;* that is, conscientious, pious, religious men; men deeply impressed with the conviction that there is a God above them, whose eye is upon them, to whom they are accountable, and by whose judgment their own will finally be tried; men who dare not do a base, mean, or unjust thing, whatever the temptation, or however secretly it might be done, because they are controlled by a holy awe of heaven. The next qualification insisted on is, that they should be *men of truth;* men whose word could be implicitly relied upon, men of approved fidelity, who would on no account utter a falsehood, or betray a trust. This is well explained in the Hebrew Canons ; 'Men of truth are such as follow after rectitude for its own sake, who out of their own minds love the truth, and hate violent wrong, and flee from every kind of injustice.' Finally, they were to be men *hating covet-*

23 If thou shalt do this thing, and God command thee *so*, then thou shalt be i able to endure, and all this people shall also go to k their place in peace.

24 So Moses hearkened to the

i ver. 18. k Gen. 18. 33. & 30. 25. ch. 16. 29. 2 Sam. 19. 39.

voice of his father-in-law, and did all that he had said.

25 And l Moses chose able men out of all Israel, and made them heads over the people, rulers of thousands, rulers of hundreds, rulers of fifties, and rulers of tens.

l Deut. 1. 15.   Acts 6. 5.

ousness, or in other words, influenced by a noble and generous contempt of worldly wealth, not only not seeking bribes, or aiming to enrich themselves, but cherishing a positive *abhorrence* of any such corruption. He only is fit to be a magistrate, who 'despiseth the gain of oppression, and shaketh his hands from the holding of bribes.' Is. 33. 15. Men of this character were to be selected, and placed over the people in regular subordination, so that each ruler of ten should be under the ruler of fifty, and so on, very much according to the order usually established in an army. These were to administer justice to the people in all smaller matters, while such as were of more importance were to be submitted to Moses as the ultimate appeal.

23. *If thou shalt do this thing, and God shall command thee so.* An entire freedom from the spirit of dictation, and a tone of the most exemplary and amiable self-distrust, is apparent in those words. Knowing that Moses had a better counsellor than he was, he gives his advice under correction, like a modest and pious man, who knows that all human counsel is to be given and received with an humble submission to the word and providence of God. He would have his suggestions followed only so far as they met with the approbation of him who is 'excellent in counsel and mighty in operation,' and infinite in both.——¶ *Then shalt thou be able to stand.* Heb. רכלת עמד *yakolta amod, thou shalt be able to stand;* i. e. to continue, to hold out; a phraseology strongly confirmatory of the sense at-

tributed to the passage Ex. 9. 16, on which see Note.——¶ *Go to their place in peace.* That is, either to the land of promise whither they are travelling ; or, shall return home in peace from the place of judicature, having obtained a speedy adjustment of their difficulties. Thus a man's *house* or *home* is called his *place*, Judg. 7. 7, 'And let all the other people go every man unto his *place;*' i. e. to his home, his place of residence. Judg. 9. 55, 'And when the men of Israel saw that Abimelech was dead, they departed every man unto his *place.*'

24, 25. *So Moses hearkened,* &c. The advice which was so discreetly and kindly given, was candidly and courteously received. A man of a different spirit would perhaps have rejected the counsel thus tendered by a stranger. But Moses was above all the selfish littleness which would have prompted such a treatment of Jethro's suggestions, and he hesitated not, on considering its reasonableness, to adopt the plan proposed. The great Jehovah did not disdain to permit his prophet to be taught by the wisdom and intelligence of a good man, though he was not of the commonwealth of Israel. It is not a little remarkable that the very first rudiments of the Jewish polity were thus suggested by a stranger and a Midianite. The ruler of Israel accordingly proceeded to make choice of able men for this purpose. But we are not to understand by the language employed, that he did this alone. 'Moses chose,' i. e. he oversaw or superintended the choosing; for the election was un-

26 And they ᵐ judged the people at all seasons: the ⁿ hard causes they brought unto Moses, but every small matter they judged themselves.

27 ¶ And Moses let his father-in-law depart: and ᵒ he went his way into his own land.

ᵐ ver. 22. ⁿ Job 29. 16. ᵒ Numb. 10. 29, 30.

CHAPTER XIX.

IN the third month, when the children of Israel were gone forth out of the land of Egypt, the same day ᵃ came they *into* the wilderness of Sinai.

ᵃ Numb. 33. 15.

---

doubtedly the act of the people. Deut. 1. 9, 13, 'And I spake unto you at that time, saying, I am not able to bear you myself alone—take you wise men, and derstanding, and known among your tribes, and I will make them rulers over you.' In like manner the deacons of the primitive church, Acts, 6. 3, were chosen by the people, and finally inducted into office by the apostles. So also Acts, 14. 23, 'And when they had ordained them elders in every church;' i. e. when they had, in conjunction with the people, and in the capacity of superintendents, seen to the appointment of elders; for the original word will not, without violence, admit of being construed as expressing the act of the apostles in contradistinction from that of the people.

26. *Judged the people at all seasons.* That is, at all times, except when they were forbidden by some paramount law requiring their attendance upon the services of public worship.

27. *And Moses let his father-in-law depart.* Heb. רשלח *yeshallah, dismissed, sent away.* That is, with the formalities usual on taking leave of an honored guest; such as accompanying him to some distance with more or less of an escort, and invoking blessings on his head. Comp. Note on Gen. 12. 20. The visit must have formed an important era in Jethro's life, and though we know of no particular authority for the statement of the Chaldee version, that he returned to make proselytes of his children, and of the people of his land, yet nothing would be more natural than

that he should endeavor to impart to others the deep religious impressions which had doubtless been made upon his own mind. From Num. 10. 29, it would appear that his son Hobab, who probably came with him to the camp, remained with Moses in compliance with his request. See Note in loc.

Chapter 19

1. *In the third month.* Heb. בחדש השלישי *bahodesh hashshelishi, in the third new (moon);* as the term proper· ly signifies, by which is to be understood, according to Jewish usage, *the first day* of the month, although for the sake of greater explicitness the phrase, 'the same day,' is added, meaning the first day of the month. This was just forty-five days after their departure from Egypt; for adding sixteen days of the first month to twenty-nine of the second, the result is forty-five. To these we must add the day on which Moses went up to God, v. 3, the next day after when he returned their answer to God, v. 7, 8, and the three days more mentioned, v. 10, 11, which form altogether just fifty days from the passover to the giving of the Law on Mount Sinai. Hence the feast which was kept in aftertimes to celebrate this event was called *Pentecost*, or the *fiftieth* day. And it was at this very feast that the Holy Ghost was given to the Apostles, Acts, 2. 1—4, to enable them to communicate to all mankind the new covenant of our Lord and Savior Jesus Christ. Such a striking coincidence of times and seasons is peculiarly worthy of note.

2 For they were departed from ᵇ Rephidim, and were come *to* the desert of Sinai, and had pitched in

the wilderness : and there **Israel** camped before ᶜ the mount.

ᵇ ch. 17. 1, 8.

ᶜ ch. 3. 1, 12.

2. *They—were come to the desert of Sinai*, &c. Having now followed the children of Israel through their desert-wanderings, to the spot, which was selected by God himself as the scene of the most signal transaction recorded in all their history, it becomes important to ascertain as accurately as possible the general features of a locality distinguished as no other region of the earth has ever been. The peninsula of Sinai, lying between the two northern arms of the Red Sea, was chosen as the theatre of that scene of grandeur which the Israelites were now called to witness, and in our remarks on the ensuing chapter we have suggested some of the reasons which may be supposed to have dictated this choice. As might naturally be expected from the character of the events that have occurred there, the region of Sinai has been for many centuries a favorite place of pilgrimage for curious and pious tourists. In modern times, in consequence of the advances of civilization and the comparative ease of access, the tide of travel has set still more strongly in that direction, and a large amount of new and important geographical information has been the result. Still we cannot say that much has been done to render this information applicable to the exact elucidation of the Scripture narrative. Several important points are, perhaps unavoidably, unsettled ; and among these is the identity of the mountain itself upon which the law was delivered. This renders it somewhat difficult to determine the precise tract which is to be understood by the 'wilderness of Sinai,' although there can be no great error in supposing it to be sufficiently extensive to embrace the range or cluster of mountains familiarly known under the title of 'Sinai' or 'Horeb.' But

that the reader may be able to judge for himself on this point, we shall so far avail ourselves of the results of modern researches in the peninsula of Sinai, as to embody a brief description of the region in which the events of the present and succeeding chapter occurred.

The breadth of the peninsula of Sinai is intersected by a chain of mountains called 'El Tih,' which run from east to west, and cut off a triangular portion of the peninsula on the south, in the very centre of which occurs the elevated group of mountains where the Sinai of the Bible is to be sought. This mountainous region, with its various valleys and ravines of different dimensions, may be described as being comprehended within a diameter of about forty miles. Its general aspect is singularly wild and dreary, being composed almost entirely of naked rocks and craggy precipices, interspersed with narrow sandy defiles, which from being seldom refreshed with rain are almost entirely destitute of vegetation. Fountains and springs of water are found only in the upper regions of the group, on which account they are the place of refuge of all the Bedouins, when the low country is parched up. From all accounts it is difficult to imagine a scene more desolate and terrific than that which constitutes this range. A recent traveller (Sir F. Henniker) describes it as a sea of desolation. 'It would seem,' says he, 'as if Arabia Petræa had once been an ocean of lava, and while its waves were running mountains high, it was commanded suddenly to stand still !' Nothing is to be seen but large peaks and crags of naked granite, composing, as far as the eye can reach, a wilderness of shaggy rocks and valleys bare of verdure. Mr Stephens, an American traveller, in his

'Incidents of Travel in Egypt, Arabia Petræa, and the Holy Land,' thus graphically describes his approach to the region in question:—'Our road now lay between wild and rugged mountains, and the valley itself was stony, broken, and gullied by the washing of the winter torrents ; and a few straggling thornbushes were all that grew in that region of desolation. I had remarked for some time, and every moment impressed it more and more forcibly upon my mind, that every thing around me seemed old and in decay: the valley was barren and devastated by torrents ; the rocks were rent ; the mountains cracked, broken, and crumbling into thousands of pieces ; and we encamped at night between rocks which seemed to have been torn asunder by some violent convulsion, where the stones had washed down into the valley, and the drifted sand almost choked the passage. At every step the scene became more solemn and impressive. The mountains became more and more striking, venerable, and interesting. Not a shrub or blade of grass grew on their naked sides, deformed with gaps and fissures ; and they looked as if by a slight jar or shake they would crumble into millions of pieces. It is impossible to describe correctly the singularly interesting appearance of these mountains. Age, hoary and venerable, is the predominant character. They looked as if their great Creator had made them higher than they are, and their summits, worn and weakened by the action of the elements for thousands of years, had cracked and fallen. The last was by far the most interesting day of my journey to Mount Sinai. We were moving along *a broad valley,* bounded by ranges of lofty and crumbling mountains, forming an immense rocky rampart on each side of us. The whole day we were moving between parallel ranges of mountains, receding in some places, and then again contracting, and about mid-day entered a nar-

row and rugged defile, bounded on each side with precipitous granite rocks more than a thousand feet high. We entered at the very bottom of this defile, moving for a time along the dry bed of a torrent, now obstructed with sand and stones, the rocks on every side shivered and torn, and the whole scene wild to sublimity. Our camels stumbled among the rocky fragments to such a degree that we dismounted, and passed through the wild defile on foot. At the other end we came suddenly upon *a plain table of ground,* and before us towered in awful grandeur, so huge and dark that it seemed close to us, and barring all further progress, the end of my pilgrimage—the holy mountain of Sinai. Among all the stupendous works of nature, not a place can be selected more fitted for the exhibition of Almighty power. I have stood upon the summit of the giant Etna, and looked over the clouds floating beneath it ; upon the bold scenery of Sicily, and the distant mountains of Calabria ; upon the top of Vesuvius, and looked down upon the waves of lava, and the ruined and half-recovered cities at its foot ; *but they are nothing compared with the terrific solitudes and bleak majesty of Sinai.* An observing traveller has well called it a perfect sea of desolation. Not a tree, or shrub, or blade of grass is to be seen upon the bare and rugged sides of innumerable mountains, heaving their naked summits to the skies ; while the crumbling masses of granite all around, and the distant view of the Syrian desert, with its boundless waste of sands, form the wildest and most dreary, the most terrific and desolate picture that imagination can conceive.' Carne, an English traveller, speaking of this district, says, 'From the summit of Sinai you see only innumerable ranges of rocky mountains. One generally places, in imagination, around Sinai, extensive plains or sandy deserts, where the camp of the hosts was placed; where the families of Israel stood at the doors of their tents, and the line was drawn round the mountain, which no one might break through on pain of death. But it is not thus. Save the valley by which we approached Sinai, *about half a mile wide and a few miles in length, and a small plain we.afterwards passed through, with a rocky hill in the middle,* there appear to be few open places round the mount. We did not, however, examine it on all sides. On putting the question to the superior of the convent, where he imagined the Israelites stood: Every where, he replied, waving his hands about,—in the ravines, the valleys, as well as the plains.'

The two most elevated and conspicuous summits of this peninsular group adjoin each other, and are respectively distinguished by the names of Djebel Katerin (Mount St. Catherine) and Djebel Mousa (Mount Moses) ; the former being for the most part locally identified with the Horeb of Scripture, and the latter with Sinai. Both terminate in a sharp peak, the planes of which do not exceed fifty or sixty paces in circumference. The former is the higher of the two, and its summit commands a very extensive prospect of the adjacent country,—the two arms of the Red Sea, a part of Egypt, and, northward, to within a few days' journey of Jerusalem. There is, however, very great confusion arising from the application of the ancient names ' Sinai' and 'Horeb' to these several summits. As both these appellations are practically unknown to the present inhabitants of the country, it has been left in great measure to the judgment or fancy of individual travellers to make the application. Professor Robinson, for instance, supposes a third still lower eminence in the same vicinity to be the true Horeb ; while the Editors of the ' Modern Traveller,' and the ' Pictorial Bible,' contend for Mount Serbal, several miles distant, as the genuine Mount Sinai.

No doubt a great portion of the difficulty on this head has been occasioned by the manner in which the Scriptures employ these names, viz. as if they were wholly convertible with each other. On this point we cannot but agree with the arguments and the conclusions of the last mentioned writers, of whom the latter speaks thus ;—'In some passages of the Pentateuch the law is described as having been delivered from Mount Horeb, and in others from Mount Sinai, and this is one of the apparent contradictions, of which scepticism has availed itself to throw doubt on the verity of the narrative, or at least to question that the books in which these seeming discrepancies occur were written by the same person. The answer to this has been by a reference to Mounts Catherine and Moses, as distinct but adjoining peaks of the *same* range of mountains ; and we have no doubt but that it was this view of the subject which occasioned the summits which now pass for Sinai and Horeb to obtain the distinction they now bear. But it does not appear to us how this answers the objection we have stated, because if Sinai and Horeb are only distinct summits of the same range, how could the same transaction take place in both at once, any more than if they were perfectly distinct mountains ? From a careful examination of the various passages in which the names of 'Horeb' and 'Sinai' occur, we think it might be easy to show that these names are different denominations of the same mountain. But it seems to us that it is susceptible of being still more distinctly shown that 'Horeb' is the name of the whole mountainous region generally, while 'Sinai' is the name of the particular summit. It appears to us that Horeb is usually spoken of as a region, the common form of expression being generally 'in Horeb,' and that where spoken of as a mountain, it is in the same general way as when we speak of *Mount* Caucasus, meaning thereby an extensive range of mountains. But 'Sinai' is usually spoken of as a distinct mountain; 'on,' or 'upon Sinai,' being the most common mode of expression, as we should speak of a particular mountain or peak in a mountainous or any other region. We believe there is no instance in which the name of Horeb occurs so as to convey the idea of ascent, descent, or standing upon it as a mountain, whereas this is invariably the idea with which the name of Sinai is associated. It is true that there are two passages which appear to militate against this view, but when carefully considered, they do in fact confirm it. Thus in Ex. 3. 1, 'Moses .. came to the mountain of God, even to Horeb;' and in 1 Kings, ·19. 8, Elijah goes 'unto Horeb, the mount of God.' In both these places it would be most obvious to understand that Horeb denotes the whole, and the 'mount of God' the part; which will be the more evident when it is recollected that the term 'mount of God' would be no distinction at all, unless the region were also mentioned; because this distinction is not peculiar to the mountain on which the law was delivered. The reader who wishes to verify the view we have taken, will moreover find further confirmation by observing that actions are mentioned as having been done 'in Horeb,' which were certainly not done on any particular mountain, but in the surrounding valleys or plains. Thus the Israelites are said to have 'made a calf in Horeb,' (Ps. 106. 19)—certainly not in a mountain, but in the wilderness of Sinai while Moses was in the mountain. The rock smitten by Moses for water is called the ' rock in Horeb' (Ex. 17. 6), which according to the view we take, is compatible with the situation we have indicated for Rephidim; whereas those who regard Horeb as a particular mountain, and determine that mountain to be Djebel Katerin, have been necessarily obliged to fix the smitten rock in a wholly unsuitable situation, in the narrow valley of El Ledja at the foot of that peak. It also deserves to be noticed, that Josephus does not mention any mount called Horeb. He speaks exclusively of Mount Sinai, and after noticing the transactions at Rephidim, says that, on leaving that station, the Israelites went on gradually till they came to Sinai.' The writer having thus adjusted the relation to each other of the terms 'Horeb' and 'Sinai,' proceeds to adduce a variety of reasons to show that Mount Serbal, and not Mount Moses, prefers the strongest claims to being the place to which God descended at the giving of the Law. We must refer the reader to the pages of the Pictorial Bible for a very elaborate canvassing of the respective claims of these two localities. The principal difficulty in regard to the present Mount Sinai, is the want of sufficient space for the encamping of so large a host as that of Israel, and the impossibility of its summit, or that of Mount St. Catherine, being seen by all the people at the same time. Mount Serbal, on the other hand, he asserts, fully meets the idea which the reader of the Scripture is naturally led to entertain of Sinai, as a detached mountain, or rather cluster of mountains, with ample open ground around the base in which the host might encamp. Some of the vallies also about Mount Serbal are fertile and well-watered; whereas at the other point it would seem to have been scarcely possible to procure sufficient forage for their cattle. Another argument is drawn by the writer from the alleged identity of Mount Serbal and Mount Paran, mentioned in Habakkuk. The valley or wady at the base of Mount Serbal is still called 'Faran,' and as p and f are letters constantly interchanged in the oriental tongues, the inference, he contends, is wholly legitimate that Paran and Faran indicate the same locality, and that this is no other than Mount

3 And ^d Moses went up unto God, and the LORD ^e called unto him out

^d ch. 20. 21.   Acts 7. 38   ^e ch. 3. 4.

Serbal. On the whole, however, we incline to adhere to the more established opinion, which assigns the region of Djebel Katerin and Mousa as the scene of the great event in question, and the following extract from Prof. Robinson's account of his visit to the spot in 1838, will go to lessen very considerably the objection founded upon the limited space for encampment :—'We approached the central granite mountains of Sinai, not by the more usual and easy route of Wady Shekh, which winds around and enters from the East ; but following a succession of Wadys we crossed Wady Shekh and entered the higher granite formation by a shorter route, directly from the N. N. W. through a steep, rocky, and difficult pass, between rugged, blackened cliffs, 800 to 1000 feet high. Approaching in this direction, we were surprised and delighted, to find ourselves, after two hours, crossing the whole length of a fine plain ; from the southern end of which that part of Sinai *now* called Horeb rises perpendicularly in dark and frowning majesty. This plain is over two miles in length, and nearly two-thirds of a mile broad, sprinkled with tufts of herbs and shrubs, like the Wadys of the desert. It is wholly enclosed by dark granite mountains,—stern, naked, splintered peaks and ridges, from 1000 to 1500 feet high. On the east of Horeb a deep and very narrow valley runs in like a cleft, as if in continuation of the S. E. corner of the plain. In this stands the convent, at the distance of a mile from the plain; and the deep verdure of its fruit-trees and cypresses is seen as the traveller approaches,—an oasis of beauty amid scenes of the sternest desolation. On the west of Horeb, there runs up a similar valley, parallel to the former. It is called El-Leja, and in it stands the deserted convent El-Erbayin, with a garden of olive and other fruit-trees, not

visible from the plain. The name *Sinai* is at present applied, generally, to the lofty ridge running from N. N. W. to S. S. E. between the two narrow valleys just described. The northern part, or lower summit, is the present Horeb, overlooking the plain. About two and a half or three miles south of this, the ridge rises and ends in a higher point ; this is the present *summit of Sinai*, the Jebel Mûsa of the Arabs ; which however is not visible from any part of the plain. West, or rather W. S. W. of the valley El-Leja, is the still higher ridge and summit of Mount St. Catharine. The plain above mentioned is in all probability the spot, where the congregation of Israel were assembled to receive the law ; and the mountain impending over it, the present Horeb, was the scene of the awful phenomena in which the law was given. As to the present summit of Sinai, there is little reason to suppose that it had any connection with the giving of the law ; and still less the higher peaks of St. Catharine. I know not when I have felt a thrill of stronger emotion, than when in first crossing the plain, the dark precipices of Horeb rising in solemn grandeur before us, I became aware of the entire adaptedness of the scene to the purposes for which it was chosen by the great Hebrew legislator.' *Bib. Repos. for April* 1839. As to the convent which is here established, and which, from the increasing resort, bids fair to become little more than a sacred caravanserai, affording its inmates but little of that holy retirement which the location was intended to secure, the reader will find a full and interesting account in the work above mentioned, by our countryman Mr. Stephens, and in fact, in nearly all the published tours of modern travellers.

3. *And Moses went up unto God.* Heb. אֶל הָאֱלֹהִים *el ha-Elohim*, *to the*

of the mountain, saying, Thus shalt
thou say to the house of Jacob, and
tell the children of Israel;
4 ᶠYe have seen what I did unto

f Deut. 29. 2.

the Egyptians, and *how* ᵍI bare
you on eagles' wings, and brought
you unto myself.

g Deut. 32. 11.   Isai. 63. 9.   Rev. 12. 14.

Elohim. That is, to the visible symbol
of God's presence, which had now doubtless taken its station on the summit of
the mount. Gr. εις το ορος του θεου, *to
the mount of God.* Chal. 'Into the presence of the Word of the Lord.' The
more attentively the sacred narrative is
scanned, the more clear is the evidence,
that wherever interviews between God
and Moses or other good men are mentioned, there we are to understand that
some *visible* manifestation of Jehovah
was present, and that this visible phenomenon is intended to be indicated by
the term 'Jehovah' or 'God.'—It will
be noticed that the object of Moses'
ascending the mount on this occasion
was simply to receive and carry back to
the people the message contained in the
verses immediately succeeding, which
was a more general intimation of the
terms on which God agreed to form the
Israelites into a distinct and peculiar
people.——¶ *Thus shalt thou say to the
house of Jacob, and tell the children
of Israel.* This two twofold denomination of the chosen people is rather
remarkable and no doubt was intended
to carry with it some special emphasis of meaning. As the mercies conferred upon them as a people extended back into the history of the past, it
was perhaps designed, by the use of
these two names, to remind them of
their humble beginnings and their subsequent increase ; to suggest to them
that they, who were once as lowly as
Jacob when he went to Padan-aram,
were now grown as great as God made
him, when he came from thence and
was called *Israel.* The mention of the
twofold appellation of their ancestor,
would tend also to excite them to obedience in conformity to his example.

4. **Ye have seen,** &c. It is a direct
appeal to themselves, to their own observation and experience, for the truth
of what is here affirmed. They could
not disbelieve God without first disbe-
lieving the testimony of their own
senses.——¶ *How I bare you on eagles'
wings* ; i. e. *as* on eagles' wings ; a
similitude denoting the speed, the security, and the tender care with which
they were, as it were, transported from
the house of bondage, and which is expanded in fuller significancy, Deut. 32,
11, 12, 'As an eagle stirreth up her nest,
fluttereth over her young, spreadeth
abroad her wings, taketh them, beareth
them on her wings ; so the Lord alone
did lead him.' In like manner, as the
church of Israel here fled from the
dragon Pharaoh, as he is termed, Ezek.
29. 3, so the Christian church in a time
of persecution is represented, Rev. 12.
14, as flying into the wilderness from
the serpent or dragon, with two wings
of a great eagle. Wings in this acceptation are a symbol of protection. The
idea of this passage is strikingly set
forth by the prophet at a long subsequent period, Is. 63. 9. 'In all their affliction he was afflicted, and the angel
of his presence saved them: in his love
and in his pity he redeemed them; and
he *bare* them, and *carried* them all the
days of old.'——¶ *Brought you unto
myself.* Delivered you from the cruel
bondage of Egypt, and graciously received you into a covenant relation to
myself and the enjoyment of my special
tutelary favor. This is the ultimate aim
of all the gracious methods of God's
providence and grace, to bring us back
to himself, to reinstate us in his lost
favor, to restore us to that relation in
which alone we can be happy. Christ

5 Now h therefore, if ye will obey
my voice indeed, and keep my co-

h Deut. 5. 2.

---

has died, 'the just for the unjust, that
he might bring us to God.'

5. *Now therefore if ye will obey,* &c.
Having briefly recounted the grounds of
their obligation to him, the Most High
now proceeds to state plainly the returns he should expect and require from
them. This was in one word *obedience*
—cordial, sincere, and unreserved obedience to the will of their best friend and
kindest benefactor, who could have nothing in view but their happiness. This
he demanded of *them*. On his own part,
he promises a profusion of blessings,
temporal, spiritual, and everlasting, of
which the crown of all is that they
should be *an appropriation to himself.*
They should enjoy a rank of higher
honor and tenderer endearment in his regard than any other people—a declaration, the scope of which will be more
apparent from a closer inspection of the
import of the particular terms.——¶ *A*
peculiar treasure. Heb. סגלה *segul-*
lah, a word of which we do not find
the verbal root סגל *sagal* in Hebrew,
but in Chaldee it signifies *to gain, to ac-*
quire to one's self, to make one's own, to
appropriate. Wherever the noun occurs in Hebrew it denotes a *peculium,*
a possession or treasure of which the
owner is peculiarly choice, one on which
his heart is set, and which he neither
shares with others nor resigns to the
care of others. It has an obvious relation to the Latin word *sigillum, seal,*
and is especially applied to such choice
possessions as were secured with a *seal,*
as gold, silver, jewels, precious stones,
&c. Thus, 1 Chron. 29. 3, 'Because I
have set my affection to the house of
my God, I have of *mine own proper*
good (Heb. of my סגלה *segullah*), of
gold and silver, which I have given,'
&c Thus too, Mal. 3. 17, 'And they

venant, then i ye shall be a peculiar

i Deut. 4. 20. & 7. 6. & 14. 2, 21. & 26. 18. &
32. 8, 9. 1 Kings 8. 53. Ps. 135. 4. Cant. 8. 12.
Isai. 41. 8. & 43. 1. Jer. 10. 16. Mal. 3 17
Tit. 2. 14.

---

shall be mine, saith the Lord of hosts,
in that day when I make up my *jewels.'*
(Heb. my סגלה *segullah).'* Eccl. 2.
8, 'I gathered me also silver and gold
and the *peculiar treasure* (סגלה) of
kings and of the provinces.' 'By סגלה
segullah,' say the Hebrew commentators, ' is signified, that they should be
beloved before him, as a desirable treasure which a king delivereth not into the
hand of any of his officers, but keepeth
it himself. And such is the case of Israel, of whom it is said, Deut. 32. 9,
'For the Lord's portion is his people.'
Thus too, Deut. 7. 6, 'Thou art an holy
people unto the Lord thy God ; the Lord
thy God hath chosen thee to be a *special*
people (סגלה) unto himself, above all
people that are upon the face of the
earth.' Ps. 135. 4, 'For the Lord hath
chosen Jacob unto himself, and Israel
for his *peculiar treasure* (לסגלתו *lis-*
gulatho).' In these cases the Greek
rendering is mostly περιουσιος, *peculiar*
precious, which occurs Tit. 2. 14, 'That
he might purify unto himself a *peculiar*
people (λαος περιουσιος), zealous of good
works.' But in 1 Peter, 2. 9, the phraseology is a little varied, 'But ye are a
chosen generation, a royal priesthood,
an holy nation, *a peculiar people* (λαος
εις περιποιησιν),' which is the Septuagint rendering of the word ' jewels,'
Mal. 3. 17. Throughout, the leading
sense is that of *select, precious, endear-*
ed; something exceedingly prized and
sedulously preserved; and it would seem
as if God would represent all the rest of
the world as comparatively worthless
lumber when viewed by the side of the
chosen race. Chal. 'Ye shall be beloved
before me.'——¶ *For all the earth is*
mine. Or, ' *though* all the earth is
mine.' The sense, however, is essentially the same by either mode of rend-

treasure unto me above all people :
for k all the earth *is* mine :

6 And ye shall be unto me a ¹ kingdom of priests, and an ᵐ holy na-

k ch. 6. 29 Deut. 10. 14. Job. 41. 11. Ps. 24.
1. & 50. 12. 1 Cor. 10 26, 28. ¹ Deut. 33. 2, 3,
4. 1 Pet. 2. 5, 9. Rev. 1. 6. & 5. 10. & 20. 6.
m Lev. 29. 24, 26. Deut. 7. 6. & 26. 19. &
28, 9. Isai. 62. 12. 1 Cor. 3. 17. 1 Thess. 5. 27.

ering. It was intended to enhance, in
their estimate, the greatness of the divine favor in making them the objects
of such a selection. Being the sovereign
and proprietor of the whole world, and
the fulness thereof, he needed them not ;
nor if he saw good to select any people
was he under the least obligation, out
of himself, to fix upon them. He might
have taken any other nation in preference to them. The parallelism, Deut.
7. 7, 8, fully confirms this sense of the
passage ; 'The Lord did not set his love
upon you, nor choose you, because ye
were more in number than any people ;
for ye were the fewest of all people :
But because the Lord loved you, and
because he would keep the oath which
he had sworn unto your fathers, hath
the Lord brought you out with a mighty
hand, and redeemed you out of the house
of bond-men, from the hand of Pharaoh
king of Egypt.'

6. *A kingdom of priests.* Heb. ממלכת
כהנים *mamleketh kohanim;* which the
Gr. renders by an inverse construction
βασιλειον ιερατευμα, *a royal priesthood,*
the phraseology adopted by the apostle,
1 Pet. 2. 9. Chal. 'Ye shall be before me
kings, priests, and an holy people.' The
true sense of the expression is perhaps
most adequately given Rev. 5. 10, where
in allusion to the passage, it is said,
'Thou hast made us unto our God *kings*
and *priests;* and we shall reign on the
earth.' They were in fact to combine
in their own persons the royal and the
sacerdotal dignity, which is figuratively
set forth in the Apocalyptic scenery by
the elders being clothed in white robes,
which was a badge of the priesthood,

tion. These *are* the words which
thou shalt speak unto the children
of Israel.

7 ¶ And Moses came and called
for the elders of the people, and
laid before their faces all these
words which the LORD commanded him.

and at the same time having crowns
upon their heads, which was an emblem
of royalty. It would be impossible
therefore to use language conveying the
promise of higher honor, of more distinguished prerogatives, than this. As
the priestly order was set apart from
the common mass of the people, and
exclusively authorised to minister in
holy things, so *all* the Israelites, compared with other nations, were to sustain this near relation to God. They
were to be, as it were, 'the first-born
from among men,' consecrated to God
from the womb, like the first-born of
their own families. And when we add
to this that they were *all* to be regarded
at the same time as *kings* also, and
none as subjects, a commonwealth of
spiritual sovereigns, what can be con
ceived more exalted and honorary ? Yet
such is undoubtedly the import of the
words, which is but little heightened
by the subsequent phrase, ' an holy nation ;' i. e. a nation hallowed, set apart,
consecrated.

7. *Moses came and called for the elders,* &c. In so immense an assembly
of people it would be necessary for Moses to treat with them through the medium of their *elders,* or the *principal
men* in the several tribes. Having convened them for the purpose, he ' laid
before their faces,' the message he had
received from God, by which is meant
that he fully explained to them what
God had given him in charge, and submitted it to their serious judgment whether they would comply with the prescribed terms. The elders of course
propounded the words to the people.

8 And ⁿ all the people answered together, and said, All that the LORD hath spoken we will do. And Moses returned the words of the people unto the LORD.

9 And the LORD said unto Moses,

ⁿ ch. 24. 3, 7. Deut. 5. 27. & 26. 17.

Lo, I come unto thee ᵒ in a thick cloud, ᵖ that the people may hear when I speak with thee, and ᑫ believe thee forever. And Moses told the words of the people unto the LORD.

ᵒ ver. 16. ch. 20. 21. & 24. 15, 16. Deut. 4 11. Ps. 18. 11, 12. & 97. 2. Matt. 17. 5
ᵖ Deut. 4. 12, 36. John 12. 29, 30. ᑫ ch. 14. 31

---

8. *And all the people answered together.* Heb. יַעֲנוּ יַחְדָּו *yaanu yahdav.* Gr. *απεκριθη ομοθυμαδον, answered with one accord,* as the term *ομοθυμαδον* is also rendered Acts, 2. 1, and often elsewhere, implying rather *unanimity of counsel* than *simultaneousness of act.* It is of course to be supposed that the elders made known the conditions to the people whom they represented, and that they unanimously signified their acceptance of them, which was again reported by Moses through their official heads. Their answer discovers indeed a commendable promptitude in acceding to the terms and availing themselves of the proffered blessings, but the sequel shows that their response was given in a spirit of overweening self-confidence. They knew comparatively little of their own spirits, and rushed precipitately into the assumption of obligations, of the full import of which they had but little idea. Their conduct strikingly illustrates that of the convinced sinner, who feels the pressure of the divine claims upon his conscience, and fondly imagines that he shall have no difficulty in keeping the whole law. But experience soon shows him his error, as it did the Israelites.

9. *Lo, I come unto thee in a thick cloud.* Heb. בְּעַב הֶעָנָן *beab hëanan, in the thickness, or density, of the cloud.* Gr. *εν στυλω νεφελης, in the pillar of the cloud.* We know that God ordinarily resided among his people and presided over them in the cloudy pillar. But as this pillar changed its aspect to a pillar of fire by night, so we can easily imagine it to have assumed a denser and darker appearance on this occasion. As it was to be accompanied with lightnings and thunders, the whole scene would be rendered more sublime and awful by the increased darkness and density of that vast mass of cloud, towering above the summit of the mountain, which was to be the *ground* of these fearful phenomena. Our conceptions on this subject will be heightened by referring to the parallel language of the Psalmist, Ps. 18. 11, 'He made darkness his secret place ; his pavilion round about him were dark waters and thick clouds of the skies ;' i. e. not literally waters in their elementary state, but such thick dark lowering clouds as are generally charged with water, and empty themselves in gushing torrents of rain ; in allusion to which it is said, Job. 26. 8, 'He bindeth up the waters in his thick clouds, and the cloud is not rent under them.' There was perhaps some reference in this mode of manifestation to the comparatively dark and obscure genius of the Mosaic dispensation. Of the ancient versions the Arab. renders this passage, ' I will manifest my Angel unto them in the thickness of clouds ;' and the Jerus. Targ. 'My Word shall be revealed unto thee in the thick cloud.'——¶ *That the people may hear when I speak with thee,* &c. This discloses one grand purpose to be accomplished by such an impressive mode of manifestation. The highest possible honor, and credence, and deference was to be secured to the person of Moses, in order that the laws and ordinances

10 ¶ And the LORD said unto Moses, Go unto the people, and r sanctify them to-day and to-morrow, and let them s wash their clothes,

r Lev. 11. 44, 45. Hebr. 10. 22. s ver. 14. Gen. 35. 2. Lev. 15. 5.

which he was to introduce among the people in the name of God might be clothed with due authority. The grandeur and solemnity of the scene in which their leader was to act such a conspicuous part would eminently tend to produce this effect. And their hearing with their own ears the voice of God speaking to his servant, would utterly cut off all future pretext for saying that Moses palmed upon them a system of laws and statutes of his own devising, or imposed upon their credulity in any way whatever. In affirming this they would be witnesses against themselves. They had an ocular demonstration that the laws to which they were required to submit, were promulgated from the highest authority in the universe, of which Moses was merely the ministering mediator. It was not, however, merely from the men of that generation that God would exact this profound deference to the official character of Moses, but it was to be perpetuated in the line of their posterity to the latest days— 'that they may believe thee for ever,' not only as long as they live, but as long as their descendants shall live. Accordingly our Savior himself recognises his authority, when he says in the parable of the rich man and Lazarus, 'They have Moses and the prophets, let them hear them,' and 'if they believe not Moses and the prophets, neither will they believe, though one rose from the dead.'

10. *Go unto the people and sanctify them*, &c. That is, command and see that they sanctify themselves, as appears from the next clause, and from v. 14. In like manner it is said that Job (ch. 1. 5.) 'Sent and sanctified his

11 And be ready against the third day : for the third day the LORD t will come down in the sight of all the people upon mount Sinai.

t ver. 16, 18. ch. 34. 5. Deut. 33. 2.

sons;' i. e. ordered them to sanctify themselves; the agent, according to Scripture usage, being said to do that which he orders or procures to be done. We see at once the propriety of their being fitted by a special preparation for such a solemn interview with the Most High as now awaited them. When but a friend or neighbor is expected somewhat formally to visit us, the natural sentiment of decorum requires that our persons, our houses, our entertainment, should be invested with an air of more than usual neatness, order, and style. How much more, when the visiter is to be no other than the King of Kings himself ! They were about to approach a holy God, a God of infinite purity, who cannot bear any unclean thing in his presence, and therefore they were to take care that no defilement was upon them. They were to wash their clothes and preserve their persons free from all impurity. They were even to abstain (v. 15) from all such innocent and lawful gratifications as might be unfavorable to the utmost degree of spirituality and abstractedness of soul in the exercises before them. Not that there was any intrinsic virtue in mere external ablutions and abstinences; they were to do this *in token* of their cleansing themselves from all sinful pollutions. While they were washing their clothes they were to think of washing their souls by repentance from the sins which they had contracted. Comp. Gen. 35. 2. Lev. 15. 5.

11. *The third day the Lord will come down*, &c. That is, will come down in the cloudy and fiery pillar, the symbol of his presence, the visible Shekinah; another of the innumerable instances in

12 And thou shalt set bounds unto the people round about, saying, Take heed to yourselves, *that ye go not* up into the mount, or touch the border of it: ᵘ whosoever toucheth the mount shall be surely put to death :

ᵘ Hebr. 12. 20.

13 There shall not a hand touch it, but he shall surely be stoned or shot through: whether *it be* beast or man, it shall not live : when the ˣ trumpet soundeth long, they shall come up to the mount.

ˣ ver. 16, 19.

which 'Lord' is used interchangeably with the term denoting his visible representative. His descent was to be in sight of all the people. We infer from this that the cloudy pillar rose to a great height in the heavens, for we believe there is no one of the several peaks of the Sinai group of mountains that could be seen from all the points where a body of two millions of men must have been encamped. Consequently, the pillar that surmounted the summit must have been very lofty.

12. *Thou shalt set bounds,* &c. Notwithstanding all the grandeurs and terrors of the scene, it was on the whole an illustrious instance of God's grace and condescension that he was pleased to vouchsafe to them such a signal display of himself on this occasion. Yet he would have them reminded of the humble awful reverence which should possess the minds of all those that worship him. Every semblance of unhallowed freedom and familiarity was to be studiously repressed. While Jehovah makes himself known as a Father, a Protector, a Guide, a Portion, he still would have his servants remember that he is 'the great and terrible God.' He therefore requires that they should worship him at a respectful and reverential distance, as being really unworthy even to lift up their eyes to the place which his footsteps were to make glorious.——
¶ *That ye go not up into the mount.* Heb. בהר *bahar, in or upon the mount.* It is important, if possible, to ascertain the exact idea, as otherwise it will be difficult to determine what is meant by the permission in the next verse, 'when

the trumpet soundeth long, they shall come up to the mount,' where the phraseology in the original is precisely the same, בהר *bahar, in or upon the mount.* It undoubtedly signifies something more than merely approaching the base of the mountain, its 'border' or extreme foot, and conveys the idea of some degree of *ascent* or *climbing* towards the summit.

13. *There shall not an hand touch it.* Heb. לא תגע בו יד *lo tigga bo yad, there shall not an hand touch him.* Our present translation evidently understands the 'mountain' as the object not to be touched with the hand. But *that* is forbidden in the clause immediately preceding, and here the true sense is doubtless that which is yielded by a literal rendering of the original. If a man or a beast should break through the prescribed limits and advance towards the mountain, they were not to rush in after him, apprehend him, and thrust him back, but on the contrary were to slay him on the spot by casting stones or shooting darts at him from a distance. Such a bold intruder upon forbidden ground, such a daring transgressor of an express divine precept, was to be regarded as so profane, execrable, and abominable, that they were not permitted to pollute their hands by touching him. What a speaking commentary upon God's estimate of presumptuous sin!——¶ *When the trumpet soundeth long they shall come up,* &c, Heb. במשך הרבל *bimshok ha-yobel, in the drawing out of the trumpet;* i. e. of the sound of the trumpet. On the true import of the word רבל *yobël* here rendered 'trumpet,

see Note on Josh. 6. 4, 5. It is the word applied to the sounding of the trumpet of *jubilee*, a term derived in fact from this very root, and supposed to denote an instrument either made of ram's horns, or constructed in that form. It was blown as a signal for the camp or congregation to assemble, or to do something in concert. Throughout the rest of the context the word for 'trumpet' is entirely different, viz., שׁפָר *shophar*, for which reason some critics have supposed that the phrase in this place denotes a signal given by order of Moses in the camp for the approach of the people to the base of the mount, whereas in the sequel the sound of the שׁפָר *shophar* was among the supernatural sounds and sights that distinguished the august occasion. This however is an interpretation which cannot well be reconciled with the context. Again, there is great uncertainty as to what is precisely to be understood by the sound of the trumpet's being *drawn out* or *prolonged;* whether it signifies a *growing intensity,* or a *remission, softening, dying away,* of the sound. The Gr. gives the latter sense, 'When the voices, and the trumpets, and the cloud are departed from the mountain, then shall ye go up.' Thus too the Syriac, 'When the trumpet shall have become silent, then it shall be permitted to you to go up.' So also the Chal. according to Fagius' version ; 'When the trumpet shall be withdrawn, then shall they have leave to go up.' But it is very doubtful whether this is correctly rendered. The original בִּמְרִגד שׁדפרא *be-migad shophara* signifies according to Cartwright, Cum protracta fuerit buccina, *when the (sound of the) trumpet shall have been prolonged;* and thus substantially agrees with the Hebrew, the root נגד *negad* answering precisely to מָשַׁךְ *mashak*, and both signifying to *draw out, extend, prolong.* The Vulg. on the other hand adopts the former, Cum cœperit clangere buccina, *when the trumpet shall begin to sound.*

A comparison of the present passage with Josh. 6. 4, 5, seems rather to confirm the first of these as the genuine sense. Then the Israelites were commanded to compass the walls of Jericho for six days in succession, the priests continually blowing the rams' horns, and on the seventh ' when they make a long blast with the ram's horn (Heb. בִּמְשֹׁךְ בְּקֶרֶן הַיּוֹבֵל *bimshok be-keren ha-yobel, in the drawing out* (of the sound made) *by the horn of the ram,* &c.—all the people shall shout.' By this is probably implied that when the sounding *shall have been long continued,* after they shall have heard it from day to day for six days, and through nearly the whole day on the seventh, then at the completion of the last circuit they should shout, and the walls would fall down. So here we are probably to understand that when the signal blast of the trumpet had been for a considerable time continued, they were to ' come up to the mount.' But this latter clause is if any thing still more difficult of explication than the preceding. Does it mean the removal of the foregoing restriction ? It would seem that our translators supposed it did not, but implied rather that at the given signal the people were to approach *to* or *towards* the mount as far as the prescribed limits would permit. But this view of the matter is not favored by the original, which has יַעֲלוּ בָהַר *yaalu bahar, come up in, into,* or *upon the mount.* The phrase is most evidently directly the reverse of the prohibition in v. 12, 'Take heed to yourselves that ye go not up into the mount (Heb. הִשָּׁמְרוּ לָכֶם עֲלוֹת בָהַר *hishshameru lakem aloth bahar, beware for yourselves of going up in, into,* or *upon the mount.*' Such is the literal rendering of the two clauses, and how are they to be reconciled ? As read in the letter they show a plain discrepancy, the one permitting what the other forbids. Some have proposed to surmount the difficulty by understand-

14 ¶ And Moses went down from the mount unto the people, and y sanctified the people ; and they washed their clothes.

15 And he said unto the people, z Be ready against the third day : a come not at *your* wives.

y ver. 10. z ver. 11. a 1 Sam. 21. 4, 5. Zech. 7. 3.   1 Cor. 7. 5.

ing the clause as an *ironical concession;* as if God had intended to intimate that before the trumpet blast was heard they should be strictly charged not to over-pass the boundaries, but that after that time, and when the sound began to wax louder and louder, then they might ascend *if they pleased, if they dared;* for then the terrors of the scene would be of themselves so tremendous and re-pulsive, that there would be no special need of any express veto to forbid a nearer approach.   But such a sense seems hardly consistent with the so-lemnity of the scene, and we are con-strained on the whole to yield our assent to the import affixed to the words by the old versions, viz., that the limitation was to be annulled and the mountain freely ascended *when the blast of the trump-et and the other supernatural sounds had been so long drawn out and pro-tracted as to have become scarcely aud-ible, and to be dying away upon the ear.* In other words we think that the Sept. rendering, though paraphrastic, gives the true sense ; 'When the voices, and the trumpets, and the cloud, are departed from the mountain, then shall ye go up.' As they were to remain encamped for a year at the base of the mountain it might be important for them to be assured of the divine permission to ascend from time to time to its top, and devoutly contemplate a spot recent-ly hallowed by the footsteps of the glory of Jehovah.

16. *And it came to pass on the third day,* &c.   The eventful day at length arrived, the sixth of the month Sivan.

16 ¶ And it came to pass on the third day in the morning, that there were b thunders and lightnings, and a c thick cloud upon the mount, and the d voice of the trumpet exceed-ing loud; so that all the people that *was* in the camp e trembled.

b Ps. 77. 18.   Hebr. 12. 18, 19.   Rev. 4. 5. & 8. 5. & 11. 19.   c ver. 9. ch. 40. 34.   2 Chron. 5. 14.   d Rev. 1. 10, & 4. 1.   e Hebr. 12. 21.

and the fiftieth after the departure from Egypt.   The morning was ushered in with terrible thunders and lightnings, and a cloud of deep lowering darkness resting upon the summit of the mount. The heavens and the earth and the ele-ments conspired to signalize, in the most impressive manner, the advent of the Creator and Lord of the universe to this part of his dominions.   Nearly every object of grandeur and awe of which we can conceive, enters into the description.   Thunder, lightning, tem-pest, the blackness of darkness, smoke, fire, earthquake, and the trumpet of God !   Never, in all probability, till the light of the last morning shall dawn, and the trump of the archangel shall peal its summons to arouse the dead, will such a spectacle be again witnessed on earth.   We have only to reflect upon the *design* of this august visitation to be satisfied that such an apparatus of awful accompaniments was in the high-est degree appropriate and seasonable. A deep moral impression in regard to the law about to be delivered was to be produced.   Every thing accordingly was so ordered as to afford the most strik-ing display of the glorious majesty of the Lawgiver, to point out the character of the law in its strictness and rigor, and its tremendous penalty, and withal to furnish a preintimation of the day of judgment, when every transgression of it will come into account.   He who has made us, and who perfectly knows our frame, knows how best to suit his dis-pensations to our condition.   It is no matter of surprise, therefore, that He

who has an unlimited control over all
the inlets to our sentient spirits should
see fit, when the occasion warrants, to
make the senses an avenue to the mind,
and to seize the conscience or overawe
the heart by speaking to the eyes or the
ears, or to both at once. Such was his
good pleasure on the delivery of the law
from Sinai; and it is a consideration
full of solemn import, that if God was
truly awful in the harmless unconsum-
ing fire at the bush of Horeb, and in the
guiding and protecting pillar of cloud;
if he was dreadful at Sinai, coming in
fierce and threatening flames to promulgate his law; what must he be ' coming
in flaming fire to take vengeance on
them that know not God, and obey not
the gospel of our Lord Jesus Christ !"
If the sound of that trumpet which proclaimed the approach of God to Israel
was almost sufficient to kill the living
with fear; what must be the trumpet
which shall awake the dead? Whatever
majesty and solemnity distinguished the
giving of the Law, the whole earth shall
eventually behold it exceeded in the consummation of the gospel.——¶ *In the
morning.* Heb. בהית הבקר *bihyoth
habboker, in the being made to be of the
morning;* implying something peculiar
and extraordinary in the atmospherical
phenomena that ushered in that memorable morn. The usual phrase for ' in
the morning' is בבקר *babboker,* and if
nothing more than that simple idea was
meant, it is not easy to account for the
present unusual phraseology.——¶ *And
there were voices and lightnings,* &c.
Heb. וירי קלת *va-yehi koloth.* Thunders are undoubtedly meant, a sense
frequently conveyed by the Heb. word
' voice,' in proof of which see Note on
Gen. 3. 8. The gloomy mass of cloud was
unquestionably the seat of the thunders
and lightnings which pealed and flashed
from its bosom. And as the pillar of
cloud was regarded as the throne of
God, we see the pertinency of the allusion to this narrative in the mystic

scenery of the Apocalypse, ch. 4. 5,
'And out of the throne proceeded lightnings and thunderings and voices.'——
¶ *The voice of the trumpet.* Heb. קל
שפר *kol shophar, the voice or sound of
a trumpet.* There is no clear authority
in the original for the use of the more
definite expression ' the trumpet,' as it
in allusion to some trumpet previously
mentioned. At the same time we are
not prepared to affirm, although the
רבל *yobel* and the שפר *shophar* were
undoubtedly different, that they may not
both refer to the same supernatural
sounds heard on this occasion. The
use of the term in either case may per
haps simply be to intimate that a sound
was miraculously produced bearing a
strong resemblance to that of a trumpet,
though immeasurably louder. Perhaps
the clangor of an unearthly trumpet was
mingled in the din of the elements to
deepen the conviction that the whole
scene was preternatural. Thunder and
lightning, and earthquake, and dark
clouds were phenomena with which they
were in some degree acquainted, and
had there been nothing more, it might
possibly have been thought, either then
or in after ages, that the spectacle witnessed was merely an extraordinary
tempest, the effect solely of natural
causes, though acting with unwonted
violence. But when a sound was heard
shrill and piercing like the notes of a
trumpet, but rising above the hoarse
peals, the roaring and the crash of the
thunder, such as was never heard before in any commotion of the elements,
and such as never could issue from an
instrument made by human hands or
blown by human breath, no wonder that
the impression upon the people was terrific beyond all conception. No wonder
that the terms ' voice of the archangel
and trump of God' should have arisen
from this incident of the dread phenomena which struck the senses of assembled Israel at the base of the holy mount.
It is undoubtedly from the circumstance

17 And f Moses brought forth the people out of the camp to meet with God ; and they stood at the nether part of the mount.

18 And g mount Sinai was altogether on a smoke, because the LORD descended upon it h in fire: i and the smoke thereof ascended

f Deut. 4. 10. g Deut. 4. 11. & 33. 2. Judg. 5. 5. Ps. 68. 7, 8. Isai. 6. 4. Hab. 3. 3. h ch. 3. 2. & 24. 17. 2 Chron. 7. 1, 2, 3. i Gen. 15. 17. Ps. 144. 5. Rev. 15. 8.

here mentioned that the Scriptures teach us to associate idea of the sound of a great trumpet with the awful occurrences of the day of judgment, of which the giving of the law from Sinai was intended to be a faint type and shadow.

17. *To meet with God.* Heb. לקראת האלהים *likrath ha-Elohim, to meet the Elohim;* i. e. the Deity, in his visible apparition. Chal. 'To meet the Word of the Lord.'——¶ *Stood at the nether part of the mount.* Without the limits fixed by Moses.

18. *And Mount Sinai was altogether on a smoke,* &c. The appearances thus far seem to have been exclusively those described in v. 16, in which we have no mention of smoke or fire. But as the solemnities proceeded, the terrors of the scene became deeper. Nature seemed to have become more conscious of the approaching God, and discovered greater commotion. Dark and pitchy volumes of smoke, intermingled with lurid flames of fire, rolled up the sides and above the summit of the mount, as if issuing from an immense furnace, and just at this time the foundations of the perpetual hills began to be moved by the throes of an earthquake, which shook the solid rocky mass to its centre.

19. *When the voice of the trumpet sounded long, and waxed louder and louder.* Heb. הולך וחזק מאד *holëk ve-hazëk meod, going and strengthening exceedingly.* It is a phrase entirely different from that v. 13, and implies a growing intensity in the loudness of

as the smoke of a furnace, and k the whole mount quaked greatly.

19 And l when the voice of the trumpet sounded long, and waxed louder and louder, m Moses spake, and n God answered him by a voice.

20 And the LORD came down upon mount Sinai, on the top of the mount : and the LORD called Moses

k Ps. 68. 8. & 77. 18. & 14. 7. Jer. 4. 24. Hebr. 12. 26. l ver. 13. m Hebr. 12. 21. n Neh. 9. 13. Ps. 81. 7.

its clang.——¶ *Moses spake and God answered him by a voice.* What Moses said on this occasion, we are not informed; at least not in this connexion. The Apostle tells us, Heb. 12. 21, that in the midst of the terrors of the scene, he said, 'I exceedingly fear and quake;' and it is not improbable that it was precisely at this stage of the transaction that these words were uttered. As to the answer which God is said to have given him, a correct view of that depends upon the construction of the next verse.

20, 21. *The Lord came down upon Mount Sinai.* As it had been already said, v. 18, that the Lord descended upon the Mount in fire, we have little hesitation in adopting the suggestion of Calvin that all the verbs here should be rendered in the pluperfect tense, ' had come down,' 'had called,' 'had gone up,' and the whole verse considered as parenthetical. The scope of it seems to be, to inform us how it happened that Moses was in a situation to hold this intercourse with Jehovah; for it does not appear that in any stage of the proceedings did God communicate with Moses while he remained among the people below. He was invariably called up to the summit, or near the summit of the mountain. But as nothing had heretofore been said of Moses since he was represented as bringing the people out of the camp to their appointed station, and he is yet here set before us as holding communion with God, it was obviously proper to interpose the notice of his having

up to the top of the mount; and
Moses went up.

21 And the LORD said unto Moses,
Go down, charge the people, lest

---

been previously called up to the top of
the mount. This is done in the twentieth
verse. If this remark be well founded,
it is perhaps to be inferred that God
answered Moses' exclamation by giving
him the order mentioned, v. 21, viz. to
go down and restrain the people from
breaking through the prescribed limits.
Otherwise we must suppose that as
Moses' words to God are not expressly
recorded, so God's words to him are for
wise reasons withheld. But however
this may be, the charge which he was
required to convey to the people leads
us to suppose, that when they saw Moses passing unharmed into the midst of
the fire, the smoke, and the lightning,
their curiosity was excited to the highest pitch to learn the nature of elements
at once so fearful to look upon, and yet
apparently so innocent in their effect,
and, accordingly, that many of them
were upon the point of breaking through
the boundaries to gaze more closely at
the spectacle. This is confirmed by the
Gr. μη ποτε εγγισωσι προς τον Θεον κατανο-
ησαι, *lest by any means they draw nigh
unto God to consider;* i. e. to contemplate, to ponder, to study, implying the
indulgence of a prying curiosity. The
word is used in this sense in Stephen's
speech, Acts, 7. 31, in reference to Moses
at the burning bush.——¶ *Charge the
people.* Heb. הָעֵד *haëd, testify unto.* Gr.
διαμαρτυραι, *bear witness to;* the same
word employed by Paul, 1 Tim. 5. 27,
' *I charge thee* (διαμαρτυρομαι) *before*
God, and the Lord Jesus Christ, and
the elect angels, &c.' So also 2 Tim.
2. 14, 'Of these things put them in remembrance, *charging them* (διαμαρτυ-
ρομενος) before the Lord that they
strive not, &c.' Again, 2 Tim. 4. 1, '*I
charge thee* (διαμαρτυρομαι) therefore,

---

they break through unto the LORD
o to gaze, and many of them perish.
22 And let the priests also which
come near to the LORD, p sanctify

o See ch. 3. 5. 1 Sam. 6. 19. P Lev. 10. 3.

before God, and the Lord Jesus Christ,
&c.' Thus the charge here appointed
to ·be given was a *solemn testimony*
of God, through Moses, of the consequences of disobedience.——¶ *Lest
they break through unto the Lord.* That
is, to the Shekinah, the visible manifestation of the Lord. The phraseology
throughout the narrative is wonderfully
in keeping with this idea.——¶ *And
many of them perish.* Heb. נָפַל מִמֶּנּוּ
רָב *naphal mimmenu rab, many of them
fall.* Gr. πεσωσιν εξ αυτων πληθος, *a multitude of them fall;* i. e. be destroyed
by being put to death in obedience
to the command, v. 12, 13. We cannot
fail to learn from this, that a prying
curiosity in relation to matters which
God does not see fit to reveal to his
creatures is not only highly presumptuous, but fraught with danger.

22. *Let the priests also which come
near to the Lord sanctify themselves.*
Heb. הַכֹּהֲנִים הַנִּגָּשִׁים אֶל יְהֹוָה *hakko-
hanim hanniggashim el Yehovah, the
priests coming near to the Lord;* i. e.
whose duty, whose function, it is, on
ordinary occasions, to come near to
the Lord. Chal. 'Which come near to
minister before the Lord.' But as the
Aaronical priesthood was not yet established it becomes a question who are
meant by the term. We learn from
Ex. 13. 2, that the *first-born* of every
family were in a special manner to be
dedicated and sanctified to God, and it
is clear, from the whole tenor of the
patriarchal history, that the honor of
the priesthood was considered as involved in the rights of primogeniture.
As this was the case, and the tribe of
Levi was afterwards substituted instead
of the first-born, we cannot well doubt
that the *eldest sons* throughout the tribes

themselves, lest the LORD ꝗ break forth upon them.

23 And Moses said unto the LORD, The people cannot come up to

ꝗ 2 Sam. 6. 7, 8.

were at this time considered as invested with so much of the priestly character as to be properly employed on all occasions when any peculiarly sacred ministrations were to be performed. We may therefore suppose that this class of the people are intended by the appellation 'priests,' and that they are the same as we afterwards, Ex. 24. 5, find denominated 'young men of the sons of Israel,' many of whom were, in all probability, at the same time *heads, chiefs,* and *elders* of the people, and so still more properly to be viewed as having the superintendence of the sacred services. These were charged in a peculiar and emphatic manner to ' sanctify themselves' on this occasion, i. e. by abstaining from presumptuous intrusion; for the nearer persons are brought to God by their office, the more dangerous and deadly are their transgressions. They had no doubt shared with the rest of the people in that previous personal sanctification which had been enjoined, v. 10, so that that cannot here be alluded to. The meaning is rather, that considering the force of their example, the obedience which they were to evince was to be so strict, so punctilious, so conscientious, that it would be considered as amounting to a ' sanctification' of themselves in the sight of God. Comp. Lev. 10. 3, ' Then Moses said unto Aaron, This is it that the Lord spake, saying, I will be sanctified in them that come nigh me, and before all the people I will be glorified.' The implication is. that while in the obedience of common persons God is *honored,* in that of his priests he is *sanctified.*
——¶ *Lest the Lord break forth upon them.* Heb. יִפְרֹץ *yiphrotz, break violently forth.* The word is not the same

mount Sinai : for thou chargedst us, saying, ʳ Set bounds about the mount, and sanctify it.

ʳ ver. 12. Josh. 3. 4.

with that applied in the preceding verse to the breaking through of the people in respect to the prescribed limits. That is a very emphatic word יֶהֶרְסוּ *yehersu,* having the import of *subverting, razing, destroying,* as of houses, walls, fortifications, &c, and therefore very well applied to the rushing and pressure of a crowd who break down, trample under foot, and obliterate, any kind of fence or barrier set up to check their progress. But the root פָּרַץ *paratz* is equally significant as spoken of God, and conveys the idea of a sudden, fearful, and destructive bursting forth of his judgments against opposers. Thus, 2 Sam. 5. 20, 'And David came to Baalperazim, and David smote them there, and said, The Lord hath *broken forth* (פָּרַץ *paratz*) upon mine enemies before me, as the breach of waters. Therefore he called the name of that place *Baal-perazim* (בַּעַל פְּרָצִים *baal peratzim,* i. e. *plain of breaches*).' So also, 2 Sam. 6. 8, 'And David was displeased, because the Lord had *made a breach* upon Uzzah : and he called the name of the place *Perez-uzzah* (פֶּרֶץ עֻזָּה *peretz Uzzah, breach of Uzzah*) to this day.' We are no doubt prone to be covetous of license beyond what God has seen fit to allow us, but we may assure ourselves that he always has conceded and always will concede as much as will be for our good, and with such precepts and such examples as we have here cited, we cannot but see that it is at our utmost peril that we presume to go beyond the salutary limits, both of knowledge and action, which he has imposed.

23. *The people cannot come up.* Not that there was any physical impossibility in the way, but Moses seems to

24 And the LORD said unto him, Away, get thee down, and thou shalt come up, thou, and Aaron with thee: but let not the priests and the people break through, to

come up unto the LORD lest he break forth upon them.
25 So Moses went down unto the people, and spake unto them.

---

have thought that by reason of the un-utterable terror and glory of the scene, it was *morally impossible* that the people should any of them be so presumptuous as to transgress an order which he had once so expressly delivered to them, and which he had guarded by setting bounds according to divine direction. Thus it is that in the consciousness of a due deference to the will of God in themselves, the good and the charitable are sometimes prone to entertain a more favorable opinion of human nature than the truth will warrant. God often sees a necessity of uttering cautions and repeating commands of which his right-minded servants are but little aware.

24. *Thou and Aaron with thee.* God does not see fit to make any direct verbal reply to Moses' remark, nor does he intimate that he had been guilty of remissness in any part of *his* duty, but he repeats the order that he should go down, not only to renew his warning to the priests and people, but also to take Aaron and bring him up with him to the top of the mount. As he was about to invest him with the honors of the high priesthood, it was fitting that he should put upon him such tokens of distinction as would inspire the people with a profound respect for his dignity and authority.——¶ *Let not the priests and the people break through to come up.* Gr. μη βιαζεσθωσαν αναβηναι προς τον Θεον, *let them not violently press to come up to God.* As if the danger were that in their anxiety to gaze they should even attempt to advance up the sides of the mountain, from which all but Moses were strictly interdicted. As the priests were ordinarily permitted to approach nearer to God than the rest of the peo-

ple in the discharge of their official duties, they might perhaps be at a loss to see why they might not follow Moses, and still more Aaron, in his near access to the Lord, and thus be emboldened to promise themselves impunity even if they went beyond the limits prescribed to the rest of the people.

25. *And spake unto them.* Heb. ויאמר *va-yomer, and said* unto them. But *what* he said unto them is not stated; for which reason some have thought that ויאמר *va-yomer* in this connexion was equivalent to וידבר *va-yedabber, and he spake,* as our translation has it. But we may still take the verb in its usual sense by supplying, with Jarchi, the objective clause; 'He said or delivered to them this admonition,' i. e. what is contained in the preceding verse. 'Moses went down and said *it* unto them.' *Ainsworth.*

Chapter 20

THE LAW.

The sacred historian, having fully detailed in the preceding chapter all the various preliminaries to the delivery of the Law, comes now to the account of the solemn transaction itself—the most remarkable event, perhaps, taken in all its bearings, that occurred in the history of the chosen people prior to the incarnation of Christ, and one of the most remarkable that ever did or will distinguish the annals of the world itself. The occasion was indeed one which had a primary reference to the nation of Israel, 'to whom,' says the apostle, 'pertaineth the adoption, and the glory, and the covenants, *and the giving of the law,* and the service of God, and the promises.' But it was not an event constituting the national distinction of that people only. It was one affecting the whole human race in its deepest interests, both temporal and eternal. God himself descended from heaven and by a supernatural voice promulgated to man the *Moral Law*, the expression of his will, the reflection of his nature, the immutable standard of right, the inflexible rule of action for his accountable creatures, containing every essential principle of duty, and embodying the grounds of all the future rewards and punishments to be enjoyed or suffered throughout the ages of eternity. These considerations impart to this event a magnitude and importance scarcely to be paralleled by any thing else which has come within the range of our expositions, so that the nature and scope of the Law itself, the various circumstances attending its promulgation, the phraseology in which it is couched, and the principles of its interpretation demand the most careful investigation. Such an inquiry will be best conducted under the several distinct heads that follow.

1. *Various Divisions and Titles of the Law.*

As the people of Israel may be viewed under a threefold aspect, so we have a foundation laid in this fact for a threefold acceptation of the word *Law*. They may be viewed, (1.) As rational and responsible creatures, depending upon God, and subject to his will as the supreme Ruler and Judge of the universe. In this capacity the *law of the ten commandments*, or the *moral law*, was given to them, which is substantially one and the same with the *law of nature*, and binding all men as such. (2.) As the church of the Old Testament, expecting the Messiah, and furnished with a system of worship embracing a great variety of rites and ceremonies, which

pointed more or less distinctly to him. Viewed in this ecclesiastical character, God bestowed upon them the *ceremonial law*, which was a body of rules and precepts regulating their religious worship. (3.) As a peculiar people, having a civil polity and constitution especially appointed for them, and distinguishing them from all other nations, their government being in fact *a theocracy*, in which God himself was their supreme magistrate. Viewed in this light a code of *civil* or *political* laws was prescribed them. The term 'the law' is sometimes applied to one of these systems, and sometimes to another, and again to the whole taken collectively; so that we must often be governed in great measure by the context in determining the precise sense in which the term is used. It is however most legitimately and emphatically employed in reference to the first of these, or the *moral law*, which was distinguished from the others by being audibly delivered by God himself and afterwards written by him upon two tables of stone. Of this Law one of the prevailing scriptural designations is 'the ten words,' or 'ten commandments,' a phraseology which is fully considered in the notes on the first verse of this chapter. The term 'Decalogue' is wholly equivalent, being derived from the Gr. δεκαλογος, from δεκα, *ten,* and λογος, *word.* The origin of this appellation is easily to be traced to such passages as the following, Ex. 34. 28, 'And he wrote upon the tables the words of the covenant, *the ten commandments* (Gr. τους δεκα λογους).' Deut. 13. 4, 'And he declared unto you his covenant, which he commanded you to perform, *were ten commandments* (Heb. עשרת הדברים *asereth haddebarim, the ten words,* Gr. τα δεκα ρηματα) ; and he wrote them upon two tables of stone.' In other connexions we find the several terms *Law, Covenant, Testimony, Statutes, Precepts, Commandments,* &c. applied as a designation of the moral code delivered at Sinai, the grounds of which are either so obvious as not to require particular exposition, or are sufficiently unfolded in the course of the ensuing notes ; so that a precise explication of them may at present be waved.

2. Classification of the Precepts of the Law.

In all ages of the church it has been admitted that the Moral Law was comprised in ten distinct commandments. Of these again a very ancient and generally recognized division is into *two tables;* the first embracing the first four, the second the last six, of the precepts ; the first containing, in a general way, the duties we owe to God, the second, those which we owe to our fellow-men. This division, which is very natural, is warranted by the express words of the Savior, Mat. 22. 37—40, who divides the Law into two great commandments, 'Thou shall love the Lord thy God with all thy heart, &c. This is the first and great commandment ; and the second is like unto it, Thou shall love thy neighbor as thyself.'

In the numerical arrangement and distinction of the several precepts of the decalogue, it is well known that the Romanists differ essentially from Protestants. Following the authority of Augustin, the Roman Church makes but one commandment of the two first, while in order to keep good the number ten, they divide the tenth into two, making the first sentence of that commandment the ninth. The consequence has been that in many professed recitals of the ten commandments in books of devotion, what *we* term the *second,* forbidding idolatry, is entirely omitted. The motive for thus abstracting the second commandment from the Decalogue is very easily imagined on the part of a church which gives so much countenance to image-worship ; and it is equally obvious that the partition of the tenth into two, is wholly with a view to compensate the mutilation by leaving the *nominal* integrity of the code unimpaired. That such a disjunction of the parts of the tenth commandment is wholly unauthorized and violent, will be evident upon a comparison of the text as it stands in the chapter before us and in Deut. 5. 21. In the present passage the coveting of a ' house' occurs *before* the coveting of a ' wife ;' whereas in the other passage the order is reversed and ' house' occurs *after* ' wife.' If then the Papal division were well founded, the *ninth* commandment according to the one reading would be, 'Thou shall not covet thy neighbor's *house,*' and according to the other, 'Thou shall not covet thy neighbor's *wife.*' Such a diversity it appears from Hallett's Notes on Scripture Texts (vol. 3. p. 55.) actually exists in some of the Catechisms and Manuals of the Roman church. But suppose, with Protestants, that ' house' and ' wife' belong to the same precept, and the change in collocation is a matter of no moment.

A difference occurs also between the Heb. and the Gr. copies in regard to the collocation of the *sixth* and *seventh* commandments. The Gr. places our seventh before the sixth, and this order is followed by such of the early Christian Fathers as used the translation of the Seventy, as also by Philo among the Jews. The Gr., however, preserves the usual order of the Heb. text in Deut. 5. 17, 18. In the New Testament a similar diversity obtains. In Mark, 10. 19, and Luke, 18. 20, the prohibition of 'adultery' comes before that of 'killing ;' while in Mat. 19. 18, the Heb. arrangement is observed. The inference is fair from this that provided the integrity of the Decalogue be preserved, and there be no addition to nor subtraction from the true number, the precise order of enumeration is not a matter of any great moment.

3. *Nature and Scope of the Law.*

It is too obvious to require proof that man was formed to be a creature of law. At his very creation, the law of God was written on his heart. Those divine fingers which so curiously wrought the physical fabric of his body, interwove also the precepts of this law with the interior frame-work of his soul. Nor are we to suppose that man had been utterly destitute of all external notices of this law from the creation to the present time. Though not previously so expressly and formally revealed, yet as sin was in the world from Adam to Moses, so we cannot doubt that that law, by the knowledge of which is the knowledge of sin, was also in the world. But nothing is more certain than that in process of time all flesh had corrupted its way, and the traces of the moral code were nearly obliterated among men. The great fundamental truths of religion were lost and buried in the abounding idolatry and immorality that every where prevailed. In these circumstances, when it pleased God to separate to himself a peculiar people, who should know his will, and be the depositaries of his truth, he saw fit to *republish* this law, and so to record it as to give it a permanent establishment in the world; and in order to convey a more suitable impression of its spirit and design, it was to be delivered in circumstances of the greatest imaginable pomp and terror. The intrinsic propriety of this will be seen at once on considering the character of the Law. As contrasted with the Gospel it was a dispensation of wrath, a ministration of condemnation and death. 'Cursed be every one that continueth not in all things that are written in the book of the law to do them,' is its inexorable language. It was a 'fiery law,' denouncing judgment without mercy for every offence, and not knowing either abatement, or intermission, or compromise of its stern demands. The circumstances of its delivery, therefore, were intended to be in keeping with its character. Being a transcript of the divine perfections, it was to be so promulgated as to impress those who heard it, and those who should hear of it, with a just sense of the greatness, majesty, glory, and terribleness of that Being from whom it emanated. It was designed to work a deep conviction of the fearfulness of Jehovah's displeasure, and to inspire alarm by awaking a sense of sin. Accordingly, as it was attended with the terrors of Sinai in its proclamation, so it comes into the conscience with the dread of God's wrath. As the mountain shook, as the people trembled, as Moses himself said, ' I exceedingly fear and quake,' so the soul when it becomes convinced of sin, is filled with dismay. Fearfulness and trembling come upon it ; it shakes with violent apprehensions of woe, and looks for instant destruction. Such is the necessary consequence. Whenever a man obtains a correct view of the Law, and feels that he has broken it ; when he sees that the Law is spiritual, and that he is carnal, sold under sin ; when he perceives that he is condemned, and every moment liable to the curse ; he cannot but experience the same kind of inward emotions and perturbations as the Israelites experienced when they saw the fires of Sinai, heard its thunders, and felt its shaking. Thus one main object of the giving of the Law was attained—the begetting a sense of native sinfulness, of distance from God, of exposedness to wrath. But this would lead directly to another of equal importance—the necessity of a Mediator. And this effect was very decidedly wrought on the present occasion. They were conscious that they could not approach to God without some kind of intervention. Accordingly, they who but just before had been with difficulty restrained from breaking through the bounds that had been assigned them, were now so alarmed that they drew back from their station, and entreated that God would no longer deliver his commands to them in that way, lest they should die. They desired that Moses might act as a mediator between God and them, and that all future intimations of the divine will should be given through that medium. They were not perhaps aware of the full meaning of their own request, nor of how much a greater mediator than Moses they stood in need. But God approved of their request, and not only complied with it, but promised another Mediator at a future period, who should resemble Moses, and whom the people were required, under the highest penalty, to obey. For it was on this occasion that the promise contained Deut. 18. 15—19, was given, 'The Lord thy God will raise up unto thee a Prophet from the midst of thee, of thy brethren, like unto me ; unto him ye shall hearken. According to all that thou desiredst of the Lord thy God in Horeb in the day of the assembly, saying, Let me not hear again the voice of the Lord my God, neither let me see this great fire any more, that I die not. And the Lord said unto me, They have well spoken that which they have spoken. I will raise them up a Prophet from among their brethren, like unto thee, and will put my words in his mouth: and he shall speak unto them all that I shall command him. And it shall come to pass, that whosoever will not hearken unto my words which he shall speak in my name, I will require it of him.' The agency of Moses, therefore, throughout the whole transaction, passing to and fro between God and the people, now ascending the mount and entering the cloud, and now again coming forth, returning to the camp, and delivering his messages, was expressly designed as a lively type of the mediatorship of Christ in effecting our acceptance and salvation. And thus it serves, as the apostle says, 'as a schoolmaster to bring us to Christ.'

With this view of the essential nature and genius of the Law before us, we cannot easily fall into the error against which the apostle Paul has so anxiously warned us, of supposing that it was given in order to man's being saved by his living up to its demands. It was not given to give life. 'By the deeds of the law shall no flesh living be justified.' It was rather designed as a divine revelation of man's religious and moral duties, as a perfect standard and rule of obedience, and one too of perpetual and universal obligation. For as every precept of it flows directly from the unchangeable perfections of God, it must for ever make the same uncompromising demand upon the obedience of its subjects. The ceremonial statutes might serve a temporary end and be abolished. But of the Moral Law our Savior says, 'Heaven and earth shall pass away, but one jot or one tittle shall in no wise pass from the law till all be fulfilled.' It must necessarily enter into the Christian dispensation, and pervade it through every period of its existence. It will even pass into heaven itself and there be the delight and govern the service of every glorified spirit and ministering angel. This will be more evident if we consider that it is the universal law of *love*. God is love, and his Law inculcates love. A compend of the whole Law is embraced in the precept, ' Thou shalt love the Lord thy God with all thy heart and all thy mind and all thy strength, and thy neighbor as thyself. On these two commandments hang all the law and the prophets.' Love therefore must be of universal and eternal obligation, immutable as the nature of God himself. God cannot divest himself of love, nor even abrogate the Law which requires it.

From all this we perceive the great ends which were to be answered by the promulgation of the Law of the ten commandments, and for the same reasons we can see why it was that such a *scene* was chosen for the purpose. The genius of the Law was severe, rigid, dark, fearful, terrific. In accordance with this the people of Israel were led into a dreary, desolate wilderness, a region of barren rocks and thirsty sands, where all nature appeared in its most wild, and rugged, and desert aspect. There, amidst bleak mountainous masses of granite, separated by narrow ravines, in which only here and there little patches of herbage, and scattered trees are found, the Law of Sinai was proclaimed, as if it were especially intended to teach them that that dispensation, compared with the gospel, was like the most desert and forbidding locality on the earth's surface contrasted with the most blooming and luxuriant paradise which the hands of nature and art ever conspired to beautify. This view of the event before us will no doubt become more and more striking, in proportion as the geological and topographical features of that region are more fully disclosed, as they are in a fair way to be, in consequence of the growing influx of travel into that memorable and interesting quarter of the globe.

4. *Principles of Interpretation.*

'Thy commandment,' says David, ' is exceeding broad ;' in which we read a clear intimation of the extent and spirituality of the divine requirements, as reaching beyond the outward actions, and taking cognizance of the inmost thoughts and intentions of the heart. With so important a portion of revelation, therefore, before us, it is evidently a matter of great moment to fix upon correct principles of interpretation, and in coming at these, nothing is more obvious than that the mode of interpretation adopted by Christ and his apostles is to be a directory for us in putting our constructions upon the precepts of the Decalogue. Referring then to our Lord's sermon on the mount, it is clear

beyond all question that the Law, properly understood, lays its demands and its prohibitions upon the inward actings of the spirit, and not merely upon the outward conduct. If we are taught by this supreme authority to regard cherished lust as adultery, and harbored hate as murder, how can we avoid the inference that all the commandments are equally extensive in their import, and address themselves directly to the *heart* as the fountain of action and the criterion of character ? To the same conclusion are we irresistibly brought by the language of Paul in his reasonings upon the Law in the Epistle to the Romans. It was only when he came to understand fully the spiritual nature of the Law and the sternness and universality of its requirements, that he became convinced of sin, and, as it were, *slain* by its killing power. The same view of the character of this deeply searching moral code is undoubtedly maintained throughout the whole tenor of the Scriptures, so that we cannot well hesitate to admit the justness of the canon laid down in the Assembly's Catechism, for interpreting the demands of the Law, ' that it binds every one to full conformity in the whole man, unto the righteousness thereof, and to entire obedience for ever ; so as to require the utmost perfection in every duty, and to forbid the least degree of every sin.' Accordingly, in putting a due sense upon the several precepts, we must admit that 'when a particular duty is commanded, the contrary sin is forbidden, with all the causes, occasions, and temptations which might lead to it ; and when a sin is forbidden, the contrary duty is commanded, together with all the requisite means to its performance.'

It may also be remarked in regard to the distinction of the precepts into *affirmative* and *negative*, that there is ground for it in the consideration that what God *forbids* is at *no time* to be done; what he *commands* is always our duty, yet every particular duty is not to be done at all times. Moreover, it must be perceived that in the negative mode of injunction, there is something more emphatic, and that leaves less room for evasion. Thus, had the first commandment, ' Thou shalt have no other gods, &c.,' been propounded affirmatively, ' Thou shalt worship one God,' the Samaritans, for instance, might still have contended that they kept this commandment, though they mixed the worship of other gods with that of the true.

On the whole, it is obvious that this momentous and immutable Law is framed with the utmost wisdom of its divine author, and that if its deep spirituality, its rigid and uncompromising demands, its perpetual authority, and its awful sanctions, were duly appreciated, it would awaken and keep alive every where the slumbering consciousness of sin, and at once lead to and endear the atonement of Christ, who was made a curse for us that he might redeem us from the curse of the violated Law.

5. *Ministry of Angels in the Delivery of the Law.*

No attentive reader of the Scriptures can fail to have been struck with the fact, that in several passages, both of the Old and New Testament, the presence and the agency of angels is expressly recognized on the occasion of the giving of the law. A somewhat extended and minute examination, therefore, of the circumstances attending this remarkable event will here be proper, in order to obtain, if possible, the true clue to the language employed by the sacred writers in describing it. It will be evident, if we mistake not, from the tenor of our annotations on the preceding chapter, that the pillar of cloud, the sublime Shekinah, which had hitherto directed the journeyings of the Israelites, now removed itself from over the place of their encampment and took its position on the mountain. Here it assumed, in the first instance, a hue of dense and pitchy darkness, which would contrast more strongly with the fiery splendors that were ere long to burst out of its bosom, and together with the earthquake, and the thunder, and the trumpet-blast, to clothe the scene with a grandeur utterly unparalleled on earth. It is true, the Shekinah is here presented in aspect different from any in which we have yet contemplated it. We have hitherto beheld it in connexion with an audible voice—as a fire burning in but not consuming the bushy thicket — as an illuminated pillar of cloud — but no where else have we seen it with the accompaniment of thunders and lightnings and the voice of a trumpet, and all the fearful array of Mount Sinai. Still that this *was* an actual exhibition of the Shekinah the narrative leaves us no room to doubt. The ancient versions plainly confirm this view. Of these one of the Chaldee Targums renders the account in the 19th chapter ;—'Moses led the people out of the camp to meet the Shekinah of Jehovah ;' another, ' to meet the Word of the Lord ;' and the Arab, ' to meet the Angel of the Lord.' Now it is to be recollected that we have previously shown that the visible Shekinah is repeatedly termed the 'Angel of the Lord,' and that this is the true object which is to be brought before the mind whenever in the books of Moses the title 'Angel of the Lord' occurs. The Shekinah was so called because it was the ordinary *medium* or *organ* through which the Most High manifested his presence and evinced his favor or disfavor towards the chosen people. Bearing this fact in mind, let us turn to Acts, 7. 37, 38, where in the speech of Stephen it is said, 'This is that Moses which said unto the children of Israel, A Prophet shall the Lord your God raise up unto you of your brethren like unto me : him shall ye hear. This is he that was in the church in the wilderness with the angel which spake to him in the Mount Sinai, and with our fathers; who received the lively oracles to give unto us.' Here it is evident that the 'Angel' mentioned is no other than he who was the great Speaker on the occasion of the delivery of the Law, and that this was Jehovah himself in his appropriate symbol of the cloudy pillar is, we think, indubitable. But here there is comparatively little difficulty, as the term 'Angel' is singular and refers plainly to a single personage. In the following passages however the term is plural, and the solution, not so directly obvious. Gal. 3. 19, 'It (the Law) was *ordained by angels* in the hand of a mediator.' Again, Heb. 2. 2, '*For if the word spoken by angels* was steadfast,' &c. No one can fail to see that in these passages the presence of *angels* is recognized as in some way connected with the sublimities and sanctities of the awful scene. It is not merely the *one Angel* of the Shekinah who is referred to, but there is a clear implication of the accompanying presence of *a multitude of the heavenly hosts*. How then is this to be understood? Moses in his narrative says nothing of such an angelic appendage to the scene, and it is an important enquiry whence such a usage of speech may be supposed to have originated. It will be seen from our Notes on Ex. 25. 18, that the Cherubim are properly to be regarded as a *symbol of multitude;* and ample proof may be adduced that *a multitude of angelic attendants* was always supposed to accompany the Shekinah. From the very first introduction of these sacred symbols into the divine economy at the garden of Eden they were always viewed in this light, and though occasionally the visible Glory might appear when the accompanying multitudes did not, yet in the minds of the chosen people they were habitually associated with it and viewed as in fact involved in it. Indeed, the

remarkable device of the Ark of the Covenant, with its appurtenances of the Glory and the Cherubim was nothing but *a sensible embodiment* of this ancient and established idea, which had been familiar to the patriarchs from the earliest ages of the world. To this ideal host, though ultimately adumbrating *men* rather than any other order of beings, yet with entire propriety they assigned the title of *angels*. That these angelic hosts should constitute a distinguishing part of the supernatural apparatus of the present scene would be a matter of course; and nothing would be more congruous to scriptural usage than to ascribe to them a special *agency* or *execution* on the occasion, from their being present, consenting, and cooperating with the divine Lawgiver. It is ascribed to them on the same grounds on which Paul affirms that the saints shall judge the world, by which at the same time nothing more is meant than that they shall be *coinciding assessors* with the great Judge himself. That this New Testament mode of speaking of the delivery of the Law is warranted by the *usus loquendi* of the Hebrew Scriptures will be evident from the following citations. Deut. 33. 2, ' The Lord came from Sinai, and rose up from Seir unto them; he shined forth from mount Paran, *and he came with ten thousands of saints:* from his right hand went a fiery law for them.' Here the ' ten thousands of saints' are ten thousands of *holy ones* or *holy myriads* (מרבבת קדש *mëribboth kodesh),*' and this is but another name for *angels*. Thus also Ps. 68. 7, 8—17, 'O God, when thou wentest forth before thy people, when thou didst march through the wilderness; The earth shook, the heavens also dropped at the presence of God: even Sinai itself was moved at the presence of God, the God of Israel. The chariots of God are twenty thousand, *even thousands of angels: the Lord is among them, as in Sinai, in the holy place.*' This, taken in its connexions, is

CHAPTER XX.

AND God spake a all these words, saying,

2 b I *am* the LORD thy God, which

a Deut. 5. 22. b Lev. 26. 1, 13. Deut. 5. 6.
Ps. 81. 10. Hos. 13. 4.

have brought thee out of the land of Egypt, c out of the house of bondage.

c ch. 13. 3.

---

a very remarkable passage, and that it has an intimate relation to the subject before, is obvious at once. The original for ' chariots' (רכב *rekeb*) is a collective singular for ' chariots,' and has an evident allusion to the same kind of symbolic scenery as that described in the vision of Ezekiel, where the Living Creatures or Cherubim are represented as forming a sort of *animated chariot* on which the Jehovah in the visible Shekinah was transported. The twenty thousand chariots of God, therefore, is but another name for twenty thousand angels supposed to be present at the giving of the Law from Sinai, on which, as on a living throne, the Glory was supported. This reminds us at once of the parallel language of the 18th Psalm, which is penned in the highest style of sanctified poetic afflatus, and which no doubt refers to the very scene at Sinai now under consideration. For although David is the speaker, yet he speaks in the person of the Jewish church, whose historical fortunes from the beginning are depicted in the boldest imagery of inspiration ; Ps. 18. 7—11, 'Then the earth shook and trembled ; the foundations also of the hills moved and were shaken, because he was wroth. There went up a smoke out of his nostrils, and fire out of his mouth devoured : coals were kindled* by it. He bowed the heavens also, and came down : and darkness was under his feet. And he *rode upon a cherub and did fly:* yea, he did fly upon the wings of the wind. He made darkness his secret place ; his pavilion round about him were dark waters and thick clouds of the skies.' That is, such dark, lowering, gloomy clouds as are usually surcharged with waters

that in a time of tempest pour themselves out in gushing torrents. 'He rode upon a cherub ;' that is, collectively, upon the Cherubim, constituting the Cherubic vehicle above mentioned. Finally we may advert to the testimony of Philo (Lib. de Decalogo), who says that ' there were present at the giving of the Law voices ; visible, animated, and splendid flames of fire ; *spirits* (πνευματα) ; trumpets ; and divine men running hither and thither to publish the Law.'

On the whole, from a collation of the various passages now adduced, we cannot but think the phraseology of the Apostles in respect to the event in question is explicable in entire consistency with the Mosaic narrative ; and it only adds another proof of the vast importance of a correct view of the Shekinah to a right understanding of this and other portions of the Scriptures.

1. *And God spake all these words.* Heb. כל הדברים אלה *kol haddebarim elleh.* That is, the words or commandments following, called ' ten commandments (דברים *debarim, words*),' Ex. 34. 28. Deut. 4. 13, whence the title ' Decalogue,' or *ten words,* and ' the voice of words,' Heb. 12. 19. That ' words' and ' precepts,' or ' commandments,' are equivalent in Scripture usage, is evident from the following passages ; Deut. 18. 19, ' I will raise them up a Prophet from among their brethren, like unto thee, and will put my *words* in his mouth ; and he shall speak unto them all that I shall *command* him. And it shall come to pass, that whosoever will not hearken unto my *words* which he shall speak in my name, I will require it of him ;'

i. e. whosoever will not hearken unto my precepts. Gal. 5. 14, 'For all the law is fulfilled *in one word;'* i. e. in one commandment, viz. that thou shalt love thy neighbor as thyself. Est. 1. 12, ' But the queen Vashti refused to come at *the king's commandment* (Heb. בדבר המלך *bidbar hammelek, at the king's word).'* Thus Mark, 7. 13, 'Making the *word* of God of none effect ;' while Mat. 15. 6, 'Made the *commandment* of God of none effect.' It would not perhaps be easy, from the letter of the present narrative, to establish conclusively the fact that these words were spoken by the Most High in an articulate voice ; as it might be maintained that they were spoken to Moses, and by him, as mediator, communicated to the people. But upon comparing other passages where this event is spoken of, the evidence, we think, is too strong to be resisted, that in delivering the Decalogue, God himself was the speaker. Thus, Deut. 5. 12, 13, 'And the Lord spake unto you out of the midst of the fire : ye heard the voice of the words, but saw no similitude ; only ye heard a voice. And he declared unto you his covenant, which he commanded you to perform, even ten commandments ; and he wrote them upon two tables of stone.' Again, in ver. 32, 33, of the same chapter, the language forces upon us the same conclusion ; 'For ask now of the days that are past, which were before thee, since the day that God created man upon the earth, and ask from the one side of heaven unto the other, whether there hath been any such thing as this great thing is; or hath been heard like it ? *Did ever people hear the voice of God speaking out of the midst of the fire,* as thou hast heard, and live ?' Add to this, that it is by no means certain, from an attentive survey of all the circumstances, that Moses was on the mount during the delivery of the Decalogue. It would seem then, that if the Law

was spoken in an audible voice at all it must have been by God himself.

PREFACE TO THE TEN COMMANDMENTS.

2. *I am the Lord thy God,* &c. Heb. יהוה אלהיך *Yehovah Elohëka, Jehovah thine Elohim.* As these words contain nothing of a preceptive nature, they are undoubtedly to be considered as a kind of *preface* to the ensuing Commandments, embracing a declaration of the grounds on which their authority rests. The Most High in proclaiming his august name Jehovah, does thereby most imperatively assert his claim to the obedience of all rational creatures to whatever he should enjoin upon them. As 'Jehovah,' the self-existent, independent, eternal fountain of all being, he has of course the most absolute right to give law to the creatures he has formed. Such a right flows by self-evident sequence from the very relation of Creator and creature. He who gives being may give law ; and no greater extrinsic sanction can be conceived to any code of laws than the supremacy, sovereignty, majesty, preeminence, and power of the source from which it emanates ; and all this is implied in the very name ' Jehovah.' It is, consequently, a ground of obligation which applies to the whole human race, as well as to the nation of Israel ; but in the accompanying title 'thy God,' there is a virtual restriction which brings home to the Israelites the import of the declaration with an emphasis and force which no other people could feel in the same degree. 'I am the Lord thy God, which brought thee out of Egypt,' are words containing a motive to obedience peculiar to the seed of Jacob, and one of which they were justly expected to feel the cogency. God was not only their God as Creator, but theirs by covenant relation, and by the signal deliverance wrought in their behalf. From whom then might he look for obedi-

3 d Thou shalt have no other gods before me.

d Deut. 5. 7. & 6. 14. 2 Kings 17. 35. Jer. 25. 6. & 35. 15.

4 e Thou shalt not make unto thee any graven image, or any likeness

e Lev. 26. 1. Deut. 4. 16. & 5. 8. & 27. 15. Ps. 97. 7.

ence, if not from them? If ' blessed is the nation whose God is the Lord, and the people whom he hath chosen for his own inheritance,' how utterly inexcusable must be *their* disobedience to the mandates of their great Lawgiver? *We* have not indeed been delivered from the literal bondage of Egypt, but the spirit of the declaration reaches to us, if Christians, as redeemed by Christ from a bondage infinitely worse, and incorporated by faith into the true Israel of God, the spiritual seed of Abraham, and made heirs of all the blessings of the covenant of grace. Consequently, as the Lord is our God, we are bound by the same inviolable bonds of love and service as rested upon the seed of Israel according to the flesh. It is to be remarked, both here and elsewhere, throughout the Decalogue, that the address is made in the *singular* and not in the *plural* number. The design of this is, undoubtedly, to render the language in the highest degree emphatic. Every individual to whom this law comes is to consider himself as being as directly and personally addressed as though it had been spoken to him alone. ' Thou art the man.' In the present passage, as the assurance conveyed is intended to be appropriated by each individual to himself personally, it is full of condescending endearment ; and the proper response to is furnished by the prophet, Zech. 13. 9, 'I will say it is my people ; and they shall say, The Lord is *my* God ;' not *our*.——¶ *Out of the house of bondage.* Heb. מבית עבדים *mibbëth abadim, out of the house of slaves;* i. e. out of the house where they themselves were slaves, and not the Egyptians ; for although we cannot doubt that a large part of the Egyptian population was in a very degraded state,

a state of vassalage and depression, yet that is not the allusion in the present passage. The words refer solely to the servile condition of the Israelites during their sojourn in the land of Egypt ; and their wonderful deliverance thence by the outstretched arm of Jehovah, is very properly insisted upon as a ground for the cordial reception of the moral and ceremonial statutes which he was now imposing upon them. The motive to obedience involved in this miraculous interposition is still more emphatically dwelt upon Deut. 6. 20—24, 'And when thy son asketh thee in time to come, saying, What mean the testimonies, and the statutes, and the judgments, which the Lord our God hath commanded you? Then thou shalt say unto thy son, We were Pharaoh's bond-men in Egypt ; and the Lord brought us out of Egypt with a mighty hand : and the Lord showed signs and wonders, great and sore, upon Egypt, upon Pharaoh, and upon all his household, before our eyes: And he brought us out from thence, that he might bring us in, to give us the land which he sware unto our fathers. And the Lord commanded us to do all these statutes, to fear the Lord our God, for our good always, that he might preserve us alive, as it is at this day.'

FIRST TABLE.

THE FIRST COMMANDMENT.

3. *Thou shalt have no other gods before me.* Heb. לא יהוה לך אלהים אחרים על פני *lo yihyeh leka Elohim aharim al panai, there shall not be to thee other gods upon or against my face;* i. e. in my sight, boldly confronting me. Chal. 'There shall not be to thee another god besides me.' Gr.

of any thing that *is* in heaven above, or that *is* in the earth be- | neath, or that *is* in the water under the earth.

ουκ εσονται σοι θεοι ετεροι πλην εμου, *there shall not be to thee other gods besides me.* But the Heb. עַל פְּנֵי no where properly signifies *besides* or *except*, but always *before, in the presence of.* The scope of the precept is evidently to make known the true and only object of worship, and to forbid the annexing of any other object of religious reverence, respect, and homage to that which they were exclusively required to serve. It requires a conduct accordant with the declaration of Jehovah himself, Is. 42. 8, 'My glory will I not give to another.' The language does not necessarily imply the *reality*, the *positive existence*, of any such adventitious deities, but they were not to have any that were *so esteemed;* or as the apostle says, 1 Cor. 8. 5, 6, 'Though there be that are called gods, whether in heaven or in earth (as there are gods many and lords many); but to us there is but one God, the Father, of whom are all things, and we in him.' The precept does not seem to be directed primarily and immediately against that idolatry which consists in the use of fabricated images, although this is virtually forbidden, but against the putting any thing else in the place of the one living and true God. This may be done mentally as well as manually. There may be idolatry without idols; and the scope of this commandment seems to be mainly to forbid the making of any other objects, whether persons or things, real or imaginary, the objects of that supreme regard, reverence, esteem, affection, and obedience which we owe to God alone. As God is the fountain of happiness, and no intelligent being can be happy but through him, whoever seeks for supreme happiness in the creature instead of the Creator, is guilty of a violation of this command. Whatever it be that sets up a rival interest in our souls, absorbing

that love and service which belongs to the true God, that is another God before him. Consequently, the proud man, who idolizes himself; the ambitious man, who pays homage to popular applause; the covetous man, who deifies his wealth; the sensualist, who lives to gratify his low appetites; the doting lover, husband, father, mother, who suffer their hearts to be supremely absorbed in the love of the creature, all come under the charge of transgressing the first commandment. In fact obedience to this precept would perfectly enthrone the Lord in our judgment and affections; and the strength of our love being thus given to him, we should love all others for his sake, and according to the measure that he had enjoined; whilst the violation of it destroys this subordination, and gives the creature the throne in our heart. With the utmost propriety therefore does it stand foremost in the tables of the Decalogue. It is the foundation of all the rest.

THE SECOND COMMANDMENT.

4. *Thou shalt not make unto thee,* &c. The second commandment, comprised in v. 4—6, differs from the first by having respect to the *mode* of worship rather than the *object.* It consists of two parts, a *precept* and a *sanction.* The precept forbids the making of any sculptured or painted images of any object in heaven or earth, to be employed in religious worship. Nothing was to be attempted of the nature of a *likeness* or *sensible representation* of the invisible Deity, nothing constructed or portrayed which should stand as an *arbitrary symbol* of Jehovah, who was to be worshipped as a pure intelligent spirit, infinitely removed beyond the possibility of any material representation. Aware of the strong idolatrous tendency in human nature, and with a view to preclude its

breaking forth among the chosen people the Most High took especial care in his manifestation at Mount Sinai that the Israelites should see 'no manner of similitude,' nothing that could afterward be represented by an image. This is particularly adverted to in the subsequent account of that transaction, Deut. 4. 12—15—23, which forms the most suitable commentary on the precept before us; 'And the Lord spake unto you out of the midst of the fire; ye heard the voice of the words, but saw no *similitude;* only ye heard a voice. Take ye therefore good heed unto yourselves; (for ye saw no manner of *similitude* on the day that the Lord spake unto you in Horeb out of the midst of the fire); lest ye corrupt yourselves, and make you a *graven image,* the *similitude* of any figure, the *likeness* of male or female. The *likeness* of any beast that is on the earth, the *likeness* of any winged fowl that flieth in the air. The *likeness* of any thing that creepeth on the ground, the *likeness* of any fish that is in the waters beneath the earth: Take heed unto yourselves, lest ye forget the covenant of the Lord your God, which he made with you, and make you a *graven image,* or the *likeness* of any thing which the Lord thy God hath forbidden thee.'

It is not to be supposed from the unqualified language of the prohibition, that sculpture or painting as branches of the fine arts are forbidden, although the Jews have for the most part been restrained by this commandment from indulging themselves to any extent in the mimetic arts. On this subject the language of Michaelis (Comment. on the Laws of Moses, Art. 250) is worthy of being quoted; 'I know not how it has happened that several writers, and among them some men of real learning, have persuaded themselves, or have, without inquiry, asserted, one after another, that the Israelites were absolutely prohibited from making, or having any image whatever, even although it

had not the most distant reference to the Deity, or to religion. But let us consider the passages in which Moses prohibits images, in their connexion with the context, and see whether any such exposition ought to be given them: We find them (for I think it best to point them all out together) in Ex. 20. 4, 5. Deut. 4. 15—18; 27. 15. Now, from the connexion, it is evident, that images of the Deity are alone spoken of in all these passages; and the man, who, from the detached clause, *Thou shalt make to thyself no image,* concludes, that no image durst have been painted, or scrawled upon a rock, or cut in wood or stone, might, with equal reason, detach from their connexion the following words, which come immediately after the prohibition of images, *Thou shalt not raise thine eyes to heaven to behold the sun, moon, and stars,* and understand them as meant to imply, that we were never to raise our eyes to heaven and contemplate the sun, moon, and stars, but rather to walk upon all fours for ever.' The scope of the precept is evidently to forbid the use of those imaged and pictured likenesses *as representations of the invisible God.* The intention of the law is obvious from the reason assigned for it, viz., that they had seen 'no manner of similitude' when God appeared and delivered the Decalogue at Horeb. As he did not *appear* to them in any shape, so he ought not to be represented in any shape. But this reason does not hold against the making graven images of men, beasts, birds, fishes, or reptiles, when they were not intended as representations of God, or to be used as objects or means of worship. Accordingly Moses was expressly commanded to construct the figures of the Cherubim of the sculptured work for the Ark of the Covenant, Ex. 25. 18—20, and also the brazen serpent as an emblematic device to aid in the production of a salutary effect on the bodies of the bitten Israelites in the wilderness, Num. 28. 8, 9. It is certain, moreover, that in the Temple of Solomon there was a great deal of sculptured work over the walls, as of flowers colocynths, palm-trees, cherubim, &c., and the brazen sea, it is well known rested upon twelve brazen oxen. In neither of these cases was there any infraction of the second commandment, because the *design* of these images did not come within the scope of its prohibition. But the making of the golden calf by the Israelites in the wilderness was in the most direct contravention of the letter and spirit of this precept, although professedly set up in honor of the true God, and was what the Scriptures expressly call *idolatry*, Acts, 7. 41, 'They made a calf in those days and offered sacrifice unto the *idol* (τῳ ειδωλῳ).' 1 Cor. 10. 7, 'Neither be ye *idolaters* as some of them were; as it is written, The people sat down to eat, and to drink, and rose up to play.' In like manner when Jeroboam set up his calves of gold and proclaimed to the people, 'Behold thy gods, O Israel, which brought thee up out of Egypt,' he was guilty of the very sin forbidden in the second commandment. That this was the idolatry condemned in this commandment, viz., worshipping the images of the true God, and not the worship of a *false* god, which is more especially pointed at in the first, is evident from this, that his sin is said to be *less* than the sin of worshipping the image of Baal, 1 Kings, 16. 31, where we read that ' it came to pass, as if it had been a light thing for Ahab to walk in the sins of Jeroboam that he went and served Baal and worshipped him;' and so in the language of the first commandment, ' had another god before Jehovah,' which Jeroboam had not, because he worshipped his idols *as images of the true God*. This we suppose to be a leading distinction between the first and second precept of the law. But the spiritual import of this commandment reaches much farther. It goes unequivocally to forbid all superstitious usages, all mere human inventions, in the matter of divine worship. The annexing of additions of our own to the institutions of heaven under the pretext of their being *significant ceremonies* calculated to excite devotion or better to promote the ends of worship, is nothing short of a bold innovation upon the prescribed worship of God. Deut. 12. 30, 'What thing soever I command you, observe to do it ; thou shalt not *add* thereto, nor *diminish* from it.' This principle accordingly condemns all such commanded practices as signing with the cross in baptism, kneeling at the sacrament, erecting altars in churches, bowing at the name of Jesus, and other things of like nature, for which the Scriptures contain no express warrant. The bare *adoption* of such usages no doubt trenches in some degree upon the spirit of this commandment ; but to *insist* upon them as terms of communion is nothing short of a downright invasion of the prerogative of the divine Lawgiver, and must incur his marked displeasure. In the minor *circumstances* of religious worship no doubt many things are left to be regulated by the dictates of human discretion, and in these the apostolic rule, ' let every thing be done decently and in order,' will always be a sufficient guide; but whenever this rule is made a plea for *imposing* things uncommanded, then a plain infraction is made upon the spirit of this precept.——¶ *Graven image.* Heb. פסל *pesel, sculptile, any thing cut, graven, or carved, a statue,* from the root פסל *pasal, to hew, to chip, to sculpture,* whether wood or stone. Gr. ειδωλον, *an idol.* Chal. 'An image.' ——¶ *Likeness.* Heb. תמונה *temunah, likeness, similitude.* The term is quite general in its import, carrying with it mainly the idea of *resemblance*, but whether this resemblance is the result of configuration or delineation is not determined by the word alone. As the previous term פסל *pesel*, more strictly

5 f Thou shalt not bow down thyself to them, nor serve them ; for I the LORD thy God *am* a g jealous God, h visiting the iniquity of the fathers upon the children unto the third and fourth *generation* of them that hate me ;

f ch. 23. 24. Josh. 23. 7. 2 Kings 17. 35. Isai. 44. 15, 19. g ch. 34. 14. Deut. 4. 24. & 6. 15. Josh. 24. 19. Neh. 1. 2.

h ch. 34. 7. Lev. 20. 5. & 26. 39, 40. Numb. 14. 18, 33. 1 Kings 21. 29. Job 5. 4. & 21. 19. Ps. 79. 8. & 109. 4. Isai. 14. 20, 21. & 65. 6, 7. Jer. 2. 9. & 32. 18.

---

denotes *statuary*, it will no doubt be proper here to understand תמונה *te-munah* of any kind of *pictorial representation* whether of real or fancied objects, which might serve as the instruments of worship.

5. *Thou shalt not bow down thyself to them.* Heb. לא תשתחוה להם *lo tish-tahavch lahem*, shalt not do obeisance to them. Gr. ου προσκυνησεις αυτοις, *shall not worship them*, a term applied to those bodily gestures, such as bowing, kneeling, falling prostrate, &c., which are used as tokens of special reverence and respect. See Note on Gen. 18. 2. Though they might not *make* nor *have* such images themselves or in their own country, yet possibly they might see them in passing through other lands, in which case they were required carefully to refrain from bowing down to them, or using any gesture which might be construed into an act of religious reverence, or as in any degree countenancing a practice so expressly forbidden.—— ¶ *Nor serve them.* Heb. תעבדם *taobdem.* Gr. μη λατρευσεις αυτοις, *nor do homage to them.* If they were forbidden to *make* or to *acknowledge* by the most casual outward gesture any such images, much less were they to go so far as to *serve* them, or unite with those that did, either by *offering sacrifice, burning incense, pouring out libations, making vows, building altars, consecrating temples*, or any other act of equivalent import. The spirit of this second commandment, like that of the whole Decalogue, is plainly ' exceeding broad.' It is undoubtedly implied that in paying our devotion to the true God we are not to employ any image or likeness for the purpose of directing, exciting, or assisting that devotion. Though it were worship designed to terminate in God, yet its being offered through such a medium would divest it of all its acceptableness in his sight. Guided solely by the dictates of our erring reason, we might suppose that the aid of bodily sense might be called in to assist our mental vision, and that the use of images, paintings, crucifixes, and other outward symbols might at least be harmless, if not positively beneficial in refreshing the memory and quickening our devotions. But God knows the downward and deteriorating tendency of our nature even in its best estate, and he sees that the employment of outward symbols of worship would gradually tend to lower the standard of pious feeling and finally to withdraw the mind from the ultimate spiritual object, and fix it upon the gross sensible medium. We have only to look at the history of the Greek and Latin churches for an abundant confirmation of this view of the subject. How palpable is it that the standard of a pure and spiritual worship is there most sadly and fearfully degraded ? that the spirit of devotion has been lost in that of downright idolatry ? From crosses and relics they proceeded to images and pictures, not only of God and Christ, and the Holy Ghost, but of the virgin and of saints and martyrs without number ; until those beings, and the paintings or carvings which represented them, originally designed as mere intercessors and aids to devotion, became, at least to the more ignorant, actual objects of worship. Now and then an individual may perhaps be found exhibiting a depth and

fervor of pious feeling that has resisted all these untoward influences. But in the general, what superstition, what profanation, what mockery, under the name of worship there prevail? Forgiveness of sin by human authority, the withholding the Bible from the people, and the grossest immorality among large portions of the priesthood are among the fruits known and read of all men, of the practical violation of the second commandment.——¶ *For I the Lord thy God am a jealous God*, &c. We have thus far considered the *precept* of the Second Commandment; the words before us bring us to its *sanction*. This is drawn from the nature of God, and the words very strikingly exhibit the peculiar feeling with which Jehovah regards all *rivalry* in the affections and homage of his subjects. This feeling is here called 'jealousy,' implying a peculiar *sensitiveness* to every thing that threatens to trench upon the honor, reverence, and esteem that he knows to be due to himself. The term will appear still more significant if it be borne in mind that *idolatry* in the Scriptures is frequently spoken of as *spiritual adultery*, and as 'jealousy is the rage of a man,' so nothing can more fitly express the divine indignation against this sin than the term in question. Those sentiments therefore which are naturally awakened by the infidelity and treachery of an espoused wife towards her husband are strongly appealed to by the use of this language.——¶ *Visiting the iniquity of the fathers*, &c. 'It is universally believed that children suffer for the iniquities of their ancestors, through many generations. 'I wonder why Tamban's son was born a cripple?' —'You wonder! why, that is a strange thing; have you not heard what a vile man his grandfather was?' 'Have you heard that Valen has had a son, and that he is born blind?'—'I did not hear of it, but this is another proof of the sins of a former birth.' 'What a wicked wretch that Venāsi is! alas for his posterity, great will be their sufferings.' 'Evil one, why are you going on in this way; have you no pity for your seed?' 'Alas! alas! I am now suffering for the sins of my fathers.' When men enjoy many blessings, it is common to say of them, 'Yes, yes, they are enjoying the good deeds of their fathers.' 'The prosperity of my house arises from the virtues of my forefathers.' In the Scanda Purāna it is recorded, 'The soul is subject to births, deaths, and sufferings. It may be born on the earth, or in the sea. It may also appear in ether, fire, or air. Souls may be born as men, as beasts or birds, as grass or trees, as mountains or gods.' By these we are reminded of the question, 'Who did sin, this man or his parents, that he was born blind?' 'Jesus answered, Neither hath this man sinned, nor his parents.' *Roberts*. To *visit* iniquity is to *punish* it; and we have here the announcement of a general principle of the divine administration or an established ordering of providence, viz., that the effects both of obedience and disobedience, or blessings and curses, remain for a long time after the original actors are no more. Universal history and experience clearly go to show that this is a distinguishing character of the divine economy, and the sentence is shielded from all charge of injustice by the terms in which it is couched—' unto the third and fourth generation of them that *hate* me;' from which it is obvious that the children were not to be thus punished for the sins of their fathers *irrespective* of their own conduct and deserts. The tokens of the divine displeasure were to flow along the line of those who continued the *haters* of God, as all idolaters are plainly considered by implication to be. This sense of the passage is distinctly recognized in the Chal. version; 'I the Lord thy God am a jealous God visiting the iniquities of the fathers upon the transgressing children, unto the third

6 And ¹ shewing mercy unto thousands of them that love me, and keep my commandments.

ⁱ ch. 34. 7. Deut. 7. 9. Ps. 89. 34. Rom. 11. 28.

and fourth generation, of those who hate me, when the children follow the iniquities of the fathers.' This natural and easy construction removes any apparent discrepancy between the rule of procedure here stated and that affirmed, Ezek. 18. 20, ' The son shall not bear the iniquity of the father, neither shall the father bear the iniquity of the son ;' for the language of the prophet is to be understood of the son who does *not* tread in the steps of his wicked father ; whereas the threatening in this precept respects those children who *do* follow the example of their evil parents. This is evident from their being said to be of those that *hate* God. The words as originally spoken undoubtedly had a primary reference to the sin of idolatry, but it cannot be doubted that they announce a general principle, to wit, that the iniquities and vices of men are punished in their posterity ; not by any arbitrary enactment, but in virtue of that constitution of things which God has adopted, and so framed, that children cannot well avoid suffering in this world in consequence of the misdeeds of their parents. From the circumstances in which they are placed and the influences that bear upon them, it is almost inevitable that they should fall into the same sinful courses with their fathers, and if so, they must necessarily experience the same punishments. It is to be observed, however, that this threatening has respect mainly to the *temporal* effects of sin, to its penal consequences in the present life, and is not to be considered as affecting the eternal salvation of individuals, any farther than as their final condition depends upon their personal conduct in this world.

7 ᵏ Thou shalt not take the name of the LORD thy God in vain : for the LORD ¹ will not hold him guiltless that taketh his name in vain.

ᵏ ch. 23. 1. Lev. 19. 12. Deut. 5. 11. Ps. 15. 4. Matt. 5. 33. ¹ Mic. 6. 11.

It is therefore an ordination or arrangement of entire equity, and one too which at the same time makes a strong appeal to the parental feelings ; as it represents the destinies of their descendants, for weal or woe, as lodged in a great measure in their hands.

6. *Shewing mercy unto thousands,* &c. So much more abundant is the Lord in mercy than in wrath, so much more congenial to his nature is the exercise of loving-kindness than punitive displeasure, that while he *punishes* to the third and fourth generation, he *shews mercy* to the thousandth. This is abundantly exemplified in the history of the posterity of Abraham, who were destined, on account of the distinguished virtues of their progenitor, to be the most illustrious nation on earth at the distance of several thousand years from his time.

THE THIRD COMMANDMENT.

7. *Thou shalt not take the name of the Lord thy God in vain.* Heb. לֹא תִשָּׂא לַשָּׁוְא *lo tissa—lashshav, thou shalt not take up* (i. e. upon thy lips) *the name of the Lord thy God to vanity,* or *falsehood.* Vulg. Non assumes, *thou shalt not assume.* The name of God signifies primarily any word or expression which denotes God ; any title or epithet which goes to distinguish him from all other beings. Of these the most peculiar and pregnant is perhaps the title 'Jehovah,' implying his absolute, eternal, and immutable existence. But besides this, he is denoted also by many other appellations of distinctive purport, such as ' God,' ' the Lord' ' the Almighty,' ' the Most High,' ' the Father,' ' the Creator,' ' the Holy One of Israel,' &c.,

some expressing what he is in himself, and some his relations to his creatures. But the 'name' of God is, from Scriptural usage, generally and properly understood in a somewhat wider sense, *of every thing by which he makes himself known*, and so including not only his various titles, but also his attributes, ordinances, word, and works. That the leading idea of 'taking the name of God' in this place is *swearing* by it, is universally conceded, and is confirmed by the three ancient versions, the Chal., the Syr., and the Arab., all which render, 'Thou shalt not swear falsely by the name of the Lord thy God.' The original term שָׁוְא *shav* signifies both *what is false* and *what is vain*, and as both senses are undoubtedly to be included in the term, it lays a foundation for a twofold view of the prohibition ; forbidding (1) All *false* swearing, all perjury, all use of the holy name of God which should go to make him witness to a lie ; (2) All *vain, light, frivolous* swearing, including all cursing and swearing in common conversation, all blasphemy, and all rash, thoughtless, irreverent use of the titles and attributes of Jehovah. As a matter of course, the worshippers of the Most High must have frequent occasion to mention his name, and the scope of this commandment is to inculcate the utmost reverence of that holy name which is but a symbol of every idea that can awaken awe, adoration, fear, and homage, in the bosoms of men or angels. If we were to indicate the point of the prohibition by specifying the directly opposite duty, it would be by adducing the words of the prophet, Is. 8. 13, '*Sanctify* the Lord of hosts himself, and let him be your fear and your dread.' In perfect consistency, however, with the tenor of this precept, appeals may be made to God, on suitable occasions, in the form of judicial oaths taken in confirmation of the truth of our statements. The example of Christ, and the

declarations of the apostles, clearly intimate the intrinsic lawfulness of oaths and the scope of the third commandment is primarily to inculcate a due degree of reverence in the use of such an invocation of the Deity. An oath is, in fact, an act of religious worship, in which God is solemnly called upon to witness the truth of the affirmations made, and to act as punisher of the crime if any perjury is committed. It imports that we acknowledge him to be the infallible searcher of hearts, and the powerful and stern avenger of all falsehood, fraud, and deceit in such a solemn transaction ; and no inference can be plainer than that it is the height of irreligion and profanity to interpose that awful name in attestation of any thing that is false, fraudulent, or hypocritical. The rule by which such an act is to be governed is expressly given, Jer. 4. 2, ' Thou shalt swear in truth, in judgment, and in righteousness,' and any deviation from this is an infraction of the precept before us, and though often accounted a trivial offence among men, yet there is scarcely a more atrocious or provoking crime in the sight of the infinitely true, and pure, and upright Jehovah. The same general remarks apply also to vows and voluntary engagements, which we assume upon ourselves and solemnly promise to fulfil. To invoke the holy name of God on such occasions, to appeal to him as the omniscient voucher of our sincerity, and then to neglect, slight, or violate the obligations we have incurred is but an impious mockery of the majesty of Jehovah, which he will not fail to punish.

But it is, perhaps, in common discourse that this command is most frequently and flagrantly disregarded. To say nothing of downright malignant blasphemy, which happily is rare in a land of Bibles and churches, and the grosser imprecations which often assail the ear from profane and impious lips the practice of interlarding our conversation with the words 'God,' 'Lord,' 'Christ,' or the expressions 'the Lord knows,' 'heaven help me,' without necessity, seriousness, or reverence, involves a measure of the guilt of transgressing the third commandment. Nor can it be denied that *profane writing* is open to the same charge with *profane speaking*. In the statement of matters of fact by way of testimony, the use of irreverent expressions may indeed be allowable, but nothing is more common than for writers of fiction to put the most revolting oaths into the mouths of their various personages; and this they seem to think harmless, provided they contrive to mask the grossness of the language by dashes and asterisks. But wherein this differs from any other profaneness, except in being more deliberate, and more pernicious in the way of example, it is not easy to see. To give currency to such profane modes of speech, under pretence of their being necessary to the faithful portraiture of character and manners, incurs we think little less guilt than that of originally uttering them. The exhibition of *such* manners, even by the greatest moral painter, can well be dispensed with.

In fine, the rule of safety in this matter is that laid down by our Lord in his commentary on the rabbinical precepts, Mat. 5. 33—37, 'Again ye have heard that it hath been said by them of old time, Thou shalt not forswear thyself, but shalt perform unto the Lord thine oaths: But I say unto you, Swear not at all: neither by heaven; for it is God's throne: nor by the earth; for it is his footstool: neither by Jerusalem; for it is the city of the great King: neither shalt thou swear by thine head, because thou canst not make one hair white or black. But let your communication be, Yea, yea; Nay, nay; for whatsoever is more than these cometh of evil.'——¶ *The Lord will not hold him guiltless,* &c. Heb. רְנַקֶּה אֹל *lo yenakkeh, will not pro-*

nounce *pure, innocent, or clean ; will not acquit.* Gr. ου μη καθαριζη, *will not cleanse;* i. e. *will not declare clean, will not absolve.* He will not let him go unpunished. It is an instance of the idiom, by no means infrequent in Hebrew, by which a negative mode of expression couches under it a strongly affirmative idea. We have then in these words a virtual assurance from Jehovah himself that this precept cannot be disregarded with impunity. Men may not discover, or they may neglect to punish, its violations, and even the hardened conscience of the sinner may fail to rebuke him on account of it; but let it not be forgotten, that God will surely detect and punish the insult thus put upon his great and glorious name. The words of inspiration clearly portray the character of those who trangress this commandment; Ps. 139. 20, 'Thine *enemies* take thy name in vain.' The profane swearer is the open and avowed *enemy* of the high and holy God, and it is no more certain that there will be a judgment seat, before which the bold transgressor must appear, than it is that he will be called to an account for his profane trifling with the most sacred things in the universe; 'And I will come near to you to judgment: and I will be a swift witness against the sorcerers, and against the adulterers, *and against false swearers,* and against those that oppress the hireling in his wages, the widow, and the fatherless, and that turn aside the stranger from his right, and fear not me, saith the Lord of hosts.' Mal. 3. 5 The remarkable passage Josh. 9. 19, 20, shows in what light the children of Israel regarded the breach of their plighted faith even to a portion of the devoted nations of Canaan ; 'But all the princes said unto all the congregation, We have sworn unto them by the Lord God of Israel: now therefore we may not touch them. This will we do to them ; we will even let them live, *lest wrath be upon us, because of the oath which we sware*

8 ᵐ Remember the sabbath-day to keep it holy.

ᵐ ch. 31. 13. 14. Lev. 19. 3, 30. & 26. 2. Deut. 5. 12.

9 ⁿ Six days shalt thou labour, and do all thy work :

ⁿ ch. 23. 12. & 31. 15. & 34. 21. Lev. 23, 3. Ezek. 20. 12. Luke 13. 14.

---

unto them.' Nor can we forbear in this connexion to advert to the fact, that the sin in question has often been followed by sudden and fearful marks of divine retribution, even in the present world. However it be accounted for, certain it is that in more than one well-attested instance men have fallen dead in the midst of the most horrid imprecations, as if God had taken them at their word in calling upon him to seal their perdition. We do not say that such cases are to be regarded as miraculous. It is very possible that the physical effects, caused by an unnatural degree of excitement of the passions, and the sudden incursion of a violent pang or panic of conscience may have been sufficient to account for the result. Still such cases should be looked upon as solemn warnings ; since it may be no less a real visitation of divine wrath for being made by the agency of natural laws acting upon the nervous system. It is to be considered also, that as this is a sin which aims perhaps more *directly* than any other at God ; one in which the inward spirit of the offender comes more immediately in collision with the spirit of God ; it is not perhaps to be wondered at that he should occasionally come out in more marked judgment against it. But however it be understood, this solemn denunciation of the Almighty ought to be to this commandment what the restraining limits were around the hallowed base of Sinai, a sacred fence to guard it from unhallowed violation.

THE FOURTH COMMANDMENT.

8. *Remember the sabbath day to keep it holy.* Heb. זכור את יום השבת *zakor eth yom hashshabboth, remember the day of cessation, or rest.* On the

import of the original word for ' Sabbath,' and on the origin, nature, and end of the institution in general, see Note on Gen. 2. 3. The term 'remember' in this connexion (זכור *zakor*), implies more than the mere mental act of memory, as it is the only Hebrew word equivalent to our *celebrate* or *commemorate,* importing that it was to be *remembered by appropriate observances.* If therefore the clause were to be rendered, 'Remember the sabbath day by way of commemoration or celebration,' it would bring us still nearer to its genuine purport. Thus Ex. 13. 3, 'Moses said unto the people, *Remember* (זכור *zakor*) this day, in which ye came out from Egypt,' where see Note. But how was it to be remembered? Not simply by mental reminiscence, but by special observance ; for it is added, ' There shall no unleavened bread be eaten.' It could not be adequately remembered without being kept in the manner prescribed. So also Ex. 12. 14, 'This day shall be unto you for a *memorial* (זכרון *zikkaron*) ;' and then the manner in which the precept should be complied with is immediately described, 'ye shall keep it a feast by an ordinance forever.' So in the present case, the Sabbath was to be *remembered by practical acknowledgment* as well as by bearing in mind, with special care, the stated season of its occurrence, and by cherishing the recollection of its early appointment as a memorial of God's rest at the close of the work of creation. Accordingly, in the parallel passage, Deut. 5. 12, the language is not 'remember the sabbath to sanctify it,' but ' keep the sabbath day,' no doubt with the design to intimate that these two terms in this connexion were equivalent. Thus too we learn, from Lev. 23. 3, that on the sabbath there was to be *a holy convocation*, or an assembly of the people, at the tabernacle, as afterwards at the temple, for the public worship of God, as if this were the appropriate mode of *remembering* the sabbath; 'Six days shall work be done ; but the seventh day is the sabbath of rest, *an holy convocation;* ye shall do no work therein: it is the sabbath of the Lord in all your dwellings.' But in addition to the 'holy convocation,' the Israelites were required to offer a greater number of sacrifices on that than on other days, Numb. 28. 9, 10, and we cannot question that these various services were understood to enter essentially into the due observance of this hallowed season. It consequently leads us to the inevitable inference, that the sabbath is not properly or adequately kept unless it be distinguished from other days by being in a special manner *devoted to the duties of public as well as private worship.*

It is doubtless true that this commandment is not so purely *moral* or *self-enforced* in its own nature as the rest. Although the consecration of a certain portion of our time to the immediate service of God may perhaps be admitted to be of *moral obligation,* yet the exact proportion, as well as the particular day, may be considered as of *positive institution,* and therefore somewhat more of a *Jewish* aspect is given to this precept than to either of the others. For this reason some in all periods of the church have been led to question whether it is properly to be considered as still remaining in force under the Christian dispensation, particularly as no express mention is made of it in the New Testament. But as it was in its substantial features no doubt in existence long before the period of the Jewish economy, as it forms an integral part of that collection of precepts which was spoken from heaven by the voice of God, and was afterwards written by the finger of God on the tables

of stone, it would not be easy to offer a stronger argument in proof of the perpetuity of its obligation. Not doubting, therefore, that an institution which was binding *before* the law is equally binding *after* it, unless distinctly repealed, we have only to remark, that the particular day in the week is not specified ; it is, 'remember the sabbath day,'—not the ' seventh day'—' to keep it holy.' All that the commandment expressly requires is, to observe a day of sacred rest after every six days of labor. The seventh day indeed is to be kept holy, but not a word is here said as to the point from which the reckoning is to begin. The ' seventh day' is not so much the seventh according to any particular method of computing the septenary cycle, as in reference to the six working days before-mentioned ; every seventh day in rotation after six of labor. The Jewish sabbath was kept on our Saturday, but we act equally in accordance with the spirit and the letter of this commandment by keeping it on Sunday; and as this was the day on which our Lord arose from the dead, it has come to be appropriately designated as 'the Lord's day,' and as such has been observed as the Christian sabbath from the earliest periods of the church.——
¶ *To keep it holy.* Heb. לקדשׁוּ *lekaddesho, to sanctify it.* On the import of this term see Note on Gen. 2. 3.

9. *Six days shalt thou labor, and do all thy work.* Heb. כל מלאכתך *kol melakteka, all thy business* or *servile work.* It comes from the ancient root לאך *laak, to send, to depute,* from which also comes מלאך *malak, a messenger,* and properly signifies all that varied service and ministry to the performance of which servants were *sent* or *despatched,* and about which they were employed. It plainly refers to the daily routine of ordinary secular employments, all which were to be diligently pursued on the six working days, and religiously suspended on the sev-

10 But the º seventh day *is* the sabbath of the Lord thy God : *in it* thou shalt not do any work, thou, nor thy son, nor thy daughter, thy man-servant, nor thy maidservant, nor thy cattle, ᴾ nor thy stranger that *is* within thy gates :

11 For �q *in* six days the Lord made heaven and earth, the sea and all that in them *is*, and rested the seventh day : wherefore the Lord blessed the sabbath-day, and hallowed it.

º Gen. 2. 2, 3. ch. 16. 26. & 31. 15. ᴾ Neh. 13. 16, 17, 18, 19.

q Gen. 2. 2.

---

enth or day of rest. As the words belong to the first table, which is not designed to teach us our duties to ourselves or our neighbors, but to God, they are not in their intrinsic import so strictly *preceptive* or *imperative*, as *permissive*. Though they do in their spirit inculcate the duty of active and exemplary diligence in the season of it, yet their primary drift is, undoubtedly, *to define that season;* to teach us within what bounds our labor is to be circumscribed, in contradistinction to the allotted time of rest. In making this disposal of time, however, the Most High of course reserved to himself the right of occasionally setting apart some one or more of those six days for religious services, and we are not to consider it as any infringement upon the original precept if extraordinary seasons of fasting, thanksgiving, and worship should occasionally be set apart in like manner, by civil or ecclesiastical authority.

10. *The seventh day is the sabbath of the Lord thy God.* Heb. שבת ליהוה אלהיך *shabboth laihovah Elohëka, a sabbath to Jehovah thy God.* That is, the sabbath appointed by and consecrated to the Lord thy God; the sabbath in which God asserts a special interest, which he peculiarly claims as his own, and which we cannot refuse to sanctify to him without being guilty of a kind of sacrilege, and appropriating to ourselves what properly belongs to another. In accordance with this phraseology we find it said, Lev. 26. 2, 'Ye shall keep *my* sabbath.' Is. 56. 4, 'For

thus saith the Lord unto the eunuchs that keep *my* sabbaths, and choose the things that please me,' &c.——¶ *In it thou shalt not do any work,* &c. .That is, no secular or servile work, nothing pertaining to a mere worldly calling. Works of piety, necessity, and charity are of course excepted, as these consist entirely with the spirit of that day, as a day of holy rest; for ' the sabbath was made for man, and not man for the sabbath.' It is obvious, however, that all works of a different character are to be excluded from the hallowed hours of the sabbath, and our affairs should be previously so arranged, that the sacred duties of the Lord's day may be interrupted as little as possible ; nor should any thing be considered as a work of necessity on that day, which can be done *before* the sabbath, or delayed till *after* it. All buying and selling, paying wages, settling accounts, gathering harvests, clearing out of vessels from port, making up, sorting, or transporting of mails, writing letters of business or amusement, reading books, papers, or pamphlets on ordinary subjects, trifling visits, journies, excursions, or conversation on topics merely secular, are inconsistent with ' keeping a day holy unto the Lord.'——¶ *Thou nor thy son, nor thy daughter, nor thy man-servant,* &c. This part of the precept goes not only to extend the obligation, but also to secure the privileges of the sabbath to every class and condition of men. The wife indeed is not mentioned, because she is supposed to be one with the husband, and as cooperating with him oɩ course in carrying into execution every commandment of God. But the rest of the family, sons and daughters, male and female servants, are specified in such a way as to throw upon heads of families the responsibility of uniting *all* their household establishment in the due observance of the day. Whatever relief, refreshment, or rest may be intended to be afforded by the institution, servants and even cattle are to be sacredly considered as entitled to its merciful provisions. It is indeed the destiny of man that he should earn his bread by the sweat of his brow, but the sabbath is graciously bestowed upon him as a relief to that destiny. His mental energy and bodily health are to be renewed by its leisure; and God who has thus bestowed upon man the substantial blessing of a periodical cessation from toil, has decreed the same privilege to the menial classes and the inferior animals. The rest therefore so kindly provided by the Creator for servants and cattle ought not to be unnecessarily broken. The domestic, on that day, should be released, as far as possible, from his ordinary labors, and the beast which has served us faithfully during the week, should not be deprived of his share of the general repose. Were this law but duly observed, the servants in many families would be spared that labor on the sabbath which now too often prevents their attending to any religious duty. Nor would the use of horses for travelling so extensively disgrace our own and other Christian lands. Many a driver and ostler, who knows no cessation from his daily task, would be found frequenting the place of worship; and many a poor animal, which now pants under the lash of the sabbath, would then be permitted to recover strength for the ensuing six days of inevitable labor.——¶ *Nor thy stranger that is within thy gates.* That is, within thy cities, as explained in the Note

on Gen. 22. 17. Gr. ὁ προσηλυτος ὁ παροικων εν σοι, *the proselyte dwelling among thee.* Even the strangers who might be resident among the Israelites, are here required to acknowledge the authority of the law sanctifying the sabbath day; which is in other words recognising the *right* of the Israelites to demand that strangers should pay a reverent respect to the institutions, civil and religious, of the people among whom they sojourned. For otherwise how could this charge be embraced in the duty of the Israelites? But the thing was in itself in the highest degree reasonable and proper. If such a stranger were a proselyte of the class called *proselytes of righteousness or justice,* it was of course incumbent upon him to conform to all the observances of the Hebrews. If he were merely a *proselyte of the gate,* who had renounced idolatry without receiving circumcision, still it was fitting that he should rest from his labors on the sabbath day, and not, by engaging in them, disturb those who were desirous at that time of quietly devoting themselves to the duties of public and private worship. It was doing as he would be done by in similar circumstances.

11. *For in six days the Lord made,* &c. We are here reminded of the origin of the sabbath, by way of enforcing its observance by an appropriate sanction. It was designed for a memorial of the creation of the world, and therefore to be observed to the glory of the Creator who made heaven and earth. All the perfections of the Godhead, accordingly, which are so conspicuously displayed in the wondrous fabric of creation, and in that providence by which it is upheld and governed, should be devoutly contemplated and adored on that solemn day. Upon comparing this passage with Deut. 5. 15, a different reason seems to be given for the observance of the sabbath; 'And remember that thou wast a

12 ¶ ʳHonour thy father and thy

ʳ ch. 23. 26. Lev. 19. 3. Deut. 5. 16. Jer.
35. 7, 18, 19. Matt. 15. 4. & 19. 19. Mark 7.
10. & 10. 19. Luke 18. 20. Ephes. 6. 2.

servant in the land of Egypt, and that the Lord thy God brought thee out thence through a mighty hand and by a stretch-ed-out arm: therefore the Lord thy God commanded thee to keep the sabbath-day.' But the two are by no means in-consistent with each other. The first, taken from the creation, was well known and continued valid of course ; but the second, taken from the deliverance from Egypt, was merely superadded to the first in order to give more force to the sense of obligation by coupling it with the memory of an important event in their national history. It would seem too that the allusion in the latter case had special respect to that clause of the precept which enjoins the duty of mas-ters in regard to their servants. While the Israelites were in Egypt in a state of slavery they were no doubt restricted by their despotic oppressors from ob-serving the sabbath as they otherwise would. But now when set at liberty and permitted to serve God according to the precepts of their religion, he just-ly expected that they should make a right use of their liberty, and deal more mercifully with their servants than the Egyptians had dealt with them ; and particularly that they should permit them to rest one day in seven, that is, as often as they did themselves.

For a more extended and elaborate view of the origin, design, obligation, and due observance of the holy sabbath, the reader is referred to Edwards' and Dwight's Theology, and to the Trea-tises of Bp. Wilson, Gurney, Humph-rey, Agnew, Waterbury, and Kings-bury, in which is accumulated an im-mense fund of argumentative and prac-tical matter relative to this divine in-stitution.

mother ; that thy days may be long upon the land which the LORD thy God giveth thee.

SECOND TABLE.

THE FIFTH COMMANDMENT.

12. *Honor thy father and thy mother,* &c. Heb. כבד *kabëd,* from כבד *ka-bad, to be heavy;* thence applied to *weight of character, dignity,* or what entitles one to *respect, honor, distin-guished esteem.* Accordingly in the Piel conjugation it signifies *to regard, treat,* or *practically declare one as worthy of honor.* It is directly opposed to the word קלל *kalal, to make light of, to set light by, to account mean, vile, or worth-less.* Accordingly we find this term em-ployed to signify a conduct the reverse of that enjoined in this precept ; as Deut. 27. 16, 'Cursed be he that *setteth light by* (מקלה *makleh*) his father or his mother.' Ezek. 22. 7, 'In thee have they *set light by* (הקלו *hëkallu*) father and mother.' From the same root כבד *kabad,* comes the original word for *glory,* כבוד *kabod,* whence the Apostle has, 2 Cor. 4. 17, 'Weight of glory,' and Peter, 2 Pet. 2. 10, denominates magis-trates δοξαι, *glories,* from the *weight of character* attached to them. Comp. Note on Gen. 31. 1. In Lev. 19. 3, and Deut. 5. 16, the word ירא *yara, to fear, to reverence* is substituted, but obvious-ly with the same import. The grand duty here inculcated is that of *filial piety,* embracing that entire class of duties which children owe to their par-ents. The foundation of these duties is laid in the nature of the relation which parents and children sustain to each other, and they are so obvious that chil-dren themselves, even at a very tender age, are capable of feeling deeply their obligation. Parents are under God the immediate authors of the being of chil-

dren. It is to their parents that they owe their preservation, sustentation, and protection during that helpless period in which they are utterly incapable of taking care of themselves. The hearts of parents are full of the kindest affection—love, tender solicitude, pity, sympathy, benevolence—towards their children, affections which show themselves in the most painful exertions, toils, watchings, privations, sacrifices of comfort and ease, of which human nature is capable. They willingly undergo hardship, encounter peril, incur expense, and jeopard their lives and their health to promote the welfare of their offspring. And children, when they are more advanced in age, come of course into the full participation of all the temporal advantages of their parents' station in life, whether of wealth, honor, or respectability. Indeed it is in great measure for their children that parents live and labor in the world.

For these and similar reasons parents most justly claim what the great Parent of all here claims for them. And as they have affections and perform actions nearly akin to those of God towards us, they may properly be deemed in a sense his representatives, the lively images of him in whom we live and move and have our being, and on that account entitled to a special veneration from their children. God himself, we know, in order to endear himself to our hearts, and to win more effectually our obedience, assumes the title of *Father*, and on this ground lays a special claim to our respect; 'If I be a father, where is mine honor?' And it is remarkable that while the duties owed to other men are termed justice, or charity, or courtesy, or liberality, or gratitude, those due to parents in most languages are comprised under the title of *piety*, implying something *divine* in the objects of them. Who indeed does not feel that it is something *more* than injustice to wrong a parent; that it is *more* than uncharit-

ableness to refuse them succor or relief; that it is *more* than incivility to be unkind to them; that it is *more* than sordid avarice to withhold aid from their necessities? Who is not prompted at once to brand such conduct as *impiety?* Indeed the language of inspiration expressly confirms this view of the subject, 1 Tim. 5. 4, 'If any widow have children or nephews (i. e. grandchildren) let them learn first *to show piety* (ευσεβειν) at home, and to requite their parents; for that is good and acceptable before God;' where the term employed is the proper one for expressing *piety* towards God.

As to the precise import of the precept, it will perhaps be more distinctly gathered from the several parallel injunctions scattered through the Old and New Testament; 'Ye shall fear every man his mother and his father, and keep my sabbath; I am the Lord your God.' 'My son, keep thy father's commandment, and forsake not the law of thy mother.' 'Children, obey your parents in the Lord; for this is right.' 'Children obey your parents in all things, for this is well pleasing unto the Lord.' In these passages the phraseology is so varied, as to make it evident that the precept implies not only an abstract sentiment, a cordial inward respect and esteem for their persons, but also obedience to their lawful commands, submission to their rebukes, instructions, and corrections, deference to their counsels, and sincere endeavors to promote their comfort, particularly in old age, when by affording them a maintenance we can in some measure requite their care of our infancy and childhood. If such are the duties of children, let parents, on the other hand, remember that correspondent duties rest upon them. Though children are not absolved from the obligation of this commandment by the misconduct of their parents, yet in the nature of things it is impossible that they should yield the same hearty respect and veneration to the unworthy as to the worthy, nor does God require a child to pay an *irrational* honor to his parents. If his parents are atheists, he cannot honor them as Christians. If they are prayerless and profane, he cannot honor them as religious. If they are worldly, avaricious, overreaching, unscrupulous as to veracity and honest dealing, he cannot honor them as exemplary, upright, conscientious, and spiritually minded. If they are intemperate and abandoned he cannot honor them as sober and virtuous, nor truly speak of them as such. But a child is obliged to think *as well as he can* of his parents, and to conceal their faults, unless the good of society obviously requires their exposure. He is to obey them in all things where their commands do not come in conflict with those of God. In that case children are not at liberty to obey; they are under an antecedent obligation; they are imperiously bound by their duty to God to adhere to truth, to honesty, to justice. But in all such cases there is need of the utmost caution, and of a positive assurance that the thing declined is as clearly forbidden by God as obedience to parents is commanded by him. Otherwise children cannot be warranted in refusing to obey parental injunctions.

That thy days may be long in the land, &c. Heb. לְמַעַן יַאֲרִכוּן *lemään yäarikun, that they may prolong.* That is, as Leclerc and some others understand it, that thy father and mother, by their prayers in thy behalf, by the blessings of heaven which they shall invoke, may be the means of prolonging thy days upon the land where thou dwellest. But the idiom of the Hebrew tongue is such that we are not required to interpret the word 'they' of parents, and from the illustration which we have given of this usage of speech in the Note on Gen. 16. 14, it will be evident that our translation presents the right rendering, 'that thy days may be

prolonged,' following herein the Gr. ινα μακρυχρονιος γενη επι της γης της αγαθης, *that thou mayest be long-lived upon the good land,* &c., where by the way, we may remark that αγαθης *good* is gratuitously inserted, but probably with a view to indicate that they understood the word 'land' of the *land of promise,* instead of 'earth' as it is frequently rendered. A similar phraseology occurs Job, 4. 19, 'Which are crushed before the moth;' Heb. They crush them before the moth. Ch. 7. 3, 'Wearisome nights are appointed to me;' Heb. They appoint to me wearisome nights. So in the New Testament, Luke 16. 9, 'That they may receive you into everlasting habitations;' i. e. that ye may be received. The parallel promise in Deut. 5. 16, has a slight additional clause, 'That thy days may be prolonged, *and that it may go well with thee,* in the land which the Lord thy God giveth thee,' and this sense of the promise is confirmed by the apostle's citation, Eph. 6. 3, 'That it may be well with thee, and that thou mayest live long on the earth.' In other cases the prolonging of the days is attributed directly and actively to the person of whose conduct it is the result. Thus Deut. 22. 7, 'But thou shalt in any wise let the dam go, and take the young to thee; that it may be well with thee, and that thou mayest prolong thy days.' This commandment is indeed cited by the apostle as the first that has a special promise annexed to it—for the promise added to the second commandment is rather general to all those that love God, or annexed to the due observance of the whole law, than of that single precept—but the promised blessing is evidently one that would in a great measure flow as a natural consequence from the due observance of the precept. God assures them that their permanence and prosperity in the land of their expected possession would depend upon their obedience to this command ; and in that he merely states what would be found to be the result of general experience in the course of his providence, that the early habit of respect and reverence to parents and superiors, would tend to the peaceful and prosperous existence of society, by removing the causes of internal discord and decay ; while, as to individuals, the salutary restraint of the passions, and the cultivation of a quiet, gentle demeanor would of itself go far towards lengthening the term of human life. But however this may be, due reverence for parents will be found to consist with reverence to God and his institutions, and where this is the case in any community he will display his favor and crown them with the blessings of long life and temporal prosperity.

That this promise had respect primarily to the chosen people, to whom God was now about to give the land of Canaan, is unquestionable; and to them it was doubtless made in a national as well as in an individual character. It was a pledge on the part of God that if they evinced a strict obedience to this command, he would grant them, as a people, a long continuance in their own land in despite of all the attempts of their enemies to conquer and dispossess them. This seems to be confirmed by the parallel language of Deut. 4. 26, 'Ye shall soon utterly perish from off the land whereunto ye go over Jordan to possess it ; *ye shall not prolong your days upon it,* but shall utterly be destroyed.' V. 33, ' Ye shall walk in all the ways which the Lord your God hath commanded you, that ye may live, and that it may be well with you, and that *ye may prolong your days in the land which ye shall possess.'* V. 40. 'Thou shalt keep therefore his statutes and his commandments, which I command thee this day, that it may go well with thee, and with thy children after thee, and *that thou mayest prolong thy*

days upon the earth (rather, upon the *land*), which the Lord thy God giveth thee, for ever.' Ch. 32. 46, 47, 'And he said unto them, Set your hearts unto all the words which I testify among you this day, which ye shall command your children to observe to do, all the words of this law. For it is not a vain thing for you: because it is your life ; and through this thing *ye shall prolong your days in the land whither ye go over Jordan to possess it.'* Accordingly we find, that when God threatens the nation with being carried captive out of their own land for their sins, he particularly mentions this among other procuring causes of their calamities; *the not honoring their parents;* Ezek. 22. 7, 12, 15, 'In thee have they set light by father and mother.—Behold therefore— I will scatter thee among the heathen, and disperse thee in the countries.' But the apostle, Eph. 6. 2, 3, cites this commandment as if the promise still held good under the Christian dispensation, and this fact is doubtless to be accounted for by supposing that *the spirit, the principle,* of the promise is still acted upon under the moral government of Jehovah. Even at the present day, it can scarcely be doubted that, as a general fact, those who are exemplary in the discharge of filial duties become the objects of *a specially rewarding providence* in the longer enjoyment of life and of those temporal blessings which make it desirable. On the other hand, what close observer of the retributive dealings of God, can question that in multitudes of cases the untimely deaths of the young have been the judicial consequences of disobedience to their parents ? In how many instances has the confession been extorted from convicted felons, that the first step in their downward career was despising the commands of parents, and the next the breach of the holy sabbath ? And it would seem as if the connexion between these two forms of transgression,

13 ⁸ Thou shalt not kill.

⁸ Deut. 5. 17.   Matt. 5. 21.   Rom. 13. 9.

14 ᵗ Thou shalt not commit adultery.

ᵗ Deut. 5. 18.   Matt. 5. 27.

was expressly recognised in the page of inspiration, from their being conjointly prohibited; Lev. 19. 3, 'Ye shall féar every man his mother and his father, and keep my sabbaths;' as if it were to be expected, as a matter of course, that he who dishonored his parents would habitually profane the sabbath.

At the same time, it is not to be considered as militating with the verity of this promise, if many children distinguished for filial piety should be cut off in their tender years. This no doubt was the case with thousands of the seed of Jacob, and the same thing happens to multitudes in every age. It is sufficient to vindicate the truth of the promise, if it holds good as a *general* fact in the divine administration. And even in the cases that constitute the apparent exceptions, the early called may be taken from the evil to come; and if the years that would have been spent on earth are spent in heaven, it cannot be said that the promise fails of its fulfilment. God is certainly *as good* as his word when he is *better*.

THE SIXTH COMMANDMENT.

13. *Thou shalt not kill.* Heb. לֹא תִרְצַח *la tirtzaha, thou shalt not murder.* Gr. ου φονευσεις, *id.* Chal. 'Thou shalt not kill a soul;' i. e. a person The original רָצַח *ratzah,* from being in several instances applied to *violent beating, breaking, contusion,* and from general usage, more properly signifies the *violent, unjust,* taking of life, which is usually denominated *murder.* In Arabic it signifies *to overwhelm with stones, to stone to death, to smash a serpent's head with a stone.* It is thus distinguished from הָרַג *harag,* also translated *to kill,* but which is more legitimately employed to designate that kind of *legal killing* which is the result

of the sentence of the magistrate. There are some few exceptions to this remark, as Num. 35. 27—30, as also vv. 11, 23, 25, of the same chapter, where it is used not only of inconsiderate and fortuitous homicide, or chance-medley, but also of killing a malefactor, which was permitted, and even commanded; but the distinction holds good in the main, and the slightest reflection will convince any one that in this precept it must have reference to an *unlawful and unjust taking of life.* The latter verb הָרַג *harag* is applied also to the *slaying of brute beasts,* which רָצַח *ratzah* never is. The scope and spirit of the injunction is therefore evident. As life is the greatest of earthly blessings, and the grand foundation of enjoying all others, God is here pleased to make known the sacredness which he would have attached to so inestimable a boon. The sixth commandment plants an inviolable guard around human life. It forbids the wanton extinction of that vital principle which was breathed into man's nostrils by the Deity himself, and the obliteration of that image of God which constituted the glory of Adam at his creation. The infliction of capital punishment for capital crimes, by the sentence of the magistrate is not here forbidden, as such a sentence is virtually involved in the Noachic precept, ' He that sheddeth man's blood, by man shall his blood be shed;' and confirmed by other passages of the Scriptures. Nor is it probably to be interpreted as prohibiting the taking life in self-defence in *lawful* war, or in a personal attack, where one *knows* that the killing of an assailant or the loss of his own life is the only alternative. In any other case we think it may be seriously doubted whether the non-resisting spirit of the New Testament precepts does not require us rather to follow the example of the martyrs, who overcame by 'not loving their lives unto death.' If man were contemplated merely in reference to his earthly existence, we do not know that there could be any doubt on the subject; but when we take into view the fact that he is to live forever, that his present state and actions are intimately connected with a system of retributions that extend into eternity, we cannot be sure that the *moral impression* of an example of meek, unresisting suffering at the hands of wicked or cruel men, may not be more important to the best interests of the universe, than that of the contrary course. The immediate effect is no doubt disastrous to him who is the victim, and it is for the time an apparent unrecompensed triumph of might over right. But still, considering how easily God can compensate in another world such a noble sacrifice for the apprehended honor of his name, and also what a tendency it has to awaken all the virtuous sensibilities of the universe in reprobation and vindication of such an outrage upon suffering innocence, we cannot satisfy ourselves that the gospel precepts, ' resist not evil,' ' avenge not yourselves,' are not to be understood in their broadest and most literal acceptation, *as far as the taking of human life in self-defence is concerned.*

As the great point aimed at in this commandment is the security of human life, it of course levels its prohibition against wilful murder, suicide, duelling, offensive war, all the slaughter flowing from sanguinary laws, oppressions, persecutions, and whatever tends directly to shorten our own lives, or those of others. The spirit of the precept plainly interdicts all those callings, occupations, and practices which are injurious to the health or safety of the community, such as the manufacture or sale of articles of diet or beverage which we have every reason to believe will be abused, to the hurt or the death of men's bodies, to say nothing of their effects on the undying soul. In like manner all incompetent practice of the medical art; all competing trials of speed in steamboats; all pugilistic combats, and whatever goes to wound, cripple, or maim the body, and thus endanger life, comes fairly within the range of what is forbidden by the sixth commandment. As far as the spiritual import of the command is concerned, it is clear, from the New Testament interpretation, that all envy, revenge, hatred, malice, or sinful anger; all that insulting language which provokes to wrath and murder; and all undue indulgence of that pride, ambition, or covetousness, which prompt to it, are virtually prohibited by the precept, 'Thou shalt not kill.' Mat. 5. 21, 22, 'Ye have heard that it was said by them of old time, Thou shalt not kill; and whosoever shall kill, shall be in danger of the judgment: But I say unto you, that whosoever is angry with his brother without a cause, shall be in danger of the judgment: and whosoever shall say to his brother, Raca, shall be in danger of the council: but whosoever shall say, Thou fool, shall be in danger of hellfire.' 1 John, 3. 15—17, ' Whosoever hateth his brother, is a murderer: and ye know that no murderer hath eternal life abiding in him. Hereby perceive we the love of God, because he laid down his life for us: and we ought to lay down our lives for the brethren. But whoso hath this world's good, and seeth his brother have need, and shutteth up his bowels of compassion from him, how dwelleth the love of God in him.'

THE SEVENTH COMMANDMENT.

14. *Thou shalt not commit adultery.* Heb. ‏לֹא תִנְאָף‎ *lo tinaph.* The original root, ‏נָאַף‎ *nâaph* in its primary and legitimate import denotes *adultery* in the strict and exclusive sense of the term, or that unlawful commerce of the **sexes**

which takes place between parties one or both of whom are married. It is thus distinguished from זנה *zanah*, the word applied to lewdness, fornication, or whoredom in general. This is plain from predominant usage. Thus Lev. 20. 10, 'And the man that *committeth adultery* (ינאף *yinaph*) with another man's wife, even he that *committeth adultery* (ינאף *yinaph*) with his neighbor's wife, the *adulterer* (נאף *noëph*) and the *adulteress* (נאפת *noäpheth*) shall surely be put to death.' Ezek. 16. 32, 'As a wife that *committeth adultery* (המנאפת *hammenäapheth*), which taketh strangers instead of her husband.' Hos. 4. 14, 'Therefore your daughters shall commit *whoredom* (תזנינה *tiznënah*), and your spouses shall *commit adultery* (תנאפנה *tenäaphnah*).' Prov. 6. 32, 'Whoso *committeth adultery* (נאף *noëph*) with a woman lacketh understanding.' That 'woman' here is equivalent to 'wife' is evident from its being immediately added; 'For jealousy is the rage of a man; therefore he will not spare in the day of vengeance;' implying that he would be prompted severely to avenge his wife's dishonor. In accordance with this we find this precept rendered in the Greek by a term (μοιχευω) which always signifies what in our language is termed *adultery*. Mat. 5. 32, 'Whosoever shall put away his wife saving for the cause of fornication, causeth her to *commit adultery* (μοιχασθαι); and whosover shall marry her that is divorced *committeth adultery* (μοιχαται).' This was because that in the eye of the divine law she was still considered as rightfully the wife of the divorcing husband. Rom. 7. 3, 'So then, if while her husband liveth, she be married to another man, she shall be called an *adulteress* (μοιχαλις): but if her husband be dead, she is free from that law; so that she is no *adulteress* (μοιχαλις) though she be married to another man.' Nor is there any other passage throughout the New Testament where μοιχεια,

adultery, is used to signify any other species of uncleanness. The appropriate Greek term for sins of lewdness in general is πορνεια usually rendered *fornication*. But this latter term in Scripture usage is of much wider import than the former; in fact it includes the former in numerous instances. Thus a *married* woman, Mat. 5. 32—19. 9, is said to be guilty of πορνεια, which our translators have rendered *fornication*, though her crime is really *adultery*. Accordingly both πορνεια and μοιχεια are used, Rev. 2. 21, 22, in reference to an *adulterous* intercourse; 'I gave her space to repent of her *fornication* (πορνεια); and she repented not. Behold, I will cast her into a bed, and them that *commit adultery* (μοιχευοντας) with her,' &c. Again, a man that has his father's wife, and so is guilty of *incest*, is said to be guilty of πορνεια, 1 Cor. 5. 1, 'It is reported commonly that there is *fornication* (πορνεια) among you, and such *fornication* (πορνεια) as is not so much as named among the Gentiles, that one should have his father's wife.' Here it is evident that the word must be understood to mean in general any unlawful kind of sexual commerce, of which *incest* is one. For it cannot be supposed that the apostle meant to say that *fornication* was not named among the Gentiles; as it was in fact very common. But what he designs to say is this, that out of many kinds of πορνεια there was one, viz., a man's having his father's wife, which was not heard of among the Gentiles, notwithstanding they were in great measure given up to fornication. Comp. to the same effect Rev. 17, 1, 2. —18. 3. Hos. 3. 3, from all which it is evident that πορνεια is a general term, including under it every species of illicit sexual connexion, and answers perhaps correctly to our English word *lewdness* or *licentiousness*.

From the scope of the foregoing remarks it cannot, we think, be questioned that the seventh commandment is pointed primarily and predominantly against the sin of *adultery*. Consequently the words of Christ, Mat. 5. 27, 28, are doubtless to be understood as referring especially to this precept thus understood; 'Ye have heard that it hath been said by them of old time, Thou shalt not commit adultery. But I say unto you, that whosoever looketh on a woman to lust after her hath *committed adultery* with her already in his heart.' Our Savior is here explaining the Law; the Law, as we have seen, employs a term in the present precept which is exclusively applied to signify *adultery;* and as *adultery*, which is here charged upon the lustful look, cannot be committed with a ' woman' who is not at the same time a ' wife,' the inference would seem to be inevitable that ' woman' (γυνη) in this passage is synonimous with ' wife' or *married* woman, it being the same term as we find used for ' wife,' v. 31, 32, and elsewhere throughout the New Testament. (See Bloomfield in loc.). But although we feel bound, as faithful expositors, to state the true sense of the terms employed in important connexions, it is not in this or any other instance with a view to lower down the standard of requisition in the divine precepts. On the same principles on which we have interpreted the other commandments, we are constrained to give this also so much latitude as to embrace a prohibition of all the sins usually included under it. These will be easily ascertained when we consider the grand design of this commandment, viz., the preservation and promotion of the general happiness of men *in their conjugal and domestic relations.* For this end God himself has instituted *marriage*. It is by means of this wise and gracious ordinance that he has provided for the regulation of those strong instinctive passions upon which the propagation of the race depends, and nothing is clearer than that a general disregard of this institution would inevitably make havoc of the peace, purity, and highest welfare of society. While therefore the *sanctity of the marriage relation* is the first object aimed to be secured by this precept, it points its prohibition at the same time against every thing that is contrary to the spirit and ends of that institution, whether in thought, word, or deed. And as *marriage* is the sole and exclusive provision made by the Creator to meet the demands of that part of our nature which the seventh commandment contemplates, every species of sensual commerce between the sexes except that which comes under its sanction, is doubtless to be viewed as a violation of this precept, as also every thing that goes by legitimate tendency to produce it. All the arts and blandishments resorted to by the seducer; all the amorous looks, motions, modes of dress, and verbal insinuations which go to provoke the passions and make way for criminal indulgence; all writing, reading, publishing, vending, or circulating obscene books; all exposing or lustfully contemplating indecent pictures or statues; all support of or connivance with the practices of prostitution, whether by drawing a revenue from houses of infamy, or winking at the abominations of their inmates; partake more or less of the guilt of violating the seventh commandment. We have only to glance at the pages of the sacred volume to perceive that sins against the law of chastity are more frequently forbidden, more fearfully threatened, and marked by more decisive tokens of the divine reprobation, than perhaps those of any other part of the Decalogue. Not only is adultery the name under which Jehovah stigmatises the sin of idolatrous apostacy from him, but fornication and uncleanness are found in almost every black catalogue of crime in the Scriptures, and the informations of history, which are but another name for the dealings of God's providence,

15 ᵘ Thou shalt not steal.

ᵘ Lev. 19. 11. Deut. 5. 19. Matt. 19. 18. Rom. 13. 9. 1 Thess. 4. 6.

make it evident that sins of this class have been the cause of more individual crime, shame, disease, misery, and death, and of more public debasement and ruin than any other. What rivers of remorseful tears, what myriads of broken hearts, what wide spread wrecks of happiness, what legacies of shame, reproach, and infamy, what fruits of perdition, have followed and are still following in the deadly train of this destroyer! The disclosures of the great day relative to this sin, its perpetrators, procurers, and consequences, will probably make the universe stand aghast. 'However it may be accounted for, says Paley, ' the criminal commerce of the sexes corrupts and depraves the mind and moral character more than any single species of vice whatsoever. That ready perception of guilt, that prompt and decisive resolution against it, which constitutes a virtuous character, is seldom found in persons addicted to these indulgences. They prepare an easy admission for every sin that seeks it; are, in low life, usually the first stage in men's progress to the most desperate villanies, and, in high life, to that lamented dissoluteness of principle which manifests itself in a profligacy of public conduct, and a contempt of the obligations of religion and moral probity.' 'These declarations,' says Dr. Dwight, 'I have long since seen amply verified in living examples.'—Would we then seek an effectual preservative against the undue predominance of those fleshly lusts which war against the soul, let us earnestly and devoutly pray for those purifying influences from above which shall 'cleanse us from all filthiness of flesh and spirit,' and makes us meet temples for the Holy Ghost to dwell in, remembering that 'he that defileth the temple of God, him will God de-

16 ʷ Thou shalt not bear false witness against thy neighbour.

ʷ ch. 23. 1. Deut. 5. 20. & 19. 16. Matt. 19. 18.

stroy.' Let us cultivate universal purity, in secret as well as openly, and feel that the strictest government over all our propensities, senses, and passions is an incumbent duty upon every one who would act upon the safe and salutary principle of the apostle, 'I keep under my body, and bring it into subjection, lest that by any means when I have preached to others, I myself should be a castaway.'

THE EIGHTH COMMANDMENT.

15. *Thou shalt not steal*, Heb. לֹא תִגְנֹב *lo tignab*. Gr. ου κλεψεις. The original גנב *ganab* is the usual word for *steal*, and has nothing peculiar in its import to require a special investigation. The scope of the commandment is to secure *the right of property*. It prescribes the mode in which love to our neighbor is to operate in this respect. The subject of property is one of great extent, and by its various relations entering largely into the elements of human happiness. While God is himself the great Proprietor, the ultimate Lord and Disposer of all things, he has established a constitution of things by virtue of which every man is not only entitled himself to the products of his own labor, but authorised also to make it over or bequeath it to his posterity or heirs. It is the wrongful abstraction or invasion of this *property* which the eighth commandment is designed to prohibit; and of all the forms of violation of this precept none is more palpable, more gross, or more highly provoking to God than that of *depriving a man of the product of his labors by depriving him of himself*. This is the most aggravated form of *stealing* of which it is possible to be guilty, or even to conceive. Whatever may be said of other possessions, a man's per-

son is his own; his life is his own; his liberty is his own. He who takes them away without his consent, and without any crime on his part, *steals* them. And surely stealing men is so much a greater crime than stealing money, as a human being holds a higher rank in the scale of existence than inert and senseless matter. The eighth commandment then forbids distinctly and peremptorily all despotic *enslaving* of our fellow-men, of whatever condition or color, or of exercising absolute lordship over them; because those acts virtually deprive human beings of that property in themselves with which the Creator endowed them. This is a usurpation of the rights of man which no usage, law, or custom can legalize in the sight of heaven. No title can make good my claim to another's person; no deed of inheritance or conveyance transmit it to a third party. There is but one Being competent to make the conveyance, and he has never done it. Every man under God *owns himself.* He has a *right* to himself which no other man can challenge. I may be lawfully restrained, punished, and even executed by just laws, but I can never be *owned.* I can never be in the sight of heaven either serf or slave. I cannot sell myself; no other can sell me. Though I may for a consideration make over to another my right to my *services*, yet the right to *myself* is no more alienable by myself than by another. God gave me myself to keep, and his ownership alone in me am I bound to recognize.

Subordinate to this are various forms of the breach of this commandment, of many of which no human laws take cognizance. The essence of dishonesty is the possessing ourselves of that which rightfully belongs to another. This may be done in an almost infinite variety of ways. Fraudulent bargains, which impose on the ignorant, the credulous, or the necessitous; contracting debts which one is unable to pay; ex-tortion and exorbitant gain; controlling the markets by stratagem, and thus obtaining inordinate prices for one's commodities; entering into combinations unduly to raise or to depress wages; taking unjust advantage of insolvent laws; exacting usurious interest for money; unnecessary subsistence on charity; evading the duties and taxes imposed by government, or in any way defrauding the public, whether by embezzling its treasures or encroaching upon its domain; using false weights and measures; removing landmarks; keeping back the wages of servants and hirelings; withholding restitution for former wrongs; refusing, when able, to pay debts from which we have obtained a legal release—all these are violations of the eighth commandment, and as such falling under the special condemnation of heaven. A slight consideration of the spirit of this precept will show that it reaches also beyond outward acts, and prohibits inordinate love of the world, covetousness, and the pride of life; that it requires industry, frugality, sobriety, submission to God's providence; in a word, a disposition to do to all others, in respect to worldly property, as we would that they should do to us.

THE NINTH COMMANDMENT.

16. *Thou shalt not bear false witness against thy neighbor.* Heb. לא תענה *lo taaneh, thou shalt not answer.* That is, more especially when cited to give testimony before a judicial tribunal. The drift of the precept, in its original import, is more fully laid open, Deut. 19. 16—19, 'If a *false witness* rise up against any man to *testify* against him, that which is wrong; then both the men, between whom the controversy is shall stand before the Lord, before the priests, and the judges, which shall be in those days; and the judges shall make diligent inquisition; and behold, if the witness be a *false witness,* and

hath *testified falsely* against his brother; Then shall ye do unto him, as he had thought to have done unto his brother: so shalt thou put the evil away from among you.' This precept differs from the three preceding in the fact that while they have respect to injuries done by *deeds* or *actions*, this has reference to wrongs done by *words*. The predominant sense of *bearing witness* is clearly recognised in the verb in this connection in the Gr. ου ψευδομαρτυρησεις, *thou shalt not falsely testify*, and in the Chal., Sam., Syr., and Arab., all which render it *testify*. Yet the term is of large import, equivalent to *utter, pronounce, declare,* and while the letter admits, the spirit of the precept requires, that it should here be understood as forbidding every thing that is contrary to strict veracity in our communications with our fellow men. We say, 'with our fellow men,' for though the phrase 'against thy *neighbor*,' might seem to limit it to the narrower circle of our immediate neighbors, yet the interpretation given to the term by our Savior, in the parable of the good Samaritan, plainly teaches us that a more extended application is to be assigned it. It is, in fact, equivalent to *other man*, whether acquaintance or stranger, friend or foe. This precept therefore constitutes the law of love as it respects our neighbor's, that is, every other man's, *good name*. And as one of the principal ways in which his interest in this respect may be injured is by having false witness borne against him in courts of justice, this is made the leading and primary, but not the exclusive, point of the prohibition. Lying in this form is denominated 'perjury,' and so far as this sin is concerned, the ninth commandment is closely related to the third, which forbids the taking of God's name in vain, as is always done in a false oath. The difference between them probably lies in this, that in the third perjury is condemned as a gross

impiety *towards God,* irrespective of any wrong done thereby to our neighbor ; while in this prohibition the head and front of the offending is the false and injurious charge preferred *against our neighbor.* This is a more heinous crime than common extra-judicial falsehood, inasmuch as it is usually more deliberate, and by the sentence to which it leads often involves in itself the guilt of robbery and murder, as well as that of calumny. Accordingly, we find the purport of this commandment otherwise, yet very emphatically expressed, Lev. 19. 16, 'Thou shalt not go up and down as a tale-bearer among thy people : *neither shalt thou stand against the blood of thy neighbor.*' That is, thou art not to stand as a false witness against thy neighbor, whereby his *blood*, his *life*, might be endangered. But if we ourselves are not permitted, in judicial matters, thus to injure our neighbor by bearing false witness against him, so neither are we to procure or encourage it in others. Consequently the suborning false witnesses is hereby condemned ; and it plainly behoves legal counsel in managing the causes of their clients to guard against a virtual perversion of the truth that shall amount to a bearing of false witness ; nor should the verdict of inspiration be forgotten, that ' he that justifieth the wicked, and he that condemneth the just, are both alike an abomination unto the Lord.'

But the scope of the prohibition embraces a multitude of aberrations from the strict law of sincerity and veracity embodied in this precept, which at the same time have nothing to do with judicial proceedings. Of this we are to judge by comparing them with those incidental explications of the ninth commandment which occur here and there both in the Old and New Testament. Nothing can be clearer than that *truth sincerity, fidelity, candor*, are required to be the governing law in all our communications with our fellow men ; and consequently, whatever is contrary to this is contrary to the spirit of this precept. 'Lying lips are an abomination to the Lord.' 'Wherefore,' says the apostle, ' putting away all lying, *speak every man the truth* with his neighbor.' '*Lie not* one to another, seeing that ye have put off the old man with his deeds.' Thus too, in the Levitical code, ' Ye shall not steal, neither deal falsely, *neither lie one to another.*' Thus also, to 'walk uprightly, to work righteousness, and *to speak the truth in his heart,*' are the first lineaments in the good man's character as portrayed by the Psalmist, Ps. 15. 2. Now if this requirement of *universal truthfulness* be not contained in the ninth commandment, it is not embraced at all in the Decalogue ; and it is scarcely to be supposed that a sin, which is every where spoken of with the most marked abhorrence, and one of which it is said, that those who are characteristically guilty of it 'shall have their part in the lake that burneth with fire and brimstone,' and that ' whatsoever worketh abomination or *maketh a lie,*' shall be excluded from the holy city, is not intended to be expressly forbidden in the perfect law of God. The commandment evidently has its foundation in that character which is given of the Most High in the words of inspiration, Deut. 32. 4, '*A God of truth,* and without iniquity, just and righteous is he.' From this view of the grounds and the tenor of the injunction, it will be evident at a glance, that not only false witness in a court, but false statements in common discourse, false promises, whether deliberate or careless, exaggerations and high colorings of facts, equivocation and deceit by word or sign, hypocritical professions and compliments, together with slandering, backbiting, tale-bearing, circulating malicious reports, imputing evil designs, or making injurious representations without sufficient proof, are all direct in-

fractions of the spirit of this command. These are all obvious methods of working ill to our neighbor, of prejudicing his reputation, and injuring or destroying his usefulness and his peace, and consequently cannot consist with the law of love.

As to such cases as those of Abraham, Jacob, Moses, the Hebrew midwives, Rahab, and David, who are often alleged, on certain occasions in their lives, to have been guilty of gross equivocation, we must refer the reader to the remarks made on those particular points of their conduct in the notes appended to their respective histories. It will there appear that an important distinction is to be made between *telling a falsehood,* and *concealing the truth,* or *a part of the truth,* from those who have no right to demand it. While the one is always wrong, the other is in some instances unquestionably right.

As a preventative or preservative, on the score of the present prohibition, nothing is more important than that parents, guardians, and teachers, should aim to check this perverse propensity in its earliest developments. Children are prone to 'go astray from the womb *speaking lies.*' A ' lying spirit' seems to be more or less indigenous to the soil of the human mind, and without the most assiduous culture is difficult to be expelled. A heedless example in this respect in parents themselves, hastily uttered and soon forgotten threats and promises, a slighter punishment for lying than almost any other fault, will be sure to confirm this evil habit in their offspring, and probably to the ultimate sorrow and affliction of their hearts.

THE TENTH COMMANDMENT.

17. *Thou shalt not covet,* &c. Heb. לֹא תַחְמֹד *lo tahmod.* The general import of the root חָמַד *hamad* is *to desire earnestly, to long for, to lust after,* or in the simpler English phrase, *to*

17 ˣ Thou shalt not covet thy neighbour's house, ʸ thou shalt not

x Deut. 5. 21. Mic. 2. 2. Hab. 2. 9. Luke 12. 15. Acts 20. 33. Rom. 7. 7. & 13. 9. Eph. 5. 3, 5. Hebr. 13. 5. y Job 31. 9. Prov. 6. 29 Jer. 5. 8. Matt. 5. 28.

covet thy neighbour's wife, nor his man-servant, nor his maid-servant, nor his ox, nor his ass, nor any thing that *is* thy neighbour's.

covet. In the parallel passage, Deut. 5. 21, this word is rendered *desire,* and another equivalent term, *covet ;* ' Neither *shall thou desire* (תחמד *tahmod*) thy neighbor's wife, neither *shalt thou covet* (תתאוה *tithavveh*) thy neighbor's house,' &c. The affection or emotion expressed by the term is not in itself sinful, but becomes so by reason of the *circumstances* or the *degree* in which it is indulged. Accordingly, it is not simply and absolutely said in this commandment, ' Thou shalt not covet,' as in the preceding commandments, ' Thou shalt not kill,' 'Thou shalt not steal,' &c., but a variety of *objects* are specified, towards which, in their relations to others, this inward emotion is not to go forth. In the present connexion, the word strictly signifies to desire to have as our own what belongs to our neighbor to his loss or prejudice, or without his consent ; and it implies that degree of propensity or appetency towards an object which usually prompts to the obtaining it, or which immediately precedes an actual volition to that effect. A simple, passing, evanescent, wish to possess any thing valuable or agreeable, which we see to belong to our neighbor, is no doubt, in thousands of cases, the mere prompting of an innate and instinctive desire, which is in itself innocent, and probably the very same feeling which prompted our neighbor himself innocently to procure it. A man may desire an increase of his property, without having a covetous or even a discontented heart. Such wishes are the moving spring to all worldly enterprise and prosperity, without which the various businesses of life would languish and die. But the longing impulse in such cases becomes sinful when

it becomes excessive, and amounts to what is termed in the Scriptures an ' evil concupiscence.' This will usually be the result where one is in the habit of setting his neighbor's possessions in contrast with his own, and of dwelling with grieved, grudging, or envious feelings upon the fancied superior advantages of his lot. There can be no harm in desiring a neighbor to *sell* me his house for the real value of it ; but it is wrong to desire to possess the house to his prejudice, or by means of injustice or violence. That coveting a man's wife also, which is here forbidden, is not so much the desire of an adulterous intercourse with her while she remains his wife, though this is expressly forbidden, as desiring that she may cease to be his wife, and become the wife of the coveting person. Among the Jews there were two ways in which this might be done ; either by a divorce, or by the death of the husband. Accordingly, he that transgressed this branch of the commandment, did really desire either that she would obtain a divorce from her husband, or wish that he was dead ; for except upon one or the other of these conditions he could not hope to enjoy her as his own. God therefore forbade this coveting, because he that earnestly desired that a divorce might ensue, would be very apt to take measures to procure its being effected ; and he that secretly cherished the desire of the death of a man, in order to possess himself of his wife, would be under a strong temptation to put him out of the way, provided he thought he could do it with impunity, of which we have a striking example in the case of David and Uriah. In like manner, coveting my neighbor's house is nothing else than earnestly wishing that it may cease to be his property and become mine. Coveting his servant too, is not merely wishing that he might now and then serve me, while he remains his, but that he should cease to be his servant, and thenceforth stand in that relation to me. As therefore we are required by the command to 'remember the sabbath day,' to *do* that which such a remembrance would naturally prompt, so the prohibition against coveting, forbids also all the *actual effects* that legitimately flow from the harboring and cherishing the interdicted affections and passions.

From this the general scope of the prohibition is manifest. It is evidently intended as a safeguard planted around all the rest. It aims to *regulate the heart*, out of which, says our Savior, 'proceed evil thoughts, murders, adulteries, fornications, thefts, false witness, blasphemies.' By forbidding the indulgence of all inordinate desires, it mounts up to the fountain head, from whence flow the manifold evils forbidden in the Decalogue. While the other precepts mainly, though not exclusively, command us to abstain from injurious actions, this requires us to repress covetous inclinations. That it is a precept comprising the utmost spirituality of the law, and effectually refuting the theory that it recognizes as violations only the gross outward act, is clear from the apostle's reference, Rom. 7. 7, 8, 'I had not known sin but by the law ; for I had not known lust, except the law had said, Thou shalt not covet.' The precept therefore reaches deep into the interior springs of action, and lays its interdict upon the very first risings of that *discontented spirit* which is the prolific germ of all unhallowed lustings. To be dissatisfied with what we have is to desire something which we have not ; and as most things which we have not are in the possession of our fellow men, there is but a step between desiring what is not our own and coveting

what is another's. How necessary then is it to cultivate a contented spirit ! Not that we are forbidden to improve our condition ; but we are required to keep our minds free from a corroding, complaining, dissatisfied feeling in view of the allotments of God's providence. There must be no envy expressed or unexpressed towards our fellow men ; no cherished habits of comparing their prosperity with our adversity, their wealth with our poverty, their blessings with our trials ; for in this there is the very essence of ingratitude and rebellion. To specify the innumerable forms in which a covetous spirit shows its pernicious effects would require a volume instead of a few paragraphs, but that the force of the subject may not lose itself in mere generalities, we may observe that *avarice*, or the sordid love of gain for its own sake, may perhaps be considered as leading the van in the train of the sins forbidden by the tenth commandment. This vile idolatry of silver and gold sets its subject in an attitude of the most direct opposition to the demands of the last precept of the Decalogue. Instead of leaving men content with a moderate sufficiency of the good things of life, or with that gradual process of accumulation which coincides with the usual order of providence, a spirit of avarice goads them on with restless eagerness to grasp at greater and greater possessions, to make haste to be rich, and to form schemes of wealth which are seldom carried into execution without fraud, chicanery, extortion, and oppression. From those measures of gain which are usually free from reproach, the transition is easy and natural to the spirit and the practices of hazardous and rash speculation, and thence to downright gaming, where the turn of a die is allowed to fix one's lot in misery for life, and entail long years of anguish upon an innocent family. Let us then pray the prayer which invokes ' neither riches nor poverty.'

Let us aim to have engraven upon the tablets of our souls the inspired declaration, that ' godliness with contentment is great gain,' and by ' coveting earnestly the best gifts,' avoid the danger of every other form of covetousness.

Such then is that remarkable code of moral duty comprised in the Ten Commandments, spoken by the great Lawgiver of the universe at Mount Sinai. In view of it, we cannot but be reminded of the solemn appeal made by Moses to Israel, Deut. 4. 8, ' What nation is there so great, that hath statutes and judgments so righteous as all this Law which I set before you this day?' Hitherto the Most High had declared the perfections of his nature by the mighty acts which he had put forth in a way of favor to his people and of vengeance to his enemies. But in the Law before us he condescended to open his mouth, and with his own majestic voice, to proclaim in their ears his name, his attributes, and his will. And what language is adequate to describe the deference, the awe, with which its every sentence should be pondered, its every demand responded to! If we look with respect and veneration upon the monuments of legislative wisdom handed down to us from a remote antiquity—if the laws of Solon and Lycurgus, and the tables and pandects of the Roman jurisprudence, are entitled to our admiration—with what profound reverence should we contemplate the enactments of the infinite Jehovah, the sovereign Lord of heaven and earth, the source of all power and dominion, 'by whom kings rule and princes decree justice.' All human codes may in one sense be considered as emanating *indirectly* from God, inasmuch as he is the author of the faculties by which they were prompted, and has, in his moral administration of the world, given them a providential sanction by requiring obedience to them in the express injunction; 'Obey the powers that be.' But in the Law of Sinai we read a system of statutes that has emanated *directly* from God, and that distinguishes itself at once from all human codes, which take cognizance of overt acts only, by pointing its requirements at the inward dispositions and affections of the heart. Every one of its several precepts condemns, not merely the outward act which it expressly prohibits, but the indulgence of all those evil passions, propensities, or sentiments, which would lead to it; enjoining at the same time an opposite conduct and the cultivation of opposite dispositions. In this extensive interpretation of the commandments we are warranted, not merely by the deductions of reason, but by the letter of the Law itself. The addition of the *last* 'Thou shalt not covet,' proves clearly that in *all*, the disposition of the heart, as truly as the immediate outward act, is the object of the divine Legislator; and thus it forms a comment on the meaning, as well as a guard for the observance of all the preceding precepts. Understood in this natural and rational latitude of import, how comprehensive and momentous is this summary of moral duty! How every way worthy of the source from whence it springs! It inculcates the adoration of the one true God who made heaven and earth, the sea and all that in them is, who must therefore be infinite in power, wisdom and goodness, and entitled to the profoundest fear, homage, and gratitude of his intelligent creatures. It prohibits every species of idolatry; whether by associating false gods with the true, or worshipping the true by symbols and images. In forbidding the taking the name of God in vain, it enjoins the observance of all outward respect for the divine authority, as well as the cultivation of inward sentiments and feelings, suited to this outward reverence. It establishes the obligation of oaths, and by consequence, that of all compacts and deliberate promises ; a principle, without which the administration of laws would be impracticable, and the bonds of society must be dissolved. By commanding to keep holy the sabbath, as a memorial of the creation, it establishes the necessity of public worship, and of a stated and outward profession of the truths of religion with a corresponding frame of heart. So kind and considerate are the provisions of this precept, that the rest of the sabbath is made to include the menial classes, the sojourning stranger, and even the laboring cattle ; thus evincing that the Creator of the universe extended his care to all his creatures ; that the humblest of mankind were the objects of his paternal care ; that no accidental differences causing alienation among different nations, would alienate any from the divine regard; and that even the brute creation shared the benevolence of the universal Father, and ought to be treated by men with gentleness and humanity.

When we proceed to the second table, comprising more especially our social duties, we find equal matter of admiration in the principles which they recognize and enforce. The precept which proclaims 'Honor thy father and thy mother,' sanctions the practice, not merely of filial obedience, but of all those duties which arise from our domestic relations, and impresses the important conviction that the entire Law proceeds from a Legislator able to search and judge the inmost actings of the heart. The subsequent commands coincide with the clearest dictates of reason, and prohibit crimes which human laws have in general prohibited as plainly destructive of social happiness. But it was of infinite importance to rest the prohibitions, 'Thou shalt not kill,' 'Thou shalt not commit adultery,' 'Thou shalt not steal,' 'Thou shalt not bear false witness,' on the weight of divine

authority, and not merely on the deductions of human reason. The depraved passions of men, idolatrous delusions, and false ideas of public good, would be an over match for the restraints which they impose without a higher sanction than their own salutary tendency. Indeed we have only to compare the precepts of the Decalogue with the tone of moral sentiment which then prevailed throughout the world, to recognize upon it at a single glance the stamp of divinity. In one country we see theft allowed, if perpetrated with address ; in another piracy and rapine allowed, if conducted with intrepredity. Sometimes we see adultery and the most unnatural crimes not only permitted and perpetrated without shame or remorse, but every species of impurity enjoined and consecrated as a part of divine worship. In others, we find revenge honored as manly spirit, and death inflicted at its impulse with savage triumph. Again we see every feeling of nature outraged, and parents exposing their helpless children to perish for deformity of body, or from mercenary or political views. Finally, we see false religions leading their deluded followers to heap their altars with human victims. The master butchers his slave, the conqueror his captive ; nay, to crown the horrors of the recital, the parent sacrifices his tender offspring, drowning their heart-rending shrieks with the noise of cymbals and the yells of fanaticism ! These abominations have disgraced ages and nations which we are accustomed to celebrate as civilized and enlightened. Babylon and Egypt, Phenicia and Carthage, Greece and Rome, have all had their legislators who enjoined, or their philosophers who defended these horrid barbarities and crimes. The same or similar enormities are still found to be practised among various heathen communities where the light of revelation has not yet penetrated. What a contrast do we behold

18 ¶ And z all the people a saw the thunderings, and the lightnings, and the noise of the trumpet, and the

z Hebr. 12. 18.   a Rev. 1. 10, 12.

in turning from these revolting outrages upon reason and humanity to the wise, just, upright, and benignant code promulgated by Jehovah in the Law of the ten commandments! Here we behold a code inculcating clearly and authoritatively the two great principles upon which all true piety and virtue depend, and which our blessed Lord recognized as having the whole Law and the Prophets hung upon them, LOVE TO GOD AND LOVE TO OUR NEIGHBOR. 'Hear, O Israel, the Lord our God is one Lord; and thou shalt *love the Lord thy God with all thy soul, with all thine heart, and with all thy might.*' Thus also, 'Thou shalt not avenge nor bear any grudge against the children of thy people, *but thou shalt love thy neighbor as thyself.*' Such is the moral constitution with which we in the providence of God are favored; by which we are to be judged; and according to which we are to frame the course of our lives and order the temper of our hearts. Under a sense of our moral impotence we cannot indeed but exclaim with the apostle, 'Who is sufficient for these things?' but thanks be to God that in the gospel of his grace he hath provided an obedience to the Law infinitely better than our own, of which every one to whom the message comes is invited, through faith, to avail himself to the joy of his heart and the salvation of his soul.

———

18. *And all the people saw the thunderings.* Heb. ראים את הקלת roim *eth hakkoloth,* (were) *seeing the voices.* Gr. εωρα την φωνην, *saw the voice;* the usual scriptural term for *thunder.* The phraseology is Hebraic, of which we have already considered a parallel specimen, Gen. 42. 1. The term appropri-

mountain b smoking: and when the people saw *it,* they removed, and stood afar off.

b ch. 19. 18.

ate to the sense of *seeing* is, from the superiority of that sense, here used in reference to objects of *hearing,* and would be more properly rendered by the English word *perceive,* which is applicable to any of the senses. Comp. Rev. 1. 12, 'And I turned *to see the voice* that spake with me.' Jer. 2. 31, 'O generation, *see the word* of the Lord;' i. e. hear, receive, apprehend appreciate it.——¶ *Lightnings.* Heb. הלפידם *hallappidim, lamps* or *torches;* so called probably because a flash of lightning somewhat resembles the light of a torch suddenly and rapidly waved to and fro by the hand. See Note on Gen. 15. 17. ——¶ *The noise of the trumpet.* Heb. קול השפר *kol hashshopher, the voice of the trumpet.* The portentous sounds of the trumpet and the thunder, which had ushered in the day and which continued to be heard while the people were assembling at the base of the mountain, probably ceased while the words of the law were pronounced in an articulate voice by Jehovah, but were again resumed, and perhaps with increased intensity, as soon as the delivery of the Decalogue was completed. The consequence was, that the phenomena of the scene were too overpowering for the people. It was a manifestation too awful for human endurance, and accordingly, as the Apostle tells us, Heb. 12. 19, 'They could not endure the things which were spoken,' and 'they which heard entreated that the word should not be spoken to them any more.' Some have supposed that had it not been for the terror and the remonstrances of the people God would, after a little interval, have proceeded and delivered the remaining laws, statutes, and judgments in the same manner. But of this we see no sufficient evidence, either from the

19 And they said unto Moses, c Speak thou with us, and we will hear: but d let not God speak with us, lest we die.

20 And Moses said unto the people, e Fear not: f for God is come

c Deut. 5. 27. & 18. 16. Gal. 3. 19, 20. Hebr. 12. 19. d Deut. 5. 25. e 1 Sam. 12. 20. Isai. 41. 10, 13. f Gen. 22. 1. Deut. 13. 3.

to prove you, and g that his fear may be before your faces, that ye sin not.

21 And the people stood afar off, and Moses drew near unto h the thick darkness where God was.

g Deut. 4. 10. & 6. 2. & 10. 12. & 17. 13, 19. & 19. 20. & 28. 58. Prov. 3. 7. & 16. 6. Isai. 8. 13. h ch. 19. 16. Deut. 5. 5. 1 Kings 8. 12.

words of the present narrative, or from the more full detail of incidents recorded, Deut. 5. 22—31, which the reader will find it interesting to compare with the account before us. The essential character and scope of the ten commandments, as compared with the rest of the Mosaic code, would make it proper that it should be promulgated in a different manner.——¶ Removed. Heb. רְנֻעֽר va-yanu-u. The root נוע nua is used not only to convey the idea of physical motion, or removal, but also of mental disturbance, agitation, or trembling. Accordingly the Gr. renders it by φοβηθεντες, affrighted, and the Chal. in the same manner; 'And the people saw and trembled and stood afar off.' So also the Lat. Vulg. 'Terrified and panic-struck.' We have little doubt that this is the genuine sense of the term. It expresses at least that degree of mental emotion which would naturally prompt to a bodily removal.

19. And they said unto Moses, &c. This it appears from Deut. 5. 23, was done through the medium of the elders and heads of the congregation, who came from the people to Moses, while he remained in his place. For he says in the passage just cited that ' they came near unto him,' when they spake these words; which implies that they were at some distance before.——¶ Lest we die. Upon this popular belief among the chosen people in ancient times, see Notes on Gen. 16. 13. Judg. 6. 22.— 13. 22.

20. And Moses said unto the people, Fear not, &c. Moses encourages and comforts them against that fear of im-

mediate death which they appear to have entertained, and at the same time assures them that from fear of another kind they were not by any means to be freed. Indeed it was one special design of the present array of terrors to inspire them with it. The language marks very clearly the distinction between the fear which has torment, which flows from conscious guilt, which genders to bondage, and which drives away from God, and that salutary fear which prompts to a deep reverence of the divine Majesty, and habitually influences the conduct.——¶ To prove you. Heb. נסות nassoth, to try, to tempt. Upon the import of this term see Note on Gen. 22. 1, respecting God's temptation of Abraham. Instead of coming to consume them, he had come to put their obedience to a fresh proof; to give them a more signal opportunity than ever before to evince their deference and devotedness to his will. All the fearful accompaniments of this august manifestation, were intended to impress them with a profound regard to the authority and majesty of Jehovah, and thus to restrain them from sinning against him.

21. Moses drew near, &c. Heb. נגש niggash, was made to draw near; the form of the verb being passive. Ot his own motion Moses would scarcely have durst to venture into the thick darkness from which ever and anon the appalling gleams of lightning burst forth; but being specially called and encouraged of God, he was virtually taken by the hand and led up into the precincts of the divine presence. The incident plainly pointed to their and our

22 ¶ And the LORD said unto Moses, Thus thou shalt say unto the children of Israel ; Ye have seen that I have talked with you i from heaven.

i Deut. 4. 36.　Neh. 9. 13.

23 Ye shall not make k with me gods of silver, neither shall ye make unto you gods of gold.

k ch. 32. 1, -2, 4.　1 Sam. 5. 4, 5.　2 Kings 17. 33.　Ezek. 20. 39. & 43. 8.　Dan. 5. 4, 23. Zeph. 1. 5.　2 Cor. 6. 14, 15, 16.

need of a Mediator in all our attempts to deal with a God of immaculate purity and inflexible justice.—— ¶ *Unto the thick darkness where God was.* Chal. 'Where the Glory of the Lord was.' Targ. Jon. 'Where the Glory of the Shekinah of the Lord was.' The original word for 'thick darkness' (עֲרָפֶל *araphel*) is rendered in the Greek of the New Testament, Heb. 12. 18, θυελλα, which properly denotes a *storm* or *tempest*, and so also it is rendered by the Sept. Duet. 4. 11, and 5. 22, in both which cases the English translation is ' thick darkness.' The idea is probably that of just such a dark, lowering, threatening cloud as is usually with us attended by raging whirlwinds, tempests, and rain.

22. *The Lord said unto Moses,* &c. There can be little doubt that this verse contains the ground and reason of the prohibition in the next ; but the exact chain of sequence which connects the two together, is not perfectly obvious from the face of the narrative. But upon referring to the parallel passage, Deut. 4. 14—16, where a more detailed account is given of the solemn transactions of Sinai, we seem to be furnished with a clue to the connexion. 'And the Lord commanded me at that time to teach you statutes and judgments, that ye might do them in the land whither ye go over to possess it. Take ye therefore good heed unto yourselves ; (for ye saw no manner of similitude on the day that the Lord spake unto you in Horeb out of the midst of the fire) ; Lest ye corrupt yourselves, and make you a graven image, the similitude of any figure, the likeness of male or female,' &c. From this we gather

that the injunction before us is equivalent to saying, 'Ye have seen the manner in which I appeared and spake with you from heaven. Ye yourselves are witnesses that no manner of similitude, no visible figure or form, nothing which could be represented by any pictorial or sculptured semblance, entered into the scenery that then struck your senses. Therefore do not think of embodying your conceptions of me in a material image. Do not dishonor and degrade me by dividing my worship with that of gods of silver or of gold. I will have no participation with images or idols, the work of your own hands.'

23. *Ye shall not make with me gods,* &c. Heb. לֹא תַעֲשׂוּן אִתִּי *lo taasun itti,* correctly rendered, *ye shall not make with me;* i. e. ye shall not make to worship in conjunction with me ; plainly implying that this could not be done without making them *rivals* with him. The Chal. has however 'before me ;' and this seems to be occasionally the force of the equivalent particle עִם *im.* Thus, Est. 7. 8, 'Then said the king, Will he force the queen also *before me* (עִמִּי *immi*) in the house ?' So 2 Sam. 6. 7, 'And then he died *by the ark* (עִם אֲרוֹן *im aron*) of God,' compared with the parallel expression, 1 Chron. 13. 10, 'And there he died *before God* (לִפְנֵי אֱלֹהִים *liphne Elohim.*)' By *gods of silver and of gold* is plainly meant *idols* made of those materials, although in accommodation to popular usages of speech he dignifies them with the title of *gods.* Thus the Israelites when they made the golden calf in the wilderness (which in Acts, 7. 41, is expressly termed an idol), are said Ex 32. 8, 31, to have ' made them gods of

24 ¶ An altar of earth thou shalt make unto me, and shalt sacrifice thereon thy burnt-offerings, and thy peace-offerings, ¹ thy sheep, and thine oxen : in all ᵐ places where I record my name I will

¹ Lev. 1, 2. ᵐ Deut. 12. 5, 11, 21. & 14. 23. & 16. 6, 11. & 26. 2. 1 Kings 8. 43. & 9. 3. 2 Chron. 6. 6. & 7. 16. & 12. 13. Ezra 6. 12. Neh. 1. 9. Ps. 74. 7. Jer. 7. 10, 12.

come unto thee, and 1 will ⁿ bless thee.

25 And ᵒ if thou wilt make me an altar of stone, thou shalt not build it of hewn stone, for if thou lift up thy tool upon it, thou hast polluted it.

ⁿ Gen. 12. 2. Deut. 7. 13. ᵒ Deut. 27. 5. Josh 8. 31.

gold,' and the idols or images of the Philistines, 2 Sam. 5. 21; 1 Chron. 14. 12, are called their 'gods.' The words of this verse are a virtual repetition of the second commandment, and point to that sin to which God foresaw the peculiar addictedness of his chosen people. Their whole subsequent history shows us that idolatry was their besetting iniquity, and consequently that against which of all others they most needed to be put upon their guard. If the true worship of the true God were corrupted, every thing would be sure to go wrong.

24. *An altar of earth thou shalt make,* &c. This was a temporary regulation, having respect to such *occasional* altars as were erected on special emergencies, of which see instances, Judg. 6. 24.— 13. 10. 1 Sam. 7. 17. They were made by heaping up a quantity of earth, and covering it with green turf. As God designed to have the worship of his people eventually concentrated at one place, he would not allow the rearing of altars of durable materials or finished workmanship elsewhere, lest his main purpose should be frustrated.——¶ *Shall sacrifice thereon—thy peace-offerings.* Heb. שלמיך *shelamëka,* lit. *pay-offerings, compensations, retributions, pacifications,* from שלם *shalam, to make up, to make good, restore, repay,* and thence *to make up a difference, to effect a reconcilation, to be at peace.* In this case the idea would perhaps be better conveyed by the phrase 'welfare-offerings,' or 'thank-offerings,' i. e. offerings elicited by a grateful sense of the divine

goodness to the offerer. The English reader might suppose, from the present rendering, 'peace-offerings,' that they were oblations presented for the purpose of securing *peace* or *reconciliation* with God ; but this was the design rather of the 'burnt-offerings,' which were strictly *propitiatory* in their nature, whereas the 'peace-offerings' were merely *eucharistical.* For the use of the word 'peace,' in the sense of 'welfare,' see Note on Gen. 29. 6.——¶ *In all places where I record my name.* Heb. אזכיר את שמי *azkir eth shemi, make my name to be remembered.* Chal. 'In every place where I shall make my Glory to dwell.' Gr. 'Where I shall name my name.' The meaning is, in all places which I shall appoint for the celebration of my name, for the performance of my worship.

25. *Thou shalt not build it of hewn stone.* The reason of this probably was, that carved and wrought stone usually expressed some kind of similitude or image which might turn to an occasion of superstition ; besides that they would be apt to be of a more durable nature, and therefore more easily converted to monuments of idolatry. It is possible, moreover, that this might be forbidden to the Israelites, in opposition to the practices of the heathen, who built their altars of hewn stones, and by having them curiously wrought and adorned, rendered them more attractive as places of worship ——¶ *If thou lift up thy tool upon it thou hast polluted it.* Not that the tool it elf had the power of pollution, but

26 Neither shalt thou go up by steps unto mine altar, that thy nakedness be not discovered thereon.

---

the work was polluted or defiled by being done *contrary to the express command of heaven.*

26. *Neither shalt thou go up by steps,* &c. The reason is subjoined. As the garments of the priests were long and flowing, their ascending a flight of steps **might** indecorously expose their persons. The ascent to the altar of the tabernacle was therefore undoubtedly by a gentle slope, and a still farther precàution against the inconvenience in question was afterwards adopted in the kind of garments prescribed to the priests.

THE SHEKINAH

As this is a term of very frequent occurrence in the Notes composing the present work, and one conveying a meaning of vast importance to the right exposition of numerous passages in the Scriptures, we have concluded to devote a few supplementary pages to its elucidation. Whatever impressions of the intrinsic moment of the subject the reader may have received from our previous allusions to it, we have no doubt they will be materially deepened by the results of the critical enquiry upon which we now enter. If it were merely a point of curious antiquarian research, of the same class with the hieroglyphics of Egypt, or even the monumental records of the chosen people themselves, we should deem its claims upon our attention comparatively slight. But involving, as we are persuaded it does, an important clue to the true nature of the *divine manifestations* recorded in the Old Testament, and their relation to the person and character of Christ, we know of no theme in the whole compass of revelation that more imperiously demands to be investigated. It is not possible indeed that our present limits should allow of full justice being done to the discussion, but we may still be able to present it in a somewhat more prominent light than is done in any of our previous or subsequent annotations.

The etymology of the term first claims our notice. The Hebrew word שכינה *shekinah* comes by the most normal mode of formation from the root שכן *shakan*, which signifies *to dwell, to dwell in, to inhabit*, but more usually spoken of that kind of dwelling common to nomade tribes, viz., in tents or tabernacles. The derivative שכינה *shekinah* is defined by Buxtorf (Lex. Rabbin. voc. שכן) to signify primarily *habitation* or *cohabitation*, but as being spoken more particularly of the divine presence, glory, and majesty, or of the Divinity itself when it is said to be present to men, or to converse with them, or to vouchsafe to them its sensible and gracious aid. He remarks, moreover, that it is commonly explained by the Rabbinical writers of *the divine glory or majesty* in its external manifestation, as something present and dwelling among men. Accordingly the following among hundreds of other passages are rendered by the Chaldee Targum of Onkelos and Jonathan conformably to this definition; Ps. 74. 2, 'Remember thy congregation which thou hast purchased of old; this mount Zion wherein *thou hast dwelt.*' Chal. 'Wherein thou hast made thy *Shekinah* to dwell.' Num. 10. 36, 'Return, O Lord, unto the many thousands of Israel.' Chal. 'Return now, O Word of the Lord, to thy people Israel, make the glory of thy *Shekinah* to dwell among them, and have mercy on the thousands of Israel.' Num. 11. 20, 'Ye have despised the Lord which is among you.' Chal. 'Ye have despised the Word of the Lord whose *Shekinah* dwelleth among you.' Hag. 1. 8, 'Go up to the mountain, and bring wood, and build the house and I will take pleasure in it, and will be *glorified*, saith the Lord.' Chal. 'And

I will make my *Shekinah* to dwell there in glory.' Ps. 85. 10, 'His salvation is nigh them that fear him, that *glory* may dwell in our land.' This is distinctly explained by Aben Ezra as meaning that the *Shekinah* may be established in the land.

It would be easy to multiply passages to the same effect ad libitum, for even the voluminous citations of Buxtorf do not embrace a tithe of the examples of the usage, which may be drawn from the Pentateuch alone. It is the current phraseology of the Chaldee Paraphrases wherever in our version we meet with any intimation of a visible display of the divine glory. Indeed the terms 'Glory' and 'Shekinah' are evidently recognised by the Targumists as convertible terms. These writers, it is well known, were Jews, and on this point we have no reason to doubt that they have transmitted, with singular fulness and accuracy, the traditions of their fathers from the earliest periods of the ancient economy. Still we should make comparatively little account of this, were it not that their interpretations on this head distinctly accord with the results which we obtain from a strict investigation of the sacred text itself. In fact, without designing it, they have yielded a most important testimony to the truth of the New Testament doctrine respecting the Messiah, as will appear more clearly from the sequel of these remarks.

In coming now to a more close examination of the subject of the Shekinah, we are met at the outset by an apparant discrepancy in the scriptural statements relative to the divine manifestations. On the one hand, we have a tolerably numerous class of texts speaking the language that follows; John, 1. 18, 'No man *hath seen* God at any time.' Col. 1. 15, 'Who is the image of the *invisible* God.' 1 Tim. 1. 17, 'Unto the king eternal, immortal, *invisible*, the only wise God.' 1 Tim. 6. 16, 'Who only hath immortality, dwelling in the light which no man can approach unto; whom *no man hath seen nor can see.*' Declarations like these establish it as an unquestionable truth, that God is a spirit, pure, incorruptible, immaterial, and in his own nature absolutely incapable of becoming an object of corporeal vision. This is to be maintained as a radical truth, not only of revelation, but of reason. But then on the other hand what can be more explicit, as far as the letter is concerned, in affirming some kind of visibility of the Deity, than the following passages? Ex. 24. 9—11, 'Then went up Moses and Aaron, Nadab and Abihu, and seventy of the elders of Israel; *and they saw the God of Israel*, and under his feet was, as it were, &c.—And upon the nobles of the children of Israel he laid not his hand; also *they saw God*, and did eat and drink.' So likewise at the delivery of the Law from mount Sinai Jehovah was in some sense certainly visible; for he announces to Moses, Ex. 19. 11, that ' on the third day he would come down *in the sight of all the people.*' And in speaking of this event afterwards, Deut. 4. 12, in an address to Israel, he says, 'Jehovah talked with you *face to face* in the mount out of the midst of the fire. The same is affirmed of Moses in person, Ex. 33. 11, 'And the Lord spake unto Moses *face to face*, as a man speaketh unto his friend.' In like manner the prophet Isaiah says of himself, ch. 6. 1, ' In the year that king Uzziah died *I saw also the Lord sitting upon a throne*, high and lifted up, and his train filled the temple;' and again in v. 5, of the same chapter; 'Then said I, Wo is me! for I am undone—for mine eyes *have seen the King, the Lord of hosts.*'

How then are these modes of speech to be reconciled? Their apparent contrariety shows at least with what confidence the book of God appeals to our reason on the ground of the general evidence of its origin, exhibiting as it does such examples of *literal* self-conflict in particular passages. A work of imposture could not *afford* to be thus seemingly indifferent to appearances. In the case before us it must be confessed, that there is something of a problem to be solved by the interpreter of the sacred text, and yet he cannot be long in coming to the conclusion, that the object seen could not be God in his essence, but some symbol, sign, token, or medium, through which he was pleased, in a unique and peculiar manner, to manifest his presence. Such an object was the Shekinah, which appears to have been a concentrated glowing brightness, a preternatural splendor, enfolded by a dark cloud, except when occasionally some faint glimpses of the imprisoned radiance were disclosed. Probably no word is so well suited to express this overpowering effulgence as the term 'glory,' and this is, in fact, the very term employed in repeated instances for the purpose. Whether this visible object, however, was in philosophical strictness material or immaterial, we hold it to be impossible to determine. For aught that appears to the contrary, it may have been a substance homogeneous with the glorified bodies of Christ and his saints. Indeed, so far as we can judge from the specimen afforded at the scene of the transfiguration, this appears to us an entirely probable supposition. But however this may be, let it suffice that it was something which came within the cognizance of the senses. It was a supernatural something which could be seen, and was seen ; and it was moreover something which God saw fit to constitute as the special indication of his presence. In this, however, we are not to conceive of the omnipresent Jehovah as foregoing the ordinary conditions of his being, or circumscribing his infinity within assignable limits. As he is every where present, and incapable of being otherwise, we cannot consider him, physically speaking—if the term may be allowed—as *really* any more present in the Shekinah than in any or every other point of the universe, which his inscrutable nature pervades. Yet nothing prevents us from supposing that he may have affixed to some sensible and miraculous phenomenon a special significancy as a medium of manifesting his will or agency to his creatures. Such a medium is usually in scriptural diction termed 'an Angel,' and this fact affords a clue to the solution of a multitude of passages where mention is made of the 'Angel of the Lord.' It is wholly unnecessary in many of these texts to suppose the presence of any *created* spiritual intelligence whatever. *The visible phenomenon was the angel, and that only.* This phraseology is peculiarly applicable to the Shekinah, which by way of eminence is again and again so denominated, as appears from the Note on Ex. 32. 34. Nothing is more common, moreover, in the ancient versions, than to meet with the phrase, 'Angel of Jehovah,' as equivalent to this visible representative of Jehovah. While therefore we are not so to think of the Shekinah as if God were really contained in it in any sense, in which we do not at the same time suppose him to be contained in every other object in the universe, and in every other portion of space, we are still to believe that he might, and that he did, in a sovereign manner, connect the manifestation of his peculiar presence with this sensible symbol. It can scarcely be necessary here to repeat, that whatever spiritual presence was associated with the visible phenomenon, it was not that which was seen or heard. 'The Father who hath sent me,' says the Savior, 'hath borne witness of me ; ye have neither heard his voice at any time, nor seen his shape.' Indeed, we have no reason to suppose that *any* spiritual being ever was or can be seen. Even in the intercourse of human beings with each other, the spirit is never seen ; it is only made known by its external manifestatións, of which the *face* is one of the most striking. Were it not so common, nothing would be more wonderful than that the inward emotions and affections of the soul, in all their variety, can be so legibly stamped upon that material organization which we behold in the eyes and other features of the human countenance. What a marvel—what a mystery—is a *smile* or a *frown*, as expressed in the movements and aspect of the face ! What an index of the hidden workings of the sentient spirit ! It is doubtless in direct allusion to this, that the Shekinah is repeatedly called the *Face* or *Presence*, or *Angel of the Face*, of Jehovah. It was a medium of expression to the thoughts and feelings and purposes of his mind precisely analogous to that which the human countenance is to the human mind. But as we have already expanded this view of the subject in our Notes on Ex. 25. 30 ; 33. 14, 15, we forbear to enlarge upon it here.

We would rather call the attention of the reader to the fact, that inasmuch as the sensuous and seen Shekinah was the adopted symbol of the divine Presence, the free and bold diction of the Scriptures denominates it, in multitudes of instances, by the very titles which are appropriated to Jehovah himself. This will have been very apparent in the quotations already made, and similar instances will be found of almost perpetual occurrence in the Notes of this and the succeeding volume.

Consequently there is no ground for the opinion, advanced by some commentators, that the spiritual being who acted in conjunction with the Shekinah, was some inferior created being, representing Jehovah, and therefore using his name and claiming his authority. The Scriptures afford not the least shadow of evidence in support of such an hypothesis. The character and titles of the supreme God are appropriated to the person concerned in these appearances in such a way that no form of speech, no principles of interpretation, will allow of their being applied to him who merely represents or personates him. The whole worship of the church is uniformly throughout the Old Testament properly and immediately directed to the person appearing, or acting in these appearances, without any intimation of a representative. So that if the person appearing in the Shekinah be a representative only, he is not only a representative speaking in the name of another, and with his authority, but he must be his representative in receiving religious worship also ; for to him was all the worship of the church directed as its immediate object. The whole scope of the language respecting the worship of the Israelitish church plainly recognises the fact, that it was addressed to Jehovah who dwelt between the Cherubim in the Most Holy place. How then can it be imagined that in a true revelation any other being than the one only God should be proposed as the object of prayer? It is well known to have been the first and fundamental article of the Jewish creed, that there is only one true God, and him only were they to worship and serve. ' If, therefore,' says Lowman, ' we consider another spirit or an angel to be the only person appearing, the whole worship of the church will then be given to that person or spirit directly and immediately, and not to the one God of Israel, and the Most High. And in this sense, as I apprehend, the whole religious service of the church must have been an express contradiction to the chief and principal doctrine of the Jewish religion, and indeed of all true religion natural as well as revealed. The worshippers of God, under the Jewish dispensation, seem very sensible of this truth, and often express how highly they were concerned never to dissent from it, or to worship any other than the one true God, on any pretence whatever. And yet throughout the whole of this dispensation all their prayers and their whole worship were addressed to the Shekinah, or to the person who appeared in it, though they never once give the least intimation, on any occasion, that the person appearing was properly an angel, and not the Most High. So that if the person appearing in the Shekinah was only an angel, or any other being than the Supreme God himself, it would seem that the whole worship of the church, for two thousand years together, was offered to one object, besides, and against the intention of every worshipper, and against the chief fundamental doctrines and rule of their religion.' We are brought, therefore, so far as we can see, irresistibly to the conclusion, that it was the Great Jehovah, the one living and true God, who appeared in the Shekinah, and who through that medium manifested his presence and communicated his will to the chosen people.

A point of equal interest and importance now invites our attention, viz., to determine the relation borne by the Shekinah to Christ. The opinion has long since become a doctrine in the Christian church, that the theophanies recorded in the Old Testament were in some sense to be referred to the Son of God, anticipating in this way his future manifestation in human flesh as the great Mediator between God and man. Still it must be confessed that a very considerable degree of vagueness has marked the views which have been entertained on this subject. It seems not to have been distinctly apprehended *in what character* precisely the Messiah is to be regarded in those manifestations. Was it the *human* or the *divine* nature which went to the constitution of his glorious person, that was made sensibly present on those occasions? If the former, how is this to be reconciled with the fact, that his human nature did not exist till he was born at Bethlehem of the virgin? If the latter, then we are forced to the conclusion, that Christ's godhead was Jehovah's godhead; that his divinity was absolutely identical with that of the Supreme God, whom we have already shown to have been exclusively concerned in these remarkable appearances. This, we have no question, is indeed the fact, and on this ground we are satisfied that an irrefragable argument may be built in proof of the real and essential deity of the Savior of men; but it is our purpose to come at this conclusion through the avenue opened before us by the usus loquendi of the Scriptures and the Jewish church relative to the Shekinah.

No one at all conversant with the Chaldee paraphrases can have failed to notice, that besides 'Shekinah,' the title which they very frequently give to the appearances of the divine being spoken of in the Hebrew records is מֵימְרָא דִּיְהֹוָה *nĕmra da-Yehovah*, which as the Greek language prevailed and acquired a fixed predominance, was translated 'The Logos, or Word of the Lord.' The Shekinah, as we have seen, was a sensible medium of the manifestation of the divine presence and the declaration of the divine will. An audible voice very frequently accompanied its visible apparition, and as it was in fact the standing organ of communication between Jehovah and his covenant people through all the periods of the ancient economy, nothing would be more natural than that it should come to be designated by the phrase 'Word of the Lord,' or by way of eminence, 'The Word.' Words, either written or spoken, are the established vehicle for conveying the thoughts and feelings of one human being to another. The Shekinah, in like manner, by addressing the senses communicated the designs and will of God to men. The two media answered the same purpose and discharged the same office. How natural, therefore, and how proper, to call the Shekinah ' the Word of the Lord'? Accordingly the evidence is superabundant, that this appellation, in reference to the Shekinah, was perfectly familiar to the Jews at and before the time of our Savior; and as used by their writers would convey an idea entirely equivalent to that couched under the ordinary terms for the divine appearances above alluded to. Out of hundreds of instances, which might be adduced to this effect, we present the following in tabellated form ; premising that in the right hand column, under the title ' Chaldee,' we give indiscriminately the renderings of Onkelos or Jonathan, as they may happen to be more or less pertinent to our purpose.

HEBREW.	CHALDEE.
Gen. 3. 8. And they heard the voice of the Lord God walking in the midst of the garden.	And they heard the voice of *the Word of the Lord* walking in the garden.
Ch. 28. 20, 21. And Jacob vowed a vow, saying, If God will be with me, and keep me, &c., then shall the Lord be my God.	And Jacob vowed a vow to the *Word*, saying, If *the Word of the Lord* will be my help, &c., then shall the Lord be my God.
Ch. 35. 9. And God appeared unto Jacob again when he came out of Padan-aram ; and blessed him.	And *the Word of the Lord* appeared to Jacob the second time, when he was coming from Padan-Aram ; and blessed him.
Ex. 16. 8. Your murmurings are not against us, but against the Lord.	Your murmurings are not against us, but against *the Word of the Lord.*
Ch. 19. 17. And Moses brought forth the people out of the camp to meet with God.	And Moses brought forth the people out of the camp to meet with *the Word of the Lord.*
Ch. 30. 6. Where I will meet with thee.	Where I will appoint for thee *my Word.*
Lev. 26. 11, 12. And I will set my tabernacle among you; and my soul shall not abhor you. And I will walk among you and be your God.	And I will set my tabernacle among you; and *my Word* shall not reject you. And I will cause my *Shekinah* to dwell among you, and be to you a God.
Num. 11. 20. Because that ye have despised the Lord which is among you.	Because ye have contemptuously rejected *the Word of the Lord,* whose *Shekinah* dwelleth among you.
Ch. 14. 9. Only rebel not ye against the Lord.	But rebel not ye against *the Word of the Lord.*
Ch. 23. 4. And God met Balaam.	And *the Word from before the Lord* met Balaam.

HEBREW.	CHALDEE.
Deut. 1. 30. The Lord your God which goeth before yon, he shall fight for you.	*The Word of the Lord thy God,* who is thy leader, shall fight for you.
Ch. 1. 32, 33. Yet in this thing ye did not believe the Lord your God, who went in the way before you, to search you out a place to pitch your tents in, in fire by night, to show you the way ye should go, and in a cloud by day.	And in this thing ye did not believe in *the Word of the Lord your God,* who went as a leader before you, &c.
Ch. 13. 18. When thou shalt hearken ،o the voice of the Lord thy God.	If thou shalt be obedient to *the Word of the Lord thy God.*

With this array of testimonies before us, it is impossible to question that the term ' Logos' or ' Word' is repeatedly employed as equivalent to the She kinah. But Jesus Christ is called by John the ' Logos' or 'Word.' ' In the beginning was the Word,' &c. And have we now obtained an adequate so lution to this title as applied to him, without going out of the bounds of the established Jewish usus loquendi ? It is not indeed to be doubted, that the Platonising fathers of the church made a very early prey of this word and wrought it into the tissue of their mystic philosophy, as a personification of the divine Reason or Wisdom—a circumstance which has led commentators to see in John's use of the term some profound allusion to the dreams and dogmas of the Gnostic heresy. But this, we conceive, is nothing else than reading inspired truth through heathen glasses. The meaning of any word or phrase, says Mr. Upham (Let. on the Logos, p. 89), is ' always to be sought, and can only be discovered, in the sources from which its use originated. 'Logos' is a Jewish expression. To the Jews must we go to ascertain its import. Inquirers and writers on this subject have, in general, failed to establish the true interpretation, by directing all their researches to the heathen systems in which the (term) Logos is used, instead of descending beyond them to the Hebrew Theology, from which they borrowed it.' With the clue before us, we are enabled without difficulty to explain this title as appropriated to Christ. He was 'The Word' in the most emphatic and preeminent sense. He was the great organ of communication between heaven and earth. He was the divine Declarer of his Father's purposes of grace and redemption to lost men. Indeed, there can be no doubt, that all previous divine communications and appearances were prospective, preparative, and preintimative in their scope, pointing to him who was subsequently to come forth from the bosom of the Godhead and *tabernacle* or *shekinize* in our nature as the incarnate 'Word.' Accordingly we are told by the apostle, Heb. 1. 1, that 'God who at sundry times and in divers manners *spake* in times past unto the fathers by the prophets, hath, in those last days, *spoken* unto us by his Son.' He was appointed to discharge between God and man in a preeminent manner the same office which *words* discharge between man and man. He was to be the proclaimer of his mercy, the revealer of his character, and at the same time, the representative, the likeness, the image of his attributes. In a word, he was to be 'God manifest in the flesh.' ' In him was to dwell all the fulness of the Godhead bodily.' And we shall have no difficulty in interpreting those lofty predicates of him which we find in the proem of John's gospel, if we bear in mind that the same or equivalent language is unreservedly used in the Old Testament of the Shekinah, the 'Word' of that dispensation. Under the dictation of the Holy Spirit the august titles Jehovah, Jehovah God, Jehovah of Hosts, Angel of the Presence, &c., are again and again applied to the visible symbol of the Shekinah, and all the acts and attributes proper to the Supreme God, the Creator of the world, and the object of all religious worship, most freely ascribed to it. So truly then as the Shekinah of the earlier economy is identified with the Jehovah of the Old Testament, and the Shekinah is the same as ' The Word' that was made flesh, so truly is Jesus Christ also the Jehovah of the inspired Scriptures, 'God over all and blessed for ever.'

To those who may be desirous of extending their inquiries on this subject, the following works will be found replete with interesting views and reasonings :— Lowman's Three Tracts on the Shekinah ; Allix's Judgment of the Ancient Jewish Church against the Unitarians ; Ben Mordecai's Letters ; and the Rev. C. W. Upham's Letters on the Logos. With several of the conclusions of this latter gentleman we find it impossible to coincide, but we feel no hesitation, nevertheless, in awarding to his little volume on the Shekinah and the Logos the praise of an elaborate and candid research into the whole subject, and of an able comparative estimate of the lights thrown upon it by sacred and ecclesiastical antiquity. But the theme is one of sufficient importance to demand a far more extended investigation than it has ever yet received. We are persuaded it is destined to furnish a key to the solution of some of the profoundest mysteries of revelation. Among English commentators we know of no one, except Patrick who seems to have had any adequate idea of what is really involved in the recorded theophanies of the Old Testament.

THE HEBREW THEOCRACY

(INTRODUCTORY TO CHAPTERS XXI.—XXIII.)

THE portion of the Book of Exodus comprised in chapters 21, 22, and 23, contains the record of what God spake to Moses, when he 'drew near to the thick darkness,' after the people had retired from their close vicinity to the sacred mount. The contents of these chapters relate for the most part to the *judicial* or *political* regulations which God was pleased to enact for his people, with the occasional intermixture of precepts pertaining to the system of worship. But in order to convey an adequate idea of this department of the Pentateuch, it will be proper to present to the reader a compendious view of the peculiar civil and ecclesiastical polity of the Hebrews, reserving to our subsequent notes, as occasion may require, a more detailed exhibition of its several distinguishing features.

The form of government which prevailed among the descendants of Abraham, prior to the time of Moses, was the *patriarchal.* Abraham, Isaac, and Jacob, governed their respective families in virtue of that paternal authority which was, in the early ages of the world, universally conceded to the fathers and heads of households. The families thus governed were the natural germs of *tribes*, every one of which obeyed its own *prince* (נשיא *nasi*), who was originally the first-born of the *founder* of the tribe, but in progress of time appears to have been elected. In proportion as the numbers of the tribes were augmented their *heads* or *patriarchs* became powerful chieftains, and under the title of *princes, elders,* and *heads of tribes*, answered very nearly to the *sheikhs* and *emirs* of the Bedouin Arabs and other nomade races of modern times spread over the regions of the East.

Such was the form of the primitive social organization of the chosen people. But after the deliverance from Egypt, when they were to be set apart, and destined to the great object of preserving and transmitting the true religion, God saw fit to bestow upon them a new civil and religious polity wisely adapted to the purposes which, as a nation, they were intended to subserve. Of these, one of the principal undoubtedly was, to keep alive the grand fundamental truth, that *there is but one living and true God, and that he only is to be worshipped and adored, loved and obeyed.* With a view to this a peculiar constitution was adopted, familiarly known as the *Theocracy ;* according to which God became *the temporal king and supreme civil magistrate of the nation.* Not that it was possible for Jehovah to sink his character of Lord and Master of the universe in his capacity as civil ruler of the Hebrews. He was still, as Creator and Judge, the God of each individual Israelite, as he is the God of each individual Christian ; but he moreover sustained, both to every *individual* Israelite, and to the whole *collective body* of the Israelitish nation, the additional relation of *temporal sovereign.* In this character he solemnly proffered himself to the people at Mount

Sinai, and in this character he was, with equal solemnity, accepted by their united voice, Ex. 19. 4—8. This polity was doubtless adopted with the design that the obedience which they rendered him as *King* might become in some measure identified with the reverence due to him as *God ;* as while they yielded the former, they would be less likely to withhold the latter. And it is to be noticed, that it was not till after the transaction recorded Ex. 19. 7—9, in which God was recognised in his character of *immediate Ruler* of that people, that he proceeded to promulgate from the clouds of Mount Sinai the system of laws and ordinances designed for them as a religious community. In this system, how-ever, the *moral code* of the Decalogue, which was both uttered and recorded in a different manner from the rest, is to be considered as given, not in his character of national king of the Israelites, but in that of the Creator and Lawgiver of the universe. A like distinction is occasionally to be made elsewhere ; but it is clear that in the chapters before us nearly every ordinance and statute can be re-ferred to some one of the ten commandments, and is to be considered as merely a developement of its sense and spirit. Yet as they are termed emphatically ' judgments,' they undoubtedly belonged more especially to the *civil* government, and formed a kind of *common law*, very analogous to the common law of other lands, having respect to matters at issue between man and man, which became the subject of *judicial* decision. Though of a *temporal* character in themselves, they still involved *moral* considerations, and were for the most part based upon some express precept of the Decalogue.

Since then the Jewish polity was strictly a Theocracy, in which Jehovah ap-peared as the immediate sovereign and the people of Israel as his immediate subjects, this relation would naturally give rise to certain important results, in the administration of that economy, which well deserve our notice. In the first place, no authority was vested, by the Mosaic constitution, in any one man or body men, nor even in the whole nation assembled, to make new laws or alter old ones ; their sovereign Jehovah reserving this power exclusively to himself. On the same grounds, the Hebrew constitution recognized no one hereditary chief magistrate, nor gave any power, even to the whole nation, to elect a su-preme governor. It was the especial prerogative of Jehovah to appoint whom-soever he pleased to preside over the people under the title of *judge*, as his own immediate vicegerent. And such men, we know, were from time to time raised up as the exigencies of the state required them, and, under a special commission from heaven, wrought the most signal deliverances for their countrymen.

Another important consequence of the Theocratic polity was, that idolatry be-came not only the transgression of a moral precept of most aggravated character, but also *an act of treason against the state.* It was a virtual rejection of the authority of their acknowledged Ruler. It was a breach of the original com-pact, an open rebellion against God, a positive casting off of sworn allegiance, and therefore, on the established principles of all governments, justly meriting capital punishment. We are not to be surprised, therefore, to find idolatry, with witchcraft, magic, necromancy, and other kindred practices connected with it, treated as a crime equal to that of murder, and subjecting all those who were guilty of committing or abetting it, to the utmost penalty of the law. The punishment of an idolatrous city was the irrevocable ban or anathema called

חרם *herem*, followed by complete destruction, Lev. 19. 31 ; 20. 6. Deut. 17, 2—
6. Nay, so strict was the prohibition on this subject, that the inciter to idolatry
was never to be pardoned, even though he should claim the character of a prophet,
and utter predictions which should be exactly fulfilled, Deut. 13. 2—12. The
nearest relations and the dearest friends were to be delivered up to just punishment if they enticed to idolatry ; and the accuser, as the first witness, was required to cast the first stone at the convicted traitor. Even a foreigner who
dwelt among the Hebrews, could not be exempted from capital punishment if he
practised idolatry himself, or tempted others to practise it ; for by so doing he
became a rebel, and a leader of rebellion, against the king, and against the whole
civil government.

Again, if it be admitted that God sustained the character of *temporal* prince and
legislator to the Israelites, nothing is more natural than that what may be termed
the *civil* or *political* laws enacted by him in that character should be enforced
by *temporal* sanctions. Accordingly, as it is beyond a doubt that the rewards
and punishments annexed to the Jewish civil code were mainly *temporal*, we find
in this view of the subject a sufficient explanation of the fact. The absence in
the books of Moses of any very explicit notice of the future existence of the soul,
or of a future state of rewards and punishments, has indeed afforded ground of
cavil to the skeptic, but there is certainly something inconsistent in the position,
that God acted as the *temporal* sovereign of Israel, and yet that while thus acting he administered the laws of the land, not by the sanction of *temporal* rewards and punishments in this world, but by the sanction of future rewards and
punishments in *another* world. Accordingly, any one has only to turn to the
declarations of the law itself in Deut. 11. 26—28 ; 28. 1—45, to be convinced that
such is not the character of its sanctions.

It is not, however, to be inferred from this, as Warburton has done, that the
fact of a future existence, and of future rewards and punishments, was *unknown*
either to Moses or to the nation of Israel. Although the doctrine of future retribution is taught rather by incidental reference than by authoritative declaration,
yet the evidence that it was known and believed under the Mosaic economy is
abundant and conclusive, as has been shown by Graves (Lect. on the Pentateuch), Faber (on the Three Dispensations), and others. Certain it is, that we
cannot suppose the nation of Israel to have enjoyed *less* of the revelation of a
future state than the patriarchs from whom they were descended, and of these
the Apostle expressly assures us, that 'they died in faith, not having received the
promises, but having seen them afar off, and were persuaded of them, and confessed that they were strangers and pilgrims on the earth, seeking and desiring a
better country, even an heavenly.' But the main purpose for which the Jewish
economy was established did not require, that any other than temporal sanctions
should be explicitly propounded under it. The laws of the Theocracy were to be
enforced by an extraordinary providence, and in accordance with this, the grand
motives placed before the Hebrews to pursue the good and to avoid the evil were
those which were derived from the benefits and calamities, the rewards and punishments of this life. The distinct and prominent exhibition of the doctrine of
future awards was reserved for the developements of that more spiritual system,

which we enjoy in the gospel of Him who 'has brought life and immortality to light.'

Once more, it is to be remarked, that in conformity with the peculiar genius of that polity, and in order that the Hebrews might have their relation to God kept constantly before their eyes, the Most High, as their King, caused a royal tent to be erected in the centre of the encampment, where the pavilions of all kings and chiefs were usually erected, and to be fitted up with all the splendor of royalty, as a moveable palace.   It was divided into three apartments, in the innermost of which was the royal throne, supported by golden cherubs ; and the foot stool of the throne, a gilded ark containing the tables of the law, the Magna Charta of church and state.   In the ante-room a gilded table was spread with bread and wine, as the royal table, and precious incense was burned.   The exterior room or court, might be considered the royal culinary apartment, and there music was performed, like the music at the festive tables of eastern monarchs. (Lev. 21. 6, 8, 17.   Num. 28. 2.   Deut. 23. 4.   Ezek. 44. 7.) God made choice of the Levites for his courtiers, state-officers, and palace guards ; and Aaron for the chief officer of the court and first minister of state.   For the maintenance of these officers, he assigned one of the tithes which the Hebrews were to pay as rent for the use of the land.   He finally required all the Hebrew males, of a suit-able age, to repair to his palace every year, on the three great annual festivals, with presents, to render homage to their king ; and as these days of renewing their homage were to be celebrated with festivity and joy, the second tithe was expended in providing the entertainments necessary for those occasions.   In short, every religious duty was made a matter of political obligation ; and all the civil regulations, even the most minute, were so founded upon the relation of the people to God, and so interwoven with their religious duties, that the Hebrew could not separate his God and his king, and in every law was reminded equally of both.   Consequently the nation, so long as it had a national existence, could not entirely lose the knowledge, or discontinue the worship of the true God.   The succeeding notes will show that this view of the drift and design of this remarkable structure is by no means inconsistent with its having been framed throughout with a *typical* import, and designed to shadow forth the leading spiritual mysteries of the gospel. But that it actually sustained the character here ascribed to it, we think there can be no doubt.

N OW these *are* the judgments which thou shalt ^a set before them.

^a ch. 24. 3, 4. Deut. 4. 14. & 6. 1.

2 ^b If thou buy an Hebrew servant, six years he shall serve: and

^b Lev. 25. 39, 40, 41. Deut. 15. 12. Jer. 34. 14.

Chapter 21

This and the two following chapters contain the record of what God spake to Moses when he 'drew near to the thick darkness,' after the people had retired from their close vicinity to the sacred mount. Their contents relate, for the most part, to the *judicial* or *political* regulations which God, as the Theocratical sovereign of the chosen people, was pleased now to enact and impose upon them. These 'judgments,' however, though in themselves mainly of a temporal character, having respect to matters between man and man, which might become the subject of *judicial* decision, still involved *moral* considerations, and were in fact based upon some one or other of the express precepts of the Decalogue. They are, therefore, very properly introduced in this connexion, immediately after the moral code, to which they have continual reference. In our estimate of the polity of which these laws form a part, we must have regard to the circumstances of the people, and the period for which they were designed, and though we may admit that it would be very possible for God to have given a code intrinsically more excellent and holy, yet we shall be ready to conclude that no better one could have been given in the then circumstances of the Jewish race.

1. *These are the judgments,* &c. Heb. מִשְׁפָּטִים *mishpotim;* from שָׁפַט *shaphat, to judge,* and here signifying the

statutes, judicial laws, or *rules of judgment*, by which their civil government was to be conducted, and according to which the magistrates were to give judgment in disputed cases or differences arising between man and man. Gr. δικαιωματα, *just judgments.* As their government was a Theocracy, their entire legislation was from God. No part of their code, whether civil or ecclesiastical, originated with themselves, or was left to be modified by the dictates of human prudence

Laws respecting Servants.

2. *If thou buy an Hebrew servant,* &c. Heb. כִּי תִקְנֶה *ki tikneh, when thou shalt purchase, procure, acquire;* a term of which the general import is that of *acquisition* or *possession* in whatever manner obtained. See Notes on Gen. 4. 1.—14. 19. The following instances of the use of the term will go to show that its sense is modified by the subjects to which it is applied, and that it does not by any means necessarily convey the idea of Hebrew servants' being bought and sold as goods and chattels, as they are under the system of modern slavery, especially in our own country. Eve said, Gen. 4. 1, 'I have *gotten* (קָנִיתִי *kanithi*) a man from the Lord.' And she accordingly named him *Cain* (קַיִן *kayin*), that is, *gotten, acquired.* Prov. 15. 32, 'He that heareth reproof *getteth* (קוֹנֶה *koneh*) understanding.' Is. 11. 11, 'The Lord

in the seventh he shall go out free for nothing.

3 If he came in by himself, he shall go out by himself: if he were

---

shall set his hand again *to recover* (לְקְנוֹת *liknoth*) the remnant of his people.' Ps. 78. 54, 'He brought them to this mountain which his right hand *had purchased* (קָנְתָה *kanethah*).' Neh. 5. 8, ' We of our ability have *redeemed* (קָנִינוּ *kaninu*) our brethren the Jews, that were sold unto the heathen.' Prov. 8. 22, ' The Lord *possessed me* (קָנָנִי *kanani*) in the beginning of his way.' Here, as the service among the Hebrews was for the most part voluntary, the 'buying an Hebrew servant' may as legitimately imply *the buying him from himself*, that is, *buying his services*, as any other mode of purchase. Indeed, as there is no positive proof that Hebrew servants were ever made such or kept in that condition by force, against their own consent, except as a punishment for crime, the decided presumption is, that such is the kind of 'buying' here spoken of. As to the term עֶבֶד *obed*, *servant*, it comes from עָבַד *abad*, *to serve*, which is applied variously to the *serving* of worshippers, of tributaries, of domestics, of Levites, of sons to a father, of subjects to a ruler, of hirelings, of soldiers, of public officers, &c. With similar latitude, the derivative noun is applied to all persons doing service for others, irrespective of the ground or principle on which that service was rendered. Accordingly it embraces in its range of application, tributaries, worshippers, domestics, subjects of government, magistrates, public officers, younger sons, prophets, kings, and the Messiah himself. To interpret it 'slave,' or to argue, from the fact of the word's being used to designate domestic servants, that they were made servants *by force*, worked without pay, and held as articles of property, would be a gross and gratuitous assumption. The meaning of the present passage undoubtedly is, ' If thou dost in any way become

possessed of a brother Hebrew, so as to have a right to command his services (in consequence of which right alone he becomes a 'servant'), retain him not in a state of servitude more that six years.'——¶ *In the seventh year.* In what sense 'the seventh year' is to be understood here is not obvious; whether as the *sabbatical year*, in which the land lay fallow, or *as the seventh year from the time when the servant was bought.* Maimonides was of the latter opinion, and this appears on the whole the most probable ; for Moses uniformly calls it ' the seventh year,' without using the term 'sabbatical year,' or apparently at all alluding to it. And besides, when he describes the sabbatical year in Lev. 25. 1—7, he says nothing about the manumission of servants. Yet it is to be presumed that if the *jubilee* year should occur before the six years' service had expired, his manumission would take place of course in virtue of the general law, Lev. 25. 40, unless he had been sold for a crime. —— ¶ *He shall go out free for nothing.* That is, without being required to pay his master any thing as a consideration for the shortened term of service. Being made free by law he was to pay nothing for his liberty. Nor was he required to pay for any thing else. Although he might during the period of his service have labored under sickness, and put his master to cost, yet no compensation was to be expected from him at the time of his release ; for a man's servant was during his servitude as his own possession for which he was bound to provide at his own charges. — One cannot but be struck with admiration at perceiving what kind provisions were made for the Hebrew bondman ; how carefully he was guarded from violence, injustice, and wrong. The circumstances under which a native He-

married, then his wife shall go out
with him.

4 If his master have given him a
wife, and she have borne him sons

---

brew might become a slave were the
following ; (1.) When under the pressure of extreme poverty he sold his
liberty to preserve himself or his family from suffering ; Lev. 25. 39, 'If thy
brother be waxen poor and be sold unto
thee,' &c. (2.) When sold for a like
reason by a father ; v. 7, 'If a man sell
his daughter to be a maid-servant,' &c.
Comp. Neh. 5. 5. (3.) Insolvent debtors might, as a punishment, be sold for
servants, or, by way of payment, put into
the hands of their creditors as slaves ;
2 Kings, 4. 1, 'My husband is dead—
and the creditor is come to take unto
him my two sons to be bondmen.' (4.)
A thief who was unable to make restitution for what he had stolen, according to the proportion required of him
by the law, was sold by way of requital to him whom he had robbed ;
Ex. 22. 3, 4, ' If he have nothing, then
he shall be sold for his theft.' (5.)
Slaves were acquired by the issue of
the marriages of slaves. The condition
of slavery, however, is undoubtedly regarded in the Scriptures as an evil, yet,
as it was an evil that had prevailed in
the world long before the establishment
of the Jewish polity, infinite wisdom
did not see fit at once to root it out, but
enacted such meliorating laws in respect to it as would tend to divest it
of its most aggravated and cruel features, and render it as tolerable as a
state of bondage could well be. In like
manner he *regulated* without *extirpating* polygamy.

3, 4. *If he came in by himself.* Heb.
בְּגַפּוֹ *begappo, with his body.* That is,
with his body only ; in his single person ; having neither wife nor children.
Gr. αυτος μονος, *himself alone.* It is
evidently used in contradistinction to
the being married in the next clause.

or daughters, the wife and her
children shall be her master's, and
he shall go out by himself.

If a free-born Hebrew, who had sold
himself for a bondman, had previously
had a wife, this relation was not disturbed by his servitude, at the expiration of which her freedom was to be restored along with her husband's. But
a different case is supposed in the next
verse. There the marriage is one that
takes place during the continuance of
the servitude, and seems to be of the
same nature with the ' contubernium,'
cohabitation, of the Romans, which, instead of ' conjugium,' *wedlock,* was the
term applied to the marriages of slaves.
A master gave his servant a wife during the period of his service, but retained her and her children after he regained his liberty, the connexion being
of course dissolved by a divorce. But
it is generally maintained by commentators, that the wife thus given was to
be a heathen or Gentile bond-maid, and
not a Hebrewess, which they gathered
from Lev. 25. 44, 'Both thy bondmen
and thy bondmaids, which thou shalt
have, shall be of the heathen that are
round about thee ; of them shall ye buy
bondmen and bondmaids.' This passage, however, does not of itself make
it certain that such was the case, although the idea is undoubtedly countenanced by v. 7—11, of the chapter before us, which would seem to intimate
that if a Jewish woman were given in
marriage at all, it must be to her master
or his son. Moreover, as it appears
from Deut. 15. 12, that Hebrew bondmen and bondmaids came under the
same law of manumission at the end of
six years, we cannot perceive on what
lawful grounds such a wife, if of the
Hebrew stock, should be detained in
servitude after the close of the allotted
time. The Jewish critics adopt the
same view. The children produced from

5 c And if the servant shall plainly say, I love my master, my wife,
and my children; I will not go out
free :
6 Then his master shall bring him

c Deut. 15. 16, 17.

unto the d judges : he shall also
bring him to the door, or unto the
door-post ; and his master shall
e bore his ear through with an awl
and he shall serve him for ever.

d ch. 12. 12. & 22. 8, 28.   e Ps. 40. 6.

---

such a *contubernium* were regarded as
being also slaves, and constituted the
class called 'born in the house,' Gen.
14. 14.—17. 23; 'sons of the house,'
Gen. 15. 3; or 'sons of the handmaid,'
Ex. 23. 12. Of those Abraham had
318; and as it might naturally be supposed that servants thus forming a part
of the household, and imbibing attach-
ments to their master from their earliest
years, would be more deserving of confidence than strangers, he puts arms into their hands, when his service required
it ; a measure, by the way, entirely inconsistent with the genius of American
slaveholding, which will not admit of
masters' putting swords or fire-arms
into the hands of their slaves.

*5, 6. And if the servant shall plainly
say,* &c. Heb. אמר יאמר *amar yo-
mar, saying shall say.* That is, shall
say it again and again, so that his purpose shall become a matter of notori-
ety. This is intimated in order that
there might be evidence of such an intention being in the highest degree voluntary and unconstrained.——¶ *Then his
master shall bring him unto the judges.*
Heb. אל האלהים *el ha-Elohim, to the
gods.* That is, to the magistrates, who
are called 'gods,' Ps. 82, 1, 6. John,
10. 34, 35. Chal. 'Before the judges.'
Gr. προς το κριτηριον του Θεου, *to the
judgment, or tribunal, of God.* The
phraseology is remarkable, but the prevalent sentiments of the Orientals in
regard to sovereignty of all sorts tend
to illustrate it. The Egyptians, according to Diodorus Siculus (B. I. c.
90), looked upon their kings in the light
of divinities ; and from the travels of
Arvieux we learn that among the modern Arabs the usual form of citation,

when one is summoned to the place of
justice is in these words, 'Thou art invited to the *tribunal of God.*' It would
seem that they regarded a judge or magistrate in the administration of justice
as such a lively image of the Deity that
they were led to apply to him in that
capacity a divine title.—It is easily
conceivable that a servant, who had a
good master, might wish to remain with
him permanently during life, particularly if he had lived *in contubernio*
with one of his master's female slaves
and had children by her, for whom he
would naturally cherish a strong affection, and from whom he must separate
if he accepted his freedom. In such a
case he was permitted to bind himself
forever to the service of the master ;
but in order to guard against all abuse
of this permission, and especially that
it might appear that he was not fraudu-
lently or forcibly detained against his
will, it was ordained that the transaction should be gone about judicially,
and with appropriate formalities. For
this purpose, after being brought before
the magistrate, and declaration probably
made of his intention, he was taken back
and his ear bored through with an awl at
the door of his master's house, in token of
his being, as it were, *affixed* to it henceforward the rest of his days. This boring of ears was in the eastern countries,
a badge of servitude. Thus Juv. Sat. 1
102, 'Why should I fear or doubt to defend the place, though born upon the
banks of the Euphrates as the *tender
perforations* in my ear* evince ?' upon
which the ancient scholiast remarks
'that this was a sign of slavery.' It is
supposed that the Psalmist, Ps. 40. 6,
speaking in the person of the Mes-

siah alludes to this custom; 'Mine ear hast thou opened.' Heb. ' dug, pierced through ;' expressive of his entire devotion to his father's service. Michaelis remarks, 'That this statute of Moses made boring the ears in some degree ignominious to a free man; because it became the sign whereby a perpetual slave was to be known, and that for this reason he would have been very glad to have procured the abandonment of the practice of servants' thus permanently adopting a state of vassalage.'——¶ *He shall serve him for ever.* That is, as long as he or his master lived. Some make it to be till the period of the next ensuing jubilee, but the other sense is probably more correct. Thus, 1 Sam. 1. 22, 'That he may appear before the Lord, and thus abide *for ever;*' i. e. as long as he lives. This will appear still more evident by supposing a case that might easily have happened. A slave was sold three years before the beginning of the jubilee. What was to be done with him at the expiration of that time ? If he were then released by the law of the jubilee, how was it possible for him to serve the six years here prescribed in the law? This brings us to so palpable an inconsistency in the law, that we are on the whole forced to the conviction that the regulation before us had no respect whatever to the jubilee. Let the grand object of that institution be considered. It was, that every man might ' return to his possession'—which could not be alienated for a longer time—and to his family; Lev. 25. 10—24. But it does not appear that the privilege extended alike to *every class* of servants. A difference would naturally be made between the case of one made a slave by his crimes, and one who became such by his misfortunes. Consequently the law contained, Lev. 25. 39—42, seems to have no reference to cases like that before us; 'And if thy brother that dwelleth by thee be waxen poor,

and be sold unto thee; thou shalt not compel him to serve as a bond-servant: But as an hired servant, and as a sojourner he shall be with thee, and shall serve thee unto the year of jubilee : and then he shall depart from thee, both he and his children with him, and shall return unto his own family, and unto the possession of his fathers shall he return. For they are my servants which I brought forth out of the land of Egypt ; they shall not be sold as bondmen.' The drift of the enactment here cited is entirely different from that of the one under consideration. The latter speaks of one who was in the fullest sense of the Jewish law a 'bond-servant' or slave; the former of one who was not to be made a ' bond-servant,' but only a ' hired-servant.' The latter relates to one who was sold for his *crimes;* the former to one who disposed of his services on account of his *poverty,* which was no crime. The term of servitude appointed by the law before us was invariably *six years;* the period fixed by the other was *till the next jubilee,* which might be any number of years from one to fifty. The design of the law in Exodus, in ordaining that the thief should be made a slave for six years, was that he might thereby be punished for his crime, and that the money given for him should make some compensation to the person he had injured ; while the object of the law in Leviticus was that the poor man should be received as a menial into an Israelitish family, not to punish him, but that he might find the means of comfortable support in his necessities. The design of the statute giving the slave his option, at the end of six years, either to leave his master or to remain with him ' forever,' could not possibly be that he should ' return to his own family and to the possession of his fathers,' for as long as he lived in bondage he could not do this, and his crime was supposed to have cut him off from

7 ¶ And if a man ᶠsell his daughter to be a maid-servant, he shall

ᶠ Neh. 5. 5.

the right to his paternal estate. But
the design of the other law in giving the
impoverished hired-servant his liberty
at the next jubilee, was expressly that
he might return to his family and again
enjoy his patrimonial inheritance. As
then these two ordinances appear to be
entirely distinct from and unrelated to
each other, there is no necessity for
interpreting the phrase ' for ever,' as
signifying the same as ' till the next
jubilee.'

7. *If a man sell his daughter,* &c.
We must still bear in mind what has
been said above respecting the import
of *selling persons* under the Mosaic law.
It was simply equivalent to *selling one's
services.* It conveyed no ownership.
It did not recognise the odious doctrine
of modern slavery that a man may become a chattel, and be held and treated
simply as an article of property. So in
the case before us, a father might be reduced to such an extreme of poverty as
to be constrained to have recourse to
the measure here mentioned, of disposing of the services of a daughter, when
of a young and tender age, for a consideration. But it is clear from the context that when this was done, it was,
usually at least, upon some engagement
or expectation that the person who
bought her would take her, when of
age, as his wife or concubine. Her purchase as a servant was her betrothal as
a wife. This is confirmed by the comment of Maimonides, who says ; 'A Hebrew handmaid might not be sold but to
one who laid himself under obligations
to espouse her to himself or to his son,
when she was fit to be betrothed.' Jarchi also on the same passage says, 'He
is bound to espouse her to be his wife,
for *the money of her purchase* is the
money of her *espousal.'* An example
of this selling of daughters by impover-

not·go out ᵍ as the men-servants
do.

ᵍ ver. 2, 3.

ished parents is related in the subse
quent history of the Jews, Neh. 5. 1—8
——¶ *She shall not go out as the men
servants do.* That is, shall not go out
upon the same conditions, but upon better. She shall be better provided for at
her departure ; inasmuch as a feeble
woman is less able to protect herself
and secure her own welfare, than a
strong and able-bodied man. There is
an apparent contradiction between this
passage, and Deut. 15. 17, where, in
speaking of the male servant's having
his ear bored in token of perpetual servitude, it is said, 'And also unto thy
maid-servant shalt thou do likewise.'
Michaelis explains this by supposing
that the Hebrew legislator, after the
lapse of forty years, made an alteration
in his laws, and added the ordinance
contained in Deuteronomy. 'He did not
patronize slavery ; at least he endeavored to mitigate its evils to native Hebrews, and to confine it within certain
limits of duration. On their departure
from Egypt, he did so with respect to
males, and availing himself of an ancient
and merciful usage, which terminated
servitude after seven years, he introduced it by a written statute, as an in-
controvertible right. After the people
had been accustomed to this piece of
clemency, he went a step farther in the
law which he gave forty years after,
and established the very same ordinance
in behalf of females.' But we think it
more probable that there was originally
a difference in the case of a woman sold
for theft, or who had sold herself because of her poverty, and of a daughter
sold by her father, in expectation of her
being espoused by her master or one of
his sons. In this last case, which is
the one here considered, she would be
entitled to peculiar tenderness, and provision is made accordingly. But in the

8 If she please not her master,
who hath betrothed her to himself,
then shall he let her be redeemed :

to sell her unto a strange nation he
shall have no power, seeing he hath
dealt deceitfully with her.

former, which seems to be contemplated
in Deuteronomy, she was to come under the same regulations with the man-
servant who declined going out free at
the end of his prescribed term. As it
is perfectly conceivable that a woman
might be influenced by the same motives
as a man to remain with her master, and
as there is no proof that such was not
the case, we think this the most natural
mode of reconciling the apparent discrepancy between the two passages.
However this may be, it is certain that
in the time of the prophet Jeremiah it
was conceived that the statutes which
gave freedom to the Hebrew slaves in
the seventh year, extended not only to
the male, but also to the female sex,
Jer. 34. 9—16, a passage which may be
very profitably read in this connexion.

8. *If she please not her master.* Heb.
אם רעה בעיני אדניה *im raah be-ainë
adonëha, if she be evil in the eyes of her
master;* a very common Hebraic idiom,
importing, however, not moral evil, but
rather the want of personal attractions.
'Good,' in like manner, is in repeated
instances used in a sense equivalent to
'goodly,' or as an attribute of the outer
man. See Note on Gen. 39. 6.——
¶ *Who hath betrothed her to himself.*
As if the purchase under these circumstances was considered as a virtual betrothal, so that no other formalities
were requisite. But it is to be noted
that the original presents here a various
reading, in which our translation has
followed the margin (לֹו *lo, to him*) instead of the text (לֹא *lo, not*). In the
one case the correct rendering is, ' who
doth *not* (לֹא) betroth her ;' in the
other, 'who hath betrothed her *to himself* (לֹו).' Either mode of reading
yields substantially the same sense,
only in the latter case 'betrothing' signifies *the preliminary engagement or affi-*

ancing, which the master is supposed
to have entered into ; in the former, *the
actual consummation of the marriage;*
that is, he hath not acted according
to the mutual understanding of the parties ; he hath not fulfilled expectation.
In doing one thing he hath not done another which was virtually implied in it.
It is obvious that according as one or
the other of these senses is assumed,
the particle employed will be לֹא *lo,
not,* or לֹו *lo, to him.* The Scriptures
present several other instances of the
same textual diversity of reading, on
which commentators have labored with
great assiduity. Of these an ample account is given in Vitringa's *Obs. Sac.
L. III. c.* 14. § 14——¶ *Then shall he
let her be redeemed.* Heb. הפדה *heph-
dah, shall cause her to be redeemed.*
Implying not merely consent to the act
of another, but positive efforts on his
own part to effect the step ; *he shall see
to her being redeemed;* i. e. by her father, or any of her kindred who has a
mind so to do. But if this were not
done, he was not allowed to marry her
to another person, or to a 'strange nation,' a phrase which has usually been
understood to mean, a stranger of the
Israelitish nation, one of a different
tribe or family, because it is supposed
no Hebrew slave could be sold to a
Gentile. But we see not why the literal
rendering may not be adhered to. The
Hebrew master must not sell her to one
of *another nation,* who might desire to
have her as a concubine, and with whom
she might be in danger of forgetting
the true religion. It was an ordinance
by which the highest welfare of the
individual was kindly consulted.——
¶ *Seeing he hath dealt deceitfully with
her.* Heb. בבגדו בה *be-bigdo bah, in
his deceitfully treating her,* i. e. as a
continuation of it. Having wronged

9 And if he have betrothed her unto his son, he shall deal with her after the manner of daughters.

10 If he take him another *wife;* her food, her ra ment, [h] and her duty of marriage shall he not diminish.

11 And if he do not these three unto her, then shall she go out free without money.

[h] 1 Cor. 7. 5.

12 ¶ [i] He that smiteth a man, so that he die, shall be surely put to death.

13 And [k] if a man lie not in wait, but God [l] deliver *him* into his hand; then [m] I will appoint thee a place whither he shall flee.

[i] Gen. 9. 6.   Lev. 24. 17.   Numb. 35. 30, 31. Matt. 26. 52.   [k] Numb. 35. 22.   Deut. 19. 4, 5. [l] 1 Sam. 24. 4, 10, 18.   [m] Numb. 35. 11. Deut. 19. 3.   Josh. 20. 2.

---

her by frustrating her hope of marriage in his own family, he was not to add one injury to another by disposing of her in a foreign connexion, where her principles and her happiness might be alike endangered.

9, 10. *He shall deal with her after the manner of daughters.* That is, he shall deal with her as a free woman ; shall give her a dowry, and bestow her in marriage as if she had been his own daughter. But whether he or his son had married her and then afterwards taken another wife, still this was not to operate to her disadvantage. She was to be suitably maintained, and her due matrimonial privileges continued to her, or else she was freely to be set at liberty.——¶ *Her duty of marriage.* Heb. עֹנָתָהּ *anothah.* Gr. την ομιλιαν αυτης, *her companying, converse, cohabitation,* which Paul, 1 Cor. 7. 3, expresses by the phrase of 'due benevolence,' equivalent to conjugal converse. ——¶ *Shall he not diminish.* Heb. לֹא יִגְרָע *to yigra, shall not keep back,* as the term is rendered Num. 9. 7, 'And those men said unto him, We are defiled by the dead body of a man: wherefore *are we kept back* (נִגְרַע *niggara*), that we may not offer an offering of the Lord in his appointed season among the children of Israel?' The Gr. in this place has ουκ αποστερησει, *shall not defraud,* whence the apostle in speaking of the same subject, 1 Cor. 7. 5, says, 'Defraud ye not one another (μη αποστερειτε αλληλους) except it be with consent, &c.' Gr. 'And he shall not de-

fraud her of necessaries, raiment, and converse.' Chal. 'And her nourishment, raiment, and communion he shall not prohibit.' Sam. 'And her habitation he shall not take away.' Arab. 'And her times he may not diminish.' Syr. 'And conjugal enjoyment he shall not lessen.'

11. *If he do not these three.* That is, either of the three things mentioned above, v. 10.——¶ *Then shall she go out free without money.* Upon coming to marriageable age, if the master neither married her himself nor disposed of her otherwise, he was not only to set her free without remuneration, but also, as appears from Deut. 15. 12—17, to furnish her liberally with gifts.

Laws respecting Murder and Manslaughter.

12. *He that smiteth a man.* That is, mortally, as is evident from what follows, and so amounting to *wilful murder.* See Note on Gen. 9. 6.——¶ *Shall be surely put to death.* Heb. מוֹת יוּמָת *moth yumath, dying shall be made to die.* The sentence is here expressed in the most emphatic language, implying that no ransom was to be taken for the life of the wilful murderer. Num. 35. 31, 'Ye shall take no satisfaction for the life of a murderer, which is guilty of death; but he shall be surely put to death.'

13. *If a man lie not in wait.* Heb. אֲשֶׁר לֹא צָדָה *asher la tzadah, whoso hath not laid in wait.* That is, whoso hath not done such a deed premeditately; who hath not waylaid another

14 But if a man come ⁿ presumptuously upon his neighbour, to slay

ⁿ Numb. 15. 30. & 35. 20. Deut. 19. 11,12. Hebr. 10. 26.

in order to take his life. The original term צָדַד *tzadah* is closely related to צוּד *tzud*, *to hunt*, and implies that *insidious watching* which hunters practice in securing their game.——¶ *But God deliver him into his hand.* Heb. אִנָּה לְיָדוֹ *innah le-yado, doth offer by chance to his hand.* Gr. παρεδωκεν, *hath delivered.* The words evidently have respect to a case where the slayer is not prompted by malice, nor endeavors by covert means to put to death a fellow being, but the catastrophe is owing solely to the special providence of God, which had put one man in the way of a deadly blow from another without any agency or design of his. This constitutes what is called in modern codes *accidental homicide* or *chance-medley,* and for which, under the Mosaic system, there was an express provision in the cities of refuge, hereafter to be described. In Deut. 19. 4—6, we have by way of illustration a specified case in which the manslayer was to be entitled to the benefit of this provision; 'And this is the case of the slayer, which shall flee thither, that he may live: Whoso killeth his neighbor ignorantly, whom he hated not in time past; as when a man goeth into the wood with his neighbor to hew wood, and his hand fetcheth a stroke with the axe to cut down the tree, and the head slippeth from the helve, and lighteth upon his neighbor, that he die; he shall flee unto one of these cities, and live; lest the avenger, of the blood pursue the slayer, while his heart is hot, and overtake him, because the way is long, and slay him; whereas he was not worthy of death, inasmuch as he hated him not in time past.'——¶ *I will appoint thee a place whither he shall flee.* This place, during the sojourn of Israel in

him with guile; º thou shalt take him from mine altar, that he may die.

º 1 Kings 2. 28,—34. 2 Kings 11. 15.

the wilderness, was the tabernacle, as appears by the mention of the altar in v. 14; but after their arrival in the land of Canaan there were six cities of refuge appointed, as we learn, from Num. 35 6, et. seq. From the case of Joab, 1 Kings, 2. 28, it would appear that the temple was occasionally resorted to for this purpose even after the cities of re fuge were established.

14. *If a man come presumptuously* &c. Heb. יָזִד *yazid, deal proudly, presumingly, high-handedly.* Chal. ' Shall do or act impiously.' The Heb. verb זוּד *zud,* which properly signifies *to deal proudly* or *presumptuously,* is applied also to the person who sins, not ignorantly or inadvertently, but wilfully, knowingly, of set purpose, inasmuch as such an offender is considered as disobeying the known law of God through the *pride, self-sufficiency,* and *presumptuous elation* of his spirit. According ly Moses, Deut. 17. 12 and 18. 22, speaks of *presumptuous sins* under the denomination of זָדוֹן *zadon,* which comes from the same root, indicating a kind of transgression entirely different from sins or errors of ignorance, inadvertence, or infirmity. Joab's murder of Abnei comes clearly within the scope of this statute, and accordingly we find that his fleeing to the sacred asylum of the altar availed him nothing. 2 Sam. 2. 19—23.—3. 26, 27. 1 Kings, 2. 28— 32.——¶ *Thou shalt take him from mine altar.* That is, if he has fled unto the altar for protection. But the Jerus. Targ. gives another turn to the expression; 'Though he be the High Priest who standeth and ministereth before me, from thence shall ye take him and kill him.' We may perhaps safely admit that both senses are included. It would certainly be important to teach

15 ¶ And he that smiteth his father, or his mother, shall be surely put to death.

16 ¶ And [p] he that stealeth a man, and [q] selleth him, or if he be [r] found in his hand, he shall surely be put to death.

p Deut. 24. 7. q Gen. 37. 28. r ch. 22. 4.

---

that no official sanctity would be allowed to screen the wilful murderer from justice.

Law respecting the Smiting of Parents.

15. *He that smiteth his father or mother*, &c. He was to be put to death even though the blow should not be fatal, but merely leave a wound or bruise; otherwise the crime mentioned in this verse is included in that specified in v. 12. The crime of parricide is not expressly mentioned in the code of Moses, any more than it was in that of Solon, and probably for the same reason; the law did not presuppose a sin of such horrid enormity.

Law respecting Man-stealing.

16. *He that stealeth a man*, &c. Gr. ὃς εαν κλεψῃ τις τινα των υιων Ισραηλ, *whosoever stealeth any one of the sons of Israel.* Chal. 'He that stealeth a soul of the sons of Israel.' And thus it is explained by Moses himself, Deut. 24. 7, 'If a man be found *stealing any of his brethren of the children of Israel*, and maketh merchandize of him,' &c. This was no doubt the primary drift of the law. It had respect to a crime committed by an Israelite upon the person of an Israelite. For this crime the punishment of death was expressly denounced; and *that* with the utmost degree of rigor. The alleviations which operated in the case of other thefts was precluded here. In other cases, if the article stolen had not been alienated, or if there was reason to look for repentance and restitution, some mitigation of the punishment ensued. But the man-stealer was absolutely doomed to die, whether he had already sold the person stolen, or whether he still had him in his own hands, neither alienated nor used for service. Comp. Deut. 24. 7. But the spirit of the interdict undoubtedly applies to all cases of man-stealing or kidnapping. In the sight of heaven it is a crime charged with the blackest guilt. This is clear from the penalty annexed to it, especially as contrasted with the penalty for stealing property, Ex. 22. 14. If a man had stolen an *ox* and killed or sold it, he was to restore five oxen; if he had neither sold nor killed it, two oxen. But in the case of stealing a *man*, the first act drew down the utmost power of punishment; however often repeated or aggravated the crime, human penalty could do no more. The fact that the penalty for *man*-stealing was death, and the penalty of *property*-stealing, the mere restoration of double, shows that the two cases were judged on totally different principles. This will appear still more evident from the remarks on this passage by Mr. Weld in his tract entitled 'The Bible against Slavery.' 'If God permitted man to hold man as property, why did he punish for stealing that kind of property infinitely more than for stealing any other kind of property? Why punish with death for stealing a very little of *that* sort of property, and make a mere fine the penalty for stealing a thousand times as much, of any other sort of property—especially if by his own act, God had annihilated the difference between man and *property*, by putting him on a level with it? The guilt of a crime, depends much upon the nature, character, and condition of the victim. To steal is a crime, whoever the thief, or whatever the plunder. To steal bread from a full man, is theft; to steal it from a starving man, is both theft and

17 ¶ And ˢ he that curseth his fa-

ˢ Lev. 20. 9.　Prov. 20. 20.　Matt. 15. 4.
Mark 7. 10.

murder. If I steal my neighbor's property, the crime consists not in altering the *nature* of the article, but in taking as *mine* what is *his*. But when I take my neighbor himself, and first make him *property*, and then my *property*, the latter act, which was the sole crime in the former case, dwindles to nothing. The sin in stealing a man, is not the transfer from its owner to another of that which is already property, but the turning of *personality* into *property*. True, the attributes of man remain, but the rights and immunities which grow out of them are annihilated. It is the first law both of reason and revelation, to regard things and beings as they are ; and the sum of religion, to feel and act toward them according to their value. Knowingly to treat them otherwise is sin ; and the degree of violence done to their nature, relations, and value, measures its guilt. When things are sundered which God has indissolubly joined, or confounded in one, which he has separated by infinite extremes ; when sacred and eternal distinctions, are derided and set at nought, then, if ever, sin reddens to its ' scarlet dye.' The sin specified in the passage, is that of doing violence to the *nature* of a *man*— to his intrinsic value as a rational being. In the verse preceding the one under consideration, and in that which follows, the same principle is laid down. Verse 15, 'He that smiteth his father or his mother shall surely be put to death.' Verse 17, 'He that curseth his father or his mother, shall surely be put to death.' If a Jew smote his neighbor, the law merely smote him in return ; but if the blow was given to a *parent*, it struck the smiter dead. The parental ralation is the *centre* of human society. God guards it with peculiar care. To violate that, is to violate all.

ther or his mother, shall surely be put to death.

18 ¶ And if men strive together,

Whoever tramples on that, shows that *no* relation has any sacredness in his eyes—that he is unfit to move among human relations who violates one so sacred and tender. Therefore, the Mosaic law uplifted his bleeding corpse, and brandished the ghastly terror around the parental relation to guard it from impious inroads. Why such a difference in penalties, for the same act ? Answer. 1. The relation violated was obvious—the distinction between parents and others self-evident, dictated by a law of nature. 2. The act was violence to nature—a suicide on constitutional susceptibilities. 3. The parental relation then, as now, was the focal point of the social system, and required powerful safe-guards. 'Honor thy father and thy mother,' stands at the head of those commands which prescribe the duties of man to man ; and throughout the Bible, the parental state is God's favorite illustration of his own relations to the human family. In this case, death was to be inflicted not for smiting a *man*, but a *parent*—a *distinction* made sacred by God, and fortified by a bulwark of defence. In the next verse, 'He that stealeth a man,' &c., the SAME PRINCIPLE is wrought out in still stronger relief. The crime to be punished with death was not the taking of property from its owner, but violence to an *immortal nature*, the blotting out of a sacred *distinction*—making men ' chattels.'——¶ *And selleth him*. Jarchi, in his comment on this stealing and making merchandize of men, gives the meaning thus : 'Using a man against his will, as a servant lawfully purchased ; yea, though he should use his services ever so little, only to the value of a farthing, or use but his arm to lean on to support him, *if he be forced so to act as a servant*, the person compelling him but

and one smite another with a stone,
or with *his* fist, and he die not, but
keepeth *his* bed :

19 If he rise again, and walk
abroad ᵗ upon his staff, then shall
he that smote *him* be quit: only he

t 2 Sam. 3. 29.

---

once to do so, shall die as a thief whether he has sold him or not.'

Law respecting the Cursing of Parents.

17. *He that curseth his father or his
mother,* &c. Heb. מְקַלֵּל *mekallël,* from
the root קָלַל *kalal,* signifying primarily to *make light of, to disparage,* and
thence in Piel *to utter violent reproaches,
to imprecate evil, to curse.* The denunciation undoubtedly applies to him who
uses light, contemptuous, or opprobrious language of his parents. Thus also
Prov. 20. 20, ' Whoso *curseth* (מְקַלֵּל
mekallël) his father or his mother, his
lamp shall be put out in obscure darkness.' Such a conduct subjected the
offender to capital punishment, because
it implied the utmost degree of depravity. He who could break the bonds of
filial reverence and duty to such a degree as in word or action to abuse his
own parents, clearly evinced thereby
that he was lost to all goodness and
abandoned to all wickedness.

Law respecting injurious Strife.

18, 19. *If men strive together,* &c.
Heb. יְרִיבֻן *yeribun,* from the root רִיב
rib, applied properly to *verbal strife,
contention, wrangling;* just that kind of
angry debate which is apt to lead to
blows. Accordingly the Gr. renders it,
εαν λοιδορωνται δυο ανδρες, *if two men
reproach.* The law evidently has respect to a case where two men begin
with a quarrel of words, and proceed to
blows, either with the fists or such weapons as come readily to hand. Provided the injury was not fatal, no further punishment was inflicted on the
injurer than that of being obliged to

---

shall pay *for* the loss of his time,
and shall cause *him* to be thoroughly healed.

20 ¶ And if a man smite his servant, or his maid, with a rod, and
he die under his hand; he shall be
surely punished.

---

pay the expenses of the other's cure, and
his 'sitting,' or 'cessation' (שִׁבְתּוֹ *shibto*),
i. e. the loss of time arising from his confinement. Gr. 'He shall pay for his ceasing from labor, and the charges of healing.' Chal. 'He shall restore his loss
in being idle from work, and pay the
hire of the surgeon.' By the phrase
'he shall be quit,' is meant that he shall
be considered *guiltless* of a capital offence.

Law respecting Injuries to Servants.

20, 21. *If a man smite his servant
&c.—he shall be surely punished.* Heb.
נָקֹם יִנָּקֵם *nakom yinnakëm, avenging
he shall be avenged.* This verb, we believe, both in this and other cases, has
at one and the same time a twofold import, viz. that of punishment to the
offender, and of vindication or avenging
to the offended. It is here, doubtless,
to be understood, both of the servant
who should be killed, and of his master
who killed him; the one was *avenged*
in the very act by which the other was
punished. The precise kind of punishment to be inflicted is here left undetermined. But as his smiting with a rod
instead of any more deadly instrument,
showed that it was his intent to correct
and not to kill him, it can scarcely
mean that he should suffer the punishment of death. This derives support
from the next verse, which enacts, that
if the servant survive a day or two, the
master shall not be punished, 'for he is
his money,' i. e. purchased with his
money, and therefore the presumption
would be, that he could not have intended to kill him, and he was considered to be sufficiently punished by

21 Notwithstanding, if he continue a day or two, he shall not be punished: for u he *is* his money.

22 ¶ If men strive, and hurt a woman with child, so that her fruit depart *from her*, and yet no mischief follow : he shall be surely punished, according as the wo-

u Lev. 25. 45, 46.

the loss which he had incurred. This remark, however, it will be observed, applies to the latter case, where the smitten servant continued a survivor a day or two ; but in the other case, when he died under his master's hand, it was to be presumed that undue severity had been used, for which he was to be punished at the discretion of the magistrate in view of all the circumstances. The law, moreover, is thought to be applicable rather to foreign servants than to Israelites, for over Hebrew servants masters were expressly forbidden to lord it harshly, Lev. 25. 39, 40.

Law respecting Injury done to Pregnant Women.

22, 23. *If men strive and hurt a Woman*, &c. Here the original word for *strive* (רצנ *yinnatzu*) is entirely different from that above remarked upon, v. 18, and implies literally *fighting*, as it is the same word with that employed to denote the 'striving together' of the two Hebrews whom Moses endeavored to separate, Ex. 2. 13. The injury of a pregnant woman in consequence of a fray between two individuals is here treated, as it deserves to be, very seriously ; first, because she was no party in the origin of the fray ; and, secondly, because the divine law would show that it protects, with preeminent care and tenderness, a woman in that helpless situation and her unborn offspring. If the consequence were only the premature birth of the child, the aggressor was obliged to give her husband a recompense in money, according to his

man's husband will lay upon him, and he shall x pay as the judges *determine*.

23 And if *any* mischief follow, then thou shalt give life for life.

24 y Eye for eye, tooth for tooth, hand for hand, foot for foot,

x ver. 30. Deut. 22. 18 19. y Lev. 24. 20. Deut. 19. 21. Matt. 5. 38.

demand ; but in order that his demand might not be unreasonable, it was subject to the final decision of the judges. On the other hand, if either the woman or her child was any way hurt or maimed, the law of retaliation at once took effect.——¶ *Then thou shalt give,* &c. That is, either thou, the offender; or thou, the judge, shalt give in passing sentence.

Lex talionis, or Law of like for like.

24. *Eye for eye, tooth for tooth,* &c. This enactment undoubtedly recognises the prevalence, in the early stages of society, of the idea that every man has a right to do himself justice and revenge his own injuries. In the infancy of all communities, when the redress of wrongs and the punishment of crimes is not yet fully settled in the hands of magistrates, this idea operates with all its force, and the principle acted upon is, that the punishment of offenders shall be an exact equivalent for the injuries sustained. This law, if it may be so termed, was undoubtedly in vogue among the Hebrews, as well as other nomade people, from the earliest periods, and the Most High accordingly, having to deal with a people but little accustomed to the restraints of settled government, and seeing it necessary to interpose the greatest obstacles in the way of the exercise of private passions, was pleased so far to consult their circumstances and notions, as to make every injury done to the *person* of another punishable by strict retaliation on the aggressor. Simple and natural as

this principle of justice seems to be, it is still a species of satisfaction verging close upon the *barbarous*, and easily perverted to wanton caprice and savage cruelty. For this reason, although the principle of the *lex talionis* was retained in the Mosaic code, yet its harsher features were softened by the exercise of it being placed, not in the hands of private individuals, but of the public magistrate. Nor does it appear that even in this form it was ever a *compulsory* mode of retribution. Although sanctioned as a general rule by which the decisions of magistrates were to be governed, yet it is probable that a pecuniary satisfaction might be made by the offender in cases of this nature provided the injured party would consent to it. When it is said, Numb. 35. 31, 'Ye shall take no satisfaction for the life of a murderer,' the inference is that for minor offences satisfaction might be taken. This is confirmed by the testimony of Josephus, who says, that the law allowed him who was injured to estimate his own damage, and to accept of a pecuniary compensation, unless he had a mind to be reckoned severe or cruel. Selden, a modern authority of great weight, says, 'This doth not mean, that if I put out another man's eye, therefore I must lose my own, (for what is he better for that?) though this be commonly received; but it means, I shall give him what satisfaction an eye shall be judged to be worth.' This is perhaps the most correct view of the *lex talionis* in its actual operation, as we find no instance on record where the law was *literally* carried into effect. The spirit of it might be, that the injuring party should in justice receive a punishment similar to the injury he had inflicted, but was allowed to redeem his eye, tooth, hand, &c., by a suitable payment to the injured person. A law of the same character was in existence among the Greeks and Romans, and was understood to admit the like commutations. In several countries of the East, moreover, we find the law of retaliation obtaining at the present day in regard to the same class of injuries as those which came under its operation in the Hebrew statute book. In some of the Indian principalities, for instance, we learn that it has been the immemorial practice, that if one person accidentally wounded another with an arrow, though ever so slightly, the sufferer, or any of his family, has a right to demand that he shall be wounded in the same manner; and a traveller in Persia mentions having met with a person who had lost one of his limbs in consequence, as he was informed, of having in a scuffle shattered the leg of his antagonist so severely that amputation was necessary. 'The practice among the Bedouins may serve in some degree to illustrate this subject, as well as the nice balancing which the law of retaliation operates in producing. In case of murder, the friends of the murdered may, at their option, either retaliate or accept a heavy blood fine. But no other offence is, in practice, liable to capital or corporal punishment. Pecuniary fines are awarded for every offence, and as they are generally heavy, in comparison with the delinquency, the dread of incurring them tends much to keep the wild natives of the desert in order; the nature and amount of the fines which immemorial usage has assigned to particular offences being well known to the Arabs. Burckhardt says, 'All insulting expressions, all acts of violence, a blow however slight, (and a blow may differ in degree of insult according to the part struck,) and the infliction of a wound, from which even a single drop of blood flows, all have their respective fines ascertained.' The kadi's sentence is sometimes to this effect :—

'Bokhyt called Djolan 'a dog.' Djolan returned the insult by a blow upon Bokhyt's arm ; then Bokhyt cut Djo-

25 Burning for burning, wound for wound, stripe for stripe.

26 ¶ And if a man smite the eye of his servant, or the eye of his maid, that it perish ; he shall let

him go free for his eye's sake.

27 And if he smite out his man-servant's tooth, or his maid-servant's tooth ; he shall let him go free for his tooth's sake.

---

lan's,with a knife. Bokhyt therefore owes to Djolan—
For the insulting expression . 1 sheep
For wounding him in the
shoulder . . . . . . 3 camels
Djolan owes to Bokhyt—
For the blow on his arm . 1 camel
Remain due to Djolan 2 camels and 1 sheep.'
Other affairs are arranged on the same principle. It is observable, that in case of theft in the home camp, or that of a friendly tribe, (for robbery and theft are not in other cases considered crimes), the criminal is condemned by an ancient law to the loss of his right hand, but custom allows him to redeem his hand on payment of five she-camels to the person he purposed to rob.' *Pict. Bib.* See on this subject the remarks of Michaelis in my 'Scripture Illustrations,' p. 83.—The purpose for which our Lord alluded to this law in his sermon on the Mount, Mat. 5. 38—40, and the construction which he put upon it, may here properly receive a passing remark. The original law, as we have intimated, did not positively bind the injured party to exact its literal execution, but left him free to forgive or to accept the commutation of a pecuniary mulct; but still if the prescribed penalty were required by him, the judge was perhaps bound to inflict it. The party injured could not be the executioner of this law, but was obliged for that purpose to repair to the magistrate ; for to the judges only were the words addressed, Deut. 19. 21, ' Thine eye shall not pity ; but life shall go for life, tooth for tooth, &c.,' nor is there any evidence that private persons in our Savior's time were in the habit of taking the redress of their wrongs into

their own hands, and making this rule a plea for the perpetration of acts of private revenge. Our Savior is evidently designing to forbid something to the Christian which was allowed to the Jews ; and this we conceive was to dissuade, or rather to inhibit them from *rigorously insisting on their right.* He forbids his disciples 'to resist evil,' by requiring *before the magistrate* the execution of this law of retaliation upon those who might have become liable to its operation. They would thus evince a merciful and forgiving spirit, the peculiar ornament of the followers of Christ. —— ¶ *Burning for burning.* That is, a brand-mark or stigma by hot iron or the like.

Further Law respecting Injuries done to Servants.

26, 27. *If a man smite the eye of his servant,* &c. Throughout these enactments it is easy to perceive that the condition of servitude among the Hebrews was marked by numerous benignant provisions, which no doubt went to render it more mild and tolerable than the same condition among any other people on earth. Here it is ordered that the loss of an eye or a tooth, through the undue violence of a master, should be compensated with the grant of liberty. Although the *eye* and the *tooth* only are mentioned, yet it is plainly to be inferred that the rule extended to every other instance of serious mutilation of the person. Moses frequently delivers general laws in the form of particular examples ; and by here specifying the noblest of our organs on the one hand, and on the other one of those that can be most easily dispensed with, and are naturally lost on the coming of

28 ¶ If an ox gore a man or a woman, that they die: then ᶻ the ox shall be surely stoned, and his flesh shall not be eaten; but the owner of the ox *shall be* quit.

29 But if the ox were wont to push

ᶻ Gen. 9. 5.

with his horn in time past, and it hath been testified to his owner. and he hath not kept him in, but that' he hath killed a man or a woman; the ox shall be stoned, and his owner also shall be put to death.

old age, he plainly gives us to understand that all the other organs, of intermediate dignity, are to be included. It is also reasonable to suppose that all slaves, whether Israelites or not, were to have the benefit of this law, though the Jewish authorities restrict it to the former.

Law respecting the pushing or goring Ox.

28, 29. *If an ox gore a man or a woman.* The present is another characteristic feature of the Mosaic code. When a man, without having himself given the fatal blow, was, in consequence of gross carelessness, the cause of his neighbor's death in any other way, he became liable to the cognizance of the law. The case of the *pushing* ox is alone here mentioned, but there can be no doubt that the regulation applied to the case of any other animal capable of inflicting a mortal injury, whether by means of his horns, feet, teeth, or otherwise. ' The Scripture,' says Maimonides, 'speaketh not of the ox but as an instance.' The design of this law was to signify the divine detestation of homicide, and to inspire the nation of Israel with the deepest horror at every species of blood-shedding, by which human life was extinguished. At the same time the ancient Asiatic notions of retributive justice are clearly to be traced in the ordinances before us. Among a people more advanced in civilization and refinement a pecuniary or other penalty would have the effect of inspiring the due degree of caution in restraining noxious animals. But for a rude people like the Hebrews in the age

of Moses, the present enactment, which inflicted punishment on the injurious beast itself, would probably be more effectual than any other in impressing their minds with a strong sense of the value of human life and the certain retribution that awaited its destroyer. Accordingly, many of the ancient legislators, who were called to institute laws to people placed in circumstances closely resembling those of the Hebrews, proceeded on the same principle as Moses; some of the wisest of them ordaining, that a dog that bit a person should be put in chains; and that if a stone, or piece of wood, iron, or the like, was thrown at a man, so as to kill him, but the perpetrator could not be discovered, the punishment appointed by the law should be forthwith inflicted on the instrument of the murder. In ancient history we read of a statue. which, by accident, had fallen down and killed a bystander, being thrown into the sea; and in modern history we meet with a singular instance of severity displayed towards a tree, in consequence of an atrocious robbery having been committed near it. Sir John Malcolm relates, that a late Persian monarch, who had signalised his reign by a laudable zeal to extirpate every species of crime, especially to make travelling through his dominions safe from the molestations of robbers, having been informed by an individual of his being waylaid and relieved of a considerable sum of money, issued a proclamation for the apprehension of the offenders. No clue, however, was found that could lead to the discovery; and the king, determined not to let such an atrocity

30 If there be laid on him a sum of money, then he shall give for ^a the ransom of his life whatsoever is laid upon him.

31 Whether he have gored a son, or have gored a daughter, accord-

^a ver. 22.   Numb. 35. 31.

ing to this judgment shall it be done unto him.

32 If the ox shall push a man-servant, or a maid-servant ; he shall give unto their master ^b thirty

^b See Zech. 11. 12, 13.   Matt. 26. 15.   Phil. 2. 7.

pass without a marked expression of his royal displeasure, sent a herald through all the neighboring towns and villages, to announce, that as the robbery was perpetrated at a certain tree, he had ordered the executioners of justice to repair on an appointed day to the spot, and punish the tree according to the utmost rigors of the law. At the period fixed, an immense crowd repaired to witness the spectacle ; the royal messenger inflicted tremendous blows on the unconscious and unoffending tree ; and the consequence was, that such a feeling was universally diffused among his subjects of the king's fixed determination to revenge the theft, that the delinquents, in the course of the next night, deposited the stolen property at the foot of the very tree at which they had taken it, and which had suffered for their crime. Instances of this description show us the wisdom and necessity of lawgivers accommodating their institutions and manner of procedure to the character and circumstances of the people over whom they preside.—— ¶ *His flesh shall not be eaten.* Both in order to inspire deeper detestation, and that the owner's loss might be greater.——¶ *The owner of the ox shall be quit.* Shall suffer no other punishment than the loss of his ox. This, however, was on condition of the owner's not having been previously acquainted with the vicious propensities of the animal. But if he had been informed of preceding instances of the same kind, and yet had neglected to take care of the ox, and through his neglect any one had lost his life, then not only must the ox be stoned, but the

owner also punished as a murderer. Mischief of this kind was provided against by the statutes or customs of most nations, but by none so studiously as those of the Hebrews. The Romans twisted hay about the horns of their dangerous cattle, as a caution to all that came in their way. Hence the saying of Horace, ' *Fœnum habet in cornu, longè fuge* !' *he has hay on his horns, flee for life!* But the Jewish law required the confinement of the beast.

30—32. *If there be laid on him a sum of money,* &c. Heb. אִם כֹּפֶר יוּשַׁת עָלָיו *im kopher yushath alav, if an atonement, or ransom, be laid upon him* This evidently supposes that in view of alleviating circumstances, the magistrates were permitted to change the punishment of death into a pecuniary mulct. The care of the ox, for instance, may have been committed to a careless servant ; or he may have broken through the cords or the inclosure by which he was secured ; or he might have been provoked and enraged by another ; all which were circumstances that should go in mitigation of the sentence. Whatever the fine were in this case, he was to submit to it, and it was to be given to the heirs of him that had been killed. This fine, in the case of a free man or woman, was left discretionary with the judge, but in the case of a male or female servant was fixed to the sum of thirty shekels of silver, or about $22 of our money. This valuation of a slave was precisely the sum for which Judas betrayed Christ ! Mat. 26. 15. Zech. 11. 12, 13.—In v. 31, the Chal. has, 'A son of Israel or a daughter of Israel.'

shekels of silver, and the c ox shall be stoned.

33 ¶ And if a man shall open a pit, or if a man shall dig a pit, and not cover it, and an ox or an ass fall therein;

34 The owner of the pit shall make *it* good, *and* give money unto the owner of them; and the dead *beast* shall be his.

35 ¶ And if one man's ox hurt another's that he die, then they shall sell the live ox, and divide the

ᶜ ver. 28.

money of it, and the dead *ox* also they shall divide.

36 Or if it be known that the ox hath used to push in time past, and his owner hath not kept him in; he shall surely pay ox for ox, and the dead shall be his own.

CHAPTER XXII.

IF a man shall steal an ox, or a sheep, and kill it, or sell it: he shall restore five oxen for an ox, and ᵃ four sheep for a sheep.

ᵃ 2 Sam. 12. 6. Luke 19. 8. See Prov. 6. 31.

Law respecting the Pit left uncovered.

33. *If a man shall open a pit*, &c. Not only were the statutes of this divine code so framed as to guard against mischief and injury arising from malice, but also against that which might be occasioned by a culpable negligence. The pits or wells from which water was procured in those countries, though usually covered when not in use, yet were very liable to be left open, thus exposing to the utmost peril the lives or limbs of the animals that chanced to fall into them. The law contemplates the two cases of opening an old pit and digging a new one. The damage accruing in either case was to be made good by the opener or digger, to whom, however, the carcase of the dead animal was to be considered as belonging.

Law respecting Injuries done to cattle.

35. *If one man's ox hurt another's.* Where cattle fought and one killed another, the owners were to adjust the matter by selling the live ox and dividing the price equally between them, and also by making an equal division of the dead ox. But it is supposed in this case, that there had been no fault on the part of the owner of the slaying ox. On the other hand, if the animal was known to be of vicious propensities and his owner had not kept him in, it

was manifestly just that he should suffer for his negligence, and was consequently required to give up his live ox and take the dead one.

Chapter 22

Law respecting Theft and Burglary.

1. *If a man shall steal an ox*, &c. The protection of person and property from the force of the violent, and from the frauds of the dishonest, is one of the chief objects of all criminal law; and this object is compassed, or at least aimed at, by means of punishments or penalties annexed to crime. Now certainly the most obvious, appropriate, and efficacious punishment for stealing is, that the thief should be compelled to restore many times the value of that which he had stolen; and in this we find the principle of the ensuing statutes concerning theft. As the property of the ancient Israelites consisted mainly in cattle, it was very natural that the principles on which the magistrates were to proceed in determining cases of theft and robbery, should be shown in instances taken from this kind of possession. From this chapter it appears that the most gentle punishment of theft was *twofold restitution to the owner*, who thus obtained a profit for his risk or loss. This punishment was applicable to every case in which the article stolen

2 ¶ If a thief be found ᵇ breaking up, and be smitten that he
  ᵇ Matt. 24. 43.

die, *there shall* ᶜ no blood *be shed*
for him.
          ᶜ Numb. 35. 27.

remained unaltered in the thief's possession; that is, was neither sold nor
slaughtered. If however either of these
were the case, and consequently all
hope of repentance and voluntary restitution precluded, the punishment was
more severe, being *fourfold restitution*
in the case of a sheep or goat, and
probably of other animals except an ox,
where it was *fivefold*. This higher
degree of penalty was annexed to the
theft of oxen on account of their great
value in the rural economy of the Israelites; for they used no horses in
their husbandry. The ox did every
thing on their farms. He plowed, he
threshed out the corn, and he drew it
when threshed to the barn or garner.
If therefore the theft of an ox was more
severely punished than that of any thing
else, it was on the same principle on
which an increase of punishment is inflicted for the crime of stealing from
the farmer his plough, or any part of
the apparatus belonging to it. It was,
however, afterward enacted, Lev. 6. 4,
5, that if the thief were touched in conscience, and voluntarily confessed his
crime and restored the stolen property,
he should only be required *to add a fifth
part to it.* Comp. Num. 5. 6, 7.

2. *If a thief be found breaking up,*
&c. Heb. במחתרת *bammahtereth, in
digging through.* Gr. εν τω διορυγματι,
id. That is, digging or breaking through
a house, as the Chal. expressly renders
it. In the eastern countries the walls
of the houses are made very thick in
order to shelter the inhabitants more
effectually from the intense heat of the
climate, and they are very frequently
made of dried mud, laid in between upright and tranverse pieces of timber.
Maundrell, speaking of Damascus, says,
'The streets here are narrow, as is usual
in hot countries, and the houses are all

built on the outside of no better a material than either sun-burnt brick, or
Flemish wall, daubed over in as coarse
a manner as can be seen in the vilest
cottages. From this dirty way of building, they experience this amongst other
inconveniences, that upon any violent
rain the whole city becomes, by the
washing of the houses, as it were a
quagmire.' As an opening therefore
was effected through dried clay, and
not through wood or stone, we perceive
the propriety of the terms employed.
The phraseology may be illustrated by
the following parallel passages: Job,
24. 16, 'In the dark they *dig through
houses* which they had marked for themselves in the daytime.' Ezek. 8. 8,
'Then said he unto me, Son of Man,
dig now in the wall,' &c. Mat. 24. 43,
'If the good man of the house had known
in what watch the thief had come, he
would have watched, and would not
have suffered his house to be *broken
up*.' Gr. 'To be *digged through*.' It
is plain also from the sequel that the
burglary is supposed to be committed
at night.——¶ *No blood for him;* as it
reads without the italics. Heb. אין
לו דמים *ain lo damim, no bloods to
him.* That is, no blood shall be imputed to him who killed him; he shall
not be held guilty of murder, inasmuch
as it could not be known in the dark
who the intruder was, or how far his designs might have carried him if not prevented. Gr. ουκ εστιν αυτω φονος, *there
shall not be slaughter for him.* Chal.,
Sam., and Vulg. 'The smiter shall not
be guilty of blood.' Syr. 'He shall not
have an action of life.' Arab. 'His
blood shall be unpunished.' The propriety of this enactment will appear
more obvious if it be considered that in
the night season men are less upon their
guard, and where the precautions are

3 If the sun be risen upon him *there shall be* blood *shed* for him: *for* he should make full restitution; if he have nothing, then he shall be ^d sold for his theft.

4 If the theft be certainly ^e found in his hand alive, whether it be ox, or ass, or sheep; he shall ^f restore double.

5 ¶ If a man shall cause a field or

^d ch. 21. 2. ^e ch. 21. 16. ^f See ver 1. 7. Prov. 6. 31.

necessarily slight, the rigor of the law should be increased. Besides, a robbery committed in the dead of night, when no spectators are by, is attended with great inconvenience for the want of witnesses, by whose testimony only the thief could be condemned. The case was directly the reverse provided the sun had risen, for then the presumption was that the thief's sole purpose was to steal and not to kill, and slaying was not the punishment for stealing. In God's code punishment is always duly proportioned to crime; and it teaches us to be tender of the lives of bad men.

3. *If the sun be risen upon him.* Chal. 'If the eye of witnesses shall have fallen upon him.' Targ. Jon. 'If it be clear by the sun's light that he did not enter for the purpose of killing.'——¶ *He should make full restitution.* This clause is designed as a statement of the reason for what goes before. The killing of the man under such circumstances were a mere act of wanton homicide, inasmuch as he could, if spared, have made complete restitution; or if too poor for this, he could have been sold as a slave, according to law, and the avails have gone to compensate the theft or the injury.——¶ *Then he shall be sold.* An unhappy rendering when strictly considered, for the housebreaker is supposed to be killed; and if so, how could he be sold as a slave? The version ought properly to have run like

vineyard to be eaten, and shall put in his beast, and shall feed in another man's field: of the best of his own field, and of the best of his own vineyard shall he make restitution.

6 ¶ If fire break out, and catch in thorns, so that the stacks of corn, or the standing corn, or the field be consumed *therewith;* he that kindled the fire shall surely make restitution.

the preceding, ' he *should* or *might have been* sold.'

4. *If the theft be certainly found in his hand alive,* &c. This is not to be understood as being at variance with what is said Prov. 6. 31, 'If he be found, he shall restore *sevenfold;*' as the 'sevenfold' here is doubtless but another term for *abundantly,* according to the common usage of the number ' seven.' Comp. Gen. 4. 24. Ps. 12. 6.—79. 12. The provision in this case seems to be based upon a mild construction of motives. The theft being found in his hand would appear to argue more hesitation and less management and decision in iniquitous practices than if he had proceeded to kill or sell it. So nice are the discriminations that are made in this wonderful code.

Law respecting Trespass.

5. *If a man shall cause a field or vineyard,* &c. This was a case of trespass upon another man's grounds, where the intruder sent in his cattle to feed upon and eat down the grass, vines, or fruit trees of his neighbor. The penalty was that he should make restitution of the best of his own.

Law respecting Conflagrations.

6. *If a fire break out, and catch in thorns,* &c. It is a plain principle running through these enactments, that men should suffer for their carelessness, as well as for their wickedness; that they are to consider themselves accountable not only for the injury they *do*, but also for that which they *occasion* through inadvertency. Here it is not necessary to suppose that he who kindled the fire *designed* the mischief that ensued. As it is a common custom in the East to set the dry herbage on fire before the descent of the autumnal rains, the fire may have been kindled on a man's own ground and by his own hand, and from want of proper attention it may have spread, and been productive of the widest ravages over the neighboring possessions. An adequate restitution is all the penalty enjoined in such a case of accidental conflagration; whereas for *wilfully* and *maliciously* kindling a destructive fire a much severer punishment was undoubtedly to be inflicted. The danger to property and loss of life arising from this source is strikingly depicted in the following note on this passage in the Pictorial Bible. 'This (law) doubtless alludes to the common practice in the East of setting fire to the dry herbage, before the commencement of the autumnal rains, under the very correct impression that this operation is favorable to the next crop. The herbage is so perfectly dry by the long summer droughts, that the fire when kindled often spreads to a great extent and cannot be checked while it finds any aliment. The operation is attended with great danger, and requires to be performed with a careful reference to the direction in which the wind blows, and to local circumstances, that nothing valuable may be consumed in the course given to the destructive element. Such a fire kindled accidentally or wilfully is sometimes attended with most calamitous consequences, destroying trees, shrubs, and standing crops, and placing in considerable danger persons who happen to be abroad on a journey or otherwise. Such accidents sometimes happen through the carelessness of travellers in neglecting, when they leave their stations, to extinguish the fires they have used during the night. The dry herbage towards the end of summer is so very combustible, that a slight cause is sufficient to set it in a blaze. Dr. Chandler relates an anecdote, which sufficiently shows the necessity and propriety of the law which the text brings to our notice. When he was taking a plan of Troas, one day after dinner, a Turk came near and emptied the ashes out of his pipe. A spark fell unobserved upon the grass, and a brisk wind soon kindled a blaze, which withered in an instant the leaves of the trees and bushes in its way, seized the branches and roots, and devoured all before it with prodigious crackling and noise. Chandler and his party were much alarmed, as a general conflagration of the country seemed likely to ensue: but after an hour's exertion they were enabled to extinguish the flames. The writer of this note can himself recollect, that when one chilly night he assisted in kindling a fire, for warmth, on the western bank of the Tigris, so much alarm was exhibited by the Arabs lest the flames should catch the tamarisks and other shrubs and bushes which skirt the river, that the party were induced to forego the enjoyment which the fire afforded. The writer has often witnessed these fires, and the appearance which they present, particularly at night, was always very striking. The height of the flame depends upon the thickness and strength of its aliment; and its immediate activity, upon the force of the wind. When there is little or no wind the fire has no other food than the common herbage of the desert or steppe; the flame seldom exceeds three feet in height, and advances slowly and steadily like a vast tide of fire backed by the smoke of the smouldering embers, and casting a strong light for a considerable height into the air, sometimes also throwing up a taller mass of flame where it meets with clumps of bushes or shrubs which

7 ¶ If a man shall deliver unto his neighbour money or stuff to keep, and it be stolen out of the man's house; g if the thief be found, let him pay double.

8 If the thief be not found, then the master of the house shall be brought unto the h judges, *to see* whether he have put his hand unto his neighbour's goods.

9 For all manner of trespass, *whether it be* for ox, for ass, for sheep, for raiment, *or* for any manner of lost thing which *another* challengeth to be his: the i cause of both parties shall come before the judges; *and* whom the judges shall

g ver. 4.   h ch. 21. 6. & ver. 28.   i Deut. 25. 1. 2 Chron. 19. 10.

condemn he shall pay double unto his neighbour.

10 If a man deliver unto his neighbour an ass, or an ox, or a sheep, or any beast to keep; and it die, or be hurt, or driven away, no man seeing *it* :

11 *Then* shall an k oath of the LORD be between them both, that he hath not put his hand unto his neighbour's goods; and the owner of it shall accept *thereof*, and he shall not make *it* good.

12 And l if it be stolen from him, he shall make restitution unto the owner thereof.

13 If it be torn in pieces; *then* let him bring it *for* witness, *and* he

k Hebr. 6. 16.   l Gen. 31. 39.

---

afford more substantial aliment. This taller mass lingers behind to complete its work after the general body of flame has continued its destructive and conquering march. A high wind throws the flames forward with great fury, while, if the ground happens to be thickly set with clumps of bushes, the tall columns of flame which start up in the advancing fiery tide, give increased intensity to the grand and appalling effect of one of the most remarkable scenes which it falls to the lot of a traveller to witness. In the steppes of southern Russia the writer has passed over tracts of ground, the surface of which had, for fifty miles or more, been swept and blackened by the flames.' *Pict. Bible.*

Law respecting Deposits.

7. *If a man shall deliver unto his neighbor money or stuff to keep.* Heb. כסף או כלים *keseph o këlim, silver or vessels ;* i. e. furniture, utensils. Perhaps the general word *articles* comes the nearest to the original. When valuable *articles* were left for safe keeping in the hands of any one, and while thus entrusted were in some way missing, if the thief were found he was to restore

double. But if the thief were not found, there was at least a suspicion that he who had them in keeping had secreted or abstracted them, and a judicial inquiry was thereupon to be instituted. The depositary was to be summoned before the magistrates and his *oath* that he knew nothing of them was to be considered as a full acquittance. The law indeed does not *expressly* mention the oath, but only says, ' he shall be brought unto the *judges* (אלהים *Elohim, gods*), to see *whether not* (אם לא *im lo*) he hath put his hand, &c.;' but the phrase אם לא *im lo, whether not,* is elsewhere so notoriously the usual formula of an oath among the Hebrews, that we can scarcely understand it otherwise than in reference to an oath ; more especially as the oath is distinctly mentioned v. 11, and in most cases no other proof of his not having retained his neighbor's property could possibly be had. This is confirmed by some of the ancient versions, as Vulg. 'And shall swear that he hath not put his hand to his neighbor's goods.' Sept. and Sam. ' Shall come before God and swear that he hath not been wicked in the whole trust of his neighbor.'

9—13. *For ox, for ass, for sheep.*

shall not make good that which was torn.

14 ¶ And if a man borrow *aught* of his neighbour, and it be hurt, or die, the owner thereof *being* not with it, he shall surely make *it* good.

15 *But* if the owner thereof *be*

The rule in the preceding verse has respect to articles of money, plate, or furniture; but in the present to *live stock* intrusted to the care of another 'to keep;' i. e. not gratuitously, as in the case above, v. 7, but for hire or upon certain considerations, as Jacob had Laban's flock to keep, Gen. 30. 31—36. That this is the true sense may be inferred from the nature of the case. The keeping of money, jewels, &c. required no care or labor, but simply a *safe place* of deposit, and therefore might be gratuitous; but not so with cattle or sheep, which must of course be fed and pastured, and would thus incur expense. If the deposit consisted of any of the animals here mentioned, and it met with any injury, or was driven away from the pasture, the depositary, if no man had seen it, was obliged to swear he had not retained it, nor applied it to his own use; and his oath to this effect the owner was bound to accept instead of payment. But if, on the other hand, it had been stolen out of the house of the depositary, he was obliged to pay for it; inasmuch as a theft in such circumstances would imply the most criminal remissness in him in whose house it had occurred, and it was just that he should suffer the loss of it. If, again, the beast was torn to pieces, the depositary was only bound to bring proof of the fact, and doing so he was under no obligation to make it good. What proof was requisite Moses does not say. The most natural proof would of course be the testimony of an eye-witness, or a remnant of the bloody skin, or carcase; Jerus. Targ. 'Let him bring of the members of it for a witness that it is killed.' But on this point nothing is specified in the text.——¶ *An oath of the Lord.* So called because to Him

the appeal was made, not only as to a Witness of truth, but as to an Avenger of falsehood and wrong. Even in the case of one who had so far broken through the bonds of moral restraint, as to offer injury to his neighbor, it might still be presumed that there was so much regard to conscience as to prevent him from profaning 'an oath of the Lord,' and calling the God of truth to be a witness to a lie.

Law respecting Things borrowed.

14, 15. *If a man borrow aught of his neighbor,* &c. In the case of a borrowed beast of burden, as an ox, an ass, or a horse, receiving any hurt, or coming by his death, the borrower was to make it good, provided the owner were not present; for it might be fairly presumed that he had injured or destroyed it by excessive labor or other cruelty. But if the owner himself were present, he would of course be presumed to have done his best to preserve it, and would at any rate be a witness to the fact, and to its not being owing to the negligence or any other fault of the borrower; consequently as the latter was not required in equity to make it good, so neither in law. As to the final clause, 'If it be an hired thing, it came for his hire,' it seems to indicate a distinction between things lent for hire, and those lent *gratis* for good will, the preceding rule applying only to the latter; whereas in the former, whether the owner were present or not, the borrower was not required to make restitution, unless indeed the owner could prove that the loss was occasioned by his culpable maltreatment or neglect. When this was not the case, but the thing were borrowed on the condition of the borrower's paying so much for the use of

with it, he shall not make *it* good : if it *be* a hired *thing*, it came for his hire.

16 ¶ And ᵐ if a man entice a maid that is not betrothed, and lie with her, he shall surely endow her to be his wife.

ᵐ Deut. 22. 28, 29.

17 If her father utterly refuse to give her unto him, he shall pay money according to the ⁿ dowry of virgins.

18 ¶ ᵒ Thou shalt not suffer a witch to live.

ⁿ Gen. 34. 12.　Deut. 22. 29.　1 Sam. 18. 25.
ᵒ Lev. 19. 26, 31. & 20. 27.　Deut. 18. 10, 11.
1 Sam. 28. 3, 9.

it, then the loss was not to be made good; 'it came for his hire ;' i. e. the loss was to be considered as balanced by the profit of the hire. The compensation agreed upon was to be regarded as an offset to the hazard run by the owner in letting out his property ; and with such a risk in view he would naturally fix his price accordingly. The more these statutes are examined, the more clearly does their reasonable, equitable, mild, and humane spirit appear.

Law respecting Seduction.

16. *If a man entice a maid*, &c. Heb. רפתה *yephatteh, enticingly persuade.* It is assumed that no *force* was used, but merely *persuasions* and *blandishments;* and that the young woman was not betrothed to another. This differences the present from the case supposed Deut. 22. 28, where it is to be understood, both that the maid was betrothed, and that some degree of violence was used. See Note in loc. The penalty prescribed for the seducer in the present case, was that he should 'endow her to be his wife,' i. e. marry her and provide for her suitably according to his station. If, however, the father did not choose to let him have her, still the seducer was obliged to pay a certain sum of money as a compensation for the injury. The amount prescribed is no more definitely fixed than by the terms, 'he shall pay money according to the dowry of virgins.' That is, according to their rank and condition in life ; having respect to their parentage, connexions, and prospects; as a

maid in humble circumstances could not reasonably look for so ample a dowry as one of a wealthy or distinguished family. It has indeed been supposed that this was a stated mulct of fifty shekels, but the passage from which this conclusion is drawn (Deut. 22. 28, 29.) refers to a *rape*, and not to simple seduction.—It might appear perhaps at first view that the law by merely appointing to the seducer marriage with the partner of his crime, and exempting her from punishment altogether, was too mild and lenient for such an offence. But it is to be considered that the woman suffered the corporeal and visible consequences, and the public disgrace of illicit intercourse ; and as to the man, although he did indeed satisfy the civil law by marrying and endowing the victim of his lust, yet in the sight of God he was not cleared from the guilt of his sin by this mode of making amends, but needed the cleansing of deep repentance before he could obtain absolution from his Judge.

Law respecting Witchcraft.

18. *Thou shalt not suffer a witch to live.* That is, a reputed or professed witch ; a woman who practised such magical arts, incantations, and sorceries, as gave her the reputation of being a witch. The use of the term, however, determines nothing as to the *reality* of the preternatural power to which such persons laid claim. The Scriptures are wont, in multitudes of instances, to speak of things not according to their absolute verity, but according to general impression and belief.

The remark of some commentators, that 'if there had been no *witches* such a law as this had never been made'— 'that the existence of the *law*, given under the direction of the Spirit of God, proves the existence of the *thing*'—is founded upon a very inadequate view of the general structure of revelation. The sacred writers speak of *false gods*, for instance, as if they were *real existences*, but we see at once how gross would be the error of such an interpretation. So likewise in regard to witchcraft, and all those arts and incantations which are based upon a supposed commerce with evil spirits. We do not consider the assumption of the *reality* of such intercourse as at all necessary to the true explication of the passages in which it seems to be implied, nor to the enactment of such laws as that under consideration. Pretended arts of this nature were common among all the idolatrous nations of antiquity, and from their intimate connexion with idolatrous rites and systems, were obviously fraught with the most pernicious effects when introduced among the chosen people, who were at best but too much addicted to superstitious practices. However false and futile in themselves, they did, in fact, involve a deep offence against the very first principles of the Mosaic dispensation, and this accounts for the severity with which they were treated by its laws. They were not only built upon systems of theology that were at war with the doctrines and worship of the Theocracy, but by imposing upon the credulity and exciting the terrors of the vulgar, they gave to individuals a very dangerous power, in a society so singularly constituted as that of the Hebrews. The practising of these arts was forbidden therefore under the severest penalties, as the mischief actually wrought was about equal, whether the supernatural power professed were a reality or a mere imposture.

This is sufficient to justify the law as here and elsewhere enounced, *under the circumstances in which it was given*, but as the subject is somewhat curious and interesting, we shall devote a little more time to the consideration of the import of the term here and elsewhere employed to designate the class of persons against whom this law is so emphatically directed. From the annexed passage, occurring Deut. 18. 9—14, it is perhaps to be inferred that the practice thus severely denounced was not one which had hitherto been common among the chosen people, but was one which they were in danger of learning from the heathen inhabitants of Canaan; ' When thou art come into the land which the Lord thy God giveth thee, thou shalt not learn to do after the abominations of those nations. There shall not be found among you any one that maketh his son or his daughter to pass through the fire, or that *useth divination*, or *an observer of times*, or *an enchanter*, or *a witch*, or *a charmer*, or *a consulter with familiar spirits*, or *a wizard*, or *a necromancer*. For all that do these things are an abomination unto the Lord: and because of these abominations the Lord your God doth drive them out from before thee. Thou shalt be perfect with the Lord thy God. For these nations, which thou shalt possess, hearkened unto observers of times, and unto diviners; but as for thee, the Lord thy God hath not suffered thee so to do.'

In the passage which we are now considering the original term is מכשפה *mekashshephah*, the fem. of מכשף *mekashsheph*, usually rendered *magician* or *sorcerer*. As to the primitive and most elementary sense of the root כשף *kashaph*, it is a point which philology has not yet clearly determined. Michaelis refers to what he considers the cognate Arabic root *kasapha*, signifying *to cut*, whence in tne time of a solar or lunar eclipse they are wont to say, 'God *cuts* the sun, or the moon ;' from a part of the luminary's appearing to be *cut off* from the remainder. Accordingly eclipses of the sun or moon are called in that language 'kusuph,' *cutting ;* while our term *eclipse* comes from a Greek word signifying *fainting* or *failing.*' Taking this derivation as a basis, Michaelis supposes that the word, in biblical usage, which had respect to the absurd and superstitious notions of the times, denotes *a person who occasions solar or lunar eclipses; that is,* from his astronomical knowledge of their approach ; making all manner of grimaces, singing songs, and so affecting to *enchant* the heavenly bodies. This, he says, corresponds with the ancient rabbinical notions of witchcraft, which was a kind of unhallowed perversion or falsification of the powers of nature, causing them to operate contrary to the true meant designs of their author. This etymology, like hundreds of others which depend upon the affinities of Arabic and Hebrew, though possibly correct, cannot be *verified,* and we are in fact thrown back upon the biblical use of the Piel form of the verb, which is universally rendered *to practise prestige, to use incantations, magic, sorcery,* in a word, *to resort to the arts of witchcraft.* The Greek renders it by φαρμακους, *poisoners,* probably because these sorcerers dealt much in *drugs* or *pharmaceutical potions,* to which potent effects were ascribed, and which were often deleterious. But it does not appear that this is a fair representation of the force of the original term. As the female sex were supposed to be more especially addicted to this kind of forbidden craft, the word here occurs in the feminine, and is rendered by a term which perhaps conveys the most adequate notion of the original. Our English word *witch* is supposed to be derived from the verb *to wit* (anciently *to weet,* i. e. to know) through its adjective form *wittigh* or *wittich,* afterwards

contracted to *witch.* A *witch,* therefore, in its etymological import, is a *knowing woman,* as *wizard (wise-ard)* is also a *knowing, cunning,* or *wise man.* But the *knowledge* implied by the terms is of a peculiar kind—a knowledge of occult and mysterious things—a skill in disclosing or foretelling matters that lie beyond the reach of ordinary human intelligence, and supposed to be acquired by means of an express or implicit compact with some evil spirit. Persons of this imputed character were accordingly invested, by popular belief, with the power of altering, in many instances, the course of nature's immutable laws, of raising winds and storms, of riding through the air, of transforming themselves into various shapes, of afflicting and tormenting those who had rendered themselves obnoxious to them, with acute pains and lingering diseases; in short, to do whatever they pleased, through the agency of the devil, who was supposed to be always obsequious to their beck and bidding. The belief in the reality of witchcraft, clothed with this kind of supernatural attributes, has been more or less prevalent in all ages and countries, and in periods of abounding ignorance and superstition, the most cruel laws have been framed against its alleged professors, and multitudes of innocent persons, male and female, many of them aged, poor, friendless, decrepid, and sick, condemned and burnt for powers they never possessed, and for crimes they neither premeditated nor committed. Happily for humanity, these sanguinary laws have been mostly abolished from the codes of enlightened modern nations, and the prevention or cure of the evils of magical imposture left to the progress of general intelligence, of science, and instructed piety among all classes. The faith in oracles and miracles, the legends of superstition, and the creations of distempered fancy have died away in Christian countries before the ad-

19 ¶ pWhosoever lieth with a beast shall surely be put to death.

p Lev. 18. 23. & 20. 15.

20 ¶ q He that sacrificeth unto

q Numb. 25. 2, 7, 8. Deut. 13. 1, 2, 5, 6, 9, 13, 14, 15. & 17. 2, 3, 5.

vancing light of revelation, and little children retire to bed without alarm, and people traverse unfrequented paths at all hours and seasons without the dread of witches or ghosts, of spells or incantations. For our highly favored exemption from these pernicious forms of superstitious belief, though they have indeed sadly darkened one period of the annals of our own country, we can never be sufficiently grateful.——¶ *Shalt not suffer to live.* Heb. לא תחיה *lo teha- yeh,* lit. *shalt not vivify.* On the pecu- liar usage of this term we have else- where commented. See Note on Gen. 6. 19. Josh. 6. 25. It implies in some way a *saving, preserving, continuing in life,* after a *virtual extinction;* and the import may be, that inasmuch as a practiser of witchcraft is to be con- sidered as *ipso facto* condemned to death by the law without any previous form- ality of trial or judicial sentence ; the forbearing to execute such an offender was a kind of *reanimation* or *resuscita- tion* of him or her in direct contraven- tion of the divine statute. This is, per- haps, the most plausible solution of a phraseology of which Michaelis inti- mates that it occasioned him no little difficulty, as the usual mode of expres- sion in the Levitical penal statutes is מות ימות *moth yamuth, he or she dy- ing shall die, shall die the death,* instead of *shall not be suffered to live.* But his proposal to read לא תהרה *shall not be,* is supported by no authority whatever ; and our interpretation renders it un- necessary.

Law respecting Beastiality.

19. *Whosoever lieth,* &c. This was a crime of such crying enormity that the earth itself was defiled by bearing such a monster of impurity as its per- petrator, and he was at once to be cut

off from among the living without mer- cy. From a comparison of this passage with Lev. ch. 18. 20, it appears that this was one of the prevalent abomina- tions of the Canaanites, from which the Israelites were to shrink with a holy horror, and in order to deepen the im- pression of its ineffable turpitude and atrocity, the abused beast was to be in- volved in the doom of the more brute- like offender.

Law respecting Idolatrous Sacrifices.

20. *He that sacrificeth,* &c. This is clearly the sin prohibited in the first commandment of the Decalogue, but it is enumerated also under the *judicial laws,* and marked with the punishment of death, not only because it was a high handed moral offence, but also a crime against the state. Under the theocracy, as we have before remarked, God was the national king of Israel, and idolatry being the virtual acknowledgment of an- other sovereign, was of course, to be ac- counted as nothing less than downright rebellion or treason against the supreme authority. Sacrificing, being the princi- pal act of religious worship among the heathen, is selected as the *overt* act of idolatry, which constituted the capital offence ; although under this name are doubtless included the various idolatrous services specified in the parallel law, Deut. 17. 2—5.——¶ *Shall be utterly des- troyed.* Heb. יחרם *yohoram, anathema- trzed,* i. e. destroyed as execrable and ac- cursed, put to death without mercy, as the original חרם *herem, a devoted thing, an anathema,* implies. Gr. εξολοθρευ- θησεται, *shall be destroyed.* Chal. 'Shall be killed.' Targ. Jon. 'Shall be killed with the sword and his goods consumed.' This law, however, is understood by the Hebrew canonists of a knowing and wilful idolater, such an one as is de-

any god, save unto the LORD only,
ne shall be utterly destroyed.

21 ¶ ʳ Thou shalt neither vex a
stranger, nor oppress him : for
ye were strangers in the land of
Egypt.

22 ¶ ˢ Ye shall not afflict any
widow, or fatherless child.

ʳ ch. 23. 9. Lev. 19. 33. & 25. 35. Deut. 10.
19. Jer. 7. 6. Zech. 7. 10. Mal. 3. 5. ˢ Deut.
10. 18. & 24. 17. & 27. 19. Ps. 94. 6. Isai. 1.
17, 23. & 10. 2. Ezek. 22. 7. Zech. 7. 10.
James 1. 27.

23 If thou afflict them in any wise,
and they ᵗ cry at all unto me, I will
surely ᵘ hear their cry ;

24 And my ˣ wrath shall wax
hot, and I will kill you with the
sword ; and ʸ your wives shall be
widows, and your children fatherless.

ᵗ Deut. 15. 9. & 24. 15. Job 35. 9. Luke
18. 7. ᵘ ver. 23. Job 34. 28. Ps. 18. 6. &
145. 19. James 5. 4. ˣ Job 31. 23. Ps. 69.
24. ʸ Ps. 109. 9. Lam. 5. 3.

---

scribed Num. 15. 27, 30, as sinning
'with a high hand.' They thus speak of
it ; 'Whoso serveth idols willingly and
presumptuously, he is exposed to cutting off (i. e. by the secret stroke of
God); and if there be witnesses that
have seen him, he is to be stoned to
death. But if he have served them ignorantly, he is to bring the sin-offering
appointed therefor.'

*Law respecting the Treatment of the
Stranger, the Widow, and the Fatherless.*

21. *Thou shalt neither vex a stranger,
nor,* &c. Heb. תּוֹנֶה *toneh, afflict, distress.* The distinction made by the
Jewish critics between ' vex' and ' oppress' is, that the former refers to up-
braiding and opprobrious *words,* while
the latter points to injurious, oppressive, and cruel *actions,* more especially
in matters of traffic and other business transactions. By ' stranger,' here
is not meant a transient passenger
through the territories of the Israelites,
but a permanent sojourner ; though not
an owner of land. That such foreign
residents dwelt among the chosen people is evident from numerous passages,
and as the somewhat exclusive genius
of the Hebrew polity might tend to subject them to vexatious or humiliating
treatment, God saw fit to protect them
by several different statutes. Accordingly we frequently find them conjoined
with other classes of mankind that are
specially entitled to compassion, as the

poor, the *widow,* and the *orphan.* It
was in fact an object of heaven to allure
strangers by kind usage to live among
the Israelites, provided they did not
practice idolatry or violate the laws ;
and in order that they might be induced
to think favorably of the true religion
and at length to embrace it, they were
to be exempted from any such harsh or
harrassing treatment as would tend to
harden their minds in prejudice or drive
them back among idolaters. The duty
of thus behaving kindly to strangers
is enforced by reminding the Israelites
of their having been themselves once
'strangers, and nothing is plainer than
that our own experience of privation and distress should school us to
a lively sympathy with the like suffering of our fellow-creatures. The oppression of strangers may well be termed ' an Egyptian sin, deserving of Egyptian plagues.'

22—24. *Ye shall not afflict any widow,*
&c. In these verses the humane and
compassionate spirit of the Mosaic law
shines very conspicuous. Jehovah here
avows himself the husband of the widow
and the father of the orphan. He virtually says of himself, what is emphatically affirmed by the Psalmist, Ps. 68.
5, 'A father of the fatherless and a
judge of the widow, is God in his holy
habitation.' In thus forbidding his people to afflict widows and orphans he
does in fact enjoin it upon them to comfort and assist them, and to be ready on
all occasions to show them kindness.

25 ¶ ᶻ If thou lend money to *any*

ᶻ Lev. 25. 35, 36, 37. Deut. 23. 19, 20. Neh
5. 7   Ps. 15. 5.   Ezek. 18. 8, 17.

Being deprived in the providence of
God of their natural guardians, and being themselves unversed in business, and
of a timorous and tender spirit, their
destitute condition laid them peculiarly
open to the deceitful arts, impositions,
and oppression of unprincipled men.
And although no one could take an unrighteous advantage of these circumstances without doing violence to some
of the strongest instinctive impulses in
his own breast, yet God is pleased by
this law to give additional force to the
native sentiments of compassion and
kindness which might be supposed to
operate in favor of the friendless and
fatherless. He declares that their case
shall come under his particular çog-
nizance. If any hardship is put upon
them from which a husband and a father
would have sheltered them, he will interpose and act the part of a vindicator
and protector. Having no one else to
complain and appeal to, if they cry unto
him he will assuredly hear and avenge
them. If men will not pity them, he
will. And this no doubt accounts for
the fact that no particular penalty is
prescribed for the violation of this statute. God himself undertakes to avenge
their cause by the retributions of his
providence; and nothing could more
impressively show the divine abhorrence
of the sin. It was no common sin, and
therefore was to be punished in no common way. The equity of the sentence
denounced is too obvious to be overlooked. The oppressors of widows and
orphans shall be punished in kind; *their*
wives shall become widows, and their
children fatherless. And even at the
present day the judgments of heaven
upon this class of men are strikingly
analogous to what is here threatened.
Those whom God makes his especial

of my people *that is* poor by thee,
thou shalt not be to him as an
usurer, neither shalt thou lay upon
him usury.

charge can never be injured or assailed
with impunity. Let the parallel monition therefore of the wise man be
reverently regarded, Prov. 23. 10, 11,
'Remove not the old landmark; and
enter not into the fields of the fatherless; for their Redeemer is mighty; he
shall plead their cause with thee.'

Law respecting Usury and Pledge.

25. *If thou lend money* to any of *my
people* that is *poor by thee.* Rather,
according to the letter of the original,
'If thou lend money to my people, *even*
to a poor man with thee.' The Israelites were a people but little engaged in
commerce, and therefore could not in
general be supposed to borrow money
but from sheer necessity; and of that
necessity the lender was not to take advantage by usurious exactions. The law
is not to be understood as a prohibition
of *interest* at any rate whatever, but of
excessive interest or *usury.* The clause,
'Thou shalt not be to him as an usurer,'
is equivalent to saying, 'Thou shalt not
domineer and lord it over him rigorous
ly and cruelly.' That this class of men
were peculiarly prone to be extortionate
and oppressive in their dealings with
debtors would seem to be implied by
the etymology of the original term for
usury (נשׁך *neshek*), which comes from
a root signifying *to bite;* and in Neh. 5.
2—5, we have a remarkable case of the
bitter and grinding effects resulting
from the exercise of the creditor's rights
over the debtor. A large portion of the
people had not only mortgaged their
lands, vineyards, and houses, but had
actually sold their sons and daughters
into bondage to satisfy the claims of
their grasping creditors. In this emergency Nehemiah espoused the cause of
the poor, and compelled the rich, against

26 [a] If thou at all take thy neighbour's raiment to pledge, thou shalt deliver it unto him by that the sun goeth down :

27 For that *is* his covering only,

[a] Deut. 24. 6, 10, 13, 17.　Job 22. 6. & 24. 3, 9.　Prov. 20. 16. & 22. 27.　Ezek. 18. 7, 16.　Amos 2. 8.

it *is* his raiment for his skin . wherein shall he sleep ? and it shall come to pass, when he [b] crieth unto me, that I will hear ; for I *am* [c] gracious.

[b] ver. 23.　[c] ch. 34. 6.　2 Chron. 30. 9.　Ps. 86. 15.

whom he called the people together, to remit the whole of their dues, and moreover exacted from them an oath that they would never afterwards press their poor brethren for the payment of those debts. This was not because every part of those proceedings had been contrary to the letter of the Mosaic law, but because it was a flagrant breach of equity under the circumstances. It was taking a cruel and barbarous advantage of the necessities of their brethren at which God was highly indignant, and which his servants properly rebuked. From this law the Hebrew canonists have gathered as a general rule, that ' whoso exacteth of a poor man, and knoweth that he hath not aught to pay him with, he transgresseth against this prohibition, Thou shalt not be to him as an exacting creditor.' (*Maimonides in Ainsworth*). We no where learn from the institutes delivered by Moses that the simple taking of interest, especially from the neighboring nations, Deut. 23. 19, 20, was forbidden to the Israelites, but the divine law would give no countenance to the griping and extortionate practices to which miserly money-lenders are always prone. The deserving and industrious poor might sometimes be reduced to such straits that pecuniary accommodations might be very desirable to them, and toward such God would inculcate a mild, kind, and forbearing spirit, and the precept is enforced by the relation which they sustained to him ; q. d., 'Remember that you are lending to *my* people, *my* poor, and therefore take no advantage of their necessities. Trust me against the fear

of loss, and treat them kindly and generously.'

26, 27. *If thou at all take thy neighbor's raiment to pledge,* &c. 'This passage, which describes a poor man as sleeping at night in his outer garment, exhibits one of the many unchanged customs of the East. The orientals generally, of whatever rank, do not undress at night. They merely throw off their outer and looser robes, unwind their turbans and vast waist-cloth, sleeping in their caps, shirt, drawers, waistcoat, and gown. The common people very often do not sleep at all in what we should call a bed. The details of their management of course depend much on the particular costume of the country ; but, speaking generally, a poor man is quite content to make his cloak and waist-cloth serve for a bed, lying on one of the two and covering himself with the other, or else making the cloak or the girdle alone serve all his purposes. A mat, rug, or piece of carpet is all he desires to render his bed more luxurious. These observations particularly apply to the Bedouin Arabs, although true also of other Asiatic countries, and is not peculiar to Asia, for, while travelling in Russia, we have often, on passing through towns and villages at night or early in the morning, seen great numbers of men lying about on the ground wrapped up in their sheepskin cloaks. The poor desert Arab, whose dress is little more than a shirt and a woollen mantle, is content to use the latter for his bed and bed-clothes when he has nothing better ;—drawing it over his head—for an Arab al-

28 ¶ ᵈ Thou shalt not revile the
ᵈ Eccles. 10. 20. Acts 23. 5. Jude 8.

gods, nor curse the ruler of thy
people.

ways covers his head whether he sleeps
by day or night—and gathering up his
feet, he sleeps with as much apparent
ease and comfort as on a down-bed, his
tough frame seeming quite unconscious
of the hardness of the ground and the
asperities of its surface. There is no
people of the East whose costume seems
to have remained with so little alteration from the most ancient times as
that of the inhabitants of the Arabian
deserts; or which is so susceptible of
being, in most cases, identified with the
dress worn by the ancient Jews. We
should therefore, perhaps, not be much
mistaken in considering the garment of
the text as nearly resembling the simple woollen mantle of the present Arabs.
It is nearly square, reaching from the
shoulders to the calf of the leg, or even
to the ancles, and about as wide as long.
A square sack, having in front a slit
from top to bottom, a hole at the top
for the neck, and a slit on each side for
the arms, would give a good idea of this
shapeless but useful article of dress.
Garments of the kind indicated are of
various qualities and texture. Some
are very light and fine, with embroidery in silk, silver, or gold, or gold on the
breast and between the shoulders; but
the common sort are coarse and heavy,
commonly with alternate stripes, a foot
wide, of blue and white, or brown and
white, but frequently all black or brown.
This robe, called an *abba*, is commonly
worn loosely on the shoulders, as the
Irish peasantry wear their great coats;
but when active exertion is required it
is either thrown aside, or is drawn close
around the body and fastened by a girdle, the arms being then necessarily
thrust through the arm-holes. This article of dress is certainly as indispensable to a poor Arab, as the garment of
the text could be to a poor Jew.' *Pict.
Bible.*——¶ *Thou shalt deliver it unto*

him by that the sun goeth down. But
it may be asked whether a formal law
would be framed in respect to articles
given in pledge but *for a single day?*
The implication undoubtedly is, that
the pledge was restored *for the night
only,* and was returned to the creditor *by day.* Here again the Hebrew
canons opportunely offer their deductions. 'When one takes a pledge of
his neighbor, if he be a poor man, and
his pledge be a thing that he hath need
of, it is commanded that he restore the
pledge at the time when he needeth it.
He is to restore him his bedding at
night, that he may sleep on it, and his
working-tools by day, that he may do
his work with them. If he do not restore the instruments of the day by
day, and the instruments of the night
by night, he transgresseth against the
prohibition, Thou shalt not sleep with
his pledge, Deut. 24. 12. (*Maimonides
in Ainsworth*).

*Law respecting the Contempt of
Authority.*

28. *Thou shalt not revile the gods.*
Heb. אֱלֹהִים *Elohim;* i. e. the judges,
rulers, magistrates. See Note on Ex.
21. 6. Thus Eccl. 10. 20, 'Curse not the
king; no, not in thy thought.' Yet it is
remarkable that both Philo and Josephus
understand this precept as prohibiting
the blaspheming or reviling of the gods
of the heathen. The former thinks that
the Deity should be to us an object of
such sacred veneration, that we ought
not even to blaspheme what is erroneously accounted divine; and that the
heathen would, out of zeal and by way
of rataliation, blaspheme the true God,
if he heard the Jew blaspheming his
gods. The latter, in detailing, in his
'Antiquities,' the laws of Moses, quotes
this as one of them; 'No man shall
blaspheme those that are accounted

gods by other cities; nor shall any man be guilty of sacrilege in strange sanctuaries, or purloin what is consecrated to a god;' and in his treatise against Apion, he has these words; 'The Jews adhere to the customs of their fathers without concerning themselves with those of strangers, or deriding them. Their legislator expressly prohibited them from deriding or blaspheming those whom others accounted gods, and that out of respect to the title *Gods*, which they love.' It may be admitted, perhaps, that there is nothing absolutely repugnant to our ideas of moral fitness in this sense of the passage, and yet there is very little reason to believe it the true sense; for the parallel clause, 'nor curse the ruler of thy people,' seems sufficiently to restrict and define the scope of the statute. But it is to be recollected that when Philo and Josephus wrote, the Jews were subjected to the Romans, a heathen people, and they would be apt, wherever it were possible, to put such a construction upon the precepts of their religion as would tend to procure for it the favorable regard of their masters, and prevent their deeming it intolerant. And there is no doubt something unreasonable and offensive in the thought of pouring contempt upon, or uttering blasphemy against, the gods and the religion, however false, of those under whose protection we live. But the laws given by Moses did not contemplate the chosen people in such a condition. They were not given to a nation subjected to foreign dominion, but to a free people, independent and isolated, among whom every approach to idolatry was strictly prohibited, and who were not required to *know* any but the true religion. And although we find no gratuitous disparaging or reviling of the gods of the heathen, yet when needs be we find Moses himself speaking contemptuously of them as *abominations* and *idols*, and in the prophets such language is of much more frequent occurrence. The

law in this place undoubtedly explains itself by the clause that follows, and a moment's reflection will convince us that the institution of magistracy cannot attain the ends for which it was designed, unless the persons of rulers be clothed with a degree of sanctity that shall shield them from popular reproach. One reason undoubtedly why the name of 'God' was applied to magistrates was, that the office might be *sanctified* in general estimation, and that the conscience of him who held the office might be duly influenced by the consideration, that he was in a sense acting as God's vicegerent and representing his person, authority, and attributes among men. Accordingly we find the apostle Paul distinctly recognising the obligation of this law even in respect to one who was in fact a most unrighteous persecutor, Acts, 23. 2—5, 'And the high priest Ananias commanded them that stood by him, to smite him on the mouth. Then said Paul unto him, God shall smite thee, thou whited wall: for sittest thou to judge me after the law, and commandest me to be smitten contrary to the law? And they that stood by, said, Revilest thou God's high priest? Then said Paul, I wist not, brethren, that he was the high priest: for it is written, Thou shalt not speak evil of the ruler of thy people.' It is observable that no penalty is annexed to the breach of this law, either because it was left to the discretion of the judges, or because it was one of those cases which distinguish this from all human codes, where God saw fit to express so much confidence in the moral sense implanted in the breasts of his creatures, as to appeal to that alone. He leaves the law in this and the ensuing verses in this chapter to their own binding force upon the consciences of those to whom they are addressed.—¶ *Nor curse.* Heb. תאר *taor*, which though usually rendered 'curse' is by Paul, Acts 23. 5, explained as equivalent to 'speak evil of.'

29 ¶ Thou shalt not delay *to offer* ● the first of thy ripe fruits, and of thy liquors: f the first-born of thy sons shalt thou give unto me.

30 g Likewise shalt thou do with thine oxen, *and* with thy sheep: h seven days it shall be with his dam; on the eighth day thou shalt give it me.

31 ¶ And ye shall be i holy men

e ch. 23. 16, 19. Prov. 3. 9. f ch. 13. 2, 12. & 34. 19. g Deut. 15. 19. h Lev. 22. 27. i ch. 19. 6. Lev. 19. 2. Deut. 14. 21.

unto me: k neither shall ye eat *any* flesh *that is* torn of beasts in the field; ye shall cast it to the dogs.

CHAPTER XXIII.

THOU a shalt not raise a false report: put not thine hand with the wicked to be an b unrighteous witness.

k Lev. 22. 8. Ezek. 4. 14. & 44. 31. a ver. 7. Lev. 19. 16. Ps. 15. 3. & 101. 5. Prov. 10. 18. See 2 Sam. 19. 27. with 16. 3. b ch. 20. 16. Deut. 19. 16, 17, 18. Ps. 35. 11. Prov. 19. 5, 9, 28. & 24. 28. See 1 Kings 21. 10, 13. Matt. 26. 59, 60, 61. Acts 6. 11, 13.

Law respecting Firstlings.

29. *Thou shalt not delay* to offer *the first*, &c. Heb. מְלֵאָתְךָ *melëatheka, thy fulness;* i. e. fruits of full maturity, ripe enough to be gathered. Gr. απαρχας αλωνος, *the first fruits of thy floor.* ——¶ *Of thy liquors.* Heb. דִּמְעֲךָ *dimaka, thy tear;* i. e. the first fruits of wine and oil, which when pressed, distil and drop as *tears.* The due observance of this law would be a general acknowledgement of the bounty and goodness of God, who had given them the early and latter rains and crowned the toils of agriculture with an ample harvest. This expression of gratitude was not to be *delayed,* for delay in rendering to God the first fruits would argue a secret unwillingness to yield him any.——¶ *The first-born of thy sons,* &c. See Note on Ex. 13. 2.

30. *Seven days it shall be with his dam.* This ordinance probably carries an allusion to the dedication of a human being to God by the rite of circumcision. As this was to take place on the eighth day, so no animal was to be presented before the eighth day from its birth. Indeed, before this the process of nutrition in a young animal can scarcely be considered as completely formed.

Law respecting Things not to be eaten.

31. *Ye shall be holy men unto me,* &c. Heb. אַנְשֵׁי קֹדֶשׁ *anshë kodesh,*

men of holiness; i. e. men separated and distinguished from others not only by inward principles, but by outward observances, among which this of abstinence from unclean meats is one. This was to be a mark of that honorable distinction which was to pertain to the chosen people, who were not to demean themselves to eat of the leavings of beasts of prey, especially as they would be apt to contain blood, which was forbidden, and might also have been torn to pieces by unclean or rabid animals. The words are perhaps to be considered moreover as carrying with them a latent intimation that the holiness of the people of God depends in great measure upon their obedience in small matters.

Chapter 23

Law respecting Slander.

1. *Thou shalt not raise a false report,* &c. Heb. לֹא תִשָּׂא שֵׁמַע שָׁוְא *lo tissa shema shav, thou shalt not take up (or receive) a hearing of vanity (or falsity).* The primary import of the original נָשָׂא *nasa,* is *to raise or lift up, to elevate;* but it occurs also in the sense of *taking, receiving, assuming.* Thus too the Gr. ου παραδεξη ακοην ματαιαν, *thou shalt not receive a vain hearsay.* Chal. ' Thou shalt not receive a false rumor.' The idea conveyed by the original term rendered 'false,' has a close affinity with that expressed by the word

2 ¶ ᶜ Thou shalt not follow a mul-

ᶜ Gen. 7. 1. & 19. 4, 7. ch. 32. 1, 2. Josh.
24. 15. 1 Sam. 15. 9. 1 Kings 19. 10. Job
31. 34. Prov. 1. 10, 11, 15. & 4. 14. Matt. 27.
24, 26. Mark 15. 15. Luke 23. 23. Acts 24.
27. & 25. 9.

'vain,' as is shown in the Note on Ex.
20. 16. And the prohibition comes obviously under that of the ninth commandment. The Hebrew word for
'raise,' is of sufficient latitude, in its
legitimate sense, to imply both the
origination and the *propagation* of a
false report. Targ. Jon. 'O my people,
ye sons of Israel, receive not lying
words from him who would calumniate
his neighbor before thee.' The precept
is no doubt of general application, equivalent to saying, Thou shalt have *nothing to do* with any false reports; yet it
seems designed to have special reference to *judicial proceedings*, where a
false report or accusation might do a
man the greatest injury. He who in-
vents a slander, and first *raises* a false
or vain report, and he who *receives* and
propagates it, are at all times very
criminal; but the iniquity is most atrocious when the calumny is advanced
and taken up in a court of justice. Yet
when we remember how many there
must have been acting in a judicial capacity amongst the Israelites, who had
judges of tens as well as of fifties and
hundreds; and when we consider also,
how generally in our own and other
Christian countries, men are occasionally called to sit as jurors, we shall
perceive how wide is its just application, and feel that no precept is of more
importance in regulating the private intercourse of individuals. 'The original
אשׂת לֹא *lo tissa* has been translated,
'thou shalt not publish.' Were there
no *publishers* of slander and calumny,
there would be no *receivers;* and were
there none to *receive* them there would
ᴅe none to *raise* them; and were there
no *raisers, receivers,* nor *propagators*
of calumnies, lies, &c., society would

titude to *do* evil; ᵈ neither shalt
thou speak in a cause to decline
after many to wrest *judgment:*

ᵈ ver. 6, 7. Lev. 19. 15. Deut. 1. 17. Ps.
72. 2.

---

be in peace.' *A. Clarke.* Prov. 17. 4,
' A wicked doer giveth heed to false
lips.'——¶ *Put not thine hand with the
wicked,* &c. Gr. ου συγκατασθησῃ, *thou
shalt not consent.* It is an allusion to
the act of joining hands as a sign of entering into a compact, or of cordially
uniting in the same enterprise; of which
the wise man, Proverbs, 11. 21, says,
'Though *hand join in hand,* the wicked
shall not be unpunished.' The primary
import of the precept probably is, 'Take
care that thou conspire not with a wicked man in his cause by giving witness
in his favor.' Vulg. 'Nec junges manum,
ut pro impio dicas falsum testimonium,'
*neither shalt thou join thine hand to say
false testimony for a wicked person.*
But like the foregoing it is of general
application.

Law requiring Impartiality in Judg-ment.

2. *Thou shalt not follow a multitude
to do evil.* Heb. רבים *rabbim, many.*
From the same root comes 'Rabbi,' *a
great man,* and some have thought the
more genuine sense of the clause to be,
'Follow not the great, the mighty, the
distinguished, to do evil,' in contradistinction from the 'poor' in the next
verse. The original word occurs in this
sense, Job, 35. 9, 'They cry out by reason of the *mighty* (רבים *rabbim*.)' We
suppose, however, that the two senses
of *multitude* and *magnitude* are both
included in the term, and that we are
taught by the passage that neither the
number, rank, nor power of those who
do evil should avail to make us follow
their example. We are to dare to be
singular, whatever it may cost, if it is
only thus that we can preserve our integrity. It is the example of the mul

3 ¶ Neither shalt thou countenance a poor man in his cause.

titude, keeping each other in countenance, that does so much for the general upholding of transgression. Did the current of public example set in the contrary direction, the *solitary* sinner would be universally shunned and detested.——¶ *Neither shalt thou speak in a cause,* &c. Heb. 'Neither shalt thou answer in a controversy to decline after many to pervert, or wrest (judgment).' The scope of the words is undoubtedly to enjoin it upon the chosen people not to be unduly influenced or carried away by the voice *of a majority* n pleading or deciding a judicial cause. They must not by any means allow themselves to be swayed or overruled by regard to the *Rabbins,* the *many,* or the *mighty,* to go against their consciences in giving judgment. They must at all events decide according to their honest convictions, and render an upright and impartial verdict. Chal. 'Neither shalt thou refrain from teaching that which thou seest to be meet in judgment.' Judges and juries especially were to guard against showing respect to the persons of their fellow-judges, as well as to those of the parties. They were not to suppose, as men are prone to do, that they could lose their own individual responsibility by merging it in the unanimous opinion of a majority. Accordingly Lyra remarks that it was decreed by the ancient Hebrews, that when the judges were numerous those of least weight and authority were required to give their sentence first, lest if they followed those of greater weight and influence, they might be unduly biassed by their verdict. This would probably not be amiss with those who needed an adventitious guaranty to the actings of sound moral principle, of whom there are no doubt too many in the world.

3. *Neither shalt thou countenance a*

4 ¶ e If thou meet thine enemy's

e Deut. 22. 1. Job 31. 29. Prov 24. 17. & 25. 21. Matt. 5. 44. Rom. 12. 20. 1 Thess. 5. 15.

poor man in his cause. Heb. לֹא דַל vedal lo tehdar, *and the poor man thou shalt not honor.* The term הדר *hadar,* has the sense of *beautifying, adorning,* and seems to refer to the arts of oratory and the sophistry of the law, by which the badness of a cause is varnished over. The word דַל *dal, attenuated, exhausted,* and here rendered *poor man,* is probably put in opposition to רבים *rabbim* in the preceding verse. If so, the meaning is, 'thou shalt neither be influenced by the *great* to make an unrighteous decision, nor by the poverty or distress of the *poor* to give thy voice against the dictates of justice and truth.' And thus the ancient paraphrasts; Chal. 'Thou shalt not pity the poor man in his judgment.' Targ. Jon 'And the poor who shall be brought into judgment thou shalt not compassionate ly respect, for there is to be no respect of persons in judgment.' Gr. και πενητα ουκ ελεησεις εν κρισει, *and the poor man thou shalt not compassionate in judgment.* In Lev. 19. 15, the like prohibition is given in regard to the rich, 'Thou shalt not respect the person of the poor, nor *honor* (תהדר *tehdar*) the person of the mighty.' In matters of right, right was always to be done, without regard to rank, character, or condition. In general there was no doubt more danger that the cause of justice would be bi assed and injury connived at in favor of the rich than of the poor, yet there might be such a thing as, under the pretence of charity or compassion, mak ing a man's poverty a shelter for his wrong-doing. This was by no means to be allowed. But on the other hand, the just rights of the poor against in fluences of an opposite character, are guarded by a special precept, v. 6.

Law inculcating Humanity.

4. *If thou meet thine enemy's ox or*

ox or his ass going astray, thou shalt surely bring it back to him again.

5 f If thou see the ass of him that hateth thee lying under his burden, and wouldest forbear to help

f Deut. 22. 4.

---

his ass going astray, &c. 'How much more his soul,' says Trapp. This precept is given with fuller details Deut. 22. 1—3, 'Thou shalt not see thy brother's ox or his sheep go astray, and hide thyself from them: thou shalt in any case bring them again unto thy brother. And if thy brother be not nigh unto thee, or if thou know him not, then thou shalt bring it unto thine own house, and it shall be with thee until thy brother seek after it, and thou shalt restore it to him again. In like manner shalt thou do with his ass; and so shalt thou do with his raiment; and with all lost things of thy brother's, which he hath lost, and thou hast found, shalt thou do likewise: thou mayest not hide thyself.' He who was in the former case termed an 'enemy' is here termed a brother,' thus teaching the Israelites that they were to regard all men, even their enemies, as brethren. This, we know, is in exact accordance with the teachings of the New Testament, and it shows very clearly that it was no more than the Pharisees' gloss, that 'they should love their friends and hate their enemies.'——¶ *Thou shalt surely bring it back.* Heb. הָשֵׁב תְּשִׁיבֶנּוּ *hashēb teshibēnu, returning thou shalt return it.*

5. *If thou see the ass of him that hateth thee,* &c. Heb. שֹׂנַאֲךָ *sonaaka, thy hater;* a different word from that standing for enemy, אֹיִבְךָ *oyibka,* in the preceding verse. The word here employed signifies *one that hates,* without implying that he is hated in return; but the other implies a *mutual enmity.* It is an easier matter to do a favor to the former than to the latter, but the design of introducing both terms is to intimate that both classes of *haters* were in this

---

him, thou shalt surely help with him.

6 g Thou shalt not wrest the judgment of thy poor in his cause.

g ver. 2. Deut. 27. 19. Job 31. 13, 21 Eccles. 5. 8. Isai. 10. 1, 2. Jer. 5. 28. & 7. 6. Amos 5. 12. Mal. 3. 5.

---

respect to be treated alike; that they were to show kindness as well where there was a reciprocal hatred, as where it was merely cherished on one side. —— ¶ *And wouldest forbear to help him,* &c. The original of this clause is, peculiarly obscure, and has given rise to a vast variety of renderings by different commentators. The original וְחָדַלְתָּ מֵעֲזֹב לוֹ עָזֹב תַּעֲזֹב עִמּוֹ *ve-hadalta maazob lo azob taazob immo,* literally signifies—'*thou shalt cease from leaving to him, thou shalt surely leave with him.*' The idea we take to be, that the man who should see his enemy's ass (or other animal) in this condition was to cease,—i. e. by no means to allow himself,—to leave the prostrated beast to his owner alone, but he was generously to go to his assistance, and not to desist but *with* the owner, when he had succeeded in raising him up, or had left him as past relief. This is perhaps the simplest construction, and it is confirmed by the parrallel passage Deut. 22. 4, ' Thou shalt not see thy brother's ass or his ox fall down by the way, and hide thyself from them: thou shalt surely help him to lift them up again.' Gr. 'Thou shalt not pass by the the same, but shalt raise up the same together with him.' Chal. 'Leaving thou shalt leave that which is in thy heart against him, and help up with him.' The scope of the precept is not only to inculcate mercy towards the brute creation, but also to engender kindly feelings among brethren. For what would tend more directly to win the heart of an alienated neighbor than such an act of well-timed benevolence ?

6. *Thou shalt not wrest the judgment of thy poor in his cause.* That is, of

7 ʰ Keep thee far from a false matter; ⁱ and the innocent and righteous slay thou not: for ᵏ I will not justify the wicked.

ʰ ver. 1. Lev. 19. 11. Luke 3. 14. Eph. 4. 25. ⁱ Deut. 27. 25. Ps. 94. 21. Prov. 17. 1**5**, 26. Jer. 7. 6. Matt. 27. 4. ᵏ ch. 34. 7. Rom. 1. 18.

thy poor neighbor (Deut. 27. 19), in whose cause thou shalt not pervert, but shalt strictly exercise, justice. Though there were cases in which there was danger lest compassion should unduly bias the course of equity in favor of a poor man, yet the instances would be far more numerous in which the magistrate would be tempted to neglect or pervert his cause, either to oblige a rich opponent, or to save trouble, or because he had not money to pay the requisite expenses. But the expression, '*thy* poor,' is supposed to be a counteractive to all such temptations : ' Remember they are *thy* poor, bone of thy bone, thy poor neighbors, thy poor brethren, and cast in providence as a special charge upon thy justice and charity.'

7. *Keep thee far from a false matter*, &c. This law seems intended as a kind of security for the due observance of the preceding. If they would guard against perversions of judgment, they must dread the thoughts of aiding or abetting a bad cause; they must have nothing to do with it; they must keep themselves at the greatest possible distance from it. And why? Because if they wilfully or incautiously hearkened to false testimony, or decided wrong in a case of life and death, they would be deemed the *murderers* of the innocent and the righteous. Indeed it may be said that God interprets as slaying the innocent and righteous that conduct which *tends* to such an issue. If then they would not *slay* with their own hands those who looked to them for justice, let them ' keep far from a false matter ;' for it might terminate in such

8 ¶ And ˡ thou shalt take no gift ; for the gift blindeth the wise, and perverteth the words of the righteous.

ˡ Deut. 16. 19. 1 Sam. 8. 3. & 12. 3. 2 Chron. 19. 7. Ps. 26. 10. Prov. 15. 27. & 17. 8, 23. & 29. 4. Isai. 1. 23. & 5. 23. & 33. 15. Ezek. 22. 12. Amos 5. 12. Acts 24. 26.

an issue as they dreamt not of, and the righteous God will not leave such wickedness to go unpunished. 'I will not justify the wicked ;' i. e. I will condemn him that unjustly condemns others. 'Cursed be he that perverteth the judgment of the stranger, fatherless, and widow. And all the people shall say, Amen.' Deut. 27. 19.

Law respecting Bribery.

8. *Thou shalt take no gift*, &c. The precepts we are now considering still have respect to the duties of those who are appointed guardians of justice. They are instructions to magistrates in the conduct of judicial cases. *They* were to keep themselves studiously free from every thing that would tend to warp or bias their judgment, or in any way mar the rectitude of their decisions. Gifts from a party to a judge are absolutely prohibited, even though not given on the condition of his pronouncing a favor· able verdict. For as human nature is constituted, *gifts* tend exceedingly to blind the understanding and to pervert the decisions of those who take them, and who would otherwise be disposed to follow equity in their sentences. The conduct of Sir Matthew Hale, when viewed by the light of this statute, is preeminently praiseworthy. Upon one of his circuits as judge, he refused to try the cause of a gentleman who had sent him the customary present of venison, until he had paid for it. He would not run the risque of suffering his feelings as a man to influence his decisions as a judge. It is worthy of note in this connexion, that in Deut. 27. 25, we find the connexion between the taking of

9 ¶ Also [m] thou shalt not oppress a stranger: for ye know the heart of a stranger, seeing ye were strangers in the land of Egypt.

10 And [n] six years thou shalt sow

thy land, and shalt gather in the fruits thereof:

11 But the seventh *year* thou shalt let it rest and lie still; that the poor of thy people may eat: and what they leave the beasts of the field shall eat. In like manner thou shalt deal with thy vineyard, *and* with thy oliveyard.

[m] ch. 22. 21. Deut. 10. 19. & 24. 14, 17. & 27. 19. Ps. 94. 6. Ezek. 22. 7. Mal. 3. 5.
[n] Lev. 25. 3, 4.

gifts and the murder of the innocent very distinctly recognized: 'Cursed be he that taketh reward to slay an innocent person.' This is an expressive commentary upon the tendency and effects of yielding to solicitations that come in the form of tempting bribes. On the contrary, how rich and emphatic the promises to those who keep themselves aloof from these abominations, Is. 33. 15, 16, 'He that walketh righteously, and speaketh uprightly; he that despiseth the gain of oppressions, that shaketh his hands from holding of bribes, that stoppeth his ears from hearing of blood, and shutteth his eyes from seeing evil; he shall dwell on high; his place of defence shall be the munitions of rocks: bread shall be given him; his waters shall be sure.'——¶ *The wise.* Heb. פקחים *pikhim, the open-eyed, the seeing.* The case of Samuel's sons, 1 Sam. 8. 1—3, affords an humiliating illustration of the effect ascribed to the conduct which is here condemned: 'And it came to pass, when Samuel was old, he made his sons judges over Israel. And his sons walked not in his ways, but turned aside after lucre, *and took bribes*, and perverted judgment.' In view of all this the wise man says, Prov. 17. 23, 'A wicked man taketh a gift out of the bosom to pervert the ways of judgment.'——¶ *Perverteth the words of the righteous.* That is, the sentence of those who are ordinarily accounted righteous, and who but for the corrupting influence of bribes would be righteous.

9. *Thou shalt not oppress a stranger.* This verse is little more than a partic-

ular application of the general precept, ch. 22. 21, introduced in this connexion in order to put the judges on their guard against the influence of prejudice in deciding causes in which foreigners were concerned. They were to be sure not to oppress them; for from their own experience of hardships and injustice in Egypt, they knew how strangers *felt* on such occasions.——¶ *Ye know the heart of a stranger.* Heb. נפש *nephesh, the soul;* the sentiments, the feelings. Knowing the griefs and afflictions of strangers, ye can the more easily put your souls into their soul's stead. Our trials and sorrows in this world go but little way towards accomplishing their true object if they do not train us to a deep sympathy with those who are called to drink of the same bitter cup.

Law respecting the Sabbatical Year.

10, 11. *Six years thou shalt sow thy land,* &c. We have here one of the most remarkable ordinances of the Jewish code. As every seventh day was to be a Sabbath, so every seventh year was to be a Sabbatical Year, and hence in the repetition of this law, Lev. 25. 4, it is called 'a Sabbath of Sabbatism to the land, a Sabbath to Jehovah.' During that year the corn-fields were neither sown nor reaped. The vines were unpruned, and there were no grapes gathered. Whatever grew spontaneously belonged alike to all, instead of being the property of any individual; and the poor, the bondman, the day-laborer, the stranger, the cattle that ranged the fields, and the very game, then left undisturbed, could assert an equal right to it. In short, during this year, the whole of Palestine continued a perfect common (Lev. 25. 1—8), and in order to render this law the more sacred, it was not only termed 'the year of the Sabbath,' its sabbatism or resting being declared holy to the Lord, but even the vines, as if under a vow, were called 'Nazarites' to which a knife must not be applied. Comp. Lev. 25. 5, with Num. 6. 5.

As to the reasons of an ordinance so remarkable, although we may perhaps admit that some regard was had to the physical benefits accruing to the soil from a periodical respite from culture for one year in seven, yet we cannot doubt that they were mostly of a *moral* nature, adapted and designed to promote the general ends of the economy to which the enactment belonged. As the Sabbath of the seventh year had the same reference as that of the seventh day to the creation of the world, it went to cherish all those pious and adoring sentiments which were awakened by the stated recurrence of the weekly day of rest. This septennial sabbatism reminded the Israelites not only of what they in common with the whole world, owed to the great and glorious Creator of the universe, but of their more especial obligations to him as their covenant God, who had made them the peculiar object of his care; and who was pleased miraculously to overrule the laws of nature in their behalf. It is scarcely possible to conceive of any more effectual mode of teaching them the duty of a continual simple-hearted reliance upon a kind and bountiful providence, than by the command to let the whole land lie fallow for one entire year, and to trust for subsistence to the provisions of that power which made the earth, and which could easily make the produce of the sixth year sufficient for the wants of the seventh or even the eighth. Were they ever tempted to cherish the slightest doubt or mis-

giving on this score, it was at once confuted by the express assurance of augmented plenty when it became requisite. Lev. 25. 20, 21, 'And if ye shall say, What shall we eat the seventh year? behold, we shall not sow nor gather in our increase: Then I will command my blessing upon you in the sixth year, and it shall bring forth fruit for three years.' This was a plain intimation that a miracle should attend the strict observation of the law in question. Had such an extraordinary increase immediately succeeded the fallow year, it might have been accounted for according to the course of nature. The land had had a respite, and would naturally bring forth with more vigor. But when after being exhausted by constant tillage for five years, it produced more instead of less on the sixth, what was this but the manifest proof of a direct intervention of Omnipotence, showing as with the light of the sun that a particular providence incessantly watched over them? And not only so; the ordinance taught them impressively upon what tenure they held their possessions. They would be forced to acknowledge God as the lord of the soil, and themselves as liege-subjects of the great Proprietor, upon whose bounty their well-being continually hung. Intimately connected with this was the lesson of humanity which they were hereby taught to the *poor*, the *enslaved*, the *stranger*, and the *cattle*. The appointment of the Sabbatical Year was a striking demonstration that all classes and conditions of men, and even the beasts of the field, were mercifully cared for by the Universal Father; and what violence must they do to every kindly sentiment, if they could evince a contrary spirit? Once in every seven years they might freely suspend all the labors of agriculture, and yet rest in perfect security of an ample supply for their wants; and what could more directly tend to work the conviction upon their

12 ° Six days thou shalt do thy work, and on the seventh day thou shalt rest : that thine ox and thine

° ch. 20. 8, 9.   Deut. 5. 13.   Luke 13. 14.

ass may rest, and the son of thy handmaid, and the stranger, may be refreshed.

minds that heaven had appointed them a higher destiny than to be always drudging in earthly toils ; that nothing would be lost by the prescribed intermission ; and that if God could, as we may say, *afford* to be thus munificent to them, they were bound to act on the like noble, liberal, and generous principles to their fellow-creatures ?

Another ordinance connected with the Sabbatical Year deserves our attention. On this year, during the feast of tabernacles, when all Israel came to appear before God the Law was to be ' read in their hearing, that they might learn, and fear the Lord their God, and observe to do all the words of this law ; and that their children which had not known any thing, might hear and learn to fear the Lord their God.' Deut. 31. 10—13. Thus once in every seven years the congregated nation had an opportunity to be instructed in the contents of the Law given by Moses ; and to render this ceremony more impressive, it is traditionally held that in after times the king in person was the reader. The season was the most eligible that could have been chosen. During this year the minds of the people were less occupied with worldly concerns than usual. They had neither to sow nor to reap. They were therefore peculiarly accessible to all the good influences connected with such an observance, and were prepared to look upon it as a striking type of heaven where all earthly labors, cares, and interests shall cease for ever.

Such was the institution of the Sabbatical Year, and such its effects in creating a sense of dependence in God, charity to man, and humanity to brutes. It was admirably adapted to be a test of the faith and obedience of the chosen people, and yet we are unhappily

obliged to record the fact, that *they did not stand the test.* Not only is there no express mention of the actual observance of the law in the historical books of the Old Testament, but in 2 Chron. 36. 21, that neglect of it is spoken of as one of the procuring causes of the seventy years captivity to which they were subjected, during which the land was to enjoy the number of Sabbaths of which it had been defrauded by the rebellion and unbelief of its inhabitants. In other words, the years of their captivity were to correspond with the number of the neglected Sabbatical years ; and as those were seventy, it would carry us back about 500 years to the close of Samuel's administration, when the observance began to go into disuse. Thus blindly and madly does depraved man war against his own interest in neglecting the salutary appointments of Heaven !

Law respecting the Sabbath day.

12. *Six days thou shalt do thy work,* &c. A repetition of the law of the fourth commandment concerning the weekly sabbath. The reason of its insertion in this connexion has divided the opinions of commentators. Some suppose it to be mainly with a view to its *civil ends,* viz. the rest and relaxation of servants and beasts, whereas in the fourth commandment, it is enjoined chiefly as a *branch of worship,* as a part of that *spiritual service* which is rendered directly to God. Others again, and we think with greater probability, suppose the design to be to guard against an erroneous inference, that might be drawn from the preceding ordinance. As the sabbatical year was a year of cessation from the ordinary labors of other years, so they might pos

13 And in all *things* that I have said unto you, ᵖ be circumspect:

ᵖ Deut. 4. 9. Josh. 22. 5 Ps. 39. 1. Eph. 5. 15. 1 Tim. 4. 16.

sibly take up the impression, that the ordinary observances of the Sabbath day were also to be suspended during that year; that it was, as it were, laid open in common with the other days of the week. But this would be a groundless and pernicious inference, and therefore the law of the Sabbath is expressly repeated, and the people reminded that the observance of that day was of perpetual and paramount obligation, and not in the slightest degree annulled by the occurrence of the Sabbatical Year. For though they might not during that year be engaged in the ordinary labors of agriculture, and the day might not be so emphatically a day of rest to them as usual, yet even during that time there were various minor occupations and cares which were to be regularly suspended as every seventh day returned.——¶ *May be refreshed.* Heb. רנפש *yinnaphesh, may be re-spirited,* or *new-souled,* from נפש *nephesh, soul;* i. e. may have a complete renewal both of bodily and spiritual health. Gr. αναψυξῃ, the same expression with that occurring Acts 3. 19, 'Repent ye, therefore, and be converted, that your sins may be blotted out when the times of *refreshing* (αναψυξεως, *re-souling*) shall come from the presence of the Lord.' The very frequent repetition of the law respecting the sabbath shows conclusively that the sanctification of that day was of great consequence in the sight of God, and that he had a special eye therein to its benign bearing physically both upon the welfare of man and beast. With this institution before us, we can no more ask the question, 'Doth God care for oxen?' So far from disregarding their well being, we find repeated provisions in his law breathing

and ᑫ make no mention of the name of other gods, neither let it be heard out of thy mouth.

ᑫ Numb. 32. 38. Deut. 12. 3. Josh. 23. 7. Ps. 16. 4. Hos. 2. 17. Zech. 13. 2.

a most tender and beneficent concern for the brute creation subjected to the uses of man. How different from the light in which they are practically regarded by multitudes of civilized and nominally Christian men! How many thousands of patient drudging cattle and noble horses, have no sabbath! They cannot remonstrate when called from their quiet stalls on the sabbath, and put to their exhausting week-day toils, but the barbarous privation of their authorized rest speaks loudly in the ears of their merciful Creator, and their meek endurance reaches one heart in the universe that is not insensible to the appeal. That heart has a hand to execute judgment adequate to the wrong done to a portion of his creatures which have a capacity to suffer, but none to complain.

Law enjoining caution against Idolatry.

13. *In all things — be circumspect.* Heb, תשמרו *tish-shameru, keep your selves.* It is a strict injunction of universal heedfulness in respect to every one of the divine precepts, but with more especial reference to those prohibiting idolatry in any of its forms; for to this sin Omniscience foresaw that they would be preeminently disposed and tempted.——¶ *Make no mention,* &c. Heb. לֹא תזכירו *lo tazkiru, ye shall not cause to be remembered.* They were to endeavor to blot out the remembrance of the gods of the heathen, and for this end their names were not to be heard from their mouths; or if mentioned at all, it must be only in a way of detestation. The Chal. terms these other gods 'idols of the peoples;' and God, by the prophet Zech. 13. 2, says, 'In that day I will cut off the

14 ¶ ʳ Three times thou shalt keep a feast unto me in the year.

15 ˢ Thou shalt keep the feast of unleavened bread : (thou shalt eat

ʳ ch. 34. 23. Lev. 23. 4. Deut. 16. 16. ˢ ch. 12. 15. & 13. 6. & 34. 18. Lev. 23. 6. Deut. 16. 8.

unleavened bread seven days, as I commanded thee, in the time appointed of the month Abib ; for in it thou camest out from Egypt • ᵗ and none shall appear before me empty :)

ᵗ ch. 34. 20. Deut. 16. 16.

names of the idols out of the land, and they shall no more be remembered.' And again, Hos. 2. 17, 'I will take away the names of Baalim out of her mouth, and they shall no more be remembered by their name.' It was in accordance with the spirit of this precept that the Israelites seem to have made a practice of 'changing the names' of idolatrous places, Num. 32. 38. And under a similar prompting David says, Ps. 16. 4, 'Their drink-offerings of blood will I not offer, nor take up their names into my lips.' In the intercourse of society, there is no more emphatical mode of indicating hatred towards a person than not mentioning his name, shrinking from even the remotest allusion to him, and striving, as far as possible, to forget even his existence. Thus would God have his people do in regard to the gods of the heathen. He says to them in effect of idolatry, as elsewhere, 'Thou shalt utterly detest it, and thou shalt utterly abhor it ; for it is a cursed thing.' The influence of a familiar acquaintance with the mythology of the ancient classics would no doubt be far more pernicious than it is, and more abhorrent to the spirit of this precept, were it not for the intrinsic absurdities of the system, and the overwhelming light of evidence which distinguishes Christianity. These are probably such as to counteract any serious injury which might otherwise result from one's being conversant with the names, characters, and alleged exploits of *Jupiter, Bacchus, Apollo, Mars, Venus,* and the other deities of Pantheon, of whom it seems to be essential to a liberal education to have some knowledge. The *practical*

evils on this score, we imagine, are a this day but slight.

Law respecting the three great Festivals.

14. **Three times thou shalt keep a** *feast,* &c. Heb. רגלים שלש *shalosh regalim, three feet;* i. e. three foot-journies. Gr. τρεις καιρους, *three times.* Chal. *id.* These three feasts were, (1.) The feast of the PASSOVER. (2.) Of PENTECOST. (3.) Of TABERNACLES ; each of which continued for a week. As we shall hereafter have occasion to consider these festivals separately in all their details, it will be sufficient at present to remark in general that this thrice-yearly concourse of all the males of Israel at the place of the sanctuary, was well calculated, (1) To counteract all the unsocial tendencies arising from their separation into distinct tribes, and to unite them among themselves as a nation of brethren. Were it not for some provision of this kind, local interest and jealousies would have been very apt to be engendered, which in process of time would probably have ripened into actual hostilities and collisions that would have broken their commonwealth to pieces. But by being frequently brought together, the acquaintances of tribes and families would be renewed, all feelings of clannish exclusiveness repressed, and the social union more effectually consolidated. (2) It was an ordinance well calculated to perpetuate the memory of the great events on which they were severally founded. As the weekly sabbath brought to remembrance the creation of the world, so did the Passover the departure

from Egypt; the Pentecost, the delivery of the Law; and the Feast of Tabernacles, the sojourning in the wilderness. Whatever of salutary religious influence was exerted by the celebration of these memorable events, it would obviously bear with most weight when it became the joint act of the whole assembled nation. Moreover, as the Law was read and instruction imparted on these occasions, the effect would naturally be, to render them faithful to their religion, and better disposed to carry out its principles in their lives and conversation. (3) Another important end which we may suppose to have been designed by these assemblages, was to afford to the people seasons of relaxation and recreation from their necessary toils. Although the weekly sabbath brought with it a welcome respite from labor, yet the Maker of our frame saw that something more than this was requisite for the highest well-being, corporeal and mental, of his creatures, and therefore ordained certain seasons of innocent hilarity in connexion with those religious observances which would tend to keep them within proper limits. It is observable, therefore, that the expression, ' rejoicing before the Lord,' is of frequent occurrence in speaking of those festive conventions which brought the Hebrews together from time to time during the year; and it is no doubt desirable that the precepts of Christianity should be so construed as to lay no chilling interdict upon those harmless amusements which the constitution of our nature seems to render occasionally requisite.

It might seem at first view that there was signal impolicy in leaving the land defenceless, while all the adult male population were congregated at a distance from their families and homes. Humanly speaking, it is indeed surprising that the hostile nations on their borders did not take advantage of their exposedness. For the matter was no secret; it was publicly known that at three set times every year they were commanded to be at Jerusalem, and that at three set times every year they actually attended. Why then were not inroads made at these seasons, to slay the old men, women, and children, to burn their cities, and carry off the spoil? How shall we account for the enmity of their foes being asleep at these particular times, when the land was defenceless; and perfectly awake at every other season, when they were at home, and ready to oppose them? Unless the Scriptures had given a solution, the matter would have been deemed inexplicable; but from this source we learn that the same Being who appointed those feasts guaranteed the security of the land while they were attending them. For thus runs the promise in Exodus 34. 23, 24, 'Thrice in the year shall all your men-children appear before the Lord God, the God of Israel. For I will cast out the nations before thee, and enlarge thy borders: neither shall any man desire thy land, when thou shalt go up to appear before the Lord thy God, thrice in the year.' Can any thing afford us a more striking instance of a particular providence? He is a wall of fire about his people as well as the glory in the midst of them. The hearts of all men are in his hands. He maketh the wrath of man to praise him and the remainder of that wrath, which will not praise him, he restraineth. During the whole period between Moses and Christ, we never read of an enemy invading the land at the time of the three festivals; the first that occurs was thirty-three years after they had withdrawn from themselves the divine protection, by embruing their hands in the Savior's blood, when Cestius the Roman general slew fifty of the people of Lydda, while all the rest were gone up to the Feast of Tabernacles, A.D. 66.

Again it is asked, how such vast multitudes could find provisions and accom-

16 ^u And the feast of harvest, the first-fruits of thy labours, which thou hast sown in the field: and ^x the feast of ingathering, *which is* in the end of the year, when thou hast gathered in thy labours out of the field.

^u ch. 34. 22. Lev. 23. 10. ^x Deut. 16. 13.

modation in the town where they congregated. The best answer will be found by a reference to the existing practice of the Mohammedans who annually repair to Mecca. The account is derived from our countryman Pitt, who was there towards the end of the seventeenth century, but the statement in its general features is equally applicable at present. After describing Mecca as a mean and inconsiderable town, he observes that four caravans arrive there every year, with great numbers of people in each. The Mohammedans say that not fewer than 70,000 persons meet at Mecca on such occasions; and although he did not think the number, when he was there, so large as this, it was still very great. Now the question recurs, how this vast multitude could find food and accommodation at so small and poor a place as Mecca? The following, from our author, is a sufficient answer:—'As for house-room, the inhabitants do straiten themselves very much, in order at this time to make their market. As for such as come last after the town is filled, they pitch their tents without the town, and there abide until they remove towards home. As for provision, they all bring sufficient with them, except it be of flesh, which they may have at Mecca; but all other provisions, as butter, honey, oil, olives, rice, biscuit, &c., they bring with them as much as will last through the wilderness, forward and backward, as well as the time they stay at Mecca; and so for their camels they bring store of provender, &c. with them.' Ali Bey confirms this account. He says, indeed, that the pilgrims often bring to Mecca rather more food than they are likely to need, and when there, they compute how much they shall want during their stay and on their return, and, reserving that, sell the remainder to great advantage. He adds, 'Every *hadji* (pilgrim) carries his provisions, water, bedding, &c. with him, and usually three or four diet together, and sometimes discharge a poor man's expenses the whole journey for his attendance upon them.' These facts no doubt apply, in a great extent, to the solution of the apparent difficulty as to the management of the Hebrews in their three annual meetings at the Tabernacle or the Temple. It will also be recollected that Jerusalem was a much larger city than Mecca, and situated in an incomparably more fertile district.

We have only farther to add, that the three great Festivals were honored with three remarkable events in the Scripture history. The feast of Tabernacles was the time when the Savior was born, and also the time when, in his thirtieth year, he was baptized. The Passover was the time when he was crucified; and the Pentecost the time when the Holy Ghost descended in a visible manner upon the apostles.

16. *The feast of harvest.* When they offered two loaves of first-fruits, Lev. 23, 17, called in Ex. 34. 22, 'the feast of weeks (or sevens'), because it was seven weeks or forty-nine days from the feast of unleavened bread, and occurring on the fiftieth day, was thence called the Pentecost, a Greek word signifying *fifty*. This was properly the *harvest* festival, in which they were to offer thanksgiving to God for the bounties of the harvest, and to present unto him the first fruits thereof in bread baked of the new corn (wheat), Lev. 23. 14—21. Num. 28. 26—31. As the period of this festival coincided with

17 y Three times in the year all thy males shall appear before the LORD God.

y cn. 34. 23. Deut. 16. 16.

that of the giving of the Law from Mount Sinai, which was fifty days after the Passover, it is usually spoken of as commemorative of that event, just as the feast of the Tabernacles is of their dwelling in tents for forty years during their sojourn in the wilderness.—— ¶ *The feast of ingathering.* Called also the 'Feast of Tabernacles,' Lev. 23. 34. Deut. 16. 13. This was the festival of gratitude for the *fruitage and vintage,* commencing on the evening of the fourteenth day of the seventh month, or October, called here ' the end of the year.' It continued seven whole days until the twenty-first, and then received the addition of the eighth day, which had probably in ancient times been the *wine-press feast* of the Israelites. During these eight days the Israelites dwelt in booths, formed of green branches interwoven together, which in the warm region of Palestine answered extremely well, as in October the weather is usually dry.—It may be remarked in regard to all these festivals, that the original term by which the appointment is expressed is חָגַג *tahag,* from חָגַג *hagag,* which signifies *to go round in a circle,* and thence in its religious application *to move round in circular dances.* As this was no doubt in early ages one of the leading features of their religious festivals, the term came in process of time to signify in a general way the *celebration of a religious feast or solemnity.* See Note on Ex. 5. 1. The idea, however, is prominent that these were to be seasons of joy and rejoicing; that a sanctified hilarity was to be regarded as a part of the duty connected with these festive seasons. The fact affords us an abundant vindication of the Mosaic system from the charge of sullen gloom and

18 z Thou shalt not offer the blood of my sacrifice with leavened

z ch. 12. 8. & 34. 25. Lev. 2. 11. Deut. 16. 4.

cheerless austerity in its rites and services.

17. *Shall appear before the Lord God.* Heb. אֶל פְּנֵי הָאָדֹן יְהֹוָה *el penë ha-Adon Yehovah, to the face of the Lord Jehovah.* This is, before the symbol of the manifested presence of Jehovah, which permanently abode on the ark and in the temple. We are still to give prominence to the idea of a *visible* exhibition which the Israelites were to regard as representing the presence of the Deity. The expression, we have no doubt, has special allusion to the ark of the covenant surmounted by the luminous cloud of glory; and though the common Israelites were not indeed permitted to go into the Holy of Holies, yet they were to offer and to worship *towards* (אֶל *el*) the sanctuary where the sacred symbols were fixed. Chal. 'All thy males shall appear before the Lord, the master or ruler of the world.' Sam. 'Before the ark of the Lord.' Arab. 'In the sanctuary of the Lord God.' This version is somewhat remarkable when viewed in connexion with Josh. 3. 11, where, as appears from our Note on that passage, the epithet, ' Lord of the whole earth,' is expressly applied to the Ark of the Covenant.

Law regulating the Offerings at the three great Feasts.

18. *Thou shalt not offer the blood,* &c. That is, the blood of the paschal lamb, called by way of emphasis the ' sacrifice.' Chal. 'Of my passover.'—— ¶ *With leavened bread.* That is, having leavened bread upon thy premises or in thy possession. All leaven was to be previously purged out, according to the statute, Ex. 12. 15, et inf.—— ¶ *Neither shall the fat of any sacrifice remain,* &c. Heb. חַגִּי *haggi, my festi-*

bread: neither shall the fat of my sacrifice remain until the morning.

19 ᵃ The first of the first-fruits of thy land thou shalt bring into the house of the LORD thy God. ᵇ Thou shalt not seethe a kid in his mother's milk.

20 ¶ᶜ Behold, I send an Angel be-

ᵃ ch. 22. 29. & 34. 26. Lev. 23. 10, 17. Numb. 18. 12, 13. Deut. 26. 10. Neh. 10. 35. ᵇ ch. 34. 26. Deut. 14. 21. ᶜ ch. 14. 19. & 32. 34. & 33. 2, 14. Numb. 20. 16. Josh. 5. 13. & 6. 2. Ps. 91. 11. Isai. 63. 9.

fore thee, to keep thee in the way, and to bring thee into the place which I have prepared.

21 Beware of him, and obey his voice, ᵈ provoke him not; for he will ᵉ not pardon your transgressions: for ᶠ my name *is* in him.

ᵈ Numb. 14. 11. Ps. 78. 40, 56. Eph. 4. 30. Hebr. 3. 10, 16. ᵉ ch. 32. 34. Numb. 14. 35. Deut. 18. 19. Josh. 24. 19. Jer. 5. 7. Hebr. 3. 11. 1 John 5. 16. ᶠ Isai. 9. 6. Jer. 23. 6. John 10. 30, 38.

val; a different word from that rendered *sacrifice* (זבח *zebah*) in the preceding clause. Yet there is no doubt that it refers to the sacrifice of the passover as the parallel passage Ex. 34. 26, has expressly, 'Thou shalt not offer the blood of my sacrifice with leaven, neither shall *the sacrifice of the feast of the passover* be left until the morning.' The fat was forbidden to remain till morning, because it was liable to corrupt and become offensive, which was very unseemly for any part of the sacred offerings. See Note on Ex. 12. 10. The *fat* was in all animal offerings accounted the choicest and most important part, and that which was preeminently devoted to God; and therefore it was required that it should be immediately consumed without any reservation. This was especially true of the fat of the paschal lamb.

19. *Thou shalt not seethe a kid in his mother's milk.* The original word for *seethe* signifies *to cook or dress by the fire, whether by boiling, roasting, or baking.* The true import of the precept is somewhat doubtful. Most commentators take it as prohibiting some kind of superstitious custom practised by the neighboring heathen, a species of magical incantation, by which they thought to secure a plentiful harvest. But perhaps the most probable interpretation of this statute is, that it forbids the killing and cooking of a kid or lamb while it was *on* its mother's milk; i. e. during the period necessary for its own

nutrition and the ease of its dam; as it is well known that all females for some time after parturition are generally oppressed with their milk. The mode of cooking alluded to in this passage, is not, it appears, wholly unknown among the Orientals at the present day. 'We alighted at the tent of the sheikh, or chief, by whom we were well received, and invited to take shelter with him for the night. Immediately after our halting a meal was prepared for us; the principal dish of which was *a young kid seethed in milk.*' *Buckingham.*

Promise of a Tutelary Angel.

20, 21. *Behold, I send an Angel before thee,* &c. Heb. הנה אנכי שלח מלאך לפניך *hinneh anoki sholah malak lepanëka,* behold me sending an angel before thee; i. e. about to send. See Note on Gen. 6. 13, 17. The reader is referred to the note on 'the Pillar of Cloud,' p. 164, for an expansion of our views on the import of the word 'Angel' in this connexion. We have there, if we mistake not, adduced satisfactory reasons for believing that the Angel here mentioned was the Shekinah, which was identical with the Pillar of Cloud, that guided the march of the children of Israel through the desert. According to this view, the *sensible phenomenon,* and not any unseen agent, whether divine or angelic, is what is primarily to be understood by the 'Angel.' This sublime and awful object they were re-

22 But if thou shalt indeed obey his voice, and do all that I speak; then g I will be an enemy unto thine enemies, and an adversary unto thine adversaries.

g Gen. 12. 3. Deut. 30. 7. Jer. 30. 20.

23 h For mine Angel shall go before thee, and i bring thee in unto the Amorites, and the Hittites, and the Perizzites, and the Canaanites, *and* the Hivites, and the Jebusites; and I will cut them off.

h ver. 20. ch. 33. 2. i Josh. 24. 8, 11.

quired to consider as the visible representative of Jehovah himself and to demean themselves towards it as obediently and reverentially as if it had been a living, intelligent, personal witness both of their outward actions and their inward thoughts, which we may not improperly say that it was, inasmuch as the Most High was pleased to *associate* his attributes of omniscience and omnipotence with it. All the language employed is such as to warrant this view of the subject. They were to beware of it, to obey its voice, to provoke it not, and that under the fearful sanction that an opposite conduct could not be evinced with impunity; that it would be sure to meet with condign punishment. Of this the grand assurance was contained in the declaration, 'My name is in him,' or rather according to the original (בקרבו *bekirbo*), *my name is in the midst of him, or it.* It is well known to the Hebrew scholar that the proper expression for *being in a person* is בו *bo, in him;* but here we find a phraseology strictly appropriate to *being within,* or in the *central parts of any gross, inanimate mass of matter.* We cannot but understand it therefore as carrying the implication that the name; i. e. the attributes—the intelligence, the power, the majesty, the glory of the Godhead—were to be considered as being mysteriously united with and abiding in the overshadowing and guiding Cloud. Arab. 'My name is with him.' Chal. 'His word is in my name;' i. e. he is clothed with my authority. Syr. and Gr. 'My name is upon him.' As we have before endeavored to show that the remarkable symbol of the

Cloudy Pillar was a preintimation of Christ's appearing in flesh, we see how naturally the apostle's words, 1 Cor. 10. 9, harmonize with this interpretation; 'Neither let us tempt Christ as some of them also tempted, and were destroyed of serpents.' By tempting the Angel that served to them as the *anticipative shadow* of Christ, they may be said to have tempted Christ himself, as nothing is more usual in the Scriptures than to apply to the *type* or *figure* the language which belongs to the *substance.* It is as proper to recognize Christ in the Angel of the Covenant before his incarnation, as it is to recognize him in 'the Lamb slain from the foundation of the world.'

22. *But if thou shalt indeed obey his voice,* &c.—*then I will be,* &c. Here the divine speaker seems imperceptibly to glide into the person of the promised Angel of whom he speaks. In the next verse the person is again changed, and he speaks as before. It is to be borne in mind that Moses was at this time on the summit of the mount, holding communion with God in the Shekinah; but we perceive nothing in this fact that militates with the view advanced above. The very *appearance* that rested upon Mount Sinai and now conversed with Moses, might be modified into the Pillar of Cloud and in that form denominated the emissary Angel that was to conduct the people on their journey to Canaan.

23. *For mine Angel shall go before thee—and I will cut them off.* Here again is another interchange of persons, similar to that above mentioned, and such as cannot fail to be frequently noticed by the attentive reader of the Scriptures.

24 Thou shalt not k bow down to their gods, nor serve them, l nor do after their works : m but thou shalt utterly overthrow them, and quite break down their images.

k ch. 20. 5. l Lev. 18. 3. Deut. 12. 30, 31. m ch. 34. 13. Numb. 33. 52. Deut. 7. 5, 25. & 12. 3.

It does not appear that the Jehovah of the Jews was a *different* being from him who is here and elsewhere termed 'the Angel.' Indeed the original phrase, מלאך יהוה *malak Yehovah*, may quite as properly be rendered 'Angel Jehovah,' as 'Angel of Jehovah,' or 'Angel of the Lord,' which is equivalent.

Idolatry to be avoided and abolished.

24. *Thou shalt not bow down to their gods.* Heb. לא תשתחוה *lo tishtahaveh*, properly signifying 'bow down,' though for the most part rendered ' worship,' and used to express, in a general way, all the various external acts and ser- vices of religious adoration. See Note on Gen. 18. 2—¶ *Nor serve them.* Heb. תעבדם *taŏbdëm*. That is, shall not pray to them, praise them, nor so conduct to- wards them as to declare thyself bound, devoted, or dedicated to them. Gr. μη λατρευσεις αυτοις, *shalt not perform ser- vice to them.* But in v. 33, the same term תעבד *taabod* is rendered in the Greek by δουλευσης, from which it would appear that the Septuagint versionists used the terms δουλευω and λατρευω, in reference to religious worship, sy- nonymously.——¶ *Nor do after their works.* It would seem from the con- struction, that the most natural antece- dent to 'their' is 'gods,' in which case the meaning is, that the Israelites were not to do after the works *which the service of the heathen gods required,* which naturally flowed out of their worship, and were incorporated with it. But Ainsworth understands ' their' as having reference to the *idolatrous wor- shippers,* and this may be admitted

25 And ye shall n serve the LORD your God, and o he shall bless thy bread, and thy water; and p I wil. take sickness away from the midst of thee.

n Deut. 6. 13. & 10. 12, 20. & 11. 13, 14. & 13. 4. Josh. 22. 5. & 24. 14, 15, 21, 24. 1 Sam. 7. 3. & 12. 20, 24. Matt. 4. 10. o Deut. 7. 13. & 28. 5. 8. p ch. 15. 26. Deut. 7. 15.

without doing any violence to the text, though we think the other sense most correct.——¶ *Thou shalt utterly over- throw them.* Here the pronoun 'them' refers to the gods, and not to the peo- ple their worshippers; which confirms the construction given above. The *sub- ject* seems to be the same throughout the verse, viz. the idol deities of the Canaanites. The idol worshippers were indeed to be destroyed, but that is not the immediate topic treated of in this verse. The divine Speaker is here com- manding the total excision of all the memorials of that vile idolatry, which would be likely to seduce his people from their allegiance to him. It was enjoining upon them the same spirit with that which afterwards prompted the convicted conjurors to ' burn their books,' Acts, 19. 19.

Farther Precepts and Promises.

25. *And ye shall serve the Lord your God.* Nothing can be more reasonable than the conditions which Jehovah im- poses upon his people—that they should serve their own God, who was indeed the only true God, and have nothing to do with the gods of the devoted nations, which were no gods, and which they had no reason to respect. In doing this they would not only be acting the part of sound reason, but would assure them- selves also of the special tokens of the divine blessing. They would be secure of the enjoyment of all desirable tem- poral prosperity. The blessing of God would crown their bread and their wa- ter, and make that simple fare more re- freshing and nutritive than the richest

26 ¶ q There shall nothing cast their young, nor be barren, in thy land: the number of thy days I will r fulfil.

27 I will send s my fear before

q Deut. 7. 14. & 28. 4. Job 21. 10. Mal. 3. 10, 11. r Gen. 25. 8. & 35. 29. 1 Chron. 23. 1. Job 5. 26. & 42. 17. Ps. 55. 23. & 90. 10. s Gen. 35. 5. ch. 15. 14, 16. Deut. 2. 25. & 11. 25. Josh. 2. 9, 11. 1 Sam. 14 .15. 2 Chron. 14. 14.

dainties without it, while wasting sickness, with its fearful train of evils, should be effectually banished from their borders.

26. *The number of thy days,* &c. That is, thou shalt not be prematurely cut off before reaching that good old age, which in the ordinary course of things thou mayest expect to attain. This is the blessing of the righteous, as is said of Job, ch. 42. 17, ' So Job died, being old, and *full of days,*' whereas 'the wicked live not half their days,' Ps. 55. 23.

27. *I will send my fear before thee.* Will strike a panic terror into the inhabitants of Canaan before thine arrival, which shall facilitate the subsequent conquests. The words of the historian Josh. 2. 9, 11, show how precisely this threatening was fulfilled. ──¶ *Will destroy all the people to whom thou shalt come.* Heb. המתי *hammothi.* But if they were previously destroyed, how could the Israelites come to them? It is evident that our translation has followed the Vulg. which has ' occidam,' *I will slay,* as if the original were the Hiph. conjug. of מות *muth, to die—to cause to die, to kill.* But the pointing on this supposition is not normal, and there is little reason to doubt that the root of the verb is not מות *to die,* but המם *to terrify, confound, discomfit,* correctly rendered by the Gr. εκστησω, *I will strike with dismay.* So also the Arab. 'I will make them astonished.' Chal. 'I will put in disorder.' In Cranmer's Bible it is

thee, and will t destroy all the people to whom thou shalt come, and I will make all thine enemies turn their backs unto thee.

28 And u I will send hornets before thee, which shall drive out the Hivite, the Canaanite, and the Hittite from before thee.

t Deut, 7. 23. u Deut. 7. 20. Josh. 24. 12.

rendered ' I will trouble,' a much better version than the present, for the context shows that the word cannot here mean to *destroy,* but to *trouble, intimidate, dismay,* so as to make them *turn their backs* to the Israelites. It is intensive of the former clause, denoting the consternation into which they should be thrown, and their consequently becoming an easy prey to their enemies.──¶ *Make all thine enemies turn their backs to thee.* Heb. ערף *oreph, neck.* In like manner Ps. 18. 40, 'Thou hast also given me the *necks* of mine enemies, that I might destroy them that hate me.'

28. *I will send hornets before thee.* Heb. את הצרעה *eth hatz-tzirah, the hornet;* collect. sing. like 'locusts,' Ex. 10. 4, for 'the locust.' The same thing is equally explicitly said, Deut. 7. 20, 'Moreover, the Lord thy God will send the *hornet* among them, &c.' As we are not expressly informed elsewhere that this annunciation was literally fulfilled, several interpreters have inferred that it is a mere metaphorical expression for enemies armed with weapons, as hornets are with stings. Bochart, however, and others, maintain that the prediction was literally accomplished, and this interpretation is said to be confirmed by the words of Joshua, ch. 24. 12, 'And I sent the *hornet* before you, even the two kings of the Amorites ; but not with thy sword nor with thy bow,' and this we consider on the whole as the most correct opinion. Some commentators, however, explain it of

29 ▼ I will not drive them out from before thee in one year; lest the land become desolate, and the beast of the field multiply against thee.

30 By little and little I will drive them out from before thee, until thou be increased, and inherit the land.

w Deut. 7. 22.

31 And ˣ I will set thy bounds from the Red sea even unto the sea of the Philistines, and from the desert unto the river: for I will ʸ deliver the inhabitants of the land into your hand: and thou shalt drive them out before thee.

x Gen. 15. 18.   Numb. 34. 3.   Deut. 11. 24.
Josh. 1. 4.   1 Kings 4. 21, 24.   Ps. 72. 8.
y Josh. 21. 44.   Judg. 1. 4. & 11. 21.

the anxieties, perplexities, and pungent stinging terrors which should seize the minds of the devoted Canaanites upon the approach of Israel. After all, the reader must be thrown upon the resources of his own judgment as to its import in this place. See the subject more fully canvassed in the Note on Josh. 24. 12.

29. *I will not drive them out from before thee in one year.* Nor in fact in four hundred years was this expulsion entirely effected. It was only in the times of David and Solomon that their enemies could be fairly said to have been driven out. The reason of this delay is stated to be, lest the land, being in a great measure left destitute of its former occupants, should be infested by great numbers of wild beasts. But it is a natural inquiry, what grounds there were to apprehend that the expulsion of the former inhabitants would leave any part of Canaan vacant, when there were at least two millions of Israelites to fill their place?—a number sufficient, it would seem, to occupy every nook and corner of the land. To this it may be answered, that the words do not respect merely the country of Canaan proper, lying between the Jordan and the Mediterranean, but the larger region embraced in the promise to Abraham, Gen. 15. 18, and the boundaries of which Moses immediately goes on to give. This was an immense territory, and it is obvious that its sudden depopulation would be attended by the consequences here stated. It was, therefore, wisely ordered that the extirpa-

tion of the Canaanites should be *gradual*, especially when we consider that the continued presence of enemies would keep them on their guard, and prevent them from settling down into that sluggish supineness to which they would otherwise be prone. Thus too in our spiritual warfare, it is no doubt ordained for our highest good that our corruptions should be subdued, not all at once, but by little and little; that our old man should be crucified gradually. We are hereby necessarily kept in an attitude of perpetual vigilance, and reminded of our constant dependence upon God, who alone giveth us the victory.

31. *I will set thy bounds,* &c. On these boundaries of the promised land see Note on Josh. 1. 4. This land, in its utmost extent, they were not to possess till the days of David. Not that there was any positive prohibition against it, or any intrinsic necessity that their occupancy should be so long deferred; but God saw that their own culpable remissness would preclude the speedier accomplishment of the promise, and according to Scripture language he is often said to order or appoint what he does not prevent.——¶ *Sea of the Philistines.* The Mediterranean, on the coast of which the Philistines dwelt ——¶ *From the desert unto the river.* From the desert of Arabia to the river Euphrates. See Note on Josh. 1. 4. Thus 1 Kings, 4. 21, 'And Solomon reigned over all kingdoms from the river to the land of the Philistines;' i. e. the river Euphrates.

32 ᶻ Thou shalt make no covenant with them, nor with their gods.

33 They shall not dwell in thy land, lest they make thee sin against me: for if thou serve their gods, ᵃ it will surely be a snare unto thee.

ᶻ ch. 34. 12, 15. Deut. 7. 2. ᵃ ch. 34. 12. Deut. 7. 16. & 12. 30. Josh. 23. 13. Judg. 2. 3. 1 Sam. 18. 21. Ps. 106. 36.

32, 33. *Thou shalt make no covenant,* &c. The import of this precept evidently is, that they should contract no such alliances, nor cherish any such intimacies with the devoted nations, as would endanger the purity of their religious worship. If they would avoid the peril of being drawn into the fatal snare of becoming worshippers of false gods, they must keep themselves aloof from all familiarity with idolaters. They must not even suffer them to sojourn amongst them, so long as they adhered to their idolatrous practices. Evil communications corrupt good manners, and by familiar converse with the votaries of idols, their dread and detestation of the sin would imperceptibly wear off, and they would find themselves, before they were aware, transferring their worship and allegiance from the true God to the vanities of the heathen. The language implies that the serving of false gods is nothing else than *making a covenant* with them, and that this is a very natural consequence of making a covenant with those who worship them.

Chapter 24

In the present chapter a transition is made from the recital of the several judicial laws embodied in the two chapters preceding, to the narrative which relates the ratification of the national covenant, the building of the Tabernacle, and the institution of the various rites and ceremonies to be observed in the permanent worship of Jehovah. The leading incidents here recorded are the solemn adoption and ratification of

CHAPTER XXIV.

AND he said unto Moses, Come up unto the LORD, thou, and Aaron, ᵃ Nadab, and Abihu, ᵇ and seventy of the elders of Israel; and worship ye afar off.

ᵃ ch. 28. 1. Lev. 10. 1, 2. ᵇ ch. 1. 5. Numb. 11. 16.

---

the foregoing law on the part of the people, the ascent of Moses and the elders to or towards the summit of the mount, and the august vision there vouchsafed them of the Divine Glory, or the Shekinah, another term for 'the God of Israel,' appearing by his appropriate symbol. The true nature and objects of this remarkable manifestation will appear more evident as we proceed in our annotations, from which the reader will probably infer, and with great justice, that the whole scene was one of far richer significance than is usually imagined.

1. *And he said unto Moses, Come up unto the Lord.* That is, God said. It would probably have been written 'the Lord said unto Moses,' were it not to prevent a repetition of the word 'Lord' in the same clause. We are still to bear in mind the remark so often made before that the 'Lord' (Jehovah) to whom they were to come up was the *visible Jehovah* now abiding in the summit of Sinai. Accordingly the Chal. has, 'Come up before the Lord;' and the Arab. 'Come up to the Angel of God.' It would seem to be unquestionable from a comparison of the context with Ex. 19, 24—20. 21, that these words were spoken to Moses while yet on the mount and before he had retired from the thick darkness into which he had entered. Consequently as he could not be commanded to ascend the mountain when he had already ascended it, and was abiding on its top, we are forced to understand the words as implying that he was to come up after having previously gone down and pre-

2 And Moses ᶜ alone shall come near the LORD: but they shall not come nigh ; neither shall the people go up with him.

3 ¶ And Moses came and told the

ᶜ ver. 13. 15, 18.

---

pounded to the people the foregoing code, obtained their assent, and performed the various covenant transactions mentioned, v. 3—9. When this was done, he and his specified company were to ascend the mountain to receive the further instructions and revelations which God designed to impart.—— ¶ *Nadab and Abihu.* These were the two sons of Aaron who came to such a fearful end for their presumptuous transgression in offering strange fire before the Lord, Lev. 10. 1, 2. When we behold *their* names in the list of the honored company selected for this near approach to God, and then cast our thoughts forward to the awful doom which they not long after brought upon themselves, we are led to the most serious reflection. How clearly does the incident show that God's outward gifts and callings are often different from his 'election according to grace !' And how forcibly is the lesson inculcated upon us, that no mere external privileges, prerogatives, professions, forms, or favors will avail us ought to the saving of our souls without an inward renewal to holiness wrought by the life-giving spirit of God!——¶ *Seventy of the elders of Israel.* That is, seventy of the aged men of the congregation ; men distinguished, respected, and venerated among the different tribes. The *official* elders mentioned Num. 11. 16, were not yet appointed. This company was selected in order that they might be witnesses of the glorious appearance about to be made, and of the communion with God to which Moses was admitted, that their testimony might confirm the people's faith in their leader and teacher. ——¶ *Worship ye afar off.* Gr. προσ-

people all the words of the LORD, and all the judgments: and all the people answered with one voice, and said, ᵈAll the words which the LORD hath said will we do.

ᵈ ver. 7. ch. 19. 8. Deut. 5. 27. Gal. 3. 19. 20.

κυνησουσι μακρωθεν τῳ Κυριῳ, *they shall worship the Lord at a distance;* from which it would appear that they understood this direction as having reference exclusively to those who accompanied Moses on this occasion. The letter of the text does not make this distinction, yet from the ensuing verse it appears not improbable. From that it appears, that, while the body of the people stood at the foot of the mountain, Aaron and his two sons, and the seventy elders, went up probably about half way, and Moses, being privileged with nearer access, went alone quite to the summit and entered the bright and fiery cloud which rested upon it. Thus in a typical manner he sustained the person of Christ, who, as our great High Priest, entered alone into the most holy place. This arrangement, which presents to us the people at the base of the mountain, the priests and the elders half the way up its sides, and Moses on its summit, affords us a striking view of the several grades which God has appointed in his church. Only it is to be remembered that the office represented in Moses is now merged in that of Christ, and the two grand distinctions of *people* and *pastors* or *elders* are all that are known under the Gospel ; the order of *deacons* being merely a kind of servants to the people, ordained to superintend the temporalities of the several congregations.

3. *And Moses came and told the people,* &c. In this and the eight following verses we have an account of the important transactions in which Moses was engaged in the interval between his descent from the mount and his subsequent ascent thither in obedience

4 And Moses e wrote all the words of the LORD, and rose up early in the morning, and builded an altar under the hill, and twelve f pillars according to the twelve tribes of Israel.

e Deut. 31. 9.

f Gen. 28. 18. & 31. 45.

to the divine injunction, v. 1, and in company with Aaron and his sons and the elders. His first business was to set before the people the body of laws, moral, civil, and ceremonial, which had been delivered from Mount Sinai, together with the promises of special blessings to be secured to them on condition of obedience. This was in fact proposing to them the terms of a *national covenant*, which was to be ratified with very solemn ceremonies, and enforced with solemn sanctions. To this covenant the people, it appears, were prompt to give their unanimous and cheerful consent, saying, 'All the words which the Lord hath said will we do.' They had before, ch. 19. 8, consented in general to come under God's government; here they consent in particular to those laws now given. The Most High might, indeed, in virtue of his sovereign authority, have enjoined his laws upon the nation without the formality of any stipulation on their part to obey them, but he condescended to give the whole affair the form of a covenant transaction, as something more calculated to win upon the generous sentiments of their hearts, and to draw forth a more affectionate obedience, than a code of precepts enjoined upon them by simple authority and appealing sternly to a bare sense of duty. God loves to endear his requisitions to the hearts of his creatures. But notwithstanding the readiness of the people thus to assume, without reservation or exception, the responsibilities of the covenant, it was no doubt done with a certain degree of precipitation and rashness, without being aware of their innate impotency to live up to the full extent of the obligations which they hereby incurred. On other occasions in the history of the chosen race we find instances of the same sanguine promptitude in making vows and promises, followed, alas, but too speedily by the grossest acts of defection and rebellion; which led one of the ancient fathers to cómpare the Israelites to locusts, 'Subito saltus dantes, et protinus ad terram cadentes,' *suddenly giving an upward spring, and forthwith falling upon the earth again.* The figure is but too fair an illustration of the halting obedience of the best of God's children in this world.

4. *And Moses wrote*, &c. Although it must have occupied a considerable part of the day, and perhaps of the night also, yet in a transaction of this solemn nature it was evidently proper that the articles of the covenant about to be entered into should be reduced to writing, that there might be no mistake, and that it might be transmitted to posterity, who are equally to come under its obligations. The fact that God himself had previously written the words of the Decalogue on tables of stone does not necessarily militate with the supposition that Moses now made a record of them in writing, to be read in the audience of the people. These tables he had not yet received. It was only when he came down from the mount, after the golden calf was erected in the camp, that he brought with him these divinely written records.—— ¶ *Builded an altar under the hill and twelve pillars;* the altar as a representative of God, as the first and principal party to this covenant; and the twelve pillars as the representatives of the twelve tribes of the people as the other party. Between these two covenanting parties Moses acted as real and typical mediator. Gr. 'He built an altar under the mountain, και δωδεκα λιθους εις· τας

5 And he sent young men of the children of Israel, which offered burnt-offerings, and sacrificed peace-offerings of oxen unto the LORD.

6 And Moses g took half of the blood, and put *it* in basons; and half of the blood he sprinkled on the altar.

7 And he h took the book of the

g Hebr. 9. 18.　h Hebr. 9. 19.

covenant, and read in the audience of the people: and they said, i All that the LORD hath said will we do, and be obedient.

8 And Moses took the blood, and sprinkled *it* on the people, and said, Behold k the blood of the covenant, which the LORD hath made with you concerning all these words.

i ver. 3.　k Hebr. 9. 20. & 13. 20. 1 Pet. 1. 2.

δωδεκα φυλας· του Ισραηλ, *and twelve stones for the twelve tribes of Israel;* as if each of the pillars consisted of a single stone, which we incline to believe was the fact; but it is not certain; they may have consisted of heaps of stones.

5. *And he sent young men,* &c. That is, the first-born, who officiated as priests and sacrificers till the Levites were appointed by substitution in their stead, Num. 3. 41. The term, as is remarked in the Note on Gen. 14. 24, does not imply persons of youthful age, but those who were qualified to act in this ministerial service, which would naturally require men of mature years. Chal. 'He sent the first-born of the sons of Israel.' The Targ. Jon. adds, 'For to this hour the business of worship was among the first-born, seeing that as yet the tabernacle of the covenant was not built, neither had the priesthood been given to Aaron.' It is observable that there was no solemn religious ceremony in any part of the Mosaic dispensation, in which there was not a sacrifice, no approach to God until he was thus propitiated. These of course were typical of that one great offering of the Son of God, afterwards to be presented, which has for ever abrogated all others. By this, peace was made between God and his sincere worshippers, who bring that sacrifice in faith, and lay it on his altar. But until the fulness of time was come, the bodies of oxen and sheep, of goats and calves, prefigured the body of Christ which he offered up, once for all, upon

the cross, expiating then the sins of men; and the people were thus taught the need of a sacrifice to propitiate as well as of a mediator to stand between them and God, and to intercede for them.——¶ *Of oxen.* From Heb. 9. 19, it appears that other animals were sacrificed on this occasion; 'He took the blood of calves and of goats,' &c. Oxen, or rather bullocks, are mentioned as being principal.

6—8. *And Moses took half of the blood,* &c. The application of the blood of the victim more explicitly demands our attention in considering the circumstances of this solemn rite. Being divided into two equal parts, one half was put into one basin, the other into another. The first was then taken, and the blood sprinkled upon the altar, the representative of God, thereby denoting that he, on his part, engaged to be faithful in the covenant relation which he now condescended to assume, performing all the promises and conferring all the blessings which their corresponding fidelity would entitle them to expect. As Moses here says the altar was sprinkled, but makes no mention of the book, and as Paul, Heb. 9. 19, speaks of the book's being sprinkled, but says nothing of the altar, the presumption is, that the book was laid upon the altar, and thus both the book and the altar partook of the sacred affusion. The import of the act was solemn and awful in the extreme, and the form of adjuration is supposed to

9 ¶ Then ¹ went up Moses, and | Aaron, Nadab, and Abihu, and

¹ ver. 1. | seventy of the elders of Israel.

have been substantially the following ; 'As the body of this victim is cloven asunder, as the blood of this animal is poured out, so let my body be divided and my blood shed, if I prove unfaithful and perfidious.' Under a stipulation of this fearful import, the people consent to the conditions of the compact, and again declare their purpose to abide steadfastly by the divine requirements. Upon this Moses took the other basin of blood, and sprinkled its contents ' on the people ;' i. e. either on the twelve pillars which stood as the representatives of the people, or upon a portion of the elders of the congregation in the name of the whole body. As the sprinklings and purifyings under the law were usually performed with water, scarlet wool, and hyssop, Lev. 14. 6. 7, such also, as we learn from the apostle, Heb. 9. 19, was the case in the present instance. The application of the blood was the seal of the covenant, giving to the whole transaction its crowning and binding sanction. It is, accordingly, with the most solemn emphasis that Moses adds, 'Behold the blood of the covenant, which the Lord hath made with you concerning all these words ;' i. e. the blood by the shedding of which the covenant is ratified and confirmed. In like manner our Savior, in instituting that ordinance which was to be a perpetual seal of the new covenant of grace, said to his disciples, ' This is my blood of the new testament, which is shed for many for the remission of sins.' And it should not be forgotten, that all those who adjoin themselves to the Lord in this sacred ordinance have the guilt of blood resting upon them if they prove unfaithful, and that the Savior probably alludes to the understood penalty of this kind of covenant-breaking, when he says, Luke, 12. 43—46, ' Blessed is that servant,

whom his lord when he cometh shall find so doing. Of a truth I say unto you, That he will make him ruler over all that he hath. But and if that servant say in his heart, My lord delayeth his coming ; and shall begin to beat the men-servants, and maidens, and to eat and drink, and to be drunken ; the lord of that servant will come in a day when he looketh not for him, and at an hour when he is not aware, and *will cut him in sunder*, and will appoint him his portion with the unbelievers.' This 'cutting asunder' alludes to the virtual imprecation of every one who entered into covenant over the divided members of the victim slaughtered on such occasions. Compare with this Heb. 9. 19, 20.——¶ *Took the book of the covenant, and read*, &c. In order that the people might be completely aware of what they were about to undertake, though they had been told before, he took the book, and read from it all that he had there written. He read it that they might be sure that what was contained in it, and what they were going, as it were, to *sign*, was the same as he had previously spoken to them, and they had promised to observe. He read it that their memories might be refreshed, and their consent given with full knowlege and due deliberation.

9. *Then went up Moses and Aaron*, &c. The several preliminary ceremonies and services mentioned above having been completed, Moses and his chosen attendants now make their ascent up the mountain, in obedience to the command before given, v. 1. From v. 13, it appears evident that Joshua constituted one of the company, though his name is not here mentioned. The omission may perhaps have been owing to the fact that he went not in a representative character, but simply as a personal attendant or minister to Mo-

10 And they ᵐ saw the God of Israel : and *there was* under his feet

ᵐ See Gen. 32. 30. ch. 3. 6. Judg. 13. 22.
Isai. 6. 1, 5. with ch. 33. 20, 23. John 1. 18.
1 Tim. 6. 16. 1 John 4. 12.

as it were a paved work of a ⁿ sapphire-stone, and as it were the ᵒ body of heaven in *his* clearness.

ⁿ Ezek. 1. 26. & 10. 1. Rev. 4. 3.   ᵒ Matt 17. 2.

ses.—In the brief narrative contained in this and the two ensuing verses, we enter upon the consideration of one of the most remarkable events recorded in the whole compass of the sacred story. The sublime and glorious spectacle to which these favored sons of Israel were now admitted is, no doubt, the germ of many of the most magnificent descriptions of the symbolical scenery of the prophets, and especially of the *theophanies*, or *visible manifestations of the Deity*, which we find subsequently recorded, and capable, if expanded into all its details, of filling a volume.

10. *And they saw the God of Israel.* Heb. אֱלֹהֵי יִשְׂרָאֵל אֵת וַיִּרְאוּ *vayiru eth Elohë Yisraël, and they saw the God of Israel.* As we are assured upon the authority of inspiration, 1 Tim. 6. 16, that 'no man hath seen or can see' God in his essential being, this language undoubtedly denotes that they were privileged to behold the visible sign, symbol, or demonstration of his presence, or in other words, the Shekinah, perhaps under a form of more distinctness, or circumstances of greater glory, than it had ever been revealed in before. It was unquestionably a similar appearance to that vouchsafed to Ezekiel, chap. 1. 26, of which he says, 'Above the firmament that was over their heads, having the appearance of a sapphire-stone, was the likeness of a throne, and upon the likeness of the throne was the likeness as the appearance of a man above upon it.' The 'firmament' here spoken of as over the heads of the living creatures was not the celestial firmament, but a splendid flooring or substratum on which the visionary throne and its occupant rested, corresponding to the 'paved work of a sapphire stone,'

mentioned by Moses. But it will be proper, in a passage of this nature to give the ancient versions, in which the reader will perceive the most distinct recognition of the Shekinah, as we have elsewhere represented it. Gr. 'And they saw the place where the God of Israel had stood, and under his feet as it were the work of a sapphire-brick, and as it were the appearance of the firmament of heaven in the purity thereof. And of the chosen of Israel there perished not one, and they were seen in the place of God, and ate and drank.' Chal. 'And they saw the glory of the God of Israel, and under the throne of his glory as the work of a precious stone, and as the aspect of heaven when it is serene. But to the princes of the sons of Israel no injury accrued ; and they saw the Glory of God, and rejoiced in the sacrifices, which were accepted, as if they had eaten and drank.' Arab. 'And they saw the Angel of the God of Israel, and under him something similar to the whiteness of adamant, and like to heaven itself in its serenity. And against the princes of the sons of Israel he sent not forth his stroke, and they saw the Angel of the Lord, and lived, and ate, and drank.' Syr. 'And they saw the God of Israel, and under his feet as it were the work of a sapphire-brick, and as it were the color of heaven when it is serene. And against the elders of the sons of Israel he did not extend his hand ; yea, they saw God, and ate and drank.' Sam. 'And they saw the God of Israel, and under his feet as it were a brick-work of sapphire, and as heaven itself in its purity. Nor yet against the elect ones of the children of Israel did he send forth his hand, but they clave unto God and ate and drank.'

It will be observed that both in the sacred text, and in these several versions, there is a studied obscurity as to the form and aspect of the object whose resting or standing place is so gorgeously described. Yet from a comparison of this passage with the vision of Ezekiel, ch. 1, of which it is unquestionably the germ, there is some reason to think it was an *approximation* to the human form, as he says, that above the firmament that was over their heads, having the appearance of a sapphire stone, there was the likeness of a throne, and ' upon the likeness of the throne the likeness as the appearance of a man above upon it.' Even here, however, the description is so worded as to leave the image in the mind of the reader designedly vague and shadowy, lest a foundation should be laid for an idolatrous abuse of the symbolical scenery depicted. While, therefore, the idea of a *distinct* personal appearance in human form is excluded, yet we may perhaps safely conceive that the luminous and glorious object presented to their view bore a *remote semblance* of such a form ; nor does it militate with this supposition that Moses says, in describing the phenomena of Sinai, 'ye saw no manner of similitude ;' for this was spoken concerning the people in general, at the time of their receiving the law in an audible voice from the mount ; but the words before us relate to a few individuals, and what they saw on a subsequent occasion. It is said of Moses, Num. 12. 8, ' the similitude of the Lord shall he behold,' and as this vision had a direct reference to Christ, who is 'the image of the invisible God,' and yet ' made in the likeness of corruptible man,' we seem to perceive an intrinsic probability in the idea of his appearing on this occasion, in at least a *faint resemblance* to that human form in which he was afterwards to manifest himself in accomplishing the work of redemption.

Still we do not insist on this interpretation. It may be sufficient to say this was a most resplendent display of the divine glory in that form in which the Shekinah usually appeared, only perhaps in a milder and more mitigated splendor ; for it seems clear that its usual aspect was that of an exceedingly bright and dazzling effulgence, increasing on some occasions to the intensity of a glowing and devouring flame. It is clear that the object seen could not have been God in the unveiled glory of his Godhead, for him no man hath seen nor can see. It must have been that *sensible manifestation* of the Deity which we have so frequently designated by the term Shekinah, and which we have endeavored to prove to be uniformly the Old Testament adumbration of Christ. It is unquestionably the same object as that mentioned by Isaiah, ch. 6. 1, 'In the year that King Uzziah died, I *saw the Lord* sitting upon a throne, high and lifted up, &c. ;' for it was only as manifested in the Shekinah that 'the Lord' (i. e. Jehovah) was ever seen under the old dispensation. It is the same object also as that described in the vision of Ezekiel, ch. 43. 1, 2, 'Afterward he brought me to the gate, even the gate that looketh toward the east ; and, behold, *the glory of the God of Israel* came from the way of the east ; and his voice was like the noise of many waters, and the earth shined with his glory.' The personage is evidently the same ; it was the 'God of Israel,' whose theophany is described by both ; and as Ezekiel is here prophetically setting forth the scenery of the New Jerusalem, we see no reason to doubt that the spectacle witnessed by Moses was the germ of that portrayed by Ezekiel, and that that depicted by John was merely a farther expansion of the same symbolical embryo. But leaving us to form our own ideas as to this part of the vision, the historian is more particular in describing the footstool upon

11 And upon the nobles of the children of Israel he p laid not his hand: also q they saw God, and did r eat and drink.

p ch. 19. 21.

q ver. 10. ch. 33. 20. Gen. 16. 13. & 32. 30. Deut. 4. 33. Judg. 13. 22. r Gen. 31. 54. ch. 18. 12. 1 Cor. 10. 18.

which the visible Divine Majesty rested. ——¶ *Under his feet as it were a paved work of a sapphire stone.* Heb. כמעשה לבנת הספיר *kemaäseh libnath hassappir, as the work of brick of sapphire.* That is, a tesselated pavement, apparently constructed of solid blocks of transparent sapphire moulded into the shape and size of bricks. The sapphire is a precious stone of a sky-colored hue, next in value and beauty to the diamond, and there seems to be an allusion to this gorgeous substratum of the throne of the divine glory in the prophet's words, Is. 54. 11, 'I will lay thy stones with fair colors, and lay thy *foundations with sapphires.*' In order to make the impression of its appearance still more distinct, it is compared to the 'body of heaven in its clearness.' That is to say, it had the aspect of the azure vault of heaven as seen in its pure native splendor, when the atmosphere is serene and unclouded. The eye then seems to behold the naked body, as it were, or the very substance of the heavenly ether. The whole spectacle, viewed merely as a sensible phenomenon, must have been beautiful and glorious beyond conception; but its glory in this respect would no doubt be far eclipsed by that of its symbolical import, could we but adequately grasp it.

11. *And upon the nobles*, &c. Heb. אצילים *otzelim, magnates, optimates, the chief men, the grandees;* evidently denoting the select and favored persons above mentioned, who are here probably called 'nobles' from the honor now conferred upon them of being admitted to witness such a spectacle; as if the splendor of the divine presence *ennobled* every thing that came within its sphere. By the 'hand' of Jehovah's 'not being laid upon them' is doubtless meant, that they received no harm from this amazing manifestation. Contrary to the usual impression in regard to the effect of such displays of the divine glory, which were thought to be fatal to the beholder, they saw God and lived. That this is the genuine sense of the phrase will appear from the following passages; Gen. 37. 22, 'And Reuben said unto them, Shed no blood, but cast him into this pit which is in the wilderness, and *lay no hand upon him;*' i. e. do no violence to him. Ps. 138. 7, 'Though I walk in the midst of trouble, thou wilt revive me; *thou shalt stretch forth thine hand against the wrath of mine enemies*, and thy right hand shall save me.' Neh. 13. 21, 'Then I testified against them and said unto them, Why lodge ye about the wall? if ye do so again, *I will lay hands on you.*' Ps. 55. 20, '*He hath put forth his hand* against such as be at peace with him.'——¶ *Also they saw God, and did eat and drink.* Heb. ויחזו את האלהים *va-yehezu eth ha-Elohim, and they saw the Elohim.* It is particularly worthy of notice, that the original here adopts a different term for 'seeing' from that which occurs in the preceding verse—'they saw (ויראו *yiru*) the God of Israel,' as if *that* were intended to refer to the mere *outward, ocular*, and *superficial* view of the object as at first beheld. Here on the other hand, the verb is חזה *hazah*, a term applied for the most part to *prophetic vision*, or that kind of inward and spiritual perception which was enjoyed by holy and inspired men when in a state of supernatural trance or extacy. In this state the exercise of the outward senses was usually suspended, and the objects seen were presented as pictures to the imagination, the full significancy of which were not

always made known to the beholder. In the present instance we cannot affirm that the ordinary functions of the eye were, after a time, superseded, but we have no doubt that their minds were gradually raised and sublimated by a special divine influence, so that they were made the subjects of a manifestation or revelation far beyond any thing which their unaided faculties were capable of attaining. They were under an illapse of the Spirit of God, and like Balaam 'saw the vision of the Almighty, falling into a trance, but (probably) having their eyes open.' In this entranced and extatic state 'they saw God ;' i. e. they had a prophetic view of the Shekinah, the symbol of the divine presence, not only in the form in which it might strike the senses, but in its hidden interior import and significancy, as pointing to that divine personage who was now involved in it and in future to be developed out of it, first in the substantiated form of human flesh, as the Son of God, humbled, suffering, and dying for the sins of men ; and secondly and chiefly as risen, glorified, and again manifested on earth in the splendor and magnificence of his second coming and his eternal kingdom. It is, we doubt not, to this future and consummated glory of the Redeemer, made again visible and taking up its abode among men, that the symbol of the Shekinah always points. Its manifestation to Israel of old was preintimative of its renewed appearance and establishment in more sublime and glorious state to the subjects of the gospel economy in its ulterior periods, as set forth in the splendid predictions of Isaiah and the Apocalypse. It is only in the realization of all that was shadowed by the Shekinah that we are to look for the fulfilment of the assurance ratified by ' a great voice out of heaven, saying. Behold, *the tabernacle of God is with men, and he will dwell with them, and* they shall be his people, and God himself shall be with them, and be their God.'

This, we are aware, is language that the Christian world have somehow come to interpret vaguely of heaven considered as a state removed to an unknown distance both of time and space from the state in which our present lot is cast; but we have greatly mistaken the drift of the oracles of God, if the conviction does not eventually grow upon the church, that it is in fact a *future* and an *earthly* state, a state to be gradually evolved out of the existing order of things, and to the developement of which every Christian is bound unceasingly and strenuously to consecrate his efforts. So far as the *heaven* of the Scriptures is identical with the New Jerusalem, the celestial city, it is certainly *future*, for *that* is future. It is a state which is to be the *result* of a great system of influences and providences, now in operation, which God has designed shall precede and introduce it. It is an economy or polity which is said to ' come down from God out of heaven,' because it is to be developed into being *in pursuance of a divine plan,—as the execution of a scheme or program of which God in his revealed word is the Author.* In like manner, it might not improperly be said that the Tabernacle and all its apparatus came down from God out of heaven, because Moses constructed it all according to the pattern shown him in the mount. We suppose that it was with a view to impart a prophetic intimation of this great futurity, that the present vision was vouchsafed and recorded; and that a similar end was contemplated in the similar disclosures made to Isaiah, to Ezekiel, to Daniel, and to John. They all point forward to the blissful period referred to in the annunciation, ' the tabernacle of God shall be with men,' that is, his Shekinah, his *manifested presence*, shall be with men ; not only with men in their raised and glorified and angelic bodies, but also with men in their human flesh, living and sojourning on the earth while this resplendent throne of Jehovah has its seat in the midst of them. And this view, we conceive, affords the true clue to the introduction of the remarkable circumstance mentioned in close connexion with that of the vision with which Moses and the elders were favored, viz., that ' they did eat and drink.' Even granting, as is very probably the case, that this eating and drinking was upon the peace-offerings and the libations which accompanied the ratification of the covenant, yet who is not struck by the juxta-position of things apparently so remote from each other in their own nature, as witnessing a vision of God and satisfying the gross appetites of the physical man? Who does not feel it to be a kind of violent transition from the Spirit to the flesh? But suppose the incident to be viewed as having, like the rest, a prophetical bearing — suppose it be a typical intimation of the fact, that eating and drinking, that is, *enjoying the conditions of our present humanity*, are not in themselves inconsistent with the visible indwelling of the Most High on earth which we are taught to expect, and do we not find a sufficient explanation of the mystery? If the vision here recorded were truly in its ultimate scope, prophetical, and pointed to an era when the glory displayed to the congregation at Sinai should be far more illustriously displayed over the face of the earth, while the race was yet sojourning upon it, would it not be natural that some hint should be afforded of the intrinsic compatibility of such a manifestation with such a mode of subsistence?

In the foregoing remarks we have stated one, and, as we conceive, a prominent one, of the designs of God in granting to his servants this signal manifestation of his glory. But this, we apprehend, was not all. Admitting that such an ultimate scope as we have now supposed was in fact couched under the vision, it would be natural that a system of rites, types, and shadows should be instituted, adapted to represent and keep vividly before the minds of the chosen people, the *grand end* which infinite wisdom thus proposed to itself eventually to accomplish. To this the Tabernacle with its various furniture and services, was eminently adapted. This sacred and symbolical structure, with all its appurtenances, was to be erected under the superintendance of Moses, and that in conformity to a model divinely given. We are expressly informed that he was to ' make every thing after the pattern shown him in the mount.' This pattern we suppose to have been shown him on this occasion; and probably one main reason of admitting Aaron and the elders to a participation of the vision, was, that by beholding the pattern they might bear witness to the fidelity of the copy. Otherwise, what evidence could Moses give to the people that he was acting in obedience to a divine command in erecting such a structure, of so strange a form and so costly a character? Would the congregation have parted so readily with their treasures, their gold and silver and jewels, unless upon the strongest assurance to their own minds that in so doing they were fulfilling an express requisition of Jehovah? The presence of the elders would give this assurance, and we therefore deem it reasonable to presume that the phenomena of the vision included the entire typical apparatus of the Tabernacle, and especially that of the Ark of the Covenant, the Mercy-seat, and the Cherubim, which were in fact the very heart and nucleus of the entire system, and of the import of which we shall speak more fully in a subsequent Note. In all probability the visible object termed the ' God of Israel' was faithfully but feebly shadowed out in the

12 ¶ And the LORD said unto Moses, ˢ Come up to me into the mount, and be there: and I will give thee ᵗ tables of stone, and a law, and commandments which I

ˢ ver. 2. 15, 18. ᵗ ch. 31. 18. & 32. 15. 16. Deut. 5. 22.

have written; that thou mayest teach them.

13 And Moses rose up, and ᵘ his minister Joshua: and Moses ʷ went up into the mount of God.

ᵘ ch. 32. 17. & 33. 11. ʷ ver. 2.

---

cloud of glory and the accompanying Cherubim which surmounted the Mercy-seat, except that the sapphire pavement was exchanged, for uniformity's sake, for one of burnished gold. As to the attendant angelic hosts, which seem to have been conceived of as an unfailing accompaniment of the Glory, and which they probably saw, since they could not be materialized in their multitude, the Cherubic device was adopted as a mystic embodiment of this order of beings. But of this more in the sequel. If our suggestions in regard to the remarkable incident here recorded be well founded, and this were the time when these 'patterns of things in the heavens' were shown to Moses, it will follow that the account here given of the vision is extremely incomplete, embracing the mention merely of the leading and most memorable object which they were favored to behold. This we infer from the fact that Moses is said to have made every thing according to the pattern shown him in the mount. But as he made many things which he is not expressly said to have seen, we may fairly conclude that he does not describe all that he did see.

12. *Come up to me into the Mount,* &c. Thus far it would appear that Moses had remained with his company at some station part way up the mountain, where the vision was vouchsafed, but he is now commanded to leave his companions, and advance towards the cloud that rested on the summit, and 'to be there,' i. e. to remain there some considerable time. The design of the summons is stated to be, that he might receive the engraved tables of the law,

containing that divine code which he was to teach to the people, for it is to the people, and not to the commandments, that the pronoun 'them' refers.

13. *And his minister Joshua.* Heb. מְשָׁרְתוֹ *mesharetho, his ministering attendant.* The root שָׁרַת *sharath* denotes a personal attendance and ministry less servile than that which is indicated by the term עָבַד *abad, to serve.* It points rather to that honorary attendance which is paid by a courtier to his sovereign or prince, than the menial obsequiousness of a slave to his master. See Note on Num. 11. 28. It was undoubtedly with a view to his future office, that Joshua was called to sustain this relation to Moses. He was to be his successor as leader of Israel, and it was fitting that he should begin by degrees to be honored before the congregation, that they might be led the more readily and cordially to render to him the deference and respect to which his station would one day entitle him. This could scarcely fail to be the result when they saw him admitted nearer to the manifested presence of God than any other individual except Moses himself. We must be strangely insensible to the tokens of the divine will not to honor those whom God himself honors. —— ¶ *And Moses went up into the mount of God.* Chal. ' Into the mountain on which the Glory of the Lord was revealed.' Targ. Jon. ' Into the mountain in which the Glorious Presence of the Lord was manifested.' Moses and Joshua went up to the higher parts of the mountain, where in all probability the lower extremities or fringes of the dark enveloping cloud

14 And he said unto the elders, Tarry ye here for us, until we come again unto you : and behold, Aaron and Hur *are* with you : if any man have any matters to do, let him come unto them.

---

embosomed them in its sombre folds. The bright interior cloud of the Glory seems to have been still higher up on the very apex of the mount, and to have been only occasionally disclosed to the sight of the congregation. The common spectacle, we suppose, was that of a dark majestic mass of cloud, within which, but invisible, the splendor of the Shekinah abode. Here it would seem that Moses and Joshua remained together for six days, pavilioned within the lower descending outskirts of the cloud, engaged in holy conference and fervent devotion, till on the seventh, perhaps the sabbath day, Moses was ordered to leave Joshua, as they had both left the elders below, and ascend up to the topmost summit of the hallowed mount, where the divine presence was more especially enthroned. So in our upward moral progress, be our attainments what they may at present, we are still to aim at something higher. Our arrival at one eminence still leaves us at the foot of another, which equally claims to be climbed, and until we reach heaven itself we must expect to see,

'Hills peep o'er hills, and Alps on Alps arise.'

14. *Tarry ye here*, &c. Aware, probably, that his absence from the people was now to be of longer duration than usual, Moses deems it necessary to make special provision for the administration of justice, and the general management of the civil affairs of the people in the interval. For this end he commissions Aaron and Hur to act as his deputies in judging causes, and tells them, moreover, to remain where they were, advanced somewhat up the mountain, patiently awaiting his and Joshua's return. It is only thus that we can understand the plain language of the text. Commentators indeed have supposed that as the people were to have constant resort to them on matters of business, and as Aaron is spoken of as engaged in the midst of the congregation in making the golden calf, the order was for the elders to remain, not in the exact spot where Moses left them, but in the camp at the base of the mountain, in the midst of the people. But this is surely doing manifest violence to the letter of the narrative ; and besides, if this were the sense, what need were there of any command at all ; for where else *should* they tarry but in the camp ? Was there any danger of their going away from it ? The truth is, if we mistake not, they were expressly required to abide in the spot where they had enjoyed the vision till Moses returned. To this spot such of the people as 'had matters to do' were permitted and directed to come as often as they had occasion for judicial decisions ; and we think that the first step in Aaron's sin was his deserting his post, and going down, contrary to Moses' direction, into the midst of the camp. He was probably infected by the contagion of the people's impatience before he yielded his consent to join in their idolatry ; thus affording us a melancholy example of the ruinous effects of a single step in the way of transgression. No man knows where he may be landed by the slightest aberration from the path of duty. Neither the foot nor the face can be safely turned away from the post assigned us. Aaron slid down the mountain both in a moral and physical sense at the same time.——¶ *Behold, Aaron and Hur are with you.* This was spoken to the elders, but to the elders as the representatives of the people, and so in a sense sustaining their persons. The people, therefore,

15 And Moses went up into the mount, and ˣa cloud covered the mount.

16 And ʸ the glory of the LORD abode upon mount Sinai, and the cloud covered it six days: and the seventh day he called unto Moses out of the midst of the cloud.

ˣ ch. 19. 9, 16. Matt. 17. 5. ʸ ch. 16. 10. Numb. 14. 10.

17 And the sight of the glory of the LORD *was* like ᶻ devouring fire on the top of the mount in the eyes of the children of Israel.

18 And Moses went into the midst of the cloud, and gat him up into the mount: and ᵃ Moses was in the mount forty days and forty nights.

ᶻ ch. 3. 2. & 19. 18. Deut. 4. 36. Hebr. 12. 18. 29. ᵃ ch. 34. 28. Deut. 9. 9.

---

were to consider themselves as addressed in the address made to their official heads. This is according to the usual analogy of the Scripture idiom, of which we shall find hundreds of examples.—— ¶ *If any man have any matters to do.* Heb. מי בעל דברים *mi baal debarim, whoso is lord or master of words* (things, matters). Gr. and Chal. 'Whoso hath a judgment or controversy.'

15. *And Moses went up into the mount,* &c. That is, Moses and Joshua together, as the whole narrative leads us to infer. For it was not till six days had elapsed that Moses was called to enter into the midst of the cloud resting on the highest peak of the mountain, and in the mean time we cannot but suppose that he and Joshua remained together. It no more follows that Joshua did not ascend with him, from his name not being mentioned, than it does that he is not to be associated with Moses in the final clause of v. 13, where any one can see that such an inference would be entirely erroneous.

16. *And the glory c͵ᷓ the Lord abode,* &c. Heb. ישכן *yishkan, tabernacled.* From the same root שכן *shakan,* comes *Shekinah,* the etymology clearly indicating the relation of the visible glory of Jehovah to some kind of *tabernacle* as its appropriate dwelling place. In the present instance, we incline to believe that the dark cloud was the tabernacle in which the Glory was enshrined, and that this is expressly intimated in the ensuing words, ' the cloud covered it six days,' i. e. covered the Glory, and

not the mountain ; for thus the original may fairly be interpreted. It is, indeed true that nearly all the ancient versions render it, 'covered him,' i. e. Moses, but the other sense is agreeable to the original, and were a *personal* object intended, we think it more probable the plural 'them' would have been employed, as there can be no doubt that Moses and Joshua were now together, and both enshrouded within the borders of the cloudy crown which covered the brow of the mountain. On the seventh day the divine summons called Moses up to the utmost heights of the mountain, and then we suppose the dark thick cloud was rent and opened in the sight of all Israel, and the inner glory broke forth like devouring fire. In the midst of this opened cloud, Moses was enabled boldly to enter, although to the multitude below it probably had the appearance of entering into the mouth of a fiery furnace, which threatened instantaneous destruction. But Moses was one whom the special favor of heaven enabled to ' dwell even with this devouring fire,' without either a hair of his head, or a thread of his garments, feeling the action of the consuming element. There he continued fasting forty days and forty nights, receiving further instructions, and no doubt enjoying the most transporting discoveries of the divine glory. The six days mentioned, v. 16, were probably not a part of the forty ; for during those six days Moses and Joshua were together, and both probably ate of manna as usual, anᵈ drank of the brook mentioned Deut. 9. 21 ; but when Moses was called into the midst of the cloud, his forty days fasting commenced, while Joshua, in the mean time, no doubt continued to eat and drink daily while waiting for Moses' return.

Chapter 25

THE TABERNACLE.

As we enter in the present chapter upon the directions given to Moses for the erection and furnishing of the sacred structure called *the Tabernacle*, it will be proper to dwell a little in the outset upon the grand design of an edifice so remarkable in itself, and holding so prominent a place in the Mosaic economy. The Tabernacle was, in fact, the central object in the Jewish system of worship, and without a tolerably correct idea of its form, uses, and ends, our view of the genius and scope of the Hebrew ritual will be essentially defective. It may perhaps be admitted, that as some of these ends were of typical import, pointing forward to a period of the Christian dispensation which fias not yet been fully devoloped, we may not be able to unfold, in all its fullness, in the present state of our knowledge, the entire reach of meaning which in the divine mind was couched under this significant structure, and its successor the Temple. Yet with the lights reflected upon it from the expositions of the New Testament and the predictions of the Old, we may doubtless attain to an interesting and edifying insight into its leading drift. We are persuaded that it is a study fraught with the most important practical results, and though generally considered, like the other symbolical portions of the Scriptures, as constituting a field of mere curious, fanciful, and speculative research, yet we cannot question that this opinion will be ere long entirely reversed by a deeper reverence for *every*

part of revelation subordinating to itself the irrepressible spirit of inquiry which is pervading every department of knowledge whether scientific or sacred, natural or supernatural. The book of revelation, like the book of nature, is designed to be of gradual development, and we know not why it is not as reasonable to look for the opening of new mines of scriptural wealth, as of new mineral treasures, that have been imbedded for ages in the bowels of the earth.—But to the point which we have more immediately in hand.

The opinion has been widely entertained, that in the early ages of the world, under the impression of the grand truth that ' God is a spirit, and that they that worship him must worship him in spirit and in truth,'—that this divine spirit filled all things, and was equally present in all parts of his creation — men had no *sacred places*, but worshipped God wherever and whenever their hearts were drawn forth towards him in veneration, gratitude, or love. To the soundness of this opinion thus broadly expressed, we are disposed to object, on the same grounds on which we object to the theory that makes the primitive state of man a *savage* state. *It is not, we conceive, in accordance with the recorded facts of inspired history.* We cannot but conclude, from the tenor of the sacred narrative, that from the creation of Adam to the present time, God has dealt with man by way of *express revelation*. The infancy of the race was cradled in the midst of supernatural disclosures, and the light of the divine *manifestations* continued to shine with brighter or dimmer beams upon its advancing youth and manhood, up to the riper age which it has now attained. With the record of Genesis before us we cannot question that Jehovah manifested himself between the Cherubims at the east of the garden of Eden, and that this earliest exhibition of the Shekinah was the *appointed place of worship* for Adam and his family, the place to which Cain and Abel *brought* their oblations, and the place from which Cain, after the murder of his brother, retired in miserable exile, when he is said to have fled from the *presence* of the Lord. True it is, that the major part of the race lapsed, by a very early defection, into the grossest idolatry, and the *visible symbols* of the divine presence, if enjoyed at all, were confined to a select few ; but we know not that we are warranted in the belief that the knowledge of the true God, or of the right mode of worshipping him, has *at any time* become entirely extinct on earth. As a matter, however, of historical fact it is unquestionable that most of the early nations of the world, under the promptings of a religious principle, rendered their worship, such as it was, in a vague and informal manner, without temple or ritual, to the invisible Deity in whom they were taught to believe. It was not unnatural that in these circumstances they should have selected the tops of mountains and the shade of groves as the seat of their worship, and there fixed their altars for sacrifice. But in process of time, as men sank deeper and deeper into idolatry, the practice of worshipping on high places and in groves became associated with so many vile abominations, that it was utterly forbidden to the Israelites, to whom God was pleased to prescribe a *localized* worship, first within the precincts of a Tabernacle, and afterwards of a Temple. The Tabernacle was little else than a portable temple ; as no other kind of structure would have suited the earlier circumstances of the chosen race. A nomade people would of course have a moveable temple ; and, among a tent-dwelling people, that temple would naturally be a tent or a portable fabric of wood. An immoveable temple could only be expected to be found among a settled race; and when a moving people become set-

tled, and exchange their tents for houses, in like manner their moveable tabernacles become fixed temples. 'See now,' said David, 'I dwell in a house of cedar, but the ark of God dwelleth between curtains.' He therefore proposed that the house of God should no longer be a tent, but a fabric of stone, in accordance with the altered circumstances of the people. But until the Israelites were settled in the land of promise, their sacred edifice, if they had one, must necessarily be such as they could easily take to pieces and transfer from place to place. The object of such a building was not, like that of our churches, as a place of shelter for the assembled worshippers, for the worshippers assembled not *in* the temples, but in the courts before or around them; nor yet as places for offering sacrifices, for the sacrifices were also offered in the courts. Its true design was as *a mansion of the Deity, a dwelling-place for the divine presence.* This was especially and preeminently the object of the Jewish Tabernacle. It was intended as a habitation of the visible symbol of Jehovah, or the Shekinah, as the God and King of the chosen people, who, as we have seen above, is emphatically designated 'the God of Israel.'

In ordering the construction of such a building, we may admit that there was an accommodation to ideas then very universally prevalent, and which from their residence in Egypt had become familiar to the minds of the Israelites. The Egyptians and other heathen nations boasted of the presence of their gods among them in their temples and tabernacles ; and as God had been pleased from the earliest periods to reveal himself to the patriarchs by visible manifestation, it was not unnatural that he should at length confer upon his people the permanent tokens of a peculiar local presence in some such striking and glorious symbol as that of the Shekinah. With this view he directed the Tabernacle to be erected as a suitable abode for his visible majesty. As such it possessed the twofold character of a *Sanctuary*, or *holy place, a place of worship;* and of a *Royal Palace;* where he would keep the state of a court, as supreme civil magistrate and king of Israel; from whence he would issue his laws and commandments as from an oracle, and where he was to receive the homage and tribute of his subjects. This idea of the Tabernacle, as in part that of *a palace for a king*, will seem perfectly clear to every one who carefully notes the terms in which this building and also the Temple are spoken of and referred to throughout the Scriptures; and we doubt not it is a view essential to the right understanding of these structures and the things which belonged to them. It is a view also which is held by the Jews themselves, who carry out the analogy and regard the utensils of the Tabernacle as *palace furniture* and the priests as its ministers of state and officers. Take, for instance, the following comment of Rab. Shem Tob on Maimonides as cited by Outram on Sacrifices, Diss. I. § 3. 'God, to whom be praise, commanded a house to be built for him resembling a royal palace. In a royal palace are to be found all the things that we have mentioned. There are some persons who guard the palace; others who execute offices belonging to the royal dignity, who furnish the banquets, and do other necessary services for the monarch; others who daily entertain him with music, both vocal and instrumental. In a royal palace there is a place appointed for the preparation of victuals, and another [nearer the Presence] where perfumes are burned. In the palace of a king there is also a table, and an apartment exclusively appropriated to himself, which no one ever enters, except him who is next in authority, or those whom he regards with the greatest affection. In like manner it was the will of God to have all these in his house, that he might not in anything give place to the kings of the earth. For he is a great king, not indeed in want of these things: but hence it is easy to see the reason of the daily provisions given to the priests and Levites, being what every monarch is accustomed to allow his servants. And all these things were intended to instruct the people that the Lord of Hosts was present among us, 'For he is a great king, and to be feared by all the nations.' These analogies will be the more apparent when it is remembered that the comparisons are to be referred to an Oriental rather than a European palace.

We do not, however, consider it sufficient to regard such a view of the Tabernacle as founded solely upon the usages of royalty as *then* existing. We are satisfied that its *typical* design is necessary to account for those features which it possessed in common with the palaces of kings. The Glory that dwelt both in the Tabernacle and the Temple was preintimative of the even yet future manifested glory of Christ, to which the 'earnest expectation of the creature' has been long looking forward, and of which the incipient dawnings begin now faintly to appear. The import of the ancient visible Shekinah and its material habitation has never yet been realized as it is destined to be in the latter day on earth; nor do we conceive it possible to gain a full and adequate idea of the *kingly* features of this typical establishment without looking forward to the time when the Savior, combining sacerdotal sanctity with royal dignity, shall sit 'a *priest* upon his *throne*,' in the earthly Zion, in accordance with the entire drift of the Old Testament prophecies. This is the state to which the anticipations of all Christians are *really* directed—a state which is to be ultimately evolved out of the present by a stupendous order of changes moral, political, and physical. The New Jerusalem of the Apocalypse is the grand object of the Christian's hope, and it is in that glorious dispensation, the theatre of which is the earth that we now inhabit, that we are to look for the *substantial realities* so strikingly figured in the ritual apparatus of the old economy. It is the state constituted by the final developement of the Kingdom of Heaven out of the regenerated and transferred dominions and dynasties of the earth, over which Jesus Christ is to reign in *visible majesty*, his redeemed people being made, in some way at present inscrutable to us, to share with him in the beatitudes and glories of his eternal kingship. It is in that dispensation, or perhaps we may say, in that stage of *this* dispensation, that the things mystically foreshown by the Tabernacle structure and the Tabernacle furniture will be made real. It will then appear how admirably adapted it was in its twofold character of Sanctuary and Palace to correspond with the twofold functions of Christ as Priest and King. But the farther unfolding of this view of the subject would carry us imperceptibly into the region of prophetic exposition, which our present plan does not embrace.

The detailed and minute account which we propose to give of every part of the Tabernacle may be prefaced with the following general description, for the most part in the words of the Editor of the Pictorial Bible. First there was the area or court in which the Tabernacle stood. This was of an oblong figure of a hundred cubits (about 150 feet) long, by fifty cubits (about 75 feet) broad; and the height of the inclosing curtain was five cubits or nearly three yards, being half the height of the Tabernacle. The inclosure was formed by a plain hanging of fine twined linen yarn, which seems to have been worked in an open or net-work texture, so that the people without might freely see the interior. The door-curtain was however of a different texture from the general hanging, being a great curtain of 'fine twined linen,' embroidered with blue, purple, and scarlet. It is described in precisely the same terms as the door-curtain of the Tabernacle itself, which was not, as commonly stated, of the same fabric with the inner covering of the Tabernacle, and the veil before the holy of holies; for in the description of the two door-curtains there is no mention of the figures of cherubim and the fancy work ('cunning work') which decorated the inner covering and vail. The door-curtain of the court was furnished with cords, by which it might be drawn up or aside when the priests had occasion to enter. The curtains of this inclosure were hung upon sixty pillars of brass, standing on bases of the same metal, but with capitals and fillets of silver. (Compare the description in this chapter with that in chap. 38.) The hooks also, to which the curtains were attached, were of silver. The entrance of the court was at the east end, opposite that to the Tabernacle; and between them stood the altar of burnt offering, but nearer to the door of the Tabernacle than to that of the court. It is uncertain whether the brazen laver was interposed between the altar and the door of the Tabernacle or not. Chap. 30. 18, certainly conveys that impression; but the Rabbins, who appear to have felt that nothing could properly interpose between the altar and Tabernacle, say that the laver was indeed nearer to the Tabernacle than was the altar, but still that it did not stand in the same line with the altar, but stood a little on one side to the south. As to the position of the Tabernacle in the court, nothing is said in the Scriptures on the subject, but it seems less probable that it stood in the centre than that it was placed towards the farther or western extremity, so as to allow greater space for the services which were to be performed exclusively in front of the Tabernacle.

The fabric properly called the Tabernacle having moveable walls of board, was of a more substantial character than a tent; but it is right to regard it as a tent, its general appearance and arrangement being the same, and its more substantial fabric being probably on account of the weight of its several envelopes which required stronger supports than are usually necessary. It was of an oblong figure, fifty-five feet in length, by eighteen feet in breadth and height. Its length extended from east to west, the entrance being at the east end. The two sides and west end consisted of a framework of boards, of which there were twenty on each side and eight at the west end. The manner in which these boards were joined to each other so as to form a wall which might be easily taken down and set up again, may be illustrated in some degree by a reference to the window-shutters of an extensive shop; but the boards of the Tabernacle did not slide in grooves, but each was furnished at the bottom with two tenons, which were received into sockets in the bases of solid silver; and to give the whole greater security, the boards were furnished each with five rings or staples of gold, by means of which they were successively run up to their proper places on horizontal poles or bars, which served as the ribs of the fabric, binding its parts together. The boards as well as the bars were of shittim wood, overlaid with thin plates of gold. The east end, being the entrance, had no boards, but was furnished with five pillars of shittim wood overlaid with gold, and each standing on a socket of brass. Four similar pillars within the Tabernacle, towards the west or further end, supported a rich hanging, which divided the interior into two apartments, of which the outer was called 'the holy place,' and the innermost and smallest

was 'the most holy place,' or the 'Holy of Holies,' in which the presence of the Lord was more immediately manifested. The separating hanging was called, by way of eminence, 'the vail;' and hence the expression 'within' or 'without the vail' is sometimes used to distinguish the most holy from the holy place. The people were never admitted into the interior of the tabernacle. None but the priests might go even into the outer chamber or holy place, and into the inner chamber the high-priest alone was allowed to enter, and that only once in the year, on the great day of atonement. To this, however, there was a necessary exception when the Tabernacle was to be taken down or set up. The outer chamber was only entered in the morning to offer incense on the altar which stood there, and to extinguish the lamps, and again in the evening to light them. On the Sabbath also the old shew-bread was taken away and replaced with new. These were all the services for which the attendance of the priests was necessary within the Tabernacle, all the sacrifices being made in the open space in front of the Tabernacle, where stood the brazen altar for burnt offerings. It will be useful to observe, that the most holy place contained only the ark with its contents; that the outer apartment contained the altar of incense, the table of shew-bread, and the great golden candlestick; while the open area in front of the Tabernacle contained the brazen laver for the ablutions of the priests, and the brazen altar for burnt offerings.

This description will give an idea of the general arrangement and substantial structure of the Tabernacle; and we may proceed to notice the various curtains which were thrown over and formed the outer coverings of the tent. The first or inner covering was of fin linen, splendidly embroidered with figures of cherubim and fancy work in scarlet, purple, and light blue. It is

CHAPTER XXV.

AND the Lord spake unto Moses, saying,

2 Speak unto the children of Israel that they bring me an offering : ª of every man that giveth it willingly with his heart ye shall take my offering.

ª ch. 35. 5, 21. 1 Chron. 29. 3, 5, 9, 14. Ezra 2. 68. & 3. 5. & 7. 16. Neh. 11. 2. 2 Cor. 8. 12. & 9. 7.

described in the same terms as the vail of the 'holy of holies,' and was doubtless of the same texture and appearance with the vail, which, according to Josephus, was embroidered with all sorts of flowers, and interwoven with various ornamented figures, excepting the forms of animals. Over this inner covering was another, made of goats' hair, which was spun by the women of the camp. Cloth made of goats' hair forms the customary covering for the tents of the Bedouin Arabs to this day, and it still continues to be spun and woven at home by the women. Over this covering was another of rams' skins dyed red, and over that the fourth and outermost covering of tahash skins (see the Note on chap. 25. 5). These curtains, after covering, or rather forming, the roof, hung down by the sides and west end of the Tabernacle, those that were outside being calculated to protect the more costly ones within, while the whole combined to render the Tabernacle impervious to the rain, and safe from the injuries of the weather.

The annexed cut will give to the reader somewhat of an adequate idea of the *frame work* of the Tabernacle, while we have reserved to a subsequent Note, ch. 26. 14, a view of the structure in its completed state with its envelope of curtains.

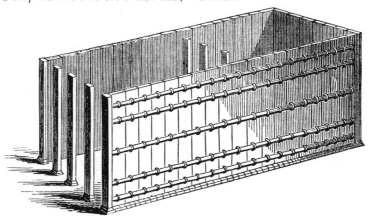

THE FRAME-WORK OF THE TABERNACLE.

2. *Speak unto the children of Israel, that they bring me,* &c. Heb. רִקְחוּ לִ *va-yikhu li, that they take for me.* The original word for 'take' very frequently has the import of *take and bring, take and give,* or *take and offer.* Thus Gen. 15. 9, '*Take* me an heifer of three years old ;' i. e. take and offer. So Ps. 68. 18, ' Thou hast *received* gifts for men ;' Heb. 'thou hast *taken;*' i. e. in order to bestow them upon men, as expounded by the apostle, Eph. 4. 8, 'gave gifts unto men.' Thus too 1 Kings, 3. 24, 'And the king said, *Bring* me a sword ;' Heb. '*take* me a sword.' 1 Kings, 17. 10, ' *Fetch* me a little water ;' Heb. '*take* me a little water.'——¶ *An offering.* Heb. תְּרוּמָה *terumah, an elevation, a heave-offering,* so called from its being *lifted up* when it was laid on

3 And this *is* the offering which
ye shall take of them; gold, and
silver, and brass,

4 And blue, and purple, and scar
let, and fine linen, and goats'
hair.

---

the altar in the act of presentation.
Chal. 'Separate a separation before me ;'
that is, such things as they should be
disposed to set apart from their effects
and consecrate to the Lord. The original term comes from רוּם *rum, to lift
up, to be lifted up*, and is generally appropriated to sacrificial offerings, which
were at least *lifted up* on the altar, if
not previously *heaved* or *waved* in the
air by way of oblation. It is elsewhere
employed as a very general term for
any thing *separated* and *made a donation* to God, and is applied, Ezek. 48.
9—20, even to the land which was to be
sacredly devoted to God and the priests
of the Temple, and which is rendered
in our version 'oblation.' In this connexion it seems to imply, that the offerings thus voluntarily made under the
promptings of a noble and liberal spirit,
were as acceptable to God, as truly
hallowed in his sight, as if they had
been real sacrifices. Thus we read of
good men offering 'sacrifices of praise.'
It is no doubt with a view to intimate
the same idea, that the Gr. and Vulg.
render it 'first-fruits ;' as if it would be
deemed the *best* and *choicest* of every
thing that they could offer. What is
done from upright motives and in a generous spirit for God will always be sure
of being rated and denominated as it
deserves.——¶ *That giveth it willingly
with his heart.* Heb. אֲשֶׁר יִדְּבֶנּוּ לִבּוֹ
*asher yiddebennu libbo, whose heart
moveth him to willingness, or liberality.*
The proposed oblation was neither to
be exacted by compulsion nor regulated
by prescription, but every one was left
to give after the promptings of his own
heart. Gr. 'Of all to whom it shall
seem good in their hearts.' Vulg. 'Of
every man that offereth of his own accord.' The original נדב *nadab* is frequently used in the sense of a *liberal*,

voluntary, and free-hearted offering,
and the correlative derivative נדבות
nedaboth occurs with a parallel meaning
Ps. 110. 3, 'Thy people shall be *willing* (נדבות *nedaboth*, lit. *willingnesses*)
in the day of the power ;' where the
drift of the Psalmist appears to be, to
compare the abundance of the free-will
offerings made to the Messiah in the
latter day for the beautifying his sanctuary (בהדרי קדש *behadrë kodesh,
with the adornments of the holy*) with
the profusion of the gifts that were so
largely poured forth at the setting up
of the Tabernacle. They shall come
forth as copiously as the drops of dew
from the womb of the morning; in a
bountifulness at least equal to that
when the dew of its noble munificence
was upon the youth of the Israelitish
church. A very appropriate commentary on the present passage is afforded
in the subsequent account of its execution, Ex. 35. 21, 22, 'And they came,
every one whose heart stirred him up,
and every one whom his spirit made
willing, and they brought the Lord's
offering to the work of the Tabernacle
of the congregation, and for all his service, and for the holy garments. And
they came, both men and women, as
many as were willing-hearted, and
brought bracelets, and ear-rings, and
rings, and tablets, all jewels of gold :
and every man that offered, offered an
offering of gold unto the Lord.' As the
Lord loves a cheerful giver, so the spirit
of a true servant of Jesus Christ prompts
him to ask not only what he *must* do
for his heavenly master, but what he
may do. See a farther consideration of
the conduct of the people on this occasion in the Note on Ex. 35. 29.

3. *Gold, and silver, and brass.* 'Here
and elsewhere we find mentioned together, the metals which were procured

the earliest, and first applied to purposes of use and ornament. No other metals were employed in the construction of the Tabernacle, nor any others mentioned but in such slight allusions as to show that they were indeed known, but not in common use. The Hebrew has the same word for both *copper* and *brass*, but our translation always renders it by *brass*, even when the context shows that the simple metal (*copper*) is intended—as in Deut. 8. 9, 'Out of whose hills thou mayest dig *brass*'— i. e. *copper*, brass being a compound factitious preparation. It is not always easy to distinguish where the word in the original denotes brass, and where copper. Perhaps we should always understand the latter in the more early passages where it occurs; and in later times we may assume that brass is intended where something refined and ornamental is implied in the text. The three metals, gold, silver, and copper, were naturally the first which men appropriated to their service; and the Scripture exhibits them as in use, and even abundant, in Egypt and Palestine a few ages after the flood. We know not precisely when these metals first became known; but at the time now immediately under our notice, the art of metallurgy had certainly attained considerable perfection; various personal ornaments, various utensils, and even images, of gold and silver, have already been often mentioned in the sacred text. It seems to our minds that a large mass of evidence in favor of the verity of the Pentateuch remains yet untouched—the evidence resulting from the perfect conformity of all its allusions to the state of the arts and the materials on which the arts operate, as well as the agreement of its statements concerning the condition of men, with the natural progress of men and of the arts they cultivate, and with the condition of things at the most early times of which profane history exhibits

any knowledge. Even the silence of the Pentateuch, as to particulars which a later writer than Moses could scarcely have failed to notice, is not the least valuable of the internal evidences which the book bears of its own antiquity and truth.'—*Pict. Bible.*

4. *Blue, and purple, and scarlet.* These are merely the names of certain colors, while no mention is made of the thing or things colored. But as we find from the apostle, Heb. 9. 19, that *scarlet wool* was employed in the sprinkling of blood, the probability is that *wool* of those colors is intended which was afterward fabricated by the women into the curtains of the Tabernacle; for however difficult it may be to conceive that they should have had in the wilderness the implements necessary to such a process, the following passage, Ex. 35. 26, puts it beyond a doubt; 'And all the women whose spirit stirred them up in wisdom *spun* goats' hair.' Thus the Heb. doctors; 'The blue spoken of in any place was wool dyed like the body of heaven; the scarlet, wool dyed in scarlet, &c.'——¶ *Blue.* Heb. תכלת *tekëleth, blue, azure, sky-color.* So Maimonides; 'This color is like the firmament.' Thus too in the Gemara (Menach. 4.) Rab. Meyr says, 'Wherein differs the תכלת *tekeleth* from the other colors? Answer, because the תכלת *tekeleth* is like the sea, and the sea like the firmament, and the firmament like the throne of glory, as it is said, Ex. 24. 10, 'Under his feet as it were sapphire bricks such as is the aspect of the serene heavens.'' Gr. ὑακινθος, *hyacinth.* This was a color distinguishing the dress of princes and potentates among the ancients, with whom the art of dyeing was carried to a high degree of perfection. The splendor and magnificence of dress seem to have consisted very much in the richness of colors, and the *blue*, which we learn from many passages of the Scriptures to have been in great request, was imported from re-

mote countries as an article of expensive and elegant luxury. It is supposed by some to have been the product of the *indigo*, a plant deriving its origin, as it doubtless does its name, from India, where its beautiful dyes have long given value to the fine linens and cottons of that ancient empire.—— ¶ *Purple*. Heb. אַרְגָּמָן *argaman*, rendered *purple* by all the ancient versions. This is the name of a very precious color extracted from the *purpura*, or *murex*, a species of shell-fish, called in English *the purple*. This color, the same with the famous Tyrian dye, and the most celebrated of all the ancient dyes, is now lost, and it is doubted by many whether the moderns have any thing which equals it in richness and brilliancy. It is known, however, that the coloring juice of the *purple* was contained in a vessel found in the throat of the *murex*, and that only one drop of liquid was obtained from each. A sacred character was very early attached to the purple, and it was the predominant color in things pertaining to the worship of God among heathen nations. In modern times, although the Tyrian purple has been long lost, yet the pride of the name is still preserved in the sacerdotal hierarchy. It was also an attribute of exalted birth and of dignities. It served as a decoration to the first magistrates of Rome, and finally became a symbol of the inauguration of the emperors. To assume the 'imperial purple' was but another name for succeeding to the throne, and the punishment of death was at length decreed against any of inferior grade who should presume to wear the royal color. To this penalty it was undoubtedly owing that the art of dyeing purple gradually disappeared from among the nations of Europe. From the epithet 'purple' being applied by Homer and Virgil to blood, it is probable that this color anciently approached much nearer to scarlet than the modern purple. Indeed the two, in the writings of the ancients, are frequently confounded together. And so also in the New Testament we find them inter changed, as Mark, 15. 17, 'they clothed him with *purple*,' compared with Mat. 27. 28, 'they put on him a *scarlet robe*.' See also John, 19. 2. 'It is important, says the Editor of the Pictorial Bible 'to understand, that the word ' purple in ancient writings does not denote one particular color. Pliny mentions the difference between some of the purples; one was faint, approaching to our scarlet, and this was the least esteemed; another was very deep approaching to violet ; and a third was of a color compared to coagulated bullock's blood. The most esteemed Tyrian purple seems to have been of this last color. We say 'the most esteemed,' because it appears that even the Tyrian purple was not one particular color, but a class of animal dyes, as distinguished from vegetable, varying in shade from the most faint to the most intense.' The purple has been styled the most sublime of all earthly colors, having the gaudiness of the red, of which it retains a shade, softened with the gravity of the blue.—— ¶ *Scarlet*. Heb. תּוֹלַעַת שָׁנִי *tolaath shani, worm of repetition*. This tincture or color is expressed by a word which signifies ' worm-color,' as ' vermillion,' comes from *vermiculus*, a little *worm*, from its being produced from a worm or insect which grew in a *coccus*, or excrescence of a shrub of the oak kind. This shrub is sometimes called the 'kermez-oak,' from 'kermez,' the Arabic word both for the worm and the color ; whence the Latin ' carmasinus,' the French ' cramoisi,' and the English ' crimson.' The color produced from the *coccus* was a lively bright red, approaching to the hue of fire. In the original of the passage before us, the Heb. word תּוֹלַעַת *tolaath*, for the *worm* or coloring matter, is connected with ' Shani,' which signifies *repeated* or *double*, implying that to strike this

color the wool or cloth was twice dipped; hence the Vulgate renders the
original 'coccum bis tinctum,' *scarlet
twice dyed.* The scarlet also was an
honorable color, being that of the Roman emperors in time of war, while the
purple was the raiment of peace. Accordingly in the book of Revelation the
scarlet color, being that of blood, is a
symbol of slaughter, and attributed especially to the woman drunk with the
blood of the saints, who is represented,
Rev. 18. 3, riding upon a beast of the
same color, another symbol of a persecuting and sanguinary power. ' Professor Tyehsen, supposing the identity of the Scripture 'scarlet' with the
kermes established, properly concludes
that the kermes dye was known before
the time of Moses;—that the dye was
known to the Egyptians in the time of
Moses; for the Israelites must have
carried it along with them from Egypt;
—that the Arabs received the name
'kermes,' with the dye, from Armenia
and Persia, where it was indigenous,
and had been long known; and that
name banished the old name in the east,
as the name 'scarlet' has in the west.
Kermes signifies always *red dye;* and
when pronounced short it becomes *deep
red.* Beckmann thinks that in later
times the Tyrian purples were superseded by the improvements of this dye;
but we do not feel satisfied with his
authorities for this conclusion. The
kermes itself has now long been superseded by the American cochineal, which
is far superior to any pigment employed in ancient times for dyeing reds. Indeed we have perhaps little cause to regret the loss or disuse of any ancient
dye, particulary in bright reds, which
owe so much to discoveries of chem-
istry, that we have every reason to conclude them infinitely superior to any
which ancient art could produce. Pliny
complains that scarlet dyes could not
be made sufficiently durable and adhesive; and the statements in ancient au-

thors as to the brilliancy of scarlet may
be admitted by recollecting that they
had nothing better with which to com
pare it.' *Pict. Bible.*——¶ *Fine linen.*
Heb. שׁשׁ *shesh;* denoting the fabric
made from the plant of that name which
grew in Egypt and Palestine, and which
is rendered by the Gr. and Chal. 'Byss,'
from the Heb. בוּץ *butz.* It was either
a species of soft, delicate, and downy
cotton, or a superior kind of flax, from
which garments were made of the most
pure and exquisite white. Moses indeed does not employ the term 'Butz'
in speaking of linen, which appears in
no author prior to the age of the books
of Esther and Chronicles, but the words
'Bad' and 'Shesh,' rendered 'Byssos,'
linen, by the Sept. appear to have been
the only ones in use in his day. That
which is of most importance in respect
to the 'Shesh' or 'Byss,' is the fact here
mentioned, that it was the material of
which the priestly garments were made
which we are told were designed for
' glory and for honor' to the wearers.
They were in fact the garments of kings
and of nobles. In Gen. 41. 42, we see
that Joseph in his exaltation was clothed in one of them, rendered by the Gr.
' stole of byss.' So likewise David appeared in a similar robe on a day of
solemnity, 1 Chron. 15. 27. In short,
the *byss* garments were the most resplendent and valuable of all the white
apparel in use among the Israelites.
Our Savior, therefore, in the parable of
the rich man describes him as clad ' in
purple and *fine linen*, Gr. 'byss.' Again,
when the marriage of the Lamb is described in the Apocalypse, ch. 19. 8, it
is said of the bride, that ' it was granted to her that she should be arrayed in
fine linen (byss) clean and white; for
the fine linen is the righteousness of
saints.' From what we have already
said the symbolical import of this will
not be of difficult solution. The *byss*
being the most valuable species of white
garments, constitutes a significant em-

5 And rams' skins dyed red, and | badgers' skins, and shittim-wood,

blem of the highest and most perfect holiness. The resurrection is the state of perfect holiness; the *byss*, therefore, is the attribute of the saints in a state of resurrection. In like manner we suppose the ' man clothed in linen,' so frequently mentioned by Ezekiel, ch. 9. and 10, to be a symbolical designation of Christ in his post-resurrection state, in which state we know he is for the most part represented as clothed in white raiment.——¶ *Goat's* hair. Heb. עזים *izzim.* That is, the down or finest part of the hair; of which much finer cloth was made in those countries than of the wool of the lamb or the sheep. The hair of the eastern goats, particularly of the Angola species, is of the most delicate and silky softness, and wrought into the kind of cloth known by the name of *camlets.* The word ' hair' does not occur in the Hebrew, but the sense evidently requires its insertion.

5. *Rams' skins dyed red.* Heb. ערת אלם מאדמים *oroth ëlim meoddamim, skins of red rams.* That is, either those which were naturally of this color, for such are found in the Levant, or those which were made so by dyeing, and thus converted to a kind of *red morocco.*——¶ *Badgers' skins.* Heb. ערת תחשים *oroth tehashin.* It is very uncertain what is intended by the original word תחש *tahash* here rendered ' badger.' The ancient versions for the most part evidently consider it as designating some kind of color, either purple or violet. But as it appears from Ezek. 16. 10, that it denotes a substance from which shoes were made, it is probably safer to consider it as the appellation of some of the animal tribes whose skins would serve for a rough exterior covering of the Tabernacle to protect the more delicate work of the inner curtains from injury by the weather. Yet that it could not have been

the animal now called ' badger,' there is the strongest reason to believe. The badger is an inhabitant of cold countries, nor can any evidence be adduced that it ever existed in Palestine, Arabia, or Egypt. Whence then could the Israelites have procured its skin to cover the Tabernacle, especially in such quantities as would be requisite? It is by no means a prolific animal, and in the countries in which it breeds, as in England, it is comparatively rare. Moreover, as it is pronounced unclean by the Mosaic law, it would scarcely have been employed for such a sacred purpose. But if it were an animal at all, of what species was it? Aben Ezra thinks, from the force of the term, that it was some animal which was *thick* and *fat,* and 'in this sense the word appears to be the same as the Arabic *dasash,* fat, oily. The conjecture, then, of those who refer the *tahash* to the seal, is every way credible; as in our own island the seal is famous for its fat or oil, which, in default of whale oil, is used for similar purposes. Moreover, sealskins, on account of their durability, are used to cover trunks and boxes, to defend them from the weather; and as the skin of the *tahash* was used for making shoes, (Ezek. 16. 10.), so the skin of the seal may be, and is, tanned into as good leather as calf-skin itself. It remains, then, to be proved that an animal, fit for the purpose, was readily procurable by the Israelites in the wilderness; for this we quote Thevenot (p. 166.), who, being at Tor, a port on the Red Sea, says, 'But they could not furnish me with any thing of a certain fish, which they call a *sea-man.* However, I got the hand of one since. This fish is taken in the Red Sea, about little isles, that are close by Tor. It is a great, strong fish, and hath nothing extraordinary but two hands, which are indeed like the hands of a man, saving that the fingers are

6 b Oil for the light, c spices for anointing oil, and for d sweet incense.

b ch. 27. 20.   c ch. 30. 23.   d ch. 30. 34.

7 Onyx-stones, and stones to be set in the e ephod, and in the f breast-plate.

e ch. 28. 4, 6.   f ch. 28. 15.

joined together with a skin like the foot of a goose ; *but the skin of the fish is like the skin of a wild goat, or chamois.* When they spy that fish, they strike him on the back with harping irons, as they do whales, and so kill him. *They use the skin of it for making bucklers, which are musket proof.*' Whether this be a species of seal must be left undetermined ; as nothing is said of its coming ashore, or being amphibious ; nevertheless, it may be the *tahash* of the Hebrews. Niebuhr says (p. 157, Fr. edit.), 'A merchant of Abushahr called *dahash* that fish which the captains of English vessels called *porpoise*, and the Germans *sea-hog*, or *dolphin*. In my voyage from Maskat to Abushahr, I saw a prodigious quantity together, near Ras Mussendom, who all were going the same way, and seemed to swim with great vehemence.' Gesenius adopts the same opinion, on account of the similarity of the Arabic name *dahash*, which means, properly, the dolphin, but is also applied to the seal genus. On many of the small islands of the Red Sea, around the peninsula of Sinai, are found seals ; (hence *insula phocarum*, Strab. 16. p. 766.) likewise, a species of seacow, called also sea-man or sea-camel, the skin of which is an inch thick, and is used by the Arabs of the present day for shoe-leather. Burckhardt remarks that he ' saw parts of the skin of a large fish, killed on the coast, which was an inch in thickness, and is employed by the Arabs instead of leather for sandals.' *Robinson's Calmet.*——¶ *Shittim-wood.* Heb. שטים עצי *atzë shittim, wood of the shittah tree,* mentioned Is. 41. 19. It is rendered by the Gr. ξυλα ασηπτα, *incorruptible wood.* Though not certainly known, it is supposed, with great probability, to be the acacia, or

species of thorn that still grows in great abundance in the deserts of Arabia ; the wood of which, according to Jerome, is extremely light, solid, strong, and smooth ; qualities rarely found together in any one wood. The tree is of the size of a large mulberry-tree, large enough, says the father above mentioned, to furnish very long planks. ' The Acacia-tree,' says Dr. Shaw, ' being by much the largest and most common tree in these deserts (Arabia Petrea), we have some reason to conjecture that the shittim-wood was the acacia.'

6. *Oil for the light.* For the lamp that was to burn continually in the sanctuary. This it appears, from Ex. 27. 20, was to be 'pure olive oil beaten.' ——¶ *Spices.* Heb. בשמים *besamim.* Gr. θυμιαματα, *incenses.* The term includes all the odoriferous ingredients which were employed in the composition of the 'anointing oil' or the ointment by which the altar of incense and all the vessels of the ark were hallowed, and lastly, in the incense which was burnt upon the altar.——¶ *For sweet incense.* Heb. הסמים לקטרת *liktoreth hassammim, for the burning of sweet odors;* i. e. upon the golden altar that stood in the holy place. Comp Ex. 30. 22—28.

7. *Onyx stones.* Heb. שהם אבני *abnè shoham, stones of shoham.* See Note on Gen. 2. 12. It is acknowledged that there is great difficulty in ascertaining what stone is meant by the 'shoham.' The Gr. translates the word in different places by no less than six different terms. In the three Chaldee Targums, as also in the Syriac, Arabic, Persic, and Ethiopic versions, it is rendered by 'beryl,' which Ainsworth adopts in his Annotations. As it was one of the jewels in the breastplate, and as two

8 And let them make me a g sanc- | tuary; that h I may dwell among them.

g ch. 36. 1, 3, 4. Lev. 4. 6. & 10. 4. & 21. 12. Hebr. 9. 1, 2.

h ch. 29. 45. 1 Kings 6. 13. 2 Cor. 6. 16. Hebr. 3. 6. Rev. 21. 3.

of them were borne on the High Priest's shoulders, each containing the names of six of the twelve tribes of Israel, it must have been a stone of very considerable size. On this account it is less likely to have been the *onyx* which is a very small stone. There were several kinds of ' beryls,' the most approved of which were of a *sea-green* color, though Pliny describes one as inclining to a hyacinthine or azure color. But of the ' beryl' see Note on Ex. 28. 9, 20.—— ¶ *Stones to be set.* Heb. אבני מלאים *abnë milluïm, stones of fillings;* i. e. stones to be set in, or, as artists say, *enchased* in the cavities of gold of the ephod. For a description of the Ephod and Breastplate, see on Ex. 28. 4, and 15.

8. *Let them make me a sanctuary.* Heb. מקדש *mikdash, a holy place;* from קדש *kadash, to sanctify, to hallow.* The term denotes a *holy habitation* expressly consecrated to the residence of the visible divine majesty in the midst of them.——¶ *That I may dwell among them.* Heb. ושכנתי *veshakanti, and I will dwell.* Gr. οφθησομαι εν ὑμιν, *I will be seen among you.* Chal. 'I will make my Glory to dwell in the midst of them.' Arab. 'That I may make my Splendor to inhabit among them.' The import plainly is, that God would dwell among them by the signal manifestations of his glory in the Shekinah, the visible token of his presence. The original word שכנתי *shakanti* comes from שכן *shakan, to dwell in a tent or tabernacle,* and from the same root comes both שכינה *shekinah,* and the Gr. σκηνοω, *to tabernacle,* from which latter is the derivative σκηνη, *a tent* or *tabernacle.* The radical consonants (*sh*)*s, k, n,* are the same in both languages, to which the vowels are mere factitious append-

ages. In express allusion therefore to the mode of the divine residence among the Israelites, it is said of Christ, John 1. 14, ' the Word was made flesh and *dwelt* (εσκηνωσε *tabernacled* or *shekinized*) among us, and we beheld his *glory;*' i. e. at the transfiguration, when the cloud or vail of his flesh, by being temporarily rent asunder, disclosed the true inner glory of his Godhead, answering to the luminous cloud of the Shekinah, which is in numerous instances called δοξα, *glory.* In like manner, in allusion to the sensible mode in which God manifested himself to his peculiar people. Christ is said to be the 'brightness of the Father's glory,' Heb. 1. 3, language which goes to identify the person of the Son with the glorious apparition of the Shekinah. The term again occurs in evident allusion to these words of Moses, Rev. 21. 3, 'And I heard a great voice out of heaven saying, Behold, the *tabernacle* of God is with men, and he will *dwell with them.*' This is the fulfilment of the prediction uttered by Ezekiel 37. 26, 27, 'And I will set my *sanctuary* in the midst of them for evermore ; my *tabernacle* also shall be with them ; yea, I will be their God, and they shall be my people,' announcing a period yet future when this earth shall again be distinguished by some visible manifestation of the divine presence under circumstances of far more glory than those in which he appeared of old to the chosen people, and answering the same purpose in respect to the whole human race which the Shekinah of the Tabernacle did in respect to a single nation. It is the period, as we have elsewhere remarked, of the New Jerusalem, of which the same prophet says, Ezek. 48. 35, 'The name of the city from that day shall ᴅᴇ, *The Lord*

9 i According to all that I shew thee, *after* the pattern of the tab-

i ver. 40.

ernacle, and the pattern of all the instruments thereof, even so shall ye make *it*.

---

is there (שמה יהוה *Yehovah shammah*).' But 'the Lord' (Jehovah) is the Shekinah, and the Shekinah is the Logos and the Lamb who is to be the Light and Glory of the heaven-descended city, and the intimation is clear that this *manifested presence* of the Deity is there to form so prominent and conspicuous an object, that the city itself is to receive from it its characteristic denomination. At the same time it is not to be forgotten that it will be a residence 'among men,' men inhabiting this terraqueous globe; for there is no greater mistake than to interpret the sublime representations of the latter part of the Apocalypse of an extramundane state of glory, having no relation to the present condition of man, or to the original scene of his existence. Time and the Providence of God will doubtless work a great change in the views of believers in reference to the genuine scope of the visions contained in this wonderful book, a portion of revelation which unfortunately has fallen into a disesteem never enough to be deplored.

9. *According to all that I shew.* Heb. אתך מראה אני אשר ככל *kekol asher ani mareh otheka, according to all that I make thee to see.* We have before remarked, Ex. 24. 10, 11, that we suppose the pattern of the Tabernacle and its furniture, but more especially the Ark, the Cherubim and the Glory, to have been shown to Moses in the presence of Aaron and his sons and the seventy elders, and the phraseology of the present passage does not militate with this idea. The designation of time by the Hebrew verbs and participles is very indefinite, and in this instance the usus loquendi will admit of the showing being understood of the past as well as the present. The whole time of Mo-

ses' sojourn on the mount, after leaving the camp with his companions, seems to be spoken of as one continuous term, not requiring to have its periods accurately distinguished. —— ¶ *After the pattern of the tabernacle.* Heb. תבנית משכן *tabnith mishkan.* We have in משכן *mishkan* another derivative from the root שכן *shakan,* rightly rendered *tabernacle.* The other term תבנית *tabnith,* comes from בנה *banah, to build,* and properly signifies in this connexion *a model, a prototype, an exemplar,* implying something *sensible, corporeal,* or *substantial* in contradistinction from דמות *demuth, a likeness,* which is applied rather in the general sense of *representation, picture,* or *image,* than of a *framed model* of any kind of structure. The distinction is very clearly indicated in 2 Kings, 16. 10, 'And king Ahaz went to Damascus to meet Tiglath-pileser, king of Assyria, and saw an altar that was at Damascus: and king Ahaz sent to Urijah the priest *the fashion* (דמות *demuth*) of the altar, and *the pattern* (תבנית *tabnith*) of it, according to all the workmanship thereof;' where תבנית undoubtedly signifies *a model,* and דמות some other kind of *representation,* either *verbal* or *pictorial.* In like manner we find a striking parallel, not only to the *phrase,* but to the *general fact* here recorded, in the history of the building of the Temple, 1 Chron. 28. 11, 12, 'Then David gave to Solomon his son *the pattern* (תבנית) of the porch, and of the houses thereof, and of the treasures thereof, and of the upper chambers thereof, and of the inner parlors thereof, and of the place of the mercy-seat, and *the pattern* (תבנית) of all he had by the Spirit, of the courts of the house of the Lord, and of all the chambers round about, of the treasuries of the house of God, and of the treasuries of the dedicated things.' David, it seems, was furnished by divine inspiration with a *visionary archetype* of the Temple which he would have Solomon build to the Lord, and in accordance with this vision he procured a *pattern* or *model* to be executed, which should answer the purpose of guiding his son in the construction of the sacred edifice. In the present instance, we do not indeed imagine that there was any miniature model in wood or stone of the Tabernacle made by Omnipotence and shown to Moses; but we do suppose that the *supernatural spectacle* presented to his view was so ordered as to convey to his mind all the impression which would have been produced by an actual objective presentation of the scenery to his outward senses in the form of substantial realities. On this strong, clear, and vivid impression of the objects seen, we suppose the use of the term *model* or *pattern* was founded. The vision was to him in the place of a *pattern*.

It may not be inapposite in this connexion to dwell somewhat upon the fact of the remarkable, and we doubt not designed, inter-relation between the general plan of the Tabernacle in its different parts, and the ideas usually entertained among the ancient Hebrews of the structure of the heavens. However it may be accounted for, we think the position is unquestionable, that the Scriptures, in their peculiar phraseology, do recognise a singular correspondence between at least the inner sanctuary, the holy of holies, both in the Tabernacle and Temple, and the supernal regions called *heaven* or *the heavens*, considered especially as the residence of God, where he sat upon the throne of his glory, surrounded by the angelic hosts. Indeed Gussetius, an eminent Hebrew Lexicographer, contends that all the 'pattern' shown to Moses on this occasion was the *heavens themselves*. This is perhaps too vague

an explanation to meet the demands of a rigid exegesis, but that there was a remarkable symbolical affinity, running occasionally into absolute identity, in the ideas of *heaven* and the *holy of holies*, may doubtless be shown beyond dispute. Such a fact, if it can be made to appear, will be of great importance in giving distinctness to our conceptions of the mystic scenery of the Apocalypse, which may be said to be almost entirely made up of elements furnished by the Tabernacle and Temple ritual. It will also go far to account for the allegorising expositions of Josephus and Philo, who evidently confounded the *symbolical* with the *philosophical* import of these sacred ordinances. Of these writers, the latter says expressly when speaking of the Tabernacle, that 'as for the inside, Moses parted its length into three partitions. At the distance of ten cubits from the most secret end, he placed four pillars, each a small matter distant from his fellow. Now the room within these pillars was The Most Holy Place; but the rest of the room was the Tabernacle, which was open for the priests. However this proportion of the measures of the Tabernacle proved to be *an imitation of the system of the world;* for that third part thereof which was within the four pillars, to which the (common) priests were not admitted, *is, as it were, an heaven peculiar to God;* but the space of the twenty cubits, is, as it were, sea and land, on which men live, and so this part is peculiar to the priests only.' Again, in accordance with this idea, he says of the Candlestick, that 'it terminated in seven heads, in one row, all standing parallel to one another; and these branches carried seven lamps, one by one, *in imitation of the number of the planets.*' In another passage, where he feels himself called upon to vindicate the wisdom of the Mosaic institutions, he remarks, 'Now here one may wonder at the ill-will which men bear to us, and which they profess to be on account of our despising that deity which they pretend to honor; for if any one do but consider the fabric of the Tabernacle, and take a view of the garments of the high priest, and of those vessels which we make use of in our sacred ministration, he will find that our legislator was a divine man, and that we are unjustly reproached by others; for if any one do without prejudice, and with judgment look upon these things, he will find *they were every one made in way of imitation and representation of the universe.* When Moses distinguished the Tabernacle into three parts, and allowed two of them to the priests, as a place accessible and common, he denoted the land and the sea, they being of general access to all; *but he set apart the third division for God, because heaven is inaccessible to men.'*

In what manner these astronomical ideas became grafted upon the peculiar fabric we are now considering, would no doubt be a difficult problem to solve, were it not for the clue afforded us in the scriptural diction which we are now about to lay before the reader. From this it will appear that it originated in a perversion or distortion of the dim intimations which were then enjoyed of the true symbolical import of these sacred institutions. And no doubt a large portion of the ancient mythological fictions could be traced by a rigid inquisition to the same source. *They are the distorted relics of an early revelation abounding in types and symbols.*

We have said that our present enquiry derives importance from its furnishing a key to the mystic scenery of the Apocalypse. Let us then take our starting point from this wonderful book, and if we should be led into somewhat of an extended array of the prophetic *usus loquendi,* we may still hope to find the result richly rewarding the time and toil of the investigation.

Probably few readers of the Revelation have failed to be struck with the fact, that while the scene of the vision is apparently laid *in heaven* (rather '*the* heaven'—ϵν τῳ ουρανῳ), yet the presence of many of the appurtenances of the Tabernacle or Temple is constantly recognised. Thus in ch. 4. 1, 2, John says, 'After this I looked, and behold a door was opened in heaven— and immediately I was in the Spirit; and behold a throne was set in heaven, and one sat on the throne.' Now as he goes on to describe a 'sea of glass' answerable to the 'brazen sea' which stood before the sanctuary; the 'four living creatures' identical with the 'cherubims' that spread their wings over the mercy-seat; and 'seven lamps of fire burning before the throne,' corresponding with the seven lamps of the candlestick placed before the vail in the holy place; how can we resist the conclusion that the 'heaven' of which he speaks is really nothing else than the *holy of holies,* and that the *throne* is the mercy-seat on which the Shekinah, the visible Glory, rested? This is confirmed by the annexed circumstance of seeing a *door,* or rather *a door-way, an entrance* (θυρα), which had been previously opened (ανεῳγμενη), and through which he was enabled to see the throne and its occupant. Now where a doorway is mentioned, the idea of an apartment or apartments naturally suggests itself to the mind, and if John saw the *throne* through the *opened entrance,* he must have been in one apartment, and the throne in another, as otherwise it is impossible to discover a reason for the mention of the door-way at all in this connexion. All this accords perfectly with the local arrangements of the Tabernacle and Temple, which consisted of two apartments, commonly separated by the vail of partition. In the outer apartment, or holy place, stood the seven-branched candlestick, **and throughout the three first chapters the** scene of John's vision is confined altogether to this first or outer room, where he beholds Christ in his priestly dress engaged about the lights of the lamp, which in the language of symbols are said to be seven stars that he holds in his right hand. Up to this time John had not seen the mercy-seat; the vail therefore was then in its place, and the θυρα or *entrance-way* was closed. But now a fresh illapse of the Spirit comes upon him, the vail is removed, and his entranced eye looks into the inner hallowed shrine of the sanctuary.

If then the scene of this vision was the *earthly sanctuary*, and not *heaven above*, as has been generally imagined, why does he call it 'the heaven?' To this we answer, because it is so called in the Old Testament, and because it was intended as a type or adumbration of the true heaven, the place of final happiness and glory of the saints. As this is a fact of some importance and one that goes to correct the interpretation of many passages in which the word 'heaven' occurs, a strict examination of the Old Testament usage in regard to this word will be necessary. And first it is clear that the *mercy-seat* is called God's *seat;* and the *sanctuary* which contained the mercy-seat God's *dwelling* or *sitting-place.* Respecting this *seat* or *throne*, God says to Moses, Ex. 25. 22, 'There will I meet with thee, and *commune* (דברתי *dibbarti*) with thee from above the mercy-seat, and from between the two cherubims which are upon the ark of the testimony,' &c. The place of the mercy-seat being intended for oral communication, it receives a name answerable to this in 1 Kings, 6 and 8, and in 2 Chron. 5, where it is called דביר *debir, word-place, speaking-place, oracle,* which term in 1 Kings, 8. 6, is plainly put in apposition with קדש הקדשים *kodesh hakkodoshim, the holy of holies,* the name given to the inner apartment of the sanctuary; 'And the priests brought

in the ark of the covenant of the Lord unto his place, into the *oracle* (דביר) of the house, to *the most holy place* (קדש הקדשים) even under the wings of the cherubims.' In the dedication of the temple by Solomon the phraseology in different passages is to be especially noticed. Thus in 1 Kings, 8. 13, he says, 'I have surely built thee a house to dwell in, *a settled place* (מכון *mekon,* lit. *a prepared place*) for thee to abide in for ever.' Here it is to be observed that Solomon calls the *house* which he had built the מכון *mekon* or *prepared place,* putting these terms in apposition; and consequently leaving us to infer that whatever other terms may in the context be found put in apposition with either of these, they are to have a similar application. With this remark premised let the phraseology in the sequel of the chapter be observed. In v. 30, it is said, 'Hearken thou to the supplication of thy servants, and of thy people Israel, when they shall pray toward this place: and hear thou *in heaven thy dwelling-place:* (אל מקום שבתך אל השמים *el mekom shibteka el hash-shamayim, in thy sitting-place, or dwelling-place, even in the heaven*): and when thou hearest forgive.' With this compare v. 39, 'Then hear thou *in heaven thy dwelling-place* (מכון שבתך *mekon shibteka, the prepared place of thy sitting, or dwelling*), and forgive,' &c. Here there is a change of terms in the original which is lost sight of in our version, but which is quite important in making out the point before us. In the one case we have מקום שבתך *mekom shibteka, the place of thy dwelling;* in the other מכון שבתך *mekon shibteka, the prepared place of thy dwelling.* But it is clear from the comparison thus made in the Hebrew text, that the terms 'heaven,' 'house,' and 'prepared place' are used as equivalents. But Solomon says, v. 13, that *he had built* the מכון *mekon* or *prepared place;* consequently he had built the *heaven* in which God is here said to dwell. It is true indeed that in other texts in this chapter 'heaven' is clearly employed in the sense of the upper regions of ether, or the celestial firmament, as it is ordinarily understood. Thus v. 23, 'And he said, Lord God of Israel, there is no God like thee *in heaven above*, or on earth beneath.' So also v. 27, 'But will God indeed dwell on the earth? behold the *heaven and heaven of heavens* cannot contain thee; how much less this house that I have builded?' But while this is admitted, it is impossible to resist the evidence that *prepared place* and *heaven* are synonimous terms in this connexion, and consequently that *the heaven* was a place which Solomon had built for the residence of the Most High by his appropriate symbol. In thinking of 'the heaven' of which Solomon here speaks we are to bring before our minds the imagery connected with the *holy of holies*, viz., the ark of the covenant, the mercy-seat or throne, the overshadowing cherubims, and the luminous cloud of the Shekinah.

This view will be confirmed by the parallel recital in 2 Chron. chps. 6 and 7, particularly 7. 1, 2, where a circumstance of great importance is noticed, which is not stated in the book of Kings; 'Now when Solomon had made an end of praying, the fire came down *from heaven* (מֵהַשָּׁמַיִם *mëhash-shamayim, from the heaven*), and consumed the burnt-offering and the sacrifices; and the glory of the Lord filled the house. And the priests could not enter into the house of the Lord, because the glory of the Lord had filled the Lord's house.' The answer thus given to the prayer of Solomon in the presence of all the worshippers, gave evidence that God had accepted *the house, the sanctuary, the heaven, the place prepared for his sitting;* for the fire here spoken of descended undoubtedly not from *heaven above*, but from the cloud which covered the mercy-seat

in the holy of holies. It is to be observed that the cloud had filled not only the inner apartment in which the priests had placed the mercy-seat, but the holy place or outer apartment, in which the priests usually officiated, so that the priests could no longer continue there (1 Kings, 8. 10). All were in the court without, in that part where the altar stood, before the sanctuary; and when Solomon had ended his prayer, fire came forth from the sanctuary, from which the priests had been expelled by the luminous cloud, *the prepared place of God's sitting, the heaven,* and fell upon and consumed the sacrifice. This is to be presumed from the analogous circumstance mentioned Lev 9. 23, 24, 'And Moses and Aaron went into the Tabernacle of the congregation, and came out and blessed the people; and the glory of the Lord appeared unto all the people. *And there came a fire out from before the Lord,* and consumed upon the altar the burnt-offering and the fat: which when all the people saw, they shouted and fell on their faces.' By this is doubtless meant that the fire came out from the presence of the Shekinah, which had now taken its station in the holy of holies, though the glorious effulgence had spread itself on this occasion over all the Tabernacle and appeared in the view of the whole congregation. Consider moreover the coincidence of the circumstances stated respecting *this heaven, the place prepared by Solomon* for the God of Israel to dwell in, and those stated by John respecting *the heaven* he describes. In Solomon's heaven there was *a seat* or *throne* (the mercy-seat); so there is in John's. Solomon's heaven was a *speaking-place* or *oracle,* and from Solomon's heaven came *fire* to consume the sacrifice; so also from the throne described by John proceeded *voices and lightnings,* Rev. 4. 5; and the seat in each is occupied by One to whom divine honors are paid.

The foregoing are not the only passages which serve to prove that 'the heaven' in which John saw the *opened entrance* and *the throne*, was the *earthly sanctuary*. In proportion as the relation which subsists between the different things mentioned in the Apocalypse is discovered, our knowledge of the particulars will be extended. At present we will simply advert to a single passage which will receive a striking light from the exposition given above. In Rev. 13. 1—10, we have the description of a symbolical beast identical with the fourth beast of Daniel, which is all but universally admitted to shadow forth the persecuting power of the Roman empire. Among the other disastrous doings of this baneful monster, it is said, v. 6, that 'he opened his mouth in blasphemy against God, to blaspheme his name, *and his Tabernacle, and them that dwell in heaven.*' That is, to blaspheme, reproach, vilify, lord it over, and persecute the true worshippers of God, represented by the Cherubims that were placed over the Ark of the Covenant, in the *holy of holies.* So that in blaspheming *the tabernacle,* he blasphemed those that dwelt in it, or in other words, those that *dwelt in heaven.*'

On the whole, we cannot question but that this idea of the import of the term 'heaven' is important to a right view of that blessed expectancy which, under the same name, sustains and fires the hope of the Christian in his toilsome pilgrimage through this vale of tears. If we conceive the subject aright, *the heavenly state is the substance of the mystery of the Most Holy Place of the Tabernacle and Temple.* This mystery is explained in the closing chapters of the Apocalypse, which affords us the only adequate clue to the prophetic purport of the Tabernacle-structure. There indeed the *inner oracle* is expanded into a glorious city, but it is enriched with the possession of the same celestial sanctities,

unfolded into their full dimensions, and shining forth in a splendor suited to their divine nature. The link of connexion between the type and the antitype, the shadow and the substance, we doubt not, is clearly disclosed in the following passages ; 'And he carried me away in the spirit to a great and high mountain, and showed me that great city the holy Jerusalem, descending out of heaven from God, *having the glory of God :* and her light was like unto a stone most precious, even like a jasper-stone, clear as crystal ; *and the city lieth four-square,* and the length is as large as the breadth : and he measured the city with the reed, twelve thousand furlongs. The length, and the breadth, and the height of it are equal.' Here we recognise in the 'Glory of God' the Shekinah of the ancient economy, and in the four-square form of the city the substantiated verity of the *holy of holies* of the Tabernacle and the Temple, in each of which this apartment was *a perfect cube.* Again it is said, 'And I saw no temple therein : for the Lord God Almighty and the Lamb are the temple of it.' By the 'temple' here is to be understood the *pronaos,* or *anterior structure,* which contained the outer room, as contradistinguished from the *sanctum sanctorum,* which in this ulterior economy of glory has absorbed within itself the distinguishing features of every previous, imperfect and shadowy dispensation, and become *the all in all.* 'And the city had no need of the sun, neither of the moon, to shine in it ; for the glory of God did lighten it, and the Lamb is the light thereof. And there shall be no night there ; and they need no candle, neither light of the sun ; for the Lord God giveth them light : and they shall reign for ever and ever.' This is language evidently borrowed from Isaiah in speaking, chap. 19. 20, of the same halcyon period ; 'The sun shall be no more thy light by day : neither for brightness

shall the moon give light unto thee :
but the Lord shall be unto thee an everlasting light, and thy God thy glory.
Thy sun shall no more go down ; neither shall thy moon withdraw itself :
for the Lord shall be thine everlasting
light, and the days of thy mourning
shall be ended.' It contains another,
and still more emphatic, recognition
of that *Resplendent Presence* which under the title of *Jehovah, Angel of Jehovah, Shekinah, Glory of the Lord,*
&c., pointed forward to Christ in his
risen and glorified *theanthropy,* when he
should be revealed, as he is here, as
the Luminary of the New Jerusalem,
superseding the sun, and throwing all
created glory into eclipse. In the idea
of this transcendent illumination we
may safely include all the *moral* elements, which in the pious mind naturally connect themselves with the manifested presence of the *God of Truth,*
and at the same time admit the sense
of the *visible personal display* which
seems to be called for by the explicitness of the letter. Still we are reminded that the scene, however magnificent
and beautiful, is sublunary. Whatever
physical changes of a renovating nature
may take place upon the surface of the
globe, or in its relation to the planet-
ary system, the locality of this state
of ' accomplished bliss' will be upon
the earth which we now inhabit, at
least for the period to which the Scriptures carry forward the heirs of life in
their revelations of eternal destiny.
What new phases of felicity may come
over their lot in the boundless tract
of time and space into which their existence is launched, revolving ages can
alone determine. But the disclosures
of revelation still retain us within the
precincts of the inhabited earth. 'And
the nations of them which are saved
shall walk in the light of it ; and the
kings of the earth do bring their glory
and honor into it.' This is strikingly
paralleled by the kindred prediction of

Isaiah, ch. 60. 2, 3—11, 'The Lord shall
arise upon thee, and his glory shall
be seen upon thee. And the Gentiles
(nations) shall come to thy light, and
kings to the brightness of thy rising.
Therefore thy gates shall be open continually ; they shall not be shut day
nor night, that men may bring unto thee
the forces (wealth) of the Gentiles, and
that their kings may be brought.' All
this supposes a scene still earthly.

A few more extracts pointing out the
identity of the heavenly city with the
substance of the *most holy place* of the
Tabernacle, and we bid a reluctant
adieu to the inspiring theme. 'And he
shewed me a pure river of water of life,
clear as crystal, proceeding *out of the
throne of God and of the Lamb.* And
there shall be no more curse ; but the
throne of God and the Lamb shall be in
it ; and his servants shall serve him :
and they shall see his face ; and his name
shall be in their foreheads.' These servants are the cherubic legions, whose appropriate device in the sanctuary looked
from the extremities of the mercy-seat
directly upon the bright cloud of the
Presence, now developed into myriads
of happy human existences, rejoicing
before the throne, and making their
perpetual oblations of service and praise.
In view of this blissful inheritance,
who does not feel involuntarily prompted to exclaim with the prophet, 'Glory
to the righteous !' And who but must
be profoundly impressed with the ineffable misery of those who shall finally
come short of this 'exceeding and eternal weight of glory?' May then the
solemn concluding intimation of the
Apocalypse sink into the deepest recesses of the souls both of the writer
and his readers ; 'Blessed are they that
do his commandments, that they may
have right to the tree of life, and may
enter in through the gates into the city.
For without are dogs, and sorcerers,
and whoremongers, and murderers, and
idolaters, and whosoever loveth and

10 ¶ k And they shall make an ark *of* shittim-wood: two cubits and a half *shall be* the length there- of, and a cubit and a half the breadth thereof, and a cubit and a half the height thereof.

k ch. 37. 1.   Deut. 10. 3.   Hebr. 9. 4.

maketh a lie. I Jesus have sent mine angel to testify unto you these things in the churches. I am the root and the offspring of David, and the bright and morning-star. And the Spirit and the bride say come. And let him that heareth say, Come. And let him that is athirst come. And whosoever will, let him take the water of life freely.'

THE ARK OF THE COVENANT.

10. *They shall make an ark of Shittim-wood.* Heb. אָרוֹן *aron.* From the identity of rendering, it might be thought that the ark of the Tabernacle and that of Noah were expressed by the same term in Hebrew. But such is not the case. The former is called אָרוֹן *aron,* and the latter תֵּבָה *tebah;* but the Greek having rendered both terms by κιβωτος, this has been followed by our own and many other versions. The object itself was properly a *chest* or *coffer* of shittim-wood, overlaid with gold, in which was deposited the tables of the ten commandments, together with Aaron's rod that budded, and the golden pot of preserved manna. This chest seems to have been of the dimensions of three feet nine inches in length, by two feet three inches in breadth and depth, according to the common cubit of eighteen inches. Around the upper edge was a rim or cornice—called in the text 'a crown'— of pure gold; and on each side were fixed rings of gold to receive the poles of shittim-wood covered with gold, by which the ark was carried from place to place. The staves always remained in the rings, even when the ark was at rest. The ark had at top a lid or cover of solid gold; for such was what the text calls 'the mercy-seat,' and which the Septuagint renders ἱλαστήριον or *the propitiatory,* by which name it is men-

tioned by St. Paul in Heb. 9. 4, and which was probably so called, because, on the great day of atonement, the blood of the expiatory sacrifice was sprinkled on or before it. Upon the two ends of this lid, and of the same matter with it, that is, solid gold, were placed two figures of cherubim which looked towards each other, and whose outstretched wings, meeting over the centre of the ark, overshadowed it completely. It was here that the Shekinah or Divine Presence more immediately rested, and both in the Tabernacle and Temple was indicated by a cloud, from the midst of which responses were delivered in an audible voice whenever the Lord was consulted in behalf of the people. Hence God is sometimes mentioned as he that 'dwelleth' or 'sitteth between the cherubim.' In its removals the ark was covered with a vail, Num 4. 6, and might only be carried on the shoulders of the priests or Levites. The Rabbins think, with some reason, that it was only carried by the priests on extraordinary occasions, being ordinarily borne by the Levites. No other form of conveyance was allowed, nor were any other persons permitted to interfere with it. The fate of Uzzah, 2 Sam. 6. 3, admonished the Israelites, in a very solemn manner, of the consequences of even a well meant officiousness in a matter where the divine will had been so clearly expressed to the contrary.

After the Israelites had passed the Jordan, the ark generally occupied its proper place in the Tabernacle, and was afterwards placed in the Temple built by Solomon. From the direction given by Josiah to the Levites, 2 Chron. 35. 3, to restore the ark to its place, it would seem to have been previously removed, but it is not known whether this was done by the priests, to preserve it from profanation, or by the idolatrous kings Manasseh or Amon, to make room for their idols. It seems that the ark, with the other precious things of the Temple, became the spoil of Nebuchadnezzar, and was taken to Babylon; and it does not appear that it was restored at the end of the captivity, or that any new one was made. What became of the ark after the captivity cannot be ascertained. Some of the Rabbins think that it was concealed, to preserve it from the Chaldeans, and that it could not again be discovered, nor will be till the Messiah comes and reveals it. Others say that it was indeed taken away by the Chaldeans, but was afterwards restored, and occupied its place in the second Temple : but the Talmud and some of the Jewish writers confess, that the want of the ark was one of the points in which the second Temple was inferior to that of Solomon : to which we may add that neither Ezra, Nehemiah, the Maccabees, nor Josephus, mention the ark as extant in the second Temple, and the last authority expressly says that there was nothing in the sanctuary when the Temple was taken by Titus. It certainly does not appear in the Arch erected at Rome in honor of that conqueror, and in which the spoils of the Temple are displayed ; although some writers have attempted to identify it with the table of shewbread which is there represented.

It is to be remarked that similar arks or chests, containing the mysteries of their religions, were common among nearly all the ancient heathen nations, the hint of which was probably taken from that of the Jews. The Egyptians, for instance, carried in solemn processions a sacred chest, containing their secret things and the mysteries of their religion, of which the following cut, from the hieroglyphic remains of that country, shows a very remarkable conformity to the Hebrew model.

EGYPTIAN ARK BORNE BY PRIESTS.

The Trojans also had their sacred chest ; and the *palladium* of the Greeks and Romans was something not very unlike. It is remarkable too, that as the Hebrew Tabernacle and Temple had a holy of holies, in which the ark was deposited, so had the heathen, in the inmost part of their temples, an *adytum* or *penetrale*, which none but the priests might enter. Something **very similar**

11 And thou shalt overlay it with pure gold, within and without shalt thou overlay it; and shalt make upon it a crown of gold round about.

12 And thou shalt cast four rings of gold for it, and put *them* in the four corners thereof; and two rings *shall be* in the one side of it, and two rings in the other side of it.

13 And thou shalt make staves *of* shittim-wood, and overlay them with gold.

14 And thou shalt put the staves into the rings by the sides of the ark, that the ark may be borne with them.

15 ¹ The staves shall be in the rings of the ark: they shall not be taken from it.

16 And thou shalt put into the ark ᵐ the testimony which I shall give thee.

1 1 Kings 8. 8. ᵐ ch. 16. 34. & 31. 18. Deut. 10. 2, 5. & 31. 26. 1 Kings 8. 9. 2 Kings 11. 12. Hebr. 9. 4.

may also be traced among barbarous and savage nations. Thus, Tacitus, speaking of the nations of Northern Germany, of whom our Saxon ancestors were a branch, says that they generally worshipped Hertham, or the Mother Earth (*Terram matrem*); believing her to interpose in the affairs of men, and to visit nations ; and that to her, within a grove in a certain island, was consecrated *a vehicle covered with a vestment,* and which none but the priests were allowed to touch. The same thing has been frequently noticed in connexion with the religious systems of other heathen nations, and among the inhabitants of Mexico and the South Sea Islands, very curious analogies with the Mosaic ark have been discovered, of which the reader will find an account in Parkhurst's Heb. Lex. Art. רן.

11. *Make upon it a crown of gold round about.* Heb. זר זהב סביב *zër zahab sabib, a golden border round about.* Gr. κυματια χρυσα στρεπτα, *golden wreathed waves round about.* This 'crown' was an ornamental cornice, moulding, or border, which went round the top, as a kind of enclosure serving to make firm the propitiatory in its place, and called a 'crown' from its encompassing the whole outer extremities of the upper side of the ark somewhat as a crown encircles the temples of the head. The term is only employed in reference to the *rims* or *crowns* of gold made round the ark of the covenant,

the table of shew-bread, and the altar of incense. From the rendering of the Greek it would appear that the work of this cornice was somehow exquisitely wrought in graceful flexures or undulations, resembling the waves of the sea.

12. *Thou shalt cast four rings of gold,* &c. Doubtless of solid gold, as they were to sustain a very considerable weight when the staves were inserted and the ark borne by the priests. Whether these rings were placed lengthwise or breadthwise of the ark is not clear. We infer the latter, however, as otherwise, when carried, the front part of the ark with its cherubim would be sideways, which is not likely. Besides we are told, 1 Kings, 8. 8, that in the Temple 'the ends of the staves were seen out in the holy place, before the oracle ;' consequently, as the ark fronted the entrance, the staves must have run along the extremity of its breadth, instead of its length.

16. *Thou shalt put — the testimony,* &c. That is, the two tables of stone on which the Law of the ten Commandments was written; called 'the testimony,' because God did in them *testify* his authority over the Israelites, his regard for them, his presence with them, and his displeasure against them in case they transgressed ; while they on the other hand by accepting and depositing this Law in its appointed place, *testified* their professed subjection and obedience to its requirements.—On the

17 And ⁿ thou shalt make a mercy-seat *of* pure gold : two cubits and a half *shall be* the length thereof,

ⁿ ch. 37. 6. Rom. 3. 25. Hebr. 9. 5.

and a cubit and a half the breadth thereof.

18 And thou shalt make two cherubims *of* gold, *of* beaten work

difficulty supposed to be created by the comparison of this passage with Heb. 9. 4, see the commentators on that text, particularly the XVIIth Excursus in Prof. Stuart's Commentary on Hebrews.

17. *Thou shalt make a mercy-seat of pure gold.* Heb. כפרת *kapporeth*, from כפר *kaphar, to cover.* The verb is, however, used for the most part in a moral sense, being applied to the *covering*, that is, the *expiation*, of sins. The Gr. version unites the two senses by rendering ἱλαστηριον επιθεμα, that is, *a propitiatory covering*, or *mercy-seat*, a rendering sanctioned by the Holy Spirit, as we find it employed, with the omission of the last word, by the apostle, Heb. 9. 5, 'And over it the cherubims of glory shadowing the *mercy-seat* (ἱλαστηριον).' The same term in Rom. 3. 25, is applied to Christ, 'whom God hath set forth to be a *propitiation* (ἱλαστηριον) through faith in his blood.' So also 1 John, 2. 2, 'He is the *propitiation* (ἱλαστηριον) for our sins.' From whence the conclusion is probably fairly to be drawn, that this mercy-seat was in some sense an adumbration of Christ as the grand medium of expiation for the sins of men. This mercy-seat, which was made of solid gold instead of wood overlaid with gold, like the rest of the ark, was the upper side of the sacred chest made to be removed entirely, or, as Josephus says, raised by hinges, when the tables of testimony were to be taken out or put in.

THE CHERUBIM.

18. *Thou shalt make two cherubims of gold,* &c. Heb. כרבים *kerubim.* Gr. χερουβιμ *Cheroubim.* Our English word is the plural untranslated of the original כרוב *kerub,* a term of which the etymology is very much of a contested

point with critics and lexicographers. According to the regular analogy of the language, it has the form of the past participle of the verb כרב *karab.* But no such verb exists among the living roots of the Hebrew. It was therefore regarded by most of the ancient Christian fathers as a compound word made up perhaps of נכר *nakar, to know* and רוב *rub, multitude,* equivalent to *multitudo scientiæ* or *multitudo cognitionis, abundance of knowledge;* or of כ *ke,* רוב *rub,* and בינה *binah, quasi multitudo cognitionis,* of equivalent import. But this mode of derivation is so utterly at variance with the laws which regulate the process of formation in Hebrew words, that it cannot be sustained for a moment when tried by the test of sound criticism. Yet it is remarkable that in nearly all the ancient interpretations the idea of *multitude* was prominent, indicating that they regarded רוב *multitudo* as beyond doubt one of its constituent elements. We have no doubt they were correct in assigning this as one of the *meanings of the symbol,* but they were unquestionably wrong in eliciting this idea from the *etymology of the term.* At the same time, although the genius of the language will not admit the legitimate developement of the sense of *knowledge* or *intelligence* from any part of the word, yet it is very possible to account for this sense being deduced from it by the philosophizing fathers of the church; for with the Platonists *wings* were deemed an emblem of *wisdom* and *knowledge,* and the same import was thought to be conveyed by the Cherubim being ' full of eyes before and behind.' Taking therefore this apprehended import of the symbol itself, and applying it reflexly to the structure of the term, they gave as the result the interpretation above-mentioned, which is no unfair specimen of patristic philology. Others again with more regard to intrinsic probability have proposed, by a transposition of letters, to trace the word to the root רכב *rakab, to ride,* as the Cherubim are described in the remarkable vision of Ezekiel, ch. 1, as forming, together with the mystic animated wheels, a kind of *living chariot* on which the symbol of the divine glory is exhibited as upborne and transported; whence the Psalmist, Ps. 18. 10, describes the Most High as ' riding upon the Cherub ;' and the Cherubim in Solomon's temple, 1 Chron. 28. 18, are called ' a chariot.'

By others various other etymologies have been suggested, but none entirely satisfactory. After a pretty extensive and elaborate investigation we have on the whole been inclined to give the preference to the root abovementioned, viz., כרב *karab,* now obsolete in Hebrew, but existing in Syriac and Arabic in the primitive sense of *ploughing* or *making furrows in the earth;* and thence, secondly, of *making incisions in metals,* or *engraving,* and finally by natural transition, of *making sculptured figures,* or *glyphs, of any kind.* This is confirmed by Rosenmuller, who remarks that as one and the same word in Syriac and Arabic is used to denote *expressing, sculpturing,* and *fabricating,* so in the verb כרב *karab* and its derivates the same complex idea is involved, as is to be inferred from the fact that the Syriac *korubo* signifies not only *a ploughman,* but also *a former of images.* It may also be observed that as *b, v,* and *f* are in all languages permutable, being letters of the same organ, this etymology presents us with some remarkable affinities. For beginning with the Heb. כרב *karab, to make incisions,* we find in the Teutonic family for *incidere, to cut* as in engraving. Germ. *kerben,* Angl. Sax. *keorfan,* Eng. *carve;* and then as *g* and *k* are inter-changeable, we have the Gr. γραφω, *grapho,* Germ. *graben,* Angl. Sax. *grafan,* Eng. *grave, engrave,* and Fr. *griffon (griffin),* an imaginary animal compounded of beast and bird, evidently derived from a distortion of the cherubic figure. In all these words the idea of *sculpturing* or *engraving* is predominant, and according to the analogy of Hebrew formations כרוב *kerub* would properly signify that which was *carved, sculptured,* or *wrought with a graving tool,* thus corresponding very well with what is said of the Cherubim as a kind of *statuary* or wrought images placed over the mercy-seat.

In the annexed cut it may be thought that we have but loosely followed the example of Moses in 'making every thing after the pattern shown in the mount,' inasmuch as Moses says nothing of the fourfold variety of faces which we have here given to the Cherubic emblem. But our design is taken from the Cherubim of Ezekiel, which are thus described, ch. 1. 4—14. 'And I looked, and behold, a whirlwind came out of the north, a great cloud, and a fire unfolding itself, and a brightness was about it, and out of the midst thereof as the color of amber, out of the midst of the fire. Also out of the midst thereof came the likeness of four living creatures. And this was their appearance; they had the likeness of a man. And every one had four faces, and every one had four wings. And their feet were straight feet; and the sole of their feet was like the sole of a calf's foot; and they sparkled like the color of burnished brass. And they had the hands of a man under their wings on their four sides; and they four had their faces and their wings. Their wings were joined one to another; they turned not when they went; they went every one straight forward. As for the likeness of their faces, they four had the face of a man, and the face of a lion, on the right side : and they four had the face of an ox on the left side; they four also had the face of an eagle. Thus were their faces: and their wings were stretched upward; two wings of every one were joined one to another, and two covered their bodies, And they went every one straight forward; whither the spirit was to go, they went; and they turned not when they went. As for the likeness of the living creatures, their appearance was like burning coals of fire, and like the appearance of lamps: it went up and down among the living creatures; and the fire was bright, and out of the fire went forth lightning. And the living creatures ran and returned as the appearance of a flash of lightning.' That these visionary beings, though here called 'living creatures,' were in fact symbolically identical with the 'cherubim,' (erroneously written 'cherubims' in our version), will appear in the sequel.

ARK OF THE COVENANT AND THE CHERUBIM.

The inquiry now arises respecting the *symbolical design* of these very remarkable creations, which, from being mere lifeless sculptured statues in the Mosaic Tabernacle, became animated, intelligent, and active agents in the mystic visions of the prophets. It is certainly one of the lowest aims of infinite wisdom in any part of its dispensations to adopt a system of symbols which should merely address themselves in beautiful or singular forms to the senses, or to the imagination. They approve themselves worthy of the divine source in which they originate only as they disclose a rich and instructive significancy under their outward aspect. That such is preeminently the case with the symbol before us, we shall hope to make appear in the remarks that follow, in the outset of which it will be necessary to show the identity of the Cherubim of Moses with the Living Creatures of Ezekiel. In order to this it is to be observed, that Ezekiel was in captivity in Babylon when this vision was vouchsafed him But it appears from Ezek. 8. 1—3 that while there he was transported in spirit to Jerusalem, and set down in the precincts of the Temple, where he beheld, among other objects, the Living Creatures and the Throne, previously described, standing in the inner court. 'Then,' says he, ch. 10. 18—22, ' the glory of the Lord (the Shekinah) departed from off the threshold of the house, and stood over the cherubims. And the cherubims lifted up their wings, and mounted up from the earth in my sight: when they went out, the wheels also were beside them, and every one stood at the door of the east gate of the Lord's house; and the glory of the God of Israel was over them above. This is the living creature (i. e. collection of living creatures) that I saw under the God of Israel by the river of Chebar; *and I knew that they were the cherubims.* Every one had four faces apiece, and every one four wings; and the likeness of the hands of a man was under their wings. And the likeness of their faces was the same faces which I saw by the river of Chebar, their appearances and themselves: they went every one straight forward.' The import unquestionably is, that although the fact was not at first made known, or the idea did not occur, to him, yet now upon farther pondering the subject, he became fully convinced and assured in his own mind that these Living Creatures were beings of the same symbolical purport with the Cherubim that stood on the Mercy-seat of the Ark in the Temple. This is an important step in the progress of our elucidation. It authorises us to set it down as a point fixed and settled beyond all debate, that *the Cherubim and the Living Creatures are, in symbolical significancy, one and the same.*

We are now prepared to consider the very remarkable usage of the sacred writers in regard both to the Hebrew and Greek original of the term rendered *living creatures* (Heb. חיות *hayoth.*

Gr. ζωα *zoa*), in each of which languages the respective roots of the words signify *to live.* Yet who would have thought *a priori* that these would have been the terms employed in the following passages? Ps. 68. 9, 10, ' Thou, O God, didst send a plentiful rain, whereby thou didst confirm thine inheritance when it was weary. *Thy congregation* (חיתך *hayatheka, thy living creature,* Gr. τα ζωα σου, *thy living creatures*) hath dwelt therein.' On what grounds, philologically, this usage is to be explained, we know not, but it is clear that it involves the idea of *multitude,* if the English equivalent, *congregation,* can be any evidence of the fact. A striking parallel occurs, 2 Sam. 23. 11, 'And the Philistines were gathered together *into a troop* (לחיה *lahayah, into a living creature.* Gr. εις θηριον, *into a wild beast*), where was a piece of ground full of lentiles: and the people fled from the Philistines.' See also, v. 13, 'And *the troop* (חיה *hayah, the living creature*) of the Philistines pitched in the valley of Rephaim.' The Gr. rendering in the latter passage does not conform, being ταγμα, *a rank, order,* and in military phrase *a battalion, a body of soldiery.* But it is clear from these citations viewed together, that the import of *numbers* actually enters into the usage of the original word for *living creature,* and as the *living creatures* and the *cherubim* are symbolically the same, the idea of *multitude* is equally common to both. This idea, however, it is to be recollected, arises wholly from the interpretation, and not from the etymology of the terms.

As then the four ζωα, *the living creatures,* of Ezekiel are identical with the *cherubim,* so they are plainly identical also with the four *beasts* (ζωα) which figure so conspicuously in the mystic machinery of the Apocalypse. Passing from the visions of the river of Chebar to those of the Isle of Patmos, we behold the following scene depicted upon the prophetic canvass, Rev. 4. 6—8, And before the throne there was a sea of glass like unto crystal : and in the midst of the throne, and round about the throne, *were four beasts,* full of eyes before and behind. And the first beast was like a lion, and the second beast was like a calf, and the third beast had a face as a man, and the fourth beast was like a flying eagle. And the four beasts had each of them six wings about him ; and they were full of eyes within: and they rest not day and night, saying, Holy, holy, holy, Lord God Almighty, which was, and is, and is to come.' As the Cherubim in this vision are nearer to the Throne and the incumbent Majesty than in the other, they are represented as having *six* wings instead of *four,* to denote the propriety of having their persons more fully vailed from the glance of that holy eye to which even the heavens are unclean. But what is the song sung by these emblematic agents? Ch. 5. 8—10, 'And when he had taken the book, the four beasts, and four and twenty elders fell down before the Lamb, having every one of them harps, and golden vials full of odors, which are the prayers of saints. And they sung a new song, saying, Thou art worthy to take the book, and to open the seals thereof : for thou wast slain, and hast redeemed us to God by thy blood out of every kindred, and tongue, and people, and nation ; and hast made us unto our God kings and priests : and we shall reign on the earth.' Can the reader have failed, from these ample quotations, to anticipate the conclusion of the whole matter? *The Cherubim of the Tabernacle and Temple, the Living Creatures of Ezekiel, and the hymning beasts of John, are all one and the same symbol.* And what is the *truth* and *mystery* of this symbol? What do we recognise in it but *human* instead of *angelic beings,* even *a multitude of the redeemed from among men?* What else is the burden

of that grateful anthem which resounds from their lips ? 'Thou hast redeemed *us* to God by thy blood out of every kindred, and tongue, and people, and nation.' Can this possibly be the language of angels ?—especially when we hear the apostle saying, Heb. 2. 16, 'For verily he took not on him the nature of angels, but he took on him the seed of Abraham,' and when, moreover, we find in this very context the angels expressly distinguished from the four beasts.

Conceiving this then as a point clearly ascertained, that the Cherubim of the Apocalypse adumbrate a *human* and not an *angelic* order of beings, let us go back and apply this result to the Cherubim of the Pentateuch. We behold them stationed on the Propitiatory, with the symbol of the Divine Presence resting between them, somewhat like Moses on the mount with Aaron and Hur supporting his arms on either side. In this position, as we have seen that they strictly represent *men* and not *angels,* what more natural than that their primary and proximate drift as symbols should be *to shadow forth the race of Israel and the great fact of God's peculiar residence among them ?* In the cherubic emblems of the Tabernacle, therefore, we behold a mystic embodiment of the congregation which, in the wilderness, was ordinarily encamped round about the holy fabric without. Accordingly the high priest who entered into the *holy of holies* and there looked upon the Ark of the Covenant and its cherubic appendages, with the Shekinah enthroned between, beheld in fact but a miniature model of what he saw on a large scale when standing in the midst of the many thousands of Israel abiding in their tents. There were the Cherubim resolved into their constituent multitudes, and over the host rested in calm majesty the Pillar of Cloud, the visible token of the Divinity permanently residing among the chosen tribes. But even this was a *typical* scene, presenting to the eye an image of that state which shall be disclosed when the last chapters of Isaiah, Ezekiel, and John shall be fulfilled, when the Tabernacle of God shall again be with men, and he shall set his sanctuary in the midst of them for ever more.

Whether Moses or Ezekiel or John were themselves aware of the true import of these hallowed hieroglyphics, is by no means essential to the validity of our conclusions respecting them. We think it highly probable, on the whole, that they did *not* understand, at least but partially, their true-meant design. They were doubtless among the things respecting which they 'enquired diligently,' but were obliged to leave their full significancy to be elicited for the edification of subsequent ages of the church. Yet even in the description quoted from Ezekiel there are occasional hints and intimations which might be supposed to lead to a strong suspicion that the Living Creatures were intended to shadow forth *men* instead of *angels.* Thus for instance, it is said, Ezek. 1. 5, 'And this was their appearance; *they had the likeness of a man;*' that is, their predominating aspect was human, notwithstanding their otherwise singular and unearthly form. Again, v. 8, 'And they had the hands *of a man* under their wings.' The same circumstance is afterwards mentioned concerning the Cherubim, ch. 10. 8, and a second time repeated, v. 21, as something peculiarly note-worthy, that 'there appeared in the cherubims the form *of a man's hand* under their wings.' These remarkable items in the description may be regarded as furnishing at least a slight inuendo as to the true solution of the symbol. But it was reserved for that pen which was to complete the sacred canon, and afford a key to the developement of so many preceding mysteries, to give to the student of revelation an inspired exposition of this remarkable symbol, about which we can no longer doubt, when we hear them ascribing their redemption to the blood of the Lamb.

It may go, moreover, to remove any lingering hesitancy on this point, to consider more closely their relation to the other parts of the typical apparatus of the Tabernacle. They were an abiding fixture upon the Ark of the Covenant; they were stationed upon the extremities of the Mercy-seat with the bright cloud of the Presence beaming between them; they were constructed of the same material with the Mercy-seat, and in every thing seemed to have the most indissoluble connexion with the latent import of this system of shadows, of which Buxtorf remarks; 'It is the opinion of the Jews, that the Ark, with the Mercy-seat and the Cherubim, form the foundation, root, heart, and marrow of the whole Tabernacle, and so of the whole Levitical service.' Now we are authorised to ask, whether it be conceivable that angels are as much interested in the truth and substance of the typical Mercy-seat or Propitiatory, as ransomed sinners, whose happiness, and song, and salvation, all centre in this grand mystery? We would detract nothing from what is justly due to angels; but we see not why, in the very heart of a system of symbols shadowing forth our recovery by a Savior, so prominent a place should be given to the hieroglyphics of a foreign race of beings, however deeply they may be interested in contemplating this work, or serviceable in promoting it. Nothing is more plainly taught in the word of God, than that it is in virtue of the atoning sacrifice of Christ that the Most High dwells amidst the children of men. And this great truth we suppose to have been visibly represented by the habitation of the Divine Glory between the Cherubim and over the Expiation cover of the Ark. But nothing of the nature of an atonement is necessary to propitiate the presence of God among the sinless angels. Why then should we assign to them, however much we love them, and prize their kind offices, a symbol so preeminently appropriate to ourselves? Until therefore we are convinced on solid grounds of the untenableness of our position, and pointed to some passage of holy writ expressly affirming or clearly implying, that the Mosaic Cherubim were emblems of angels, we shall hold them to be representatives of human beings, and of no others.

At the same time we find no difficulty in admitting, in perfect consistency with this theory, that the Cherubim were *popularly regarded* by the ancient Jews, as they still are by modern Christians, as a current designation of some portion at least of the angelic order of beings. Nor do we doubt that Peter, in saying that the things of redemption were things ' which the angels desired to look into,' had direct allusion in his own mind to the position of the Cherubim on the Ark of the Covenant, which stood as if intently poring upon the mysteries couched under both it and the surmounting Glory. Angels usually appeared as *winged* messengers ; and *wings* were a striking appendage of the Cherubim. Angels too were always considered as a race of beings abiding near to the Divine Presence in heaven, and as an accompaniment of the Shekinah, whenever and wherever it appeared ; the Cherubim, also, in their relation to the Cloud of Glory, were regarded as a *materialized representation* of this great fact, and the Holy of Holies in which they stood was dimly conceived of *as a type of heaven.* Under these circumstances it was natural that the idea of angelic beings should attach to the symbol, and that this idea should be traditionally perpetuated, at least until a more rigid research into the nature and genius of the symbolical language should bring to light its genuine import. That

the Cherubim do actually in their true intent represent *human beings* instead of *angels,* is a conclusion to which we seem to be brought irresistibly by the chain of scriptural induction in the foregoing remarks ; and if it should still remain problematical in the mind of the reader on what grounds a device so strikingly *angelic* should have been adopted to represent a *human* reality, we do not hesitate to suggest that the true clue is to be found in the fact, that *the cherubic symbol, in its ultimate scope, pointed forward to that condition of regenerate, redeemed, risen, and glorified men, when they shall have assumed an angelic nature.* Our Savior declares of the happy sons of the resurrection that they shall neither marry nor be given in marriage, but shall be as the angels of God in heaven ; and when John fell down before the revealing angel of the Apocalypse, and was about to worship him, he was met by the rebuke, 'See that thou do it not ; for I am thy fellow-servant, and of thy brethren the prophets, and of them which keep the sayings of this book.' Such, we doubt not, is the final destination of the children of God in that future economy to which the eye of faith looks forward ; and in the mean time, if the visions of the prophets should portray the scenes of that coming dispensation, where the actors were to be truly men in their post-resurrection natures, how should such actors be symbolically represented but by angels? The Cherubim then may be considered as representatives of angels, so far as angels themselves are representatives of men ; but, in our opinion, no farther.

If then our main position in regard to the representative character of the Cherubim, may be considered as established, it only remains to make use of this proof by way of explication of the strange, anomalous, and, we had almost said, monstrous, diversity of forms and faces of which the symbol was composed. Were the Cherubim *men*—men standing in covenant relation with God—men possessed of renewed spiritual life, and thus enjoying the divine favor—then may we not conclude, that this unique combination of forms *represents some marked and definable attributes in the character of those whom the symbol adumbrates?* What then are the distinguishing traits in the character of the people of God, which may be fitly represented by emblems so unique? How shall the hieroglyphic be read? The face of the Ox reminds us of the qualities of the ox, and these, it is well known, are patient endurance, unwearied service, and meek submission to the yoke. What claims has he to the title of a man of God who is not distinguished by these ox-like attributes? The Lion is the proper symbol of undaunted courage, glowing zeal, triumph over enemies, united with innate nobleness, and magnanimity of spirit. The Man, as a symbol, we may well conceive as indicating intelligence, meditation, wisdom, sympathy, philanthropy, and every generous and tender emotion. And, finally, in the Eagle we recognise the impersonation of an active, vigilant, fervent, soaring spirit, prompting the readiest and swiftest execution of the divine commands, and elevating the soul to the things that are above.

We admit the affixing of these interpretations to be in a great measure arbitrary, and we hope they may be rejected or improved upon, according as the evidence for or against them may weigh in the mind of the reader. They certainly mean *something;* they have not been adopted without wise reasons; and we would wish to fix upon such a solution as shall carry with it the highest intrinsic probability. In the nature of the case, much must be left to the private judgment, perhaps we might say fancy, of expositors in tracing analogies and assigning meanings to symbols which we yet know in the main to be possessed of meaning.

In adverting, however, to the symbolical import of the straight forward motion of the Cherubim, we have perhaps a more explicit warrant of the Scriptures for our explication. In speaking of this peculiarity, Ezekiel says, 'They went every one straight forward; whithersoever the spirit was to go, they went; they turned not as they went.' Their locomotive progress was directly and undeviatingly *forward.* They turned neither their faces, nor their wings, nor their bodies. There was no digression, regression, wandering, or circuitous wheeling in their movements. In the direction in which their eyes or faces were fixed, their progress tended. Is it not then a rational supposition that by this is indicated that steady and undeviating course of obedience, that determined adherence to the right ways of the Lord, from which the faithful are not to be seduced? Is not *rectitude* the prevailing tenor of a good man's life, and is not his course onward, according to the Apostle's motto, 'forgetting the things which are behind and reaching forth unto those things that are before, I press toward the mark for the prize of the high calling of God in Christ Jesus.' Again, let the following passages be noticed in this connexion. Prov. 4. 25—27, 'Let thine eyes look right on, and let thine eyelids look *straight before thee.* Ponder the path of thy feet, and let all thy ways be established. *Turn not to the right hand nor to the left:* remove thy foot from evil.' Ps. 125. 5, 'As for such as *turn aside unto their crooked ways,* the Lord shall lead them forth with the workers of iniquity.' Heb. 12. 13, '*Make straight paths for your feet* lest that which is lame be turned out of the way.' Thus plainly are we taught the teaching of the rectilinear course of the Cherubim, i. e. of the people of God.

Upon the various other items of the

shalt thou make them, in the two ends of the mercy-seat.

19 And make one cherub on the one end, and the other cherub on the other end: *even* of the mercy-seat shall ye make the cherubims on the two ends thereof.

20 And ᵒ the cherubims shall stretch forth *their* wings on high, covering the mercy-seat with their wings, and their faces *shall look* one to another; toward the mercy-seat shall the faces of the cherubims be.

ᵒ 1 Kings 8. 7.   1 Chron. 28. 18.   Hebr. 9. 5.

---

prophet's description of these visionary creations, it will scarcely be necessary in this connexion to enlarge. Sufficient has probably been said to establish our main position, that *the Cherubim of the Scriptures are a symbol of holy men, and not, primarily, of holy angels.* The importance of this clue to the mystic device will be obvious to every reader, and will no doubt justify the adaptation of our figure to Ezekiel's rather than to Moses' description. We could not otherwise so well have expanded our remarks in the form of a systematic inquiry into the genuine scope and design of this extraordinary symbol, of which Josephus says, 'They (the Cherubim) are flying creatures, but their form is not like to that of any of the creatures which men have seen; though Moses said he had seen such beings near the throne of God.' The field of investigation, however, in reference to this sacred hieroglyphic is but just entered, and the most enriching results still await the future explorer.—We now return to the material construction of these mystic appendages of the Ark.

Of beaten work shalt thou make them. Heb. מקשה *mikshah, hard work shalt thou make it.* Gr. χρυσοτορευτα, *golden-turned-work.* This is generally explained as importing, that the Cherubim were to be beaten out with the hammer from the same solid mass of gold with the Mercy-seat, but no such meaning can be gathered from the genuine sense of the original. The term מקשה *mikshah,* from קשה *kashah, to be hard,* implies simply that the materials of the Propitiatory and the Cherubim were to be of solid massive gold

in contradistinction from being hollow inside, or made of wood overlaid with gold. Besides, it must be evident to the slightest reflection that such a mode of construction is utterly beyond the art or power of man; it must have been nothing short of a miracle. The cherubic figures were doubtless either cast in a mould or sculptured by the engraver's tool, as the Greek renders the word, and then permanently attached by soldering to either extremity of the Mercy-seat.

19. *Of the mercy-seat shall ye make the cherubims,* &c. A marginal reading, designed to be explanatory of this, is here given, which rests upon no sufficient authority, viz., 'of the matter of the Mercy-seat.' The meaning is simply, that when finished the Cherubim should be seen shooting up from the ends of the Mercy-seat, not that they should be continuously fabricated out of the same mass by a process of beating, which in the nature of the case was absolutely impossible. Of this any man may be convinced who shall take the most plastic and malleable piece of lead, and, with no other instrument than a hammer, endeavor to work it into the shape of a human head or body, or that of a bird or beast, much more into the complex configuration of the cherub. The common interpretation of this passage respecting the formation of the mercy-seat and the Cherubims has been derived from the groundless conceits and puerile glosses of the Rabbinical critics, who wished to multiply as much as possible the number of miracles pertaining to their economy.

20. *Covering the mercy-seat with their wings.* Gr. συσκιαζοντες εν ταις πτερυξιν

21 ᵖ And thou shalt put the mercy-seat above upon the ark; and ᵠ in the ark thou shalt put the testimony that I shall give thee.

22 And ʳ there I will meet with thee, and I will commune with thee from above the mercy-seat, from ˢ between the two cherubims which *are* upon the ark of the testimony, of all *things* which I will give thee in commandment unto the children of Israel.

23 ¶ ᵗ Thou shalt also make a table *of* shittim-wood: two cubits *shall be* the length thereof, and a cubit the breadth thereof, and a cubit and a half the height thereof.

24 And thou shalt overlay it with pure gold, and make thereto a crown of gold round about.

25 And thou shalt make unto it a border of an hand-breadth round about, and thou shalt make a golden crown to the border thereof round about.

26 And thou shalt make for it four rings of gold, and put the rings in the four corners that *are* on the four feet thereof.

27 Over against the border shall the rings be for places of the staves to bear the table.

28 And thou shalt make the staves *of* shittim-wood, and overlay them

p ch. 26. 34. q ver. 16. r ch. 29. 42, 43. & 30. 6. 36. Lev. 16. 2. Numb. 17. 4. s Numb. 7. 89. 1 Sam. 4. 4. 2 Sam. 6. 2. 2 Kings 19. 15. Ps. 80. 1. & 90. 1. Isai. 37. 16. t ch. 37. 10. 1 Kings 7. 48. 2 Chron. 4. 8. Hebr. 9. 2.

αυτων επι του ἱλαστηριου ***shadowing over the propitiatory with their wings***. This word 'shadowing,' instead of 'covering,' is adopted by the apostle, Heb. 9. 5, 'Over it the cherubims of glory *shadowing* the mercy-seat;' where it is to be noted that the phrase 'cherubims of glory' might perhaps be rendered cherubims of *the* glory;' i. e. the glory of the Shekinah, the luminous splendid appearance which was visibly enthroned between them, the mystery or substance of which is disclosed to us in the visions of the Apocalypse, ch. 5, where we learn that the symbol of the divine glory dwelling between the Cherubim was the hieroglyphic of *the Son of God dwelling in the midst of his redeemed people, receiving their adorations and bestowing upon them the tokens of his complacency.*——¶ Shall look *one to another.* Heb. איש אל אחיו *ish el ahiv, a man to his brother;* a common Hebrew idiom for expressing the idea of our version.

22. *There I will meet with thee.* Heb. נועדתי לך שם *nöadti leka sham, I will convene with thee there.* Gr. *γνωσθησομαι σοι εκειθεν, I will be known to thee there.* Chal. 'I will appoint my Word to thee there.' That is, on the mercy-seat, between the cherubim. Here the visible Glory of Jehovah was to reside and to give audience, as a sovereign on his throne, having the ark as his footstool, as it seems to be termed, Ps. 99. 5—132. 7. From the same root with נועדתי *nöadti*, viz. יעד *yäad, to meet by appointment*, comes מועד *möad appointed meeting or convention*, whence the Tabernacle is called אהל מועד *ohel möad, tabernacle of Convention.* See Note on Ex. 33. 7.

THE TABLE OF SHEW-BREAD.

23—28. *Thou shalt also make a table,* &c. This part of the sacred furniture keeps up still farther the analogy with a royal palace, to which we have before adverted as pervading the entire structure of the Tabernacle. Yet a purely spiritual drift is at the same time sufficiently discernible in the typical aliment with which it was provided, and which pointed to the nourishment of the soul, and not of the body. As to the table itself, it was constructed of the same material with the Ark, viz. shittim-wood overlaid with gold. It was also furnished with rings or sta-

with gold, that the table may be borne with them.

29 And thou shalt make ᵘ the

ᵘ ch. 37. 16. Numb. 4. 7.

dishes thereof, and spoons thereof, and covers thereof, and bowls thereof, to cover withal: *of* pure gold shalt thou make them.

---

ples, through which were passed the staves by which it was carried, in the same way as the Ark. These staves, however, did not remain in the rings when at rest, like those of the Ark, v. 15, but were, as Josephus informs us, removed, that they might not be in the way of the priests in their weekly ministrations at the table. The table was inferior to the Ark in breadth by half a cubit; but it was of the same height, and stood lengthwise, east and west, at the north side of the Holy Place. From the obscurity of the ancient terms there is some difficulty in determining with precision the details of its form; but what we seem to learn from the text is, that the platform or surface of the table had its edges faced with a perpendicular border, or enclosure, somewhat resembling a window-frame before it is inserted into the wall of a building or the

sashes put in. This border was to be of a hand's breadth and ornamented on its upper and lower edge with a beautiful golden cornice or moulding, which is here also, as in the case of the Ark, called a 'crown.' The upper rim of the border rose of course somewhat above the superficial level of the table, and was well adapted to prevent what was deposited thereon from falling off. The Table, as seen in the Arch of Titus at Rome, on which the spoils of the Temple are represented, shows but very little of the ornamental work described in the text; but this, it is supposed, was not the Table of the Tabernacle. It is generally agreed that this was among the spoils carried away by Nebuchadnezzar, and that when the Jews were restored to their own land, they made a new Table. The view given in the cut is deduced from the text.

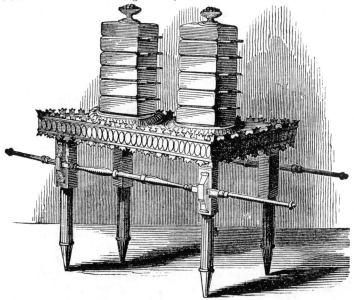

TABLE OF SHEW BREAD.

30 And thou shalt set upon the ta- | ble ^w shew-bread before me alway.

w Lev. 24. 5, 6.

---

29. *Dishes.* Heb. קְעָרֹת *ke-aroth,*
dishes, or *chargers,* as the word is
translated Num. 7. 13. Gr. τρυβλια,
plates or *platters,* on which it is supposed by some, that the loaves of bread
were placed. Others, however, assign
different uses to these dishes. It is a
point which cannot be positively determined.——¶ *Spoons.* Heb. כַּפֹּת *kap-*
poth, more properly *cups* or *censers* of
concave form like spoons, or like the
hollow of the hand, which is the primitive meaning of the original כַּף *kaph.*
They were for holding incense (Num.
7. 14), which it is evident from Lev. 24.
7, was employed in conjunction with
the holy bread. It is supposed there
were two of them, one placed on each
pile of loaves.——¶ *Covers.* Heb.קְשָׂוֹת
kesoth; probably for covering both the
loaves and the incense. The Gr. renders the word wherever it occurs by
σπονδεια, *libation-vessels.*——¶ *Bowls.*
Heb. מְנַקִּית *menakkiyoth.* Gr. κυαθοι,
wine-cups. 'For though we do not read
that any wine was set upon this table,
yet as libations were made to God by
pouring out wine before him in the
Holy Place, there is nothing improbable
in the Jewish tradition, that a bowl of
excellent wine was always kept upon
the table ; and that once a week, when
the bread was changed, the contents
were poured out as a libation before the
Lord. Josephus confirms this tradition
by relating that when Pompey went
into the Holy Place, he saw there cups
for libation among the sacred vessels.'
Pict. Bible.——¶ *To cover withal.* Heb.
אֲשֶׁר יֻסַּךְ בָּהֵן *asher yussak bahën,*
with which it was poured out ; with
which the drink-offerings were made.
This sense agrees better with the meaning of the original נָסַךְ *nasak,* and with
the probable uses of the 'bowls.' There
is no sufficient authority for rendering
the original by 'cover.'

30. *Show-bread.* Heb. לֶחֶם פָּנִים *le-*
hem panim, bread of faces, or ' bread of
presence (presence bread).' This title
is usually supposed to be derived from
its being continually set before the *face*
or *presence* of God, as manifested in his
visible symbol in the sanctuary, and
that too although they were deposited
in the Holy, and not in the Most Holy
place. But the true grounds of the appellation will be fully considered in the
sequel. The Gr. of the Sept. renders it
by αρτους ενωπιους, *fore-placed loaves,*
and that of Sym. αρτους της προθεσεως,
loaves of proposition, which is the constant reading of Jerome in the Latin
Vulgate. Twelve cakes or loaves of
this bread answering to the twelve
tribes, were set upon the table in two
separate rows of six each, which were
renewed every sabbath ; when the old
were taken away and eaten by the
priests. This is not particularly mentioned in the present text, supplementary to which is the information more
expressly given, Lev. 24. 5—9, 'And
thou shalt take fine flour, and bake
twelve cakes thereof: two tenth-deals
shall be in one cake. And thou shalt
set them in two rows, six on a row, upon the pure table before the Lord. And
thou shalt put pure frankincense upon
each row, that it may be on the bread
for a memorial, even an offering made
by fire unto the Lord. Every sabbath
he shall set it in order before the Lord
continually, being taken from the children of Israel by an everlasting covenant. And it shall be Aaron's and his
sons' ; and they shall eat it in the holy
place ; for it is most holy unto him of
the offerings of the Lord made by fire
by a perpetual statute.'

Of the spiritual or typical design of
this part of the apparatus of the Tabernacle, we cannot speak with much confidence, because we consider the full

realization of its import, like most other things pertaining to the Tabernacle and Temple, to be yet future. They look forward, as we conceive, to that final earthly consummation of the Gospel economy which is announced in the predictions of Scripture under the title of the New Jerusalem. This state, we consider as one in which the terrestrial and the celestial are to be merged together in a manner which we cannot at present adequately understand. It is only, therefore, by studying profoundly what is vaguely and mystically intimated of that coming glorious dispensation, that we can attach their proper significancy to the various symbols of the Mosaic economy. It is a period when Christ's kingdom is to be fully manifested, and he himself says, Luke 22. 30, that he has a table in his kingdom, at which all his saints shall for ever eat and drink with him. He will then sup with them and they with him, and they shall be abundantly satisfied with the goodness of the Lord's house. As to any more distinct application of these emblems to the particular features, institutions, or ordinances, of the present Gospel economy, which may seem to afford their counterparts, we are not disposed to object to it, or deny that it may be well founded, but for the full and complete substantiation of the Mosaic shadows we look to the future.

But we will enter into a little fuller examination of the subject, and in order to give as much precision as possible to our inquiries, it will be necessary to weigh with the utmost practical accuracy the import of the title לחם הפנים *lehem happanim, the bread of the face or presence.* This, as intimated above, is usually understood as equivalent to *the bread set before God's face.* But whether this was mainly with the ideal purpose of *being seen by God,* i. e. the Shekinah, dwelling in the holy of holies, or *by men,* is not entirely obvious. Accord-

ing to the first supposition, it would be viewed either merely as a kind of offering presented in token of gratitude for the daily bread by which life is sustained, and upon which Jehovah might be considered as looking down from his throne on the mercy-seat with special complacency; or as directly the apparent food of God himself regarded as theocratic king of Israel, having his abode in a palace richly furnished with all the common necessaries and comforts of life. According to the second hypothesis, the Shew-bread was something which was to be viewed by the people as a sign of the divine care and providence in their behalf, intended to awaken a thankful recollection of the source from whence flowed the daily bread which went to the sustentation of their natural life. This is the view taken by Lightfoot and Carpzov. But to this whole mode of exposition it is justly objected, that there is no sufficient authority for ascribing to הפנים *happanim* when standing alone the sense of *before* or *in the sight or presence of any thing,* as if it were equivalent to לחם לפני יהוה *lehem liphnë Yehovah, bread before the Lord.* It will be observed that the original in the passage before is, 'and thou shalt set upon the table לחם פנים לפני *lehem panim liphnai, bread of face before me* alway.' Here then as that which the interpretation we are considering understands by פנים *panim, face* or *presence,* is actually expressed by לפני *liphnai, before me,* it follows that פנים *panim* must necessarily convey some other idea than merely that of *proposition* or *setting before.* The same consequence follows also from the denomination of the Table, Num. 4. 7, viz., שלחן הפנים *shilhan happanim, table of face or presence.* If this article were called *the table of the presence,* simply from its position, what reason can be assigned why the Candlestick, and more especially the Altar of Incense which stood between the Table and the Candlestick and still more directly in front of the throne than either, should not equally be distinguished by the same epithet? Yet we nowhere find them so denominated, though it is said of the Altar, Lev. 16. 18, אֲשֶׁר לִפְנֵי יְהוָה *asher liphnë Yehovah, which is before the Lord;* from which it appears how the original expresses itself, when it would convey the idea so erroneously attributed to הַפָּנִים *happanim.*

On the same grounds, we are constrained to reject the idea of the Shewbread's being intended as an offering and sign of national thankfulness for national favors. For if it received on this account the predicate הַפָּנִים, the question immediately occurs, as before, why this predicate is applied to the Table and not to the Altar of Incense, which no less than the Table *stood before* the Lord in the holy place? And as to its serving as a *visible remembrancer* of the divine providence towards the chosen people, how is this consistent with the circumstance of its being placed in the sacred apartment, entirely hidden from public view, and visible only to the priests in the discharge of their offices? How could that be a visible sign which was not *seen?* And why should that bread which, from its symbolic relations, might be readily presumed to point forward to a *future spiritual sustenance,* be understood as emblematic of a *present physical aliment* daily supplied by a bounteous providence?

We are thrown then upon another interpretation of the phrase before us, and though the idea which we suppose to be conveyed by it is somewhat complex, yet we flatter ourselves with being able to make it intelligible. It is clear that the expression in the original לֶחֶם פָּנִים *lehem panim, bread of the presence,* is strikingly analogous with מַלְאַךְ פָּנִים *malak panim, angel of the presence,* Is. 63. 9, 'In all their affliction he was afflicted, and the *angel of his presence*

(מַלְאַךְ פָּנָיו) saved them,' &c. So also Ex. 33. 14, 15, 'And he said, *My presence* (פָּנַי *panai*) shall go with thee, and I will give thee rest. And he said unto him, if *thy presence* (פָּנֶיךָ *panëka*) go not with me, carry us not up hence.' Compare with this Deut. 4. 37, 'And because he loved thy fathers, therefore he chose their seed after them, and brought thee out *in his sight* (בְּפָנָיו *bepanav, with, by, or through his presence;* i. e. the angel of his presence), with his mighty power out of Egypt.' But the Angel of the divine Face or Presence, of whom God says, 'my name is in him,' we have before shown to be no other than the Shekinah or the *visible manifestation* of Jehovah, as he was anciently pleased to make himself known to his people. His essential being will no doubt for ever remain inscrutable to created intelligences. If he reveals himself it must be through some medium which will bring him measurably within the comprehension of his creatures. This medium he denominates his *face* or *presence;* and as the human face is the principal means of revealing the inward being and character of a man, so the Shekinah is called the *face of God,* inasmuch as it is through this medium that the Divinity comes within the sphere of human cognition. Now let it be borne in mind that the Shekinah, i. e. the Angel of the Presence, is but the Old Testament designation of Christ, and the phrase לֶחֶם פָּנִים *lehem panim, bread of the presence,* is brought into immediate identity of import with *bread of Christ,* who was the *true presence* indicated by the term. But what is the bread of Christ but that divine spiritual sustenance which maintains the inner, higher, and eternal life of his believing followers? In order then to gain a full apprehension of the purport of the Table of Shew-bread and its mystic loaves, we must have recourse to such passages as the following; John, 6. 32—58, 'Then

31 ¶ ˣ And thou shalt make a can-
ˣ ch. 37. 17. 1 Kings, 7. 49. Zech. 4. 2.
Hebr. 9. 2. Rev. 1. 12. & 4. 5.

dlestick *of* pure gold : *of* beaten
work shall the candlestick be made:

Jesus said unto them, Verily, verily, I say unto you, Moses gave you not that bread from heaven ; but my Father giveth you the true bread from heaven. For the bread of God is he which cometh down from heaven, and giveth life unto the world. Verily, verily, I say unto you, He that believeth on me hath everlasting life. I am that bread of life. Your fathers did eat manna in the wilderness, and are dead. This is the bread which cometh down from heaven, that a man may eat thereof, and not die. I am the living bread which came down from heaven: if any man eat of this bread, he shall live for ever : and the bread that I will give is my flesh, which I will give for the life of the world. The Jews therefore strove among themselves, saying, How can this man give us his flesh to eat? Then Jesus said unto them, Verily, verily, I say unto you, Except ye eat the flesh of the Son of man, and drink his blood, ye have no life in you. Whoso eateth my flesh, and drinketh my blood, hath eternal life ; and I will raise him up at the last day. For my flesh is meat indeed, and my blood is drink indeed. He that eateth my flesh, and drinketh my blood, dwelleth in me, and I in him. As the living Father hath sent me, and I live by the Father: so he that eateth me, even he shall live by me. This is that bread which came down from heaven : not as your fathers did eat manna, and are dead: he that eateth of this bread shall live for ever.'

Now it is well known that this is the great evangelical truth which is significantly shadowed forth in the sacramental bread of the Lord's Supper, the lively emblem of that spiritual aliment which he gives to his faithful household. *The mystery of the Table of Shew-bread is substantially the same with that of the Table spread with the emblems of the*

Lord's body and blood. It was a sensible and lively, though still inadequate 'shew' of the nourishment of that holy, hidden, spiritual life which is to be consummated in that coming world of glory, where the face of God will be revealed without a cloud, in joyful foresight of which the Psalmist exclaims Ps. 17. 15, 'As for me, I shall behold *thy face* in righteousness ; I shall be satisfied, when I awake with thy likeness,'—a plain allusion to the beatific vision in heaven. Then shall his servants 'see his face,' and because they shall 'see him as he is,' therefore shall they 'be like him.' 'In his presence is fullness of joy, and at his right hand are pleasures for evermore.' This ravishing and transforming view of the glorious presence of the Lord shall be an eternal *feast* to the blessed beholders, and it is doubtless from the intimate ideal relation between this *seeing* and *eating* that the bread of the Tabernacle is called the *bread of the face or presence.* The whole points directly to Christ, and is fulfilled only in him when he shall come the second time without sin unto salvation, shedding the *light of his countenance* in one endless and *soul-satisfying* blaze upon his redeemed ones. Their *vision* shall be eternal *fruition.* Thus we have obtained a view of the subject which shows the intimate connexion of the ideas of 'Bread' and 'Face' or 'Presence,' and with how much propriety the adjunct פנים *panim* is applied to the Tabernacle-table, while it is withheld from any other article of the sacred furniture.

THE CANDLESTICK.

31. *Thou shalt make a candlestick.* Heb. מנרת *menorath, a candelabrum, a lamp-bearer.* As 'candlestick' with us imports but a single upright shaft, the term fails to give us an idea at all

adequate of the construction of this article of the Tabernacle furniture. It consisted of a base or shaft, with seven branches, three on each side, and one in the middle. These branches were all parallel to one another, and were worked out in bowls, knobs (knops), and flowers, placed alternately, of which we shall shortly give a more particular description. On the extremity of each branch was a golden lamp, whose light was supplied by pure olive oil, prepared in a peculiar way, as will be seen by the Note on Ex. 27. 20. This Candlestick, which is affirmed by Josephus to have been hollow within, was wholly of pure gold, and weighed a talent (about 125 lbs.), although nothing is said of its height, thickness, or any of its dimensions. Nor is mention made of any kind of foot or pediment on which it rested, though we cannot doubt that it had one. The Jewish writers suppose that its height was about double that of the Table of Shew-bread and of the Altar of Incense, which would give it a very majestic appearance, and probably require a stool for lighting and trimming it, while at the same time it was not so much raised as to endanger the curtain-roof of the Tabernacle. It was placed on the south or left hand side of the holy place, as one entered, the row of lamps being probably parallel with the wall, though Lightfoot thinks that that described, Rev. 1. 12, 13, was perpendicular to it. It is a point, however, which it is difficult to determine, and about which the Rabbinical writers are not agreed. The oil for the seven lamps was to be supplied in such quantities as to keep them always burning. It is indeed imagined by some expositors that they did not perpetually burn, but were lighted every evening and went out one after another in the morning, an opinion which is no doubt favored at first view by several passages in the sacred writers. Thus for instance in 1 Sam. 3. 3, mention is

made of the lamp of God going out in the Temple; and in 2 Chron. 13. 11, we read of 'setting in order the candlestick of gold with the lamps thereof, *to burn every evening.*' So also in Ex. 30. 7, 8, it is mentioned as the duty of the priest to 'dress' the lamps every morning, and to 'light' them every evening But then on the other hand in the paralle text, Lev. 24. 2, it is said that the lamps were to burn continually, and though this term is not in itself absolutely decisive of the fact, as *continually* is often used in the sense of *regularly, statedly,* yet when we add the authority of Josephus, who was himself a priest, and not likely to be ignorant on this subject, it would seem to put the matter beyond question. He says expressly that the lamps continued to burn day and night. And there would seem in fact to have been a necessity for this, unless the priests ministered in the dark; for as there were no windows in the Tabernacle, light could only be admitted through the curtained entrance at the east or unboarded end; and unless that entrance were left open, which we do not learn that it was, the holy place might have been so dark as to render artificial light not less requisite by day than by night. At any rate, it is obvious that the most holy place, where the Ark lay, was entirely dependent for light, when it had any, upon the lamps of the golden Candlestick. This fact explains another allusion in reference to the heavenly city in the Apocalypse, the connexion of which with the holy of holies we have endeavored to show on a preceding page. In Rev. 22. 5, it is said, 'And there shall be no night there; and *they need no candle,* neither light of the sun; for the Lord God giveth them light.' In this respect the *substance* differed from the *shadow.* The typical heaven needed the artificial light of the lamps of the Candlestick; the *anti-typical* did not. 'The Lamb is the light thereof.'

his shaft, and his branches, his | bowls, his knops, his flowers, shall be of the same.

Having thus given a general view of the plan and uses of the golden Candlestick, we enter upon the more minute description of its individual parts.

Of beaten work. Heb. מקשה *mik-shah, of hard or solid work;* i. e. made of the solid material, having no wood-work about it, though Josephus represents it as being hollow. Our present rendering 'beaten work' is peculiarly unfortunate, as it leads the reader to suppose that several of the most exquisite fabrics of the Tabernacle were wrought out by a process of 'beating' with a hammer, than which nothing, we conceive, can be farther from the fact, as they were undoubtedly cast in moulds. So far as the present term is concerned, which is used several times in the narrative, it is designed to acquaint us solely with the *character of the material,* and not with the *process of formation.* See the remarks above on the use of the term, v. 18, in reference to the construction of the Cherubim.——¶ *His shaft.* Heb. ירכה *yerëkah, her shaft;* and so in all the following terms, קנה *kanah, her branches,* &c., instead of 'his.' The original term ירך *yerek,* properly signifies *a thigh,* but here is understood by the Rabbins of the *base* or *thick lower part* on which the main branch (קנה) rested and from which it rose. We suppose, therefore, the term ירך *yerek* to have been applied to that thick and massive portion of the stock which extended upwards from the foot or bottom to the point where the lowermost pair of branches separated.——¶ *His branches.* Heb. קנה *kanah, her branch.* The word properly signifies a *reed* or *cane,* which each of the branches probably somewhat resembled; indeed nothing is more remarkable, as we shall soon see, throughout this description of the Candlestick, than the employment of terms evidently drawn from the distinguishing parts of plants and trees, indicating a striking affinity in its structure, with the forms of the *vegetable* world. The reason of this singular fact we shall hope to elucidate in our remarks on the typical import of the Candlestick. In the present case the original term, though singular in form, has really a plural import, being intended to denote *all* the branches collectively, as appears from the next verse, and from the Greek rendering καλαμισκοι, *little reeds* or *canes.* Of these the middle one, constituting the main trunk of it, was of course the most important. And hence in v. 33, 34, and Chron. 3. 20, it is actually called by the name (מנרה *menorah*) of the whole Candlestick. It is not indeed expressly so distinguished in the present text, and the reason we suppose to be, that all the lower part of the stock or trunk up to the point where the different arms branched off, three on either side, was called ירך *yerek,* or *thigh.* Of the thickness of the central or the side branches we have no intimation, but Jarchi and Abenezra agree with Josephus, who denominates them λεπτους, *slender.*——¶ *His bowls.* Heb. גביע *gebia, calyx* or *cup;* so called from its resemblance to that part of the plant from which the flower springs. The Gr. however has κρατηρες, *bowls,* and the Vulg. *scyphos, cups,* from which the English rendering has flowed. The appendages here called 'bowls,' 'knops,' and 'flowers,' were mere ornamental devices, intended, it would seem, to give to each of the branches the appearance of a succession of *fruits* and *flowers.* As to the form of the 'bowls,' it is clear from v. 33, that they had some relation to the 'almond,' but in what respect, it is not easy to determine. The phrase in the original is גבערם משקדים *gebiim meshukkadim.*

which is to be literally rendered *cups made* or *figured almond-wise*, by which perhaps is to be understood nothing more than that this calyx-shaped ornament was to be fashioned in imitation of the calyx of the almond, rather than of any other plant. The expression is less likely to have denoted the *flower of the almond*, because the flower-work is denoted by another term, and because the term 'almond-wise' is in some way inseparably connected with the original for *cups* or *bowls*, as if to indicate their form. For this purpose the calyx would be much more suitable than the corolla. But it may be asked whether the bowls were not shaped like the *fruit* or *nut* of the almond, the shell of which when divided into its halves presents the appearance of small scolloped vessels like our spoons. To

this we can only say, that if such appendages were intended as *containing vessels*, they would not only be *useless* in the place which they occupied,—for what were they to hold?—but would be very unsightly and out of keeping as ornaments. If, moreover, they were intended to represent the *fruit* of the almond, then besides the intrinsic inappropriateness of the term, they would trench upon what we suppose to have been the design of the 'knops,' which is soon to be explained. On the whole, therefore, we seem to be shut up to the conclusion stated above, that the 'bowls' were exquisitely wrought ornaments in the shape of the *calyx of the almond flower;* and the annexed cut of the blossoms, flowers, and fruit of this plant may essentially aid our conception of this part of the workmanship.

THE ALMOND.

***His* knops.** Heb. כפתרים *kaphtorim.* Gr. σφαιρωτηρες, *spheres.* Vulg. *sphærulas, little spheres.* The term here employed receives but little light from

biblical usage. It is only in Amos, 9. 1, and Zeph. 2. 14, that כפתר *kaphtor,* occurs, in the first of which it is rendered 'door' and in the other 'lin tel,' and doubtless erroneously in both. It is probably to be understood in each case of some *round moulding, rows of knobs*, or other architectural ornaments of spherical form about the heads of pillars. The Rabbins with somewhat remarkable unanimity interpret it here by 'apple,' and Josephus expressly likens it to the 'pomegranate' (granate-apple), of which a cut and a full account is given hereafter; and we learn from 1 Kings, 7. 18, that the chapiters of the pillars in Solomon's Temple were adorned with pomegranates. Maimonides says, 'The *kaphtor* had the figure of a little globe, yet not exactly round, but somewhat oblong, like an egg.' He does not, however, it will be observed, recognise any allusion to the form of the pomegranate, and as the proper Hebrew for pomegranate is not כפתר *kaphtor*, but רמון *rimmon*, we incline to think that the *shelled fruit* of the almond itself is intended, which the reader will perceive bears a striking resemblance to the form of an egg, and was well calculated for a decoration of such a fabric as the Candlestick. We understand then by the term in this connexion those *rounded spherical swells* or *knobs* occurring alternately with the calyxes and flowers, along the length of the several branches, and which were expressly intended to represent some kind of *fruit;* and that fruit, if we rightly conceive of the matter, was the *nut of the almond.* —— ¶ *His flowers.* Heb. פרחיה *perahë-hah.* Gr. κρινα, *lillies.* Vulg. *lilia;* and so also Maimonides and Josephus. But the word in the original is the general word for *flowers*, or rather for *the blossoms of trees;* and we have nothing to guide us, in fixing upon any particular species. Yet as the other connected terms have a dominant reference to the *almond tree*, we seem to discover an intrinsic probability that the allusion is the same in the case before us; and this suggestion receives perhaps an in-

direct support from what is said Num. 17. 8, of the budding and blossoming of Aaron's rod; 'And it came to pass on the morrow Moses went into the tabernacle of witness; and, behold, the rod of Aaron for the house of Levi *was budded* (פרח *parah*), and *brought forth buds* (ויצא פרח *yotzë perah*), and bloomed blossoms, and yielded almonds.' In both passages we find פרח *perah* used in connexion with the *almond*, and we shall see in the sequel that the evidence in favor of this interpretation is much increased by what will be shown to have been the spiritual or typical uses of the Candlestick.

As to the manner in which this threefold variety of ornament was arranged relatively to each other on the branches, the text is not free from ambiguity. If our conception of the form were governed solely by what is said v. 33, we should perhaps infer that there was but one knop and one flower to the three bowls on each of the branches, as the two former are expressed by words in the singular, while 'bowls' is in the plural. Yet upon comparing the subsequent verses, and making up our idea of the whole, we cannot well resist the conclusion, that the bowls, knops, and flowers formed together one complex ornament which was three times repeated on each of the six side-branches, and four times on the central one. And thus we have represented them in the annexed original draft of the Candlestick, in which the reader will recognise the results of the foregoing researches and reasonings. It will be found to differ very considerably from the model given in the Candlestick represented on the Arch of Titus. But it is to be remembered that the utensils carried away by Vespasian were not the same with those made by Moses; and Josephus says the Candlestick was especially altered from its original form. The Mosaic Candlestick was transferred to the Temple and lost in the Babylonish captivity.

32 And six branches shall come out of the sides of it ; three branches of the candlestick out of the one side, and three branches of the candlestick out of the other side :
33 Three bowls made like unto almonds, *with* a knop and a flower in one branch ; and three bowls made like almonds in the other branch, *with* a knop and a flower : so in the six branches that come out of the candlestick.

THE GOLDEN CANDLESTICK.

As the Candlestick of the Tabernacle forms a constituent part of a system preeminently symbolical and typical, no good reason can be assigned why it should not, like the other sacred things with which it is connected, possess a *meaning* suited to the economy of which it formed a part. Its adaptation to its *primary* or *material* uses is evident ; and equally obvious, if we mistake not, will appear its fitness to the *spiritual* ends which it was intended to answer. In the attempt to ascertain and settle these upon satisfactory grounds, it will be important to draw largely upon various portions of holy writ, through which the light of the Tabernacle-lamps shines more or less distinctly, and from the concentrated rays of which we are to deduce its ultimate scope. The inquiry naturally divides itself into two distinct heads, the one in reference to the typical purport of the Lights, the other, that of the Candlestick viewed as a whole composed of its shaft and branches.

(1.) *The Lights.* As our grand object in this part of the investigation is, to obtain the unequivocal sanction of the Scriptures themselves for the solution which we propose to give to the symbol before us, we are naturally referred to those passages where an express mention of the Candlestick occurs, or which contain such allusions to its mystical import as will serve to guide us to correct conclusions. Several such places may be cited from which it will appear that *Light*, in its most genuine usage as a symbol, stands for *knowledge*, or rather that kind of *sacred intelligence* or *moral illumination*

34 And in the candlestick *shall be* four bowls made like unto al- | monds, *with* their knops and their flowers.

which has for its object *the things of God,* and for its author *the Holy Spirit,* the great fountain of all *spiritual light.* The remarks of Pres. Edwards in his 'Notes on the Bible' may be pertinently cited in this connexion. 'In the golden Candlestick that stood before the throne, on the left side was a representation both of the Holy Spirit and of the Church. The pure oil olive that fed the lamps is indisputably a type of the Holy Ghost; and it is evident, from Rev. 4. 5, compared with chap. 1. 4, and v. 6, and Zech. 3. 9, and 4. 2, 6, 10. The burning of the lamp represents that divine, infinite, pure energy and ardor wherein the Holy Spirit consists. The light of the lamps filling the Tabernacle with light which had no windows, and no light but of those lamps, represents the divine, blessed communication and influence of the Spirit of God, replenishing the church and filling heaven with the light of divine knowledge in opposition to the darkness of ignorance and delusion, with the light of holiness in opposition to the darkness of sin, and with the light of comfort and joy in opposition to the darkness of sorrow and misery.'

As this light however is communicated for the most part through the intervention of certain agencies set apart for that purpose, it is quite natural that it should be symbolically exhibited in concentrated form, in those artificial luminaries with which all men are familiar. The light of the Tabernacle answers to the light of the church; and the light of the church is the light of the Spirit of God dispensed through such media as it has pleased infinite wisdom to adopt. Of these the *sacred ministry* is perhaps the chief; and though the ministers of Christ shine with a borrowed lustre, merely *reflecting,* like mirrors, the rays of the great fountain

of light, yet we see a peculiar propriety and felicity in their being symbolised by the *lamps* or *lights* of the golden Candlestick. This will appear more strikingly evident by recurrence to the mystic scenery of the Apocalypse. In the opening vision of that book, chap. 1. John, hearing a voice behind him turns and beholds seven golden candlesticks and in the midst of them one like unto the Son of Man clothed with a long priestly tunic or robe, and girt about the breast with a golden girdle. This indicated that the character in which he now appeared was a priestly character, and that the action which he performed was a priestly action. What this action was and what it was designed to shadow forth, will be easily inferred from the circumstances of the vision. The scene of it is undoubtedly laid in the outer room or holy place of the Tabernacle, where the priests were wont to officiate, and where among other things it was the duty of some one of the number to see to the lighting, trimming, and snuffing the lamps of the golden Candlestick, which was done just as it began to grow dark in the evening. Imagine the apostle then, about the hour of twilight, standing without, near the entrance of the holy place, and looking in to the further end of the room, and there beholding the Great High Priest of the Christian Church occupied about the lights of the seven distinct golden candlesticks into which the one large candelabrum of the Tabernacle is multiplied under the New Testament economy. These lights thus seen from a distance in a room otherwise dark would have very much the appearance of *stars,* and it would be scarcely a stretch of language to say that the person employed in trimming and dressing the lamps, with his hand passing to and fro from one to the other, *held the stars in his right hand.* Such at any rate we doubt not was the imagery presented to the entranced perception of the seer, and as the action was unquestionably symbolic, our next object is to ascertain its meaning. But to this we have a luminous clue in the words of the divine hierophant himself v. 19, 20, 'Write the things which thou hast seen, and the things which are, and the things which shall be hereafter; the mystery of the seven stars which thou sawest in my right hand, and the seven golden candlesticks. The seven stars are the angels of the seven churches: and the seven candlesticks which thou sawest are the seven churches.' Here then we learn that the seven stars are the seven angels of the seven churches, while the seven Candlesticks are the churches themselves. But the *angels* of the churches are, in symbolical diction, the *ministers*, the *elders*, the *collective pastorship*, of the churches; and as we have shown the *stars* and the *lights* or *lamps* to be equivalent symbols, it follows that the lights set upon the respective Candlesticks are the *spiritual teachers*, the *moral luminaries*, appointed to impart spiritual and moral light to the churches. Viewed in connexion with this, how striking is our Savior's language, Mat. 5. 15, as applied to ministers of the gospel, to whom it was no doubt *primarily* intended to apply, 'Neither do men light a candle and put it under a bushel, but on a candlestick; and it giveth light to all that are in the house.' But the Apocalyptic visionings referred to require still farther explication. John not only saw the emblematic objects and action described, but he received a command also which disclosed the drift of the whole. He was ordered to address, in the name of Christ, seven epistles to the seven Asiatic Churches filled with reproofs, counsels, admonitions, and urgent exhortations, the design of which was to revive the decaying light, or in other words to quicken the lan-

guishing graces, both of the pastors and people of those churches, which from being embraced in the number of universality (seven) appear to have stood as representatives of *all* Christian churches down through the successive periods of time to the era of his second coming. This work, therefore, put forth by John in the name of Christ upon the churches by these epistles was the very work which was symbolically represented by the action of the Savior in trimming and dressing the lamps of the golden candlesticks. Each epistle was the application of the symbolical snuffers to each of the churches; but in a more especial manner to the *ministers* or *teachers* of the churches.

We gather from this explanation the clearest evidence of the truth of our main position, that the material lights of the Candlestick represented the spiritual lights of the church. The same view of this symbolical fabric applies to the object presented under some circumstantial varieties of form and aspect in the vision of Zechariah, ch. 4. 1—3, 'And the angel that talked with me came again, and waked me, as a man that is wakened out of his sleep, and said unto me, What seest thou? And I said, I have looked, and behold a candlestick, all of gold, with a bowl upon the top of it, and his seven lamps there on, and seven pipes to the seven lamps, which are upon the top thereof; and two olive-trees by it, one upon the right side of the bowl, and the other upon the left side thereof.' The candlestick seen by the prophet differed from that made by Moses by being surmounted by a bowl, out of which, as from a reservoir the oil was conducted through golden pipes to each of the lamps; and this bowl was moreover supplied by oil that flowed in a peculiar manner through two branches of two olive-trees standing on either side of the Candlestick, v. 11—14. This part of the vision especially attracted the curiosity and interest of the prophet. 'Then answered I, and said unto him, What are these two olive-trees upon the right side of the candlestick and upon the left side thereof? And I answered again, and said unto him, What be these two olive branches which through the two golden pipes empty the golden oil out of themselves? And he answered me and said, Knowest thou not what these be? And I said, No, my lord. Then said he, These are the two anointed ones (Heb. 'sons of oil'), that stand by the Lord of the whole earth.' These variations from the Mosaic model are certainly very remarkable; still in general significancy we have no doubt the symbol in each case is the same. The Candlestick with its branches and its lighted lamps, represents the church in its multiplied unity, as a medium for shedding abroad the beams of revealed truth amidst the darkness of a benighted world. But as the natural light of lamps is sustained by oil, so spiritual light is sustained by *truth*. Truth is its appropriate and genuine pabulum; and in the imagery of the vision before us, the obvious design is to represent the manner in which the churches are furnished with the nourishment of truth. Is not this from the Scriptures of truth, and are not the Old and New Testaments strikingly and adequately shadowed forth by the two olive-trees out of which the mystic oil was elaborated and conveyed to its golden receptacles? Here then we have the true clue to the 'two witnesses' of the Revelation, ch. 11. 3, 4. 'And I will give power unto my two witnesses, and they shall prophesy a thousand two hundred and threescore days, clothed in sackcloth. These are the two olive-trees, and the two candlesticks standing before the God of the earth.' The two witnesses are *two kinds of witnesses*, one of each, but most intimately related to each other, and their symbolical identity with the two olive-trees and the two candlesticks is here *expressly asserted by the Holy Ghost.* How vain then must be every attempt to settle the significancy of these mystic agents of the Apocalypse without first determining the genuine import of the Old Testament imagery here depicted? This we have endeavored to do in the foregoing remarks, and just in proportion to the evidence there adduced of the truth of our explanation is the evidence that by the 'two witnesses' of John is meant the *Scriptures* and the *Churches*—that is, the true, genuine, duly constituted apostolical churches—which have in fact been in all ages, except when suppressed, the main *witnesses* of God to the eyes and ears of corrupt and apostate christendom. In the prophecy of the Apocalypse it is clearly announced that the evil predominance of a great Antichristian power, called the Beast, should avail to cause these witnesses to prophesy in sackcloth, or in an embarrassed condition, for the space of twelve hundred and sixty years, and at last for a short period to suppress them altogether; after which they were again to rise from their extinction and recommence in an open, public, and acknowledged manner the exercise of their suspended functions. This is undoubtedly the great *truth* which the imagery was intended to shadow forth, and for the verification of this truth we are thrown upon the resources of history. But this process we must necessarily leave to be followed out by others. It constitutes the appropriate province of the expositor of the Apocalypse.

To the reader who would desire a more full expansion of the idea here advanced respecting the typical import of the Lights of the golden candlestick, we have great pleasure in recommending 'Stonard's Commentary on the Vision of Zechariah,' Lond. 1824, an abstract of which will be found in Robinson's edition of Calmet, under the article 'Candlestick.' This work exhibits one of the most admirable specimens of the sober and scriptural interpretation of prophetic symbols to be found in the English or any other language. The German treatise also of Bähr, entitled ' Symbolik des Mosaischen Cultus,' will be found an important auxiliary in this field of Biblical exposition. It is exceedingly desirable that both these works should be made accessible to the mass of English readers of the Scriptures. Our own conclusions, however, have been arrived at by a process conducted for the most part independently of either.

(2.) *The Candlestick.* To the symbolical purport of the Candlestick, considered more particularly in reference to its construction with ornamented shaft and branches, we have already obtained a clue in the express declaration of the Savior to John ; 'The mystery of the seven candlesticks is the seven churches.' Since then a candlestick in general is the scriptural symbol of a church, a candlestick with seven branches must be the symbol of the universal church, spread abroad through all its numerous particular congregations, each one in its allotted station, shining through both its members and ministers, and giving light to the world. For the number *seven* being used by the sacred writers to denote not merely an indefinite multitude, but *totality* and *perfection*, the seven branches are doubtless to be understood as denoting *all* the various and dispersed congregations of the great spiritual body ; while their all proceeding from one shaft plainly implies, that all those congregations are united in the one body of the universal church. ' In this character,' says Stonard, ' the church began to show itself, when the children of Israel, grown into a numerous people, were first collected and incorporated into a regularly formed body of believers in the true God, obeying, serving, and worshipping him according to his known will ; and

yet more conspicuously, when they were planted in the land of Canaan and spread over it, presenting to view many congregations of religious persons, spiritually united in one general community. The unity thereof was sufficiently guarded by the unity of the tabernacle, and afterwards of the temple in ' the place, which God had chosen to put his name there.' At the same time, there were doubtless many synagogues scattered over the whole country, somewhat in the nature of our parish churches, wherein the several congregations met to celebrate divine worship and receive religious instruction. The Jewish church still more completely answered to this symbol, on the return from the Babylonian captivity, when in almost all cities, towns, and populous villages, synagogues were erected and numerous congregations assembled, professing the belief, service, and worship of the true God, reading, teaching, preaching, and hearing his holy word ; and that not within the narrow bounds of Palestine only, but through almost every part of the civilized world. But doubtless the real, proper, perfect antitype of the Candlestick is to be found in the Christian church, when the gospel was published and its light diffused among all the nations of the world, illuminating its dark corners with the knowledge of truth and salvation.'

As to the *material* of this remarkable fabric, it is described to be of pure gold in all its parts and appendages ; and in the vision of Zechariah the oil by which its light was supplied is termed 'golden oil,' from its perfectly pure consistency, which resembled it to liquid gold. Now it is well known that gold is the most beautiful and precious of all metals, and no one needs to be reminded of the happy adaptation of this substance to represent the church, that object which of all others that the earth contains, is beyond comparison the most excellent, precious, and glorious in the sight of

God, whose judgment is according to truth.

It only remains to account for the stock and branches being wrought in such exquisite resemblance to the leading parts of the almond-tree, from which the model of its fruits and flowers appears to have been derived. The mention of the almond-tree is not of infrequent occurrence in the Scriptures, and it would seem, from its peculiar physical properties, to be well adapted to stand among moral emblems as symbolical of that *spiritual prosperity,* *thrift, vigor,* and *early productiveness,* which we naturally associate with our ideas of the operations of divine principles in the souls of the righteous. Its Hebrew name שָׁקֵד *shakëd* comes from שָׁקַד *shakad, to make haste, to be in a hurry,* and thence especially *to awake early, to be vigilant, to watch.* The almond-tree therefore is called שָׁקֵד *shakëd,* 'quia prima inter arbores evigilat,' *because it awakes before all other trees* from its winter's repose. In southern climates it flowers often in the month of January, and by March brings its fruit to maturity. Such a tree, of which it is said Eccl. 12. 5, ' the almond-tree shall flourish,' naturally forms a very suitable emblem of the vigorous vitality of the people of God, who are like ' a tree planted by the rivers of waters, which bringeth forth his fruit in his season, and his leaf doth not fade.' We do not indeed find it any where *expressly affirmed* that such is the designed import of figures and illustrations drawn from this member of the vegetable kingdom, but we do find it introduced into *the sacred things* for some reason or other, and this reason we are doubtless left to deduce from the intrinsic adaptedness of its properties to the end in view. Thus we are told, Num. 17. 6—8, that 'Moses spake unto the children of Israel, and every one of their princes gave him a rod apiece, for each prince one, accord-

ing to their fathers' house, even twelve rods: and the rod of Aaron was among their rods. And Moses laid up the rods before the Lord in the tabernacle of witness. And it came to pass, that on the morrow Moses went into the tabernacle of witness; and behold, the rod of Aaron for the house of Levi *was budded, and brought forth buds, and bloomed blossoms, and yielded almonds.'* By this was shadowed forth the fact, that the priestly office, in the fruits and flowers of its functions, should bloom and flourish in the family of Aaron; and we have here only to transfer the essential significancy of the symbol to the body of Christians to see its applicability to the work of the golden Candlestick. But waving all attempts to account with assurance for the employment of the almond-tree rather than any other in this relation, the main fact remains indisputable, that *blossoms, flowers,* and *fruits* were wrought into the ornamental work of the branches, and that a symbolical intention governed this part of the workmanship. Now we have seen that the Candlestick, in its New Testament bearings, represents the Churches of Christ. But the churches are composed of Christians, and Christians are a *flower-decked* and *fruit-bearing* people. They are distinguished by the *beautifying graces* of the Holy Spirit, fitly represented by *flowers,* and by the *substantial fruits* of holy living. 'Every branch in me that beareth fruit, he purgeth it, that it may bring forth more fruit.' A multitude of passages will at once occur to the reader, in which comparisons drawn from plants are made use of in order to portray more vividly the leading attributes of the Christian character. Why then should not a similar device, addressed to the eye, have been inwrought into the structure of a symbol expressly designed to adumbrate the churches of the saints? Is it a mere work of fancy to recognise a meaning worthy

35 And *there shall be* a knop under two branches of the same, and a knop under two branches of the same, and a knop under two branches of the same, according to the six branches that proceed out of the candlestick.

36 Their knops and their branches shall be of the same : all of it *shall be* one beaten work *of* pure gold.

37 And thou shalt make the seven lamps thereof : and ʸ they shall light the lamps thereof, that they may ᶻ give light over against it.

ʸ ch. 26. 21. & 30. 8. Lev, 24. 3, 4. 3 Chron. 13. 11.   ᶻ Numb. 8. 2.

of the subject and worthy of its divine Author in the unique decoration of this remarkable portion of the Mosaic apparatus ? It was, at any rate, a view of the subject which commended itself to the gifted mind of Edwards, who thus comments upon the passage before us ; ' The Candlestick was like a tree of many branches, and bearing flowers and fruit, agreeable to the very frequent representations of the church by a tree, an *olive-tree, a vine, a grain of mustard-seed that becomes a tree, the branch of the Lord, a tree whose substance is in it,* &c. The continuance and propagation of the church is compared to the propagation of branches from a common stock and root, and of plants from the seed. In this Candlestick, every flower is attended with a knop, apple, or pomegranate, representing a good profession attended with corresponding fruit in the true saints. Here were rows of knops and flowers one after another, beautifully representing the saints' progress of religious attainments, their going from strength to strength. Such is the nature of true grace and holy fruit, that it bears flowers that promise a further degree of fruit, the flowers having in it the principles of new fruit, and by this progress in holiness, the saint comes to shine as a light in the world.' *Notes on the Bible,* p. 265. For a still further confirmation of the truth of this solution, see Notes on Ex. 28. 33—35, respecting the pomegranates and bells on the robe of the ephod of the high priest.—We now resume the thread of our annotations.

35. *A knop under two branches,* &c. From this being thrice repeated it would seem to import that, beginning from the bottom pair of branches, there was to be on the main shaft one knop under each pair, near where it branched out, which would leave one knop with its bowl and flower to ornament the upper part of the shaft, between the upper pair of branches and the middle lamp.

36. *Shall be of the same.* That is, of the same material; all pure solid gold.

37. *Thou shalt make the seven lamps thereof.* Shalt cause to be made. By ' lamps' here is meant the *lamp-sconces* or *receptacles* for holding the oil, attached to the upper extremity of the shaft and each of the branches. This is rendered in the Gr. by λυχνοι, *lamps.* ——¶ *And they shall light,* &c. Heb. הֶעֱלָה *healah, he shall cause to ascend;* i. e. he, the priest ; whose duty it was to attend the Candlestick. Yet the phrase is collective implying the succession of priests, and therefore properly enough rendered in the plural in oui translation. The rendering ' shall light' is rather a paraphrase than a literal version. The meaning of the original will be plain if we bear in mind that the ' lamps' or *sconces* were to be detached and taken down from their sockets in the top of the Candlestick. When they were cleaned, filled with oil, and lighted, they were to be *put up* again in their places, and this is the exact sense of the Heb. הֶעֱלָה *to make to ascend,* i. e. *to raise, to elevate.* Gr. επιθησεις τους λυχνους, *thou shalt put on the lamps.* So also the Vulg ' Thou

38 And the tongs thereof, and the snuff-dishes thereof, *shall be of* pure gold.

39 *Of* a talent of pure gold shall he make it, with all these vessels.

40 And [a] look that thou make *them* after their pattern, which was shewed thee in the mount.

[a] ch. 26. 30. Numb. 8. 4. 1 Chron. 28. 11, 19 Acts 7. 44. Hebr. 8. 5.

shalt set them upon the Candlestick.' As the lamps were thus *put up* in a *lighted* state, it is easy to see how the term came to be rendered by the verb *to light.* When the lamps were all lighted below, and duly *raised up* to their proper places, the Candlestick might be said to be lighted.——¶ *Give light over against it.* Heb. עֵל עֵבֶר פָּנֶיהָ *al ëber panëha, over against the face thereof;* i. e. right forward, or straight before it, as the phrase signifies Ezek. 1. 9, 12. As the Candlestick stood near the wall on the south side of the Holy Place, its light would naturally fall in the opposite direction, more especially upon the Table of Shewbread, which faced it on the north. Comp. Num. 8. 2, 3.

38. *The tongs thereof.* Heb. מֶלְקָחֶיהָ *malkahëha,* literally *takers* from לָקַח *lakah, to take, to receive;* supposed to be a kind of *scissars* or *snuffers* for trimming the lamps. Chal. 'Forceps.'—— ¶ *Snuff-dishes thereof.* Heb. מַחְתֹּתֶיהָ *mahtothëha,* probably a kind of vessels or pans for receiving the snuffings of the lamps after they had been cut off by the 'tongs' above mentioned. Their precise form cannot now be determined.

39. *A talent of pure gold,* &c. That is, a talent of gold in weight was used in making the Candlestick, and the different vessels and instruments belonging to it; and this according to the most approved estimates of the value of Jewish coins amounted to not less than $30,000.

40. *Look that thou make them after their pattern, which was shewed thee,* &c. Heb. אֲשֶׁר אַתָּה מָרְאָה *asher attah morëh, which thou wast caused to see.* The command here given to Moses, enjoining upon him a scrupulous adher-

ence to the model proposed, undoubtedly carries with it an intimation that God regards his own appointments in matters of worship as of the utmost importance, and at the same time of a tendency in man to vary from his patterns and trust to his own inventions. Probably some more latitude is allowed under the Christian dispensation to the dictates of human wisdom in regard to externals, provided certain great fundamental *principles* be adhered to, and no onerous impositions be laid upon the conscience; but the Tabernacle service was throughout a sytem of *instituted worship,* which derived all its authority from the express appointment of Jehovah. On this account it was manifestly proper that every item of the apparatus should be fashioned according to the model set before Moses on the mount. It is to be observed, therefore, that this order was given to him *repeatedly,* and with very peculiar force and emphasis; and his strict adherence to it is, in the last chapter in this book, noticed no less than eight times, once after the mention of every separate piece of furniture that was made. In the New Testament also his compliance with the command is repeatedly adverted to, and the very order itself expressly quoted, Acts, 7. 4, Heb. 8. 5. What then was the reason of such minute particularity? Why must such and such things only be made, and they too of such precise materials and shape? Undoubtedly because the whole was intended to be of a *typical* character, shadowing the leading features of the gospel dispensation. Now as none but God could know all the things that were to be prefigured, so none but he could know how to adjust and designate them in the way

CHAPTER XXVI.

MOREOVER,[a] thou shalt make the tabernacle *with* ten cur-

ᵃ ch. 36. 8.

tains *of* fine twined linen, and blue, and purple, and scarlet : *with* cherubims of cunning work shalt thou make them.

---

best adapted to their end. Had Moses been left to contrive any thing from his own ingenuity, there might have wanted a correspondence between the type and the antitype. But when a model of every thing was shown him by God himself, the whole must of necessity accord most perfectly with the mind and purpose of the divine Designer.

Chapter 26

THE CURTAINS OF THE TABERNACLE.

1. *Thou shalt make the tabernacle with ten curtains*, &c. Heb. המשכן *hammishkan, the habitation.* It will be observed, that as nothing is said of the frame-work of wood till we arrive at the 15th verse, and yet the term 'tabernacle' is here employed, the original משכן *mishkan* must be understood in somewhat of a restricted sense as denoting the *inner set of curtains.* From this is distinguished the second or goats' hair set, expressly called אהל *ohel*, a *tent*, and from both, the other two which are called simply by the more general term מכסה *mikseh, covering.* There is no doubt that the two first of these terms משכן *mishkan* and אהל *ohel* elsewhere occur as a designation of the *whole tabernacle* without special reference to its several parts, yet it is always important to notice the minutest shades of peculiarity in the use of Scriptural terms ; and we shall see as we proceed, that the distinction now adverted to is amply supported. See Note on Ex. 40. 19. The ten curtains which the sacred writer goes on to describe did not, as we have remarked above, form the whole envelope of the Tabernacle, but simply one set, of which there were four in all. Of these the inner set, here described, was by far the richest and

most exquisite. They were made of the finest linen, dyed of the most beautiful colors, blue, purple, and scarlet, and curiously embroidered all over with Cherubim, as if it were intended to intimate that the beings which they represented were vitally interested in the great truths shadowed forth by the most recondite and central mysteries of the Tabernacle. This is evidently a relation too intimate to be sustained by angels, and therefore we are to look to men, men redeemed by the blood of the Lamb, for the substance of the symbol But as the symbol points more especially to men in their saved and glorified state, there is less impropriety in giving them an angelic emblem, because they will then be raised to an angelic condition. Our Savior's words, Mark, 12. 25, 'They shall be as the angels in heaven,' we have no doubt when rightly understood go rather to *identify* than to *assimilate* the sons of the resurrection with the angels of heaven.——¶ *Fine twined linen;* by which is meant linen made of threads *finely twisted* in the process of spinning. Hence in the Hebrew canons it is said, 'Wheresoever fine linen twisted is spoken of in the law, it must be six-double thread.' It is conjectured that this is the reason why this exquisite kind of linen, the Byss, is called שש *shesh* in the original, which properly signifies ' six.'—— ¶ *Cherubims of cunning work.* Heb. מעשה חשב *maaseh hoshĕb, the work of an exquisite craftsman.* Gr. εογασια υφαντον, *with the work of a weaver.* Chal. 'With the work of the artificer.' Arab. 'A picture of the most sagacious art.' Vulg. 'Variegated with embroidered work.' The meaning is, that figures of the Cherubim were to be embroidered into the tapestry of which the linen

2 The length of one curtain *shall be* eight and twenty cubits, and the breadth of one curtain four cubits : and every one of the curtains shall have one measure.

3 The five curtains shall be coupled together one to another; and

other five curtains *shall be* coupled one to another.

4 And thou shalt make loops of blue npon the edge of the one curtain from the selvedge in the coupling ; and likewise shalt thou make in the uttermost edge of *another*

---

curtains were composed. Considering that the inner set of curtains here described was ornamented *throughout* with this splendid coloring and embroidery, we are on the whole strongly inclined to adopt the opinion of Bähr (Symbolik des Mosaischen Cultus, p. 64.), that no part of it hung on the *outside* of the structure, but that it served as an *interior lining* to both the outer and inner rooms of the Tabernacle. To say nothing of the fact that otherwise it is not easy to conceive why the linen curtains were not as much an אֹהֶל or *tent* as the goats' hair, it follows from the ordinary interpretation, that all that part of the beautiful embroidered work which fell outside of the walls was entirely concealed from view ; that is to say, that out of 1120 square cubits of this exquisitely wrought tapestry, only 300, or the portion over-head were visible, leaving 820, or about three-fourths of the whole, entirely excluded from the eye, either within or without, except when the Tabernacle was taken down or set up ; and then they would be exposed to the general gaze, which was equally abhorrent to the sacredness of their design. It may then be safely asked, whether this is probable? Would infinite wisdom have authorised such a superfluous expense of workmanship, such a prodigal waste of splendid imagery? Suppose this curtain-work, on the other hand, to be wholly suspended *within* the rooms, and the whole of the embroidery was or might be visible. And in accordance with this, we find that in the Temple, which was modelled after the Tabernacle, the figures of the Cherubim were carved on the in-

side *walls* all round about the Holy and Most Holy Place, 1 Kings, 6. 29. It is true indeed that this view of the subject requires us to suppose that these curtains were attached by some kind of fastenings to the upper extremity of the boards, after passing across and forming the roof; but as the separating vail, v. 32, was suspended from the pillars by means of hooks and loops, so nothing is easier than to imagine that a similar expedient was adopted here. The more the matter is considered, the more probable we think will this suggestion appear ; although we have in the figure below represented the inner set of curtains as hanging without ; but this is simply with a view to display the difference of their texture from that of the others.

2, 3. *The length of one curtain* shall be *eight and twenty cubits,* &c. That is, about fourteen yards in breadth, and two in width. These ten curtains were to be formed into two separate hangings, five breadths in each, which were probably sewed together, while the two hangings were coupled by loops and golden clasps. With one of these large and gorgeous pieces of tapestry the Holy Place was covered, with whose dimensions it very exactly corresponded, and with the other the Most Holy. This was doubtless the reason of the twofold division. But as the Most Holy Place was only five yards long, there remained a surplus of five yards, which hung down on the west end of that room, being just sufficient to cover it.

4. *And thou shalt make loops of blue.* That is, of blue tape. These loops did not themselves interlace with each

curtain, in the coupling of the second.

5 Fifty loops shalt thou make in the one curtain, and fifty loops shalt thou make in the edge of the curtain that *is* in the coupling of the second; that the loops may take hold one of another.

6 And thou shalt make fifty taches of gold, and couple the curtains together with the taches: and it shall be one tabernacle.

7 ¶ And ᵇthou shalt make curtains *of* goats' *hair* to be a covering upon the tabernacle: eleven curtains shalt thou make.

8 The length of one curtain *shall*

ᵇ ch. 36. 14.

be thirty cubits, and the breadth of one curtain four cubits: and the eleven curtains *shall be all* of one measure.

9 And thou shalt couple five curtains by themselves, and six curtains by themselves, and shalt double the sixth curtain in the forefront of the tabernacle.

10 And thou shalt make fifty loops on the edge of the one curtain *that is* outmost in the coupling, and fifty loops in the edge of the curtain which coupleth the second.

11 And thou shalt make fifty taches of brass, and put the taches into the loops, and couple the tent together, that it may be one.

---

other, and thus connect the curtains, but they were brought near together and then coupled by the 'taches' or *clasps.* As to the precise manner in which this coupling was effected we are thrown upon our own conjectures. Horsley's account of it is as follows, (Bibl. Crit. vol. 1. p. 103): 'Since the two sheets were fastened together, whenever the Tabernacle was set up by the loops and the hooks, and there were fifty hooks upon each sheet, but only fifty hooks in all, it is obvious that one hook must have served each pair of loops. And this is remarked by all commentators. But how this was effected, I have nowhere found explained in an intelligible manner. I think it must have been thus. The fifty hooks were all set upon one sheet. Each hook was set immediately behind a loop. Then the loop immediately before the hook was passed through the opposite loop on the other sheet, and being drawn back, was hitched upon the hook behind it. Thus the edge of the sheet on which the hooks were not set, would be made to lap a little over the edge of the other, and a close, firm, neat joining would be formed.' The coupling of the two main hangings together in this

manner made it, as it were, 'one tabernacle' (משׁכן), i. e. one continuous awning or pavilion. It was such, moreover, or rather is spoken of as such, independent of the wood work, which is subsequently mentioned.

7—11. *Curtains of goats'* hair. The nature of this material, as a coarse kind of *camlet,* we have already considered, ch. 25. 4. The curtains made of it were designed as a protection to the finer fabric of the inner set, which seems to be more especially alluded to in the term 'tabernacle'—a sense confirmed by the usage of the Heb. משׁכן before remarked upon. There was one more piece of this camlet covering than of the linen, and it was also two cubits, or a yard, longer. The breadth of each piece was the same as that of the former, but as there was one more of the camlet than of the linen, it made the whole covering when coupled together two yards longer and one yard broader than the interior one. For this reason it hung down near to the bottom of the side-walls, and one yard in front over the entrance, which part of it was ordinarily doubled back. The coupling of the parts was managed in the same way as that of the other, except that

12 And the remnant that remaineth of the curtains of the tent, the half curtain that remaineth, shall hang over the back-side of the tabernacle.

13 And a cubit on the one side, and a cubit on the other side of that which remaineth in the length of the curtains of the tent, it shall hang over the sides of the tabernacle on this side and on that side, to cover it.

14 And c thou shalt make a covering for the tent *of* rams' skins dyed red, and a covering above *of* badgers' skins.

c ch. 36. 19.

one division consisted of five pieces and the other six, and in this instance the taches were of brass instead of gold.—— ¶ *Couple the tent together.* Heb. אֹהֶל *ohel.* This phraseology keeps up the distinction adverted to above between 'tabernacle' and 'tent' in this part of the history.

13. *The remnant that remaineth,* &c. The disposal of this surplus part of the curtains has been already intimated above. From the additional particulars here given, we learn, that it went to furnish the greater length of hanging on the sides, the front, and the west end of the Tabernacle. Still it did not depend quite to the ground, but left the foundation work of silver sockets exposed to view.

14. *Thou shalt make a covering,* &c. Of the third and fourth of these involopes, which were made of skins, as they were of a still coarser fabric, the account is very brief. Nothing is said of the dimensions of either, but it is to be presumed that each was somewhat larger than the one immediately next it, and to which it served as a ' covering.' It is not expressly stated whether the curtains lay flat or sloping on the top of the Tabernacle; if flat, there was more need of so many distinct coverings to prevent the rain from soaking through and injuring the inner and finer set, or from dropping into the sanctuary. It is probable, however, that the successive layers would of themselves sufficiently round the top of the Tabernacle to carry off the water, of which but little would be expected to fall in

that arid region. It may also be supposed that in g'ood weather, and on more solemn occasions, the exterior and coarser hangings were folded up on the sides so as to let the inner and finer appear in all their beauty ; and as it is certain that neither of the inner hangings came lower than to the upper side of the silver ground-sill, that splendid foundation would be thus exposed to view, and the whole together would present to the eye of the beholder a magnificent spectacle. In bad weather, or at night, the skin-coverings were probably let down to their full length, which was sufficient to cover the silver sleepers, and thus protect them from rain or snow. The remark of Scott on the typical design of the several curtain-layers is very appropriate ; 'The whole represents the person and doctrine of Christ, his true church, and all heavenly things ; which are outwardly, and to the carnal eyed, mean, but are inwardly and in the sight of God, exceedingly glorious and precious. The secure protection which he prepares for those who are inwardly precious in his sight, may also be denoted ; and the unity of the whole, formed of so many pieces and of such different materials, into one covering of the sanctuary, represents the spiritual temple formed of persons of different nations, dispositions, abilities, and attainments, compacted together into one church, by the uniting influence of the spirit of love.' The annexed cut is a probable approximation to a correct view of the curtains.

15 ¶ And thou shalt make boards for the tabernacle *of* shittim-wood standing up.

16 Ten cubits *shall be* the length of a board, and a cubit and a half *shall be* the breadth of one board.

17 Two tenons *shall there be* in one board, set in order one against another: thus shalt thou make for all the boards of the tabernacle.

18 And thou shalt make the boards for the tabernacle, twenty boards on the south side southward.

THE CURTAINS OF THE TABERNACLE.

THE BOARDS.

15. *Thou shalt make boards*, &c. Heb. קְרָשִׁים *kerashim*, *boards* or *planks*. The appropriate root קָרַשׁ *karash* does not occur in Hebrew, but in Chaldee the verb signifies to *coagulate, congeal, condense*, as קְרַס *keres* likewise does in Arabic, and the Syriac uses קַרְשָׁא *karsha* as a noun for *contignation*, or *coupling together*. The radical idea of the Heb. קָרַשׁ *karash* seems to be *to compact, contignate, or fasten together*, as in the frame-work of a building. Such a frame-work was necessary to support the curtains, and to give more stability to the sacred tent. Of the 'shittim-wood,' or acacia, we have already spoken ; the remaining particulars will be considered as we proceed.

16. *Ten cubits shall be the length of a board*. As the length of the boards constituted the height of the Tabernacle, it follows from this, according to the common computation of the cubit, that it was five yards or fifteen feet high. As there were twenty of these on each side, each of which were a cubit and a half, or twenty-seven inches in breadth, it made the whole length thirty cubits, or fifteen yards. Nothing, however, is said of the thickness of the boards, which Lightfoot fixes at nine inches, and which we have every reason to believe did not fall short of that estimate, though the Rabbins make it an entire cubit. This inference is confirmed by the fact that the Sept renders the original קְרָשִׁים by στύλοι *pillars*, and this they would scarcely have done had they understood it to mean only *boards*, which would certainly be a very inadequate material for such a structure.

17. *Two tenons*. Heb. יָדוֹת *yadoth, hands;* so called probably from their *holding fast* in the sockets into which they were mortised. These 'tenons' are generally understood to have been affixed to the bottom of each board, and to have been precisely the same with those mentioned below, v. 19. But we are rather of opinion that the two tenons here spoken of projected from the *side* of each board, and were inserted into corresponding receptacles in the adjoining board, in order to give more con-

19 And thou shalt make forty sockets of silver under the twenty boards: two sockets under one board for his two tenons, and two sockets under another board for his two tenons.

20 And for the second side of the

pactness to the wall. With this substantially agrees the rendering of the Vulg. ' In the sides of the boards shall be made two mortises, whereby one board may be joined to another board.' The original for ' set in order' (מְשֻׁלָּבֹת *meshallaboth*) properly signifies ' set ladderwise,' and it is perfectly easy to conceive that where two boards were brought near together, and yet not quite closed up, the connecting tenons would

tabernacle on the north side *there shall be* twenty boards.

21 And their forty sockets *of* silver; two sockets under one board, and two sockets under another board.

22 And for the sides of the tab-

look like the rounds of a ladder. The tenons at the bottom of each board we suppose to have been additional to these. Still it must be admitted that this interpretation is not quite certain. The matter is left to the judgment of the reader. The annexed cut may be considered as a probable approximation to a correct idea of the position of the boards, tenons, and sockets. The different parts will be readily distinguished

BOARDS AND SOCKETS.

19. *Forty sockets of silver.* Heb. אַדְנֵי כָסֶף *adnë keseph, bases of silver;* implying doubtless the *supporting* sockets of the tenons, as the true import of אֶדֶן *eden* is a *base* or *supporter*. Each of these sockets was composed of a talent of silver, and every two of them joined together equalled in length the width of one of the planks, and so formed, when united, one entire foundation, which, in the technical language of the architects, may be termed a *silver ground-sill.*

20, 21. *And for the second side, &c* These two verses amount to nothing more than a direction, that the construction of the north side of the Tabernacle should exactly correspond with that of the south.

22. *For the sides of the tabernacle westward.* Heb. יַרְכֹת *yarkoth.* This term when applied to things inanimate usually denotes *an end, a term, an extremity,* and is doubtless so to be understood here, as we find it occasionally rendered in the Gr. εσχαρα, *extreme*

ernacle westward thou shalt make six boards.

23 And two boards shalt thou make for the corners of the tabernacle in the two sides.

24 And they shall be coupled together beneath, and they shall be coupled together above the head of it unto one ring: thus shall it be for them both; they shall be for the two corners.

25 And they shall be eight boards, and their sockets *of* silver, sixteen sockets; two sockets under one board, and two sockets under another board.

26 ¶ And thou shalt make bars

of shittim-wood; five for the boards of the one side of the tabernacle,

27 And five bars for the boards of the other side of the tabernacle, and five bars for the boards of the sides of the tabernacle, for the two sides westward.

28 And the middle bar in the midst of the boards shall reach from end to end.

29 And thou shalt overlay the boards with gold, and make their rings *of* gold *for* places for the bars, and thou shalt overlay the bars with gold.

30 And thou shalt rear up the tab-

---

parts. The idiomatic plural term 'sides' therefore is here equivalent to ' end.' So it is distinctly interpreted both in the Targum of Onkelos and Jonathan.

23, 24. Two boards shalt thou make for the corners. These two verses are involved in an obscurity which we have endeavored in vain to penetrate. The reader must be thrown upon his own resources to imagine such a construction of the corners as the general plan and objects of the building would admit or require. The original word for ' coupled' literally signifies ' twinned' or ' made like twins,' i. e. exactly alike ; but beyond this we are unable to afford him any light. Should he obtain it from other commentators, he will be more fortunate than ourselves. Our inability, however, to make out satisfactorily this part of the structure detracts nothing from the accuracy of the explanations of the rest.

25. They shall be eight boards. The two corner boards being added to the six others made up the complement of eight.

26. Thou shalt make bars. The south and north sides, and the west end of the Tabernacle had five gold-covered bars, each of which were carried through rings or staples of gold, but what the

length of these bars was, is not said. The middle ones, indeed, on the different sides and end, were appointed to be of the whole length, or thirty cubits on the north and south sides, and ten cubits at the west end ; which was probably sunk into the boards, and ran along a groove from end to end, at five cubits from the ground. The other four bars, which Josephus says were each five cubits long, were perhaps variously disposed on the sides and end of the structure in such a way as to conduce at once most effectually to its beauty and strength. Having no certain information as to the precise manner in which the four were disposed along the sides we have represented them in our cut as arranged uniformly with the middle one. It is obviously a matter of little importance. In the phrase, ' for the two sides westward,' the plural is probably put for the singular, as it was the end in which the two sides terminated.

29. Thou shalt overlay the boards with gold. We are thrown upon our own conjectures as to the thickness of the metal by which the boards and bars were overlaid. If it were done with *gold plates,* they must have been extremely thin, as otherwise the weight would have been altogether too great to

ernacle d according to the fashion
thereof which was shewed thee in
the mount.

31 ¶ And e thou shalt make a
vail *of* blue, and purple, and scar-
et, and fine twined linen of cun-

<small>d ch. 25. 9, 40. & 27. 8. Acts 7. 44. Heb. 8.
5. e ch. 36. 35. Lev. 16. 2. 2 Chron. 3. 14.
Matt. 27. 51. Hebr. 9. 3.</small>

allow of their having been carried but
with the utmost difficulty. We presume, therefore, that they were rather
gilded than *plated.* Such a thin coat-
ing would no doubt have been liable to
be easily worn off, but it could as easily
be repaired.

THE PARTITION-VAIL.

31. *Thou shalt make a vail,* &c. Heb.
פֶרֹכֶת *paroketh.* Gr. καταπετασμα, *a
vail, a spreading.* The etymology of
the original term is doubtful, though
we find in the Chaldee פְרָךְ *perak, to
break, rend apart, forcibly separate,*
and פֶרֹכֶת according to Parkhurst is
applied to the inner Vail from its *breaking, interrupting,* or *dividing* between
the Holy and Most Holy Place. This
Vail was undoubtedly of the same material with the inner set of curtains,
and figured and embroidered in the same
manner. And as it constituted, when
hanging down, the *lining* of one side of
both the Holy and Most Holy Place, it
goes somewhat, perhaps, to confirm our
suggestion above relative to the position of the wrought linen curtains of
the Tabernacle, as hanging *within* the
edifice instead of *without;* for this
would make the adorning of the whole
interior uniform throughout. The Vail
was to be suspended from golden hooks
attached to four pillars of shittim-wood
resting, like the boards, upon an equal
number of silver sockets. And this, by
the way, leads us to remark, that the
punctuation of our English Bibles conveys an idea entirely erroneous, viz.,
that the hooks were to be placed upon
the silver sockets. But these sockets

ning work: with cherubims shall
it be made.

32 And thou shalt hang it upon
four pillars of shittim-*wood* overlaid with gold: their hooks *shall
be of* gold upon the four sockets of
silver.

33 ¶ And thou shalt hang up the

were unquestionably at the bottom of
the pillars, and the clause, 'their hooks
shall be of gold,' ought to be inclosed
in a parenthesis, as it is in the old Geneva
version; 'And thou shalt hang it upon
four pillars of shittim-wood covered
with gold (whose hooks shall be of
gold), standing upon four sockets of
silver.' It was the pillars and not
the hooks that stood upon the silver
sockets.

33. *Shalt hang up the vail under the
taches.* That is, under the golden clasps
that connected the two larger hangings
of the inner curtain, spoken of above,
v. 6. These were joined just over the
dividing line between the two rooms of
the Tabernacle, so that this separating vail hung exactly under the taches
or clasps. It does not appear from any
express passage of Scripture, in what
proportions the interior of the Tabernacle was divided. But as Solomon's
Temple, of sixty cubits in length, was
divided into two parts of forty and
twenty, so it is highly probable that
the thirty cubits in length of the Tabernacle was divided into similar proportions of twenty cubits for the Holy, and
ten for the Most Holy Place, making
the latter a perfect cube of ten cubits
every way. This accounts, as we have
before intimated, for the remarkable
feature in the description of the heavenly city, mentioned Rev. 21. 16, to wit,
that *it lay four square,* the length,
breadth, and height of it being equal.
This was because it answered to its
type the Holy of Holies. In the Holy
Place, into which none but the priests
were allowed to enter, were stationed

vail under the taches, that thou mayest bring in thither within the vail f the ark of the testimony: and the vail shall divide unto you between g the holy *place* and the most holy.

34 And h thou shalt put the mer-

f ch. 25. 16. & 40. 21. g Lev. 16. 2. Hebr. 9. 2, 3. h ch. 25. 21. & 40. 20. Hebr. 9. 5.

cy-seat upon the ark of the testimony in the most holy *place*.

35 And i thou shalt set the table without the vail, and k the candlestick over against the table on the side of the tabernacle toward the south: and thou shalt put the table on the north side.

i ch. 40. 22. Hebr. 9. 2. k ch. 40. 24.

the Candlestick, the Table of Shewbread, and the Altar of Incense. In the Most Holy, into which none but the High Priest could enter, and he but once a year, was deposited only the Ark of the Covenant or Testimony, with its surmounting Mercy-seat.

The special design of this Vail was to debar the people from entering, or even looking, into the Most Holy Place, or place of the Ark, and the reason of this rigid exclusion acquaints us at once with the general mystical import of Vail, as a part of the apparatus of the Tabernacle. On this point we have happily the apostle Paul as the *angelus interpres.* Heb. 9. 6—9, 'Now when these things were thus ordained, the priests went always into the first tabernacle (the first or outer room), accomplishing the service of God: but into the second went the high priest alone once every year, not without blood, which he offered for himself, and for the errors of the people: the Holy Ghost this signifying, that the way into the holiest of all was not yet made manifest, while as the first tabernacle was yet standing: which was a figure for the time then present.' In other words, the way into the true heaven, of which the inner sanctuary was a type, was not laid open under the old economy, or by means of any of its services, but remained to be opened by Christ, of whom it is said, v. 24, that he 'is not entered into the holy places made with hands, which are the figures of the true; but into heaven itself, now to appear in the presence of God for us.'

But this does not yet exhaust the pregnant import of the Mosaic symbols. Still farther light is thrown upon it, Heb. 10. 19, 20, 'Having therefore, brethren, boldness to enter into the holiest by the blood of Jesus, by a new and living way, which he hath consecrated for us, through the vail, that is to say, his flesh, let us draw near.' Here it is clear that the Vail is represented as in some way shadowing forth the *flesh* or *body* of Christ, although it is perhaps at first view difficult to avoid an impression of incongruity in the imagery. What is Christ's *flesh* or *body* but *himself?* And how can he be described as the *person entering*, and yet *he himself* the *medium* through which the entrance is made? But a right view of the glorious constitution of Christ's person as God-man Mediator, and of the prominent place which he holds as the soul and centre and substance of nearly *every part* of the typical economy, will afford a clue to the solution of the problem. We have previously shown, if we mistake not, in our remarks upon the Cloudy Pillar, and upon the Shekinah in general, that that splendid symbol pointed directly to Christ as the central mystery which it involved. As the sombre folds of the guiding Cloud in the wilderness enshrouded the Glory of Jehovah, except when occasional displays of it were made, so the human nature or body of Christ, while he *tabernacled* on earth, served as a kind of temporary *invelope* or *vail* of the divine nature which dwelt within. This mystic *cloud* or *vail* of

36 And ¹ thou shalt make an hanging for the door of the tent, *of* blue,

¹ ch. 36. 37.

and purple, and scarlet, and fine twined linen, wrought with needle-work.

his flesh we suppose to have been transiently rent or cloven at his transfiguration, and a momentary display made of the indwelling glory of his Godhead. But this was not designed to be permanent ; it was only an evanescent gleam vouchsafed to the outward senses, for the greater inward assurance, of his select disciples, in respect to the essential dignity and divinity of his character, and to connect his person not only with the *truth* of the ancient visible Shekinah, but also with that future foretold *theophany*, which is to constitute the beatific vision in heaven. It was only at his death, when his ' body was broken' for the sins of the world, that this intervening *cloud* or *vail* was entirely rent, dissolved, and done away, and a way thus opened for the free manifestation of his glory and majesty to all believers, whether Jews or Gentiles. Now it is well known that after the Cloudy Pillar was removed from the sight of Israel, subsequent to the rearing of the Tabernacle, and the indwelling Shekinah had taken up its abode in the Holy of Holies, the separating Vail served to conceal the supernatural Brightness from the view, just as the dark mass of the Cloud had done prior to that event. Consequently as the Vail of the Tabernacle was to the inner abiding Glory what the Savior's flesh was to his indwelling Divinity, it was ordered that at the same time that the vail of his flesh was rent upon the cross, the corresponding Vail of the Temple was ' rent in twain from the top to the bottom,' implying that a blessed way of access was now provided into the interior of the heavenly sanctuary, of which the grand characteristic is, that it is to have ' the Glory of God,' and from thence to receive its denomination, 'Jehovah-Shammah,' *the Lord is there.* The truth is, that Christ sus-

tains so many offices in the plan of redemption, and he is presented to us in the ancient symbols in such a manifold variety of aspects, that we are not to be surprised if we should find in the apostolic explanations a blending of import that even approximates to something like confusion. Who can doubt that in the priestly service the High Priest himself, the Sacrifice, and the Altar, all found their substance in Christ ? In like manner, may not the Vail and the inner Presence both point also to him ?

THE ENTRANCE-VAIL.

36. *Thou shalt make an hanging for the door.* Heb. מסך *masak, from* סכך *sakak, to overspread, to cover,* denoting in general *tegumentum, operimentum, a covering, any thing spread over;* but here applied to the vail or curtain which hung over the entrance to the Tabernacle, and formed its outer-door. Oriental usages still furnish something analogous to this. 'We passed Lahar,' says Morier, ' close to a small valley, where we found several snug encampments ot the Eelauts, at one of which we stopped to examine the tent of the chief of the *obah*, or family. It was composed of a wooden frame of circular laths, which were fixed on the ground, and then covered over with large felts, that were fastened down by a cord, ornamented by tassels of various colors. A curtain, curiously worked by the women, with coarse needle-work of various colors, was suspended over the door. In the king of Persia's tents, magnificent *perdahs*, or hangings of needle-work, are suspended, as well as on the doors of the great mosques in Turkey.' This Vail was suspended on five pillars, overlaid with gold, at the east end of the sanctuary ; and though of the same

37 And thou shalt make for the nanging ᵐ five pillars *of* shittim-wood, and overlay them with gold,

ᵐ ch. 36. 38.

and their hooks *shall be of* gold: and thou shalt cast five sockets of brass for them.

---

rich material with the inner Vail, yet it seems to have been less highly orna-mented, as the Jewish writers affirm that there was a difference between the work of the 'cunning workman' men-tioned v. 1, and that of the 'embroider-er' mentioned here, which consisted in this; that in the former, the figures were so wrought, perhaps in weaving, that they might be seen on both sides of the work; but in the latter, being wrought by needle-work, they were on-ly visible on one side. Accordingly, while the Cherubic figure was wrought in one, we find no intimation of it in the other. As it was solely by raising or turning aside this Vail, that the priest entered the Tabernacle, it is obvious that the term 'door' in our translation is not to be taken in its ordinary sense, nor is the original strictly equivalent to 'thou shalt make a hanging *as a door* for the tent;' for the Heb. פתח *pethah*, as remarked in the Note on Gen. 19. 6, signifies properly the *open space* or *passage-way* which is usually closed by the *door*, and the meaning here is simply, 'thou shalt make a hanging *for the entrance-way.*' 'This is the more material,' says Wells (Intro-duction to Paraphrase, p. 47), 'to be tak-en notice of, because the said rendering of the Hebrew word by a *door*, not only gives the reader a wrong notion of the entrance itself into the Tabernacle, but also thereby hinders him from having a clear perception of the reason of several rites and expressions referring to the said entrance of the Tabernacle. For instance, what was done at the entrance of the Tabernacle, is expressly said in many places of Scripture to be done 'before the Lord,' as Ex. 29. 11—42. Lev. 1. 3, &c. Insomuch, that where a thing is said to be done only 'before

the Lord,' thereby expositors under-stand it generally of its being done *at the entrance of the Tabernacle* or the like, justly looking on these expressions as equivalent generally in Scripture, be-cause they are often so joined together as one and the same thing. Now the reason, why these two expressions came to be thus equivalent I take to be this. It was looked on as a piece of state and majesty by the eastern princes, seldom to vouchsafe the honor of com-ing near to their presence to any but their great courtiers; and when they were pleased to vouchsafe the great honor of coming into their presence or before them to any others on special and extraordinary occasions, they them-selves were wont then to sit on their thrones, which was covered with a can-opy over it, and encompassed all round with fine curtains; not drawn quite close, but so as that they could see easily those that were admitted thus into their presence, through the small spaces left between the curtains; but the others could have but a small, if any, glimpse, of their majesties or the inside of the thrones they sat on. Agree-ably hereto the whole Tabernacle in this case was to be looked on as the *throne of the Divine Majesty* here on earth. And consequently when any were to be admitted to the honor of ap-pearing more immediately *before the Lord,* he was to appear *at the entrance of the Tabernacle,* as before the throne of the Divine Majesty; from within which the Divine Majesty was conceiv-ed in a special and gracious manner to see or look on the person that so ap-peared before him; though the said per-son could not see the Divine Majesty, or have any more than perhaps a glimpse of the inside of his throne or of the

CHAPTER XXVII.

A ND thou shalt make ᵃ an altar *of* shittim-wood, five cubits

ᵃ ch. 38. 1. Ezek. 43. 13.

Tabernacle, by reason of the Vail hanging afore the entrance of it. And whereas it is one piece of reverence not to *turn one's back,* but to *stand with one's face,* toward any great person, especially kings; in like manner he that appeared *before the Lord,* stood *with his face toward the entrance of the Tabernacle,* as being the forepart of the throne of the Divine Majesty, and consequently by so doing he was conceived to stand with his face toward the Divine Majesty itself. But now all this agreement between the manner of appearing *before the Lord,* as it is called in Scripture, and of appearing before earthly princes, in those eastern countries, to which the former referred, is much obscured by representing the entrance into the Tabernacle as through a *door.'* Josephus informs us that besides the Vail of linen here described there was another of coarser fabric hung over the first to defend it from injuries of the weather, and that upon festival occasions this was drawn aside or rolled up that the people might see the exquisite beauty of the workmanship of the first; a suggestion which we deem altogether probable.

Chapter 27

THE ALTAR OF SACRIFICE.

1. *Thou shalt make an altar.* Heb. מזבח *mizbeah.* Gr. θυσιαστηριον, *sacrificatory;* both appellations being derived from a term signifying to *sacrifice.* On the general import of the term see Note on Ex. 20. 24. This altar was a sort of square chest of shittim wood overlaid with brass. It was five cubits long by five broad, and three in height (about three yards square and five feet high), and had a horn or

long, and five cubits broad; the altar shall be four square: and the height thereof *shall be* three cubits.

2 And thou shalt make the horns

projection at each corner. It was hollow within, and in the middle of its surface was a sunk grating of brass to support the fire, which was furnished with four rings, that it might be taken out and carried separately from the body of the altar. The ashes from the fire sunk through the grating, and were taken thence in a pan made for the purpose. The altar had four rings or staples at the sides, into which poles of shittim wood covered with brass were inserted when the altar was to be moved from place to place. This is the account which seems to agree best with the text, although some of the details have been differently understood by various expositors. It is thought that both this altar and the larger one made by Solomon, by which it was superseded, had the lower part of the hollow filled up either with earth or stones, in compliance with the injunction in chap. 20. 24, 25. Josephus says, that the altar used in his time at the Temple was of unhewn stone, and that no iron tool had been employed in its construction. None of the altars which the Scripture assigns to either the Tabernacle or Temple were of this construction, but that erected at Mount Ebal by Joshua was so (Josh. 8. 31), and apparently others which were set up in different parts of the land of promise.——

¶ *Thou shalt make the horns of it.* Heb. קרנת *karnoth.* Gr. κερατα. The horns of the Altar have given scope to voluminous discussion, both as regards their form and their design. They were certainly projections of some kind or other at the four corners, but their precise shape, or even the direction in which they projected, cannot be distinctly collected from the sacred text. By many it is supposed that they were

of it upon the four corners thereof:
his horns shall be of the same: and
ᵇ thou shalt overlay it with brass.
3 And thou shalt make his pans

ᵇ See Numb. 16. 38.

to receive his ashes, and his shovels, and his basons, and his flesh-
hooks, and his fire-pans: all the
vessels thereof thou shalt make
of brass.

actually *horn-shaped,* and this opinion
is supported by the authority of Josephus as to the Altar used in his time.
But the opinion seems preferable that
they were square risings, or *pinnacles,*
from each corner of the Altar ; or square
to half their height, and terminating
pyramidically in a sharp tip or point.
The descriptions given by the Rabbins,
and the pictures of the most ancient
altars go to confirm this view of their
form. We are no more certain as to
the *use* of this appendage to the Altar,
than as to its form. It is inferred by
some from Ps. 118. 27, ' bind the sacrifice with cords to the horns of the Altar,' that these appendages were designed for the purpose of fastening the
victim to the Altar before it was slain.
But of this there is little probability,
as the incense-altar, at which no bloody
sacrifices were offered, also had horns ;
and there is nothing in all Jewish antiquity to favor the idea of the victims
being ordinarily thus secured and slain
immediately contiguous to the Altar.
Of the passage just cited the best interpretation is perhaps that of Rabbi D.
Kimchi, given in the following paraphrase ; ' Bring the sacrifices bound
with cords until (from their great number) they shall have reached even to
the horns of the Altar.' The Psalmist
is supposed to have commanded so large
a sacrifice, that the victims should even
crowd the outer court, and press up
against the very Altar. The Chaldee
gives a somewhat different construction ; 'Tie the lamb, that is to be offered, with cords, till ye come to offer
him ; and sprinkle his blood upon the
horns of the Altar.' Either of them,
however, are preferable to the sense
yielded by our translation. The prob-

ability on the whole is, that these pro-
tuberances had some connexion with the
use of horns as symbols of sovereignty,
glory, power, strength. Hab. 3. 4, 'He
had *horns* coming out of his hands, and
there was the biding of his *power.*' But
we shall have more to say upon this
point in the sequel.

3. *His pans to receive his ashes.* Heb.
סירתיו *sirothauv;* a word which signifies either *pots* or *pans,* but which is
here doubtless to be taken in the latter
sense, as appears from the specified use
to which they were applied. The original term, however, rendered ' to receive his ashes' (לדשנו *ledashsheno*),
signifies rather *to remove, to carry out*
the ashes which fell from the grate to
the earth within the compass of the
Altar. The pans were employed for
the purpose of taking up these ashes
and carrying them to a clean place, as
we learn from Lev. 4. 12.——¶ *His
shovels.* יעיו *yaauv.* The radical יעה
yaäh has a sense so near that of *col-
lecting together by scraping,* that some
of the older interpreters have rendered
the present word by *besoms* or *brooms.*
But as they were made of brass, that
rendering is obviously untenable, and
we are warranted in understanding by
the term the *fire-shovels* by which the
ashes were *scraped together in a heap,*
and then thrown into the pans. ——
¶ *His basons.* Heb. מזרקתיו *mizre-
kothauv, sprinkling vessels.* Gr. τας
φιαλας αυτου, *his vials.* The term comes
from זרק *zarak, to sprinkle,* and properly denotes the vessels or bowls into
which the blood of the sacrifices was
received, that it might thence be
sprinkled on the people, on the horns
of the Altar, &c.——¶ *His flesh-hooks.*
Heb. מזלגתיו *mizlegothauv.* Gr. τας

4 And thou shalt make for it a grate of net-work *of* brass; and upon the net shalt thou make four brazen rings in the four corners thereof.

5 And thou shalt put it under the

κρεαγρας αυτου, defined by the Lexicons *hooked instruments for drawing out the meat;* i. e. for picking up and replacing any portion of the sacrifice which may have fallen out of the fire, or off from the Altar. Probably no more suitable word could be adopted by which to render it than the one chosen by our translators, *flesh-hooks.* By its being rendered *tridents* in some of the old versions, we infer that it was a *three-pronged* instrument in the form of *a curved fork.* We may gather somewhat more respecting its use from 1 Sam. 2. 13, 14, 'And the priest's custom with the people was, that when any man offered sacrifice, the priest's servant came, while the flesh was in seething, with a *flesh-hook* (מזלג *maz-leg*) of three teeth in his hand; and he struck it into the pan, or kettle, or caldron, or pot; all that the *flesh-hook* (מזלג *mazleg*) brought up the priest took for himself. So they did in Shiloh unto all the Israelites that came thither.' The Heb. זלג *zalag* has the general import of *curvature* or *crookedness of form,* and it is a little remarkable that, as Bochart has observed, the ancient name of Messina in Sicily was *Zanklé* (*Ζαγκλη*) from its resemblance to a *sickle* which Thucydides says they called *zanklon* (*ζαγκλον*); whence Ovid (Trist. L. IV.) speaking of the same city, says,

Quique locus *curvœ nomina falcis* habet.

The place that's from *the crooked sickle* named.

The Greek word is no doubt of Punic or Phœnician and not Sicilian origin, formed by transposing the letters ג (g) and ל (l). To the same root is probably to be traced the Gr. *σκολιος crooked* and *σκαληνος scalene,* and also the English *sickle.*—¶ *His fire-pans.* Heb. מהתתיך *mahtothauv.* Gr. *το πυρειον αυτου, his fire-receptacle.* Bp. Patrick's explanation of this term is perhaps the most probable. He supposes it to have been 'a larger sort of vessel, wherein the sacred fire, which came down from heaven (Lev. 9. 24,) was kept burning whilst they cleansed the Altar and the grate from the coals and ashes; and while the Altar was carried from one place to another, as it often was in the wilderness.' The root חתה *hathah* has the import of *keeping fire alive* or *glowing,* and from this root probably comes the Gr. *αιθω, to burn,* and Eng. *heat* and *hot.*

4, 5. *Thou shalt make for it a grate of net-work of brass,* &c. From the phraseology of the text it would appear, that this brazen grating was let into the hollow of the Altar, and sunk so far below the upper surface that its bottom, which was probably convex, reached to midway of the height of the Altar; 'that the net may be even to the midst of the Altar.' Being thus made of net-work like a sieve, and hung hollow, the fire would burn the better, and the ashes would sift through into the hollow of the Altar, from whence they were removed through a door constructed for the purpose. The four rings attached to the corners of this grated partition were for the purpose of lifting it out and putting it in. Some of the elder commentators have suggested that these rings were connected by chains with the horns of the Altar, which thus served an important purpose in suspending the grate. However this may be it is altogether probable that the rings fell within the compass of the Altar below the top, and were not seen without. Some writers have been much censured by a fancied difficulty in seeing how the wood-work of the Altar could be kept from being burnt, when exposed

compass of the altar beneath, that the net may be even to the midst of the altar.

6 And thou shalt make staves for the altar, staves *of* shittim-wood, and overlay them with brass.

7 And the staves shall be put into the rings, and the staves shall be upon the two sides of the altar to bear it.

8 Hollow with boards shalt thou make it: c as it was shewed thee in the mount, so shall they make *it*.

c ch. 25. 40. & 26. 30.

to such a constant heat. But nothing forbids the supposition, that it was cased both *within* and *without* with plates of metal; and for further security a lining of stone might easily have been laid within against the sides of the frame, and as the grate was *sus*-pended by the rings, and the fire no-where in contact with the frame, besides the whole being under the continual inspection of the priests, the danger of combustion was very slight. The annexed cut will supersede any more minute description.

THE ALTAR OF SACRIFICE.

In pursuance of our general plan, it will be requisite here to endeavor to ascertain the typical import of the Altar of Offering. The *a priori* presumption that it possessed such a character will be seen to be abundantly confirmed by the evidence now to be adduced. This evidence, it is true, is seldom found in the Scriptures in the form of *direct assertion*, but in the way of *pointed allusion* and *inference* it is perhaps equally unequivocal. And this remark holds good in respect to many of the typical objects, persons, and institutions of the Mosaic economy. While they are not *expressly affirmed* to have represented corresponding realities under the gospel dispensation, yet we find our Lord and his apostles arguing in such a way as to recognise the truth of this principle of typical or spiritual interpretation. That the principle, in its practical application, may be and has been carried to the wildest and most extravagant extent by writers of imaginative temperament, is but too obvious to admit of question. But we see not why this fact should be allowed to invalidate the soundness of the principle itself. Under the control of a subdued and sober judgment, it is a principle which may be safely and profitably recognised, and in nothing more so than in reference to those great and paramount features of the Mosaic ritual which we are now considering. Among these the Altar of Sacrifice holds too prominent a place not to partake in large measure of that typical character which pertained to the sacrifices themselves, and which no one in that relation thinks of questioning. Let us see then what may be gathered as to the spiritual bearing of this part of the legal shadows.

Of the preeminent *sanctity* which attached to the Altar by divine appointment nothing can be a stronger proof than the words of God himself, Ex. 29. 37, ' Seven days thou shalt make an atonement for the altar, and *sanctify it;* and it shall be an altar *most -holy:* whatsoever toucheth the altar *shall be holy;*' or rather *shall become holy, shall be sanctified.* Hence the declaration of our Savior, that ' the altar *sanctifieth* the gift.' This then is an important item in our consideration of the typical design of this structure ; it pointed to something sustaining a character of paramount *holiness*, and this character is evidently sustained by the subject of it in connexion with some kind of *mediatorial function*, which was, with one consent attributed by the ancient Jewish writers to the Altar of Burnt-offerings, as a part of its typical uses. Indeed they expressly denominated it מזבח המצצע *mizbëah hammetzëah, the mediator altar*, and as *intercession* is one of the principal offices of a mediator, it was also called פרקלרט *peraklit, παρακλητος, paraclete, advocate*, the same word which Christ applies to the Holy Spirit as the *comforting advocate* whom he would send to his people to supply the lack of his own presence, and which is explained in the Gemara to mean ' an interpreter, daysman, or kind intercessor in behalf of a person with the king.' This view of the subject does not, it is true, rest upon express

scriptural authority, but it is altogether consistent with it, and rises naturally out of the ideas which its local position between the Presence in the Tabernacle and the people in the Court, and its office as a *sacrificatory* suggested. Among the ancient Orientals, the usages of royalty forbade the access of subjects of common rank to the person of the king without the offices of a mediator, and more especially to those who had in any way incurred the monarch's displeasure, of which a striking illustration is to be seen in the case of Absalom, 2 Sam. 14. 32, 33. That the Israelites habitually ascribed this *mediating* or *reconciling* virtue to the Altar, there can be no doubt, although we may be constrained to admit that, confounding the type with the antitype, they blindly ascribed this efficacy to the material fabric, instead of recognising its ulterior reference to another Mediator ' of higher name,' who was to open the way of access to the Father by the sacrifice of himself. For that this was in fact the real typical purport of the Altar of sacrifice, cannot for a moment be questioned by any one who considers its intrinsic adaptedness to shadow forth the divine substance in its mediatory relations to a holy God and offending sinners. It is indeed certain that this typical design both of the Altar and Sacrifices offered upon it points to a *common* substance which we recognise in the person and offices of Christ, but a discrimination may still be made between what is more immediately applicable to the one and to the other respectively.

Taking it for granted that the idea of *mediatorship* is fundamental in the typical institute of the Altar, we are naturally led to investigate the points of analogy in this respect between the shadow and the substance. Now it is obvious that one of the leading offices of a mediator is the *procurement of peace*, or the *reconciliation of offended and contending parties*, and we have the decided evidence of heathen antiquity in favor of connecting this effect with the symbolical uses of altars. Thus Virgil (Æn. IV. 56.) says,

Principio delubra advent, *pacemque per aras Exquirunt.*

'First they repair to the shrines and *through the medium of altars solicit peace*.' The same office is attributed to the Mosaic Altar and its offerings by Rabbi Menahem ; 'And an altar was made that *it might conciliate peace* between the Israelites and their Father in heaven through the mysteries of sacrifice.' This point is made still more evident if we connect with the Altar the *act of expiation* in which it was mainly instrumental, as we learn from the most express Rabbinical authority. 'This is that Altar,' says the Midrash Rabboth, 'which was in the temple and *expiated* the children of Israel.' Another also of the Jewish authorities says, that 'when the sprinkled blood touches the Altar, then those *are expiated* who offer the sacrifice.' Closely connected with the *conciliatory* or *peace-procuring* design of the Altar was that which it subserved as a *table* or *board of feasting* to the parties which were thus brought to mutual fellowship ; as it is well known that, except in the case of the *holocaust*, the priests and some times the offerer too feasted upon a portion of the offerings. Accordingly the sacrifices offered upon the Altar are expressly spoken of, Num. 28. 2, as *bread* or *food* laid upon a table, and in Mal. 1. 7, it is said, 'Ye offer polluted *bread upon mine altar;* and ye say, Wherein have we polluted thee ? In that ye say, The *table of the Lord* is contemptible.' Eating together at the same table has ever been accounted among the Orientals the most unequivocal *pledge of amity, union,* and *common interest*, and accordingly the Apostle conveys the idea of the closest possible relation and fellowship when he says, 1 Cor. 10. 18, 'Are not they which eat of the sacrifices *partakers of the altar ?*' That is, they were bound in most solemn covenant ties to him whose table the altar was. Consequently they could not eat of the sacrifices of idol altars without virtually eating at the table of idols, and thus entering into fellowship with them. But Christ is the true altar of fellowship for Christians, and its import both as an *altar* and a *table* is fulfilled in him.

We remark again that *affording succor and protection* to the weak, the pursued, the endangered, is another idea naturally connected with the mediatory uses of an altar. And such a purpose we find answered by the Altar of Burnt-offerings in the case of Adonijah and Joab, who both flew to it as an asylum when the guilt of treason and blood had put their lives in peril. The same character was ascribed by the heathen to their altars, as we learn from numerous passages in the classics. Flying to and sitting down by an altar was a significant mode of claiming protection from vengeance. How perfectly the *succoring* and *saving* offices of Christ towards the guilty fulfil these typical uses of the Altar is too obvious to require elucidation.

This use of the Altar as a place of refuge seems to be intimately connected with the *horns* by which it was distinguished. The culprit who fled to it seized hold of its *horns,* and it was from thence that Joab was dragged and slain. Now the *horn* was one of the most indubitable symbols of *power,* as we learn from the frequent employment of it in this sense by the sacred writers. In Hab. 3. 4, for instance, it is said, 'He had *horns* coming out of his hand, and there was the hiding of his *power*.' The '*horn* of David' is the power and dominion of David, and Christ is called a '*horn* of salvation,' from his being a *mighty* Savior, invest-

9 ¶ And ^d thou shalt make the court of the tabernacle: for the south side southward *there shall be*

^d ch. 38. 9.

hangings for the court *of* fine twined linen of an hundred cubits long for one side:

---

ed with royal dignity, and able to put down with triumph and ease all his enemies. It is probably in real, though latent allusion to the *horned altar* and its *pacifying* character that God says through the prophet, Is. 27. 5, 'let him take hold of my *strength*, that he may *make peace with me;* and he shall make peace with me;' let him fly to the horns of the mystic Altar, and find security and peace in that *reconciled omnipotence* of which it was the sign. As the Altar then is primarily an adumbration of Christ in his mediatorial office, the *horns* may very suitably denote those attributes of his character which as symbols they are adapted and designed to shadow forth. As the *strength* of all horned animals, that strength by which they defend themselves and their young, is concentrated mainly in their horns, so in the ascription of horns to Christ we recognise the symbol of that *divine potency* by which he is able to subdue all things to himself, and to afford complete protection to his people. In accordance with this, the visions of the Apocalypse represent him as ' a Lamb *having seven horns,*' as the mystic insignia of that irresistible power with which he effects the discomfiture of his adversaries and *pushes* his spiritual conquests over the world. This view of the typical import of the Altar and its appendages might doubtless be much enlarged, but sufficient has been said to show, that the same rich significancy and the same happy adaptation, pervades this as reigns through every other part of the Mosaic ritual.

THE COURT OF THE TABERNACLE.

9. *Thou shall make the court of the Tabernacle.* This court or open enclosure, in which the Tabernacle stood,

was of an oblong figure of a hundred cubits (about fifty-eight yards) in length by half that breadth, and the height of the enclosing fence or curtain was five cubits, or nearly three yards, being half the height of the Tabernacle. The enclosure was formed by a plain hanging of fine twined linen yarn, which seems to have been worked in an open or network texture, so that the people without might freely see the interior. The door-curtain was however of a different texture from the general hanging, being a great curtain of ' fine twined linen,' embroidered with blue, purple, and scarlet. It is described in precisely the same terms as the door-curtain of the Tabernacle itself, and was of the same fabric with the inner covering of the Tabernacle and the vail before the Holy of Holies. It was furnished with cords, by which it might be drawn up or aside when the priests had occasion to enter. The curtains of this enclosure were hung upon sixty pillars of brass, standing on bases of the same metal, but with capitals and fillets of silver. (Compare the description in this chapter with that in chap 38.) The hooks also, to which the curtains were attached, were of silver. The entrance of the Court was at the east end opposite that to the Tabernacle, and between them stood the Altar of Burnt-offering, but nearer to the door of the Tabernacle than to that of the Court. It is uncertain whether the brazen laver was interposed between the Altar and the door of the Tabernacle or not. Chap. 30. 18, certainly conveys that impression ; but the Rabbins, who appear to have felt that nothing could properly interpose between the Altar and Tabernacle, say that the laver was indeed nearer to the Tabernacle than was the Altar. but still

10 And the twenty pillars thereof and their twenty sockets *shall be of* brass: the hooks of the pillars and their fillets *shall be of* silver.

11 And likewise for the north side in length *there shall be* hangings of a hundred *cubits* long, and

his twenty pillars and their twenty sockets *of* brass: the hooks of the pillars and their fillets *of* silver.

12 ¶ And *for* the breadth of the court on the west side *shall be* hangings of fifty cubits: their pillars ten, and their sockets ten.

---

that it did not stand in the same line with the Altar, but stood a little on one side to the south. As to the position of the Tabernacle in the Court, nothing is said in the Scriptures on the subject, but it seems less probable that it stood in the centre than that it was placed towards the farther or western extremity, so as to allow greater space for the services which were to be performed exclusively in front of the Tabernacle. Within the precincts of this Court any Israelite might enter, but none but the

priests were permitted to go into the outer room of the Tabernacle, and into its inner recess admission was forbidden to all but the high priest. A view of the Tabernacle with its curtained enclosure will hereafter be given.

10. *The twenty pillars thereof, and their twenty sockets,* &c. These pillars, which were probably made of shittim-wood, were placed at five cubits distance from each other, in sockets of brass, in the manner represented in the cut.

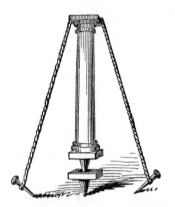

PILLAR AND SOCKET, WITH CORDS AND STAKES.

¶ *Fillets.* Heb. חשוקים *hashukim,* from the root חשק *hashak* which has the sense of *connecting, conjoining,* whence Rosenmuller and others with much probability understand by the term the connecting rods of silver between the heads of the pillars, on which the curtains were suspended. Otherwise it is rendered as in our version *fillets,* by which is meant raised ornamental bands or mouldings encircling the tops of the pillars.

12. *Breadth, fifty cubits.* The breadth of the Court was therefore equal to one half its length; the whole area being of an oblong square, one hundred cubits in length and fifty in breadth. The form and proportions of the Tabernacle itself were nearly the same, being thirty cubits in length and twelve in breadth.

14. *Fifteen cubits.* As twenty out of the fifty cubits which measured the breadth of the Court on the eastern side

13 And the breadth of the court on the east side eastward *shall be* fifty cubits.

14 The hangings of one side *of the gate shall be* fifteen cubits: their pillars three, and their sockets three.

15 And on the other side *shall be* hangings, fifteen *cubits:* their pillars three, and their sockets three.

16 ¶ And for the gate of the court *shall be* a hanging of twenty cubits, *of* blue, and purple, and scarlet, and fine twined linen, wrought with needle-work: *and* their pillars *shall be* four, and their sockets four.

17 All the pillars round about the court *shall be* filletted with silver: their hooks *shall be of* silver, and their sockets *of* brass.

18 ¶ The length of the court *shall be* an hundred cubits, and the breadth fifty every where, and the height five cubits *of* fine twined linen, and their sockets *of* brass.

19 All the vessels of the tabernacle in all the service thereof, and all the pins thereof, and all the pins of the court, *shall be of* brass.

20 ¶ And ᵉ thou shalt command the children of Israel, that they bring thee pure oil olive beaten for the light, to cause the lamp to burn always.

21 In the tabernacle of the congregation ᶠ without the vail, which *is* before the testimony, ᵍ Aaron and his sons shall order it from evening to morning before the Lord: ʰ *It shall be* a statute for ever unto their generations on the behalf of the children of Israel.

ᵉ Lev. 24. 2. ᶠ ch. 26. 31, 33. ᵍ ch. 30. 8. 1 Sam. 3. 3. 2 Chron. 13. 11. ʰ ch. 28. 43. & 29. 9, 28. Lev. 3. 17. & 16. 34. & 24. 9. Numb. 18. 23. & 19. 21. 1 Sam. 30. 25.

---

were to be appropriated to the gate or entrance-way, this would leave of course fifteen cubits on each side.

19. *The pins of the court.* The nails or small stakes which were driven into the ground that the hangings, attached to them by cords, might be made fast at the bottom. They are represented in the cut above. In allusion to these and in view of its future glorious enlargement, the prophet thus apostrophizes the church, Is. 54. 1—3, 'Sing, O barren, thou that didst not bear ; break forth into singing, and cry aloud, thou that didst not travail with child : for more are the children of the desolate than the children of the married wife, saith the Lord. Enlarge the place of thy tent, and let them stretch forth the curtains of thy habitations ; spare not, *lengthen thy cords, and strengthen thy stakes;* For thou shalt break forth on the right hand and on the left ; and thy seed shall inherit the Gentiles, and make the desolate cities to be inhabited.' See Mr. Barnes's Note on the passage.

THE OIL FOR THE CANDLESTICK.

20. *Pure oil olive beaten.* The Lamp was to be fed with pure oil, prepared from olives which were bruised with a pestle, and so free from the sediment and dregs which were apt to mar that that was obtained from an oil-press or mill. 'By the expression *oil olive,* this oil is distinguished from other kinds. The addition *beaten,* indicates that it is that oil obtained from olives pounded in a mortar, and not pressed from olives in the oil-mill. The oil obtained from pounded olives is, according to Columella's observation, much purer and better tasted, does not emit much smoke, and has no offensive smell.' *Burder.* ——¶ *To cause the lamp to burn always.* To light it regularly every night. That is said, according to Scripture usage, to be *always* done, which never fails to be done at the appointed season. Thus a ' continual burnt-offering' is one which is continually offered *at the stated time.*

21. *In the tabernacle of the congre*

CHAPTER XXVIII.

A ND take thou unto thee [a]Aaron thy brother, and his sons with

him, from among the children of Israel, that he may minister unto

[a] Numb. 18. 7. Hebr. 5. 1, 4.

gation. Heb. אהֶל מוֹעֵד *ohel moëd, tabernacle of appointment,* or of *stated meeting.* The common rendering, 'tabernacle of the congregation,' implies that it was so called merely from the fact of the peoples' there *congregating* to attend upon the worship of God, whereas the genuine force of the original expression imports not only the *meeting* of the people with each other, a general assembling of the host, but the *meeting of God* also with them, according to his promise, v. 43. '*And there will I meet with* the children of Israel, and the Tabernacle shall be sanctified with my glory.' The Hebrew מוֹעֵד *moëd,* the term in question, strictly signifies a *meeting by appointment, a convention at a time and place previously agreed upon by the parties.* The Chaldee both of Onkelos and Jonathan render this by מַשְׁכַּן זִמְנָא *mishkan zimna, tabernacle of appointed time,* implying that at *stated seasons* the children of Israel were to have recourse thither.——¶ *Which is before the testimony.* That is, before the Ark of the testimony. See ch. 25. 21, 22. ——¶ *Aaron and his sons shall order it from evening to morning.* Josephus, in speaking of the duty of the priests (Ant. L. III. ch. 8.), says, 'They were also to keep oil already purified for the lamps; three of which were to give light all day long, upon the sacred Candlestick before God, and the rest were to be lighted at the evening.' It is not unreasonable to suppose that this was the case, although the authority of Josephus cannot be considered as *decisive* of any point of Jewish antiquity. Still as he was nearer the source of tradition, his testimony is always worthy of being carefully weighed, although the whole ritual had no doubt undergone great changes before his time.

The following detailed account of the manner of ' ordering' the lamps is given by Ainsworth from Maimonides. As a Rabbinical relic exhibiting a striking specimen of the scrupulous exactness with which every part of the Tabernacle service was performed, it is not without its interest. 'Of every lamp that is burnt out, he takes away the wick, and all the oil that remaineth in the lamp, and wipeth it, and putteth in another wick, and other oil by measure, and that is an half a log (about a quarter of a pint); and that which he taketh away he casteth into the place of ashes by the altar, and lighteth the lamp which was out, and the lamp which he findeth not out, he dresseth it. The lamp which is middlemost, when it is out, he lights not it but from the altar in the court; but the rest of the lamps, every one that is out he lighteth from the lamp that is next. He lighteth not all the lamps at one time; but lighteth five lamps, and stayeth, and doth the other service; and afterwards cometh and lighteth the two that remain. He whose duty it is to dress the candlestick cometh with a golden vessel in his hand (called Cuz, like to a great pitcher) to take away in it the wicks that are burnt out, and the oil that remaineth in the lamps, and lighteth five of the lamps, and beareth the vessel there before the Candlestick, and goeth out; afterwards he cometh and lighteth the two lamps, and taketh up the vessel in his hand, and boweth down to worship, and goeth his way.' *Treat. of the Daily Sacrifice,* C. III. Sect. 12—17.

Chapter 28

THE PRIESTLY GARMENTS.

As full and ample directions had now

me in the priest's office, *even* | Aaron, Nadab and Abihu, Eleazar and Ithamar, Aaron's sons.

been given in respect to rearing and furnishing the Tabernacle as a place of worship, we have in the present chapter an intimation of the setting apart an order of men to officiate as ministers of this worship, and a minute description of the vestment by which they were to be distinguished. Previous to this time the patriarchal mode of service had no doubt obtained, every master of a family being a priest to his own household ; but now as a Tabernacle of the congregation was about to be erected, as a visible centre of unity to the nation, God saw fit to order the institutions of a public priesthood, and according to previous intimation, Ex. 27. 21, Aaron and his sons are here fixed upon as candidates for the high distinction.

1. *Take thou unto thee.* Heb. הַקְרֵב *hakrёb, cause to come nigh.* Gr. προσαγαγου, *bring near.* The original root קרב *karab* is of the most frequent occurrence in relation to sacrifices, and is the ordinary term applied to the *bringing near* or *presenting* the various offerings which were enjoined under the Mosaic ritual. It is wholly in keeping with this usage to employ it, as here, in reference to *persons* who by their dedication to the service of the sanctuary, were in a sense *sacrificially offered up* and *devoted* to God. Before entering upon the description of the sacerdotal dresses, the historian prefaces a few words respecting those who were to wear them, viz., Aaron and his sons ; of whose solemn consecration to office a full account is given in the next chapter. God is introduced as especially designating and appointing these individuals to the sacred function of the priesthood ; and this would have the effect at once to show that this was an honor too great to be assumed by men without a call from heaven, according to the Apostle's statement, Heb. 5. 4,

and also to free both Moses and Aaron from the charge of grasping this distinction for the purpose of aggrandizing their own family.——¶ *That he may minister.* Heb. לְכַהֲנוֹ *lekahano,* from the root כהן *kahan,* of which Kimchi says the primary meaning is the *rendering of honorable and dignified service,* such as that of officers of state to their sovereign. In accordance with this it is used concerning the sons of David, 2 Sam. 8. 18, who could not. strickly speaking, be priests ; and on the same grounds the substantive כהנים *kohanim* is in several places in the margin rendered 'princes.' See Note on Gen. 14. 18. But as *princes* or courtiers wait on the king, and are honored by nearer access to him than others ; so the priests under the law were assumed into this near relation to the King of Israel, and for this reason the term in its ordinary acceptation is applied more especially to the duties of priests in ministering before God at his altar. The remark is no doubt well founded, that wherever the word is connected with any of the names of God, it always denotes a *priest;* but when standing alone it usually means a *prince,* or some person of eminence. Comp. Ex. 2. 16. Of the duties pertaining to the priestly office we shall have occasion to speak in detail in subsequent notes ; but we may here observe briefly, that although as high functionaries in the court of the Great King, many of their duties were of a civil nature, as might be expected under a system in which *church* and *state* were united, yet those that more properly belonged to them in their sacerdotal character were mainly the following : They were to pronounce the benediction upon the people and to conduct the whole service of the holy place. Their's was the business of sacrificing,

2 And ᵇ thou shalt make holy

ᵇ ch. 29. 5, 29. & 31. 10. & 39. 1, 2. Lev. 8. 7, 30. Numb. 20. 26, 28.

in all its rites, in all offerings upon the alter of burnt-offerings. The government and ordering of the sanctuary and of the house of God lay upon them. They kept the table of show-bread properly supplied; they attended to the lamps of golden candelabrum every morning: at the same time they burnt the daily incense, which prevented any offensive scent from the dressing of the lamps from being perceived. It was their duty to keep up the fire upon the brazen altar, that the fire originally kindled from heaven might never be extinguished. It was their office to make the holy anointing oil; and their's to blow the silver trumpets at the solemn feasts, and also before the Ark at its removals. While their numbers were few, there was occupation enough to keep them all employed; but when they afterwards became numerous, they were divided into twenty-four bands, or courses, each of which undertook weekly, in rotation, the sacred services. But this regulation belongs to the time of David, and remains to be considered in another place. Although the Most High had before, Ex. 19. 6, said of Israel in general, 'that they should be to him a kingdom of priests,' yet this did not militate with his *concentrating* the office, in its active duties, in a single family, as he now saw fit to do. It was only in this way that the great ends of the institution could be attained. Of the four sons of Aaron here selected, the two eldest, Nadab and Abihu, unfortunately showed themselves ere long unworthy of the honor now conferred upon them, and perished miserably in consequence of their presumptuous levity in the discharge of their office. The succession then reverted to the line of Eleazar and Ithamar, in which it was perpetuated down to the latest period of the Jewish polity.

garments for Aaron thy brother, for glory and for beauty.

2. *Holy garments.* Heb. בגדי קדש *bigdë kodesh, garments of holiness.* Gr στολη ἀγια, *a holy stole,* or perhaps collectively *a quantity of holy stoles.* These garments are called 'holy' because they were designed for holy men, and because they formed part of an establishment whose general character was *holy.* Indeed, whatever was separated from common use, and consecrated to the immediate service of God, acquired thereby a *relative holiness;* so that we see the amplest ground for the bestowment of this epithet upon the sacred dresses. In ordinary life, when not engaged in their official duties, the priests were attired like other Israelites of good condition; but when employed in their stated ministrations, they were to be distinguished by a peculiar and appropriate dress. Of this dress, which was kept in a wardrobe somehow connected with the Tabernacle, and which was laid aside when their ministration ceased, and returned to the wardrobe, the Jewish writers have much to say. According to them the priests could not officiate without their robes, neither could they wear them beyond the sacred precincts. Under the Temple, where the usages were no doubt substantially the same as in the Tabernacle, when the priests arrived to take their turns of duty, they put off their usual dress, washed themselves in water, and put on the holy garments. While they were in the Temple, attending upon their service, they could not sleep in their sacred habits, but in their own wearing clothes. These they put off in the morning, when they went to their service, and after bathing, resumed their official dress.—But we shall treat of the details in their order.——¶ *For glory and for beauty.* Heb. לכבד ולתפארת *le-kabod u-letiphareth, for glory,* or *honor,*

3 And c thou shalt speak unto all *that are* wise-hearted, d whom I have filled with the spirit of wisdom, that they mav make Aaron's garments to consecrate him, that he may minister unto me in the priest's office.

4 And these *are* the garments

c ch. 31. 6. & 36. 1. d ch. 31. 3. & 35. 30, 31.

which they shall make; e a breastplate, and f an ephod, and g a robe, and h a broidered coat, a mitre, and a girdle: and they shall make holy garments for Aaron thy brother, and his sons, that he may minister unto me in the priest's office.

e ver. 15. f ver. 6. g ver. 31. h ver. 39.

and for *beauty, ornament, decoration.* The expression is very strong, leading us to the inference that a special significancy and importance attached to these garments. They were to be made thus splendid in order to render the office more respected, and to inspire a becoming reverence for the Divine Majesty, whose ministers were attired with so much grandeur. As every thing pertaining to the sanctuary was to be made august and magnificent, so were the dresses of those who ministered there. Yet we cannot doubt that a typical design governed the fashion and appearance of these gorgeous robes, and that they pointed forward to the ' glory' and ' beauty' both of the internal character and the outward display of the ' great High Priest' of the church, in his yet future manifestation. We may perhaps recognise also a secondary allusion to the beautiful spiritual investment both of his ministers and people, in that bright period when they shall have laid aside the ' filthy garments' of their captivity and degradation, and shall shine forth as the ' perfection of beauty in the whole earth,' being clothed in that ' clean linen which is the righteousness of saints.' Accordingly it is said, Is. 51. 1, 'Put on thy *beautiful garments* (Heb. בגדי תפארתך *bigdë tipharthëk, garments of thy beauty*),' the very word here employed.

3. *Speak unto all* that are *wise-hearted.* Heb. אל כל חכמי לב *el kol ḥakmë lëb, to all wise of heart.* Gr. πασι τοις σοφοις τη διανοια, *to all wise in understanding.* That is, skilful, ex-

pert, ingenious, as artists. It is clearly intimated, however, by the connected phrase, ' whom I have filled with the spirit of wisdom' that the epithet implies more than the mere native gifts and endowments which might be possessed by any in this line. Whatever mechanical skill might be evinced by any of the people, yet here was a work to be executed which required something still higher, and therefore God was pleased to impart a special inspiration to endow them with the requisite ability. Compare this with Is. 28. 23—29, where even the necessary skill for rightly conducting the occupations of husbandry are referred to the same source. To the right-minded it is pleasant as well as proper to ascribe to the Father of lights, from whom cometh down every good and perfect gift, the glory of whatever talents may give us eminence or success in any of the lawful or honorable callings of life. ——¶ *To consecrate him.* To render him consecrated; to be a badge and sign of his consecration.

4, 5. *These are the garments,* &c. Of the garments here appointed to be made of these rich materials four were common to the high priest and the inferior priests; viz., the linen breeches, the linen coat, the linen girdle, and the bonnet or turban; that which the high priest wore is called a mitre. The remaining four were peculiar to the high priest, viz., the ephod with its curious girdle, the breast-plate, the long robe with its bells and pomegranates, and the golden plate on his forehead. These

5 And they shall take gold, and blue, and purple, and scarlet, and fine linen.

6 ¶ [1] And they shall make the ephod *of* gold, *of* blue, and *of* purple, *of* scarlet, and fine twined linen, with cunning work.

7 It shall have the two shoulder-

pieces thereof joined at the two edges thereof; and *so* it shall be joined together.

8 And the curious girdle of the ephod, which *is* upon it, shall be of the same, according to the work thereof; *even of* gold, *of* blue, and purple, and scarlet, and fine twined linen.

[1] ch. 39. 2.

---

last are frequently termed by the Rabbinical writers, by way of distinction, the בגדי זהב *bigdë zahab, garments of gold* while the others, made of linen, are called בגדי לבן *bigdë laban, garments of white*. We shall consider each of them in order. We may here remark, however, that on one day in the year, viz., the great day of atonement, or fast of annual expiation, the High Priest wore none of the *golden garments*, but appeared, like the rest of the priests, simply in habiliments of *white linen*. Even his mitre was then made of linen. The reason of this was, that the day of atonement was a day of *humiliation;* and as the High Priest was then to offer sacrifices for *his own* sins, as well as those of the people, he was to be so clad as to indicate that he could lay claim to no exemption on the score of frailty and guilt; that he recognised the fact that in the need of expiation, the highest and the lowest, the priest and the Levite, stood on a level before God, with whom there is no distinction of persons.

THE EPHOD.

6. *They shall make the ephod*, &c. Heb. אפוד *ëphod.* Gr. επωμιδα, *shoulder-piece.* The original comes from אפד *aphad, to bind or gird on,* and therefore signifies in general *something to be girded on;* but as to the precise form of the vestment itself it is difficult to gather from the words of the narrative a very distinct notion ; and even if we succeed in this, we must still depend mainly upon a pictured representation to convey an adequate idea of it to the

reader. From an attentive comparison of all that is said of the Ephod in the sacred text, commentators are for the most part agreed in considering it as approaching to the form of *a short double apron,* having the two parts connected by two wide straps united on the shoulders. These are called, v. 7, the two *shoulder-pieces,* which were to be joined at the two edges thereof; i. e. on the very apex of the shoulders. This junction was effected in some way under the two onyx-stones and at the precise point where they rested upon the shoulders. These stones are said by Josephus (who calls them 'sardonyx-stones') to have been very splendid, and Bähr thinks that the symbolical significancy of the Ephod was mainly concentrated in these ' shoulder-pieces,' which, like our modern *epaulettes*, were a badge of dignity, authority, command—an idea to which we shall advert in the sequel. The two main pieces or lappets of the Ephed hung down, the one in front, the other behind, but to what depth is not stated, although Josephus says it was a cubit, which would bring their lower extremity about to the loins. It seems to us probable on the whole that the posterior portion hung down from the shoulders considerably lower than the anterior. But without some other appendage these dorsal and pectoral coverings would hang loose upon the person, to prevent which a ' curious girdle,' forming an integral part of the Ephod itself, and composed probably of two distinct bands issuing from the sides of either the frontal or hinder portion, passed round the body just under the arms so as to encircle it over the region of the heart. The annexed cut will aid the reader's conception. The open space in the front piece is designed for the insertion of the Breast-plate. The appendant straps when brought around the body formed the ' curious girdle of the Ephod.'

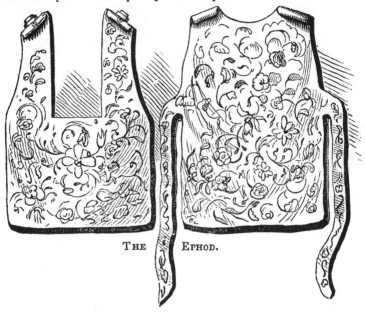

THE EPHOD.

In this representation we have mainly followed Braunius in his celebrated work on the Dresses of the Jewish Priests, as that which we regard as on the whole the most probable ; but Gussetius, one of the ablest of the Hebrew Lexicographers, contends for a form approaching nearer to that of a belt or girdle for the whole Ephod, and there is so much that is plausible in his view, that we are induced to give a copy of his engraving.

Such appears to have been the general form of the Ephod, and the manner in which it was made to be fitted close to the body. As to the material of which

9 And thou shalt take two onyx-stones, and grave on them the names of the children of Israel:

10 Six of their names on one stone, and *the other* six names of the rest on the other stone, according to their birth.

11 With the work of an engraver

in stone, *like* the engravings of a signet, shalt thou engrave the two stones with the names of the children of Israel: thou shalt make them to be set in ouches of gold.

12 And thou shalt put the two stones upon the shoulders of the ephod *for* stones of memorial unto

---

it was made, this was evidently the same with that of the interior curtains and the separating vail of the Tabernacle, and wrought like it, except that in this ephod-tapestry the figures of cherubim were wanting, and instead of them there was a rich interweaving of threads of gold, which together with the beautiful colors embroidered, must have given it an air of inexpressible richness. On this point the Jewish writers say, 'The gold that was in the weaving of the ephod and breast-plate was thus wrought: He (the cunning workman) took one thread of pure gold and put it with six threads of blue and twisted these seven threads as one. And so he did one thread of gold with six of purple, and one with six of scarlet, and one with six of linen. Thus these four threads of gold and twenty-eight threads in all.' *Maimonides in Ainsworth.* This is a very probable account of the mode of texture, though the proportion of gold strikes us as very small. From the allusion in the description of our Savior's dress, Rev. 1. 13, 'Clothed with a garment down to the foot, and girt about the paps with a *golden girdle,*' it is reasonably to be inferred that it contained a pretty copious insertion of gold in its texture, from which fact the curious girdle of the Ephod was usually distinguished by this epithet. Though properly and primarily a vestment of the High Priest, yet it appears that garments of the same name were worn by the inferior priests, but they were plain ones of linen. It does not appear that even these were worn at first by the common priests. But we after-

wards read of common priests wearing Ephods; and indeed Samuel, who was only a Levite, wore one; and David, who was not even a Levite, did the same when he danced before the ark. On one occasion Saul consulted the Lord by Urim, and consequently used the Ephod of the high priest, 1 Sam. 28. 6; and on another occasion David did the same, 1 Sam. 30. 7. It is thought by some, however that Saul and David did not themselves use the Ephod, but directed the priest to use it.

9—12. *Thou shalt take two onyx-stones,* &c. On each of the connecting pieces that went across the shoulders was set an arch or socket of gold, containing an onyx-stone (Chal. 'Beryl-stone') on which the names of the tribes of Israel were engraved, as in a seal, six on each shoulder. Thus Maimonides; 'He set on each shoulder a beryl-stone four-square, embossed in gold; and he graved on the two stones the names of the tribes, six on one stone and six on the other, according to their births. And the stone whereon Reuben was written, was on the right shoulder, and the stone whereon Simeon was written, was on the left.' The Rabbins say, moreover, that the letters were so equally divided in these two inscriptions that Joseph's name was written 'Jehoseph' in order to make just twenty-five letters in each stone.——

¶ *According to their birth.* Heb. כתלדתם *ketholedotham, their births* or *generations.* That is, according to the order of their respective births or ages The arrangement is diversely understood by Josephus and most of the

the children of Israel: and [1] Aaron shall bear their names before the LORD upon his two shoulders [m] for a memorial.

13 ¶ And thou shalt make ouches *of* gold;

14 And two chains *of* pure gold at the ends; *of* wreathen work

[1] ver. 29. ch. 39. 7. [m] See Josh. 4. 7. Zech. 6. 14.

Rabbinical writers, according to the latter of whom the order was as follows:

Left.	Right.
Gad,	Reuben,
Asher,	Simeon,
Issachar,	Levi,
Zebulon,	Judah,
Joseph,	Dan,
Benjamin,	Naphtali.

The former, having a special view to their several mothers, arranges them thus;

Simeon,	Reuben,
Judah,	Levi,
Zebulon,	Issachar,
Dan,	Naphtali,
Asher,	Gad,
Benjamin,	Joseph.

It is a matter of little moment which we consider as the most correct.

12. *For stones of memorial unto the children of Israel.* That is, as a memorial *for* or in *behalf of* the children of Israel; a remembrancer to Aaron and to Israel that he appeared. before God in the priestly office as a representative of the whole people. The meaning is in fact explained in· the next clause.

THE BREAST-PLATE.

15. *Thou shalt make the breast-plate of judgment,* &c. Heb. חשׁן משׁפט *hoshen mishpat.* This would perhaps be better rendered in our version *pectoral* or *breast-piece of judg-*

shalt thou make them, and fasten the wreathen chains to the ouches.

15 ¶ And [n] thou shalt make the breast-plate of judgment with cunning work; after the work of the ephod thou shalt make it; *of* gold, *of* blue, and *of* purple, and *of* scarlet, and *of* fine twined linen shalt thou make it.

[n] ch. 39. 8.

ment, as *breast-plate* conveys the idea of a *military accoutrement,* which is not implied in the original. Greek λογειον των κρισεων, the *rationale of judgments,* as it is also rendered in the Lat. Vulg. The etymology of the original term חשׁן *hoshen,* is entirely unknown. Gesenius indeed refers to the Arabic *hashna, to be fair, beautiful, splendid,* as perhaps having affinity with its root, with which he compares the Germ. *scheinen, to appear, schön, fair,* and Eng. *shine.* But though it is equally a matter of conjecture, we for ourselves prefer the suggestion of Aven arius (Lex. ad rad. חשׁן) that it comes by transposition of letters from נחשׁ *nahash, to augur, to divine,* a sense very nearly akin to that of *seeking information by consulting an oracle.* Yet we are still unable to *establish* this or any other as the legitimate formation of the word, and are compelled therefore to content ourselves with such a view of the material, form, and uses of the חשׁן *hoshen* as can be deduced from the text independent of philological or collateral aid. It was called ' breast-plate of judgment' from its being worn by the High Priest when he went into the Most Holy Place to consult God respecting those matters of *judgment* which were too hard for the inferior judges, and which had reference to the more important civil or religious concerns of the nation. Comp. Deut. 17. 18, 19. The cloth which formed the ground of the Breast-plate was of the same rich embroidered stuff or

16 Four-square it shall be, *being* doubled; a span *shall be* the length thereof, and a span *shall be* the breadth thereof.

17 º And thou shalt set in it settings of stones, *even* four rows of stones; *the first* row *shall be* a sar-

º ch. 39. 10, &c.

dius, a topaz, and a carbuncle: *this shall be* the first row.

18 And the second row *shall be* an emerald, a sapphire, and a diamond.

19 And the third row a ligure, an agate, and an amethyst.

20 And the fourth row a beryl,

---

brocade as the Ephod, of two spans in length and one in breadth. Consequently when doubled it was just a span or eighteen inches square. For what reason it was doubled is not apparent. Some suppose it was to give it more strength in bearing the precious stones appended to it. But for ourselves we are unable to see how the back fold could have aided in supporting the weight of the stones in front. Far preferable therefore to us seems the opinion, that it was doubled thus in order that being sewed together on three sides and left open on one it might form a kind of sack, pocket, or bag, as a receptacle of something which was to be put in it. But of this more in the sequel. At each corner of the Breast-plate thus made into a square form was a golden ring. To the two upper ones were attached two golden chains of wreathen work, i. e. chains made of golden threads or wires braided together, which passed up to the shoulders and were there somehow fastened to the shoulder-pieces or to the onyx-stones. By means of these chains it was suspended on the breast. But to render it still more firm in its position, two laces or ribbons of blue were passed through the two rings at the two lower corners of the Breast-plate, and also through two corresponding rings in the Ephod, and then tied together a little above the girdle of the Ephod. This rendered the Breast-plate and Ephod inseparable, so that the latter could not be put on without being accompanied by the former, and the punishment of stripes was decreed against him who

should attempt to divide the one from the other.

17. *Thou shalt set in it settings of stones.* Heb. מִלֵּאתָ בוֹ מִלֻּאַת אֶבֶן *millëtha bo milluath eben, thou shalt fill in it fillings of stones.* The import undoubtedly is that these stones were to be *set* or *enchased* in sockets of gold or some other metal, and they are called *fillings* because the stones when inserted *filled up* the cavities prepared for their reception. The precise manner in which these twelve precious stones, which had the names of the twelve tribes engraved upon them, were attached to the Breast-plate is not expressed in the text, though it is usually understood by commentators to have been upon the outside, and that they were fully exposed to view when worn upon the High Priest's bosom. This, however, is not asserted in the text, and we shall soon suggest several reasons for doubting whether it were the fact. It is certain that the stones were in some way appended to the Breast-plate, and that they were arranged in four rows, three in each, but as to the peculiar manner in which they were adjusted to the supporting ground of the tapestry, this is a point which is to be *inferred* from an attentive consideration of all the circumstances relating to the fabric itself, and upon this we shall be more full in a subsequent note. At present we shall devote a page or two to the consideration of the stones themselves, in relation to which we are constrained to remark that after all the research expended by antiquarians upon the subject much uncertainty still rests

upon it. They cannot be satisfactorily identified. We can only approach a *probability*, more or less strong, that the gems which we now call the topaz, emerald, sapphire, carbuncle, &c., do truly answer to the original terms which they are thus made to represent in English. Our explanations must be taken therefore by the reader subject to the necessary abatement on this score.

1. SARDIUS. Heb. אדם *odem,* from the radical אדם *adam, to be ruddy or red.* Chal. סמקן *samkan,* and סמקתא *samketha, red.* Gr. σαρδιον, *sardine,* a name supposed to be taken from *Sardis* or *Sardinia,* where it was originally found. It was a stone of the *ruby* class, and answers to the *carnelian* of the moderns. The finest specimens now come from Surat, a city near the gulf of Cambay in India.

2. TOPAZ. Heb. פטדה *pitdah.* Etymology unknown. Gr. τοπαζιον, *topazion,* a name which Pliny says is derived from *Topazos,* an island in the Red Sea. Chal. ירקן *yarkan* and ירקתא *yarketha,* signifying *green.* It is supposed to be the modern *chrysolite,* and its color to have been a transparent *green-yellow.* It comes now from Egypt, where it is found in alluvial strata.

3. CARBUNCLE. Heb. ברקת *bareketh,* from ברק *barak, to lighten, glitter,* or *glister;* answering to the ανθραξ *anthrax,* of the Greeks, so called because when held to the sun it resembles a piece of *bright burning charcoal.* Indeed its name *carbuncle* means *a little coal,* and refers us at once to a *lively coal-red.* Its modern name is the *garnet.* The Septuagint, Josephus, and Lat. Vulgate have rendered in this place by σμαραγδος *smaragdos, emerald.* But this is more properly the rendering of the next in order. The *carbuncle* and the *emerald* have in fact in some way become transposed in the Greek version.

4. EMERALD. Heb. נפך *nophek.* Gr. ανθραξ. This gem is undoubtedly the same with the ancient *smaragdos,* or *emerald,* one of the most beautiful of all the precious stones. It is characterised by a *bright green* color, with scarcely any mixture, though differing somewhat in degrees. The true Oriental emerald is now very scarce. The best that are at present accessible are from Peru. In the time of Moses they came from India.

5. SAPPHIRE. Heb. ספיר *sappir.* Gr. σαπφειρος *sapphiros.* The word is very nearly the same in all known languages, and as to the sapphire itself it is, after the diamond, the most valuable of the gems, exceeding all others in lustre and hardness. It is of a *sky-blue,* or *fine azure* color, in all the choicest specimens, though other varieties occur. Indeed among practical jewellers it is a name of wider application perhaps than that of any of the rest of the precious stones. Pliny says that in his time the best sapphires came from Media. At present they are found in greater or less perfection in nearly every country.

6. DIAMOND. Heb. יהלם *yahalom,* from הלם *halam, to beat, to smite upon,* so called from its extraordinary hardness, by which like a hammer it will *beat to pieces* any of the other sorts of stones. Thus the Greeks called the diamond αδαμας, *adamas,* from Gr. *a, not* and δαμαω, *damao, to subdue,* on account of its supposed *invincible hardness.* Accordingly Pliny says of diamonds, that ' they are found to resist a stroke on the anvil to such a degree that the iron itself gives way and the anvil is shattered to pieces.' This is no doubt exaggerated and fabulous, but it is sufficient to justify the propriety of the Hebrew name, that diamonds are *much harder* than other precious stones, and in this all are agreed. This quality of the diamond, together with its incomparable brilliancy, renders it by far the most valuable of all the gems. The Gr. here has ιασπις *jaspis,* or *jasper.*

7. LIGURE. Heb. לשם *leshem.* Gr

and an onyx, and a jasper: they shall be set in gold in their enclosings.

21 And the stones shall be with the names of the children of Israel, twelve, according to their names, *like* the engravings of a signet; every one with his name shall they be according to the twelve tribes.

22 ¶ And thou shalt make upon the breast-plate chains at the ends *of* wreathen work *of* pure gold.

23 And thou shalt make upon the breast-plate two rings of gold, and shalt put the two rings on the two ends of the breast-plate.

24 And thou shalt put the two wreathen *chains* of gold in the two rings *which are* on the ends of the breast-plate.

25 And *the other* two ends of the two wreathen *chains* thou shalt fasten in the two ouches, and put *them* on the shoulder-pieces of the ephod before it.

26 ¶ And thou shalt make two rings of gold, and thou shalt put them upon the two ends of the breast-plate in the border thereof, which *is* in the side of the ephod inward.

27 And two *other* rings of gold thou shalt make, and shalt put them on the two sides of the ephod underneath, toward the fore-part thereof, over against the *other* coupling thereof, above the curious girdle of the ephod.

28 And they shall bind the breast-plate by the rings thereof unto the

---

λιγυριον, *ligurion.* This is one of the most doubtful of the precious stones as to color. It is supposed to be closely related to the *hyacinth* (*jacinth*) of the moderns, which is *a red strongly tinged with orange-yellow.*

8. AGATE. Heb. שבו *shebo.* Gr. αχατης, *achates, agate.* This is a stone of a great variety of hues, which is thought by some to be identical with the *chrysopras,* and if so it is probably that a *golden green* was the predominant color.

9. AMETHYST. Heb. אחלמה *ahlamah.* Gr. αμεθυστος, *amethystos,* from *a, not,* and μεθυστος, *drunken,* because wine drank from an amethyst cup was supposed by the ancients to prevent *inebriation.* The oriental amethyst is a transparent gem, the color of which seems to be composed of a *strong blue* and a *deep red*; and according as either prevails, affording different tinges of *purple,* and sometimes even fading to a *rose color.* It comes from Persia, Arabia, Armenia, and the East Indies.

10. BERYL. Heb. תרשיש *tarshish.* Gr. χρυσολιθος, *chrysolithos.* A pellucid gem of *a sea* or *bluish green.* But

if, as many mineralogists and critics suppose, the *beryl* is the same as the *chrysolite,* it is a gem of *yellowish green* color, and ranks at present among the *topazes.*

11. ONYX. Heb. שהם *shoham;* called *onyx* from Gr. ονυξ, *onyx,* from its resemblance of its ground color to that lunated spot at the base of the human *nail,* which the Greek word signifies. It is a semi-pellucid stone of a fine flinty texture, of a *waterish sky-colored* ground, variegated with bands of *white* and *brown,* which run parallel to each other. It is here rendered by the Gr. βηρυλλιον, *beryllion, beryl,* from some apparent confusion in the order of the names. See Note on Gen. 2. 12.

12. JASPER. Heb. ישפה *yashepheh.* Gr. ονυχιον, *onuchion.* The similarity of the Hebrew name has determined most critics to consider the *jasper* as the gem intended by this designation. This is a stone distinguished by such a vast variety of hues, that it is extremely hazardous to fix upon any one as its distinguishing color. The brown Egyptian variety is conjectured to have been the one selected for the Breast-plate.

The annexed cut, conformed to the usual model, will convey a tolerably correct idea of the general form and appearance of the Breast-plate. The Eng- lish name we consider as unfortunately chosen. Pectoral, i. e. *breast-plate* is decidedly preferable. Josephus calls it *Essen*.

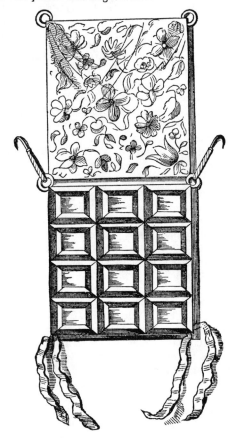

THE BREAST-PLATE.

21. *And the stones shall be with the names.* Heb. עַל שְׁמֹת *al shemoth, upon the names.* The more natural and direct phraseology would be—'the names shall be upon the stones,' but the expression is idiomatic, and probably implies that the stones should be *accompanied* or *distinguished by* the names; or we may adopt the coustruction of Noldius (De Heb. Partic. sub voc. עַל) and all the ancient versions, and render it—'the stones shall be *according to* the names* of the children of Israe , which probably involves the complex idea of the stones *corresponding* with the names in number, and also of having the names actually *sculptured* upon them.

28. *Unto the rings of the ephod.* Of these two rings nothing was said in the account of the construction of the Ephod above; probably because the use of them would not so fully appear till the Breast plate and its position came to

rings of the ephod with a lace of blue, that *it* may be above the curious girdle of the ephod, and that the breast-plate be not loosed from the ephod.

29 And Aaron shall bear the names of the children of Israel in the breast-plate of judgment upon his heart, when he goeth in unto the holy *place*, P for a memorial before the LORD continually.

P ver. 12.

be described as is done in the present context.

29. *Aaron shall bear the names*, &c., *in the breast-plate of judgment upon his heart.* The phrase ' upon his heart' is not properly to be understood in this connexion in a *physical* sense, as if equivalent to ' upon his breast,' ' upon his bosom.' This is not the usage of the Hebrew in regard to the word ' heart.' After a pretty thorough examination of the many hundreds of cases in which the term occurs in the sacred writers, we have not been able to find *a single instance*, apart from the present, in which it is unequivocally employed in a physiological sense, to denote that grand organ of the human body which anatomists call ' the heart.' The passage which comes nearest to such a sense is that in Is. 1. 5, ' The whole head is sick, and the whole *heart* faint.' Yet even here the metaphorical sense is predominant; for as the *sickness* is not corporeal, but moral, so the *members* affected are to be considered as equally figurative. According to the prevailing usage of Scripture, the *heart* is regarded as the seat of intelligence and emotion. The feelings of love, hope, fear, joy, sorrow, &c., are referred to the *heart;* and in the present case we cannot question that although as a matter of fact the Breast-plate was worn over the region of the *heart*, yet the dominant idea conveyed by the phrase is, that Aaron was to bear these names of the tribes *in his kind and affectionate remembrance* whenever he went into the holy place. The beautiful sculptured gems were to be *to him* a memorial or memento of the fact that the interests of the whole people were committed to him as their representative, and that he should never cease to feel burdened in soul with this grave responsibility, especially whenever he was called to act in his capacity as *sacerdotal judge* of the chosen tribes. In this fact we are no doubt at liberty to read one very interesting feature of the typical intent of the jewelled Breastplate. The priesthood of Aaron shadowed forth the infinitely greater and more glorious priesthood of Christ. In the execution of his office as the great High Priest of the Church, he was ordained to enter into the holy place, there to appear in the presence of God for us. This he has done. He ascended to heaven after his resurrection, that he might there complete the work he had begun on earth. On his heart are engraven the names of all his people, and not one of them is overlooked or forgotten. He presents them all before his Father, as the objects of his own kind and solicitous sympathy and care, and they are dear to the Father, because they are dear to the Son. As he thus bears these his jewels on his heart while they are toiling and travailing here below, so will he finally transfer them from his bosom to his head, making them to adorn his diadem forever in the kingdom of his glory.

But this does not forbid the supposition, that *in relation to God* the stones of the Breast-plate may have subserved still another purpose. Certain it is that the whole scope of the context leads us to view them as indicating not only the *subjects*, but also the *instruments*, of those *judicial decisions* about which they were employed. They were in some way made use of as a *medium of the oracular responses* which the High Priest obtained by consultation from Jehovah in behalf of the Jewish people. But as this presents them in a distinct point of view, as intimately connected, if not absolutely identified, with the Urim and Thummim, we shall defer the sequel of our remarks on the Breast-plate till we come to the consideration of that very interesting but abstruse subject.

In the mean time, we cannot forbear presenting the reader with the following translated extract from the work of Bähr before mentioned, in relation to the joint symbolical uses of the Ephod and the Breast-plate.

' The Ephod and the Hoshen or Pectoral, which formed the third general division of the High Priest's vestments, and signified the *kingly dignity,* do not stand in subordinate relation the one to the other, so that the Hoshen was merely an appendage to the Ephod, but they are both treated in the original as independent articles, yet at the same time making together one whole. The dignity also which they represent, must be in some way of a two-fold nature, or which exhibits itself under a double aspect ; and thus in fact was the kingly dignity, both among the Hebrews and all oriental antiquity conceived of, viz., as uniting in itself the two grand prerogatives of *lordship* and *judgment.* Thus, 1 Sam. 8. 5, 6, 'And said unto him, Behold, thou art old, and thy sons walk not in thy ways: now make us *a king to judge us* like all the nations. But the thing displeased Samuel, when they said, Give us *a king to judge us:* and Samuel prayed unto the Lord.' So also 20, 'That we also may be like all the nations ; and that *our king may judge us,* and go out before us, and fight our battles.' 2 Sam. 15. 4, 'Absalom said moreover, Oh that I were *made judge* in the land, that every man which hath any suit or cause might come unto me,

and *I would do him justice!*' 1 Kings, 3. 9, 'Give therefore thy servant an understanding heart *to judge thy people,* that I may discern between good and bad : for who is able *to judge* this thy so great a people ?' So Artemidorus the Oneirocritic remarks, κρινειν το αρχειν ελεγον οἱ παλαιοι, *the ancients said that reigning was judging.* Now the *reigning dignity* is plainly indicated by the Ephod, inasmuch as we have already observed, that its distinguishing feature was the *shoulder-piece* (Gr. επωμις), and the *shoulder* both in sacred and profane antiquity is considered as the *seat of sovereignty.* Thus Isaiah says of the Messiah, ch. 9. 5, 'And the *government* shall be upon his *shoulder.*' So also according to an Indian myth, when the different castes came forth from the body of Brahma, *kings* and *warlike heroes* issued from the *shoulder.* That the same idea was familiar among the Romans would appear from the words of Pliny (Panegyr. 10.), 'Cum abunde expertus esset pater, quam bene humeris tuis sedet imperium,' *since (thy) father hath abundantly proved how well dominion sits upon thy shoulders.* The symbolical import is the same when upon the shoulder of a statue of the Egyptian king Sesostris the inscription was read ; Εγω τηνδε χωρην ωμοισι τοισι εμοισι εκτησαμην, *I have acquired this province by my shoulders.* In accordance with this, the usual insignia of *ruling,* viz., sword and keys, were suspended from the shoulder. Thus, Is. 22. 22, 'And the *key* of the house of David will I lay upon his *shoulder; so* he shall open, and none shall shut ; and he shall shut, and none shall open.' That the sword hung from the *shoulder* among the Greeks and Romans, will be seen by reference to Hom. Il. 2. 45. Lipsius in Tac. Annal. 1. 35. As to what relates to the *judicial prerogative,* we need not go beyond the designation given in the original to the Breast-plate, viz., חשן

30 ¶ And ᑫ thou shalt put in the breast-plate of judgment the Urim and the Thummim; and they shall

ᑫ Lev. 8. 8.   Numb. 27. 21.   Deut. 33. 8. 1 Sam. 28. 6.   Ezra, 2. 63.   Neh. 7. 65.

be upon Aaron's heart, when he goeth in before the LORD: and Aaron shall bear the judgment of the children of Israel upon his heart before the LORD continually.

מֹשֶׁפֵּט *hoshen mishpat, breast-plate of judgment,* to show its symbolical bearing.' *Symbol. des Mos. Cult.,* vol. II. p. 127—9. If this view of the subject be well founded, we think there is strong reason to believe, that the use of *epaulettes* as a badge of *authority* and *imperatorial command* is to be traced back through the line of past centuries to the Shoulder-piece of the ancient *Ephod.* This article of military accoutrement forms at any rate a subject of very curious historical interest, which might well demand a thorough investigation.

THE URIM AND THUMMIM.

30. *Thou shalt put in the breast-plate of judgment the Urim and Thummim.* Heb. אוּרִים וְאֵת הַתֻּמִּים *urim ve-eth hattummim, the Lights and the Perfections.* Gr. τὴν δήλωσιν και αληθειαν, *the manifestation and the truth.* Aq. ' Enlightenings and Certainties.' Sam. ' Elucidations and Perfections.' Syr. ' the Lucid and the Perfect.' Arab. ' Illuminations and Certainties.' Lat. Vulg. ' Doctrine and Verity.' Luth. 'Light and Right.' The Hebrew terms signify primarily *fires* or *lights,* and *perfections* or *truth. Perfection* and *truth* are in Scripture style virtually equivalent in import, because what is *perfected* is *truly* done, neither false, vain, or *unexecuted,* but *accomplished.* The sacred writers, therefore, who often conjoin synonymous terms, have brought these epithets together in several instances, as Josh. 24. 14, 'Fear the Lord and serve him *in perfection and truth* (בְּתָמִים וּבֶאֱמֶת *betummim ubeëmeth*);' i. e. really and perfectly. Thus also ' according to truth,' Rom. 2. 2, is the same as *most certainly to be*

accomplished; wherefore εργον *work* or *deed,* and αληθεια *truth,* 1 John, 3. 18, are synonymous; 'My little children let us not love in word or in tongue, but in *deed* and in *truth.*' That the divine oracles were *perfect* or *truth* no one will doubt who reflects a moment on their source, and who recals the expression of the Psalmist, Ps. 119. 130, ' The entrance (Gr. δηλωσις, *the manifestation*) of thy word giveth light.' Others, however, understand the phrase as an instance of *hendiadys,* denoting under a double denomination one and the same thing, or as equivalent to *most perfect light or illumination.* The same figure occurs Deut. 16. 18. Mat. 4. 16. comp. with Job, 10. 21. John, 3. 5.

In the Urim and Thummin, a subject of great interest, and at the same time of great difficulty, opens upon us. Various and voluminous have been the speculations of learned men in respect to what is meant by these objects, and the precise manner in which they were made instrumental in obtaining oracular responses from God. We cannot, in consistency with our general plan of exposition, avoid entering somewhat minutely into the investigation of both these points; and yet we are unable to assure ourselves of presenting the evidence under either head in such a light as to command the entire assent of our readers to the resulting conclusions. Should we fail of success in this, we shall at least but share the defeat of most of our predecessors in the same field of enquiry, yet we are not without hope that our usual method of rigid philological analysis and parallel induction may conduct us to results of a somewhat satisfactory character;

and as this is the last point connected with the Hebrew ritual which will require a very elaborate discussion, we shall with more confidence bespeak the reader's indulgence for a train of remark more than usually extended.

I. The first question respecting the Urim and Thummim regards their *nature*. What were they? Certain it is, that we find no previous mention of them; no order given for their construction; and no intimation that these names were ever applied to any of the articles which Moses *was* directed to make. The obscurity in which the subject is involved in the sacred text, together with the infinite conjectures to which it has given rise, has led some commentators to the conclusion that the matter is, and was intended to be, one of inscrutable mystery, which it is vain to think of penetrating. In this they virtually subscribe to the opinion of the learned Kimchi, who remarks, that ' he is on the safest side who frankly confesses his ignorance ; so that we seem to need a priest to stand up with Urim and Thummim to teach us what the Thummim were.' The question, however, may be properly narrowed down to a single point, which perhaps admits of solution, viz., were the Urim and Thummim identical with the stones of the Breast-plate, or something distinct from them? On this question the mass of commentators divide. Several of the Jewish Rabbis among the ancients, and Spencer, Michaelis, Jahn, and Gesenius among the moderns contend that they were something entirely distinct from the Pectoral, and deposited within the pocket or bag made of its folds. Some of the earlier Hebrew doctors say that what is called the Urim and Thummim were nothing else than an inscription upon a plate of gold of the Tetragrammaton or four-lettered name of God (רהוה *Yehovah*), by the mystic virtue of which the High Priest was enabled to pronounce *luminous* and *perfect* ora-

cles to the people. But this is a conceit which may be safely passed to the account of the wild and childish figments of the Talmudical Rabbins, which it would require the same weakness to refute as to adopt.

A theory coming from a far higher source, and yet almost equally extravagant, is that proposed by Spencer in his voluminous and in many respects valuable work on the Laws of the Hebrews. He supposes that the Urim were the same with the Teraphim, and that they were nothing more than small divining images, put into the lining of the Breast-plate, which were miraculously made to speak with an articulate voice and utter oracles from God. But it would be scarcely possible to have introduced into the service of the sanctuary any thing more directly idolatrous and pagan in its tendencies than such a device ; and when we consider how carefully the whole Mosaic system guards against that propensity to image-worship which the Israelites evidently brought with them from Egypt, we cannot but be surprised that a theory so utterly abhorrent to the genius of Judaism should have been proposed by a Christian writer. It is but justice, however, to the erudite Spencer to say, that he is far more successful in urging objections to the common theories than in establishing his own. His dissertation on the Urim and Thummim is preeminently able and learned, notwithstanding the obvious error of his main position, nor is it by any means an easy task to dispose of the philological and critical arguments by which he aims to prove, that the objects so called, whatever they were, were something *put into* the lining or folds of the Breast-plate, instead of being externally attached to it. We are on the whole constrained to yield a qualified assent to the force of his reasonings on this head, while at the same time the sequel will show, that this admission is perfectly consistent with maintaining the main view which he is induced to reject.

We may observe, moreover, while adverting to the work of Spencer, that we are firmly of opinion that much more weight is due to the grand idea pervading it, of the conformity in many features of the Jewish to the Egyptian system of worship, than has usually been conceded. Certain it is that within the last fifty years new sources of evidence have been opened upon this subject, by which the state of the question has been entirely altered, from one of *argument* to one of *fact.* These sources are found in the ancient paintings and sculptures of Egypt, which exhibit with great minuteness of detail not only the usages of that extraordinary nation in peace and war, but portray also the rites and ceremonies of their religion, with the various acts performed, the utensils employed, the dresses and ornaments worn, by the Egyptian priesthood in the services of their gods. The result of the comparison will set the question of inter-conformity between the two systems at rest. It is impossible to deny that the most remarkable similarities obtain in the ceremonial observances and the forms and apparatus of divine worship established among the two people. The reader has only to turn back to a preceding page, and compare the cut of an Egyptian Ark borne by priests with Moses's account of the Ark of the Covenant and the manner in which it was carried, for a striking specimen of this coincidence. How the coincidence originated—whether it was accidental; or whether the Jews borrowed from the Egyptians, or the Egyptians from the Jews; or whether both are to be traced to a common origin in the patriarchal practice—is a question not easily decided, though for ourselves we consider the latter supposition as by far the most probable. We have little question that an antediluvian ritual existed, some of

the main features of which were transmitted, through the family of Noah, to all the different nations of antiquity, and which are still traceable in their various superstitions, though sadly deformed, defaced, and perverted by the foul admixture of corruptions subsequently introduced. In giving the Levitical system to the chosen people, God was pleased to retain, purified from their idolatrous associations, many of the peculiarities which marked the Egyptian worship, not because they *were* Egyptian, or because God would unduly consult the weaknesses and prejudices of the chosen people, but because they were primitive and patriarchal, common in their elementary forms to all nations, and perhaps originally of divine institution. This we consider a view of the subject sufficient to account for all the facts, not liable to any serious objection, and one which will afford us essential aid in the explication of the present and many other features of the Hebrew ritual.

The other and much more probable opinion relative to the Urim and Thummim is, that they were in fact identical with the stones of the Breast-plate, but called by this name from the *instrumental uses* which they were made to subserve in the symbolical economy of the priesthood. This opinion, which is held by Josephus, Philo, and most of the ancient Jewish doctors, and has been generally adopted by the moderns, is supported by the following considerations:

(1.) If the words Urim and Thummim be regarded as *epithets*, rather than *names*, applied to the stones, nothing could be more appropriate. From their intrinsic properties of splendor, brilliancy, and *luminousness*, they might very properly be termed *Lights* and *Perfections*, an expression supposed by many to be grammatically equivalent to *most perfect lights.* This is the view of Braunius, who says that not only were precious stones to be employed, but they were to be the most *shining* and *perfect* of the kind. Accordingly, v. 30 may be considered as in fact an emphatic repetition of v. 29, intimating that the work commanded should be executed in the most exact and scrupulous manner; that such stones should be provided and so exquisitely polished and set, as to present the most brilliant appearance, and be entitled to the significant designation of *Lights* and *Perfections*.

(2.) If the Urim and Thummim were not the same with the gems of the Breast-plate, it is wholly inexplicable that the sacred narrative gives us no account of them. While every other part of the ritual is described with the most scrupulous minuteness, as if not a pin of the Tabernacle or a thread of the priestly garments were to be made without express direction, how comes it that nothing is said of an article which, in obtaining responses from God, was absolutely indispensable and which was in every respect among the most important items of the whole apparatus? The silence of the historian, therefore, on this point must be regarded as strong evidence that the Urim and Thummim were identical with the stones.

(3.) It will be observed upon comparing Ex. 39. 8—21, with Lev. 8. 8, that in the description of the Breast-plate, given in the former, while the rows of stones are mentioned, nothing is said of the Urim and Thummim; while in the latter, which speaks of the investiture of Aaron with the pontifical habit, the Urim and Thummim are mentioned, but the stones are passed over in silence. What inference more obvious than that these objects were in fact one and the same?

In order to concentrate still farther all possible collateral light on this point, we shall adduce the various passages in which the Urim and Thummim are mentioned throughout the Scriptures.

Lev. 8. 8, 'And he put the breast-plate upon him; also *he put in the breast-plate the Urim and Thummim.*'

Num. 27. 21. 'And he shall stand before Eleazar the priest, who shall ask counsel for him *after the judgment of Urim* before the Lord.'

Deut. 33. 8, 'And of Levi he said, *Let thy Thummim and Urim be with thy holy one.*'

1 Sam. 28. 6, 'And when Saul inquired of the Lord, the Lord answered him not, neither by dreams, *nor by Urim*, nor by prophets.'

Ezra, 2. 63, and Neh. 7. 65, 'And the Tirshatha said unto them, that they should not eat of the most holy things, *till there stood up a priest with Urim and with Thummum.*'

In neither of these passages is the language any more decisive than the text before us of the question at issue. The first of them does indeed speak very expressly of the Urim and Thummim being *put into* the Breast-plate, and this also would seem to be the unequivocal sense of the words in the verse upon which we are now commenting; 'Thou shalt *put in the breast-plate of judgment* (נתת אל חשן המשפט *nathatta el hoshen hammishpat*) the Urim and Thummim.' Chal. בחשן *bahoshen, in or into the breast-plate*. The phraseology is precisely similar to that Ex. 25. 16, 21, 'And thou shalt *put into the ark* (אל נתת הארון *nathatta el haäron*) the testimony,' &c. Nor is it by any means unusual to find the particle אל *el* interchanged with ב *b*, in the sense of *in, into*. Thus Gen. 49. 29, 'Bury me with my fathers *in* (אל) the cave that is in field, of Ephron.' Ps. 104. 22, 'The sun ariseth, they gather themselves together, and lay them down *in* (אל) their dens.' 1 Sam. 10. 22, 'And the Lord answered, Behold, he hath hid himself *among* (אל) the stuff.' It would seem that in point of local position the Urim and Thummim bore the same relation to the Breast-plate which the Tables of Testimony did to the Ark of the Covenant; and accordingly R. Levi ben Gerson in Buxtorf remarks thus upon the passage before us; 'Because Moses, after inserting the precious stones in the Pectoral, was commanded to put the Urim and Thummim into the same, we cannot help believing that these were something which Moses put into the Pectoral in the same manner in which he put tables into the Ark, inasmuch as he expresses both by the same phrase (נתת אל).'

With this philological evidence before us we know not how to avoid the conclusion, that the Urim and Thummim were actually *put into* the fold or lining of the Breast-plate, and the only question is, how this idea can be reconciled with the above position, that the Urim and Thummim and the precious stones were identical. The single solution which, as far as we see, *can* reconcile two positions so apparently in conflict is, that the stones, instead of being *outwardly* attached to the embroidered work of the Pectoral, and thus made visible to the beholder, were in fact placed upon its *inside*, or in other words lodged *within* the lining of the Breast-plate, and entirely out of sight to any eye but that of Omniscience. We do not perceive that there is any thing in the text, however rigidly scanned, which necessarily requires us to understand the attachment of the stones as *external* to the Breast-plate, nor can we resist the belief that the main use of the Pectoral was that of a *bag* or *pocket* in which *something* was to be deposited. If it served merely as a *ground* for supporting the precious stones, the greater part of it would necessarily be concealed by them, and what then were the use of such an exquisite and costly material? Would not a coarser fabric or a metallic plate have better answered the purpose? Rabbi Solomon, as quoted by Buxtorf,

remarks that 'both in the command to place the inscribed stones upon the shoulder of Aaron, and in the account of its execution, the preposition על *al*, *upon*, occurs in order to teach us that they were placed *exteriorly* to the Ephod, whereas ·in speaking of the stones of the Pectoral the preposition ב *b* or אל *el*, *in*, is uniformly employed, as Ex. 28. 17, מלאת בו *millëtha bo*, *thou shalt fill in it.* Ex. 39. 10, וימלאו בו *va-yemalleü bo*, *and they filled in it.* As to the subjoined phrase על לבו *al libbo*, *upon his heart*, that is used to signify that they were to be hidden.'

But it is not by philological considerations alone that we deem this view of the subject sustained. We have already adverted to the fact of a very remarkable coincidence between the religious rites and usages of the Egyptians and Israelites. The extent to which these affinities exist, as shown by the monumental sculptures and paintings of Egypt, can be but imperfectly appreciated by those who are not somewhat conversant with the works containing the fac-similes of these wonderful remains. Nearly every article of the sacred costume prescribed by God to Moses has its counterpart in the pictured dresses of the Egyptian priests; and in regard to the objects now under consideration and some other peculiarities of the Mosaic system, we are strongly inclined to the opinion, that so few particulars are given, because *it is taken for granted that they were sufficiently known before*. Nahmanides observes that whenever the mention of any of the sacred things is introduced by the use of the definite or emphatic article ה *h, the*, it implies that it was something previously designated or known. Thus it is ordered in general terms, 'they shall make *an* ark,' 'thou shalt make *a* table,' 'thou shalt make *a* candlestick,' &c., but when we come to the text before us it is said, 'thou shalt put in the breast-plate of judgment *the* Urim and

Thummim,' as something which would *of course* be adequately understood from other sources. In like manner, says he, we are told, in Gen. 2. 24, that 'God placed *the cherubims* (הכרבים *hak-kerubim*) at the east of the garden of Eden,' as something too well known to need a particular description. Now if we could obtain evidence that any similar usage prevailed among the ancient Egyptians, especially in the matter of delivering oracles, it would obviously go far to countenance the idea, that the jewelled appendage to the Pectoral was a matter with which both Moses and the people had already become familiar in the land of their bondage. By a singular fortuity it so happens, that we are possessed of just the evidence that we want in relation to this point. Not only do the Egyptian paintings exhibit the pectoral ornament answering to the Jewish *hoshen* or *breast-plate*, but in two of the Greek historians, viz., Diodorus Siculus and Ælian we find the express record which Mr. Wilkinson has embodied in the following passage (Man. and Cust. of Anc. Egypt, vol. 2. p. 26.), ' When a case was brought for trial, it was customary for the arch-judge to put a golden chain around his neck, to which was suspended a small figure of *Truth* or ornamented with precious stones. This was in fact a representation of the goddess who was worshipped under the double character of *truth* and *justice*, and whose name, *Thmei*, appears to have been the origin of the Hebrew *thummim*, a word according to the Septuagint translation, implying *truth*, and bearing a further analogy in its plural termination. And what makes it more remarkable is, that the chief priest of the Jews, who, before the election of a king, was also the judge of the nation, was alone entitled to wear this honorary badge ; and the *thummim* of the Hebrews, like the Egyptian figure, was studded with precious stones.' It is

moreover affirmed by the traveller Peter du Val that he saw a mummy at Cairo, round the neck of which was a chain having a golden plate suspended from it, which lay on the breast of the person, and on which was engraved the figure of a bird. This person was supposed to have been one of the supreme judges ; and in all likelihood the bird was the emblem of truth, justice, or innocence.

This is certainly a remarkable set of coincidences, and the force of it in the argument is not to be weakened by the intimation, that this official badge was worn by *civil* magistrates among the Egyptians. The truth is, the religion of that people was so interwoven with their laws and government that their *kings* were of the *sacerdotal* order, and the *judicial* functions were exercised by the *priests*. As in nearly all the governments of that early period of the world, so among the Egyptians, the people were taught to regard their rulers as clothed with *divine* authority, as the immediate delegates and vicegerents of the gods ; and especially in the administration of justice, it was their object to beget the universal belief that their decisions were in fact *divine oracles*. As scarcely any thing of moment in private life was undertaken without consulting oracles, so especially was this the case in matters of government It was of the highest importance that the impression should prevail that it was done with the concurrence of the gods.

Now that precious stones were instrumentally employed in this kind of divination which had respect to the administration of justice, or the delivery of *judicial oracles*, is very largely and lucidly proved by Daubuz in his invaluable 'Commentary on the Apocalypse,' ch. 21, when treating of the twelve foundations of precious stones of the heavenly Jerusalem. By a learned array of citations from ancient authors he shows that a peculiar mystic virtue was attributed to gems as amulets and charms, and as a medium of converse in general with demons and spirits of the invisible world. Thus Pliny says that the *jasper* was worn every where over the East for amulets; and of the *amethyst* he remarks, that according to popular belief if the name of the sun and moon be written on this kind of stones, and they be suspended from the neck by the feathers of certain birds, they will resist the effect of poison, and avert hail, locusts, &c.; and the same virtue he ascribes to *emeralds* provided they have the figure of an eagle or scarabæus inscribed upon them. We may agree with him in the remark that such things cannot well be written without exciting the contempt and derision of the human race; but however vain were such notions, it is clear that they influenced the practice of the ancients; and they enable us better to understand the reason and origin of their sacred symbolical use. Epiphanius also, in speaking of the gems on the High Priest's Breast-plate, takes notice of the virtues assigned to them by the magicians. Of the *emerald* he says it is accounted to possess a prognosticating power; of the *jasper*, that it drives away spectres and delusions which were attributed to demons; and the same of the *ligure* and *hyacinth*. As therefore these magical and mystical notions respecting the virtues of gems did beyond question prevail among the ancient pagans, especially the Egyptians and the Chaldeans; as they were undoubtedly employed in their *judicial* and *oracular* transactions, we cannot but deem it altogether probable that there was a certain degree of assimilation, or latent inter-relation, between the Hebrew Breast-plate with its Urim and Thummim, and the jewelled collar or pectoral of the Egyptian judge. But although thus related in general as a medium of *oracular* revelation, yet they

would of course differ according to the different scope and genius of their respective institutions. While with the Egyptians these sacred instruments were subservient to the grossest superstition, to magic, and idolatry, with the Hebrews they were instituted for a purpose directly the reverse. They were designed to call them away from the practice of all unhallowed divinations and auguries, and fix their dependence upon the true God. That people were indeed permitted to avail themselves of an oracle on great emergencies; but that oracle was *divine*. It was the true God, Jehovah, omniscient, omnipotent, and infallible. And though he was pleased, in accommodation to their mental condition and capacities to retain and incorporate into his ritual certain usages, to which they had been familiar in other connexions, yet they were henceforth *hallowed* usages, and never to be associated with any idolatrous sentiments or aims. The use of precious stones by those that ministered at heathen temples was nothing but deceit, delusion, and fraud. They were instrumental in uttering oracles which were enigmatical, ambiguous, and false. In God's worship they were *Urim* and *Thummim, clearness* and *certainty, light* and *perfection,* lacking nothing in explicitness of enunciation, nothing in truth of accomplishment. ' To show how all this is suitable,' says Daubuz, ' to the principles of the symbolical language, by which alone the true notion and full force of the word *Urim* is to be understood, we need only to remember that God was the king and ruler of Israel, and that his *oracles* were the special orders and commands which he gave to that people to govern and guide them. Now all kind of government, according to the style of those ages, which were acquainted with symbolical notions, was represented by *light;* because the lights or luminaries direct and show the way, and by consequence *govern* men, who otherwise should not know what to do or whither to go. The word *thummim* joined to the *urim*, and showing this *light* to be *true* and *perfect*, implied that whatsoever God should by the *urim* foretel, would certainly come to pass. So that when God gave his *urim*, or *lights of direction*, to the Israelites, it was in order to bring to *perfection* all those counsels which he then discovered to them. It was upon this account that Christ is called, John, 8. 12, 'the *light* of the world,' and also, John, 14. 6, ' the *way*, the *truth*, and the *life*.' For these titles signify his dominion and power to rule all the world ; and he is the *Urim* and *Thummim*, the disposer of the *oracles* of God to guide and rule men, and to bring to *perfection* all the mystery of God, which is to bring men to eternal life. Hence in the New Jerusalem, wherein that mystery is *perfected*, he is with the Father the *Luminary* thereof. So that this New Jerusalem being founded or begun upon the *oracles* and *light* of the apostles of Jesus Christ, shall be completed by having therein the great Urim and Thummim, which gives *light* to all that are therein.' This New Jerusalem state, therefore, is one in which all the will, counsel, and promises of God from the beginning of the world are to be *perfected*. It is in that glorious state that their accomplishment is to result ; but more especially those which have been made from the beginning of the Gospel dispensation by the apostles of the Lamb, who laid the first foundation of an universal church, and have consequently their names written on the symbols of that foundation.

We have enlarged thus fully in the preceding train of remark on the origin and primitive notions of the Urim and Thummim, not only on account of its intrinsic importance, but also in order to gain still stronger confirmation of the view advanced above in relation to their identity with the precious stones and their true position in the Breast-plate. From an attentive consideration of the whole, we cannot but deem the inference very fair, that the gems, though perhaps permanently attached to the Pectoral, were yet placed in the *inside* of its folds when doubled, and thus in a still more emphatic sense borne ' upon the heart' of the High Priest. Yet as we cannot claim an entire certainty for this explanation we have represented the Breast-plate in the preceding cut as having the form and appearance usually ascribed to it. The matter is left to the enlightened judgment of the reader.

II. We have now to devote a few sentences to the discussion of the *manner* in which responses were given to the consultations made by the High Priest through the medium of the Urim and Thummim. And here the cloud, in which a remote antiquity has inveloped the question, is made still denser by the mists of conflicting conjectures. Among the Rabbinical writers there is a pretty general agreement as to the *occasions* on which those consultations were resorted to, viz., that they were of a *public* and not of a *private* nature. As the High Priest appeared before God in such cases with the names of all the twelve tribes on his Breast-plate, so they suppose that the counsel sought must be sought in the name and on the behalf of *all* the tribes, as having relation to interests which concerned them all ; as for instance matters of peace and war, the election of rulers, the duties of the king on special emergencies, &c. But as to the precise *mode* of the responses, their diversities of opinion show that they were as little furnished with a clue to it as ourselves. The prevalent belief seems to have been, that the letters engraved on the precious stones were effected in some extraordinary manner, so that the dimness or lustre, depression or elevation, of the successive letters composing the

31 ¶ And ʳ thou shalt make the robe of the ephod all *of* blue.

ʳ ch. 39. 22.

32 And there shall be an hole in the top of it, in the midst thereof. it shall have a binding of woven

answer enabled the High Priest to read the response in, or reflected from, his Breast-plate. But this in most cases would have been impossible, as the names of the twelve sons of Jacob do not contain all the letters of the Hebrew alphabet, nor can we conceive how the letters should have been raised or illuminated in such order as to convey an intelligible answer. A far more probable opinion is, that the Urim and Thummim were merely a *requisite circumstance* in the consultation; that they simply *put the High Priest into a condition to receive responses,* and that these responses when duly sought *were given in an audible voice from between the Cherubim.* This seems supported by the fact, that this method of obtaining the divine response is described as ' asking *at the mouth* of the Lord.' ' Whatever was the precise medium through which the response was conveyed, the mode in which the priest acted is sufficiently plain. When any national emergency arose for which the law had made no provision, the High Priest arrayed himself in his Breast-plate and pontifical vestments, and went into the holy place, and standing close before the vail, but not entering within it, stated the question or difficulty, and received an answer. Several instances will occur of this manner of consulting the Lord. It is an opinion which has at least the tacit sanction of Scripture, that the mode of consulting the Lord by Urim and Thummim only subsisted under the theocracy, and while the Tabernacle still remained. Spencer strongly urges that the Urim and Thummim were essentially connected with the theocratic government of the Hebrews. While the Lord was their immediate governor and king, it was necessary that they should be enabled to consult

him on important matters, and obtain his directions on occasions of difficulty. This method was also established for the purpose of consulting God in matters that concerned the common interest of the entire nation. On both these grounds the oracle might well cease when the theocracy terminated by the kingdom becoming hereditary in the person and family of Solomon ; and still more, when the division of the nation into two kingdoms at his death rendered the interests of the nation no longer common. This is but an hypothesis : but it is certain that there are no traces in the sacred books of consulting the Lord by Urim and Thummim from the time of the erection to the demolition of Solomon's Temple : and that it did not *afterwards* exist is on all hands allowed.' *Pict. Bible.*

THE ROBE OF THE EPHOD.

31, 32. *Thou shalt make the robe of the ephod,* &c. This is a garment distinct from any that has yet been mentioned. It is called the ' robe of the ephod,' simply because it was worn immediately under it. Its Hebrew name is מְעִיל *meïl,* rendered in the Gr. ὑποδυτην ποδηρη, an *under-garment reaching down to the feet.* Vulg. 'Tunic of the Ephod.' Arab. 'A rain-shedding cloak.' Luth. 'A silk robe.' Belg. 'A mantle. Jun. and Trem. ' Pallium, *a cloak.*' The *meïl* was a distinguishing priestly vestment, and therefore Christ appears, Rev. 1. 13, ' clothed with *a garment down to the feet* (ποδηρη),' to show himself the Great High Priest of the church. It was a long linen gown of sky blue color, reaching to the middle of the leg. It was all of one piece, and so formed as to be put on, not like other garments which are open in front, but like a surplice, over the head, having a hole at

work round about the hole of it, as it were the hole of an habergeon, that it be not rent.

33 ¶ And *beneath*, upon the hem of it thou shalt make pomegranates *of* blue, and *of* purple, and *of* scar-

the top for the head to pass through, which was strongly hemmed round with a binding or welt to prevent it from rending, and with openings or arm-holes in the sides in place of sleeves. Round its lower border were tassels made of blue, purple, and scarlet, in the form of pomegranates, interspersed with small gold bells, in order to make a noise when the High Priest went into or came out from the holy place, the reason of which is given below. We are not in-

formed of the exact number of the pomegranates and bells. The Rabbinical writers are mostly unanimous in saying, there were 72 in all, which is doubtless as probable as any other conjecture on the subject. It will be observed, that while the body of the Robe was entirely of blue, this ornamental appendage in the skirts was richly dyed of variegated hues, and must have rendered the whole a vestment of exquisite beauty.

THE ROBE OF THE EPHOD.

33. *Thou shalt make pomegranates.* רִמֹּן *rimmon.* The term '*pomegranate*' is compounded of *poma, apple,* and *granata, grained,* from its resemblance, when opened, to *an apple full of grain.* It grows wild in Palestine, and in other parts of Syria, as well as in Persia, Arabia, Egypt, and the southern parts of Europe, and in some portions of our own country. The fruit is the size of an orange, flattened at the end like an apple; and when cultivated is of a beautiful color and highly grateful flavor. The rind is at first green; but in August

and September when the fruit is ripe, it assumes a brownish-red color, becomes thick and hard, yet easily broken. The inside of the pomegranate is of a bright pink, with skinny partitions like those of the orange, filled with a subacid juice and a great multitude of white and purplish red seeds. The flower, which is of a scarlet color, is peculiarly beautiful, and it is probably to the flower that allusion is had, Cant. 4. 3, where the royal bridegroom compares the cheeks of his bride to a 'piece of pomegranate,' though others understand by this a *section* of the fruit itself, the cheeks being called in the Talmudic language, *the pomegranates of the face.* The annexed cut will give an idea of the form of the fruit and flower of this plant, both which are among the most striking objects of the vegetable world.

THE POMEGRANATE.

The Pomegranate abounds more particularly in Syria and the ancient As-syria, where it was held sacred and entered into the symbols of the heathen worship, as is plainly to be inferred from its giving name to an idolatrous temple, 2 Kings, 5. 18, called 'the house of Rimmon,' i. e. the Pomegranate. In Persia the heads of sceptres and honorary staves were formed in the shape of a Pomegranate. It was also held sacred in Egypt; and in all countries where it was not to be found, the poppy, which also abounds in seeds, was chosen in its stead. Both were dedicated by the pagans to the *generative* powers, their numerous seeds rendering them an apt emblem of *prolific properties.* Hence at marriages the bride was crowned with a chaplet in which were inserted the flowers of pomegranates and poppies as an omen of *fruitfulness.* As then the idea of *fruitful increase* is prominent among the symbolical notions attached to this plant and its fruit, there is perhaps ample ground for the suggestion, that this singular appurtenance to the High Priest's dress, in conjunction with the bells, was designed to intimate that the *sound* of the gospel should not be in vain; that wherever the *sound* of the doctrine of Christ and the apostles should come, then it should *bear fruit,* or that churches should be gathered bringing forth the *fruits* of righteousness; the *preaching* of the gospel should be the means of begetting *a* spiritual progeny zealous of *good works.* The remarks of Prof. Edwards are too pertinent to this point not to be cited in the present connexion. 'The golden bells on the Ephod, by their precious matter and pleasant sound do well represent the good profession that the saints make; and the pomegranates the fruit they bring forth. And as in the hem of the (robe of the) Ephod, bells and pomegranates were constantly connected, as is once and again observed,—' a golden bell and a pomegranate, a golden bell and a pomegranate'—so it is in the true saints. Their good '*profession,* and their good *fruit,* do constantly accompany one another. The fruit they bring in life answers the pleasant sound of their profession.' *Treat. on Affect,* Part III. p. 395.——
¶ *Of blue, purple, scarlet,* &c. Although the body of this garment was of

let, round about the hem thereof; and bells of gold between them round about:

34 A golden bell and a pomegranate, a golden bell and a pomegranate, upon the hem of the robe round about.

35 And it shall be upon Aaron, to minister: and his sound shall be heard when he goeth in unto the holy. *place* before the LORD, and when he cometh out, that he die not.

36 ¶ And ᵗ thou shalt make a plate *of* pure gold, and grave upon it *like* the engravings of a signet, HOLINESS TO THE LORD.

t ch. 39. 30. Zech. 14. 20.

---

one uniform color, a beautiful blue, yet the skirts were ornamented with this parti-colored fringe-work, wrought somewhat like the silken balls, or ball-tassels, of modern upholstery, into the shape of the fruit here mentioned.——
¶ *Bells of gold.* Of the suggesting origin of this part of the dress of the High Priest it is difficult to give any account. That bells were not unknown in the costume of the East is evident from the Targum on Est. 6. 10, where Ahasuerus says to Haman ' Go to my wardrobe, and take one of my best purple cloaks, and of the best silk vests, with gems at the four corners of it, and *golden bells and pomegranates hanging round about.*' Michaelis conjectures that the Oriental kings of that period were accustomed to wear little. bells upon some part of their robes in order to give notice that that they were near by, and that the people might retire. Hence perhaps the use of bells as a symbol of the reverence due to holy places. This idea is favored by the strong language, v. 35, where the punishment of death is threatened upon the neglect of this ceremony ; which would seem to imply that as in the etiquette of an Eastern court, no one would rush rudely, or without some kind of annunciation, into the presence of the sovereign, so the High Priest was not to be guilty of the irreverence of approaching the Oracle without some kind of signal of his coming. Another use of this appendage of the mantle, as inferred from Ecclus. 45. 7 9, was, that the people collected in the court around the sanctuary might be admonished of the High Priest's entrance into the Holy Place, and so unite their prayers with his incense offering, ' An everlasting covenant he made with him (Aaron), and gave him the priesthood among the people ; he beautified him with comely ornaments, and clothed him with a robe of glory. He put upon him perfect glory ; and strengthened him with rich garments, with breeches, with a long robe, and the ephod. And he compassed him with pomegranates, and with many golden bells round about, that as he went there might be a sound, and a noise made that might be heard in the temple, for a memorial to the children of his people.' If this be well founded, and the sound of the bells had principal reference to the people, to remind them of the proper spirit and deportment to be observed on the occasion, then it may be suggested that the phrase, ' that he die not,' is perhaps to be understood not of Aaron, but to be rendered impersonally, ' that *one* die not,' ' that there be no dying,' i. e. that no one may presumptuously lay aside the becoming reverence and thus expose himself to death. The original will no doubt admit of this construction, but whether it be the true one, we are not prepared to decide.

THE GOLDEN PLATE AND MITRE.

36. *Thou shalt make a plate of pure gold,* &c. Heb. צִיץ *tzitz.* Gr. πεταλον, *petal, leaf.* Vulg. ' Lamina,' *plate,* Arab. 'Fillet.' Luth. 'Forehead-plate.' The original word עִיץ *tzitz,* from

צוּץ *tzutz, to flourish,* is generally understood to signify *a flower,* and the Greek rendering *petal* would seem to be founded upon this sense, implying either that the plate was itself of the form of a flower, or was curiously wrought with flower-work. Such also was plainly the opinion of Josephus, who gives a minute description of the particular kind of flower or calyx which was figured upon the plate. Rosenmuller, however, contends that this rendering in this place is founded upon a false interpretation of צִיץ, which does not, he says, legitimately signify *a flower,* nor has it any relation to *flowers* or *flower-work,* but properly denotes something *glistening, radiant, effulgent,* and is here applied to the plate on the Mitre, from the *flashing splendors* which beamed from it. But the ideas of *flourishing* and of *emitting splendor* are somewhat closely related in all languages, as nothing is more common with us for instance than to speak of the *brightness* or *splendid hues* of flowers, and from the usus loquendi of the term it cannot at all be questioned that the dominant sense of צִיץ is that of *flowers* or *flowering plants.* Yet it is very possible that the two ideas of *efflorescence* and *shining* may be combined in this passage, especially if we suppose, as we think was undoubtedly the case, that some kind of *floral ornament* was wrought upon the *glistening* gold plate of the Mitre. In describing the execution of this order, Ex. 39. 30, it is said, ' they made the *plate of the holy crown* (צִיץ נֵזֶר הַקֹּדֶשׁ *tzitz nëzer hakkodesh*) of pure gold,' &c., where נֵזֶר *nëzer* comes from a verb signifying *to separate,* and hence denoting a *crown* as a mark of *separation* or *distinction.* So also the original word for mitre occurs Job, 29. 14, where it is rendered ' diadem,' leading us to the inference that the sacerdotal mitre is closely allied with the kingly crown. **Thus too Lev. 8. 9,** ' and he put the

mitre upon his head; also upon the mitre, even upon his fore-front, did he put the golden plate, *the holy crown;* as the Lord commanded Moses.' In like manner we find it said Ps. 132, 18, ' upon himself *shall his crown flourish* (יָצִיץ נִזְרוֹ *yatzitz nizro*).' Here it is difficult to account for the idea of *a crown's flourishing,* except upon the suppostion of some kind of *floral* appendages being connected with it in the mind of the writer; and this might have arisen from the fact, that the earliest crown was merely a chaplet, garland, or wreath bound around the head; or from the beautiful wrought flower-work on the priestly Mitre of Aaron. But whatever uncertainty may otherwise envelope the subject, this is clear beyond question, that the Plate was the principal part of the Mitre, and that the badges of the *priestly* are closely interwoven with those of the *kingly* dignity in the appointed vesture of the Jewish pontiff. For this fact a twofold reason may be assigned. In the first place, the entire nation of Israel was in a sense concentrated in the person of the High Priest, their head and representative. It was the high prerogative of this favored people to be chosen as a ' royal priesthood,' a ' kingdom of priests,' and the unity of the nation, in this exalted character, was made visible in the person of him who was ordained as their supreme dignitary. Nothing therefore would be more natural or appropriate than that corresponding symbols or badges of this twofold distinction should appear on the head-dress of the High Priest, as we here learn to have been the fact. Indeed the Jewish tradition amplifies this idea somewhat, and affirms a *threefold* dignity of their race, which they say was indicated by a triplet of crowns, viz., the crown of the priesthood, the crown of the kingdom, and the crown of the law.—Secondly, this conjunction of *sacerdotal* and *royal* symbols in the

37 And thou shalt put it on a blue lace, that it may be upon the mitre; upon the fore-front of the mitre it shall be.

Mitre was intended to serve as a typical intimation of the union of these two offices in the person of Christ, who was to sit as 'a *priest* upon his *throne*,' being made a *priest* after the order of Melchizedek, *king* of righteousness. ·

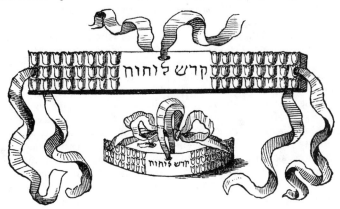

THE GOLDEN PLATE OF THE MITRE.

¶ *Like the engravings of a signet.* It is probable that the Jewish writers are correct in supposing that the letters were not *cut* or *grooved into* the plate, but were rather *embossed* or *made to stand in relief* upon it. The precise manner in which this was done, cannot at present be determined, but Maimonides says that in working the inscription, the instruments were applied to the *inside* and *not to the outside* of the plates, so as to make the letters stand out. —— ¶ HOLINESS TO THE LORD. Heb. קֹדֶשׁ לַיהֹוָה *kodesh la-Yehovah, holiness to Jehovah,* or *the holiness of Jehovah,* according to the Gr. which has ἁγίασμα κυρίου, *the holiness,* or *sanctification, of the Lord.* This was perhaps the most conspicuous object of the High Priest's dress, and was in fact a significant memento of the character of the entire service in which he sustained so prominent a part. By this inscription the wearer became 'as a city set on a hill, which cannot be hid;' the bright memorial incessantly, though silently, proclaiming to the eye, to the heart, to the conscience, 'a holy God, a holy service, a holy minister, a holy people, and a holy covenant.' The children of Israel could not look upon it without being reminded of the great principle which Jehovah would have to pervade all his worship, and which is elsewhere so solemnly announced, 'I will be *sanctified* in all them that draw nigh unto me.' And to the saints in all ages it should serve as a remembrancer of the equivalent intimation, that as 'he which hath called us is holy, so are we to be holy in all manner of conversation.'

37. *And thou shalt put it on a blue lace.* An idiomatic expression for 'put upon it.' It was to hang by a ribbon of blue upon the Mitre, as is intimated in the words following, and as represented in the cut. The Talmudists however say, there were three ribbons, one at each ear, and one in the middle, passing over the head. We have accordingly so represented it on the smaller figure in the cut, as there is no inconsistency in supposing it to have

38 And it shall be upon Aaron's forehead, that Aaron may [u] bear

[u] ver. 43. Lev. 10. 17. & 22. 9. Numb. 18. 1. Isai. 53. 11. Ezek. 4. 4, 5, 6. John 1. 29. Hebr. 9. 28. 1 Pet. 2. 24.

the iniquity of the holy things, which the children of Israel shall hallow in all their holy gifts; and it shall be always upon his fore-

been the case.——¶ *That it may be upon the mitre.* Heb. מצנפת *mitznepheth,* from צנף *tzanaph, to wrap, to enwrap, to roll round.* The term applies itself at once to the style of head-dress common among the Arabs, Turks, Persians, and other Oriental nations, called *the turban,* and formed of a number of swathes or foldings of cloth. As nothing is said of the *precise form* of the High Priest's Mitre, we are doubtless at liberty to suppose it justly represented in the main by an eastern turban, though perhaps of more than usual amplitude. By the ancient Greeks this kind of covering for the head was called *tiara,* and *cidaris,* and sometimes *diadema;* and that it was not unusual to have it made of *fine linen,* as in the present case, is clear from the fact that Justin relates of Alexander the Great,

that he took the *diadem* from his head to bind up the wounds of Lysimachus. From these titles we perceive new evidence that the priestly Mitre carried at the same time a *kingly* import; and it is even supposed that the inveterate predilection of the Orientals for the turban arises from the belief of some mystic virtue emblematic of *sovereignty* still clinging to it. The Mitre of Aaron merely covered the crown and upper part of the head without descending low upon the forehead, which was left bare for the golden Plate to lie upon it below the edge of the Mitre. In this respect the Mitre of the High Priest differed from the bonnets of the common priests, which having no plate sunk lower on the forehead. In other points the general resemblance was very striking.

THE HIGH PRIEST'S MITRE.

38. *That Aaron may bear the iniquity,* &c. The implication plainly is, that there might be, unconsciously perhaps to the offerers, some defects in the oblations presented, which were graciously *pardoned*—a frequent sense of *borne* or *carried* in the Scriptures—by the intercession of the High Priest ap-

pearing before God perfectly attired and crowned in the manner presented. The efficacy, however, of this intermediation on the part of Aaron appears to be in some way more especially concentrated in this resplendent inscribed plate upon his forehead, and this we think can only be understood by refer-

head, that tney may be ʷ accepted before the LORD.

39 ¶ And thou shalt embroider

ʷ Lev. 1. 4. & 22. 27. & 23. 11. Isai. 56. 7.

the coat of fine linen, and thou shalt make the mitre *of* fine linen, and thou shalt make the girdle *of* needle-work.

---

ence to the typical character which the High Priest sustained. Christ, we well know, is represented as ' bearing the sins,' i. e. the *punishment* due to the sins of men. Aaron in his office was a type of Christ, and accordingly is represented not only as *making an atonement* in general for the sins of the people, by the sacrifices offered, but also as making an atonement for the *imperfections of the atonement itself.* This was done, it appears, by what we may term the memorial and typical virtue of the shining plate of the Mitre, upon the inscription of which God is supposed to look and thereby be reminded of that perfect ' holiness to the Lord' which should so preeminently distinguish the great Mediator whom Aaron represented. The following passages must be taken in this connexion in order fully to convey the import of the language, Ps. 84. 9, 'Behold, O God our shield, and *look upon the face of thine anointed.*' Ps. 132. 9, 10, ' Let thy priests be clothed with righteousness;

and let thy saints shout for joy. For thy servant David's sake, *turn not away the face of thine anointed.*' i. e. be propitious by looking upon the face; regard the significance of the golden plate. The prayers embracing this expression appear to have a special allusion to *the imperfections of the holy things* of the people of God.

THE COAT OR TUNIC.

39. *Thou shalt embroider the coat of fine linen,* &c. Heb. כְּתֹנֶת *kethoneth.* This was the innermost of the sacerdotal vestments, being a long robe with sleeves to the wrists, which sat close to the body, and extended down to the feet. This garment was not peculiar to the High Priest, but was similar to that worn by the other priests while officiating. What became of the tunic of the High Priests we do not know; but that of the common priests was unravelled when old, and made into wicks for the lamps burnt in the feast of tabernacles.

THE COAT, OR TUNIC.

40 ¶ ˣ And for Aaron's sons thou shalt make coats, and thou shalt make for them girdles, and bonnets shalt thou make for them, for glory and for beauty.

41 And thou shalt put them upon

ˣ ver. 4. ch. 39. 27, 28, 29, 41. Ezek. 44. 17. 18.

Aaron thy brother, and his sons with him: and shalt ʸ anoint them, and ᶻ consecrate them, and sanctify them, that they may minister unto me in the priest's office.

ʸ ch. 29. 7. & 30. 30. & 40. 15. ᶻ ch. 29. 9, &c. Lev. ch. 8. Hebr. 7. 28.

THE GIRDLE.

¶ *Girdle of needle-work.* Heb. אבנט *abnet.* This was a piece of fine twined linen, embroidered with blue, purple, and scarlet, and which went round the body. Josephus says it was embroidered with flowers; and also states that it was four fingers broad, and that, after being wound twice around the body, it was fastened in front, and the ends allowed to hang down to the feet, on ꞏꞏꞏꞏ occasions; but that, when offi- ꞏ altar, the priest threw left shoulder. Maimoni-

des says the Girdle was three fingers broad, and thirty-two cubits long; being, as its length necessarily implies, wound many times round the body. As this Girdle was so narrow, its length, if this statement be correct, will not seem extraordinary to those who are acquainted with the ordinary length of Oriental girdles, and the number of times they are carried around the body. The Girdle was worn over the embroidered coat by the common priests, to whom this coat, unlike the attire of the High Priest, formed the outer garment.

THE GIRDLE.

THE BONNETS.

40. *Bonnets.* Heb. מגבעת *migbaoth.* Gr. κιδαρεις, *tiaras.* Vulg. 'Tiaras.' As a different term is used to designate the article here mentioned from that which is applied to the Mitre of the High Priest, there was probably some difference in the form; but what

it was precisely it is difficult to say. According to the Jewish writers the Bonnets came down lower upon the forehead than the Mitre, and rose up higher like an hillock, as the original is derived from גבע *geba,* a hillock, a knoll. In other words they were of a more *conical* shape than the Mitre

42 And thou shalt make them ᵃ linen breeches to cover their nakedness: from the loins even unto the thighs they shall reach:

43 And they shall be upon Aaron, and upon his sons, when they come in unto the tabernacle of the congregation, or when they come near ᵇ unto the altar to minister in the holy *place;* that they ᶜ bear not iniquity and die. ᵈ *It shall be* a statute for ever unto him, and his seed after him.

ᵃ ch. 39. 28. Lev. 6. 10. & 16. 4. Ezek. 44. 18.

ᵇ ch. 20. 26. ᶜ Lev. 5. 1. 17. & 20. 19, 20. & 22. 9. Numb. 9. 13. & 18. 22. ᵈ ch. 27. 21. Lev. 17. 7.

This, however, does not convey a very distinct idea, and we must refer the reader to the accompanying cut for a view, which is at best conjectural, of the probable difference between them. ——¶ *For glory and for beauty.* Nothing is more obvious than that the priestly attire was to be so ordered as to present an air of impressive splendor and gorgeousness, that a becoming reverence might be inspired towards the persons of those who wore them. But to *us,* they present merely a gaudy spectacle, a showy pageant, except so far as we fix our eye upon their *typ-*ical import. Here, and here only, in the *glory of grace* and the *beauty of holiness,* which they shadowed forth, do we behold the true *glory* and *beauty* of these sacred robes. It is only as the light of the *substance* is reflected upon the *symbol,* that the symbol itself can at all *shine* in our eyes. But when we discern in these beauteous robes an image of the spiritual attire of the saints, the true royal hierarchy, who are made at once kings and priests unto God, we feel no restraint in letting our admiration go forth towards the external adornments.

THE BONNETS.

THE LINEN DRAWERS.

42. *Thou shalt make them linen breeches.* Heb. מכנסי בד *miknesë bad;* more properly *linen drawers,* which though last mentioned were the first put on. 'The ancient Jews, like the modern Arabs and some other Orientals, did not generally wear drawers or trowsers. Maimonides says that the drawers worn by the priests reached from above the navel to the knee, and had no opening before or behind, but were drawn up around the body by strings, like a purse. This resembles the linen drawers worn by the Turks and Persians at the present day, ex-

cept that they reach rather below the knee. They are very wide altogether, and when drawn on are fastened very tight around the body by means of a string or girdle, which runs through a hem in the upper border.' *Pict. Bible.*

THE DRAWERS.

In concluding this account of the priestly robes, it may be useful to repeat that the robes common to all were —the Drawers, the Embroidered Coat, the Girdle, and the Turban; but, besides this, the High Priest wore the Ephod, the Robe of the Ephod with its Bells and Pomegranates, the Breast-plate over the Ephod, the Shoulder-pieces of onyx-stone, and the engraved ornament of pure gold in front of his turban. The Rabbins seem to have the sanction of the Scripture for their opinion, that the robes were so essential a part of the priestly character, that without them a priest had no more right than private persons, or even foreigners, to officiate at the altar. It seems that the old robes of the priests, as already mentioned in the Note on v. 39, were unravelled, to be burnt as wicks for the lamps at the feast of tabernacles. What was done with those of the High Priest is not known; but analogy would seem to render it probable that they were similarly used for the lamps in the tabernacle. We may remark also that as no shoes or sandals are mentioned among the sacred vestments, it is supposed the priests always ministered barefoot. This is perhaps confirmed by the fact that Moses, before the symbol of Jehovah at the burning bush, was commanded to put off his shoes.

43. *That they bear not iniquity and die.* That is, that they do not expose themselves to be cut off by a sudden stroke of vengeance for the profanity of appearing before God without their holy garments. Gr. και ουκ επαξονται προς ἑαυτους ἁμαρτιαν, ινα μη αποθανωσι, *and they shall not bring sin upon themselves that they die not.* This caution, as the Hebrew writers have gathered, was intended to apply not to the linen drawers only, but to all the garments. Their language is as follows: ' The High Priest that ministereth with less than these eight garments, or the inferior Priest that ministereth with less than these four garments, his service is unlawful, and he is guilty of death by the hand of God, even as a stranger that ministereth. When their garments are upon them, their priesthood is upon them; if their garments be not upon

CHAPTER XXIX.

A ND this *is* the thing that thou shalt do unto them to hallow them, to minister unto me in the

priest's office: a Take one young bullock, and two rams without blemish,

a Lev. 8. 2.

---

them, their priesthood is not upon them, but, lo, they are as strangers; and it is written, Num. 1. 51, ' The stranger that cometh nigh shall be put to death.'' *Maimonides in Ainsworth.*

Chapter 29

THE CONSECRATION OF THE PRIESTS.

As God had said, v. 41, of the preceding chapter respecting Aaron and his sons, 'Thou shalt anoint them and consecrate them and sanctify them, that they may minister unto me in the priest's office,' he proceeds in the present chapter to prescribe, with great minuteness, the manner in which this solemn ceremony should be performed. As the office which they were to sustain was in itself one of the utmost importance to themselves and the people, it was proper that the mode of their induction into it should be in the highest degree august and impressive; and as nothing of the kind had been done before, and as a permanent form of inauguration was now to be fixed upon, we see abundant reason for the express appointment of the various ceremonies by which the procedure was to be marked. These were of such a nature as was calculated to affect the incumbents with the greatness and sacredness of the work to which they were called, and also to lead the people to magnify and reverence an office in which their interests were so deeply involved. The whole transaction was to be so conducted that there should be ample evidence that Aaron and his sons did not 'glorify themselves to be made priests,' but that they were 'called of God' to exercise the sacerdotal functions. The Most High did, as it were, in this ceremony put his hand upon them, distinguish

them from common men, set them apart from common services, and make them the fixed organ of communication between himself and the chosen race. ' The consecration of God was upon their heads.' But while they were thus made to feel that they were invested with an office of the highest sanctity, and one in which they were to expiate the sins of the people by typical sacrifices, they were not suffered to forget that they also were themselves sinners, and needed an expiation as much as any of those for whom they ministered. Accordingly the very first step in the ceremony of consecration was the providing of a bullock, rams, &c., as a sin-offering for themselves, to keep them perpetually reminded of the fact that the ' law made men priests that had infirmity, who needed first to offer up sacrifices for their own sins, and then for the people's,' Heb. 7. 27, 28. The typical reference of the office itself to the Savior Jesus Christ, the Messiah or Anointed One, the great High Priest of the Church, is very obvious, although those parts of the consecrating ceremony which implied sinful infirmity in its subjects could have no bearing in relation to him who was in himself 'holy, harmless, undefiled, separate from sinners, and made higher than the heavens.' He needed not to be sanctified by the blood of rams and bullocks, or made perfect by the death of others, inasmuch as he has by his one offering of himself upon the cross satisfied for ever all the demands of the law upon himself and his believing people.

1. *And this is the thing that thou shalt do.* Heb♦ הַדָּבָר *haddabar, the word.* Gr. και ταυτα εστιν, *and these are the things.* See Note on Gen. 15. 1.
——¶ *To hallow them.* Heb. לְקַדֵּשׁ

2 And ᵇ unleavened bread, and
cakes unleavened tempered with
　ᵇ Lev. 2. 4. & 6. 20, 21, 22.

אתם *lekaddësh otham, to sanctify them,
to set them apart.* This is here a term
denoting that *general* consecration to
the priestly office which is expanded in
fuller detail in the sequel of the chapter. The subsequent expression ' consecrate,' v. 9, 29, has respect rather to
one particular part of the ceremonies
enjoined on the occasion.——¶ *To
minister in the priest's office.* This
is expressed in Hebrew by the single
term לכהן *lekahën,* from כהן *kohën,
a priest,* and signifying literally *to
act the priest, to discharge the priestly functions.* See Note on Ex. 28. 1.
——¶ *Take one young bullock.* Heb.
פר אחד בן בקר *par ehad ben bakar,
one bullock a son* (i. e. a youngling) *of
the herd.* The Heb. פר *par,* from which
comes the German ' Farre,' *a young
bull, a bullock,* is a generic term equivalent to the Lat. ' pullus,' *a foal,* denoting the young of cattle, and yet not
at the youngest age. It is perhaps most
properly rendered, as here, by *bullock,*
as is the fem. פרה *parah* by *heifer.* Gr.
μοσχαριον εκ βοων, *a youngling or calf
of the oxen.* Some of the Hebrew doctors suppose that בן בקר *ben bakar* implies a bullock of not less than three
years old; but this cannot be made to
appear, though it doubtless denotes one
that has been sometime weaned.——
¶ *Without blemish.* Heb. תמימם *te-
mimim, perfect;* i. e. without defect,
superfluity, or deformity. The animal
and the other articles mentioned in this
connexion were to be the first which
were to be provided, but they were not
to be used till various other preliminary ceremonies, such as washing, rob-
ing, &c., had been performed. In fact
the consecration itself here ordered did
not take place till after the tabernacle
was erected. See Lev. 8. 9, 10.
　2. *Unleavened bread, and cakes,* &c.

oil, and wafers unleavened annoint.
ed with oil: *of* wheaten flour shalt
thou make them.

It is important to bear in mind, in reference to the Jewish ritual generally,
that the ideas of *sacrificing* and of
feasting are very intimately related to
each other. We are doubtless much in
the habit of regarding the offerings of
the Mosaic law as pertaining wholly to
one party, and as a purely expiatory
act on the part of the offerer, in which
nothing of a *mutual* nature was implied.
But the truth is, these sacrifices actually partook more or less of the character
of a *mutual entertainment,* for with the
exception of the *holocaust,* or *whole-
burnt-offering,* and of certain parts
which were offered and consumed upon
the altar, the rest were eaten by the offerers and the priests, and this fact will account for some of the oblations consisting of articles which were and always
have been articles of diet. The Most
High could not be expected of course to
make a party at a *literal table,* but at
the same time such viands *as would be
set upon a table* might be offered to him,
and the fire of his altar as his representative might consume them. Considering therefore the character and relation of the parties, the disposal of
the sacrificial offerings came as near
perhaps to the semblance of a *mutual
feast* as the nature of the case would
allow. If this view of the subject be
admitted, it will account for the requirement of such offerings on the pres-
sent occasion as unleavened cakes and
wafers mingled with oil. In our ordinary meals *flesh* and *bread* go together;
and so in the present case, although the
ram was to be a holocaust, yet the bullock was to be part offered and part
eaten, constituting with its annexed
meat or meal-offering, the matter of an
entertainment in which God and they
might feast together in token of friendship and fellowship. In this there was

3 And thou shalt put them into one basket, and bring them in the basket, with the bullock and the two rams.
4 And Aaron and his sons thou shalt bring unto the door of the tabernacle of the congregation, cand shalt wash them with water.

c ch. 40. 12. Lev. 8. 6. Hebr. 10. 22.

5 d And thou shalt take the garments, and put upon Aaron the coat, and the robe of the ephod, and the ephod, and the breastplate, and gird him with e the curious girdle of the ephod:
6 f And thou shalt put the mitre

d ch. 28. 2. Lev. 8. 7. e ch. 28. 8. f Lev 8. 9.

a distinct allusion to the prevalent custom in the East of ratifying every important covenant transaction by an entertainment of which the covenanting parties partook together. In like manner, the Lord's supper is often properly represented as *a feast upon a sacrifice*. While it commemorated the sacrifice made by the death of the divine victim it betokened at the same time the *pacification* and covenant fellowship of Christ and his followers. The vegetable offering here prescribed as an accompaniment to the animal sacrifice constituted a מנחה *minhah* or *mincha*, as it is usually termed, of the nature of which see Note on Gen. 4. 3. The two first, the bread and the cakes, were mixed with oil (i. e. oil of olives) before baking ; the last, the wafers, were merely smeared with oil after they were baked. The original term for 'wafers' רקיקים *rekikim* comes from רקק *rakak*, *to be* or *to be made thin*, and is applied to signify a *thin kind of cakes* similar to what are known among us by the name of 'pan-cakes.' The Ital. version has 'fritella' *fritters*. These were all to be put into a basket as constituting one מנחה *minhah* or *breadoffering*, and brought along with the bullock and the rams to the door of the tabernacle, and there presented to the Lord.
4. *Shalt bring unto the door of the tabernacle.* To the open space in the court in front of the tabernacle, and near the entrance. It was here that the altar and the laver stood, and where all the ordinary sacrificial services were

performed. Moreover, as God was pleased to dwell by his Shekinah in the tabernacle, and the people attended in the court, it was peculiarly appropriate that those who were to act as mediators between these two parties should be consecrated in some intervening spot between them ; and such a spot was here appointed where the sacerdotal daysman might, as it were, 'lay his hand upon both.'——¶ *Shalt wash them with water.* That is, with the water of the laver, which was made, anointed, and set in the court of the tabernacle before the priests were consecrated. It is reasonably supposed, though not expressly asserted, that on this occasion their whole bodies were washed, whereas at other times when engaged in their ministrations they only washed their hands and feet ; and to this our Savior perhaps alludes, John, 13. 10, 'He that is washed needeth not save to wash his feet, but is clean every whit.' The object of this preliminary oblation cannot well be mistaken. It was emblematical of that inward spiritual cleansing which so obviously becomes those who minister in holy things. 'Be ye clean that bear the vessels of the Lord,' is the fixed decree of heaven.
5. *Thou shalt take the garments,* &c. The entire person having duly undergone the prescribed ablution, the next step was the putting on the priestly garments so particularly described in the preceding chapter. By this was implied that not only were they to put away the impurities of the flesh, but to

upon his head, and put the holy crown upon the mitre.

7 Then shalt thou take the an-

ointing g oil, and pour *it* upon his head, and anoint him.

g ch. 28. 41. & 30 35. Lev. 8. 12. & 10, 7, & 21. 10. Num. 35. 25.

clothe themselves also with the graces of the Spirit, significantly shadowed forth by the splendid robes in which they were to officiate. The original word for 'gird' is אָפַד *aphad, to bind, girdle, enclose,* from which 'Ephod' is a derivative. The act of girding seems to denote readiness and preparation for active service. So the ministers of Christ, prompt to do his will, are symbolically represented, Rev. 15. 6, by 'angels coming out of the temple clothed in pure and white linen, and having their breasts *girded with golden girdles.*' ——¶ *The holy crown.* That is, the plate of gold with the blue lace above mentioned, Ex. 28. 36, 37. It is here called נֵזֶר *nezer, separation,* from its being a badge of the wearer being separated from his brethren. It is elsewhere used as a denomination of the diadems of kings, 2 Sam. 1. 19. Ps. 89. 40. The mention of the linen drawers is here omitted, because they were put on privately before they came to the more public vestry at the door of the tabernacle.

7. *Thou shalt then take the anointing oil,* &c. Heb. שֶׁמֶן הַמִּשְׁחָה *shemen hammishshah, oil of unction;* the peculiar mode of compounding which for sacred purposes is afterwards detailed, Ex. 30. 23—33. This was perhaps the most important, because the most significant, part of the ceremony of the consecration. As the High Priest was a type of Christ, whatever part of the ceremonies represented the most eminent endowments and attributes of the great Antitype were certainly of paramount import to all others. Now the ineffable *sanctity* of the Savior, the measureless possession of the gifts and graces the Holy Spirit conferred upon him, was one of those divine qualifi-

cations which went preeminently to constitute the greatness, the fitness, and glory of his sacerdotal character; and so far as the communication of this plenary gift of the Spirit could be shadowed forth by any physical act, it was done by the process of anointing. Thus, Is. 61. 1, 'The Spirit of the Lord God is upon me, because the Lord hath *anointed* me to preach,' &c. Indeed it is from the import of this act that our Lord receives his most familiar designation. The Heb. term for *anoint* is מָשַׁח *mashah,* from which comes מָשִׁיחַ *mashiah* or *Messiah.* Greek Χριστος, *Christ,* i. e. *the Anointed One,* the preeminent and distinguishing appellation of the Savior of men. The consecration of the High Priest to his office was a type of that of Christ, and of this the pouring out of the holy oil was a most beautiful emblem. As oil insinuates itself into and diffuses itself over the body to which it is applied, so the divine nature, the informing Spirit of God, possessed wholly the human person of Jesus, communicating to him all those attributes and perfections which exalted the 'name of Jesus above every name,' and qualified him to act as Mediator between God and man. In the consecration of the Aaronic order, the *inferior* priests were only *sprinkled* with this oil mixed with the blood of the sacrifice, but in the unction of the High Priest the oil was so *copiously poured forth* as to 'run down upon the beard, and even to the skirts of his garments.' It was like 'the dew of Hermon,' says the Psalmist, 'descending upon the mountains of Zion.' This was because it pointed to him who received the Spirit 'without measure.' *He* was 'anointed with the oil of gladness above his fellows;' i. e. above those who pos-

8 And ^h thou shalt bring his sons, and put coats upon them.

9 And thou shalt gird them with girdles (Aaron and his sons) and

^h Lev. 8. 13.

put the bonnets on them; and ⁱ the priest's office shall be theirs for a perpetual statute: and thou shalt ^k consecrate Aaron and his sons.

ⁱ Num. 18. 7. ^k ch. 28. 41. Lev. 8. 22. &c. Hebr. 7. 28.

---

sessed with him a *fellowship* or similarity of office, as types of himself. Aaron was anointed high priest; Saul was anointed king; Elisha was anointed prophet; Melchizedek, king and priest; Moses, priest and prophet; David, king and prophet; yet none was ever anointed to the joint possession of all these dignities together save the *Christ* of God, the antitype of them all. *Christians* derive the *name* of *Christians* from their profession of *Christ*, and the *nature* and *character* of *Christians* from their union to *Christ*. It is their peculiar privilege and distinguishing joy, 'to have the *unction* from the Holy One, and to know all things,' that are necessary for them to know. As the oil which was poured upon Aaron was so copiously effused as to run down to the 'skirts of his clothing,' so the unction of the Holy One was so abundant, that from him as the Head, it ever has and ever will run down to the meanest and weakest believers. And this 'anointing which they receive of him, abideth in them, and teacheth them.' What distinguished honor then, what strong consolation, pertain to them, who are made one with Christ, and who feel the heavenly influences of his Spirit in their souls! They obtain a life from him with which they were not born; and which because it is *his* life can never be destroyed!

8. *And thou shalt bring.* Heb. תקריב *takrib, shalt bring near, shalt cause to approach.* But whether the term is to be understood in a general sense of their being *set apart* or *devoted* to the service of God, or more strictly of their being *brought near* to the door of the Tabernacle, where these consecration-cere-

monies were to be performed, is not certain. They were to be immediately robed in their sacred garments, as the *anointing rite* was to be confined to Aaron as High Priest. These garments were the drawers or breeches, the coat, the girdle, and the bonnet. The first two were like those of the High Priest. The bonnet was probably the same as the mitre worn by the high priest with the slight difference before mentioned. The girdles of the inferior priests were of the same form as that of the high priest; but less costly and of less elegant texture. These four garments were of linen, such as were worn by the Egyptian priests as emblems of innocence. Cicero has observed from Plato, that 'white is a color peculiarly becoming the Deity.'

9. *Put bonnets on them.* Heb. חבשת להם *habashta lahem, shalt bind to them;* a phraseology adapted to the act of *wrapping* a head-dress upon one, whereas our term 'put' is more obviously conformed to the usages with which we are familiar in loosely and lightly covering the head with a cap, hat, or bonnet.——¶ *For a perpetual statute.* Heb. לחקת עולם *lehukkath olam, for a statute of eternity;* i. e. they shall enjoy that office in uninterrupted succession as long as the Aaronical Priesthood itself continued.——¶ *Thou shalt consecrate Aaron and his sons.* This, as we have before remarked, is not the term for the *general act* of consecration here described, but for a *particular ceremony* forming a part of it. The original is מלאת יד *millētha yad, thou shalt fill the hand* of Aaron and his sons; an expression alluding to the fact of some part of the sacrifice being put

10 And thou shalt cause a bullock to be brought before the tabernacle of the congregation; and [1]Aaron

[1] Lev. 1. 4. & 8. 14.

and his sons shall put their hands upon the head of the bullock.

11 And thou shalt kill the bullock before the LORD, *by* the door of the tabernacle of the congregation.

---

into their hands to be waved and then borne to the altar. As sacrificing was a very prominent part of the sacerdotal office, this was a ceremony strikingly significant of the nature of the functions which they were called to discharge; and as it was the first or initiating action that marked their entrance upon the performance of the priestly services, the idea of *consummation* or *perfection* is attached to it, for which reason it is rendered in English by the term *consecrate*, as if it were the crowning ceremony of the whole. So also the Gr. τελειωσεις Ααρων τας χειρας αυτου, και τας χειρας των 'υιων αυτου, *thou shalt consummate, or perfect, the hands of Aaron and the hands of his sons*; i. e. thou shalt do to him, through the medium of his hands, that which shall be virtually the *perfecting* act of investiture upon his person. Arab. 'Thou shalt complete, or perfect, the glory of Aaron and the glory of his sons.' Accordingly in allusion to this the apostle, Heb. 7. 28, says, 'The law maketh men high priests which have infirmity; but the word of the oath, which was since the law, maketh the son who is *consecrated* (τετελειωμενον *perfected*) for evermore. The allusion is probably the same in other cases where the term ' perfect' is applied to Christ, implying an *official* instead of *personal* perfection, or in other words that *fulness of endowment*, and that *completeness of initiation*, which so signally marked the preeminence of his mediatorial character. The usage which elsewhere obtains in regard to the Hebrew phrase may serve to give a still clearer view of its import in this connexion, 1 Chron. 29. 3, 5, 'I have prepared for the holy house—the gold for things of gold, and the silver

for things of silver, and for all manner of work to be made by the hands of artificers. And who then is willing *to consecrate his service* (לְמַלֹּאת יָדוֹ *lemalloth yado, to fill his hands*) this day unto the Lord.' This is obviously an exhortation to a liberal giving to a sacred purpose; and whoever proposes to make a donation takes his gift in his hand, and the larger it is, the more is his hand filled with it. Again, Ex. 32. 28, 29, 'And the children of Levi did according to the word of Moses; and there fell of the people that day about three thousand men. For Moses had said, *Consecrate yourselves* (מִלְאוּ יֶדְכֶם *milu yedkem, fill your hands*) to day to the Lord, even every man upon his son and upon his brother.' This was a kind of *initiating* or *inaugurating* act on the part of the tribe of Levi—a specimen of such thoroughgoing obedience to the divine mandate as to amount to an installing of themselves in the official dignity to which they were destined. It is easy to perceive from all this the true force of the expression. 'The filling of the hands,' says Rab. Solomon, ' is nothing else than an *initiation* when one enters upon any business that he may be confirmed in it from that day forward.' In a somewhat like manner it is said to have been formerly customary in the English church, when a minister was ordained, for the Bishop to put into his hand a Bible indicative of the nature of the work upon which he had now entered, and of which his *hands*, as well as his *head* and his *heart*, were to be *full*.

The Bullock for a Sin-offering.

10. *And thou shalt cause a bullock to be brought*, &c. The due completion

12 And thou [m] shalt take of the blood of the bullock, and put *it*

[m] Lev. 8. 15.

of the various ceremonies above described was followed by the oblation of their sacrifices for Aaron and his sons; (1.) A sin-offering; (2.) A burnt-offering; (3.) A peace-offering. The sin-offering, which here consisted of a bullock, was a kind of expiation by which they were first of all to be purified. By the ceremony of putting their hands upon the head of the victim was signified, (1.) that the offerer had need of a sacrifice to atone for his sins; (2.) that he symbolically transferred his sins to the victim; (3.) that he confided in faith and hope that although he deserved himself to die, yet the death of the animal, which he thus devoted to God, would be accepted as an expiation for his sins, so as to avert from him the punishment which they had righteously incurred. The same ceremony of imposition of hands was enjoined upon every one who brought a sacrifice for his sins, Lev. 4. 24, 29, and the manner of it, as practised by the Jews, is thus particularly described by Maimonides in his Treatise on the Sacrificial Offerings; 'There is no imposing of hands but in the court. If he lay on hands without, he must lay them on again within. None may impose hands but a clean person. In the place where hands are imposed, there they kill the beast immediately after the imposition. He that imposeth must do it with all his might, with both his hands upon the beast's head, not upon the neck or sides; and there may be nothing between his hands and the beast. If the sacrifice be of the most holy things, it standeth on the north side (as Lev. 1. 11.), with the face to the west; the imposer standeth eastward with his face to the west, and layeth his two hands between the two horns, and con-

upon [n] the horns of the altar with thy finger, and pour all the blood beside the bottom of the altar.

[n] ch. 27. 2. & 30. 2.

fesseth sin over the sin-offering and trespass over the trespass-offering, &c., and saith, 'I have sinned; I have committed iniquity; I have trespassed, and done thus and thus, and do return by repentance before thee, and with this I make atonement,'' And what could more strikingly represent the fact that, in the economy of redemption, the sins of men are imputed to Christ, 'upon whom the Lord hath laid the iniquity of us all,' Is. 53. 6—8. With this solemn rite before us, how evangelic and happy the familiar strain of the Christian psalmist;

> My faith would lay her hand
> On that dear head of thine,
> While like a penitent I stand,
> And there confess my sin.

> My soul looks back to see
> The burden thou didst bear,
> When hanging on the cursed tree,
> And hopes her guilt was there.

11. *And thou shalt kill the bullock before the Lord.* That is before the Shekinah. 'Thou shalt kill' is doubtless equivalent to 'thou shalt cause to have killed.' It is not necessary to suppose that Moses, who was not strictly a priest, killed the bullock in person.

12. *Put it on the horns of the altar.* The first sin-offering differed from those ordinarily presented by the priests, in which the blood was carried into the Tabernacle, and applied to the horns of the golden altar of incense, Lev. 4. 3, 7, whereas in the present instance the blood was put upon the horns of the brazen altar of burnt-offering which stood in the court. But the design of this first oblation was to make atonement for the altar itself, and to sanctify it, that it might afterward be fit to sanctify the

13 And ᵒ thou shalt take all the fat that covereth the inwards, and the caul *that is* above the liver, and the two kidneys, and the fat that *is* upon them, and burn *them* upon the altar.

ᵒ Lev. 3. 3.

offerings of the people laid upon it, as is intimated v. 36, 37, and still more plainly taught, Ezek. 43. 25, 26. Besides this, the ceremony did not in this respect differ at this time from that observed by common persons, inasmuch as Aaron and his sons did not become full priests till the period of their seven days' consecration was ended.——¶ *And pour all the blood.* That is, all the rest of the blood.——¶ *Beside the bottom of the altar.* Where there was a trench into which the blood of the sacrifices was poured.

13. *The fat that covereth the inwards.* By the fat that covereth the inwards is meant the thin fatty membrane extended over the intestines, called in Lev. 9. 19, simply ' that which covereth,' and technically denominated the *omentum*—supposed to have been so called from the fact that the heathen diviners derived the good or bad *omens* from the observation of this part of the animal. Although in many instances the ' fat' is said to denote the *best* or *choicest part* of any thing, as is observed upon Gen. 4. 4, yet in other cases it is evidently used as equivalent to that which is *evil*, from the fact that fatness is naturally understood to imply an obtuseness of sensibility. Thus it is said of the wicked, Ps. 119. 70, ' Their heart is as *fat* as grease.' So Deut. 32. 15, 'But Jeshurun *waxed fat* and kicked: thou art waxen fat, thou art grown thick, thou art covered with *fatness;* then he forsook God which made him.' Again, Is. 6. 10, ' Make the heart of this people *fat*, &c., lest they understand,' &c. The ' fat' therefore, as a signal of man's corruption, God ordered to be consumed with fire on the altar, teaching perhaps the necessity of the mortification of our earthly members

by the work of the Spirit of Christ.—— ¶ *The caul that is above the liver.* Heb יתרת על הכבד *yothereth al hakkabëd the redundance of the liver.* Gr. τοͅ λοβον τον ἥπατος, *the lobe of the liver;* i. e. the greater lobe of the liver, which, although a part of the liver itself, may very properly be rendered ' the lobe over or *by* the liver.' As the gall-blad. der is attached to this part of the liver it is probably to be included in the precept of consumption. Parkhurst remarks; 'If the great excellence of this *billious juice*, and its importance to the well-being of the animal, together with its influence and instrumentality in the passions, both concupiscible and irascible, are duly considered, we shall see the reasons why the *gall-bladder* was especially ordered by God to be taken off and consumed on the altar.' Of the moral design of this part of the Jewish ritual the early Jewish commentators say; 'Therefore the kidneys and the fat which is on them, and the caul that covereth the liver, were burnt unto God to make atonement for the sins of men, which proceedeth out of the thoughts of the reins, and the lust of the liver, and the fatness of the heart, for they all consent in sin.'——¶ *And burn them upon the altar.* Heb. הקטרת *hiktarta*, *burn.* The original here is not the word usually employed to signify *consuming by fire.* The Heb. קטר *katar*, in its native import, implies *the making a fume by incense*, and when applied to sacrifices denotes the rising up of their smoke as the vapor of incense, from their peculiar acceptableness to him to whom they were offered. From the same root comes מקטרת *miktoreth*, *a censer, an instrument for fuming incense;* and in the participle נקטר *niktar, perfumed*, we trace the origin of

14 But p the flesh of the bullock, and his skin, and his dung shalt thou burn with fire without the camp: it *is* a sin-offering.

p Lev. 4. 11, 12, 21. Heb. 13. 11.

15 ¶ q Thou shalt also take one ram; and Aaron and his sons shall r put their hands upon the head of the ram.

q Lev. 8. 18. r Lev. 1. 4,—9.

the classic *Nectar*, the fabled beverage of the gods, from their inhaling the perfumed odor of incense as if it were a delightful drink. It was probably to convey a somewhat similar idea that the word is employed in the present connexion, viz., that these bloody sacrifices, rightly and reverently presented, were as *acceptable* as if they had been an offering of incense.

14. *But the flesh, &c., shalt thou burn with fire without the camp.* Here the word for ' burning' is intirely different from that in the former verse, implying a consumption by a *strong fire* and excluding the idea of that grateful incense-like odor which was conveyed by the sacrifice of the fat. It appears to have been ordained with a view to inspire a greater detestation of sin in those sustaining the priestly office. The language of the action was, 'Let all iniquity be *far* from them that bear the vessels of the Lord.' In the case of a sin-offering for the prince or any other person, this usage of burning without the camp was not observed, but as the iniquities of the priests were of a more heinous character, a corresponding brand of reprobation was stamped upon them by this enactment. It was doubtless with a view to indicate that Christ was made a sacrifice under circumstances of the greatest possible ignominy that the apostle, Heb. 13. 12, 13, alludes to this precept of the law; 'Wherefore Jesus also, that he might sanctify the people with his own blood, suffered *without the gate*. Let us go forth, therefore, unto him *without the camp*, bearing his reproach.'——¶ *It is a sin-offering.* Heb. אוּה חַטָּאת *hat-tath hu, it is a sin.* This strong language implied that it must be treated

with abhorrence and consumed by the fire, as if it were *sin* itself. Judging from the usage of the Greek it would seem that the phrase is accurately enough translated, but the expression throws a decided light upon the emphatic language of the apostle, 2 Cor. 5. 21, ' Christ was made *sin* for us, who knew no sin ; that we might be made the righteousness of God in him.'

The Ram for a Burnt-offering.

15. *Thou shalt also take one ram.* That is, one of the two commanded to be taken, v. 1. The remark of Rabbi Levi ben Gerson respecting the design of these several victims may here be appropriately given. 'It is proper to notice the order in which these sacrifices were offered. For first of all an atonement for sins was made by the *sin-offering;* of which nothing but the fat was offered to God (to whom be praise) ; because the offerers were not yet worthy of God's acceptance of a gift and present from them. But after they had been purified, to indicate their being devoted to the sacred office, they immolated to God (to whom be praise) a *holocaust*, which was entirely consumed upon the alter. And after the holocaust they offered a sacrifice resembling a *peace-offering*, of which part used to be given to God, part to the priests, and part to the offerers, and which was to indicate their being now received into favor with God, so as to use one common table with him.' *Outram.* To this we may add, that the ram was *wholly* burnt to the honor of God, in token of the dedication of themselves wholly to God and to his service, as *living sacrifices*, kindled with the fire and ascending in the flame of holy

16 And thou shalt slay the ram, and thou shalt take his blood, and sprinkle *it* round about upon the altar.

17 And thou shalt cut the ram in pieces, and wash the inwards of him, and his legs, and put *them* unto his pieces, and unto his head.

18 And thou shalt burn the whole ram upon the altar: it *is* a burnt-offering unto the LORD: it *is* a ⁵ sweet savour, an offering made by fire unto the LORD.

⁵ Gen. 8. 21.

---

19 ¶ ᵗ And thou shalt take the other ram; and Aaron and his sons shall put their hands upon the head of the ram.

20 Then shalt thou kill the ram, and take of his blood, and put *it* upon the tip of the right ear of Aaron, and upon the tip of the right ear of his sons, and upon the thumb of their right hand, and upon the great toe of their right foot, and sprinkle the blood upon the altar round about.

ᵗ ver. 3. Lev. 8. 22.

---

love.——¶ *Shall put their hands upon the head*, &c. The general import of this action was always the same, viz., to indicate the sinfulness of the offerers, and to prefigure the vicarious sufferings of Christ, the Lamb slain from the foundation of the world. It was done on the present occasion, though the ram offered was a *ram of consecration*, to convey the same impressive lesson that it ordinarily did to those concerned. Upon the priests' initiation into their office they were to be taught the full significancy of the various sacrifices which they were henceforth to be employed in offering.

16. *Shalt take his blood, and sprinkle it*, &c. As nothing is said of any other disposition of any part of the blood, we may suppose it was *all* to be sprinkled about the altar; or, as others conjecture, *poured on the altar round about*, to be consumed or 'licked up' by the fire along with the flesh.

18. *It is a sweet savor.* Heb. רֵיחַ נִיחֹחַ *rëha nihovah, a savor of rest;* i. e. an *appeasing* odor, from its supposed efficacy in *quieting* and *pacifying* the divine displeasure, and rendering the offerer acceptable. Chal. 'That it may be received with favorable acceptation.' Gr. εις οσμην ευωδιας, *for a savor of sweet smell;* an expression adopted by the apostle, Eph. 5. 2. See Note on Gen. 8. 21.

The Ram for a Peace-offering.

20. *Take of the blood, and put it upon the tip*, &c. That the ram now to be offered, and called, v. 22, 'the ram of consecration,' was truly a *peace-offering* will be obvious from what is said in v. 28, 32. It is doubtless called *the ram of consecration* because there was more in this sacrifice that was peculiar to the present occasion than in either of the others. The ceremonies, therefore, were more numerous and significant. The blood instead of being merely sprinkled on the horns of the altar or effused round about it, was shared, as it were, between God and them; part of it being sprinkled, and part put upon them, upon their bodies, and upon their garments. The parts of their persons to which it was applied were no doubt selected with a view to render the rite most replete with instruction relative to the duties of their station. It was intended to imply that they ought to devote diligently their *ears*, their *hands*, and their *feet*, or in other words, all their faculties of mind and body, to the discharge of their ministerial office. By the blood's being applied to the *extreme* parts of the body, they could not but understand that the *whole* person in all its entirety, from the tip of the ear to the toe of the foot, was to be sanctified and set apart to the service of God.

21 And thou shalt take of the blood that *is* upon the altar, and of ^u the anointing oil, and sprinkle *it* upon Aaron, and upon his garments, and upon his sons, and upon the garments of his sons with him: and ^w he shall be hallowed, and

^u ch. 30. 25, 31. Lev. 8. 30. ^w ver. 1. Hebr. 9. 22.

his garments, and his sons, and his sons' garments with him.

22 Also thou shalt take of the ram the fat and the rump, and the fat that covereth the inwards, and the caul *above* the liver, and the two kidneys, and the fat that *is* upon them, and the right shoulder: for it *is* a ram of consecration:

---

21. Upon the garments. This was merely to carry out in all its completeness, and in reference to every thing about them, the significant rite of the sprinkled blood. The apostle tells us, Heb. 9. 22, that ' almost all things were by the law purged with blood'; and as the sacred garments were the badge of that office which enabled them to be instrumental in sanctifying and purifying others, it was manifestly proper that they should themselves receive fully the sign of the same cleansing and consecrating influence. 'We reckon,' says Henry, 'that the blood and oil, sprinkled upon garments, spotted and stained them; yet the holy oil and the blood of the sacrifice, sprinkled upon their garments, must be looked upon as the greatest adorning imaginable to them, for they signified the blood of Christ, and the graces of the Spirit, which constitute and complete the beauty of holiness, and recommend us to God. We read of robes ' made *white* with the blood of the Lamb.' '

22. The fat and the rump. Heb. אַלְיָה *alyah*, defined by Gesenius and Rosenmuller the *thick fatty tail* of the Syrian sheep. Russell in his Natural History of Aleppo, p. 51, after observing that they are in that country much more numerous than those with smaller tails, adds, 'This tail is very broad and large, terminating in a small appendix that turns back upon it. It is of a substance between fat and marrow, and is not eaten separately, but mixed with the lean meat in many of their dishes, and also often used instead of butter.

A common sheep of this sort, without the head, feet, skin, and entrails, weighs about twelve or fourteen Aleppo roto-loes (a rotoloe is five pounds), of which the tail is usually three rotoloes or upwards; but such as are of the largest breed, and have been fattened, will sometimes weigh above thirty rotoloes, and the tail of these ten. These very large sheep being about Aleppo kept up in yards, are in no danger of injuring their tails: but in some other places, where they feed in the fields, the shepherds are obliged to fix a piece of thin board to the under part of their tail, to prevent its being torn by bushes and thistles, as it is not covered underneath with thick wool like the upper part. Some have small wheels to faciliate the dragging of this board after them.' This contrivance is at least as old as Herodotus, who expressly mentions it (Lib. III. c. 115.), where, speaking of the Arabian shepherds' management to prevent this kind of sheep from having their tails rubbed and ulcerated, he says, 'They make little *cars*, and fasten one of these under the *tail* of each sheep.' The Abbe Mariti in his Travels through Cyprus (vol. I. p. 36.) confirms this account of the extraordinary size of the tails of some species of eastern sheep; ' The mutton is juicy and tender. The tails of some of the sheep, which are remarkably fine, weigh *upwards of fifty pounds.*'——¶ *It is a ram of consecration.* Heb. אֵיל מִלֻּאִים הוּא *ēl milluim hu*, *it is a ram of fillings.* Gr. εστι γαρ τελειωσις αυτη, *for this a perfection.* That is, a consecrat-

23 ˣAnd one loaf of bread, and one cake of oiled bread, and one wafer out of the basket of the unleavened bread, that *is* before the LORD.

24 And thou shalt put all in the hands of Aaron, and in the hands of his sons; and shalt ʸwave them *for* a wave-offering before the LORD.

25 ᶻAnd thou shalt receive them of their hands, and burn *them* upon the altar for a burnt-offering, for a sweet savour before the LORD: it *is* an offering made by fire unto the LORD.

ˣLev. 8. 26. ʸLev. 7. 30. ᶻLev. 8. 28.

26 And thou shalt take ᵃthe breast of the ram of Aaron's consecration, and wave it *for* a wave-offering before the LORD: and ᵇit shall be thy part.

27 And thou shalt sanctify ᶜthe breast of the wave-offering, and the shoulder of the heave-offering, which is waved and which is heaved up, of the ram of the consecration, *even* of *that* which *is* for Aaron, and of *that* which *is* for his sons:

28 And it shall be Aaron's and his sons' ᵈby a statute for ever,

ᵃLev. 8. 29. ᵇPs. 99. 6. ᶜLev. 7. 31. 34.
Numb. 18. 11, 18. Deut. 18. 3. ᵈLev. 10. 15.

---

ing initiation by which the incumbents were *perfected* in their official character. The sense of the term is governed by that which we have already assigned to the root in our remarks above, v. 9. Whether it is implied at the same time that *the hands were filled with pieces of the sacrifice*, as an intimation of their duties, cannot be ascertained. However this may be, the explanation given above is sufficient to account for the form of the expression.

23, 24. *And one loaf of bread*, &c. The Note on v. 2, of this chapter will sufficiently explain the reason of the order respecting the articles here mentioned. As to the 'waving' of the whole to and fro, which was ordinarily done by the priests' putting his hand under theirs, and then lifting them first upwards, and then round about in every direction, it was probably intended as a significant mode of dedicating the offering to Him ' whose is the earth and the fulness thereof;' who is the Possessor of heaven, as well as the earth, and claims a universal homage. If, however, we keep up the idea of a *mutual feast* in connexion with the peace-offering, this ceremony of *waving* may perhaps be considered as a virtual act of *offering* or *presenting* a dish to an hon-

ored guest who sits at the table. This God could not do in person, but he would still have that kind of fellowship recognised, and he made the altar his substitute for devouring his part of the sacrifice. The Gr. renders by ἀφοριεῖς, *thou shalt separate*, and Paul uses this term in speaking of his designation to the ministry, Rom. 1. 1, as if he had been made in that office a kind of *wave-offering* to the Lord.——¶ *Shalt wave them for a wave-offering.* Heb. הנפת אתם תנופה *hēnaphta otham tenuphah, thou shalt wave them a waving.* The original root נוף *nuph* signifies properly to *shake, agitate, move to and fro,* or *up and down.*

25. *Burn them upon the altar for a burnt-offering.* Although it is undoubted that this was not a whole burnt-offering, but a peace-offering, yet as some of it was burnt on the altar, that part of it is called *a burnt-offering.* Compare Lev. 3. 5, where all that was to be burnt of the peace-offerings is commanded to be ' burnt upon the burnt sacrifice,' in reference to which act it might very properly be called *a burnt-offering.*

26—28. *And thou shalt take the breast*, &c. These three verses are probably to be regarded as a parenthe-

from the children of Israel: for it *is* an heave-offering: and e it shall be an heave-offering from the children of Israel of the sacrifice of their peace-offerings, *even* their heave-offering unto the LORD.

29 ¶ And the holy garments of Aaron f shall be his sons' after him, g to be anointed therein, and to be consecrated in them.

e Lev. 7. 34. f Numb. 20. 26, 28. g Numb. 18. 8. & 35. 25.

30 *And* h that son that is priest in his stead shall put them on i seven days, when he cometh into the tabernacle of the congregation to minister in the holy *place.*

31 ¶ And thou shalt take the ram of the consecration, and k seethe his flesh in the holy place.

32 And Aaron and his sons shall eat the flesh of the ram, and the

h Numb. 20. 28. i Lev. 8. 35. & 9. 1, 8. k Lev. 8. 31.

---

sis fixing the law for all future time, in relation to the priests' part of the peace-offering, viz., the breast and shoulder. It is true, that on the present occasion these were divided, and the shoulder burnt on the altar with God's part, v. 22, but ever after they were both to go together as the allotted portion of the priests. This, if we may admit the suggestion of Ainsworth, was intended to intimate to them ' how with all their *heart,* and with all their *strength,* they should give themselves unto the service of the Lord in his church.' As to the precise distinction between *wave-offering* (תנופה *tenuphah*) and *heave-offering* (תרומה *terumah*), it is not easy to ascertain it, as we are furnished with no clue in the original, except what we find in the import of the terms; of which we may say in general that the former more properly denotes *horizontal* and the latter *perpendicular* motion. This fact has led Houbigant and some others to imagine that by this twofold movement in the act of oblation we are to recognise a dim and shadowy *figure of the cross,* on which the great Peace-offering between God and man was offered, in the person of the blessed Redeemer. But as this conjecture rests upon no positive *authority,* we build nothing upon it, leaving the reader to deduce his own inferences from the etymology of the words.

29, 30. *And the holy garments of*

Aaron shall be, &c. Another general law is here given, viz., that all the successors of Aaron in the high priesthood should be set apart to the office in the same garments, by the same unction, and, as we learn from v. 36, with the same sacrifices, as those which were prescribed on the present occasion. Accordingly it is said, Num. 20. 28, 'And Moses stripped Aaron of his garments, and put them upon Eleazer his son; and Aaron died there in the top of the mount.' For seven successive days was the high priest to be robed in these sacred vestments, and during that time to abide without intermission at the door of the tabernacle ' keeping the charge of the Lord,' Lev. 8. 35. As the number seven is the Scripture number of *perfection,* and is often used to denote the *completion, consummation,* or *fulness* of any thing, so the act of consecration was to last seven days that it might signify a *perfect* consecration, and to intimate to the priest that his *whole life* was to be devoted to his ministry. It afforded the opportunity also for one Sabbath to pass over him in his consecration, in reference to which the Jewish writers say, ' Great is the Sabbath day; for the high priest entereth not upon his service, after he is anointed, till the Sabbath pass over him, as it is written, Ex. 29. 30, 'Seven days shall he that is priest,' &c.

31, 32. *Seethe his flesh in the holy place.* That is, *boil* his flesh, in order

¹bread that *is* in the basket, *by* the door of the tabernacle of the congregation.

33 And ᵐthey shall eat those things wherewith the atonement was made, to consecrate *and* to sanctify them: ⁿbut a stranger shall not eat *thereof*, because they *are* holy.

34 And if aught of the flesh of the consecrations, or of the bread, remain unto the morning, then ᵒthou shalt burn the remainder

with fire: it shall not be eaten, because it *is* holy.

35 And thus shalt thou do unto Aaron, and to his sons, according to all *things* which I have commanded thee: ᵖseven days shalt thou consecrate them.

36 And thou shalt ᑫoffer every day a bullock *for* a sin-offering for atonement; and thou shalt cleanse the altar, when thou hast made an atonement for it, ʳand thou shalt anoint it, to sanctify it.

---

¹Matt. 12. 4. ᵐLev. 10. 14, 15, 17. ⁿLev. 22. 10. ᵒLev. 8. 32.

ᵖExod. 40. 12. Lev. 8. 33, 34, 35. ᑫHebr. 10. 11. ʳch. 30. 26. 28, 29. & 40. 10.

---

to render it edible. The phrase ' holy place' is here used in a wider sense than ordinary. The next verse shows that it means the outer court of the sanctuary near the door. This is still more expressly affirmed Lev. 8. 31. This requisition as to the place of eating was peculiar to the present occasion. In ordinary cases the allotted parts of the peace-offering might be taken home and there eaten by the offerers and their families, but this was to be eaten in God's own house, as it were, where his ministers officiated and neither sons nor daughters could share with them in it.

33. *A stranger shall not eat thereof because they are holy.* Heb. בִּי קֹדֶשׁ הֵם *ki kodesh hëm, because they are holiness;* i. e. the bread and meats. Or the pronoun ' they' may refer to Aaron and his sons, who are called *holy* because they were *consecrated* to the service of God. ' Stranger' here signifies one that is not of the family of Aaron. Holy things for holy men was the motto of the Levitical economy.

36. *For atonement.* Heb. עַל הַכִּפֻּרִים *al hakkippurim,* pl. *for expiations, propitiations, reconciliations;* meaning for Aaron and his sons, and the altar. The original term implies both the *pacification* of God's wrath on account of sin, and the merciful *covering* of trans-

gression, which enter so essentially into the idea of *atonement.* See Note on Gen. 32. 20.——¶ *Thou shalt cleanse the altar.* Heb. חִטֵּאתָ *hittëtha.* Leclerc well remarks that this word in Piel when spoken of *persons* signifies to *expiate, to atone for,* but when applied to things *to purge, cleanse, purify,* as here. Gr. καθαριεῖς, *thou shalt purify.* It is not to be supposed that this period of seven days allotted to the consecration of the altar was *distinct* from the seven days of consecrating the priests, or that the atonements in the one case were different from those in the other. They were in fact one and the same. The atoning virtue of the sacrifices applied itself at the same time both to the persons sanctified and to the altar. The phrase ' when thou hast made atonement *for* it,' should rather be rendered ' when thou hast made an atonement *upon* it,' and the meaning is, that during all the time in which they were engaged from day to day in offering the prescribed sacrifices, they were to be careful to keep the altar duly cleansed, to have the ashes removed, and the unction applied to it, so that at the end of the time it should be an altar duly consecrated, like those who had been ministering at it, so that henceforth it should be so preeminently holy as to confer a

37 Seven days thou shalt make
an atonement for the altar, and
sanctify it; [s] and it shall be an altar most holy: [t] whatsoever toucheth the altar shall be holy.
38 ¶ Now this *is that* which thou
shalt offer upon the altar; [u] two
lambs of the first year [w] day by
day continually.
39 The one lamb thou shalt offer
[x] in the morning: and the other
lamb thou shalt offer at even:

[s] ch. 40. 10. [t] ch. 30. 29. Matt. 23, 19. [u] Numb. 28. 3. 1 Chron. 16. 40. 2 Chron. 2. 4. & 13. 11. & 31. 3. Ezra 3. 3. [w] See Dan. 9. 27. & 12. 11. [x] 2 Kings 16. 15. Ezek. 46. 13, 14, 15.

40 And with the one lamb a tenth-
deal of flour mingled with the
fourth part of an hin of beaten oil:
and the fourth part of an hin of
wine *for* a drink-offering.
41 And the other lamb thou shalt
[y] offer at even, and shalt do thereto
according to the meat-offering of
the morning, and according to the
drink-offering thereof, for a sweet
savour, an offering made by fire
unto the LORD.
42 *This shall be* [z] a continual burnt-

[y] 1 Kings 18. 29, 36. 2 Kings 16. 15. Ezra 9. 4, 5. Ps. 141. 2. Dan. 9. 21. [z] ver. 38. ch. 30. 8. Numb. 28. 6. Dan. 8. 11, 12, 13.

---

relative holiness upon the gifts laid upon it. 'Whatsoever toucheth it shall be holy,' upon which our Savior's brief and pithy comment is, 'The altar sanctifieth the gift.' Like a magnetized bar of iron or steel, it was first to receive itself a sanctifying influence from the oblations presented upon it, and then for ever after to impart it.

Law of the Daily Offering.

38—44. *This is that which thou shalt offer*, &c. Two lambs of the first year were to be offered daily, the one in the morning, the other in the afternoon, for a burnt-offering. These were generally termed the *morning* and *evening daily sacrifice*, and were never on any account to be intermitted. Other additional sacrifices were appointed for Sabbaths and festivals on various occasions, but they were never to be allowed to displace, supersede, or interfere with this stated and constant offering, which was binding in its observance inasmuch as it typified the never-ceasing necessity and efficacy of the atonement made by the 'Lamb of God which taketh away the sins of the world.' It conveyed also to the people of God of that age and of every age a significant intimation of the duty of daily morning and evening worship. As regularly as the sun rises and declines in his daily round, the spiritual sacrifices of prayer and praise are to be offered upon the altar of our domestic or private devotion; and not only should no business be suffered to jostle them out of their appropriate seasons, but they should be regarded as a sacred feast to the soul, for which we should long as earnestly as for the food that sustains our bodies. It was probably with a view to render this idea more familiar to their minds that the several particulars requisite to a feast accompanied the sacrifice. Bread and wine for a meat and drink-offering formed a part of the commanded oblation, as a continual remembrance of the privilege of fellowship and communion with God to which they are admitted. The word rendered *tenth-deal* (עשרון *issaron*) means a *tenth of an ephah*, or about three quarts wine-measure, being the same as an omer A *hin* contained a gallon and two pints; the fourth part of this was consequently about one quart and a quarter of a pint wine-measure.——¶ *Where I will meet you* (pl.) *to speak there unto thee* (sing.). As if he spake unto all the congregation when he spake to Moses, their representative. Yet as if this might appear to indicate something unduly *exclusive* —a privilege vouchsafed to Moses but denied to them—he gives the assurance in the next verse in the most uni

offering throughout your generations *at* the door of the tabernacle
of the congregation before the
LORD: a where I will meet you to
speak there unto thee.

43 And there I will meet with
the children of Israel; and *the tabernacle* b shall be sanctified by my
glory.

a ch. 25. 22. & 30. 6, 36. Numb. 17. 4. b ch.
40. 34. 1 Kings 8. 11. 2 Chron. 5. 14. & 7.
1, 2, 3. Ezek. 43. 5. Hag. 2. 7, 9. Mal. 3. 1.

44 And I will sanctify the tabernacle of the congregation, and the
altar: I will c sanctify also both
Aaron and his sons, to minister to
me in the priest's office.

45 And d I will dwell among the
children of Israel, and will be their
God.

c Lev. 21. 15. & 22. 9, 16. d Exod. 25. 8.
Lev. 26. 12. Zech. 2. 10. John 14. 17, 23
2 Cor. 6. 16. Rev. 21. 3.

versal terms—' There I will meet with
the children of Israel;' with *all* of
them; they shall *all* have the benefit
of this high distinction. Chal. 'And
I will appoint my Word unto you, that
he may speak with you there.' This
promise is still farther amplified in
what follows; 'And the tabernacle shall
be sanctified by my glory.' Heb. נקדש
בכבדי *nikdash bikbodi;* where the verb
has no specific nominative, leaving us
to understand the expression in its
largest sense, as implying that *every
thing*, people, tabernacle, altar, and
priesthood, should be illustriously hallowed by the glory of the divine presence, the visible symbol of which was
to be seen in the Shekinah enthroned
in the Most Holy Place. It will be observed that the marginal reading of the
English Bible is, '*Israel* shall be sanctified.' This is very admissible grammatically, and is no doubt favored by
the parallel promise, Ezek. 37. 28, to
which the present has clearly an ultimate or typical reference, 'And the
heathen shall know that I the Lord do
sanctify Israel, when my sanctuary shall
be in the midst of them for evermore.'
As the *glory* of God is in a great measure identified with his *tabernacle* in
which it dwelt, the *sanctifying* virtue of
the one was that of the other, so that the
two passages are plainly of kindred import. But this interpretation makes no
less true or pertinent the remark of Henry, that ' what is sanctified *to* the glory
of God, shall be sanctified *by* his glory.'

45. *And I will dwell among the children of Israel*, &c. Heb. ושכנתי *veshakanti, and I will tabernacle.* Chal.
' I will make my majesty (שכנתי *shekinti, my shekinah*) to dwell in the
midst of the children of Israel.' The
'Shekinah' here is the same as the
Word of v. 42, according to the same
version. On the peculiar force of this
word and its etymological relations,
see Note on Ex. 25. 8, where we have
expounded at some length what we
conceive to be the genuine import of
this promise. Its primary fulfilment
was the grand central fact in the history of the Jewish people for century
after century, as long as their national
polity continued. To this peculiar indwelling among the chosen race the
tabernacle and the temple were entirely
subservient. They were each in its
turn the palace of the Great King. It
was not simply a *spiritual* but a *sensible* residence of the Deity, which hallowed those sacred structures. That
this mode of habitation and manifestation was indeed typical of a future indwelling of God by his enlightening
Spirit in the hearts of men, cannot be
questioned. It is a view of the subject
expressly recognised by the apostle,
2 Cor. 6. 16, 'For ye are the temple of
the living God; as God hath said, I
will dwell in them and walk in them;
and I will be their God, and they shall
be my people.' But nothing is clearer
from the prophecies, than that this form
of fulfilment does not *exhaust* the rich

46 And they shall know that e I *am* the LORD their God, that brought

e ch. 20. 2.

them forth out of the land of Egypt, that I may dwell among them: I *am* the LORD their God.

---

purport of the promise. It is a promise no less made to Israel in their *future restoration,* than at their *original adoption;* and in that relation is no less literally to be understood, though far more gloriously, than in the present annunciation. So far as we are able to see, the literal restoration and return of the Jews are assured to us by no other principles of interpretation, than those which require us to admit the literal return and re-establishment of the manifested glory of Jehovah, the true Shekinah, in visible communication with the children of men on earth. Let the following passages, for instance, be taken as a specimen: Zech. 2. 10—12, ' Sing and rejoice, O daughter of Zion: for lo, I come *and I will dwell in the midst of thee* (שכנתי *shakanti*), saith the Lord. And many nations shall be joined to the Lord in that day, and shall be my people: *and I will dwell in the midst of thee* (שכנתי *shakanti*), and thou shalt know that the Lord of hosts hath sent me unto thee. And the Lord shall inherit Judah his portion in the holy land, and shall choose Jerusalem again.' Ezek. 37. 21—28, 'And say unto them, Thus saith the Lord God ; Behold, I will take the children of Israel from among the heathen, whither they be gone, and will gather them on every side, and bring them into their own land: And I will make them one nation in the land upon the mountains of Israel ; and one king shall be king to them all: and they shall be no more two nations, neither shall they be divided into two kingdoms any more at all: Neither shall they defile themselves any more with their idols, nor with 'heir detestable things, nor with any of their transgressions; but I will save them out of all their dwelling-places, wherein they have sinned, and will

cleanse them: so shall they be my people, and I will be their God. And David my servant shall be king over them; and they all shall have one shepherd: they shall also walk in my judgments, and observe my statutes, and do them. And they shall dwell in the land that I have given unto Jacob my servant, wherein your fathers have dwelt, and they shall dwell therein, even they, and their children, and their children's children for ever: and my servant David shall be their prince for ever. Moreover I will make a covenant of peace with them ; it shall be an everlasting covenant with them ; and I will place them, and multiply them, and *will set my sanctuary in the midst of them for evermore. My tabernacle* (משכן *mishkan*) *also shall be with them: yea, I will be their God, and they shall be my people.* And the heathen shall know that I the Lord do *sanctify Israel, when my sanctuary shall be in the midst of them for evermore.*' We have given this extract at full length, because there is scarcely in the whole compass of the Scriptures a more direct and unequivocal prediction of the *literal* return of the Jews to their own land, than is to be found in these words. That it is a return yet future is clear from the fact ; (1.) That the two grand divisions of the nation, the houses of Judah and Israel, are both to be restored, which it is well known was not the case at the return from Babylon. No past period can be assigned when this prediction can be fairly said to have been fulfilled. (2.) They are to be gathered under the headship of 'David their king,' which is undoubtedly the mystical denomination of the Messiah. He is probably here called 'David' more especially because he shall reign over the two united nations of Judah and Israel, as did the

CHAPTER XXX.

AND thou shalt make ᵃan altar ᵇto burn incense upon: *of* shittim-wood shalt thou make it.

ᵃ ch. 37. 25. & 40. 5. ᵇ See ver. 7. 8, 10.
Lev. 4. 7, 18. Rev. 8. 3.

2 A cubit *shall be* the length thereof, and a cubit the breadth thereof; four-square shall it be; and two cubits *shall be* the height thereof: the horns thereof *shall be* of the same.

---

literal David before the kingdom was divided. That Christ will ever rule over his people *by this title* in any other world than the present, we can gather no evidence from the Scriptures. Accordingly Newcome remarks upon the passage, that ' it favors the supposition that Christ will hereafter assume royal state on earth among the converted Jews.' (3.) It is said, v. 25, 'They shall dwell therein, even they, and their children, and their children's children, *for ever;* and my servant David shall be their prince *for ever.*' Even though this language should be taken to mean something short of absolute eternity, yet it is clear that it has never yet been fulfilled. Consequently its fulfilment is still future ; and we are utterly unable to see why it is not quite as certain that the *visible glory* will be restored to the land of promise as that the *chosen people* will. If further evidence of this be necessary we find it in Ezek. 43, 1—4, which is a prediction having respect to the destinies of the Jewish race in the latter day, after their re-establishment in the land of their fathers ; ' Afterward he brought me to the gate, even the gate that looketh toward the east: And behold, *the glory of the God of Israel* came from the way of the east: and his voice was like a noise of many waters: and the earth shined with his glory. And it was according to the appearance of the vision which I saw, even according to the vision that I saw when I came to destroy the city: and the visions were like the visions that I saw by the river Chebar ; and I fell upon my face. And the *glory of the Lord* came into the house by the way **of the gate whose prospect is toward**

the east.' This is no other, as will appear upon strict examination, than the glory of the Shekinah which dwelt between the Cherubim in the Temple, and which on account of the sins of the nation had forsaken its ancient dwelling-place, Ezek. 10. 18—20, but which is here announced as again returning to its vacated habitation. This glory, however, will be the glory of the person of Christ, in whom the shadow of the Shekinah is turned into substance. It is this which constitutes the criterion of identity between the prophetic Jerusalem of Ezekiel and that of John in the Apocalypse ; ' And he showed me that great city the holy Jerusalem, descending out of heaven from God, *having the glory of God.*' But in regard to this sublime annunciation we must for the present rest contented with the simple *fact* assured to us. The *manner* of its accomplishment is hidden by a vail which only the developements of time and providence can remove.

Chapter 30

THE ALTAR OF INCENSE.

1, 2. *Thou shalt make an altar to burn incense upon.* Heb. מזבח מקטר קטרת *mizbëah miktar ketoreth, an incense-altar of incense;* or, *an altar, a perfumatory of perfume.* Gr. θυσιαστηριον θυμιαματος, *an altar of incense.* Chal. 'Thou shalt make an altar to offer upon it incense of sweet spices.' The original implies an altar on which odorous substances were to be burnt and resolved into a fragrant and grateful fume. In the subsequent account of its construction, Ex. 37. 25, it is called simply an 'altar of incense,' as

3 And thou shalt overlay it with pure gold, the top thereof, and the sides thereof round about, and the horns thereof; and thou shalt make unto it a crown of gold round about.

---

rendered by the Greek here, and in Num. 4. 11, 'the golden altar,' as the other covered with brass was called 'the brazen altar.' But as the Hebrew term for *altar* (מזבח *mizbëah,* from זבח *zabah, to slay*), legitimately carries with it the idea of *slain sacrifices,* and as no such service was performed upon this, it is for distinction sake termed מקטר *miktar,* from קטר *katar, to fume, to fumigate, to make to smoke.* The practice of burning incense upon altars as a religious rite is to be traced to a very remote antiquity ; but we have nothing *more* ancient in the way of historic record relative to this custom than what the present chapter contains. It seems scarcely probable, however, that the custom originated on this occasion in the order here prescribed. Incense altars appear in the most ancient Egyptian paintings, and when it was required to be compounded 'after the art of the apothecary (perfumer),' it would seem to be implied that this was an art which was practised, and which the Israelites had learned, in Egypt. Plutarch moreover assures us, that the Egyptians offered incense to the sun—resin in the morning, myrrh at noon, and about sunset an aromatic compound which they called *kypi.* But the custom was in ancient times•by no means confined to Egypt. It pervaded all the religions of antiquity, and like many other features of the Hebrew worship may have been derived from an antediluvian origin. Nor are we disposed to overlook the circumstance in this connexion of incense being burnt among the Orientals by way of honorary tribute to kings, princes, and persons of distinction. It is one of the usages peculiar to palaces, and the houses of the wealthy and great, and as God in the character of Theocratic

Ruler of Israel saw fit to be honored in modes analogous to those which were common in reference to eastern sovereigns, so he would not have *his* palace, the Sanctuary, to be lacking in a usage of such striking significancy. But we shall hope to evince in the sequel that this came far short of fulfilling *all* the symbolical purposes which were answered by this remarkable portion of the furniture of the Tabernacle. Of the remark of Maimonides that incense was burnt in the Tabernacle to counteract the offensive smell of the sacrifices, we can only say, that although this may have been to a very limitted degree the *effect* of the ordinance, it fell altogether short of being its main *object.* As to its materials and form this Altar was made like the Ark of shittim-wood overlaid with plates of gold. When it is said to have been ' four-square,' the meaning is, not that it was, as a whole, of a cubical form, but that upon its upper and under surface it showed four equal sides. It was, however, twice as *high* as it was *broad,* being twenty-one inches broad, and three feet six inches high. From the four corner posts arose four *horns* or *pinnacles,* doubtless of similar form to those of the altar of sacrifice, which were covered with gold like the rest, and its top was surrounded with an ornamental ledge or border of solid gold, here called ' a crown,' like that which adorned the upper edges of the Ark of the Covenant and of the Table of Shewbread. Beneath this were placed two golden rings, probably on the opposite corners, for the conveniency of carrying it on staves during the marches of Israel in the wilderness, and afterwards when removed to different places in Canaan.

3. *The top thereof.* Heb. גגּ *gaggo, his*

roof; implying that its top was fashioned like the flat roofs of eastern houses. These were furnished with parapets, battlements, or balustrades, to which the border or crown of the altar bore, on a small scale, a striking resemblance. The rendering of the Gr. εσχαραν, *hearth,* and the Lat. Vulg. 'Craticula' *grate,* is entirely erroneous, as the original word is different from that applied to the *grate* of the brazen altar (מכבר)

mikbar), and there is not the least mention made of cleansing the Altar from ashes, or of any thing to receive them. The incense was not burnt upon a grate, but in a golden censer which was placed, filled with coals, upon the Altar, so that no ashes or refuse whatever fell upon the Altar.——¶ *The sides thereof.* Heb. קירתיו *kirothauv, his walls;* in continued analogy with the structure of a house.

THE ALTAR OF INCENSE.

The mystical design of the Altar of Incense now demands attention. Its primary use is sufficiently evident from its name, and from what is said in the subsequent verses. As the Table was for the Bread, the Candlestick for the Lights, and the brazen Altar for the Sacrifices, so the golden Altar was for the Incense which was to be burnt upon it. Now that the general import of *incense* as a symbol was that of *prayer,* cannot be questioned by any one who casts his eye over the following passages; Ps. 141. 2, 'Let my *prayer* be set forth before thee (as) *incense;* and the lifting up of my hands as the evening sacrifice. Rev. 5. 8, 'And when he had taken the book, the four beasts and four and twenty elders fell down before the Lamb, having every one of them lamps and golden vials full of odors, *which*

are the prayers of saints.' Again, Rev. 8. 3, 4, 'And another angel came and stood at the altar, having a golden censer; and there was given unto him much incense, that he should offer it *with the prayers of all saints* upon the golden altar which was before the throne. And the smoke of the incense, which came with the prayers of the saints, ascended up before God out of the angel's hand.' Here it is evidently implied that while the sacerdotal angel was officiating at the golden Altar, the saints were to be at the same time engaged in offering up prayers which might, as it were, mingle with the fragrant incense, and both come up in a grateful and acceptable cloud before God. In like manner it is said, Luke, 1. 9, 10, that while Zechariah was 'executing the priest's office according to the custom, his lot was 'o burn incense when he went into the temple of the Lord. And the whole multitude of the people *were praying without at the time of incense.*' Here the two services were performed together, the one being an emblem of the other. As then the idea of *prayer* is prominent in the symbolical purport of the act of offering incense, we may safely consider the *intercessory* office of Christ in heaven as primarily shadowed forth by the golden Altar and its Levitical uses. As the brazen Altar which was placed *without* the sanctuary typified his *sacrifice*, which was made on earth, so the Altar of Incense stationed *within* the sanctuary represented his *interceding* work above, where he has gone to appear in the presence of God for us, and where his intercession is as sweet-smelling savor. This is to be inferred from the fact that it occupied a *place*—directly before the mercy seat—which represented the appropriate sphere of the Savior's *present* mediatorial functions. Whatever service was performed by the priests *within the precincts of the Tabernacle* had a more special and emphatic reference to Christ's work *in heaven;* whereas their duties in the outer court had more of an *earthly* bearing, representing the oblations which were made on *the part* of sinners, and on behalf of sinners, *to* the holy majesty of Jehovah. As, however, scarcely any of the objects or rites of the ancient economy had an *exclusive* typical import, but combined many in one, so in the present case, nothing forbids us to consider the prayers and devotions of the saints as also symbolically represented by the incense of the golden Altar. As a matter of fact, they *do* pray below while Christ intercedes above ; their prayers mingle with his ; and it is doing no violence to the symbol to suppose their spiritual desires, kindled by the fire of holy love, to be significantly set forth by the uprising clouds of incense, which every morning and evening filled the holy place of the sanctuary with its grateful perfume.

Still it may be doubted whether the full and complete design of the golden Altar as a symbol can be reached, without assigning to it, as well as to the Candlestick and the Table, a *prospective* reference. Can it be in keeping with the rest of the furniture of the Tabernacle, unless it points to the heavenly state as yet to be developed ? *There* no Altar of sacrifice is found, because the one offering of the Savior was consummated in his oblation of himself upon the cross. But the Altar of Incense is there, and it bears a name (מזבח *mizbēah*), the leading idea of which is that of *slain sacrifice.* Why is this idea to be carried forward into the upper sanctuary in connexion with a structure intended mainly as a shadow of *prayer, thanksgiving,* and *praise?* Why, but to intimate that there is still, and is ever to be, to the saints a real and indissoluble connexion between the *atonement* of Christ and the *praises* and *doxologies* in which they are engaged in heaven? — between *acquittal from guilt* and *acceptance to favor ?* Were it not for the virtue of his *atoning sacrifice* how could they be in heaven to *praise* him at all? In the ministrations of the earthly sanctuary, the coals on which the incense was burnt on the golden Altar were to be taken from the brazen Altar. This taught the Israelite from whence the efficacy and acceptableness of their prayers and praises was derived. So in the heavenly sanctuary, the instrument of incense is called by the otherwise inappropriate name of *altar* (sacrificatory) to keep its blessed inhabitants in mind of the fact, that the *blood of atonement* and the *fire of sacrifice,* must be for ever that which imparts all its grateful fragrance to the songs, ascriptions, and hallelujahs of the ransomed throng in glory.

4 And two golden rings shalt thou make to it under the crown of it, by the two corners thereof, upon the two sides of it shalt thou make it; and they shall be for places for the staves to bear it withal.

5 And thou shalt make the staves of shittim-wood, and overlay them with gold.

6 And thou shalt put it before the vail that is by the ark of the testimony, before the c mercy-seat that is over the testimony, where I will meet with thee.

c ch. 25. 21, 22.

7 And Aaron shall burn thereon d sweet incense every morning when e he dresseth the lamps, he shall burn incense upon it.

8 And when Aaron lighteth the lamps at even, he shall burn incense upon it; a perpetual incense before the LORD, throughout your generations.

9 Ye shall offer no f strange incense thereon, nor burnt-sacrifice, nor meat-offering; neither shall ye pour drink-offering thereon.

d ver. 34. 1 Sam. 2. 28. 1 Chron. 23. 13. Luke 1. 9. e ch. 27. 21. f Lev. 10. 1.

6. *Thou shalt put it before the vail*, &c. That is, before the separating vail suspended between the Holy and Most Holy Place of the Tabernacle. It would of course be 'before the mercy-seat,' though the Vail interposed. It was stationed about midway between the Candlestick and Table of Shew-bread, though considerably nearer to the Vail than either.

7, 8. *Aaron shall burn thereon sweet incense every morning.* Heb. קטרת סמים *ketoreth sammim, incense of spices.* Gr. θυμιαμα συνθετον λεπτον, *incense delicately campounded.* It might seem from the letter, that Aaron or the High Priest alone was entitled to burn incense on this Altar. But the word 'Aaron' is often used to designate *the whole priestly order.* There is no doubt that Aaron did in person perform this service on the present occasion, and the High Priest, whoever he was, did the same on other great occasions; but it was ordinarily executed by the inferior priests in their courses. Whatever priest was appointed by lot to be in waiting during the week, he every morning and evening filled his censer with fire from the brazen Altar, and introducing the sacred incense went into the holy place and set the censer upon the Altar. As the *daily sacrifice* represented the perpetual efficacy of Christ's

atonement, so the *burning of incense morning and evening* typified his *continual intercession* for us. This offered incense was called a 'perpetual incense' because it was regularly offered at the appointed time without cessation. By a like phraseology we are exhorted to 'pray without ceasing,' i. e. to continue in the daily practice of prayer without omitting it. The command to have the incense burnt at the same time that the lamps were dressed gives occasion to Henry to remark in his ordinary spiritualizing vein, that it was designed 'to teach us, that the reading of the Scriptures, which are our light and lamp, is a part of our daily work, and should accompany our prayers and praises. When we speak to God, we must hear what God says to us, and thus the communion is complete.'—— ¶ *When Aaron lighteth.* Heb. בהעלת *be-haäloth, when he causeth to ascend;* a phraseology the ground of which is explained in the Note on Ex. 27. 20.—— ¶ *At even.* Heb. בין הערבים *bën ha-arbayim, between the two evenings.* See Note on Ex. 12. 16.

9. *Ye shall offer no strange incense thereon.* That is, incense of a different composition from that prescribed, v. 34. Gr. θυμιαμα ἑτερον, *another incense.* Chal. 'Incense of strange spices.' The incense was to be that alone which God

10 And ᵍ Aaron shall make an atonement upon the horns of it once in a year, with the blood of the sin-offering of atonements: once in the year shall he make

ᵍ Lev. 16. 18. & 23. 27.

atonement upon it throughout your generations: it *is* most holy unto the LORD.

11 ¶ And the LORD spake unto Moses, saying,

---

had appointed; and special care was to be taken to make no confusion between the offerings belonging to the respective altars, of which the one kind was for *atonement*, the other for *acceptance* only. So when drawing nigh to God in prayer, we are not to bring the fervor of mere animal spirits, which may easily be mistaken for true devotion; but a broken and a contrite heart, which alone sends forth an odor that is well-pleasing to God. Nor are we to imagine that by our *prayers*, or by any thing else that we can bring to God, we can *atone* for sin, or contribute in the least degree towards the efficacy of Christ's atonement. These must be kept quite distinct; and whilst our prayers are offered on the Altar of Incense, our pleas must be taken solely from the Altar of Burnt-offering.

10. *Aaron shall make atonement upon the horns of it once in a year.* This was to be upon what was called the great day of Atonement, of which a full account is given Lev. 10. 1—28. The ordinance was peculiarly striking, as it intimated that all the services performed at it were imperfect, that the Altar itself had contracted a degree of impurity from the sinfulness of those who ministered there, and that even the very odors of the daily incense needed to be sweetened by a fresh infusion of the savor of the blood of sprinkling.—This mention of atonement made upon the horns of the Altar affords a fair occasion for an attempted explication of a passage in the Apocalypse, c. 9. 13, 14, which commentators have for the most part passed over with a very superficial notice; 'And the sixth angel sounded, and I heard a voice from the four horns

of the golden Altar which is before God, saying to the sixth angel who had the trumpet, Loose the four angels which are bound in the great river Euphrates.' The question is, What is implied in the fact of this voice being represented as proceeding from the four 'horns of the golden Altar?' In answer to this it may be observed, that the cases mentioned Ex. 21. 24. 1 Kings, 1. 50. 1 Kings, 2. 28, clearly evince that the horns of the Altar were constituted an asylum for those who had been guilty of undesigned transgressions. It is true indeed that in these instances allusion seems to be had more especially to the Altar of holocausts standing in the court of the Tabernacle, but as the blood of atonement was sprinkled in like manner upon the horns of both the brazen and the golden altar, it is to be inferred, we imagine, by a parity of reasoning that the horns of the Altar are in general a symbol of divine protection, or of a secure sanctuary for those whose crimes are of a remissible nature. But as the sin to be punished by the voice of the sixth trumpet was that of idolatry, as appears from Rev. 9. 20, 21, which in a whole people is less pardonable in the sight of God than any other, the voice issuing from the four horns of the golden Altar, is a virtual proclamation that God was about to withdraw his protection from a portion of idolatrous Christendom, and to send upon it a plague of far more desolating character than that of the locusts which had preceded. For in the case of the locust-wo, commandment was given that men should be tormented, but not killed. But in that of the sixth trumpet, the Euphratean horsemen were appointed t-

12 h When thou takest the sum of the children of Israel after their number, then shall they give every man i a ransom for his soul unto the LORD, when thou numberest them: that there be no k plague among them when *thou* numberest them.

13 l This they shall give, every one that passeth among them that are numbered, half a shekel, after the shekel of the sanctuary: (m a shekel *is* twenty gerahs:) n an half shekel *shall be* the offering of the LORD.

h ch. 38. 25. Numb. 1. 2, 5. & 26. 2. 2 Sam. 24. 2. i Job 33. 24. & 36. 18. Ps. 49. 7. Matt. 20. 28. Mark 10. 45. 1 Tim. 2. 6. 1 Pet. 1 18, 19. k 2 Sam. 24. 15. l Matt. 17. 24. m Lev. 27. 25. Numb. 3. 47. Ezek. 45. 12. n ch. 38. 26.

---

ed to *slay* the third part of men. The voice therefore in this vision of the prophet is to be understood as a sign that neither atonement nor protection were any longer to be afforded by the horns of the Altar to those who were the destined victims of the impending judgments. The consequence was that a great part of degenerate Christendom was speedily overrun by myriads of the Turkish cavalry, carrying wasting and destruction in their progress.

THE ATONEMENT-MONEY, OR RANSOM-TAX.

12—16. *When thou takest the sum,* &c. That is, when thou makest a census; which Moses is not indeed here expressly *commanded* to do, but which it is supposed, from its intrinsic utility and propriety, he *would* do, as would also his successors in the government of Israel in after ages. It seems to be a general direction as to the mode of raising the requisite revenues for supporting the expenses of the Tabernacle worship. The original *building* and *furnishing* the sanctuary was provided for by the voluntary contributions of

14 Every one that passeth among them that are numbered, from twenty years old and above, shall give an offering unto the LORD.

15 The o rich shall not give more, and the poor shall not give less than half a shekel, when *they* give an offering unto the LORD to make an p atonement for your souls.

16 And thou shalt take the atonement-money of the children of Israel, and q shalt appoint it for the service of the tabernacle of the congregation; that it may be r a memorial unto the children of Israel before the LORD, to make an atonement for your souls.

o Job 34. 19. Prov. 22. 2. Ephes. 6. 9. Col. 3. 25. p ver. 12. q ch. 38. 25. r Numb. 16. 40.

---

the people; but the necessary charges for *sustaining* the worship now to be established were to be defrayed from other sources, and the present order seems to come in as a kind of reply to the question which would be naturally but tacitly asked, 'How are the inevitable expenses of such a system of worship to be met?' The passage before us contains the desired information. The Most High foreseeing that the custom of taking a census, not annually perhaps, but occasionally, would obtain among the chosen people, now orders that an assessment, or poll-tax, of half a shekel each, should be grafted upon this custom, and that this should be the ordinary revenue for the support of the ritual. But why is this tax called a 'ransom or atonement (כֹּפֶר ke-phor) for the soul?' The word 'atonement' naturally suggests the idea of *expiation for sin;* but can silver or gold or any thing short of the blood of the 'Lamb slain from the foundation of the world,' avail to propitiate the justice of God, and serve as a 'ransom for the soul?' The true answer to the question depends upon a correct inter-

17 ¶ And the LORD spake unto Moses, saying,

18 ˢ Thou shalt also make a

ˢ ch. 38. 8. 1 Kings 7. 38.

pretation of the language. The term 'soul' in this connexion is equivalent to 'life,' 'person,' 'self,' as explained in the Note on Gen. 14. 21. It was therefore *a ransom for their lives*, or in other words, a tribute paid to God by way of acknowledgment that they had originally received their lives from him, that they had forfeited their lives to him, and that their continued preservation in being under these circumstances was owing to his more sovereign forbearance and patience; and that consequently he might most justly claim from them whatever he might see fit to demand, for the support of institutions of which they themselves at the same time were to reap the great advantage. The payment of the tax of half a shekel, therefore, was an act of homage to their sovereign Lord, by which they would express their dependence upon him for their spared lives and continued mercies, and deprecate those plagues and judgments which their sins had deserved. This tax was to be assessed upon those who were twenty years old and upward, women, minors, and probably very old men being exempted; and by the same sum being fixed for all, rich and poor, it was strongly intimated that all lives, or persons, were in the sight of God of *equal value*. So in the higher atonement which Christ has wrought, the same price had to be paid for the soul of the lowest, weakest, meanest believer, as for the greatest philosopher, prince, or potentate that shall taste of his salvation.——¶ *Every one that passeth among them*. In allusion perhaps to the customary mode of numbering and marking flocks of sheep, which were made to *pass* before the numberer that he might count them one by one. See Note on Lev. 27. 32. Comp. Jer. 33. 13.——¶ *Shekel of the*

sanctuary. So called, it is supposed, from the fact of the standard of weights and measures being kept in the sanctuary. This might have been the case under the Temple, but it seems in the highest degree unlikely that such a custom obtained at this early period. And yet we know of no *other* reason for the use of this peculiar designation. On the name and value of the ancient Hebrew shekel see Note on Gen. 20. 16. A half a shekel was not far from twenty-five cents of our money.—— ¶ *That it may be a memorial unto the children of Israel before the Lord.* That is, a memorial at once *of* them and *for* them; a memorial testifying to their obedience, and reminding them of what they owed to their heavenly Benefactor. We read of different memorials in the sacred Scriptures. The censers in which Korah and his company offered incense were taken out of the fire in which the offerers perished, and made into plates to be a covering of the altar; ' to be a *memorial* that none but the seed of Aaron come near to offer incense before the Lord.' The jewels and bracelets of which the Israelites spoiled the slaughtered Midianites were presented to the Lord ' as a *memorial* unto the children of Israel,' that not one of their army fell, though the whole Midianitish kingdom was utterly destroyed. So the half shekels at the numbering of the people would serve as a remembrancer of all the interesting facts connected with the occasion of their past deliverance, of the fulfilment of the divine promises, and of their future preservation and blessedness under the favor of heaven.

THE LAVER.

18. *Thou shalt make a laver of brass*, &c. Heb. כִּיּוֹר *kiyor*, rendered ' caldron,' 1 Sam. 2. 14, but usually spoken

.aver *of* brass, and his foot *also of* brass, to wash *withal :* and thou shalt [t]put it between the taber-

[t] ch. 40. 7, 30.

nacle of the congregation and the altar, and thou shalt put water therein.

---

of a large basin or other vessel for washing. In respect to none of the sacred articles is the information of the text more brief than in respect to this, as nothing is said of its form or dimensions. It is reasonable, however, to infer, that as Solomon modelled the furniture of the Temple after that of the Tabernacle, only on a vastly larger scale, and as his Laver was an immense vat or reservoir, called ' a sea,' and of a circular form, so the form of the Tabernacle-laver was also circular. De Dieu infers the same from the fact, that the analogous Arabic word is used to denote vessels of that form, and to this inference we have nothing to object. The original word rendered *foot* (כֵּן *kën*) has a meaning not easily determined. Some interpreters understand it of a *lid* or *cover*, but as the root has the sense of *establishing, fixing, founding* any thing, we prefer to consider it as importing in this connexion a *basis, pediment,* or *supporter* upon which the Laver rested. As the cut which we have given below is substantially the same with that of the Pictorial Bible, and adopted for a like reason, we cite the words of the Editor as conveying on the whole that view of the subject which we consider the most correct. ' Our impression is, that the Laver, whatever were. its shape, stood upon another basin, more wide and shallow, as a cup on a saucer ; and that the latter received, from cocks or spouts in the upper basin, the water which was allowed to escape when the priests washed themselves with the water which fell from the upper basin. If by the under basin we understand the ' foot' of the text, the sense is clear. The text does not say that the priests were to wash themselves *in* the basin,

but *at* it. *In* it they could not well wash their hands and feet if the Laver was of any height. The Rabbins say the Laver had several cocks, or, ' nipples,' as they call them, from which the water was let out as wanted. There were several such spouts, but the number is differently stated. How the priests washed their hands and feet at the Laver seems uncertain. That they did not wash in either the Laver or its base seems clear, because then the water in which they washed would have been rendered impure by those who washed before or with them ; and as we know that Orientals do not like to wash in a basin, after our manner, in which the water with which we commence washing is clearer than that with which we finish, but at a falling stream, where each successive affusion is of clean water, we incline to think that the priests either washed themselves with the stream as it fell from the spouts into the base, or else received in proper vessels so much water as they needed for the occasion. The Orientals, in their washings, make use of a vessel with a long spout, and wash at the stream which issues from thence, the waste water being received in a basin which is placed underneath. This seems to us to illustrate the idea of the Laver with its base, as well as the ablutions of the priests. The Laver had thus its upper basin, from which the stream fell, and the under basin for receiving the waste water ; or it is quite compatible with the same idea and practice to suppose that, to prevent too great an expenditure of water, they received a quantity in separate vessels, using it as described, and the base receiving the water which in washing fell from their hands and feet. This ex-

19 For Aaron and his sons u shall wash their hands and their feet thereat:

20 When they go into the tabernacle of the congregation, they shall wash with water, that they die not: or when they come near

u ch. 40. 31, 32. Ps. 26. 6. Isai. 52. 11. John 13. 10. Heb. 10. 22.

to the altar to minister, to burn offering made by fire unto the LORD:

21 So they shall wash their hands and their feet, that they die not: and w it shall be a statute for ever to them, *even* to him and to his seed throughout their generations.

w ch. 28. 43.

planation, although it seems to us probble, is, necessarily, little more than conjectural. Our cut exhibits another view more in conformity with the usual interpretations. The Jewish commentators say that any kind of water might be used for the Laver; but that the water was to be changed every day. They also state that ablution before

entering the Tabernacle was in no case dispensed with. A man might be perfectly clean, might be quite free from any ceremonial impurity, and might even have washed his hands and feet before he left home, but still he could by no means enter the Tabernacle without previous ablution at the Laver.'

THE LAVER.

The typical design of the Laver flows so naturally out of its primary uses, that but little room is left for a formal discussion of the subject. The external ablution of the body with water, either in whole or in part, was a significant mode of teaching the necessity of an inward purification of the spirit. Those who were officially engaged in the services of the Sanctuary were especially to be reminded of the duty of preserving purity in all their ministrations, and of dreading the pollutions of sin. It was only thus that their functions could be available to themselves. Their *feet* trod the hallowed precincts of the Holy Place, and their *hands* offered the sacrifices upon the altar, and to these members, therefore, in lieu of their whole bodies, was this washing to be especially applied. The position of the Laver was between the Tabernacle and the Altar, as an intermediate something which had an important relation to the entrance within the outer vail. In passing from the Altar of Sacrifice to the interior of the Sanctuary, the priest was, as it were, arrested by the

22 ¶ Moreover, the LORD spake unto Moses, saying,

23 Take thou also unto thee ˣprincipal spices, of pure ʸmyrrh five hundred *shekels*, and of sweet cinnamon half so much, *even* two

ˣ Cant. 4. 14. Ezek. 27. 22. ʸ Ps. 45. 8. Prov. 7. 17.

Laver, at which he was previously to pause and perform the requisite personal cleansings. Thus too there is no entering into heaven, the upper sanctuary, without a previous washing in the *laver of regeneration.* The renewing and purifying influences of the Holy Spirit, not only at the outset, but through the whole course of the Christian life, are most significantly shadowed forth by this feature of the ancient economy. Indeed, we may say in brief that as the Altar on which the victims were offered was a symbol of *justification,* so the Laver, with its cleansing fountain, was a symbol of *sanctification;* and among the moral truths so impressively taught by the sensible emblems of the Mosaic ritual, none was perhaps more pertinently or palpably set forth than the strict connexion between the *atoning blood* of Christ and the *sanctifying efficacy* of the Holy Spirit in this mutual relation of these articles standing in the outer court. It is a relation which seems to be expressly recognised by David when he says, Ps. 26. 6, ' I will wash mine hands in innocency, so will I compass thine altar, O Lord.' The same truth is taught in the New Testament, where we are told that Christ came both by *water* and by *blood.* —the one to *atone* and the other to *purify*—and beyond this it is not needful to seek for the typical mystery of the Laver.

THE HOLY ANOINTING OIL.

23, 24. *Take thou unto the principal spices,* &c. Heb. בשמרם ראש *besamim rosh,* *head spices;* intimating that the

hundred and fifty *shekels*, and of sweet ᶻcalamus two hundred and fifty *shekels.*

24 And of ᵃcassia, five hundred *shekels,* after the shekel of the sanctuary, and of oil-olive an ᵇhin:

ᶻ Cant. 4. 14. Jer. 6. 20. ᵃ Ps. 45. 8. ᵇ ch. 29. 40.

several spices which formed the ingredients of the anointing oil were to be of the very best kinds then known and valued. These we may consider in their order.——¶ *Pure myrrh.* Heb. מר דרור *mar deror, myrrh of freedom;* i. e. myrrh which flowed freely and spontaneously, instead of being drawn by incision, and was therefore of the purest kind.——¶ *Sweet cinnamon.* Hebrew קנמן בשם *kinnemon besem, aromatic cinnamon,* a well-known article of spicery deriving its name directly from the Hebrew. The word is ordinarily used to denote the second or inner bark of the cinnamon-tree which grows in great abundance in the island of Ceylon. But as the bark of the root has a stronger flavor than that of the trunk, Scheuzer conjectures that that which was employed in the composition of the holy anointing oil was of the former kind.——¶ *Sweet calamus.* Heb. קנה בשם *kenëh bosem, spiced cane.* This term denotes an aromatic reed growing in moist places in Egypt, in Judea near lake Gennesareth, and in several parts of Syria. It grows to about two feet in height; bearing from the root a knotted stalk, quite round, containing in its cavity a soft, white pith. The whole is of an agreeable aromatic smell ; and the plant is said to scent the air with fragrance, even while growing. When cut down, dried, and powdered, it makes an ingredient in the richest perfumes. —— ¶ *Cassia.* Heb. קדה *kiddah;* but as the Shemitic *d* and *z* are closely related in sound, the word is otherwise written *kitzia,* from which comes the Gr. κασσια, and thence the

25 And thou shalt make it an oil of holy ointment, an ointment compound after the art of the apothecary: it shall be c an holy anointing oil.

26 d And thou shalt anoint the tabernacle of the congregation therewith, and the ark of the testimony.

27 And the table and all his ves-

c ch. 37. 29. Numb. 35. 25. Ps. 89. 20. & 133. 2. d ch. 40. 9. Lev. 8. 10. Numb. 7. 1.

sels, and the candlestick and his vessels, and the altar of incense.

28 And the altar of burnt-offering with all his vessels, and the laver and his foot.

29 And thou shalt sanctify them, that they may be most holy: e whatsoever toucheth them shall be holy.

30 f And thou shalt anoint Aaron

e ch. 29. 37. f ch. 29. 7, &c. ' Lev. 8. 12. 30.

English, *cassia*. We find in the Scriptures no mention of this article except here and Ezek. 27. 19, where it is joined with calamus and enumerated among the precious things which were brought from the mart of Tyre.

25—28. *Thou shalt make it an oil of holy ointment.* The quantity of oil was sufficient to retain the compound in a *liquid* state, which was probably much improved by straining off the dreggy parts and leaving the residuum defecated and pure. With this holy oil was the Tabernacle, with its priesthood and its furniture, to be anointed, as the last and crowning act of consecration. By this sacred unction the whole was sanctified and set apart to the uses for which it was designed. And as every thing to which it was applied became thereby *most holy*, so a peculiar sanctity attached to the anointing oil itself, which imparted this, and it was on peril of death that any of the same composition was made for any other purpose. But the tradition of the Jews, founded upon the phraseology of v. 31, 'throughout your generations,' that the very oil now prepared by Moses was preserved till near the captivity, and that none was to be made like it, not even for the same purpose, is undoubtedly erroneous. It is perfectly reasonable to suppose that under the inspection of the High Priest it was made as often as it was wanted ; nor do we see any objection to the idea that not only the

priests but also the kings of Judah were anointed with it, although as that form of government was not especially contemplated at this time, nothing is said on this subject.

29. *Whatsoever toucheth them shall be most holy.* The two leading attributes of the anointing oil were its *preciousness* and its *sanctity*. The spices of which it was composed were peculiarly rare and odoriferous, and the oil with which they were blended was most pure. This was doubtless intended to shadow forth the excellency of the gifts of the Holy Spirit, whose distinguishing emblem under the old economy was *oil*. And what is to be compared with the preciousness of those divine influences which emanate from this source? Upon whomsoever they are poured forth, they impart light to the understanding, pliancy to the will, purity to the affections, tenderness to the conscience, and holiness to the entire man. There is nothing beside them to be so earnestly coveted or so advantageously possessed. They are the true riches of the soul, and the sealing title to an eternal inheritance. Wherever enjoyed they constitute the subject of them, ' a new creature,' and so far sanctify every offering which he presents, that ' God smells a sweet savor from it,' and is well pleased. And not only so. It is a diffusive blessedness which is thus conferred. As every vessel that was anointed with the holy ointment, im-

and his sons, and consecrate them, that *they* may minister unto me in the priest's office.

31 And thou shalt speak unto the children of Israel, saying, This shall be an holy anointing oil unto me throughout your generations.

32 Upon man's flesh shall it not be poured, neither shall ye make *any other* like it, after the composition of it : g it *is* holy, *and* it shall be holy unto you.

g ver. 25. 37.

33 h Whosoever compoundeth *any* like it, or whosoever putteth *any* of it upon a stranger i shall even be cut off from his people.

34 ¶ And the LORD said un'o Moses, k Take unto thee sweet spices, stacte, and onycha, and galbanum; *these* sweet spices with pure frankincense: of each shall there be a like *weight:*

h ver. 38. i Gen. 17. 14. ch. 12. 15. Lev. 7. 20, 21. k ch 25. 6. & 37. 29.

---

parted a sanctity to every thing with which it came in contact, so every true Christian communicates to others, as far as his influence extends, the same divine principles which he has imbibed. As was said in mystic language of the Savior, so may it be said of all his anointed ones, 'Their garments smell of myrrh, aloes, and cassia,' and wherever they go they diffuse around them ' the savor of the knowledge of Christ.' Let us seek then this ' unction from the Holy One,' the ' crown of the anointing oil,' which sanctifies and separates all those upon whom it comes. Let us guard against any thing that would reflect dishonor upon the Holy Spirit. Let us bear in mind the striking admonition conveyed in the figurative style of Solomon ; ' Dead flies cause the *ointment of the apothecary* to send forth a stinking savor ; so doth a little folly him that is in reputation for wisdom and honor.' There is a sanctity about the Christian character which should be kept inviolate, and he that dishonors his calling puts fire to the oil of his consecration to his own consuming.

32. *Upon man's flesh shall it not be poured.* That is, upon common men, upon any who were not priests ; equivalent to which is ' stranger' in the next verse.

THE HOLY PERFUME.

34. *Take unto thee sweet spices,* &c.

This order has respect to the composition of the Incense which was to be burnt upon the golden Altar. This also was prepared of sweet spices, though not of so rare or precious a quality as those of which the anointing oil was compounded. But concerning both preparations the same law is given that nothing like them should be made for common use. This would tend to beget among the Israelites a reverence for whatever was of divine institution, and a sedulous care to guard against its profanation or abuse, and as to us, who are privileged to look deeper into the spiritual drift of the Mosaic economy, it may well admonish us to beware ot any ' counterfeit presentment,' or any unhallowed prostitution, of those ordinances, gifts, or graces which emanate from the Spirit of God and in which his honor is especially concerned.——— ¶ *Stacte.* Heb. נטף *netaph* from נטף *nataph,* to drop. Gr. στακτη, from σταζω, to distil. This was a fine kind of gum which was produced from the myrrh-tree, but differing from that substance mentioned v. 23, by retaining a waxy or resinous form, instead of flowing out as a liquid. It is supposed to have been the same with what was afterwards called ' opobalsam' or ' the balm of Jericho.'——— ¶ *Onycha.* Heb. שחלת *shehĕleth,* a word which occurs only in this place, and of which the true sense is consequently very difficult to be de-

35 And thou shalt make it a perfume, a confection [l] after the art of the apothecary, tempered together, pure *and* holy:

36 And thou shalt beat *some* of it very small, and put of it before the testimony in the tabernacle of the congregation, [m] where I will meet with thee: [n] it shall be unto you most holy.

[l] ver. 25. [m] ch. 29. 42. Lev. 16. 2. [n] ver. 32. ch. 29. 37. Lev. 2. 3.

37 And *as for* the perfume which thou shalt make, [o] ye shall not make to yourselves according to the composition thereof: it shall be unto thee holy for the Lord.

38 [p] Whosoever shall make like unto that, to smell thereto, shall even be cut off from his people.

[o] ver. 32. [p] ver. 33.

---

termined. In Syriac שׁוחלתא *shehelta,* is *a tear, a distillation,* and the Hebrew word would seem therefore to mean *something that exuded,* some vegetable gum of odorous qualities. The Gr. indeed has ονυχα, *onycha,* from ονυξ, *nail,* and several learned critics have supposed it to be the external covering (nail) of the shell-fish *purpura* or *murex,* which possessed aromatic properties and was thence called *unguis odoriferans, odoriferous onyx.* This, according to Rumphius, was the basis of the principal perfumes employed in India, just as *aloes* is the basis of all their pills. But as India was too distant for drugs to be brought from thence to Judea or Arabia, where the Israelites now were, and as the context and the etymology seem to require some *vegetable* substance, the opinion is far preferable that makes it the gum of some aromatic plant; and as the Arabic version has 'Ladana,' it is not improbable that *gum-ladanum,* the produce of the 'Cistus ladaniferus,' was the drug in question. This is a secretion from the leaves, which is swept off by the beard of the browzing goats, from whence it was collected. The shrub is a native of the Levant, the isles of the Mediterranean, and Arabia.
——¶ *Galbanum.* Heb. חלבנה *helbenah,* which Michaelis supposes to be a compound of חלב *heleb, milk* or *gum* and לבן *leben, white,* denoting the *white milk* or *gum* of some plant, as it is common with us to call the white

juice which exudes from certain plants the 'milk,' and the phraseology is retained in medical nomenclature 'gum lac, &c. The 'galbanum' is supposed to have been the gum-resin or thickened sap of the 'Bubon Gummiferum,' an umbelliferous plant of Turkey, which yields this gum in softish, pliant, and pale cream-colored masses, whenever a wound is made in any part of it. It is of a strong piercing smell, and of a bitterish taste.——¶ *Frankincense.* Heb. לבנה *lebonah,* a term of which the root also is לבן *labën* and conveying the idea of *whiteness.* The English word 'frankincense' is supposed to have the prefixed epithet ' frank,' *free,* from the *liberal* and *ready* distribution of its odors. This drug, otherwise called ' olibanum,' is a dry resinous substance of a yellowish white color, a strong fragrant smell, and bitter acrid taste. It is produced from the ' Boswellia serrata,' a native of India, and a fine tree belonging to the family of the turpentine-bearing trees. The ' pure frankincense' is that which is first obtained from the tree, and for that reason considered the best. When laid upon burning coals, or a hot iron, it sends forth a vapor of most delicious fragrance.

35. *Tempered together.* Heb. ממלח *memullah, salted,* from מלח *melah, salt.* The Chal. and Gr., however, have set the example of rendering by *mixed* or *tempered,* as if their idea was that

CHAPTER XXXI.

AND the LORD spake unto Moses, saying,

2 a See, I have called by name Bezaleel the b son of Uri, the son of Hur, of the tribe of Judah:

3 And I have c filled him with the

a ch. 35. 30. & 36. 1. b 1 Chron. 2. 20.
c ch. 35. 31. 1 Kings 7. 14.

spirit of God, in wisdom, and in understanding, and in knowledge, and in all manner of workmanship,

4 To devise cunning works, to work in gold, and in silver, and in brass,

---

the different ingredients were to be mixed together just as salt is mixed with any substance on which it is sprinkled. Ainsworth contends for the liberal rendering, inasmuch as the law, Lev. 2. 13, expressly says, 'With all thine offerings *thou shalt offer salt.*' In support of this he quotes Maimonides, who affirms that ' there was not any thing offered on the Altar *without salt,* except the wine of the drink-offerings, and the blood, and the wood;' and of the incense he says still more expressly, that ' they added to it the fourth part of a kab of *salt.*' In accordance with which, it is supposed, our Savior says, Matt. 9. 49, 'Every sacrifice shall be *salted with salt.*' We feel incompetent to decide the question, but confess a leaning towards the view of Ainsworth, who further remarks very appropriately, that ' if our *speech* is to be always with grace, seasoned with salt, as the apostle teaches, Col. 4. 6, how much more should our incense, our *prayers* unto God, be therewith seasoned ?'

Chapter 31

The Workmen called.

2. *I have called by name Bezaleel the son of Uri.* That is, I have especially designated, appointed, and set apart to the superintendance of this work Bezaleel the son of Uri. His name signifies ' under the shadow of God,' but that it has any particular significancy in this connexion we see no evidence. He was the seventh in descent from

Judah, and the reader will find his genealogy expressly detailed, 1 Chron. 2. 5—20.

3. *I have filled him with the Spirit of God,* &c. That is, with those *intellectual* gifts and endowments which are immediately specified, and which amounted to something like a *divine inspiration,* but at the same time not implying any thing of a *moral* character, the usual result of the operation of the Spirit of God. Both he and his associates in the work were to be the subjects of an influence which should improve their faculties and endow them with an ingenuity and skill far beyond the utmost stretch of their unassisted powers. This extraordinary ability now to be imparted, infinite wisdom doubtless saw to be indispensable on the present occasion. The children of Israel had in Egypt been condemned to a hard bondage in brick and in mortar, and in all kinds of coarse, rough, and degrading labor, and consequently could not be supposed to be qualified for the curious workmanship which was now required. To engrave and to embroider, to work gold, to cut diamonds, and to mount jewels, would of course demand a degree of tact and dexterity for which, as they had served no previous apprenticeship at it, they must be indebted to a supernatural teaching. But he who had designed the work was abundantly able to qualify the workmen.

4. *To devise cunning work.* Heb לחשב מחשבת *lahashob mahashoboth, to think thoughts,* or *to ponder devices*

5 And in cutting of stones to set
them, and in carving of timber, to
work in all manner of workmanship.
6 And I, behold, I have given
with him [d]Aholiab the son of
Ahisamach, of the tribe of Dan;
and in the hearts of all that are
[e]wise-hearted I have put wisdom;
that they may make all that I
have commanded thee:
7 [f]The tabernacle of the congregation, and [g]the ark of the testimony, and [h]the mercy-seat that *is*
thereupon, and all the furniture of
the tabernacle,
8 And [i]the table and his furniture, and [k]the pure candlestick
with all his furniture, and the
altar of incense,
9 And [l]the altar of burnt-offering with all his furniture, and [m]the
laver and his foot,
10 And [n]the clothes of service,
and the holy garments for Aaron
the priest, and the garments of his
sons, to minister in the priest's
office,
11 [o]And the anointing oil, and
[p]sweet incense for the holy *place;*
according to all that I have commanded thee shall they do.
12 ¶ And the LORD spake unto
Moses, saying,
13 Speak thou also unto the children of Israel, saying, [q]Verily my
sabbaths ye shall keep: for it *is* a
sign between me and you throughout your generations; that *ye* may
know that I *am* the LORD that
doth sanctify you.

[d]ch. 35. 34. [e]ch. 28. 3. & 35. 10, 35. & 36. 1. [f]ch. 36. 8. [g]ch. 37. 1. [h]ch. 37. 6. [i]ch. 37. 10. [k]ch. 37. 17. [l]ch. 38. 1. [m]ch. 38. 8. [n]ch. 39. 1 41. Numb. 4. 5, 6, &c. [o]ch. 30. 25, 31. & 37. 29. [p]ch. 30. 34. & 37. 29. [q]Lev. 19. 3, 30. & 26. 2. Ezek. 20. 12, 20. & 44. 24.

Gr. *αρχιτεκτονησαι*, lit. *to architectonize.* Chal. 'To teach artificers;' i. e. to act in the capacity of chief designer, director, and overseer, in executing the various works prescribed. The term does not, however, in this connexion imply that Bezaleel or any of his assistants were to exercise their ingenuity in *contriving* or *originating* any of the utensils or decorations of the Tabernacle. They were merely to execute the plans of the divine Draughtsman. But in doing this there was still room for the display of much mechanical tact, or *device*, in accomplishing every thing with exactness, readiness, and elegance.

5—11. *In carving of timber*, Heb. בחרשת *baharoshith*, from חרש *harash*, which has the general sense of *making incisions*, or *furrows*, whether by a *ploughshare in the soil*, or by a *graving tool in metal*, *wood*, or *stone*. It is the same word with that rendered 'cutting' in the preceding clause, which has reference mainly to the *engraving* of the names on the gems of the breastplate. We do not indeed read elsewhere expressly of there having been any 'carved work' about the Tabernacle, which has led Patrick to suppose that the term indicated merely the common work of carpenters and joiners. But we deem it altogether probable that there was some ornamental carved work about the pillars; and if, as we have hinted above, several of the utensils were made from *moulds*, there can be little doubt that these were carved out of wood.——¶ *The furniture.* Heb. כלי *keli, vessels, implements, utensils.* See Note on Gen. 24. 53.——¶ *Clothes of service.* That is, the various vails and coverings of cloth which were used for wrapping the holy things whenever the people broke up from their encampments, and moved on their journeys. Comp. Numb. 4. 5—12.

The Observance of the Sabbath re enjoined.

13. *Verily my sabbaths ye shall keep*

14 ^rYe shall keep the sabbath therefore: for it *is* holy unto you. Every one that defileth it shall surely be put to death: for ^s whosoever doeth *any* work therein, that soul shall be cut off from among his people.

15 ^t Six days may work be done,

^r ch. 20. 8. Deut. 5. 12. Ezek. 20. 12. ^s ch. 35. 2. Numb. 15. 35. ^t ch. 20. 9.

This command is here repeated from the divine foresight of its necessity under the circumstances. It is as if he had said, 'You are indeed about to be employed in an important and sacred work, one requiring great assiduity and despatch; nevertheless let it not be thought that this circumstance affords sufficient ground for encroaching upon holy time with the work in which you are engaged. Let the most urgent business come to a pause during the hallowed hours of the Sabbath.'——

¶ *The Lord that doth sanctify you.* That is, by an external consecration of the race of Israel to himself, as a sign and token of which the Sabbath was ordained as a day of worship and of rest from secular labor. The institution of the weekly Sabbath as a *sanctified* season, was an expressive indication of the character of the covenant relation which was to subsist between God and Israel. They were continually reminded by it that they were to be a *sanctified* people, chosen, separated, and distinguished from the rest of the world, with whom all traces of the primitive Sabbath had become nearly extinct. Consequently this institution would not be a sign to the Israelites only, but to the surrounding nations. They would be taught the same truth by the same medium. As the religious rites and ceremonies of all people are an index of the character of the deities whom they serve, so the stated observance of the Sabbath in a holy manner

but in the ^u seventh *is* the sabbath of rest, holy to the Lord: whosoever doeth *any* work in the sabbath-day he shall surely be put to death.

16 Wherefore the children of Israel shall keep the sabbath, to observe the sabbath throughout their generations, *for* a perpetual covenant.

^u Gen. 2. 2. ch. 16. 23. & 20. 10.

---

would testify to all the world the holy attributes of that God whom they worshipped and with whom they were in covenant.

14. *It is holy unto you.* Heb. קדש הוא לכם *kodesh hi lakem, it is holiness or sanctification unto you.——* ¶ *Shall surely be put to death.* Heb. מות רדמת *moth yumath, dying shall be made to die.* That is, by the hands of the magistrate if the iniquity could be proved; if not, by premature death at the hand of God himself, which seems, from the Rabbinical writers, to have been understood as the penalty denounced against daring crimes when there were no human witnesses to bear testimony to the fact. See Note on Gen. 17. 14.

15. *Sabbath of rest, holy to the Lord.* Heb. שבת שבתון קדש ליהוה *shabbath shabbathon kodesh laihova, a sabbath of sabbatism, holiness to Jehovah.* Gr. αναπαυσις αγια τῳ κυριῳ, *a rest holy to the Lord.* The phrase is peculiarly intensive in the original. Upon comparing this with the preceding verse, it is clear that the two parties, God and Israel, were each to hold the Sabbath holy to the other; and upon this ground the observance of it is called v. 16, a ' perpetual covenant.'

16. *To observe the sabbath.* Heb. לעשות את השבת *laäsoth eth hash-shab-bath*, lit. *to do or make the sabbath.* The expression in the original is peculiar, and conveying an idea not easily transferable into English. Our phrases ' keep

17 It *is* ˣ a sign between me and the children of Israel for ever: for ʸ *in* six days the LORD made heaven and earth, and on the seventh day he rested and was refreshed.
18 ¶ And he gave unto Moses,

ˣ ver. 13.   Ezek. 20. 12, 20,   y Gen. 1. 31.
& 2. 2.

the Sabbath' and ' observe the Sabbath' are hardly to be distinguished in import from each other, carrying with them mainly the idea of *cessation from secular work*. But the Hebrew formulary ' to do the Sabbath' has the additional involved sense of the *active doing* or *performing* of certain acts and exercises essential to the due sanctification of a day which was yet emphatically *a day of rest*. The same phrase occurs Deut. 5. 15, 'And remember that thou wast a servant in the land of Egypt, and that the Lord thy God brought thee out thence through a mighty hand and by a stretched-out arm: therefore the Lord thy God commanded thee *to keep the sabbath-day*. (לַעֲשׂוֹת אֶת רוֹם שׁבת, *to do the day of rest*).' So also, Deut. 16. 1, 'Observe the month of Abib, and *keep the passover* (עֲשׂית פסח *asitha pesah, do the passover*) unto the Lord thy God.' Comp. Mat. 26. 18, 'The Master saith, My time is at hand; *I will keep the passover* (ποιω το πασχα *I will do or make the passover*) at thy house with my disciples.' Again Deut. 16. 13, 'Thou shalt *observe the feast of tabernacles* (חג הסכת תעשׂה *hag hassukkoth taäseh, the feast of tabernacles thou shalt do or make*) seven days,' &c.
17. *A sign between me and the children of Israel for ever.* Chal. 'Between my Word and the sons of Israel.'——
¶ *Was refreshed.* Heb. ינפשׁ *yinnaphesh, fetched breath.* Of course to be understood as spoken of God after the manner of men, on the principle of *anthropomorphism*, of which a very expanded detail is given in Rev. J. P.

when he had made an end of communing with him upon mount Sinai, ᶻ two tables of testimony, tables of stone, written with the finger of God.

ᶻ ch. 24. 12. & 32. 15, 16. & 34. 28, 29,
Deut. 4. 13. & 5. 22. & 9. 10, 11. 2 Cor
3. 3.

Smith's Comparative View of Scriptur and Geology.

The Delivery of the Tables of th
Law.

18. *When he had made an end oₜ communing with him.* At the close of the forty days' sojourn upon the mount, during which time all the preceding laws and ordinances had been delivered to him. The clause occurs at a point where it forms a very suitable transition in the progress of the narrative. In the ensuing chapter he is about to relate the fact of his having broken the tables under the impulse of a holy indignation at the sins of the people, and he accordingly here premises the necessary information respecting the tables themselves, what they contained, and whence they were received.——¶ *Two tables of testimony.* The grounds of this appellation have already been explained, ch. 25. 16. The laws written on them *testified* the will of God as to the duties of his creatures, and by being received and deposited in the Ark, they were a *testimony* on the part of Israel that they had covenanted to receive and obey them upon the penalty of incurring all the judgments and curses by which they were enforced. They were written on tables of stone to denote their perpetual and unchangeable obligation; ard they were written not by the *commandment*, but by the immediate *power* of God himself, here termed his ' finger,' which is elsewhere used in the same sense, Ps. 8. 3. Luke, 11. 20. As however, the ' finger of God' is spoken of by our Savior as equivalent to the ' Spirit of

God,' the power by which devils were cast out, some have supposed that all that is meant here is, that these tables were written by Moses indeed, but still by the direct *prompting* and *dictation* of the Spirit of God, so that it was more entitled to be considered as a divine than a human work. But the following passages would seem to be too explicit to allow of any other than the common explication. Ex. 24. 12, 'And the Lord said unto Moses, Come up to me into the mount, and be there: and I will give the tables of stone, and a law, and commandments *which I have written; that* thou mayest teach them.' Ex. 32. 15, 16, 'And Moses turned, and went down from the mount, and the two tables of the testimony were in his hand: the tables were written on both their sides; on the one side and on the other were they written. And the tables *were the work of God,* and the writing *was the writing of God,* graven upon the tables.' Deut. 5. 22, 'These words the Lord spake unto all your assembly in the mount, out of the midst of the fire, of the cloud, and of the thick darkness with a great voice; and he added no more: and *he wrote them in two tables of stone,* and delivered them unto me.' 'Of the Decalogue, above all other holy writ, God seems to say, as Paul, Philem. 19, 'Behold, I have written it with mine own hand.'' *Trapp.*

Chapter 32

The Golden Calf.

If ever a situation occurred in the history of man in which we were authorised to expect the presence and prevalence of a deep and awful sense of the majesty of Jehovah, together with a grateful acknowledgment of his goodness, and a trembling solicitude to avoid every thing which might offend him, it was that in which the race of Israel was now placed at the base of the hallowed mount. They had ex-perienced the most incontestible and astonishing proofs the divine power, favor, and love. Little more than thirty days had passed since they had witnessed a scene of grandeur and glory such as had never before been accorded to mortal eyes. Jehovah had delivered to them his holy law in the midst of thunder, lightning, earthquake, fire, and the presence of the ministering angels. The terms of a sacred binding covenant had been proposed to them, to which they with one voice acceded, and indeed the last thing which is related of them prior to the present chapter is, that 'Moses came and told the people all the words of the Lord, and all the judgments; and all the people answered with one voice, and said, All the words which the Lord hath said we will do, and be obedient.' Even now Moses was gone up into the mount to commune with God on their behalf; as their faithful representative, he had transacted all their great concerns; the forty days were almost completed; and he was just upon the point of coming down, bearing the sacred tables in his hand, and fully instructed and authorised to set up the Tabernacle-worship among them; when lo, the innate depravity of the human heart breaks out with a virulence utterly astounding, and unbelieving impatience ripens at once into an act of gross idolatry! Who could have thought it? Daily fed by manna from heaven; daily refreshed by water from the smitten rock; surrounded by miracles of might and benignity against which it would seem impossible that their eyes should be closed, who could have anticipated, that in utter defiance of the commandment to which they had so lately and so solemnly avowed obedience, they should have ordered the fabrication of other gods, and 'changed their glory into the likeness of an ox, that eateth grass?' Yet this is the mournful scene which we are now called to contem-

CHAPTER XXXII.

AND when the people saw that Moses ᵃ delayed to come down out of the mount, the people gathered themselves together unto Aaron, and said unto him, ᵇ Up, make us

ᵃ ch. 24. 18. Deut. 9. 9.   ᵇ Acts 7. 40.

gods which shall ᶜ go before us: for *as for* this Moses, the man that brought us up out of the land of Egypt, we wot not what is become of him.

ᶜ ch. 13. 21.

---

plate! No wonder that Josephus should have felt this transaction to be such a stain on the character of his people as to make him ashamed to record it; although its disgracefulness cannot justify him, as an honest historian, in omitting it.

1. *When the people saw that Moses delayed,* &c. Heb. משה בשש כי *ki boshesh Mosheh,* lit. *that Moses caused shame.* The idiom of the original in regard to this word is peculiar. The radical בוש *bosh* signifies primarily *to be ashamed, abashed, to blush for shame,* whether through fear, modesty, or disappointment; and as long tarrying or waiting in vain for one's coming is apt to be attended with a sensation of shame or displacency, as Judg. 3. 25, 'they *tarried* till they were *ashamed,*' the word is thence easily applied as here to *tarrying* or *delaying,* the effect being put, by a usual rhetorical figure, for the cause. See this ideal connexion between *delay* and *shame* in the diction of the Hebrew more fully unfolded in the Note on Judg. 3. 25. The Gr. has κεχρονικε from χρονιζω, *to procrastinate,* a derivative from χρονος, usually rendered *time,* but in many cases more legitimately signifying *delay.* Thus Rev. 10. 5—7, 'And the angel which I saw stand upon the sea and upon the earth, lifted up his hand to heaven, And sware by him that liveth for ever and ever, who created heaven, and the things that therein are, and the earth, and the things that therein are, and the sea, and the things which are therein, that *there should be time* (χρονος *delay*) *no longer:* But in the days of the voice of the seventh

angel, when he shall begin to sound, the mystery of God should be finished, as he hath declared to his servants the prophets, Here the meaning undoubtedly is, that there should be *no longer delay than until* the days of the voice of the seventh angel, when the events predicted should come to pass. As there can be no question, from the computation of prophetic chronology, that we are brought, in the evolutions of providence, to the very borders of this period, it should be no matter of surprise to witness the most stupendous changes, moral, intellectual, and political in the affairs of the world. The 'finishing of the mystery of God' is a much greater event, or order of events, than the occurrence of the anticipated Millennium.

——¶ *Gathered themselves together unto Aaron.* Heb. ארן על יקהל *yikkahël al Aaron, were assembled upon or against, Aaron.* The usual term in Hebrew for *to* is אל *el* instead of על *al,* which latter has more the sense of *contra, against,* and the idea intended to be conveyed is probably that they *beset* him in a violent and tumultuous manner, clamorously demanding of him that he should yield to their wishes. It is perhaps but justice to Aaron to suppose that he at first earnestly opposed the measure, but that he was at length overcome by the importunity and menaces of the people. Still nothing can excuse his ultimate compliance.——¶ *Up, make us gods,* &c. Heb. עשה אלהים לנו *asëh lanu elohim, make for us Elohim.* The term itself leaves it somewhat doubtful whether a unity or plurality of idea is intended by it, as it admits of either. From Neh. 9. 18, it would seem that the former was the meaning; 'Yea, when they had made them a molten calf, and said, *This is thy God* that brought thee out of Egypt.' The same is doubtless also to be inferred from the fact that Aaron made only one calf. Stephen indeed, Acts, 7. 40, uses the plural number, but this is probably merely in imitation of the Hebrew form, which very often has a singular import. Comp. Gen. 25. 13. 35. 7. We are not to suppose that a people who only six weeks before had witnessed such amazing demonstrations of the existence and glory of the true God had suddenly sunk to such a pitch of mad infatuation and brutish stupidity, as to imagine that human fabrication could 'make a god that should go before them.' Their meaning was that an image, a visible sign or symbol of Jehovah, should be made, something which should answer to them in place of the Shekinah which had hitherto conducted them in the pillar of cloud. This visible symbol, which they had hitherto enjoyed, and which had now become apparently immoveable on the summit of the mount, is frequently denominated 'glory,' or 'glory of thê Lord,' and as they proposed to form to themselves so vile a substitute for this as a brute animal, therefore it is that the Psalmist calls it a 'changing of their *glory* into the likeness of an ox that eateth grass.' That the measure was prompted at bottom by a disrelish of a purely spiritual worship, and a desire to be furnished with some *sensible sign* of a divine presence in the midst of them, is, we think, quite manifest; and that the forms of Egyptian idolatry, to which they had been previously familiarised, had tended to infuse this leaven into their minds, is, in our view, equally unquestionable. We are inclined, therefore, to give no little weight to the following extracts from the Rabbinical writers cited by Bishop Patrick. In the Pirke Elieser (c. 55.) we are told that ' they said unto Aaron, The Egyptians extol their gods; they sing and chant before them; for they behold them with their eyes. Make us such gods as theirs are, that we may see them before us.' So also R. Jehudah (Cosri, P. 1. § 97.) 'They desired a sensible object of divine worship to be set before them; not with an intention to deny God, who brought them out of Egypt, but that something in the place of God might stand before them, when they declared his wonderful works.' ——¶ *We wot not what is become of him.* They evidently had no sufficient reason to warrant them in supposing that he was lost, or that he delayed his return longer than was necessary. They knew that he had made arrangements for a somewhat protracted stay. They had seen him ascend the mount and enter the cloud; they knew his errand, for they had themselves, when shrinking under a sense of guilt and terror from converse with the Most High, delegated him to be their representative. Had they not then every reason to be persuaded of his safety? Yet they *affect* to consider him as lost to them, as no more to come among them; nor any more to guide them towards the promised land! Yet even if they were sincere in this, how little respect do they show to his memory! How lightly do they speak of the apparent loss of their faithful leader, of their kind benefactor! 'We wot not what is become of him!'—evidently implying that they *cared* as little as they pretended to *know.* Alas! how true is it, as evinced by this transaction, that the highest services, the greatest merits, the richest benefactions, cannot secure their subjects from the vilest indignities, aspersions, and ingratitude of their objects!

2. *Aaron said unto them, break off the golden ear-rings,* &c. The very jewels, without doubt, of which they

2 And Aaron said unto them, Break off the ᵈgolden ear-rings which *are* in the ears of your wives, of your sons, and of your daughters, and bring *them* unto me.

3 And all the people brake off the golden ear-rings which *were* in their ears, and brought *them* unto Aaron.

ᵈ Judg. 8. 24, 25, 26, 27.

4 ᵉAnd he received *them* at their hand, and fashioned it with a graving tool, after he had made it a molten calf: and they said, These *be* thy gods, O Israel, which brought thee up out of the land of Egypt.

ᵉ ch. 20. 23. Deut. 9. 16. Judg. 17. 3, 4
1 Kings 12. 28. Neh. 9. 18. Ps. 106. 19.
Isai. 46. 6. Acts 7. 41. Rom. 1. 23.

had despoiled their oppressors at their departure from Egypt, and at the Red Sea. But what shall be said of the conduct of Aaron on this emergency? We have no intimation in the text that he remonstrated at all against the monstrous suggestion, or endeavored in the least to convince the people of their sin and folly in the measure they proposed; and yet we would fain, if possible, find some extenuation of the course pursued by so good a man on this occasion. There is perhaps a shadow of ground, on which to erect a charitable apology for Aaron in this part of the transaction. The proposal that they should break off and give up their ear-rings *may* have been made in the secret hope, that they would be unwilling to devote their choicest treasures to this object, and that while they were wavering in reference to the project, Moses might return and by his presence crush the growing evil in the bud. But the result showed that it is not safe to try experiments upon the readiness of sinners to make sacrifices for their lusts, and that his true course was at once to have stood up and boldly resisted their insolent and impious demands, even at the hazard of his life. His not taking this resolute stand, and in humble trust in God braving all consequences, but pusillanimously yielding to their importunities, gave a kind of *public* and *official* sanction to the whole proceeding, in consequence of which the people would naturally rush on with ten-

fold violence in their chosen way. How fearful the example of a great and good man succumbing to the urgency of a lawless mob! How deplorable the issues when the appointed *barriers* to iniquity become, by their yielding, its *abettors!*

3. *All the people brake off*, &c. The sequel shows that the phrase 'all the people' is not to be taken in its most literal sense, for there were some that still refused to give in to the general act of rebellion; but the majority were unanimous, and promptly resigned their ornaments; thus teaching us that the impulse of a mad and foolish superstition is sometimes sufficiently powerful to overrule the principles of pride and avarice, and that the charges of idolatry are more cheerfully met than the expenses of the true religion. Alas! how is the niggardliness of the people of God in maintaining the services of his worship rebuked by the liberality and self-sacrifices of the votaries of idols!

4. *Fashioned it with a graving-tool, after,* &c. But if it were run or cast in a mould, as is implied by the word 'molten,' how could it properly be said to have been *fashioned* afterward? The literal rendering of the original is, ' He fashioned it with a graving-tool, and made it a calf of molten-work;' by which we may understand either, that he first formed a model of wood, with the instrument here mentioned, by means of which a mould was construct-

5 And when Aaron saw *it*, he built an altar before it; and Aaron made [f] proclamation, and said, To-morrow *is* a feast to the LORD.

[f] Lev. 23. 2, 4, 21, 37.   2 Kings 10. 20.   2 Chron. 30. 5.

---

ed, and in the mould the calf was cast, or that the carved image was itself made into the idol by having the melted metal poured over it. It is a point difficult to be determined, and one that has given rise to much diversity of interpretation among commentators. This we forbear to recite, as it is needless to swell the accumulation of uncertainties. ⸺¶ *Made it a molten calf.* The motive for giving this form to a representation of the Deity, is doubtless to be proximately traced to their familiarity with the idol worship of Egypt. That people were in the habit of paying divine honors to Apis in the form of an ox or bull, and this probably offered the hint to the Israelites on the present occasion. Whether Apis was in himself an original and independent God, or merely a living and visible representation of another, is still questionable. The most general and probable opinion is, that he was regarded as a symbol of their chief god Osiris, or the Sun; and if so, we can see more reason for the remark made above, that the object of the Israelites in this proceeding was to make a *symbol* or *sign* of the Most High, or something to represent to the senses his real presence among them. But although the allusion to the Egyptian mythology now recognised might, without going any farther, be deemed a sufficient explanation of the fact, we are still induced to express the opinion that there was, moreover, at the same time a latent and ultimate reference to the cherubic symbol, of which the ox was one of the leading elements. We know no reason to doubt that from the earliest ages the Cherubim, as an accompaniment of the Shekinah, had been revealed under the fourfold variety of aspect which is as-signed to them in Ezekiel; and as this device was consequently closely connected in the Israelitish mind with the visible manifestation of the Deity, it would not be unnatural that, having come recently from Egypt, they should have chosen it as the most appropriate medium of representing Jehovah.⸺ ¶ *These be thy gods, O Israel,* &c That is, this is thy god, O Israel; in ac cordance with what we have already said above of the import of the phrase The tenor of the observations just made must be our clue to the right construction of this language. Aaron did not intend to say that this molten image was the *real* and *veritable* God who had brought them out of Egypt, but simply that it was his visible symbol; and not improbably his secret hope was, that on this account they would make the due mental discrimination, and not be so sottish as to worship it. But the act was in direct contravention of the second commandment, and that it was regarded by the Spirit of God as an in stance of downright, unequivocal idol atry, we are assured upon the testimony of the apostle, 1 Cor. 10. 7, 'Neither be ye *idolaters*, as were some of them.' So also Ps. 106. 19, 'They made a calf in Horeb and *worshipped the molten image.*' 'How oft, alas! have we abused God's mercy; taking his jewels, and making a golden calf of them!' *Trapp.*

5. *When Aaron saw it,* &c. Heb. וירא אהרן *va-yar Aaron, and Aaron saw;* i. e. saw the result; saw how the affair was regarded by the people; saw and considered the issue of his own conduct. The word 'it,' supplied by our translators, does not refer to the calf, but in a wider sense to what oc-curred upon its formation.⸺¶ *And*

6 And they rose up early on the morrow, and offered burnt-offerings, and brought peace-offerings: and the ᵍpeople sat down to eat and to drink, and rose up to play.

7 ¶ And the LORD said unto Mo-

ᵍ 1 Cor. 10. 7.

Aaron made a proclamation, and said, To-morrow is a feast to the Lord. Heb. הַג לַיהוָֹה *hag laihovah, a feast to, for,* or *of Jehovah.* By Aaron's building an altar and proclaiming this feast to the true God, it would seem that he still proposed within himself to lead the thoughts of the people through the outward medium and fix them upon Jehovah himself, the only proper object of adoration. But such a mixture of *divine* and *idolatrous* worship never fails to mislead the mass of men, and though the *priests* of a corrupt religion, in imitation of Aaron, may plead that the use of paintings, images, and sacrifices, is intended merely as a help, by sensible media, to spiritual worship, yet there can be no doubt that its practical effects are always just the same with those here recorded, and that it comes under the same condemnation. Whatever were Aaron's private views or wishes, the transaction is thus again characterised by the Holy Ghost, Acts, 7. 41, 'And they made a calf in those days, and *offered sacrifices unto the idol,* and rejoiced in the work of their hands.' So Jehu, led away by the same delusion, could boast of his zeal for the Lord of hosts, while yet he was a worshipper of the golden calves of Jeroboam, 2 Kings, 10. 16, 29.

6. *And they rose up early,* &c. Eagerly intent upon their idolatrous service, and apparently uneasy at its being delayed so long as until the morrow, they lost no time on the ensuing morning in bringing their burnt-offerings and peace-offerings, although of sin-offerings, which they most needed, we find no mention. They thought-

ses, ʰGo, get thee down: for thy people, which thou broughtest out of the land of Egypt, ⁱhave corrupted *themselves:*

ʰ Deut. 9. 12, ver. 1. ch. 33. 1. Dan. 9. 24. ⁱ Gen. 6. 11, 12. Deut. 4. 16. & 32. 5. Judg. 2. 19. Hos. 9. 9.

---

lessly exulted in the celebration of a festival which was soon to prove so fatal to them.——¶ *Sat down to eat and to drink.* That is, upon the remainder of the oblation of peace-offerings, to a share of which the offerers were entitled. The burnt-offerings were wholly consumed as holocausts. By thus partaking of these offerings they were brought into forbidden fellowship with the idol, as is clear from the reasonings of Paul, 1 Cor. 10. 17—21. The sad consequences of this apostacy they were soon made to experience. God's jealousy burns very fiercely about his altar.—— ¶ *Rose up to play.* Heb. לְצַחֵק *letzahëk.* A word of ominous import, implying not only such sports as singing, dancing, and merry-making in general, but in some cases also a species of conduct which the epithet *wanton* as correctly defines as any·term which we deem it proper to employ. Compare the use of the same original word, rendered 'mock,' Gen. 39. 14. Compare also Num. 25. 1, 2. In like manner it appears that the ancient sacrificial feasts among the Gentiles were so frequently turned into scenes of voluptuous revelling and drunkenness, that Athenæus informs us, that by the early Greeks, the word μεθυειν, *to be drunk,* was supposed to be derived from μετα το θυειν, *after the sacrifices,* when they gave themselves up to large drinking.

7. *And the Lord said unto Moses Go, get thee down,* &c. As if the urgency of the occasion would naturally give the utmost intensity to the language, the Greek here adds the word 'quickly,' as does Moses indeed himself in speaking of the incident, Deut

8 They have turned aside quickly out of the way which k I commanded them: they have made them a molten calf, and have worshipped it, and have sacrificed thereunto, and said, l These *be* thy

k ch. 20. 3, 4, 23. Deut. 9. 16. l 1 Kings 12. 28.

gods, O Israel, which have brought thee up out of the land of Egypt.
9 And the LORD said unto Moses, m I have seen this people, and behold, it *is* a stiff-necked people:

m ch. 33. 3, 5. & 34. 9. Deut. 9. 6. 13. & 31. 27. 2 Chron. 30. 8. Isai. 48. 4. Acts 7. 51.

9. 12, 'Arise, get thee down quickly.' The people, abandoning themselves to unhallowed revelry, thought neither of God, before whom they had so recently trembled, nor of Moses, their venerable leader and friend, nor of the ten commandments to which they had a few weeks since so solemnly sworn obedience, and one of which in the most express terms forbade the very crime of which they were now guilty. Giving themselves up to licentious mirth, they thought only of the present moment. But here we learn how the matter was viewed *on the mount*. This ought in fact to have been their chief concern—not how *they* regarded it, but how it was looked upon *from above*. But this was neglected, and the same neglect is continually evinced by heedless transgressors intent upon sensual pleasures. Ah, did they but reflect that there is an unsleeping eye ever watchful over their career, and a true estimate incessantly making up of their conduct, which will finally come to them in the form of a fearful indictment, what a salutary damper would it throw upon their profane hilarities! How needful is it for us often while sporting *on the plain*, to think of the judgment formed of our conduct *on the mount!*——¶ *Thy people.* A tone of indignation breathes through this language, as if the offending people had forfeited all right to be longer considered *God's* people, and he had utterly cast them off; ' for *thy* people have corrupted themselves.' The effect of sin is to write 'Lo-ammi,' *not my people*, upon the most chosen servants of Jehovah. ' But in this mode of

speech something gracious was concealed. A hint was, as it were, given him to gainsay the Lord, and to put him upon the *thine* and the *thou*. Of this he immediately availed himself and said, 'Why doth thy wrath wax hot against *thy* people, which *thou* hast brought forth out of the land of Egypt, with great power, and with a mighty hand?' *Krummacher.* The original term for ' corrupted' implies both their *idolatry* and the *consequent judgments* which they had brought upon themselves, according to the twofold sense of the same word, Gen. 6. 11—13, on which see Note.

8. *They have turned aside quickly,* &c. This language might properly be used considering the very short time that had passed since they heard the law from mount Sinai, and promised obedience, and were afterwards warned not to ' make to them gods of silver or of gold.' They *quickly* forgot his works; but the punishment which their sudden defection incurred admonishes us, that nothing is more provoking in the eyes of heaven than a speedy backsliding after solemnly renewing our covenant with God, or receiving special mercies at his hand.

9. *I have seen this people,* &c. Targ Jon. ' The pride of this people is revealed before me.' The meaning is, I have long noted, observed, and studied, as it were, their disposition. I know their genius, and the character which I am constrained to give of them is, that they are a stiff-necked people. This is a metaphor taken from stubborn and intractable bullocks whose necks are

10 Now therefore [n] let me alone, that [o] my wrath may wax hot against them, and that I may consume them: and [p] I will make of thee a great nation.

11 [q] And Moses besought the LORD his God, and said, LORD, why doth thy wrath wax hot against thy people, which thou hast brought forth out of the land of Egypt, with great power, and with a mighty hand?

12 [r] Wherefore should the Egyptians speak and say, For mischief did he bring them out, to slay them in the mountains, and to consume them from the face of the earth? Turn from thy fierce wrath, and [s] repent of this evil against thy people.

[n] Deut. 9. 14, 19.   [o] ch. 22. 24.   [p] Numb. 14. 12.   [q] Deut. 9. 18, 26, 27, 28, 29.   Ps. 74. 1, 2. & 106. 23.

[r] Numb. 14. 13.   Deut. 9, 28. & 32. 27
[s] ver. 14.

brought with the greatest difficulty to submit to the yoke. Compare the equivalent allusion, Is. 48. 4, 'Thy neck is an iron sinew,' which would not bend. Jer. 5. 5, 'But these (the great men) have altogether broken the yoke and burst the bonds.'

10. *Now therefore let me alone*, &c. Chal. 'Leave off thy prayer before me.' Do not interpose by prayers and deprecations in their behalf. Moses had not yet opened his mouth, but God foresaw the holy violence with which his importunity would besiege his throne, and *apparently* desires him not to intercede for them. What greater or more significant proof could be given of the divine condescension to the petitions of a mortal? 'God is fain to bespeak his own freedom; as if Moses' devotion were stronger than God's indignation. Great is the power of prayer; able, after a sort, to transfuse a dead palsy into the hand of Omnipotence.' *Trapp.* The words, however, which *seemed* to forbid, were *really* intended to encourage Moses in his suit. They are not indeed a positive command to him to pray in behalf of Israel, but they indicated what it was that would stay the divine hand from punishing; and were equivalent to saying, 'If you intercede for them, my hands are tied, and I cannot execute the deserved vengeance.' Of this hint Moses would not be slow to avail himself.——¶ *And I will make of thee a great nation.* As

if the Most High would bribe the forbearance of his servant. The words evidently disclose a secret purpose to try the spirit of Moses, as if to see whether the prospect of becoming great and distinguished himself, would outweigh his regard for the interests of his people. He assaults him in a point where most men are most vulnerable, but the noble disinterestedness of Moses was proof against the power of this appeal to the selfish principles of his nature, and the apparent dissuasives from intercession only urged him on with more vehemence in his suit.

11. *Why doth thy wrath wax hot against thy people*, &c. This is not probably to be understood as an expostulation, as if there were not sufficient cause for God to be angry; but rather as an earnest entreaty that he would not in wrath consume them. The same usage of speech is common both in the prophets and the Psalms. Thus Ps. 44. 23, 24, 'Awake, *why* sleepest thou, O Lord? arise, cast us not off for ever. *Wherefore* hidest thou thy face, and forgettest our affliction and our oppression?' See also the interrogative and optative modes of expression interchanged, Mat. 5. 39, and Luke. 8. 52. Mat. 8. 29, and Luke, 8. 28.

12. *Wherefore should the Egyptians speak and say*, &c. The prayer of Moses on this occasion contains a threefold plea; (1.) That God would not reflect upon his own wisdom by so soon

13 Remember Abraham, Isaac, and Israel, thy servants, to whom thou t swearest by thine own self, and saidst unto them, u I will multiply your seed as the stars of hea-

t Gen. 22. 16.　Hebr. 6. 13.　u Gen. 12. 7. & 13. 15. & 15. 7. 18.　& 26. 4. & 28. 13. & 35, 11, 12.

ven, and all this land that I have spoken of will I give unto your seed, and they shall inherit *it* for ever.

14 And the LORD w repented of

w Deut. 32. 26.　2 Sam.　24. 16.　1 Chron. 21. 15.　Ps. 106. 45.　Jer. 18. 8. & 26. 13, 19 Joel 2. 13.　Jonah 3. 10. & 4. 2.

destroying what he had employed so much power to preserve. (2.) That he would not give advantage to the Egyptians to glory over the ruin of a race whom they so much hated. (3.) That he would remember his covenant promises to Abraham, Isaac, and Jacob. The second of these arguments he prosecutes in the passage before us, and in doing so shows that he had the glory of God quite as much at heart as the welfare of Israel. Aware that the eyes and the tongues of Egypt and the surrounding nations were intent on finding matter of malicious triumph over a people so signally delivered from bondage, so miraculously sustained, so wondrously conducted, he would at all hazards preclude every ground and occasion upon which the divine glory could be blemished in the estimate of his enemies. Should the chosen people now after such illustrious displays of divine power in their behalf perish under the stroke of deserved wrath, what would be more natural than that fickleness or impotence should be imputed to their covenant God, and thus his holy name be blasphemed on every side? All that had been thus far done would go for nothing, and to human appearance the Most High would ' disgrace the throne of his glory.' But this was a consequence which the pious heart of Moses could not endure to contemplate, and therefore is he so emphatic in urging the question, 'What will the Egyptians say?' Whatever petitions we offer to God, the glorifying his great name should ever be the grand prompting motive and the ultimate scope.——

¶ *For mischief.* Heb. ברעה *beraah,*

in evil, in malice; i. e. maliciously. Gr. μετα πονηριας, *with maliciousness* ——¶ *Repent of this evil against thy people.* Heb. על הרעה לעמך *al haraah le-ammeka, over the evil to thy people.* Gr. επι τη κακια του λαου σου, *upon the evil of the people.* The original doubtless implies both the evil of *crime* committed by the people, and the evil of *punishment* suffered, or about to be suffered, by them. The latter idea of the two was so prominent in the mind of the Chaldean translator that he has rendered it, 'Repent of the evil which thou purposedst to do unto thy people.' This of course is spoken after the manner of men on the principles explained in the Note on Gen. 6. 6. The simple meaning is, 'Relent from inflicting this threatened evil.'

13. *Remember Abraham, Isaac,* &c. This was doubtless the great argument of all, the promise made to the fathers. To the fulfilment of this promise the veracity of God would have been pledged, had it been given simply in the form of a plain declaration; but there was more than this; it was a promise confirmed by an oath, and an oath sworn by himself, than whom he could swear by no greater. Consequently nothing could be conceived more binding by which the honor of divine truth could be engaged to the performance of its stipulations. It is as if he had said, 'Lord, if thy people be now destroyed, shall not thy promise fail for evermore? And shall their unbelief be allowed to make thy truth of none effect? God forbid.'

14. *And the Lord repented,* &c. Heb וינחם יהוה *va-yinnahem Yehovah.* Gr.

the evil which he thought to do unto his people.

15 ¶ And ˣ Moses turned, and went down from the mount, and the two tables of the testimony *were* in his hand: the tables *were* written on both their sides; on the one side and on the other *were* they written.

ˣ Deut. 9. 15.

16 And the ʸ tables *were* the work of God and the writing *was* the writing of God, graven upon the tables.

17 And when Joshua heard the noise of the people as they shouted, he said unto Moses, *There is* a noise of war in the camp.

ʸ ch. 31. 18.

ἱλασθη κυριος, *the Lord was propitiated;* the same term which occurs in the prayer of the publican, Luke, 18. 13, 'God, *be merciful* (ἱλασθητι, *be propitiated*) to me a sinner;' i. e. by the intervention of a mediator. The publican therefore does not rely upon the absolute mercy of God irrespective of an atonement.—The suit of Moses prevails with Jehovah. He so redoubles and multiplies the obstacles which he would fain throw in the way of the execution of vengeance, that God virtually acknowledges himself overcome, and accordingly the Psalmist says, Ps. 106. 23, 'He would have destroyed them had not Moses his chosen stood before him in the breach.'

15. *The two tables of testimony were in his hand.* The reason of this denomination has been previously explained. See Note on Ex. 25. 16. These tables, as we are elsewhere informed, were of stone; by which we are perhaps to understand a substance similar to that of the precious stones; beautiful and splendid in a high degree, as well as durable, that it might correspond with the remaining articles of the tabernacle-furniture. Thus the Jewish writers; 'The first tables were hewn out of the sapphire of the throne of God's glory.' The two tables were probably designed to close together like the lids of a book, and by their being written on both sides is meant that their right and left hand leaf or side were each of them to be occupied with letters.

16. *The tables were the work of God,* &c. That is, the preparation of the materials, the stony tablets, by which they were brought into a state suitable for receiving the purposed inscription, was as purely the work of Jehovah himself, as the engraving of the characters which appeared upon them.

17. *And when Joshua heard,* &c. The ignorance of Joshua respecting the real nature of the uproar in the camp evinces that he had not, after ascending the mount with Moses, ch. 24. 13, as yet returned thither again; so that the inference is obvious that Joshua, as well as Moses, was forty days in the mount, though not in the same part of it. How he was sustained or employed we are not informed. He was now probably waiting for Moses at some distance from the top of the mountain, at the point whither Moses 'went down,' v. 15, and upon his re-appearance addressed him in the words that follow. His calm and quiet waiting during all the time of Moses' absence stands in very strong and, to him, creditable contrast with the rash, impatient, and unbelieving temper of the people during the same period.——¶ *As they shouted.* Targ. Jon., 'When they shouted with the noise of jubilee before the calf.'——¶ *A noise of war in the camp.* Heb. קוֹל מִלְחָמָה *kol milhamah;* a phrase rendered in Jer. 50. 22, ' the sound of battle.' The sounds that struck his ear were so different from those with which the camp had thus far been familiar, that he seems at once

18 And he said, *It is* not the voice of *them that* shout for mastery, neither *is it* the voice of *them that* cry for being overcome: *but* the noise of *them that* sing do I hear.

19 ¶ And it came to pass as soon as he came nigh unto the camp, that [z] he saw the calf, and the dancing: and Moses' anger waxed hot, and he cast the tables out of his hands, and break them beneath the mount.

[z] Deut. 9. 16, 17.

to have concluded that an attack had been made upon the host by some of the wandering tribes of the desert, and that what he heard was the cry or shout of onset, such as was usually made by an eager soldiery rushing into combat. But this erroneous report of his senses was soon corrected.

18. *It is not the voice,* &c. Heb. ' It is no voice of the crying of strength (prowess), and it is no voice of the crying of weakness.' Chal. ' It is not the voice of strong men which overcome in the war, neither is it the voice of weak men which are discomfited'—a correct paraphrase.——¶ *But the noise of them that sing do I hear.* That sing in alternate or responsive strains, one choir *answering* (עֲנוֹת *annoth*) another, as the original properly implies. Gr. 'The voice of them that sing for wine ;' in allusion to their revelling and riot. As Moses had been instructed of God as to what the people were now doing, he could easily correct the mistaken apprehensions of Joshua.

19. *And it came to pass,* &c. The first effects of this fearful apostasy are here related. They show themselves in the conduct of their returning leader. It is recorded as a high character of Moses that he was pre-eminent in meekness. Yet in his, as in every other case of *true* meekness, this spirit wrought in harmonious cooperation with a lively and glowing *zeal* for the Lord of hosts. With all his gentleness and patience he could tolerate nothing that reflected or cast a stain upon the divine glory. His own insults and injuries, the ingratitude and disrespect shown to himself during his absence, he could

easily pass by. But not so the offence committed against God. This was too gross, daring, and high-handed an insult to the majesty of heaven not to draw from him the tokens of a holy indignation. Accordingly as he approached the camp and beheld the congregation giving themselves up to bacchanalian revelries and dancing around the idol which they had formed, he cast the precious tables out of his hand and brake them to pieces at his feet. This was not done in a paroxysm of intemperate wrath, but as a significant emblem representing the crime which they had now committed. He was undoubtedly inwardly moved to it by a prompting from above. God had condescended to enter into a covenant with them to be their God, and they had covenanted to be his people. These tables of stone contained, as it were, the terms of agreement ; and were a pledge, that God would fulfil to them all that he had spoken. This covenant they had entirely annulled, and consequently all their expectations from God were utterly destroyed. Such a mode therefore of representing the transaction, on the part of Moses, was perfectly lawful and right. Indeed, so far was his conduct on this occasion from being a sudden transport or sally even of *pious* wrath in view of the enormity of Israel's sin, that there is every reason to regard it as the result of a deliberate purpose executed indeed by a roused and energetic spirit. It is to be recollected that he did not first come to the knowledge of the people's crime, when he first came within sight of the camp. God had previously informed him of it,

20 ᵃ And he took the calf which they had made, and burnt *it* in the fire, and ground *it* to powder, and

ᵃ Deut. 9. 21.

strewed *it* upon the water, and made the children of Israel drink *of it.*

---

and it was no doubt under divine dictation that he resolved as he descended upon the manner in which he should most significantly express his own and Jehovah's sense of the fearful consequences of their guilt. This was to be done by some action performed in the sight of the host. Accordingly instead of being ordered to leave the tables behind him on the mount, he was directed to take them along with him, that when they were broken before their eyes they might be more deeply affected, and filled with confusion to think what blessings they had lost. They had broken the covenant itself, and Moses as a sensible sign of the awful fact breaks the monumental tables in which it was inscribed. Nothing could more solemnly indicate that their covenant standing was wrecked, and that they now lay exposed to the severest vengeance of an angry God. It is doubtless in this view of the transaction that we find no censure passed upon Moses, nor does he afterward, Deut. 9. 17, speak of it with any regret.

20. *And he took the calf,* &c. The zeal with which he was inspired enabled him to face the congregation with majestic authority, and to seize and reduce to powder the vile fabrication of their hands. They appear to have been too much overawed by his presence to attempt any resistance, and he proceeded at once in a very striking manner both to convince them of their sin, and to punish them for it. He gives them a demonstration of the vanity of the idol which they had so stupidly worshipped by virtually annihilating it, except as a portion of it remained as an instrument of correction.——¶ *Ground it to powder.* Heb. רטדן *yithan.* The original denotes any mode of com-

minuting or reducing to small particles a hard substance, whether by filing, grinding, or any other process of abrasion. As to the precise manner in which the effect was produced in the present instance, we are not informed. We must be left to our own conjectures, aided only by the dim light of the parallel passage, Deut. 9. 21, 'And I took your sin, the calf which ye had made, and burnt it with fire, and stamped it, and ground it very small, even until it was as small as dust: and I cast the dust thereof into the brook that descended out of the mount.' By its being ' stamped' we are probably to infer that it was *beat* or *hammered* out into thin plates, and from that form reduced to the condition of a fine dust, which might easily be strewed upon the water. The process would no doubt require considerable time and labor; but he would have numbers to assist him, and no hypothetical difficulties in the way of the result are to be allowed to countervail the express testimony of revelation that *such was the fact.*—— ¶ *Made the children of Israel to drink of it.* Not perhaps that he *constrained* them to this; but having no other water for their daily use than that of the brook which descended out of the mount, Ex. 17. 6. Deut. 9. 21, they could not avoid, when they drank at all, drinking this mixture. How suitable the punishment to the sin! What greater indignity could be offered to the worthless idol? What more humiliating punishment could be inflicted upon the people, than to be thus compelled to *swallow their god,* and to ' cast him out into the draught' with their common food. But this, like the breaking the tables, was an *emblematical* action. It not only showed them how utterly con-

21 And Moses said unto Aaron, b What did this people unto thee, that thou hast brought so great a sin upon them ?

b Gen. 20. 9. & 26. 10.

22 And Aaron said, Let not the anger of my lord wax hot : c thou knowest the people, that they *are* set on mischief.

c ch. 14. 11. & 15. 24. & 16. 2, 20, 28. & 17. 2. 4.

temptible was the idol, which could thus be reduced so near to nothing, but taught them also in a most impressive manner, that ' the backslider in heart shall be filled with his own ways.' The powder mixed with their drink ' signified to them that the curse they had thereby brought upon themselves, would mingle itself with all their enjoyments, and embitter them ; that it would enter into their bowels like water, and like oil into their bones.' *Henry.*

21. *And Moses said unto Aaron*, &c. Another painful duty still remained to be performed by Moses. His own brother had been ' chief in the transgression,' and he is now to be called to account and interrogated with a holy sternness. The language in which Moses addressed him might seem at first view to involve a latent vein of irony or satire, as if he had inquired what offence they had committed against him, that he should think of avenging himself by leading them into so great wickedness. This would imply that so enormous in his eyes was the guilt of the transaction, that it must have required some *violent motive* on the part of Aaron to prompt him to engage in it. On the common principles by which a servant of God might be supposed to be actuated, it seemed to him impossible to account for his conduct, and he therefore asks if there were not some *personal* consideration which moved him to the deed. This is the view taken of the passage by Scott and other commentators, who understand Moses as insinuating that the spirit of *retaliation* or *revenge* was at the bottom of his conduct. But we prefer on the whole a simpler construction of the

speaker's meaning. We believe the scope of the question is simply to inquire, what were the influences and inducements brought to bear upon him by the people, which could prevail to gain his consent to such an abominable measure. If it were possible for him to advance any thing which should stand him instead of an excuse, he was willing and anxious to hear it. 'Did they importune, or cajole, or threaten thee ? Make a free confession, and solve the problem of thy conduct.' Yet it is not to be supposed that Moses anticipated any answer from Aaron that could *really* excuse him, or explain away the fact that *a great sin* had been actually committed. Whatever were his motives, *he had led the people into sin*, not perhaps by being the first mover of it, but by consenting to it, aiding and abetting it, when, as a magistrate, he should have resisted and put it down. He might justly be said, therefore, to have ' brought it upon them' by giving them his countenance in it. Such is the tenfold power of evil, which attaches itself to the example of those who stand high in authority and repute ! In the estimate of Scripture Aaron's conduct was a virtual *hatred* of his people which was not to have been expected except from an *enemy.* Lev. 19. 17, ' Thou shalt not *hate* thy brother in thine heart ; thou shalt in any wise rebuke thy neighbor, and shalt not *suffer sin upon him.*' This text is an humbling commentary upon the proceedings of Aaron in this sad affair.

22. *And Aaron said, Let not*, &c. The reasons assigned by Aaron for his conduct are honest, but frivolous. He makes a candid statement of the facts

23 For they said unto me, ^d Make us gods which shall go before us: for *as for* this Moses, the man that brought us up out of the land of Egypt, we wot not what is become of him.

24 And I said unto them, whosoever hath any gold, let them break

^d ver. 1.

it off. So they gave *it* me: then I cast it into the fire, and there ^e came out this calf.

25 ¶ And when Moses saw that the people *were* ^fnaked, (for Aaron ^g had made them naked unto *their* shame among their enemies,)

^e ver. 4. ^f ch. 33. 4, 5. ^g 2 Chron. 28. 19.

---

but leaves himself wholly unjustified in the premises, as may easily be inferred from the circumstance, that Moses does not seem to regard it as deserving of a reply. He passes by the lame apology without a single word of comment.—— ¶ *Thou knowest the people, that they are set on mischief.* Heb. ברע הוא *bera hu,* that *they are in evil;* an emphatic mode of expression indicating that they are, as it were, settled, sunk, immersed in evil or in sin. So, 1 John, 5. 19, 'The whole world lieth *in wickedness* (in evil) ;' a phrase equivalent to *being very evil,* as when it is said, Ps. 33. 4, (Heb.) 'his words are *in truth,*' the meaning is, that his words are *pre-eminently true* and *faithful.* Gr. 'Thou knowest the violent force of this people.' Yet how obvious even to a child, that the perverseness of the people was no apology for the pusillanimity of their leader. Were they given to evil?—So much the more needful was it for him to stem the torrent, and by inflexible firmness withstand the workings of their corruptions. Our instinctive sentiments at once respond to the justice of the divine judgment respecting this affair as recorded, Deut. 9. 20, 'And the Lord was very angry with Aaron to have destroyed him: and I prayed for Aaron also the same time.'

24. *And there came out this calf.* It might perhaps appear from the letter that Aaron intended to insinuate, that the calf was produced by accident, or by some invisible or magical operation, and that he was as much surprised at

the result as any one else could be. The Targ. Jon. takes the same view of it ; 'And I said unto them, whosoever hath gold let him break it off and give, it to me ; and I cast it into the fire, *and Satan entered into it,* and it came out in the form of this calf.' But it is scarcely possible to conceive that a man like Aaron should have resorted to such a silly and ridiculous subterfuge. We therefore take it as a brief and rather garbled account of the process of formation, upon the details of which he did not like to dwell, though he would not deny his agency in the affair. He confesses that he took the gold and melted it, and that the calf was the result ; but he excuses himself from reciting all the particulars of the process.

25. *And when Moses saw that the people were naked.* Heb. פרע *parua,* from פרע *para, to free, to set loose, to let break away,* and thence *to fall into disorder, confusion,* and *exposedness,* a state in which one is *naked of defence.* This is probably the leading idea ; not so much that they were denuded of their garments or ornaments, as that they were deprived by their impious act of the favorable presence and protection of heaven, which was their glory and their strength, so that they now stood as *naked unarmed men* liable to be surprised and put to flight by the weakest enemy. It was doubtless a conduct strikingly exemplifying the truth of the apothegm of one of the Latin fathers ; 'Non est nudus nisi quem culpa nudaverit,' *he only is naked whom*

26 Then Moses stood in the gate of the camp, and said, Who *is* on the LORD's side? *let him come* unto me. And all the sons of Levi gathered themselves together unto him.

27 And he said unto them, Thus saith the LORD God of Israel, Put

every man his sword by his side, *and* go in and out from gate to gate throughout the camp, and h slay every man his brother, and every man his companion, and every man his neighbor.

h Numb. 25, 5.   Deut. 33. 9.

---

crime hath made so. As the import, however, of the original word is not settled with absolute precison, it may be that it more properly denotes a dissipated, dissolute, disorderly state, in which the people had thrown off discipline and restraint, and given themselves up to every excess of revelling and riot. Thus the Gr. ' were *dissipated,* for Aaron had *dissipated* them.' Parkhurst renders it *to break loose,* or *start aside,* as from the true religion and worship; parallel to which he says is the usage of the term, Prov. 29. 18. 'Where there is no vision the people *perish* (יפרע *yipparä*) ;' rather, ' the people *break away or apostatize,*' or as the Vulg. renders, *will be dissipated.* So 2 Chron. 27. 19, ' For the Lord brought Judah low because of Ahaz king of Israel; for he made Judah *naked.*' Gr. 'Because he *utterly apostatized* from the Lord.' —— ¶ *Unto their shame.* Heb. לשמצה *leshimtza, to infamy;* i. e. when the report of their foul revolt should spread abroad. Chal. 'To blot them with an evil name in their generations. Gr. 'For Aaron had dissipated them for a rejoicing to their adversaries ;' i. e. so as to give their enemies cause of exultation and triumph over them.

26. *Then Moses stood in the gate of the camp,* &c. Some place probably about the outskirts of the camp, answering in a rude way to the gate of a city, where courts of judgment were wont to sit, hear causes, and give sentence.—— ¶ *Who is on the Lord's side ? let him come to me.* Heb. מי לירהוה אלי *mi laihovah ëli, whosoever* (is) *for the*

Lord—to me !—where the words ' let him come' are omitted through the impassioned earnestness of the speaker. ¶ *All the sons of Levi gathered themselves together unto him.* This can hardly be understood literally, as it is clearly implied, Deut. 33. 9, that some of the Levites were slain, and consequently that some of them were involved in the guilt of this transaction. By 'all' therefore we are to understand, perhaps, that all who did assemble were sons of Levi, and that of them there was a very large number.

27. *Put every man his sword by his side,* &c. Judgment was here to be executed by commission, and not by the immediate hand of God himself, as in some other instances of aggravated transgression. It was indeed a trying test to which the fidelity of the faithful was now to be submitted in becoming the executioners of their own brethren, and without distinction of sex, age, or relation, to imbrue their hands in the blood of those that were most dear to them. But the offence was one of the most aggravated character ; one by which the honor of God's great name had been sadly tarnished; and in order to a more effectual vindication of it, judgment was to be executed with terrible severity.—— ¶ *Go in and out from gate to gate throughout the camp.* This is no doubt to be understood as a commission to slay every one whom they should meet in the open places of the camp, let him be relation, friend, or neighbor, while they were not required to enter into any of the tents, inasmuch as those who were sensible of the divine

28 And the children of Levi did according to the word of Moses: and there fell of the people that day about three thousand men.

29 i For Moses had said, Consecrate yourselves to-day to the LORD, even every man upon his son, and upon his brother; that he

i Numb. 25. 11, 12, 13. Deut. 13. 6,—11. & 33. 9, 10. 1 Sam. 15. 18, 22. Prov. 21. 3. Zech. 13. 3. Matt. 10. 37.

displeasure might be presumed to be there employed in secret in bemoaning their own or the iniquity of their brethren. None were executed but those who openly and boldly stood forth.——

¶ *Slay every man his brother*, &c. That is, let those who are on the Lord's side slay all the rest who have apostatized, even their nearest relations.

28. *The children of Levi did according to the word of Moses.* Their numbers were incomparably less than those of the rest of the people, yet acting under and animated by a divine commission, they hesitated not to encounter them sword in hand. Their victims, on the other hand, were probably so disheartened by conscious guilt, and so confounded and intimidated by the authority of Moses, that they made no resistance.

29. *For Moses had said*, &c. This discloses the reason of the zeal and alacrity of the Levites in this trying service. They had been informed by Moses that the inflicting of vengeance on their guilty brethren would be a service so acceptable to God, that they would by performing it secure his 'blessing' by being confirmed in the sacerdotal office, and should by this act, as it were, 'consecrate' and initiate themselves unto God as by an offering of sacrifice. Accordingly it is said to the same purpose, Deut. 33. 8—10, 'And of Levi he said, Let thy Thummim and thy Urim be with thy holy one, &c., who said unto his father and

may bestow upon you a blessing this day.

30 ¶ And it came to pass on the morrow, that Moses said unto the people, k Ye have sinned a great sin: and now I will go up unto the LORD; l peradventure I shall m make an atonement for your sin.

k 1 Sam. 12. 20, 23. Luke 15. 18. l 2 Sam. 16. 12. Amos 5. 15. m Numb. 25. 13.

to his mother, I have not seen him; neither did he acknowledge his brethren, nor know his own children; for they have observed thy word and kept thy covenant. They shall teach Jacob thy judgments, and Israel thy law; they shall put incense before thee, and whole burnt sacrifice upon thine altars.' This act of obedience was a kind of inauguration, though a fearful one, of the tribe into their holy office. They thus wiped away as it were the stain which adhered to the escutcheon of their tribe from the conduct of their father Levi, who had wielded his sword unto sin in the affair of the Shechemites, Gen. 34. 25, in consequence of which he lost the blessing which would otherwise have been conferred upon him, and which the faithful and devoted conduct of his sons may be said to have regained.——

¶ *Consecrate.* Heb. מלאו ידכם *milu yedkem, fill your hands.* On the appropriate significancy of this term, see Note on Ex. 29. 9.——¶ *That he may bestow upon you a blessing.* The blessing of preferment to the rank of God's special ministers in the service of his house.

30. *Ye have sinned a great sin.* From this it appears that *all* the guilty were not cut off by the sword of the executioners. But those who *were* destroyed were probably the individuals who headed the rebellion, and of whom it was fit to make a signal example in order to inspire the rest with a salutary dread. The fact of their exemption

31 And Moses [n] returned unto the LORD, and said, Oh, this people have sinned a great sin, and have [o] made them gods of gold.

32 Yet now, if thou wilt forgive

[n] Deut. 9. 18.   [o] ch. 20. 23.

their sin: and if not, [p] blot me, I pray thee, [q] out of thy book which thou hast written.

[p] Ps. 69. 28. Rom. 9. 3.   [q] Ps. 56. 8. & 139. 16.   Dan. 12. 1.   Phil. 4. 3.   Rev. 3. 5. & 13. 8. & 17. 8. & 20. 12, 15. & 21. 27. & 22. 19.

from the fatal stroke might possibly beget, in their minds, the persuasion that their guilt was not of a very deep dye ; but Moses here acquaints them to the contrary. He assures them that they —even *they*—had ' sinned a great sin ;' and not only so, he even expresses himself as if he deemed it somewhat questionable whether it would be consistent with the honor of God to grant them forgiveness. ' I will go up unto the Lord ; *peradventure* I shall make an atonement for your sin.' He thought he might perhaps be made *an instrument of reconciliation;* for in no other sense could *atonement* be properly predicated of Aaron's agency on this occasion. He was not without hope, nor yet was he destitute of fear ; accordingly his words were calculated to preserve the people in a due medium between desponding dread and presumptuous confidence. Such is the usual style of the Scriptures in their addresses to flagrant sinners. Amos, 5. 15, ' *It may be* that the Lord God of hosts will be gracious unto the remnant of Joseph.' Jonah, 1. 6, 'What meanest thou, O sleeper? arise, call upon thy God, *if so be* that God will think upon us, that we perish not.' Acts, 8. 22, 'Repent therefore of this thy wickedness, and pray God, *if perhaps* the thought of thine heart may be forgiven thee.'

31. *And Moses returned.* From a comparison of this with the subsequent parts of the narrative we infer that this withdrawment from the people was not the same with that of forty days' duration of which Moses thus speaks, Deut. 9. 18, 'And I fell down before the Lord, as at the first, forty days and forty

nights ; I did neither eat bread, nor drink water, because of all your sins which ye sinned, in doing wickedly in the sight of the Lord, to provoke him to anger.' The train of events is not very clearly detailed, but we are forced to the conclusion that Moses retired for a short time to consult the Most High once or twice in the interval between the first and second protracted term of forty days. See the remarks upon the order of occurrences in the next chapter.——¶ *Oh, this people have sinned a great sin,* &c. The impassioned and pathetic tone in which he begins his prayer is very remarkable. He speaks like one who is overwhelmed with horror at the enormity of the sin, for the pardon of which he pleads. The Scriptures deal but sparingly in such interjectional phrases as the present, and wherever they occur they indicate the most profound emotion in the speaker. But Moses knew well, as do all other saints, that nothing is so efficacious in obtaining mercy as deep humiliation before God.

32. *Yet now, if thou wilt forgive their sin.* This is an imperfect sentence, and ought undoubtedly to be printed as it is in many English editions of the Bible—'Yet now if thou wilt forgive their sin— ; if not,' &c. The Gr. has, 'If thou wilt forgive them the sin, forgive them.' Several modern versions propose to supply the ellipsis in like manner ; but the suspension of the meaning by such an expressive break is far more significant than any word which could be introduced to fill it up.——¶ *Blot me, I pray thee, out of thy book;* called Ps. 69. 29, ' the book of the living ;' Phil. 4. 3, 'the book of life ;' Ezek. 13

33 And the LORD said unto Moses, ʳ Whosoever hath sinned against me, him will I blot out of my book.

34 Therefore now go, lead the people unto *the place* of which I

ʳ Lev. 23. 30. Ezek. 18. 4.

have spoken unto thee: ˢ Behold, mine Angel shall go before thee: nevertheless, ᵗ in the day when I visit, I will visit their sin upon them.

ˢ ch. 33. 2, 14, &c. Numb. 20. 16. ᵗ Deut. 32. 35. Amos 3. 14. Rom. 2. 5, 6.

9, 'the writing of the house of Israel.' The meaning is, let my name be no more in the number of those whom thou hast destined to live; let me die with my people. For as the phrase, Is. 4. 3, 'to be written with the living,' signifies to be preserved alive while others die, so to be blotted out of the book of the living is tantamount to being taken out of life while others survive. There is no intimation in these words of any secret book of the divine decrees, or of any thing involving the question of Moses' final salvation or perdition. He simply expressed the wish rather to die than to witness the destruction of his people. The phraseology is in allusion, probably, to the custom of having the names of a community enrolled in a register, and whenever one died, of erasing his name from the number.

33. *Whosoever hath sinned against me*, &c. This seems intended to declare a general rule of proceeding in the divine government, in which an assurance is given that the innocent shall not be confounded with the guilty, but that punishment should fall where it was justly due, and nowhere else. It was in the present case a clear intimation of mercy to the people, assuring their leader that they should not be destroyed in a body, but those only who had merited cutting off by their sin.

34. *Behold mine Angel shall go before thee.* As the term 'Angel' is in several cases in this narrative used as synonimous with the Pillar of Cloud, we should naturally be led to suppose, if the sequel were not inconsistent with it, that the meaning here was, that notwithstanding their recent high handed

iniquity, this guiding signal, this protecting Presence, should still go with them. But upon comparing the passage before us with the words of Moses, ch. 33. 12—16, it appears obvious that he took the word in a more general sense as simply indicating *some kind of providential agency* which should be exerted in their behalf while pursuing their journey through the wilderness. That this is a legitimate sense of the word 'Angel' any one may be convinced by referring to the scriptural use of the term as fully detailed in the Note on Ex. 3. 2. The promise, therefore, though consoling was yet vague. It left Moses in doubt as to the real character of the Angel, i. e. agency, which he was taught to expect. Accordingly in his prayer in the ensuing chapter he earnestly beseeches for more precise information, and desires that no other than the particular 'Angel of the presence' the majestic Shekinah, should accompany them. —— ¶ *Nevertheless, in the day when I visit, I will visit their sin upon them.* That is, when I have occasion to visit them in judgment for other offences, I will remember their sin on this occasion, and increase their punishment on account of it. Accordingly it has always remained as a tradition among the Jews, even to the present day, that in whatever afflictions they have been made to experience there was mingled at least an ounce of the powder of the golden calf. The intimation conveys an important practical lesson to the people of God in all ages. The effects of one sin may go to enhance the punishment of another, and so we may have constant memorials

35 And the LORD plagued the people, because ᵘ they made the calf which Aaron made.

CHAPTER XXXIII.

AND the LORD said unto Moses, Depart *and* go up hence,

ᵘ 2 Sam. 12. 9.   Acts 7. 41.

---

of a particular offence throughout the chastening discipline of a whole life.

35. *And the Lord plagued the people,* &c. It is not clear that this statement refers to any particular plague or pestilence which occurred *at this time* among the people. It may be understood of the subsequent scourges and calamities which they suffered during their sojourn in the wilderness as long as Moses lived. In this case it is but another mode of saying that the threatening denounced in the preceding verse was actually fulfilled in their after experience as a nation. At the same time, as there is no doubt that the order of events is very much transposed in this part of the narrative, there is nothing actually to forbid the supposition that the plague or stroke here mentioned is no other than the slaughter of the three thousand recorded in the next chapter. Indeed we think this on the whole the preferable interpretation.——¶ *Because they made,* &c. That is, because they caused or procured to be made; a phraseology of very frequent occurrence. Thus, Acts, 1. 18, Judas is said to have purchased a field, which in fact, was purchased by the priests, but it is attributed to Judas because his receiving and then returning the money, was the occasion of its being bought. The originators and procurers of evil are not to promise themselves impunity because they have prevailed upon others to become their tools in its execution. The consequences will ' return to plague the inventors.' God's judgment is always according to truth, and he will charge home guilt where it properly belongs.

thou ᵃ and the people which thou hast brought up out of the land of Egypt, unto the land which I sware unto Abraham, to Isaac, and to Jacob, saying, ᵇ Unto thy seed will I give it:

ᵃ ch. 32. 7.   ᵇ Gen. 12. 7. ch. 32. 13.

' Deos qui rogat, ille facit,' *he who asks for gods makes them.*

Chapter 33

The right adjustment of the events of this chapter in the chronological order of the narrative, is a matter attended with some difficulty. From the rendering of our established version it would seem, that what was now said to Moses was posterior in point of time to the incidents recorded in the close of the preceding chapter; but from an attentive consideration and collation of the tenor of the whole, we are persuaded, with Calvin and other critics of note, that the proper rendering of v. 1, is in the pluperfect—' the Lord *had* said'—and that the appropriate place for the interview and incidents here related is *prior* to the order and the promise contained v. 34 of ch. 32. In that verse God declares his purpose of sending his angel before the people, and we naturally enquire how it happens that such an assurance was necessary? Was there any danger that an angel would *not* be sent ? Had any intimation been given that his guiding and protecting presence would be withdrawn? To this the correct answer undoubtedly is, that all that is related in ch. 33, had occurred *anterior* to the promise made in ch. 32. 34. God had threatened to send Moses and the people forward without the accompanying presence of the Angel of the Shekinah, and it was only in consequence of the fervent intercession of Moses that he was induced to retract this dread determination. In the foregoing chapter, therefore, the historian merely

2 c And I will send an angel before thee; d and I will drive out the Canaanite, the Amorite, and the Hittite, and the Perizzite, the Hivite, and the Jebusite:

c ch 32. 34. & 34. 11. d Deut. 7. 22. Josh. 24. 11

states in a summary way the fact of his earnest prayer and the concession made to it; in the present, he goes back and relates minutely the train of circumstances which preceded and led to the declaration above mentioned. In doing this he virtually makes known to us one main ground of the urgency of his supplications. He was afraid that God would withdraw thé tokens of his visible presence. As a punishment for the mad attempt of the people to supply themselves with a *false* symbol of his presence, he was apprehensive he might be provoked to take from them the *true*, and hence his impassioned entreaty that God would not visit them with so sore a judgment. But the particulars will disclose themselves as we proceed.

1. *And the Lord said.* Heb. וידבר יהוה *va-yedabber Yehovah, and Jehovah had said;* as the like phrase is often elsewhere to be translated. It is only the context in such cases that determines the true mode of rendering.—— ¶ *Depart and go up hence,* &c. These words, and what immediately follows, appear to have been spoken by God to Moses during his first sojourn upon the summit of the mount, and upon the occasion of the making of the golden calf. In sovereign displeasure he turns the people over, as it were, upon Moses, whom he represents as having brought them out of Egypt, rather than himself; and though he promises to make good his covenant with Abraham, and give them the land of Canaan, yet he intimates that they shall go forward without the extraordinary tokens of his

3 e Unto a land flowing with milk and honey: f for I will not go up in the midst of thee; for thou *art* a g stiff-necked people: lest h I consume thee in the way.

e ch. 3. 8. f ver. 15. 17. g ch. 32. 9. & 34. 9. Deut. 9 6, 13. h ch. 23. 21. & 32. 10. Numb. 16. 21. 45.

presence which they had hitherto enjoyed, and which would have been continued to them but for their sin. Such language imports, however, a reserved prerogative of change in the dispensation announced if adequate reasons for it should occur.

2. *And I will send an angel before thee.* This clause is not to be understood as spoken to Moses, but is to be read in connexion with the preceding, v. 1, as a part of the promise to the fathers and their seed, which God is here reciting. The promise of the emissary angel was not, indeed, expressly made to either of the patriarchs here mentioned, but it was expressly made to the Israelites, Ex. 23. 20, and the whole is here brought together as one integral promise.

3. *For I will not go up in the midst of thee,* &c. Chal. 'I will not make my Shekinah (שכנתי *shekinti*) to go up in the midst of thee.' Arab. 'I will not make my Light (or Splendor) to go up among you.' Having recited the promise formerly made of conducting them into Canaan by the medium of the Angel of his presence, or the Shekinah, the Lord here ostensibly retracts his promise and announces a contrary intention. So perverse, stiff-necked, and rebellious had they proved, that they were to consider themselves as having forfeited the favor of such a presence, and as being righteously exposed to be left in utter destitution of the symbol of their glory. Yet the well-grounded remark of Scott is ever to be borne in mind, that 'such declarations rather express what God justly might do, what

4 ¶ And when the people heard these evil tidings, i they mourned: k and no man did put on him his ornaments.

5 For the LORD had said unto Moses, Say unto the children of

i Numb. 14. 1, 39.   k Lev. 10. 6.   2 Sam. 19. 24. 1 Kings 21. 27. 2 Kings 19. 1. Esther 4. 1, 4.   Ezra 9. 3.   Job 1. 20. & 2. 12.   Isai. 32. 11.   Ezek. 24. 17, 23. & 26. 16.

Israel, l Ye *are* a stiff-necked people: I will come up m into the midst of thee in a moment, and consume thee: therefore now put off thy ornaments from thee, that I may n know what to do unto thee.

l ver. 3.   m See Numb. 16. 45, 46.   n Deut. 8. 2.   Ps. 139. 23.

it would become him to do, and what he would do, were it not for some intervening consideration, than his *irreversible* purpose; and always imply a reserved exception, in case the party offending were truly penitent.' —— ¶ *Lest I consume thee in the way.* Lest I should be constrained, by a just regard to my own glory, to come out in consuming wrath against your iniquities.

4, 5. *When the people heard these evil tidings, they mourned.* The announcement was probably made to the people when Moses first came down from the mount, and after breaking the tables of stone. Their humiliation, therefore, took place in the interval between the first and second period of forty days, during which Moses withdrew himself from the congregation for the purpose of prayer and fasting. The effect produced showed that they were deeply sensible of the value of the blessing which they were likely to lose. They were at once filled with grief, which expressed itself by the usual external badges of 'mourning,' viz., divesting themselves of their ornaments, although it appears from v. 5, that this was at the same time in obedience to an express command of Jehovah. This was not only in order that they might evince the appropriate tokens of sorrow and humiliation, but also that they could make sacrifices to God as well as to a golden calf. While thus disrobed of their festive garments and precious jewels, and clad in the habit of penitents, God represents him-

self as deliberating how to act towards them. But when God speaks of himself in this language, as if perplexed and wavering in his mind, it is not to be understood as intimating that such things *actually* exist; for 'known unto God are all his works from the beginning of the world;' nor can any occasion possibly arise in which he can be at a loss how to act. But he is pleased to speak in this way of himself in order to accommodate himself to our feeble apprehensions. Compare Hos. 6. 4. and Jer. 3. 19, where also the Most High speaks as if perplexed in his mind about the line of conduct he should pursue, and as wishing to show mercy, but not knowing how to do it consistently with his own honor. All this is plainly capable of a sense entirely consistent with the reverence due to the Supreme Being. But while it is intimated that so long as impenitence continues *he knows not how* to exercise mercy to the sinner, it is at the same time implied, that when once humbled for their iniquities he is at no loss how to act towards them; he can then give free scope to the merciful and compassionate disposition of his own heart. So it is clear that the language in the present case implied a design of mercy, provided they showed signs of repentance and as they *did* demean themselves as those who were conscious of their delinquencies and sincerely mourned, we may suppose that this fact added its weight to the fervency of Moses' prayers to give them prevalence with God in their behalf.

6 And the children of Israel stripped themselves of their ornaments by the mount Horeb.

7 And Moses took the tabernacle, and pitched it without the camp afar off from the camp, ° and

° ch. 29. 42, 43.

called it the Tabernacle of the Congregation. And it came to pass, *that* every one which ᴾ sought the LORD, went out unto the tabernacle of the congregation, which *was* without the camp.

ᴾ Deut. 4. 29. 2 Sam. 21. 1.

6. *By the mount Horeb.* Heb. מֵחַר חֹרֵב *mëhar Horëb, from mount Horeb.* That is, at a considerable distance from it, as not worthy to stand in immediate proximity to it. The form of the expression, however, in that sense is so singular, that we are strongly inclined to regard the preposition ' from' as a particle of *time* rather than of *place,* implying that from the time of the occurrence of this transaction at Horeb, they divested themselves of their ornaments, and continued to dispense with them during the remainder of their sojourning. Thus it is said, Num. 14. 19, 'As thou hast forgiven this people *from Egypt* even until now;' i. e. from the time of their being in Egypt. Why may not the phrase ' from Horeb' in the one instance be equivalent to ' from Egypt' in the other? See this usage of speech more fully illustrated in the Note on Gen. 2. 10.

7. *And Moses took the tabernacle,* &c. Heb. הָאֹהֶל *ha-ohel, the tent.* It is evident that the tabernacle or tent here mentioned could not be that concerning which Moses had before received directions, for that was not yet built; nor is it at all probable that the private tent of Moses is to be understood, for it appears v. 8, that Moses himself went back and forth to and from this tabernacle as well as the rest of the congregation, from which it is to be inferred that he, as well as they, ordinarily resided within the camp. The probability therefore is that the Israelites, previous to the erection of the prescribed tabernacle, had some kind of sacred tent or portable temple for the public performance of religious rites, which Moses, as an argument of God's displeasure against Israel, on this occasion, ordered to be removed from a camp so grossly profaned by idol-worship. It is indeed objected to this, that this tabernacle now first began to be honored with a new designation, and called אֹהֶל מוֹעֵד *ohel moëd, the tabernacle of convention,* which is inconsistent with the idea of its having *previously* been employed for such a purpose. But to this it may be replied, that nothing forbids the rendering the clause in the pluperfect, and considering it as introduced parenthetically—' And took the tabernacle and pitched it without the camp afar off from the camp (for he had called it the Tabernacle of Convention) ; and it came to pass,' &c. It was so called because such was its object and use. It had hitherto served this purpose in the midst of the camp; but now as a sign of the divine alienation and displeasure, and in order to quicken and deepen their penitence, it was to be removed from its former position, and stationed at a distance from a locality which had forfeited its longer continuance upon it. The withdrawment was an intimation to their senses of the fact announced by Moses of their purposed dereliction by Jehovah's presence. He had before promised, ch. 25. 8, to dwell among them, in the midst of them, and as the oracular presence of the Deity was supposed to be especially connected with a *tent* or *tabernacle,* it may be supposed that this temporary erection had been prepared with that view, until the larger and more magnificent one designed by God himself should be built. But so

8 And it came to pass when Moses went out into the tabernacle, *that* all the people rose up, and stood every man ᑫ *at* his tent-door, and looked after Moses, until he was gone into the tabernacle.

ᑫ Numb. 16. 27.

9 And it came to pass, as Moses entered into the tabernacle, the cloudy pillar descended and stood *at* the door of the tabernacle, and *the LORD* ʳ talked with Moses.

ʳ ch. 25. 22. & 31. 18. Ps. 99. 7.

aggravated and enormous had been the offence recently committed, that the Most High proceeds now to indicate in a visible manner the retraction of his gracious promise, and instead of fixing the symbols of his presence in the camp, to cause them to be removed and planted far away from the places which had contracted such foul defilement. —— ¶ *Every one which sought the Lord.* Chal. 'Every one which sought doctrine .(or information) from before the face of the Lord—went forth to the tabernacle of the house of doctrine which was without the camp.' The removal of the tabernacle took away of course the facilities which the people had formerly enjoyed for consulting the divine oracle. This they could no more do in the camp, but were obliged for the purpose to go abroad to the place where God was henceforth pleased to manifest his presence. It is evident, therefore, that it was not a *total* withdrawment of the tokens of the divine favor. The Most High still proclaimed himself willing to be sought unto. Intimations of mercy were thus mingled with the signs of displeasure, ' lest the spirit should faint before him and the souls which he had made.' It may still, however, be regarded as probable that the people here spoken of did not actually enter *into* the tabernacle—a privilege apparently reserved for Moses alone—but only approached *towards* it themselves, while Moses acted as their advocate in the business which had brought them out.

8. *It came to pass when Moses went out*, &c. The particulars here mentioned are not. as we suppose, to be un-

derstood as having occurred on one special occasion only, but as being the ordinary accompaniments, for several days together, of Moses' ingress into the sacred tent whenever he entered it. His ordinary residence was doubtless in the camp with his family, but in his office of intercessor, mediator, and judge, he had repeated occasions to go forth to this tent to hold interviews with Jehovah ; and whenever this was the case, as he was acting on the behalf of the people, it was natural that they should watch with intense solicitude the visible indications of the issue of the affair. Thus the disciples ' looked after' our Lord Jesus, when he ascended on high to enter into the holy place not made with hands, till ' a cloud received him out of their sight, as Moses here.' *Henry.* The station of the tabernacle, we think it probable, was somewhere on the side of the mountain, far indeed below the summit, and yet in some conspicuous locality, that might be seen by most of the multitude below. The topographical features of the region are such that if the tent were *without* the camp it must necessarily be upon some elevated ground, as all the valleys or wadys would of course be occupied by the tents of the congregation.

9. *The cloudy pillar descended and stood at the door of the tabernacle,* &c. It descended from the summit to the less elevated part of the mountain where the Tabernacle stood. As the sublime object had probably remained entirely stationary for at least forty days, we can easily imagine that it must have produced a deep sensation

10 And all the people saw the cloudy pillar stand *at* the tabernacle-door: and all the people rose up and ˢworshipped, every man *in* his tent-door.

ˢ ch. 4. 31.

among the people to see it now again majestically moving from its place, and transferring itself down the mountain to the spot where the tent was fixed, and where Moses had now repaired. This would indeed verify the claim of the sacred structure to the title of ' Tabernacle of Meeting,' when Jehovah by his symbol was thus pleased to *meet* with his servant in this open and honorary manner, in the sight of the awe-struck host. The effect would naturally be to inspire additional reverence for the person and authority of Moses, as one whom God saw fit to distinguish by the indubitable seal of his own selection, and to endow with the highest prerogatives of a human mediator. The descent of the cloudy pillar at the door of the tent would also tend to assure them that the rupture between God and his people was not utterly past healing. Though withdrawn, in the withdrawing of the Tabernacle, from the midst of them, he was still accessible. With due reverence and patience and prostration of spirit they might still approach him, notwithstanding his offended majesty maintained a lofty and awful reserve which could not but engender some measure of trembling suspense. Nor is such an attitude unwonted to the Holy One of Israel. He often hides his face from sinners that he may the more effectually incite them to seek him with broken hearts. Under his fatherly chastisement, therefore, we are not to give way so far to the promptings of terror or conscious guilt as to forbear to seek him, but even though from afar to make our earnest suit towards him. So long as the tokens of his presence are not entirely removed, we are not permitted to nourish our despair.——¶ *And* the Lord *talked with Moses.* The words ' the Lord' are evi-

dently supplied, as if there were in the original an ellipsis of the proper subject of the verb. But we have no doubt that the correct rendering is yielded by the omission of this phrase. The writer *intended* to say that the cloudy pillar talked with Moses ; nor is any thing farther necessary to justify the expression than a reference to the view, so often repeated in the preceding Notes, of the Shekinah of the Old Testament economy. The aerial column, as the enclosing receptacle of the inner 'Glory' was the symbol of the Lord's presence to his people, and was the visible organ of the communication of his will. In this character it bore the name, displayed the attributes, and claimed the honors, of Jehovah himself. Nothing can be more pertinent to this point than the language of the Psalmist, Ps. 99. 7, 'He spake to them in the cloudy pillar.' It would be easy to enlarge upon this explanation, and to show its immense importance as a clue to the solution of a multitude of passages which speak of the divine manifestations, but the extended Note at the close of chapter 14, to which the reader is referred, will preclude the necessity of any fuller discussion of the text before us.

10. *All the people rose up and worshipped, every man in his tent door.* This is sometimes erroneously interpreted of the more civil respect and homage paid by the people to Moses as he passed by the doors of their tents on his way to the Tabernacle of the Congregation. It was unquestionably a worship rendered to God in token of their devout and grateful acknowlegement of his goodness in restoring to them, even though at a distance, the symbol of his gracious presence. It was a virtual profession that, whatever had been their past obliquities, they

11 And ᵗ the LORD spake unto Moses face to face, as a man speaketh unto his friend.   And he

ᵗ Gen. 32. 30. Numb. 12. 8. Deut. 34. 10.

turned again into the camp; but ᵘ his servant Joshua the son of Nun, a young man, departed not out of the tabernacle.

ᵘ ch. 24. 13.

now considered him as the only proper object of adoration, and would hence-forth pay their homage to him alone. It was an act of humble reverence very naturally prompted by the circumstances in which they were placed. How must their hearts have beat with tremulous anxiety as they stood at their tent-doors and ' looked after Moses un-til he had gone into the Tabernacle !' Their encampment they had so sadly defiled by their sin that they could not but have deep misgivings whether Je-hovah would any more return to them or accept their sacrifices, or listen to their prayers and praises. They could not but ask themselves, whether he would indeed meet Moses and them that sought him at the Tabernacle without the camp. What a relief then to such doubts as these to see the cloudy pillar descend ! How gladdening to their souls to behold even this partial intimation of the reconcileableness of their offended sovereign ! In the honor thus put upon their leader and advocate they could not but read a token of good to themselves. They had put off their ornaments in obedience to the divine injunction, and now doubtless stood with tears of repentance awaiting the indications of mercy or wrath. To the joy of their hearts they behold the signal of favor and forgiveness, and see themselves spared in that they feared ! How then could they fail to give vent to the admiring and adoring sentiments of their bosoms by falling down, as prostrate worshippers, and acknowledging the clemency of the Most High !

11. *And the Lord spake unto Moses face to face, as a man speaketh unto his friend.*   That is, familiarly and plain-ly, not in visions, dreams, or dark ora-

cles — a privilege peculiar to Moses; Num. 12. 6—8, ' If there be a prophet among you, I the Lord will make my-self known unto him in a vision, and will speak unto him in a dream.   My servant Moses is not so, who is faith-ful in all my house.   With him will I speak mouth to mouth, even apparently and not in dark speeches ; and the sim-ilitude of the Lord shall he behold.' It is clear however, that this must be understood in such a way as not to con-flict with what is said, v. 20, 'Thou canst not see my face ; for there shall no man see me and live.'   There is a sense in which God never has been nor can be seen.   Comp. John 1. 8. Col. 1. 15. 1 Tim. 6. 16.   Indeed we have no reason to suppose that a purely spirit-ual being can in the nature of things be made visible to mortal eyes.   We do not even see each other's spirits.   We only see the outward material forms through which, as a medium, the in-ward spirit manifests itself.   So in the present case.   What Moses saw and held communion with was not God in his intimate essence, but God in his sensible symbol of the Shekinah, and this as we have before remarked is re-peatedly called his 'Face' or 'Presence.' See Note on Ex. 25. 30.   Understood in this sense all difficulty vanishes at once, and leaves the two passages in entire harmony with each other.—Chal. ' And God spake unto Moses word to word.'   Gr. ενωπιον ενωπιω, *presence to presence.*——¶ *His servant Joshua, the son of Nun, a young man, departed not out of the tabernacle.*   As it is difficult to conceive for what purpose Joshua could have been required to remain in the Tabernacle after Moses had left it, there seems to be good ground for

12 ¶ And Moses said unto the Lord, See, ˣ thou sayest unto me, Bring up this people: and thou hast not let me know whom thou wilt send with me. Yet thou hast said, ʸ I know thee by name, and thou hast also found grace in my sight.

ˣ ch. 32. 34.

ʸ ver. 17. Gen. 18. 19. Ps. 1. 6. Jer. 1. 5. John 10. 14, 15. 2 Tim. 2. 19.

adopting the rendering of Junius and Tremellius, approved by Pool, Patrick, Rivet, Scott, and others, which runs thus ;—'He turned again into the camp, (he) and his servant Joshua, the son of Nun, a young man; but he (i. e. the Lord, as appearing in the cloud) departed not out of the Tabernacle.' The original will not only admit of this version, but the disposition of the accents seems rather to require it. Add to this, that the phrase ' out of the tabernacle,' is in the Hebrew ' out of the midst of the tabernacle,' which is more correctly applicable to the symbol of the Presence, for we have no intimation that any other person than Moses went into the Tabernacle, who seems to have been alone admitted to the honor of conversing with the divine Majesty. We have little hesitation therefore, on the whole, in adopting this as the true sense.—As to the epithet ' young man' applied to Joshua, it cannot be predicated of his age, for he was now about fifty-three years old; but he was a young man compared with Moses, and the original term נַעַר *naar* is often applied to one on the ground of his acting in a *ministerial* or *servile* capacity, as is clearly shown in the Note on Gen. 14. 24.

12. *And Moses said unto the Lord,* &c. There are few portions of the entire Pentateuch where it is so difficult to settle with precision the order of events as in the narrative before us. As to the present interview, there can be but little doubt that it took place before Moses went to pass the second forty days in the mount, but whether it is to be referred to the time when he interceded with God before coming down with the tables, or to some subsequent date in the interval between the two forty-days' sojourns, is questioned by commentators. For ourselves, as before remarked, we incline to the opinion which supposes a transposition of events, and that this prayer of Moses was really offered at the time when he returned unto the Lord, ch. 32. 31, and obtained the promise of an emissary angel, ch. 32. 34. But 'Angel,' is a term of large and somewhat indefinite import, implying *any kind of providential agency* by means of which Omnipotence might see fit to execute its plans. Moses therefore was desirous of *more particular* information. He wished to have the accompanying presence not merely of *an* Angel, but of *the* Angel, i. e. the Angel of the divine Face; the same Angel which had hitherto conducted their march in the Cloudy Pillar. In urging his plea for the bestowment of this blessing, he avails himself of the interest which he himself had with God as a special object of his favor, as one whom he ' knew by name,' i. e. as a particular friend and confidant, rendered in the Gr. 'I know thee above all ;' and in the Arab. 'I have ennobled thy name.' God had offered to destroy the whole nation of Israel, and raise up another from Moses' loins, and this token of good-will he lays hold of as a ground of hope that the object of his entreaty would not be denied him. It is not indeed to be supposed that in using this language Moses claimed a degree of personal merit sufficient to be the foundation of such a request, but he knew that one favor on the part of God was a pledge and precursor of others, and probably the

13 Now therefore, I pray thee, ᶻif I have found grace in thy sight, ᵃshew me now thy way, that I may know thee, that I may find grace in thy sight: and consider that this nation *is* ᵇthy people.

14 And he said, ᶜMy presence shall go *with thee*, and I will give thee ᵈrest.

ᶻch. 34. 9. ᵃPs. 25. 4. & 27. 11. & 86. 11. & 119. 33.

ᵇDeut. 9. 26, 29. Joel 2. 17. ᶜch. 13. 21. & 40. 34,—38. Isai. 63. 9. ᵈDeut. 3. 20. Josh. 21. 44. & 22. 4. & 23. 1. Ps. 95. 11.

---

very fact that he, notwithstanding his unworthiness, had been so graciously dealt with, was the moving cause of his earnest petition for still farther manifestations of his kindness and care. As God had been good to him in despite of his deserts, why might he not sue for augmented acts of clemency?

13. *Shew me now thy way.* That is, show me the way in which thou wouldst have thy people conducted to their inheritance. Show me thy views and purposes, thine *intended ways* of acting and thy requirements of me in reference to this great object. Gr. εμφανισον μοι σεαυτον, *discover thyself to me.* Chal. 'Show me the way of thy goodness.' Arab. 'Show me the ways of thy good-will.' Sam. 'Show me thy ways.'——¶ *That I may know thee, that I may find grace in thy sight.* It will be observed that the plea here is peculiar, and the logic such as can be fully appreciated only by a pious heart. He makes the fact of his having found grace already an argument for his finding still more. 'Lord, if it be so that I have indeed found acceptance with thee, then may I not confidently implore of thee that thou wouldst manifest thy mind and will to thy servant, so that in obeying it, I may continue to experience the uninterrupted and growing exhibitions of thy favor towards me. Grant me *light* that I may continue to yield thee *love.*'——¶ *Consider that this nation is thy people.* In the spirit of true prayer he presses into his service every argument that can increase the cogency of his plea. He does not beg the desired favor merely on the ground of what he might be permitted to urge on his own account, but he reminds the Most High that the people of whom he was constituted leader stood in a peculiar relation to him their covenant God and Portion. He had chosen their fathers, he had delivered *them* from bondage, he had adopted them as his own, he had crowned them with precious promises, and by all the ties which bound them to himself he beseeches that he would not leave nor cast them off. Though utterly unworthy, yet consider that they are *thine.*

14. *And he said, My presence shall go* with thee. Heb. פני ילכו *panai yёlïku, my face shall go.* Chal. 'My Majesty (שכנתי *shekinti, my Shekinah*) shall go.' Arab. 'My Light (or Splendor) shall walk with thee until I cause thee to rest.' The prayer of Moses at length prevails. Jehovah vouchsafes to him a definite assurance, that the object of his suit, viz., the same visible symbol of the divine presence which they had hitherto enjoyed, should be granted to accompany the host in their onward march to Canaan. More than this they did not need, and less than this could never satisfy one who had thus experienced the divine guidance and protection. This Presence was in truth no other than what is called, Is. 63. 9, 'the Angel of God's presence,' who saved, sustained, and guided the chosen people all the days of old. As to the relation which this Presence-angel bore to Christ in his human manifestation, see the Note on the Cloudy Pillar at the close of the thirteenth

15 And he said unto him, e If thy presence go not *with me*, carry us not up hence.

16 For wherein shall it be known here that I and thy people have found grace in thy sight? f *Is it not in that thou goest with us?*

So g shall we be separated, I and thy people, from all the people that *are* upon the face of the earth.

17 And the Lord said unto Moses, h I will do this thing also that thou hast spoken: for thou hast

e ver. 3.   ch. 34. 9.   f Numb. 14. 14.

g ch. 34. 10.   Deut. 4. 7, 34.   2 Sam. 7. 23
1 Kings 8. 53.   Ps. 147. 20.   h Gen. 19. 21.
James 5. 16.

---

chapter.——¶ *And I will give thee rest.* That is, by subduing all thine enemies and planting thee in triumph in the land of promise—a promise made, however, not to Moses in person, but to the collective people. It is in fact the Presence who is speaking, for it was with the Shekinah that Moses held intercourse throughout the whole of the time embraced in this narrative.

15. *If thy presence go not,* &c. Heb. אם אין פניך הלכים *im ën panëka holekim, if thy face do not go.* If we have not the peculiar *manifestation* of thy presence through the wonted medium, carry us not up hence. Without this it were better that they should remain, even at the hazard of eventually wasting away, in the desert. With several commentators we take this and the following verse to have been uttered by Moses *before* God gave him the promise in the verse preceding. The proper translation of the opening clause we have little doubt is, 'For Moses *had* said, &c.' The words are intended to discover to us the *reason* of God's giving him the specific promise. It was because Moses had made a specific request to that effect. Otherwise, we cannot see a sufficient ground for his so urgently renewing the petition when God had just engaged to grant it. Was it decorous in him to speak as if he doubted whether Jehovah were really in earnest in what he promised? As to v. 17, which might seem at first view to conflict with this suggestion, we regard it as merely Moses' own record,

slightly varied, of what God had said, v. 14. As that answer had come in a little out of place, he here recites the substance of it again. We feel on the whole quite satisfied that all the conversation we are now considering transpired before Moses came down from the interview recorded, ch. 32. 31—35 It was on the same occasion also that he besought a view of the divine glory, though the mention of it was omitted in its proper connexions. Nothing is more common than a similar usage of transposition among the sacred writers.——¶ *So shall we be separated.* Heb. נפלינו *niphlinu, gloriously or marvellously separated;* as the term is explained at length in the Note on Ex. 8. 22. Gr. ενδοξασθησομαι εγω τε και ὁ λαος σου, *I shall be glorified and also thy people.* The guidance of the Pillar of Cloud, as the sensible representative of the God of Israel, was the grand and glorious prerogative that distinguished them from all other people. The daily supply of manna was indeed a miraculous token of the divine regard, but it was not so strikingly, so signally, supernatural as the mystic aerial column brightening into a fiery pillar by night, and darkening into a majestic cloud by day. It was not, however, merely as a splendid visible phenomenon that Moses prized its presence. It was because Jehovah was in it. The virtue of his ineffable name; the efficacy of his attributes; the demonstration of his godhead; the preintimative shadow and symbol of his Son, was in it, and it

found grace in my sight, and ¡I know thee by name.

i ver. 12.

was mainly this which gave it value in his eyes.

18. *And he said, I beseech thee, show me thy glory.* Heb. הראני נא את כבדך *harëni na eth kebodeka, make me I pray thee to see thy glory.* Gr. εμφανισον μοι σεαυτον, *manifest or display thyself to me.* Arab. 'Show me even thy Light (or Splendor).' The request of Moses, couched in these words, involves considerations of a deep and mysterious nature, before which we are instinctively prompted to shrink back abashed, with covered face and a soul filled with awe. Yet as it forms a part of the sacred record, and was doubtless intended to be understood by those for whose benefit it was written, we may humbly essay to ascertain the true import of the request, together with that of the answer made to it. In stating then our impressions of the drift of these words, we do not hesitate to believe, that Moses, in beseeching that God would grant him a view of his glory, had respect primarily to a *visible glory*, something which could be seen with the bodily eyes, and not merely to a perception of the divine essence or an inward, mental, or spiritual apprehension of the divine attributes. We do not say that the object of his request was *exclusive* of such an inward sense or discovery of the divine perfections as we should perhaps most naturally connect with a sight of the glory of God; but we are still satisfied from the context that the prominent idea conveyed in the words of Moses' request is that of a *sensible manifestation* of the divine glory. From what he had already seen of the previous theophanies vouchsafed to him, and probably also from what he had heard of similar discoveries made to others, he was no doubt led to suppose that there was something still behind—some

18 And he said, I beseech thee, shew me ᵏthy glory.

k ver. 20.　1 Tim. 6. 16.

ineffable brightness, or beauty, or majesty,—immensely transcending all that he had hitherto been permitted to witness. He doubtless felt that he had not yet been favored to behold or understand all that was involved in the wondrous symbol of the Shekinah. With its daily sombre aspect and its nightly effulgence his senses were indeed familiar; but he was assured within himself that he had never been enabled to penetrate fully its hidden recesses. Neither his eyes nor his mind had pierced to its central mystery. Accordingly he here expresses an earnest wish to be favored with a deeper insight into this marvellous and mystic object. He would be made acquainted with the nucleus enwrapped in such a splendid envelope. And having thus far prevailed with God by his fervent intercession on behalf of the people, he is emboldened to go still farther in his request, making one concession an argument for seeking another. Whether he conceived that any corporeal semblance would be developed to his vision, we have no means of ascertaining; but we believe he had some dim and shadowy impression that the mystery of the Shekinah had a close relation to the mystery of redemption, and that a preintimation of the future glorious manifested person of the Messiah was in some way couched in this sublime symbol. And in this we cannot question that he was right. The glory of the Shekinah was the Old Testament manifestation of Christ. He was its inner essence. It was he who was the true Face or Presence of Jehovah, and as we have before remarked vol. I. p. 167, one grand object of the Savior's transfiguration on the mount was to afford evidence to the senses of the identity of his glory with that of the

19 And he said, ¹I will make all my goodness pass before thee, and I will proclaim the name of the Lord before thee; ᵐand will be

ⁿgracious to whom I will be gracious, and will shew mercy to whom I will shew mercy.

¹ ch. 34. 5, 6, 7. Jer. 31. 14. ᵐ Rom. 9. 15, 16, 18.

ⁿ Rom. 4. 4, 16.

ancient Shekinah. Of this truth Moses had undoubtedly a very vague and inadequate conception, and yet the little that he did apprehend of it only stimulated his desire for fuller disclosures. In the answer which God returned, and the partial compliance which he yielded, we seem to read a virtual allowance of the justness of his main impression, grounded no doubt upon the fact, that it was God's design from all eternity to appear to the bodily eyes of his saints in a visible external glory in the person of Christ as God-man mediator. Of this fact all the sensible manifestations which he had made to Moses and other holy men were presages and pledges. Their full import indeed had never been understood, nor was it possible that it should be; yet Moses was led to think it possible that he might be more largely informed upon the subject than he had ever yet been, and God seems not to have been displeased with his desire. Yet he is told that so long as he was in the flesh it could not be gratified to its full extent. The revelation vouchsafed must be governed by the measure of his ability to receive it, and by the useful ends to be answered by it. Accordingly in the reply Jehovah says;

19. *I will make all my goodness pass before thee.* Heb. כָּל טוּבִי *kol toobi.* Gr. παραλευσομαι προτερος σου τη δοξη μου, *I will pass by before thee with my Glory;* from which it would appear that the Seventy regarded the expression as having reference to a *sensible* and not merely a *mental manifestation.* So also the Arab. 'I will make all my Light (or Splendor) to pass by in thy presence.' The Syriac, however, has ' all my *bless-*

edness,' and the Chal. retains the Heb. ' goodness.' The true import of the original, therefore, remains to be accurately weighed; and this can only be done by a reference to dominant usage. The radical טוֹב *tob, good,* as an adjective is expressly used in reference to personal qualities which address themselves to the eye, and to which in English we apply the epithet *goodly.* Thus it is said of Joseph, Gen. 39. 6. that he was ' *goodly* and well-favored,' and so of Moses, Ex. 2. 2, that he was ' a *goodly* child.' Indeed one of the most common applications of the word in this form is to those properties of objects which come within the cognisance of the outward senses, as any one may be satisfied who will refer either to a Hebrew or English Concordance. The same idea is perhaps still more prominent in the abstract substantive טוּב *toob, goodness,* which is a designation for whatever strikes the senses as *pleasant, agreeable, beautiful, precious.* Thus Gen. 24. 10, 'And the servant took ten camels of the camels of his master, and departed; for all the *goods* (טוּב) of his were in his hand;' where we have endeavored to show in our Note that the term is used to denote the *rich, choice,* and *precious things* which the servant took from his master's effects for a present to Rebekah and her family. Gen. 45. 18, ' I will give you the *good* (טוּב) of the land of Egypt;' i. e. the choicest and best parts. Deut. 6. 10, 11, 'To give thee great and *goodly* (טבת) cities which thou buildedst not, and houses full of all *good things* (טוּב) which thou filledst not,' &c. Is. 1. 19, ' If ye be willing and obedient, ye shall eat *the good* (טוב) of the land.' In all these cases it is evident that the leading import of the term is that of *sensible* or *physical good*, and not of a *moral attribute* so denominated, which is more frequently expressed by the term חסד *hesed*, as in ch. 34. 6,—' the Lord God, merciful and gracious, long-suffering, and abundant in *goodness* (חסד) and truth,' &c. Nor, in reference to the present passage, does it by any means appear how a moral attribute could be properly said to *pass by* or *before* any one. Yet it cannot be questioned that in other connexions, though of rare occurrence, the sense of *moral goodness* or *benignity* is conveyed by the term, or more properly the *fruits* of such an attribute, as Ps. 31. 20.—145. 7. Is. 63. 7. Now in the present instance, if the answer of Jehovah might be supposed to be governed by the tenor of Moses' request, we should naturally expect that the favor promised to be granted would be something which should in some way address itself to the *senses* of the petitioner; for it was doubtless mainly a *sensible revelation* which he desired to have made to him. His request was 'make me *see* thy glory;' and in the answer to this, v. 22, it is said, 'It shall come to pass, while *my glory* passeth by,' &c., but in the verse before us God says, 'I will make all *my goodness* pass before thee.' It is evident, therefore, that the display of the 'goodness' and the 'glory' is identical, and as the latter implies something addressed to the senses, so also does the former. We infer then that the leading idea conveyed by the term טוב *goodness* in the connexion is that of something superlatively *fair, beautiful, exquisite, excellent, splendid* —whatever in fine could enter the conception of the most transcendant and glorious *visible* display which the Deity could make of himself to human vision. At the same time, it must be granted that the mental transition from this grosser sense of the term 'goodness,' in its present connexion, to that of the combination of *moral qualities* so denominated, is easy and natural, and almost necessary. The most gorgeous and dazzling exhibition of a merely *sensible glory* would leave the mind unsatisfied, except so far as it could be regarded as a kind of outward reflection of mental and moral attributes of corresponding character. In like manner, the external forms of beauty in the works both of nature and art produce a powerful effect upon us only as we see reflected in them the emanations of intellectual and moral properties.

We doubt not, therefore, that there was in these words of Jehovah a latent implication, that the exhibition about to be made to his servant should involve something *more* than a splendid phenomenon addressed to the outward eye. A glorious though partial disclosure should indeed be made to his sight; but he should withal be enabled by means of a supernatural illumination to pierce beyond the sensuous imagery, and comprehend its interior meaning. He should have a mental perception of those divine perfections which were so illustriously displayed in connexion with the sublime spectacle of the Shekinah, and the objects for which it was granted to the chosen people. The record of the *facts*, as given in the ensuing chapter, show conclusively that this is the true import of the declaration before us.——¶ *I will proclaim the name of the Lord before thee.* Heb. קראתי בשם יהוה לפניך *karathi beshēm Yehovah lepanēka, I will call in the name of Jehovah before thee.* The sense is no doubt substantially given in our version, viz., that he would proclaim the name, or in other words would declare the nature, the character, which was always to be associated in their minds with the august denomination, JEHOVAH. He would make it known as implying or carrying with

20 And he said, Thou canst not see my face: for ᵒ there shall no man see me and live.

ᵒ Gen. 32. 30. Deut. 5. 24. Judg. 6. 22 & 13. 22. Isai. 6. 5. Rev. 1. 16, 17. See ch. 24. 10.

it the exercise of a holy sovereignty in the bestowment of grace and mercy upon such objects as to him seemed good. The meaning therefore is ; ' I will proclaim myself in passing by thee as the Lord whose prerogative it is to be gracious to whom I will be gracious, and to have mercy upon whom I will have mercy. This shall be the substance of what I will proclaim respecting the import of that great and fearful name.' The clause thus understood is therefore a mere brief compend of the more expanded declaration, ch. 34. 6, 7. It is to be observed, however, that some critics take these words simply as yielding a reason for compliance with Moses' request As such a supernatural manifestation of himself to any person was a special favor on the part of Jehovah, to which no one could lay claim as a right ; therefore the scope of the clause they think is to preclude any objection to his thus distinguishing Moses rather than any other of the Israelites, or the Israelites themselves, rather than any other nation. With them accordingly the ' and' is equivalent to ' for.' ' I will make all my goodness to pass before thee, &c., *for* it is my prerogative to show favors of this kind to whomsoever I will.' For ourselves we prefer the former interpretation.

20. *Thou canst not see my face,* &c. That is, thou canst not *fully* and *adequately* see ; thou canst not, in thy mortal state, receive the full unclouded blaze of glory which constitutes the visible symbol of my face or presence. It is remarkable that one of the Rabbinical writers speaks thus upon the text before us ; ' Of that divine glory mentioned in the Scriptures, there is one degree

21 And the LORD said, Behold *there is* a place by me, and thou shalt stand upon a rock:

22 And it shall come to pass, while my glory passeth by, that I

which the eyes of the prophets were able to explore ; another which all the Israelites saw, as the cloud and consuming fire ; the third is so bright and so dazzling, that no mortal is able to comprehend it ; but should any one venture to look on it, his whole frame would be dissolved.' *R. Jehudah, Sepher Cosri,* P. 4. § 9. In such in conceiveable splendor is the divine Majesty revealed to the inhabitants of the celestial world, where he is said to ' dwell in the light which no man can approach unto' — an intimation which was probably suggested to the mind of Paul by the very incident we are now considering. That Moses had previously been favored, *in some degree,* with the vision of God's face in the bright cloud of the Presence, is clear from v. 11, where it is expressly said that ' the Lord spake unto Moses *face to face,* as a man speaketh unto his friend.' But that was a limited degree of disclosure compared with that which he now sought, and of which the Most High predicates the impossibility of granting it. The implication is obvious that the display of that uncreated splendor which pertained to Christ as the 'brightness of the Father's glory,' would be altogether too overpowering for a tenant of flesh, and could be accorded only to those who were translated into the world of light. At the scene of the Savior's transfiguration on the mount, some measure of this glory was displayed, but even then we have reason to believe it was a mitigated manifestation, or the powers of life in the disciples would have been utterly extinguished. It is only in a future state, when this mortal shall put on immor-

will put thee ᴾin a cleft of the
rock; and will ᑫ cover thee with
my hand while I pass by :

ᴾ Isai. 2. 21.   ᑫ Ps. 91. 1, 4.

23 And I will take away mine
hand, and thou shalt see my back
parts: but my face shall ʳnot be
seen.

ʳ ver. 20.   John 1. 18.

tality, that the desire which prompted
Moses' petition can be gratified. Then,
if his, 'we shall see him as he is,'
without a medium and without a cloud.
——¶ *There shall no man see me, and
live.* Or perhaps more literally, 'there
shall no man see me, and *be alive;*'
this vision is impossible to men in
their present state of existence ; they
must first pass through death, or be
translated, before they are capable of
beholding it. This sense is somewhat
milder than the common one, as it removes the idea of *arbitrary destructiveness* from the expression, and substi-
tutes that of *intrinsic*, or perhaps we
may say, *physical impossibility.* At
the same time it is unquestionable,
that it was the received opinion among
the ancient Israelites, which no one can
show to have been false, that a full
view of the divine glory would at once
be fatal to the beholder. Comp. Gen.
16. 13. Judg. 6. 22, 23, and 13. 22. And
it is somewhat confirmatory of this that
when the Shekinah, or divine glory,
filled the tabernacle, Ex. 40. 35, Moses
was not able to enter into it, i. e. he could
not make the attempt with safety to his
life. So also afterwards at the dedication of the temple, 2 Chron. 7. 1, 2, it
is said, 'The glory of the Lord filled
the house, and the priests could not enter into the house, because the glory of
the Lord had filled the Lord's house.'
The difficulty in both cases was the
same. The glory was too splendid for
human endurance. God must ' hold back
the face of his throne,' if he would spare
the visual and vital powers of feeble
worms. Even the partial display that
was made to Paul on his way to Damascus struck him with a blindness of
some days continuance. But in heaven

the difficulty is removed. It is the
blessed prerogative of the tenants of
that world of light, that they are prepared to enjoy what is prepared to be
enjoyed. Rev. 22. 4, 'His servants shall
see his face.'

21—23. *And the Lord said, Behold,
there is a place by me,* &c. It is clear
that God was not displeased with the
petition of his servant. He saw that it
was not prompted by an idle curiosity
or a vain presumption, but from a fervent desire to enjoy more of the brightness of his presence. He was willing,
therefore, to comply with it as far as
would be either safe or profitable for
him. But in order to this the imbecility
of his nature required that certain
precautions should be adopted. The
splendor of a full display of his glory
would be wholly insufferable, and means
must be resorted to to soften and mitigate the manifestation so that his feeble
powers would be able to bear it. Accordingly he informs him that there is
a rocky recess in some part of the
mount near where the Cloud was abiding, into which he should enter, and after
being still farther overshadowed by the
divine hand, (Arab. ' I will overshadow
thee with my cloud') should be permitted to behold a transient glimpse of
the overpowering brightness of Jehovah. But even this was not to be a
view of his *face.* The interposing medium was to screen the vision from his
sight till it had passed by, and then he
was to look upon it and behold his *back
parts,* as one might behold the back of
a royal personage as he moved along
in majestic state in front of his train.
Arab. 'I will then take away my cloud,
that thou mayst see the back parts of
my Angel, for his face is not to be

seen.' The language of Elihu in Job, ch. 36. 32, is peculiarly applicable to this part of the narrative ; 'With clouds he covereth the light, and commandeth it not to shine, by the cloud that cometh betwixt.' The language of the description is necessarily borrowed from human things, though we see no reason to doubt that it was as literally correct as the nature of the case would allow. Even if it be granted that Omnipotence *could* so have softened the *front aspect* of the glory as to make it tolerable to Moses' eyes, and displayed it in a stationary-form without passing by, yet nothing could be more expressive than the mode adopted to convey the intimation, that while a *lower* degree of disclosure could be made to him, a *higher* could not. This would be still more indubitable from the effect produced. Partial and moderated as the revelation was, yet the face of Moses caught a supernatural lustre from the glory as it passed, which remained with him when he came down from the mount, and which was so overpowering to the beholders that, from a regard to their weakness, he veiled himself before them. If then a more *reflected* radiance from the countenance of Moses, and that too coming from the *hinder part* of the resplendent phenomenon, was so transcendantly glorious, what must have been the effect of the unclouded light of Jehovah's *face!* Yet let us repeat in reference to this whole gracious manifestation, that the glory beheld was unquestionably the glory of Christ. Nor are we prepared to deny that a resplendent human form, preintimative of the Divine Man, Christ Jesus, was vaguely presented to his view. At any rate we would have the following passage attentively considered in this connexion, Num. 12. 6—8, 'And he said, Hear now my words: If there be a prophet among you, I the Lord will make myself known unto him in a vision, and will speak unto him in a dream. My servant Moses is not so, who is faithful in all mine house. With him will I speak mouth to mouth, even apparently, and not in dark speeches ; *and the similitude of the Lord shall he behold:*' What can be meant by Moses' beholding ' the similitude of the Lord' but his being favored with the display here recorded ? And what is the similitude of the Lord but he who is the ' brightness of the Father's glory and the *express image* of his person.' At the same time it was not, we believe, a view of Christ's glory in his state of humiliation and suffering, as the man of sorrows, that was accorded to Moses, but of the glory of his post-resurrection state of exaltation and honor, when he shall be revealed from heaven in a splendor that shall darken the light of the sun. For a somewhat more adequate view of this state we must have recourse to the scene of the Savior's transfiguration, when a cloud also overshadowed the disciples, as it doubtless did Moses ; and when Moses and Elias were present in glorified forms, probably because they had both in the very same place been favored with a remarkable manifestation of the Deity, a coincidence by the way that has generally been overlooked, but about which there can be no doubt. As to Moses, the present narrative is sufficiently explicit, and as to Elijah we are told, 1 Kings, 19. 8—11, that he arose and went in the strength of his supernatural supply of food ' forty days and forty nights unto Horeb, the mount of God. And he came thither unto a cave and lodged there.' This was probably the same cave into which Moses was made to enter on the present occasion. Elijah, however, was commanded to go forth, and to stand upon the mount before the Lord ; 'And behold, the Lord *passed by,*' as he had done in the case of Moses, though in a different mode of manifestation. Still it was a real theophany with which he was favored, and

CHAPTER XXXIV.

AND the Lord said unto Moses, ªHew thee two tables of stone like unto the first: ᵇ and I will write upon *these* tables the words that were in the first tables which thou brakest.

2 And be ready in the morning, and come up in the morning to

ª ch. 32. 16, 19. Deut. 10. 1. ᵇ ver. 28. Deut. 10. 2, 4.

Mount Sinai, and present thyself there to me ᶜ in the top of the mount.

3 And no man shall ᵈ come up with thee, neither let any man be seen throughout all the mount: neither let the flocks nor herds feed before that mount.

ᶜ chap. 19. 20. & 24. 12. ᵈ ch. 19. 12, 13, 21.

---

one that doubtless had a prospective reference to Christ; so that we can see sufficient reason from these historical facts for Moses and Elijah's appearing at the scene of transfiguration. It was natural that they should be associated with that display of the Savior's glory which was so similar to what they had seen in the days of their flesh. Add to this that Elijah was translated, and in all probability assimilated at once, as the saints will hereafter be, to this very glory.

Chapter 34

1. *And the Lord said unto Moses, Hew thee,* &c. Heb. פְּסָל לְךָ *pesal leka, hew for thyself;* whereas the former tables, both as to matter and form, were the work of God himself. Ex. 32. 16. The English word 'hew' denotes a rougher process than is legitimately implied by the original, which signifies *to cut with a graving tool, to chisel, to execute a piece of sculpture.* The divine benignity here shows itself ready to renew the covenant which Israel had broken, but at the same time gives a command which indicated that favor was restored with some abatement. God would not allow the facility of pardon to beget a presumptuous levity of spirit or slight apprehension of the evil of sin. Some memento of punishment therefore adheres to the renewed expression of favor. The wound is healed, but a scar remains. The former tables were throughout of divine

workmanship, both the material and the writing; in the present, the writing only. But it is enough if the writing be his; for that is the life of the covenant. The circumstance affords well grounded comfort if we are touched with genuine compunction after having proved unfaithful to our Christian vows. God is willing to renew the covenant, if we devoutly desire the favor at his hands. He is still virtually saying, 'I will write upon those (fleshly) tables (of the heart) the words that were in the first tables (in the state of innocence) which thou brakest (in the fall of Adam).'

2, 3. *Come up in the morning unto mount Sinai, and present thyself there to me.* Heb. נִצַּבְתָּ לִּי שָׁם *nitz-tzabta li sham, stand for me there.* That is, take your station there and await my coming down, as appears from v. 5. It would seem therefore that by 'the top of the mount' is not meant absolutely the highest summit, but some elevated point in the neighborhood of the summit. For as the cloud of the Shekinah usually abode on the apex of the mount, and yet in v. 5, is said to have 'descended,' the inference is inevitable that Moses was to station himself at a point somewhat *below* the topmost brow of the mountain. Here he was to stand alone, and the flocks and herds were forbidden to approach the base of the mount, in order that the law might be a second time received with the solemnity and sanctity which marked its first delivery. The

4 ¶ And he hewed two tables of stone, like unto the first; and Moses rose up early in the morning, and went up unto mount Sinai, as the LORD had commanded him, and took in his hand the two tables of stone.

5 And the LORD descended in the cloud, and stood with him there, and e proclaimed the name of the LORD.

6 And the LORD passed by before him, and proclaimed, The LORD, The LORD f God, merciful and gra-

e ch. 33. 19. Numb. 14. 17. f Numb. 14. 18. 2 Chron. 30. 9. Neh. 9. 17. Ps. 86. 15. & 103. 8. & 111. 4. & 112. 4. & 116. 5. & 145. 8. Joel 2. 13.

cious, long-suffering, and abundant in g goodness and h truth,

7 i Keeping mercy for thousands, k forgiving iniquity and transgression and sin, and l that will by no means clear *the guilty;* visiting the iniquity of the fathers upon the children, and upon the children's children, unto the third and to the fourth *generation.*

g Ps. 31. 19. Rom. 2. 4. h Ps. 57. 10. & 108. 4. i ch. 20. 6. Deut. 5. 10. Ps. 86. 15. Jer. 32. 18. Dan. 9. 4. k Ps. 103. 3. & 130. 4. Dan. 9. 9. Eph. 4. 32. 1 John 1. 9. l ch 23. 7, 21. Josh. 24. 19. Job. 10. 14. Mich 6. 11. Nah. 1. 3.

whole transaction was to be so ordered as to impress the congregation with an awful sense of the holiness of Jehovah, and of their own unworthiness, and with a deep conviction that it was a matter of no trifling moment thus to have subjected the Most High to the necessity of *deuteronomising,* as we may say, the law of the ten commandments.

4. *And Moses rose up early in the morning,* &c. To show his alacrity and zeal in yielding obedience to the divine command. ' The morning is, perhaps, as good a friend to the *graces* as it is to the *muses.'* Henry.——¶ *And took in his hand the two tables of stone.* Which it is consequently to be inferred were thin and light and of no very great dimensions. This is also to be inferred from their having been deposited in the ark, which was three feet nine inches in length, by two feet three inches in breadth. We can easily conceive what an impression it must have conveyed to the people of the dignity of the law to see these smooth and empty tables returned from the mount re-inscribed with the ten commandments, when they well knew that no graving-tool or other instrument was there to be found with which Moses could have executed the work. They would of course refer it

at once not to the act of man, but to the finger of God; and if he had *written* it, they might be sure that he would *maintain* it.

5. *And the Lord descended in the cloud.* The cloud's descending was the Lord's descending. According to the usage so frequently adverted to in previous Notes, the title of Jehovah is applied to the symbol by which he was represented. Not that the cloud was an arbitrary and empty emblem of a distant God, but the divine presence was most intimately, though mysteriously, united with it, so that for all designed purposes it was God manifest to the outward senses—a shadow and preintimation of ' God (subsequently) manifest in the flesh.' Arab. 'And the Angel of God appeared in the clouds, and his Light (or Splendor) stood with him there.' The Most High descended in this manner in fulfilment of his promise before made, ch. 33. 19—23, and accordingly proclaimed, in an audible voice, his NAME, that is, the character and perfections denoted by his name.

6, 7. *And the Lord passed by,* &c. Chal. 'And the Lord made his Shekinah to pass before his face.' Arab. 'And when the Angel of God passed before him,' &c. The Hebrew writers, therefore, comparing this passage with Ex. 33. 19, 22, say, 'The Shekinah, or Divine Majesty, called I, passed by;' thus denoting that they regarded the Shekinah as mysteriously one with the Father. But what was the import of the proclamation?——¶ *The Lord, the Lord God, gracious and merciful*, &c. The reader who may chance to be familiar with the Hebrew will at once perceive that our mode of interpunction in this passage does not agree with that of the original. The proper reading is the following, 'And the Lord passed by before him and proclaimed Jehovah, Jehovah: God, merciful and gracious,' &c. The august title ' Jehovah' is reduplicated by way of emphasis, as that pre-eminent designation which was designed to come home to the soul with the utmost fulness of awful import. To this the name ' God' (אֵל *ël*) is subjoined, of which the leading idea is that of *strength, might, potency*, and which in this connexion would naturally convey the idea of *all-sufficient protection* to all his people and of *formidableness* to all their enemies. 'He is *mighty in strength;* who hath hardened himself against him, and prospered?' This proclamation of his name as *almighty* would serve as a very suitable preface to the announcement of his *moral attributes* just about to follow; for it becomes us to think and to speak even of his grace and goodness in a spirit of holy awe, as deeply conscious how fearful and terrible is that Being who wields *omnipotence*. His mercies are not the mercies of a frail feeble creature like ourselves, but of a God of infinite resources ; and they are on this account unspeakably endeared to the subjects of them. 'His *greatness* and *goodness* illustrate and set off each other. That the terror of his greatness may not make us afraid, we are told how *good* he is ; and that we may not presume upon his *goodness*, we are told how *great* he is.' *Henry.*—The attributes

that follow require to be considered a little more in detail.——¶ *Merciful* Heb. רחום *rahum*. The import of the term is that of *tenderly kind, pitiful, compassionate*, whence the term רחמים *rahamim, bowels of mercies or compassions*, Gen. 43. 14. This is that perfection of Jehovah's nature with which we, as sinners, have the most immediate and intimate concern, and therefore it very properly stands first in this enumeration. It is this that constitutes the moving spring in the great machinery of benevolence, which is to be seen in the scheme of redemption. It is the disposition which prompts to the pity and relief of the miserable ; which renders the possessor propense to acts of kindness and clemency, like those of a father to a child, wherever the objects of them are found. It is an attribute of the Godhead which is incessantly celebrated by the inspired writers. The Psalmist, whose pious songs are so instinct with the praises of God, says of him that he is ' plenteous in *mercy*,' speaks again and again of the ' multitude of his *mercies*,' and assures us that his ' *tender mercies* are over all his works.' But it is those who live under the gospel who see its brightest displays, nor was it possible for any of the Old Testament saints to speak in such eulogy of it as the apostles Peter and Paul, for example, in the citations which follow ; 1 Pet. 1. 3, 'Blessed be the God and Father of our Lord Jesus Christ, which, according to his *abundant mercy*, hath begotten us again unto a lively hope by the resurrection of Jesus Christ from the dead,' Eph. 2. 4—7, 'But God, who is *rich in mercy*, for his great love wherewith he loved us, even when we were dead in sins, hath quickened us together with Christ ; (by grace ye are saved ;) and hath raised us up together, and made us sit together in heavenly places, in Christ Jesus: That in the ages to come he might shew the exceeding riches of his grace in his kindness towards us, through Christ Jesus.'——¶ *Gracious.* Heb. חַנּוּן *hannun;* from the root חָנַן *hanan,* signifying *to be kindly or graciously affectioned towards a person.* In Scripture usage this term as applied to God and as denoting his dispositions and dealings towards men, carries with it the leading import of *unmerited favor or kindness.* 'We call that חֲנִנָה *haninah,*' says Maimonides, ' which we bestow upon any man to whom we owe nothing.' In this sense does God bestow grace upon the sinning children of men. He is rich in the donation of favors to which they have no claim. His abounding benignity triumphs over their ill desert, and causes heaven to be peopled with those who were justly the heirs of hell.—— ¶ *Long suffering.* אֶרֶךְ אַפִּים *erek appim, long of anger,* or more literally, *long of nostrils,* from the ideal connexion between the passion of anger and its effects in inflating the nostrils. This ' long suffering' on the part of God is the first-fruit of his mercy and grace. He bears long with sinners; he delays the execution of justice; he waits to be gracious in despite of their iniquities. Nothing is more wonderful than the patience of God when we consider the provocations which he continually receives at the hands of the ungodly. How long did he bear with the antediluvian world! What forbearance did he exercise towards the murmuring and rebellious Israelites during their sojourn in the wilderness, and indeed throughout all their generations! Nay, to bring the matter home to ourselves, who is not forced to acknowledge that he is himself a monument of the same long-suffering and tender mercy? Have we not provoked him to anger every day of our lives? Yet to the praise of his patience here we still find ourselves, standing on praying ground, and favored with the offers and opportunities of pardon. Ah, how different would be our lot had he dealt with us

after our sins, or rewarded us according to our iniquities!—— ¶ *Abundant in goodness and truth.* Heb. רַב חֶסֶד וֶאֱמֶת *rab hesed ve-emeth, much in goodness,* or *benignity, and truth.* The idea is that of *exuberant benevolence.* So rich, so bounteous, so multitudinous, are the expressions of the divine favor, that we may be said to be almost overflown with them. And not only so, not only does his goodness abound above our deserts and above our powers of acknowledgment, but being a God of *truth,* who will not and cannot deceive, we are assured that every promise of further and future good will be strictly fulfilled, and that nothing will prevent the realization of those eternal blessings which he has reserved for them that put their trust in him! 'Faithful is he who hath called us, who also will do it.' He may not indeed in all cases *speedily* accomplish his word. His ways are often directly contrary to those of reason, and a long time elapses, and many difficulties are overcome, but finally his truth comes without fail to a triumphant fulfilment.—— ¶ *Keeping mercy for thousands.* Heb. נֹצֵר חֶסֶד *notzër hesed.* The original term חֶסֶד *hesed, mercy,* here is precisely the same with that which in the preceding clause is rendered 'goodness.' In the former passage, therefore, reference is had to the *plenitude* of the divine mercy, in the present to its *perpetuity.* Chal. 'Keeping goodness to a thousand generations.' God *keeps* or *preserves* mercy by continually showing it in all its various exercises to thousands of sinners in all ages and to the end of time. His *keeping* it implies that it is inexhaustible; that whatever measures of it may yet have been dispensed, an infinite sufficiency still remains behind. He *keeps* it notwithstanding the crying provocations which might move him to cast it away. He *reserves* it for his chosen people through all the days of their unregeneracy; ne *keeps* it for his backsliding Davids, and his denying

Peters, against the time in which they shall penitently exclaim, 'I have sinned!' Nay, who can tell but he may have 'kept mercy' for him whose eye is now perusing these pages—kept it year after year unto the present hour? And shall he not accept of it? But let us remember that although this mercy is inexhaustible for those that shall come after us, yet for each of us individually its day has a close. If we embrace it not while the day lasts, the night is not far distant when its door will be shut against us for ever.——

¶ *Forgiving iniquity and transgression and sin.* Heb. נשא עון ופשע וחטאה *nosë avon vapesha vehattaah,* *taking or bearing away* (i. e. forgiving) *iniquity, trespass, and sin.* This is the climax of the present proclamation of the divine perfections. *Pardoning* mercy is specified, not only because it is in this form that the glory of this attribute pre-eminently shines, but because it is pardoning mercy that opens the way for the exercise of all other mercy. It was all important therefore for the consolation of sinners, that this peculiar aspect of the divine goodness should be distinctly displayed. Hence we find the terms expressive of the sins forgiven so remarkably varied and multiplied, in order to imply that *all sorts and degrees* of offences come within the scope of its benign operation. In order then that our hearts may be duly affected by this declaration, let us refer both to history and to experience for a confirmation of its truth. See in the sacred records what multiplied acts and what aggravated forms of iniquity the divine clemency has graciously passed by! What sins before conversion! what sins after conversion! And then if we attempt, each for himself to enumerate his own transgressions, will they not be found more in number than the sands on the sea-shore, and sufficient, if visited according to their desert, to overwhelm the soul at once in perdition! Yet if believers in Christ these our sins are all forgiven! How many iniquities then is God continually pardoning in every quarter of the globe! What an idea does it give of the divine indulgence to think that his remissions keep pace with our provocations!——¶ *That will by no means clear the guilty.* Heb. נקה לא ינקה *nakkëh lo yenakkëh, that clearing will not clear;* i. e. acquit, absolve, hold guiltless. This is a clause of exceedingly difficult interpretation, as will be evident from the diversity of ancient renderings, which we give before attempting to settle the genuine sense. Chal. 'Sparing those who are converted to his law, and not justifying those who are not converted.' Gr. και ου καθαριει τον ενοχον, *and will not purify the guilty.* Arab. 'Who justifies and is not justified.' Sam. 'With whom the innocent shall not be innocent.' Vulg. 'And no person is innocent by or of himself before thee,' which gives a sound theological sense, viz., that no man can make an atonement for his own sins, or purify his own heart; inasmuch as all have sinned and come short of the glory of God. But whether this is the idea intended to be conveyed in this passage, is another question. Jerus. Targ. 'He will not clear sinners in the day of the great judgment.' Most of these versions yield substantially, though not very explicitly; the sense of ours; and yet it is certain that the language of the English text at first blush seems to stand at least in verbal contrariety to that of the preceding declaration; for how can it be said that God 'forgiveth iniquity, transgression, and sin,' if at the same time 'he will by no means clear the guilty?' If it were possible, therefore, on legitimate grounds, to assign to the words a sense which should more nearly accord with the drift of the foregoing expressions, it would seem to give more unity of import to the whole address. This we think may be very easily done without doing the least violence to the text, or slurring over, with some critics, the intimation doubtless intended to be conveyed, that God is a God of justice as well as a God of mercy. From comparing this form of expression with the usus loquendi in other cases, we are satisfied that the true rendering is, ' who will not wholly, entirely, altogether clear ;' i. e. who, although merciful and gracious in his dispositions, strongly inclined to forgive, and actually forgiving in countless cases and abundant measure, is yet not unmindful of the claims of justice. He will not always suffer even the pardoned sinner to escape with entire impunity. He will mingle so much of the penal in his dealings as to evince that his clemency is not to be presumed upon. Accordingly a proof of this would be seen in his visiting the iniquity of the fathers upon the children and their descendants unto several generations; for this clause is to be taken in immediate connexion with what goes before, and as a kind of complement to its sense. That this is philologically the true import of the phrase ' clearing will not clear,' the following parallel citations we think will put beyond question. Is. 30. 19, 'For the people shall dwell at Zion in Jerusalem ; *thou shalt weep no more* (בכו לא תבכה *bako lo thibkah, weeping thou shalt not weep*).' The meaning, according to Gesenius, is, not that their weeping should utterly and absolutely cease, but that they should not incessantly weep ; they should not weep as if they had nothing to do *but* to weep ; though weeping had hitherto been prevailingly their lot, yet it should not always continue so. They should have a respite and remission to the effusion of their tears. So also still more pertinently, Jer. 25. 29, 'For lo, I begin to bring evil on the city which is called by my name, and *should ye be utterly unpunished* (הנקה תנקו *hinnakëh tin-*

naku, *clearing should ye be cleared ?*)?' That is, should ye be entirely and altogether exempted? Jer. 30. 11, ' Though I make a full end of all nations whither I have scattered thee, yet will I not make a full end of thee : but I will correct thee in measure, and *will not leave thee altogether unpunished* (נקה לֹ אנקך *nakkëh lo anekkeka, clearing I will not clear thee*).' In this case the parallelism is perfect. If the version— ' will not leave thee altogether unpunished'—is correct in the one case, why should not *precisely the same words*— with only the personal variation — be rendered in the present passage, ' I will not utterly or altogether acquit, absolve, exempt from punishment?' So also Jer. 49. 12, 'Behold, they whose judgment was not to drink of the cup, have assuredly drunken ; and art thou he *who shall go altogether unpunished* (הוא hu nakoh tinnakëh, *who shall clearing be cleared ?*) ?' Where the sense given in our translation is undoubtedly correct. On the whole, therefore, there seems no room to question that God intended in these words to intimate, that the preceding declaration of a readiness to forgive all manner of transgression was not to be understood in so absolute and unqualified a sense as to preclude all ideas of penal justice. Though prone to pardon, yet it was to be known that he could and would punish, whenever his wisdom saw that the occasion required, even in those cases where, on the whole, his mercy was predominant. Thus in the case of David, while his great sin was forgiven, and matter of praise and thanksgiving throughout eternity administered to him, yet in ' clearing he was not wholly cleared.' A series of chastisements and afflictions followed him to his dying day, that he might learn how bitter and evil a thing it was to turn away from God as he had rashly done. And so in multitudes of other instances. Let us then beware that we do not lose our

8 And Moses made haste, and
ᵐ bowed his head toward the earth,
and worshipped.

9 And he said, If now I have
found grace in thy sight, O Lord,
ⁿ let my Lord, I pray thee, go

m ch. 4. 31. n ch. 33. 15, 16.

among us (for ᵒ it *is* a stiff-necked
people), and pardon our iniquity
and our sin, and take us for ᵖ thine
inheritance.

o ch. 33. 3. p Deut. 32. 9. Ps. 28. 9. & 23.
12. & 78. 62. & 94. 14. Jer. 10. 16. Zech.
2. 12.

---

selves and endanger our souls in erroneous and unauthorized views of the
pardoning mercy of the Most High.
Though inclined to forgive and to blot
out the multitudinous transgressions of
his sinful creatures, yet he would never
have them lose sight of the fact, that
no one can absolutely promise himself
impunity in doing wrong.——¶ *Visiting the iniquity of the fathers.* An
ample exposition of the drift of this
language has already been given in the
Note on Ex. 20. 5. The Chal. supplies
what is necessarily to be understood in
this connexion; 'Visiting the iniquities
of the fathers upon the children, and
the children's children *of the wicked,*
to the third and fourth generation.' So
also the Targ. Jerus. 'Remembering
the sins of the wicked fathers upon the
rebellious sons, unto the third generation and the fourth generation.'

8, 9. *And Moses made haste, and
bowed,* &c. No doubt the effect of this
overpowering display at once upon the
senses and the soul of Moses was a
kind of rapture, which while it left him
in the possession of his reason, still
prompted him with the utmost expedition suitably to acknowledge and improve the amazing manifestation of mercy now vouchsafed to him. He not only
falls down in prostrate adoration on the
earth, but seizes the encouraging words
from the mouth of the Lord, and pleads
them as a fresh argument for the forgiveness of Israel, and the continuance
of his presence among them.——¶ *O
Lord, let my Lord, I pray thee, go among
us.* Chal. 'Let I pray thee, the Shekinah of the Lord go among us.' Arab.
'Let thine Angel walk among us.' The

recent discovery made to him of what
was involved in the symbol redoubled
his anxiety as to its continuance among
them. Hence the repetition of the request. It should be remarked that in
the address the original is not יְהֹוָה
Yehovah, but אֲדֹנָי *adonai,* which is a
term of less significant but perhaps in
this relation of more endearing import,
and approaching more nearly to the
sense of *Master.* It is more properly
a term applicable to a *restricted lordship,* founded upon a peculiar relation,
subsisting by covenant or some special mode of acquisition, between the
ruler and the ruled. The fact that Israel were Jehovah's 'inheritance' would
make him their אֲדֹנָי *adonai,* while the
fact that they were his *creatures* would
make him their יְהֹוָה *Yehovah.* So in
the New Testament phrase, 2 Pet. 2. 1,
'denying the Lord that bought them,'
the original is δεσπότης *despotes* instead
of κυριος *kurios,* the usual word for
Lord and the common translation of
יְהֹוָה *Yehovah;* implying that their denial was the denial of a *federative* or
rectoral lord and governor, who had acquired a right, growing out of covenant
or pactional relations, to their homage
and loyalty. They had *professed,* by
assuming the Christian name, to belong
to the number of those whom Christ
had *bought, possessed,* or *inherited,* and
consequently their defection was a *trea-
sonable outrage* upon their most sacred
obligations. To say that *true Christians* should become false teachers and
bring in damnable heresies and deny
the Lord who had *really* bought them
with his blood and endowed them with
his spirit, and thus bring swift destruc-

10 ¶ And he said, Behold ᑫ I make a covenant: before all thy people I will ʳ do marvels, such as have not been done in all the

ᑫ Deut. 5. 2. & 29. 12, 14.   ʳ Deut. 4. 32.
2 Sam. 7. 23. Ps. 77. 14. & 78. 12. & 147. 20.

earth, nor in any nation: and all the people among which thou *art* shall see the work of the Lord: for it *is* ˢ a terrible thing that I will do with thee.

ˢ Deut. 10. 21.   Ps. 145. 6.   Isai. 64. 3.

tion upon themselves, seems scarcely a supposable mode of speech. But it would be very applicable to those who were only *professedly* Christians, and proved recreant to their assumed character.——¶ *For it is a stiff-necked people.* Heb. פר עם קשה ערף הוא *ki am keshëh oreph hu*, which may with equal propriety be rendered, 'THOUGH *this be a people hard of neck*.' Notwithstanding they have proved so refractory and rebellious, that I scarcely know how to bespeak thy favor for them, yet pardon their iniquity and forsake them not. Continue to vouchsafe to them the tokens of thy presence.' See on Gen. 8. 21.——¶ *Take us for thine inheritance.* Heb. נחלתנו *nehaltanu, inherit or possess thou us.* Gr. εσομεθα σοι, *we shall be to thee,* i. e. thine. Arab. 'Elect us.' The Targ. Jon., which is followed by Le Clerc, gives a causative sense to the term, 'Make us to inherit the land which thou didst promise to our fathers, that thou mayst not exchange us for another people.' The common rendering, however, is more simple, and such as finds an echo in numerous passages like the following; Deut. 32. 9, 'The Lord's portion is his people; Jacob is the *lot of his inheritance*.' Ps. 28. 9, 'Save thy people, and bless thine *inheritance*.' Ps. 33. 12, 'Blessed is the nation whose God is the Lord; and the people whom *he hath chosen for his own inheritance*.' Ps. 78. 62, 'He gave his people over also unto the sword; and was wroth with *his inheritance*.' The favors which Moses bespeaks in this verse are indeed the favors which God already explicitly promised to grant, and yet he here renews his supplication for them with redoubled earn-

estness; thus teaching us that the certainty of receiving good at the hand of the Lord should never relax, but always quicken, our prayers and endeavors to secure it.

10. *Behold I make a covenant,* &c. In such language is God pleased to signify his acceptance of and compliance with the prayer of Moses. In that prayer he had virtually pleaded with God the verification of his own words respecting his own attributes, as a God forgiving iniquity, transgression, and sin. He beseeches him to remember and perform all the good he had promised to the chosen race, unworthy as they were, and instead of casting them off, to confirm them as his own inheritance, his peculiar treasure, among the nations of the earth. To this prayer the Lord not only lends a favoring and consenting ear, but in order to give him the fullest possible assurance, he renews his promise under the form of a covenant engagement, than which nothing could be conceived more binding. Infinite veracity seems disposed to puʋ itself under additional obligations. In deed upon an attentive view of the whole context we can scarcely consider it as any thing short of an actual and formal renewal of the covenant which the people had broken, and the blessings of which they had forfeited by their late transgression. Although the word 'covenant' is repeatedly used by the sacred writers in the sense of *solemn promise, purpose, pledge, stipulation,* announced by one party only, yet here it seems to imply something *mutual,* as God goes on to state in the first place what he himself engages to do, and then to command what he would

11 t Observe thou that which I command thee this day: Behold, u I drive out before thee the Amorite, and the Canaanite, and the Hittite, and the Perizzite, and the Hivite, and the Jebusite.

12 x Take heed to thyself, lest thou make a covenant with the inhabitants of the land whither thou goest, lest it be for y a snare in the midst of thee:

13 But ye shall z destroy their altars, break their images, and a cut down their groves:

14 For thou shalt worship b no other god: for the LORD, whose c name *is* Jealous, *is* a d jealous God:

15 e Lest thou make a covenant with the inhabitants of the land, and they f go a whoring after their gods, and do sacrifice unto their gods, and *one* g call thee, and thou h eat of his sacrifice;

t Deut. 5. 32. & 6. 3, 25. & 12. 28, 32. & 28. 1. u ch. 33. 2. x ch. 23 32. Deut. 7. 2. Judg. 2. 2. y ch, 23. 33. z ch. 23. 24. Deut. 12. 3. Judg. 2. 2.

a Deut. 7. 5. & 12. 2. Judg. 6. 25. 2 Kings 18. 4. & 23. 14. 2 Chron. 31. 1. & 34. 3, 4 b ch. 20. 3. 5. c So Isai. 9. 6. & 57. 15. d ch 20. 5. e ver. 12. f Deut. 31. 16. Judg. 2. 17 Jer. 3. 9. Ezek. 6. 9. g Numb. 25. 2. 1 Cor 10. 27. h Ps. 106. 28. 1 Cor. 8. 4, 7, 10.

---

have them, on their part, observe; in which he repeats in fact the leading points that formed the conditions of the former national compact. Compare chapters twenty-three and twenty-four. —— ¶ *Before all thy people I will do marvels, such as have not been done.* Heb. נפלאת אשר לא נבראו *niphlaoth asher lo nibreü, marvellous things which have not been created.* The phraseology affords another instance of that peculiar use of the Hebrew term for *create* which we have so fully illustrated in our Note on Gen. 1. 1. The allusion is doubtless to the wonderful display of power which marked the introduction of Israel into the promised land, and their subsequent series of conquests, such as the dividing the waters of Jordan, the causing the walls of Jericho to fall down, making the sun and moon to stand still, &c., all which would amount to precisely that *marvellous* and *glorious discrimination* for which Moses had prayed, Ex. 33. 16, where the original verb נפלינו *niphlinu* is from the same root with נפלאת *niphlaöth, marvels,* in the passage before us.—— ¶ *All the people among which thou art.* That is, all thine own people; the nation of Israel in contradistinction from the heathen races round about.—— ¶ *It is a terrible thing that I*

will do with thee. Heb. עמך *immeka.* That is, not *towards* thee, but in thy sight, in thy presence, and, as it were, in conjunction with thee; making thee not only a witness, but also in some sense a medium, an instrumental agent. The words seem to be spoken to Moses personally.

11. *Observe thou that which I command thee this day.* What follows from this verse to the end of v. 26, is to be considered as a collection of the most prominent precepts, forming the conditions of the covenant on the part of the people. But before reciting them God very briefly repeats the substance of his own engagement, as a motive to stimulate them to the performance of theirs, to wit, that he would drive out before them the devoted nations, and put them in triumphant possession of the promised land. As if he should say, 'You see what I have pledged my self to do; now let me see that you will not be wanting in what I require of you.'

12—17. *Take heed to thyself,* &c. The grand prohibition which God saw to be most needful for his people was that against idolatry; and this accordingly occupies the series of verses from the 12th to the 17th. The interdiction of a covenant with the inhabitants of

16 And thou take of i their daughters unto thy sons, and their daughters k go a whoring after their gods,

i Deut. 7. 3. 1 Kings 11. 2. Ezra 9. 2. Neh. 13. 25. k Numb. 25. 1, 2. 1 Kings 11. 4.

and make thy sons go a whoring after their gods.

17 l Thou shalt make thee no molten gods.

l ch. 32. 8. Lev. 19. 4.

the land, to which they were going, was but the planting of a safeguard around the main precept. It was scarcely possible that they should form treaties and alliances of any kind with those idolatrous nations without being inveigled into a participation of their sin. Such connexions would be sure to be a snare to them, and how reasonable was it that they should be forbidden to make peace with those with whom God was making war? So far indeed from tolerating these abominations, they were to hold themselves bound utterly to destroy all their altars, images, and groves, and as far as in them lay to efface every vestige of their foul and odious worship. For this a reason full of awful import is given;——¶ *For the Lord, whose name is Jealous, is a jealous God.* That is, whose *nature* is jealous; who can bear no rival. The *names* of God designate his attributes. This is mentioned here with peculiar propriety. The covenant made with Israel was virtually a marriage-covenant, and consequently idolatry was adultery. Every approach to this sin, therefore, would be sure to provoke him to jealousy, just as the infidelity of a wife stirs up the same passion in the bosom of the injured husband. We are not indeed to transfer in our minds human passions to the bosom of the Deity; but the Scriptures, as we have before remarked, are constructed on the plan of ascribing the attributes of humanity to God, because he often *acts* in his dealings with men *as they act* when under the influence of certain passions. To convey, therefore, an intelligible idea, the passions themselves are affirmed of God when his conduct resembles the effect of those im-

pulses in men. 'Jealousy,' says Solomon, Prov. 6. 34, 35, ' is the rage of a man; therefore he will not spare in the day of vengeance; he will not regard any ransom, neither will he rest content though thou givest many gifts.' This is human jealousy. What is said of divine? Deut. 32. 21 — 23, 'They have moved me to jealousy; and a fire is kindled in mine anger, and it shall burn to the lowest hell, and shall consume the earth with her increase, and set on fire the foundations of the mountains. I will heap mischiefs upon them, and will spend mine arrows upon them.' Compare Nahum. 1. 2.——¶ *And one call thee, and thou eat of his sacrifice.* This the apostle informs us, 1 Cor. 10. 20, 21, was equivalent in the sight of God to one's professing himself to be of the idolatrous communion which feasted upon the sacrifices of their demongods. The reason of this is obvious. When the covenant people feasted upon a sacrifice, the meat was supposed to be God's, and to be set upon his table. The feasters were accordingly considered as his guests, entertained at his table in token of reconciliation and friendship. This act confirmed in the strongest possible manner the covenant relation supposed to exist between the parties. Consequently, all those who ate of the sacrifices offered to *other gods*, virtually professed themselves thereby to be the worshippers and servants of such false deities, which they could not be without renouncing the worship and service of the true God. See Note on Ex. 27. 4, 5. The subsequent history, Num. 25. 1—3, shows but too clearly how intimate is the connexion between the sins here mentioned, and how needful, though unavail-

18 ¶ The feast of ᵐunleavened bread shalt thou keep. Seven days shalt thou eat unleavened bread, as I commanded thee, in the time of the month Abib: for in the ⁿmonth Abib thou camest out from Egypt.

19 ᵒAll that openeth the matrix *is* mine: and every firstling among thy cattle, *whether* ox or sheep, *that is male.*

ᵐ ch. 12. 15. & 23. 15.   ⁿ ch. 13. 4.   ᵒ ch. 13. 2, 12. & 22. 29.   Ezek. 44. 30.   Luke 2. 23.

20 But ᵖ the firstling of an ass thou shalt redeem with a lamb: and if thou redeem *him* not, then shalt thou break his neck. All the first-born of thy sons thou shalt redeem. And none shall appear before me ᑫ empty.

21 ¶ ʳSix days thou shalt work, but on the seventh day thou shalt rest: in earing-time and in harvest thou shalt rest.

ᵖ ch. 13. 13.   Numb. 18. 15.   ᑫ ch. 23. 15. Deut 16. 16.   1 Sam. 9. 7, 8.   2 Sam. 24. 24. ʳ ch. 20. 9. & 23. 12. & 35. 2.   Deut. 5. 12, 13. Luke 13. 14.

---

ing, was the caution now administered; 'And Israel abode in Shittim, and the people began to commit whoredom with the daughters of Moab. *And they called the people unto the sacrifices of their gods:* and the people did eat, and bowed down to their gods. And Israel joined himself unto Baal-peor: and the anger of the Lord was kindled against Israel.' Compare also the melancholy case of Solomon, 1 Kings, 11. 1—10.

18. *The feast of unleavened bread shalt thou keep.* See Notes on Ex. 12. 15, 16.—13. 6, 7.—23. 15. The following precepts, which have been for the most part explained in the Notes on ch. 23. 1—17, relate to such points of their religion as were peculiar to it, and such as they would be most apt to neglect; not such as in themselves and morally considered were of the greatest importance.

19. *All that openeth the matrix,* &c. See Notes on Ex. 13. 2, 12.—22. 29.

20. *The firstling of an ass thou shalt redeem with a lamb.* That is, with a living lamb, either of the sheep or goat, which was to be given to the priest, Num. 18. 15. Comp. Ex. 13. 13. On this precept the Hebrew writers say, 'It might be redeemed with a lamb, whether male or female, unblemished or blemished, small or great. If a man have no lamb to redeem it with, he may redeem it with the value of it, and give

the price to the priest. The law commandeth not a lamb to make it heavier upon him, but lighter   For if he have the firstling of an ass which is worth ten shekels, he may redeem it with a lamb worth a quarter of a shekel.' *Ainsworth.*

21. *In earing-time and in harvest shalt thou rest.* That is, in the busiest seasons of the year, the seasons of ploughing and sowing and harvesting. They were not to consider the urgency of business as affording a sufficient excuse for neglecting the religious observance of the day. 'This commandment is worthy of especial note. Many break the Sabbath on the pretence of åbsolute necessity, because, if in harvest time, the weather happens to be what is called *bad,* and the Sabbath day be *fair* and *fine,* they judge it perfectly lawful to employ that day in endeavoring to save the fruits of the field, and think that the goodness of the day is· an indication from providence that it should be thus employed. But is not the command above pointed directly against this? I have known this law often broken on this pretence, and have never been able to discover a single instance, where the persons who acted thus succeeded one whit better than their more conscientious neighbors, who availed themselves of no such favorable circumstances, being deter-

22 ¶ ˢ And thou shalt observe the feast of weeks, of the first-fruits of wheat-harvest, and the feast of ingathering at the year's end.

23 ¶ ᵗ Thrice in the year shall all your men-children appear before the Lord GOD, the God of Israel.

ˢ ch. 23. 16. Deut. 16. 10, 13. ᵗ ch. 23. 14, 17. Deut. 16. 16.

24 For I will ᵘ cast out the nations before thee, and ˣ enlarge thy borders: ʸ neither shall any man desire thy land, when thou shalt go up to appear before the LORD thy God thrice in the year.

ᵘ ch. 33. 2. Lev. 18. 24. Deut. 7. 1. Ps. 78 55. & 80. 8. ˣ Deut. 12. 20. & 19. 9. 8. ʸ See Gen. 35. 5. 2 Chron. 17. 10. Prov. 16. 7. Acts 18. 10.

---

mined to keep God's law even to the prejudice of their secular interests; but no man ever yet suffered loss by a conscientious attachment to his duty to God. He who is willing and obedient shall eat the good of the land; and God will ever distinguish those in his providence, who respect his commandments.' *A. Clarke.*

22. *Thou shalt observe the feast of weeks.* Heb. חג שבעת תעשה לך *hag shabuoth taaseh leka, the feast of sevens shalt thou do unto thee.* That is, keep and celebrate by appropriate *doings.* So the Gr. ποιησεις μοι, *thou shalt do or make to me.* See the phraseology amply illustrated in the Note on Ex. 31. 16. This 'feast of weeks' was a feast to be observed seven weeks after the passover, called otherwise the 'feast of Pentecost,' Lev. 23. 15, 16. Acts, 2. 1. It was held at the same time with the feast of the first-fruits of the wheat-harvest.——¶ *At the year's end.* Heb. תקופת השנה *tekuphath hashshanah, at the circumvolution, or circuit, of the year;* i. e. at its *return;* which was in the seventh month, corresponding with our September. The phraseology is illustrated by a comparison of the two following passages relative to the invasion of Israel by Benhadad, king of Syria. 2 Chron. 24. 23, 'And it came to pass *at the end of the year* (לתקופת השנה *lithkuphath hashshanah*), that the host of Syria came up, &c.' 1 Kings, 20. 26. 'And it came to pass *at the return of the year* (לתשובת השנה *lith-shubath hashshanah, at the turning of*

the year), that Benhadad numbered the Syrians, and went up to Aphek, to fight against Israel.'

23, 24. *Thrice in the year shall all your men-children,* &c. See Note on Ex. 23. 14, 17. Deut. 16. 16. Scarcely any feature of the religion of Israel was more remarkable than this, or more signally declarative of a particular providence watching over the covenant race. To the eye of reason it would no doubt seem that the observance of this ordinance would expose them to the incursions of the surrounding nations, who would be sure to take advantage of their absence, and rob or capture the country. To human reason too it might appear to have been sufficiently perilous to be cruel, to leave the women, the children, the aged, and the sick, in such a defenceless state. Would it not have been better, it might be asked, that certain delegates should have been appointed to repair to the place of worship in the name of all the rest of the people? But God would not be served by proxy. He commanded, therefore, *all the males* to keep the feasts at the place prescribed; and to remove all apprehensions as to the safety of their property or their families, he pledged himself to protect their frontier and so to overrule the minds of their enemies, that they should not even ' *desire*' to invade their land at any of those seasons. Accordingly we look in vain throughout the whole course of their subsequent history for an instance of foreign aggression made under these

25 ᶻ Thou shalt not offer the blood of my sacrifice with leaven, ᵃ neither shall the sacrifice of the feast of the passover be left until the morning.

26 ᵇ The first of the first-fruits of thy land thou shalt bring unto the house of the LORD thy God.

ᶻ ch. 23. 18.   ᵃ ch. 12, 10.   ᵇ ch. 23. 19.
Deut. 26. 2, 10.

ᶜ Thou shalt not seethe a kid in his mother's milk.

27 And the LORD said unto Moses, Write thou ᵈ these words: for after the tenor of these words I have made a covenant with thee, and with Israel.

ᶜ ch. 23. 19. Deut. 14. 21.   ᵈ ver. 10. Deut 4. 13. & 31. 9.

circumstances. The way of duty is the way of safety.

25, 26. *Thou shalt not offer the blood,* &c. See Note on Ex. 23. 18.—12. 10.—23. 19. Deut. 26. 2.

27. *And the Lord said unto Moses, Write thou these words,* &c. There is some difficulty attending the exposition of this command to Moses respecting the writing the words of the covenant. It is clear from v. 1, of this chapter that God promised to write *with his own hand* the ten commandments on the tables prepared by Moses. The execution of this promise we conceive is expressly recorded in v. 28, 'And he (i. e. God) wrote upon the tables the words of the covenant, the ten commandments.' The parallel narrative, Deut. 10. 1—4, puts this beyond question, 'At that time the Lord said unto me, Hew thee two tables of stone like unto the first, and come up unto me into the mount, and make thee an ark of wood. *And I will write on the tables the words that were in the first tables which thou brakest,* and thou shalt put them in the ark. And I made an ark of shittim wood, and hewed two tables of stone like unto the first, and went up into the mount, having the two tables in my hand. *And he wrote on the tables, according to the first writing the ten commandments, which the Lord spake unto you in the mount, out of the midst of the fire, in the day of the assembly:* and the Lord gave them unto me.' What then were the words which Moses wrote? Certainly that summary of

judicial and ceremonial precepts comprised in the verses immediately preceding from v. 11th to v. 26th, which were an appendage to the moral law, and which formed, in all their details, the conditions of the national covenant on the part of the nation. But did Moses write them on the present occasion? This we think may justly be questioned. By recurrence to chap. 24. 3—8, we learn that when Moses came down from the mount he wrote out in a book the collection of laws and precepts, additional to the Decalogue, which form the contents of chapters 21, 22, and 23, and which include every one of the items recited in the present context. Now these laws were not inscribed on the tables which were broken; consequently there was no occasion, on this score, for their being re-written; and if the book already written were preserved, was there any occasion for another copy of the precepts being made at all at this time? It is indeed possible that the short compend here recited may have been transcribed in pursuance of a direction now given to that effect, but on the whole we prefer to consider the verse as more correctly rendered in the pluperfect—'And the Lord *had* said unto Moses, Write thou these words,' &c. This refers the writing back to the occasion just mentioned, of which it is said, 'And Moses came and told the people all the words of the Lord, and all the judgments: and all the people answered with one voice, and said, All the words which the Lord

28 e And he was there with the
Lord forty days and forty nights;
he did neither eat bread nor drink

e ch. 24. 18. Deut. 9. 9, 18.

water. And f he wrote upon the
tables the words of the covenant,
the ten commandments.

f ver. 1. ch. 31. 18. & 32. 16. Deut. 4. 13
& 10. 2, 4.

hath said will we do. *And Moses
wrote all the words of the Lord,* and
rose up early in the morning, and builded an altar under the hill, and twelve
pillars according to the twelve tribes of
Israel. And he took the book of the
covenant, and read in the audience of
the people; and they said, All that the
Lord hath said will we do, and be
obedient. And Moses took the blood,
and sprinkled it on the people, and
said, Behold the blood of the covenant,
which the Lord hath made with you
concerning all these words.' This construction removes, as far as we can perceive, all appearance of discrepancy
between the different parts of the narrative. Having repeated the leading
specifications of the compact formerly
entered into, it was natural to advert to
the fact, that Moses had been required
to write them down at the time they
were first delivered and formally accepted and ratified. If, however, it
should still be thought probable that
some kind of writing was *now* enjoined
upon Moses, we are by no means disposed to join issue with such a conclusion. It is no doubt very supposable, that as they had in their recent
transgression broken both the *table-sta-
tutes* and the *book-statutes*—the *moral*
and the *ceremonial* part of the covenant
—God may have seen fit, that the renewal of both these departments of the
covenant should be marked by a similar
proceeding. As he himself was pleased
to restore by re-inscribing the Decalogue, so Moses *may* have been ordered to re-write on parchment the prominent points of the ceremonial law, as
a token that both were again in force
in their covenant relations.

28. *And he was there with the Lord*

forty days and forty nights. Being of
course miraculously sustained by the
power of God without food or drink, as
in the former case, ch. 24. 18. 'It was
not long since Moses' former fast of
forty days. When he then came down
from the hill his first question was not
for meat; and now going up again to
Sinai, he takes not any repast with him.
There is no life to that of faith. 'Man
lives not by bread only.' The vision
of God did not only satiate, but feast
him. What a blessed satiety shall there
be when we shall see him as he is,
and he shall be all in all to us; since
this very frail mortality of Moses was
sustained and comforted but with representations of his presence! I see
Moses, the receiver of the law, Elias,
the restorer of the law, Christ, the ful-
filler of the old law, and author of the
new, all fasting forty days; and these
three great fasters I find together glorious in mount Tabor. Abstinence merits
not, but it prepares for good duties.
Hence solemn prayer takes ever fasting to attend it, and so much the rather
speeds in heaven when it is so accompanied. It is good so to diet the body,
that the soul may be fattened.' *Bp.
Hall.* In Deut. 9. 18, this second sojourn is thus alluded to; 'And I fell
down before the Lord, as at the first,
forty days and forty nights: I did
neither eat bread, nor drink water, because of all your sins which ye sinned,
in doing wickedly in the sight of the
Lord, to provoke him to anger.' If we
enquire into the *design* of this second
forty days' withdrawment and seclusion, the passage now cited seems to
disclose one at least of the grand ends
which were to be answered by it; viz.,
to convey to the people a deeper im-

pression of the guilt of their recent iniquitous proceedings. What must they think of the heinousness of their conduct when a period of forty days' earnest intercession, on the part of Moses, accompanied by fasting and prayer, was none too much in which to deprecate the deserved vengeance of heaven? Could they ever after venture to deem sin a light matter? Could they delude themselves with the idea that God was very *easily pacified* in view of a highhanded transgression? Alas, how little aware are most men of the aggravated nature of sins committed against covenant vows and engagements! It is only those who live very near to the light of the throne, and gaze like Moses upon the burning brightness of the divine purity that can appreciate it aright! They see the awful turpitude of rebellion against God, and how difficult it is to recover the lost tokens of his favor. This lesson was now to be taught to the sinning congregation, and nothing would do it more effectually than this long period of fasting and prayer. Again, the same honor was to be secured for the second tables as for the first, and though the thunders and lightnings that marked the first delivery of the law were not repeated, yet the forty days' fasting of Moses *was*, and the tables were to be brought forth, in that respect, 'as at the first.' All the circumstances, in fine, were to be so ordered that the deepest moral impression should be produced upon the general mind of the people.

The remarks of Calvin upon this passage are well worthy of being appended in the present connexion. 'Moses was exempted from the common lot of men that he might usher in a law evidently from heaven. Had he been detained but a few days upon the mount, his authority would not have been sanctioned by so illustrious a miracle. The forty days, therefore, thus spent gave a full attestation to his commission as a

divine legate: for the endurance of so long a fast evidently exceeded the powers of human nature. In order that the majesty of the law might be unquestioned, its minister was distinguished by an angelical glory. He expressly asserts of himself that he neither drank water nor tasted of bread, that by being thus distinguished from ordinary mortals his official dignity might be superior to exception. We are to understand the fast, therefore, here mentioned not as one of mere temperance or sobriety, but of singular privilege, in which a temporary immunity from the infirmity of the flesh was granted, that his condition might be shown to be super-human. He was unconscious of thirst, nor did he struggle any more with the appetite for food than one of the angels. Therefore this abstinence was never drawn into a precedent by any of the prophets, nor did any one think of imitating what all knew was not intended for themselves. I except the case of Elijah, who was sent to renew the law which had almost perished from Israel, and who, as a second Moses, abstained from food and drink for forty days.'——¶ *And he wrote upon the tables*, &c. That is, God wrote, as is evident from the proof adduced under the foregoing remarks, v. 27. 'Moses heard, and God wrote. Our true Moses repairs that law of God which we, in our nature, had broken; he revives it for us, and it is accepted of God, no less than if the first character of his law had been still entire. We can give nothing but the table; it is God that must write in it. Our hearts are but a bare board till God by his finger engrave his law in them. Yea, Lord, we are a rough quarry; hew thou us out, and square us fit for thee to write upon. *Bp. Hall.*

29. *And it came to pass when Moses came down*, &c. Notwithstanding the slight air of confusion in the statement of this verse, the meaning of the writer

29 ¶ And it came to pass when Moses came down from mount Sinai (with the ᵍ two tables of testimony in Moses' hand, when he came down from the mount) that Moses wist not that ʰ the skin of his face shone, while he talked with him.

ᵍ ch. 32. 15.

ʰ Matt. 17. 2. 2 Cor. 3. 7. 13.

is yet too obvious to be misunderstood. The time of Jehovah's 'talking with him' was indeed prior to his coming down from the mount, and it was then that his face began to shine; but he had not become conscious of the fact till after he had descended. The reason why his countenance shone now, and not when he came down the first time from the mount undoubtedly was, that during the second time he had been favored with far more glorious views of the divine character and perfections than before. The original for 'wist not that the skin of his face shone' is לֹא יָדַע כִּי קָרַן עוֹר פָּנָיו *lo yada ki karan, or panauv*, were the verb קָרַן *karan* signifies *to irradiate, to shoot forth or emit rays of light;* whence, from the idea of *shooting forth*, comes the noun קֶרֶן *keren, a horn.* This fact throws an important light upon the well-known passage in the sublime description of the Most High, Hab. 3. 3, 4, 'God came from Teman, and the Holy One from mount Paran. Selah. His glory covered the heavens, and the earth was full of his praise. And his brightness was as the light; he had *horns* coming out of his hands; and there was the hiding of his power.' It is not perhaps to be confidently affirmed that this rendering is erroneous, inasmuch as the original word is that which is usually and properly translated *horns.* Yet we think that scarcely any one can help being conscious of some slight incongruity in the imagery. The head, and not the hands, is the proper place for the outgrowth of *horns.* But suppose the term to be rendered 'rays,' and to have reference to the *streaming* or *flashing splendors* which emanated from the hands of the personified glory of Jehovah, and the image is far more grand and impressive Conceive the word, in fact, to be but another term for *lightnings*, and we see at once with what propriety it is added, 'And there was the hiding of his power.' What more striking emblem could be imagined of the resistless might of Omnipotence? Here too we are not improbably enabled to trace the origin of the ancient Greek mythologic device, which represents Jupiter, the father of the gods, as grasping the *lightnings* or *thunderbolts* in his right hand, as a symbol of his power over the elements. We suggest this, however, as rather probable than certain. Whatever may be thought of it, no doubt can remain as to the etymological affinity between 'rays' and 'horns,' and with this fact before us, we can easily account for the strange rendering of the Lat. Vulgate; 'Ignorabat quod *cornuta* esset facies sua,' *he knew not that his face was* HORNED, which is evidently as improper as it would be to translate the word 'rayed' when applied to an ox or a goat. Yet in accordance with this error, the Italian painters, who were unacquainted with any other version, have for the most part represented Moses with the uncouth appendage of *horns!* These pictures have been copied into engravings, and thus it is that in ancient biblical cuts we often see him thus depicted. This circumstance of 'rays' and 'horns' having a common radical has led moreover to a *verbal* as well as a *pictorial* confounding the two. Thus the eloquent Jeremy Taylor in his 'Holy Dying,' p. 17, describes the rising sun as 'peeping over the eastern hills, thrusting out his *golden horns.*'

The Gr. version renders nearer to the sense of the original by δεδόξασται, *was glorified, or made glorious*, whence the apostle, 2 Cor. 3. 7, says, 'The children of Israel could not steadfastly behold the face of Moses for *the glory* (δοξα) of his countenance, i. e. the exceeding brightness. Chal. 'Moses knew not that the brightness of the glory of his face was multiplied.' Sir Thomas Brown, according to the Editor of the Pictorial Bible, is probably correct in his understanding of the matter, after Tremellius and Estius; 'His face was radiant, and dispersing beams, like many horns or cones about his head; which is also consonant unto the original signification, and yet observed in the pieces (pictures) of our Savior and the Virgin Mary, who are commonly drawn with scintillations or radiant halos, about their head; which, after the French expression, are called, the Glory.'ʼ He remarks, moreover, that the custom among painters of putting 'glories' around the heads of sacred persons no doubt arose from this fact concerning Moses. 'We are not aware,' says he, ' of any other authority, except that the *raiment* of Christ became shining at the transfiguration. The ancient heathen considered an irradiation or lambent flame about the head, as a manifestation of the divine favor and protection. But whether this arose from any tradition concerning Moses it is impossible to determine.' The notions of the Mohammedans on this subject, which are very curious, and which probably arose from a Scriptural source, may be seen detailed in my ' Life of Mohammed.'——¶ *Wist not that the skin of his face shone.* What was visible to others was hidden to himself. Although from the effects of his transforming communion with the divine presence he had become in a measure 'changed into the same image, from glory to glory,' yet he remained in perfect unconsciousness of the fact! How

this could have happened, we feel but little interest to inquire. Calvin thinks it not improbable, that the miraculous effulgence may have been restrained from bursting forth until Moses came into the immediate presence of Aaron and the people, that they might have an impressive view of the phenomenon. But however this may be, it is a theme of more profitable contemplation as viewed in its emblematical applications. 'He wist not that the skin of his face shone;' nor is it ever found that those who bear much of the divine image are conscious of the moral glory which has passed upon them. Their minds are so fixed upon their own defects; they are so deeply convinced of the corruption of their nature; they are so profoundly penetrated with the sense of their ill desert, that so far from recognising any peculiar tokens of divine favor in themselves, they are rather prone to say with Job, ' If I had called, and he had answered me; yet would I not believe that he had hearkened unto my voice.' Instead of realizing the possession of distinguished graces, they still count themselves as ' less than the least of all saints.' To others their spiritual excellencies shine forth with great lustre, but they are blind to them themselves; and the nearer they attain to the view of the divine glory; the more familiar their converse with infinite excellence, the more unconscious do they become of its effects upon them. Has one been recently on the mount in beatific fellowship with God, the evidence of it will appear when he comes down. It will show itself in the heightened meekness and sweetness of his temper, in the sanctity of his demeanor, in the quickened zeal of his efforts to do good, and in the subdued, heavenly, and Christ-like spirit that breathes through all his deportment. But to all this he will be himself unconscious. 'Whatever beauty God puts upon us, we should still be filled with such an

30 And when Aaron and all the children of Israel saw Moses, behold, the skin of his face shone; and they were afraid to come nigh him.

31 And Moses called unto them; and Aaron and all the rulers of the congregation returned unto him: and Moses talked with them.

humble sense of our own unworthiness and manifold infirmities, as will make us even overlook and forget that which makes our faces shine.' *Henry.*

30. *And they were afraid to come nigh him.* The circumstance of their being strangely repelled from his presence, was probably the first intimation that Moses had of there being any thing preternatural or peculiar in his appearance. How must he have been surprised to find himself the unsuspecting cause of a dispersion among his friends, somewhat similar to that which took place among the band that came under the conduct of Judas to apprehend the Savior, when a supernatural something in his aspect struck them so overpoweringly that 'they went backward and fell to the ground?' But why this intimidation at this time? What made Israel to shrink from the face of their leader, intercessor, and friend? What could render the presence of his affectionate brother formidable to Aaron? Moses had come to them with his heart overflowing with good will, and exulting in the thought of having procured pardon and reconciliation for their offences. Why then do they avoid his presence, instead of greeting him with a cordial welcome? Alas, the same inward impulse which led the first transgressors to 'hide themselves from the presence of the Lord,' is at work in their bosoms. It is conscious guilt that is driving them away from unconscious goodness. Under the awful terrors of the glory of Jehovah a few weeks before they had earnestly besought, saying, 'Let Moses speak to us and we will hear.' But now even the bare look of Moses fills them with dismay, and they flee from the sight of it! An ac-

cusing conscience has so disturbed their perception, that the beaming radiance of his countenance has converted him into a flaming minister of heaven prepared to execute vengeance upon them! 'That which should have comforted, affrights them; yea, Aaron himself, that before went up into the mountain to see and speak with God, now is afraid to see him that had seen God! Such a fear there is in guiltiness — such confidence in innocency. When the soul is once cleared from sin, it shall run to that glory with joy, the least glimpse whereof now appals it, and sends it away in terror. How could the Israelites now choose but think, How shall we abide to look God in the face, since our eyes are dazzled with the face of Moses? And well may we still argue, if the image of God which he hath set in the fleshly forehead of authority daunt us, how shall we stand before the dreadful tribunal of heaven!' *Bp. Hall.*

31. *And Moses called unto them*, &c. Whatever might have been the cause of their fleeing, he was conscious that it was nothing in the state of his feelings towards them. The real cause, however, was soon disclosed to him, and far from being elated with the honor conferred upon him or desirous to make his authority felt in keeping his people at a distance, his disposition is quite the reverse. Considered in itself, the phenomenon would tend greatly to enhance his authority among the congregation. There could not be a more striking attestation to the divine commission which he had received, as their leader and law-giver, than this supernatural appearance. It invested him with a badge of honor such as no dia-

dem could have conferred. It was in fact a crown of light to his head; and decisively marked him out as one who was appointed of God to fill the place which he occupied. Yet he is far from priding himself upon this distinction, or from a desire to overawe his brethren. On the contrary he is exceedingly anxious to reassure their confidence. Accordingly in all the simplicity of a kind and affectionate spirit, he invites them to come near. And in order to remove all let or hindrance to their returning, he covers his face with a veil, which he continued to wear all the time that he was speaking to them, but laid aside whenever he went into the tabernacle to appear before the Lord. In doing this, he set a noble example of condescending meekness, of modesty, of self-renunciation. Had he been a man of another mould, he would probably have stood upon his prerogative, and said, 'If God has been pleased miraculously to distinguish me, am I responsible for the effects of it? If there is a supernatural splendor about my face, God put it there; and it is not probable that he would have made it so conspicuous had he intended it should be concealed. It is much more proper that you should hide your guilty heads, than that I should, draw a veil over mine.' But so spake not Moses. He chose rather to hide from their view the wonderful work of God upon his person than to forego the opportunity of declaring his will to the people—a conduct which fully warrants the remark of Bp. Hall, that 'Moses had more glory by his veil than by his face.' Vain glory always defeats the ends at which it aims, while humility gains the point of which it little thought, for which it was least of all anxious. Who does but esteem Moses, modestly shrouded in a veil, infinitely more than he does the most loquacious boaster and exhibitor of himself, who ever sought to shine in the eyes of men,

while he heeded not how he might appear in the eyes of God? In this incident we learn what kind of spirit should ever mark the deportment of him, who is favored with high spiritual attainments and revelations. It is indeed scarcely possible to converse much with God without appearing more glorious in the eyes of man. But nothing can be more foreign to the temper of such a man than an ostentatious blazoning of what God has done for his soul. He will not be forward to talk of remarkable discoveries, to exhibit the shining of his face, to abash and confound a less favored brother. On the contrary, he will be meek, modest, and retiring. He will be more anxious to do good to others, than to gain eclat for himself. He will accommodate himself to the weakness of those whose progress may not have kept pace with his own. He will strive to abate envy by condescension and courtesy, nor will he be forward to make his experiences the theme of discourse, unless, as in the case of Paul, a supreme regard to the glory of God may compel him to bear witness to extraordinary manifestations, in order to put to shame and silence the disparaging reflections of gainsayers. Even then it will be a reluctant disclosure that is made. It will be made only because it is extorted by a paramount regard to the interests of truth. He will say, or at least feel, with the apostle, 'I am become a fool in glorying; ye have compelled me.'

Again, the incident before us is a plain and striking lesson to all who undertake to instruct others. It is a pitiful ambition, to seek merely to shine. The great aim of a moral teacher should be to communicate most effectually useful and saving knowledge. In doing this he is to think little of what immediately concerns himself, or the impression which he may personally make. If the minds of men, if the church of God, be enlightened, what matters it if he is

32 And afterward all the children of Israel came nigh: [i] and he gave them in commandment all that the LORD had spoken with him in mount Sinai.

[i] cn. 24. 3.

33 And *till* Moses had done speaking with them, he put [k] a vail on his face.

[k] 2 Cor. 3, 13.

---

himself somewhat obscured? He is required to consult the condition and capacities of those for whose good he labors. He is to accommodate himself to their weakness; he is not to oppress their minds with a *burden* even of truth; he is in all things to study their edification. So doing he may safely leave his reputation to God. He will take care of it. Let his mind be intent upon usefulness; let him be willing joyfully to give up fame for the sake of doing good, and he need not fear but as much celebrity will crown his name as will benefit the cause to which he is devoted, and more he will not desire.

But the veil which Moses constantly wore in his intercourse with the people, he laid aside whenever he went to commune with God, and to receive instruction from him. There the lustre of his face would be renewed and brightened again in the beams of that splendor from which it had been first received; and doubtless on every return from such visits, the Israelites would perceive that he had been with God. And so the truth will generally evince itself to others whenever any one has been favored with near approaches to God in prayer and communion. His face will shine brighter upon every renewed access to the throne of grace, and the beauty of the Lord his God will be upon him. He will be perceptibly more and more transformed into the image of that with which he is familiar. His very exterior will be meliorated and improved. The exercises of the closet will be seen and felt in the serenity of his countenance, in the benignity of the eye, in the gentle tones of the voice, and in the in-

creased affability and graciousness of the whole deportment. The world itself will take knowledge of the disciple who has been with Jesus. Yet the main remark suggested by this part of the narrative is, that when we come to present ourselves before God every veil must be laid aside, and no disguise or concealment attempted before the eyes of him with whom we have to do, and to whom all things are naked and open. As we do in fact appear then in the unveiled truth of our character, it is folly to act as if it were not so; as if any illusion could be practised upon Omniscience. 'When Moses went to speak with God, he pulled off his veil. It was good reason he should present to God that face which he had made; there had been more need of his veil to hide the glorious face of God from him, than to hide his from God; but his faith and thankfulness serve for both these uses. Hypocrites are contrary to Moses. He showed his worst to men, his best to God; they show their best to men, their worst to God; but God sees both their veil and their face; and I know not whether he more hates their veil of dissimulation, or their face of wickedness.' *Bp. Hall.*

33. *And* till *Moses had done speaking with them, he put a veil on his face.* The sense is undoubtedly correctly rendered, although the idiom of the original requires the insertion of 'till' in our translation. Rosenmuller and some few others do indeed contend that the true rendering requires the omission of all supplementary words, inasmuch as Moses intended to say that he had finished speaking before he assumed a veil. But this construction goes so decidedly

34 But ¹ when Moses went in before the LORD to speak with him, he took the vail off, until he came out.   And he came out and spake unto the children of Israel *that* which he was commanded.

¹ 2 Cor. 3. 16.

35 And the children of Israel saw the face of Moses, that the skin of Moses' face shone : and Moses put the vail upon his face again, until he went in to speak with Him.

against the whole current of ancient interpreters, and the manifest drift of the context, that it will be superfluous labor to confute it. We have no hesitation in taking the passage as it reads, and thus understood we are led to view it in connexion with the typical application made of it by the apostle, 2 Cor. 3. 6—18. He evidently employs the incident as shadowing forth in a typical way the relative glories of the legal and evangelical dispensations. We give the passage at length. ' But if the ministration of death, written and engraven in stones, was glorious, so that the children of Israel could not steadfastly behold the face of Moses for the glory of his countenance ; which glory was to be done away: How shall not the ministration of the Spirit be rather glorious? For if the ministration of condemnation be glory, much more doth the ministration of righteousness exceed in glory. For even that which was made glorious had no glory in this respect, by reason of the glory that excelleth. For if that which is done away was glorious, much more that which remaineth is glorious. Seeing then that we have such hope, we use great plainness of speech: And not as Moses, which put a veil over his face, that the children of Israel could not steadfastly look to the end of that which is abolished: But their minds were blinded: for until this day remaineth the same veil untaken away in the reading of the old testament ; which veil is done away in Christ. But even unto this day, when Moses is read, the veil is upon their heart. Nevertheless, when it shall turn to the Lord, the veil shall be taken

away. Now the Lord is that Spirit : and where the Spirit of the Lord is, there is liberty. But we all, with open face beholding as in a glass the glory of the Lord, are changed into the same image from glory to glory, even as by the Spirit of the Lord.' Here it is obvious that Moses appearing with his face veiled stands as a symbol of his own dispensation, which was in fact only the gospel under a veil. Whether Moses himself was conscious that any such mystic or spiritual import was couched under the incident may well be doubted ; but we can have no doubt that the Spirit of God by the hand of Paul has sanctioned this allegorical use of the fact in question. It is plainly set before us as having a three-fold phasis of emblematic meaning.

(1.) It is represented as being symbolical of the *intrinsic* glory or excellence of that dispensation, notwithstanding it is the special drift of the apostle to show that however glorious or excellent that dispensation was, it had no glory *compared* with the superior glory of the gospel. The law was glorious in the pure and holy nature of its precepts, which reflected the attributes of a glorious God, and it was glorious in the circumstances of its delivery. But as the glory of Moses' face was absorbed and lost in the splendor of God when he went into his presence in the tabernacle or on the mount, so the brightness and excellence of the Mosaic dispensation are eclipsed and swallowed up in the transcendant brightness of the gospel. The one is the shadow, the other the substance. The one is a ministration of condemnation the other of justification. Let us not then undervalue our distinguished privileges. We should no doubt be prone to think ourselves highly favored had we, like the Jews, a minister of God's word, in whose very face we could see a miraculous and divine light shining continually to prove him a man of God; but we have in fact a far greater privilege in the glorious gospel of the blessed God, which is constantly shedding forth the light of life, and irradiating men's minds with its spiritual beams.

(2.) It is used by the apostle to represent the *comparative obscurity* of the Mosaic dispensation. The veil intimated the indistinct view which the Israelites had of the ultimate scope of their law. Theirs was a system of rites and ceremonies, under which was *wrapped up* or *covered* a variety of spiritual subjects that their minds did not penetrate. They did not lift the veil so as to obtain a sight of the spiritual treasures which it concealed. They did not look to the 'end of the commandment,' which was to be ' abolished,' but rested in the mere letter, or literal meaning, which was comparatively meagre and barren.

(3.) It represents the *blindness and ignorance* under which the Jewish mind labored down to the time when Paul wrote, and which is not even yet, after the lapse of eighteen hundred years, removed. Age after age the inveterate prejudice and obduracy of the Jewish heart has prevented them from discerning the true sense of their own law, of its figures, types, and institutions, just as effectually as the veil on the face of Moses prevented them from beholding the beauty of his countenance. They read the books of their lawgiver, but in the sacrifices and services there prescribed they see no intimation of that Lamb of richer blood and that Priest of higher name, whom *we* are taught to recognise as foreshadowed by them. They read the predictions of the prophets, but they do not see them pointing to the Savior Christ, the true Messiah, in whom all their oracles are fulfilled. The thick veil of error and unbelief is upon their minds, and until that is taken away, as we learn it eventually shall be, the light of the glory of God in the gospel of his Son will not shine into them.

But let it not be forgotten that this veil of darkness and unbelief is not confined to the Jewish people. The natural man, whether Jew or Gentile, does not receive the things of the Spirit of God. We see it and wonder at it in *them*, but are unconscious of it in *ourselves*. Yet we are in fact monuments of greater obduracy than they, because there was in the very nature of the case, a veil cast over their dispensation which is removed from ours. Let us be reminded then that ' if the gospel be *hid* (Gr. κεκαλυμμενον, *veiled*) it is *hid* to them that are lost, in whom the god of this world hath blinded the minds of them which believe not. The prevailing power of a *worldly spirit* may as effectually tend to *judaize* our minds and thus obscure our spiritual vision, as the strictest adherence to the traditions of Rabbinical elders. How earnestly then should we strive to divest ourselves of every interposing medium that would prevent the free admission of the glorious light of the gospel into our souls ! With what a transforming power does it come ! To what a height of privilege and blessedness does it exalt its possessor ! 'We all, with open face, beholding as in a glass the glory of the Lord, are changed into the same image from glory to glory, even as by the Spirit of the Lord.' These words contain an evident allusion to the Old Testament narrative which we are now considering. The apostle is drawing a contrast between the genius of the two dispensations as it relates to the privilege of their respective subjects. When Moses was favored with a partial view of the glory of God as he passed by him, he was not only stationed in a cave, a cleft in the rock, but a cloud was interposed between him and the resplendent object of his vision, lest its brightness should be too dazzling for his visual powers. Yet notwithstanding this precaution, so much of the splendor of the divine glory was communicated to his countenance that he was obliged to veil himself when he appeared before the people. As he could not see God without the medium of a cloud, so they could not see *him* without the medium of a veil. The one was the counterpart of the other. But under the gospel the case is entirely changed. We can now look upon the moral glory of God ' with open face,' without any intervening cloud or veil. And when he says we behold this glory ' as in a glass' (κατοπτριζομενοι), the allusion is doubtless to the effect produced by looking into a highly burnished mirror. Macknight renders it, ' we all reflecting as mirrors the glory of the Lord.' If a strong light were thrown upon the polished surface of a mirror, the rays would be cast by reflection upon the face of the beholder, which would consequently be strongly illuminated. Such was the case to some extent with Moses. The radiation that came upon him from the glory of the Shekinah, and so wondrously illumined his face, was a kind of flashing reflection from the transcendant brightness of the Deity. But still more signally does this occur under the gospel. The glory of God, the splendor of the divine perfections, is thrown on the gospel, so to speak, like a bright light on a polished mirror, and that glory is so reflected on him that believingly contemplates it, that he appears to be transformed into the same image. Nothing can be more significant or happy than the figure employed ; and we should at least draw from it the inference, that we are not to rest satisfied unless we find that the view which we take of the

divine character in the gospel is *assimilating.* No visible effect analogous to that wrought upon Moses is indeed to be expected to be produced upon our bodies, but the character of our minds will be affected, the graces of our souls will be quickened, by habitual intercourse and converse with the glorious realities of the gospel of Christ. Nor should any thing short of this content those who are hoping at last to ' awake in his likeness.'

Again, we learn from this incident as used by the apostle, how much the Old Testament and the New serve mutually to explain each other. Very often what is obscure in the former becomes luminous in the latter ; and again, what is dark or indistinct in the New Testament often receives a flood of light from some kindred passage in the Old. No sentiment more injurious to the interests of truth could possibly come into vogue, than that the Old Testament is superseded by the New, and therefore that the study of it has but slight claims upon the Christian. The Old and the New Testament form one continuous system of revelation, the latter being merely the developement of the interior sense, and the substantiation of the typical shadows, of the former. He who sees in the books of Moses and the other writings of the Old Testament, nothing but the histories of certain events long since past, and a mass of religious usages and ceremonies practised by a particular people, with none of which we have any special concern, may be said to look not merely with a *veil*, but with a *bandage*, upon his eyes, and as he reads without understanding, he reads without profit. Such an one is not only unfaithful to the true interests of his own soul, but he is guilty of downright disparagement of the oracles of God, which are able to make us wise unto salvation. Let us then pray the prayer of David in reference to the same Scriptures, 'Open thou mine eyes

CHAPTER XXXV.

AND Moses gathered all the congregation of the children of Israel together, and said unto them, ª These *are* the words which the LORD hath commanded, that *ye* should do them.

ª ch. 34. 32.

---

that I may behold wondrous things out of thy law.'

Finally, let the suggestion come home to us in all its power, that if we belong to the true Israel of God we shall not always see thus through a glass darkly. The glimpses of the heavenly glory which we catch here below from time to time are indeed refreshing and precious to the soul. But they are transient and evanescent. God reveals himself as he did to Moses, *in passing by.* We see him for a moment, and he is gone. But the time is at hand when the beatific vision will be at once perfect and perpetual. In what lustre and glory will the children of the kingdom then shine forth! What will be the blissful state of those who shall be admitted into the paradise of God, when they shall each of them appear in a splendor not like that which invested Moses at mount Sinai, but rather like that which enrobed him as a garment of light at the transfiguration-scene of mount Tabor! How different from our present state! Now we see but vaguely, and know but in part. There we shall see face to face, and know as we are known; for no cloud will intercept the enraptured vision. Was Moses made honorable in the sight of the chosen tribes, by converse with Jehovah at Sinai? What then will be their glory, who shall enjoy a communion with him as uninterrupted as the flowings of his love, as endless as the days of eternity! Behold, and wonder; behold, and rejoice in the hope of the glory of God! Then shall the ransomed 'shine forth as the

2 ᵇ Six days shall work be done, but on the seventh day there shall be to you an holy day, a sabbath of rest to the LORD: whosoever doeth work therein shall be put to death.

ᵇ ch. 20. 9. & 31. 14, 15. Lev. 23. 3. Numb. 15. 32, &c. Deut. 5. 12. Luke 13. 14.

---

sun in the kingdom of their Father,' a blessed spectacle to each other, and to all the kindreds of heaven! It will be the eternal day of Christ's and his saint's transfiguration, when *they* shall say, with a rapture which Peter could not feel, even on the holy mount, 'Master, it is good for us to be here!'

Chapter 35

The Offerings for the Tabernacle.

1, 2. *And Moses gathered all the congregation of the children of Israel,* &c. God having now become reconciled to his people, and the covenant which they had, on their part, annulled by their recent transgression, having been graciously renewed, the delayed work of building the Tabernacle is ordered to go on. This edifice was to be constructed and furnished of materials supplied by the liberality of the people; and they were now gathered together to receive afresh the intimation of the Lord's will respecting the undertaking. The directions now given are prefaced with a repetition of the law of the Sabbath. As the sanctification of the seventh day is all along represented as a point of prime moment in the system of religious service ordained by God, we are not to be surprised to find it again and again insisted on and enforced in a great variety of ways. In the original the command is given in terms of peculiar emphasis;—'On the seventh day there shall be to you holiness, a sabbath of sabbatism to the Lord.' On that day no work was to be done, not even the work of the tabernacle. The

3 e Ye shall kindle no fire throughout your habitations upon the sabbath-day.
4 ¶ And Moses spake unto all
the congregation of the children of
Israel, saying, d This *is* the thing

c ch. 16. 23.   d ch. 25. 1, 2.

---

sanctity of the Sabbath was greater
than that of the sanctuary, and its holy
rest must not be invaded under any pretence whatever. However important the
outward apparatus of worship, it was
of less consequence than the spiritual
necessities of the soul. One day in
seven was none too much to be devoted
to a hallowed recess from secular business, and to a devout meditation upon
those themes which the Sabbath was
intended to familiarise to their minds.
It was a day commemorative of a rest
that was past, and typical of one that
was to come. Its peculiar designation,
' sabbath of sabbatism,' points to a *special plenitude* in the degree of rest
which it implied, as if it were a designed shadow of that rest, spiritual
and eternal, which remains for the people of God.——¶ *Whosoever doeth work
therein shall be put to death.* The clear
and explicit declaration of this precept
and its frequent repetition, could leave
room for no possible doubt as to the
will of God respecting it; and consequently the guilt of violating it would
be enhanced in proportion. On these
grounds, therefore, the severe penalty
of death is annexed to the command,
from which it is evident that it was
considered in this relation as a *judicial
statute.*

3. *Ye shall kindle no fire,* &c. Not,
probably, that fires in their private
dwellings were absolutely forbidden at
all seasons, for the winters in Judea
are often very cold, but the design
seems to have been mainly to prohibit
fires being made for the purpose of carrying on the work of the sanctuary,

---

which the LORD commanded, saying,
5 Take ye from among you an offering unto the LORD: e whosoever
is of a willing heart, let him bring
it, an offering of the LORD; gold,
and silver, and brass,

e ch. 25. 2.

---

just about to be commenced, the importance and sacredness of which they
might interpret as constituting a license
for a breach of the Sabbath. By this
precept they were taught, on the other
hand, that no plea of this kind would
avail; that none of the various pro-
cesses of fusing or moulding the gold,
or silver, or brass appointed for the
work of the tabernacle would be allowed to interfere with the devout observance of holy time, when every thing
but the duties of worship were to come
to a solemn pause. The spirit of the
precept probably applies to many species of employment which, under the
plea of necessity, are at the present day
prosecuted on the Sabbath.

5. *Take ye from among you an offering unto the Lord.* Heb. תרומה *terumah, a heave-offering,* from רום *rum,
to be lifted up, exalted, elevated.* Gr.
and Chal. ' a separation;' i. e. a gift
separated and set apart to the service
of God, from their other possessions.
See Note on Ex. 29. 28. In the requisition for their offerings or gifts it will
be observed that Moses put no compulsion upon the people, nor did he give
any directions as to the quantity of
the different articles which they should
bring. The whole was to be left to the
promptings of their own willing and
generous hearts. God loves a cheerful
giver, and instead of imposing a tax,
he offered them an opportunity of showing, by spontaneous expressions, how
much they were disposed to do for him
who had laid them under such infinite
obligations. The most costly offering
was not too precious, nor was the mean-

6 And blue, and purple, and scarlet, and fine linen, and goats' *hair*,

7 And rams' skins dyed red, and badgers' skins, and shittim-wood.

8 And oil for the light, ᶠand spices for anointing oil, and for the sweet incense,

f ch. 25. 6.

---

9 And onyx-stones, and stones to be set for the ephod, and for the breast-plate.

10 And ᵍ every wise-hearted among you shall come, and make all that the LORD hath commanded;

g ch. 31. 6.

---

est too small for him who accepteth according to that a man hath, and not according to that he hath not. To the same principle God now addresses himself in making his demands for the charitable contributions of his people. *We* have not indeed any such *material* building to raise, and therefore may be sometimes prone to imagine that the same occasion for the display of liberality does not exist. But is there not a *spiritual* temple which God designs to have erected for himself, wherein he may be glorified? And is not that temple infinitely more dear to him than any which can be formed by human hands? Should not the manifestation of his presence, and the establishment of his kingdom in the world, call forth our zeal, as much as the erection of that fabric in the wilderness did the zeal of the Israelites? The material tabernacle was only a shadow of that better habitation wherein God delights to dwell. To the erection of this spiritual house every true christian Israelite is called to contribute according as God hath given him ability. And let it be ever remembered that the blessing will go with our contributions according to the free, cordial, generous spirit with which they are made. It is not the amount given, but the motive of the giver, which is of account in God's sight. Even the poor widow who casts in her two mites will receive an equal plaudit with Araunah, of whom it is said, 'All these things did Araunah, *as a king*, give unto the king.' They who do what they can show evidently that they would do more if they could.——

¶ *Of a willing heart.* Heb. נדיב לבו *nedib libbo, willing (in) his heart.* The original term נדיב *nadib*, signifying *free, spontaneous, liberal,* and sometimes rendered *noble*, is more frequently employed as a designation of *princes*, from the *generosity*, and *nobleness*, and *largeness of soul* by which they are supposed to be characterised. In its substantive form it occurs Ps. 68. 9, 'Thou, O God, didst send a *plentiful rain*, whereby thou didst confirm thine inheritance when it was weary.' Heb. 'a rain of liberalities;' which Chandler in his Life of David, vol. 2. p. 61, renders, 'a shower, as it were voluntarily falling,' and refers it to the abundant supply of manna and quails which descended upon the Israelites like a falling rain from heaven; an interpretation which seems to be confirmed by Ps. 78. 24, 27, 'He opened the doors of heaven, and *rained* down manna upon them to eat. He *rained* flesh also upon them as dust, and feathered fowls like as the sand of the sea.'

6. *Blue, and purple, and scarlet*, &c. As the principal items contained in this chapter have already been largely considered in the Notes on chapters 25—31, the reader is referred to them and to the parallel texts in the margin for the requisite explanations.

10. *Every wise-hearted.* Heb. כל חכם לב *kol hakam lēb*, every one *wise of heart;* i. e. apt, skilful, ingenious in the various kinds of workmanship now required. The same term is applied to the women, v. 25, 26. The Heb. word חכמה *hokmah* is used variously, according to Maimonides; some-

11 [h] The tabernacle, his tent, and his covering, his taches, and his boards, his bars, his pillars, and his sockets;

12 [i] The ark, and the staves thereof, *with* the mercy-seat, and the vail of the covering;

13 The [k] tables, and his staves, and all his vessels, [l] and the shew-bread;

14 [m] The candlestick also for the light, and his furniture, and his lamps, with the oil for the light;

15 [n] And the incense-altar, and his staves, [o] and the anointing oil, and [p] the sweet incense, and the hanging for the door at the entering in of the tabernacle;

16 [q] The altar of burnt-offering, with his brazen grate, his staves, and all his vessels, the laver and his foot;

17 [r] The hangings of the court, his pillars, and their sockets, and the hanging for the door of the court;

18 The pins of the tabernacle, and the pins of the court, and their cords;

19 [s] The clothes of service, to do service in the holy *place*, the holy garments for Aaron the priest, and the garments of his sons, to minister in the priest's office.

20 ¶ And all the congregation of the children of Israel departed from the presence of Moses.

21 And they came, every one [t] whose heart stirred him up, and every one whom his spirit made willing, *and* they brought the LORD's offering to the work of the tabernacle of the congregation, and for all his service, and for the holy garments.

[h] ch. 26. 1, 2, &c. [i] ch. 25. 10, &c. [k] ch. 25. 23. [l] ch. 25. 30. Lev. 24. 5, 6. [m] ch. 25. 31, &c. [n] ch. 30. 1. [o] ch. 30. 23. [p] ch. 30. 34. [q] ch. 27. 1.

[r] ch. 27. 9. [s] ch. 31. 10. & 39. 1, 41. Numb. 4, 5, 6, &c. [t] ver. 5. 22, 36, 29. ch. 25. 2. & 36. 2. 1 Chron. 28. 2, 9. & 29. 9. Ezra 7. 27. 2 Cor. 8. 12. & 9. 7.

---

times for a deep knowledge of divine things; sometimes for moral virtue; sometimes, as here, for skill in mechanical arts; and sometimes for craft and subtlety. A passage in Homer, quoted by Aristotle, remarkably coinciding with this, shows that this sense of the term is not unknown to classical usage; 'The gods neither made him a ditcher, nor a plowman, nor any other sort of *wise man.*' Upon this Aristotle observes, 'We ascribe *wisdom* in arts to those who excel in them.' Indeed the character given of Wisdom by Solomon, Prov. 8. 12, would seem to carry with it an allusion to this sense of the term, 'I Wisdom dwell with prudence, and find out the knowledge of *witty inventions.*' The word לב *lëb, heart,* is used in accordance with the popular notions of that age and people, that the heart is the seat of the understanding.

11. *The tabernacle, his tent, and his covering.* These three terms evidently import in this connexion the three exterior sets of curtains. Compare Note Ex. 26. 1, where this sense of 'tabernacle' and 'tent' is confirmed.

18. *The pins of the tabernacle,* &c. These were not particularly mentioned before, though we have previously given a cut of them under ch. 27. 10. Josephus says that to every board of the tabernacle, and to every pillar of the court, there were ropes or cords fastened at the top, having the other end secured to a πασσαλος, *nail* or *pin,* which at a good distance off was driven into the ground up to the head, a cubit deep It was a nail or pin of this description which Jael drove into the temples of Sisera. See Note on Judg. 4. 21.

20, 21. *And all the congregation—departed,* &c. Having had the will of God now fully explained to them, they proceed deliberately to *act* in accord-

22 And they came, both men and women, as many as were willing-hearted, *and* brought bracelets, and ear-rings, and rings, and tablets, all jewels of gold : and every man that offered, *offered* an offering of gold unto the LORD.

23 And ᵘ every man with whom was found blue, and purple, and scarlet, and fine linen, and goats' *hair*, and red skins of rams, and badgers' skins, brought *them*.

ᵘ 1 Chron. 29. 8.

ance with the instructions received. They retire from the assembly to their tents, but only to return again with their offerings in their hands. They had no bibles at home with which to compare the requisitions of their leader, and 'see if these things were so,' but his commands they regarded as imperative and ultimate, and would not allow their zeal to cool before obeying them. There was no doubt, in view of their recent transgression, the working of a spirit very much akin to that awakened by the apostle and described in his second epistle to the Corinthian church; 'For behold this self-same thing, that ye sorrowed after a godly sort, what carefulness it wrought in you, yea, what clearing of yourselves, yea, what indignation, yea, what fear, yea, what vehement desire, yea, what zeal, yea, what revenge ! In all things ye have approved yourselves to be clear in this matter.' The idea of having once done evil ought to operate as a powerful incentive to ever after doing good.—— ¶ *Every one whose heart stirred him up.* Heb. לבו נשאו אשר *asher nesaü libbo, whose heart lifted him up.* Chal. 'Whose heart was spontaneous.' Every one whose heart was raised to a free and cheerful promptitude ; and such undoubtedly was the case with the congregation *en masse.* We do not consider the language as intended to bear invidiously upon some by implying that they were *not* thus iberal ; that they either did not offer at all or at best but grudgingly. It is rather an intimation of the general spirit which actuated the whole body of the people. Possibly individual ex-

ceptions might have been found, but they are not regarded in the comprehensive estimate of the Spirit.

22. *And they came, both men and women.* Heb. האנשים על הנשים *haanashim al hannashim, the men upon, over and above, in addition to, the women ;* a peculiar phraseology, which implies, according to the Jewish critic Abrabanel, that the women came first and presented their offerings, and were then followed by the men. This sense is approved by Cartwright, one of the soundest commentators who have ever undertaken to illustrate the Scriptures from Rabbinical sources. Nor has the prompt and forward obedience of woman ever belied this character in any age of the world.—— ¶ *And brought bracelets, and ear-rings,* &c. Their offerings were various according to their various possessions. They show themselves, if any thing, more forward to give to the service of God than they had before been to contribute to the fabrication of the golden calf. There we read of *ear-rings* only having been offered, but here of all kinds of precious articles, as if nothing was too good or too rich to be parted with for the honor of God. Indeed it would seem from the final clause of v. 22, that the spirit of the offerers was so acceptable in the sight of God that he regarded every offering, whatever it was, as an offering of gold. Even the goats' hair and rams' skins acquired so high a value in his esteem from the motives which prompted the givers, that they were accounted as oblations of pure gold ! —— ¶ *Tablets.* Heb. כומז *kumaz.* This is a very doubtful word, occurring

24 Every one that did offer an of-fering of silver and brass brought the Lord's offering: and every man with whom was found shittim-wood for any work of the service, brought *it*.

25 And all the women that were w wise-hearted did spin with their hands, and brought that which they had spun, *both* of blue, and of purple, *and* of scarlet, and of fine linen.

26 And all the women whose heart stirred them up in wisdom spun goats' *hair*.

27 And x the rulers brought onyx stones, and stones to be set, for the ephod, and for the breast-plate;

28 And y spice, and oil for the light, and for the anointing oil, and for the sweet incense.

29 The children of Israel brought a z willing offering unto the Lord, every man and woman, whose heart made them willing to bring, for all manner of work which the Lord had commanded to be made by the hand of Moses.

30 ¶ And Moses said unto the children of Israel, See, a the Lord

w ch. 28. 3. & 31. 6. & 36. 1. 2 Kings 23. 7. Prov. 31. 19, 22, 24.

x 1 Chron. 29. 6. Ezra 2. 68. y ch. 30. 23. z ver 21. 1 Chron. 29. 9. a ch. 31. 2, &c.

---

only here and in Num. 31. 50. Geddes, Boothroyd, and others render it by 'lockets,' answering to the Roman 'bulla,' or the 'baccatum monile' of Virgil, which was a necklace formed of gems or precious stones, resembling *berries*. Such trinkets are still worn by the Arabians. Bochart supposes it was a kind of supporting girdle worn by the wo-men round the bosom. The Editor of the Pictorial Bible, on the other hand, sup-poses it to have been an ornamented *hoop* or *band* surrounding the head. His plates represent such an ornament among the articles of Egyptian cos-tume. They were at any rate prob-ably a part of the spoils obtained from the Egyptians.——¶ *Every man that offered.* Heb. הניף *hëniph, that waved;* from the circumstance of their obla-tions being *heaved up* and *waved* when offered to the Lord; consequently call-ed, Ex. 38. 24, 'a wave-offering.'

25. *And all the women that were wise-hearted*, &c. The sense in which 'wis-dom' is predicated of all these various arts and handicrafts has been already explained above on v. 10. Here it ap-pears that the women were as forward in the good work as the men. They were not only willing to *give*, but to *make*. They not only resigned their

ornaments, but went immediately to work by spinning and weaving to fabri-cate such articles of tapestry as were needed for the tabernacle. As all are interested in the worship of God, so all should bear a part in it. The well-being and happiness of woman is in a special manner vitally involved in the existence and maintenance of religious institutions, and why should she not be active in promoting them? So in the early history of the church, the Chris-tian tabernacle, there were 'women which labored in the gospel,' Phil. 4. 3, and of whom Paul again says, Rom. 16. 12, that they 'labored in the Lord.'

29. *The children of Israel brought a willing offering, every man and wo-man*, &c. Heb. נדבה *nedabah, a free-will gift.* The same word is rendered in v. 3, of the ensuing chapter, 'free-offering.' No other impulse was needed than the generous promptings of their own bosoms to draw from them the most liberal donations to the good work in hand. Even the maidens, who are not prone to forget their ornaments, now readily divested themselves of their bracelets, pendants, and jewels to swell the amount of the general contribution, as if more anxious for the beautifying of the sanctuary than the

nath called by name Bezaleel, the son of Uri, the son of Hur, of the tribe of Judah;

31 And he hath filled him with the spirit of God, in wisdom, in understanding, and in knowledge, and in all manner of workmanship;

32 And to devise curious works, to work in gold, and in silver, and in brass,

33 And in the cutting of stones, to set *them*, and in carving of wood, to make any manner of cunning work.

34 And he hath put in his heart that he may teach, *both* he, and b Aholiab, the son of Ahisamach, of the tribe of Dan.

b ch. 31. 6.

35 Them hath he c filled with wisdom of heart, to work all manner of work, of the engraver, and of the cunning workman, and of the embroiderer, in blue, and in purple, in scarlet, and in fine linen, and of the weaver, *even* of them that do any work, and of those that devise cunning work.

CHAPTER XXXVI.

THEN wrought Bezaleel and Aholiab, and every a wisehearted man, in whom the LORD put wisdom and understanding to know how to work all manner of work for the service of the b sanctuary, according to all that the LORD had commanded.

c ver. 31. ch. 31. 3, 6. 1 Kings 7. 14. 2 Chron. 2. 14. Isai. 28. 26. a ch. 28. 3. & 31. 6. & 35. 10, 35. b ch. 25. 8.

decoration of their own persons. One spirit seems to have pervaded the whole people. Whatever any one possessed that could be applied to the projected structure, he instantly wrote upon it 'Corban,' and dedicated it to the service of God. Each doubtless thought himself rich, not in proportion to what he retained for his own use, but to the supplies he was able to contribute. In this way the genuine influence of the gospel always operates. Its converts in every age are represented as coming unto God, 'their gold and their silver with them.' However dear may have been their earthly treasures to their hearts, yet the love of Christ will relax their tenacious grasp upon them, and they will be willing, at the call of duty, to part with that which they most value, and deem it a privilege to give up their *all* to him who has bought them with his blood. How little is to be lost by a liberal policy and how heartily we are to adopt it, is clearly taught in the words of Paul, 2 Cor. 9. 6, 7, 'But this I say, he which soweth sparingly, shall reap also sparingly; and he which soweth bountifully, shall reap also boun-

tifully. Every man according as he purposeth in his heart, so let him give; not grudgingly, or of necessity: for God loveth a cheerful giver.' O what might not be done for the honor of God and the welfare of man, if this noble spirit every where prevailed, and men gave to the utmost of their ability! How easy would it be to erect places of worship, to maintain a settled ministry, to supply the wants of the poor, to send the gospel to the heathen, to administer instruction to the ignorant, consolation to the troubled, relief to the distressed! Well may it shame the world and the church that a concern for trifles crowds out these great objects from their minds; that their own petty interests take precedence of the infinite and eternal interests of God and his kingdom!

Chapter 36

1. *Then wrought Bezaleel and Aholiab, and every wise-hearted man,* &c. Heb. חכם לב *hakem lëb, wise of heart.* Wherever this epithet occurs the reader is to consider it as an Hebraism, even though it should be met with in the New Testament, as 1 Cor 3. 10, 'Ac-

2 And Moses called Bezaleel and Aholiab, and every wise-hearted man, in whose heart the LORD had put wisdom, *even* every one ᶜ whose heart stirred him up to come unto the work to do it:

3 And they received of Moses all the offering which the children of Israel ᵈ had brought for the work of the service of the sanctuary, to make it *withal*. And they brought yet unto him free-offerings every morning.

4 And all the wise men, that wrought all the work of the sanctuary, came every man from his work which they made;

ᶜ ch. 35. 2, 26. 1 Chron. 29. 5.　ᵈ ch. 35. 27.

5 ¶ And they spake unto Moses, saying, ᵉ The people bring much more than enough for the service of the work which the LORD commanded to make.

6 And Moses gave command ment, and they caused it to be pro claimed throughout the camp, say ing, Let neither man nor woman make any more work for the offer ing of the sanctuary. So the peo ple were restrained from bringing.

7 For the stuff they had was sufficient for all the work to make it, and too much.

ᵉ 2 Cor. 8. 2, 3.

cording to the grace of God which is given unto me as a *wise* master-builder, I have laid the foundation.' Strictly speaking, a man may be replete with wisdom, and yet be a poor artificer; and here perhaps a better version would have been ‘ ingenious,' ‘skilful,' or some such term; or ‘wise-hearted' may be exchanged for ‘wise-minded,' as ‘heart,' in the modern acceptation, is the seat neither of wisdom, nor skill, nor in genuity; but of love, hatred, pride, revenge, and other similar passions; whereas in the *mind* lodges not only wisdom, properly so called, but pru dence, foresight, genius, contrivance, invention, and other kindred faculties. Our previous explanations, however, on the scriptural sense of this epithet have been too full to leave the reader under any mistake as to its meaning.

2. *And Moses called*, &c. Rather, ‘ For Moses *had* called,' according to very common usage.

3. *And they received of Moses all the offering*, &c. Heb. כל התרומה *kol hatterumah, all the heaving,* or *heave-offering.*——¶ *And they brought yet unto him free-offerings every morning.* Heb. בקר בקר *boker boker, morning, morning.* They kept it up from day to

day, and how long they would have gone on, if not restrained, no one can tell. But we are not left merely to *ad mire* their conduct. ‘We should always make it our morning's work to bring our offering unto the Lord, even the spiritual offerings of prayer and praise, and a broken heart surrendered entirely to God. This is that which the duty of every day requires. God's compas sions are new every morning, and so should our offerings be, our free offer ings: God's grace to us is free, and so should our duty to him be.' *Henry.*

4—7. *And all the wise men.— came every man from his work*, &c. The ‘wise men' here mentioned were evident ly the *artificers* or *artisans* who took charge of the different departments of the work. Although their several tasks were not yet completed, yet from the best judgment they could form of the amount of materials requisite, they did not hesitate to assure Moses that the supply exceeded the demand. This re port was alike creditable to the artists and to the people. It showed con clusively the exemplary honesty of the former. Had they been governed by any thing but the strictest principles of integrity, they would scarcely have

8 ¶ ᶠAnd every wise-hearted man among them that wrought the work of the tabernacle made ten

ᶠ ch. 26. 1.

curtains *of* fine twined linen, and blue, and purple, and scarlet: *with* cherubims of cunning work made he them.

failed to seize the opportunity of enriching themselves by appropriating the overplus of the offerings to their own use as perquisites of their place. When we consider that it was impossible to determine beforehand precisely how large an amount of materials would be necessary for any particular province of the work, and how desirous most men are of having the handling and the discretionary control of precious things, though they may not actually use them, it was certainly a rare example of disinterestedness and probity that was now exhibited. With every thing to favor peculation, they scorn to entertain the thought for a moment of turning the public liberality to their private advantage. On the contrary, they determine to cut themselves off from a liability to temptation by declining to receive any more than they were confident of having occasion for. Accordingly upon their statement to Moses he immediately issued his command in a proclamation that the contributions should cease. Here again it is impossible to conceive a more emphatic testimony than this to the profuse generosity of the people. 'Let neither man nor woman make any more work for the offering of the sanctuary!' Moses might well adopt the language of Paul respecting the churches of Macedonia; 'Their deep poverty abounded unto the riches of their liberality. For to their power, I bear record, yea, and beyond their power, they were willing of themselves; praying us with much entreaty that we would receive the gift.' It would almost seem that they had heard ' the words of the Lord Jesus, how he said, It is more blessed to give than to receive.' Alas, are we not constrained to acknowledge that this con-

duct stands in mortifying contrast with that of the great mass of the Christian world! Instead of giving 'too much,' where do they ever give enough? And where do we now find men acting so fully on the *voluntary* principle? How small a proportion of the benevolent offerings of Christians are *brought* to the Lord's treasury? Instead of this they must be *sent for*. Numerous, expensive, and laborious agencies must be employed, which of themselves absorb a considerable portion of the funds raised. Collectors must go from house to house, and even then are often esteemed unwelcome visitors; nay, so prone is the worldly heart to evasion, that many will consider it a good excuse for not giving to a well-known object of benevolence, if they can say, *they have not been called on!* Ah, how different from the full-souled and spontaneous promptings of the Israelitish donors on this occasion! They needed simply to have a want stated, and then without waiting for duty to be inculcated, appeals urged, a precise amount prescribed, or a messenger sent, they become the carriers of their own gifts and pour them in without stint till checked by a public proclamation! God be praised, however, that this spirit is not entirely lacking in the church at this day. Some there are who only require the slightest signal of the Lord's finger, not to be behind the most forward Israelite in contributing to the up-building of his kingdom on the earth. Their record is on high. ——¶ *Make any more work.* That is collect, accumulate, make ready any more materials to work with. See this sense of the word 'make' illustrated in the Note on Gen. 12. 5.

8—38. *Made ten curtains of fine*

9 The length of one curtain *was* twenty and eight cubits, and the breadth of one curtain four cubits: the curtains *were* all of one size.

10 And he coupled the five curtains one unto another: and *the other* five curtains he coupled one unto another.

11 And he made loops of blue on the edge of one curtain from the selvedge in the coupling: likewise he made in the uttermost side of *another* curtain, in the coupling of the second.

12 g Fifty loops made he in one curtain, and fifty loops made he in the edge of the curtain which *was* in the coupling of the second: the loops held one *curtain* to another.

13 And he made fifty taches of gold, and coupled the curtains one unto another with the taches. So it became one tabernacle.

14 ¶ h And he made curtains *of* goats' *hair* for the tent over the tabernacle: eleven curtains he made them.

15 The length of one curtain *was* thirty cubits, and four cubits *was* the breadth of one curtain: the eleven curtains *were* of one size.

16 And he coupled five curtains by themselves, and six curtains by themselves.

17 And he made fifty loops upon the uttermost edge of the curtain in the coupling, and fifty loops made he upon the edge of the curtain which coupled the second.

18 And he made fifty taches *of* brass to couple the tent together, that it might be one.

19 i And he made a covering for the tent *of* rams' skins dyed red, and a covering *of* badgers' skins above *that*.

20 ¶ k And he made boards for the tabernacle *of* shittim-wood, standing up.

21 The length of a board *was* ten cubits, and the breadth of a board one cubit and a half.

22 One board had two tenons, equally distant one from another: thus did he make for all the boards of the tabernacle.

23 And he made boards for the tabernacle; twenty boards for the south side southward:

24 And forty sockets of silver he made under the twenty boards; two sockets under one board for his two tenons, and two sockets under another board for his two tenons.

25 And for the other side of the tabernacle *which is* toward the north corner, he made twenty boards,

26 And their forty sockets of

g ch. 26. 5.   h ch. 26. 7.   i ch. 26. 14.   k ch. 26. 15.

twined *linen*, &c. We find scarcely any thing in the sequel of this chapter but what has been mentioned and fully commented on in preceding Notes. Both this and the remaining chapters of the book are little more than a bare repetition of the contents of the previous chapters from ch. 25th to 31st inclusive. We shall find nothing to surprise or weary us in this extended recital of minute circumstances, if we bear in mind, that it is doubtless intended as a tacit intimation to us of the duty of ful- filling to the letter, and with the most scrupulous exactness, every jot and tittle of the word of God. Of this the narrative before us affords so striking an instance, that it may well stand as a grand and paramount illustration of a general principle. Indeed it may be said, that the whole mass of Scripture consists chiefly of two corresponding parts, viz., *precept* and *example*; on the one hand the directions as to what we are to do to fulfil the divine will, and on the other, the example of those who

silver; two sockets under one board, and two sockets under another board.

27 And for the sides of the tabernacle westward he made six boards.

28 And two boards made he for the corners of the tabernacle in the two sides.

29 And they were coupled beneath, and coupled together at the head thereof, to one ring: thus he did to both of them in both the corners.

30 And there were eight boards; and their sockets *were* sixteen sockets of silver, under every board two sockets.

31 ¶ And he made ¹ bars *of* shittim-wood; five for the boards of the one side of the tabernacle,

32 And five bars for the boards of the other side of the tabernacle, and five bars for the boards of the tabernacle for the sides westward.

33 And he made the middle bar to shoot through the boards from the one end to the other.

34 And he overlaid the boards

---

¹ ch. 26. 26.

---

with gold, and made their rings *of* gold *to be* places for the bars, and overlaid with bars of gold.

35 ¶ And he made ᵐ a vail *of* blue, and purple, and scarlet, and fine twined linen: *with* cherubims made he it of cunning work.

36 And he made thereunto four pillars *of* shittim-*wood*, and overlaid them with gold: their hooks *were of* gold; and he cast for them four sockets of silver.

37 ¶ And he made a ⁿ hanging for the tabernacle-door *of* blue, and purple, and scarlet, and fine twined linen, of needle-work;

38 And the five pillars of it, with their hooks: and he overlaid their chapiters and their fillets with gold: but their five sockets *were of* brass.

CHATER XXXVII.

AND Bezaleel made ᵃ the ark *of* shittim-wood: two cubits and a half *was* the length of it, and a cubit and a half the breadth of it, and a cubit and a half the height of it:

ᵐ ch. 26. 31.   ⁿ ch. 26. 36.   ᵃ ch. 25. 10.

---

have actually fulfilled it. The comparison of the two cannot but be admonitory to us, that in all things we are to work for God according to the pattern shown to us. In all our conduct, whether it be in the world's estimation a great matter or a small, it is of the first importance that there be neither a nail nor a pin, a loop nor a hook, otherwise than God has commanded. To do his will makes every matter great. Nothing can be a trifle that promotes his glory. 'Blessed is that servant whom his Lord when he cometh shall find *so doing*' as he hath ordered.

Chapter 37

There is little in the present chapter

that requires additional exposition. We have already considered its various items in minute detail in our remarks upon the previous chapters. The execution of each particular part, in exact conformity with the directions given, is punctiliously recited, not only for the general reason mentioned above, but also to intimate with what serious and profound consideration the form, furniture, uses, and typical design of this remarkable structure deserved to be studied. We can scarcely suppose that so much space would have been allotted to it, had it not been intended to shadow forth some of the central mysteries of redemption. What these were we have endeavored partially to unfold in our previous annotations. How far they

2 And he overlaid it with pure gold within and without, and made a crown of gold to it round about.

3 And he cast for it four rings of gold, *to be set* by the four corners of it: even two rings upon the one side of it, and two rings upon the other side of it.

4 And he made staves *of* shittim-wood, and overlaid them with gold.

were or could he understood by Moses and his cotemporaries, it is not easy to determine; but as the finer ornaments of the tabernacle were not to be seen by the common people, but only by the priests, and as the Scriptures were intended for the people at large, we can see a peculiar propriety in the verbal description being given at great length. In the same manner, many of the events in the life of Christ are in the New Testament related by two, and three, and some by four of the Evangelists, for the same reason.

For the ensuing extended note on a point of antiquarian interest, we have drawn upon the treasures of the Pictorial Bible.

2. *He overlaid it with pure gold.* Heb. צפה *tzippah*. 'The question here arises whether here and elsewhere gilding, or actual overlaying with plates of metal, is intended. It is observable that the word 'gilding' never occurs in our translation, but 'overlaying' often; and yet there is no reason to question that the Hebrews were at some time or other acquainted with gilding, and it is therefore difficult to conclude that in all cases where the word צפה *tzaphah* occurs it means only overlaid with plates of metal; and this may be the rather questioned, since the Septuagint renders it by καταχρυσοω, *to gild*, and is followed in this by the Vulgate. Modern translators have, however, generally adopted the ambiguous expression, 'to overlay;' yet one of them, Michaelis, uses the term 'to gild' in application to the boards of the tabernacle. When Beckmann was writing his article on gilding, he applied to Professor Tychsen to furnish him with some information as to the Scriptural notices on the subject. The professor, in his reply, states the instances in which gilding or overlaying are mentioned. They are, in the works of the tabernacle:—the ark, which was covered with gold within and without, and also the staves which belonged to it—the table of shew-bread, with its staves—the altar of burnt incense—the boards which formed the sides and the west end of the tabernacle; these were forty-eight in number, each having a surface of about forty-three feet and a half: besides which, there were the five bars on each side, which bound the whole together, and the pillars at the east end, which were also overlaid with gold. Then in Solomon's temple, the parts overlaid with gold were:—the whole inside of the house (1 Kings, 6. 21, 22): the altar of incense (ver. 20—22): the wooden cherubim, above seventeen feet in height (ver. 28): the floor (ver. 30): the doors of the oracle, on which were carved cherubim, palm-trees, and open flowers, so that the covering gold accurately exhibited the figures of the carved work (ver. 32—35). 'Now,' proceeds the professor, 'the question is, whether all these were gilt, or covered, or overlaid with plates of gold. I am acquainted with no work in which this subject is professedly discussed, and therefore I submit the following remarks to your consideration: The expression continually used for overlaying is צפה *tzaphah*, the original meaning of which in the Arabic, צפא *tzapha, clear, to be bright*, seems still to remain. The signification therefore is, *to make clear, to render bright;* but, as is commonly the case, nothing decisive can be obtained from this etymology, for it is equally applicable to gilding as to overlaying with

5 And he put the staves into the rings by the sides of the ark, to bear the ark.

6 ¶ And he made the b mercy-seat *of* pure gold : two cubits and a half *was* the length thereof, and one cubit and a half the breadth thereof.

7 And he made two cherubims *of* gold, beaten out of one piece made he them, on the two ends of the mercy-seat ;

8 One cherub on the end on this side, and another cherub on the *other* end on that side : out of the mercy-seat made he the cherubims on the two ends thereof.

9 And the cherubims spread out *their* wings on high, *and* covered with their wings over the mercy-seat, with their faces one to another ; *even* to the mercy-seat-ward were the faces of the cherubims.

10 ¶ And he made c the table *of* shittim wood : two cubits *was* the length thereof, and a cubit the breadth thereof, and a cubit and a half the height thereof :

b ch. 25. 17.   c ch. 25. 23.

11 And he overlaid it with pure gold, and made thereunto a crown of gold round about.

12 Also he made thereunto a border of an hand-breadth round about ; and made a crown of gold for the border thereof round about.

13 And he cast for it four rings of gold, and put the rings upon the four corners that *were* in the four feet thereof.

14 Over against the border were the rings, the places for the staves to bear the table.

15 And he made the staves *of* shittim-wood, and overlaid them with gold, to bear the table.

16 And he made the vessels which *were* upon the table, his d dishes, and his spoons, and his bowls, and his covers to cover withal, *of* pure gold.

17 ¶ And he made the e candle-stick *of* pure gold ; *of* beaten work made he the candlestick ; his shaft, and his branch, his bowls, his knops, and his flowers were of the same :

d ch. 25. 29.   e ch. 25. 31.

gold.' In some following observations the professor omits to avail himself of the important corroboration of his own view (that the word translated ' to over-lay' means only ' to render bright'), which is afforded by the fact, that when overlaying is undoubtedly intended, as in overlaying the altar of burnt-offering with plates of copper, quite another word is used, נחשת *nehosheth*, than that which refers to the covering of the wood-work with gold. Upon the whole, Tychsen concludes, from a comparison of the different passages, that gilding is sometimes intended rather than over-laying with plates of metal. He considers that the drying of the wood, and the softness of gold, which, in regard to staves, floors, &c., would soon be rubbed off, occasions some difficulty in

the notion that plates of metal were employed ; but even admitting that such plates could be made sufficiently fast to smooth surfaces of wood, he doubts whether any plates, however thin, could be so applied as to fit and exhibit accurately carved wooden fig-ures and flower-work, as in 1 Kings, 6. 35. And, with regard to the parts of the tabernacle, had they been covered with plates of gold, would they not have been too heavy for transportation, particularly as several of them were to be carried on the shoulders of men ? He also states his impression, that the twenty-nine talents and odd shekels ot gold, could scarcely have been sufficient to cover with plates of gold all the arti· cles above enumerated after so many vessels and other things had been made

18 And six branches going out of the sides thereof; three branches of the candlestick out of the one side thereof, and three branches of the candlestick out of the other side thereof:

19 Three bowls made after the fashion of almonds in one branch, a knop and a flower; and three bowls made like almonds in another branch, a knop and a flower: so throughout the six branches going out of the candlestick.

20 And in the candlestick *were* four bowls made like almonds, his knops and his flowers:

21 And a knop under two branches of the same, and a knop under two branches of the same, and a knop under two branches of the same, according to the six branches going out of it.

22 Their knops and their branches were of the same: all of it *was* one beaten work *of* pure gold.

23 And he made his seven lamps, and his snuffers, and his snuff-dishes *of* pure gold.

24 *Of* a talent of pure gold made he it, and all the vessels thereof.

25 ¶ f And he made the incense-altar *of* shittim-wood: the length of it *was* a cubit, and the breadth of it a cubit; *it was* four-square; and two cubits *was* the height of it; the horns thereof were of the same.

26 And he overlaid it with pure gold, *both* the top of it, and the sides thereof round about, and the horns of it: also he made unto it a crown of gold round about.

27 And he made two rings of gold for it under the crown thereof, by the two corners of it, upon the two sides thereof, to be places for the staves to bear it withal.

28 And he made the staves *of* shittim-wood and overlaid them with gold.

29 ¶ g And he made the holy anointing oil, and the pure incense of sweet spices, according to the work of the apothecary.

f ch. 30. 1. g ch. 30. 23, 34.

---

with pure gold. Upon the whole, Professor Tychsen thinks that the Hebrews understood both the arts of gilding and of overlaying with plates of metal, and that we must be left to infer from analogy and probability which process of the two was employed in particular cases. Some of these arguments seem to us to deserve great attention, and we have little hesitation in allowing their application to the temple of Solomon in the instances to which Professor Tychsen adverts; and, although with somewhat more hesitation, we may allow that collateral considerations give some probability to their application even to a structure so much more ancient and so different as the tabernacle. One of these considerations is, that gilding did not in ancient times imply as much inferiority to overlaying with plates as at present; for the ancient gold-beaters had not the art of reducing the gold-leaf to any thing like the tenuity which may now be produced, and hence the ancient gilding was thick, durable, and rich. Another is, that the art of gilding was of very high antiquity in Egypt, although it is of course impossible to say that the art existed there previous to the exodus of the Israelites. Herodotus mentions Egyptian statues ornamented with gilding; and he also mentions that he saw in the palace at Sais a cow of richly gilded wood, which had been made, in times long anterior to his own, by Mycerinus (the son of Cheops, the pyramid-builder) to enclose the mummy of his daughter. Even at this day we find traces of gilding on mummies and mummy-cases, and in some instances the mummies appear to have

CHAPTER XXXVIII.

AND ª he made the altar *of* burnt-offering *of* shittim-wood: five cubits *was* the length thereof, and five cubits the breadth thereof; *it was* four-square; and three cubits the height thereof.

2 And he made the horns thereof on the four corners of it; the horns thereof were of the same: and he overlaid it with brass.

3 And he made all the vessels of the altar, the pots, and the shovels, and the basons, *and* the flesh-hooks, and the fire-pans: all the vessels thereof made he *of* brass.

4 And he made for the altar a brazen grate of net-work under the

ª ch. 27. 1.

compass thereof beneath unto the midst of it.

5 And he cast four rings for the four ends of the grate of brass, *to be* places for the staves.

6 And he made the staves *of* shittim-wood, and overlaid them with brass.

7 And he put the staves into the rings on the sides of the altar, to bear it withal; he made the altar hollow with boards.

8 ¶ And he made ᵇ the laver *of* brass, and the foot of it *of* brass, of the looking-glasses of *the women* assembling, which assembled *at* the door of the tabernacle of the congregation.

ᵇ ch. 30. 18.

been gilt all over. (See 'Egyptian Antiquities,' vol. ii. p. 144.) Goguet thinks, indeed, that gilding was not known to the Greeks in the time of Homer. We do not feel that this position is fairly established by the instance he adduces; and if it were so, it is not only easy to conceive, but is certainly true, that the Egyptians had at that time long been acquainted with many arts which were not yet known to the Greeks. Goguet's instance is, that when the heifer which Nestor was about to offer to Minerva had, according to custom, its horns ornamented with gold, the process followed by the operator, who came with anvil, hammer, and pincers, is evidently not that of gilding, but of overlaying with plates of metal. (See 'Origine des Lois,' t. 2. p. 209.)' *Pictorial Bible.*

Chapter 38

8. *He made the laver of brass—of the looking-glasses of the women assembling,* &c. 'As the laver was of brass or copper, it is evident that the 'looking-glasses,' with which it was made, were of the same metal. The word 'mirror' should have been used in the

place of 'looking-*glass*,' in the various passages where it occurs, and which are all incompatible with the idea of *glass.* Thus Job (chap. 37. 18), 'Hast thou with him spread out the sky, which is strong, and *as a molten looking-glass?*' and an apocryphal writer (Ecclus. 12. 11.) says, 'Thou shalt be unto him as if thou hadst wiped *a looking-glass,* and thou shalt know that his *rust* hath not been altogether wiped away.' In all these passages a metallic mirror is obviously intended. The word מַרְאֹת *maroth,* considered to denote mirrors in the present text, does not, however, any where else occur in that sense, and Dr. Boothroyd, taking it in its most usual sense, considers the text to mean that the laver was made *under the inspection* of the women, not *with their mirrors.* This explanation seems to us to involve greater difficulties than those which it is designed to obviate. The common translation is perfectly consistent with the context, and with the early history of mirrors; besides which, all the ancient versions, as well as the Jewish writers, understand mirrors to be intended. We may understand either that the stock of copper in the camp was so comparatively small, as to have been exhausted in the other works for the tabernacle, or else that the mirrors of the women were particularly required for the laver as being of a superior sort of metal. As the women who assembled at the tabernacle are especially mentioned, it is not improbable that they followed the example of the Egyptian women who took their mirrors with them when they went to the temples. Moses may have required them for the laver, in order to put a stop to a practice of which he did not approve.

'Artificial mirrors seem to have been made as soon as men began to exercise their ingenuity on metals and stones. Every solid body capable of receiving a polish would be more or less suitable for this purpose; hence the earliest mirrors of which we possess any information were of metal. Stone mirrors are also noticed very early; but as such mirrors could not have been in any degree equal to those of polished metal, they are rarely mentioned by ancient authors, and then seem to be chiefly used for purposes of ornament, being polished slabs or panels fixed in the walls of wainscoted apartments. For this purpose the Romans preferred what Pliny calls the obsidian stone, which Beckmann identifies with the species of vitrified lava now called Icelandic agate. Plane, concave, and convex mirrors of a similar substance were in use among the Americans when the Spaniards came among them; and they had also others made with a mineral called the Inca's stone, which seems to have been a compact marcasite or pyrites, susceptible of a fine polish, and calculated to form mirrors apparently superior to any of stone which the ancient nations of Europe and Asia seem to have possessed. The Americans had also mirrors of silver, copper, and brass. When men began to work metals, it must soon have been discovered that the hardest white metals reflected more

distinct images, when polished, than any others. Of all the metals known to the ancients, steel was the best calculated for the purpose; but Beckmann says that he can discover no indications that steel mirrors were in use among them; and he thinks that its liability to contract rust and to become tarnished, prevented this otherwise desirable metal from being employed for the purpose. We rather differ from him in this particular. The mention of *rust* in the above quotation from the Apocrypha seems to imply that the mirror there in view was of steel; and although it be true that the Greeks and Romans did not use such mirrors, it does not follow that they were not employed in the East, where, in most parts, the dryness of the atmosphere exposes polished steel to the least possible danger from rust. In fact steel mirrors, although in some degree superseded by looking-glasses, continue to be extensively used in the East. After steel, in eligibility for mirrors, comes silver; and we find that silver mirrors are those most generally mentioned among the Greeks and Romans. 'In the Roman code of laws,' says Beckmann, 'when silver plate is mentioned, under the heads of heirship and succession by propinquity, silver mirrors are rarely omitted; and Pliny, Seneca, and other writers, who inveigh against luxury, tell us, ridiculing the extravagance of that age, that every young woman in their time must have a silver mirror. These polished silver plates may however have been very slight, for all the ancient mirrors preserved in collections, which I have seen, are only covered with a thin coat of that expensive metal.' There was also in use for the same purpose a mixture of copper and tin, producing a white metal which would seem to have been better adapted for mirrors than silver, although, on some account or other, it was not so much esteemed for the purpose. One reason probably was, tha this metal was more liable to be tarnished than those of silver, requiring to be frequently brightened before being used. Hence it seems that a sponge with pounded pumice-stone was generally suspended near the ancient mirrors. Mirrors of copper, brass, and gold, do not appear to have been much in use after the superior fitness of silver was discovered; yet there is no question that copper and brass were soonest applied to this purpose, and doubtless continued to be used by those who could not afford silver or silvered mirrors. The use of metallic mirrors is now, in Europe, almost entirely confined to reflecting telescopes. The mode of compounding the metals of which these mirrors are made, and of polishing them of a proper form, is an art of great nicety.

There is some difficulty in determining when glass mirrors were invented. Pliny alludes to attempts made at Sidon to form mirrors with glass, but in what manner does not appear; and if the attempts had produced any approximation to our mirrors, they would surely have superseded those of metal, which they were so far from doing that, whatever they were, they never came into use. With the exception of this notice in Pliny, there is no trace of glass mirrors till the the thirteenth century, after which they are spoken of in the clearest manner, and continued to be mentioned in every century, and at last mirrors of metal passed entirely out of notice. That the practical invention of glass mirrors cannot be much earlier than the date here assigned, seems to be evinced by the fact, mentioned by Beckmann, that glass mirrors continued to be very scarce in France in the fourteenth century. Those of metal were still in common use, and the mirror of even the queen, Anne of Bretagne, consort of Louis XII., was of this description.—On the history of mirrors, see further in Beckmann's ' Hist. of Inventions,' vol. iii. See also Goguet, 'Origine des Lois.' t. i. p. 371; Harmer vol. iv. p. 332—334; Burder's 'Oriental Customs,' vol. i. p. 37; vol. ii. p. 52, &c. *Pict. Bib.*

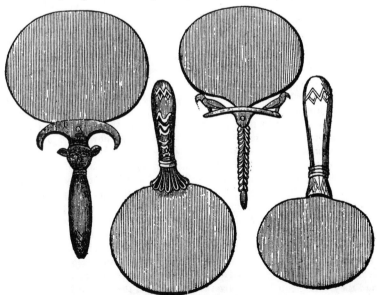

ANCIENT EGYPTIAN MIRRORS.

9 ¶ And he made c the court: on the south side southward the hangings of the court *were of* fine twined linen, a hundred cubits:

10 Their pillars *were* twenty, and their brazen sockets twenty; the hooks of the pillars, and their fillets, *were* of silver.

11 And for the north side, *the hangings were* an hundred cubits, their pillars *were* twenty, and their sockets of brass twenty: the hooks of the pillars, and their fillets, *of* silver.

12 And for the west side *were* hangings of fifty cubits, their pillars ten, and their sockets ten; the hooks of the pillars, and their fillets, *of* silver.

c ch. 27. 9.

13 And for the east side eastward fifty cubits.

14 The hangings of the one side *of the gate were* fifteen cubits; their pillars three and their sockets three.

15 And for the other side of the court-gate, on this hand and that hand, *were* hangings of fifteen cubits; their pillars three, and their sockets three.

16 All the hangings of the court round about *were* of fine twined linen.

17 And the sockets for the pillars *were of* brass; the hooks of the pillars, and their fillets, *of* silver and the overlaying of their chapiters *of* silver; and all the pillars of the court *were* filleted with silver.

¶ *Assembling.* Heb. צֹבְאֹת *tzobeoth assembling in troops.* The Heb. word here rendered ' assembling' is properly a military term applied to the *orderly mustering or marshalling of an army.* The verb from which it is derived, צבא *tzaba,* has the signification of *warring* or *going forth upon a military expedition,* and the corresponding substantive is for the most part rendered 'host,' 'hosts ;' sometimes 'war,' or 'warfare.' But as the regu'arity and order which marked the services of the sanctuary resembled those which prevail in a well-disciplined army, one party succeeding and relieving another in the discharge of their appropriate duties, the term became at length applied to the orderly course of ministration in the matter of the worship of God, as may be seen from the following passages; Num. 4. 23, 'All that enter in *to perform the service* (צבא לצבא *litzbo tzaba, to war the warfare ;)* i. e. perform the service, to do the work of the tabernacle; Gr. λειτουργειν, *to minister.* Num. 8. 24, 'From twenty and five years old and upward they will go in *to wait upon the service* (צבא לצבא *litzbo tzaba, to war*

the warfare) of the tabernacle.' So with probably a like sense Paul says to Timothy, 'that thou mightest *war a good warfare ;'* as if it were a usual phrase to signify the service of God. In the present instance accordingly we suppose the word is applied to certain women of the congregation who had devoted themselves, from the promptings of a peculiar spirit of piety, to various functions pertaining to the tabernacle service, for the same or a similar reason to that for which the term is applied to men when busied in the like employment. In strict parallelism with this we find the word occurring 1 Sam. 2. 22. 'And how they lay with the women that *assembled* (הצבאת *hatztzobeoth*) at the door of the congregation ; i. e. who were convened there as female ministers for pious purposes. So it is said of Anna, the prophetess, Luke 2. 26, that she 'departed not from the temple, but served God with fastings and prayers night and day.' With this mode of interpretation—the assembling for purposes of pious ministry—several of the ancient versions strikingly accord. Thus, the Chal. 'Of the mir-

18 And the hanging for the gate of the court *was* needle-work, *of* blue, and purple, and scarlet, and fine twined linen : and twenty cubits *was* the length, and the height in the breadth *was* five cubits answerable to the hangings of the court.

19 And their pillars *were* four, and their sockets *of* brass four ; their hooks *of* silver, and the overlaying of their chapiters and their fillets *of* silver.

20 And all the d pins of the tabernacle, and of the court round about, *were of* brass.

21 ¶ This is the sum of the tabernacle, *even* of e the tabernacle of testimony, as it was counted, according to the commandment of Moses, *for* the service of the Levites, f by the hand of Ithamar, son to Aaron the priest.

d ch. 27. 19.   e Numb. 1. 50. 53. & 9. 15. & 10. 11. A 17. 7, 8. & 18. 2.   2 Chron. 24. 6. Acts 7. 44.   f Numb. 4. 28. 33.

22 And g Bezaleel the son of Uri, the son of Hur, of the tribe of Judah, made all that the Lord commanded Moses.

23 And with him *was* Aholiab, son of Ahisamach, of the tribe of Dan, an engraver, and a cunning workman, and an embroiderer in blue, and in purple, and in scarlet, and fine linen.

24 All the gold that was occupied for the work in all the work of the holy *place*, even the gold of the offering, was twenty and nine talents, and seven hundred and thirty shekels after h the shekel of the sanctuary.

25 And the silver of them that were numbered of the congregation *was* a hundred talents, and a thousand seven hundred and threescore and fifteen shekels, after the shekel of the sanctuary :

g ch. 31. 2, 6.   h ch. 30 13, 24.   Lev. 5. 15 & 27. 3, 25.   Numb. 3. 47. & 18. 16.

---

rors of the women which came *to pray* at the door of the tabernacle.' Gr. 'Of the women that *fasted*, which *fasted* at the door of the tabernacle of witness.' *Fasting* is here specified because it was a usual accompaniment of *praying*. Targ. Jon. ' Of the brazen mirrors of modest women, who, when they came to pray in the portal of the tabernacle stood by their heave-offering, and offered praises and made confessions.'

18. *The height in the breadth was five cubits.* The phrase is Hebraic, denoting the height of the hanging of the gate, which was five cubits, corresponding with that of the rest of the hangings of the court. Suppose this piece of tapestry, which was twenty cubits in length, to be lying spread out upon the ground ; it is evident that what constitutes its *breath* in this situation becomes its *height* when hung up ; and this is what is meant by the text. Its height as composed of its breadth was five cubits.

21. *This is the sum of the tabernacle.* That is, the sum, enumeration, or inventory of the various particulars of the tabernacle furniture. These were reckoned up by the Levites over whom Ithamar, the son of Aaron, presided. In the clause, ' for the service of the Levites,' the word 'for' does not occur in the original, and the meaning probably is, that it was counted *by the labor* or *ministry* of the Levites. The words are a preface to what follows extending to the end of the chapter.

24. *And all the gold*, &c. Although the tabernacle, as a *portable* structure, cannot, from its known proportions and general appearance, have been a very grand or imposing structure, yet we may safely say, that probably the world never saw so small a fabric composed of such rich materials, and reared at so vast a cost. As the quantities of the precious metals employed are stated, some idea of its surpassing richness may be formed. The *gold* weighed 29

26 ᶦ A bekah for every man, *that*
half a shekel, after the shekel
of the sanctuary, for every one that
went to be numbered, from twenty
years old and upward, for ᵏ six hundred thousand and three thousand
and five hundred and fifty *men.*

27 And of the hundred talents of
silver were cast ᶩ the sockets of the

ᶦ ch. 30. 13, 15.　ᵏ Numb. 1. 46.　ᶩ ch. 26.
19, 21, 25, 32.

sanctuary, and the sockets of the
vail; a hundred sockets of the hundred talents, a talent for a socket.

28 And of the thousand seven
hundred seventy and five *shekels*
he made hooks for the pillars, and
overlaid their chapiters, and filleted them.

29 And the brass of the offering
was seventy talents, and two thousand and four hundred shekels.

---

talents and 730 shekels, if we allow
3000 shekels to the talent of 125 lbs. ;
and this at £4 the ounce would be
equal to £175,000 sterling, or nearly
$877,000. The silver was 100 talents
and 1775 shekels, being a half shekel
from all the males above twenty years
of age when they came out of Egypt,
whose number was 603,550 ; the whole
value of this would, at 5s. the ounce, be
£39,721, or nearly $188,605. The *brass,*
or rather *copper,* was 70 talents and
24,000 shekels, which if valued at 1s. 3d.
the pound avoirdupois would be worth
£138, or $690. The amount of these
several sums would not be less than
£213,320, or $1,066,600. But this amount
does not include the curtains of the inclosure, the coverings of the tabernacle,
the dress of the high priest and its jewels, the dresses of the common priests,
or the value of the skill and labor employed in the work, the whole of which
may be fairly taken to have raised its
value to the immense sum of £250,000,
or $1,250,000 !

It may perhaps be difficult for some
to imagine how the Israelites should
have been possessed of so much wealth
in the desert. But it is to be recollected that they had come out of Egypt
with great spoil, which was no doubt
very much augmented by what they obtained from the dead bodies of their
enemies, cast upon the shores of the
Red Sea. The subsequent victory over
the Amalekites, probably increased still
further their predatory treasures. Add

to this, that there is no reason to question that they trafficked more or less
with the wandering tribes of the desert,
on their way to Canaan, though we are
no where expressly informed that this
was the case.

The grand reason for employing so
great an amount of riches in the construction of the tabernacle and its furniture was undoubtedly two-fold, (1.)
To impress the minds of the chosen
people with the glory and dignity of the
Divine Majesty, and the importance of
his service ; and (2.) To convey through
the gorgeousness and splendor of the
external ritual an intimation of the
essential and transcendent beauty, excellence, and glory of the spiritual things
that were shadowed out by it. In this
there was a wise adaptation to the
mental condition of the Israelites. They
were in a sense like children, whose
minds must be reached through the medium of their senses. But little capable
of high abstract apprehensions of spiritual subjects, it was only by means of
such a sensuous apparatus of worship
that they could receive the inner essential truths which it involved. To us,
favored as we are with a higher state
of intellectual advancement, such a system is not necessary, and consequently
it is done away.

26. *A bekah for every man.* The
value of the bekah is immediately defined to be half a shekel. The original
בֶּקַע *bekah* comes from בָּקַע *baka, to divide, to cleave, to separate into two.* It

30 And therewith he made the sockets to the door of the tabernacle of the congregation, and the brazen altar, and the brazen grate for it, and all the vessels of the altar,

31 And the sockets of the court round about, and the sockets of the court-gate, and all the pins of the tabernacle, and all the pins of the court round about.

CHAPTER XXXIX.

AND of ᵃ the blue, and purple, and scarlet, they made ᵇ clothes of service, to do service in the holy◦

ᵃ ch. 35. 23. ᵇ ch. 31. 10. & 35. 19.

place, and made the holy garments for Aaron; ᶜ as the LORD commanded Moses.

2 ᵈ And he made the ephod *of* gold, blue, and purple, and scarlet, and fine twined linen.

3 And they did beat the gold into thin plates, and cut *it into* wires, to work *it* in the blue, and in the purple, and in the scarlet, and in the fine linen, *with* cunning work.

4 The made shoulder-pieces for it, to couple *it* together: by the two edges was it coupled together.

5 And the curious girdle of his

ᶜ ch. 28. 4. ᵈ ch. 28. 6.

seems to signify, not a particular coin, but a shekel *broken* or *cut in two.* So, according to A. Clarke, the English penny was anciently cut into four parts, and the fourth part called *a fourthing*, corrupted into *farthing*.

Chapter 39

The Work of the Tabernacle continued.

I. *They made clothes of service.* This phrase is previously used, Ex. 31. 10, for the coverings which were thrown over or wrapped about the various articles of the sacred furniture, when the camp was removed. But it is here applied to the priestly garments, importing that they were not made for mere display, nor to be worn abroad, but only in the sanctuary. The ensuing clause, 'to do the service in the holy place,' is probably to be understood as determining the use of them to the one place and purpose for which they were intended, and for nothing else. 'Those upon whom honor is put, from them service is expected. It is said of those who are arrayed in white robes, Rev. 7. 13, 15, that 'they were before the throne and serve him day and night in his temple.'' *Henry.*——¶ *As the Lord commanded Moses.* It is observable that all the six paragraphs from this to

v. 31, giving an account of the making of the high priest's garments, conclude with these words. As this is not the case in the previous statements, it would seem that they had in the preparation of these articles a peculiarly strict regard to the divine appointment; and this was perhaps owing to the fact that the high priest in his appropriate dress was the most prominent type of Christ of any thing in the whole establishment.

3. *They did beat the gold into thin plates, and cut it into wires.* We here again avail ourselves of the result of the researches of our usual guide in matters of this nature. 'This is the most ancient notice of the preparation of gold in wires, or extended threads to be interwoven in cloths, and it is quite in conformity with all the information we can collect from ancient writings on the subject. Works made with threads of metal are rarely mentioned at all, and whenever they are spoken of, the wire appears to have been wholly made on the anvil. The metals were beaten with a hammer into thin plates, then cut with a pair of scissors or other instrument, into narrow slips, which were afterwards rounded with the hammer and file, so as to form wires or threads. Most of this process is described in the

ephod, that *was* upon it, *was* of the same, according to the work thereof; *of* gold, blue, and purple, and scarlet, and fine twined linen; as the Lord commanded Moses.

6 ¶ ᵉ And they wrought onyx stones enclosed in ouches of gold, graven as signets are graven, with the names of the children of Israel.

ᵉ ch. 28. 9.

text. A very similar process of fabrication is described by Homer as being used by Vulcan, who repaired to his forge and formed upon his anvil a net so fine, that it could be perceived by no one, not even by the gods, being more delicate than the web of a spider. Abating the hyperbole, we gather from this, as well as from the fact that the threads of metal were, in the instance before us, interwoven with, or employed to embroider cloths, that very fine wire was formed by this tedious and laborious process. It is not exactly clear how the gold threads were applied to ornament the ephod of the high priest. We rather think they were not interwoven in the cloth, as in ch. 35. 34, it seems to be said that the colors in the rich cloth were the work of the embroiderer as distinguished from the weaver, who is afterwards mentioned. So also the robe of the ephod, which was all of blue, is said to have been of woven work (v. 22.), probably to denote its simplicity. The same is also said of the innermost coat (v. 27.); while in speaking of the ephod, the girdles, &c., which were highly ornamented, embroidery and needlework are mentioned. Beckman thinks that the earliest application of gold to dress was to sew on slips of the metal, particularly on the seams, as is now done with gold lace. As there is no mention in the text of any process subsequent to that of cutting the metallic plate into slips, necessarily flat, it is possible that they were embroidered on the dress or otherwise applied without being rounded into wires or threads. Beckmann supposes that gold stars and other figures cut from thin plates of the metal were very early applied to dresses, much in the same manner as

spangles at present, being either sewed to the cloth, or fastened by some adhesive composition. To this would seem to have succeeded the arts of embroidering and interweaving with threads of gold and ultimately the progress of uncomfortable luxury led to the formation of clothes entirely of threads of gold without any other material. This was indeed 'cloth of gold'—a name which in more modern times has been given to cloth, the threads of which are of silk wound about with silver wire flattened and gilded. Silver does not seem for a long time to have been employed for similar purposes, and accordingly it is not mentioned in Scripture as being so applied. Beckmann, in evidence of its being unknown at so comparatively late a period as the time of Aurelian, quotes a passage from Vopiscus, who states that this emperor was desirous of entirely abolishing the use of gold in gilding and weaving, because, though there was more gold than silver (this is in itself a curious fact), the former had become scarcer, as much of it was continually lost by being applied to such purposes, whereas every thing that was silver continued so. This seems to render it clear that silver was not used for such purposes. Yet, as Beckmann himself observes in a note, it is barely possible that Vopiscus speaks of gilt silver; for as the ancients were not acquainted with the art of separating these metals, the gold would be entirely lost when they melted the silver. He adds, however, that he had met with no passage in any ancient authors where weaving or embroidering in threads of gilt silver is mentioned. Neither have we. There is no notice of silver thread being interwoven in cloth ear-

7 And he put them on the shoulders of the ephod, *that they should
be* stones for a ᶠmemorial to the
children of Israel; as the LORD
commanded Moses.

8 ¶ ᵍ And he made the breast-
plate *of* cunning work, like the
work of the ephod; *of* gold, blue,
and purple, and scarlet, and fine
twined linen.

9 It was four-square; they made
the breast-plate double: a span
was the length thereof, and a span
the breadth thereof, *being* doubled.

10 ʰ And they set in it four rows
of stones: *the first* row *was* a sardius, a topaz, and a carbuncle:
this *was* the first row.

f ch. 28. 12.   g ch. 28. 15.   h ch. 28. 17. &c.

11 And the second row, an emerald, a sapphire, and a diamond.

12 And the third row, a ligure,
an agate, and an amethyst.

13 And the fourth row, a beryl,
an onyx, and a jasper: *they were*
enclosed in ouches of gold in their
enclosings.

14 And the stones *were* according to the names of the children of
Israel, twelve, according to their
names, *like* the engravings of a signet, every one with his name, according to the twelve tribes.

15 And they made upon the
breast-plate chains at the ends, *of*
wreathen work *of* pure gold.

16 And they made two ouches
of gold, and two gold rings, and

---

lier than the times of the Greek later
emperors.

'It is really surprising to find so much
use made of threads of precious metals
while it continued to be formed by the
hammer. Beckmann declares himself
unable to determine when attempts
were first made to draw into threads
metal, cut or beat into small slips, by
forcing them through holes in a steel
plate placed perpendicularly on a table.
But the art was not known in Italy in
the time of Charlemagne; and our author, from the best evidence he was
able to obtain, is disposed to attribute
the invention of the drawing-plate to
the fourteenth century. Since then the
arts of forming and applying threads of
gold have received much improvement.
It is not known when wire first began
to be spun round thread, as it now usually is in application to dress. This
branch of the art is not ancient. The
threads found among the ruins of Her-
culaneum are of massy gold. When
the fine wire first began to be spun
round the thread it was round; the art
of first flattening the wire, by means of
which tassels and other ornaments have
teen rendered much cheaper—in conse-

quence of much less metal being re
quired to cover the silk—and at the
same time more brilliant and beautiful,
is of modern but uncertain date. The
different degrees of ductility of gold
and silver have led to the beautiful invention of plating silver wire with gold.'
Pict. Bible.

6. *Onyx-stones enclosed in ouches of
gold, graven as signets are graven.*
'There can be no doubt but that mankind were at this time well acquainted
with the art of polishing and engraving
precious stones; and the various texts
relating to the jewelled ornaments of
Aaron's dress are very interesting indications of the progress which had been
made in lapidary and stone-engraving.
It is to observed, that the shoulders
of the ephod were ornamented with
two onyx-stones mounted on gold, and
that these stones were engraved with
the names of twelve tribes—six in each
stone; and we may therefore suppose
the work to have been of a rather minute
character. Then from the breast-plate
we learn that twelve other sorts of precious stones were known, as well as the
brilliant effect which they would produce by a proper arrangement on the

put the two rings in the two ends of the breast-plate.

17 And they put the two wreathen chains of gold in the two rings on the ends of the breast-plate.

18 And the two ends of the two wreathen chains they fastened in the two ouches, and put them on the shoulder-pieces of the ephod, before it.

19 And they made two rings of gold, and put *them* on the two ends of the breast-plate, upon the border of it, which *was* on the side of the ephod inward.

20. And they made two *other* golden rings, and put them on the two sides of the ephod, underneath, toward the forepart of it, over against the *other* coupling thereof, above the curious girdle of the ephod:

21 And they did bind the breast-plate by his rings unto the rings of the ephod with a lace of blue, that it might be above the curious girdle

of the ephod, and that the breastplate might not be loosed from the ephod; as the LORD commanded Moses.

22 ¶ i And he made the robe of the ephod *of* woven work, all *of* blue.

23 And *there was* a hole in the midst of the robe, as the hole of a habergeon, *with* a band round about the hole, that it should not rend.

24 And they made upon the hems of the robe pomegranates *of* blue, and purple, and scarlet, *and* twined *linen.*

25 And they made k bells *of* pure gold, and put the bells between the pomegranates upon the hem of the robe, round about between the pomegranates;

26 A a bell and a pomegranate, a bell and a pomegranate, round about the hem of the robe to minister *in;* as the LORD commanded Moses.

ι ch. 28. 31.　ᵏ ch. 28. 33.

same surface. Each of these stones also contained the name of a tribe; and, altogether, we are led to form no mean idea of the progress which art had thus early made in the treatment of precious stones. Any one at all acquainted with the arts is well aware that the engraving of precious stones demands no common measure of address, precision, and knowledge. There must be a considerable number of very fine and delicate tools, and great decision of hand and practice. It is indeed true that the engraving of names admits of no comparison with the skill and delicacy of execution required in cutting the figures of men and animals; but still, as to the essentials of the art, the process is the same in both, and the difference is only a question of more or less perfection. Goguet is astonished to see that, in the time of Moses, and doubtless earlier, men had made so

much progress in art as to be able to execute such works. Considering the number of previous discoveries which it is necessary to suppose, as well as the degree of knowledge and attainment which it involves, the same author, not without reason, is disposed to regard the engraving of precious stones as a most marked evidence of the general progress which the arts had made, in certain countries, at a very early period. With regard to this particular branch of art, we may observe also, that in the course of time it attained such an advanced state among the ancients that the moderns have never been able to equal them in the exquisite delicacy and beauty of their performances on precious stones. The engraved gems which have been preserved are still the unapproached models of the art. *Pict. Bible.*

23. *As the hole of an habergeon.* The

27 ¶ ¹And they made coats *of* fine linen, *of* woven work, for Aaron and for his sons,

28 ᵐAnd a mitre *of* fine linen, and goodly bonnets *of* fine linen, and ⁿlinen breeches *of* fine twined linen.

29 ᵒAnd a girdle *of* fine twined linen, and blue, and purple, and scarlet, *of* needle-work; as the LORD commanded Moses.

30 ¶ ᴾAnd they made the plate of the holy crown *of* pure gold, and wrote upon it writing, *like to* the engravings of a signet, HOLINESS TO THE LORD.

31 And they tied unto it a lace of blue, to fasten *it* on high upon the mitre; as the LORD commanded Moses.

32 ¶ Thus was all the work of the tabernacle of the tent of the congregation finished: and the children of Israel did ᑫaccording to all that the LORD commanded Moses, so did they.

33 ¶ And they brought the tabernacle unto Moses, the tent, and all his furniture, his taches, his boards, his bars, and his pillars, and his sockets;

<small>l ch. 28. 39, 40. m ch. 28. 4, 39. Ezek. 44. 18. n ch. 28. 42. o ch. 28. 39. p ch. 28. 36, 37. q ver. 42, 43. ch. 25. 40.</small>

34 And the covering of rams' skins dyed red, and the covering of badgers' skins, and the vail of the covering;

35 The ark of the testimony, and the staves thereof, and the mercy-seat;

36 The table, *and* all the vessels thereof, and the shew-bread;

37 The pure candlestick, *with* the lamps thereof, *even with* the lamps to be set in order, and all the vessels thereof, and the oil for light;

38 And the golden altar, and the anointing oil, and the sweet incense, and the hanging for the tabernacle-door:

39 The brazen altar, and his grate of brass, his staves, and all his vessels, the laver and his foot.

40 The hangings of the court, his pillars, and his sockets, and the hanging for the court-gate, his cords, and his pins, and all the vessels of the service of the tabernacle, for the tent of the congregation;

41 The clothes of service to do service in the holy *place*, and the holy garments for Aaron the priest, and his sons' garments, to minister in the priest's office.

42 According to all that the LORD

---

habergeon or *hauberk* was a small coat of mail, made of little iron rings curiously united together. It covered the neck and breast, was very light, and resisted the stroke of a sword. The 'band' is what we should now call *a binding*.

27. *And they made coats of fine linen.* The order for making these coats is given above, ch. 28. 40, but the material is not there mentioned. Here they are said to have been made of fine linen, and there is good evidence that pure white linen garments were anciently used by all nations in the service of God. This usage the Most High was

pleased to retain in his worship. The Jewish priests, however, wore this raiment only while officiating in the sanctuary; whereas in Egypt, for instance, the priests of Isis went every where clothed in white.

30. *They made the plate of the holy crown of pure gold.* To the explanations on this subject made above, ch. 28. 36, we have only here to add, that the priests generally among the heathen nations of antiquity were distinguished by the epithet στεφανοφοροι, *crown-bearers*, from the crowns worn upon their heads, which were usually made either of a laurel wreath, or of a rayed or

commanded Moses, so the children of Israel r made all the work.

43 And Moses did look upon all the work, and behold, they had

r ch. 39. 10.

done it as the LORD had command-ed, even so had they done it: and Moses s blessed them.

s Lev. 9. 22, 23. Numb. 6. 23. Josh. 22. 6. 2 Sam. 6. 18. 1 Kings 8. 14. 2 Chron. 30. 27

serrated band of gold.—We here ap-pend a view of the high priest in his

full costume, the details of which have been already given

THE HIGH PRIEST.

43. *And Moses blessed.* After having thoroughly examined the work in all its various items, and found it executed precisely according to the directions given, he confirms his acceptance of it at the hands of the people by solemnly invoking the blessing of God upon them. This teaches us, at the conclusion of every enterprise undertaken for a good object devoutly to acknowledge the good hand of the Lord in enabling us to carry it forward to completion, and to implore his benediction upon the results. We are reminded also that those who serve the cause of religion have a claim to our prayers, even as if they were our own personal benefactors ; for that cause we are bound to consider as our own.

CHAPTER XL.

AND the LORD spake unto Moses, saying,

2 On the first day of the ᵃ first month shalt thou set up ᵇ the tabernacle of the tent of the congregation.

3 And ᶜ thou shalt put therein the ark of the testimony, and cover the ark with the vail.

4 And ᵈ thou shalt bring in the table, and ᵉ set in order the things that are to be set in order upon it; ᶠ and thou shalt bring in the candlestick, and light the lamps thereof.

5 ᵍ And thou shalt set the altar of gold for the incense before the ark of the testimony, and put the hanging of the door to the tabernacle.

6 And thou shalt set the altar of the burnt-offering before the door of the tabernacle of the tent of the congregation.

7 And ʰ thou shalt set the laver between the tent of the congregation and the altar, and shalt put water therein.

8 And thou shalt set up the court round about, and hang up the hanging at the court-gate.

9 And thou shalt take the anointing oil, and ᶦ anoint the tabernacle, and all that *is* therein, and shalt hallow it, and all the vessels thereof: and it shall be holy.

10 And thou shalt anoint the altar of the burnt-offering, and all his vessels, and sanctify the altar : and ᵏ it shall be an altar most holy.

11 And thou shalt anoint the laver and his foot, and sanctify it.

12 ˡ And thou shalt bring Aaron and his sons unto the door of the tabernacle of the congregation, and wash them with water.

ᵃ ch. 12. 2. & 13. 4. ᵇ ver. 17. & ch. 26. 1, 30. ᶜ ver. 21. ch. 26. 33. Numb. 4. 5. ᵈ ver. 22. ch. 26. 35. ᵉ ver. 23. ch. 25. 30, Lev. 24. 5, 6. ᶠ ver. 24. 25. ᵍ ver. 26.

ʰ ver. 30. ch. 30. 18. ᶦ ch. 30. 26. ᵏ ch. 29. 36, 37. ˡ Lev. 8. 1,—13.

Chapter 40

The Tabernacle set up.

2. On the first day of the fifth month thou shalt set up the tabernacle. From an attentive survey of all the incidents recorded to have happened after the exodus from Egypt, it appears that about six months intervened between that event and the commencement of the work of the tabernacle. Consequently they were about six months employed in the work itself; for the tabernacle was set up at the beginning of the second year, or one year lacking fifteen days after they had left Egypt. Considering the vast amount of curious and costly workmanship that was requisite, the undertaking was carried through with great expedition. But the hearts of the people were in this work, and this made all their labor light ; and the union of men's hands, and much zeal will necessarily bring to a speedy accomplishment any work that is undertaken.

3. And cover the ark with the vail That is, hang up the separating vail so as to *hide* the ark from the public view. For this reason the vail is called, Num. 4. 5, ' the covering vail.'

9. And thou shalt take the anointing oil and anoint, &c. Every thing having been duly brought and disposed in its proper place, the consecration of the whole by sacred unction follows. In allusion to this it is said, Dan. 9, 24, ' Seventy weeks are determined upon thy people and upon thy holy city, to finish the transgression, and to make an end of sins, and to make reconciliation for iniquity, and to bring in everlasting righteousness, and to seal up the vision and prophecy, and *to anoint the Most Holy.*' The ' most holy' here is but another name for the *Christian*

13 And thou shalt put upon Aaron the holy garments, [m] and anoint him, and sanctify him; that he may minister unto me in the priest's office.
14 And thou shalt bring his sons, and clothe them with coats:
15 And thou shalt anoint them, as thou didst anoint their father, that they may minister unto me in the priest's office: for their anointing shall surely be an [n] everlasting priest-hood throughout their generations.
16 Thus did Moses; according to all that the LORD commanded him, so did he.
17 ¶ And it came to pass in the first month, in the second year, on the first *day* of the month, *that* the [o] tabernacle was reared up.
18 And Moses reared up the tabernacle, and fastened his sockets. and set up the boards thereof, and put in the bars thereof, and reared up his pillars.
19 And he spread abroad the tent over the tabernacle, and put the covering of the tent above upon it; as the LORD commanded Moses.
20 ¶ And he took and put [p] the testimony into the ark, and set the staves on the ark, and put the mercy-seat above upon the ark:
21 And he brought the ark into the tabernacle, and [q] set up the vail of the covering, and covered the ark of the testimony; as the LORD commanded Moses.
22 ¶ [r] And he put the table in the tent of the congregation upon the side of the tabernacle northward, without the vail.
23 [s] And he set the bread in order upon it before the LORD; as the LORD had commanded Moses.
24 ¶ [t] And he put the candlestick in the tent of the congregation, over against the table, on the side of the tabernacle southward.
25 And [u] he lighted the lamps before the LORD, as the LORD commanded Moses.
26 ¶ [y] And he put the golden altar in the tent of the congregation, before the vail:
27 [z] And he burnt sweet incense thereon; as the LORD commanded Moses.
28 ¶ [a] And he set up the hanging *at* the door of the tabernacle.
29 [b] And he put the altar of burnt-offering *by* the door of the tabernacle of the tent of the congregation, and [c] offered upon it the burnt-offering, and the meat-offering; as the LORD commanded Moses.
30 ¶ [d] And he set the laver between the tent of the congregation

[m] ch. 28. 41. [n] Numb. 25. 13. [o] ver. 1. Numb. 7. 1. [p] ch. 25. 16.

[q] ch. 26. 33. & 35. 12. [r] ch. 26. 35. [s] ver. 4. [t] ch. 26. 35. [u] ver. 4. ch. 25. 37. [y] ver. 5. ch. 30. 6. [z] ch. 30. 7. [a] ver. 5. ch. 26. 36. [b] ver. 6. [c] ch. 29. 38. &c. [d] ver. 7 ch. 30. 18.

Church which was to be established at the end of the seventy weeks, and which was anointed at its setting up by the Holy Spirit in his miraculous effusion on the day of Pentecost.

15. *Their anointing shall be an everlasting priesthood.* The meaning is, that as far as the common priests were concerned, the efficacy of this first anointing should extend to the whole future line, so that they need not from one generation to another receive successively the consecrating unction. With the High Priest the case was different. As he was elected, it was fit that he should, upon entering into office, be anointed; but in regard to the ordinary priests, who inherited their office as their birthright, the same necessity did not exist.

26. *And he put the golden altar in the tents of the congregation.* Of the gen

and the altar, and put water there, to wash *withal*.

31 And Moses, and Aaron, and his sons, washed their hands and their feet thereat:

32 When they went into the tent of the congregation, and when they came near unto the altar, they washed; e as the LORD commanded Moses.

33 f And he reared up the court round about the tabernacle and the altar, and set up the hanging of the court-gate: so Moses finished the work.

e ch. 30. 19.   f ver. 8. ch. 27. 9. 16.

---

eral aspect of the interior of the tabernacle, when all its furniture was properly arranged, a tolerably correct idea may be formed from the accompanying cut.

THE INTERIOR OF THE TABERNACLE.

33. *And he reared up the court round about the tabernacle,* &c. As all the particulars have been formerly explained, nothing more is here necessary than to present to the eye the general appearance of the tabernacle with the court, altar, and laver; the whole surmounted by the pillar of cloud.

34 ¶ g Then a cloud covered the tent of the congregation, and the glory of the LORD filled the tabernacle.

g ch. 29. 43. Lev. 16. 2. Numb. 9. 15. 1 Kings 8. 10, 11. 2 Chron. 5. 13. & 7. 2. Isai. 6. 4. Hag. 2. 7, 9. Rev. 15. 8.

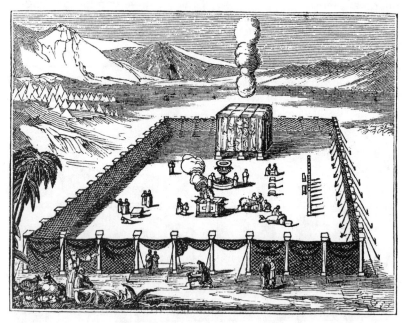

THE TABERNACLE AND COURT.

34. *Then a cloud covered the tent of the congregation.* Rather according to the Hebrew literally translated, 'the cloud' (הֶעָנָן *hëanan*) that is, the cloudy pillar, or cloud of the Shekinah, which had previously abode for many weeks on the summit of the mountain, and which had subsequently descended upon Moses' tent and stood before the door of it, as mentioned, ch. 33. 9. This sublime cloud now removed from its former station and stood at first not only over, but around the tabernacle, completely covering or enwrapping it in its sombre folds while inner unseen Glory, after first filling the outer room, entered and took its station in the Most Holy Place between the Cherubim.—— ¶ *The glory of the Lord filled the tabernacle.* That is, the visible sign or symbol of the Lord's glorious presence 'By this Glory was signified,' says Maimonides 'a certain created splendor which God caused miraculously to dwell any where for the purpose of manifesting forth his majesty.' Abrabanel on this passage speaks still more distinctly; 'Behold, it is clear that the Glory of the Lord was not a cloud, but something in respect to light and splendor like unto fire. A cloud, however, was round about it, as smoke is always about a fire; and as burning lamps (or lightnings) appear from the midst of clouds, so was the Glory of the Lord like to fire in the midst of the cloud and the darkness.' In this august manner God took formal possession of the house which had been prepared for his residence. All things having been duly

made ready, the great and glorious Occupant now makes a solemn entry into the habitation in which he had promised to dwell, and of which he now virtually says, 'This is the place of my throne, and the place of the soles of my feet, where I will dwell in the midst of the children of Israel for ever.' By this act Jehovah not only testified the restoration of his forfeited favor to the people, and his gracious acceptance of their services, but also gave typically a pledge of the future *tabernacling* of Christ, the true Shekinah, in human flesh, and of an ulterior visible manifestation of the divine glory in the latter days on the earth. This latter great event is distinctly foreshown in the following passages in language bearing evident allusion to that of Moses in the narrative before us; Ezek. 43, 4, 5, 'And the *Glory of the Lord* came into the house by the way of the gate whose prospect is toward the east.—So the Spirit took me up and brought me into the inner court; and behold the *Glory of the Lord* filled the house.' John also in the Revelation, chap. 21. 10, 11, alluding to the same illustrious period of the church, says, 'And he carried me in the spirit to a great and high mountain, and showed me that great city, the holy Jerusalem, descending out of heaven from God; *having the Glory of God.*' For ourselves we think it deserving of the most serious and profound enquiry, whether this 'glory to be revealed' be not a another term for the whole heavenly world composed of the glorified spiritual bodies of Christ and his saints, together with his holy angels, coming down to enter into a new and abiding connexion with the church on earth in its latter-day prosperity. To what else can it refer? Our Savior expressly assured his disciples that 'hereafter they should see heaven opened, and the angels of God ascending and descending, upon the Son of Man.' Equally explicit is the declara-

tion of John in the Apocalypse, ch. 21. 3, 'And I heard a great voice from heaven saying, Behold, the tabernacle of God is with men, and he shall dwell with them, and they shall be his people; and God himself shall be with them, and shall be their God.' As the glory of the Shekinah came in all its effulgence and took possession of the tabernacle when it was prepared for its reception, so when the earth, by the previous outpouring of the Spirit and the universal diffusion and establishment of the gospel shall have become fitted for the divine inhabitation, are we not taught to expect that the glorified Savior and the glorified saved—the substance of the resplendent Cloud and the shining Cherubim of the most holy place—shall come and fix themselves in permanent sojourn in the temple thus prepared for them? Not that we are to understand this as implying that the glorified saints will ever be promiscuously mingled together with the tenants of earth, the dwellers in houses of clay and houses of wood or stone, but simply that there will be a visible communication and an intimate relation between these two great departments of the Lord's family. We have no reason to suppose that spiritual bodies will ever inhabit material tenements on the earth, but as there was at the birth of Christ a sudden and glorious manifestation of a multitude of the heavenly host in the air, so we are perhaps taught that a similar developement of the invisible world will be made and become permanent in the latter day, abiding in immediate proximity to our globe, and thus giving its ultimate fulfilment to the dream of Jacob of an angelic intercourse between heaven and earth. In this state of things, the separating veil between the holy and the most place, will be done away. The cherubim will be 'living creatures' and pass freely out into the outer room. Sure we are, that if these predictions do not announce the

35 And Moses ^h was not able to enter into the tent of the congre-

^h Lev. 16. 2. 1 Kings 8. 11. 2 Chron. 14. 5.

gation, because the cloud abode thereon, and the glory of the LORD filled the tabernacle.

---

sublime event now suggested, as they plainly point to *some* fulfilment of stupendous character, it behoves the interpreters of the oracles of God to inform an inquiring world what they *do* mean. It is impossible to be faithful to the entrusted truth of heaven, and permit its most sublime revelations to lie shrouded in obscurity under the idle plea that they are a part of prophecy, and that prophecy was not designed to be understood till it is accomplished. Not indeed that we would maintain that prophecy can be *equally well* understood before and after its accomplishment, but if it be unintelligible, why are we exhorted to study it ? The truth is, the prophecies touch the very vital doctrines of Christianity. Its grand sanctions—its promises of bliss and its threatenings of woe—the judgment, the resurrection, and the New Jerusalem— are inseparably interwoven with the fulfilment of the great chain of scriptural prophecy; and we doubt not the time is not far distant when the interests of truth will *imperiously demand* that the mysteries of the Apocalypse shall be unfolded.

35. *And Moses was not able to enter into the tent of the congregation*, &c. The glory of the Shekinah shone so bright and dazzling, that it was absolutely insufferable to the sight. Indeed, as the phenomenon was in effect the same with that which appeared on the summit of Sinai, and of which it is said, Ex. 24. 16, that the part of it covered by the cloud, when partially exposed to view, was like unto ‘ devouring fire,’ the tabernacle could not now be entered for the same reason that the cloud could not then have been entered, even by Moses, without a special summons to that effect from Jehovah himself. Precisely the same thing happened at the

dedication of the temple of Solomon, when, we are told, 1 Kings, 8. 10, 11, ‘The cloud filled the house of the Lord ; so that the priests could not stand to minister because of the cloud, for the glory of the Lord had filled the house of the Lord.’ A palpable allusion to this incident is also to be recognised in Rev. 15. 7, 8, although the meaning of the prophecy is too profound to be hastily decided upon ; ‘And one of the four beasts gave unto the seven angels seven golden vials full of the wrath of God, who liveth for ever and ever. And the temple was filled with smoke from the glory of God, and from his power ; and no man was able to enter into the temple, till the seven plagues of the seven angels were fulfilled.’ Moses was obliged to wait till the overwhelming brightness had somewhat abated, and the Glory had retired within the veil. That these circumstances were designed to point forward to some grand accomplishment of far more illustrious character, in the state described in the closing chapters of Ezekiel and John, when the divine Glory shall again take up its abode on earth, we have no doubt. But as the *precise manner* of its ultimate fulfilment appears to be hidden by a veil at present inscrutable, we are thrown upon a *moral* improvement of the occurrence, upon which no mystery rests. It affords another intimation how awful and terrible is the majesty of Jehovah when he is pleased to reveal himself to human eyes. How impossible it was for Moses to behold it without a screen, we have already had occasion to notice. The greatest and the best of men are utterly unable to stand before it. ‘Our God is a consuming fire.’ How thankful then are we called to be, that we may contemplate the softened glories of the Godhead in

36 ᶦAnd when the cloud was taken up from over the tabernacle, the children of Israel went onward in all their journeys:

37 But ᵏ if the cloud were not

1 Numb. 9. 17. & 10. 11.   Neh. 9. 19.
ᵏ Numb. 9. 19,—22.

taken up, then they journeyed not till the day that it was taken up.

38 For ˡthe cloud of the Lᴏʀᴅ *was* upon the tabernacle by day, and fire was on it by night, in the sight of all the house of Israel, throughout all their journeys.

1 ch. 13. 21.   Numb. 9. 15.

Jesus Christ, who has drawn nigh and entered as our forerunner into the holy place not made with hands, that we might in due time be admitted to a participation of the same honor and joy.

36, 37. *And when the cloud was taken up,* &c. Thus the cloud was a guide to the camp of Israel in their march through the wilderness. While the cloud remained upon or over the tabernacle, they rested abiding in their tents; when it removed, they removed and followed their aërial conductor. This is more fully detailed Num. 9. 15—23, and long afterwards mentioned with grateful remembrance by the Psalmist, Ps. 78. 14, —105. 39; and Nehemiah notices its continuance as an extraordinary mercy notwithstanding their great provocation in the matt'r of the golden calf; ch. 9. 19, 'Yet thou in thy manifold mercies forsookest them not in the wilderness; the pillar of cloud departed not from them by day, to lead them in the way; neither the pillar of fire by night, to show them light and the way wherein they should go.'

38. *For the cloud of the Lord was upon the tabernacle, by day,* &c. Chal. and Targ. Jon. 'The cloud of the Glory of the Lord.' Targ. Jerus. 'The cloud of the Glory of the Shekinah of the Lord.' That same mysterious cloud which had led them up from Egypt, and which had all along been pregnant with wonders, now settled upon the tabernacle and hovered over it, even in the hottest and clearest day; for this was not a cloud of which it could be said that the sun 'wearieth the thick cloud; he scattereth the bright cloud.' It was

a cloud that served as a remarkable token of the Divine Presence, constantly visible day and night to all Israel, and to those who were situated in the remotest corners of the camp, so that they could never have occasion to propose the question, 'Is the Lord among us, or is he not?' They could not doubt it, unless they could doubt the evidence of their own senses.——¶ *And fire was on it by night in the sight of all the house of Israel,* &c. The fire and the cloud were not, as we have before remarked, two different and distinct things. It was one and the same pillar which was a dark cloud by day and a shining fire by night. Indeed, as the original for ' on it ' is בֹּו *bo, in it,* it is contended by Fagius and others that the true meaning is, that the fire was *in the cloud* by night, i. e. that the cloud was the seat of it, that it did not emanate from any source different from the cloud; not that the fire was so inveloped in the cloud as to be invisible, for on that supposition, the fire was in it by day as well as by night. It is possible that the term 'fire' is to be understood merely of a phosphorescent glow which the exterior of the cloud was made to assume at night, and thus to be viewed as entirely distinct from the inner enwrapped glory, which Moses so ardently desired to see. These are particulars in respect to the cloud which it is exceedingly difficult to determine; but the general image can easily be brought before the mind, and we can see at once how express is the allusion to this incident in the words of the prophet, Is. 4. 5, 'And the Lord will create upon every dwelling-place of Mount Zion, and upon her assemblies, a cloud and smoke by day, and the shining of a flaming fire by night ; for upon all the glory shall be a defence.' The dwelling-places of Mount Zion here spoken of are doubtless *Christian churches*, and the intimation seems to be, that in the times of the gospel each individual church, or congregation of believers, should be as complete in itself in its endowments, and prerogatives ; that it shall be as truly distinguished by the tokens of the Divine presence, guidance, and guardianship, as was the one congregation of Israel with its one tabernacle, surmounted by the pillar of cloud and of fire. The Jewish nation formed but one church, having its unity concentrated in one place and one system of worship. As such it was not so properly a type of the whole collective body of Christian churches, nor of any one great sectarian division of the church, as of each particular single church, duly organized and furnished. All such churches the Scriptures represent as complete and independent in themselves, and subject to no jurisdiction save that of Christ administered by his word, spirit, and officers.

——¶ *Throughout all their journeys.* This circumstance is so prominent in the history of the wanderings of Israel, and so replete with interest in itself, that we know not how to forbear enlarging somewhat more at length upon it. Whatever may have been the impression produced by it upon the minds of those to whose senses it was present, it soars majestically before *our* minds as a threefold token of the divine *presence, protection,* and *guidance.* In this sublime symbol the journeying host could but feel that God was always nigh them, resting with them when they rested, and moving with them when they moved. Never could they cast their eyes upon that towering pillar, ever

dark by day and bright by night, always maintaining its position, and not, like other clouds, changing, breaking, and dissipating into the surrounding air ; never, we say, could they look upon this august object without being reminded that 'a God at hand, and not afar off, was the Lord in his holy habitation.' But not only so ; it was a source of *protection.* It shaded them, as a pleasant pavilion, from the rays of the noon-tide sun, and under its canopy they could rest as under the shadow of a great rock in a weary land. Nor less did it serve as a defence from their enemies, than as a shade from the beams of the sultry sun. Its descending and interposing folds placed a wall of adamant between them and their Egyptian pursuers, beyond which they could no more penetrate than they could have broken through the granite barriers of Sinai and Horeb. But last, though not least, they had in the cloudy pillar a constant *guide and director.* It conducted them in all their movements, and indicated to them all their rests. They rose up and journeyed whenever it began to move ; they stopped at the moment when it became stationary. When it rose they knew not whither it would go, but it led them constantly in the right way ; and they had no inquiries to make, no doubts or fears to cherish, nothing to do but to yield themselves implicitly to its guidance. What a wondrous mercy to be thus conducted in all their way ! Travellers, especially in desert and inhospitable climes, like that which now lay before the children of Israel, are prone to be concerned about their route and about their safety. They lie down at night with planted guards around them, and look with fearful solicitude to the events of the coming day, lest perchance they should lose their way, or their water become exhausted, or their strength fail. But no misgivings of this nature could trouble the peace of the favored hosts of Israel.

They could lay them down to rest without any care how far or whither they should go on the morrow, or whether they should move at all. No anxiety as to food or drink could afflict their minds, for without any care or thought of theirs, 'their bread would be given and their water would be sure,' and if they journeyed, an unerring guide would mark out their place of rest. 'Happy, thrice happy, ye highly favored of heaven!' we are prone to exclaim in view of this distinguished lot of the chosen tribes. Thrown often ourselves into the greatest perplexity as to the decisions we shall make, and the conduct we shall pursue in life, we naturally feel how great would be the blessing of being ever thus sensibly directed by the Lord.

But let us not disparage our own privileges compared with those of the seed of Jacob. As to the *presence* of Jehovah with us, encompassing our ways, we are not left destitute of that. If we have not the Shekinah in *shadow* we have it in *substance*, in him who is 'the brightness of the Father's glory, and the express image of his person.' His *tabernacling* has already, in one sense, been with men in human flesh, and he is the proper object to bring before our thoughts, whenever we would have an equivalent for the visible symbol of Jehovah. In him the promise is, 'I will dwell in (among) them, and walk in (among) them, and they shall be my people.' 'I will never leave you nor forsake you.' By his spirit he is present with his whole church and with every individual member of it. By that Spirit he will abide with them for ever, cheering their hearts and renewing their strength by the light of his countenance.

Do we desire *protection* as real and as effectual as that which spread its panoply over the chosen race? The consoling strain in which, if his, we are assured of it, is uttered in the language of the Psalmist, 'The Lord is thy keeper: the Lord is thy shade upon thy right hand. The sun shall not smite thee by day, nor the moon by night. The Lord shall preserve thee from all evil: he shall preserve thy soul. The Lord shall preserve thy going out and thy coming in from this time forth, and even for ever more.'

Finally, do we desire *guidance*, an *infallible light* to direct us in all the mazes and perplexities of our path—something which shall stand to us instead of the luminous pillar that, in the dark night poured its splendors upon the shifting sands and the rocky roughnesses of the Arabian desert? Doubtless, *secret intimations of Providence* are sometimes given to this end, especially if sought in earnest prayer and humble watchfulness. But however this may be, we have a more sure directory of duty. The Bible is *our* pillar of cloud and of fire. Let us look to the pages of that inspired word which is a light to our feet, and a lamp to our path,' and we shall cease to desiderate the guiding glory which aided only the outward eye, and directed only a local sojourn. We have all and abound. We have the oracles of truth and life; we have the proffer of the illuminating Spirit; we have the promise of a better Canaan than that which smiled beyond Jordan; and if we can sincerely say with the Psalmist, in respect to the divine leading on earth, 'Thou shalt guide me with thy counsel,' we may confidently add the supplementary clause, 'And afterward receive me to glory.'